SCHOOL DICTIONARY

A
B
C
D
E
F
G
H
I
J
K
L
M
N
O
P
Q
R
S
T
U
V
W
X
Y
Z

A DORLING KINDERSLEY BOOK
www.dk.com

Produced for Dorling Kindersley by
Rigby Heinemann, 22 Salmon Street,
Port Melbourne, Victoria, Australia

First published in Great Britain in 1999
by Dorling Kindersley Limited,
9 Henrietta Street, London, WC2E 8PS

2 4 6 8 10 9 7 5 3 1

A CIP catalogue record for this book is
available from the British Library.

ISBN 0 7513 5800 2

Printed in Italy by Printer Trento

CONTENTS

INTRODUCTION

Welcome to the *DK School Dictionary.* It has been specially written and designed for pupils like you to use in the classroom, or at home when you are doing homework or your own writing.

We have made this dictionary clear and straightforward because we want you to feel comfortable using it. It has many features that you'll find useful, such as *Homophones.* It is important that you really understand what dictionaries do so that you can use one whenever you need help finding the meaning of a word or spelling the word you need. We have chosen a wide range of words to include in the dictionary. You'll find some very common words that you probably know something about already. There are also many less common words – these often have a pronunciation guide next to them so that you'll know how to say them as well as write them. You'll also find some interesting new words that most other dictionaries don't have yet. Some of these have to do with computing, such as the *Internet*; some have to do with food we are eating nowadays, such as *kebab*; while others have to do with popular culture, especially music and clothing, such as *rave* and *techno.*

We hope you enjoy reading and using this dictionary as much as we enjoyed writing it for you.

USING THE DICTIONARY

Page letter indicator

Headword

Definition

B C D E F G H I J K L M N O P Q R S T U V W X Y Z

(*say* ad-**vize**) *verb*
to recommend or give advice to someone: *She advised me to get a haircut.*
•***Word Family:*** **advisable** *adjective* sensible or safe **advisory** *adjective* giving advice: *an advisory speed limit* **adviser** *noun*

(*say* **ad**-va-kate) *verb*
1 to urge or support something, especially by arguing: *to advocate freedom of speech*
advocate (*say* **ad**-va-kit) *noun*
2 someone who recommends or supports a person or cause: *She's an advocate of the green movement.*

or (*say* **ee**-on) *noun*
an immensely long period of time
•***Word Origins:*** from a Greek word meaning "an age"

(*say* **air**-i-al) *noun*
1 a wire rod that receives radio or television signals
aerial *adjective*
2 from the air: *aerial bombardment*

(*say* air-**o**-biks) *plural noun*
vigorous physical exercises you do to music to stimulate your breathing and the circulation of blood through your body
•***Word Family:*** **aerobic** *adjective*

(*say* **air**-o-drome) *noun*
a small airfield for planes

(*say* air-o-**naw**-tiks) *noun*
the study of flight, especially of aircraft
•***Word Family:*** **aeronautical** *adjective*

(*say* **air**-o-plane) *noun*
an aircraft driven by jet engines or propellers

(*say* **air**-o-sol) *noun*
a can or container for storing a liquid under pressure and releasing it as a spray: *aerosol paint*

(*say* es-**thet**-ik) *adjective*
to do with the appreciation of beauty: *The old building was saved for aesthetic rather than practical reasons.*
•***Word Family:*** **aesthetics** *noun* the study of beauty, especially in art **aesthetically** *adverb*

noun
1 a particular event or matter: *Have you heard about the kidnapping affair?* 2 **affairs** business: *She wanted to put her affairs in order before she died.* 3 a sexual relationship between two people who are not married to each other: *They're having an affair.*

verb
to influence: *Witnessing the accident really affected me.*
•***Word Family:*** **affecting** *adjective* moving

verb
to pretend or imitate: *He affected complete innocence about the stink bombs. / She affects a cockney accent.*
•***Word Family:*** **affected** *adjective* artificial or put on **affectation** (*say* af-ek-**tay**-shin) *noun* artificial behaviour

noun
warm feelings of love and care: *She greeted her mother with affection.*
•***Word Family:*** **affectionate** *adjective* showing affection **affectionately** *adverb*

noun
a feeling of mutual attraction or close similarity between people or groups: *an affinity between friends*
•***Word Family:*** the plural is **affinities**

verb
to firmly declare or confirm: *The prime minister affirmed that he would act.*
•***Word Family:*** **affirmative** *adjective* agreeing: *He gave an affirmative answer.* **affirmation** *noun*

verb
to trouble or cause distress: *He's afflicted with asthma.*
•***Word Family:*** **affliction** *noun*

(*say* **af**-loo-ence) *noun*
wealth, especially measured by your possessions: *The size of their house is a sign of their affluence.*
•***Word Family:*** **affluent** *adjective*

verb
1 to have enough money to buy something: *I can't afford those new jeans.* 2 to have enough of something for a particular purpose: *We can't afford to miss another class or we won't pass the exam.*

noun
the covering of land with forest so that animals can return to their homes, soil erosion is slowed down, the soil is enriched and the trees can produce more oxygen
•***Word Family:*** **afforest** *verb*

adjective
1 frightened or feeling fear: *I'm afraid of the dark.* 2 feeling sorry or regretful: *I'm afraid I can't stay at your place tonight.*

preposition
1 later than: *after tea* 2 behind: *She came here after me.* 3 in honour or imitation of: *Who are you named after? / He paints after Nolan's style.* 4 about: *They asked after you.* 5 in agreement with: *a man after my own heart* 6 **after all** in spite of everything: *We are able to come after all.*
after *adverb*
7 behind: *The dog trotted after.* 8 later: *They arrived a day after.*

8

Word Origin

Word Family

(*say* ka-**nal**) *noun*
a waterway built for boats and ships

(*say* ka-**nair**-ree) *noun*
a small, yellow finch, often kept in a cage as a pet
•***Word Family:*** the plural is **canaries**
•***Word Origins:*** these birds first came from the *Canary* Islands

(*say* **kan**-sul) *verb*
1 to call off or stop something: *to cancel a match / to cancel an order* 2 to cross out something so that it can't be used: *to cancel a ticket*
•***Word Family:*** other forms are **cancels, cancelled, cancelling** □ **cancellation** *noun*

(*say* **kan**-sa) *noun*
a disease in which a group of cells multiplies, destroying nearby tissue. The growth may spread throughout the body.
•***Word Family:*** **cancerous** *adjective*

adjective
open or honest: *a candid opinion*
•***Word Family:*** **candidly** *adverb* **candidness** *noun* **candour** *noun*

(*say* **kan**-di-date) *noun*
someone who wants to do or get a certain job or prize: *He is a candidate for school captain.*

noun
a stick of wax with a wick through it which gives a light when you burn it

noun
a hard sweet made by boiling sugar
•***Word Family:*** the plural of the noun is **candies**

noun
1 the long, hollow, jointed stems of some plants such as bamboo 2 a stick used to beat someone with
cane *verb*
3 to hit with a stick as a punishment

(*say* **kay**-nine) *adjective*
1 to do with dogs
canine *noun*
2 any animal in the dog family: *a fox is a canine*
3 a short form of **canine tooth**
•***Word Origins:*** from a Latin word meaning "dog"

noun
one of the four pointed teeth that you have, two on each jaw

(*say* **kan**-is-ta) *noun*
a tin or jar used to store food: *a canister for tea*

noun
another name for **marijuana**
•***Word Origins:*** form a Greek word meaning "hemp"

noun
an animal or a human being that eats other animals like itself
•***Word Family:*** **cannibalistic** *adjective* **cannibalism** *noun*

noun
a large gun, often on wheels
•***Word Family:*** the plural is **cannon** or **cannons**

(*say* ka-**noo**) *noun*
a light, narrow boat that you move by paddles
•***Word Family:*** the plural is **canoes** □ **canoeist** *noun*

(*say* **kan**-un) *noun*
1 a law or rule, especially a religious one 2 music in which the same tune is played or sung by two or more instruments or voices overlapping
•***Word Family:*** **canonize** or **canonise** *verb* to declare someone to be a saint

(*say* **kan**-un) *noun*
a clergyman who works from a cathedral

(*say* **kan**-a-pee) *noun*
a cover that hangs over something: *a bed canopy / the forest canopy*
•***Word Family:*** the plural is **canopies**
•***Word Origins:*** from a Greek word meaning "bed with a mosquito net"

(*say* kan-**tank**-a-rus) *adjective*
bad-tempered or quarrelsome

(*say* kan-**teen**) *noun*
1 a cafeteria in a factory, office or school 2 a box holding a set of cutlery 3 the set of things for eating and drinking used by a soldier, especially a water-bottle

noun
the way a horse moves, faster than a trot but slower than a gallop
•***Word Family:*** **canter** *verb*

noun
someone who leads the singing in a church service, especially in a Jewish synagogue

(*say* **kan**-vus) *noun*
1 a heavy cloth made from flax or cotton and used for tents and sails 2 a piece of canvas used by an artist to paint on

(*say* **kan**-vus) *verb*
to ask people for their opinions: *The politician canvassed the district before the election.*
•***Word Family:*** **canvasser** *noun*

noun
a narrow, steep-sided river valley

noun
1 a soft, round hat with no brim, usually with a peak at the front 2 the top of a pen or jar that

A B C D E F G H I J K L M N O P Q R S T U V W X Y Z

WHAT IS A HEADWORD?

THE WORD YOU LOOK FOR in a dictionary is called a headword. All the headwords in a dictionary are arranged in alphabetical order to help you find the word you need.

Two running headwords are shown in the top left- and top right-hand corners of each page. The running headword in the top left-hand corner tells you this is the first entry on this page. The running headword in the top right-hand corner tells you this is the last word on the page. You can use these running headwords to help you find your word. Simply look to see if the word you are looking for lies in alphabetical order between the two running headwords.

Sometimes you will see two entries for the same headword. These headwords are spelt the same but have diffferent histories. They may have come into English from different languages or at different times. When this happens each word is listed separately and has a small number next to it.

calf (1) *noun*
a young cow, whale or seal
• ***Word Family:*** the plural is **calves**

calf (2) *noun*
the back of your leg, below the knee
• ***Word Family:*** the plural is **calves**

Sometimes headwords are shown with two different spellings like *organise* and *organize*. This means that although either spelling can be used, the first entry in this dictionary is the most common spelling.

WHY DO I NEED A PRONUNCIATION GUIDE?

SOMETIMES UNFAMILIAR WORDS can be difficult to pronounce. To help you, a pronunciation guide has been given for these words so that you pronounce them correctly.

The *DK School Dictionary* uses two different ways to pronounce words.

compromise (*say* **kom**-pra-mize)

This style divides the word up into syllables and spells it exactly as you would say it. The part in thick bold type is the part that you say more strongly than the rest.

doubt (*rhymes with* out)

This style shows you that the unfamiliar word rhymes with a familiar word.

WHERE WILL I FIND THE PART OF SPEECH?

THE PART OF SPEECH for each headword comes after the pronunciation guide. It is always written in italics. If there is a change in the part of speech the headword is repeated.

> erect (*say* e-**rekt**) *adjective*
> 1 upright
> **erect** *verb*
> 2 to build something: *We erected a monument in his honour.*
> •***Word Family:*** **erectly** *adverb* **erectness** *noun*

THE PARTS OF SPEECH YOU WILL SEE IN THIS DICTIONARY ARE:

Noun A noun is a word that names something. There are common nouns, such as "girl" or "dog", proper nouns such as "Tom" and "Newcastle", abstract nouns such as "beauty" and "anger", or collective nouns such as "herd" and "flock".

Pronoun A pronoun is a word used in the place of a noun. "It", "that", "they" and "she" are examples of pronouns.

Adjectives An adjective is a word that describes a noun or a pronoun. In the sentence *The young boy bought a big book,* "young" and "big" are adjectives.

Verb A verb is a word that tells you what someone or something does or feels, such as "sang" and "cleaned" in *The boy sang as he cleaned his bike.*

Adverb An adverb is a word that adds to the meaning of a verb or an adjective or other adverb, by telling you how, why, when, or where an action takes place. In the sentence *The girl walked quickly,* "quickly" is an adverb.

Preposition A preposition is a word used before a noun or pronoun to show how it connects with other words in the sentence. In the sentence *The book is on the table,* "on" is a preposition.

Conjunction A conjunction is a word that joins together parts of a sentence, for example "and", "but", or "because".

Prefix A prefix is a small word which is added to a root word to change its meaning. For example, the prefix "un-" always changes the meaning of a word to its exact opposite, as in "unbelievable".

A B C D E F G H I J K L M N O P Q R S T U V W X Y Z

Why is the definition important?

The definition tells you what the word means. Some headwords have more than one definition. When this happens each definition is numbered.
Sometimes a phrase or sentence is written in italics to show the correct use of the word. If there is more then one example they are separated by a slash, "/".

What is a secondary headword?

A secondary headword is a phrase with the headword in it but which has a special meaning. It always appears in bold letters and it is followed by a definition.

horse *noun*
1 a four-legged mammal with hoofs and a long mane and tail, used for riding or pulling a cart
2 **horse around** to play roughly or noisily

What other information do the entries give?

Under the definition there is often more information about the word.
A heading in bold italic tells you what kind of information it is. The different types of information are described below.

Word Family This section lists other words that can be made from the headword, such as the plural of a noun or other verb, adverb, or adjective forms. Sometimes a definition or a phrase is used to show the correct use of the word.

con (2) *verb*
•***Word Family:*** other verb forms are **cons, conned, conning**

calculate *verb*
•***Word Family:*** **calculating** *adjective* slyly clever

Word Origins Many words in the English language have come to it from other languages. Brief explanations about the origins of a word are provided for headwords that have interesting histories.

alto *noun*
•***Word Origins:*** from an Italian word meaning "high"

Sometimes these languages are still used today, such as "Italian". Sometimes they are ancient forms of the language, such as "Old English" and "Old French" that died out a long time ago and are no longer spoken.

WHAT TO DO WHEN YOU CAN'T FIND A WORD

SOMETIMES IT CAN BE difficult to find a word. This might be because it starts with a silent letter or begins with a letter or a blend of letters that create a different sound from what you are expecting.

When in doubt, turn to this chart for help.

The sounds the word begins with	The way the word might begin	Example
ch	c	cello
f	ph	phone
g	gh	gherkin
g	gu	guitar
h	wh	wholesome
j	g	gentle
k	ch	character
k	qu	quoits
k	kh	khaki
kw	qu	quite
n	gn	gnaw
n	kn	know
n	pn	pneumonia
r	rh	rhythm
r	wr	wreath
s	c	celery
s	ps	psychiatrist
s	sc	science
sh	s	sugar
sh	sch	schedule
sh	ch	chauffeur
sk	sch	school
t	th	thyme
t	tw	two
w	wh	whinge
z	x	xylophone

b c d e f g h i j k l m n o p q r s t u v w x y z

abacus (*say* **ab**-a-kus) *noun*
a frame with thin rods and sliding beads used for counting
• ***Word Family:*** the plural is **abacuses** or **abaci**

abandon (1) *verb*
1 to leave without intending to return: *We abandoned our school bags and fled.* 2 to stop going on with: *The rescue squad abandoned the search after four days.*
• ***Word Family:*** **abandonment** *noun*

abandon (2) *noun*
freedom from control or care: *The class cheered with great abandon.*

abattoir (*say* **ab**-a-twar) *noun*
a place where cattle, sheep and other animals are killed for food
• ***Word Family:*** the plural **abattoirs** is often used: My *father worked at the abattoirs.*

abbey (*say* **ab**-ee) *noun*
the place where monks or nuns live
• ***Word Family:*** **abbot** *noun* the male head of an abbey **abbess** *noun* the female head of an abbey

abbreviate (*say* a-**bree**-vi-ate) *verb*
to shorten a word or words by leaving out letters: *you can abbreviate the words "I shall" to "I'll"*
• ***Word Family:*** **abbreviation** *noun* a shortened form of a word

abdicate *verb*
to give up your position or privileges, usually a claim to the throne: *King Edward VIII abdicated when he married the divorced Mrs Simpson.*
• ***Word Family:*** **abdication** *noun*

abdomen (*say* **ab**-do-men) *noun*
1 the main part of your body below your chest, which contains your stomach and intestines
2 the section of an insect's or spider's body furthest from its head
• ***Word Family:*** **abdominal** (*say* ab-**dom**-i-nal) *adjective*

abduct *verb*
to take a person away illegally or by force: *to abduct a baby in its pram*
• ***Word Family:*** **abductor** *noun* someone who abducts another person **abduction** *noun*

abide *verb*
1 to tolerate: *I can't abide racist comments.*
2 **abide by** to keep to: *I'll abide by my promise to tidy my room.*

ability *noun*
1 the power to do something: *Superman has the ability to leap tall buildings with a single bound.*
2 skill or talent: *sporting ability*
• ***Word Family:*** the plural is **abilities**

ablaze *adjective*
on fire or lit up: *The whole house was soon ablaze. / The skyscraper is ablaze with lights.*

able *adjective*
1 having the opportunity or being allowed to do something: *Are you able to start work tomorrow?*
2 competent or skilled: *an able driver*
• ***Word Family:*** **ably** *adverb*

abnormal *adjective*
different from what is usual or normal: *an abnormal pulse rate*
• ***Word Family:*** **abnormality** *noun* **(abnormalities) abnormally** *adverb*

aboard *adverb*
on a ship, train or aircraft: *How many passengers are aboard?*

abolish (*say* a-**bol**-ish) *verb*
to put an end to something: *It took many years to abolish the slave trade.*
• ***Word Family:*** **abolition** *noun*

abominable (*say* a-**bom**-in-a-bul) *adjective*
dreadful or shocking: *abominable behaviour*
• ***Word Family:*** **abominate** *verb* to detest **abomination** *noun* a person or thing that is abominable **abominably** *adverb*

Aborigine (*say* ab-o-**rij**-i-nee) *noun*
1 a descendant of the race of tribal people who have lived in Australia for thousands of years
2 **aborigine** an original inhabitant of a country
• ***Word Family:*** **Aboriginal** *adjective* to do with the Australian Aborigines: *Aboriginal languages* **aboriginal** *adjective*
• ***Word Origins:*** from a Latin word meaning "from the beginning"

abortion (*say* a-**bor**-shin) *noun*
1 the removal of a baby from its mother's womb before it is big enough to live on its own, usually before its 28th week of growth
2 anything that is a failure
• ***Word Family:*** **abortive** *adjective* unsuccessful **abort** *verb* **abortionist** *noun*

about *preposition*
1 concerning or on the subject of: *a song about love* 2 around: *He looked about the park as he walked.* 3 approximately: *a friend about my height* 4 **about to** just going to: *She's about to jump.*

about *adverb*
5 nearly or close to: *about halfway there / about time for lunch* 6 close by: *The kittens are somewhere about.*

above *adverb*
1 at or to a higher place: *Stand on the step above.*
2 more than: *a temperature of above 40°C*
above *preposition*
3 higher than: *The sun rose above the horizon.*

abrasive *adjective*
1 used for scraping off or wearing away by rubbing: *an abrasive soap* 2 harsh, irritating or annoying: *an abrasive personality*
• ***Word Family:*** **abrasion** *noun*

abreast *adverb*
1 side by side: *to walk two abreast* 2 keeping up with the latest developments: *Doctors like to stay abreast of new research.*

abridge *verb*
to shorten a book or piece of writing: *The magazine editor abridged the book for publication in serial form.*
• ***Word Family:*** **abridged** *adjective* **abridgement** or **abridgment** *noun*

abroad *adverb*
in or to a country other than your own: *to go abroad for holidays*

abrupt *adjective*
1 sudden or unexpected: *an abrupt movement*
2 rude and unfriendly: *an abrupt phone call*
• ***Word Family:*** **abruptly** *adverb* **abruptness** *noun*

abscess (*say* **ab**-ses) *noun*
a painful, infected swelling in your body, that contains pus
• ***Word Family:*** the plural is **abscesses**

abscissa (*say* ab-**sis**-a) *noun*
the horizontal distance on a graph

abscond (*say* ab-**skond**) *verb*
to leave suddenly or secretly, especially when you have done something wrong: *She absconded with the chess club's money.*

abseil (*say* **ab**-sail) *verb*
to lower yourself down a mountain or cliff, using a double rope

absent (*say* **ab**-sent) *adjective*
1 away: *She's absent today.*
2 missing or not present: *The money was absent from my wallet.*
• ***Word Family:*** **absentee** (*say* ab-sen-**tee**) *noun* **absence** *noun* **absently** *adverb*

absent-minded *adjective*
vague or forgetful
• ***Word Family:*** **absent-mindedly** *adverb*

absolute (*say* **ab**-so-loot) *adjective*
complete, perfect or with no limits: *The day was an absolute success. / The dictator had absolute power.*
• ***Word Family:*** **absolutely** *adverb*

absorb *verb*
1 to take in liquid or soak it up: *The sponge absorbed the water.* 2 to interest you very much: *She was completely absorbed by the book.*
• ***Word Family:*** **absorbent** *adjective*: *absorbent tissues* **absorbing** *adjective* interesting: *an absorbing film* **absorption** *noun*

abstract (*say* **ab**-strakt) *adjective*
1 to do with thoughts and ideas rather than things 2 based on theory: *abstract arguments*
3 not representing lifelike people or things, but expressing yourself using colour and form: *an abstract painting*
abstract *noun*
4 a summary
• ***Word Family:*** **abstracted** *adjective* preoccupied or lost in thought **abstractly** *adverb* **abstraction** *noun*

absurd *adjective*
foolish or ridiculous: *an absurd song / an absurd idea*
• ***Word Family:*** **absurdity** *noun* **absurdly** *adverb*

abundance (*say* a-**bun**-dance) *noun*
a full or ample supply or amount of something: *an abundance of Easter eggs*
• ***Word Family:*** **abundant** *adjective* **abundantly** *adverb*

abuse (*say* a-**bewz**) *verb*
1 to speak insultingly to someone: *The drunk abused the barman.* 2 to use something wrongly: *Don't abuse your chisel by using it as a screwdriver.*
3 to treat someone in a cruel or violent way
abuse (*say* a-**bewce**) *noun*
4 insults or cruel language 5 wrong or harmful use of something: *drug abuse* 6 cruel or violent treatment
• ***Word Family:*** **abusive** *adjective* **abusively** *adverb*

abysmal (*say* a-**biz**-mal) *adjective*
very bad indeed: *I thought the performance was abysmal.*
• ***Word Family:*** **abysmally** *adverb*

abyss (*say* a-**biss**) *noun*
a deep hole or chasm
• ***Word Origins:*** from a Greek word meaning "bottomless"

acacia (*say* a-**kay**-sha) *noun*
a small tree or shrub with very small, yellow flowers massed together into balls or rods: *Wattle is a type of acacia.*

academic (*say* ak-a-**dem**-ik) *adjective*
1 to do with a university or college: *an academic gown* 2 to do with theory and ideas rather than practical things: *an academic problem*
academic *noun*
3 someone who teaches or does research in a university or college
• ***Word Family:*** **academically** *adverb*

academy (*say* a-**kad**-a-mee) *noun*
1 a school or college for learning practical subjects: *a naval academy* 2 a scientific or artistic association: *the British Academy*
• ***Word Family:*** the plural is **academies**
• ***Word Origins:*** from the Greek word *Akademeia*, the garden where the philosopher Plato taught

accelerate (*say* ak-**sel**-er-ate) *verb*
to move faster or speed up
• ***Word Family:*** **acceleration** *noun*

accelerator (*say* ak-sel-a-**ray**-tor) *noun*
the pedal that you press to make a car or other motor vehicle go faster

accent (*say* **ak**-sent) *noun*
1 your particular way of speaking: *She speaks French with an American accent.* 2 the stronger tone or stress you give to part of a word or a musical note, to make it stand out from the rest: *The accent on each word pronounced in this dictionary is shown as* **bold**. 3 any of the marks used with letters to change their sound or to indicate stress

accentuate (*say* ak-**sen**-choo-ate) *verb*
to emphasise or highlight: *The skintight dress accentuates her slender figure.*
• ***Word Family:*** **accentuation** *noun*

accept (*say* ak-**sept**) *verb*
to receive, especially with good feelings: *Please accept my apologies.*
• ***Word Family:*** **acceptable** *adjective* welcome or worth accepting **acceptance** *noun* **accepted** *adjective*

access (*say* **ak**-sess) *noun*
1 a way of entering or approaching a place: *The only access to the island is by boat.* 2 the right or opportunity of seeing someone: *Our dad has right of access to us even though our parents are divorced.*
access *verb*
3 to gain entry to the memory of a computer: *to access a file* 4 to obtain data from a computer
• ***Word Family:*** **accessible** *adjective* able to be reached or obtained **accessibility** *noun*

accessory (*say* ak-**ses**-a-ree) *noun*
1 any extra item that is not really necessary: *Some cars today have CD players as an accessory.* 2 **accessories** any extra items, such as shoes, belts, scarves or handbags, that go well with your clothes 3 someone who helps a criminal before or after a crime
• ***Word Family:*** the plural is **accessories**

accident (*say* **ak**-si-dent) *noun*
1 anything unexpected or unplanned: *We bumped into our friends by accident.* 2 any unfortunate event, especially one involving injury: *a shocking car accident*
• ***Word Family:*** **accidental** *adjective* **accidentally** *adverb*

acclaim (*say* a-**klaim**) *verb*
to express sounds of approval: *The Rolling Stones were acclaimed with screams as they came on stage.*
• ***Word Family:*** **acclamation** *noun*

acclimatize or **acclimatise** (*say* a-**klime**-a-tize) *verb*
to get used to something new: *He soon acclimatized to the tropical heat.*

accommodate (*say* a-**kom**-a-date) *verb*
1 to provide something, often as a favour: *Can you accommodate me with a loan?* 2 to adapt to something: *It took a few minutes for my eyes to accommodate to the dark.* 3 to have rooms or beds for someone: *The hotel accommodates 14 guests.*
• ***Word Family:*** **accommodation** *noun*

accompaniment *noun*
a part written to go with a melody: *piano accompaniment*

accompany (*say* a-**kum**-pa-nee) *verb*
1 to go with someone or something: *We'll accompany you to the airport./We had rice to accompany the curry.* 2 to sing or play with someone: *The piano will accompany the violin.*
• ***Word Family:*** other forms are **accompanies, accompanied, accompanying** □ **accompanist** *noun* someone who accompanies

accomplice (*say* a-**kum**-plis) *noun*
a partner in crime or wrongdoing

accomplish (*say* a-**kum**-plish) *verb*
to bring something about or complete it successfully: *We accomplished our project ahead of time.*
• ***Word Family:*** **accomplished** *adjective* skilled: *an accomplished singer* **accomplishment** *noun*: *His many accomplishments include horseriding.*

accord (*say* a-**kord**) *noun*
1 agreement or harmony: *The warring countries are in accord at last.* 2 **of your own accord** willingly: *The politician resigned of her own accord.*

according *adverb*
1 **according to** in someone's opinion: *According to the forecast, it's going to rain./According to him*

the meeting is at 6.00 p.m. **2 according to** in a way that agrees or suits something: *You will be put in groups according to your ability.*

accordion *noun*
a musical instrument that you strap to your body, with keys, bellows and two sets of metal reeds
• ***Word Family:*** **accordionist** *noun*

account *noun*
1 the money you have in a bank or building society 2 a description or explanation of something: *The radio announcer gave a full account of the rugby match./She gave an interesting account of why she was late.* 3 a statement recording the money spent or saved by a person or business: *The clerk kept the financial accounts.* 4 importance: *Her feelings are of no account.*
account *verb*
5 to explain: *I can't account for her tantrum.*

accountant *noun*
someone with the job of recording and analysing the money that a person or business earns and spends
• ***Word Family:*** **accountancy** *noun* an accountant's work **accounting** *noun*

accumulate (*say* a-**kew**-mew-late) *verb*
to gather or pile up: *Dust accumulates in the corners. / We accumulated a stack of travel brochures.*

accurate (*say* **ak**-yoo-rate) *adjective*
correct or exact: *My new watch is more accurate than my old one. / What an accurate guess.*
• ***Word Family:*** **accuracy** *noun* **accurately** *adverb*
• ***Word Origins:*** from a Latin word meaning "prepared with care"

accuse (*say* a-**kewz**) *verb*
to blame someone outright for doing something wrong: *They accused me of stealing the money.*
• ***Word Family:*** **accused** *noun* the defendant in a criminal court case **accusation** *noun*

accustom *verb*
to become familiar with something by using it or through habit: *You'll have to accustom yourself to our strange ways.*
• ***Word Family:*** **accustomed** *adjective* usual or customary: *our accustomed breakfast* **accustomed to** *adjective* familiar with or used to: *He was accustomed to seeing her every day.*

ace *noun*
1 a playing card with a single spot, the highest or lowest card in its suit 2 someone who excels at something: *an ace at flying* 3 a serve in tennis which your opponent cannot even touch: *The tennis champ served an ace.*
ace *verb*
4 sensational or great: *That new band is ace!*

acetylene (*say* a-**set**-a-leen) *noun*
a colourless, inflammable gas that burns with such a hot flame that it is used for cutting and welding metal

ache (*rhymes with* take) *noun*
1 a dull, continuous pain: *an ear ache*
ache *verb*
2 to hurt: *My back had begun to ache.*

achieve (*say* a-**cheev**) *verb*
to attain or accomplish something through hard work: *to achieve all your goals*
• ***Word Family:*** **achiever** *noun* someone who achieves **achievement** *noun*

acid *noun*
a chemical substance that releases hydrogen when dissolved in water and that can eat away metals
acid *adjective*
sharp or bitter: *an acid taste / an acid comment*
• ***Word Family:*** **acidic** *adjective* **acidity** *noun*
• ***Word Origins:*** from a Latin word meaning "sour"

acid rain *noun*
rain that can harm the environment because it contains acids from polluted air

acknowledge (*say* ak-**nol**-ij) *verb*
1 to confess or accept responsibility for something: *I acknowledge the error of my ways.* 2 to mention that you have received something: *to acknowledge a letter / to acknowledge a smile*
• ***Word Family:*** **acknowledgement** or **acknowledgment** *noun*

acne (*say* **ak**-nee) *noun*
a skin complaint, common among teenagers, that causes pimples and spots on your face and back

acorn (*say* **ay**-korn) *noun*
the fruit of an oak tree, consisting of a nut with a cup-shaped base

acoustics (*say* a-**koo**-stiks) *noun*
1 the science of sound 2 the qualities of a room that make it good or bad for hearing sounds, especially music: *Our school hall has great acoustics.*
• ***Word Family:*** **acoustic** *adjective* with sound not electronically amplified: *an acoustic guitar*

acquaintance *noun*
1 someone you know slightly, rather than a friend: *a passing acquaintance* 2 familiarity or knowledge: *We've no acquaintance with Japanese.*

acquire (*say* a-**kwire**) *verb*
to get or obtain something
• ***Word Family:*** **acquisition** *noun*: *What do you think of my latest acquisition?* **acquisitive** *adjective* keen to acquire things

acquit (*say* a-**kwit**) *verb*
1 to declare someone free of guilt, especially in a court of law 2 **to acquit yourself** to perform: *She acquitted herself well as the daughter in the play*
•***Word Family:*** other forms are **acquits, acquitted, acquitting** □ **acquittal** *noun*

acre (*say* **ay**-ka) *noun*
an area of land equal to slightly less than half a hectare
•***Word Family:*** **acreage** *noun* an area expressed in acres: *What's the acreage of the farm?*

acrid *adjective*
sharp or biting: *The acrid smell of burning rubber.*

acrobat (*say* **ak**-ro-bat) *noun*
a skilled entertainer who performs tricks on a tightrope or trapeze
•***Word Family:*** **acrobatics** *plural noun* the daring tricks of an acrobat or any behaviour like this **acrobatic** *adjective*

acronym (*say* **ak**-ro-nim) *noun*
a word formed from the first letter or letters of several words, such as RSPCA from Royal Society for the Prevention of Cruelty to Animals

acrostic (*say* a-**kros**-tik) *noun*
a poem in which the first or last letters of each line form a word, a phrase or the alphabet

acrylic (*say* a-**kril**-ik) *noun*
1 a quick-drying paint that can be dissolved in water 2 synthetic material used to make clothes, sheets, and so on

act *noun*
1 anything you do: *an act of great bravery* 2 a law or decree: *an act of Parliament* 3 one of the main divisions in a play or opera 4 a single item in a programme: *The next act is a juggler.*
act *verb*
5 to do or perform something: *He acted wisely.* 6 to take part in a play or film, especially when you imitate or represent a particular character 7 **act up** to misbehave: *He's bound to act up if you ignore him.*
•***Word Family:*** **acting** *noun* the profession of being an actor **acting** *adjective* being a substitute for: *the acting Prime Minister* **actor** *noun* **actress** *noun*

action *noun*
1 the process of acting or doing: *Is the machine in action yet?* 2 fighting or combat: *The soldiers were trained for action overseas.* 3 a way of moving: *Watch that racehorse's graceful action!* 4 any legal proceedings: *The tennis star started a libel action against the newspaper.* 5 lively or exciting events: *They cruised the streets looking for some action.*

activate *verb*
to make something work: *Press this button to activate the alarm.*

active *adjective*
1 in action: *Only one engine is active.* 2 busy or lively: *She leads an active life.* 3 currently running and able to be used: *That computer file is active.*
•***Word Family:*** **actively** *adverb*

activity *noun*
1 the state of being active: *Her life is a whirlwind of activity.* 2 something you do: *Swimming is our favourite summer activity.*
•***Word Family:*** the plural is **activities**

actor *noun*
someone who performs a role in a play or film

actress *noun*
a girl or woman who performs a role in a play or film

actual *adjective*
real or existing
•***Word Family:*** **actually** *adverb*

acupuncture (*say* **ak**-yoo-punk-cher) *noun*
the Chinese technique of puncturing the skin with needles, used to treat and cure illness
•***Word Family:*** **acupuncturist** *noun* someone who performs acupuncture

acute *adjective*
1 sharp or keen: *acute pain* 2 less than 90°: *an acute angle in maths* 3 intense, severe and usually not lasting long: *an acute shortage of blood doners* 4 needing immediate treatment: *The accident victim needs acute care.*
acute *noun*
5 a mark (´) over a letter in languages such as French, used to mark a stress

AD *abbreviation*
short for anno domini, *Latin words meaning* "in the year of our Lord": *Princess Diana died in AD 1997.*

adagio (*say* a-**dah**-jee-o) *adverb*
played or sung slowly or in a leisurely manner
•***Word Origins:*** from Italian

adamant (*say* **ad**-a-mant) *adjective*
stubborn or not willing to change: *We were adamant in our decision.*

adapt (*say* a-**dapt**) *verb*
1 to alter or adjust something: *We adapted the sheets to make ghost costumes.* 2 **adapt to** to become used to something: *I'm sure you'll adapt to the new situation*
•***Word Family:*** **adaptable** *adjective* easily adapted **adaptation** *noun* anything adapted: *The film is an adaptation of a novel.* **adaptor** *noun* any

a b c d e f g h i j k l m n o p q r s t u v w x y z

A B C D E F G H I J K L M N O P Q R S T U V W X Y Z

added device that lets you use a machine or tool in a new way

add *verb*
1 to find the sum of two or more numbers 2 to join one thing to another: *to add an extension to a house / to add some advice* 3 **add up** to make sense: *Your tale just doesn't add up.*

adder *noun*
a small venomous snake

addict (*say* **ad**-ikt) *noun*
someone who cannot stop a particular habit, such as smoking or taking drugs
• *Word Family:* **addiction** *noun* **addictive** *adjective*

addition *noun*
adding, or the thing that is added
• *Word Family:* **additional** *adjective* **additionally** *adverb*

additive *noun*
something added to food, to preserve, flavour or colour it

address *noun*
1 the details of the place where you live or may be contacted 2 a formal talk made to an audience 3 a number that shows where information is stored in the memory of a computer 4 the special code of letters or numbers used as identification when sending messages or asking for information on the Internet
address *verb*
5 to speak to someone: *The head teacher addressed the whole school* 6 to write an address on a letter or parcel
• *Word Family:* the plural form of the noun is **addresses**

adenoids (*say* **ad**-a-noyds) *plural noun*
the soft tissue at the back of your nose, which may affect your breathing and speech if swollen and inflamed

adequate (*say* **ad**-a-kwit) *adjective*
sufficient or enough: *an adequate supply of food for the camping trip*
• *Word Family:* **adequacy** *noun* **adequately** *adverb*

adhere *verb*
to stick: *The label adheres to the bottle. / We must adhere to our plans.*
• *Word Family:* **adherent** *noun* a person who follows or supports a cause **adherence** *noun* **adherent** *adjective*

adhesive *noun*
1 a substance, such as cement, used for sticking two surfaces together
adhesive *adjective*
2 sticky: *adhesive tape*

adjacent (*say* a-**jay**-sent) *adjective*
next to or near: *They occupied adjacent seats.*

adjective (*say* **aj**-ek-tiv) *noun*
a word that describes a noun or pronoun. In the sentence *The young boy bought a big book* "young" and "big" are adjectives.
• *Word Family:* **adjectival** (*say* a-jek-**tie**-val) *adjective* **adjectivally** *adverb*

adjourn (*say* a-**jern**) *verb*
to break off or postpone: *The judge adjourned the case.*
• *Word Family:* **adjournment** *noun*

adjudicate (*say* a-**joo**-di-kate) *verb*
to judge a competition or settle an argument
• *Word Family:* **adjudicator** *noun* someone who adjudicates **adjudication** *noun*

adjust (*say* a-**just**) *verb*
1 to change the position of something, so that it fits: *to adjust a car's brakes / to adjust the angle of a picture* 2 to get used to new circumstances: *It takes time to adjust to a new school.*
• *Word Family:* **adjustable** *adjective* **adjustment** *noun*

administer *verb*
1 to manage or have charge of something: *The local council administers this park.* 2 to give or apply: *to administer first aid* 3 **administer to** to help: *The nurses administered to the wounded.*
• *Word Family:* **administrate** *verb* **administration** *noun* **administrator** *noun*

admiral (*say* **ad**-mi-ral) *noun*
the highest ranking commissioned officer in the navy
• *Word Family:* **admiralty** *noun* the top level of administration in the navy

admire *verb*
to approve of or have a high regard for someone or something: *I admire the way she makes friends easily.*
• *Word Family:* **admirable** *adjective* worth admiring **admirably** *adverb* **admiration** *noun*
• *Word Origins:* from a Latin word meaning "to wonder at"

admit *verb*
1 to allow in: *Dogs are not admitted to this restaurant.* 2 to say that you are responsible for something: *Okay, I admit to guzzling all the ice-cream.* 3 to agree that something is true: *I admit that you've got a good point there.*
• *Word Family:* other forms are **admits, admitted, admitting** □ **admission** *noun* the act of entering, or the entrance fee **admittance** *noun* the right to enter **admittedly** *adverb* without denial

admonish *verb*
to advise or warn in a firm but gentle way
• ***Word Family:*** **admonition** *noun* **admonitory** *adjective*

adolescent (*say* ad-o-**les**-ent) *noun*
someone who is no longer a child but is not yet an adult
• ***Word Family:*** **adolescence** *noun*
• ***Word Origins:*** from a Latin word meaning "to grow up"

adopt *verb*
1 to make someone a member of your family by legal means: *to adopt a child* 2 to make something your own: *to adopt the customs of a new country* 3 to accept by vote: *The class council adopted both my suggestions.*
• ***Word Family:*** **adoptive** *adjective* related by adopting: *an adoptive parent* **adoption** *noun*

adore *verb*
to worship or love devotedly
• ***Word Family:*** **adorable** *adjective* enchanting or lovable **adoration** *noun* **adoringly** *adverb*

adorn *verb*
to decorate or make beautiful: *Her arms were adorned with bracelets.*
• ***Word Family:*** **adornment** *noun* adorning, or something that adorns

adrenal gland (*say* a-**dree**-nal gland) *noun*
one of the two small glands forming a cap over each of your kidneys and releasing chemicals called hormones

adrenalin (*say* a-**dren**-a-lin) *noun*
a hormone in your body, that affects a wide range of body functions such as your heart beat, your blood pressure and your response to stress

adult *noun*
a fully grown, mature animal or plant
• ***Word Family:*** **adulthood** *noun*

adulterate (*say* a-**dul**-ter-ate) *verb*
to spoil something or make it impure, especially by adding inferior substances: *to adulterate milk with water*
• ***Word Family:*** **adulteration** *noun*

adultery (*say* a-**dul**-ter-ree) *noun*
the act of a married person having sexual intercourse with a person other than their husband or wife
• ***Word Family:*** **adulterer** *noun* **adulterous** *adjective*

advance *verb*
1 to move forward: *The cat advanced slowly towards the mouse. / How far have you advanced with your music lessons?* 2 to give money before it is actually due: *Can you advance me some of my pocket money?*
advance *noun*
3 progress or forward movement: *Have you made any advance in your quest?* 4 a loan or an early payment of a wage 5 **advances** attempts to establish friendly relations: *I discouraged his advances.* 6 **in advance** ahead of time: *Rent must be paid one month in advance.*

advantage *noun*
1 anything that favours or helps you: *My height gives me an advantage in basketball.* 2 the first point after a score of deuce in tennis 3 **take advantage of** (a) to make use of: *We took advantage of the cave for shelter.* (b) to exploit: *to take advantage of someone's weakness*
• ***Word Family:*** **advantageous** *adjective*

Advent *noun*
the four weeks before Christmas

adventure *noun*
a dangerous or exciting activity or experience
• ***Word Family:*** **adventurous** *adjective* willing to seek or risk danger **adventurer** *noun*

adverb *noun*
a word that adds to the meaning of a verb, adjective or other adverb, by telling how, why, when or where an action takes place. In the sentence *The boy walked slowly home*, "slowly" is an adverb
• ***Word Family:*** **adverbial** *adjective*: *an adverbial phrase*

adversary *noun*
someone you fight or compete with
• ***Word Family:*** the plural is **adversaries** □ **adverse** *adjective* unfavourable or against your interests

adversity *noun*
misfortune: *In times of adversity we ask our friends for help.*
• ***Word Family:*** the plural is **adversities**

advertise *verb*
to tell the public about something for sale or a coming event: *The rock concert was advertised in several newspapers.*
• ***Word Family:*** **advertiser** *noun* someone who advertises **advertising** *noun* the use and making of advertisements

advertisement (*say* ad-**vert**-is-ment) *noun*
a public notice or announcement offering jobs, services or goods for sale, or telling you about a coming event

advice (*say* ad-**vice**) *noun*
an opinion or suggestion that helps you decide what to do: *My best friend gave me advice about what to wear to the disco.*

advise (*say* ad-**vize**) *verb*
to recommend or give advice to someone: *She advised me to get a haircut.*
• ***Word Family:*** **advisable** *adjective* sensible or safe **advisory** *adjective* giving advice: *an advisory speed limit* **adviser** *noun*

advocate (*say* **ad**-va-kate) *verb*
1 to urge or support something, especially by arguing: *to advocate freedom of speech*
advocate (*say* **ad**-va-kit) *noun*
2 someone who recommends or supports a person or cause: *She's an advocate of the green movement.*

aeon or **eon** (*say* **ee**-on) *noun*
an immensely long period of time
• ***Word Origins:*** from a Greek word meaning "an age"

aerial (*say* **air**-i-al) *noun*
1 a wire rod that receives radio or television signals
aerial *adjective*
2 from the air: *aerial bombardment*

aerobics (*say* air-**o**-biks) *plural noun*
vigorous physical exercises you do to music to stimulate your breathing and the circulation of blood through your body
• ***Word Family:*** **aerobic** *adjective*

aerodrome (*say* **air**-o-drome) *noun*
a small airfield for planes

aeronautics (*say* air-o-**naw**-tiks) *noun*
the study of flight, especially of aircraft
• ***Word Family:*** **aeronautical** *adjective*

aeroplane (*say* **air**-o-plane) *noun*
an aircraft driven by jet engines or propellers

aerosol (*say* **air**-o-sol) *noun*
a can or container for storing a liquid under pressure and releasing it as a spray: *aerosol paint*

aesthetic (*say* es-**thet**-ik) *adjective*
to do with the appreciation of beauty: *The old building was saved for aesthetic rather than practical reasons.*
• ***Word Family:*** **aesthetics** *noun* the study of beauty, especially in art **aesthetically** *adverb*

affair *noun*
1 a particular event or matter: *Have you heard about the kidnapping affair?* 2 **affairs** business: *She wanted to put her affairs in order before she died.* 3 a sexual relationship between two people who are not married to each other: *They're having an affair.*

affect (1) *verb*
to influence: *Witnessing the accident really affected me.*
• ***Word Family:*** **affecting** *adjective* moving

affect (2) *verb*
to pretend or imitate: *He affected complete innocence about the stink bombs. / She affects a cockney accent.*
• ***Word Family:*** **affected** *adjective* artificial or put on **affectation** (*say* af-ek-**tay**-shin) *noun* artificial behaviour

affection *noun*
warm feelings of love and care: *She greeted her mother with affection.*
• ***Word Family:*** **affectionate** *adjective* showing affection **affectionately** *adverb*

affinity *noun*
a feeling of mutual attraction or close similarity between people or groups: *an affinity between friends*
• ***Word Family:*** the plural is **affinities**

affirm *verb*
to firmly declare or confirm: *The prime minister affirmed that he would act.*
• ***Word Family:*** **affirmative** *adjective* agreeing: *He gave an affirmative answer.* **affirmation** *noun*

afflict *verb*
to trouble or cause distress: *He's afflicted with asthma.*
• ***Word Family:*** **affliction** *noun*

affluence (*say* **af**-loo-ence) *noun*
wealth, especially measured by your possessions: *The size of their house is a sign of their affluence.*
• ***Word Family:*** **affluent** *adjective*

afford *verb*
1 to have enough money to buy something: *I can't afford those new jeans.* 2 to have enough of something for a particular purpose: *We can't afford to miss another class or we won't pass the exam.*

afforestation *noun*
the covering of land with forest so that animals can return to their homes, soil erosion is slowed down, the soil is enriched and the trees can produce more oxygen
• ***Word Family:*** **afforest** *verb*

afraid *adjective*
1 frightened or feeling fear: *I'm afraid of the dark.* 2 feeling sorry or regretful: *I'm afraid I can't stay at your place tonight.*

after *preposition*
1 later than: *after tea* 2 behind: *She came here after me.* 3 in honour or imitation of: *Who are you named after? / He paints after Nolan's style.* 4 about: *They asked after you.* 5 in agreement with: *a man after my own heart* 6 **after all** in spite of everything: *We are able to come after all.*
after *adverb*
7 behind: *The dog trotted after.* 8 later: *They arrived a day after.*

aftermath *noun*
the time or conditions after something: *They discovered much damage in the aftermath of the storm.*

afternoon *noun*
the time of day between noon and sunset

afterwards *adverb*
later: *I'm too busy now, but I'll speak to you afterwards.*

against *preposition*
1 not in favour of: *I'm against killing whales.* 2 in collision with: *He fell heavily against the chair.* 3 in contrast with: *The trees stood out against the sky.*

age *noun*
1 the length of time during which something has existed: *She's 12 years of age.* 2 a particular period of time in history: *the Ice Age / the Middle Ages* 3 a long time: *I've been waiting here for ages.*
age *verb*
4 to become or appear older: *He's aged a lot since we last saw him.*
•*Word Family:* other verb forms are **ages, aged, ageing** or **aging** □ **aged** *adjective* old **ageing** or **aging** *adjective* growing or seeming to grow old **ageless** *adjective*

agency (*say* **ay**-jen-see) *noun*
a business organization that provides a particular service: *an employment agency*
•*Word Family:* the plural is **agencies**

agenda (*say* a-**jen**-da) *noun*
the list of matters to be dealt with or introduced, especially at a meeting

agent (*say* **ay**-jent) *noun*
1 anything that produces an effect or result: *Rats are an agent of disease.* 2 a person who is allowed to act for another person, company or a government: *a travel agent/a secret agent*

aggravate (*say* **ag**-ra-vate) *verb*
1 to make something worse or more intense: *Eating hot dogs will only aggravate your indigestion.* 2 to annoy: *Don't aggravate the dog by teasing him.*
•*Word Family:* **aggravation** *noun*

aggregate (*say* **ag**-ra-gat) *noun*
1 the total or number of separate things brought together in a group 2 a mixture of different materials used in making concrete
•*Word Family:* **aggregation** *noun* any collection or total forming a unified whole

aggression *noun*
violent and threatening behaviour
•*Word Family:* **aggressive** *adjective* feeling or showing aggression **aggressor** *noun* someone or something that is aggressive **aggressively** *adverb* **aggressiveness** *noun*

aghast (*say* a-**gahst**) *adjective*
amazed and horrified: *I'm aghast at the tales she's told about me.*

agile (*say* **aj**-ile) *adjective*
quick or nimble: *an agile hurdler*
•*Word Family:* **agilely** *adverb* **agility** *noun*

agitate (*say* **aj**-a-tate) *verb*
1 to shake something or move it rapidly from side to side: *to agitate clothes in soapy water* 2 to disturb or excite: *She became agitated after the accident.* 3 to arouse public feelings about something, especially politics: *The speaker tried to agitate the crowd.*
•*Word Family:* **agitator** *noun* **(a)** a machine for stirring or shaking **(b)** someone who agitates: *a political agitator* **agitatedly** *adverb* **agitation** *noun*

agnostic (*say* ag-**nos**-tik) *noun*
someone who believes that you cannot know whether God exists
•*Word Family:* **agnosticism** *noun*

agony (*say* **ag**-a-nee) *noun*
extreme pain or suffering
•*Word Family:* the plural is **agonies** □ **agonize** or **agonise** *verb* to suffer agony or intense worry **agonizing** *adjective*

agoraphobia (*say* ag-ra-**fo**-bi-a) *noun*
an abnormal fear of open spaces
•*Word Family:* **agoraphobic** *adjective*

agrarian (*say* a-**grair**-ri-an) *adjective*
to do with farming land or with agriculture
•*Word Origins:* from a Latin word meaning "field"

agree *verb*
1 to decide in favour of or say yes: *I hope Dad will agree.* 2 to have the same idea or opinion: *We all agreed that the fudge was disgusting.* 3 arrange: *We agreed to meet at the big tree at midnight.* 4 **agree with** to suit: *Spicy foods don't agree with me.*
•*Word Family:* **agreement** *noun*

agreeable *adjective*
1 to your liking: *Is your new job agreeable?* 2 willing or ready to agree: *I'm agreeable to either plan.*

agriculture (*say* **ag**-ri-kul-cher) *noun*
the use of land for planting and growing crops, rather than for raising animals
•*Word Family:* **agricultural** *adjective* **agriculturally** *adverb*

ahead *adverb*
forwards or in front: *Don't run too far ahead.*

aid *noun*
1 help or assistance: *We need the aid of a doctor.* 2 something that helps: *teaching aids/a hearing aid*
• ***Word Family:*** **aide** *noun* an assistant

AIDS *noun*
a disease caused by a virus (HIV) that enters the blood stream and destroys the body's infection-fighting, white blood cells, usually resulting in death
• ***Word Origins:*** an acronym from the first letter of the words Acquired Immune Deficiency Syndrome

aim *verb*
1 to point or direct towards: *He aimed his gun at the target.* 2 to have as your purpose or intention: *Where do you aim to go first?*
aim *noun*
3 a purpose or target

aimless *adjective*
without purpose: *aimless wandering*
• ***Word Family:*** **aimlessly** *adverb*

air *noun*
1 the gases surrounding the earth 2 a particular appearance or feeling: *an air of excitement* 3 a simple tune or melody 4 **up in the air** uncertain: *The decision is still up in the air.*
air *verb*
5 to expose to the air: *to air a stuffy room* 6 to test or make known: *to air new ideas*
• ***Word Family:*** **airing** *noun: to give the sheets an airing* **airless** *adjective* having no fresh air

air-base *noun*
an airfield used as a base for military aircraft

airborne *adjective*
1 flying: *The balloon was soon airborne.* 2 carried in the air: *airborne diseases*

aircraft *noun*
a flying machine, such as a helicopter or aeroplane

airforce *noun*
the armed forces of a country that fight in the air

airline *noun*
an organization that provides regular air transport between places for people and cargo
• ***Word Family:*** **airliner** *noun* any large passenger or cargo-carrying aircraft

airport *noun*
a large field with runways, hangars, workshops and passenger terminals

airship *noun*
a large air balloon which has engines and can carry passengers

airtight *adjective*
not allowing air to pass through: *an airtight jar*

airy *adjective*
1 letting air move through: *an airy bedroom* 2 carefree: *an airy wave*
• ***Word Family:*** other forms are **airier, airiest** □ **airily** *adverb* **airiness** *noun*

aisle (*rhymes with* **file**) *noun*
a passage between the blocks of seats in a church or theatre

ajar (*say* a-**jar**) *adverb*
partly open: *I like the door ajar.*

aka *adverb*
an abbreviation of the words also known as: *Batman, aka Bruce Wayne, jumped into the Batmobile and sped off.*

akin (*say* a-**kin**) *adjective*
similar or related: *Lions are akin to tigers.*

alarm *noun*
1 any noise or signal used as a warning: *a fire alarm* 2 sudden fear caused by becoming aware of danger: *The earth tremor filled us with alarm.*
alarm *verb*
3 to make someone feel alarm: *I didn't mean to alarm you.*
• ***Word Family:*** **alarming** *adjective* **alarmist** *noun*
• ***Word Origins:*** from Italian words meaning "to arms!"

albatross *noun*
a large, white seabird with very long wings
• ***Word Family:*** the plural is **albatrosses**

albino *noun*
a person or animal with pale skin, white hair and pink eyes due to lack of pigment
• ***Word Family:*** the plural is **albinos**

album *noun*
1 a book for storing things like stamps and photographs 2 a long-playing record or CD

alcohol (*say* **al**-ka-hol) *noun*
a colourless liquid made by fermenting sugar with fruit, which can make you drunk

alcoholic (*say* al-ka-**hol**-ik) *noun*
1 someone who is addicted to drinking alcohol
alcoholic *adjective*
2 made from or containing alcohol: *alcoholic lemonade*
• ***Word Family:*** **alcoholism** *noun*

alcove *noun*
a section of a room or other space set back from the main part

alderman (*say* **awl**-der-man) *noun*
a member of a local council
• ***Word Family:*** the plural is **aldermen**

ale *noun*
a type of beer

alert *adjective*
1 wide-awake or paying attention: *Always stay alert when you drive.*
alert *noun*
2 a warning or alarm: *an air-raid alert*
•*Word Family:* **alertness** *noun*
•*Word Origins:* from Italian words meaning "to the watch-tower"

A level *noun*
an examination that you can take after your GCSEs, usually at the age of eighteen
•*Word Family:* the plural form is **A levels**

algae (*say* **al**-jee) *plural noun*
simple plants growing in the sea or in ponds
•*Word Origins:* from the Latin word for "seaweed"

algebra (*say* **al**-ji-bra) *noun*
the branch of maths that uses symbols such as letters to stand for numbers
•*Word Family:* **algebraic** *adjective* **algebraically** *adverb*

algorithm (*say* **al**-ga-ri-dhum) *noun*
a clear way of solving a particular problem in maths
•*Word Origins:* from the name of a Persian mathematician

alias (*say* **ay**-lee-as) *noun*
1 a false name: *He travelled under an alias.*
alias *adverb*
2 also called: *Batman, alias Bruce Wayne*
•*Word Family:* the plural is **aliases**
•*Word Origins:* from a Latin word meaning "at another time or place"

alibi (*say* **al**-i-by) *noun*
a defence by an accused person that he or she was somewhere else at the time a crime was committed
•*Word Family:* the plural is **alibis**

alien (*say* **ay**-li-an) *noun*
1 someone who was not born in the country they live in and has not become a naturalized citizen there 2 a creature from outer space
alien *adjective*
3 foreign or strange
•*Word Origins:* from a Latin word meaning "belonging to another"

alienate (*say* **ay**-lee-a-nate) *verb*
to turn away or make hostile: *to alienate your friends by your behaviour*
•*Word Family:* **alienation** *noun*

alight *verb*
to get out of or down from a vehicle: *to alight from a train*

align (*say* a-**line**) *verb*
to arrange things in a line: *to align fence posts*
•*Word Family:* **alignment** *noun*

alike *adverb*
1 in the same way: *He treats all his dogs alike.*
alike *adjective*
2 similar: *All politicians are alike.*

alimentary canal *adjective*
the passage in your body, including the mouth, oesophagus, stomach, intestines and anus, which takes in food, digests it and gets rid of the remains

alive *adjective*
living: *The plant is still alive.*

alkali (*say* **al**-ka-lie) *noun*
a chemical that lessens the effects of acids or combines with them to produce salts
•*Word Family:* **alkaline** *adjective* **alkalinity** *noun*
•*Word Origins:* from an Arabic word meaning "limed ashes"

Allah
the name for God that is used by Muslim people

allege (*say* a-**lej**) *verb*
to declare or assert, often without proof: *I allege my innocence.*
•*Word Family:* **allegation** *noun* **allegedly** *adverb*

allegiance (*say* a-**lee**-jens) *noun*
a loyalty or duty, especially to a government or ruler of a country

allegory (*say* **al**-a-gree) *noun*
a story or poem which seems simple but in which the events and characters are meant to represent a deeper meaning
•*Word Family:* the plural is **allegories** □ **allegorical** *adjective*

allegro (*say* a-**leg**-ro) *adverb*
played or sung in a fast and lively manner
•*Word Origins:* from Italian

allergy (*say* **al**-a-jee) *noun*
an abnormal sensitivity to substances most people find harmless, such as dust, bee stings, certain fruit and pollen
•*Word Family:* the plural is **allergies** □ **allergen** *noun* any substance that can cause an allergy **allergic** (*say* a-**ler**-jik) *adjective* having an allergy: *I'm allergic to cat hair.*

alley (*say* **al**-ee) *noun*
a narrow path or street, usually between buildings
•*Word Family:* the plural is **alleys**

alliance (*say* a-**lie**-ance) *noun*
a friendly association or union, usually made by formal agreement between countries: *a trade alliance between European nations*

alligator (*say* **al**-i-gay-ta) *noun*
a large reptile, similar to a crocodile, that lives in fresh water and has a broad, rounded snout, a strong tail and powerful jaws
•***Word Origins:*** from Spanish words meaning "the lizard"

alliteration (*say* a-lit-a-**ray**-shon) *noun*
the repetition of the same letter or sound, usually a consonant, to begin a series of closely connected words, as in "*P*eter *P*iper *p*icked a *p*eck of *p*ickled *p*epper"
•***Word Family:*** **alliterative** *adjective*

allocate (*say* **al**-a-kate) *verb*
to set something aside for a particular purpose: *The librarian has allocated money for new books.*
•***Word Family:*** **allocation** *noun*

allot (*say* a-**lot**) *verb*
to share out or distribute: *I've allotted you several tickets.*
•***Word Family:*** other forms are **allots, allotted, allotting**

allotment *noun*
an area of land: *an allotment for growing vegetables*

allow *verb*
1 to permit: My *parents won't allow me out tonight.* 2 to give or provide with: *She's allowed £15 a week for clothes.* 3 **allow for** to take into consideration: *We'll have to allow for the train being late.*

allowance *noun*
a sum of money given for particular needs

alloy (*say* **al**-oy) *noun*
a metal mixed from two or more other metals: *Brass is an alloy made from zinc and copper.*

all right *adjective*
1 safe or in good order: *Are you all right?*
2 satisfactory: *Your new story is all right, but the last one was more exciting.*

allure (*say* a-**loor**) *noun*
attraction or charm: *the allure of the bright lights of the city*
•***Word Family:*** **alluring** *adjective* very attractive

alluvial (*say* a-**loo**-vi-al) *adjective*
made of soil or sand deposited by flowing water: *an alluvial plain*

ally (*say* **al**-eye) *noun*
1 a country or group united with another, especially by signing a formal agreement: *Britain's trade allies.* 2 any close friend or supporter
ally (*say* a-**lie**) *verb*
3 to unite or connect
•***Word Family:*** the plural of the noun is **allies** □ other verb forms are **allies, allied, allying** □ **alliance** *noun*

almanac (*say* **al**-ma-nak) *noun*
a yearly calendar giving information about the sun, moon, tides and other useful things

almighty (*say* awl-**my**-tee) *adjective*
1 having absolute power 2 very great: *What an almighty noise!* 3 **the Almighty** God

almond (*say* **ah**-mond) *noun*
a brown, oval-shaped nut with a mild, sweet taste

alms (*say* ahms) *plural noun*
any money or gifts given to the poor

alone *adverb*
1 by yourself: *Don't leave the baby alone.* 2 **let alone** not to mention: *He can hardly walk, let alone run.*
•***Word Family:*** **alone** *adjective*

aloof *adjective*
1 proud and keeping to yourself: *She's so aloof that I don't dare to speak to her.*
aloof *adverb*
2 apart or at a distance, especially from people: *He stands aloof from family quarrels.*
•***Word Family:*** **aloofness** *noun*

aloud *adverb*
1 in a voice people can hear: *Recite the poem aloud.* 2 loudly: *He cried aloud for joy.*

alp *noun*
1 a high mountain or a field high on a mountain 2 **the Alps** a mountain range in Europe
•***Word Family:*** **alpine** *adjective* to do with the alps: *alpine streams*

alphabet (*say* **al**-fa-bet) *noun*
the letters or signs of a particular language, set in their usual order
•***Word Family:*** **alphabetical** *adjective* being in the order of the alphabet, as in a dictionary **alphabetically** *adverb*
•***Word Origins:*** Greek *alpha* A + *beta* B

alright *adverb*
another spelling of **all right**

Alsatian (*say* al-**say**-shin) *noun*
a large, strong, smooth-haired dog, often used as a police-dog
•***Word Origins:*** from *Alsace*, a region of France

altar (*say* **awl**-ta) *noun*
a table where religious rites and ceremonies are performed in a church or where sacrifices were offered in a temple

alter (*say* **awl**-ta) *verb*
to make or become different: *We must alter our*

plans. / Our plans have altered due to the weather.
•***Word Family:*** **alteration** *noun* a change or modification

alternate (*say* **awl**-ter-nayt) *verb*
1 to replace each other by turns: *Her mood alternates between joy and depression.*
alternate (*say* awl-**ter**-nit) *adjective*
2 every second one: *We play squash on alternate Saturdays.*
•***Word Family:*** **alternately** *adverb* **alternation** *noun*

alternating current *noun*
an electric current that changes direction, with the electrons travelling one way and then the other

alternative (*say* awl-**ter**-na-tiv) *noun*
1 a choice between two possibilities: *The alternatives are red or green boots.* 2 any choice: *Are there no other alternatives?*
alternative *adjective*
3 giving a choice: *an alternative plan* 4 different from what is usual or standard: *alternative medicine*

although (*say* awl-**dho**) *conjunction*
even though: *I'll go although I'd rather not.*

altitude *noun*
the height of anything, especially above sea-level

alto (*say* **al**-toe) *noun*
1 the range of musical notes sung by a contralto, the lowest female singing voice, or a countertenor, highest adult male singing voice 2 any singer or musical instrument having this range: *She's singing alto.*
•***Word Family:*** the plural is **altos** □ **alto** *adjective: an alto saxophone*
•***Word Origins:*** from an Italian word meaning "high"

altogether (*say* awl-to-**ge**-dha) *adverb*
1 entirely or completely: *He's altogether nasty.* 2 in total: *It adds up to £400 altogether.* 3 on the whole: *Altogether, we had an exciting time.*

aluminium (*say* al-oo-**min**-yum) *noun*
a lightweight, silvery-white metal which is soft enough to be rolled into sheets of silver foil and is used to make soft drink cans and utensils

always *adverb*
1 at all times: *She'll always be my friend.*
2 continually: *She always wears makeup to school.*

Alzheimer's Disease (*say* **alts**-high-mers diz-**eez**) *noun*
a brain disease making it hard to think, remember and act normally, usually affecting old people

a.m. *abbreviation*
short for ante meridiem, *Latin words meaning* "before noon": *I don't start school until 9 a.m.*

amalgamate (*say* a-**mal**-ga-mate) *verb*
to combine or mix: *The two schools amalgamated last month.*
•***Word Family:*** **amalgamation** *noun*

amateur (*say* **am**-a-ter) *noun*
1 an athlete who does not play sport for money 2 a person who takes part in an activity for enjoyment rather than for making money 3 a person who lacks skill or ability
•***Word Family:*** **amateur** *adjective: an amateur boxer* **amateurish** *adjective* unskilled
•***Word Origins:*** from a Latin word meaning "lover"

amaze *verb*
to surprise or astonish: *His wide general knowledge amazed us.*
•***Word Family:*** **amazement** *noun* **amazing** *adjective*

amazon (*say* **am**-a-zon) *noun*
1 **Amazon** a member of a legendary race of female warriors and hunters who kept men out of their country 2 a physically strong or powerful woman
•***Word Family:*** **amazonian** *adjective*

ambassador *noun*
1 the chief representative of a government, sent to a foreign country 2 any famous person, often a sports star or an actor, who carries messages of goodwill from their country to another

amber *noun*
1 the yellow, reddish or brown fossilized resin of pine trees, polished and used in jewellery 2 the orange colour used on a traffic light

ambergris (*say* **am**-ber-grees) *noun*
a grey waxy substance obtained from the intestine of the sperm whale and formerly used in making perfume

ambidextrous *adjective*
able to use both hands equally well

ambiguous (*say* am-**big**-yew-us) *adjective*
having two or more possible meanings: *an ambiguous smile/The message was ambiguous.*
•***Word Family:*** **ambiguity** *noun* **ambiguously** *adverb*
•***Word Origins:*** from a Latin word meaning "changing sides"

ambition *noun*
1 a strong desire for success or fame: *to be filled with ambition* 2 the thing that you want to do more than anything else: My *ambition is to be a singer like Madonna.*
•***Word Family:*** **ambitious** *adjective*

A B C D E F G H I J K L M N O P Q R S T U V W X Y Z

ambivalent (*say* am-**biv**-a-lent) *adjective*
having opposite and conflicting feelings about someone or something: *I like him, but I'm ambivalent about going out with him.*

amble *verb*
to walk at a relaxed or easy pace: *The cattle ambled across the field.*
• ***Word Family:*** **amble** *noun* **ambling** *adjective*

ambulance (*say* **am**-bew-lance) *noun*
a vehicle equipped to carry sick or injured people

ambush (*say* **am**-bush) *verb*
1 to lie in wait in order to make a surprise attack
ambush *noun*
2 a surprise attack

amen *interjection* (*say* **ay**-men *or* **ah**-men)
a word that you say after a prayer
• ***Word Origins:*** from a Hebrew word meaning "let it be so"

amend *verb*
1 to make changes in a law: *The committee has amended the rule.* 2 to correct or improve: *to amend a piece of writing*
amends *plural noun*
3 **make amends** to make up for a wrong done: *How can I make amends for my carelessness?*
• ***Word Family:*** **amendment** *noun: an amendment to a law / amendments to a film script*

amenity *noun*
anything which adds to your comfort, ease or pleasure: *a campsite with cooking amenities and running water*
• ***Word Family:*** the plural is **amenities**

amino acid *noun*
an acid that is in proteins

ammeter *noun*
an instrument that you use to measure electric current

ammonia (*say* a-**mo**-nee-a) *noun*
a colourless, strong-smelling gas, often dissolved in water and used to make cleaning products, explosives and fertilizers
• ***Word Origins:*** from the Temple of *Ammon* in Libya, where it was first found

ammunition (*say* am-yoo-**nish**-on) *noun*
shot, shells, bullets and powder used in firing guns

amnesia *noun*
a loss of memory: *A blow to the head can cause amnesia.*

amnesty (*say* **am**-nes-tee) *noun*
a general pardon, especially for crimes against a government: *Many people handed in weapons when a gun amnesty was announced.*

amoeba (*say* a-**mee**-ba) *noun*
a one-celled animal that moves by changing its shape and reproduces by dividing in two, which can only be seen with a microscope
• ***Word Family:*** the plural is **amoebae** (*say* a-**mee**-bee) or **amoebas** ☐ **amoebic** *adjective*
• ***Word Origins:*** from a Greek word meaning "change"

among or **amongst** *preposition*
1 surrounded by: *He stood among the crowd.*
2 between: *to settle a fight among yourselves / to divide chocolates among a group*

amorous (*say* **am**-or-rus) *adjective*
showing or feeling love, especially sexual love: *an amorous glance / an amorous girl*
• ***Word Family:*** **amorously** *adverb* **amorousness** *noun*

amount *noun*
1 the extent or total of anything: *The job only took a small amount of effort.*
amount *verb*
2 **amount to** to add up or be equal to: *Our debts amounted to £20. / Her fine words amount to nothing.*

ampere (*say* **am**-pair) *noun*
the unit for measuring the flow of electrical current
• ***Word Origins:*** named after André *Ampère*, a French physicist

ampersand *noun*
the sign "&", meaning "and"

amphibian (*say* am-**fib**-i-an) *noun*
1 an animal, with a backbone, that develops in water but spends most of its adult life on land, such as a frog or toad 2 a vehicle that can travel on land or water
• ***Word Family:*** **amphibious** *adjective* able to live or move in water and on land
• ***Word Origins:*** from a Greek word meaning "living a double life"

amphitheatre (*say* **am**-fi-thear-ta) *noun*
a circular or oval area with sloping sides rising around it, such as a theatre gallery or sports arena

ample *adjective*
large or plentiful: *A house with ample space for all of us.*
• ***Word Family:*** **amply** *adverb*

amplify (*say* **am**-pli-fie) *verb*
to make louder: *to amplify the violin*
• ***Word Family:*** other forms are **amplifies, amplified, amplifying** ☐ **amplification** *noun*

amputate (*say* **am**-pew-tate) *verb*
to cut off by a surgical operation: *They had to amputate his leg.*
• ***Word Family:*** **amputee** *noun* someone who has had a limb amputated **amputation** *noun*

amuse (*say* a-**mewz**) *verb*
1 to make someone smile or laugh 2 to make time pass pleasantly: *You can amuse yourself until we return.*
• ***Word Family:*** **amusement** *noun* the feeling of being amused, or anything that amuses **amusingly** *adverb*

anaemia (*say* a-**nee**-mi-a) *noun*
a shortage of red blood cells which causes weakness and pale skin
• ***Word Family:*** **anaemic** *adjective* pale or weak: *an anaemic complexion*
• ***Word Origins:*** from Greek words meaning "without blood"

anaesthetic (*say* an-is-**thet**-ik) *noun*
a substance, such as ether or chloroform, that makes you lose your sense of feeling or pain
• ***Word Family:*** **anaesthesia** *noun* loss of feeling, especially of pain **anaesthetist** (*say* a-**nees**-tha-tist) *noun* a doctor trained to give an anaesthetic **anaesthetize** or **anaesthetise** (*say* a-**nees**-tha-tize) *verb*

anagram (*say* **an**-a-gram) *noun*
a word made by rearranging the letters of another word: *"March" is an anagram of "charm".*

analgesic (*say* an-al-**jee**-zik) *noun*
a substance that relieves pain

analogue (*say* **an**-a-log) *adjective*
showing a measurement by means of a pointer or needle, such as the hands on clocks and watches

analogy (*say* a-**nal**-a-jee) *noun*
a likeness or agreement between things that you can compare: *There's an analogy between the heart and a pump.*
• ***Word Family:*** **analogous** *adjective* comparable in several respects **analogously** *adverb*

analyse (*say* **an**-a-lize) *verb*
1 to examine something critically in order to find out its meaning: *to analyse motives / to analyse a work of art* 2 to divide something into the parts and examine each part: *to analyse a chemical compound*

analysis (*say* a-**nal**-a-sis) *noun*
1 the process of examining something critically 2 division into parts
• ***Word Family:*** the plural is **analyses** □ **analyst** (*say* **an**-a-list) *noun* someone skilled in analysis **analytical** *adjective* **analytically** *adverb*

anarchy (*say* **an**-a-kee) *noun*
1 disorder or lack of established government or control 2 a general state of confusion or uproar: *Anarchy reigned in the school during the teachers' strike.*
• ***Word Family:*** **anarchist** *noun* someone who believes in anarchy **anarchic** *adjective* **anarchism** *noun*
• ***Word Origins:*** from Greek words meaning "without a ruler"

anatomy (*say* a-**nat**-a-mee) *noun*
1 the inside structure of a human or an animal body 2 the study of the structure of humans and animals
• ***Word Family:*** **anatomist** *noun* a scientist who studies anatomy **anatomical** *adjective*

ancestor (*say* **an**-ses-tor) *noun*
a relative from whom you are descended and who can be traced through either of your parents
• ***Word Family:*** **ancestral** (*say* an-**ses**-tral) *adjective*: *The duke still lived in his ancestral home.* **ancestry** *noun*: *She was proud of her ancestry.*

anchor (*say* **an**-ka) *noun*
a heavy object attached to a ship by a rope or chain and lowered into the seabed to stop the ship from drifting
• ***Word Family:*** **anchorage** *noun* an area where ships may anchor **anchor** *verb*

ancient (*say* **ayn**-shent) *adjective*
1 happening or living long ago: *ancient history / the ancient Greeks* 2 very old: *an ancient wizard*
• ***Word Family:*** **ancient** *noun* someone who lived in ancient times

andante (*say* an-**dan**-tay) *adverb*
played or sung slowly and smoothly
• ***Word Origins:*** from an Italian word meaning "walking"

anecdote (*say* **an**-ek-dote) *noun*
a short, interesting or amusing story about a person or event

anemone (*say* a-**nem**-a-nee) *noun*
1 a small garden plant that looks like a poppy, with red, purple and white flowers 2 a sea creature that uses its tentacles to catch food

angel (*say* **ayn**-jel) *noun*
1 a messenger of God, pictured as a beautiful human with golden hair and wings 2 any beautiful or kind person: *You're an angel for helping me.*
• ***Word Family:*** **angelic** (*say* an-**jel**-ik) *adjective* **angelically** *adverb*

anger *noun*
a strong feeling of being not at all pleased with

someone, caused when you have been treated cruelly or unfairly: *Her rudeness increased the teacher's anger.*
•***Word Family:*** **anger** *verb: The rude names they shouted angered me.*

angle *noun*
1 the pointed space between two straight lines or planes which begin at the same point 2 an aspect or point of view: *We must consider the matter from all angles.*
angle *verb*
3 to place, bend or move something at an angle: *They angled the roof steeply to allow snow to slide off.* 4 to bias or slant something: *He angled the question so that only one answer was possible.*

angler *noun*
a person who goes fishing with a fishing rod
•***Word Family:*** **angling** *noun*

angora (*say* an-**gaw**-ra) *noun*
1 a cat, goat or rabbit with long, silky hair
2 the yarn or fabric made from the coat of one of these animals
•***Word Origins:*** from *Angora*, the former name of Ankara, the capital of Turkey

angry *adjective*
full of anger: *an angry child / an angry glare*
•***Word Family:*** the other forms are **angrier, angriest** □ **angrily** *adverb*

anguish (*say* **ang**-gwish) *noun*
extreme pain or suffering: *The decision caused them great anguish.*

animal *noun*
1 any living organism that is not a plant and can feel and move about for at least part of its life 2 any creature that is not a human
3 someone with beast-like behaviour or rough manners
•***Word Family:*** **animal** *adjective*

animate *verb*
1 to bring something alive or make it lively: *Her smile animates her face.* 2 to make something move as if it is living: *to animate a cartoon by photographing a series of drawings*
•***Word Family:*** **animate** *adjective* alive
animation *noun*

animosity (*say* an-ni-**mos**-i-tee) *noun*
a strong feeling that makes you want to act like an enemy: *He looked at the bully with animosity.*

ankle *noun*
the joint, made up of seven bones, connecting your lower leg to your foot

anklet *noun*
an ornamental band or chain worn around the ankle

annals *plural noun*
the historical records of events kept year by year
•***Word Family:*** **annalist** *noun*

annex (*say* a-**neks**) *verb*
to take over and attach to something you already own: *The country annexed several smaller territories during the war.*
•***Word Family:*** **annexation** *noun*

annexe (*say* **an**-eks) *noun*
a building or structure added to a larger one

annihilate (*say* a-**nigh**-a-late) *verb*
to completely destroy or defeat: *to annihilate an army*
•***Word Family:*** **annihilation** *noun*

anniversary (*say* an-i-**ver**-sa-ree) *noun*
the annual celebration or remembering of an event that took place on the same date in a past year: *a wedding anniversary*
•***Word Family:*** the plural is **anniversaries**

announce *verb*
to state or make known publicly: *The head teacher announced the winner.*
•***Word Family:*** **announcer** *noun* someone who announces or narrates, especially on radio or television **announcement** *noun*

annoy (*say* a-**noy**) *verb*
to displease or irritate someone
•***Word Family:*** **annoyance** *noun*

annual *adjective*
1 occurring once a year: *the annual fair*
annual *noun*
2 a book published once a year 3 a plant that lives for one season or one year
•***Word Family:*** **annually** *adverb*

anoint *verb*
to put oil or ointment on someone, especially in a religious ceremony
•***Word Family:*** **anointment** *noun*

anonymous (*say* a-**non**-i-mus) *adjective*
having an author who is unknown: *an anonymous poem*
•***Word Family:*** **anonymity** (*say* an-a-**nim**-i-tee) *noun* **anonymously** *adverb*

anorak (*say* **an**-a-rak) *noun*
a warm, waterproof jacket, usually with a hood
•***Word Origins:*** from an Inuit language

anorexia (*say* an-a-**rek**-si-a) *noun*
an eating disorder or illness during which someone refuses to eat normally because they think they are too fat
•***Word Family:*** **anorexic** *adjective* being extremely thin from anorexia
•***Word Origins:*** from a Greek word meaning "no appetite"

another (*say* a-**nuth**-er) *adjective*
1 an additional: *Pass me another biscuit.* 2 a different: *another day.*
• *Word Family:* **another** *pronoun*

answer (*say* **ahn**-sa) *noun*
1 a reply or response: *Please give me an answer to my request.* 2 a solution to a problem: *What was your last answer in the test?*
answer *verb*
3 to respond: *He answered with a wink.* 4 to reply to: *Answer the invitation.* 5 to correspond to: *The boy answers your description.*
• *Word Family:* **answerable** *adjective* responsible or accountable: *Who's answerable for this child's behaviour?*

ant *noun*
a small insect that builds, and lives in, a community or colony

antagonize or **antagonise** (*say* an-**tag**-a-nize) *verb*
to make someone hostile: *His movements antagonized the guard dog.*
• *Word Family:* **antagonism** *noun* open opposition or hostility **antagonistic** *adjective*

Antarctica *noun*
1 the continent around the South Pole, almost entirely covered by a vast ice sheet
antarctic *adjective*
2 to do with the icy region near the South Pole

ante- *prefix*
before in space or time: *antecedent*
• *Word Origins:* from Latin

anteater *noun*
an animal that feeds on ants and termites using its long, sticky tongue

antelope (*say* **an**-ta-lope) *noun*
a fast-running animal with horns, similar to deer

antenna (*say* an-**ten**-a) *noun*
1 one of two jointed feelers found on the heads of insects. 2 a radio or television aerial
• *Word Family:* the plural for definition 1 is **antennae** (*say* an-**ten**-ee) □ the plural for definition 2 is **antennas**

anthem *noun*
1 a short, solemn hymn or song of praise
2 **national anthem** a ceremonial song adopted by a country to express patriotism and loyalty

anthology (*say* an-**thol**-a-jee) *noun*
a collection of poems, songs, stories or plays written by different authors and published in one book
• *Word Family:* the plural is **anthologies**

anthropology (*say* an-thra-**pol**-a-jee) *noun*
the study of human beings and their customs
• *Word Family:* **anthropological** (*say* an-throp-a-**loj**-i-kal) *adjective* **anthropologist** *noun*

anti- *prefix*
against, opposite or opposed to: *anticlockwise*
• *Word Origins:* from Greek

antibiotic (*say* an-ti-by-**ot**-ik) *noun*
a drug, such as penicillin, used to kill bacteria or cure infections
• *Word Family:* **antibiotic** *adjective*

antibody (*say* **an**-ti-bod-ee) *noun*
a protein produced when any foreign substance enters your body to help it fight against disease
• *Word Family:* the plural is **antibodies**

anticipate (*say* an-**tis**-i-pate) *verb*
1 to expect or act beforehand: *Try to anticipate what your opponent will do./Police don't anticipate any trouble at the match.* 2 to foresee or mention before other people: *Jules Verne anticipated modern technology by 50 years.*
• *Word Family:* **anticipation** *noun*

anticlimax *noun*
something that lets you down or disappoints you: *The end of the film was rather an anticlimax.*
• *Word Family:* the plural is **anticlimaxes**

anticlockwise *adjective*
turning in the opposite direction to the hands on a clock

antics *plural noun*
silly or strange behaviour: *Journalists love to write about the antics of public figures.*

anticyclone *noun*
an area of high pressure

antidote *noun*
any substance that will work to stop the effects of a poison or disease: *the antidote for a spider bite*

antipodes (*say* an-**tip**-a-deez) *plural noun*
1 any two points directly opposite each other on a globe, such as the North and South Poles
2 **the Antipodes** Australia and New Zealand in relation to Britain
• *Word Family:* **antipodean** (*say* an-tip-a-**dee**-en) *adjective*

antiquated (*say* **an**-ti-kway-tid) *adjective*
old-fashioned, quaint or out of date: *Antiquated machinery is often valued as a collector's item.*
• *Word Family:* **antiquarian** *adjective*: *an antiquarian bookshop*

antique (*say* an-**teek**) *noun*
1 any rare or valued object from the past
antique *adjective*
2 dating from past times
• *Word Family:* **antiquities** *plural noun* any works

of art or ruins from the distant past: *Greek antiquities* **antiquity** (*say* an-**tik**-wi-tee) *noun* any ancient time or remote period
•***Word Origins:*** from a Latin word meaning "ancient"

anti-Semitic (*say* an-ti-sem-**it**-ik) *adjective*
unfriendly to Jewish people or discriminating against them
•***Word Family:*** **anti-Semite** *noun* **anti-Semitism** *noun*

antiseptic (*say* an-ti-**sep**-tik) *noun*
a substance that kills germs

antler *noun*
a bony, branching horn on the skull of deer

antonym (*say* **an**-ta-nim) *noun*
a word with the opposite meaning to another: *"Good" is an antonym of "bad".*

anus (*say* **ay**-nus) *noun*
the ring of muscle at the lower end of the alimentary canal, through which solid waste matter from the bowel is excreted
•***Word Family:*** **anal** *adjective*

anvil *noun*
a heavy iron block on which red-hot metals are hammered into shape by a blacksmith

anxiety (*say* ang-**zy**-a-tee) *noun*
worry or nervousness: *anxiety about public speaking*
•***Word Family:*** the plural is **anxieties**

anxious (*say* **ang**-shus) *adjective*
1 suffering from anxiety: *anxious about an exam*
2 eager: *anxious to be finished*
•***Word Family:*** **anxiously** *adverb*

Anzac *noun*
1 a soldier fighting in the Australian and New Zealand Army Corps during World War 1
2 the name given to these soldiers
•***Word Origins:*** an acronym from the first letter of the words Australian and New Zealand Army Corps

aorta (*say* ay-**or**-ta) *noun*
the largest artery in your body, arching out of your heart and carrying blood down through your diaphragm into your abdomen

apart *adverb*
1 separated into pieces: *to take an engine apart*
2 at a distance: *Keep the fighting children apart.*
apart *adjective*
3 separate or independent

apartheid (*say* a-**part**-hite) *noun*
a policy of keeping black and white people separated in a country

apartment *noun*
a flat or set of rooms in a large building: *holiday apartments*

apathy (*say* **ap**-a-thee) *noun*
a lack of interest or enthusiasm: *My suggestion of a picnic met with apathy.*
•***Word Family:*** **apathetic** (*say* ap-a-**thet**-ik) *adjective* **apathetically** *adverb*

ape *noun*
1 a large monkey with no tail, such as the chimpanzee, gibbon, gorilla and orang-outang
ape *verb*
2 to imitate or mimic: *She couldn't help aping her teacher.*

aperture (*say* **ap**-a-cher) *noun*
1 a gap or opening 2 the size of the adjustable opening in a camera that lets in light

apex (*say* **ay**-peks) *noun*
the highest point or summit: *The apex of a triangle is opposite its base.*
•***Word Family:*** the plural is **apexes** or **apices**

apiary (*say* **ape**-ya-ree) *noun*
a place where beehives are kept
•***Word Family:*** the plural is **apiaries** □ **apiarian** *adjective* having to do with the breeding and care of bees **apiarist** *noun* someone who keeps bees

aplomb (*say* a-**plom**) *noun*
the ability to do something difficult with great confidence

apocalypse (*say* a-**pok**-a-lips) *noun*
any revelation or remarkable disclosure, such as the end of the world as revealed in the last chapter of the Bible
•***Word Family:*** **apocalyptic** *adjective*

apology (*say* a-**pol**-a-jee) *noun*
something you say or write in order to say sorry
•***Word Family:*** the plural is **apologies** □ **apologize** or **apologise** *verb* **apologetic** *adjective*

apostle (*say* a-**pos**-al) *noun*
1 one of the twelve original disciples of Christ, chosen by him to teach his message to others
2 someone who believes strongly in a cause or idea and tries to convince everyone else about it: *an apostle of computerization*

apostrophe (*say* a-**pos**-tra-fee) *noun*
1 a punctuation mark (') used to show that something is owned, as in *John's book* / *the boys' father* 2 a punctuation mark used to show that letters or numbers have been left out, as in *I'll tell him* and *the summer of '76*

appal (*say* a-**pawl**) *verb*
to shock or fill with horror: *to be appalled at bad news*
•***Word Family:*** other forms are **appals, appalled, appalling**

appalling *adjective*
1 shocking you or filling you with horror: *an*

appalling accident 2 of very poor quality: *Her handwriting is appalling.*

apparatus (*say* ap-a-**ray**-tus) *noun*
equipment you need for a particular task: *scientific apparatus*
• ***Word Family:*** plural is **apparatus** or **apparatuses**

apparent (*say* a-**par**-ent) *adjective*
1 easily seen or understood: *It's quite apparent that you don't want to come.* 2 seeming true or real, without being so: *her apparent confidence.*
• ***Word Family:*** **apparently** *adverb*

apparition (*say* ap-a-**rish**-on) *noun*
a sudden or frightening vision, especially a ghost

appeal (*say* a-**peel**) *verb*
1 to make an urgent call or request for something: *He appealed for calm.* 2 **appeal to** to interest or attract: *Does that book appeal to you?* 3 to apply for a legal case to be heard again by a higher court
• ***Word Family:*** **appealing** *adjective* attractive and interesting **appeal** *noun*

appear (*say* a-**peer**) *verb*
1 to become clear or visible: *The sun appeared at last.* 2 to seem: *Try not to appear frightened.* 3 to attend a court of law as part of a court case: *She will be appearing next Thursday.* 4 to take part in a film or play: *He has appeared in six Dracula films.*

appearance *noun*
1 what your face looks like, or the way you dress: *I described his appearance to the police.* 2 becoming clear or visible 3 the way something seems to be 4 attendance at a court of law as part of a court case 5 taking part in film or play

appendicitis (*say* a-pen-di-**sigh**-tis) *noun*
a very painful inflammation of the appendix, which may require it to be removed
• ***Word Family:*** **appendectomy** *noun* an operation to remove the appendix

appendix (*say* a-**pen**-diks) *noun*
1 extra material added at the end of a book, such as lists or tables 2 a small tube on the right side of your abdomen, which joins onto your bowel
• ***Word Family:*** the plural is **appendices** or **appendixes**
• ***Word Origins:*** from a Latin word meaning "something added on"

appetite (*say* **ap**-a-tite) *noun*
a desire or craving, especially for food

appetizing or **appetising** *adjective*
stimulating your appetite by smelling or looking good to eat: *an appetizing smell from the kitchen*
• ***Word Family:*** **appetizer** *noun* a small snack or drink served before a meal to stimulate your appetite

applaud (*say* a-**plawd**) *verb*
to express approval or praise, for example by clapping
• ***Word Family:*** **applause** *noun*

apple *noun*
a round fruit with crisp, firm flesh and a green or red skin

appliance (*say* a-**ply**-ance) *noun*
a device or tool designed for a special use, especially in the home: *An iron is an essential household appliance.*

applicant (*say* **ap**-li-kant) *noun*
a person who is applying for something such as a job

application *noun*
1 a formal or written request: *We regret to inform you that your application has been unsuccessful.* 2 hard work and concentration: *She shows great application.*

apply (*say* a-**ply**) *verb*
1 to put on or into use: *to apply glue sparingly / to solve a mystery by applying common sense* 2 to request or ask to be given: *A hundred people applied for the job.* 3 **apply yourself** to work hard and concentrate 4 **apply to** to concern or affect: *These rules do not apply to pupils who bring a packed lunch.*
• ***Word Family:*** other forms are **applies, applied, applying** □ **applied** *adjective* put into or designed for practical use: *applied maths*

appoint *verb*
to select a person for a job: *to appoint a lunch monitor*
• ***Word Family:*** **appointed** *adjective* fixed or arranged: *We met at the appointed time.* **appointee** *noun* someone who is appointed

appointment *noun*
1 an arrangement to meet or visit: *I have an appointment with the dentist after school.* 2 a job to which someone is appointed: *His new appointment is with the Skateboard Association.*

appreciate (*say* a-**pree**-shi-ate) *verb*
1 to value highly: *I really appreciate your help.* 2 to understand: *We appreciate your concern.* 3 to rise in value: *The houses in our street have appreciated considerably in the past year.*
• ***Word Family:*** **appreciable** *adjective* noticeable, or fairly large **appreciably** *adverb* **appreciation** *noun* **appreciative** *adjective*

apprehend (*say* ap-ree-**hend**) *verb*
1 to arrest or seize: *The police apprehended him a week after the robbery.* 2 to understand the

A B C D E F G H I J K L M N O P Q R S T U V W X Y Z

meaning of: *She was quick to apprehend the extent of the disaster.*

apprehensive (*say* ap-ree-**hen**-siv) *adjective*
worried or nervous about what might go wrong: *apprehensive about starting school*
•***Word Family:*** **apprehension** *noun* **apprehensively** *adverb* **apprehensiveness** *noun*

apprentice (*say* a-**pren**-tis) *noun*
someone who is learning how to do something
•***Word Family:*** **apprentice** *verb* **apprenticeship** *noun*

approach *verb*
1 to move nearer to, or come near: *We approached the house cautiously. / As dawn approached we got ready to leave.* 2 to make a request to: *You should approach your local Member of Parliament about this problem.* 3 to deal with a problem: *I'd approach it like this.*
•***Word Family:*** **approach** *noun*

approachable *adjective*
friendly and easy to talk to

appropriate (*say* a-**pro**-pree-it) *adjective*
1 suitable or right for the situation: *an appropriate dress for a party*
appropriate (*say* a-**pro**-pree-ate) *verb*
2 to take something for yourself, especially without permission: *I have appropriated my brother's guitar.*
•***Word Family:*** **appropriation** *noun* **appropriately** *adverb* **appropriateness** *noun*
•***Word Origins:*** from a Latin word meaning "made your own"

approve (*say* a-**proov**) *verb*
1 to agree to: *The committee has officially approved our request.* 2 **approve of** to consider as good or right: *We don't approve of your selfish behaviour.*
•***Word Family:*** **approval** *noun*

approximate (*say* a-**prok**-si-mit) *adjective*
1 more or less right, but not exactly: *Tell us the approximate price.*
approximate (*say* a-**prok**-si-mate) *verb*
2 to be almost as much as or nearly equal to: *My athletics score approximates hers.*
•***Word Family:*** **approximately** *adverb* **approximation** *noun*

apricot (*say* **ay**-pri-kot) *noun*
1 a small, round fruit with soft orange flesh and a hard stone 2 a yellowish-orange colour
apricot *adjective*
3 having an apricot colour

April *noun*
the fourth month of the year, with 30 days

apron *noun*
a loose piece of clothing worn over the front of other clothes to protect them, usually tied at the back

aptitude *noun*
a natural ability or skill to learn something quickly and well: *an aptitude for sport*

aqualung (*say* **ak**-wa-lung) *noun*
a tank of air that a diver uses to breathe underwater through a tube attached to a mouthpiece

aquarium (*say* a-**kwair**-i-um) *noun*
a tank or building in which fish or other water-living animals are kept and displayed
•***Word Family:*** the plural is **aquariums** or **aquaria**

aquatic (*say* a-**kwot**-ik) *adjective*
1 living or growing in water: *an aquatic plant.* 2 taking place in or on water: *aquatic sports*

aqueduct (*say* **ak**-wa-dukt) *noun*
a bridge for carrying water across a valley

aquiline (*say* **ak**-wa-line) *adjective*
curved or hooked like the beak of an eagle: *an aquiline nose*
•***Word Origins:*** from a Latin word meaning "eagle"

arable (*say* **ar**-a-bel) *adjective*
suitable for growing crops: *arable land*

arachnid (*say* a-**rack**-nid) *noun*
a creature such as a spider or scorpion, that has eight legs

arbitrary (*say* **ar**-ba-tree) *adjective*
based on your own feelings rather than being properly worked out or carefully planned: *an arbitrary decision*
•***Word Family:*** **arbitrarily** *adverb* **arbitrariness** *noun*

arbitrate *verb*
to officially judge, decide or settle a dispute
•***Word Family:*** **arbitrator** or **arbiter** *noun* someone appointed to settle disputes **arbitration** *noun*

arboreal (*say* ar-**baw**-ree-al) *adjective*
of, like or adapted to living in trees: *A koala is an arboreal marsupial.*

arbour or arbor (*say* **ar**-ba) *noun*
a shady place among trees, especially in a garden

arc *noun*
1 a curved line: *the arc of a circle* 2 anything shaped like an arc: *the arc of a rainbow*
•***Word Family:*** **arc** *verb*
•***Word Origins:*** from a Latin word meaning "a bow or arch"

arcade *noun*
a hall or passage, often with shops or video games along its sides: *an amusement arcade*

arch *noun*
1 a curved structure that supports an overlying weight such as the roof of a building or the roadways of a bridge 2 something shaped like an arch: *the arch of your foot*
arch *verb*
3 to form an arch or curve

archaeology or **archeology** (*say* ar-ki-**ol**-a-jee) *noun*
the study of ancient cultures by digging up and examining things they have left behind, such as buildings, pots or coins
•***Word Family:*** **archaeologist** *noun* **archaeological** *adjective*

archaic (*say* ar-**kay**-ik) *adjective*
from long ago and not used any more: *an archaic word*

archangel (*say* **ark**-ayn-jel) *noun*
a head or chief angel

archbishop *noun*
a head or chief bishop

archer *noun*
someone who shoots with a bow and arrow, especially for sport
•***Word Family:*** **archery** *noun*

architecture (*say* **ar**-ki-tek-cher) *noun*
1 the art or science of designing buildings 2 a particular style of building: *Gothic architecture*
•***Word Family:*** **architect** *noun* someone trained in architecture **architectural** *adjective*

archives (*say* **ar**-kives) *plural noun*
1 a collection of documents or historical records 2 the place where these are stored
•***Word Family:*** **archival** *adjective*: *archival material* **archivist** (*say* **ar**-ki-vist) *noun* someone who looks after archives **archive** *verb*

arctic *adjective*
1 at or near the North Pole 2 icy cold: *arctic conditions*
arctic *noun*
3 **the Arctic** the region around the North Pole

ardent *adjective*
full of passion or enthusiasm
•***Word Family:*** **ardently** *adverb*

ardour (*say* **ar**-da) *noun*
enthusiasm or passion: *He sings with great ardour.*

arduous (*say* **ard**-yew-us) *adjective*
needing great effort or energy: *Marathon running is an arduous sport.*
•***Word Family:*** **arduously** *adverb* **arduousness** *noun*

area (*say* **air**-ee-a) *noun*
1 the total surface measurement: *What's the area of our garden?* 2 a particular part of a place or piece of land: *a rural area* 3 a subject or topic: *This is an area we haven't looked at yet*

arena (*say* a-**ree**-na) *noun*
a field or space set aside for sports or contests

arguable *adjective*
1 able to be doubted or disputed: *an arguable opinion* 2 able to be supported by reasons: *It is arguable that this is the best one of all.*
•***Word Family:*** **arguably** *adverb*

argue (*say* **ar**-gew) *verb*
1 to exchange angry words: *to argue about the money* 2 to give reasons for or against something: *to argue in favour of nuclear power*
•***Word Family:*** other forms are **argues, argued, arguing**

argument (*say* **ar**-gew-ment) *noun*
1 a disagreement or quarrel 2 a reason given to explain or prove: *a good argument for wearing seat belts*
•***Word Family:*** **argumentative** *adjective* fond of arguing

aria (*say* **ar**-i-a) *noun*
a song for one of the leading singers in an opera or other choral work

arid *adjective*
very dry: *the arid Sahara desert*
•***Word Family:*** **aridity** (*say* a-**rid**-i-tee) *noun*

arise *verb*
1 to appear or come into existence: *New problems may arise.* 2 to get up or move upwards
•***Word Family:*** other forms are **arises, arose, arisen, arising**

aristocracy (*say* ar-is-**tok**-ra-see) *noun*
the people belonging to the most powerful or wealthy group in a country, usually by birth or marriage
•***Word Family:*** **aristocrat** *noun* a member of the aristocracy **aristocratic** *adjective*

arithmetic (*say* a-**rith**-ma-tik) *noun*
the branch of maths that studies numbers and the use of addition, subtraction, multiplication and division
•***Word Family:*** **arithmetical** *adjective* **arithmetician** *noun*

ark *noun*
the boat built by Noah in order to survive the Flood written about in the Bible

arm (1) *noun*
1 the part of your body between your shoulder and your wrist 2 the part of a garment covering

A B C D E F G H I J K L M N O P Q R S T U V W X Y Z

the arm 3 something that is shaped like or works like an arm: *the arm of a chair*

arm (2) *verb*
to equip with weapons

armada (*say* ar-**mah**-da) *noun*
a large fleet of ships, especially warships

armaments (*say* **ar**-ma-ments) *plural noun*
the weapons used to equip a tank, bomber or warship

armed *adjective*
having weapons, especially guns: *the armed forces / They were held up by two armed robbers.*

armistice (*say* **arm**-i-stis) *noun*
a temporary peace agreement between countries involved in a war

armour *noun*
1 protective covering, such as chain mail for the body or steel plating on tanks or battleships
2 anything that protects or keeps something safe
armour *verb*
3 to fit with armour
•***Word Family:*** **armoured** *adjective: an armoured car* **armourer** *noun* someone who makes or sells armour or weapons **armoury** *noun*

armpit *noun*
the place under the arm where it joins the body

arms *plural noun*
weapons

army *noun*
1 an organized group trained and equipped to fight on land 2 a large, organized group: *an army of cleaners*
•***Word Family:*** the plural is **armies**

aroma (*say* a-**ro**-ma) *noun*
a strong or pleasant smell: *the aroma of coffee*
•***Word Family:*** **aromatic** (*say* ar-a-**mat**-ik) *adjective* having a sweet or pleasant smell
•***Word Origins:*** from a Greek word meaning "spice"

around *preposition*
1 on all sides of: *There were people around us.*
2 from one part or place to another of: *We walked around the city.* 3 at approximately the time and place talked about: *I'll meet you around one o'clock.*

arouse (*say* a-**rowz**) *verb*
to wake or stir up: *to arouse from sleep / His odd behaviour aroused her suspicions.*
•***Word Family:*** **arousal** *noun*

arpeggio (*say* ar-**pej**-i-o) *noun*
the playing of the notes of a musical chord one after the other instead of all at once
•***Word Family:*** the plural is **arpeggios**

arrange *verb*
1 to set in order: *to arrange chairs around a table* 2 to prepare or organize: *to arrange a trip* 3 to adapt: *to arrange a song for the piano* 4 to agree: *to arrange to meet later*
•***Word Family:*** **arrangement** *noun*

arrears (*say* a-**rears**) *plural noun*
1 money that should already have been paid to someone, for example rent that you owe 2 **in arrears** still owing money after it should have been paid: *in arrears with the rent / to pay in arrears*

arrest (*say* a-**rest**) *verb*
1 to officially stop or catch someone because they have broken the law 2 to stop: *to arrest the spread of a disease*
•***Word Family:*** **arresting** *adjective* surprising or startling **arrest** *noun*

arrive (*say* a-**rive**) *verb*
1 to come to the end of a journey: *to arrive at your destination* 2 to come: *Her birthday finally arrived.*
•***Word Family:*** **arrival** *noun*

arrogant (*say* **ar**-a-gant) *adjective*
behaving as if you are better than everyone else: *His arrogant manner made him unpopular.*
•***Word Family:*** **arrogance** *noun* **arrogantly** *adverb*

arrow *noun*
1 a long, slender shaft with a point at one end and feathers at the other, shot from a bow 2 a sign in the shape of an arrow used to point the direction

arsenal (*say* **ar**-sa-nal) *noun*
a place where weapons and ammunition are manufactured or stored

arsenic (*say* **ar**-se-nik) *noun*
a very poisonous chemical, used in insecticides and weedkillers

arson *noun*
the deliberate burning or setting fire to something, especially a building
•***Word Family:*** **arsonist** *noun*

art *noun*
1 the creation or production of something that expresses your feelings or ideas, for example by painting, sculpture or composing music 2 the works that artists produce 3 a particular skill or technique: *the art of cookery*

artefact (*say* **ar**-ta-fakt) *noun*
an object made by humans, such as a tool or work of art

artery (*say* **art**-a-ree) *noun*
1 one of the thick-walled tubes carrying blood

away from the heart to other parts of the body 2 a major road or railway in a transport system
•**Word Family:** the plural is **arteries** ☐ **arterial** *adjective*

artesian well (*say* ar-**tee**-zhan well) *noun*
a well in which water rises, under pressure, above the level of the water-bearing rock to the earth's surface

artful *noun*
1 good at tricking or deceiving people
2 skilfully done or made: *an artful film*

arthritis (*say* ar-**thrie**-tis) *noun*
a disease or condition that inflames and swells the joints, making it painful and difficult to move
•**Word Family: arthritic** (*say* ar-**thrit**-ik) *adjective*

arthropod (*say* **ar**-thra-pod) *noun*
an animal with a segmented body, jointed legs, sometimes a hard, external skeleton and with no backbone, such as an insect or a spider

artichoke *noun*
1 **globe artichoke** a thistle-like plant with a flower head consisting of many small, fleshy, tightly-folded leaves that is eaten as a vegetable
2 **Jerusalem artichoke** a type of sunflower with an underground stem you can eat

article *noun*
1 an individual thing or object: *They stole several valuable articles.* 2 a word, such as "a", "an" and "the", used before a noun to indicate any person or thing, or one particular person or thing 3 a piece of writing that gives information or an opinion in a magazine or newspaper: *an article on gardening*

articulate (*say* ar-**tik**-yoo-lit) *adjective*
1 clear in your speech or expression 2 able to speak
articulate (*say* ar-**tik**-yoo-late) *verb*
3 to pronounce clearly: *to articulate your words so that people at the back of the hall can hear*
•**Word Family: articulated** *adjective* having joints **articulation** *noun*
•**Word Origins:** from a Latin word meaning "to divide into joints"

artificial (*say* ar-ti-**fish**-al) *adjective*
made by people, rather than occurring in nature: *artificial flowers*
•**Word Family: artificiality** *noun* **artificially** *adverb*

artillery (*say* ar-**til**-a-ree) *noun*
1 large guns such as cannons 2 the branch of an army that uses such guns

artisan (*say* **ar**-ti-zhan) *noun*
a trained or skilled worker who makes things using hand tools rather than machinery

artist *noun*
1 someone who creates works of art, especially a painter or sculptor 2 an entertainer, especially a singer or dancer
•**Word Family: artistic** *adjective* able to create works of art as artists do **artistically** *adverb* **artistry** *noun*

as *adverb*
1 to the amount or degree that: *Hard as he tries, he never wins.* 2 for example: *Cities such as London and Sydney.*
as *conjunction*
3 when or while: *As we approached, the door opened.* 4 because: *As he was late, we couldn't start.* 5 like or in the manner of: *quick as lightning*
as *pronoun*
6 in the function or position of: *Let this serve as a warning.*

asbestos (*say* az-**bes**-tos) *noun*
a grey, fireproof material now known to cause lung diseases and cancer

ascend (*say* a-**send**) *verb*
to rise or climb: *to ascend a ladder*
•**Word Family: ascent** *noun* **(a)** a climb: *the ascent of Everest* **(b)** an upward slope: *a steep ascent*

ascetic (*say* a-**set**-ik) *noun*
someone who has a strict and simple way of life, denying themselves the pleasures of everyday living
•**Word Family: ascetically** *adverb* **asceticism** *noun*
•**Word Origins:** from the Greek word for a "hermit"

ash (1) *noun*
1 the powdery remains of anything that has been burnt: *cigarette ash* 2 **ashes** the remains of a human body after cremation

ash (2) *noun*
a tree with grey bark and hard, tough wood used for timber

ashamed *adjective*
1 feeling shame or guilt: *I'm ashamed of laughing at him.* 2 unwilling through fear of shame: *Don't be ashamed to say you're sorry.*

ashen *adjective*
pale or grey: *ashen-faced refugees*

ashore *adverb*
towards or onto the shore from the sea: *He swam ashore in the dark.*

aside *adverb*
1 on or to one side: *to turn aside at the last moment / Put aside some money for the holiday.*

A B C D E F G H I J K L M N O P Q R S T U V W X Y Z

aside *noun*
2 a remark spoken quietly so that only certain people will hear

ask *verb*
1 to seek a reply or response from someone or about something: *Don't ask me! / May I ask how old you are?* 2 to invite: *We asked them home after school.*

askew (*say* as-**kew**) *adverb*
crooked or out of position: *We wear our baseball caps askew.*

asleep *adverb*
1 in or into a state of sleep: *to fall asleep*
asleep *adjective*
2 sleeping: *Is the baby asleep?* 3 numb: *My foot's asleep.*

asp *noun*
a small venomous snake, such as the Egyptian viper

asparagus (*say* a-**spar**-a-gus) *noun*
a plant related to the lily, with long soft green shoots which are eaten as a vegetable

aspect *noun*
1 a part of a situation or problem: *It's an aspect of his personality that I don't like.* 2 the look or appearance of anything: *the pale aspect of his face after the accident* 3 the direction something faces: *The front rooms have a northerly aspect.*

aspersions (*say* a-**sper**-shons) *plural noun*
unkind or damaging criticism: *to cast aspersions on someone's good name*

asphalt (*say* **ash**-felt) *noun*
a black, sticky substance made by mixing bitumen, oil and small stones, used to make road surfaces, runways and playgrounds

aspirin (*say* -**ass**-prin) *noun*
1 a drug used to reduce pain, fever or swelling
2 a tablet of this drug: *take a couple of aspirin*

ass *noun*
1 a donkey 2 a stupid person
• ***Word Family:*** the plural is **asses**

assassin (*say* a-**sas**-in) *noun*
someone who murders an important person such as a politician or religious leader
• ***Word Family:*** **assassinate** *verb* to kill an important person such as a politician or religious leader **assassination** *noun*

assault (*say* a-**salt**) *verb*
1 to attack violently
assault *noun*
2 an attack

assemble (*say* a-**sem**-bul) *verb*
1 to meet or gather: *We'll assemble outside the hall.* 2 to put together: *to assemble a model aeroplane*

assembly (*say* a-**sem**-blee) *noun*
1 a group of people gathered together for a particular purpose: *a school assembly* 2 the putting together of something, especially parts of machines
• ***Word Family:*** the plural is **assemblies**

assert (*say* a-**sert**) *verb*
1 to state firmly: *to assert your innocence*
2 **assert yourself** to speak up firmly or strongly to support your wishes or beliefs
• ***Word Family:*** **assertion** *noun* a strong statement **assertive** *adjective* speaking out forcefully **assertively** *adverb* **assertiveness** *noun*

assess (*say* a-**ses**) *verb*
1 to examine or judge: *Let's assess the situation.*
2 to work out or estimate a price for goods or services
• ***Word Family:*** **assessor** *noun* someone appointed to assess or advise **assessment** *noun*

asset *noun*
1 anything that is useful or valuable: *He is a great asset to the football team.* 2 **assets** all the property and other things you own and could sell to raise money

assignment (*say* a-**sine**-ment) *noun*
a particular task or duty: *The reporter was given an assignment overseas.*
• ***Word Family:*** **assign** *verb* to appoint or allocate: *She's been assigned to the company's Newcastle office.*

assimilate (*say* a-**sim**-i-late) *verb*
to absorb or take in: *to assimilate information*
• ***Word Family:*** **assimilation** *noun*

assist *verb*
to help: *The mountain rescue team was assisted by several volunteers.*
• ***Word Family:*** **assistance** *noun* help **assistant** *noun* a helper

associate (*say* a-**so**-see-ate) *verb*
1 to connect in your mind: *to associate swimming with summer* 2 **associate with** to spend your time with someone: *He associates with some odd people.*
associate (*say* a-**so**-see-it) *noun*
3 a partner or colleague

association *noun*
1 a group of people joined or organized together for a common purpose: *the National Association of Head Teachers* 2 the link or connection you make between things: *an association of ideas in your mind*

assonance (*say* **ass**-a-nunce) *noun*
a similarity between sounds, especially the

repeating of vowel sounds in the words of a line of poetry
•**Word Family:** **assonant** *adjective*

assume (*say* ass-**yoom**) *verb*
1 to suppose to be true, especially without proof: *Let's assume you are right.* 2 to take on: *She assumed command of the group.*
•**Word Family:** **assumption** *noun* something assumed: *That's an assumption, not a fact.*

assure (*say* a-**sure**) *verb*
1 to convince: *He assured us that he would return.* 2 to make sure or secure: *Our victory is assured.*
•**Word Family:** **assurance** *noun* a promise **assured** *adjective*: *an assured manner* **assuredly** *adverb* certainly or definitely

asterisk (*say* **ast**-a-risk) *noun*
a mark (*) used beside a word in writing or printing to show the reader that extra information appears at the bottom of the page
•**Word Origins:** from a Greek word meaning "small star"

asteroid (*say* **ast**-a-royd) *noun*
one of the small planets, all less than 500 kilometres in diameter, found between Mars and Jupiter

asthma (*say* **as**-ma) *noun*
a breathing disorder due to the narrowing of the air passages, causing wheezing and shortness of breath
•**Word Family:** **asthmatic** *adjective* suffering from asthma **asthmatic** *noun* someone who suffers from asthma
•**Word Origins:** from a Greek word meaning "panting"

astonish *verb*
to surprise very much: *The news astonished us.*
•**Word Family:** **astonishing** *adjective* **astonishingly** *adverb* **astonishment** *noun*

astound *verb*
to surprise, confuse or shock: *We were astounded at his bad behaviour.*
•**Word Family:** **astounding** *adjective* **astoundingly** *adverb*

astray (*say* a-**stray**) *adverb*
1 **go astray** to disappear, be lost or stolen: *Several library books have gone astray.* 2 **lead astray** to encourage someone to behave badly or wrongly: *He was led astray by the older boys.*

astringent (*say* a-**strin**-jent) *adjective*
1 causing the pores of your skin to tighten and tingle: *an astringent lotion* 2 harsh and severe: *Such astringent comments made us flinch.*

astrology (*say* a-**strol**-a-jee) *noun*
the study of the influence the stars are supposed to have on human lives and events
•**Word Family:** **astrologer** *noun* **astrological** *adjective* **astrologically** *adverb*

astronaut (*say* **ast**-ra-nawt) *noun*
someone trained to operate and travel in spacecraft
•**Word Family:** **astronautics** *plural noun* the study of space flight

astronomical (*say* as-tra-**nom**-i-kul) *adjective*
1 to do with astronomy 2 immensely large: *an astronomical rise in the price of petrol*
•**Word Family:** **astronomically** *adverb*

astronomy (*say* a-**stron**-a-mee) *noun*
the scientific study of planets and stars, their movements, positions and what they are made of
•**Word Family:** **astronomer** *noun*

astute (*say* as-**tewt**) *adjective*
clever and quick at understanding things: *astute comments*
•**Word Family:** **astutely** *adverb* **astuteness** *noun*

asunder (*say* a-**sun**-da) *adverb*
apart or into separate pieces: *The storm tore the roof asunder.*

asylum (*say* a-**sigh**-lum) *noun*
1 a hospital or refuge, often providing care for people with mental illness 2 protection or shelter, especially given to political refugees fleeing from their own country

atheist (*say* **ay**-thee-ist) *noun*
someone who does not believe in God
•**Word Family:** **atheism** *noun* **atheistic** *adjective*

athlete (*say* **ath**-leet) *noun*
someone trained to take part in sporting events such as running, jumping and throwing
•**Word Family:** **athletic** *adjective* **athletics** *noun*

atlas *noun*
a book of maps
•**Word Family:** the plural is **atlases**

atmosphere (*say* **at**-mos-fear) *noun*
1 the mixture of gases surrounding the earth, a star or a planet 2 the feeling or mood of a situation: *There was a crazy atmosphere at the disco.*
•**Word Family:** **atmospheric** *adjective*: *atmospheric pressure*

atoll (*say* **at**-ol) *noun*
a circular coral island, usually enclosing a lagoon

atom (*say* **at**-om) *noun*
the smallest part of a chemical element that can take part in a chemical reaction
•**Word Family:** **atomic** (*say* a-**tom**-ik) *adjective*

atomic bomb *noun*
a powerful bomb that explodes by splitting atoms, releasing nuclear energy

atomic energy *noun*
the power produced by splitting or forcing together atoms

atonal (*say* ay-**toh**-nal) *adjective*
not written in any particular musical key: *atonal music*

atone *verb*
to show you are sorry and try to make things better: *I helped him with his homework to atone for my unkindness.*
• ***Word Family:*** **atonement** *noun*

atrocious (*say* a-**tro**-shus) *adjective*
1 extremely cruel or wicked: *an atrocious act of terrorism* 2 very bad: *atrocious violin playing*
• ***Word Family:*** **atrocity** *noun* (**atrocities**) an atrocious act **atrociously** *adverb*

attach *verb*
1 to connect or fasten: *The shelves attach to the wall.* 2 **be attached to** to like strongly or be very fond of: *She's very attached to her cat.*
• ***Word Family:*** **attachment** *noun* a bond of affection between people

attack *verb*
1 to set upon with great force or violence: *The enemy attacked the fort at nightfall.* 2 to criticize strongly: *He attacked the newspaper for false reporting.* 3 to begin with energy: *to attack a meal*
• ***Word Family:*** **attack** *noun* **attacker** *noun*

attempt *noun*
1 an effort to achieve something: *an attempt at the world record* 2 an attack: *The assassin made an attempt on her life.*
attempt *verb*
3 to try to do something

attend *verb*
1 to be present at: *Did you attend school yesterday?* 2 to help or look after: *An army of doctors attended the victims of the blast.* 3 to pay attention: *Please attend to your work.*
• ***Word Family:*** **attendance** *noun* the number of people present **attendant** *noun* someone who helps to look after people

attention *noun*
1 concentrating or directing your thoughts on something: *Pay attention!* 2 consideration: *Your letter will receive early attention.* 3 **at attention** the position when you stand with your feet together and your arms at your sides
• ***Word Family:*** **attentive** *adjective* helpful **attentively** *adverb* **attentiveness** *noun*

attic *noun*
the room or space immediately under the roof of a house

attire *noun*
your clothes, especially the ones you wear to something special: *to put on formal attire for the wedding*

attitude *noun*
1 your views on a particular subject: *What's your attitude to gambling?* 2 the way you speak and behave: *I don't like your attitude.*

attorney (*say* a-**ter**-nee) *noun*
1 an American word for a lawyer 2 **power of attorney** the legal authority given by one person to another, to act on his or her behalf
• ***Word Family:*** the plural is **attorneys**

attract (*say* a-**trakt**) *verb*
1 to pull or cause to move towards: *The magnet attracts pins.* 2 to arouse interest or attention: *The show attracted a large audience.*
• ***Word Family:*** **attractive** *adjective* pleasing: *an attractive woman / an attractive proposal* **attraction** *noun* **attractively** *adverb*

attribute (*say* a-**trib**-yewt) *verb*
1 to consider as belonging to or created by: *This painting is attributed to Monet. / remarks attributed to the Prime Minister*
attribute (*say* **at**-rib-yewt) *noun*
2 a quality or characteristic: *the powerful attributes of intelligence and beauty*
• ***Word Family:*** **attributable** *adjective* able to be attributed to **attribution** *noun*

auburn (*say* **aw**-burn) *noun*
a rich, reddish-brown colour
• ***Word Family:*** **auburn** *adjective: auburn hair*

auction (*say* **ok**-shon) *noun*
a public sale at which goods are sold to the highest bidder
• ***Word Family:*** **auctioneer** *noun* someone who sells goods at an auction **auction** *verb*

audacious (*say* aw-**day**-shus) *adjective*
daring or recklessly bold: *an audacious bank robbery*
• ***Word Family:*** **audacity** *noun* **audaciously** *adverb*

audible (*say* **aw**-di-bul) *adjective*
loud enough to be heard: *an audible reply*
• ***Word Family:*** **audibility** *noun* **audibly** *adverb*

audience (*say* **aw**-di-ence) *noun*
1 the people attending or listening to something, especially a play, concert or lecture 2 a formal meeting held by a high official or ruler: *an audience with the Pope*

audiovisual (*say* **aw**-dio-**vish**-ual) *adjective*
using sound and picture together: *audiovisual equipment / an audiovisual display*

audit *noun*
an official examination of financial records
• ***Word Family:*** **auditor** *noun* someone appointed to make an audit

audition (*say* aw-**dish**-on) *noun*
a trial performance to test whether someone is suitable for a part in a play, to play in an orchestra, and so on
•*Word Family:* **audition** *verb: to audition for a film role*

auditorium (*say* aw-di-**taw**-ri-um) *noun*
the area in a large theatre or concert hall where the audience sits

auditory (*say* **or**-da-tree) *adjective*
having to do with hearing or the ears: *two auditory nerves*

augment (*say* awg-**ment**) *verb*
to increase or add to: *doing odd jobs to augment your pocket money*
•*Word Family:* **augmentation** *noun*

August (*say* **aw**-gust) *noun*
the eighth month of the year, with 31 days
•*Word Origins:* named after the Roman Emperor *Augustus*

aunt (*say* **arnt**) *noun*
1 a sister of one of your parents 2 your uncle's wife

au pair (*say* oh-**pair**) *noun*
1 a person, usually a young woman, who comes from another country to stay with a family in their home and helps to look after the children
au pair *verb*
2 to work as an au pair

aura (*say* **or**-a) *noun*
the particular atmosphere or feeling surrounding something: *The end of term has an aura of excitement.*

aural (*say* **aw**-ral) *adjective*
to do with or heard by the ear: *an aural test.*

aurora (*say* a-**raw**-ra) *noun*
a coloured glow seen high in the sky near the two poles, caused by particles from the sun hitting the earth's atmosphere

auspicious (*say* aws-**pish**-us) *adjective*
likely to be successful: *an auspicious start to the year*

Aussie (*say* **oz**-ee) *noun*
an Australian

austere (*say* **os**-teer) *adjective*
1 morally strict or restrained: *the austere life of a monk* 2 not comfortable or decorated: *They worked in austere surroundings.*
•*Word Family:* **austerely** *adverb* **austerity** *noun*

authentic (*say* aw-**then**-tik) *adjective*
1 genuine: *an authentic Roman necklace*
2 accurate or true: *an authentic account of what happened*
•*Word Family:* **authenticate** *verb* to prove to be genuine **authentically** *adverb* **authenticity** *noun*

author (*say* **aw**-tha) *noun*
1 someone who writes something, such as a book or article 2 someone who originates or creates something: *Who was the author of this scheme?*
•*Word Family:* **authorial** *adjective* **authorship** *noun*

authoritarian (*say* aw-thor-i-**tair**-i-an) *adjective*
in favour of obedience to authority, rather than individual freedom
•*Word Family:* **authoritarianism** *noun*

authority (*say* aw-**thor**-i-tee) *noun*
1 the power or right to give orders and make others obey: *the authority of the law / to speak with authority* 2 permission: *Who gave you the authority to do this?* 3 an expert or reliable source: *He's an authority on road safety.* 4 an organization or group having control over public affairs: *the local authority*
•*Word Family:* the plural is **authorities** □ **authoritative** *adjective* having or using authority **authoritatively** *adverb*

authorize or **authorise** (*say* **aw**-tha-rize) *verb*
1 to give legal authority to: *I'll authorize my solicitor to contact you.* 2 to give official permission for: *to authorize a cheque to be paid*
•*Word Family:* **authorization** *noun*

autistic (*say* **aw**-tis-tik) *noun*
born with an illness in which you cannot respond to or communicate normally with other people
•*Word Family:* **autism** *noun*

autobiography (*say* aw-to-bi-**og**-ra-fee) *noun*
the story of your own life, written by yourself
•*Word Family:* the plural is **autobiographies** □ **autobiographer** *noun* **autobiographical** *adjective*

autocracy (*say* aw-**tok**-ra-see) *noun*
1 the absolute power that some people have over others, especially a ruler 2 a country ruled by someone with absolute power
•*Word Family:* the plural is **autocracies** □ **autocrat** *noun* a ruler with absolute power **autocratic** *adjective* **autocratically** *adverb*

autograph (*say* **aw**-ta-graf) *noun*
a famous person's signature
•*Word Family:* **autograph** *verb*

automatic (*say* aw-ta-**mat**-ik) *adjective*
1 done without thinking: *an automatic smile*
2 programmed to operate by itself, without direct human control: *an automatic washing machine / automatic weapons*

A B C D E F G H I J K L M N O P Q R S T U V W X Y Z

automatic *noun*
3 a car that changes gear by itself and does not need a clutch 4 a weapon that reloads itself over and over again
•***Word Family:*** **automatically** *adverb*

automation (*say* aw-ta-**may**-shon) *noun*
the use of machines rather than people, especially to do dangerous or repetitive factory jobs
•***Word Family:*** **automate** *verb* to supply with machines

automobile (*say* **aw**-ta-mo-beel) *noun*
a motor car

automotive (*say* aw-ta-**mo**-tiv) *adjective*
having to do with motor vehicles: *the automotive industry*

autonomous (*say* aw-**ton**-a-mus) *adjective*
1 self-ruling: *an autonomous country* 2 free or independent
•***Word Family:*** **autonomy** *noun* independence

autopsy (*say* **aw**-top-see) *noun*
the medical examination of a dead body to find out how death happened
•***Word Family:*** the plural is **autopsies**
•***Word Origins:*** from a Greek word meaning "seeing with your own eyes"

autumn (*say* **aw**-tum) *noun*
the season of the year between summer and winter
•***Word Family:*** **autumnal** (*say* aw-**tum**-nal) *adjective*

auxiliary (*say* awg-**zil**-i-a-ree) *adjective*
1 kept in reserve in case it is needed: *auxiliary troops* 2 doing work which helps other people to do their jobs, for example in a school or hospital: *auxiliary staff*

available (*say* a-**vay**-la-bul) *adjective*
suitable or ready for use: *There are no more seats available for the concert.*
•***Word Family:*** **availability** *noun*

avalanche (*say* **av**-a-lahnch) *noun*
a sudden fall or movement of a large amount of snow, rock or mud down a slope

avant-garde (*say* **av**-on-gard) *adjective*
leading or at the forefront of the latest trends in music, art and literature: *an avant-garde painter*
•***Word Origins:*** from a French word meaning "vanguard"

avenge (*say* a-**venj**) *verb*
to punish severely the person responsible for something: *to avenge a murder*
•***Word Family:*** **avenger** *noun: the masked avenger*

avenue (*say* **av**-a-new) *noun*
a street or road, especially one that is wide and lined with trees

average (*say* **av**-rij) *noun*
1 the result obtained by dividing the sum of several quantities by the number of quantities added: *The average of 2, 4 and 6 is 4.* 2 the most common or usual amount, quality or kind: *Her singing is way above average.*
average *verb*
3 to calculate the average of

aversion *noun*
1 an extreme dislike: *an aversion to spiders*
2 someone or something that is disliked

avert (*say* a-**vert**) *verb*
1 to turn away: *to avert your eyes* 2 to avoid: *to avert disaster*

aviary (*say* **ave**-ya-ree) *noun*
a large cage or enclosure in which birds are kept
•***Word Family:*** the plural is **aviaries**

aviation (*say* ay-vee-**ay**-shon) *noun*
the science or skill of flying aircraft
•***Word Family:*** **aviator** *noun* a pilot
•***Word Origins:*** from a Latin word meaning "bird"

avid (*say* **av**-id) *adjective*
1 very enthusiastic or keen: *an avid bird watcher*
2 greedy: *avid for power*
•***Word Family:*** **avidity** *noun* **avidly** *adverb*

avocado (*say* av-a-**kah**-do) *noun*
a tropical fruit with a dark green or black skin, creamy yellowish flesh and a large seed, often used in salads
•***Word Family:*** the plural is **avocados**

avoid (*say* a-**voyd**) *verb*
to keep away from: *to avoid the dangerous road / to avoid an unpleasant job*
•***Word Family:*** **avoidable** *adjective* **avoidance** *noun*

await *verb*
1 to wait for or expect: *We await your decision.*
2 be ready for: *Your taxi awaits you.*

awake *adjective*
1 not asleep 2 alert: *awake to danger*
awake *verb*
3 to wake from sleep 4 to arouse or stir up: *to awake feelings of guilt*
•***Word Family:*** other forms are **awakes, awoke, awoken, awaking** □ **awaken** *verb* to wake up or alert **awakening** *noun* an arousing of interest

award *verb*
1 to give or grant something officially: *to award prizes*
•***Word Family:*** **award** *noun*

aware *adjective*
having knowledge or understanding of: *to be aware of a problem*
• ***Word Family:*** **awareness** *noun*

awe *noun*
respect mixed with fear: *to be in awe of your head teacher*
• ***Word Family:*** **awesome** *adjective* inspiring awe

awful (*say* **aw**-ful) *adjective*
1 extremely bad or unpleasant: *What an awful day!* 2 very great: *She has an awful lot of money.*
• ***Word Family:*** **awfully** *adverb* **awfulness** *noun*

awkward *adjective*
1 lacking grace or skill: *awkward with his hands* 2 causing problems or embarrassment: *an awkward time for me to come / caught in an awkward situation*
• ***Word Family:*** **awkwardness** *noun*

awning *noun*
a roof-like cover, usually canvas, above a doorway or window

axe *noun*
1 a tool with a long, wooden handle and a sharp, wedge-shaped metal head, used for cutting down trees or chopping wood 2 **give the axe** to dismiss: *to give someone the axe from their job* 3 **have an axe to grind** to have private or selfish reason's for doing something
axe *verb*
4 to get rid of: *400 jobs are to be axed.*
• ***Word Family:*** the plural of the noun is **axes**

axis *noun*
1 the imaginary line that something rotates or turns around: *The earth rotates on its axis.* 2 a line that divides something in half: *the axis of symmetry*
• ***Word Family:*** plural is **axes** (*say* **ak**-seez)

axle (*say* **ak**-sel) *noun*
a supporting shaft on which a wheel or wheels turn

axolotl (*say* axe-o-**lot**-ul) *noun*
a Mexican salamander with a long tail and short legs, often kept with goldfish in a tank

ayatollah (*say* eye-a-**tol**-a) *noun*
a title of respect given to some important Muslim religious leaders in Iran

azalea (*say* a-**zay**-li-a) *noun*
a garden shrub with bright flowers

azure (*say* **ay**-zher) *noun*
a clear, sky-blue colour
• ***Word Family:*** **azure** *adjective*

Bb

babble *verb*
1 to make garbled or meaningless sounds: *The baby babbled happily in its cot.* 2 to talk for a long time without being serious or sensible: *to babble on for hours*
babble *noun*
3 a babbling sound
• ***Word Family:*** **babbling** *adjective: a babbling brook* **babbler** *noun*

baboon (*say* ba-**boon**) *noun*
a large monkey found in Africa and Arabia
• ***Word Origins:*** from an Old French word meaning "a stupid person"

baby *noun*
1 a very young child or animal
baby *adjective*
2 like or made for a baby: *a baby face / a baby seat*
• ***Word Family:*** the plural is **babies**

babysit *verb*
to look after a young child while its parents are out
• ***Word Family:*** other forms are **babysits, babysat, babysitting** □ **babysitter** *noun*

bachelor (*say* **batch**-a-la) *noun*
1 an unmarried man 2 someone who holds the first degree awarded by a university: *a Bachelor of Arts*

back *noun*
1 the rear part of the body between the shoulders and the bottom 2 the rear side or part of anything: *the back of the shop* 3 a defending player in games such as football
back *verb*
4 to reverse: *to back a car / He backed into the driveway.* 5 to bet on or support: *to back a horse in a race / to back your local soccer team*
back *adverb*
6 at or towards the rear: *Please move back.* 7 in or towards a place or time from the past: *to go back home / to think back to last week* 8 in return: *to send back / to write back*
• ***Word Family:*** **backer** *noun* someone who supports a business with money

backbone *noun*
1 the set of bones found in all mammals and in some other animals such as fish 2 strength of character: *He didn't have the backbone to admit he was wrong.*

backfire *verb*
1 to make a loud noise because of an explosion in an engine's exhaust pipe, as a result of a build-up of unburnt fuel 2 to go wrong: *Our plans backfired because the teacher didn't turn up.*

backgammon *noun*
a game for two people who take turns to move their pieces around a specially marked board after throwing dice

background *noun*
1 the part of a view or picture which is furthest away: *We could see the lake, with the mountains in the background.* 2 the events surrounding or causing: *the background to the French Revolution* 3 the things you have done, or that have happened to you: *a background in politics*

backhand *noun*
a stroke in tennis made across the body with the back of the hand facing forwards

backing *noun*
1 support, promotion or assistance: *The film will never go ahead without proper backing.* 2 a supporting or strengthening back part: *The backing on this furniture isn't very strong.* 3 the music played while someone is singing, especially in a pop song: *a backing track*

backlash *noun*
a strong reaction against something that has until now been popular: *the backlash against modern farming methods*

backlog *noun*
a build up of work that needs to be done: *a backlog of mail to be answered*

backside *noun*
your buttocks or bottom

backspace *verb*
to move the computer cursor back to text you've already keyed in, especially to insert or delete words

backstage *noun*
1 the area in a theatre behind or at the sides of the stage, containing the dressing-rooms, props and other equipment
backstage *adjective*
2 private or behind the scenes

backstroke *noun*
a swimming stroke in which the swimmer lies face up in the water, reaching back and pulling with each arm in turn

backup *noun*
1 help or support: *Other team members provided him with backup.* 2 a spare part kept in case you need it: *Take an extra torch as a backup.* 3 an extra copy of a computer file or disk made in case the original becomes corrupted or lost
• ***Word Family:*** **back up** *verb* to copy onto a computer disk: *to back up a file or program*

backward *adjective*
1 towards the back or in reverse: *She left without a backward glance.* 2 a long way behind others in your ability to learn
• ***Word Family:*** **backwards** *adverb: to lean backwards* **backwards** *adjective*

bacon *noun*
a cut of meat from the back or sides of a pig, usually salted or smoked

bacteria (*say* bak-**teer**-ee-a) *plural noun*
a tiny one-celled organism that helps plants and animals decay, helps wine to ferment and cheese to mature and causes diseases, such as typhoid and tetanus
• ***Word Family:*** the singular is **bacterium** □ **bacteriology** *noun* the study of bacteria **bacterial** *adjective* **bacteriologist** *noun*
• ***Word Origins:*** from a Greek word meaning "a small stick"

bad *adjective*
1 evil: *a bad man* 2 unpleasant, disagreeable or upsetting: *a bad dream* 3 severe or serious: *a bad toothache / a bad accident* 4 sour or spoiled: *bad milk* 5 **not bad** rather good
• ***Word Family:*** the other forms are **worse, worst** □ **badly** *adverb* **badness** *noun*

badge *noun*
an emblem showing your rank or membership in an organization or that you support something

badger *noun*
1 a mammal of Europe and North America, that has a striped face and lives in a burrow
badger *verb*
2 to pester: *Stop badgering me with questions.*

badminton *noun*
a game similar to tennis but which uses a higher net and is played using a shuttlecock
• ***Word Origins:*** named after *Badminton* House in England, where the game was first played

badmouth *verb*
to criticise or say something nasty about: *Don't badmouth my friend in front of me.*

baffle *verb*
to confuse or puzzle: *He was clearly baffled by these questions.*
• ***Word Family:*** **baffling** *adjective*

bag *noun*
1 a container made from paper, cloth, leather, and so on: *a bag of sweets / your school bag*
2 **bags** a large quantity: *He has bags of money.*
3 an ugly woman: *an old bag*

bag *verb*
4 to seize or catch
•***Word Family:*** other verb forms are **bags, bagged, bagging**

bagel (*say* **bay**-gel) *noun*
a ring-shaped bread roll
•***Word Origins:*** this word comes from Yiddish

baggage (*say* **bag**-ij) *noun*
any luggage for taking on a journey

baggy *adjective*
bulging or hanging loosely: *baggy trousers*
•***Word Family:*** other forms are **baggier, baggiest**

bagpipes *plural noun*
a musical instrument which makes a sound when air is squeezed from a bag held under the arm and then out through a number of pipes

Baha'i (*say* ba-**high**) *noun*
a follower of a religion founded in 1863 by Mirza Husain 'Ali, with the world centre in Haifa, Israel
•***Word Family:*** the plural is **Baha'is**
•***Word Origins:*** named after the Persian title of the founder meaning "Glory of God"

bail (1) *noun*
the money paid to a court to guarantee that someone accused of a crime will appear in court for trial if they remain free until then

bail (2) *noun*
one of the two small pieces of wood that sit across each set of cricket stumps to form the wicket

Bairam (*say* by-**ram**) *noun*
a Muslim festival, either at the end of Ramadan or at the end of the Islamic year.

bait *noun*
1 the food used in an animal trap or attached to a fish hook 2 anything that attracts or entices: *The police use unlocked cars as bait to catch the thieves.*
bait *verb*
3 to prepare a fish hook or trap by attaching bait 4 to anger someone by teasing them
•***Word Origins:*** from an Old Norse word meaning "to hunt"

bake *verb*
1 to cook or heat in an oven 2 to harden by heating: *to bake pottery in a kiln*

baker *noun*
someone who bakes and sells bread and cakes
•***Word Family:*** **bakery** *noun*

baker's dozen *noun*
thirteen

baklava (*say* **bak**-lar-va) *noun*
a pastry filled with honey and nuts
•***Word Origins:*** this word comes from Turkish

balaclava (*say* bal-a-**klah**-va) *noun*
a woollen hood that covers your head, ears and neck
•***Word Origins:*** named after the caps worn by British soldiers to keep out the cold at the battle of *Balaclava* in 1854

balalaika (*say* bal-a-**lie**-ka) *noun*
a triangle-shaped, musical instrument related to the guitar, with three strings for plucking or strumming

balance *noun*
1 steadiness, especially when two opposing forces are equal: *Try to keep your balance when you ride the bike.* 2 a weighing instrument, especially one with two pans hanging from an arm 3 the difference between the debit and credit sides of an account
balance *verb*
4 to bring into or keep in a steady condition or position: *I can balance a book on my head. / The acrobat balanced on one hand.* 5 to be equal in weight, amount or force: *His good points probably balance his bad.*

balcony (*say* **bal**-ka-nee) *noun*
1 a platform that sticks out from a building, usually with a railing or wall for safety 2 a raised gallery with seats, in a theatre or public building
•***Word Family:*** the plural is **balconies**

bald (*say* bawld) *adjective*
1 with no hair: *a bald head / a bald person*
2 blunt or plain: *a bald statement of the facts*
•***Word Family:*** **baldly** *adverb* **baldness** *noun*

bale (1) *noun*
a large, compact package or bundle held together by wires, cord or cloth: *a bale of hay*
•***Word Family:*** **baler** *noun*

bale (2) *verb*
1 to scoop out water from the bottom of a boat
2 **bale out** (a) to parachute from an aircraft in an emergency (b) to leave a dangerous or embarrassing situation
•***Word Origins:*** from an Old French word meaning "bucket"

baleful *adjective*
menacing or evil: *to give someone a baleful stare*
•***Word Family:*** **balefully** *adverb* **balefulness** *noun*

balk (*say* bawlk) *verb*
1 to stop and refuse to continue: *The horse balked at the jump. / She balked at the idea of marriage.* 2 to prevent: *The huge advertising campaign was balked by a newspaper strike.*

A B C D E F G H I J K L M N O P Q R S T U V W X Y Z

ball (1) *noun*
1 a round object, either hollow or solid, such as the one you hit in cricket or tennis 2 a rounded part of something: *to balance on the balls of your feet*

ball (2) *noun*
1 a large social gathering, usually formal, with dancing, eating and drinking 2 **have a ball** to enjoy yourself very much
• ***Word Origins:*** from an Old French word meaning "to dance"

ballad *noun*
1 a simple poem that tells a story and is often set to music for singing: *the ballad of Robin Hood*
2 a popular, romantic song

ballast (*say* **bal**-ast) *noun*
any heavy material, such as lead or bags of sand, placed in the hold of a ship to make sure that it is stable

ballet (*say* **bal**-ay) *noun*
a dance with formal steps, movements and gestures performed by a group of dancers who act out a story to music
• ***Word Family:*** **ballet-dancer** *noun* **ballerina** *noun* a female ballet-dancer
• ***Word Origins:*** from an Italian word meaning "little dance"

ballistics (*say* ba-**list**-iks) *noun*
the study of the movement of projectiles, such as bullets or missiles
• ***Word Family:*** **ballistic** *adjective* to do with projectiles and their movement
• ***Word Origins:*** from a Greek word meaning "to throw"

balloon (*say* ba-**loon**) *noun*
1 a coloured, rubber bag designed to be blown up, used as a toy or for decoration 2 an aircraft that is lighter than air and consists of a large bag filled with hydrogen, helium or hot air, and a basket underneath to carry people
balloon *verb*
3 to swell up like a balloon, or go up in a balloon
• ***Word Family:*** **balloonist** *noun* a traveller in a balloon

ballot *noun*
1 a system of secret voting in an election 2 the piece of paper you use to record the name of the candidate for whom you wish to vote before placing it in a ballot-box
• ***Word Family:*** **ballot** *verb* (**ballots, balloted, balloting**) to vote by ballot
• ***Word Origins:*** from an Italian word meaning "a little ball", because the first votes were cast by dropping a ball into a box

ballpoint pen *noun*
a pen containing a supply of ink and a point with a metal ball that turns to allow ink to be applied

balm (*rhymes with* calm) *noun*
1 a sweet-smelling, soothing ointment made from the scented gum of certain trees
2 anything that heals or soothes: A *good night's rest was balm after so many sleepless nights.*
• ***Word Family:*** **balmy** *adjective* (**balmier, balmiest**)

baloney (*say* ba-**lo**-nee) *noun*
rubbish or nonsense: *Stop talking baloney.*

balsa (*say* **boll**-sa) *noun*
a tropical, South American tree with very light, soft wood, used for timber in rafts or for making model planes

balsam (*say* **bawl**-sam) *noun*
1 the fragrant gum of certain trees, used as a soothing ointment 2 a common garden plant with red, pink or white flowers

balustrade (*say* **bal**-a-strade) *noun*
a series of upright supports or pillars with a rail on top, such as is used in a stone balcony or as part of a staircase
• ***Word Family:*** **baluster** *noun* one of the upright supports used in a balustrade

bamboo *noun*
a tropical, woody grass with long, hollow, jointed stems growing up to 10 metres or more in height
• ***Word Family:*** the plural is **bamboos**

bamboozle *verb*
to trick or deceive: *to bamboozle someone with card tricks*

ban *verb*
1 to prohibit or put a stop to something: *to ban a book*
ban *noun*
2 an official order stopping something: *a ban on whaling*
• ***Word Family:*** other verb forms are **bans, banned, banning**

banana (*say* ba-**nah**-na) *noun*
a tropical fruit shaped like a finger, with a yellow skin and growing in bunches called hands

band (1) *noun*
1 a small group of people doing something together: *a band of soldiers* 2 a group of musicians: *a pop band / a brass band*
band *verb*
3 to unite or join together

band (2) *noun*
1 a flat strip of any material for binding or trimming: *to strengthen a box with metal bands*

2 a broad stripe crossing any surface: *a fish with bands of red and silver*
band *verb*
3 to stripe or mark with bands
•***Word Family:*** **banded** *adjective* striped

bandage (*say* **ban**-dij) *noun*
1 a strip of fabric, used to bind a wound
bandage *verb*
2 to put a bandage on

bandit *noun*
a robber or outlaw

bandwagon *noun*
jump on the bandwagon to join in or start doing something just because everyone else is

bandy *verb*
1 to pass a story or rumour back and forth: *to bandy a story about* 2 **bandy words** to argue
•***Word Family:*** other verb forms are **bandies, bandied, bandying**

bandy-legged *adjective*
having legs that curve outwards at the knees

bang *noun*
1 a sudden loud noise 2 a violent blow or knock: *a nasty bang on the head / a bang on the door*
bang *adverb*
3 with a bang
bang *verb*
4 to close or hit with a bang

bangle *noun*
an ornamental band or chain without a clasp, worn around your wrist
•***Word Origins:*** from a Hindi word meaning "a glass bracelet"

banish *verb*
1 to send someone away as a punishment: *to banish the man from his homeland* 2 to get rid of or drive away: *to banish fear*
•***Word Family:*** **banishment** *noun*

banister *noun*
the rail and its supports running down the side of a staircase

banjo *noun*
a musical instrument with strings, a narrow neck and a round body, that you pluck with your fingers or with a plectrum
•***Word Family:*** the plural is **banjos** or **banjoes**

bank (1) *noun*
1 a slope, pile or solid mass: *a bank of tyres / a bank of clouds hiding the sun* 2 the sloping land at the edge of a river or creek: *a river bank*
bank *verb*
3 to form into a bank: *The earth is banked up near the construction site.* 4 to tilt an aircraft sideways during flight

bank (2) *noun*
1 an organization whose business is keeping money and valuables safe, lending and borrowing money, and sometimes giving out and exchanging foreign money 2 any storage place: *a blood bank*
bank *verb*
3 to deposit in a bank: *to bank a cheque* 4 **bank on** to rely on: *to bank on someone to help*
•***Word Family:*** **bankbook** *noun* a book given to you by a bank to record hwo much money you have there **banker** *noun* someone who controls or supervises the business of a bank

bank (3) *noun*
a set of objects arranged in a line: *a bank of spotlights*

banknote *noun*
a piece of paper money, rather than a coin

bankrupt *noun*
1 someone who cannot pay their debts
bankrupt *adjective*
2 unable to pay people the money you owe them: *His business failed and he went bankrupt.*
bankrupt *verb*
3 to make bankrupt
•***Word Family:*** **bankruptcy** *noun* being bankrupt

banner *noun*
1 a flag, especially of a country or army 2 a piece of cloth with a slogan written on it, held up on a pole in a demonstration or procession

banquet (*say* **bang**-kwit) *noun*
a feast or formal dinner for many guests

bantam (*say* **ban**-tam) *noun*
a small domestic fowl, with the male having brightly coloured feathers
•***Word Origins:*** named after *Bantam*, a village in Indonesia, where these birds probably came from

banter *noun*
playfully teasing or mocking talk: *Their banter was a sign of their friendship.*

baptism *noun*
a Christian ceremony in which someone is sprinkled with, or bathed in, water as a sign that they are ready to be accepted as a member of the church
•***Word Family:*** **baptize** *verb* to perform the ceremony of baptism **baptismal** *adjective: baptismal robes*
•***Word Origins:*** from a Greek word meaning "to dip"

bar *noun*
1 a piece of some solid material, usually longer than it is wide: *a bar of chocolate / the bars of a cage* 2 a barrier or obstruction which stops you going somewhere or getting something you

A B C D E F G H I J K L M N O P Q R S T U V W X Y Z

want 3 the group of beats which music is divided into, separated from similar groups by a vertical line on a music score 4 a counter in a hotel or pub where drinks are served 5 a place where drinks and food are served
bar *verb*
6 to block or obstruct: *Police barred the door of the building.*
• ***Word Family:*** other verb forms are **bars, barred, barring**

barb *noun*
1 a sharp backward point at the end of a fish hook or harpoon 2 a sharp or cutting remark: *She ignored my barbs.*
• ***Word Family:*** **barbed** *adjective* spiteful: *a barbed comment*

barbarian (*say* bar-**bair**-i-an) *noun*
someone who is crude, coarse, cruel or uncivilized
• ***Word Family:*** **barbarian** *adjective: invading barbarian hordes* **barbaric** *adjective* extremely cruel **barbarity** *noun* the brutal or cruel behaviour of a barbarian: *Poisoning civilians with gas is sheer barbarity.*
• ***Word Origins:*** from a Greek word meaning "foreign" or "speaking without making sense"

barbecue (*say* **bar**-ba-kew) *noun*
1 a metal frame or fireplace for grilling food over an open fire 2 an outdoor meal at which food is grilled on a barbecue
• ***Word Family:*** **barbecue** *verb*

barbed wire *noun*
a type of wire with sharp points or barbs at intervals, used for fences

barber *noun*
someone whose job is cutting men's hair and trimming or shaving their beards
• ***Word Origins:*** from a Latin word meaning "beard"

barbiturate (*say* bar-**bit**-yoo-rit) *noun*
a drug used to calm someone down or make them feel sleepy, with the side-effect that you can become addicted to it

bar chart *noun*
a graph on which amounts are shown as different sized stripes or bars

bar code *noun*
a series of vertical stripes, able to be scanned by a computer and used to identify items in a shop, books in a library, and many other different products
• ***Word Family:*** **bar coding** *noun*

bard *noun*
a poet or singer
• ***Word Family:*** **bardic** *adjective*

bare *adjective*
1 naked, empty or without covering: *bare feet / a bare room / bare floorboards* 2 plain, simple or unadorned: *the bare facts*
bare *verb*
3 to make bare
• ***Word Family:*** **barely** *adverb* only, just or not quite **bareness** *noun*

bareback (*say* **bear**-back) *adjective*
without using a saddle or stirrups: *bareback horse riding*
• ***Word Family:*** **bareback** *adverb: to ride bareback*

bargain (*say* **bar**-gin) *noun*
1 an agreement between two people, especially about the price of something they are buying or selling, or about a business deal 2 something bought or offered for sale at a low price: *There are always good bargains in the shops after Christmas.*
bargain *verb*
3 to argue about the price of something

barge (*rhymes with* large) *noun*
1 a long flat-bottomed boat, sometimes without an engine, used for transporting heavy goods on rivers and canals
barge *verb*
2 to move clumsily or heavily: *to barge through the crowd* 3 to rush in rudely or intrude: *to barge into the room without knocking*
• ***Word Origins:*** from a Greek word meaning "an Egyptian boat"

baritone (*say* **ba**-ri-tone) *noun*
1 the range of musical notes sung by a man with a fairly low voice: *to sing baritone* 2 any singer or instrument having this range
• ***Word Family:*** **baritone** *adjective: a baritone saxophone*

bark (1) *verb*
1 to make the sound of a dog or similar animal 2 to speak sharply or roughly: *The general barked out his orders.*

bark (2) *noun*
1 the outer covering of the trunk and branches of a tree
bark *verb*
2 to scrape or skin: *to bark your shins on the edge of a chair*

barley (*say* **bar**-lee) *noun*
a cereal or grain used as food and for making malt and beer

bar mitzvah (*say* bar **mits**-vah) *noun*
the service and celebration held for a Jewish boy of thirteen to show he has become an adult
• ***Word Origins:*** from a Hebrew word meaning "son of the commandment"

barmy *adjective*
stupid or mad: *You're barmy.*
• ***Word Family:*** **barmier, barmiest**

barn *noun*
a farm building used to store hay or shelter animals

barnacle (*say* **bar**-na-kul) *noun*
a small shellfish that clings firmly to rocks, floating timber and the bottoms of ships

barometer (*say* ba-**rom**-i-ta) *noun*
an instrument for measuring air pressure, working out how high you are above sea-level and showing when the weather is likely to change
• ***Word Family:*** **barometric** *adjective*

baron *noun*
1 a powerful nobleman who, in the Middle Ages, owned a castle and land and was expected to support the king or queen 2 a powerful person who owns a lot of large businesses or companies: *a media baron*
• ***Word Family:*** **baroness** *noun* the feminine form of baron, or the wife of a baron **baronial** (*say* ba-**ro**-nee-al) *adjective*

barracks *plural noun*
the group of buildings where soldiers live
• ***Word Origins:*** from an Italian word meaning "a soldier's tent"

barracouta (*say* bar-a-**koo**-ta) *noun*
a fish found in the Southern Hemisphere, usually with long needle-like teeth

barrage (*say* **ba**-rahzh) *noun*
1 heavy gunfire intended to keep the enemy from moving 2 an overwhelming number: *The Prime Minister faced a barrage of questions from reporters.*
• ***Word Family:*** **barrage** *verb*

barrel *noun*
1 a large round container with flat ends, used to hold liquids such as beer 2 the tube-like part of a gun
• ***Word Family:*** **barrel** *verb* **(barrels, barrelled, barrelling)**

barren *adjective*
1 with nothing growing or able to grow: *barren land* 2 not able to have children: *a barren woman*

barricade *noun*
1 a temporary barrier or wall, usually across a street
barricade *verb*
2 to block or defend a place with a barricade
• ***Word Origins:*** from a Spanish word meaning "cask"

barrier *noun*
1 anything that blocks or keeps back: *a police barrier to control the crowd.* 2 anything that separates things or people: *a language barrier*

barrister *noun*
a lawyer who is allowed to argue cases for people in the higher courts of law

barrow (1) *noun*
a handcart, such as a wheelbarrow, or a street cart where vegetables and fruit are sold

barrow (2) *noun*
a mound of earth or stones built over a grave, usually dating from prehistoric times

barter *verb*
to trade by exchanging food and other goods instead of paying money: *to barter ten bags of grain for one pig*
• ***Word Family:*** **barter** *noun*

base *noun*
1 the bottom part of something, especially the part that supports it: *a vase with a narrow base* 2 the most important part: *Meat is the base of this soup.* 3 one of the four places in baseball or rounders around which the player must run after hitting the ball 4 a place where work is carried out and where equipment is kept: *a military base* 5 a number that is used to organize a counting system in maths, such as ten in the decimal system and two in the binary system
base *verb*
6 to use as the most important part or starting point: *He based his story on careful research.*
• ***Word Family:*** the plural is **bases** □ **baseless** *adjective* having no base or support

baseball *noun*
1 a game played between two teams of nine on a diamond formed by four bases. Having hit the ball, the striker tries to score by running round the diamond before the ball is thrown home 2 the ball used to play this game

basement *noun*
the level of a building which is below the ground: *Many large stores have a bargain basement.*

bash *verb*
1 to hit someone or something violently 2 to criticize someone very strongly: *She's always bashing the unions.*
bash *noun*
3 a try: *Tim will have a bash at anything.*

bashful *adjective*
timid or easily embarrassed
• ***Word Family:*** **bashfully** *adverb* **bashfulness** *noun*

A B C D E F G H I J K L M N O P Q R S T U V W X Y Z

basic (1) (*say* **bay**-sik) *adjective*
essential or most important: *It's easy to learn the basic principles of chess.*
• ***Word Family:*** **basically** *adverb* essentially

basic (2) *noun*
a widely used computer language with many uses
• ***Word Origins:*** from *b*(eginners) *a*(ll) *s*(ymbolic) *i*(nstruction) *c*(ode)

basil (*say* **baz**-il) *noun*
an aromatic herb used in cooking
• ***Word Origins:*** from a Greek word meaning "royal"

basin (*say* **bay**-sin) *noun*
1 a deep, round container with sloping sides, used to hold water for washing in 2 a deep bowl used for mixing or cooking 3 land around a river and its tributaries 4 an area of water enclosed by land, where boats are kept

basis (*say* **bay**-sis) *noun*
1 the foundation at the base of something: *This point forms the basis of my argument.* 2 the essential part or ingredient
• ***Word Family:*** plural is **bases** (*say* **bay**-seez)
• ***Word Origins:*** from a Greek word meaning "a step" or "pedestal"

bask (*rhymes with* ask) *verb*
1 to sit or lie in the sun and enjoy the warmth: *to bask in the sun* 2 to enjoy having someone think well of you: *to bask in someone's approval*

basket *noun*
a stiff container, usually with handles, made of woven canes, plastic or metal
• ***Word Family:*** **basketry** *noun* **basketwork** *noun*

basketball *noun*
1 a game played on a rectangular court between two teams of five, six or seven players whose aim is to throw a leather ball through a net suspended from an iron ring at either end of the court 2 the ball used in this game

bass (*say* base) *noun*
1 the range of musical notes sung by a man with a very low voice: *to sing bass* 2 any singer or instrument with this low range
• ***Word Family:*** **bass** *adjective: a bass guitar*

bassinet *noun*
a basket, sometimes with a hood, used as a baby's cradle
• ***Word Origins:*** from a French word meaning "a basin"

bassoon (*say* ba-**soon**) *noun*
a woodwind instrument with a deep rich tone, made from a long wooden tube that doubles back on itself
• ***Word Family:*** **bassoonist** *noun*

bastard (*say* **bah**-stud) *noun*
1 a horrible person who is selfish or uncaring: *a mean bastard* 2 a child whose parents were not married when he or she was born

baste *verb*
to pour cooking liquid, especially melted fat, over food cooking in the oven

bastion (*say* **bast**-i-on) *noun*
1 the protecting part of a rampart in a fortification 2 an organization or place that protects or supports something: *The army is a bastion of authority.*

bat (1) *noun*
1 a stick, usually wooden, used to hit the ball in games such as cricket or baseball 2 someone in cricket who is batting
bat *verb*
3 to hit the ball with a bat, in games such as table tennis or cricket
• ***Word Family:*** other verb forms are **bats, batted, batting**

bat (2) *noun*
a flying, mouse-like mammal with membranes joining the front and hind legs to form wings

bat (3) *verb*
to blink
• ***Word Family:*** other forms of the verb are **bats, batted, batting**

batch *noun*
a number of things together: *a batch of scones*
• ***Word Family:*** the plural is **batches**
• ***Word Origins:*** from an Old English word meaning "to bake"

bath (*rhymes with* path) *noun*
1 a large container of water in which you sit to wash your whole body 2 an occasion when you wash yourself in a bath 3 the water you use in a bath 4 **baths** a public swimming pool
bath *verb*
5 to wash someone in a bath: *He's bathing the baby.*

bathe (*say* bayth) *verb*
1 to wash or cover something with liquid: *to bathe a wound with antiseptic / Tears bathed her face.* 2 to swim
• ***Word Family:*** **bather** *noun*

bathroom *noun*
a room for washing in with a basin and bath or shower, and often a toilet

batik *noun*
1 a method of printing on fabric using wax and dyes to make a pattern 2 the fabric printed in this way
• ***Word Origins:*** from a Malay word meaning "painting"

bat mitzvah (*say* bart-**mits**-vah) *noun*
a bar mitzvah for a girl

baton (*say* **bat**-on) *noun*
a short stick or rod: *The conductor raised her baton and the orchestra began to play.*

battalion (*say* ba-**tal**-yun) *noun*
1 an army unit consisting of three or more companies of soldiers 2 any large group: *a battalion of cleaners*
• ***Word Origins:*** from an Italian word meaning "a battle"

batten *noun*
1 a thin strip of wood or plastic slipped into a sail to keep it flat 2 a light strip of wood for fastening or joining things such as fence wires
• ***Word Family:*** **batten down** *verb* to fasten a ship's hatches with battens

batter (1) *verb*
to strike or beat something many times: *The ship was battered against the rocks.*

batter (2) *noun*
a mixture of water or milk with flour and eggs, used in cooking to coat foods for frying or to make food such as pancakes

battering ram *noun*
a long, heavy beam, used as a weapon for breaking down walls or gates in the past

battery *noun*
1 a group of electric cells connected together in order to produce or store electricity: *a car battery / a radio battery* 2 a group of heavy guns firing together 3 a group of similar machines or parts: *a battery of computers* 4 an attack on someone by striking or wounding them: *to be charged with assault and battery*
• ***Word Family:*** the plural is **batteries**

battery hen *noun*
a hen kept with hundreds of others in a group of small cages and mechanically fed throughout its life, to make it lay as many eggs as possible

batting *noun*
any cotton or wool fibre padded together and used to fill bed covers and other things like this

battle *noun*
1 a fight, especially one between organized forces or armies 2 any struggle: *the battle against poverty*

battlements *plural noun*
the upper edge of a castle wall containing a series of openings that arrows can be shot through

battleship *noun*
a powerful and heavily armoured warship

batty *adjective*
slightly mad

bauble (*say* **baw**-bul) *noun*
a pretty ornament that is not valuable: *baubles for the Christmas tree*

baulk (*say* bawlk) *verb*
another spelling for **balk**

bauxite (*say* **bawk**-site) *noun*
a mixture like clay which comes from rock and is used to make aluminium
• ***Word Origins:*** named after *Les Baux*, the place in France where it was first found

bawl *verb*
1 to cry or sob noisily: *The baby turned red and bawled.* 2 to shout or yell out loudly: *She bawled my name from across the street.*

bay (1) *noun*
a sheltered area of water almost enclosed by land but opening onto the sea

bay (2) *noun*
a special area separated off from the rest of a place: *a loading bay*

bay (3) *noun*
1 the deep, drawn-out bark of a hound when it's hunting 2 **keep at bay** stop something from affecting you or coming too close: *This medicine will keep the pain at bay.*
bay *verb*
3 to howl like a dog

bay (4) *noun*
a tree that has dark green, scented leaves used as a herb in cooking
• ***Word Family:*** **bay leaf** the dried leaf of a bay tree, often used for cooking

bay (5) *noun*
a dark brown horse, usually with a black mane and tail

bayonet (*say* **bay**-o-net) *noun*
a sharp blade attached to the end of a rifle, used to stab or slash an enemy
• ***Word Family:*** **bayonet** *verb* (**bayonets, bayoneted, bayoneting**) to stab someone with a bayonet
• ***Word Origins:*** named after *Bayonne* in France, where these weapons originally came from

bazaar (*say* ba-**zar**) *noun*
1 a marketplace in India and Middle Eastern countries 2 a sale of goods to raise money for charity: *the church bazaar*

BC *abbreviation*
short for "before Christ": *Augustus Caesar, the first Roman Emperor, was born in 63 BC.*

A B C D E F G H I J K L M N O P Q R S T U V W X Y Z

beach *noun*
1 the sandy or pebbly land at the water's edge, formed by the waves
beach *verb*
2 to bring a boat onto a beach from the water
• ***Word Family:*** the plural is **beaches**

beacon (*say* **bee**-kon) *noun*
any signal used as a guide or warning, such as a fire on a hilltop, a flashing light from a lighthouse, or a radio signal

bead *noun*
1 a small ball of glass, wood or other material, pierced so that you can thread it on a string
2 a drop or bubble: *beads of sweat*
• ***Word Origins:*** from a Middle English word meaning "a prayer" or "rosary bead"

beady *adjective*
small, round, and bright: *beady eyes*

beagle *noun*
a small, smooth-haired dog used for hunting hares
• ***Word Origins:*** from an Old French word meaning "a noisy person"

beak *noun*
the horny part of a bird's mouth

beaker *noun*
1 a large cup, usually made of plastic 2 a glass container, usually with a lip for pouring liquids, used in laboratories

beam *noun*
1 a long, thick piece of wood, steel or concrete, used as a support 2 a line of light or radiation 3 a big smile 4 the widest part of a ship
beam *verb*
5 to transmit by satellite 6 to smile

bean *noun*
1 a seed from a climbing plant or the pod in which such a seed grows, which is eaten as food: *runner beans / broad beans* 2 a dried bean: *baked beans* 3 **spill the beans** let out information: *Don't spill the beans before the surprise party.* 4 **full of beans** energetic and cheerful

bear (1) (*say* bair) *verb*
1 to support the weight of something: *That branch is sure to bear my weight.* 2 to show a particular mark or sign: *The document bore her signature.* 3 to give birth to a baby: *She bore three daughters.* 4 to put up with: *to bear pain / Bear with me until I've finished.* 5 to accept responsibility: *He bears the blame for his mistakes.* 6 **can't bear** dislike very strongly: *I can't bear celery.* 7 **bear out** confirm: *His story bears out what you said.* 8 **bear up** to keep up your spirits or strength when under a strain
• ***Word Family:*** other forms are **bears, bore, borne, bearing** □ **bearable** *adjective* endurable

bear (2) (*say* bair) *noun*
a large mammal with a shaggy coat and a short tail: *the brown grizzly bear of America*

beard (*say* beerd) *noun*
1 the hair that grows on a man's face on or below the chin
beard *verb*
2 to oppose or defy: *to beard the lion in his den*

bearing (*say* **bair**-ing) *noun*
1 the way you behave or stand: *to have a confident bearing* 2 part of a machine on which another part slides or turns 3 **have a bearing on** have relevance to: *The new evidence has no bearing on the case.* 4 **bearings** the direction or relative position of something: *to lose your bearings*

beast *noun*
1 a four-footed animal 2 a cruel or nasty person: *I hate that beast!*
• ***Word Family:*** **beastly** *adjective* nasty or unpleasant: *What beastly weather!* **beastliness** *noun*

beat *verb*
1 to hit or strike something repeatedly: *The rain beat against the windows.* 2 to make the same movement many times: *The bird beat its wings against the glass.* 3 to pump blood regularly through your body: *His heart is beating.* 4 to stir or mix something thoroughly: *to beat six eggs* 5 to defeat a person or a team in a competition: *Our team beat them by two points.* 6 **beat it** leave: *Beat it! We didn't invite you.* 7 **beat up** to hit or kick someone repeatedly until they are seriously hurt: *She was beaten up and robbed.*
beat *noun*
8 a regular, repeated movement or sound: *the beat of my heart* 9 a steady rhythm in music 10 a regular route or area: *The policeman's beat covered most of the suburb.*
• ***Word Family:*** other verb forms are **beats, beat, beaten, beating** □ **beater** *noun*

beat-up *noun*
an exaggerated or sensationalised news story written by a journalist: *Did you read the beat-up about the movie star's arrest for drunk driving.*

Beaufort scale (*say* **bo**-fort skale) *noun*
a scale and description of wind in which 0 is calm and force 12 is a hurricane
• ***Word Origins:*** named after its inventor, Sir Francis *Beaufort*, 1774 to 1857, a British admiral

beautician (*say* bew-**tish**-an) *noun*
someone whose job is to care for the body, using massage, manicure and facials

beautiful (*say* **bew**-ti-ful) *adjective*
pleasing or lovely to look at, hear, smell, touch or taste: *a beautiful face / beautiful music / beautiful skin*
• ***Word Family:*** **beautify** *verb* (**beautifies, beautified, beautifying**) to make something more beautiful **beautifully** *adverb*

beauty (*say* **bew**-tee) *noun*
1 being beautiful: *The mountain scenery is renowned for its beauty.* 2 a beautiful person or thing: *That grey horse is a beauty.* 3 **the beauty of** the good thing about: *The beauty of this watch is that it wakes me up in the morning.*
• ***Word Family:*** the plural is **beauties**

beaver *noun*
a small mammal with webbed hind feet, thick fur and a paddle-like tail, that lives in the north of the United States and builds dams across streams

beckon *verb*
to signal or summon someone by waving your finger: *He beckoned us to follow.*

become (*say* be-**kum**) *verb*
1 to come to be: *Biting her nails has become a habit. / He becomes angry quite easily.* 2 to suit someone well: *That dress becomes you.*
• ***Word Family:*** other forms are **becomes, became, become, becoming**

becoming *adjective*
1 proper or suitable: *Such behaviour is not becoming for a teacher.* 2 attractive: *Those earrings are rather becoming.*

bed *noun*
1 a piece of furniture that you sleep on, usually with a frame, mattress, pillow and coverings
2 any flat base on which something rests: *benches set into a bed of concrete* 3 the bottom of the sea or a river: *The sunken ship rested on the sea bed.*
4 an area of soil in a garden for growing plants
5 a layer of a particular kind of rock
• ***Word Family:*** **bedding** *noun* sheets, blankets and so on that you use for making your bed

bedclothes *noun*
sheets, blankets and duvets

bedlam *noun*
a scene of noisy uproar and confusion: *There was bedlam in the classroom after the fire broke out.*
• ***Word Origins:*** a corrupted abbreviation of Hospital of St Mary of *Bethlehem*, a notorious 15th-century lunatic asylum at Bishopsgate, London

Bedouin (*say* **bed**-oo-in) *noun*
an Arab who travels about the deserts of North Africa and Arabia
• ***Word Origins:*** from an Arabic word meaning "desert dwellers"

bedraggled (*say* be-**drag**-eld) *adjective*
limp, wet and dirty: *a bedraggled kitten*

bedridden *adjective*
forced to remain in bed because you are too ill to get up

bedrock *noun*
1 the solid rock under the top layers of soil
2 the ideas or people which something is based on or most depends on: *She thinks that families are the bedrock of our society.*

bedspread *noun*
a decorative cover which goes on top of the sheets and blankets on a bed

bee *noun*
a stinging insect that gathers nectar and makes honey

beech *noun*
a tree with shiny leaves it loses in winter, small triangular nuts and smooth bark, whose timber is used for furniture
• ***Word Family:*** the plural is **beeches**

beef *noun*
the meat from a cow, bull or ox
• ***Word Family:*** **beefy** *adjective* (**beefier, beefiest**)

beehive *noun*
a structure in which bees are kept and from which their honey can be collected

beeper *noun*
a small electronic device that makes a high-pitched sound when you are wanted by someone

beer (*rhymes with* ear) *noun*
an alcoholic drink brewed from malt and flavoured with hops

beet *noun*
a plant with a thick root that is used to make sugar or fed to animals

beetle *noun*
a flying insect whose front wings have become hard to protect the delicate back wings underneath
• ***Word Origins:*** from an Old English word meaning "a biting thing"

beetroot *noun*
1 a round, dark red root of a plant, used as food
beetroot *adjective*
2 crimson like beetroot: *Her face was beetroot with embarrassment.*

befall (*say* be-**fawl**) *verb*
to happen or occur: *Whatever befalls, let's remain friends.*
• ***Word Family:*** other forms are **befalls, befell, befallen, befalling**

a b c d e f g h i j k l m n o p q r s t u v w x y z

beforehand *adverb*
earlier

beg *verb*
1 to ask for money from people: *Homeless people are begging on the streets.* 2 to ask for earnestly: *to beg forgiveness*
•**Word Family:** other forms are **begs, begged, begging**

beggar *noun*
someone who lives by begging

begin *verb*
to start: *We'll begin work after lunch. / It began to rain.*
•**Word Family:** other forms are **begins, began, begun, beginning** □ **beginner** *noun* someone who is learning or hasn't had much experience

beginning *noun*
the start or first part of anything: *You must read the beginning of that story.*

begrudge (*say* be-**gruj**) *verb*
to resent someone because of what they have got: *I don't begrudge him his wealth.*

beguile (*say* be-**gile**) *verb*
1 to trick someone: *to beguile someone into giving you money* 2 to charm: *He beguiled his little sister with fairy stories.*
•**Word Family: beguiling** *adjective* charming

behalf *noun*
on someone's behalf for someone as their representative: *I'm acting on my brother's behalf.*

behave (*say* be-**hayv**) *verb*
1 to act in a particular way: *She was behaving rather oddly / The car behaved perfectly.* 2 **behave yourself** to act in an acceptable or proper way
•**Word Family: behaviour** *noun* the way you behave

behead (*say* be-**hed**) *verb*
to cut off someone's head: *The axeman beheaded the King.*

beige (*say* bayzh) *noun*
a light, brownish-yellow colour
•**Word Family: beige** *adjective*

being *noun*
1 existence or life: *A new leader has come into being.* 2 a person or animal: *a human being*

belated (*say* be-**lay**-tid) *adjective*
late: *a belated birthday present*
•**Word Family: belatedly** *adverb*

belch *verb*
1 to pass out wind noisily from your stomach through your mouth 2 to gush or burst out: *The volcano belched out lava and smoke.*
•**Word Family: belch** *noun* **(belches)**

belfry (*say* **bel**-free) *noun*
the part of a church tower in which the bell hangs
•**Word Family:** the plural is **belfries**

belief (*say* be-**leef**) *noun*
1 the feeling of certainty you have that something is real, true or worthwhile: *belief in God* 2 ideas that you believe: *religious beliefs*

believe (*say* be-**leev**) *verb*
1 to accept that something is real or true: *I really believed she'd stolen my jacket. / Do you believe in ghosts?* 2 **believe in** to have faith or trust in something: *Why not believe in me?*
•**Word Family: believer** *noun* someone who believes in something, especially a particular religion **believable** *adjective*

belittle *verb*
to make something seem unimportant or less valuable: *Don't belittle his efforts.*
•**Word Family: belittlement** *noun*

bell *noun*
1 a hollow metal cup, usually with a tongue or hammer inside, that makes a ringing sound when you hit or shake it 2 the sound a bell makes 3 something that rings like or has the shape of a bell: *a door bell*

belligerent (*say* be-**lij**-a-rent) *adjective*
angry and ready for a fight
•**Word Family: belligerence** *noun*

bellow (*say* **bel**-o) *verb*
to make a loud cry or roar: *The bull bellowed with rage and pain. / He bellowed a reply down the garden.*
•**Word Family: bellow** *noun* **bellowing** *noun*

bellows (*say* **bel**-oze) *plural noun*
a device for pumping a stream of air, used to make a fire blaze more strongly or to produce sound from the pipes of an organ or similar musical instrument

belly *noun*
the part of your body containing your stomach and intestines
•**Word Family:** the plural is **bellies**

belong *verb*
1 to be owned by someone: *Those pens belong to Ken.* 2 to go in a particular place where it always goes: *The spoons belong in the top drawer.*

belongings *plural noun*
possessions, especially your own personal ones

below *adverb*
1 beneath: *The lift descended to the floor below.*
below *preposition*
2 lower than: *The sun sank below the horizon.*

belt *noun*
1 a strip of fabric or leather you wear around your waist or hips to keep your clothes in place 2 a long narrow area of land that has a particular feature: *a belt of trees* 3 a strip of tough, flexible material in a machine that transmits power or moves parts along: *a conveyor belt*
belt *verb*
4 to hit someone or something very hard 5 to go very fast: *The sports car belted around the corner.* 6 **belt up** to be quiet
• ***Word Family:*** **belting** *noun* a thrashing

bemused (*say* be-**mewzd**) *adjective*
1 confused and slightly puzzled: *a bemused frown* 2 lost in thought
• ***Word Family:*** **bemuse** *verb*

bench *noun*
1 a long, hard seat for several people 2 a long, narrow work table: *a carpenter's bench* 3 a long seat where members of parliament sit in the House of Commons or House of Lords: *the Opposition benches* 4 the seat or position of a judge in court: *The prisoner will stand before the bench.*
• ***Word Family:*** the plural is **benches**

bend *verb*
1 to turn or force something into a curved direction or shape: *The road bends sharply here. / He bent the wire into a loop.* 2 to stoop: *to bend over* 3 **bend over backwards** to try very hard
bend *noun*
4 a curve in something: *a sharp bend in the road*
• ***Word Family:*** **bendy** *adjective*

bends *noun*
the formation of nitrogen bubbles in your blood when the pressure outside your body changes too quickly, such as when a diver ascends to the surface too rapidly

bene- *prefix*
well: *beneficial*
• ***Word Origins:*** this prefix comes from Latin

beneath *adverb*
1 under: *He stood on the bridge and watched the motorway traffic beneath.*
beneath *preposition*
2 below or lower than: *She could feel the ground beneath her feet.*

benefactor (*say* **ben**-a-fak-tor) *noun*
someone who gives help, money or support to others
• ***Word Family:*** **benefaction** *noun* a good deed or charitable gift **beneficence** *noun*

beneficiary (*say* ben-a-**fish**-a-ree) *noun*
someone who receives a benefit or advantage, often money or property in a will
• ***Word Family:*** the plural is **beneficiaries**

benefit *noun*
1 something that helps you: *I hope the holiday will be of benefit.* 2 a payment: *unemployment benefit given by the government to people who are unemployed, ill or poor* 3 a concert held to raise money for charity
• ***Word Family:*** **benefit** *verb* (**benefits, benefited, benefiting**) □ **beneficial** *adjective*

benevolent (*say* be-**nev**-a-lent) *adjective*
kind or wishing well to others: *a benevolent attitude to others / a benevolent organization*
• ***Word Family:*** **benevolence** *noun* **benevolently** *adverb*

Bengali *noun*
the language spoken in Bangladesh and West Bengal

benign (*say* be-**nine**) *adjective*
1 gentle and kind: *a benign smile* 2 not causing you serious harm: *a benign tumour*
• ***Word Family:*** **benignly** *adverb*
• ***Word Origins:*** from a Latin word meaning "kind-hearted"

bent *adjective*
1 crooked or curved out of shape 2 dishonest: *a bent shopkeeper* 3 **bent on** determined to: *She was bent on learning to ride.*
bent *noun*
4 a natural talent: *a bent for writing*

bequeath (*say* be-**kweeth**) *verb*
to hand down or leave to people who come after you, for example in a will: *knowledge bequeathed to us by the ancient Greeks*
• ***Word Family:*** **bequest** *noun* a gift from someone who has died

berate (*say* be-**rate**) *verb*
to scold angrily

bereaved (*say* be-**reevd**) *adjective*
made sad because someone has died: *the bereaved family*
• ***Word Family:*** **bereave** *verb* (**bereaves, bereft** or **bereaved, bereaving**) **bereavement** *noun* your experience when someone close to you has died

beret (*say* **ber**-ay) *noun*
a soft, round, flat cap

berry *noun*
a small, soft, juicy fruit
• ***Word Family:*** the plural is **berries**

berserk (*say* ber-**zerk**) *adjective*
wild and uncontrollable: *The horse went berserk at the smell of blood.*
• ***Word Origins:*** from an Icelandic word meaning "wild warrior"

berth *noun*
1 a bunk or bed in a ship or train 2 a place

A B C D E F G H I J K L M N O P Q R S T U V W X Y Z

where a ship may be moored 3 **give a wide berth to** to avoid: *I'll give her a wide berth.*
berth *verb*
4 to come to a mooring or dock

beseech *verb*
to ask earnestly and urgently: *I beseeched him not to be angry.*
•***Word Family:*** other forms are **beseeches, beseeched** or **besought, beseeching** □ **beseechingly** *adverb*

beside *preposition*
1 next to 2 **beside yourself** feeling something extremely strongly: *She was beside herself with rage.*

besides *preposition*
1 as well as: *There were twenty five people in the classroom besides the teacher.*
besides *adverb*
2 also: *I can't go now and besides, I'm going tomorrow.*

besiege (*say* be-**seej**) *verb*
1 to surround a place with an army: *The troops besieged the city for four months.* 2 to surround someone and keep asking for their attention: *Reporters besieged the star with questions.*

best *adjective*
1 finest: *my best clothes* 2 closest or favourite: *your best friend* 3 most successful: *the best reader in the class*
best *adverb*
4 most: *I like these chocolates best.*
best *verb*
5 to outdo or defeat someone: *She has never been bested.*
•***Word Family:*** the other adjective forms are **good, better** □ the other adverb forms are **well, better**

best man *noun*
the friend of the bridegroom who looks after him at his wedding

bet *noun*
1 an agreement that, if you guess right about the likely outcome of an uncertain fact or event, you are paid money and if you guess wrong you pay money 2 **a good bet** or **a safe bet** something that is likely to be successful: *That horse is a good bet to win the race.*
bet *verb*
3 to make a bet 4 to be certain: *I bet I'm right.*
•***Word Family:*** other verb forms are **bets, bet** or **betted, betting**

betray *verb*
1 to be disloyal or treacherous towards someone: *to betray someone's trust* 2 to show your feelings without intending to: *Her shaking hand betrayed her nervousness.* 3 to reveal a secret: *to betray a confidence*
•***Word Family:*** **betrayer** *noun* someone who betrays **betrayal** *noun*

betrothed (*say* be-**trothd**) *adjective*
engaged to be married
•***Word Family:*** **betroth** *verb* **betrothal** *noun*

better *adjective*
1 of greater quality or value: *This violin has a better sound than my last one.* 2 no longer ill: *I hope you are better now.*
better *adverb*
3 in an improved way: *She read better today.*
better *verb*
4 to do something better: *His record in long-distance races has never been bettered.*
•***Word Family:*** the other adjective forms are **good, best** □ the other adverb forms are **well, best**

between *preposition*
1 within the given limits of: *Come between 1 and 2 o'clock. / a mountain range between here and the sea* 2 connecting: *love between two people / similarity between two things* 3 shared among: *We own the house between us.* 4 when comparing: *There's not that much difference between onions and shallots.*
between *adverb*
5 between two given limits: *We have maths in the morning and then science, but we get lunch in between.*

beverage (*say* **bev**-a-rij) *noun*
a drink

bevy (*say* **bev**-ee) *noun*
a gathering or group, especially of girls or women
•***Word Family:*** the plural is **bevies**

beware *verb*
be careful: *Beware of the dog.*

bewilder *verb*
to make someone feel puzzled and confused

bewitch *verb*
1 to put a magic spell on someone 2 to fascinate: *The young pianist bewitched the audience with his playing.*
•***Word Family:*** **bewitching** *adjective*

beyond *preposition*
1 on the far side of something: *The river is beyond the church.* 2 too difficult for you to understand: *This physics book is beyond me.*

bi- (*say* by) *prefix*
1 two: *bicycle* 2 twice: *biannual*
•***Word Origins:*** this prefix comes from Latin

biannual (*say* by-**an**-yew-al) *adjective*
happening twice a year

bias (*say* **by**-us) *noun*
1 a tendency to prefer one person or group to another: *There is a bias in favour of younger people in the chess club.* 2 a slanting line or direction
bias *verb*
3 to prejudice or influence someone unfairly: *Don't say that, you might bias him against us.*
•*Word Family:* other verb forms are **biases, biased, biasing** □ **biased** *adjective* prejudiced

bib *noun*
1 a piece of cloth or plastic to tie around the neck of a young child to protect their clothes while they eat 2 the part of an apron or overalls above the waist

Bible *noun*
the holy book of the Christian religion, consisting of the Old and New Testaments
•*Word Family:* **biblical** *adjective*
•*Word Origins:* from a Greek word meaning "book"

bibliography (*say* bib-li-**og**-ra-fee) *noun*
1 a list of all the books or sources used by a writer when writing a book or essay 2 a list of everything written about a particular topic, or by a particular writer: *a bibliography of underwater creatures / a bibliography of the books of Roald Dahl*
•*Word Family:* the plural is **bibliographies** □ **bibliographer** *noun* **bibliographic** *adjective* **bibliographical** *adjective*

bicentenary (*say* by-sen-**tee**-na-ree) *noun*
a 200th anniversary: *Australia's bicentenary was in 1988.*
•*Word Family:* the plural is **bicentenaries** □ **bicentennial** *adjective*

biceps (*say* **by**-seps) *noun*
a large muscle in the front of your upper arm that you use when you move your elbow and lower arm

bicycle *noun*
a two-wheeled vehicle for one rider who steers with handlebars and propels it along by turning the pedals with his or her feet

bid *verb*
1 to make an offer to buy something, especially at an auction: *to bid for a chair* 2 to say how many tricks you think you can win in a card game 3 to say: *We bade the travellers farewell.*
bid *noun*
4 an attempt to get or do something: *she made a bid for the presidency.*
•*Word Family:* other forms for definitions 1 and 2 are **bids, bid, bidding** □ other forms for definition 3 are **bids, bade** (*sounds like* **bad**), **bidden, bidding** □ **bidder** *noun* someone who bids **bidding** *noun* an order or command

biennial (*say* by-**en**-i-al) *adjective*
1 happening every two years: *a biennial event*
biennial *noun*
2 a plant that lives for two years, producing flowers and seed in its second year
•*Word Family:* **biennially** *adverb*

big *adjective*
1 large: *a big boy / a big dinner* 2 important: *big business* 3 elder: *my big sisters*
•*Word Family:* other forms are **bigger, biggest**

bigamy (*say* **big**-a-mee) *noun*
the crime of marrying someone when you are already married to another person
•*Word Family:* **bigamist** *noun* **bigamous** *adjective*

bigot (*say* **big**-et) *noun*
an intolerant person with strong and unreasonable opinions about things like religion or race
•*Word Family:* **bigoted** *adjective* **bigotry** *noun*

bike *noun*
1 a bicycle, tricycle or motorcycle
bike *verb*
2 to ride a bike
•*Word Family:* **biking** *noun*

bikini (*say* be-**kee**-nee) *noun*
a woman's swimming costume in two parts which are like a bra and pants
•*Word Origins:* named after *Bikini* Atoll in the Pacific Ocean made bare by US atomic bomb tests

bilateral (*say* by-**lat**-a-ral) *adjective*
to do with two sides or groups: *Britain and France had a bilateral agreement.*
•*Word Family:* **bilaterally** *adverb*

bile *noun*
the bitter yellow liquid produced by the liver, and stored in the gall bladder which is essential for digesting fat

bilge (*say* bilj) *noun*
1 the lowest parts inside a boat 2 the water that collects in these parts

bilingual (*say* by-**ling**-gwel) *adjective*
able to speak two languages fluently
•*Word Family:* **bilingualism** *noun* **bilingually** *adverb*

bilious (*say* **bil**-yus) *adjective*
1 having too much bile 2 feeling nauseous or sick in the stomach
•*Word Family:* **biliousness** *noun*

bill (1) *noun*
1 a statement showing how much money you owe for goods you have bought or jobs done for

you 2 a suggested or proposed law that has not yet been passed by parliament 3 a list of the performers and the pieces of music, films and so on being put on at a concert, film showing or theatre
•***Word Family:*** **bill** *verb*

bill (2) *noun*
a bird's beak

billabong *noun*
a pool or waterhole formed when the branch of a river was cut off or separated from the main stream
•***Word Origins:*** from words in an Aboriginal language meaning "dead river"

billet *verb*
to board or lodge for a while: *The students were billeted at private homes in the town.*
•***Word Family:*** other forms are **billets, billeted, billeting** □ **billet** *noun*

billiards *noun*
a game for two played on a rectangular table using a long cue and three balls, with the aim of hitting balls into pockets at the side

billion (*say* **bill**-yon) *noun*
a thousand times a million (1000 000 000)
•***Word Family:*** **billionaire** *noun* someone who owns a billion dollars, pounds and so on **billionth** *noun* **billionth** *adjective*

billow *verb*
1 to move upwards in large clouds: *Smoke billowed out of the chimney.* 2 to get pushed outwards by a gust of air: *The curtains billowed in the wind.*

billy-cart *noun*
a home-made, children's cart consisting of planks or a box on four wheels, steered with a rope tied to the front axle

billy-goat *noun*
a male goat

bin *noun*
a container, usually with a lid, for holding food or rubbish: *a bread bin / Could you put those sweet wrappers in the bin?*

binary (*say* **by**-na-ree) *adjective*
1 using only the numbers 0 and 1: *The binary system is used in computing.* 2 having two parts: *a binary star system*

bind (*rhymes with* kind) *verb*
1 to tie something or someone with string or rope so that it is held firmly 2 to fasten the pages of a book together in a cover: *to bind a book in leather*
bind *noun*
3 an annoying situation or a boring activity
•***Word Family:*** other forms are **binds, bound, binding** □ **binding** *noun* a book cover

binge (*say* binj) *noun*
a time when you drink or eat much more than you should, or you spend too much money

bingo *noun*
a game in which contestants match numbers on a card with numbers drawn at random

binoculars (*say* bi-**nok**-yoo-lerz) *plural noun*
an instrument with lenses for each of your eyes, used for making distant objects appear closer
•***Word Family:*** **binocular** *adjective* using both your eyes

bio- *prefix*
life or living things: *biology*
•***Word Origins:*** this prefix comes from Greek

biodegradable (*say* by-o-de-**grade**-a-bul) *adjective*
able to be broken down into natural substances by bacteria and therefore not contributing to pollution: *biodegradable washing powder*

biography (*say* by-**og**-ra-fee) *noun*
the life story of a person written by someone else
•***Word Family:*** the plural is **biographies** □ **biographer** *noun* someone who writes biographies **biographical** *adjective*

biology (*say* by-**ol**-a-jee) *noun*
the study of living things
•***Word Family:*** **biological** *adjective* **biologist** *noun*

bionic (*say* by-**on**-ik) *adjective*
with parts of the body working electronically, giving a person superhuman strength

biopsy (*say* **by**-op-see) *noun*
the removal and study of a tiny piece of your body tissue, to help doctors see if it is normal or diseased
•***Word Family:*** the plural is **biopsies**

biplane (*say* **by**-plane) *noun*
an old-fashioned type of aeroplane with two pairs of wings, one above the other

birch *noun*
a tall tree with thin branches and smooth bark, used for timber
•***Word Family:*** the plural is **birches**

bird *noun*
1 a two-legged animal with feathers and wings that lays eggs 2 a person, especially an odd one 3 a young woman

birth *noun*
1 being born or the time of being born: *The baby weighed 4 kilograms at birth.* 2 the beginning of something: *the birth of Islam*

birth control *noun*
ways of preventing a woman from becoming pregnant

birthday *noun*
1 the day or date of your birth 2 the anniversary of your birth celebrated each year

birthmark *noun*
a coloured mark that is on a person's skin when they are born

biscuit (*say* **bis**-kit) *noun*
a small, flat, crisp cake

bisect (*say* by-**sekt**) *verb*
to divide something into two equal parts
•*Word Family:* **bisector** *noun* a line that bisects an angle **bisection** *noun*

bisexual *adjective*
1 sexually attracted to both sexes, male and female 2 with both male and female sex organs: *Earthworms are bisexual.*
•*Word Family:* **bisexual** *noun* **bisexually** *adverb*

bishop *noun*
1 a Christian clergyman of high rank who is in charge of a diocese or district 2 a chess piece that may move any number of squares diagonally
•*Word Family:* **bishopric** *noun* the office or district of a bishop

bison (*say* **by**-son) *noun*
a large buffalo living in the United States, with a shaggy mane, short horns and high, humped shoulders
•*Word Family:* the plural is **bison** as well

bisque (*rhymes with* risk) *noun*
a smooth, creamy soup, often made of shellfish

bistro *noun*
a small restaurant with a casual style
•*Word Family:* the plural is **bistros**
•*Word Origins:* this word comes from French

bit (1) *noun*
1 a metal bar in a horse's mouth that the reins are attached to 2 the cutting part of a drill

bit (2) *noun*
a small piece or amount of something: *a bit of apple / a bit of money*

bit (3) *noun*
a number, either 0 or 1, which is the smallest unit of information in a computer and is used to convey instructions and write data

bitch *noun*
1 a female dog, fox or wolf 2 a nasty or unpleasant woman: *She's such a bitch.*
bitch *verb*
3 to complain about someone unkindly: *I can't help bitching about him.*
•*Word Family:* the plural form of the noun is **bitches** □ **bitchiness** *noun* **bitchy** *adjective* **(bitchier, bitchiest)**

bite *verb*
1 to cut into something with your teeth 2 to prick your skin sharply: *A mosquito bit me.* 3 to take the bait or hook on a fishing line and get caught: *The fish are biting well tonight.*
bite *noun*
4 an injury caused when an animal or insect bites you 5 a mouthful: *a bite of cake* 6 a small meal or snack
•*Word Family:* other forms are **bites, bit, bitten, biting**

bitter *adjective*
1 having a sharp, unpleasant taste 2 extremely cold: *Don't go out in that bitter wind without your scarf.* 3 filled with anger or hatred: *bitter words*
bitter *noun*
4 a type of strong tasting beer
•*Word Family:* **bitterly** *adverb* **bitterness** *noun*

bitumen (**bit**-yoo-men) *noun*
a sticky black mixture, similar to tar that is found in the ground or obtained from petrol and used to make roads
•*Word Family:* **bituminous** *adjective*

bizarre (*say* ba-**zar**) *adjective*
extremely strange or odd
•*Word Family:* **bizarrely** *adverb*
•*Word Origins:* this word comes from French

blab *verb*
to tell a secret: *I trusted you not to blab.*
•*Word Family:* other forms are **blabs, blabbed, blabbing** □ **blabbermouth** *noun* someone who blabs

black *noun*
1 the darkest colour, reflecting almost no light 2 someone with a naturally dark skin
black *adjective*
3 of the colour black 4 having a naturally dark skin 5 humble and upsetting: *It was a black day for all concerned.* 6 angry: *a black look* 7 without milk or cream: *black coffee* 8 evil or wicked: *to commit black deeds*

black belt *noun*
a sign of rank awarded to a grade of mastership in judo or karate

blackberry *noun*
a sweet, dark purple berry that grows on a thorny bush
•*Word Family:* the plural is **blackberries**

blackbird *noun*
a common bird whose male has black feathers and an orange beak

A B C D E F G H I J K L M N O P Q R S T U V W X Y Z

blackboard *noun*
a board painted black, that you can write on it with chalk

blackcurrant *noun*
a small, black fruit that grows on a shrub

blacken *verb*
1 to make something black or to turn black: *Grill the peppers until the skin starts to blacken.* 2 to say nasty things about someone so other people believe he or she is a bad person: *to blacken someone's reputation*

blackguard (*say* **blag**-ard) *noun*
a scoundrel

blackhead *noun*
a black spot on your face caused by a skin pore becoming blocked and filling with dark grease

black hole *noun*
a place in space that scientists think could exist, where the gravity is so strong that nothing can escape from it, not even light

blackmail *noun*
the crime of demanding payment from someone in return for keeping quiet about secrets they don't want revealed
• ***Word Family:*** **blackmail** *verb* **blackmailer** *noun*

black market *noun*
a system of buying and selling things which are illegal

blackout *noun*
1 a power failure 2 the concealing of lights during enemy air attacks at night 3 a sudden, temporary loss of memory or consciousness
• ***Word Family:*** **black out** *verb* to lose consciousness for a short time

blacksmith *noun*
someone who makes iron objects, such as horseshoes, by beating red-hot metal on an anvil using a hammer

bladder *noun*
a small bag-like part inside your body where urine is stored until it passes out of your body

blade *noun*
1 the flat cutting part of a sword or knife 2 the thin, flat part of an oar or propeller 3 a single plant leaf: *a blade of grass*

blame *verb*
to think that something bad is a particular person's fault
• ***Word Family:*** **blame** *noun*

blanch (*rhymes with* branch) *verb*
1 to suddenly turn pale because you are very shocked or frightened 2 to dip vegetables, fruits or nuts in boiling water in order to remove their skins or before freezing them: *to blanch almonds*
• ***Word Origins:*** from a French word meaning "white"

bland *adjective*
1 mild and tasteless: *This sauce is a bit bland.* 2 polite but dull or not giving away what you think: *a bland smile*
• ***Word Family:*** **blandly** *adverb* **blandness** *noun*

blank *adjective*
1 without anything written or drawn: *Put your name in the blank space.* 2 without expression: *He gave me a blank look.*
blank *noun*
3 an empty space on a piece of paper where you are supposed to write something 4 the cartridge of a gun that contains powder but no bullet
• ***Word Family:*** **blankly** *adverb* **blankness** *noun*

blanket *noun*
1 a piece of soft material on a bed used as a covering 2 a layer of something thick and soft: *There was a blanket of snow over the fields.*
blanket *verb*
3 to cover a place as if with a blanket
blanket *adjective*
4 affecting everyone in a group or every one of a type: *a blanket ban on meat products*

blare *verb*
to make a loud unpleasant noise: *The hi-fi next door was blaring all night.*

blasé (*say* **blah**-zay) *adjective*
uninterested in or bored by the things that other people find exciting

blaspheme (*say* blas-**feem**) *verb*
to speak disrespectfully about God or religion
• ***Word Family:*** **blasphemer** *noun* someone who blasphemes **blasphemous** *adjective* **blasphemy** *noun* (**blasphemies**)

blast (*say* blahst) *noun*
1 a strong gust of wind or jet of air 2 a short loud sound made by a horn, whistle or wind instrument 3 an explosion 4 **full blast** at full power: *The heater was going full blast.*
blast *verb*
5 to blow something up with explosives 6 to tell someone off very angrily: *She blasted me for being late.*

blatant (*say* **blay**-tunt) *adjective*
very obvious and without shame: *blatant advertising / a blatant lie*

blaze (1) *noun*
1 a strongly burning fire: *Firemen rushed to the blaze.* 2 a bright show of light or colour: *a blaze of light* 3 a sudden outburst: *a blaze of anger*
blaze *verb*
4 to burn or shine brightly

blaze (2) *noun*
1 a white mark on the face of a horse or cow
blaze *verb*
2 **blaze a trail** to be the first to discover or do something

blazer *noun*
a jacket, usually with a school or club badge sewn on the breast pocket

bleach *verb*
1 to make something become white or colourless or to turn white or colourless: *The sun bleached his hair.*
bleach *noun*
2 a chemical used to bleach clothes or to kill germs

bleak *adjective*
1 cold or windswept: *a bleak hillside* 2 cheerless, dismal or dreary: *a bleak future*

bleary (*say* **bleer**-ee) *adjective*
blurred and watery: *bleary eyes*
•*Word Family:* other forms are **blearier, bleariest**

bleat *verb*
to make a sound like a sheep or goat
•*Word Family:* **bleat** *noun*

bleed *verb*
1 to lose blood from an artery or vein 2 to ooze: *The sap bled from the tree.*
•*Word Family:* other forms are **bleeds, bled, bleeding** □ **bleeder** *noun* **bleeding** *adjective*

bleep *noun*
a short, high sound made by something electronic such as a digital watch or a computer
•*Word Family:* **bleep** *verb*

blemish *noun*
1 a stain or ugly mark: *a blemish on your skin* 2 a flaw in something that is otherwise good: *a blemish on my driving record*
blemish *verb*
3 to spoil the way something looks
•*Word Family:* the plural of the noun is **blemishes**

blend *verb*
1 to mix or join different things together so that they can no longer be thought of as separate: *The soup is blended from carrot and celery juice.*
blend *noun*
2 a mixture of several things
•*Word Family:* **blender** *noun* a machine for chopping and mixing food until it's smooth

bless *verb*
1 to ask God to look after someone or something: *The archbishop blessed the new church.* 2 **Bless you** thank you for being so kind or generous
•*Word Family:* other forms are **blesses, blessed** or **blest, blessing** □ **blessed** *adjective* favoured by **blessedly** *adverb* **blessedness** *noun*

blessing *noun*
1 a prayer for God's protection 2 something to be grateful for: *It's a blessing we were inside when the storm broke.*

blight *noun*
1 something that destroys or spoils something else: *the blight of pollution* 2 a plant disease, usually caused by fungi
•*Word Family:* **blight** *verb*

blind *adjective*
1 unable to see 2 unquestioning: *blind faith in his friends* 3 hidden from view: *a blind corner* 4 uncontrolled: *He murdered him in a blind fit of passion.* 5 **turn a blind eye to** to pretend not to notice
blind *verb*
6 to make someone blind or temporarily unable to see: *He was blinded in the explosion. / The headlights blinded her for a moment.*
blind *noun*
7 a roll of fabric or other material that you pull down over a window to keep light out
•*Word Family:* **blindly** *adverb* in a blind way **blindingly** *adverb* **blindness** *noun*

blindfold *verb*
to cover a person's eyes with a strip of fabric so that they cannot see
•*Word Family:* **blindfold** *noun*

blink *verb*
to close your eyes and open them again

bliss *noun*
great happiness and contentment
•*Word Family:* **blissful** *adjective* **blissfully** *adverb*

blister *noun*
1 a swelling like a bubble on your skin that has a watery liquid inside, caused where your skin has been rubbed or burned: *My new shoes have given me blisters on my feet.* 2 a swelling like a blister in old paint
•*Word Family:* **blister** *verb* **blistering** *adjective*

blithe *adjective*
cheerful and carefree
•*Word Family:* **blithely** *adverb*

blitz *noun*
1 a sudden attack by enemy aircraft 2 a sudden, energetic effort to get a job done: *I had a blitz on tidying up my room.*
•*Word Family:* **blitz** *verb*
•*Word Origins:* a short form of the German word *Blitzkrieg* meaning "lightning war"

blizzard *noun*
a fierce storm of wind and snow

bloat *verb*
to swell up with gas or liquid

blob *noun*
a large drop of something thick or sticky: *a blob of glue*

bloc (*say* blok) *noun*
a group of parties or countries who agree to act together

block *noun*
1 a solid piece of something, especially wood or stone 2 an area in a city or town bounded by four roads 3 a large building containing flats or offices
block *verb*
4 to prevent something from getting past or from happening: *The angry boy blocked his way.*
• ***Word Family:*** **blockage** *noun*

blockade *noun*
1 the surrounding of a place with ships and soldiers so that goods and people cannot get in or out 2 an obstruction that stops things from getting past: *The workers put up a blockade at the building site.*
• ***Word Family:*** **blockade** *verb*

blockbuster *noun*
a very popular and successful film or book

bloke *noun*
a man

blond *adjective*
with fair hair: *blond hair*
• ***Word Family:*** **blonde** *noun* a woman with blond hair **blond** *noun* **blondness** *noun*
• ***Word Origins:*** from a Latin word meaning "yellow"

blood (*say* blud) *noun*
1 the red fluid pumped through your body's arteries and veins by your heart 2 the family you belong to: *They are related by blood.* 3 **in cold blood** deliberately and cruelly
• ***Word Family:*** **bloodless** *adjective*

bloodbath *noun*
the violent killing of many people

bloodcurdling *adjective*
terrifying and horrible: *a bloodcurdling movie about a wicked killer*

blood donor *noun*
someone who gives blood so that it can be used in transfusions or operations

bloodhound *noun*
a large, strong dog, with smooth hair and a good sense of smell, used for tracking and hunting

bloodshed *noun*
the killing of people in a war or other violent situation: *There were calls for peace and an end to the bloodshed.*

bloodshot *adjective*
reddened with burst blood vessels: *bloodshot eyes*

bloodstream *noun*
the blood flowing round your body

bloodthirsty *adjective*
violent or willing to kill people: *Bloodthirsty bandits wait for passing travellers.*
• ***Word Family:*** **bloodthirstily** *adverb* **bloodthirstiness** *noun*

bloody (*say* **blud**-ee) *adjective*
1 stained with blood: *a bloody handkerchief*
2 killing many people: *a bloody battle*
3 complete or awful: *a bloody pain in the neck*
bloody *verb*
4 to stain something with blood
• ***Word Family:*** other adjective forms are **bloodier, bloodiest** □ other verb forms are **bloodies, bloodied, bloodying** □ **bloodily** *adverb* **bloodiness** *noun*

bloom *noun*
1 a flower
bloom *verb*
2 to produce flowers
• ***Word Family:*** **blooming** *adjective* glowing with health

bloomers *plural noun*
a pair of soft, loose, women's underpants
• ***Word Origins:*** named after Mrs Amelia *Bloomer*, 1818 to 1894, an American feminist and magazine publisher who helped promote these pants

blossom (*say* **blos**-om) *noun*
1 a flower, especially the flower of a fruit tree
blossom *verb*
2 to flower 3 to develop successfully: *He blossomed into a top basketball player.*

blot *noun*
1 a spot or stain, especially of ink 2 something that makes other people think badly of you: *The silly things he did last term are still a blot on his reputation.*
blot *verb*
3 to use a soft cloth or paper to dry unwanted liquid 4 **blot out** to try to forget something terrible: *She tried to blot out the awful memory.*
• ***Word Family:*** other verb forms are **blots, blotted, blotting**

blotch *noun*
a large coloured patch or stain: *There were red blotches on his cheeks.*
• ***Word Family:*** the plural is **blotches** □ **blotchy** *adjective* (**blotchier, blotchiest**): *blotchy skin*

blouse (*rhymes with* cows) *noun*
a woman's shirt, especially a pretty one that you tuck into a skirt or trousers

blow (1) (*rhymes with* slow) *noun*
1 a hard, sudden hit using your hand or a weapon: *She received a painful blow on the head.* 2 a shock or disappointment: *Her death was a great blow to the family.*

blow (2) (*rhymes with* slow) *verb*
1 to be moving as air: *The wind blows hard in the winter.* 2 to push air out through your mouth: *She blew on her cold hands.* 3 to move or be moved because of the wind: *The wind blew the tree down.* 4 to produce sound by blowing into a wind instrument: *to blow a trumpet* 5 to melt because the electric current is too strong: *The fuse has blown.* 6 to spend a lot of money or all your money: *to blow your fortune at the horse races* 7 to fail at: *Trust you to blow a simple job like that!* 8 **blow out** to put out a flame by blowing at it: *to blow out a candle* 9 **blow up** (a) to explode: *to blow up a bridge* (b) to enlarge: *to blow up a photograph* (c) to fill something with air: *to blow up a balloon*
•***Word Family:*** other forms are **blows, blew, blown, blowing** □ **blown** *adjective*

blowfly *noun*
a fly that usually lays its eggs or larvae on meat and other food scraps on which the larvae feed
•***Word Family:*** the plural is **blowflies**

blowhole *noun*
the breathing hole of a whale

blown *adjective*
1 inflated or swollen: *a horse with a blown stomach from eating too much clover* 2 out of breath 3 **blown away** amazed with delight: *I'm blown away by the band's new lead singer.*
•***Word Family:*** **blow** *verb* **blow** *noun*

blubber *noun*
1 the thick layer of fat under the skin of sea mammals, such as whales and seals
blubber *verb*
2 to cry noisily

bludgeon (*say* **bluj**-en) *verb*
to hit someone repeatedly with something heavy

blue (*say* bloo) *noun*
1 the colour of a clear sky 2 **out of the blue** suddenly or unexpectedly: *She arrived out of the blue, we thought she was in Africa.*
blue *adjective*
3 of the colour blue: *blue eyes* 4 depressed or unhappy: *a blue mood* 5 about sex: *blue movies*
•***Word Family:*** other adjective forms are **bluer, bluest**

bluebell *noun*
a plant with small, blue flowers shaped like bells

bluebottle *noun*
a large blue and green fly

blueprint *noun*
1 a photographic copy of an architect's or engineer's plan, printed in white on blue paper 2 a detailed outline or plan of how something is expected to work

blues *plural noun*
1 feelings of sadness or depression: *to have the blues* 2 a type of jazz music that developed from the slow, sad songs that early African Americans used to sing: *to sing the blues*

bluey *noun*
the swag or bundle of possessions carried by a bushman

bluff (1) *noun*
1 a steep headland or cliff
bluff *adjective*
2 hearty and outspoken
•***Word Family:*** **bluffness** *noun*
•***Word Origins:*** from a German word meaning "flat"

bluff (2) *verb*
to mislead people by pretending that you know something or can do something when it is not true: *to bluff your way into a building by pretending to be someone else*
•***Word Family:*** **bluff** *noun*

blunder *noun*
1 a stupid mistake
blunder *verb*
2 to make a stupid mistake 3 to move awkwardly and clumsily: *to blunder past, treading on toes*

blunt *adjective*
1 with a dull, rounded edge or tip: *a blunt knife* 2 honest and direct in what you say without trying to be polite or kind: *I was hurt by his blunt criticism.*
•***Word Family:*** **blunt** *verb* **bluntly** *adverb* **bluntness** *noun*

blur *verb*
to make something unclear or fuzzy or to become unclear or fuzzy: *Bitter tears blurred her vision. / Her eyes blurred with tiredness.*
•***Word Family:*** other forms are **blurs, blurred, blurring** □ **blurry** *adjective* (**blurrier, blurriest**) **blur** *noun* **blurred** *adjective*

blurb *noun*
a description of a book printed on its jacket which aims to make you want to read the book
•***Word Origins:*** made up by Gelett Burgess, an American who died in 1951

A B C D E F G H I J K L M N O P Q R S T U V W X Y Z

blush *verb*
to go red in the face

bluster *verb*
1 to blow in loud, violent gusts: *The wind blustered through the leaves.* 2 to speak or behave noisily but with little result
• ***Word Family:*** **blustery** *adjective*

BMX *noun*
a strong bicycle specially designed for rough riding
• ***Word Origins:*** short for Bicycle Motocross, with X taking the place of *cross*

boa (*say* **bo**-a) *noun*
a large snake that coils around its prey and crushes it to death
• ***Word Family:*** the plural is **boas**

boar *noun*
a male pig

board *noun*
1 a long, flat piece of timber, used in building 2 a thin, flat piece of wood or stiff card: *an ironing-board / a chess board* 3 a group of people who control the business affairs of a company
board *verb*
4 to get on a train, ship or plane 5 to pay to live in someone's house and have meals that they cook for you: *to board with a friend*
• ***Word Family:*** **boarder** *noun* someone who pays for food and lodgings

boarding school *noun*
a school where pupils live during term time

board shorts *plural noun*
shorts with extra-long legs, originally designed to protect surfers riding waxed surfboards

boardwalk *noun*
a wide path beside the beach or the water

boast (*rhymes with* post) *verb*
1 to speak about yourself or the things you own with too much pride
boast *noun*
2 something you boast about

boat *noun*
1 a vehicle built to float and travel on water 2 **in the same boat** all in the same unpleasant situation
• ***Word Family:*** **boating** *noun*

boater *noun*
a straw hat with a flat, round top and brim

bob (1) *verb*
1 to move up and down: *We could see the ball bobbing in the water.* 2 **bob up** to appear suddenly
• ***Word Family:*** other forms are **bobs, bobbed, bobbing**

bob (2) *noun*
1 a woman's haircut in which the hair is cut evenly at chin level
bob *verb*
2 to cut short: *to bob a horse's tail*
• ***Word Family:*** other verb forms are **bobs, bobbed, bobbing**

bobbin *noun*
an object around which thread is wound for use in weaving or sewing

bobsleigh *noun*
a vehicle like a large sledge with long blades underneath used for racing downhill on ice

bodice (*say* **bod**-iss) *noun*
the top part of a dress above the waist

body *noun*
1 the whole physical structure of a person or animal 2 the central part of a person or animal without the head, arms or legs 3 a dead person or animal: *The body was found in the boot of the car.* 4 the main part: *the body of the poem* 5 a group of people: *a body of troops* 6 a large quantity of something: *a body of water*
• ***Word Family:*** the plural is **bodies** □ **bodily** *adjective*

bodyguard *noun*
a person whose job is to protect someone from being attacked

bog *noun*
an area of ground that is always wet and spongy, often formed by decaying plants
• ***Word Family:*** **boggy** *adjective* (**boggier, boggiest**)

bogey (*say* **bo**-gee) *noun*
something frightening that doesn't really exist: *Children are often afraid of bogeys under the bed.*

bogie (*say* **bo**-gee) *noun*
1 a trolley or truck used by railway workmen 2 a wheeled undercarriage for supporting a railway locomotive

boggle *verb*
to be startled and find something difficult to grasp: *The mind boggles at the idea.*

bogus *adjective*
not real or genuine: *A bogus workman got into the building. / a bogus claim for money*
• ***Word Origins:*** named after a machine that produced counterfeit money

boil (1) *verb*
1 to make a liquid so hot or to get so hot that it bubbles and starts to change into steam: *I boiled her bedtime milk. / The milk boiled.* 2 to cook something by boiling it in liquid
• ***Word Family:*** **boil** *noun: Bring the milk to the boil slowly.* **boiling** *adjective* very hot: *the boiling sun*

boil (2) *noun*
a large painful spot on the skin, often filled with pus

boiler *noun*
a container in which water is stored, heated by burning fuel and circulated, to be used for heating or power

boiling point *noun*
the temperature at which a liquid begins to boil

boisterous (*say* **boy**-ste-rus) *adjective*
noisy, rough and full of energy: *boisterous puppies*
•***Word Family:*** **boisterously** *adverb*

bold *adjective*
1 fearless and ready to take risks: *a bold adventurer* 2 confident and a bit daring: *a bold reply* 3 clear and distinct: *bold handwriting* 4 thicker, and darker than ordinary printing: *a bold typeface*
•***Word Family:*** **boldly** *adverb* **boldness** *noun*

bollard *noun*
a short, strong post which a ship is tied to at a dock or that stops a car going off the road

bolster (*say* **bohl**-ster) *noun*
1 a long, narrow pillow
bolster *verb*
2 to build up or support someone or something: *to bolster your courage*

bolt *noun*
1 a sliding metal bar for fastening a door or window 2 a heavy metal pin with a thread at one end, used with a nut for holding things together 3 a flash: *a bolt of lightning* 4 a sudden swift dash: *They made a desperate bolt for the door.*
bolt *verb*
5 to fasten a door or window with a bolt 6 to run away very quickly and suddenly: *The horse bolted after its jockey fell.* 7 to eat too fast: *Please don't bolt your food.*

bomb (*say* bom) *noun*
1 a container filled with an explosive charge and used as a weapon to blow things up
bomb *verb*
2 to attack or destroy something with bombs

bombard *verb*
1 to repeatedly attack a place with bombs or gunfire 2 to ask questions or say things to someone repeatedly and with great energy: *to bombard someone with questions*
•***Word Family:*** **bombardment** *noun*

bombastic *adjective*
using a lot of impressive-sounding long words but not making much sense
•***Word Family:*** **bombast** *noun* important-sounding words **bombastically** *adverb*

bomber *noun*
1 someone who places a bomb so that it will go off 2 an aeroplane that carries and drops bombs

bombshell *noun*
a sudden or shocking surprise: *The criticism came as a complete bombshell.*

bonanza *noun*
a source of good luck or wealth: *The discovery of an oil well was a bonanza.*
•***Word Origins:*** from a Spanish word meaning "fair weather"

bonbon *noun*
a small sweet

bond *noun*
1 a feeling or experience that people share that makes them very close: *a bond of affection*
bond *verb*
2 to join or be stuck together firmly

bondage *noun*
being a slave or a prisoner: *The men were sold into bondage.*

bone *noun*
1 one of the separate hard pieces of a skeleton: *a knee bone* 2 **have a bone to pick** to have a subject you want to complain or argue about: *I've got a bone to pick with you.*
bone *verb*
3 to remove the bones from meat or fish: *to bone a chicken* 4 **bone up on** to study and learn all about something
•***Word Family:*** **bony** *adjective* (**bonier, boniest**) thin so you can see the bones under the skin: *a bony face*

bone-idle *adjective*
extremely lazy

bonfire *noun*
a large fire built outside in the open

bongos *plural noun*
a pair of small drums played by hitting them with your hands

bonnet *noun*
1 a soft hat, with its sides pulled down over the ears and tied with ribbons under the chin 2 the metal cover for a car engine

bonsai (*say* **bon**-suy) *noun*
1 the art of pruning the roots and branches of certain trees to keep them tiny, dwarfed and beautifully shaped 2 a tree grown like this
•***Word Origins:*** from the Japanese words for "pot" and "plant"

bonus *noun*
something given in addition to what is usual or

expected, such as extra money given to an employee in return for good work
•*Word Family:* the plural is **bonuses**

booby trap *noun*
1 a trap designed to trick someone 2 a hidden bomb set to go off when someone touches something connected to it

boogie board *noun*
a small, light, flexible surfboard that you ride lying on your belly
•*Word Origins:* a trademark; *boogie* is the name of the first of this type of board

book (*say* buk) *noun*
1 a number of sheets of paper bound or fastened together between covers, to be read or written in: *I'll have that book for my bedtime story. / a chequebook* 2 **be in somebody's good books** to have someone thinking good things about you
book *verb*
3 to write someone's name in police records along with the crime they are being charged with: *The police booked her for speeding.* 4 to reserve something in advance: *to book tickets for a play*
•*Word Family:* **booking** *noun* an advance reservation

book-keeping *noun*
the process or job of recording all the money received and spent in a business
•*Word Family:* **book-keeper** *noun*

booklet *noun*
a book with just a few pages that gives information about something

bookmaker *noun*
someone who takes people's bets on horse races or other competitions

bookworm *noun*
someone who reads a lot

boom (1) *verb*
1 to make a loud, hollow sound 2 to flourish or progress surprisingly fast: *Business boomed in the big city.*
•*Word Family:* **boom** *noun*

boom (2) *noun*
1 a long pole attached to the bottom of a sail and often by one end to the mast 2 a movable arm from which a microphone or floodlight hangs down over actors being filmed in a studio

boomerang *noun*
1 a curved, wooden throwing stick that is used by Australian Aborigines to kill animals for food, and is designed to return to the thrower
boomerang *verb*
2 to rebound with harmful effects upon the person who started something
•*Word Origins:* from an Aboriginal language

boon *noun*
something that makes your life much more pleasant or comfortable: *Her friendship is a real boon to me.*

boor *noun*
someone who is rude and without manners
•*Word Family:* **boorish** *adjective* **boorishly** *adverb*
•*Word Origins:* from a Dutch word meaning "peasant"

boost *verb*
1 to increase something or improve its success: *to boost sales by advertising* 2 to help something improve: *That should boost her confidence.*
boost *noun*
3 an increase or improvement

booster *noun*
1 a rocket that gives extra power to a spacecraft 2 an extra dose of vaccine given after the main dose to make sure you are still protected from getting an illness

boot (1) *noun*
1 a heavy shoe that covers your ankle and sometimes part of your leg 2 a space usually at the back of a car for carrying luggage 3 **give someone the boot** to dismiss someone from their job: *We had to give him the boot for stealing.*

boot (2) *verb*
to turn on a computer and start it loading its operating system

booth *noun*
a small, enclosed place, for one person to use at a time: *a telephone booth*

bootleg *adjective*
illegally made, sold or smuggled: *bootleg whisky*

booty *noun*
something stolen or captured in war or by robbery

booze *noun*
1 alcoholic drink: *We'll buy some booze at the off-licence on the way home.*
booze *verb*
2 to drink a lot of alcohol
•*Word Family:* **boozer** *noun* someone who drinks a lot of alcohol **boozy** *adjective*: *a boozy lunch*

boppy *adjective*
easy to dance to: *The DJ is playing boppy music tonight.*
•*Word Family:* other forms are **boppier, boppiest**

border *noun*
1 the line or area that separates one country, state or place from another: *We crossed the border between France and Germany.* 2 a strip

around the edge of something: *The tablecloth has a lace border.*
border *verb*
3 to share a border with another country or place: *Italy borders France and Austria.*

borderline *adjective*
close to the line which separates people who pass from those who fail or something which is acceptable from something which isn't: *He got a borderline pass in the test.*

bore (1) *verb*
1 to make a deep, round hole
bore *noun*
2 the diameter inside a gun barrel

bore (2) *verb*
1 to be dull and make people feel uninterested: *He bored us with his long tales.*
bore *noun*
2 someone or something that bores you
•***Word Family:*** **bored** *adjective* uninterested in, and impatient with, something dull **boredom** *noun* **boring** *adjective*

borer *noun*
an insect that burrows into timber or trees and does damage with the holes it makes

borough *noun*
a town or part of a city that has its own council

borrow *verb*
to take something belonging to someone else which you are going to return later: *He let me borrow his guitar.*
•***Word Family:*** **borrower** *noun*

borsch (*say* borsh) *noun*
a Russian soup made from beetroot and served hot or cold

bosom (*say* **booz**-em) *noun*
1 someone's breast, usually thought of as a woman's 2 the warmth or affection of a group of people who accept you as one of them: *He was welcomed into the bosom of the family.*
bosom *adjective*
3 close or intimate: *bosom buddies*

boss *noun*
1 a person who other people work for
boss *verb*
2 to order someone around
•***Word Family:*** the plural of the noun is **bosses** □ **bossy** *adjective* (**bossier, bossiest**) liking to boss people
•***Word Origins:*** from a Dutch word meaning "master"

botany (*say* **bot**-a-nee) *noun*
the study of plants
•***Word Family:*** **botanist** *noun* someone who studies plants **botanic** *adjective* **botanical** *adjective*

botch *verb*
to spoil something by doing it badly or clumsily
•***Word Family:*** **botch** *noun* (**botches**): *I've made a real botch of this map.*

bother (*say* **both**-a) *verb*
1 to annoy you: *Stop bothering me while I'm reading.* 2 to take the trouble to do something: *She never bothers to check her spellings.* 3 to worry or upset you: *The noise of the tap dripping bothered him.*

bottle *noun*
1 a glass or plastic container for holding liquid, usually with a narrow neck and a lid or cork
bottle *verb*
2 to put liquid into a bottle 3 **bottle up** to keep your feelings or thoughts inside you without letting anyone know how you feel

bottle-brush *noun*
1 a brush for cleaning bottles 2 an Australian shrub with red or pink flower spikes that look like brushes

bottleneck *noun*
a narrow bit of road that becomes easily congested when traffic slows down to go through it

bottom *noun*
1 the lowest part of something 2 the part of your body that you sit on

botulism (*say* **bot**-yoo-liz-um) *noun*
a disease of your nervous system caused by eating bad food, and making you see double and become paralysed
•***Word Origins:*** from a Latin word meaning "sausage" and first used to describe food poisoning from contaminated sausage

bough (*rhymes with* cow) *noun*
a large tree branch, usually starting at the trunk

bouillon (*say* **boo**-yon) *noun*
a clear broth
•***Word Origins:*** from a French word meaning "to boil"

boulder (sounds like bolder) *noun*
a very large, rounded stone

boulevard (*say* **bool**-a-vard) *noun*
a wide city street lined with trees
•***Word Origins:*** this word comes from French

bounce *verb*
1 to spring back after hitting something: *The ball bounced on the concrete.* 2 to make something bounce: *Bounce the ball on the floor.* 3 to move in a lively manner: *She bounced into the room.* 4 to be returned unpaid from a bank due to lack of money in the account: *My cheque bounced.*

bounce *noun*
5 the movement that a ball makes when it bounces
•*Word Family:* **bouncing** *adjective* large and healthy: *a bouncing baby* **bouncy** *adjective* lively and full of energy

bound (1) *adjective*
1 certain: *Their plan is bound to fail.* 2 unable to get away from or get to because of a particular situation: *snowbound* 3 obliged: *I feel bound to explain why I didn't come.*
bound *verb*
4 the past tense and past participle of the verb **bind**

bound (2) *verb*
to move in leaps: *He bounded energetically into the room.*

bound (3) *noun*
1 a limit or boundary: *There are no bounds to his ambition.* 2 **out of bounds** forbidden: *That street is out of bounds.*
bound *verb*
3 to limit or form the limit of something
•*Word Family:* **boundless** *adjective* unlimited

boundary *noun*
1 anything that marks the edge: *Those trees mark the boundary of our property.* 2 a strike in cricket that counts for four or six runs and sends the ball beyond the field boundary
•*Word Family:* the plural is **boundaries**

bountiful *adjective*
1 generous: *a bountiful giver* 2 plentiful: *a bountiful supply of corn*

bounty *noun*
1 generosity 2 a bonus or reward, especially one given by a government: *a bounty for capturing the escaped prisoner*
•*Word Family:* the plural is **bounties**

bouquet (*say* bo-**kay** *or* boo-**kay**) *noun*
1 a bunch of flowers 2 the special smell of a wine
•*Word Origins:* from an Old French word meaning "little wood"

bout *noun*
1 a short but intense period: *a bout of flu / a frantic bout of packing* 2 a contest: *a boxing bout*

boutique (*say* boo-**teek**) *noun*
a small, fashionable shop usually selling women's clothing or gifts

bouzouki (*say* boo-**zoo**-kee) *noun*
a musical instrument with strings and a long neck, played by plucking
•*Word Origins:* this word comes from Greek

bovine (*say* **bo**-vine) *adjective*
1 to do with cows, bulls and oxen 2 dull or stupid

bow (1) (*rhymes with* cow) *verb*
1 to bend down or sideways: *The branches bowed in the wind. / He bowed politely to the Queen.*
2 to give way: *You must bow to their wishes.*

bow (2) (*rhymes with* go) *noun*
1 a weapon made from a length of wood which has string stretched tightly between its two ends, used to shoot arrows 2 a knot used as a decoration: *to wear a bow in your hair* 3 a stick with horsehairs stretched along it, used to play stringed instruments, such as a violin or cello

bow (3) (*rhymes with* cow) *noun*
the front end of a boat

bowel (*rhymes with* towel) *noun*
1 a tube in the lower part of your body that carries food, while it is being digested, from your stomach to your anus 2 the innermost part of something: *in the bowels of the earth*

bower (*rhymes with* flower) *noun*
a shady, leafy shelter

bowl (1) (*say* bohl) *noun*
1 a deep, round dish 2 a rounded, hollow object shaped like this: *the bowl of a pipe*

bowl (2) (*say* bohl) *verb*
1 to throw or roll 2 to move along smoothly and rapidly 3 to throw the ball for the batsman to hit in cricket
bowl *noun*
4 a heavy ball used in the game of bowls or for tenpin bowling
•*Word Family:* **bowling alley** *noun* a long, indoor wooden alley for tenpin bowling or skittles **bowler** *noun*

bowler hat (*say* **bohl**-er hat) *noun*
a man's hat with a rounded crown and narrow brim, usually made of felt

bowls (*say* bohls) *noun*
a game played on a green or lawn by players who try to roll heavy balls as close as possible to a small white ball (jack)

box (1) *noun*
1 a container with a lid, made of cardboard or wood 2 a separate compartment, container or enclosure: *the glove box of a car / a witness box*
3 something shaped like a box: *a box kite*
box *verb*
4 to put something in a box or something like a box
•*Word Family:* the plural is **boxes**

box (2) *verb*
to fight with your fists
•*Word Family:* **boxer** *noun* someone who boxes **boxing** *noun* the sport of someone who boxes

boxer shorts *plural noun*
men's underwear similar to loose-fitting shorts

box office *noun*
the place where tickets are sold in a theatre
•***Word Family:*** **box office** *adjective: a box office hit*

box seat *noun*
the best position

boy *noun*
a male child
•***Word Family:*** **boyhood** *noun* **boyish** *adjective*

boycott *verb*
to stop buying a product or dealing with a company, as a way of making a protest: *to boycott imported goods*
•***Word Origins:*** named after Captain Charles *Boycott*, 1832 – 97, a land agent for an Irish earl, who was boycotted by his tenants when he would not lower their rents

boyfriend *noun*
the boy or man that a girl or woman regularly goes out with

bra *noun*
close-fitting underwear that supports the breasts

brace *noun*
1 something that holds parts together or acts as a support, such as wires and bands fitted against teeth to straighten them 2 **braces** the straps that you wear over your shoulders to hold up trousers
brace *verb*
3 to steady yourself: *to brace yourself against the wall* 4 to prepare or summon up courage: *to brace yourself to hear bad news*
•***Word Family:*** **bracing** *adjective* invigorating: *bracing sea breezes*

bracelet *noun*
a decorative band or chain that you wear around your wrist

bracken *noun*
a large, coarse fern or clump of ferns

bracket *noun*
1 a support for a shelf or rack 2 either of the marks, [ ] or ( ), used to add information to a sentence or to show that everything inside is to be treated as a separate unit, as in *Jason (the boy I love) gave me a sloppy kiss.* 3 a grouping: *People in the high income bracket.*
•***Word Family:*** **bracket** *verb*

brackish *adjective*
slightly salty: *This brackish water isn't much good for drinking.*

brag *verb*
to boast
•***Word Family:*** other forms are **brags, bragged, bragging** □ **braggart** *noun* someone who boasts or brags

brahmin *noun*
a breed of cattle with a humped back, bred from Indian zebus

braid *noun*
1 a band of fabric made of woven threads and used for trimming or decoration 2 a plait
braid *verb*
3 to weave or plait

braille (*say* brale) *noun*
a system of printing for blind people, using raised dots that they can read by touching them
•***Word Origins:*** invented by Louis *Braille*, who lived from 1809 to 1852

brain *noun*
1 the soft mass of nerve cells inside your skull, that controls the way your body thinks, moves and feels 2 intelligence: *You need a good brain to solve that problem.* 3 an intelligent person: My *sister's a real brain.*
brain *verb*
4 to hit on the head: *He brained me with a stick!*
•***Word Family:*** **brainy** *adjective* (**brainier, brainiest**) intelligent

brainwave *noun*
a sudden clever idea

braise *verb*
to cook meat or vegetables by browning in fat and then stewing in a covered pot

brake *noun*
something for slowing or stopping the speed of a wheel, motor or vehicle
•***Word Family:*** **brake** *verb*

bramble *noun*
a coarse prickly shrub, especially the blackberry bush
•***Word Family:*** **brambly** *adjective*

bran *noun*
the ground husks of wheat after the flour has been removed: *Wholemeal bread has bran in it.*

branch *noun*
1 an offshoot of the main stem of a tree or shrub 2 a smaller division or section: *a branch of a bank / the branch of a river*
branch *verb*
3 to divide or separate: *Our road branches off here.*
•***Word Family:*** the plural is **branches**

brand *noun*
1 a trademark or name used to identify a product: *What brand of soap do you use?* 2 the mark put on something to show where it comes from or how good it is: *The cattle have a brand burnt onto their skin to show who they belong to.*

a b c d e f g h i j k l m n o p q r s t u v w x y z

brand *verb*
3 to mark something with a brand: *to brand cattle* 4 to be known or have a reputation for: *He's been branded a loser.*

brandish *verb*
to wave about: *She brandished her tennis racquet.*

brandy *noun*
an alcoholic drink made from wine or fruit juice: *cherry brandy*
• ***Word Family:*** the plural is **brandies**

brash *adjective*
too bold and confident: *The brash new student told the rest of the class what to do.*
• ***Word Family:*** **brashly** *adverb*

brass (*rhymes with* grass) *noun*
1 a goldish metal made from a mixture of zinc and copper 2 the family of metal musical instruments, such as trumpets and horns, which you blow through a mouthpiece
• ***Word Family:*** **brass** *adjective: a member of the brass family* **brassy** *adjective* (**brassier, brassiest**)

brasserie (*say* **brass**-er-ee) *noun*
a restaurant that serves plain, cooked food

brat *noun*
a child, especially an irritating one

bratwurst (*say* **brat**-werst) *noun*
a type of German sausage

bravado (*say* bra-**vah**-do) *noun*
a display of bravery or courage, especially bravery you don't really feel: *His bravado turned to terror when it was his turn to parachute.*

brave *adjective*
1 having or showing courage: *a brave girl / a brave deed*
brave *verb*
2 to meet or face with courage: *to brave the storm*
• ***Word Family:*** **bravely** *adverb* **bravery** *noun*

bravo (*say* brah-vo) *interjection*
well done! or good!

brawl *noun*
a noisy quarrel or fight
• ***Word Family:*** **brawl** *verb*

brawn *noun*
1 muscles, or the strength of muscles: *The giant used his brawn to pull up the tree.* 2 boiled and moulded meat
• ***Word Family:*** **brawny** *adjective* (**brawnier, brawniest**) muscular or strong
• ***Word Origins:*** from an Old French word meaning "slice of meat"

bray *noun*
1 the harsh, noisy cry of a donkey 2 a similar sound: *a bray of laughter*
• ***Word Family:*** **bray** *verb*

brazen *adjective*
1 bold or cheeky: *a brazen remark* 2 like brass or made of brass
• ***Word Family:*** **brazenly** *adverb* **brazenness** *noun*

brazier *noun*
a metal container for holding burning fuels such as coal

breach *noun*
1 a gap or break: *a breach in the opponent's defence* 2 the breaking of an agreement or rule: *a breach of promise*
• ***Word Family:*** the plural is **breaches** □ **breach** *verb*

bread (*say* bred) *noun*
1 a shaped, baked food made of flour, liquid and usually yeast to make it rise 2 food: *to earn your bread* 3 money
bread *verb*
4 to coat with breadcrumbs: *breaded cutlets*

breadth (*say* bredth) *noun*
1 the width of something or the distance from one side to the other 2 extent: *He showed great breadth of knowledge.*

breadwinner *noun*
someone who earns the money for a family or household

break (*rhymes with* cake) *verb*
1 to divide into parts, usually by force: *to break a vase* 2 to stop: *to break a habit* 3 to fail to keep: *to break a promise* 4 to outdo: *to break a world record* 5 to change in range or tone: *His voice is about to break.* 6 to crack a bone of: *to break your arm* 7 **break down** (a) to collapse or become very upset (b) to stop working correctly 8 **break up** (a) to separate: *to break up with your girlfriend* (b) to end a school term
break *noun*
9 an opening made by breaking: *a break in the wall* 10 the beginning: *the break of day* 11 an attempt to escape: *a jail break* 12 a rest: *a morning tea break*
• ***Word Family:*** the other verb forms are **breaks, broke, broken, breaking** □ **breakage** *noun* breaking, or something broken **breakable** *adjective*

breakdown *noun*
1 a collapse or failure to work: *the breakdown of law and order / We had a breakdown on the motorway.* 2 becoming so depressed that you become mentally ill: *to have a mental breakdown* 3 an analysis or summary of important points: *a breakdown of what we spend money on*

breakfast (*say* **brek**-fast) *noun*
1 the first meal of the day
• ***Word Family:*** **breakfast** *verb*

breakthrough (*say* **brake**-throo) *noun*
a sudden, new development in our knowledge or the discovery of a new way of doing something: *a breakthrough in AIDS research*

breakwater *noun*
a jetty built out from a beach or river bank, to protect the beach from being eroded by heavy waves

breast (*say* brest) *noun*
1 one of the two fleshy parts on a woman's chest that produce milk when she has a baby 2 the chest 3 **make a clean breast of** to confess

breast stroke *noun*
a swimming style in which you lie face-down in the water with both arms moving out and back to your chest and the feet kicking like a frog

breath (*say* breth) *noun*
1 the air that goes into and out of your lungs 2 taking in and letting out this air: *Take a deep breath.* 3 a small amount of something: *There was not a breath of wind.* 4 **under your breath** in a whisper 5 **out of breath** unable to breathe freely 6 **take your breath away** to astonish
•***Word Family:*** **breathless** *adjective* out of breath

breathalyser (*say* **breth**-a-lighz-er) *noun*
an instrument that measures the amount of alcohol in your breath as you breathe out
•***Word Family:*** **breathalyse** *verb*

breathe (*say* breedh) *verb*
1 to take in and give out air 2 to relax: *to breathe freely again* 3 to speak: *Don't breathe a word about what I've said.*
•***Word Family:*** **breather** *noun* a pause or rest

breathtaking *adjective*
amazing or wonderful: *a breathtaking view*

breech *noun*
the rear part of a gun, behind the barrel

breeches (*say* **brit**-chiz) *plural noun*
trousers reaching to just below the knee: *riding breeches*

breed *verb*
1 to produce offspring or young: *Many animals breed in the spring.* 2 to keep animals in order to produce and raise more: *to breed bantams* 3 to cause: *Hatred breeds violence.*
breed *noun*
4 a type or species of animal: *a breed of dog*
•***Word Family:*** other verb forms are **breeds, bred, breeding** □ **breeder** *noun* someone who breeds animals

breeze *noun*
1 a light, steady wind 2 something very easy: *The test was a breeze.*
breeze *verb*
3 to move lightly and easily: *He breezed past, grinning as he went.*
•***Word Family:*** **breezy** *adjective* (**breezier, breeziest**) **breezily** *adverb* **breeziness** *noun*

brethren (*say* **bredh**-rin) *plural noun*
brothers

brevity *noun*
being short or brief: *The brevity of their visit was unexpected.*

brew (*say* broo) *verb*
1 to make or prepare beer, tea or coffee 2 to make or form: *Trouble's brewing between the workers.*
brew *noun*
3 a drink made by brewing
•***Word Family:*** **brewer** *noun* someone who brews **brewery** *noun* (**breweries**) a place where beer and similar drinks are brewed

briar *noun*
a prickly bush, such as a rosebush

bribe *noun*
money or gifts given to someone in return for doing something for you that they shouldn't do
•***Word Family:*** **bribe** *verb* **bribery** *noun*

bric-a-brac *noun*
any odd pieces of furniture, jewellery or ornaments that are not worth much
•***Word Origins:*** from Old French words meaning "at random"

brick *noun*
a block made of baked clay or a similar substance, used for building
•***Word Family:*** **bricklayer** *noun* someone who builds with bricks

bride *noun*
a woman who is about to be married or has been married recently
•***Word Family:*** **bridal** *adjective* to do with a bride or a wedding

bridegroom *noun*
a man who is about to be married or has been married recently

bridesmaid *noun*
a girl or unmarried woman who looks after the bride at her wedding

bridge (1) *noun*
1 a structure built over a road, railway line or water, usually to provide a crossing from one side to the other: *a bridge across the river*
2 something like a bridge, such as a thin support for the strings of a musical instrument: *the bridge of a violin* 3 the bony, upper line of your nose

A B C D E F G H I J K L M N O P Q R S T U V W X Y Z

4 a raised platform over the deck of a ship, used by the captain or officers
bridge *verb*
5 to cross or extend across: *to bridge a gap*

bridge (2) *noun*
a card game for four players in which one pair of players attempts to win the number of tricks that it has bid for

bridle *noun*
1 the leather straps, with a bit and reins, fitted around the head of a horse to guide or control it
bridle *verb*
2 to put a bridle on a horse

brie (*say* bree) *noun*
a soft, white cheese
•***Word Origins:*** named after *Brie*, a district in northern France where it was first made

brief (*say* breef) *adjective*
1 short: *a brief talk / a brief skirt*
brief *noun*
2 information and instructions given about a project or job: *a barrister's brief about a legal case*
3 **in brief** in a few words: *the news in brief*
brief *verb*
4 to give a brief to: *The spy was briefed about his next mission.*
•***Word Family:*** **briefly** *adverb* **briefness** *noun*

briefcase *noun*
a flat case, often leather, for carrying books and papers

briefs *plural noun*
short underpants

brigade *noun*
1 a group of people, usually wearing a uniform, trained to perform special duties: *a fire brigade*
2 a large group of soldiers consisting of three battalions or armoured units
•***Word Family:*** **brigadier** *noun* the army officer in charge of a brigade, ranking between a colonel and a major-general
•***Word Origins:*** from an Italian word meaning "a troop"

bright *adjective*
1 shining or giving out light: *a bright star*
2 cheerful: *a bright smile* 3 strong or vivid: *bright red* 4 clever: *a bright pupil*
•***Word Family:*** **brighten** *verb* to make more bright or cheerful: *Sunlight brightened the room.* **brightly** *adverb* **brightness** *noun*

brilliant *adjective*
1 very bright or sparkling: *brilliant sunshine*
2 very clever: *He's brilliant at maths*
•***Word Family:*** **brilliance** *noun* **brilliantly** *adverb*

brim *noun*
1 the upper or outer edge of anything: *a cup filled to the brim with orange juice* 2 the wide projecting part at the bottom of a hat
brim *verb*
3 to be full to overflowing: *Chopping onions made her eyes brim with tears.*
•***Word Family:*** other verb forms are **brims, brimmed, brimming** □ **brimful** or **brimfull** *adjective* completely full

brindled *adjective*
brownish-grey with darker streaks or spots: *a brindled cow*
•***Word Family:*** **brindle** *noun*

brine *noun*
salty water used for preserving meat and other food
•***Word Family:*** **briny** *adjective* salty

bring *verb*
1 to make someone come with you: *Do bring your friends to the disco.* 2 to make something come: *What brought that to mind?* 3 to carry: *Bring some sausages.* 4 to make or persuade someone: *I couldn't bring myself to squash the spider.* 5 **bring off** to do successfully: *How on earth did you bring it off?* 6 **bring round** (a) to help someone become conscious again (b) to convince 7 **bring up** (a) to raise or educate: *to bring up children* (b) to mention: *to bring up an unpopular subject* (c) to vomit
•***Word Family:*** other forms are **brings, brought, bringing**

brink *noun*
the very edge of something dangerous: *brink of a cliff / the brink of disaster*

brisk *adjective*
quick or lively: *a brisk stroll / a brisk manner*
•***Word Family:*** **briskly** *adverb* **briskness** *noun*

bristle (*say* **bris**-ul) *noun*
1 a short, coarse, stiff hair: *a brush bristle / bristles on your chin*
bristle *verb*
2 to stand on end like a bristle: *The hair on the back of my neck bristled with fear.* 3 to react with horror and anger: *Grandma bristled at the suggestion.*
•***Word Family:*** **bristly** *adjective*

brittle *adjective*
hard but fragile and easily broken: *a brittle piece of pottery*
•***Word Family:*** **brittleness** *noun*

broad (*say* brawd) *adjective*
1 wide or large: *a broad smile / someone with a broad knowledge of world affairs* 2 full or complete: *in broad daylight* 3 general: *a broad outline of the story* 4 strong: *a broad Yorkshire accent*
•***Word Family:*** **broaden** *verb* **broadly** *adverb*

broadcast *verb*
1 to send out by television or radio: *They usually broadcast the news at 7 o'clock.* 2 to spread: *Please don't broadcast the gossip.*
broadcast *noun*
3 a programme sent out by television or radio
•***Word Family:*** other verb forms are **broadcasts, broadcast** or **broadcasted, broadcasting**

broad-minded *adjective*
being tolerant of other people's ideas and having a mind open to new things
•***Word Family:*** **broad-mindedly** *adverb* **broad-mindedness** *noun*

broadside *noun*
1 the firing of all the guns on one side of a ship at the same time 2 a strong verbal attack on someone

brocade (*say* bro-**kade**) *noun*
a woven cloth, originally made of silk but now often made of cotton or synthetic fibre, with raised patterns on it
•***Word Family:*** **brocaded** *adjective: a brocaded dressing-gown*

broccoli (*say* **brok**-a-lee) *noun*
a vegetable with green stalks and tightly bunched green or purple flower heads, similar to a cauliflower
•***Word Origins:*** from an Italian word meaning "little sprouts"

brochure (*say* **bro**-sher) *noun*
a small book or booklet filled with pictures and useful information: *a travel brochure*

brogue (*rhymes with* rogue) *noun*
1 a strong leather shoe 2 a broad, soft accent, especially an Irish one
•***Word Origins:*** from an Irish Gaelic word meaning "shoe"

broke *adjective*
having no money
•***Word Family:*** **broke** is a past form of the verb **break**

broken *adjective*
1 shattered or smashed into pieces: *broken glass* 2 with injured or damaged parts: *a broken leg / a broken heart / a broken CD player* 3 disobeyed or not kept: *a broken school rule / a broken promise* 4 spoken incorrectly: *broken English* 5 **a broken home** a family in which the parents have separated and live apart
•***Word Family:*** **broken** is a past form of the verb **break**

broker *noun*
someone who makes money from buying and selling goods or shares for other people: *an insurance broker*

brolly *noun*
an umbrella
•***Word Family:*** the plural is **brollies**

bronchitis (*say* brong-**kigh**-tis) *noun*
an illness in which the lining of the air passages connecting your windpipe to your lungs becomes red and swollen

brontosaurus (*say* bron-ta-**saw**-rus) *noun*
a giant, plant-eating dinosaur with a long neck and tail, that became extinct millions of years ago
•***Word Family:*** the plural is **brontosauruses**
•***Word Origins:*** from Greek words meaning "thunder lizard"

bronze *noun*
1 a yellowish-brown metal mixed from a large amount of copper and a smaller amount of tin or aluminium
bronze *adjective*
2 bright yellowish or reddish-brown
•***Word Family:*** **bronzed** *adjective* deeply suntanned: *bronzed skin*

brooch (*rhymes with* coach) *noun*
a piece of jewellery that fastens onto your clothes by a pin at the back
•***Word Family:*** the plural is **brooches**

brood *noun*
1 a group of young animals, especially birds, hatched at the same time
brood *verb*
2 to sit over eggs or young offspring 3 **brood on** to think resentfully about something: *The prisoner brooded on his fate.*
•***Word Family:*** **broody** *adjective: a broody hen* **broodily** *adverb* **brooding** *adjective*

brook (*rhymes with* book) *noun*
a small stream

broom *noun*
a long-handled brush for sweeping floors

broth *noun*
a thin soup made with meat, fish or vegetable juices

brothel *noun*
1 a place where prostitutes work 2 a messy place: *Your room looks like a brothel.*

brother (*say* **brudh**-er) *noun*
1 a boy or man who has the same parents as another person 2 a man belonging to a religious order
•***Word Family:*** **brotherhood** *noun* **brotherly** *adjective*

brother-in-law *noun*
1 the brother of your husband or wife 2 the husband of your sister
• ***Word Family:*** the plural is **brothers-in-law**

brow (*rhymes with* cow) *noun*
1 the part of your face between the top of your eyes and your hair 2 an eyebrow

browbeat *verb*
to bully or force: *They tried to browbeat him into signing the contract.*
• ***Word Family:*** other forms are **browbeats, browbeaten, browbeating**

brown *noun*
1 the dark colour of wood, formed by mixing colours such as red, black and yellow
brown *adjective*
2 of a brown colour: *brown hair*
brown *verb*
3 to make something brown: *to brown meat by cooking it quickly in a pan*
• ***Word Family:*** **brownness** *noun*

brownie *noun*
1 a little brown elf or goblin in fairytales, who is said to help about the house at night 2 a small, flat chocolate cake with nuts 3 **Brownie** a junior Girl Guide

browse (*rhymes with* cows) *verb*
1 to graze or nibble on grass or leaves: *The sheep browsed by the stream.* 2 to glance at random through the pages of a book or at the goods in a shop
browse *noun*
3 a casual look: *I enjoy a good browse in the bookshop.*

bruise (*say* brooz) *noun*
1 a mark on your skin, from an injury that damaged the blood vessels beneath it
bruise *verb*
2 to get a bruise or make something bruised: *to bruise your leg when you fall / The apples were bruised.* 3 to hurt: *His feelings are easily bruised.*
• ***Word Family:*** **bruiser** *noun* a tough person

brunch *noun*
a midmorning meal that you have instead of breakfast and lunch
• ***Word Family:*** the plural is **brunches**
• ***Word Origins:*** formed by joining the first letters of *br*eakfast with the last letters of l*unch*

brunette (*say* broo-**net**) *noun*
a woman with dark, especially dark brown, hair: *My mother's a brunette but her sister is a blonde.*

brunt *noun*
the main strength or force of something: *The town took the brunt of the storm.*

brush (1) *noun*
1 an object made of hair or bristles set into a solid base with a handle: *a hair brush / a paint brush / a dustpan and brush* 2 a short fight or hostile encounter: *The demonstrators had a brush with the police.*
brush *verb*
3 to use a brush on something: *Brush your hair!* 4 to sweep or touch something as if with a brush: *They brushed his fears aside.* 5 to touch lightly in passing: *He brushed past us.*
• ***Word Family:*** the plural of the noun is **brushes**

brush (2) *noun*
a dense growth of bushes or shrubs

brusque (*say* broosk) *adjective*
blunt or abrupt in the way you speak or behave: *a brusque reply*
• ***Word Family:*** **brusquely** *adverb* **brusqueness** *noun*

brussels sprout *noun*
a small, green vegetable like a tiny cabbage, growing in clusters on a stalk
• ***Word Family:*** the plural is **brussels sprouts**

brutal (*say* **broo**-tal) *adjective*
savage or cruel: *a brutal attack*
• ***Word Family:*** **brutalize** or **brutalise** *verb* to make or become brutal: *Years of abuse had brutalized him.* **brutality** *noun* **brutally** *adverb*

brute *noun*
1 a four-legged animal or beast 2 a strong or cruel person
brute *adjective*
3 animal-like strength: *brute force*
• ***Word Family:*** **brutish** *adjective* like an animal: *brutish behaviour*

bubble *noun*
1 a small ball of gas rising through a liquid: *a bubble of air* 2 a light, clear ball of liquid with air inside it
bubble *verb*
3 to rise in bubbles or make the sound of bubbles: *The stew bubbled on the stove.* 4 to be active and full of vigour: *The children bubbled with excitement.*

bubblegum *noun*
chewing gum that you can blow into bubbles

bubonic plague (*say* bew-**bon**-ik plague) *noun*
a disease spread by the fleas on rats which can cause epidemics and death
• ***Word Origins:*** from a Greek word meaning "groin"

buccaneer (*say* buk-a-**neer**) *noun*
a pirate or bold adventurer

buck (1) *noun*
a male rabbit or deer

buck (2) *verb*
to leap in the air with the head down, back arched and all four feet off the ground: *The horse bucked when I tried to saddle him.*

bucket *noun*
1 a round container with a flat bottom and no lid, for holding or carrying liquids 2 **kick the bucket** to die
•***Word Family:*** **bucketful** *noun*

buckle *noun*
1 a clasp for fastening a belt or strap
buckle *verb*
2 to fasten with a buckle 3 to bend or give way suddenly from pressure or heat: *the plastic buckled in the hot sun / My legs buckled and I fell flat on my face.* 4 **buckle down** to start to work seriously: *We must buckle down to work now.*

buckteeth *plural noun*
any of your top teeth that stick out
•***Word Family:*** the singular is **bucktooth** □ **bucktoothed** *adjective*

bucolic (*say* bew-**kol**-ik) *adjective*
having to do with the country or country life

bud *noun*
a tightly closed flower or leaf: *The tree was covered in sticky buds.*

Buddhism (*say* **bood**-iz-um) *noun*
a world religion teaching that the way to end pain and suffering is through meditating and living a good life
•***Word Family:*** **Buddhist** *adjective: a Buddhist monk* **Buddhist** *noun*
•***Word Origins:*** from a Sanskrit word *Buddha* meaning "the enlightened one", the title given to an Indian teacher living in the 6th century BC, on whose ideas Buddhism is based

budge *verb*
to move or give way slightly: *We pulled and pushed the donkey but it would not budge.*

budgerigar (*say* **buj**-a-ree-gar) *noun*
a small Australian parrot that may be kept as a pet
•***Word Origins:*** from words in an Aboriginal language meaning "good cockatoo"

budget (*say* **buj**-it) *noun*
1 a plan that shows what you expect to earn and how much you expect to spend 2 the sum of money put aside for a particular purpose: *The film was made on a very small budget.*
budget *verb*
3 to plan the use of money in advance: *We try to budget for a holiday every year.*

buff *noun*
1 a pale brownish-yellow colour 2 someone who knows a lot about something: *a film buff*
buff *adjective*
3 a pale yellow
buff *verb*
4 to polish or shine: *to buff your shoes*

buffalo (*say* **buf**-a-lo) *noun*
1 a kind of ox, with broad, flat horns that curve downwards 2 a bison
•***Word Family:*** plural is **buffaloes** or **buffalo**
•***Word Origins:*** from a Greek word meaning "wild ox"

buffer *noun*
1 anything that softens the shock of a collision, especially the bumper on the ends of a railway carriage 2 a part of the memory in a computer used to store information for a short time until it can be transferred to another place in the memory or onto a disk

buffet (1) (*say* **buf**-et) *verb*
to strike, knock, shake or toss about: *Huge waves buffeted the sides of the boat.*
•***Word Family:*** other verb forms are **buffets, buffeted, buffeting**

buffet (2) (*say* **buf**-ay) *noun*
1 an informal meal at which guests stand and serve themselves 2 a refreshment bar at a railway station or on a train
•***Word Origins:*** from an Old French word meaning "stool"

buffoon *noun*
someone who acts the fool
•***Word Family:*** **buffoonery** *noun*
•***Word Origins:*** from an Italian word meaning "jester"

bug *noun*
1 an insect 2 an infection: *There's a tummy bug going around.* 3 a hidden microphone used to record other people's conversations secretly 4 a mistake in the design or working of a computer or the software that runs it
bug *verb*
5 to irritate: *You're really bugging me.* 6 to install or use a hidden microphone: *to bug a hotel room*
•***Word Family:*** other verb forms are **bugs, bugged, bugging**

buggy *noun*
1 a light, four-wheeled passenger vehicle pulled by one horse 2 a light wheeled chair for conveying babies
•***Word Family:*** the plural is **buggies**

bugle (*say* **bew**-gul) *noun*
a brass instrument like a trumpet used by armies to sound signals
•***Word Family:*** **bugler** *noun*

build (*say* bild) *verb*
1 to join or put together parts to make a whole structure: *to build a house* 2 to establish or develop over time: *to build a business from nothing*
build *noun*
3 the shape of your body: *Our sheepdog has a heavy build.*
•***Word Family:*** other verb forms are **builds, built, building** □ **builder** *noun* someone who builds or makes things

building *noun*
a built structure, such as a house or office

building society *noun*
a business organization that lends money to people buying houses and offers interest to people who save with them
•***Word Family:*** the plural is **building societies**

bulb *noun*
1 the rounded, root-like stem of plants such as the onion, planted underground and sending shoots up to the surface: *a tulip bulb* 2 a pear-shaped or bulb-shaped object: *an electric light bulb*
•***Word Family:*** **bulbous** *adjective* shaped like a bulb: *a bulbous nose*

bulge (*say* bulj) *noun*
1 a rounded swelling or part
bulge *verb*
2 to swell or stick out: *His stomach bulged after the meal.*

bulk *noun*
1 the size or volume of anything: *the bulk of an elephant* 2 the main amount: *I do the bulk of my shopping at the supermarket.* 3 **in bulk** in large quantities: *to buy in bulk*
•***Word Family:*** **bulky** *adjective* (**bulkier, bulkiest**) very large or awkward **bulkiness** *noun*

bull *noun*
1 the male of beef or dairy cattle, oxen and buffaloes 2 the male of various other mammals, especially the elephant, whale or seal
3 anything you think is nonsense: *You're talking bull.*
•***Word Family:*** the female of definition 1 and 2 is **cow** □ definition 3 is colloquial

bulldog *noun*
a low, sturdy, short-haired dog, originally bred for baiting bulls

bulldozer *noun*
a powerful tractor with a wide blade at the front for moving earth
•***Word Family:*** **bulldoze** *verb* to use a bulldozer

bullet *noun*
a small metal cylinder fired from a rifle or pistol

bulletin *noun*
a news report: *The next bulletin is at 6 o'clock.*

bulletin board *noun*
an electronic directory on a computer network where users can exchange messages

bullfight *noun*
a public entertainment in an arena, in which skilled fighters dodge a charging bull and usually try to kill it
•***Word Family:*** **bullfighter** *noun* someone trained to bullfight **bullfighting** *noun*

bullion (*say* **bool**-yen) *noun*
gold or silver bars

bullock *noun*
a young castrated bull

bull's-eye *noun*
the centre of a target

bully *noun*
someone who frightens or hurts another person who is smaller or weaker than themselves
•***Word Family:*** the plural is **bullies** □ **bully** *verb* other forms are **bullies, bullied, bullying**

bulrush (*say* **bool**-rush) *noun*
a large reed found in swampy areas, with coarse leaves used to make mats and other similar things
•***Word Family:*** the plural is **bulrushes**

bumblebee *noun*
a large type of bee with a loud buzz

bump *verb*
1 to strike or collide with: *My arm bumped her head. / The pram bumped into the fence.* 2 to move with jolts or jerks: *The motorbike bumped over the rough field.*
bump *noun*
3 the act or sound of bumping 4 the raised mark left by a collision or blow: *a large bump on your forehead*
•***Word Family:*** **bumpy** *adjective* (**bumpier, bumpiest**)

bumper *noun*
a rounded bar along the front and back of a car or truck, that protects it in a collision

bumpkin *noun*
an awkward, clumsy person who is unsure of how to behave in polite company: *a country bumpkin*

bumptious (*say* **bump**-shus) *adjective*
unpleasantly conceited and self important: *a bumptious mayor*
•***Word Family:*** **bumptiousness** *noun*

bun *noun*
1 a type of sweet bread roll, usually round and containing spices or fruit 2 a long bunch of

hair wound into a bun shape on the back of your head

bunch *noun*
1 a group of things attached or collected together: *a bunch of grapes / a bunch of friends*
bunch *verb*
2 to form into bunches or folds
•*Word Family:* the plural of the noun is **bunches**

bundle *noun*
1 a number of things fastened or carried together: *a bundle of firewood*
bundle *verb*
2 to carry or tie in a bundle: *Bundle these parcels together.* 3 to send away in a hurry: *to bundle someone out of the house* 4 **bundle up** to dress warmly: *He bundled the baby up in a warm coat.*

bung *noun*
1 a stopper for closing a hole in a barrel or cask
bung *verb*
2 to block or close with a bung or something like a bung 3 to put or throw something quickly or carelessly: *Bung it on the chair!*

bungalow (*say* **bung**-ga-lo) *noun*
a single-storey house

bungle *verb*
to do something clumsily or without success: *to bungle a job*
•*Word Family:* **bungler** *noun* **bunglingly** *adverb*

bunion (*say* **bun**-yon) *noun*
a painful swelling at the base of your big toe

bunk (1) *noun*
a single bed with a matching one built above it

bunk (2) *noun*
do a bunk to run away: *The culprits had done a bunk and could not be found.*

bunker *noun*
1 a large container for storing fuel such as coal 2 an obstacle on a golf course consisting of a pit filled with sand, backed by a grassy ridge 3 an underground shelter where you can go in wartime to be safe from bombs

bunting *noun*
the coloured fabric used to make the flags that line streets during a parade

bunyip *noun*
a monster told of in Aboriginal legends, said to live in billabongs and swamps

buoy (*rhymes with* toy) *noun*
1 an anchored float used to mark a channel or obstruction in the water, or used to mark the course in a yacht race
buoy *verb*
2 to encourage or support: *She was buoyed up by the hope of winning the record.*

buoyant (*say* **boy**-ant) *adjective*
1 able to float: *The boat remained buoyant even though it was damaged.* 2 lively or cheerful: *She was buoyant after she passed her violin exam.*
•*Word Family:* **buoyancy** *noun* **buoyantly** *adverb*

burden *noun*
1 a heavy or difficult load to carry: *The donkey carried its burden patiently. / The burden of responsibility is on your shoulders.*
burden *verb*
2 to load with a burden: *I'm sorry to burden you with my problems.*
•*Word Family:* **burdensome** *adjective*

bureau (*say* **bure**-o) *noun*
1 an office or department with particular duties: *the weather bureau* 2 a writing desk with drawers
•*Word Family:* plural is **bureaus** or **bureaux**

bureaucracy (*say* byew-**rok**-ra-see) *noun*
1 an official organization with too much power or having too many rules 2 the system of rules made by public officials rather than by elected politicians
•*Word Family:* the plural is **bureaucracies** □ **bureaucrat** *noun* a member of the bureaucracy **bureaucratic** *adjective* too official or attached to rules **bureaucratically** *adverb*

burger (*say* **ber**-ger) *noun*
a short form of hamburger

burghul (*say* **ber**-gool) *noun*
crushed wheat that has been hulled, cooked, dried and ground for use in Lebanese and other similar cooking
•*Word Origins:* from a Persian word meaning "bruised grain"

burglar *noun*
someone who breaks into a house in order to steal
•*Word Family:* **burglary** *noun* (**burglaries**) □ **burgle** *verb: to burgle a house*

burial (*say* **ber**-i-ul) *noun*
putting a dead person into a grave
•*Word Family:* **bury** *verb*

burly *adjective*
big and strong: *A burly attendant grabbed his arm.*
•*Word Family:* other forms are **burlier, burliest** □ **burliness** *noun*

burn (1) *verb*
1 to set something on fire or to be on fire: *to burn coal in the grate / These wet matches will not burn.* 2 to injure yourself or mark something with extreme heat or fire: *to burn your hand in the oven* 3 to turn black or red from too much heat: *Dad burnt the chops. / Make sure you don't get burnt at the beach.* 4 to use something as

fuel: *The stove burns wood.* 5 to be hot: *Her face burnt with embarrassment.* 6 to be alight: *The lights burn all night.*
burn *noun*
7 an injury produced by extreme heat
•***Word Family:*** other verb forms are **burns, burnt** or **burned, burning**

burn (2) *noun*
a Scottish word for a small stream

burnish *verb*
to polish something or make it shiny by rubbing: *to burnish a saucepan*
•***Word Family:*** **burnished** *adjective* shiny or glossy

burp *verb*
1 to let wind out of your stomach noisily, through your mouth 2 to help a baby to burp after feeding by patting it on the back
•***Word Family:*** **burp** *noun*

burr (1) *noun*
the round, prickly case covering the seeds of some plants: *the burr of the chestnut tree*

burr (2) *noun*
1 a rough pronunciation, especially of the letter "r" 2 a low or muffled buzzing or whirring sound

burrow *noun*
1 a hole made in the ground by a rabbit or other animal
burrow *verb*
2 to dig a burrow: *The dog tried to burrow under the fence.* 3 to search: *Mum had to burrow in her bag for some money.*

bursary (*say* **ber**-sa-ree) *noun*
a scholarship given to a student by a school or college to help pay for fees, textbooks and so on
•***Word Family:*** the plural is **bursaries**

burst *verb*
1 to explode or break open suddenly: *The balloon burst loudly. / The buds burst into flower.* 2 to be full to overflowing: *Their pockets were bursting with conkers. / The kids are bursting with excitement.* 3 to enter loudly or suddenly: *to burst into the room*
burst *noun*
4 a sudden or violent explosion: *There was a burst of gunfire and then silence.* 5 a sudden display of energy or activity: *He cleaned the car in a burst of enthusiasm.*
•***Word Family:*** other verb forms are **bursts, burst, bursting**

bury (*say* **ber**-ee) *verb*
1 to place a dead body in a grave 2 to hide or cover from view: *to bury your face in your hands / The dog buried his bone in the garden.* 3 **bury yourself in** to give all your attention to: *to bury yourself in a book*
•***Word Family:*** other forms are **buries, buried, burying** □ **burial** *noun*

bus *noun*
1 a long motor vehicle, containing seats for passengers
bus *verb*
2 to take schoolchildren by bus: *They bussed pupils in from the other side of town.*
•***Word Family:*** the plural of the noun is **buses** □ other verb forms are **buses, bussed, bussing**
•***Word Origins:*** from a Latin word meaning "for all"

bush *noun*
1 a small woody shrub with branches that begin growing near the ground 2 the natural countryside in Australia or Africa, where there are no crops 3 **beat about the bush** to take too long getting to the point of what you are saying
•***Word Family:*** the plural is **bushes** □ **bushy** *adjective* (**bushier, bushiest**) thick like a bush: *a bushy tail*

bushel *noun*
1 an old-fashioned unit of volume for large amounts of goods such as grain or fruit 2 **hide your light under a bushel** to be modest about your good qualities or talents

bushfire *noun*
a fire in uncleared bush or forest land

bushranger *noun*
a bandit in Australia who hid in the bush, robbing people who passed on the roads: *Ned Kelly and his band of bushrangers*
•***Word Family:*** **bushranging** *noun*

bushwalk *verb*
to hike in the bush
•***Word Family:*** **bushwalking** *noun*

business (*say* **biz**-ness) *noun*
1 your occupation or work: *My business is selling cars.* 2 an organization or institution such as a shop or factory, that sells or produces things to make money: *He is in the advertising business.* 3 affair: *What she does is no longer your business.* 4 trade: *The shop did good business last year.* 5 **mean business** to be serious in what you intend to do: *Those thugs look as if they mean business.*
•***Word Family:*** the plural is **businesses** □ **businesslike** *adjective* practical and well-organized in your approach **businessman** *noun* **businesswoman** *noun*

busker *noun*
a street entertainer who performs in order to earn money from people passing by
•***Word Family:*** **busk** *verb* **busking** *noun*

bust (1) *noun*
1 a woman's breasts 2 a sculpture of someone's head and shoulders

bust (2) *verb*
1 to break or burst: *to bust a toy / to bust a balloon* 2 to arrest: *to bust someone for stealing*
3 **go bust** to become bankrupt: *His record business went bust.*
bust *adjective*
4 broken

bustard (*rhymes with* custard) *noun*
a large, shy, fast-running brown and white bird living in open, grassy country in Australia, Europe and Africa

bustle (*say* **bus**-ul) *verb*
to move or act with energy or fuss: *The waiters bustled about among the guests.*

busy (*say* **biz**-ee) *adjective*
1 doing a lot of things or having a lot to do: *He's busy this morning so come back tonight.*
2 full of activity: *a busy city* 3 being used: *The phone is busy at the moment.*
busy *verb*
4 to make yourself busy or keep busy: *He busied himself raking the autumn leaves.*
•***Word Family:*** other adjective forms are **busier, busiest** □ other verb forms are **busies, busied, busying** □ **busily** *adverb* **busyness** *noun*

busybody *noun*
someone who interferes or meddles in other people's affairs
•***Word Family:*** the plural is **busybodies**

butcher *noun*
1 someone who prepares and cuts up meat to be sold 2 someone who kills people cruelly
butcher *verb*
3 to kill and prepare meat for food 4 to kill a person or animal cruelly: *The killer butchered his victims.*
•***Word Family:*** **butchery** *noun*

butler *noun*
the head male servant in a large house

butt (1) *noun*
1 the end of anything, especially the thicker end: *the butt of a rifle* 2 the unused end: *the butt of a cigarette*

butt (2) *noun*
someone who is an object of ridicule: *I'm tired of being the butt of all their jokes.*

butt (3) *verb*
1 to hit a person or animal with the head or horns: *Our goat butted him in the back.* 2 **butt in** to interrupt or interfere: *I can't talk to her if you keep butting in.*
butt *noun*
3 a hit or nudge with the head

butter *noun*
1 the yellow food made from churning cream, used in cooking or on bread 2 any similar spread: *peanut butter*
butter *verb*
3 to spread with butter: *to butter a baking dish*
4 **butter up** to flatter: *She always butters me up when she wants something.*
•***Word Family:*** **buttery** *adjective*

buttercup *noun*
a bright yellow wild flower

butterfly *noun*
1 an insect with short feelers and large, often brightly coloured wings 2 a swimming style in which you lift both arms out of the water at the same time, bringing them strongly forward and down
•***Word Family:*** the plural is **butterflies**

butterscotch *noun*
a flavouring, toffee or sauce made with brown sugar, vanilla essence and butter
•***Word Family:*** the plural is **butterscotches**

buttock *noun*
either of the two rounded fleshy parts of the body that you sit on

button *noun*
1 a small disc or knob attached to clothing to fasten two parts together or as decoration
2 a knob or switch for an electrical appliance
button *verb*
3 to fasten with a button or buttons
•***Word Family:*** other verb forms are **buttons, buttoned, buttoning**

buttonhole *noun*
1 a slit in your clothing where a button goes when you do it up 2 a single flower worn as a decoration on the lapel of a coat
buttonhole *verb*
3 to stop someone so that you can talk to them for a long time

buttress *noun*
1 a structure built into or against a wall to support or strengthen it
buttress *verb*
2 to provide a structure with a buttress
•***Word Family:*** the plural of the noun is **buttresses** □ other verb forms are **buttresses, buttressed, buttressing**

buxom (*say* **buk**-som) *adjective*
plump and healthy-looking: *a buxom young lady*

buy (*rhymes with* fly) *verb*
1 to get something by paying money: *We are*

buying a new car. 2 to accept the truth of something: *I can't buy that story.*
buy *noun*
3 something you buy: *The strawberries are a good buy.*
•***Word Family:*** other verb forms are **buys, bought, buying** □ **buyer** *noun*

buzz *verb*
1 to make a low, humming sound: *Flies buzzed noisily in the kitchen.* 2 to move rapidly or busily: *Reporters buzzed around the scene of the accident.* 3 to communicate by telephone or an intercom system: *I'll buzz his office.*
4 **buzz off** to go away: *Buzz off and don't come back!*
buzz *noun*
5 a low, humming sound: *the buzz of bees / the buzz of eager gossip*
•***Word Family:*** the plural of the noun is **buzzes** □ **buzzer** *noun*

buzzard *noun*
a large, heavy bird of the falcon family

buzzword *noun*
a fashionable word used by people in a particular job or group to impress listeners or readers

by *preposition*
1 near to: *Sit by me.* 2 past: *He walked right by me without saying a word.* 3 using as a way: *Enter by the front door. / We'll travel by bus. / You can come by the beach.* 4 during: *We'll travel by day.* 5 not later than: *Come by 5 o'clock.*
by *adverb*
6 near: *The shop is close by.*

bye *noun*
a run scored in cricket when a ball passes the batsman and the wicket without touching either of them

by-election *noun*
an extra election called to fill the seat of a member of parliament who retires or dies

bygone (*say* **by**-gon) *adjective*
1 past: *In bygone days people believed the world was flat.*
bygone *noun*
2 **let bygones be bygones** forgive and forget past disagreements

by-line *noun*
an author's name printed above or below an article printed in a newspaper or magazine

bypass *noun*
1 a road that passes around or avoids a busy area such as a city centre 2 an operation which makes an alternative route for blood, to avoid a diseased heart
bypass *verb*
3 to avoid something by using a bypass: *to bypass traffic*
•***Word Family:*** the plural is **bypasses**

by-product *noun*
a less important product of an activity, especially manufacturing: *Whey is a by-product of cheese-making.*

bystander *noun*
someone standing near to, but not taking part in, what is happening

byte (*say* bight) *noun*
a unit of information, usually consisting of eight bits, used for storing information in a computer

Cc

cab *noun*
1 a taxi 2 the part of a lorry where the driver sits

cabanossi (*say* ka-ba-**no**-see) *noun*
a thin, seasoned, beef sausage that is cooked when you buy it
•***Word Origins:*** from a Turkic Tartar word meaning "boar"

cabaret (*say* **kab**-a-ray) *noun*
a form of entertainment consisting of songs and dances, usually performed in a restaurant or nightclub
•***Word Origins:*** from a French word meaning "tavern"

cabbage *noun*
a large vegetable, with its broad leaves arranged in a tight bunch

cabin *noun*
1 a small, simple house, often in the country
2 a room where passengers sleep on a ship 3 the space for passengers or crew on an aircraft

cabinet *noun*
1 a piece of furniture with shelves and drawers to show or store things 2 a group in parliament who help the Prime Minister govern a country

cable *noun*
1 a thick, strong rope or chain 2 a bundle of insulated wires for carrying electricity 3 an overseas telegram

cable television *noun*
a way of broadcasting TV programmes by sending them directly down a linking cable to your TV

cache (*say* kash) *noun*
1 a hiding-place 2 things hidden or stored in a secret place
• ***Word Origins:*** from a French word meaning "to hide"

cackle *verb*
1 to make a shrill, broken sound similar to that of a hen after it lays an egg 2 to laugh or chatter noisily
• ***Word Family:*** **cackle** *noun*

cacophonous (*say* ka-**kof**-a-nus) *adjective*
having a harsh sound
• ***Word Family:*** **cacophony** *noun*
• ***Word Origins:*** from Greek words meaning "bad sound"

cactus *noun*
a desert plant that stores water in its fleshy, spike-covered stem
• ***Word Family:*** the plural is **cacti** or **cactuses**

cadaver (*say* ka-**dah**-va *or* ka-**dav**-a) *noun*
the body of someone who has died
• ***Word Family:*** **cadaverous** *adjective* pale and haggard

caddie *noun*
1 someone who helps a golfer by carrying the golf bag and often helps choose which club to use
caddie *verb*
2 to act as a caddie
• ***Word Family:*** other verb forms are **caddies, caddied, caddying**

caddy *noun*
a small tin or box for holding tea

cadence (*say* **kay**-dunce) *noun*
the rise and fall of sounds in the pitch of a voice when someone is speaking

cadet (*say* ka-**det**) *noun*
someone being trained to work in an organization such as the armed forces or the police

cadge *verb*
to get food, money and so on by asking someone for it: *Can I cadge a sandwich?*

cafe (*say* **kaf**-ay) *noun*
a restaurant where coffee and light meals are served
• ***Word Origins:*** from a French word meaning "coffee"

cafeteria (*say* kaf-a-**tear**-ree-a) *noun*
a self-service restaurant, especially in a school, an office building or a department store
• ***Word Origins:*** from a Spanish word meaning "coffee shop"

caffeine (*say* **kaf**-een) *noun*
a drug found in tea and coffee, which can keep you awake

caftan *noun*
a long, loose gown or dress with long, wide sleeves

cage *noun*
1 an enclosure with wires or bars in which birds or animals are kept 2 anything like a cage, such as a lift in a coalmine

cagey (*say* **kay**-jee) *adjective*
careful or secretive in the way you act: *He was cagey about where he'd been.*
• ***Word Family:*** other forms are **cagier, cagiest** □ **cagily** *adverb* **caginess** *noun*

cagoule *noun*
a lightweight waterproof jacket

cajole (*say* ka-**jole**) *verb*
to coax or persuade someone

cake *noun*
1 something that you bake using flour, eggs, sugar and butter: *a chocolate cake / fairy cakes*
2 something shaped like a cake: *a potato cake*
cake *verb*
3 to cover with something soft that has become hard: *My boots were caked with mud.*

calamari (*say* kal-a-**ma**-ree) *noun*
squid which can be eaten

calamity (*say* ka-**lam**-a-tee) *noun*
a terrible or unfortunate event
• ***Word Family:*** the plural is **calamities** □ **calamitous** *adjective* **calamitously** *adverb*

calcium (*say* **kal**-see-um) *noun*
a soft, whitish metal found in limestone, chalk, teeth and bones

calculate (*say* **kal**-kyoo-late) *verb*
1 to solve a problem using mathematics: *We calculated how long our trip would take.* 2 to intend or mean something: *Her rudeness was calculated to annoy me.*
• ***Word Family:*** **calculating** *adjective* slyly clever **calculation** *noun* the result of calculating **calculator** *noun* a person or machine that calculates

calendar (*say* **kal**-en-da) *noun*
a list of the days, weeks and months of a particular year

calf (1) *noun*
a young cow, whale or seal
• ***Word Family:*** the plural is **calves**

calf (2) *noun*
the back of your leg, below the knee
• ***Word Family:*** the plural is **calves**

calibre (*say* **kal**-i-ba) *noun*
1 the measurement across a tube or the inside of the barrel of a rifle 2 the character or ability of a person: *He is a man of great calibre.*

calico *noun*
a coarse, cotton fabric, usually off-white in colour
• ***Word Family:*** the plural is **calicoes** or **calico**
• ***Word Origins:*** this material was first made in *Calicut*, India

call *verb*
1 to say loudly or clearly: *She called for help.* 2 to attract or bring: *Try not to call attention to her mistakes.* 3 to pay a visit or telephone: *May I call tomorrow?* 4 to give a name to or consider: *It was hardly what you would call a success.* 5 to describe as: *They called him a hero.*
call *noun*
9 a shout or cry: *Her calls for help were not heard.* 10 a telephone conversation
• ***Word Family:*** **caller** *noun*

calligraphy (*say* ka-**lig**-ra-fee) *noun*
the art of fine handwriting
• ***Word Origins:*** from Greek words meaning "beautiful writing"

calling *noun*
your job or career, especially one you feel that you have to do

calliper *noun*
a brace or support, such as one worn to straighten an injured arm or leg

callous *adjective*
cruel or unfeeling: *His callous treatment of animals shocked us.*
• ***Word Family:*** **callously** *adverb* **callousness** *noun*
• ***Word Origins:*** from a Latin word meaning "thick-skinned"

calm *adjective*
1 quiet or feeling easy in your mind: *She remains calm in any crisis.* 2 without wind: *Today is calm and sunny.*
calm *verb*
3 to make someone or become calm
• ***Word Family:*** **calmly** *adverb* **calmness** *noun*

calorie (*say* **kall**-a-ree) *noun*
a measurement of heat or the energy given by the food we eat

calypso (*say* ka-**lip**-so) *noun*
a kind of music from the West Indies which has a strong rhythm
• ***Word Family:*** the plural is **calypsos**

camcorder *noun*
a video camera that you can use to record sound and pictures

camel *noun*
a tall animal with long legs and one or two humps on its back, used to carry people and goods and found in the desert regions of Africa, Asia and Australia

cameo (*say* **kam**-ee-o) *noun*
1 a piece of jewellery, usually a brooch, that shows a head in a lighter colour than the background 2 a small, but important role in a play or a film

camembert (*say* **kam**-em-bear) *noun*
a soft, rich, ripened cheese made in small, flat rounds and covered with white rind
• ***Word Origins:*** named after *Camembert*, a town in Normandy, France

camera (*say* **kam**-ra) *noun*
a machine or instrument that takes photographs or films

camouflage (*say* **kam**-a-flahzh) *noun*
a way of colouring or covering something so that it is hard to see against the things around it
• ***Word Family:*** **camouflage** *verb*

camp (1) *noun*
1 a group of tents or caravans in one place 2 a place where there are shelters: *a refugee camp*
camp *verb*
3 to live in tents for a short time
• ***Word Family:*** **camper** *noun*

camp (2) *adjective*
1 in an exaggerated or unnatural manner
2 homosexual

campaign (*say* **kam**-pane) *noun*
1 a series of battles especially at one time 2 a planned series of activities for a special purpose: *a political campaign*
• ***Word Family:*** **campaigner** *noun*

campus *noun*
the grounds of a university or college
• ***Word Origins:*** from a Latin word meaning "a field"

can (1) *verb*
1 to be able to: *Can you lift the suitcase?* 2 to be allowed to: *You can only enter if you have a pass.*
• ***Word Family:*** this verb helps other verbs and another form is **could**

can (2) *noun*
1 a container for food or drink
can *verb*
2 to put or seal something in a container: *to can peaches*
• ***Word Family:*** other verb forms are **cans, canned, canning** □ **cannery** *noun* (**canneries**) *noun* a factory where food is put into cans

canal (*say* ka-**nal**) *noun*
a waterway built for boats and ships

canary (*say* ka-**nair**-ree) *noun*
a small, yellow finch, often kept in a cage as a pet
•***Word Family:*** the plural is **canaries**
•***Word Origins:*** these birds first came from the *Canary* Islands

cancel (*say* **kan**-sul) *verb*
1 to call off or stop something: *to cancel a match / to cancel an order* 2 to cross out something so that it can't be used: *to cancel a ticket*
•***Word Family:*** other forms are **cancels, cancelled, cancelling** □ **cancellation** *noun*

cancer (*say* **kan**-sa) *noun*
a disease in which a group of cells multiplies, destroying nearby tissue. The growth may spread throughout the body.
•***Word Family:*** **cancerous** *adjective*

candid *adjective*
open or honest: *a candid opinion*
•***Word Family:*** **candidly** *adverb* **candidness** *noun* **candour** *noun*

candidate (*say* **kan**-di-date) *noun*
someone who wants to do or get a certain job or prize: *He is a candidate for school captain.*

candle *noun*
a stick of wax with a wick through it which gives a light when you burn it

candy *noun*
a hard sweet made by boiling sugar
•***Word Family:*** the plural of the noun is **candies**

cane *noun*
1 the long, hollow, jointed stems of some plants such as bamboo 2 a stick used to beat someone with
cane *verb*
3 to hit with a stick as a punishment

canine (*say* **kay**-nine) *adjective*
1 to do with dogs
canine *noun*
2 any animal in the dog family: *a fox is a canine*
3 a short form of **canine tooth**
•***Word Origins:*** from a Latin word meaning "dog"

canine tooth *noun*
one of the four pointed teeth that you have, two on each jaw

canister (*say* **kan**-is-ta) *noun*
a tin or jar used to store food: *a canister for tea*

cannabis *noun*
another name for **marijuana**
•***Word Origins:*** form a Greek word meaning "hemp"

cannibal *noun*
an animal or a human being that eats other animals like itself
•***Word Family:*** **cannibalistic** *adjective* **cannibalism** *noun*

cannon *noun*
a large gun, often on wheels
•***Word Family:*** the plural is **cannon** or **cannons**

canoe (*say* ka-**noo**) *noun*
a light, narrow boat that you move by paddles
•***Word Family:*** the plural is **canoes** □ **canoeist** *noun*

canon (1) (*say* **kan**-un) *noun*
1 a law or rule, especially a religious one 2 music in which the same tune is played or sung by two or more instruments or voices overlapping
•***Word Family:*** **canonize** or **canonise** *verb* to declare someone to be a saint

canon (2) (*say* **kan**-un) *noun*
a clergyman who works from a cathedral

canopy (*say* **kan**-a-pee) *noun*
a cover that hangs over something: *a bed canopy / the forest canopy*
•***Word Family:*** the plural is **canopies**
•***Word Origins:*** from a Greek word meaning "bed with a mosquito net"

cantankerous (*say* kan-**tank**-a-rus) *adjective*
bad-tempered or quarrelsome

canteen (*say* kan-**teen**) *noun*
1 a cafeteria in a factory, office or school 2 a box holding a set of cutlery 3 the set of things for eating and drinking used by a soldier, especially a water-bottle

canter *noun*
the way a horse moves, faster than a trot but slower than a gallop
•***Word Family:*** **canter** *verb*

cantor *noun*
someone who leads the singing in a church service, especially in a Jewish synagogue

canvas (*say* **kan**-vus) *noun*
1 a heavy cloth made from flax or cotton and used for tents and sails 2 a piece of canvas used by an artist to paint on

canvass (*say* **kan**-vus) *verb*
to ask people for their opinions: *The politician canvassed the district before the election.*
•***Word Family:*** **canvasser** *noun*

canyon *noun*
a narrow, steep-sided river valley

cap *noun*
1 a soft, round hat with no brim, usually with a peak at the front 2 the top of a pen or jar that

A B C D E F G H I J K L M N O P Q R S T U V W X Y Z

you can take off 3 a small explosive used to make a noise in a toy gun
cap *verb*
4 to put a cap on something 5 to do better than something: *Can you cap his performance?*
• ***Word Family:*** other verb forms are **caps, capped, capping**

capable (*say* **kay**-pa-bul) *adjective*
1 skilful or able to do something: *a capable student* 2 **be capable of** to have the ability or possibility: *He is capable of murder.*
• ***Word Family:*** **capability** *noun* **capably** *adverb*

capacity (*say* ka-**pas**-i-tee) *noun*
1 an ability: *She has a great capacity for learning.* 2 the amount something can hold: *The capacity of this jug is one litre.* 3 the position someone holds: *in his capacity as leader*
• ***Word Family:*** the plural is **capacities**

cape (1) *noun*
a short, sleeveless cloak fastened at the neck and hanging around the shoulders

cape (2) *noun*
a piece of land jutting out into the sea

caper *noun*
1 a playful leap or skip 2 a prank
caper *verb*
3 to jump or dance about
• ***Word Origins:*** from a Latin word meaning "a goat"

capillary (*say* ka-**pil**-a-ree) *noun*
one of the smallest blood vessels in your body, that joins your arteries to your veins
• ***Word Family:*** the plural is **capillaries**
• ***Word Origins:*** from a Latin word meaning "a hair"

capital *noun*
1 the main city of a country or state where the parliament is: *Paris is the capital of France.* 2 a capital letter 3 the amount of money or property owned by a business
capital *adjective*
4 capital or main: *a capital city*

capitalism *noun*
a system where businesses are owned and controlled by private individual people or groups
• ***Word Family:*** **capitalist** *noun*

capital letter *noun*
a large letter that you use at the beginning of a sentence and for names and places

capital punishment *noun*
punishment of criminals by death

capitulate (*say* ka-**pit**-yoo-late) *verb*
to surrender or give in: *The enemy capitulated.*
• ***Word Family:*** **capitulation** *noun*

cappuccino (*say* kap-a-**chee**-no) *noun*
a cup of coffee made with frothy milk
• ***Word Family:*** the plural is **cappuccinos**
• ***Word Origins:*** from an Italian word meaning "hood"

caprice (*say* ka-**preece**) *noun*
a change of mind without a good reason
• ***Word Family:*** **capricious** *adjective*

Capricorn *noun*
Tropic of Capricorn an imaginary line around the globe between the equator and the South Pole

capsicum (*say* **kap**-si-kum) *noun*
a long or bell-shaped, green or red pepper that can taste sweet and mild or hot

capsize *verb*
to overturn or make something overturn, especially a ship or boat: *The ferry capsized when it hit the rock. / The big wave capsized the boat.*

capsule (*say* **kaps**-yool) *noun*
1 a small container that holds a dose of medicine 2 the part of a spacecraft holding the instruments and crew

captain *noun*
1 someone who leads others: *She is the captain of the team.* 2 an officer in the army or the navy
• ***Word Family:*** **captaincy** *noun*

caption (*say* **kap**-shon) *noun*
a heading over a newspaper article or a title under a picture or illustration

captivate (*say* **kap**-ti-vate) *verb*
to hold someone's attention: *The class was captivated by Rosa's poetry reading.*
• ***Word Family:*** **captivation** *noun* **captivating** *adjective*

captive (*say* **kap**-tiv) *noun*
someone who is captured or made a prisoner
• ***Word Family:*** **captive** *adjective* **captivity** *noun*

capture (*say* **kap**-cher) *verb*
1 to take a person or animal prisoner
• ***Word Family:*** **capture** *noun* **captor** *noun*

car *noun*
1 a motor car 2 a railway carriage or tram: *the buffet car*
• ***Word Origins:*** from a Latin word meaning "a four-wheeled wagon"

carafe (*say* ka-**rahf** *or* ka-**raf**) *noun*
a glass jug used to serve drinks at a table

caramel (*say* **ka**-ra-mel) *noun*
1 burnt sugar used for colouring or flavouring food 2 a sweet with this taste 3 a pale, golden-brown colour
• ***Word Family:*** **caramelize** or **caramelise** *verb*

carat (*say* **ka**-ret) *noun*
a metric unit used for measuring how pure gold is or the weight of jewels

caravan (*say* **ka**-ra-van) *noun*
1 a van in which people may live and which is pulled by a car or horses 2 a group of people travelling together, usually across a desert

carbohydrate (*say* kar-bo-**high**-drate) *noun*
a chemical, such as sugar or starch, which is present in all living things

carbon *noun*
a common element found in all living things as well as in diamonds, graphite, petroleum and coal

carbon dioxide *noun*
a colourless gas which has no smell, does not burn and is used in fizzy drinks

carbon monoxide *noun*
a poisonous gas with no colour and no smell

carbuncle *noun*
an infection in the skin like a large boil

carburettor (*say* **kar**-ba-ret-a) *noun*
the part of an engine that mixes fuel and air in the correct amounts

carcass (*say* **kar**-kus) *noun*
the dead body of an animal

card (1) *noun*
1 a piece of stiff paper or thin cardboard, often printed for a particular purpose: *a Christmas card / a pack of playing cards* 2 **cards** any games played with playing cards 3 **on the cards** likely

card (2) *noun*
a kind of comb used to separate fibres of wool or cotton before spinning

cardboard *noun*
a thick, stiff sheet of paper

cardiac arrest *noun*
a serious condition in which the heart stops pumping blood through the body, often resulting in death
•*Word Family:* **cardiac** *adjective* to do with the heart

cardigan (*say* **kar**-di-gun) *noun*
a knitted jacket that fastens down the front

cardinal (*say* **kar**-di-nul) *noun*
an important clergyman in the Roman Catholic church who helps elect and advise the Pope

cardinal number *noun*
any whole number such as "1", "2" or "3"

cardinal points *noun*
one of the four main directions of the compass: north, south, east or west

care (*rhymes with* hair) *noun*
1 worry or problems: *She hasn't a care in the world.* 2 close attention: *He takes great care in everything he does.* 3 supervision: *She left the children in the care of an aunt.* 4 **care of** at the address of: *We wrote to her care of the Post Office.*
care *verb*
5 to be concerned or interested: *Parents care about their children.* 6 **care for** (a) to look after: *The government should care for the poor.* (b) to like: *I don't care for chocolates.*
•*Word Family:* **carer** *noun* **caring** *adjective*

career (*say* ka-**rear**) *noun*
1 your job or occupation: *a career in medicine*
career *verb*
2 to move rapidly: *The car careered down the hill.*

careful *adjective*
1 cautious and paying attention: *Be careful when you cross the road.* 2 thorough: *a careful study of the situation*
•*Word Family:* **carefully** *adverb* **carefulness** *noun*

careless *adjective*
not taking enough care or paying enough attention: *a careless remark / careless work*
•*Word Family:* **carelessly** *adverb* **carelessness** *noun*

caress (*say* ka-**res**) *verb*
1 to touch or hug someone in a loving manner
caress *noun*
2 an action, such as a hug or kiss, that shows affection
•*Word Origins:* from a Latin word meaning "dear"

caretaker *noun*
a person employed to look after a building: *a school caretaker*

cargo *noun*
the goods carried on a ship or an aircraft
•*Word Family:* the plural is **cargoes**

caricature (*say* **ka**-rik-a-ture) *noun*
a drawing of a person which is funny because it makes their nose, ears and so on more noticeable: *a caricature of the Prime Minister*
•*Word Family:* **caricature** *verb* **caricaturist** *noun* someone who draws caricatures

carillon (*say* ka-**ril**-yun) *noun*
a set of bells in a tower on which tunes are played by people or machinery
•*Word Family:* **carillonist** *noun* someone who plays a carillon

carnage (*say* **kar**-nij) *noun*
the killing of many people

carnal (*say* **kar**-nul) *adjective*
to do with the body
•*Word Origins:* from a Latin word meaning "of flesh"

A B C D E F G H I J K L M N O P Q R S T U V W X Y Z

carnation (*say* kar-**nay**-shun) *noun*
a garden plant with sweet-smelling, rose-like flowers

carnival *noun*
1 a noisy happy party held out of doors, often with people dressing up in costumes 2 a fair

carnivore (*say* **kar**-niv-or) *noun*
an animal that eats meat
•***Word Family:*** **carnivorous** *adjective*

carob (*say* **ka**-rub) *noun*
the pod of a Mediterranean tree that can be used instead of chocolate

carol (*say* **ka**-rul) *noun*
a song sung at Christmas

carousel (*say* ka-ra-**sel**) *noun*
1 a merry-go-round 2 a moving platform from which you collect your baggage at an airport

carp *noun*
a type of freshwater fish that you can eat
•***Word Family:*** the plural is **carp** as well

carpenter *noun*
someone who builds or repairs the wooden parts of buildings
•***Word Family:*** **carpentry** *noun*

carpet (*say* **kar**-pit) *noun*
1 a thick, soft covering for the floor, made from wool or other materials
carpet *verb*
2 to cover a floor with carpet
•***Word Family:*** other verb forms are **carpets, carpeted, carpeting**

carriage (*say* **ka**-rij) *noun*
1 a vehicle on wheels pulled by a horse and used for carrying passengers 2 one of the separate parts of a train used for carrying passengers

carrion (*say* **ka**-ri-un) *noun*
dead or rotting flesh

carrot *noun*
a plant with a cone-shaped, orange root which is used as a vegetable

carry *verb*
1 to take something or someone from one place to another: *Carry the milk bottles inside. / I carried the baby upstairs.* 2 to travel or be carried: *His voice carries well.* 3 to have or offer: *This shop carries a wide range of goods.* 4 to support or bear: *Will that branch carry your weight?* 5 to hold: *Carry your head high.* 6 **carry on** to keep doing: *Carry on with your work.* 7 **carry out** to do something: *to carry out a plan / He never carries out his threats.*
•***Word Family:*** other forms are **carries, carried, carrying** □ **carrier** *noun*

cart *noun*
1 a vehicle with wheels, sometimes pulled by a horse, used to carry goods or passengers
cart *verb*
2 to carry something by cart 3 to carry something heavy: *Do I have to cart all of these bags home?*

cartilage (*say* **kar**-ta-lij) *noun*
tough, elastic tissue that forms the ends of bones and parts of the ears and nose

cartography (*say* kar-**tog**-ra-fee) *noun*
the drawing and study of maps
•***Word Family:*** **cartographer** *noun*

carton (*say* **kart**-un) *noun*
a cardboard box or container: *a carton of juice*

cartoon *noun*
1 an amusing drawing 2 a film made of a series of drawings that seem to move when shown through a projector
•***Word Family:*** **cartoonist** *noun*

cartridge (*say* **kar**-trij) *noun*
1 a case holding the powder and bullet or shot for a gun 2 an ink container for a fountain pen

cartwheel *noun*
1 the wheel of a cart 2 a somersault you do sideways with your hands and legs stretched out

carve *verb*
1 to cut into a shape: *He carved a statue from stone.* 2 to slice: *Who will carve the turkey?*
•***Word Family:*** **carving** *noun* a carved object

cascade (*say* kas-**kade**) *noun*
1 a waterfall or series of waterfalls
cascade *verb*
2 to fall like a cascade: *The water cascaded over the road. / Ivy cascaded over the wall.*

case (1) *noun*
1 an event or example: *In that case I will not come.* 2 something to be thought about: *This is a case requiring attention.* 3 a state of affairs: *Whatever you may think, that is not the case.* 4 a disease or the person who has it: *a case of measles* 5 a matter being judged in a court of law: *a murder case*

case (2) *noun*
1 a box or a covering: *a case of oranges* 2 a suitcase: *to pack your case*

cash *noun*
1 money in the form of banknotes or coins rather than cheques or credit cards 2 payment made straight away: *I will pay cash for the furniture.*
cash *verb*
3 to give or get cash in exchange for a cheque: *She cashed the cheque at the bank.*

cash dispenser *noun*
a machine, usually outside a bank, from which people can take money out of their bank accounts using a special card

cashew (*say* **kash**-oo) *noun*
a small, kidney-shaped nut you can eat

cashier (*say* kash-**eer**) *noun*
someone who receives and pays out money in a bank or shop

cashmere (*say* **kash**-mear) *noun*
soft goats' hair used to make material for clothing
• ***Word Origins:*** named after the *Kashmir* goats of India

cash register *noun*
a machine in a shop used to keep count of cash sales, and which has a drawer for banknotes and coins

casino (*say* ka-**see**-no) *noun*
a place where gambling games are played
• ***Word Family:*** the plural is **casinos**

cask (*rhymes with* ask) *noun*
a barrel

casket (*rhymes with* basket) *noun*
1 a small box for storing jewels or other valuable things 2 a coffin

casserole (*say* **kas**-a-role) *noun*
1 a dish with a lid, used for baking 2 the food cooked in such a dish, usually a mixture of meats and vegetables: *lamb casserole*

cassette (*say* ka-**set**) *noun*
a small plastic box containing the recording tape for videos and tape-recorders: *a cassette player*

cassock *noun*
a long robe, usually black, worn by priests

cassowary (*say* **kas**-a-wair-ree) *noun*
a large, blue-black bird found in Australia and New Guinea, which runs but cannot fly
• ***Word Family:*** the plural is **cassowaries**

cast *verb*
1 to throw: *She cast her line into the water.* 2 to pour liquid into a mould and let it set: *to cast a statue in bronze* 3 to choose actors for the roles in a play, film and so on
cast *noun*
4 all the actors in a play or film 5 something shaped into a mould such as plaster for a broken limb

castanets (*say* **kas**-ta-nets) *plural noun*
a musical instrument used by Spanish dancers, consisting of two shell-shaped pieces of wood which they click together with their fingers
• ***Word Origins:*** from a Spanish word meaning "little chestnuts"

castaway (*say* **kahst**-a-way) *noun*
someone who has been shipwrecked

caste (*say* kahst) *noun*
a social group into which someone is born, such as the Hindu castes in India
• ***Word Origins:*** from a Portuguese word meaning "pure"

castigate (*say* **kas**-ti-gate) *verb*
to speak sternly to or punish severely
• ***Word Family:*** **castigation** *noun* **castigator** *noun*

castle (*say* **kah**-sel *or* **kas**-el) *noun*
1 a large strongly-built building which rulers and nobles used to live in and fight from in the olden days 2 a castle-shaped piece used in chess

castor oil *noun*
a thick oil made from the seeds of a plant and used in some medicines

castor sugar *noun*
a fine white sugar

castrate (*say* **kass**-trate) *verb*
to remove the testicles from an animal: *to castrate a bull*
• ***Word Family:*** **castration** *noun*

casual (*say* **kazh**-yew-ul) *adjective*
1 happening by chance: *a casual meeting* 2 careless: *a casual attitude towards work* 3 informal: *casual dress* 4 not regular or permanent: *casual employment*
• ***Word Family:*** **casually** *adverb*

casualty (*say* **kazh**-yew-ul-tee) *noun*
1 someone who has been injured or killed in an accident or in war 2 a place in a hospital where people with severe injuries are taken for emergency treatment: *She was rushed to casualty.*
• ***Word Family:*** the plural is **casualties**

cat *noun*
1 a small animal often kept as a pet 2 an animal of the cat family such as a lion or a tiger
• ***Word Family:*** **catty** *adjective* **(cattier, cattiest)** spiteful

cataclysm (*say* **kat**-a-kliz-um) *noun*
any sudden terrible upset or change
• ***Word Family:*** **cataclysmic** *adjective*

catacombs (*say* **kat**-a-koom *or* **kat**-a-kome) *plural noun*
a set of underground tunnels and rooms, once used for burying bodies

catalogue (*say* **kat**-a-log) *noun*
1 a list of names, paintings or articles on display or for sale: *a catalogue of artists in an exhibition*

A B C D E F G H I J K L M N O P Q R S T U V W X Y Z

catalogue *verb*
2 to list things in a catalogue
• ***Word Family:*** other verb forms are **catalogues, catalogued, cataloguing** □ **cataloguer** *noun*

catalyst (*say* **kat**-a-list) *noun*
1 a substance that doesn't change itself but makes other substances change 2 something or someone that makes a change happen
• ***Word Family:*** **catalytic** *adjective*

catamaran (*say* **kat**-a-ma-ran) *noun*
a boat or raft with two hulls, side by side, which are joined above the water

catapult (*say* **kat**-a-polt) *noun*
1 something that throws objects, such as a Y-shaped stick for shooting stones
catapult *verb*
2 to hurl or be hurled, as if from a catapult: *She was catapulted to stardom.*

cataract *noun*
1 a waterfall or series of waterfalls 2 an eye disease that causes blindness unless you have an operation

catastrophe (*say* ka-**tas**-tra-fee) *noun*
a sudden or terrible disaster
• ***Word Family:*** **catastrophic** *adjective* **catastrophically** *adverb*

catch *verb*
1 to stop and hold a moving object: *Throw the ball and I'll catch it.* 2 to become sick with: *I hope I don't catch flu.* 3 to see someone in the act of doing something: *Mother caught him stealing.* 4 to get someone's attention: *He caught my eye and winked.* 5 **catch up** to come up to someone or overtake them
catch *noun*
6 catching something 7 anything that is caught: *a good catch of fish* 8 a difficulty or drawback: *What's the catch?*
• ***Word Family:*** other verb forms are **catches, caught, catching** □ the plural of the noun is **catches**

catechism (*say* **kat**-a-kiz-um) *noun*
a book of questions and answers that teaches you about your religion

category (*say* **kat**-a-garee) *noun*
a division or group: *The books were sorted into categories.*
• ***Word Family:*** the plural is **categories**

cater (*say* **kay**-ter) *verb*
to supply food: *That firm only caters for weddings and other large parties.*
• ***Word Family:*** **caterer** *noun*

caterpillar (*say* **kat**-a-pil-a) *noun*
the larva of a butterfly or moth

cathedral (*say* ka-**thee**-drul) *noun*
the most important church in an area, which has a bishop in charge of it
• ***Word Origins:*** from a Greek word meaning "chair"

catholic (*say* **kath**-a-lik) *adjective*
1 covering or including a very wide area of things: *She has catholic tastes in music.* 2 **Catholic** (a) to do with the whole Christian church (b) Roman Catholic: *a Catholic priest*
Catholic *noun*
3 **Catholic** a member of the Roman Catholic Church
• ***Word Family:*** **Catholicism** *noun* the beliefs of the Roman Catholic Church
• ***Word Origins:*** from a Greek word meaning "universal"

cattle *plural noun*
cows and bulls: *cattle grazing in the paddock*

catwalk *noun*
a long narrow platform that models walk along to show new clothes

caucus (*say* **kaw**-kus) *noun*
a committee, especially one made up of the members of a political party in parliament

cauldron (*say* **kawl**-drun) *noun*
a large iron pot for cooking: *a steaming cauldron of soup / a witch's cauldron*
• ***Word Origins:*** from a Latin word meaning "a hot bath"

cauliflower (*say* **kol**-i-flow-er) *noun*
a large vegetable with a round head of tight, white flowers

cause *noun*
1 anything that makes something happen: *A virus was the cause of his illness.* 2 a purpose or aim: *They are working for a good cause.* 3 reason: *You have no cause to complain.*
cause *verb*
4 to make something happen: *What caused the explosion?*
• ***Word Family:*** **causation** *noun*

causeway *noun*
a raised road or path across wet or swampy ground

caustic (*say* **kos**-tik *or* **kaw**-stik) *adjective*
1 able to eat away living matter: *caustic soda* 2 sarcastic or biting: *a caustic remark*
• ***Word Family:*** **caustically** *adverb*
• ***Word Origins:*** from a Greek word meaning "capable of burning"

caution (*say* **kaw**-shon) *noun*
1 taking care, especially to avoid danger: *Drive with caution.* 2 a warning: *The policeman let the driver off with a caution.*

caution *verb*
3 to warn or advise someone
•***Word Family:*** **cautious** *adjective* wary or careful

cavalcade (*say* **kav**-ul-kade) *noun*
a procession of horses and riders or other vehicles: *A cavalcade of official cars followed the President's car.*

cavalry (*say* **kav**-ul-ree) *noun*
a group of soldiers fighting on horseback
•***Word Family:*** the plural is **cavalries**

cave *noun*
1 a hollow space under the ground or in the side of a cliff or hill
cave *verb*
2 to fall or collapse: *The ground caved in under us.* 3 to explore caves

caveman *noun*
a man in prehistoric times who lived in a cave
•***Word Family:*** the plural is **cavemen**

cavern (*say* **kav**-un) *noun*
a large cave
•***Word Family:*** **cavernous** *adjective* deep or hollow

cavewoman *noun*
a woman in prehistoric times who lived in a cave
•***Word Family:*** the plural is **cavewomen**

cavity (*say* **kav**-i-tee) *noun*
a hole or hollow: *a cavity in a tooth*
•***Word Family:*** the plural is **cavities**

CBD *noun*
the central business district of a city
•***Word Origins:*** formed from the first letters of central business district

CD *noun*
the short form of **compact disc**

CD-ROM *noun*
a compact disc which reads text in digital form and displays it on a computer screen

cease *verb*
to stop or come to an end: *Fighting has ceased.*
•***Word Family:*** **ceaseless** *adjective* without end **ceaselessly** *adverb*

cedar (*say* **see**-da) *noun*
a kind of tree, whose wood is used in buildings or to make furniture

cede (*say* seed) *verb*
to give up or surrender something to someone: *The property was ceded to the government.*

ceiling (*say* **seel**-ing) *noun*
1 the flat surface of a room above your head: *Can you reach the ceiling?* 2 the highest point something can go to: *You'll have to put a ceiling on your spending.*

celebrate (*say* **sel**-a-brate) *verb*
1 to hold a party in honour of a person or a festival: *We celebrated my birthday at a restaurant. / Do you celebrate Passover?* 2 to conduct a religious service: *The priest celebrated mass.* 3 to praise: *Her beauty was celebrated in poetry.*
•***Word Family:*** **celebrated** *adjective* famous **celebration** *noun* a party **celebrant** *noun*

celebrity (*say* se-**leb**-ra-tee) *noun*
a famous person
•***Word Family:*** the plural is **celebrities**

celery (*say* **sel**-a-ree) *noun*
a vegetable with long pale green stalks that you eat

celestial (*say* se-**les**-ti-ul) *adjective*
1 to do with the sky: *celestial bodies* 2 to do with heaven: *celestial happiness*

celibacy (*say* **sel**-i-ba-see) *noun*
the state of being unmarried and not having sexual intercourse, especially because of religious vows
•***Word Family:*** **celibate** *adjective*

cell *noun*
1 a small room, usually for one person, in a prison or convent 2 one of the smallest parts of all living things: *a blood cell / a plant cell* 3 one of the parts of a battery
•***Word Family:*** **cellular** *adjective* having a cell or cells
•***Word Origins:*** from a Latin word meaning "storeroom"

cellar (*say* **sel**-a) *noun*
a room under a building: *a wine cellar*

cello (*say* **chel**-o) *noun*
a musical instrument like a large violin which you play sitting down
•***Word Family:*** **cellist** *noun* a cello player

cellophane (*say* **sel**-o-fane) *noun*
a transparent, waterproof paper used for wrapping presents, food or other things
•***Word Origins:*** this word is a trademark

cellulose (*say* **sel**-yoo-lohs) *noun*
a substance that makes up the cell walls of plants

Celsius (*say* **sel**-see-us) *adjective*
using a scale of temperature with 0°C set at the melting point of ice, and 100°C set at the boiling point of water
•***Word Origins:*** named after Anders *Celsius*, 1701 to 1744, a Swedish astronomer

cement (*say* si-**ment**) *noun*
1 a mixture of limestone and clay which, when mixed with water, sets to form concrete 2 a type of glue
cement *verb*
3 to cover or join something with cement

A B C D E F G H I J K L M N O P Q R S T U V W X Y Z

cemetery (*say* **sem**-a-tree) *noun*
an area of land where dead people are buried
•***Word Family:*** the plural is **cemeteries**

cenotaph (*say* **sen**-a-tahf) *noun*
a monument, especially as a war memorial, in memory of a person or people whose bodies are buried elsewhere

censor (*say* **sen**-sa) *noun*
a person whose job it is to cut out any parts of a film or book that they think other people shouldn't see or read
•***Word Family:*** **censor** *verb* **censorship** *noun*

census (*say* **sen**-sus) *noun*
an official count of all the people living in a country

cent (*say* sent) *noun*
a coin used in the United States, Canada and Australia which is worth one hundredth of a dollar

centaur (*say* **sen**-taw) *noun*
a creature in Greek legend, thought to be half man and half horse

centenary (*say* sen-**teen**-a-ree) *noun*
a one hundredth anniversary
•***Word Family:*** the plural is **centenaries** □ **centenarian** *noun* a person who is 100 years old **centennial** *adjective*

centi- *prefix*
showing one hundredth part of a unit: *centimetre*

centimetre *noun*
a hundredth part of a metre

centipede (*say* **sen**-ti-peed) *noun*
a small creature with a long body and many legs
•***Word Origins:*** from two Latin words meaning "a hundred feet"

central (*say* **sen**-trul) *adjective*
1 at or near the centre: *The rooms in the house opened onto the central passage.* 2 principal or chief: *the central figure in a story*
•***Word Family:*** **centrally** *adverb*

central locking *noun*
a system in which all your car doors, and sometimes the boot, are automatically locked from a single key or other operating control

centre (*say* **sen**-ta) *noun*
1 a middle point: *the centre of a circle* 2 the main place for something: *a shopping centre*
centre *verb*
3 to place in the centre: *Centre your picture on the screen.*
•***Word Origins:*** from a Greek word meaning "a sharp point"

centrefold *noun*
the two facing pages in the centre of a magazine which have a picture you can take out and pin up

centrifugal (*say* **sen**-tri-few-gul *or* sen-**trif**-a-gul) *adjective*
moving away from the centre

centurion (*say* sen-**tew**-ree-on) *noun*
an officer commanding one hundred soldiers in the army of ancient Rome

century (*say* **sen**-cha-ree) *noun*
1 a period of one hundred years 2 one hundred
•***Word Family:*** the plural is **centuries**

ceramics (*say* se-**ram**-iks) *plural noun*
1 the art of making pottery from clay 2 objects made from clay
•***Word Family:*** **ceramic** *adjective: a ceramic vase*

cereal (*say* **seer**-i-al) *noun*
1 a grain plant such as wheat, rice or corn 2 a breakfast food made from these plants
•***Word Origins:*** named after *Ceres*, a goddess in Roman myths

cerebral (*say* **ser**-i-brul) *adjective*
to do with the brain

cerebral palsy *noun*
an illness caused by damage to the brain which makes a person partly paralysed or makes them suffer from muscle spasms they cannot control

ceremony (*say* **ser**-a-mu-nee) *noun*
the formal actions and words performed on certain sacred or important occasions: *a wedding ceremony / a medal ceremony*
•***Word Family:*** the plural is **ceremonies** □ **ceremonial** *adjective* to do with a ceremony **ceremonious** *adjective* very polite and formal

certain (*say* **sir**-tun) *adjective*
1 sure or free from doubt: *I am certain he won't forget a second time.* 2 not named but known: *Everyone knows a certain person stole the money.*
•***Word Family:*** **certainly** *adverb* without doubt **certainty** *noun* **(certainties)**

certificate (*say* sir-**tif**-a-kit) *noun*
a printed statement telling you something is true: *a birth certificate*

certify (*say* **sir**-ti-fie) *verb*
to state in writing or declare that something is true
•***Word Family:*** other forms are **certifies, certified, certifying**

cervix (*say* **sir**-viks) *noun*
the opening to the womb
•***Word Family:*** the plural is **cervixes** or **cervices** □ **cervical** *adjective*
•***Word Origins:*** from a Latin word meaning "neck"

CFC *noun*
the short form of **chlorofluorocarbon**

chafe *verb*
1 to make something sore by rubbing it: *The new shoes chafed his feet.* 2 to become impatient: *She chafed at the idea of waiting so long.*

chaff (*say* chahf) *noun*
1 the husks separated from the grain by threshing 2 finely chopped hay used as food for animals

chain *noun*
1 a series of metal rings or links joined together
2 a connected series of things: *a mountain chain / a chain of motels*
chain *verb*
3 to bind or fasten something with a chain: *Chain your bike to the railings.*

chainsaw *noun*
a saw that has a moving chain with teeth set on it and is driven by a small motor

chain store *noun*
one of a number of similar shops in different towns that are owned by the same company

chair *noun*
1 a seat for one person, usually having four legs, a support for your back and sometimes arms
2 someone who is in charge of a meeting: *Direct your questions to the chair.*
chair *verb*
3 to be in charge of a meeting

chairperson *noun*
the person in charge of a meeting
•***Word Family:*** **chairman** *noun* **chairwoman** *noun*

chalet (*say* **shal**-ay) *noun*
a house in the mountains, particularly where there is snow

chalk (*rhymes with* walk) *noun*
1 soft, white limestone 2 a stick made from this substance for drawing on blackboards or for artwork
•***Word Family:*** **chalky** *adjective* **chalkiness** *noun*

challenge *noun*
1 an invitation to take part in a contest: *He issued a challenge to a game of chess.* 2 something that is hard for you to do: *Learning a new language is a challenge.*
challenge *verb*
3 to invite someone to take part in a contest: *I challenge you to a race.* 4 to question whether something is true
•***Word Family:*** **challenger** *noun*

chamber (*say* **chaym**-ber) *noun*
1 an old-fashioned word for a room, especially a bedroom 2 **chambers** the rooms where judges or barristers work when they are not in court

chamber music *noun*
music composed for a small group of instruments

chameleon (*say* ka-**mee**-lee-on) *noun*
a kind of lizard that can change colour to blend with its surroundings

champagne (*say* sham-**pane**) *noun*
a bubbly white wine
•***Word Origins:*** named after *Champagne* in France, where the wine comes from

champion *noun*
1 someone or something that wins first prize in a competition 2 someone who supports or fights for a good cause: *She is a champion of human rights*
champion *verb*
3 to support or fight for a cause
•***Word Family:*** **championship** *noun*

chance (*rhymes with* dance) *noun*
1 the unexpected way things can happen: *Their careful preparations left nothing to chance.*
2 possibility: *Is there no chance of recovery?* 3 an opportunity: *This is your chance to win.* 4 risk: *Take no chances when riding your bike.*
chance *verb*
5 to risk: *In spite of my warning he said he would chance it.*
•***Word Family:*** **chancy** *adjective* risky or uncertain

chandelier (*say* **shan**-da-lear) *noun*
an ornamental holder for two or more lights, which hangs from a ceiling
•***Word Origins:*** from a French word meaning "candlestick"

change *verb*
1 to make something different or to become different: *Sunset changed the colour of the sky. / The weather changed as we drove south.* 2 to exchange: *Will you change places with me?* 3 to exchange for smaller notes or coins: *Can you change a £50 note for me?* 4 to put on different clothes: *Shouldn't you change before you go out?*
change *noun*
5 anything that is changed or different
6 money in the form of coins 7 the money you are given back when you pay more money than something costs: *Don't forget your change!*
•***Word Family:*** **changeability** *noun* **changeable** *adjective* **changeless** *adjective*

channel *noun*
1 the deepest part of a river or harbour: *a boat channel* 2 a stretch of water joining two seas
3 a passage along which something is carried or

a b c d e f g h i j k l m n o p q r s t u v w x y z

A B C D E F G H I J K L M N O P Q R S T U V W X Y Z

moved: *He dug a channel along the fence.* 4 the wave or frequency band used by a television or radio station
channel *verb*
5 to form or cut a channel in something: *The river channelled its way to the sea.*
•***Word Family:*** other verb forms are **channels, channelled, channelling**

chant *noun*
1 a repeated tune sung in some church services: *a Gregorian chant* 2 a singsong way of speaking
chant *verb*
3 to sing 4 to speak in a singsong manner: *The crowd chanted "we want jobs".*

chaos (*say* **kay**-os) *noun*
total confusion or disorder: *There was chaos in the city when the traffic lights failed.*
•***Word Family:*** **chaotic** *adjective*

chap (1) *verb*
to become cracked or roughened as a result of cold or wind: *Her hands were chapped at the end of the day's hike.*
•***Word Family:*** other forms are **chaps, chapped, chapping**

chap (2) *noun*
a man: *He's a very pleasant chap.*

chapatti (*say* cha-**pah**-tee) *noun*
flat, round Indian bread

chapel *noun*
a small church or part of a larger one

chaperone (*say* **shap**-a-rone) *noun*
an older person who accompanies young, unmarried or inexperienced people to social events
•***Word Family:*** **chaperone** *verb*

chaplain (*say* **chap**-lin) *noun*
a clergyman who works in a school, hospital or the armed services

chapter *noun*
a division or section of a book

char *verb*
to scorch or burn with fire: *to char steak*
•***Word Family:*** other forms are **chars, charred, charring**

character (*say* **ka**-rak-ta) *noun*
1 the qualities that make one person or thing different from another: *It is not in her character to be bad-tempered.* 2 the quality of being brave and honest: *Teachers try to help children build character.* 3 an odd or unusual person: *Our old postman is a real character.* 4 one of the people in a novel, play or film: *Which character did you like best?* 5 a symbol or letter, as in an alphabet

characterize or characterise
(*say* **ka**-rak-ta-rize) *verb*
to mark or show something to be different: *His work is characterized by carefulness.*
•***Word Family:*** **characteristic** *adjective* typical **characterization** *noun*

charade (*say* sha-**rahd**) *noun*
1 **charades** a game in which a player mimes a word or phrase which others try to guess 2 an act or pretence: *Stop this charade—you aren't hurt at all.*

charcoal *noun*
1 partly burnt wood 2 a stick of charred willow used for drawing

charge *verb*
1 to accuse someone of committing a crime: *He was charged with burglary.* 2 to ask for an amount of money as payment: *They charge very high prices for all their goods.* 3 to write down as a debt to be paid: *Please charge it to my account.* 4 to attack by rushing forward: *The bull charged as soon as we climbed the fence.*
charge *noun*
5 an attack made by rushing forward: *The bull's charge scared us.* 6 an amount that is charged: *What is the charge for delivering goods to my home?* 7 anyone or anything in the care of someone else: *The teacher and his charges crowded into the museum.* 8 an explosive: *The engineers set off a charge to demolish the building.* 9 **in charge** in command: *Who is in charge of this class?*
•***Word Origins:*** from a Latin word meaning "load"

chariot *noun*
an open, two-wheeled carriage pulled by horses and used in ancient times in wars
•***Word Family:*** **charioteer** *noun* the driver of a chariot

charisma (*say* ka-**riz**-ma) *noun*
a special quality some people have to attract people
•***Word Family:*** **charismatic** *adjective*
•***Word Origins:*** from a Greek word meaning "a divine gift"

charity (*say* **cha**-ri-tee) *noun*
1 helping poor or helpless people 2 an organization or fund that does this
•***Word Family:*** the plural is **charities** □ **charitable** *adjective* showing charity **charitably** *adverb*

charm *noun*
1 a magic formula or spell 2 an object worn or carried because it is believed to have magic powers 3 a trinket worn on a bracelet 4 the power or quality of attracting or pleasing: *She has charm, wit and poise.*

charm *verb*
5 to please or attract someone greatly: *We were charmed by her friendliness.*
•***Word Family:*** **charmer** *noun* **charming** *adjective* delightful **charmingly** *adverb*

chart *noun*
1 a sheet or record showing special information, often with lists or diagrams: *a weather chart* 2 a map of the sea and coasts
chart *verb*
3 to make a map of an area or a chart of information

charter *noun*
1 a written or printed statement of rights granted by a ruler or government 2 the leasing or hiring of an aeroplane or boat
charter *verb*
3 to grant a charter to someone 4 to hire or lease: *They chartered a boat to sail to the island.*

chase *verb*
1 to follow or run after someone or something, especially when you are hunting or trying to catch them: *The police chased the suspect's car.*
chase *noun*
2 chasing or hunting: *The owner of the stolen car joined the chase.*

chasm (*say* **kaz**-um) *noun*
a deep narrow valley or split in the earth's surface

chassis (*say* **shas**-ee) *noun*
the frame of a motor vehicle on which the body, wheels and other fittings are mounted
•***Word Family:*** the plural is also **chassis**

chaste (*say* chayst) *adjective*
1 not having sexual intercourse until marriage
2 pure and decent: *chaste behaviour*
•***Word Family:*** **chastity** *noun* the quality of being chaste **chastely** *adverb*

chastise (*say* **chas**-tize) *verb*
1 to scold or tell someone off 2 to punish, usually by beating
•***Word Family:*** **chastisement** *noun*

chat *verb*
to have a friendly talk
•***Word Family:*** other verb forms are **chats, chatted, chatting** □ **chat** *noun*

chatter *verb*
1 to talk very quickly, often about unimportant things 2 to utter short, garbled sounds: *Squirrels chattered in the trees.* 3 to click together rapidly: *His teeth chattered with cold.*

chauffeur (*say* **sho**-fa) *noun*
someone whose job is to drive a car
•***Word Family:*** **chauffeur** *verb*

chauvinism (*say* **sho**-va-niz-um) *noun*
1 believing strongly that your country is better than all others 2 the belief that some men have that women are inferior to men
•***Word Family:*** **chauvinist** *noun* **chauvinistic** *adjective*

cheap *adjective*
1 not costing very much money 2 not of good quality: *Don't use cheap material if you want your dress to last.* 3 mean: *That was a cheap trick.*
•***Word Family:*** **cheapen** *verb* **cheaply** *adverb* **cheapness** *noun*

cheat *verb*
1 to trick someone or be dishonest in order to get something: *She always cheats at cards. / He cheated her of £5.*
cheat *noun*
2 someone who cheats

check *verb*
1 to stop something or hold it back: *The government are trying to check inflation.* 2 to make sure that a sum is correct: *Add these figures and then check your answer.*
check *noun*
3 anything that stops, controls or holds something back: *You must keep your temper in check.* 4 a way of making sure something is correct: *We use a pocket calculator as a check on our sums.* 5 a pattern of squares, like those on a chessboard
•***Word Family:*** **checked** *adjective*: *checked curtains*

checkmate *noun*
the winning move in chess, in which your opponent's king can't escape
•***Word Origins:*** from Persian words meaning "the king is dead"

cheek *noun*
1 the side of your face, below your eye
2 boldness or rudeness
•***Word Family:*** **cheeky** *adjective* (**cheekier, cheekiest**) impudent **cheekily** *adverb* **cheekiness** *noun*

cheer *verb*
1 to shout out encouragement or praise 2 to make someone happy or hopeful: *The news cheered him greatly.*
cheer *noun*
3 a shout of encouragement and praise: *The crowd gave a great cheer.* 4 feelings of happiness: *She was full of good cheer.*
•***Word Family:*** **cheerful** *adjective* happy or making you feel happy: *She's always cheerful. / We chose a cheerful colour for the curtains.* **cheerfully** *adverb* **cheerfulness** *noun*

cheese *noun*
food made from the curd of milk

cheetah *noun*
a long-legged animal of the cat family, that lives in Africa and Asia and is the fastest animal on land

chef (*say* shef) *noun*
a cook, especially the head cook in a restaurant

chemical (*say* **kem**-i-kul) *adjective*
1 to do with the science of chemistry
chemical *noun*
2 a substance used or produced in a chemical process
•***Word Family:*** **chemically** *adverb*

chemist (*say* **kem**-ist) *noun*
1 a scientist who studies or researches chemistry
2 someone who has studied drugs and medicine
3 a shop where drugs and medicines are sold

chemistry (*say* **kem**-i-stree) *noun*
the study of how substances are made up and their effect upon each other

chemotherapy (*say* keem-o-**the**-ra-pee) *noun*
the treatment of diseases such as cancer, using chemicals

cheque (*say* chek) *noun*
a printed form telling a bank they can pay the amount written on it and take that amount from the account of the person who signed it
•***Word Family:*** **chequebook** *noun*

chequered (*say* **chek**-erd) *adjective*
marked with squares

cherish *verb*
to treasure or care for something tenderly

cherry *noun*
1 a small, round, juicy red fruit with a stone 2 a bright purplish-red colour
•***Word Family:*** the plural is **cherries**

cherub (*say* **che**-rub) *noun*
1 an angel, often pictured as a child with wings
2 a well-behaved child often with a chubby face
•***Word Family:*** the plural for definition 1 is **cherubim** and for definition 2 is **cherubs** □ **cherubic** *adjective* angelic

chess *noun*
a game played by two players on a chequered board with each player having 16 pieces
•***Word Family:*** **chessboard** *noun* **chessman** *noun* a piece used in chess

chest *noun*
1 the front part of your body between your neck and your abdomen 2 a large, strong box with a lid, used for storing things: *a treasure chest*

chestnut *noun*
1 a large brown nut which is often roasted on coals 2 the tree that chestnuts grow on 3 a reddish-brown horse, with a slightly darker mane and tail 4 a reddish-brown colour

chew *verb*
to crush or grind with your teeth
•***Word Family:*** **chewy** *adjective*

chic (*say* sheek *or* shik) *adjective*
elegant and stylish, especially in the way you dress
•***Word Origins:*** this word comes from French

chick *noun*
a young bird, especially a chicken

chicken *noun*
1 a young domestic hen or rooster, or its meat
2 a coward: *You're a chicken to run away.*
chicken *verb*
3 **chicken out** to refuse to do something because you are afraid

chickenpox *noun*
a disease causing fever and small itchy spots, most common in children

chide *verb*
to scold someone or find fault with them: *Her last letter chided me for not writing.*
•***Word Family:*** other forms are **chides, chided** or **chid, chided** or **chidden, chiding**

chief (*say* cheef) *noun*
1 the head or ruler of a group
chief *adjective*
2 most important: *Our chief complaint is about the heat.*
•***Word Family:*** **chiefly** *adverb*

chieftain (*say* **cheef**-tun) *noun*
the leader of a clan or tribe

chiffon (*say* shi-**fon**) *noun*
a thin cloth made from silk, nylon or rayon: *a chiffon scarf*

child *noun*
1 a boy or girl 2 a son or daughter
•***Word Family:*** the plural is **children** □ **childhood** *noun* the time when you are a child

child abuse *noun*
the harming of a child by a parent or guardian, using violence, neglect or sexual acts

childish *adjective*
sulky or immature: *His outburst was quite childish.*
•***Word Family:*** **childishly** *adverb* **childishness** *noun*

chill *noun*
1 coldness: *The fire took the chill off the room.*
2 the shivery feeling you get at the beginning of an illness
chill *verb*
3 to make something cold or to become cold: *Chill the wine.*

chill *adjective*
4 cold enough to make you shiver: *a chill wind*
• ***Word Family:*** **chilling** *adjective* frightening **chilly** *adjective* (**chillier, chilliest**) **chilliness** *noun*

chilli *noun*
a hot-tasting small capsicum
• ***Word Family:*** the plural is **chillies**

chime *noun*
1 a bell with a musical sound: *a door chime*
2 **chimes** a set of bells or tubes that are tuned
chime *verb*
3 to ring bells or to make the sound of bells

chimney (*say* **chim**-nee) *noun*
a tall hollow structure that carries smoke from a fire out through the roof of a building

chimpanzee *noun*
an African ape that is very intelligent
• ***Word Origins:*** from a Bantu word

chin *noun*
the lower part of your face, below your mouth

china (*rhymes with* finer) *noun*
cups, plates and other such articles made from porcelain clay: *to use the best china*

chintz *noun*
a shiny cotton material with printed flowery designs, used for curtains and chair covers
• ***Word Family:*** the plural is **chintzes**

chip *noun*
1 a small piece broken or cut from something larger: *a wood chip* 2 a long thin piece of fried potato 3 a mark where a small piece has been broken off: *This cup has a chip in it.* 4 a thin slice of silicon used in a computer
chip *verb*
5 to make a chip or chips in something: *Be careful not to chip that plate.* 6 **chip in** to give money as your share: *We all chipped in to buy the present.*
• ***Word Family:*** other verb forms are **chips, chipped, chipping**

chipmunk *noun*
a small squirrel-like animal with a striped back, found in forests in northern America

chiropody (*say* ki-**rop**-a-dee) *noun*
the treatment of foot complaints, such as corns
• ***Word Family:*** **chiropodist** *noun*

chiropractic (*say* **kie**-ra-prak-tik) *noun*
the treatment of disease and injuries, especially to the back, by adjusting the spinal column
• ***Word Family:*** **chiropractor** *noun*

chirp *verb*
to make a short, high-pitched sound like a bird
• ***Word Family:*** **chirp** *noun* **chirpy** (**chirpier, chirpiest**) *adjective* lively or chatty **chirpily** *adverb*

chisel (*say* **chiz**-ul) *noun*
1 a tool with a finely sharpened edge, used for cutting and shaping
chisel *verb*
2 to cut with a chisel
• ***Word Family:*** other verb forms are **chisels, chiselled, chiselling** □ **chiselled** *adjective*

chivalry (*say* **shiv**-ul-ree) *noun*
1 polite or courteous behaviour especially of a man to a woman 2 the qualities of honour, courage and duty which were valued by knights in the Middle Ages
• ***Word Family:*** **chivalrous** *adjective*

chive *noun*
a small plant of the onion family used as a herb

chlorine (*say* **klaw**-reen) *noun*
a poisonous gas with a choking, irritating smell, used as a bleach and to purify water

chlorofluorocarbon (*say* klor-o-floo-ro-**kar**-bon) *noun*
a chemical compound used in refrigerators and aerosols. Manufacturers are using this less now as it is dangerous to the environment

chlorophyll (*say* **klor**-a-fil) *noun*
the green colouring found in most leaves and plants, that traps energy from sunlight to help them grow

chock *noun*
a block of wood or other material used as a wedge to stop something moving

chocolate (*say* **chok**-lit) *noun*
1 a sweet or flavouring made from the seeds of a small, tropical tree 2 a dark brown colour

choice (*rhymes with* voice) *noun*
1 choosing: *The choice between the two candidates was very difficult.* 2 something that you choose: *What is your choice for dinner?* 3 a number of things from which to choose: *There is a wide choice of subjects to study.*
choice *adjective*
4 excellent or fine

choir (*say* kwire) *noun*
a group of trained singers

choke *verb*
1 to stop someone breathing or to be unable to breathe because of something pressing on your windpipe: *The tight leash choked the dog. / He choked on the lolly.* 2 to become clogged or overgrown: *The garden is choked with weeds.*
choke *noun*
3 a device which increases the amount of air mixing with the petrol when you start an engine

A B C D E F G H I J K L M N O P Q R S T U V W X Y Z

cholera (*say* **kol**-a-ra) *noun*
an infectious disease causing severe stomach upset, which can kill you

cholesterol (*say* ka-**les**-ta-rol) *noun*
a fatty substance found in your body or in such foods as egg yolk. Although it is necessary for good health, you are more likely to suffer from heart disease if you have too much in your bloodstream

choose (*say* chooz) *verb*
to decide on or pick from a number of things
•*Word Family:* other forms are **chooses, chose, chosen, choosing** □ **choosy** *adjective* (**choosier, choosiest**) fussy or difficult to please: *choosy about what you eat*

chop *verb*
1 to cut with heavy strokes
chop *noun*
2 a cutting stroke or movement: *He made a wild chop at his opponent's neck.* 3 a small piece of lamb or pork containing a bone
•*Word Family:* other verb forms are **chops, chopped, chopping**

chopper *noun*
1 a person or thing that chops, such as a cleaver for chopping meat 2 a helicopter

choppy *adjective*
rough, with small uneven waves: *a choppy sea*
•*Word Family:* other forms are **choppier, choppiest**

chopsticks *plural noun*
a pair of fine sticks made of ivory, bamboo or plastic used to pick up food

choral (*say* **ko**-ral) *adjective*
to do with music sung by a choir

chord (*say* kord) *noun*
three or more musical notes played together

chore *noun*
a small job that you think is boring or unpleasant

choreography (*say* ko-ree-**og**-ra-fee) *noun*
the planning of movements for ballets
•*Word Family:* **choreographer** *noun*

chorister (*say* **ko**-ris-ta) *noun*
a singer in a choir

chorus (*say* **kaw**-rus) *noun*
1 a group of singers or dancers who perform together 2 a song or part of a song which is sung by a number of singers and is often repeated after each verse
chorus *verb*
3 to sing or speak in a chorus

chow mein (*say* chow **main**) *noun*
a dish of fried noodles with shredded vegetables and finely chopped meat, chicken or shrimps

Christ *noun*
a religious teacher, who lived in Judaea about 2000 years ago and who taught that we should all love one another

christen (*say* **kris**-un) *verb*
1 to give a name to someone, especially at baptism 2 to use something for the first time
•*Word Family:* **christening** *noun*
•*Word Origins:* from an Old English word meaning "to make Christian"

Christian (*say* **kris**-tee-un) *adjective*
1 to do with Christ and the religion based on his teachings
Christian *noun*
2 a follower of Christ
•*Word Family:* **Christianity** *noun* the Christian religion or beliefs

Christian name *noun*
your first name or names apart from your surname or family name

Christmas (*say* **kris**-mus) *noun*
the time of the year when Christians celebrate the birth of Christ
•*Word Family:* **Christmas Day** 25 December, the main day of Christmas **Christmas Eve,** the day and night before Christmas

chromatic (*say* kro-**mat**-ik) *adjective*
1 having to do with colour 2 having to do with a musical scale that moves by small steps called semitones
•*Word Family:* **chromatically** *adverb*

chrome (*say* krome) *noun*
a hard, silver-coloured metal which is used to coat other metals

chromosome (*say* **kro**-ma-some) *noun*
the part of a living cell that determines what the organism will be like

chronic (*say* **kron**-ik) *adjective*
lasting for a long time: *chronic bronchitis*
•*Word Family:* **chronically** *adverb*

chronicle (*say* **kron**-i-kul) *noun*
a history or record of events in the order in which they happened
•*Word Family:* **chronicle** *verb* **chronicler** *noun*

chronological (*say* kron-a-**loj**-i-kul) *adjective*
arranged in the order in which things happen
•*Word Family:* **chronologically** *adverb*

chrysalis (*say* **kris**-a-lis) *noun*
the protective cover a caterpillar makes round itself before it changes into a butterfly or moth
•*Word Family:* plural is **chrysalises** or **chrysalides**

chrysanthemum (*say* kri-**san**-tha-mum) *noun*
a plant with large, brightly coloured flowers

chuck (1) *verb*
1 to throw 2 to pat or tap lightly: *The old lady chucked the baby under the chin.*

chuck (2) *noun*
a cut of beef between the neck and the shoulder-blade

chuckle *verb*
to laugh softly, often to yourself
•***Word Family:*** **chuckle** *noun*

chunk *noun*
a thick or large rough piece: *a chunk of meat*
•***Word Family:*** **chunky** *adjective* (**chunkier, chunkiest**) thick and muscular

church *noun*
1 a building where Christians worship 2 **Church** all Christians thought of as a whole or any group of Christians: *the Presbyterian Church*

churn *noun*
1 a machine that turns cream into butter 2 a large metal milk-can
churn *verb*
3 to stir or beat in order to make butter 4 to move violently: *My stomach churns when I have to sing in public.*

chute (*say* shoot) *noun*
a sloping passage for carrying things to a lower level: *We slid down the chute into the water.*

chutney (*say* **chut**-nee) *noun*
a thick, spicy sauce made from mangoes or other fruit or vegetables

cicada (*say* se-**kah**-da) *noun*
a large insect with four wings, which makes a very long, shrill noise in hot weather

cider (*say* **sigh**-da) *noun*
an alcoholic drink made from apple juice

cigar *noun*
a roll of tobacco leaves that people smoke

cigarette *noun*
a narrow roll of cut tobacco in thin paper that people smoke

cinder (*say* **sin**-da) *noun*
a small burnt piece of wood or coal

cinema (*say* **sin**-i-ma) *noun*
a public theatre where films are shown on a screen

cinnamon (*say* **sin**-a-mun) *noun*
a sweet spice made from the bark of some tropical trees

cipher (*say* **sigh**-fa) *noun*
a secret way of writing, especially using codes or symbols
•***Word Origins:*** from an Arabic word meaning "empty"

circle (*say* **sir**-kul) *noun*
1 a round shape 2 anything in the shape of a circle: *We sat in a circle around the teacher.* 3 a group of people: *He has a nice circle of friends.*
circle *verb*
4 to move in or make the shape of a circle: *The plane circled above the airport before landing.*

circuit (*say* **sir**-kit) *noun*
1 a circular line or path: *He ran five circuits of the track.* 2 a set of wires that are joined to carry electricity for a special purpose: *a power circuit*
•***Word Family:*** **circuitry** *noun* system of electrical circuits

circular (*say* **sir**-kyoo-la) *adjective*
1 shaped like or moving in a circle
circular *noun*
2 a notice or letter sent to several people

circulate (*say* **sir**-kyoo-late) *verb*
1 to go round continuously: *Blood circulates around your body.* 2 to pass from place to place: *The rumour circulated rapidly in the small town.*
•***Word Family:*** **circulatory** *adjective*: *Your heart is part of your circulatory system.*

circum- (*say* **sir**-kum) *prefix*
moving around or on all sides: *circumnavigate*

circumcise (*say* **sir**-kum-size) *verb*
to cut away the foreskin at the end of the penis
•***Word Family:*** **circumcision** *noun* the act or ceremony of circumcising

circumference (*say* sir-**kum**-fer-ence) *noun*
1 the outer line of a circle 2 the length of this line

circumnavigate (*say* sir-kum-**nav**-i-gate) *verb*
to sail around: *Captain Flinders circumnavigated Australia.*
•***Word Family:*** **circumnavigation** *noun* **circumnavigator** *noun*

circumspect *adjective*
cautious and watchful: *Be circumspect when you are talking to people who gossip.*
•***Word Family:*** **circumspectly** *adverb* **circumspection** *noun*

circumstance (*say* **sir**-kum-stance) *noun*
1 something that affects, or happens at the same time as, a particular event 2 **circumstances** financial position

circumvent (*say* **sir**-kum-vent) *verb*
to avoid or find a way around: *It was impossible to circumvent the rules.*

circus (*say* **sir**-kus) *noun*
a form of entertainment consisting of acrobats, clowns and trained animals

cirrus (*say* **si**-rus) *noun*
a high feathery cloud
•***Word Origins:*** from a Latin word meaning "ringlet"

cistern (*say* **sis**-tun) *noun*
a raised tank for holding water, such as one above a toilet

citadel (*say* **sit**-a-del) *noun*
a fortress guarding a city

cite (*say* site) *verb*
to quote or refer to something: *The coach cited the rule book to settle the argument.*
•***Word Family:*** **citation** *noun*

citizen (*say* **sit**-i-zun) *noun*
someone who lives in a city or country and who has certain rights and duties
•***Word Family:*** **citizenship** *noun*

citrus (*say* **sit**-rus) *noun*
an evergreen tree or shrub including the lemon, orange and grapefruit
•***Word Family:*** **citrus** *adjective*

city *noun*
1 a large or important town 2 the people who live in a city: *The whole city watched the fireworks on New Year's Eve.*
•***Word Family:*** the plural is **cities**

civic (*say* **siv**-ik) *adjective*
to do with a city or citizens: *The town hall is in the civic centre.*

civil (*say* **siv**-ul) *adjective*
1 to do with citizens or citizenship: *civil law* 2 to do with citizens rather than military or religious matters: *a civil marriage* 3 polite: *Although she was extremely angry she gave a civil reply.*
•***Word Family:*** **civility** *noun* **civilly** *adverb*

civilian (*say* si-**vil**-yen) *noun*
someone who is not a member of the armed forces

civilization or **civilisation** (*say* siv-i-lie-**zay**-shon) *noun*
1 a society that is well-organized and advanced in art, science and so on 2 people or societies that have reached this stage 3 areas where many people live: *It was a relief to get back to civilization after the camping trip.*
•***Word Family:*** **civilize** or **civilise** *verb* to refine or educate someone

claim *verb*
1 to demand something that is your right: *to claim unemployment benefit* 2 to say as if you are sure: *He claims he saw a ghost.*
claim *noun*
3 a demand: *There are many claims on a teacher's time.* 4 something you state is your right: *He has no claim to fame.* 5 something that you claim, such as land for mining
•***Word Family:*** **claimant** *noun* someone who makes a claim

clairvoyance (*say* klair-**voy**-ance) *noun*
being able to see or know things that have not yet happened
•***Word Family:*** **clairvoyant** *noun*

clam *noun*
a type of large shellfish with two shells

clamber *verb*
to climb using your hands and feet

clammy *adjective*
cold and damp
•***Word Family:*** other forms are **clammier, clammiest**

clamour or **clamor** *noun*
1 a loud noise or fuss made by many people when they are angry: *There was an angry clamour about the referee's decision.*
clamour *verb*
2 to make a loud noise: *The children clamoured for ice-cream.*

clamp *noun*
1 a tool that presses or holds things together
clamp *verb*
2 to fasten with or hold in a clamp 3 to press firmly: *A hand was clamped over his mouth.*

clan *noun*
a large family or group of related families
•***Word Family:*** **clannish** *adjective* very loyal as if you are family

clang *verb*
to make a noise like loud bells

clank *verb*
to make a harsh sound like metal banging on metal

clap *verb*
1 to strike your hands together loudly: *The children clapped at the end of the play. / We all clapped the clown.* 2 to slap or grasp, often in a friendly way: *to clap someone on the back* 3 to put away immediately: *He was clapped into jail.*
clap *noun*
4 the act or sound of clapping: *The audience gave the actors a clap.* 5 a sudden loud noise: *A clap of thunder frightened us.*
•***Word Family:*** other verb forms are **claps, clapped, clapping** □ **clapper** *noun* a person or thing that claps, such as the tongue of a bell

clarinet *noun*
a musical instrument of the woodwind family
•***Word Family:*** **clarinettist** *noun* someone who plays the clarinet

clarity (*say* **kla**-ri-tee) *noun*
clearness: *the clarity of water*

clash *verb*
1 to hit with a loud, harsh sound: *The cymbals clashed dramatically.* 2 to fight or come into conflict: *The gangs clashed in the playground.* 3 to look ugly together: *The red shirt clashed with her orange blouse.* 4 to coincide or be at the same time: *His party clashed with the tennis match.*
clash *noun*
5 the act or sound of clashing

clasp (*say* klahsp) *noun*
1 something with a catch, used to fasten two things together 2 a hold or grasp: *a firm clasp of the hand*
clasp *verb*
3 to fasten with a clasp 4 to hold or grasp tightly

class *noun*
1 a group of people or things that are similar 2 a group of students who are taught together 3 one of the groups in society in which people are said to belong according to their education, income or the kind of work they do: *working class*
class *verb*
4 to arrange or rate things or people according to type, quality and so on
• ***Word Family:*** the plural of the noun is **classes**

classic *adjective*
1 thought by many people to be important or of very good quality: *a classic novel* 2 serving as a model or guide: *Here is a classic example of bad architecture.*
classic *noun*
3 someone or something of the highest standard or quality: *This novel is a classic.* 4 **classics** the literature of ancient Greece and Rome

classical *adjective*
1 to do with the art, literature or civilization of ancient Greece and Rome 2 traditional or of lasting artistic value, such as a symphony or concerto: *classical ballet / classical music*

classified advertisement *noun*
a small advertisement printed in a magazine or newspaper under particular headings

classify (*say* **klas**-i-figh) *verb*
1 to arrange things in classes or similar groups: *to classify plants* 2 to declare that a government or military document must be kept secret
• ***Word Family:*** other forms are **classifies, classified, classifying** □ **classification** *noun*

clatter *verb*
1 to make harsh, rapid, rattling sounds: *The plates clattered against each other.*
clatter *noun*
2 a noise of things banging together

clause (*say* klawz) *noun*
a group of words containing a subject and a verb and which can be part of a sentence or a whole sentence, as in *"The girl was called Claudine" and was born in France.*

claustrophobia (*say* klos-tra-**foh**-bee-a) *noun*
a terrible fear of being shut in a small space
• ***Word Family:*** **claustrophobic** *adjective*

clavicle (*say* **klav**-i-kul) *noun*
one of the two long bones that join your chest to your shoulder

claw *noun*
1 a hard, sharp, usually curved nail on the paw of an animal or the leg of a bird 2 the jointed grasping part of a crab or lobster
claw *verb*
3 to scratch, tear or pull with claws or nails

clay *noun*
a kind of thick wet soil which is used for making bricks and pottery

clean *adjective*
1 not dirty or stained: *Put on a clean shirt.* 2 not written on yet: *Give me a clean sheet of paper.* 3 neat and simple: *I like the clean lines of our new car.* 4 not rude: *a clean joke*
clean *verb*
5 to make something clean: *Clean your shoes.*
• ***Word Family:*** **cleaner** *noun* **cleanliness** *noun* (*say* **klen**-lee-nes) **cleanly** *adverb*

cleanse (*say* **klenz**) *verb*
to make clean or pure: *to cleanse your skin*

clear *adjective*
1 able to be seen through: *clear water* 2 not cloudy: *a clear sky* 3 plain or easy to understand: *She gave me clear directions on how to come here.* 4 open or free of blockages: *Keep the hall clear of school bags.* 5 certain or sure: *Are you clear about what you have to do?* 6 complete: *We had a clear win over the other team.*
clear *verb*
7 to make something clear or to become clear or clearer: *The sky cleared and the sun shone brightly.* 8 to pass over without touching: *She cleared the high jump bar.* 9 to say that someone is not guilty: *He was cleared of all blame.*
• ***Word Family:*** **clearly** *adverb* without doubt

clearance *noun*
1 a clear space or distance, especially between things: *The sign on the bridge showed how much clearance there was for ships.* 2 a clearing away: *slum clearance* 3 permission to do something: *The journalist was given clearance to enter the naval base.*

clearing *noun*
a piece of land cleared of trees, within a forest area

a b c d e f g h i j k l m n o p q r s t u v w x y z

A B C D E F G H I J K L M N O P Q R S T U V W X Y Z

cleavage (*say* **klee**-vij) *noun*
a division or split

cleave *verb*
to split or separate, especially by cutting: *The ramblers had to cleave a path through the tall weeds.*
•***Word Family:*** other forms are **cleaves, cleft, cleaved** or **clove, cleft, cleaved** or **cloven, cleaving** □ **cleaver** *noun* a heavy chopper used to divide large sections of meat

clef *noun*
a sign on lines of music which shows the name and pitch of the notes which follow it: *the bass clef*
•***Word Origins:*** from a French word meaning "key"

cleft *noun*
a division or split

cleft palate *noun*
a defect in which a child is born with a lengthwise slit along the roof of the mouth, making it hard to speak

clench *verb*
to close or clasp tightly: *He clenched his teeth in pain.*

clergy (*say* **kler**-jee) *noun*
people who are priests or ministers in a Christian church

clerk (*say* klark) *noun*
someone who keeps records of accounts or deals with correspondence in a business
•***Word Family:*** **clerical** *adjective: clerical assistants*

clever *adjective*
1 quick or intelligent: *a clever solution / a clever child* 2 skilful: *His clever hands repaired the clock.*
•***Word Family:*** **cleverly** *adverb* **cleverness** *noun*

cliché (*say* **klee**-shay) *noun*
an idea or saying which has been used so often it is boring
•***Word Family:*** **clichéd** *adjective*
•***Word Origins:*** this word comes from French which is why there is an accent over the "e"

click *noun*
1 a short, sharp, snapping sound: *the click of a key in the lock*
click *verb*
2 to make a click or clicks: *The door clicked shut behind them.*

client (*say* **klie**-ent) *noun*
someone who is a customer of a professional person or business: *The social worker advised her client to see a solicitor.*

cliff *noun*
a very steep, rocky slope, especially at the edge of the land where it meets the sea

cliff-hanger *noun*
anything that is full of suspense or uncertainty, such as a film or serial

climate (*say* **klie**-mit) *noun*
the weather conditions of a place: *a tropical climate / a cold climate*
•***Word Family:*** **climatic** *adjective* **climatically** *adverb*

climax (*say* **klie**-maks) *noun*
the highest or most exciting point of anything: *The play reached its climax in the second act.*
•***Word Family:*** **climactic** *adjective* **climax** *verb*
•***Word Origins:*** from a Greek word meaning "a ladder" or "staircase"

climb (*say* klime) *verb*
1 to move or go upwards: *The plane climbed above the clouds.*
climb *noun*
2 the act of climbing: *We went for a climb on the mountain.* 3 a high place that you can climb: *That hill would be a good climb.*
•***Word Family:*** **climber** *noun* someone or something that climbs

cling *verb*
to hold on tightly: *The child clung to its mother.*
•***Word Family:*** other forms are **clings, clung, clinging**

clinic *noun*
a medical centre, sometimes in a hospital, where you can get specialized treatment, such as X-rays: *a dental clinic*

clip (1) *verb*
1 to cut or trim, especially with scissors or shears: *The hedge was clipped in the shape of a bird.* 2 to hit sharply or quickly: *The car clipped the edge of the fence.*
clip *noun*
3 the act of clipping 4 a short, sharp blow: *a clip over the ear* 5 a short extract from a film or video
•***Word Family:*** other verb forms are **clips, clipped, clipping**

clip (2) *noun*
1 something that holds or grips: *a paper clip*
clip *verb*
2 to fasten with a clip
•***Word Family:*** other verb forms are **clips, clipped, clipping**

clique (*say* kleek) *noun*
a small group of people who don't welcome others
•***Word Family:*** **cliquy** or **cliquey** *adjective*

cloak *noun*
1 a long, loose piece of clothing like a coat without sleeves, which you fasten at the neck

cloak *verb*
2 to cover or hide: *Darkness cloaked their movements.*

clobber *verb*
to hit someone

clock *noun*
1 an instrument for measuring and showing time
clock *verb*
2 to test or measure the time of a person or vehicle: *His run was clocked at 13.56 seconds.*

clockwise *adjective*
turning in the same direction as the hands of a clock

clockwork *noun*
1 the working parts of a clock 2 **like clockwork** smoothly or perfectly: *The plan went like clockwork.*

clod *noun*
a lump of earth or clay

clog *noun*
1 a heavy shoe with a thick wooden or cork sole
clog *verb*
2 to block or become blocked: *The sink is clogged with dirt.*
•***Word Family:*** other verb forms are **clogs, clogged, clogging**

cloister (*say* **kloy**-sta) *noun*
1 a monastery or convent 2 a path with a roof joined to a church or other building and usually going around an open courtyard
•***Word Family:*** **cloistered** *adjective* quiet or sheltered

clone *noun*
an animal or plant that grows from a single cell rather than from two parent cells as is most usual
•***Word Family:*** **clone** *verb*

close (*say* kloze) *verb*
1 to shut: *Please close the door.* 2 to bring to an end: *We will close the meeting.*
close (*say* klose) *adverb*
3 near: *Don't go too close to the edge.*
close (*say* klose) *adjective*
4 complete and careful: *Pay close attention to what you are doing.* 5 loyal and loving: *a close family / a close group of friends* 6 not having fresh air: *The air in here is very close.* 7 having very little difference: *It was a very close competition.* 8 **close call** a narrow escape
close *noun*
9 (*say* kloze) an end or finish: *at the close of the day* 10 (*say* klose) a road closed at one end
•***Word Family:*** **closely** *adverb* **closeness** *noun*

closet (*say* **kloz**-it) *noun*
1 a room or cupboard where you store clothing and other things
closet *verb*
2 to shut up in a private room for talks: *The staff have been closeted away since lunch.*

closure *noun*
1 when something is shut or closed: *We must fight the closure of our swimming pool.*
2 something that is used to close or shut something: *a wire closure*

clot *noun*
1 a mass or lump: *a blood clot* 2 a stupid person
clot *verb*
3 to thicken or form into clots: *the cream started to clot*
•***Word Family:*** other verb forms are **clots, clotted, clotting**

cloth *noun*
1 a material made from wool, cotton or other yarn 2 a piece of cloth used for a particular purpose: *a tablecloth*

clothe (*say* klothe) *verb*
to dress someone
•***Word Family:*** **clothing** *noun*

clothes *plural noun*
anything you wear on your body, except jewellery

cloud *noun*
1 a dense mass of water drops or ice crystals that floats high in the air 2 a similar dark mass: *a cloud of smoke*
cloud *verb*
3 to become dark or make something dark: *His eyes clouded with tears.*
•***Word Family:*** **cloudy** *adjective* (**cloudier, cloudiest**) **cloudiness** *noun*

clout *noun*
1 a blow or knock, especially with the hand: *The bully gave him a clout on the head.* 2 power or influence especially in politics or business
clout *verb*
3 to hit or knock

clove *noun*
a sweet spice made from the dried flower bud of a tropical tree

clover *noun*
1 a plant, usually with three leaves on each stalk, grown as food for cattle and sheep
2 **in clover** in great comfort or luxury

clown *noun*
1 an actor in a circus or pantomime who is usually dressed in funny clothes and make-up
2 a funny or clumsy person
clown *verb*
3 to act like a clown
•***Word Family:*** **clownish** *adjective*

club *noun*
1 a thick, heavy stick, used as a weapon 2 a stick with a shaped wooden or metal head, used in golf 3 a group of people who have the same interests and meet regularly: *a chess club* 4 a meeting-place for a group where the members can eat, drink and play games
club *verb*
5 to hit with a club 6 to join together to pay for something: *We all clubbed together to buy a boat.*
• **Word Family:** other verb forms are **clubs, clubbed, clubbing**

clue (*say* kloo) *noun*
something that helps you solve a problem or mystery: *The police have found no clue to the identity of the thief.*
• **Word Family: clueless** *adjective* stupid

clump *noun*
a cluster or mass of things growing together: *a clump of rose bushes*

clumsy (*say* **klum**-zee) *adjective*
1 ungraceful or awkward in your movements: *The clumsy workman dropped a load of cement.* 2 done without skill or tact: *She made a clumsy attempt to apologize.*
• **Word Family:** other forms are **clumsier, clumsiest** □ **clumsiness** *noun*

cluster *noun*
1 a number of things grouped or moving together: *The guests stood in clusters at the gate.*
cluster *verb*
2 to gather in tight groups

clutch (1) *verb*
1 to seize and hold tightly: *The rider clutched the saddle for support.*
clutch *noun*
2 a tight hold 3 the part of a motor that is needed to change gears while it is operating 4 control or power: *in the clutches of the enemy*

clutch (2) *noun*
1 a number of eggs 2 a brood of chickens hatched at the one time

clutter *verb*
to make a place untidy or confused: *The room was cluttered with old newspapers.*
• **Word Family: clutter** *noun*

coach *noun*
1 a bus used for long journeys 2 a railway carriage 3 someone who teaches or trains others for a particular purpose: *a tennis coach*
coach *verb*
4 to train or teach: *She coaches us in swimming.*

coal *noun*
a black or dark brown rock formed underground from ancient trees and burned for fuel

coalition (*say* ko-a-**lish**-un) *noun*
a joining together of two or more things: *Two political parties formed a coalition.*

coarse (*rhymes with* horse) *adjective*
1 made up of large particles: *coarse sand* 2 rude or vulgar: *There was coarse language in the play.* 3 rough or harsh: *coarse cloth*
• **Word Family: coarsely** *adverb* **coarsen** *verb* **coarseness** *noun*

coast *noun*
1 the land by the side of the sea 2 the seaside: *We are going to the coast for our holidays.*
coast *verb*
3 to move without working at it: *The bicycle coasted down the hill.*
• **Word Family: coastal** *adjective* to do with a coast

coastguard *noun*
an officer or group of officers who patrol a coast looking for smugglers or ships in trouble

coat *noun*
1 a piece of clothing, with sleeves and a collar or lapels, which you fasten down the front and wear over other clothes 2 an outer covering: *a coat of paint* 3 an animal's fur: *a dog's wiry coat*
coat *verb*
4 to put on a coat or cover: *Coat the cake with icing.*
• **Word Family: coating** *noun* a layer

coat of arms *noun*
a design in the shape of a shield with pictures representing the historical events or characteristics of a family or nation
• **Word Family:** the plural is **coats of arms**

coax (*say* cokes) *verb*
to flatter or persuade gently: *He coaxed the toddler to take the nasty medicine.*

cob *noun*
1 the centre part of an ear of corn, on which the kernels or corn seeds grow 2 a male swan

cobalt (*say* **ko**-bolt) *noun*
a hard, silvery-white metal, similar to iron, used in alloys and to produce blue dye

cobble *verb*
1 to make or mend shoes 2 to make or put together clumsily: *I cobbled together a folder of work.*
• **Word Family: cobbler** *noun* someone who mends shoes

cobble-stone *noun*
a smooth, round stone used for paving
• **Word Family: cobbled** *adjective*: *cobbled streets*

cobra *noun*
a poisonous snake that spreads out its neck to form a hood of skin when it is angry

cobweb *noun*
a thin thread spun by spiders into different shapes to catch insects for food

cocaine (*say* ko-**kane**) *noun*
a powerful addictive drug that is sometimes used as an anaesthetic and is also taken illegally by some people

cochlea (*say* **kock**-lee-a) *noun*
a small spiral structure in the innermost part of your ear

cock (1) *noun*
1 a male adult bird, especially a domestic fowl
2 the hammer of a gun
cock *verb*
3 to pull back and set the hammer of a gun before firing

cock (2) *verb*
to turn something upwards or to the side in a cheeky or defiant manner: *He cocked an eyebrow at me.*

cockatoo (*say* kok-a-**too**) *noun*
a large, crested parrot, found in Australia and New Guinea

cockerel (*say* **kok**-a-rul) *noun*
a young male hen

cocker spaniel *noun*
a small, long-haired dog with long drooping ears

cockle *noun*
a small edible shellfish with a ribbed shell

cockney (*say* **kock**-nee) *noun*
1 someone who comes from London, especially the East End area 2 their way of speaking: *a cockney accent*
•*Word Family:* the plural is **cockneys**

cockpit *noun*
the space for the pilot and crew flying an aircraft

cockroach *noun*
a brown oval-shaped insect that lives in warm, dark places and comes out at night looking for food
•*Word Family:* the plural is **cockroaches**

cocktail *noun*
1 a strong, alcoholic drink made of one or more spirits, often with fruit juice and ice 2 a dish of seafood or fruit served as a starter: *prawn cocktail*

cocky *adjective*
too confident or pleased with yourself
•*Word Family:* **cockily** *adverb* **cockiness** *noun*

cocoa (*say* **ko**-ko) *noun*
1 the powdered seeds of the cacao tree 2 a drink made from this

coconut (*say* **ko**-ku-nut) *noun*
1 the large seed of a palm tree, with a hard shell, a white, fleshy lining and a milky liquid
2 the white lining which is often grated and used in cooking
•*Word Origins:* from a Spanish word meaning "grinning face", which the base of the shell looks like

cocoon (*say* ka-**koon**) *noun*
1 a silky case spun by an insect larva to protect it while it is growing into its next stage
cocoon *verb*
2 to cover or protect someone or something: *We slept cocooned in our sleeping bags.*

cod *noun*
a kind of large sea fish that you can eat

coda (*say* **koh**-da) *noun*
the part at the end of a piece or section of music

code *noun*
1 a set of rules about a particular subject: *the highway code* 2 a secret way of writing using symbols or letters of the alphabet differently from the normal way: *morse code / The general sent a message to the army in code.*
code *verb*
3 to put something in code: *to code messages*

coerce (*say* ko-**erse**) *verb*
to force or compel someone: *He coerced his brother into helping him.*
•*Word Family:* **coercion** *noun* **coercive** *adjective*

coffee *noun*
1 the roasted and ground seeds of a tropical, evergreen shrub 2 a drink made from this

coffin *noun*
the box into which a dead body is placed before it is buried or cremated
•*Word Origins:* from a Greek word meaning "basket"

cog *noun*
1 a tooth or sharp projection on a wheel that fits with a matching tooth on another wheel so that when one wheel is turned it makes the other wheel turn too 2 a person or department that is part of a large organization: *a cog in the machinery of government*

cognac (*say* **kon**-yak) *noun*
a type of brandy
•*Word Origins:* first made in Cognac, France

cohere (*say* ko-**heer**) *verb*
1 to stick together 2 to agree or go well together
•*Word Family:* **coherent** *adjective* making sense: *a coherent conversation* **coherence** *noun* **coherently** *adverb* **cohesion** *noun* **cohesive** *adjective*

A B C D E F G H I J K L M N O P Q R S T U V W X Y Z

coil *noun*
1 a continuous series of rings or spirals: *a coil of rope* 2 a single ring in such a series
coil *verb*
3 to wind something round and round into loops

coin (*say* koyn) *noun*
1 a metal disc we use as money
coin *verb*
2 to make coins 3 to make or invent: *to coin a phrase*
•***Word Family:*** **coinage** *noun*

coincide (*say* ko-in-**side**) *verb*
to happen at the same time: *My holidays coincide with yours.* 2 to agree: *Her opinions usually coincide with mine.*

coincidence (*say* ko-**in**-si-dunce) *noun*
something that happens unexpectedly at the same time as something else: *It was a complete coincidence that we both caught the same train.*
•***Word Family:*** **coincidental** *adjective*

coke *noun*
a hard, dark grey fuel that is made from coal

colander (*say* **kul**-un-da) *noun*
a bowl with lots of small holes, for draining cooked vegetables or pasta

cold *adjective*
1 having no heat or a very low temperature: *cold toes / a cold morning* 2 unfriendly: *a cold stare*
cold *noun*
3 an absence of heat or warmth: *I dislike the cold.* 4 an infectious disease causing fever, a sore throat and a blocked nose
•***Word Family:*** **coldly** *adverb* **coldness** *noun*

cold-blooded *adjective*
1 extremely cruel: *a cold-blooded act* 2 having a body temperature which is always similar to the temperature of the surrounding air or water: *Fish and reptiles are cold-blooded animals.*
•***Word Family:*** **cold-bloodedly** *adverb*

coleslaw *noun*
a salad made from raw, shredded cabbage, carrots, onions and mayonnaise
•***Word Origins:*** from Dutch words meaning "cabbage salad"

colic (*say* **kol**-ik) *noun*
sudden, frequent pains in your stomach
•***Word Family:*** **colicky** *adjective*

collaborate (*say* ku-**lab**-a-rate) *verb*
to work together: *Two classes collaborated on this project.*
•***Word Family:*** **collaborator** *noun* someone who collaborates **collaboration** *noun*

collage (*say* kul-**ahzh**) *noun*
a picture made by sticking pieces of paper, cloth, string or other things onto paper or cardboard

collapse *verb*
1 to fall or break down: *The building collapsed.* 2 to come to a stop: *The plan collapsed because no-one could agree.* 3 to break down emotionally or physically: *They collapsed in shock at the terrible news.* 4 to be designed to fold up: *This bed collapses.*
•***Word Family:*** **collapsible** *adjective* designed to fold up

collar *noun*
1 something worn or tied around the neck: *a dog's collar* 2 the part of a shirt, coat or dress that fits around the neck
collar *verb*
3 to seize by the collar or neck

collarbone *noun*
one of the two bones that join your chest to your shoulder

colleague (*say* **kol**-eeg) *noun*
someone you work with, usually in the same profession or job

collect (*say* kol-**lekt**) *verb*
1 to gather money or things together: *to collect for charity* 2 to fetch or call for something to take it away: *When will the mail be collected?* 3 to gather and keep examples of a particular type of thing: *He collects butterflies.*
•***Word Family:*** **collected** *adjective* self-possessed **collector** *noun* someone who collects

collection (*say* kol-**lek**-shun) *noun*
1 collecting or gathering together: *the collection of information for a survey* 2 an attempt to raise money: *a collection for famine victims* 3 a group of things, or the things themselves: *a stamp collection / a collection of fossils* 4 the time when something such as mail or rubbish is taken away: *Is there a collection this afternoon?*

collective *adjective*
1 combined or united: *A collective effort will get the job done quickly.*
collective *noun*
2 a group of people who share everything they own, and the work that has to be done, and who live together by their own rules
•***Word Family:*** **collectively** *adverb*

collective noun *noun*
the term given to nouns which name groups of things, such as *crowd, bunch* or *herd*

college (*say* **kol**-ij) *noun*
1 a school or institution you can go to once you are over sixteen 2 a name used by some schools 3 a group of people who belong to the same profession: *the Royal College of Surgeons*

collide *verb*
to crash together
•***Word Family:*** **collision** *noun*

collie *noun*
a wavy-haired, Scottish sheep-dog

colliery (*say* **kol**-yer-ee) *noun*
a coal mine, with its buildings and machinery

colloquial (*say* ko-**lo**-kwee-al) *adjective*
to do with everyday speech rather than formal writing or speech
•***Word Family:*** **colloquialism** *noun* a colloquial expression **colloquially** *adverb*

colon (1) (*say* **ko**-lon) *noun*
a punctuation mark (:) that is used before a quotation, a list or a statement

colon (2) (*say* **ko**-lon) *noun*
the large, thin-walled tube that forms the lower part of your digestive system, ending in the rectum and the anus

colonel (*say* **ker**-nul) *noun*
a high-ranking officer in the army

colonize or **colonise** (*say* **kol**-a-nize) *verb*
to make somewhere into a colony: *Australia was colonized by Great Britain.*
•***Word Family:*** **colonization** *noun*

colony (*say* **koll**a-nee) *noun*
1 a country or area settled and governed or controlled by another country 2 a group of people who leave their home to settle in a new land 3 a group of similar people who live together: *a leper colony* 4 a group of the same kind of plants or animals that live close together: *a termite colony*
•***Word Family:*** the plural is **colonies** □ **colonial** *noun* someone who lives in a colony **colonial** *adjective* **colonist** *noun* someone who lives in or establishes a colony

colossal (*say* ku-**los**-ul) *adjective*
extremely large: *a colossal statue*

colour or **color** (*say* **kul**-a) *noun*
1 the sensation produced in your eye by the way light is reflected from what you are looking at: *the colours of the rainbow* 2 a paint, pigment or dye 3 someone's skin colour: *A person's colour is not important.* 4 something that adds interest or brightness: *The tour guide's information added some colour to the trip.* 5 **flying colours** great success: *She passed her exams with flying colours.* 6 **off colour** not well: *He seemed a bit off colour.*
colour *verb*
7 to add colour to something 8 to blush or go red: *She coloured when I mentioned his name.* 9 to influence or change: *Her story was coloured by her anger.*
•***Word Family:*** **colourful** *adjective* **colourfully** *adverb* **colourfulness** *noun*

colt *noun*
a young male horse, especially one up to three years old

column (*say* **kol**-um) *noun*
1 a tall upright support, usually made of brick or stone 2 something with a similar shape: *This page has two columns. / a thin column of smoke* 3 a short magazine or newspaper article that appears regularly, usually written by the same person: *the sports column* 4 a line of soldiers or vehicles following one after another
•***Word Family:*** **columnar** (*say* ku-**lum**-na) *adjective* **columnist** *noun* someone who writes a magazine or newspaper column

coma (*say* **ko**-ma) *noun*
a state like a very deep sleep in which you are unconscious, usually due to injury or disease
•***Word Family:*** the plural is **comas** □ **comatose** *adjective* affected with or seeming to be affected with a coma

comb (*say* kome) *noun*
1 an object of bone or plastic with a row of long, narrow teeth, that is used for smoothing or untangling your hair 2 the fleshy growth on the head of a hen or rooster
comb *verb*
3 to arrange or untangle your hair with a comb 4 to search a place or area thoroughly: *Police combed the district for the missing child.*

combat (*say* **kom**-bat) *noun*
1 a fight or battle
combat (*say* kum-**bat**) *verb*
2 to fight against something or someone: *to combat crime*
•***Word Family:*** **combatant** *noun* someone taking part in a combat

combination (*say* kom-bi-**nay**-shon) *noun*
a mixture of different things: *The soup was made from a combination of meat and vegetables.*

combine (*say* kom-**bine**) *verb*
1 to join or mix several things together: *Combine the eggs with a little flour.*
combine (*say* **kom**-bine) *noun*
2 a group consisting of people or businesses joining together to make themselves more powerful or effective

combustion (*say* kom-**bus**-chon) *noun*
burning
•***Word Family:*** **combustible** *adjective* able or likely to burn **combust** *verb* to burn

come (*say* kum) *verb*
1 to approach or move towards: *Come and sit beside me.* 2 to arrive or reach: *They came to a*

small, deserted house. 3 to occur or happen: *My birthday comes after yours.* 4 to change from one state into another: *The parcel came undone.* 5 **come across** to find or meet someone or something by chance 6 **come from** to be born in: *He comes from a wealthy family.* 7 **come in** to be: *This money will come in handy.* 8 **come of** to be the result of a particular way of behaving: *See what comes of carelessness.* 9 **come over** to happen to someone, making them change: *What has come over her?* 10 **come to** to add up to: *The bill for lunch came to £20.* 11 **come up with** to suggest an idea or plan
• ***Word Family:*** other forms are **comes, came, coming**

comedian (*say* ku-**mee**-di-an) *noun*
someone who performs in a comedy or comic act
• ***Word Family:*** **comedienne** *noun* a female comedian

comedy (*say* **kom**-a-dee) *noun*
a play, film or other entertainment that is meant to make you laugh
• ***Word Family:*** the plural is **comedies**

comet *noun*
an object in space that moves around the sun and has a bright centre and a long tail
• ***Word Origins:*** from a Greek word meaning "long-haired"

comfort (*say* **kum**-fut) *verb*
1 to make someone feel less sad or upset: *Her kindness comforted us in our grief.*
comfort *noun*
2 freedom from worry or unhappiness: *They live in great comfort.* 3 something that removes your pain, worry or unhappiness: *It was a comfort to see the lights of the city.*
• ***Word Family:*** **comforter** *noun* **comforting** *adjective* **comfortingly** *adverb*

comfortable (*say* **kum**-fut-a-bul) *adjective*
1 having or giving you comfort: *a comfortable old armchair* 2 in a state of comfort: *I'm nice and comfortable here.*
• ***Word Family:*** **comfortably** *adverb*

comic *adjective*
1 to do with comedy: *a comic actor*
comic *noun*
2 a magazine full of stories told using pictures
3 a funny person or actor
• ***Word Family:*** **comical** *adjective*

comma *noun*
a punctuation mark (,) used between words, phrases or clauses to show there is a short pause

command (*say* ku-**mahnd**) *verb*
1 to have control over people or a place: *He commands two thousand troops.* 2 to order someone: *She commanded us to shoot them.* 3 to deserve and be given special treatment: *His experience commands great respect. / His paintings command very high prices.*
command *noun*
4 an order given: *He ignored the command to stop.* 5 power or control: *Who is in command here?* 6 an ability to use something: *a good command of German*
• ***Word Family:*** **commandeer** *verb* to take something with official approval **commander** *noun*

commandment (*say* ku-**mahnd**-munt) *noun*
1 a command 2 a holy law, such as one of the Ten Commandments in the Bible

commemorate (*say* ku-**mem**-a-rate) *verb*
to honour the memory of something or someone, especially by a ceremony or celebration
• ***Word Family:*** **commemoration** *noun* **commemorative** *adjective*

commence *verb*
to start or begin: *The game will commence after lunch.*
• ***Word Family:*** **commencement** *noun*

commend *verb*
to praise someone or something: *The pilot was commended for her bravery.*
• ***Word Family:*** **commendable** *adjective* worthy of praise **commendation** *noun* praise or approval **commendatory** *adjective* giving praise or approval

comment *noun*
1 a remark: *The teacher's comments on my project were very helpful.*
comment *verb*
2 to make a comment

commentary (*say* **kom**-un-tree) *noun*
1 a description of an event while it is happening, for example on TV or the radio 2 a piece of writing that has been written to explain or help you understand another piece of writing: *a commentary on the poems of Robert Burns*
• ***Word Family:*** the plural is **commentaries** □ **commentate** *verb* to describe an event on TV or the radio **commentator** *noun*

commerce *noun*
the buying and selling of goods

commercial (*say* ko-**mer**-shul) *adjective*
1 to do with commerce 2 made so that it can be sold at a profit: *a commercial product* 3 paid for by advertisers: *commercial radio*
commercial *noun*
4 an advertisement on radio or television

• *Word Family:* **commercialize** or **commercialise** *verb* to turn something into a business or moneymaking project **commercialization** *noun* **commercialism** *noun*

commiserate (*say* ku-**miz**-a-rate) *verb*
to express to someone the sorrow or pity you feel for them: *We commiserated with him about the accident.*
• *Word Family:* **commiseration** *noun*

commission (*say* ku-**mish**-on) *noun*
1 a group of people officially appointed to do a particular job: *the Commission for Racial Equality* 2 money paid to someone for buying or selling goods as part of their job: *a 10% commission* 3 the act of doing something: *The commission of such a crime is unthinkable.*
commission *verb*
4 to officially arrange for a job or piece of work to be done: *to commission a film*

commissioner (*say* ku-**mish**-on-er) *noun*
1 someone who is appointed to be in charge of a government department: *a police commissioner* 2 a member of an official commission

commit *verb*
1 to do something, especially something bad such as a crime: *The police believe he committed the murders.* 2 to officially arrange for someone to do something, or for something to happen: *She was committed to a mental institution.* 3 **commit yourself** to promise: *Don't commit yourself to spending more than you can afford.*
• *Word Family:* other forms are **commits, committed, committing** □ **commitment** *noun* a promise to do something **committal** *noun* the act of committing **committed** *adjective*

committee *noun*
a small group of people chosen from a larger group to discuss things and make decisions

commodity (*say* ku-**mod**-i-tee) *noun*
anything useful, especially something which can be bought or sold
• *Word Family:* the plural is **commodities**

common *adjective*
1 shared by two or more people: *The story is common knowledge.* 2 happening often: *a common event* 3 regular or ordinary: *a common weed* 4 impolite or vulgar: *She has very common table manners.* 5 **in common** shared or alike: *They have very little in common.*
common *noun*
6 a piece of land that can be used by everyone: *Wimbledon Common*
• *Word Family:* **commonly** *adverb*

Common Market *noun*
a group of European countries including Britain that trades together and makes its own laws and trade agreements

common noun *noun*
a noun that you use to name an ordinary thing and that does not have a capital letter, such as *person, banana,* or *cow*

common sense *noun*
good sense or judgment

Commonwealth *noun*
1 a country made up of several states that each have their own parliament as well as a parliament for the whole country: *the Commonwealth of Australia* 2 an association of self-ruling countries: *the British Commonwealth*

commotion (*say* ku-**mo**-shon) *noun*
a noisy or violent disturbance

commune (1) (*say* ku-**mewn**) *verb*
to talk to someone so that you both understand each other's thoughts and feelings

commune (2) (*say* **kom**-yoon) *noun*
a group of people who live together and share their money, their possessions and all the work that needs doing
• *Word Family:* **communal** *adjective*

communicate (*say* ku-**mew**-ni-kate) *verb*
1 to pass on or share information: *Who communicated the news to you?* 2 to speak to people in a way that shows you want to understand them or get on with them: *She finds it easy to communicate with young people.*
• *Word Family:* **communication** *noun* **communicative** *adjective* willing to communicate **communicator** *noun*

communion (*say* ku-**mewn**-yon) *noun*
1 a sharing or exchange of thoughts or feelings 2 a Christian ceremony in which bread and wine are blessed by a clergyman and shared among the congregation

communism (*say* **kom**-yoo-niz-um) *noun*
1 the belief that everyone should share equally in the ownership of all property and in the profits from their work 2 a way of governing a country in which the state controls all property and industry
• *Word Family:* **communist** *noun* **communist** *adjective*

community (*say* ku-**mew**-ni-tee) *noun*
a group of people who live in one place or have similar interests: *The community must look after homeless people. / a religious community*
• *Word Family:* the plural is **communities**

commute (*say* ku-**mewt**) *verb*
1 to alter or make less severe: *The prisoner's death sentence was commuted to life imprisonment.*

A B C D E F G H I J K L M N O P Q R S T U V W X Y Z

2 to travel between home and your daily workplace
•*Word Family:* **commuter** *noun* someone who commutes

compact (*say* **kom**-pakt) *adjective*
1 closely packed or fitted together: *a compact chess set*
compact *noun*
2 a container for face powder
compact (*say* kom-**pact**) *verb*
3 to fit or pack things firmly together
•*Word Family:* **compactly** *adverb* **compactness** *noun*

compact disc *noun*
a plastic and metal disc on which music or information is digitally recorded and can be played back on a compact disc player or a computer

companion (*say* kum-**pan**-yon) *noun*
1 someone who is a friend or helper: *a travelling companion* 2 a guide or reference book
•*Word Family:* **companionship** *noun*

company (*say* **kum**-pa-nee) *noun*
1 a group of people who are together for a special reason: *a ship's company* 2 friends or the presence of friends: *I get lonely without company.* 3 guests: *We have company for tea.* 4 an organization of people who run a business: *a manufacturing company* 5 a part of an army
•*Word Family:* the plural is **companies**

comparative (*say* kom-**pa**-ra-tiv) *adjective*
1 to do with the form of an adjective or adverb that expresses a greater degree: "Bigger" is the comparative form of "big" and "more loudly" is the comparative form of "loudly" 2 to do with comparison: *a matter of comparative importance*
•*Word Family:* **comparatively** *adverb*

compare *verb*
1 to decide how certain things are similar or different by looking carefully at them: *Let us compare our answers.* 2 to describe as being similar or like: *You could compare me with Einstein.* 3 **compare with** be as good as
•*Word Family:* **comparable** (*say* **kom**-pra-bul) *adjective* able or suitable to be compared

compartment *noun*
1 a separate part or division of something, for example on a train: *a luggage compartment*

compass (*say* **kum**-pus) *noun*
1 an instrument which has a magnetized needle which always points north, used to help you find directions 2 an instrument for drawing circles that consists of two rods, one pointed and the other holding a marker, hinged together at one end

compassion (*say* kum-**pash**-on) *noun*
a strong feeling of understanding, pity or sympathy for what other people are suffering
•*Word Family:* **compassionate** *adjective* **compassionately** *adverb*

compatible (*say* kum-**pat**-i-bul) *adjective*
1 well suited or able to exist together peacefully: *Our political ideas are not compatible.* 2 able to be used together: *compatible computers*
•*Word Family:* **compatibility** *noun* **compatibly** *adverb*

compatriot (*say* kum-**pat**-ri-ut) *noun*
someone from the same country as yourself

compel *verb*
to force someone to do something interesting or moving, and making you want to pay attention: *a compelling film / Heavy rain compelled us to cancel the picnic.*
•*Word Family:* other forms are **compels, compelled, compelling** □ **compelling** *adjective*

compensate (*say* **kom**-pen-sate) *verb*
to make up for something: *Payment could not compensate for the damage.*
•*Word Family:* **compensation** *noun*

compere (*say* **kom**-pair) *noun*
someone who introduces the performers in a radio or television programme or variety show
•*Word Family:* **compere** *verb*

compete (*say* kom-**peet**) *verb*
to take part in a competition: *I am going to compete in the long jump.*
•*Word Family:* **competitor** *noun*

competent (*say* **kom**-pa-tunt) *adjective*
able to do something well or properly: *a competent driver*
•*Word Family:* **competence** *noun* **competency** *noun*

competition (*say* kom-pa-**tish**-on) *noun*
1 an activity in which you try to do better than other people 2 the people you are trying to do better than: *Your competition in this race is very weak.* 3 the feeling of being in a competition: *There is a lot of competition between the two local schools.*
•*Word Family:* **competitive** *adjective* **competitively** *adverb*

compile *verb*
to collect and order information, for example into a list
•*Word Family:* **compilation** *noun*

complain *verb*
to talk about things that are annoying or worrying you

complaint *noun*
1 a statement in which you complain about something: *I wish to make a complaint.* 2 an illness

complement (*say* **kom**-ple-munt) *noun*
1 the full amount needed: *The ship has its full complement of crew members.*
complement *verb*
2 to go well together with something else: *Those curtains really complement the furniture.*
•*Word Family:* **complementary** *adjective*

complete *adjective*
1 having all its parts: *a complete set of cutlery* 2 finished: *The story is now complete.* 3 total or thorough: *He is a complete fool.*

complex *adjective*
1 difficult to follow or understand: *a complex design*
complex *noun*
2 anything made up of different or connected parts: *a shopping complex*
•*Word Family:* the plural of the noun is **complexes** □ **complexity** *noun*

complexion (*say* kom-**plek**-shon) *noun*
1 the appearance or colour of your skin especially on your face: *a rosy complexion.* 2 nature or character: *The quarrel changed the complexion of their relationship.*

complicate (*say* **kom**-pli-kate) *verb*
to make something difficult to do or understand: *Do not complicate the situation with more new ideas.*
•*Word Family:* **complicated** *adjective* **complication** *noun*

compliment (*say* **kom**-pli-munt) *noun*
1 words of praise or respect: *The chef received many compliments for the delightful meal.*
compliment *verb*
2 to pay a compliment to: *to compliment the winner on his skill*
•*Word Family:* **complimentary** *adjective* free of charge: *complimentary drinks*

comply (*say* kom-**ply**) *verb*
to do what someone asks or demands: *You must comply with the rules.*
•*Word Family:* other forms are **complies, complied, complying** □ **compliant** *adjective* willing to comply **compliantly** *adverb* **compliance** or **compliancy** *noun*

component (*say* kum-**po**-nent) *noun*
something that is part of a whole system or thing: *An engine has many components.*

compose (*say* kum-**poze**) *verb*
1 to make up or form: *The class is composed of 24 students.* 2 to make up music or poetry: *Who composed "Yellow Submarine"?* 3 to control someone's feelings or make them feel calm: *You must compose your thoughts before answering the question.*
•*Word Family:* **composer** *noun* someone who composes music

composition (*say* kom-pa-**zish**-on) *noun*
1 making up music or poetry: *The composition of the third symphony took three years.* 2 a piece of music 3 the way something is formed: *the composition of the earth's atmosphere* 4 an essay

compost (*say* **kom**-post) *noun*
a mixture of rotting leaves, vegetable peelings and manure you put in the soil to fertilize it

composure (*say* kom-**pohzh**-er) *noun*
calmness or self-control: *Her composure in the face of danger helped save her life.*

compound (1) (*say* **kom**-pound) *adjective*
1 made up of two or more parts: *Blackberry is a compound word.*
compound *noun*
2 a mixture, such as a chemical substance made up of two or more elements
compound (*say* kom-**pound**) *verb*
3 to put parts together to form a whole 4 to make a bad situation even worse: *He compounded his crime by lying about it.*

compound (2) (*say* **kom**-pound) *noun*
an area containing buildings and surrounded by a fence or wall: *a prison compound*

comprehend (*say* **kom**-pre-hend) *verb*
to understand or know something fully: *Can you comprehend the importance of what has happened?*

comprehension (*say* kom-pre-**hen**-shun) *noun*
1 understanding or the ability to understand: *Some modern poetry is beyond my comprehension.* 2 a written exercise with questions to answer, that tests how well you read and understand

comprehensive (*say* kom-pre-**hen**-sive) *adjective*
meant to include or deal with everything or everyone: *a comprehensive insurance policy*

comprehensive school *noun*
a secondary school that all the children who live in a particular area can go to

compress (*say* kom-**press**) *verb*
1 to press something closely together or force it into a smaller space
compress (*say* **kom**-press) *noun*
2 a soft pad of material held firmly against a wound
•*Word Family:* **compression** *noun* **compressor** *noun*

comprise (*say* kom-**prize**) *verb*
to consist or be made up of: *The book comprises twelve chapters.*

A B C D E F G H I J K L M N O P Q R S T U V W X Y Z

compromise (*say* **kom**-pra-mize) *verb*
1 to settle a disagreement by each side giving up something and receiving less than it asked for: *We compromised by taking turns.* 2 to expose to danger or suspicion: *Don't compromise your safety.*
compromise *noun*
3 a settlement by compromising 4 anything which is halfway between two other things: *Watching a video was a compromise between seeing the film and reading the book.*

compulsion (*say* kom-**pul**-shun) *noun*
1 compelling or forcing: *There is no compulsion for you to come with us.* 2 a feeling of being compelled or forced: *She felt a great compulsion to sneeze.*

compulsory (*say* kum-**pul**-sa-ree) *adjective*
forced or required: *English lessons are compulsory for all pupils.*

compute (*say* kum-**pewt**) *verb*
to find an answer by calculating, using maths
• ***Word Family:*** **computation** *noun*

computer (*say* kum-**pewt**-a) *noun*
1 an electronic machine that stores and organizes large amounts of information and can do calculations very fast 2 someone or something that computes
• ***Word Family:*** **computerize** or **computerise** *verb*

comrade (*say* **kom**-rad *or* **kom**-rade) *noun*
a close or loyal friend
• ***Word Family:*** **comradeship** *noun*

con (1) *noun*
an argument or person against something: *Let's think about the pros and cons in this argument.*

con (2) *verb*
1 to trick or cheat someone
con *noun*
2 a trick
• ***Word Family:*** other verb forms are **cons, conned, conning**
• ***Word Origins:*** a short form of **confidence trick**

concave *adjective*
curved inwards like the inside of a hollow ball: *a concave lens*

conceal (*say* kun-**seel**) *verb*
to hide or keep someone or something from sight: *The cupboard concealed a hole in the wall.*
• ***Word Family:*** **concealment** *noun*

concede (*say* kun-**seed**) *verb*
1 to admit that something is true: *I concede that rain affected the result of the game.* 2 to accept that something is going to happen whether you like it or not: *to concede defeat*
• ***Word Family:*** **concession** *noun*

conceit (*say* kun-**seet**) *noun*
a very high opinion of yourself or your abilities: *He is full of conceit.*
• ***Word Family:*** **conceited** *adjective* **conceitedly** *adverb* **conceitedness** *noun*

conceive (*say* kun-**seev**) *verb*
1 to think of or believe in: *It is difficult to conceive of such wealth.* 2 to become pregnant: *to conceive a child*
• ***Word Family:*** **conceivable** *adjective* able to be imagined or believed **conceivably** *adverb*

concentrate (*say* **kon**-sen-trate) *verb*
1 to keep your thoughts on one thing: *to concentrate on doing your homework* 2 to bring or come towards one point: *The general concentrated his forces around the palace. / A magnifying glass concentrates the sun's rays.*
• ***Word Family:*** **concentrated** *adjective* made stronger or purer, especially by removing water: *concentrated orange juice* **concentration** *noun*

concentration camp *noun*
a place where prisoners, refugees and so on are held, especially the Nazi camps of World War II

concentric (*say* kon-**sen**-trik) *adjective*
having the same centre: *concentric circles*

concept (*say* **kon**-sept) *noun*
an idea: *He has no concept of right and wrong.*
• ***Word Family:*** **conceptual** *adjective* **conceptualize** or **conceptualise** *verb* **conceptually** *adverb*

conception (*say* kon-**sep**-shon) *noun*
1 conceiving a child or becoming pregnant
2 an idea or thought: *They had little conception of the importance of the news.*

concern (*say* kon-**sern**) *verb*
1 to be of interest or importance to particular people: *It is a problem which concerns everyone.* 2 to be about a particular subject: *The film concerns a magic crystal.* 3 to cause worry or unhappiness to people: *Her illness has concerned us for some time.* 4 to be worried or unhappy about someone or something: *We are very concerned about her.*
concern *noun*
5 something of interest or importance: *His problems are no concern of mine.* 6 an anxiety or worry: *She was full of concern for me when I was ill.* 7 a business or company
• ***Word Family:*** **concerning** *preposition* about

concert (*say* **kon**-sert) *noun*
1 a public performance by musicians, singers, and so on
concert (*say* kon-**sert**) *verb*
2 to do something together or in agreement: *We concerted our efforts to defeat the enemy.*

•*Word Family:* **concerted** *adjective* planned or decided in union: *a concerted effort*

concertina (*say* kon-sa-**teen**-a) *noun*
a small accordion, played by pressing buttons at each end

concerto (*say* kon-**cher**-toe) *noun*
a musical composition for one or more solo instruments
•*Word Family:* the plural is **concertos** or **concerti**

concession (*say* kon-**sesh**-on) *noun*
1 conceding or giving in 2 something that you have given in on or allowed: *The government has already made concessions to the union on their wage claim.* 3 a right or privilege you are given: *student concessions for cheap travel*
•*Word Family:* **concessionary** *adjective* specially reduced in price: *concessionary fares*

concise (*say* kon-**sise**) *adjective*
giving a lot of information using only a few words: *a concise answer*
•*Word Family:* **concisely** *adverb* **conciseness** *noun*

conclude *verb*
1 to bring or come to an end: *The meeting concluded with a short speech.* 2 to come to a decision: *The judge concluded that the prisoner was guilty.* 3 to work out by thinking about something
•*Word Family:* **conclusion** *noun* (a) the ending of something (b) the result of an investigation

concoct (*say* kon-**kokt**) *verb*
1 to make by mixing in a new or unusual way: *She concocted a fish sandwich.* 2 to think up or invent: *He concocted a plan to escape from the kidnapper.*
•*Word Family:* **concoction** *noun*

concrete (*say* **kon**-kreet) *noun*
1 a mixture of cement, sand, water and minerals that sets very hard and is used for building
concrete *adjective*
2 made of this mixture: *a concrete path* 3 able to be seen and touched: *Trees are concrete objects but ideas are not.*
concrete *verb*
4 to lay concrete

concur (*say* kon-**ker**) *verb*
to agree: *Our opinions on books usually concur.*
•*Word Family:* other forms are **concurs, concurred, concurring** □ **concurrence** *noun* **concurrent** *adjective*

concussion (*say* kon-**kush**-on) *noun*
a temporary injury to the brain caused by a fall or blow to the head
•*Word Family:* **concuss** *verb*

•*Word Origins:* from a Latin word meaning "shaken violently"

condemn (*say* kon-**dem**) *verb*
1 to judge someone to be guilty: *The jury condemned the accused man.* 2 to say officially that something is unfit to be used: *The council condemned the old house.* 3 to say you disapprove of: *His parents condemned his rowdy behaviour.*
•*Word Family:* **condemnation** *noun* **condemnatory** *adjective*

condense *verb*
1 to make a story or book shorter 2 to change or be changed into a liquid: *The steam condensed into water.*
•*Word Family:* **condensed** *adjective* made thicker and smaller in volume, especially by boiling away some of the water: *condesed soup / condensed milk* **condensation** *noun:* water that has condensed, for example on a cold window
•*Word Origins:* from a Latin word meaning "crowded"

condescend (*say* kon-di-**send**) *verb*
1 to do something kindly and willingly for someone less important than yourself: *The Prime Minister condescended to open our school fete.* 2 to do something even though you think you are too important: *He finally condescended to wash the dishes.*
•*Word Family:* **condescending** *adjective* **condescension** *noun*

condition (*say* kon-**dish**-on) *noun*
1 the state of someone or something: *The house is in a very neglected condition.* 2 something that another thing depends on: *To be aged 12 or over is one of the conditions of entering the competition.*
condition *verb*
3 to affect or make a difference to something: *Climate can condition the way people live.* 4 to make you or a part of your body fit or healthy: *Some shampoos condition your hair*
•*Word Family:* **conditioner** *noun* someone or something that conditions **conditional** *adjective*

condolences *plural noun*
words of sympathy: *Please accept our condolences on your father's death.*

condom *noun*
a thin sheath of rubber worn over the penis in sexual intercourse, used as a contraceptive and to prevent people catching sexual diseases

condone *verb*
to pardon, forgive or overlook: *We cannot condone violence.*

conduct (*say* **kon**-dukt) *noun*
1 your behaviour or way of acting: *Your good conduct makes your parents proud.*

conduct (*say* kon-**dukt**) *verb*
2 to behave: *He conducted himself very badly at the party.* 3 to control, direct or manage: *to conduct a business / to conduct an orchestra* 4 to lead or direct: *Latecomers were conducted to the back seats.* 5 to carry or transmit electricity, heat and so on: *Electricity is conducted along cables to each house.*

conduction *noun*
the process by which heat is carried through solid objects

conductor *noun*
1 someone who conducts, directs or leads: *the conductor of an orchestra* 2 someone who collects fares and looks after passengers on public transport: *a bus conductor* 3 something that conducts electricity, heat and so on

cone *noun*
1 a solid or hollow shape with a circular base which narrows to a point 2 any object with this shape: *an ice-cream cone*
•*Word Family:* **conical** *adjective*

confectionery *noun*
sweets
•*Word Family:* **confectioner** *noun*

confederacy (*say* kon-**fed**-a-ra-see) *noun*
a group of people or nations joined together for a common cause: *All building trade unions have formed a confederacy.*
•*Word Family:* the plural is **confederacies** □ **confederate** *noun* supporter **confederation** *noun*

confer *verb*
1 to give or award something: *The mayor conferred a medal of bravery on her.* 2 to discuss or talk about something together
•*Word Family:* other forms are **confers, conferred, conferring**

conference *noun*
a meeting for discussing things or exchanging opinions: *a business conference in Glasgow*

confess *verb*
to own up to or admit something: *He confessed to having stolen £50.*
•*Word Family:* **confession** *noun*

confetti *plural noun*
the small pieces of coloured paper thrown into the air at weddings, celebrations and so on
•*Word Origins:* from an Italian word meaning "a sweet or candy"

confide (*say* kon-**fide**) *verb*
to tell someone a secret knowing they won't tell anyone else: *I confided to my friend that I was making a surprise gift for my mother.*
•*Word Family:* **confidant** or **confidante** *noun* someone you confide in **confidential** *adjective* secret or private
•*Word Origins:* from a Latin word meaning "trust"

confidence (*say* **kon**-fi-dence) *noun*
1 a firm trust: *We have confidence in our doctor.* 2 a belief in your own ability: *He went to the music exam with a feeling of confidence.* 3 a secret: *She doesn't exchange confidences.*

confident *adjective*
sure or certain: *She was confident of success.*

confirm *verb*
1 to show something as being true or correct: *There were no facts to confirm his story.* 2 to approve something formally or officially: *The Director's letter confirmed her appointment as supervisor.* 3 to make certain or sure about something: *We confirmed our booking at the hotel.* 4 to make someone a full member of the Christian church in a special ceremony: *He's being confirmed next Sunday.*
•*Word Family:* **confirmed** *adjective* **confirmation** *noun* (a) confirming something (b) the Christian ceremony at which someone is confirmed

confiscate (*say* **kon**-fi-skate) *verb*
to take and keep: *The teacher confiscated our comics.*
•*Word Family:* **confiscation** *noun*

conflict (*say* **kon**-flikt) *noun*
1 a battle, struggle or disagreement: *Two hundred soldiers died in the conflict.*
conflict (*say* kon-**flikt**) *verb*
2 to be or come into disagreement: *His ideas conflict with the old-fashioned policies of the school.*
•*Word Origins:* from a Latin word meaning "dashed together"

conform *verb*
to follow the rules or do what most other people do: *If you conform you will keep out of trouble.*
•*Word Family:* **conformist** *noun* **conformity** *noun*
•*Word Origins:* from a Latin word meaning "to shape"

confound *verb*
to confuse or puzzle someone completely: *The unexpected news confounded her.*

confront (*say* kon-**frunt**) *verb*
1 to come face to face with someone in a disagreement: *The detective confronted the suspect with the stolen goods.* 2 to deal with something rather than ignoring it: *We must confront the problem now.*
•*Word Family:* **confrontation** *noun* **confrontational** *adjective* hostile or aggressive in the way you deal with other people

confuse (*say* kon-**fewz**) *verb*
1 to puzzle or bewilder someone: *Complicated road maps always confuse me.* 2 to mistake one thing for another: *He confused question 6 with question 7 in the exam.*
• **Word Family: confusingly** *adverb* **confusion** *noun*
• **Word Origins:** from a Latin word meaning "mixed or jumbled"

congeal (*say* kon-**jeel**) *verb*
to set, or change from a liquid to a solid or semi-solid state: *The blood soon congealed.*

congenial (*say* kon-**jeen**-nee-al) *adjective*
pleasant or agreeable: *The family next door are congenial company.*

congenital (*say* kon-**jen**-i-tal) *adjective*
to do with an illness which you have when you are born, but which is not hereditary: *a congenital heart complaint*

congest (*say* kon-**jest**) *verb*
to make or become overcrowded or too full: *Traffic congests the city streets during the rush hour.*
• **Word Family: congestion** *noun*
• **Word Origins:** from a Latin word meaning "heaped up"

congratulate (*say* kon-**grat**-yoo-late) *verb*
to tell someone you are pleased at their success or good luck: *He congratulated her on her exam results.*
• **Word Family: congratulatory** *adjective*

congregate (*say* **kon**-gri-gate) *verb*
to come together in a group: *A crowd congregated at the scene of the accident.*

congregation *noun*
1 a gathering together 2 all the people at a church service

congress *noun*
1 a formal meeting of people to discuss similar interests, problems, and so on: *a world congress of scientists* 2 **Congress** the name of the government or parliament of the United States

congruent (*say* **kon**-groo-ent) *adjective*
identical in shape and size: *Congruent triangles overlap exactly if one is placed on top of another.*
• **Word Family: congruence** *noun*

conifer (*say* **kon**-if-a) *noun*
an evergreen tree with cones and needle-like leaves, such as the pine or fir
• **Word Family: coniferous** *adjective*
• **Word Origins:** from a Latin word meaning "cone-bearing"

conjunction (*say* kon-**junk**-shon) *noun*
1 a word that joins parts of a sentence, such as *and* or *because.* 2 **in conjunction with** together with: *We wrote the report in conjunction with the architects.*

conjure *verb*
to do magic tricks
• **Word Family: conjurer** *noun*

conker *noun*
1 a hard shiny brown nut that grows in a spiky green case on horse chestnut trees 2 **conkers** a game played using conkers hanging on pieces of string

connect *verb*
1 to join or be joined: *Connect the wires to the plug and switch the radio on.* 2 to meet something else: *The bus connects with the train.* 3 **be connected** to be associated or involved
• **Word Family: connection** *noun* **connector** *noun*

connoisseur (*say* kon-a-**sir**) *noun*
someone who knows a lot about a particular subject: *a music connoisseur*

conquer (*say* **kong**-ka) *verb*
to defeat or overcome people, a place or something you are afraid of: *The German army conquered France. / He conquered his fear of water.*
• **Word Family: conqueror** *noun*

conquest (*say* **kon**-kwest) *noun*
conquering: *The conquest of Europe was Hitler's plan.*

conscience (*say* **kon**-shunce) *noun*
your sense of right and wrong

conscientious (*say* kon-shee-**en**-shus) *adjective*
particularly or painstakingly careful: *She is a conscientious worker.*
• **Word Family: conscientiousness** *noun*

conscious (*say* **kon**-shus) *adjective*
1 awake: *The mother wanted to stay conscious during her baby's birth.* 2 aware: *She was conscious of a faint smell of burning.* 3 deliberate or intentional: *His action was a conscious attempt to conceal the truth.*
• **Word Family: consciousness** *noun*

conscript (*say* kon-**skript**) *verb*
1 to force people to join the army, navy or airforce by law
conscript (*say* **kon**-skript) *noun*
2 someone who has been conscripted
• **Word Family: conscription** *noun*

consecrate (*say* **kon**-si-krate) *verb*
to officially declare that a place can be used for a religious purpose: *The bishop consecrated the chapel.*
• **Word Family: consecration** *noun*

consecutive (*say* kon-**sek**-yoo-tiv) *adjective*
one after the other: *She missed school on four consecutive days.*
• **Word Family: consecutively** *adverb*

consensus *noun*
a general agreement: *There was a consensus of opinion that the minister should resign.*

consent *verb*
1 to agree or allow: *The principal consented to the pupils playing in the hall.*
consent *noun*
2 permission or agreement

consequence (*say* **kon**-si-kwence) *noun*
1 an effect or result: *Lung cancer is a possible consequence of smoking.* 2 importance or distinction: *It was a decision of some consequence.*

consequent *adjective*
following or happening as a result of something else: *Consequent upon the sale of our house we will be moving.*
•***Word Family:*** **consequential** *adjective* **consequently** *adverb*

conservation (*say* kon-sa-**vay**-shon) *noun*
1 saving and keeping things from being spoiled or wasted 2 the preservation of the environment, especially by the wise use of resources, the control of pollution, recycling and so on
•***Word Family:*** **conservationist** *noun*

conservative (*say* kon-**ser**-va-tiv) *adjective*
1 opposed to any great or sudden change: *conservative ideas about education* 2 moderate or careful: *a conservative estimate / conservative style of dress*
•***Word Family:*** **conservatism** *noun*

conservatorium (*say* kon-serv-a-**taw**-ree-um) *noun*
a school of music

conservatory (*say* kon-**ser**-va-tree) *noun*
a glass room on a house or other building, in which plants are often grown
•***Word Family:*** the plural is **conservatories**

conserve (*say* kon-**serve**) *verb*
1 to keep or prevent something from being wasted or used up
conserve (*say* **kon**-serve) *noun*
2 a kind of jam

consider (*say* kon-**sid**-a) *verb*
1 to think carefully about a particular thing: *We need some time to consider your offer.* 2 to believe or think: *They consider her to be in great danger.*

considerable (*say* kon-**sid**-er-a-bull) *adjective*
large or important: *a considerable amount of money / his considerable sporting talents*
•***Word Family:*** **considerably** *adverb* greatly

considerate (*say* kon-**sid**-a-rut) *adjective*
kind or thoughtful

consideration (*say* kon-sid-a-**ray**-shun) *noun*
1 serious thought: *After careful consideration we decided to emigrate.* 2 respect or thoughtfulness: *She shows no consideration for others.*
3 something that you take into account before making a decision: *Our main consideration in coming to live here was the climate.*

consist *verb*
to be made up of: *Jam consists of fruit and sugar.*

consistency *noun*
1 an agreement or similarity between things: *Your statement shows no consistency with what you said yesterday.* 2 the thickness or feel of something: *Her gravy had the consistency of glue.*

consistent *adjective*
1 in agreement: *What we heard was consistent with the newspaper report.* 2 always acting or thinking the same way: *Good teachers are consistent in the way they discipline pupils.*

consolation (*say* kon-so-**lay**-shun) *noun*
comfort or support

consolation prize *noun*
a special prize which is given to someone who did not win anything, but deserved to

console (1) (*say* kon-**sole**) *verb*
to comfort: *He tried to console his friend when her dog died.*

console (2) (*say* **kon**-sole) *noun*
a panel of keys and switches from which a computer, machine and so on is operated

consolidate (*say* kon-**sol**-i-date) *verb*
to strengthen or support what you have learned or done earlier: *Homework helps you consolidate what you learn at school.*
•***Word Family:*** **consolidation** *noun*

consonant (*say* **kon**-sa-nant) *noun*
any letter of the alphabet except *a*, *e*, *i*, *o* or *u*

consortium (*say* kon-**sor**-tee-um) *noun*
a group of companies that have combined to carry out a big business deal
•***Word Origins:*** from a Latin word meaning "partnership"

conspicuous (*say* kon-**spik**-yew-us) *adjective*
easily seen or standing out very clearly: *His height made him conspicuous in the crowd.*

conspire *verb*
to plan secretly, especially to do something unlawful: *They conspired to kill the king.*
•***Word Family:*** **conspiracy** *noun* a secret plan, or plot **conspirator** *noun* someone involved in a conspiracy
•***Word Origins:*** from a Latin word meaning "to breathe together"

constable (*say* **kun**-sta-bul) *noun*
an ordinary police officer
•***Word Family:*** **constabulary***noun*

constant *adjective*
1 going on all the time: *the constant noise of the drills at the building site* 2 loyal or faithful: *a constant friend*
•***Word Family:*** **constancy** *noun*

constellation (*say* kon-sta-**lay**-shon) *noun*
a group of stars which forms a shape and which has a name, such as The Plough

consternation (*say* kon-sta-**nay**-shon) *noun*
shock or fear: *To her great consternation she saw a policeman standing on the doorstep.*

constipation (*say* kon-sti-**pay**-shon) *noun*
difficulty in emptying your bowels
•***Word Family:*** **constipate** *verb* **constipated** *adjective*

constituency (*say* kon-**stit**-yoo-en-see) *noun*
an area that elects a Member of Parliament to represent it
•***Word Family:*** the plural is **constituencies**

constituent (*say* kon-**stit**-yoo-unt) *noun*
1 someone who lives in a particular constituency
2 a part or ingredient of something

constitute (*say* **kon**-sti-tewt) *verb*
to make up or form something: *the nations that constitute the European Community*

constitution (*say* kon-sti-**tew**-shon) *noun*
1 your bodily health or strength: *He has the constitution of an ox.* 2 a set of rules or laws: *the American Constitution*
•***Word Family:*** **constitutional** *adjective*

constrict *verb*
to squeeze or press together: *The tight collar constricted his throat.*
•***Word Family:*** **constriction** *noun*

construct *verb*
to build: *Engineers have constructed a new bridge.*
•***Word Family:*** **construction** *noun*

constructive *adjective*
useful or helpful: *constructive advice*

consul (*say* **kon**-sul) *noun*
an official sent to live in a foreign country to look after the people from his or her own country that live there
•***Word Family:*** **consular** *adjective* **consulate** *noun*

consult *verb*
1 to seek advice from: *to consult a doctor* 2 to discuss or exchange views: *We consulted for several hours before reaching a decision.*
•***Word Family:*** **consultation** *noun*

consultant (*say* kon-**sul**-tunt) *noun*
1 an expert who provides advice, especially for businesses or companies 2 a senior doctor in a hospital

consume *verb*
1 to eat: *We consumed all the ice-cream.* 2 to use up: *The job consumed all his strength.* 3 to destroy: *Fire consumed the forest.*

consumer *noun*
someone who buys goods or uses services: *an electricity consumer*

contact *noun*
1 communicating with or meeting: *The sisters have had no contact with each other for years.*
2 touching or hitting: *His head made contact with the road and he passed out.* 3 someone you know through one of your interests: *a business contact*
4 a device that completes or breaks an electrical circuit
contact *verb*
5 to put or bring into contact

contact lenses *plural noun*
small, thin discs of glass or plastic worn in your eyes to improve your sight

contagious (*say* kon-**tay**-jus) *adjective*
catching or easily spread or passed on from one person to another: *Colds are contagious. / contagious laughter*
•***Word Family:*** **contagion** *noun*

contain *verb*
to have inside it: *This book contains ninety pages.*
•***Word Family:*** **container** *noun*

contaminate (*say* kon-**tam**-i-nate) *verb*
to dirty something or make it impure
•***Word Family:*** **contaminated** *adjective* dirty or impure: *contaminated drinking water*
contamination *noun*

contemplate (*say* **kon**-tem-plate) *verb*
to look at or think about something: *to contemplate a painting / to contemplate dying*
•***Word Family:*** **contemplation** *noun* **contemplative** *adjective*

contemporary (*say* kon-**temp**-a-ra-ree) *adjective*
1 existing or happening in the same period: *Nelson and Napoleon were contemporary historical figures.* 2 of the present time: *contemporary art*
contemporary *noun*
3 someone living at the same time as another
•***Word Family:*** the plural of the noun is **contemporaries**

contempt *noun*
a feeling of dislike because someone or something is completely worthless or useless
•***Word Family:*** **contemptible** *adjective* **contemptibly** *adverb*

A B C D E F G H I J K L M N O P Q R S T U V W X Y Z

contemptuous (*say* kon-**temp**-tew-us) *adjective*
showing contempt: *a contemptuous smile*
•***Word Family:*** **contemptuously** *adverb*

contend *verb*
1 to struggle or fight: *Which teams will be contending for the cup?* 2 to state or claim: *I still contend that I was right.*
•***Word Family:*** **contender** *noun* **contention** *noun*

content (*say* kon-**tent**) *adjective*
1 happy or satisfied: *She is content with her job.*
content *verb*
2 to make someone happy or satisfied: *He contented himself with a good book on a rainy day.*
•***Word Family:*** **contented** *adjective* happy or satisfied **contentedly** *adverb* **contentment** *noun*

contents (*say* **kon**-tents) *plural noun*
1 anything that is contained in something: *the contents of a parcel* 2 a list of topics or chapters in a book

contest (*say* **kon**-test) *noun*
1 a competition: *a swimming*
contest (*say* kon-**test**) *verb*
2 to object to or argue against something: *The team contested the referee's decision.* 3 to fight for something: *to contest a prize*
•***Word Family:*** **contestant** *noun*

context (*say* **kon**-tekst) *noun*
1 the situation in which something is done or in which it happens: *In what context did he make that statement?* 2 the words or phrases that come before and after a particular word or passage

continent (*say* **kon**-ti-nent) *noun*
1 a large mass of land, such as Europe, Africa or Asia 2 **the Continent** Europe, not including the British Isles
•***Word Family:*** **continental** *adjective*
•***Word Origins:*** from a Latin word meaning "continuous land"

contingency (*say* kon-**tin**-jun-see) *noun*
something that might happen and affect other plans or decisions: *We must plan for all contingencies.*
•***Word Family:*** the plural is **contingencies**

continual (*say* kon-**tin**-yew-ul) *adjective*
happening all the time or only with short breaks: *She has continual attacks of asthma.*
•***Word Family:*** **continually** *adverb*

continue (*say* kon-**tin**-yoo) *verb*
1 to go on and on without stopping: *It continued to rain all day.* 2 to start again after a break: *We will continue the meeting after lunch.*
•***Word Family:*** **continuation** *noun* **continuous** *adjective* **continuously** *adverb*

contort *verb*
to twist or bend out of its normal shape: *His face contorted with rage.*
•***Word Family:*** **contorted** *adjective* bent or twisted **contortion** *noun*

contortionist (*say* kon-**tor**-shon-ist) *noun*
an acrobat who performs gymnastic tricks involving unusual or contorted body positions

contour (*say* **kon**-toor) *noun*
1 the outline or shape of something: *the contours of the landscape* 2 a line on a map joining points which are an equal height above sea-level

contra- *prefix*
against or opposite: *contraception*, *contradict*

contraband *noun*
articles smuggled into or out of a country

contraception (*say* kon-tra-**sep**-shon) *noun*
a way of preventing a woman from getting pregnant, such as by using a condom
•***Word Family:*** **contraceptive** *noun* a way of preventing pregnancy, such as a condom **contraceptive** *adjective*

contract (*say* kon-**trakt**) *verb*
1 to make or become smaller: *Elastic contracts after being stretched.* 2 to get or bring upon yourself: *to contract measles / to contract debts* 3 to make a legal agreement with someone to do a particular job: *We are contracted to clean the offices, but not the stairs.*
contract *noun*
4 a legal agreement you make with someone: *a contract to build a house*
•***Word Family:*** **contraction** *noun* **contractual** *adjective* **contractor** *noun*

contradict (*say* kon-tra-**dikt**) *verb*
1 to say the opposite of, or deny: *She contradicted my story of what happened.* 2 to be opposite of: *His behaviour often contradicts what he tells other people to do.*
•***Word Family:*** **contradiction** *noun* **contradictory** *adjective*

contralto (*say* kon-**trahl**-toe) *noun*
1 the range of musical notes sung by a woman with the lowest female singing voice 2 a singer or musical instrument having this range
•***Word Family:*** the plural is **contraltos** □ **contralto** *adjective*

contraption (*say* kon-**trap**-shon) *noun*
a strange or complicated device or machine

contrary *adjective*
1 (*say* **kon**-tra-ree) opposite or opposed: *Contrary to all advice she left school.* 2 (*say* kon-**trair**-ree) difficult or stubborn: *She is very contrary and refuses to do what she is told.*

contrary (*say* **kon**-tra-ree) *noun*
3 the opposite of something **4 on the contrary** the opposite of what has been said: *Is it sunny here? On the contrary; it's pouring.*
• ***Word Family:*** **contrarily** *adverb*

contrast (*say* kon-**trahst**) *verb*
1 to compare two things by showing their differences: *to contrast two poems*
contrast (*say* **kon**-trahst) *noun*
2 an easily seen difference

contribute (*say* kon-**trib**-yoot) *verb*
1 to give something as your share: *Have you contributed to the farewell gift?* 2 to add: *His jokes contributed to the laughter in the room.*
• ***Word Family:*** **contribution** *noun* **contributor** *noun* **contributory** *adjective*

contrite *adjective*
sorry about having done something wrong
• ***Word Family:*** **contrition** *noun*

control *verb*
1 to be in charge of: *The Principal controls the staff and pupils of a school.* 2 to keep in check: *Control your temper!* 3 to regulate: *The trigger on the nozzle controls the flow of petrol into a car.*
control *noun*
4 check or restraint: *Keep your temper under control.*
• ***Word Family:*** other verb forms are **controls, controlled, controlling** □ **controllable** *adjective*

controversy (*say* kon-**trov**-a-see *or* **kon**-tra-ver-see) *noun*
an argument or difference of opinion that goes on for a long time
• ***Word Family:*** the plural is **controversies** □ **controversial** *adjective*

conundrum (*say* ko-**nun**-drum) *noun*
a puzzle or riddle

convalescence (*say* kon-va-**les**-ence) *noun*
the time during which you get stronger after an accident, illness or operation
• ***Word Family:*** **convalesce** *verb* **convalescent** *adjective* **convalescent** *noun*

convection (*say* kon-**vek**-shon) *noun*
the spreading of heat in a liquid or gas, caused by warm liquid or gas rising and cold liquid or gas sinking

convene *verb*
to call or bring a group of people together: *The committee will convene on Friday.*
• ***Word Family:*** **convener** *noun*

convenience *noun*
1 something that is convenient, such as a particular time: *Come at your convenience.* 2 something that is useful: *Our holiday house had many conveniences.* 3 a toilet

convenient (*say* kon-**veen**-i-ent) *adjective*
easy to reach or use: *a convenient bus-stop*
• ***Word Family:*** **conveniently** *adverb*

convent (*say* **kon**-vent) *noun*
1 a group of nuns or the place where they live
2 a school run by nuns

convention (*say* kon-**ven**-shon) *noun*
1 a formal meeting of people with the same interests: *a science convention* 2 a rule or way of behaving that everyone accepts as being right
• ***Word Family:*** **conventional** *adjective* accepted as the right or proper way to do something

converge (*say* kon-**verj**) *verb*
to meet at one point: *We all converged on the picnic area.*
• ***Word Family:*** **convergence** *noun* **convergent** *adjective*

conversation (*say* kon-va-**say**-shon) *noun*
a chat or talk between two or more people

convert (*say* kon-**vert**) *verb*
1 to change into a different form: *Convert a mile into metres.* 2 to change someone to another way of life or religious belief
convert (*say* **kon**-vert) *noun*
3 someone who has been converted: *a convert to Buddhism*
• ***Word Family:*** **conversion** *noun*

convex *adjective*
curved outwards like the outside of a ball or a bump: *a convex lens*

convey (*say* kon-**vay**) *verb*
to carry: *to convey passengers / to convey a message*
• ***Word Family:*** **conveyance** *noun*

conveyor belt *noun*
a long belt or strip which carries goods along in a factory

convict (*say* kon-**vikt**) *verb*
1 to find someone guilty of a crime, especially after a trial
convict (*say* **kon**-vikt) *noun*
2 someone who has been found guilty of a crime, and has been sent to prison

conviction (*say* kon-**vik**-shon) *noun*
1 a strong belief or opinion: *It is my conviction that the report is not true.* 2 the state of being convicted: *He has had eight convictions for burglary.*

convince *verb*
to persuade someone about something by giving strong arguments or evidence: *to convince someone of the truth.*
• ***Word Family:*** **convincing** *adjective* **convincingly** *adverb*

A B C D E F G H I J K L M N O P Q R S T U V W X Y Z

convoy *noun*
a group of ships or vehicles travelling together

convulsion (*say* kon-**vul**-shon) *noun*
1 a fit: *The baby became ill and had a convulsion.* 2 laughter or a sudden burst of anger: *She looked so funny we went into convulsions.*
•***Word Family:*** **convulse** *verb* **convulsive** *adjective*

cooee *interjection*
a call used as a signal in Australia and New Zealand
•***Word Origins:*** originally used by Aboriginal people and then by settlers

cook *verb*
1 to prepare something for eating by heating it: *to cook food in an oven*
cook *noun*
2 someone who cooks
•***Word Family:*** **cookery** *noun*

cooker *noun*
a device used for cooking food

cool *adjective*
1 not very warm 2 not very friendly: *We received a cool welcome.* 3 pleasing or fashionable: *That's cool!*
cool *verb*
4 to make or become less warm
•***Word Family:*** **coolly** *adverb* **coolness** *noun*

coop *noun*
1 a cage for hens and chickens
coop *verb*
2 to shut people or animals in a small space or area

cooperate (*say* ko-**op**-a-rate) *verb*
to work together: *If we cooperate we'll get a lot more done.*
•***Word Family:*** **cooperation** *noun* **cooperative** *adjective*

cooperative (*say* ko-**op**-er-a-tiv) *noun*
a company or business in which everyone shares the work equally and is paid equally, and which is owned by everyone that works there

coordinate (*say* ko-**or**-di-nate) *verb*
1 to manage things so that they work well: *to coordinate a class timetable / to coordinate your clothes* 2 to make parts of your body work together smoothly: *Babies have to learn to coordinate their hands and eyes.*
coordinate (*say* ko-**or**-din-ut) *noun*
3 one of the numbers that shows the position of something on a map, a graph and so on
•***Word Family:*** **coordination** *noun* **coordinator** *noun*

cop *noun*
1 a police officer
cop *verb*
2 to receive: *She copped a terrible blow on the head.* 3 **cop out** to avoid making a difficult or unpopular decision 4 **cop it** to get into trouble
•***Word Family:*** other verb forms are **cops, copped, copping**

cope *verb*
to manage: *The new pupil coped very well on her first day.*

copper (1) *noun*
1 a reddish-brown metal 2 a coin made from or containing copper 3 a shining, reddish-brown colour

copper (2) *noun*
a police officer

copulation (*say* kop-yoo-**lay**-shon) *noun*
sexual intercourse
•***Word Family:*** **copulate** *verb*

copy *noun*
1 something which has been made to be the same as something else: *an exact copy of a Roman coin* 2 one of a particular book, magazine or newspaper: *a copy of a "Superman" comic*
copy *verb*
3 to make a copy of 4 to imitate: *The toddler copied everything his father did.*
•***Word Family:*** the plural of the noun is **copies** □ other verb forms are **copies, copied, copying** □ **copier** *noun*
•***Word Origins:*** from a Latin word meaning "plenty"

copyright *noun*
the legal right composers and writers have to stop other people using their work without permission

coral *noun*
1 the hard, coloured skeletons of tiny sea animals living in tropical waters, that often form reefs 2 a pinkish-orange colour

cord *noun*
1 a strong, thick string made by weaving or twisting several strands together 2 corduroy 3 a wire covered by plastic, that you plug in to supply power to an electrical appliance

cordial *adjective*
1 polite or friendly: *a cordial greeting*
cordial *noun*
2 a sweet thick liquid you add water to in order to make a drink
•***Word Family:*** **cordially** *adverb* **cordiality** *noun*
•***Word Origins:*** from a Latin word meaning "from the heart"

corduroy (*say* **kor**-da-roy *or* **kord**-yu-roy) *noun*
material with fine raised lines running along it

core (*say* kor) *noun*
1 the central or inner point: *an apple core*
core *verb*
2 to cut out the core of something such as an apple
• ***Word Family:*** **corer** *noun*

corgi *noun*
a small, short-legged dog with short pointed ears
• ***Word Family:*** the plural is **corgis**
• ***Word Origins:*** from a Welsh word meaning "dwarf dog"

cork *noun*
1 the lightweight bark of a tree, used to make tiles, bottle corks and so on 2 a specially shaped piece of this, used to seal bottles of wine and so on

corkscrew *noun*
a pointed, spiral-shaped piece of metal for pulling the cork out of a bottle

cormorant (*say* **kor**-mer-unt) *noun*
a sea-bird with a long neck and dark feathers

corn (1) *noun*
the seed of a cereal plant, especially wheat

corn (2) *noun*
a hard area of skin on your foot, caused by pressure or rubbing

cornea (*say* **kaw**-nee-a) *noun*
the transparent skin that covers the coloured part of your eye

corner *noun*
1 the point at which two edges or surfaces meet: *the corner of a table / a street corner* 2 an area or region: *a quiet corner of the world*
corner *verb*
3 to turn a corner, especially in a vehicle 4 to trap or get into a difficult situation: *The cat cornered the mouse.*

cornet *noun*
1 a brass wind instrument that looks like a small trumpet 2 an ice-cream cone

cornflour *noun*
a fine flour made from wheat or maize, used in cooking, especially to thicken sauces

coronation (*say* kor-a-**nay**-shon) *noun*
the crowning of a king or queen, usually at a special ceremony

coroner (*say* **ko**-ra-na) *noun*
an official appointed by the government to find out about any strange or suspicious deaths, either accidents or murders

corporal *noun*
a non-commissioned officer in the armed forces, just below a sergeant

corporal punishment *noun*
any physical punishment such as smacking or caning

corporation (*say* kor-pa-**ray**-shon) *noun*
a company, business or similar organization

corps (*say* kor) *noun*
1 an army unit 2 an organized group: *the diplomatic corps*
• ***Word Family:*** the plural is **corps**
• ***Word Origins:*** from a French word meaning "body"

corpse *noun*
a dead body

corpuscle (*say* **kor**-pus-ull) *noun*
a red or white blood cell

corral (*say* cor-**ral**) *noun*
a fenced area where cattle, horses and so on are kept
• ***Word Family:*** **corral** *verb*

correct *adjective*
1 free from mistakes 2 according to what is considered to be right and proper: *correct behaviour*
correct *verb*
3 to make right or free from mistakes
• ***Word Family:*** **correction** *noun* **corrective** *adjective* **correctness** *noun*

correspond (*say* ko-ri-**spond**) *verb*
1 to match: *His actions do not correspond with his ideas.* 2 to write letters: *to correspond with a penpal*
• ***Word Family:*** **corresponding** *adjective*

correspondence (*say* ko-ri-**spon**-dunce) *noun*
1 agreement or similarity: *There is no correspondence between what she says and what she does.* 2 letters you write to people

correspondent *noun*
1 someone who writes letters 2 someone who reports for newspaper, radio or TV news from a particular place or on a particular subject: *the BBC's New York correspondent*

corridor *noun*
a long passage with rooms along its sides

corroboree (*say* ka-**rob**-a-ree) *noun*
an Aboriginal gathering or ceremony at which dances are performed

corrode (*say* ka-**rode**) *verb*
to eat something away gradually, especially the surface of a metal
• ***Word Family:*** **corrosion** *noun* **corrosive** *adjective*

corrugate *verb*
to bend or form into ridges or furrows
• ***Word Family:*** **corrugation** *noun: a corrugation on the surface of a road*

corrugated iron *noun*
a sheet of iron or steel with rounded ridges or ripples used in buildings, especially roofs

corrupt (*say* ka-**rupt**) *adjective*
1 dishonest or having taken bribes
corrupt *verb*
2 to make someone dishonest, for example by paying them bribes: *to corrupt a judge* 3 to spoil or make impure: *A bug in the program has corrupted all the files we saved.*
•***Word Family:*** **corruptible** *adjective* **corruption** *noun*
•***Word Origins:*** from a Latin word meaning "broken in pieces"

corset *noun*
underwear that shapes or supports your waist, abdomen or upper legs, worn mostly by women
•***Word Family:*** **corsetry** *noun*
•***Word Origins:*** from an Old French word meaning "little body"

cosmetics (*say* koz-**met**-iks) *plural noun*
beauty products such as lipstick or mascara

cosmic *adjective*
to do with the universe: *cosmic radiation*

cosmonaut (*say* **koz**-ma-nawt) *noun*
a Russian astronaut
•***Word Origins:*** Greek words meaning "universe sailor"

cosmopolitan (*say* koz-ma-**pol**-it-an) *adjective*
1 involving people, ideas, food and so on from many different parts of the world: *Glasgow is a very cosmopolitan city.* 2 feeling at home in all parts of the world: *a cosmopolitan outlook*

cosmos *noun*
the whole universe

cost *noun*
1 the amount of money you have to pay for something: *the cost of an ice-cream* 2 a loss: *The battle was won at the cost of many lives.*
cost *verb*
3 to have a particular amount as a price: *It cost £40.* 4 to lose something as a result of what you do or the way you behave: *His foolishness cost him his life.*
•***Word Family:*** **costly** *adjective*

costume *noun*
a type of clothing that is suitable for a particular time or place: *The actors all wore peasant costumes for the play. / a swimming costume*

cosy *adjective*
1 warm and comfortable: *a cosy room*
cosy *noun*
2 a padded cover for a teapot to keep it warm
•***Word Family:*** other adjective forms are **cosier, cosiest** □ the plural of the noun is **cosies** □ **cosily** *adverb* **cosiness** *noun*

cot *noun*
a small bed for babies, especially one with high sides

cottage (*say* **kot**-ij) *noun*
a small simple house, especially one in the country

cottage cheese *noun*
a soft, white curdled cheese made from skimmed milk

cotton *noun*
1 a soft white material that grows around the seeds of the cotton plant 2 a type of thin thread made from this material 3 cloth woven from this thread

cotton wool *noun*
fluffy cotton that has not been spun and is used to clean wounds and so on

couch *noun*
1 a sofa 2 a flat narrow bed with a headrest, used by doctors for their patients

cough (*say* koff) *verb*
1 to force air suddenly from your lungs with a loud, harsh sound
cough *noun*
2 an occasion when you do this, or the sound it makes: *I heard a cough behind me.* 3 an illness which makes you cough a lot: *I've got a bad cough.*

could *verb*
1 *the past tense of* **can (1)**
2 *a polite form of* **can**: *Could you help me?*

council *noun*
a group of people who meet regularly for discussion and to make decisions: *the city council*
•***Word Family:*** **councillor** *noun* a member of a council

counsel *noun*
1 advice 2 a barrister or barristers who represent a client in court
counsel *verb*
3 to give advice
•***Word Family:*** other verb forms are **counsels, counselled, counselling**

counsellor *noun*
1 an adviser 2 a lawyer, especially a barrister in the United States

count *verb*
1 to name numbers in order: *Can you count to 100?* 2 to add up: *to count votes* 3 to include: *There are 300 people in the town not counting babies.* 4 to consider: *Count yourself lucky you weren't hurt.* 5 to matter: *Every run counts in*

cricket. 6 **count on** to rely on or expect: *You can count on me to help.*

countenance (*say* **kown**-tin-ance) *noun*
your face, especially its appearance or expression: *His fierce countenance hides a gentle nature.*

counter (1) *noun*
1 a long table or bar where goods are sold or food and drink is served in a shop 2 a small piece of wood, plastic or metal used to play snakes and ladders, ludo and so on

counter (2) *adverb*
1 in the opposite direction: *The result went counter to his hopes.*
counter *verb*
2 to meet or move against: *We countered their plan with one of our own.*

counterattack *noun*
1 an attack you make in reply to someone else's attack on you
•***Word Family:*** **counterattack** *verb*

counterfeit (*say* **kown**-ta-fit *or* **kown**-ta-feet) *adjective*
1 made to imitate, especially to deceive: *counterfeit money* 2 false or insincere: *a counterfeit smile*
counterfeit *verb*
3 to make a counterfeit version of something such as money
•***Word Family:*** **counterfeiter** *noun*

counterpart *noun*
someone or something that matches or looks like another thing: *The Prime Minister had a meeting with his Japanese counterpart.*

countless *adjective*
very many, or too many to count: *the litter left by countless tourists*

country (*say* **kun**-tree) *noun*
1 an area of land made separate from others, with its own government: *the countries of Europe* 2 the land outside a city or town: *We live in the country.* 3 a particular type of land: *desert country*
•***Word Family:*** the plural is **countries**

county *noun*
one of the regions or areas that a country is divided into: *the county of Yorkshire*
•***Word Family:*** the plural is **counties**

coup (*say* koo) *noun*
1 an unexpected or clever victory: *The new deal was a coup for the government.* 2 a sudden revolt that overthrows a government
•***Word Origins:*** from a French word meaning "blow"

couple (*say* **kup**-ul) *noun*
1 two people or things together: *a married couple / a couple of sweets*
couple *verb*
2 to join two things together: *The train carriages were coupled by heavy metal links.*

couplet (*say* **kup**-lit) *noun*
a pair of rhyming lines in a poem

coupon (*say* **koo**-pon) *noun*
a form or ticket that you have to fill in to enter a competition or to buy or receive things advertised in a magazine and so on
•***Word Origins:*** from a French word meaning "a piece cut off"

courage (*say* **ku**-rij) *noun*
the strength to face danger or pain even when you are frightened: *She had the courage to admit her guilt.*
•***Word Family:*** **courageous** *adjective*

courier (*say* **koo**-ri-a) *noun*
1 someone who delivers messages or parcels
2 a person whose job is to look after a group of holiday-makers while they are on holiday
•***Word Origins:*** from a Latin word meaning "to run"

course (*rhymes with* horse) *noun*
1 a path or direction: *The ship changed course to avoid the storm. / a course of action* 2 an area on which a sport is played: *a golf course* 3 one of the parts of a meal: *the main course* 4 a series, especially of lessons: *a course of Italian lessons*
5 **of course** certainly: *Of course we will help you.*

court (*say* kort) *noun*
1 a level area marked with lines where you play certain sports: *a tennis court* 2 a place where law cases are heard 3 the home of a king or queen and all the people who live or work there
court *verb*
4 to try to win the love of: *Your father courted me for three years.*
•***Word Family:*** **courtier** *noun* **courtly** *adjective* **courtship** *noun*

courteous (*say* **ker**-ti-us) *adjective*
polite and well-mannered

courtesy (*say* **ker**-ti-see) *noun*
polite behaviour: *The guards saluted in courtesy to the Queen.*

court martial *noun*
1 the court of military officers that tries someone in the armed forces who has broken military law
court-martial *verb*
2 to try by court martial
•***Word Family:*** the plural is **court martials** or

A B C D E F G H I J K L M N O P Q R S T U V W X Y Z

courts martial □ other verb forms are **court-martials, court-martialled, court-martialling**

courtyard *noun*
an open area surrounded by walls and usually paved, often at the centre of a large house or other building

couscous (*say* **koos**-koos) *noun*
a North African dish made of steamed semolina, meat and spices

cousin (*say* **kuz**-in) *noun*
the child of your aunt or uncle

cove *noun*
a small bay

covenant (*say* **kuv**-a-nant) *noun*
an agreement or promise

cover (*say* **kuv**-a) *verb*
1 to put something over or around something else to protect it or decorate it: *to cover a cake with icing* 2 to get news of an event for newspapers, television programmes and so on: *Two reporters covered the carnival for the local radio station.* 3 to protect: *Our insurance policy covers us against fire.* 4 to deal with or include: *The second book only covers the Roman Empire.* 5 to be enough for: *My pocket money covers the bus fare to school.* 6 to travel: *We covered 30 kilometres on our bikes today!*
cover *noun*
7 something that covers or protects: *This book has a hard cover.* 8 shelter: *We ran for cover as soon as the rain started.*
•***Word Family:*** **covering** *noun*

coverage (*say* **kuv**-a-rij) *noun*
the amount by which something is covered, for example on the television or radio: *There will be extensive radio coverage of the cricket.*

covet (*say* **kuv**-it) *verb*
to want something belonging to someone else
•***Word Family:*** **covetous** *adjective*

cow *noun*
the female of cattle or some other large animals, such as the elephant or whale

coward *noun*
someone who is afraid and tries to avoid danger or pain: *I'm a complete coward about having injections.*
•***Word Family:*** **cowardice** *noun* **cowardly** *adjective*

cowboy *noun*
a man who looks after cattle in the United States

cower *verb*
to crouch back in fear: *The dog cowered in the corner every time the doorbell rang.*

cowrie (*say* **kow**-ree) *noun*
a smooth shiny seashell

cox *noun*
1 someone who steers a boat, especially in rowing
cox *verb*
2 to act as a cox

coy *adjective*
shy or modest, or pretending to be so
•***Word Family:*** **coyly** *adverb* **coyness** *noun*

coyote (*say* **koy**-ote *or* koy-**o**-tee) *noun*
a wild dog that lives in western North America

crab *noun*
a sea animal with a hard flat shell, four pairs of legs and two strong pincers

crack *verb*
1 to make a sharp sound: *to crack a whip* 2 to break without falling into pieces: *The cup cracked when I dropped it.* 3 to solve: *He cracked the mystery.* 4 to tell: *He cracked some terrible jokes.* 5 to change sharply in pitch: *His voice cracked with emotion.*
crack *noun*
6 the result of cracking: *a crack in a cup* 7 a slight opening: *a crack in the wall* 8 a hard blow: *She got a crack on the head in the accident.*

cracker *noun*
1 a firework that explodes 2 a tube of paper, often containing a gift or joke, which explodes harmlessly when you pull the ends 3 a dry or savoury biscuit

crackle *verb*
to make small, cracking sounds: *The fire crackled away in the grate.*
•***Word Family:*** **crackle** *noun*

cradle (*say* **kray**-dul) *noun*
1 a small bed for a baby, usually set on rockers 2 a frame used to support something, such as the wooden framework supporting a ship in a dry dock
cradle *verb*
3 to hold or protect something as if it is in a cradle: *to cradle a baby in your arms*

craft *noun*
1 a trade or art, especially one needing skill with your hands: *a potter's craft* 2 cunning or deceit 3 a boat or aircraft
•***Word Family:*** the plural for definition 3 is **craft** □ **craftsman** *noun* **craftswoman** *noun* **craftsmanship** *noun*

crafty *adjective*
cunning or sly
•***Word Family:*** other forms are **craftier, craftiest** □ **craftily** *adverb* **craftiness** *noun*

crag *noun*
a steep, rough rock
• ***Word Family:*** **craggy** *adjective* (**craggier, craggiest**) rugged or rough

cram *verb*
to stuff things into a space that is too small for them: *He crammed his clothes into a tiny suitcase.*
• ***Word Family:*** other forms are **crams, crammed, cramming**

cramp *noun*
a sudden painful tightening of one of your muscles, especially in your legs

cramped *adjective*
crowded, or not big enough to hold everything in it: *a cramped room.*

cranberry *noun*
a small, red, sour berry used in jams and sauces
• ***Word Family:*** the plural is **cranberries**

crane *noun*
1 a large wading bird with long legs 2 a mechanical device with a long arm for lifting and moving heavy objects
crane *verb*
3 to stretch out your neck

crane fly *noun*
a flying insect with a thin body and extremely long legs
• ***Word Family:*** the plural is **crane flies**

cranium (*say* **kray**-ni-um) *noun*
the area of bone that surrounds your brain
• ***Word Family:*** **cranial** *adjective* to do with the cranium

crank *noun*
1 a bar that sticks out from a wheel or shaft in an engine and works another part of the engine 2 a handle you use when turning something by hand 3 an unusual or odd person
crank *verb*
4 to cause something to move by using a crank handle

crankshaft *noun*
the main shaft in an engine, that is made to turn by the up-and-down movement of the pistons

cranky *adjective*
bad-tempered
• ***Word Family:*** other forms are **crankier, crankiest**

cranny *noun*
a small hollow place or an opening, for example in a wall or cliff
• ***Word Family:*** the plural is **crannies**

crash *verb*
1 to come together and break with a loud noise: *The cars crashed into each other.* 2 to fall on to land or into the sea: *The plane ran out of fuel and crashed.*
crash *noun*
3 an accident: *a car crash* 4 the sound of crashing: *the crash of waves on the seashore*

crate *noun*
a wooden box in which you pack goods to be carried away or stored

crater *noun*
1 a large hole or hollow in the top of a volcano 2 a large hole in the ground caused by an explosion: *a bomb crater*
• ***Word Origins:*** from a Greek word meaning "mixing-bowl"

crave *verb*
to want very badly: *On hot days I crave cold orange juice.*
• ***Word Family:*** **craving** *noun* a strong desire

crawl *verb*
1 to move along the ground on your hands and knees 2 to be nice to someone just to get something you want: *She crawls to the teacher hoping for good marks.* 3 to move slowly, for example in a queue: *The car crawled up the hill.* 4 **be crawling** to be full of or covered with insects, spiders and so on: *The garden was crawling with ants.*
crawl *noun*
5 a crawling movement 6 a swimming style in which you are face down in the water and you move your arms alternately over and forward and back

crayfish *noun*
a lobster-like creature with a hard shell, that lives in fresh water
• ***Word Family:*** the plural is **crayfish** or **crayfishes**

crayon *noun*
a stick of coloured wax or chalk for writing or drawing

craze *noun*
1 a popular fashion: *Long skirts are the craze this year.*
craze *verb*
2 to make or become mad or insane

crazy (*say* **kray**-zee) *adjective*
insane or mad
• ***Word Family:*** other forms are **crazier, craziest** □ **crazily** *adverb* **craziness** *noun*

creak *verb*
to make a squeaking or grating sound: *The door creaked as it opened.*
• ***Word Family:*** **creaky** *adjective* (**creakier, creakiest**)

A B C D E F G H I J K L M N O P Q R S T U V W X Y Z

cream *noun*
1 the fatty part of milk which rises to the top when the milk is left to stand 2 anything that looks or feels like cream, such as cosmetics or some desserts 3 the best part of anything: *the cream of our scholars* 4 a yellowish-white colour
cream *adjective*
5 yellowish-white: *a cream blouse*
•***Word Family:*** **creamy** *adjective* (**creamier, creamiest**)

crease *noun*
1 a line or mark made when you fold something
crease *verb*
2 to fold or wrinkle something
•***Word Family:*** **creased** *adjective*

create (*say* kree-**ate**) *verb*
to make: *According to the Bible, God created the world in six days.*
•***Word Family:*** **creative** *adjective* good at making things or having new ideas **creativity** *noun* **creator** *noun*

creation *noun*
1 creating 2 something that has been created: *This dress is one of his latest creations.* 3 **Creation** the making of the world or universe by God
•***Word Family:*** **the Creator** *noun* God

creature (*say* **kree**-cha) *noun*
a living thing, especially an animal

creche (*say* kraysh) *noun*
a nursery for babies and young children
•***Word Origins:*** from an Old French word meaning "crib"

credit *noun*
1 belief or trust: *You should not give credit to everything you hear.* 2 someone's belief in your ability to repay a loan: *Is my credit good?* 3 the amount of money you have in a bank account 4 **in credit** having money in your bank account: *We're still £400 in credit.* 5 **on credit** using a credit card or a loan: *We bought the car on credit.* 6 someone who makes those around them proud of them: *She's a credit to the school.* 7 **credits** a list of the people who took part in making a film or TV programme
credit *verb*
8 to believe: *I couldn't credit what I heard him say.* 9 to believe someone to have a particular quality: *I credited her with more sense.* 10 to put money into a person's bank account
•***Word Family:*** **creditable** *adjective* deserving praise: *a creditable effort*

credit card *noun*
a card you use to buy things without using cash, that are later charged to your account

creditor (*say* **kred**-it-er) *noun*
a person or organization that you owe money to

creed *noun*
a statement of beliefs, especially of a religion

creek *noun*
1 a small stream 2 **up the creek** in trouble

creep *verb*
1 to move or crawl close to the ground 2 to move slowly, quietly or secretly: *to creep around the room*
creep *noun*
3 **the creeps** a feeling of fear and disgust: *This place gives me the creeps.* 4 an unpleasant person
•***Word Family:*** other verb forms are **creeps, crept, creeping** □ **creepy** *adjective* (**creepier, creepiest**) horrible or frightening

creeper *noun*
a plant that grows along the ground or up walls, such as ivy

cremate (*say* kre-**mate**) *verb*
to burn to ashes, especially a dead body
•***Word Family:*** **cremation** *noun* the act of cremating **crematorium** *noun* a place where dead bodies are cremated

crepe (*say* krape) *noun*
a thin fabric with a wrinkled surface, made from cotton or silk

crescendo (*say* kre-**shen**-doe) *noun*
a gradual increase in the loudness of music or a noise
•***Word Origins:*** an Italian word

crescent (*say* **kres**-unt) *noun*
1 a curved shape or figure whose two ends each taper to a point: *the crescent of the new moon* 2 a curved street: *We live at 24 Mornington Crescent.*
•***Word Origins:*** from a Latin word meaning "increasing"

cress *noun*
a herb, with small sharp-tasting leaves that are used in salads and on sandwiches

crest *noun*
1 the highest part of something: *the crest of a hill* 2 a growth of hair or feathers on the top of a bird's or animal's head 3 a design on a coat of arms, notepaper and so on: *a family crest*
•***Word Family:*** **crested** *adjective*

crestfallen *adjective*
sad or disappointed: *He looked a bit crestfallen but he soon cheered up.*

crevasse (*say* kre-**vas**) *noun*
a deep crack, especially in a glacier

crevice (*say* **krev**-is) *noun*
a narrow deep crack such as one in a wall or rock

crew *noun*
the people who work on a ship or aircraft: *The captain and crew wish to welcome you aboard.*

crib *noun*
1 a baby's cradle 2 a rack in a stable that holds food for horses or cattle
crib *verb*
3 to copy something in order to cheat
• ***Word Family:*** other verb forms are **cribs, cribbed, cribbing**

cricket (1) *noun*
an insect like a grasshopper that makes a loud noise by rubbing its wings on its abdomen

cricket (2) *noun*
a game played by two teams of 11 players with a bat and ball

crime *noun*
1 an act that is against the law 2 a foolish or wicked act: *It would be a crime to close down the swimming pool.*

criminal *noun*
1 someone who has been convicted of a crime
criminal *adjective*
2 to do with crime or criminals
• ***Word Family:*** **criminally** *adverb*

crimson (*say* **krim**-zon) *noun*
a deep purplish-red colour

cringe *verb*
1 to bend or crouch down in fear: *The small boy cringed from the bully's clenched fist.* 2 to feel extremely embarrassed or uncomfortable: *Her singing makes me cringe.*

crinkle *verb*
to wrinkle: *The baby's face crinkled into a smile.*
• ***Word Family:*** **crinkly** *adjective* (**crinklier, crinkliest**)

cripple *noun*
1 someone who has lost the use of one or more limbs
cripple *verb*
2 to cause someone to become a cripple: *The accident crippled her.*

crisis (*say* **kry**-sis) *noun*
a time or situation that is important, difficult or dangerous: *a political crisis*
• ***Word Family:*** the plural is **crises** (*say* **kry**-seez)
• ***Word Origins:*** from a Greek word meaning "decision"

crisp *adjective*
1 firm but easily broken: *a crisp wafer* 2 brisk, fresh or sharp: *crisp air / a crisp manner*
crisp *noun*
3 a very thin fried slice of potato
crisp *verb*
4 to make or become crisp

critic *noun*
1 someone who makes expert judgments on something: *an art critic* 2 someone who points out faults or mistakes: *We will show the critics of our school that we can behave.*

critical *adjective*
1 finding fault: *critical remarks* 2 serious and important: *a critical period in his life*
• ***Word Family:*** **critically** *adverb*

criticize or **criticise** (*say* **krit**-i-size) *verb*
1 to find fault with someone or something: *He criticizes me all the time.* 2 to judge the good and bad points of something
• ***Word Family:*** **criticism** *noun*

critique (*say* kri-**teek**) *noun*
an essay or review in which you judge the good and bad points of something: *The magazine contains a critique of the film.*
• ***Word Origins:*** this word comes from French

croak *verb*
to make a low, hoarse sound like a frog
• ***Word Family:*** **croaky** *adjective* (**croakier, croakiest**)

crochet (*say* **kro**-shay) *noun*
1 a type of needlework using a hooked needle to make loops that join together to make something
crochet *verb*
2 to make something by crochet
• ***Word Family:*** other forms are **crochets, crocheted, crocheting**

crockery *noun*
earthenware or china objects such as cups, saucers and plates

crocodile (*say* **krok**-a-dile) *noun*
1 a large reptile with a tough skin, a long tail and very big jaws, that lives in the rivers of tropical countries 2 a long line of people walking in pairs
• ***Word Origins:*** from a Greek word meaning "a lizard"

croft *noun*
a small farm, found in parts of Scotland
• ***Word Family:*** **crofter** *noun* someone who farms a croft

croissant (*say* **krwa**-son) *noun*
a flaky pastry roll baked in a crescent shape
• ***Word Origins:*** from a French word meaning "crescent"

crook *noun*
1 a criminal or dishonest person 2 a curved or hook-shaped stick: *a shepherd's crook*

A B C D E F G H I J K L M N O P Q R S T U V W X Y Z

croon *verb*
to sing or hum softly
• ***Word Family:*** **crooner** *noun*

crop *noun*
1 something that is grown in the ground for food: *a crop of wheat* 2 a short riding whip
crop *verb*
3 to cut off or cut short: *I let the hairdresser crop my hair.*
• ***Word Family:*** other verb forms are **crops, cropped, cropping**

croquet (*say* **kro**-kay) *noun*
a game played on a lawn using mallets to hit balls through small hoops set in the ground

cross *noun*
1 a mark or sign you make by putting one line through another, such as "×" or "+" 2 the result of mixing two or more types of animals or plants: *Our dog is a cross between a collie and a labrador.* 3 a post with another piece of wood fixed across it, on which people were executed in ancient times
cross *verb*
4 to go from one side of something to the other: *to cross the road* 5 to put a line through something: *We have crossed your name off the list.* 6 to put one part of something across another part: *to cross your legs*
cross *adjective*
7 angry or annoyed: *Don't be cross with Ann for breaking the window.*
• ***Word Family:*** the plural of the noun is **crosses** □ **crossly** *adverb* **crossness** *noun*

crossbar *noun*
a bar that runs across part of something, for example on a bike

crossbow *noun*
a short, powerful bow held like a gun and used in the Middle Ages

cross-examine *verb*
to question someone carefully, for example in a court of law: *to cross-examine a witness*
• ***Word Family:*** **cross-examination** *noun* **cross-examiner** *noun*

cross-eyed *noun*
having eyes that look as though they turn inwards towards the nose

crossing *noun*
a place where you can cross a road or track: *The cars lined up at the railway crossing.*

crossroads *noun*
a place where roads cross each other

cross-section *noun*
1 a line or piece made by cutting across through the middle of something 2 a drawing of what something would look like if it had been cut through in this way 3 a sample of people who are taken to be typical of a much larger group: *We interviewed a cross-section of people to see what they thought.*

crotchet *noun*
a musical note which is a quarter of a semibreve
• ***Word Origins:*** from a French word meaning "a small hook"

crotchety (*say* **krot**-cha-tee) *adjective*
cross or bad-tempered

crouch (*rhymes with* ouch) *verb*
to lower your body with your legs bent, such as when starting a race

crouton (*say* **kroo**-ton) *noun*
a small cube of fried bread you eat with soup
• ***Word Origins:*** from a French word meaning "crust"

crow (1) (*say* kro) *noun*
a bird with shiny black feathers and a harsh cry

crow (2) (*say* kro) *verb*
1 to make the harsh, loud cry of a crow or rooster 2 to boast or express glee
• ***Word Family:*** the other forms are **crows, crowed** or **crew, crowed, crowing**

crowbar *noun*
a long metal bar that you use as a lever

crowd (*rhymes with* loud) *noun*
1 a large group of people: *A crowd gathered in the square.*
crowd *verb*
2 to come together in a crowd or large group: *We all crowded around the television.*

crown *noun*
1 an ornamental headdress, especially one worn by a king or queen 2 the top or highest part of something: *The crown of his hat was dented.*
crown *verb*
3 to officially make someone into a king or queen by putting a crown on them: *The Archbishop crowned the Queen.* 4 to reward something, or end it successfully: *Success crowned his hard work.*

crucial (*say* **kroo**-shul) *adjective*
the most important: *The crucial moments of the game were just after half-time.*

crucifix (*say* **kroo**-si-fiks) *noun*
a cross with a figure of Christ on it

crucify (*say* **kroo**-si-fie) *verb*
to put someone to death by nailing them to a cross
• ***Word Family:*** other forms are **crucifies, crucified, crucifying** □ **crucifixion** *noun*

crude *adjective*
1 not manufactured or changed from its natural state: *crude oil* 2 incomplete or not carefully done: *a crude drawing* 3 vulgar or rude: *crude behaviour / a crude joke*
•*Word Family:* **crudeness** *noun* **crudity** *noun*

cruel (*say* **kroo**-el) *adjective*
deliberately causing pain or suffering to others: *cruel remarks*
•*Word Family:* **cruelly** *adverb*

cruise (*say* krooz) *verb*
1 to sail from place to place 2 to travel at a moderate speed: *The jet cruised above the clouds.*
cruise *noun*
3 a pleasure trip on a boat
•*Word Family:* **cruiser** *noun* a motor boat

crumb (*say* krum) *noun*
a tiny piece or flake of something: *She left only a few crumbs of cake on her plate.*

crumble *verb*
1 to break or fall into tiny pieces: *She crumbled the soil between her fingers.*
crumble *noun*
2 a baked dessert made of fruit topped with a mixture of flour, fat and sugar
•*Word Family:* **crumbly** *adjective*

crumpet *noun*
a small, spongy, bread-like cake that you toast and spread with butter and honey or jam

crumple *verb*
to make something such as clothing very creased, or to become very creased
•*Word Family:* **crumpled** *adjective*

crusade (*say* kroo-**sade**) *noun*
1 a strong campaign in support of a cause: *a campaign against cigarette smoking* 2 **Crusade** a military campaign during the Middle Ages carried out by European Christians in the Holy Land against native Muslims
•*Word Family:* **crusader** *noun* **crusade** *verb*
•*Word Origins:* from a Spanish word meaning "the Cross"

crush *verb*
1 to press or squeeze something out of shape: *His car was crushed by a falling tree.* 2 to break something into small pieces: *to crush apples for cider* 3 to defeat someone, especially when this embarrasses them: *She felt crushed by their cruel remarks.*
crush *noun*
4 a feeling of love that doesn't last: *She has a crush on him.*

crust *noun*
1 a hard, outer layer or surface: *Cut the crusts off the bread.*
crust *verb*
2 to form a crust
•*Word Family:* **crusty** *adjective* (**crustier, crustiest**)

crustacean (*say* krus-**tay**-shon) *noun*
an animal with a hard shell such as a prawn or crab, that usually lives in water

crutch *noun*
a padded stick that fits under the armpit and is used to support an injured person and help them walk

cry *verb*
1 to shout: *She cried out for help.* 2 to shed tears: *The baby began to cry as soon as its mother left.*
cry *noun*
3 a loud shout or call: *a cry for help*
•*Word Family:* other verb forms are **cries, cried, crying** □ the plural of the noun is **cries**

crypt (*say* kript) *noun*
an underground room, especially one under a church and used as a burial place

cryptic (*say* **krip**-tik) *adjective*
having a hidden meaning, and seeming mysterious or secret: *a cryptic message*
•*Word Family:* **cryptically** *adverb*

crystal (*say* **kris**-tal) *noun*
1 a clear mineral that looks like glass
2 something made from good quality glass: *Wash the crystal glasses carefully.* 3 a grain or small piece of something that has a regular or symmetrical shape: *an ice crystal*
•*Word Family:* **crystalline** *adjective* like or containing crystals
•*Word Origins:* from a Greek word meaning "ice"

crystallize or **crystallise** (*say* **kris**-ta-lize) *verb*
to form into crystals: *The honey has crystallized in the jar*
•*Word Family:* **crystallization** *noun*

cub *noun*
the young of some wild animals, such as a lion, wolf, and so on

cube (*say* kewb) *noun*
1 a solid or hollow boxlike shape with six square sides 2 the result of multiplying a number by itself twice: *The cube of 2 is 2 × 2 × 2, or 8*
cube *verb*
3 to cut or make into cubes

cubic (*say* **kew**-bick) *adjective*
relating to volume, rather than to area or length. A **cubic centimetre** is the volume of a cube whose sides all measure one centimetre

cubicle (*say* **kew**-bi-kul) *noun*
a small room: *a toilet cubicle*
•*Word Origins:* from a Latin word meaning "bedchamber"

A B C D E F G H I J K L M N O P Q R S T U V W X Y Z

cuckoo *noun*
a bird that lays its eggs in the nests of other birds

cucumber (*say* **kew**-kum-ba) *noun*
a long, green-skinned, fleshy fruit you use in salads

cud *noun*
food that an animal such as a cow brings back from its stomach into its mouth to chew again

cuddle *verb*
to hold someone closely and lovingly: *We love to cuddle our new baby.*
•***Word Family:*** **cuddly** *adjective* (**cuddlier, cuddliest**)

cue (1) (*say* kew) *noun*
a word or action that is a signal for another actor in a play to act his or her part

cue (2) (*say* kew) *noun*
a long rod used to hit the ball in snooker

cuff *noun*
a fold or band at the bottom of your trousers or sleeve

cuisenaire rods (*say* kwee-za-**nair** rodz) *plural noun*
coloured wooden blocks of different lengths, used to help children learn to count
•***Word Origins:*** named after the Belgian inventor Georges *Cuisenaire*

cuisine (*say* kwi-**zeen**) *noun*
a particular type of cooking: *Italian cuisine.*
•***Word Origins:*** from a French word meaning "kitchen"

culinary (*say* **kul**-in-ree) *adjective*
to do with the kitchen, food or cooking

cull *verb*
1 to gather a crop of fruit 2 to kill some of a group of animals, for example if there are too many in a herd
•***Word Family:*** **cull** *noun: a seal cull*

culminate (*say* **kul**-mi-nate) *verb*
to reach the highest point or climax: *The argument culminated in a fight.*
•***Word Family:*** **culmination** *noun*

culprit *noun*
someone who has done something wrong

cult (*say* kult) *noun*
1 a religion 2 a thing or person that is popular only with a small group of people: *a cult film*

cultivate (*say* **kul**-ti-vate) *verb*
1 to prepare and work land in order to plant and raise crops 2 to make something stronger and better: *to cultivate friendships*
•***Word Family:*** **cultivation** *noun*

cultivated (*say* **kul**-ti-vay-ted) *adjective*
1 produced by or using cultivation: *cultivated land* 2 well-educated and well-behaved

culture (*say* **kul**-cher) *noun*
1 the ideas, knowledge and beliefs of a particular society or group of people: *Aboriginal culture* 2 art, literature, music and so on

cumbersome (*say* **kum**-ba-sum) *adjective*
clumsy or difficult to manage: *a cumbersome parcel*

cumulus (*say* **kew**-mya-lus) *noun*
a cloud that has a rounded top and a flat base
•***Word Origins:*** from a Latin word meaning "a heap"

cuneiform (*say* **kew**-ni-form) *noun*
an early form of writing, using wedge-shaped symbols carved on pieces of clay or stone

cunning *adjective*
cleverly getting what you want, usually by tricking people
•***Word Family:*** **cunningly** *adverb*

cup *noun*
1 a small, open container with a handle, that you use for drinking 2 an ornamental cup used as a prize: *the World Cup*
cup *verb*
3 to form into the shape of a cup: *He cupped his hand over the match to keep it alight.*
•***Word Family:*** other verb forms are **cups, cupped, cupping**

cupboard (*say* **kub**-ud) *noun*
an enclosed set of shelves or drawers you use to store things in

curate (*say* **kew**-rit) *noun*
a clergyman who helps a parish priest
•***Word Family:*** **curacy** *noun* the position of a curate

curator (*say* kew-**ray**-tor) *noun*
someone who looks after the things in a museum, art gallery and so on

curb *noun*
1 something that holds back or controls: *The new rules will put a curb on bad behaviour.*
curb *verb*
2 to control or hold back: *Curb your temper.*

curd *noun*
the soft, white substance that forms when milk turns sour, used as a food or to make cheese

curdle *verb*
to turn into curd: *to curdle milk*

cure *verb*
1 to bring back to health 2 to preserve meat or fish by drying, smoking or salting it

cure *noun*
3 anything that cures you

curfew *noun*
an official order stopping people going out on the streets after a set time at night, usually during a war or an emergency

curious (*say* **kew**-ri-us) *adjective*
1 wanting to know and learn 2 unusual, strange or interesting: *That's a curious bracelet.*
•***Word Family:*** **curiosity** *noun* **curiously** *adverb*

curl *verb*
1 to form into a curve, ring or spiral: *to curl your hair*
curl *noun*
2 anything in the shape of a curl: *a curl of hair*
•***Word Family:*** **curly** *adjective* (**curlier, curliest**)

curlew *noun*
a bird with a down-curved beak, that lives on the seashore

currant *noun*
a small, dark seedless raisin

currency (*say* **ku**-ren-see) *noun*
the money used in a particular country

current *adjective*
1 to do with or existing in the present time: *current affairs*
current *noun*
2 a flow or stream of water, air or electricity

curriculum (*say* ka-**rik**-yoo-lum) *noun*
the subjects or courses usually taught in a school, university and so on
•***Word Family:*** the plural is **curricula**

curry (1) *noun*
a dish of meat or vegetables cooked with spices
•***Word Family:*** the plural is **curries**

curry (2) *verb*
to groom a horse with a special comb
•***Word Family:*** other forms are **curries, curried, currying**

curse (*say* kerse) *noun*
1 a prayer or spell which is meant to bring harm or evil to another person. 2 something that brings harm: *the curse of poverty* 3 a swear word or blasphemy
curse *verb*
4 to swear, or use rude words 5 to put a curse on someone
•***Word Family:*** **cursed** *adjective*

cursor (*say* **ker**-sa) *noun*
a moving dot or symbol on a computer screen to show you where the next word will appear

curt *adjective*
rudely brief or abrupt
•***Word Family:*** **curtly** *adverb* **curtness** *noun*
•***Word Origins:*** from a Latin word meaning "shortened"

curtail (*say* ker-**tale**) *verb*
to reduce something or cut it short: *We must try to curtail our spending this month.*
•***Word Family:*** **curtailment** *noun*

curtain (*say* **ker**-tin) *noun*
a length of cloth hung at a window or door to shut out light or for decoration

curtsy (*say* **kert**-see) *noun*
1 a respectful bow a woman makes by bending one knee behind the other and lowering her body slightly
curtsy *verb*
2 to make a curtsy
•***Word Family:*** the plural is **curtsies** □ other verb forms are **curtsies, curtsied, curtsying**

curve *noun*
1 a line or shape that bends and has no straight or flat parts
curve *verb*
2 to form a curve
•***Word Family:*** **curvy** *adjective* (**curvier, curviest**)

cushion (*say* **kush**-on) *noun*
1 a bag with a soft filling such as feathers or rubber, used to support your back in a chair
cushion *verb*
2 to lessen the effect or force of something: *The soft snow cushioned his fall.*

custard (*say* **kus**-tid) *noun*
a sweet yellow sauce made by mixing eggs, sugar and milk or by mixing milk, sugar and custard powder

custody (*say* **kus**-ta-dee) *noun*
the care or keeping of someone or something: *The father was given custody of the children.*
•***Word Family:*** **custodian** *noun* someone who has custody of something

custom *noun*
1 a habit, practice or way of behaving: *It is the custom to send people cards at Christmas time.* 2 **customs** (a) a tax paid on goods that are brought into a country (b) the place where you pay this tax, for example at an airport

customary (*say* **kus**-tom-ree) *adjective*
based on custom or usual practice: *It is customary to wear a uniform at our school.*
•***Word Family:*** **customarily** *adverb*

customer *noun*
someone who buys goods or services from someone else

cut *verb*
1 to make an opening using something sharp: *to*

A B C D E F G H I J K L M N O P Q R S T U V W X Y Z

cut your finger 2 to separate or divide something using a knife, scissors and so on: *to cut an apple in half* / *to cut a piece of string* 3 to reduce something or make it lower: *to cut the price* 4 to go across: *We cut through the field to save time.* 5 **cut in** to interrupt someone
cut *noun*
6 the result of cutting: *a cut on your finger* / *a cut of meat* 7 a reduction: *a wage cut* / *a price cut*
•***Word Family:*** other verb forms are **cuts, cut, cutting**

cute *adjective*
attractive or pleasing: *a cute child* / *a cute smile*

cuticle (*say* **kew**-ti-kul) *noun*
the skin that covers the base of your fingernails and toenails

cutlass (*say* **kut**-lus) *noun*
a short, heavy sword with a curved blade and one cutting edge

cutlery (*say* **kut**-la-ree) *noun*
the knives, forks and spoons you use for eating

cutlet *noun*
a cut of meat, usually lamb or veal, containing a rib, and eaten grilled or fried

cyanide (*say* **sigh**-a-nide) *noun*
an extremely poisonous chemical

cyberspace (*say* **sy**-ber-space) *noun*
an imagined space in which communication using computers or the Internet takes place

cycle (*say* **sigh**-kul) *noun*
1 a series of events that are repeated in a regular order: *the cycle of the seasons* 2 a bicycle
cycle *verb*
3 to ride a bicycle
•***Word Origins:*** from a Greek word meaning "a circle"

cyclist (*say* **sigh**-klist) *noun*
someone who rides a bicycle or motorcycle

cyclone (*say* **sigh**-klone) *noun*
a tropical storm with strong winds
•***Word Family:*** **cyclonic** *adjective*

cygnet (*say* **sig**-nut) *noun*
a young swan

cylinder (*say* **sil**-in-da) *noun*
1 a tube-shaped object with circular ends, that can be solid or hollow 2 the part of an engine where the mixture of petrol and air is fired by a spark from a spark plug
•***Word Family:*** **cylindrical** *adjective* shaped like a cylinder

cymbals (*say* **sim**-bals) *plural noun*
a pair of thin brass discs that are struck against each other to make music

cynical (*say* **sin**-i-kal) *adjective*
refusing to believe that people can ever be good, kind or honest
•***Word Family:*** **cynic** *noun* **cynically** *adverb* **cynicism** *noun*

cypress (*say* **sigh**-pris) *noun*
a type of evergreen tree with dark, small, needle-like leaves and hard wood

cyst (*say* sist) *noun*
a swelling or lump on your body, which usually contains some kind of fluid

czar (*say* zar) *noun*
an emperor of Russia before the Revolution in 1917

Dd

dab *verb*
1 to touch with, or put on, something lightly: *My sister dabbed make-up on her cheeks.*
dab *noun*
2 a small amount: *a dab of perfume on your wrists*
•***Word Family:*** other verb forms are **dabs, dabbed, dabbing**

dabble *verb*
1 to splash in water, especially with your hands or feet 2 **dabble in** to do something only as a hobby or casual interest: *I dabble in pottery during my spare time.*
•***Word Family:*** **dabbler** *noun*

dachshund (*say* **daks**-und) *noun*
a small, short-legged dog with a long body
•***Word Origins:*** from German words meaning "badger" and "dog"

daffodil *noun*
a plant with yellow or creamy white trumpet-shaped flowers, growing from a bulb in spring

daft *adjective*
foolish or silly: *What a daft thing to say.*

dagger *noun*
1 a weapon like a small sword, with a short pointed blade 2 **look daggers** to glare at someone in an angry or threatening way

daily *adjective*
1 happening every day: *the daily weather report*
daily *noun*
2 a newspaper published every day
daily *adverb*
3 every day: *The milk is delivered daily.*

dainty *adjective*
very delicate or neat: *a dainty eater / dainty napkins*
•*Word Family:* other forms are **daintier, daintiest** □ **daintily** *adverb* **daintiness** *noun*

dairy *noun*
a place where milk and cream is stored or made into butter and cheese ready to be sold
•*Word Family:* the plural is **dairies** □ **dairy cattle** cattle bred or kept to produce milk rather than meat

dais (*say* **day**-is) *noun*
a raised platform at the end of a hall, for a speaker to stand on to address an audience

daisy (*say* **day**-zee) *noun*
a small plant whose flowers have a yellow centre with many white petals surrounding it
•*Word Family:* the plural is **daisies**
•*Word Origins:* from a Middle English word meaning "day's eye", because it opens at dawn when the world wakes

dale *noun*
a valley, especially in northern parts of the United Kingdom

dalmatian *noun*
a large, short-haired, white dog, usually with black spots
•*Word Origins:* named after *Dalmatia*, a region of the former Yugoslavia

dam (1) *noun*
1 a wall built across a river valley to hold back a large amount of water or make a reservoir
dam *verb*
2 to hold back water by building a dam
•*Word Family:* other verb forms are **dams, dammed, damming**

dam (2) *noun*
a horse's mother

damage (*say* **dam**-ij) *noun*
1 injury or harm: *damage to your leg / earthquake damage* 2 **damages** the money you claim in court if you are hurt or lose something
damage *verb*
3 to harm or injure: *to damage your car in an accident*
•*Word Family:* **damagingly** *adverb*

dame *noun*
1 **Dame** the title used to address a woman of high rank 2 a comic woman character in a pantomime, played by a man

damn (*say* dam) *verb*
1 to curse someone or something: *Damn this traffic!* 2 to criticize or condemn something: *The film was damned by almost all the critics.*
damn *interjection*
3 something you say when you are angry or annoyed: *Damn! I've forgotten my wallet.*
•*Word Family:* **damnation** *noun* eternal punishment in hell **damned** *adjective* very annoying: *a damned nuisance* **damning** *adjective* proving that someone is guilty: *damning evidence*

damp *adjective*
1 moist or slightly wet: *a damp towel*
damp *verb*
2 to moisten: *to damp clothes before ironing* 3 to discourage or dull: *to damp your enthusiasm*
damp *noun*
4 moisture: *patches of damp on the wall*
•*Word Family:* **dampen** *verb* **damply** *adverb* **dampness** *noun*

dance *noun*
1 a series of steps and movements, usually performed in time to music 2 a social event or party where you are expected to dance: *a school dance*
dance *verb*
3 to perform a dance 4 to move quickly or nimbly
•*Word Family:* **dancer** *noun*

dandelion (*say* **dan**-dee-li-on) *noun*
a weed with jagged leaves and bright yellow flowers that form soft white balls of seeds
•*Word Origins:* from French words meaning "lion's tooth", because of the shape of the leaves

dandruff *noun*
small pieces of dead skin that come off your scalp

danger (*say* **dayn**-ja) *noun*
1 the possibility of being hurt or killed: *to put someone in danger* 2 **in danger of** likely to: *The fence is in danger of collapsing. / We were in danger of being found out.*
•*Word Family:* **dangerous** *adjective* **dangerously** *adverb*

dangle *verb*
to swing or hang loosely

dank *adjective*
unpleasantly damp: *a dank cellar*
•*Word Family:* **dankness** *noun*

dapper *adjective*
neat and smart: *My father is a dapper dresser.*

A B C D E F G H I J K L M N O P Q R S T U V W X Y Z

dappled *adjective*
having spots of different colours: *a dappled grey pony*
• ***Word Family:*** **dapple** *verb* to mark with spots **dapple** *noun* a spot or marking

dare *verb*
1 to be brave enough to do a particular thing: *He dared not contradict his teacher.* 2 to challenge: *I dare you to jump off the diving board.* 3 **dare say** to suppose: *I dare say we'll win.*
dare *noun*
4 a challenge
• ***Word Family:*** **daring** *adjective* brave

dark *adjective*
1 with little or no light: *a dark cellar* 2 not pale or light in colour: *dark blue* 3 angry: *a dark look* 4 sad or evil: *dark thoughts* 5 **a dark horse** someone who has hidden talents
dark *noun*
6 an absence of light: *to be afraid of the dark* 7 nightfall: *Be home before dark.* 8 **in the dark** in ignorance or without knowledge
• ***Word Family:*** **darken** *verb* to make or become dark or darker **darkly** *adverb* **darkness** *noun*

darkroom *noun*
a room sealed so that no light gets in, for developing and printing films

darling *noun*
someone you love very much
• ***Word Origins:*** from *dearling*, meaning "dear little thing"

darn *verb*
1 to repair something by sewing over the hole rather than joining it together: *to darn a hole in your jumper*
darn *noun*
2 a patch you have darned in your clothes
• ***Word Family:*** **darning** *noun* anything that needs to be darned: *to do the darning*

dart *noun*
1 a small, sharp, metal arrow with feathers at one end 2 **darts** a game in which each player throws a series of darts at a dartboard 3 a tuck sewn in clothing to alter its shape
dart *verb*
4 to move swiftly and suddenly: *to dart across the lawn*

dash *verb*
1 to throw or strike something violently against something else: *The boat was dashed against the rocks during the storm.* 2 to rush: *He dashed across the road.* 3 to ruin or frustrate: *His hopes were dashed when his skateboard lost a wheel.* 4 **dash off** to write quickly: *to dash off a letter*
dash *noun*
5 a sudden rush or violent movement: *The ambulance made a dash to the hospital.* 6 a small quantity added to something: *I'd like a dash of cordial in my soda water.* 7 a punctuation mark (—), used to introduce a break in a sentence or in speech, as in *If your story is true — and I believe it is — we must act immediately.* 8 a sprint or short race: *the 100 metre dash*
• ***Word Family:*** the plural of the noun is **dashes**

dashing *adjective*
lively and well dressed: *a dashing young woman in a sports car*

data (*say* **day**-ta *or* **dah**-ta) *plural noun*
facts or information
• ***Word Family:*** the singular is **datum**

database *noun*
a large collection of data stored in a computer and organized so that you can find and use it quickly

date (1) *noun*
1 a particular point or period of time: *The meeting has been put off until a later date.* 2 the day, month and year: *What's the date today? / your date of birth* 3 a particular year: *What is the date on that coin?* 4 an appointment to meet a particular person: *We went to a film on our last date.* 5 **out of date** old-fashioned
date *verb*
6 to give a date to: *to date an ancient manuscript* 7 to put or have a date on: *All letters must be dated correctly.*
• ***Word Family:*** **dated** *adjective* old-fashioned

date (2) *noun*
the small, sweet-tasting, brown fruit of the date palm, widely grown in Africa and the Middle East and eaten fresh or dried

daub (*say* dawb) *verb*
to cover something with paint, mud, or anything sticky like this: *to daub paper with paint*

daughter (*say* **daw**-ta) *noun*
someone's female child: *My parents have two sons and one daughter.*

daughter-in-law *noun*
the wife of your son
• ***Word Family:*** the plural is **daughters-in-law**

daunt (*say* dawnt) *verb*
to discourage someone or make them feel less eager: *We were daunted by the sight of the mountain but we kept walking.*
• ***Word Family:*** **daunting** *adjective*

dawdle *verb*
to waste time or fall behind by going slowly: *If you dawdle you'll make me late for work.*
• ***Word Family:*** **dawdler** *noun*

dawn *noun*
1 the first appearance of daylight: *We woke at dawn.* 2 the beginning: *the dawn of time*
dawn *verb*
3 to begin: *The day dawned.* 4 **dawn on** to start to become clear to someone: *It slowly dawned on him that everyone else had left.*

day *noun*
1 the period of light from dawn to dusk 2 the 24-hour period from one midnight to the next 3 the time you are awake or active: *I've had a tiring day.* 4 a particular period: *School hours were much longer in my grandfather's day.*

daybreak *noun*
the dawn

daydream *noun*
imagining something pleasant while you are awake
•*Word Family:* **daydream** *verb* **daydreamer** *noun*

daylight *noun*
1 the light of the sun during the day: *I could see daylight through the cracks in the wall.* 2 dawn: *We left for work before daylight.*

daylight-saving *noun*
a system of putting the clock forward one or more hours, usually in summer, to increase the number of hours of daylight in the working day

daze *verb*
1 to stun or bewilder someone: *The accident dazed him.*
daze *noun*
2 a state of confusion: *to stumble about in a daze*
•*Word Family:* **dazed** *adjective* stunned

dazzle *verb*
1 to blind someone for a short time with bright light 2 to impress people because you do something so well: *Her acrobatic skill dazzled the audience.*
•*Word Family:* **dazzling** *adjective*

deacon (*say* **dee**-kun) *noun*
1 a member of the clergy in the Christian Church, who assists bishops and priests with their duties 2 someone who assists in worship and has other duties in some Protestant churches but who is not a member of the clergy
•*Word Family:* **deaconess** *noun*

dead (*say* ded) *adjective*
1 without life or no longer living: *The dead leaves fell from the tree.* 2 numb or without feeling: *My foot is dead because I've been sitting on it.* 3 no longer used or working: *The phone's dead.* 4 complete or absolute: *dead silence* 5 exhausted: *I'm really dead by Friday.*
dead *noun*
6 people who are dead: *A memorial was erected to the dead of World War II.* 7 the middle or quiet part: *in the dead of night*
dead *adverb*
8 completely: *You're dead wrong.* 9 abruptly: *to stop dead in your tracks*
•*Word Family:* **deaden** *verb* to reduce pain, noise and so on: *The doctor gave him medicine to deaden the pain.*

deadline *noun*
the time by which you must do something

deadlock *noun*
a point people reach in an argument when they cannot agree and refuse to change their opinions

deadly *adjective*
1 tending to cause death: *a deadly poison / deadly weapons* 2 intending to destroy or kill: *deadly enemies*
•*Word Family:* other forms are **deadlier, deadliest** □ **deadliness** *noun*

deadpan *adjective*
looking serious when you are actually joking: *a deadpan expression / deadpan humour*

deaf (*say* def) *adjective*
1 unable to hear or hear well 2 refusing to pay attention: *He was deaf to her pleas.*
•*Word Family:* **deafen** *verb* to make deaf, or overwhelm with noise **deafening** *adjective* extremely loud **deafeningly** *adverb* **deafness** *noun*

deal *verb*
1 to do business with: *I always deal with that cycle shop.* 2 to distribute or hand out something, such as playing cards: *I'll deal the next hand.* 3 to deliver: *The boxer dealt his opponent a heavy blow.* 4 **deal with** (a) to manage or sort out: *Let's deal with this problem first.* (b) to be about: *The new TV show deals with cooking.*
deal *noun*
5 an agreement or arrangement: *We made a deal not to say anything.* 6 someone's turn to give out playing cards: *It's my deal.*
•*Word Family:* other verb forms are **deals, dealt, dealing** □ **dealer** *noun* a trader or merchant **dealings** *plural noun* relations, especially business ones with people or organizations

dean *noun*
1 a teacher or official in charge of students and the day-to-day running of a college or part of a university 2 the head priest who runs a cathedral or a number of parishes
•*Word Family:* **deanery** *noun* (**deaneries**) the home or the job of a dean
•*Word Origins:* from a Latin word meaning "someone in charge of ten people"

A B C D E F G H I J K L M N O P Q R S T U V W X Y Z

dear *adjective*
1 much loved or highly regarded: *a dear friend*
2 expensive: *Strawberries are dear at the moment.*
3 **Dear** the way you begin a letter: *Dear Sir*
dear *noun*
4 someone you love or like a lot: *Hello, dear.*
•***Word Family:*** **dearly** *adverb*

death (*say* deth) *noun*
1 dying or the end of life: *His death occurred last week.* 2 **put to death** to execute or kill someone
•***Word Family:*** **deathly** *adverb* like death: *deathly quiet*

debate *noun*
1 a formal discussion: *a debate about law and order* 2 an organized contest in which two teams of speakers argue opposite points of view
debate *verb*
3 to argue about or discuss a subject
•***Word Family:*** **debatable** *adjective* open to question **debater** *noun* someone who debates

debit (*say* **deb**-it) *noun*
1 an amount of money taken out of someone's bank account or a record of this
debit *verb*
2 to take money from someone's account

debonair (*say* deb-a-**nair**) *adjective*
polite, cheerful and charming
•***Word Origins:*** from French words meaning "of good disposition"

debris (*say* deb-**ree** *or* **day**-bree) *noun*
the remains of something which has been broken or destroyed: *The road was covered with debris after the accident.*

debt (*say* det) *noun*
1 something that one person owes to another: *I always pay my debts. / a debt of friendship* 2 **bad debt** a debt that is unlikely to be paid: *to be owed £200 of bad debts* 3 **in debt** owing money: *to be in debt / to be £500 in debt*
•***Word Family:*** **debtor** *noun* someone who owes money

debug (*say* dee-**bug**) *verb*
to remove the faults from a computer program or system

debut (*say* **day**-bew *or* **day**-boo) *noun*
your first public appearance as a performer: *her TV debut / his Wimbledon debut*
•***Word Origins:*** from a French word meaning "to make the first stroke in a game"

deca- *prefix*
ten times a given unit: *decathlon / decade*

decade (*say* **dek**-ade) *noun*
a period of ten years: *We've been married for a decade.*

decaffeinated (*say* de-**kaf**-a-nay-ted) *adjective*
with the caffeine removed: *decaffeinated coffee*

decagon (*say* **dek**-a-gon) *noun*
a flat shape with ten straight sides
•***Word Family:*** **decagonal** (*say* dek-**ag**-a-nal) *adjective*

decahedron (*say* dek-a-**hee**-dron) *noun*
a solid or hollow body with ten flat faces
•***Word Family:*** the plural is **decahedrons** or **decahedra** □ **decahedral** *adjective*

decanter *noun*
a special flask or bottle for serving wine, juice or water
•***Word Family:*** **decant** *verb* to pour liquid from one container into another

decapitate (*say* de-**kap**-i-tate) *verb*
to cut someone's head off

decathlon (*say* de-**kath**-lon) *noun*
a contest in which athletes compete for the highest total score in ten separate events

decay *verb*
1 to rot away or go bad: *The fallen leaves slowly decayed. / the smell of decaying food*
decay *noun*
2 the process of rotting away

deceased *adjective*
1 dead
deceased *noun*
2 the dead person

deceive (*say* de-**seev**) *verb*
to trick or mislead someone, often by telling lies
•***Word Family:*** **deceit** *noun* **deceitful** *adjective* **deceitfully** *adverb* **deceiver** *noun*

December (*say* de-**sem**-ba) *noun*
the twelfth month of the year, with 31 days
•***Word Origins:*** from the Latin word for "ten", because December was the tenth month of the Roman calendar

decent (*say* **dee**-sent) *adjective*
1 honest and respectable: *a decent family* 2 fair or reasonable: *The workers demanded decent wages.* 3 kind: *It was decent of you to lend me your car.*
•***Word Family:*** **decency** *noun* (**decencies**) **decently** *adverb*

deception (*say* de-**sep**-shon) *noun*
1 deceiving someone: *to use deception to get what you want* 2 a trick or something similar that deceives someone: *a cruel deception*
•***Word Family:*** **deceptive** *adjective* deceiving or misleading **deceptively** *adverb*

deci- (*say* **des**-ee) *prefix*
one tenth of a given unit: *decimal*

decibel (*say* **des**-i-bel) *noun*
a unit used to measure how loud a sound is

decide (*say* de-**side**) *verb*
1 to make a choice: *She decided to continue although her friend advised her to stop.* 2 to settle a question or conflict: *The election will not be decided until all votes are counted.*
•***Word Family:*** **decided** *adjective* definite: *a decided difference between two people* **decidedly** *adverb* definitely **decision** *noun*

deciduous (*say* dee-**sid**-yew-us) *adjective*
losing its leaves every autumn: *a deciduous tree*
•***Word Origins:*** from a Latin word meaning "to fall down"

decimal (*say* **des**-i-mal) *adjective*
1 based on tenths or ten: *decimal currency* 2 able to be expressed in tenths: *a decimal fraction*
decimal *noun*
3 a fraction in which the bottom number or denominator is 10, 100, 1000, 10 000 and so on, but which is usually written with just the top number after a dot or decimal point, as in $0.5 = \frac{5}{10}$ or $0.05 = \frac{5}{100}$
•***Word Family:*** **decimalize** or **decimalise** *verb* to express in decimals **decimally** *adverb*
•***Word Origins:*** from a Latin word meaning "tenth"

decimate (*say* **des**-i-mate) *verb*
to kill or destroy a large part of: *The air-raids decimated the population.*
•***Word Family:*** **decimation** *noun*
•***Word Origins:*** from a Latin word meaning "to kill every tenth man", as punishment in a disgraced army

decipher (*say* de-**sigh**-fer) *verb*
to find or work out the meaning of something: *to decipher a code*
•***Word Family:*** **decipherable** *adjective*

decision (*say* de-**sizh**-on) *noun*
1 making a choice: *Our decision was to continue.* 2 a judgment reached or given: *The principal's decision on our new uniform will be announced soon.* 3 firmness or lack of hesitation: *to act with decision*
•***Word Family:*** **decider** *noun* **decisively** *adverb*

decisive (*say* de-**sye**-siv) *adjective*
1 important because of settling or ending something such as a dispute: *a decisive court case* 2 acting confidently because you have made up your mind: *a decisive person*

deck *noun*
1 the floor of a ship or bus 2 the turntable of a record player 3 a pack of cards

declare *verb*
1 to announce something formally or officially: *to declare war* 2 to record all the goods you are bringing into a country on which tax must be paid 3 to close a cricket innings before all ten wickets have fallen
•***Word Family:*** **declaration** *noun*

decline *verb*
1 to refuse politely: *He declined our offer of help.* 2 to become weaker, less or smaller: *to decline in strength as you grow old / Profits declined in the first six months of the year.*
decline *noun*
3 a falling or weakening: *a decline in prices / a decline in health*

decompose (*say* dee-kom-**poze**) *verb*
to decay or break down: *The corpse had begun to decompose by the time the police found it.*
•***Word Family:*** **decomposition** *noun*

decorate (*say* **dek**-a-rate) *verb*
1 to make somewhere or something look more attractive by painting it, putting ornaments on it and so on: *to decorate the living room / to decorate the Christmas tree* 2 to honour someone by awarding them a medal or badge: *My grandfather was decorated for bravery during World War II.*
•***Word Family:*** **decorator** *noun* someone whose profession is to decorate houses **decoration** *noun* **decorative** *adjective* **decoratively** *adverb*

decoy (*say* **dee**-koy) *noun*
1 someone or something used to tempt another into a trap or into danger: *The rabbit was used as a decoy to trap the fox.*
decoy *verb*
2 to lure or trap a person, animal and so on by using a decoy
•***Word Origins:*** from a Dutch word meaning "the cage"

decrease (*say* dee-**kreese**) *verb*
1 to make or become less: *to decrease the amount of coffee you drink / The popularity of football has decreased.*
decrease (*say* **dee**-kreese) *noun*
2 a lessening in the amount of something: *a decrease in the number of cases of German measles*
•***Word Family:*** **decreasingly** *adverb*

decree (*say* de-**kree**) *noun*
1 an official order or decision: *a government decree to free all prisoners*
decree *verb*
2 to say formally that something will happen
•***Word Family:*** other verb forms are **decrees, decreed, decreeing**

decrepit (*say* de-**krep**-it) *adjective*
broken down by old age or ill health: *a decrepit house / a decrepit old lady*
•***Word Family:*** **decrepitly** *adverb* **decrepitude** *noun*

A B C D E F G H I J K L M N O P Q R S T U V W X Y Z

dedicate *verb*
1 to devote yourself to doing a particular thing: *to dedicate yourself to your work* 2 to write someone's name on something you have written as a sign of your affection, thanks or respect: *The author dedicated the novel to his son.*
•*Word Family:* **dedicated** *adjective* devoted **dedication** *noun* (a) hard work and enthusiasm (b) the message written on a book when you dedicate it to someone

deduce (*say* de-**dewce**) *verb*
to reach a conclusion by working it out from what you already know: *The detective deduced that the intruder was a child from the size of the footprints.*
•*Word Family:* **deductive** *adjective*

deduct *verb*
to take an amount away from a total amount: *to deduct money from a bill*
•*Word Family:* **deductible** *adjective*

deduction *noun*
1 an amount taken away from a total: *a deduction from the bill* 2 a conclusion you reach by putting together facts you already know
•*Word Family:* **deductive** *adjective* arguing or reasoning by deduction **deductively** *adverb*

deed *noun*
1 something done: *Lifesavers perform many deeds of bravery.* 2 a signed document kept as proof of who owns a property

deep *adjective*
1 going a long way down, inwards or back: *a deep breath / deep water / a deep shelf* 2 low in pitch: *a deep voice* 3 great or intense: *to have a deep mistrust of strangers / a deep feeling of guilt* 4 strong and dark: *deep red*
deep *noun*
5 a deep place, especially in the ocean: *the monsters of the deep*
•*Word Family:* **deepen** *verb* to make or become deep or deeper **deeply** *adverb* **deepness** *noun* **depth** *noun*

deer *noun*
a large mammal with hoofs, the males of which have antlers
•*Word Family:* the plural is **deer**

deface *verb*
to deliberately damage or spoil something by writing or drawing on it: *to deface a library book*
•*Word Family:* **defacement** *noun*

de facto (*say* day-**fak**-toh) *adjective*
really existing or occurring but not legally recognised: *They have a de facto relationship although they aren't married.*
•*Word Origins:* from Latin words meaning "from the fact"

defame (*say* de-**fame**) *verb*
to damage the good name and reputation of someone
•*Word Family:* **defamation** *noun* the wrong of damaging someone's good name **defamatory** *adjective*: *a defamatory remark*

defeat (*say* de-**feet**) *verb*
1 to win a victory over someone: *to defeat an enemy / to defeat a champion sprinter*
defeat *noun*
2 defeating: *His defeat of the World Champion made him a star.* 3 a loss: *The football team suffered four major defeats.*

defecate (*say* de-**deff** a-cate) *verb*
to empty your bowels
•*Word Family:* **defecation** *noun*

defect (*say* **dee**-fekt) *noun*
1 a fault or flaw: *a defect in the new TV / a defect in someone's character*
defect (*say* de-**fekt**) *verb*
2 to abandon a cause or desert your country, especially for political reasons: *The spy attempted to defect to the enemy.*
•*Word Family:* **defection** *noun* **defective** *adjective* faulty **defectiveness** *noun* **defector** *noun* someone who defects

defence (*say* de-**fence**) *noun*
1 action taken to protect against attack: *The defence of the city cost many lives.* 2 something that protects you: *high walls built as a defence against the sea* 3 an argument to support something or explain it: *He can offer no defence for what he did.* 4 what you say to convince the jury that you are not guilty in court: *He conducted his own defence at the trial.*
•*Word Family:* **defenceless** *adjective* **defensible** *adjective* **defensive** *adjective*

defend *verb*
1 to protect a person or place from danger or attack: *to defend yourself with a stick / to defend your homeland* 2 to argue in support of a person, belief or opinion: *How can you defend experimenting on animals?* 3 to represent someone in court and argue their case for them
•*Word Family:* **defendant** *noun* someone accused of a crime in a law court **defendable** *adjective* **defender** *noun*

defer (1) (*say* de-**fir**) *verb*
to delay or postpone something until a better time: *The surgeon deferred the operation until he could check the results of all the tests.*
•*Word Family:* other forms are **defers, deferred, deferring** □ **deferment** *noun*

defer (2) (*say* de-**fir**) *verb*
to give way to someone who knows more than

you do about a particular subject: *to defer to your friend when it comes to football*
• ***Word Family:*** other forms are **defers, deferred, deferring** □ **deference** *noun* great respect **deferential** *adjective* **deferentially** *adverb*

defiance (*say* de-**fie**-ence) *noun*
refusal to give way when you are told to or when you are expected to: *He expressed his defiance by wearing an earring to school.*
• ***Word Family:*** **defiant** *adjective* **defiantly** *adverb*

deficiency *noun*
something lacking: *a vitamin deficiency*
• ***Word Family:*** the plural is **deficiencies** □ **deficient** *adjective* **deficiently** *adverb*

deficit (*say* **def**-i-sit) *noun*
the amount by which the money received is less than the money spent: *The country has a billion pound deficit this year.*

define (*say* de-**fine**) *verb*
1 to state or describe the meaning or nature of something: *to define a word / to define what is real* 2 to determine or show the limits or form of something: *to define the area of a triangle / to define a shape in art*
• ***Word Family:*** **definition** *noun* **definitive** *adjective* **definitively** *adverb*

definite (*say* **def**-a-nit) *adjective*
1 clear or with only one meaning: *She didn't give me a definite answer either way.* 2 sure or certain: *She was definite that she had seen his face before.*
• ***Word Family:*** **definitely** *adverb*

definition *noun*
the meaning of a particular word in a dictionary

deflate *verb*
1 to release gas or air from something: *to deflate a balloon / to deflate a tyre* 2 to reduce or lower economic inflation 3 to make someone feel less confident or less important
• ***Word Family:*** **deflated** *adjective* **deflation** *noun* **deflationary** *adjective*

deflect (*say* de-**flekt**) *verb*
to make something turn aside or travel in a different direction: *The tree deflected the golf ball from its course.*
• ***Word Family:*** **deflection** *noun*

defoliate (*say* dee-**fole**-ee-ate) *verb*
to make trees lose their leaves, especially by using a chemical spray
• ***Word Family:*** **defoliant** *noun* a chemical used to strip plants of their leaves **defoliation** *noun*

deforestation (*say* dee-for-es-**tay**-shon) *noun*
the cutting down of trees or forests

deform *verb*
to spoil or change the natural shape or appearance of a person or a part of their body: *A large swelling deformed his leg.*
• ***Word Family:*** **deformed** *adjective* out of shape **deformity** *noun* (**deformities**) something that deforms a person or a part of their body

defraud (*say* de-**frawd**) *verb*
to cheat a person or organization, especially out of property or money

deft *adjective*
quick and skilful: *Her deft fingers neatly bandaged the wound.*
• ***Word Family:*** **deftly** *adverb* **deftness** *noun*

defuse (*say* dee-**fewz**) *verb*
1 to make an unexploded bomb safe so it won't explode 2 to make a situation much more calm or safe

defy (*say* de-**fie**) *verb*
1 to ignore or resist what you are supposed to do, without hiding it or apologizing: *If you continue to defy me, you'll be in serious trouble.* 2 to annoy or puzzle people: *His behaviour defies explanation.* 3 to challenge someone to do something: *I defy you to stop me!*
• ***Word Family:*** other forms are **defies, defied, defying** □ **defiance** *noun* **defiant** *adjective* **defiantly** *adverb*

degenerate (*say* de-**jen**-a-rate) *verb*
1 to become worse than it was before: *The meeting degenerated into an argument.*
degenerate (*say* de-**jen**-a-rut) *adjective*
2 corrupt: *a degenerate ruler*
degenerate (*say* de-**jen**-a-rut) *noun*
3 a corrupt person
• ***Word Family:*** **degeneracy** *noun* **degenerately** *adverb* **degeneration** *noun* **degenerative** *adjective*

degrade *verb*
1 to humiliate someone 2 to make something poorer or worse in quality: *fertilizers which degrade the soil*
• ***Word Family:*** **degradation** *noun* the process of degrading: *soil degradation* **degrading** *adjective* humiliating or embarrassing

degree *noun*
1 a unit of measurement for angles, temperature or latitude and longitude 2 a qualification awarded by a university when a student completes a course of study 3 a level or amount: *I agree with you to some degree. / the degree of danger involved in these experiments*

dehydrate (*say* dee-**high**-drate) *verb*
to lose water or make someone or something lose it: *The heat dehydrated many of the runners.*
• ***Word Family:*** **dehydrated** *adjective* **dehydration** *noun*

A B C D E F G H I J K L M N O P Q R S T U V W X Y Z

deity (*say* **dee**-a-tee) *noun*
a god or goddess
•***Word Family:*** the plural is **deities**

déjà vu (*say* day-zha-**voo**) *noun*
the feeling you have when encountering a completely new scene or experience that you have been there or done that before
•***Word Origins:*** this expression comes from French

dejected *adjective*
sad and depressed: *a dejected look*
•***Word Family:*** **dejectedly** *adverb* **dejection** *noun*

delay (*say* de-**lay**) *verb*
1 to put something off until later: *We'll delay our holiday until next week.* 2 to make someone or something late: *Having a flat tyre delayed us for several hours.*
delay *noun*
3 a hold-up: *The accident caused a delay.*

delegate (*say* **del**-i-gate) *verb*
1 to give part of your own work to someone else: *She delegated the project to her assistant.*
delegate (*say* **del**-i-gut) *noun*
2 someone who acts for or represents a particular country, organization and so on: *a delegate at the United Nations*
•***Word Family:*** **delegation** *noun*

delete (*say* de-**leet**) *verb*
to cross out or remove something or part of something: *to delete scenes from a film / to delete words from a sentence*
•***Word Family:*** **deletion** *noun*

deliberate (*say* de-**lib**-a-rut) *adjective*
1 done on purpose: *a deliberate act of cruelty*
2 slow and cautious: *a deliberate manner*
deliberate (*say* de-**lib**-a-rate) *verb*
3 to think or talk about something carefully: *The jury deliberated for several days.*
•***Word Family:*** **deliberately** *adverb* **deliberation** *noun*

delicacy (*say* **del**-ik-a-see) *noun*
a delicious and rare or expensive kind of food: *Many people think caviar is a delicacy.*
•***Word Family:*** the plural is **delicacies**

delicate (*say* **del**-i-kit) *adjective*
1 fine: *delicate features / delicate skin* 2 fragile: *a delicate vase* 3 often becoming ill: *a delicate child* 4 needing great care to avoid embarrassment or danger: *a delicate situation*
•***Word Family:*** **delicately** *adverb* **delicateness** *noun*

delicatessen (*say* del-ik-a-**tes**-en) *noun*
a shop selling cooked meat, cheese and other prepared food, especially ones that are unusual or come from other countries
•***Word Origins:*** from a German word meaning a "delicacy"

delicious (*say* de-**lish**-us) *adjective*
very pleasing, especially in its taste or smell: *a delicious meal*
•***Word Family:*** **deliciousness** *noun*

delight *noun*
1 a great pleasure or joy: *to receive the news with delight* 2 something that gives pleasure: *He is a delight to be with.*
delight *verb*
3 to give someone pleasure or be pleased with something: *to delight people with your singing / to delight in your friend's company*
•***Word Family:*** **delighted** *adjective* **delightedly** *adverb* **delightful** *adjective* **delightfully** *adverb*

delinquent (*say* de-**ling**-kwent) *noun*
someone, especially a young person, who keeps getting into trouble or breaking the law: *a juvenile delinquent*
•***Word Family:*** **delinquency** *noun*

delirious (*say* de-**lear**-ree-us) *adjective*
1 imagining things that aren't there, as when you have a fever 2 wildly excited or enthusiastic: *delirious with happiness*
•***Word Family:*** **deliriously** *adverb* **delirium** *noun*

deliver *verb*
1 to take something to someone else: *to deliver a letter* 2 to help with the birth of a baby or a young animal: *to deliver a baby* 3 to aim or send something towards someone: *to deliver a punch / to deliver a ball in cricket* 4 to save or rescue someone: *to deliver someone from certain death* 5 to give or announce something: *to deliver a speech / The jury delivered its verdict.*
•***Word Family:*** **deliverance** *noun* release or rescue **delivery** *noun* **(deliveries)**

delta *noun*
the low, flat area shaped like a triangle, where a river meets the sea
•***Word Origins:*** from the name of a triangular-shaped letter in the Greek alphabet

delude (*say* de-**lood**) *verb*
to deceive or mislead someone
•***Word Family:*** **delusion** *noun* a mistaken idea, especially one that means you might be mentally ill

deluge (*say* **del**-yooj) *noun*
1 a flood or very heavy fall of rain 2 a huge number: *a deluge of questions*
deluge *verb*
3 to overwhelm you with lots of things: *to be deluged with replies*

deluxe (*say* de-**luks**) *adjective*
luxurious or of a high quality: *a deluxe hotel*

•*Word Origins:* from French words meaning "of luxury"

demand (*say* de-**mahnd**) *verb*
1 to ask for something, leaving no chance of being refused: *to demand more money* 2 to need or require a particular thing: *This work demands your full concentration.*
demand *noun*
3 a request: *a demand for more money* 4 a need: *There's a great demand for ice-cream at this time of year.* 5 a requirement: *I've many demands on my time.*
•*Word Family:* **demanding** *adjective*

demean *verb*
to lower yourself or someone else in dignity: *Don't demean yourself by paying him any attention.*

demeanour (*say* de-**mee**-na) *noun*
your behaviour or manner: *His proud demeanour kept people away.*

demented (*say* de-**men**-ted) *adjective*
acting as if you were mad: *demented with rage*
•*Word Family:* **dementia** *noun* madness

democracy (*say* de-**mok**-ra-see) *noun*
1 the system in which the people of a country choose their leaders and their government by voting for them 2 a country governed like this
•*Word Family:* the plural for definition 2 is **democracies** □ **democrat** *noun* **democratic** *adjective* to do with democracy
•*Word Origins:* from the Greek words for "people" and "rule"

demolish (*say* de-**mol**-ish) *verb*
to pull down or destroy something: *to demolish a house / to demolish a weak argument*
•*Word Family:* **demolition** *noun*

demon (*say* **dee**-mon) *noun*
1 an evil spirit or devil 2 someone with great energy: *He's a demon for work.*
•*Word Family:* **demonic** *adjective*
•*Word Origins:* from a Greek word meaning "a god"

demonstrate (*say* **dem**-on-strate) *verb*
1 to prove or show a particular thing: *to demonstrate that a problem can be solved / to demonstrate how a machine works* 2 to hold a march or public meeting: *to demonstrate against airport noise*
•*Word Family:* **demonstrable** *adjective* **demonstrably** *adverb* **demonstrator** *noun*

demonstration *noun*
1 a showing or explanation of how to do or work something 2 a meeting or march held to show that people support or do not support a particular thing or idea: *a demonstration against the new motorway*

demoralize or **demoralise** (*say* de-**mor**-a-lize) *verb*
to make someone feel less confident: *Failing the driving test again has demoralized my sister.*
•*Word Family:* **demoralization** *noun*

demote *verb*
to make someone lower in rank: *He was demoted from sergeant to corporal.*
•*Word Family:* **demotion** *noun*

demure (*say* de-**mew**-er) *adjective*
quiet, modest and rather shy: *a demure young person*
•*Word Family:* **demurely** *adverb* **demureness** *noun*

den *noun*
1 a wild animal's home, often a cave or burrow: *a lion's den* 2 a quiet, cosy and private room or other place

denim *noun*
a strong, cotton fabric used to make jeans, jackets and other clothes
•*Word Origins:* named after the French city of *Nîmes* where it was first made

denomination *noun*
a religious movement or group who share the same beliefs: *The Church of England is one denomination within the Christian Church.*

denominator (*say* de-**nom**-i-nay-ta) *noun*
the number in a fraction in maths that is below the line, showing how many equal parts a quantity is divided into: *The 4 is the denominator in the fraction* $\frac{1}{4}$.

denote *verb*
to mean or be a sign of a particular thing: *A country's flag flying at half-mast denotes the death of an important public figure.*

denounce *verb*
to speak strongly against a person or thing: *He was denounced as a traitor.*
•*Word Family:* **denunciation** *noun*

dense *adjective*
1 thickly or closely packed together: *The airport was closed owing to dense fog.* 2 stupid or dull 3 having a high density: *a very dense liquid / Is water denser than oil?*
•*Word Family:* **densely** *adverb* **denseness** *noun*

density *noun*
1 thickness 2 the scientific measurement which shows the mass of a particular volume of a particular substance, usually in grams per cubic centimetre
•*Word Family:* the plural of definition 2 is **densities**: *Compare the densities of these two metals.*

A B C D E F G H I J K L M N O P Q R S T U V W X Y Z

dent *noun*
1 a hollow in a surface, usually from a blow: *He backed into my car and made a dent.*
•*Word Family:* **dent** *verb*

dental *adjective*
to do with teeth

dentist *noun*
someone trained to care for people's teeth
•*Word Family:* **dentistry** *noun* a dentist's work

denture (*say* **den**-cher) *noun*
a plate that fits into your mouth, with false teeth attached to it

deny (*say* de-**nigh**) *verb*
1 to say that a particular thing is untrue: *He denied being involved in the robbery.* 2 to refuse to let someone do or have what they want: *They denied him the right to see a lawyer.*
•*Word Family:* other forms are **denies, denied, denying** □ **denial** *noun*

deodorant (*say* dee-**o**-da-rent) *noun*
a substance for preventing or covering bad smells

depart *verb*
to leave or go away: *to depart for school*
•*Word Family:* **departure** *noun*

department *noun*
one of the sections into which a large organization is divided: *The shoe department is in the basement. / the government department for education*
•*Word Family:* **departmental** *adjective*

depend *verb*
1 to rely on or trust a particular person or thing: *I depend on him for support.* 2 **depend on** to be decided or controlled by something: *It all depends on the weather.*
•*Word Family:* **dependability** *noun* **dependable** *adjective* **dependably** *adverb*

dependant *noun*
someone who depends on another person for help or support: *My young son is still a dependant.*

dependent *adjective*
needing support from or relying on someone or something else: *a dependent relative*
•*Word Family:* **dependence** *noun* **dependency** *noun*

depict (*say* de-**pikt**) *verb*
1 to represent something in pictures: *photographs depicting the horror of war* 2 to describe something: *a book depicting life in Victorian Britain*
•*Word Family:* **depiction** *noun*

deplete (*say* de-**pleet**) *verb*
to reduce the amount of something until not much is left: *Stocks of the band's new CD were depleted by the fire at the warehouse.*
•*Word Family:* **depletion** *noun*

deplore *verb*
to dislike something very strongly because it annoys or upsets you: *I deplore bad language.*
•*Word Family:* **deplorable** *adjective* bad or terrible: *deplorable behaviour*

deploy *verb*
to spread out troops to carefully chosen positions as part of an overall plan
•*Word Family:* **deployment** *noun*

deport *verb*
to officially expel someone from a country: *The government says it will deport all illegal immigrants.*
•*Word Family:* **deportee** *noun* someone who is deported **deportation** *noun*

deposit (*say* de-**poz**-it) *verb*
1 to put or lay something down somewhere: *to deposit a load of sand on the driveway* 2 to put money or valuables in a safe place, for example a bank: *to deposit £200 in your account / to deposit jewels in the hotel safe*
deposit *noun*
3 a payment you make towards the cost of something you intend to buy: *to pay the deposit on a house* 4 an area or layer of a particular mineral in the ground
•*Word Family:* **depositor** *noun*

depot (*say* **dep**-oh) *noun*
1 a place where things are unloaded or stored: *a grain depot* 2 a place for keeping trains and buses: *a bus depot*

depress *verb*
1 to make someone very unhappy or gloomy: *Her illness depressed her.* 2 to lower or press down on something: *Depress this lever to operate the machine.* 3 to lower or lessen something in value, price and so on: *Demand for other metals will depress the price of gold.*
•*Word Family:* **depressed** *adjective* **depressing** *adjective* making you feel very sad **depressive** *adjective*

depression *noun*
1 a feeling of great sadness or hopelessness 2 a period when a lot of people lose their jobs and a lot of companies lose money 3 a shallow hole or dip in the ground or in the surface of something 4 an area of cold air which often brings rain with it

deprive *verb*
to keep or take away from someone: *to deprive him of his pocket money*
•*Word Family:* **deprived** *adjective* **deprivation** *noun*

depth *noun*
1 deepness or distance downwards, inwards or backwards: *The exact depth of this pool is unknown. / What is the depth of this shelf?* 2 intensity: *the depth of your feelings / the depth of a colour* 3 **depths** a deep or distant part: *the depths of the sea*

deputy (*say* **dep**-yoo-tee) *noun*
1 someone appointed or elected to act for or assist someone else: *The managing director's deputy took over when he was overseas.*
deputy *adjective*
2 assistant: *a deputy prime minister*
•***Word Family:*** the plural is **deputies** □ **deputize** *verb* to act as a deputy

derail *verb*
to make a train leave the tracks on which it is travelling

derby (*say* **dar**-bee) *noun*
1 a match between two teams from the same place or area: *the Liverpool-Everton derby* 2 **the Derby** a horse race held every year at Epson in Surrey
•***Word Family:*** the plural is **derbies**

derelict (*say* **der**-i-likt) *adjective*
1 abandoned and ruined: *a derelict house*
derelict *noun*
2 a poor, ill person, especially someone who is homeless
•***Word Family:*** **dereliction** *noun* neglect

derive (*say* de-**rive**) *verb*
1 to come or develop from a source or origin: *Many English words derive from ancient Greek.* 2 to get a particular feeling: *He derives great pleasure from reading.*
•***Word Family:*** **derivative** *adjective* copied from something else **derivation** *noun*

dermatitis (*say* der-ma-**tie**-tis) *noun*
an allergy of the skin that makes it become dry, red and sore
•***Word Family:*** **dermatologist** *noun* a skin doctor **dermatology** *noun* the study of skin diseases

derogatory (*say* de-**rog**-a-tree) *adjective*
insulting or critical: *a derogatory remark*
•***Word Family:*** **derogatorily** *adverb*

derrick *noun*
1 a type of crane 2 a tower that holds the drill in an oil well

descant (*say* **des**-kant) *noun*
a high part in music, sung or played above the main tune

descend (*say* de-**send**) *verb*
1 to come or go down: *He descended the ladder carefully. / The road descends steeply to the lake.* 2 to have a particular person or family as your ancestor or ancestors: *to be descended from convicts* 3 to lower yourself: *She would not descend to such nastiness.*
•***Word Family:*** **descendant** *noun* someone who is descended from a particular person or family **descent** *noun*

describe *verb*
to say what a person or thing is like: *Can you describe the man who attacked you?*

description *noun*
1 words or writing that describe a particular person or thing: *Give me a description of your dog.* 2 sort or variety: *The vintage car rally was attended by old cars of every description.*
•***Word Family:*** **descriptive** *adjective*: *descriptive poetry*

desert (1) (*say* **dez**-ert) *noun*
rocky or sandy land where few plants grow because little rain falls

desert (2) (*say* de-**zert**) *verb*
to leave a person or place, especially without intending to return: *to desert your wife and children*
•***Word Family:*** **deserted** *adjective* abandoned **deserter** *noun* someone who leaves and runs away from the army, navy or air force **desertion** *noun* the crime that a deserter commits

deserts (*say* de-**zerts**) *plural noun*
something you really deserve such as a punishment or reward: *I hope the thief gets his just deserts.*

deserve (*say* de-**zerv**) *verb*
to earn something or have a right to it: *He deserves to win because he tries so hard.*
•***Word Family:*** **deserving** *adjective* worthy of help

design (*say* de-**zine**) *verb*
1 to invent or plan a particular thing, especially by preparing drawings: *to design a new way of purifying water / A young architect designed their house.*
design *noun*
2 the shape and style of a painting, building and so on 3 a plan or scheme

designate (*say* **dez**-ig-nate) *verb*
to mark or point out something clearly in order to use it for a particular purpose

designer *noun*
1 someone who creates and produces designs: *a fashion designer*

desire *verb*
1 to want or hope for a particular thing very much: *to desire peace*

a b c d e f g h i j k l m n o p q r s t u v w x y z

A B C D E F G H I J K L M N O P Q R S T U V W X Y Z

desire *noun*
2 a strong wish or hope: *a desire for peace*
•***Word Family:* desirable** *adjective* worth having

desist (*say* de-**zist**) *verb*
to cease or stop: *Please desist from swearing.*

desk *noun*
1 a table you use for reading at or writing on
2 a counter at the front of a hotel or office where a receptionist answers the phone, makes bookings and provides information

desktop *adjective*
having a size suitable for use on a table or desk: *a desktop computer*

desktop publishing *noun*
the use of a computer to arrange the way the words and pictures look in magazines, books, newspapers and so on before they are printed

desolate (*say* **des**-a-lut) *adjective*
1 deserted and bare: *It's a bleak and desolate part of the country.* 2 sad and lonely: *What a desolate life she leads now that her friends have all died.*
•***Word Family:* desolation** *noun*

despair *noun*
1 the complete loss of hope: *to weep in despair*
despair *verb*
2 to lose hope: *to despair over her chances of getting well*

desperate (*say* **des**-pa-rit) *adjective*
1 ready to take any risk: *The bank clerk made a desperate attempt to tackle the thieves.* 2 violent and dangerous: *desperate criminals* 3 very serious: *a desperate shortage of food*
•***Word Family:* desperation** *noun* great despair **desperately** *adverb*

despise *verb*
to feel scorn or contempt for: *to despise bullying*
•***Word Family:* despicable** *adjective* nasty, and deserving contempt

despite *preposition*
in spite of: *We had a great time despite the rain.*

despondent *adjective*
sad and depressed: *The players were despondent at losing the game.*
•***Word Family:* despondency** *noun* **despondently** *adverb*

dessert (*say* de-**zert**) *noun*
a sweet food served at the end of a meal
•***Word Family:* dessertspoon** *noun* an oval spoon between a teaspoon and a tablespoon in size

destination *noun*
the place or point to which you are going, or to which something is being sent: *Their final destination was London.*

destiny (*say* **des**-ti-nee) *noun*
fate, or the things that happen to you that seem to be beyond human control: *His destiny was to die young.*
•***Word Family:*** the plural is **destinies** □ **destined** *adjective* meant to happen **destine** *verb*

destitute (*say* **des**-ti-tewt) *adjective*
lacking money and everything else you need: *Last century, destitute children lived on the street.*
•***Word Family:* destitution** *noun*

destroy *verb*
1 to ruin something or make it useless: *Fire destroyed our school.* 2 to kill an injured animal: *to destroy a horse*
•***Word Family:* destroyer** *noun* **(a)** someone or something that destroys **(b)** a small, fast warship **destruct** *verb* **destruction** *noun*

detach *verb*
to separate something or take it off: *to detach a coupon from a page by cutting along the dotted line*
•***Word Family:* detachable** *adjective*

detached *adjective*
1 not interested or involved in what's going on
2 not joined to or built onto anything else: *a detached house*

detail (*say* **dee**-tale) *noun*
1 one of the small but important parts that make up a whole: *the minute detail in a painting / Tell us all the details.*
detail *verb*
2 to describe something fully: *Let me detail my plans.*

detain *verb*
1 to keep someone in a place or make them stay there: *The police detained three men for questioning.*
2 to make someone late by going on too long: *Don't try to detain me—I'm late already!*

detect *verb*
to discover or notice a particular thing: *I detected the smell of burning in the kitchen.*
•***Word Family:* detection** *noun*: *crime detection*

detective *noun*
a police officer or private investigator who investigates crimes and criminals

detention *noun*
being made to stay or being kept in a particular place, especially as a punishment: *an hour's detention after school / a detention centre*

deter (*say* de-**ter**) *verb*
to discourage or prevent you from doing something: *to be deterred from speaking by their hostile threats*
•***Word Family:*** other forms are **deters, deterred, deterring** □ see also **deterrent**

detergent (*say* de-**ter**-jent) *noun*
a powder or liquid used for washing or cleaning things

deteriorate (*say* de-**tear**-ree-a-rate) *verb*
to become worse: *His hearing deteriorated after his accident.*
• ***Word Family:*** **deterioration** *noun*

determine (*say* de-**ter**-min) *verb*
1 to establish or control the way things are: *My parents' views determine the way I think.* 2 to settle or decide on what to do: *Three judges were appointed to determine the outcome of the dispute.*
• ***Word Family:*** **determination** *noun: your determination to win* **determined** *adjective*

deterrent (*say* de-**terr**-unt) *noun*
something that is meant to put people off doing something that is wrong: *He believes prison sentences act as a deterrent to vandals.*

detest *verb*
to dislike someone or something very much: *She detests being called a baby.*
• ***Word Family:*** **detestable** *adjective* deserving to be detested

detonate (*say* **det**-a-nate) *verb*
to explode something or cause it to explode: *to detonate a bomb*
• ***Word Family:*** **detonator** *noun* a small explosive device used to make something else explode **detonation** *noun*

detour (*say* **dee**-toor) *noun*
another way to get to a particular place, for example because the road is closed

detract *verb*
to make something seem less good or valuable: *Her scrawly writing detracts from her essay.*
• ***Word Family:*** **detraction** *noun* **detractor** *noun*

detrimental (*say* det-ri-**men**-tal) *adjective*
harmful or damaging: *Smoking is detrimental to your health.*
• ***Word Family:*** **detriment** *noun* harm or damage **detrimentally** *adverb*

deuce (*say* dewce) *noun*
a stage in a tennis game where the scores are equal at 40 all and one player must win two points in a row to win the game

devalue (*say* dee-**val**-yoo) *verb*
1 to make something seem less important, for example by criticizing it: *to devalue someone's hard work* 2 to officially reduce the value of money in a particular country compared to other currencies
• ***Word Family:*** **devaluation** *noun*

devastate (*say* **dev**-a-state) *verb*
to ruin somewhere or make it barren: *Nuclear testing devastated the island.*
• ***Word Family:*** **devastated** *adjective* shocked and upset **devastating** *adjective* shocking or destructive **devastation** *noun*

develop (*say* de-**vel**-up) *verb*
1 to grow something, or become bigger, stronger and so on: *The chicks are developing wings.* / *to develop a stammer* 2 to improve something: *to develop your knowledge of computing* 3 to build on new land: *to develop farmland* 4 to treat a film or a photograph with chemicals to make it come out

developer *noun*
1 a company or business person involved in developing land 2 a chemical used for developing films and photographs

developing country *noun*
a country which is quite poor and needs to build more roads, houses, hospitals and so on

development *noun*
1 something that changes things in a particular situation: *There have been no developments since you phoned me.* 2 building houses, factories and so on: *There's been a lot of development in this area* 3 an area of new houses, factories and so on: *a luxury development consisting of thirty houses*

deviate (*say* **dee**-vi-ate) *verb*
to change from the usual route or way of doing something: *The bus deviated from its usual route.*
• ***Word Family:*** **deviant** *adjective* different from what is usual or accepted **deviant** *noun* someone who behaves wrongly

device (*say* de-**vice**) *noun*
1 a mechanical tool: *a device for slicing vegetables* 2 **to leave someone to their own devices** to let someone get on with something, without giving them any help or advice

devil *noun*
1 **the Devil** Satan, the chief spirit of evil opposed to God 2 a very evil person 3 an unlucky or unfortunate person: *Poor devil!*
• ***Word Family:*** **devilish** *adjective* **devilishly** *adverb* **devilment** *noun* **devilry** *noun*

devious (*say* **dee**-vi-us) *adjective*
1 tricky or dishonest: *I think he makes his money in devious ways.* 2 not straight or direct: *to come by a devious route*
• ***Word Family:*** **deviously** *adverb* **deviousness** *noun*

devise (*say* de-**vize**) *verb*
to make or think up something: *to devise a scheme for making money*

devolution (*say* de-vo-**loo**-shun) *noun*
handing power over from the central government to local government: *devolution for Scotland*

A B C D E F G H I J K L M N O P Q R S T U V W X Y Z

devote (*say* de-**vote**) *verb*
to spend all your time or energy on something or someone: *to devote his time to reading / to devote herself to her mother*
• ***Word Family:*** **devoted** *adjective: a devoted grandparent* **devotee** *noun: a devotee of football* **devotion** *noun*

devour (*say* de-**vow**-a) *verb*
to eat or swallow something greedily: *The lion devoured its kill.*

devout *adjective*
devoted to your religion: *a devout Catholic*
• ***Word Family:*** **devoutly** *adverb* **devoutness** *noun*

dew *noun*
small drops of water that form on the ground and on other cool outdoor surfaces during the night
• ***Word Family:*** **dewy** *adjective* **(dewier, dewiest)**

dexterity (*say* dex-**te**-ri-tee) *noun*
skill or quickness in using your hands or mind
• ***Word Family:*** **dextrous** or **dexterous** *adjective*

dhoti (*say* **doe**-tee) *noun*
a long piece of cloth worn by Hindu men around the lower part of their body
• ***Word Family:*** the plural is **dhotis**

diabetes (*say* die-a-**bee**-teez) *noun*
a disease caused when too much sugar builds up in someone's blood, due to a lack of the hormone insulin
• ***Word Family:*** **diabetic** *noun* someone with diabetes

diagnosis (*say* die-ag-**no**-sis) *noun*
finding out what disease a sick person has by studying the symptoms, signs and results of tests
• ***Word Family:*** the plural is **diagnoses** □ **diagnose** *verb* to make a diagnosis **diagnostic** *adjective*

diagonal (*say* die-**ag**-a-nal) *adjective*
1 having a slanted direction: *a diagonal line*
diagonal *noun*
2 a slanted or sloping line joining two opposite corners of a square or rectangle
• ***Word Family:*** **diagonally** *adverb*

diagram (*say* **die**-a-gram) *noun*
a simple drawing that explains or shows something: *a diagram of how food moves through the body / a diagram of the layout of the theatre*
• ***Word Family:*** **diagrammatic** adjective **diagrammatically** *adverb*

dial *noun*
1 the front part or face of a clock, meter or gauge with numbers for showing the time or a measurement 2 the part of a radio, time switch or heater for tuning or controlling it
dial *verb*
3 to press buttons or turn the numbered circle on a phone in order to call someone: *to dial* 999
• ***Word Family:*** other forms are **dials, dialled, dialling**

dialect (*say* **die**-a-lekt) *noun*
the version of a language spoken in a particular part of a country or by a particular group of people

dialogue (*say* **die**-a-log) *noun*
a conversation, especially one in a play or film

diameter (*say* die-**am**-a-ter) *noun*
1 the straight line across a circle, that passes through its centre 2 the length of this line

*diamond** *noun*
1 a gem made of pure, colourless carbon, which is the hardest known substance in the world 2 the red shape with four sides on some playing cards

diarrhoea (*say* die-a-**ree**-a) *noun*
a stomach illness that makes you want to go to the toilet a lot and makes the waste matter from your bowel too runny
• ***Word Origins:*** from a Greek word meaning "flowing through"

diary (*say* **die**-a-ree) *noun*
1 a book in which you write down what happens to you every day 2 a book for writing down all the things you need to do each day
• ***Word Family:*** the plural is **diaries** □ **diarist** *noun* someone who keeps a diary

dice *noun*
1 a small cube with dots marked on its side, used in some games
dice *verb*
2 to cut something into small pieces: *to dice vegetables*
• ***Word Family:*** strictly speaking, **dice** is the plural form of the noun, while the singular form is **die**

dictate (*say* dik-**tate**) *verb*
1 to read or say something out loud for someone else to write down 2 to command or order people to do things
dictate (*say* **dik**-tate) *noun*
3 an order that must be obeyed
• ***Word Family:*** **dictation** *noun*

dictator *noun*
a ruler with unlimited power, especially one who has taken control by force
• ***Word Family:*** **dictatorial** *adjective* **dictatorially** *adverb* **dictatorship** *noun*

dictionary (*say* **dik**-shon-ree) *noun*
a book which lists words of a language in alphabetical order with their meanings
• ***Word Family:*** the plural is **dictionaries**

didgeridoo (*say* dij-a-ree-**doo**) *noun*
a tube-shaped, Aboriginal wind instrument made of wood

die (1) *verb*
1 to stop living 2 to stop: *The engine died at the traffic lights.* 3 **die down** to become much less or fade away: *The noise died down gradually.* 4 **die out** to disappear from the earth: *Dinosaurs died out millions of years ago.*
• ***Word Family:*** other forms are **dies, died, dying**

die (2) *noun*
1 a tool used for cutting or shaping metal 2 a dice 3 **the die is cast** the decision or situation cannot be changed

diesel engine (*say* **dee**-zel) *noun*
an engine which burns oil instead of petrol and has no spark plugs
• ***Word Origins:*** invented by R. *Diesel*, a German engineer, who lived from 1858 to 1913

diet (1) (*say* **die**-ut) *noun*
1 the food that you usually eat 2 specially chosen food to cure disease or keep your weight steady: *a low-fat diet*
diet *verb*
3 to eat food specially chosen to help you lose weight or get healthy
• ***Word Family:*** other verb forms are **diets, dieted, dieting** □ **dietician** *noun* someone trained to plan balanced diets **dietary** *adjective*
• ***Word Origins:*** a Greek word meaning "a way of life"

diet (2) (*say* **die**-ut) *noun*
a formal congress of the states of an empire, to discuss or carry out its business

differ *verb*
1 to be different from someone or something else: *He and his brother differ in many ways.* 2 to disagree: *We differed about which film to see.*

difference *noun*
1 the way in which people or things are unlike each other: *The differences between us do not stop us being good friends.* 2 an argument or disagreement 3 the amount by which one number is greater or less than another: *The difference between 10 and 6 is 4.*

different *adjective*
1 not alike 2 separate: *We rang on three different occasions.* 3 unusual: *Let's do something different today.*
• ***Word Family:*** **differently** *adverb*

difficult *adjective*
1 hard to do or understand: *a difficult task / a difficult problem* 2 being hard to please or get along with: *a difficult child*
• ***Word Family:*** **difficulty** *noun* (**difficulties**)

diffuse (*say* dif-**yooz**) *verb*
1 to spread out and mix with everything else: *The gas from the broken container diffused into the air.*
• ***Word Family:*** **diffusion** *noun*

dig *verb*
1 to break up, remove or turn over earth with a spade or similar tool 2 to make something in this way: *to dig a hole / to dig a flower bed* 3 to poke someone: *to dig someone in the ribs*
dig *noun*
4 a poke 5 a place where archaeologists are digging to uncover things that are buried in the ground 6 a sly remark
• ***Word Family:*** other verb forms are **digs, dug, digging**

digest (*say* die-**jest**) *verb*
1 to break food down in your stomach and intestines so that it can be absorbed into your body: *to digest food* 2 to take in and understand what you have been told: *The judge had to digest all the facts before making a decision.*
digest (*say* **die**-jest) *noun*
3 a shortened version of a book, report or article
• ***Word Family:*** **digestion** *noun* the function or process of digesting food **digestible** *adjective* **digestive** *adjective*

digger *noun*
1 someone who digs, especially for gold 2 an Australian or New Zealand soldier, usually from World War I

diggings *plural noun*
a place, such as a mine or excavation, where people dig

digit (*say* **dij**-it) *noun*
1 a finger or toe 2 a number between 0 and 9 in the Arabic counting system
• ***Word Family:*** **digitize** or **digitise** *verb* to change pictures, sounds and so on into numbers so that you can store them as information on a computer

digital (*say* **dij**-i-tal) *adjective*
1 storing information in the form of numbers like a computer: *digital stereo / a digital camera* 2 using numbers rather than a pointer to display information: *a digital watch*
• ***Word Family:*** **digitally** *adverb*

digital computer *noun*
a computer that uses data or information represented by numbers

dignitary (*say* **dig**-na-tree) *noun*
someone of high rank or great importance in the church or in government
• ***Word Family:*** the plural is **dignitaries**

dignity *noun*
a noble or serious quality in someone's character

or manner that makes others respect them: *She received her award for bravery with great dignity.*

dilapidated (*say* de-**lap**-i-day-ted) *adjective*
in ruins: *a dilapidated old house*
•***Word Family:*** **dilapidation** *noun*

dilate (*say* die-**late**) *verb*
to make or become larger or wider, especially the pupils of your eyes
•***Word Family:*** **dilated** *adjective: dilated pupils*

dilemma *noun*
a situation requiring you to choose between difficult or unpleasant alternatives: *I'm in a dilemma because going on holidays means I miss the rock concert.*

diligent (*say* **dil**-i-jent) *adjective*
careful and hard-working: *a diligent student*
•***Word Family:*** **diligence** *noun* **diligently** *adverb*

dill *noun*
a herb whose seeds and leaves are used in medicine and for cooking or pickling food

dilute (*say* die-**loot**) *verb*
to make a liquid weaker or thinner, by adding water: *to dilute orange squash*
•***Word Family:*** **dilute** *adjective* **dilution** *noun*

dim *adjective*
1 faint or unclear: *a dim light / a dim cellar*
2 stupid: *He's really dim.*
dim *verb*
3 to make something less bright: *to dim the lights*
•***Word Family:*** other adjective forms are **dimmer, dimmest** □ other verb forms are **dims, dimmed, dimming** □ **dimmer** *noun: a dimmer for lights* **dimly** *adverb* **dimness** *noun*

dimension (*say* de-**men**-shon) *noun*
the size of something, especially its length, width or height

diminish *verb*
to make or become smaller: *Drought diminished the country's food supply. / His fame diminished as he got older.*
•***Word Family:*** **diminution** *noun* the process of diminishing

diminuendo (*say* dim-in-yoo-**en**-doh) *adverb*
gradually lessening in strength or loudness

diminutive (*say* di-**min**-yoo-tiv) *adjective*
1 very small
diminutive *noun*
2 a word that shows you that something is smaller than usual: *"Piglet" is the diminutive of "pig".*

dimple *noun*
a small hollow or fold, usually in your cheek

dim sum *noun*
small dumplings in Chinese cooking, filled with savoury or sweet fillings and prepared by steaming or frying

din *noun*
a loud noise: *Will that awful din never end?*

dine *verb*
to eat a meal, especially the main meal of the day
•***Word Family:*** **diner** *noun* a railway dining car or a roadside snack-bar

dinghy (*say* **ding**-gee) *noun*
a small boat that you can row or sail
•***Word Family:*** the plural is **dinghies**

dingo *noun*
an Australian wild dog with sandy-coloured fur, pointed ears and a bushy tail
•***Word Family:*** the plural is **dingoes**
•***Word Origins:*** from an Aboriginal language

dingy (*say* **din**-jee) *adjective*
dark, dull or shabby: *a dingy shack with damp, peeling walls*
•***Word Family:*** other forms are **dingier, dingiest** □ **dinginess** *noun*

dinkum *adjective*
1 true or honest: *a dinkum Aussie*
dinkum *adverb*
2 honestly or truly

dinner *noun*
1 the main meal of the day, eaten at midday or in the evening 2 a formal meal: *a dinner in honour of the president*

dinosaur (*say* **die**-na-sor) *noun*
one of a group of huge reptiles, the largest land animals ever known, that lived millions of years ago
•***Word Origins:*** from Greek words meaning "terrible lizard"

diocese (*say* **die**-a-sis) *noun*
a district under the religious control of a bishop or archbishop
•***Word Family:*** **diocesan** *adjective: a diocesan newspaper*

diode (*say* **die**-ode) *noun*
a small electronic part that allows current to pass in only one direction, used in many electronic devices

diorama *noun*
a miniature scene with modelled, painted figures and a painted background
•***Word Family:*** **dioramic** *adjective*

dip *verb*
1 to put or lower something briefly into a liquid: *to dip fish in batter* 2 to drop or point something downwards: *He dipped his headlights.*

dip *noun*
3 anything into which you dip something: *a sheep dip / a savoury dip for biscuits* 4 a plunge or swim: *a dip in the sea* 5 a downward slope or movement: *a dip in the road*
•***Word Family:*** other verb forms are **dips, dipped, dipping** □ **dipper** *noun*

diphtheria (*say* dif-**thear**-ree-a) *noun*
a serious infectious disease causing a high fever and making your throat so swollen that swallowing and breathing is difficult

diphthong (*say* **dif**-thong) *noun*
a sound made when a speaker's tongue slides smoothly from one vowel sound to another in the same syllable, such as *oy* in *boy* or *ue* in *fuel*

diploma (*say* di-**plo**-ma) *noun*
a certificate awarded when a student finishes a particular course of study: *a teaching diploma*

diplomacy (*say* di-**ploh**-ma-see) *noun*
skill in keeping friendly with other countries and people: *The Australian ambassador's diplomacy in Japan helped trade relations between the two nations.*
•***Word Family:*** **diplomat** *noun* someone employed or skilled in diplomacy **diplomatic** *adjective*

dire *adjective*
very serious or disastrous: *in dire need of medical treatment / dire consequences*

direct *verb*
1 to guide or control the way something is done: *Who directed the film "ET"?* 2 to show someone the way to somewhere
direct *adjective*
3 straight or uninterrupted: *a direct flight to Spain / a direct hit* 4 exact or absolute: *a direct quote from a play / the direct opposite*
•***Word Family:*** **directly** *adverb* without delay **directness** *noun* □ see also **director**

direction (*say* di-**rek**-shon) *noun*
1 guidance or control: *He acted under the direction of his boss.* 2 the point or position that something faces or moves towards: *He drove off in the direction of the city.* 3 information about how to get to a particular place or how to do something: *We need directions to the zoo.*

director *noun*
1 a person who manages a company: *the managing director / the board of directors* 2 a person who controls how a film is made or how a play is performed

directory *noun*
a book with an alphabetical list of names, subjects or numbers: *a street directory / a telephone directory*
•***Word Family:*** the plural is **directories**

dirt *noun*
1 something which is unclean: *Please wash that dirt off your hands before you have lunch.* 2 earth or soil: *He dug in the dirt.*
dirt *adjective*
3 made of earth: *a dirt road into the rainforest*
•***Word Family:*** **dirty** *adjective* (**dirtier, dirtiest**) covered with dirt **dirtiness** *noun*

disability (*say* dis-a-**bil**-i-tee) *noun*
a lack of ability to do things that most people can do: *She has a serious reading disability.*
•***Word Family:*** the plural is **disabilities**

disable (*say* dis-**ay**-bul) *verb*
to take away or destroy the ability or power of something: *Strong winds disabled the yacht so that its sails could not be used.*

disabled *adjective*
having an injury or illness which makes it difficult to move around or do things as easily as other people

disadvantage (*say* dis-ad-**vahn**-tij) *noun*
1 something that makes things more difficult for you: *The speaker's soft voice was a disadvantage in the large hall.*
disadvantage *verb*
2 to make things more difficult for someone: *Lack of cheap housing disadvantages poor families.*

disagree (*say* dis-a-**gree**) *verb*
1 to have a different opinion or view: *I disagree with what you just said.* 2 **disagree with** to make you feel unwell: *Rich food disagrees with me.*
•***Word Family:*** other forms are **disagrees, disagreed, disagreeing** □ **disagreement** *noun* an argument

disagreeable *adjective*
unpleasant or offensive: *a disagreeable job*
•***Word Family:*** **disagreeably** *adverb*

disappear *verb*
1 to go out of sight or get lost: *My gloves have disappeared from the table.* 2 to stop happening or existing: *My cough has disappeared.*
•***Word Family:*** **disappearance** *noun*

disappoint *verb*
1 to fail to live up to someone's hopes or expectations: *The new movie disappointed me.* 2 to make someone unhappy: *We were disappointed that you couldn't come.*
•***Word Family:*** **disappointment** *noun*

disapprove (*say* dis-a-**proov**) *verb*
to dislike someone or something, or have a poor opinion of them: *The family disapproves of his new friends.*
•***Word Family:*** **disapproval** *noun*: *to look at someone with disapproval* **disapproving** *adjective* **disapprovingly** *adverb*

A B C D E F G H I J K L M N O P Q R S T U V W X Y Z

disarm *verb*
1 to take away weapons from someone: *The police disarmed the two men.* 2 to overcome someone's suspicion or anger: *Her frankness in chatting about her drug problem disarmed the reporters.*
• ***Word Family:*** **disarmament** *noun* the reduction or disbanding of a country's weapons and armed forces **disarming** *adjective* tending to charm or win over **disarmingly** *adverb*

disaster (*say* di-**zah**-sta) *noun*
a sudden shocking accident or event that causes great grief and suffering: *The train disaster killed one hundred passengers.*
• ***Word Family:*** **disastrous** *adjective* causing ruin or disaster
• ***Word Origins:*** from Italian words meaning "not having a lucky star"

disbelief *noun*
a refusal or inability to believe someone or something: *We stared at her with disbelief.*
• ***Word Family:*** **disbelieve** *verb*

disc *noun*
a flat, round object 2 a gramophone record 3 a flat, round piece of plastic that holds sound, pictures or other information, such as a compact disc 4 a computer disk

discard *verb*
to put or throw something away: *We discard all bruised or damaged fruit before cooking.*

discern (*say* dis-**sern**) *verb*
to be able to see or recognize something clearly: *She discerned from our silence that we were angry.*
• ***Word Family:*** **discernible** *adjective* able to be seen or recognized **discerning** *adjective* able to judge or see clearly **discernment** *noun*

discharge (*say* dis-**charj**) *verb*
1 to officially release someone or let them out of where they are being kept: *to be discharged from hospital* 2 to send out something or release it, especially something unpleasant: *The waste is discharged into the sea. / lorries discharging clouds of black smoke* 3 to dismiss someone from a job: *The company discharged the driver for stealing.*
discharge (*say* **dis**-charj) *noun*
4 something which is discharged: *a yellow discharge from a wound*

disciple (*say* de-**sigh**-pul) *noun*
a follower, companion or student: *the disciples of Christ / a disciple of the Green movement*
• ***Word Family:*** **discipleship** *noun*
• ***Word Origins:*** from a Latin word meaning "a learner"

discipline (*say* **dis**-a-plin) *noun*
1 training or rules to make people do what they're told or what they ought to do 2 the control a person has over the way he or she behaves: *I practise for an hour a day now that I've learnt some discipline.* 3 punishment
discipline *verb*
4 to punish someone
• ***Word Family:*** **disciplinarian** *noun* someone who uses or encourages discipline **disciplinary** *adjective*: *to take disciplinary measures*

disclose *verb*
to reveal something or allow it to be seen or known by other people: *The solicitor disclosed the contents of the will.*
• ***Word Family:*** **disclosure** *noun*

disco *noun*
1 a club or similar place for dancing, usually to records or taped music 2 the type of music played in discos
• ***Word Family:*** the plural is **discos**

discomfort (*say* dis-**kum**-fut) *noun*
1 a lack of comfort or peace: *The crowded bus caused them great discomfort.* 2 embarrassment and uneasiness: *I shifted about with discomfort when the teacher called me.*

disconcert (*say* dis-kon-**sert**) *verb*
to upset someone or make them feel embarrassed: *His stare disconcerted her.*
• ***Word Family:*** **disconcerted** *adjective* **disconcerting** *adjective* **disconcertingly** *adverb*

disconnect *verb*
1 to take something apart or detach it: *to disconnect the vacuum cleaner hose* 2 to cut off the telephone or the electricity, gas or water supply: *They'll disconnect us if we don't pay the electricity bill.*
• ***Word Family:*** **disconnected** *adjective*

discontent *noun*
unhappiness about your life or things around you
• ***Word Family:*** **discontented** *adjective* **discontentedly** *adverb* **discontentment** *noun*

discord *noun*
1 a disagreement or difference of opinion 2 a group of musical notes played together, that have a harsh sound
• ***Word Family:*** **discordant** *adjective*: *Their discordant opinions lead to many arguments.*

discotheque (*say* **dis**-ko-tek) *noun*
a place for dancing, usually with records or taped music
• ***Word Origins:*** a French word meaning "record library"

discount (*say* **dis**-count) *noun*
1 a reduction or lessening in price: *a 40% discount / We give a discount for cash purchases.*

discount (*say* dis-**count**) *verb*
2 to reduce the price of something, often by a set amount or percentage: *The store discounted last season's clothes in the sale.* 3 to ignore something or refuse to believe it: *Please discount all the stories that you hear about him.*

discourage (*say* dis-**kur**-ij) *verb*
1 to take away someone's hope or confidence: *Their constant criticism discourages me.* 2 to try to prevent something or make it less likely to happen: *to discourage rust by using a special paint*
•*Word Family:* **discouragement** *noun* **discouraging** *adjective* **discouragingly** *adverb*

discover *verb*
1 to find out or realize something: *to discover a new way of solving a problem* 2 to find something: *Who discovered America?*
•*Word Family:* **discovery** *noun* (**discoveries**)

discredit *verb*
1 to destroy people's confidence in someone or something: *The fact that he stole the money discredited him.* 2 to cause someone or something to be doubted or not believed: *to discredit a scientist's theory*
•*Word Family:* **discreditable** *adjective*

discreet *adjective*
1 tactful and careful to avoid making mistakes or embarrassing people: *discreet comments* 2 able to keep secrets: *You can trust her, she's very discreet.*
•*Word Family:* **discreetly** *adverb* **discreetness** *noun*

discrepancy (*say* dis-**krep**-an-see) *noun*
a difference between things you would expect to be similar: *Did you notice the discrepancy between what we ate and the final bill?*
•*Word Family:* the plural is **discrepancies**

discrete *adjective*
separate: *The hall was divided into discrete offices.*
•*Word Family:* **discretely** *adverb*

discretion (*say* dis-**kresh**-un) *noun*
1 the ability to be discreet or tactful: *Please use your discretion in this delicate matter.* 2 the freedom to act or decide for yourself: *Just use your discretion.*
•*Word Family:* **discretionary** *adjective* allowed or not allowed depending on the situation: *a discretionary grant*

discriminate (*say* dis-**krim**-i-nate) *verb*
1 to notice a difference: *to discriminate between the taste of two different brands of orange juice*
2 **discriminate against** to treat someone badly or unfairly because their sex, race or religion is different to yours: *That company still discriminates against women.*
•*Word Family:* **discriminating** *adjective* showing good taste or judgment **discrimination** *noun* **discriminatory** *adjective* unfair

discus (*say* **dis**-kus) *noun*
a heavy round plate or disc you throw as far as you can in an athletic competition
•*Word Family:* the plural is **discuses**

discuss (*say* dis-**kus**) *verb*
to all speak about a particular thing together and say what you think
•*Word Family:* **discussion** *noun* a talk to exchange opinions or views

disease (*say* diz-**eez**) *noun*
an illness or sickness
•*Word Family:* **diseased** *adjective* affected by disease

disembark (*say* dis-em-**bark**) *verb*
to go ashore from a ship or plane
•*Word Family:* **disembarkation** *noun*

disfigure (*say* dis-**fig**-a) *verb*
to spoil the appearance of someone or something: *Burns disfigured his hands. / Vandals had disfigured the sculpture.*
•*Word Family:* **disfigurement** *noun*

disgrace *noun*
1 shame 2 something that is shameful or causes disgrace: *This room is an absolute disgrace!*
3 **in disgrace** regarded with disapproval: *You are in disgrace for telling such a lie.*
disgrace *verb*
4 to bring shame to someone or the place they come from: *Bad conduct on the bus disgraces your school.*
•*Word Family:* **disgraceful** *adjective* **disgracefully** *adverb*

disgruntled *adjective*
displeased or in a bad mood: *He was disgruntled at being woken up.*

disguise (*say* dis-**gize**) *verb*
1 to change the appearance of something in order to conceal its identity: *to disguise yourself as a tramp*
disguise *noun*
2 the clothes you put on or the changes you make to do this: *This red wig is part of my disguise.*

disgust *noun*
1 a strong feeling of dislike: *Watching violent movies fills me with disgust.*
disgust *verb*
2 to cause strong dislike in someone: *Cruelty to animals disgusts me.*
•*Word Family:* **disgusting** *adjective: a disgusting smell* **disgustingly** *adverb*

a b c d e f g h i j k l m n o p q r s t u v w x y z

A B C D E F G H I J K L M N O P Q R S T U V W X Y Z

dish *noun*
1 a shallow container with a flat bottom, from which food may be served or eaten 2 a particular kind of food or way of preparing it: *Roast chicken is my favourite dish.*
dish *verb*
3 **dish out** or **dish up** to serve food to people: *to dish out the pasta*
•***Word Family:*** the plural of the noun is **dishes**

dishevelled (*say* dish-**ev**-uld) *adjective*
untidy in the way you look: *dishevelled hair / dishevelled clothes*
•***Word Family:*** **dishevel** *verb* (**dishevels, dishevelled, dishevelling**)

dishonest (*say* dis-**on**-ist) *adjective*
not honest or truthful: *a dishonest person / a dishonest act*
•***Word Family:*** **dishonestly** *adverb* **dishonesty** *noun*

dishonour or **dishonor** (*say* dis-**on**-a) *noun*
1 shame or disgrace: *His crime brought dishonour upon his family.* 2 a lack of respect: *Their remarks show dishonour to their country.*
dishonour *verb*
3 to bring dishonour on or to someone or something
•***Word Family:*** **dishonourable** *adjective* **dishonourably** *adverb*

disinfect *verb*
to clean something or somewhere in order to kill all the germs: *to disinfect the toilet*
•***Word Family:*** **disinfectant** *noun* a chemical that destroys germs

disintegrate (*say* dis-**in**-ti-grate) *verb*
to break into small pieces: *The vase disintegrated when it fell onto the floor.*
•***Word Family:*** **disintegration** *noun*

disinterested *adjective*
not involved in what's going on, and so not biased: *a disinterested onlooker / a disinterested judge*
•***Word Family:*** **disinterest** *noun* **disinterestedly** *adverb*

disjointed *adjective*
not connected or fitting together properly: *a disjointed account of the accident*

disk *noun*
a thin round object used for storing computer data or programs. A *floppy disk* is made of plastic and comes in a flat square case; a *hard disk* is inside a computer and is made of metal
•***Word Family:*** another spelling is **disc**

dislocate (*say* **dis**-la-kate) *verb*
to put one of your bones or joints out of its proper place: *to dislocate your elbow*
•***Word Family:*** **dislocation** *noun*

dislodge *verb*
to make something move from its place: *His coughing dislodged the fish bone in his throat.*

dismal (*say* **diz**-mal) *adjective*
sad or gloomy: *dismal news / dismal weather*
•***Word Family:*** **dismally** *adverb*
•***Word Origins:*** from Latin words meaning "unlucky days"

dismantle *verb*
to take something to pieces: *to dismantle an engine*

dismay *noun*
1 a feeling of worry, alarm or discouragement
dismay *verb*
2 to fill with dismay

dismiss *verb*
1 to send someone away or allow them to leave: *to dismiss a class* 2 to remove or reject someone or something: *to dismiss someone from a job / to dismiss an idea as silly* 3 to get someone out in cricket: *Our fast bowler dismissed the first batsman.*
•***Word Family:*** **dismissal** *noun* **dismissive** *adjective*

dismount *verb*
to get down off something you are riding, such as a horse or motorbike

disobey (*say* dis-o-**bay**) *verb*
to fail or refuse to do what you are told: *to disobey your parents / to disobey an order*
•***Word Family:*** **disobedient** *adjective*: *a disobedient dog* **disobedience** *noun*

disorder *noun*
1 untidiness or lack of order: *After the party our house was in complete disorder.* 2 an illness: *a stomach disorder* 3 rioting in the streets: *Troops were called in to put down the disorder in the capital.*
•***Word Family:*** **disordered** *adjective* **disorderly** *adverb*

disorganized or **disorganised** *adjective*
confused or lacking in organization: *disorganized behaviour in the streets / a disorganized piece of writing*

dispatch *verb*
1 to send something off: *to dispatch an urgent telegram* 2 to kill someone: *The gladiator quickly dispatched his opponent.*
dispatch *noun*
3 a story sent in to a newspaper or magazine by a reporter based overseas
•***Word Family:*** the plural of the noun is **dispatches**

dispel (*say* dis-**pel**) *verb*
to drive away fear, doubt and so on: *The bright sunshine dispelled all fears of rain.*
•***Word Family:*** other forms are **dispels, dispelled, dispelling**

dispensary (*say* dis-**pens**-a-ree) *noun*
the place in a hospital or chemist's shop where medicine is given out
• ***Word Family:*** the plural is **dispensaries**

dispense *verb*
1 to give something out: *to dispense food and medicine to refugees* 2 to mix, measure and give out medicine: *The chemist dispenses medicine on prescription.* 3 **dispense with** to do without or get rid of someone or something
• ***Word Family:*** **dispensable** *adjective* able to be done without **dispenser** *noun* a device for dispensing something: *a soap dispenser* **dispensation** *noun*

disperse *verb*
1 to scatter: *The demonstrators dispersed when the police arrived.* 2 to drive away something: *The wind dispersed the morning mists.*
• ***Word Family:*** **dispersal** *noun* **dispersion** *noun*

displace *verb*
1 to put someone or something out of their usual place: *to displace your hip* 2 to take the place of: *Bob has displaced Rick in Cathy's affections.*
• ***Word Family:*** **displacement** *noun*

display *verb*
1 to show or arrange something: *to display fear / to display goods in a shop window*
display *noun*
2 a show: *a breathtaking display of diving*
3 information shown on something such as a computer screen

displease *verb*
to offend or annoy someone: *Her constant lateness displeased them.*
• ***Word Family:*** **displeasing** *adjective* **displeasure** *noun*

disposable *adjective*
meant to be thrown away after being used only once: *disposable nappies*

disposal *noun*
1 getting rid of something: *a waste disposal pipe*
2 **at your disposal** ready for you whenever you want: *A company car is at your disposal.*

dispose *verb*
1 to make someone willing to do a particular thing: *The offer of higher pay disposed her to accept the job.* 2 to make someone or something able to be more easily affected by a particular problem: *His weak heart disposes him to illness.*
3 **dispose of** to get rid of something: *to dispose of your old clothes*

disposition (*say* dis-pa-**zish**-on) *noun*
your natural way of acting or thinking: *She has a cheerful disposition.*

dispute *verb*
1 to argue or debate 2 to question the truth of something: *He disputed her account of the incident. / to dispute a claim for insurance money*
dispute *noun*
3 an argument

disqualify (*say* dis-**kwol**-if-eye) *verb*
1 to remove someone from a competition, for example for cheating 2 to make someone unsuitable for or unable to do something: *His weak heart disqualified him from serving in the army.*
• ***Word Family:*** other forms are **disqualifies, disqualified, disqualifying** □ **disqualification** *noun*

disrupt *verb*
to break something up or stop it running smoothly: *The hecklers succeeded in disrupting the meeting.*
• ***Word Family:*** **disruptive** *adjective* **disruption** *noun*

dissect *verb*
to cut something up in order to examine it: *to dissect a rat*
• ***Word Family:*** **dissection** *noun*

dissent *verb*
to differ from other people in your opinion: *He dissented again when we decided to watch the football.*
• ***Word Family:*** **dissent** *noun* difference of opinion **dissenter** *noun* someone who dissents **dissenting** *adjective*

dissipate (*say* **dis**-i-pate) *verb*
1 to disappear without a trace: *By mid-morning the fog had dissipated.* 2 to waste foolishly or fritter away: *to dissipate your energy by worrying for no reason*
• ***Word Family:*** **dissipation** *noun*

dissolute (*say* **dis**-a-loot) *adjective*
behaving in a self-indulgent and immoral way
• ***Word Family:*** **dissolutely** *adverb* **dissoluteness** *noun*

dissolve (*say* di-**zolv**) *verb*
1 to mix or become mixed with a liquid: *First dissolve the sugar in the milk. / Sugar dissolves in coffee.* 2 to bring to or come to an end: *to dissolve a marriage / to dissolve parliament*
• ***Word Family:*** **dissolution** *noun*: *The President ordered the dissolution of parliament so that an election could be held.*

dissonance *noun*
1 a sound that is unpleasant and grating 2 a group of musical notes that sound harsh when played together
• ***Word Family:*** **dissonant** *adjective*

dissuade *verb*
to persuade someone not to do something

distance *noun*
1 the amount of space between two points or things: *the distance from London to Liverpool is about 300 km* 2 a long way away: *The city looked quite pleasant from a distance.*
distance *verb*
3 to try to have as little as possible to do with someone or the things they say: *The Prime Minister was quick to distance himself from this disagreement.*

distant *adjective*
far away: *a distant star / the distant past / a distant relative*
•***Word Family:*** **distantly** *adverb*

distemper *noun*
an easily spread disease in young dogs, that causes coughing and sometimes death

distend *verb*
to make something expand or swell: *Overeating distended their bellies.*
•***Word Family:*** **distended** *adjective*

distil (*say* dis-**til**) *verb*
1 to make something pure by heating, evaporating and cooling: *to distil water* 2 to separate substances in this way: *to distil petrol from crude oil*
•***Word Family:*** other forms are **distils, distilled, distilling** □ **distillery** *noun* (**distilleries**) a place for making whisky or other alcoholic spirits by distilling **distillation** *noun*
•***Word Origins:*** from a Latin word meaning "to drip down"

distinct *adjective*
1 plain or clear: *Everything looks more distinct when I wear my glasses.* 2 definite: *She showed a distinct improvement in her work.* 3 different or separate: *two distinct species of animal*
•***Word Family:*** **distinctive** *adjective* easy to recognize or notice: *a distinctive accent / a distinctive uniform* **distinctly** *adverb* **distinctness** *noun*

distinction *noun*
1 a difference: *to make a distinction between two different shades of green* 2 great worth or quality: *a car of distinction* 3 an award: *a distinction for athletics*

distinguish *verb*
1 to recognize two things as being different or separate: *to distinguish butter from margarine* 2 to hear or see something clearly: *to distinguish the actor's words from the back of the theatre* 3 to make a particular person famous: *to distinguish yourself as a sporting hero*
•***Word Family:*** **distinguished** *adjective* famous or well-known

distort *verb*
1 to pull or twist something out of its usual shape: *Her face distorted with rage.* 2 to change something so that it becomes incorrect or misleading: *to distort the truth*
•***Word Family:*** **distorted** *adjective* **distortion** *noun*

distract *verb*
to stop someone from concentrating, or make them concentrate on something else: *The radio distracts me from my homework.*
•***Word Family:*** **distracted** *adjective* confused or troubled **distraction** *noun* something that distracts you **distractedly** *adverb*

distress *noun*
1 great suffering or trouble 2 serious difficulty or danger: *We picked up the radio signals of a ship in distress.*
distress *verb*
3 to cause distress to: *His suspension from school distressed his parents.*
•***Word Family:*** **distressful** *adjective* **distressing** *adjective* **distressingly** *adverb*

distribute (*say* dis-**trib**-yoot) *verb*
1 to divide things and share them out: *to distribute blankets to the homeless* 2 to spread something out: *to distribute flea powder all over the dog* 3 to deliver things or hand them out: *to distribute leaflets*
•***Word Family:*** **distribution** *noun: the distribution of presents / the distribution of plants in an area*

district *noun*
an area or region: *the business district of a city / a postal district*

distrust *verb*
to not trust someone or something
•***Word Family:*** **distrust** *noun* a lack of trust

disturb *verb*
1 to destroy someone's peace or rest: *The noise of screeching cats disturbed our sleep. / Does the noise from the TV disturb you?* 2 to put things out of order or interfere with them: *Who disturbed the papers on my desk?*
•***Word Family:*** **disturbing** *adjective* upsetting **disturbance** *noun* **disturbingly** *adverb*

disuse (*say* dis-**yoos**) *noun*
lack of use: *The door latch fell into disuse and rusted when the owner died.*
•***Word Family:*** **disused** *adjective*

ditch *noun*
1 a long narrow trench dug in the earth, usually to drain away water

ditch *verb*
2 to get rid of someone or something quickly: *to ditch a stolen car*
• ***Word Family:*** the plural of the noun is **ditches**

dither (*say* **didh**-a) *verb*
to fuss about: *He dithered about which way to go.*

ditto marks *plural noun*
marks (") used in writing or printing lists, and so on to show that you are repeating the word or words used above

dive *verb*
1 to jump headfirst into the water 2 to go deep under water: *to dive for pearls* 3 to drop sharply: *Gold prices have dived.* 4 to leap: *to dive into the bushes*
dive *noun*
5 a jump downwards, especially into water
• ***Word Family:*** **diver** *noun* **diving** *noun*

diver *noun*
1 a swimmer who dives into water 2 a person who works underwater and wears a diving suit 3 a bird which catches fish by diving for them

diverge *verb*
to branch off in different directions: *The road and railway line diverge at the bottom of the hill.*
• ***Word Family:*** **divergence** *noun* **divergent** *adjective*

diverse *adjective*
having different kinds or forms: *The kids in my class come from diverse backgrounds.*
• ***Word Family:*** **diversely** *adverb* **diversify** *verb* **diversity** *noun*

divert *verb*
1 to change direction, or make something change direction: *to divert traffic* 2 to amuse or entertain someone
• ***Word Family:*** **diversion** *noun*

divide *verb*
1 to separate something into parts or share it: *to divide a cake between four people / to divide sweets equally* 2 to disagree: *We remain divided over the issue.* 3 to calculate how many times one number contains another: *12 divided by 4 is 3*
• ***Word Family:*** **divisible** *adjective* able to be divided: *21 is divisible by 7 and 3* **divisive** *adjective* causing disagreement among people who usually agree

dividend (*say* **div**-i-dend) *noun*
1 the number to be divided by another number: *If we divide 20 by 5, 20 is the dividend.* 2 a share of something that has been divided, such as money paid to shareholders from a company's profits

divine (*say* de-**vine**) *adjective*
1 to do with God 2 sacred: *the divine sacrament of communion* 3 excellent: *What a divine meal!*
divine *verb*
4 to learn or discover something by guessing, inspiration or magic: *to divine what will happen in the future*
• ***Word Family:*** **divination** *noun* the telling of future events **divinely** *adverb*

divinity (*say* di-**vin**-i-tee) *noun*
1 a god, goddess or other divine being 2 the study of religion or scriptures
• ***Word Family:*** the plural for definition 1 is **divinities**

division *noun*
1 the process of dividing one number by another in maths 2 a separation into parts: *the division of the class into reading groups* 3 a department of a large organization: *He was sent to the spare parts division. / an army division*
• ***Word Family:*** **divisional** *adjective*

divisor (*say* di-**vie**-zor) *noun*
the number by which another number is to be divided: *If we divide 20 by 5, 5 is the divisor.*

divorce *noun*
1 the official ending of a marriage by a law court
divorce *verb*
2 to officially end your marriage to someone
• ***Word Family:*** **divorcee** *noun* someone who is divorced

divulge (*say* die-**vulj**) *verb*
to reveal: *He refused to divulge information to the press.*
• ***Word Family:*** **divulgence** *noun*

Diwali (*say* dih-**wah**-lee) *noun*
a Hindu festival held in October or November, over the Hindu New Year

dizzy *adjective*
having or causing a feeling of spinning or giddiness: *to experience a dizzy spell / to watch from a dizzy height*
• ***Word Family:*** other forms are **dizzier, dizziest** □ **dizzily** *adverb* **dizziness** *noun*
• ***Word Origins:*** from an Old English word meaning "silly"

DJ *noun*
someone who plays records in a club or on the radio
• ***Word Origins:*** from the initials of disc jockey

do *verb*
1 to perform or finish: *She still hasn't done her homework.* 2 to attend to: *to do the dishes / to do your teeth / to do the flowers for the wedding* 3 to cause: *His attitude can do harm.* 4 to travel at: *The car will do 200 km per hour.* 5 to study: My

A B C D E F G H I J K L M N O P Q R S T U V W X Y Z

sister does French at school. 6 to be good enough for: *This dress will do me.* 7 to work at: *What will you do when you leave school?*
do *noun*
8 a party or celebration: *Are you going to the do tonight?*
•***Word Family:*** other verb forms are **does, did, done, doing**

dob *verb*
1 **dob on** to inform or report on, usually for doing something bad: *to dob on someone for smoking in the toilets* 2 **dob in** to suggest someone do something, especially something unpleasant: *to dob him in for peeling potatoes*
•***Word Family:*** other forms are **dobs, dobbed, dobbing**

docile (*say* **doe**-sile) *adjective*
easy to control or give orders to: *a docile dog*
•***Word Family:*** **docilely** *adverb* **docility** *noun*

dock (1) *noun*
1 a place with equipment for loading, unloading or repairing ships 2 the place in a building where large trucks can unload
dock *verb*
3 to bring a ship into a dock for repair or loading 4 to join together with another space ship while in orbit: *The rocket docked with the space platform.*
•***Word Family:*** **docker** *noun* someone employed to work on the docks

dock (2) *verb*
1 to cut off part of an animal's tail 2 to take away part of something such as your wages or pocket money: *to dock your allowance as a punishment*

dock (3) *noun*
the place in a courtroom where the person accused of a crime is kept during a trial

docket *noun*
1 a label on a package listing its contents 2 a receipt that shows you have paid for the goods you are carrying

doctor *noun*
1 someone who has studied medicine and is allowed by law to treat sick people and prescribe drugs for them 2 someone who has received the highest university degree, usually after several years of research or study
doctor *verb*
3 to tamper with or alter something: *to doctor his drink*
•***Word Family:*** **doctoral** *adjective: a doctoral student* **doctorate** *noun*
the degree received by a doctor (definition 2)
•***Word Origins:*** from a Latin word meaning "teacher"

doctrine (*say* **dok**-trin) *noun*
something you believe: *a religious doctrine*
•***Word Family:*** **doctrinal** (*say* dok-**try**-nal) *adjective*

document (*say* **dok**-yoo-ment) *noun*
1 a piece of paper with information written or printed on it: *When you apply for a passport you must supply certain documents, including your birth certificate.*
document *verb*
2 to supply someone with or support something using documents: *You need to document your case if you want them to believe you.*
•***Word Family:*** **documentation** *noun*

documentary (*say* dok-yoo-**men**-tree) *noun*
1 a television or radio programme which gives information about real people and events: *a documentary about the police*
documentary *adjective*
2 written or official: *documentary evidence used in court*
•***Word Family:*** the plural of the noun is **documentaries**

dodge *verb*
1 to move aside or change position suddenly, especially to avoid something: *to dodge an oncoming car*
dodge *noun*
2 a cunning trick

dodgem (*say* **doj**-em) *noun*
a small, low-powered, electric car driven in special rinks at amusement parks

doe *noun*
a female deer or rabbit

dog *noun*
1 a four-legged, meat-eating mammal that barks and is often kept as a pet 2 the male of this animal
dog *verb*
3 to follow or chase someone without stopping: *Ill health dogged him through his teenage years.*
•***Word Family:*** other verb forms are **dogs, dogged, dogging** □ **dogged** *adjective* determined to continue **doggedly** *adverb*

dogma *noun*
a strong system of beliefs or principles held by a group of people: *religious dogma / political dogma*
•***Word Family:*** plural is **dogmas** □ **dogmatic** *adjective* stating your opinions in a positive or overbearing way **dogmatism** *noun* **dogmatically** *adverb* **dogmatist** *noun*

doily *noun*
a small, ornamental mat made of paper or lace and placed under a glass or vase on a table or under a cake on a plate

•*Word Family:* the plural is **doilies**
•*Word Origins:* named after *Doily*, a draper living in London in the 1600s

dole *noun*
1 **the dole** the money paid by the government to unemployed people 2 **on the dole** receiving unemployment payment
dole *verb*
3 **dole out** to give something out among a group, especially in small amounts: *to dole out praise / to dole out pizza slices*

doleful *adjective*
sad or full of grief: *The funeral was a doleful affair.*
•*Word Family:* **dolefully** *adverb*

doll *noun*
1 a toy that looks like a person
doll *verb*
2 **doll up** to dress smartly or showily

dollar *noun*
1 the basic unit of money, equal to 100 cents and used in the United States, Australia and certain other countries 2 a coin or banknote worth one dollar
•*Word Origins:* from a German word meaning "a silver coin"

dolphin (*say* **dol**-fin) *noun*
a large intelligent sea mammal with a long nose, similar to whales and porpoises

domain *noun*
1 an area which is ruled or controlled by someone: *That stretch of sea is the domain of pirates.* 2 something that a person is involved in or good at: *The gardening is her domain.*

dome *noun*
a rounded roof like half of a ball: *the dome of a cathedral*
•*Word Family:* **domed** *adjective*

domestic (*say* de-**mes**-tik) *adjective*
1 to do with the home or family: *domestic chores / a domestic argument* 2 tame: *domestic animals* 3 inside your own country, not abroad: *a domestic flight*
domestic *noun*
4 someone employed to do household chores
•*Word Family:* **domestically** *adverb* **domesticate** *verb* to train an animal to live in the home **domesticity** *noun*

dominant *adjective*
1 most powerful or important: *the dominant gorilla in the group* 2 main or major: *the dominant peak in a range of mountains*
•*Word Family:* **dominate** *verb* to control **dominance** *noun* **domination** *noun*

domineering *adjective*
arrogant and bossy
•*Word Family:* **domineer** *verb* **domineeringly** *adverb*

dominion (*say* de-**min**-yon) *noun*
1 the power to govern or control a particular place or area: *to have dominion over a country* 2 the area governed by a person or government: *the dominions of the king*

domino *noun*
a small, flat, oblong piece with spots on one side, used to play a game
•*Word Family:* the plural is **dominoes** and this is also the name of the game

don *verb*
to put on clothing: *to don your coat and hat*
•*Word Family:* other forms are **dons, donned, donning**

donate (*say* doe-**nate**) *verb*
to give a particular amount as a gift: *She donated £100 to the appeal.*
•*Word Family:* **donation** *noun* a gift

donkey *noun*
1 a long-eared mammal that looks a bit like a horse 2 a silly person

donor (*say* **doe**-nor) *noun*
someone who donates something: *a blood donor*

doom *noun*
1 something terrible in the future, especially death and suffering: *A feeling of doom hung over us.*
doom *verb*
2 to condemn a person or place to ruin or destruction: *The city was doomed from the moment they decided to drop the bomb.*
•*Word Family:* **doomed** *adjective*

door *noun*
something that opens or closes across the way in to a room, house or cupboard

dope *noun*
1 an illegal drug, especially marijuana 2 a stupid person 3 secret or private information: *Give us the dope on the meeting.*
dope *verb*
4 to give drugs to a person or animal, especially to make them sleep or to make them run faster in a race: *to dope a racehorse*
•*Word Origins:* from a Dutch word meaning "a sauce"

dormant *adjective*
1 not active, or as if asleep: *Squirrels remain dormant all through the winter.* 2 not erupting: *a dormant volcano*
•*Word Family:* **dormancy** *noun* the state of being dormant

A B C D E F G H I J K L M N O P Q R S T U V W X Y Z

dormitory (*say* **dor**-ma-tree) *noun*
a room or building with enough beds in it for several people to sleep there
•***Word Family:*** the plural is **dormitories**

DOS *noun*
a computer program that controls the way the disk works and what you can do with it
•***Word Origins:*** this word is an acronym from disk operating system

dose *noun*
1 the amount of medicine you are meant to take at one time: *The dose is written on the bottle.* 2 a bit of something you didn't want: *a dose of the flu*
dose *verb*
3 to give medicine to someone: *to dose yourself with antibiotics*
•***Word Family:*** **dosage** *noun* the amount of medicine given
•***Word Origins:*** from a Greek word meaning "a gift"

dossier (*say* **dos**-ee-a) *noun*
a collection of information about a particular person or subject: *The secret service have a dossier on him.*

dote *verb*
dote on to love someone very much: *She dotes on her son and carries his picture everywhere.*
•***Word Family:*** **doting** *adjective* **dotingly** *adverb*

double (*say* **dub**-el) *adjective*
1 twice as big: *a double portion of chips* 2 having two of something: *a double-breasted jacket / a double-barrelled shotgun* 3 made for two people: *a double room / a double bed*
double *noun*
4 an amount or size that is twice as big: *12 is the double of 6.* 5 someone who looks exactly like someone else 6 **on the double** quickly: *Pick them up on the double.*
double *verb*
7 to make or become twice as great: *to double a bet / The cake doubled in size as it rose in the oven.* 8 to bend or fold: *to double up with pain / to double towels as you fold them* 9 to serve or be used in two ways: *He doubles as bass player and pianist in the band.* 10 **double back** to turn and go back in the direction from which you came

double bass *noun*
a very large, low-pitched, stringed instrument you play with a bow
•***Word Family:*** the plural is **double basses**

double click *verb*
to click a computer mouse or trackball button twice quickly and without moving the mouse or trackball, to open a document or work some other feature

double-cross *verb*
to cheat someone while you are supposed to be helping them

doubt (*rhymes with* out) *noun*
1 a feeling of worry because you are not very sure about something: *to have doubts about moving house*
doubt *verb*
2 to feel worry because you are not sure about something: *I doubt whether we will get there before 7 o'clock.*
•***Word Family:*** **doubtful** *adjective*

dough (*say* doe) *noun*
1 a thick paste of flour and water, used to make bread, pizza and so on 2 money
•***Word Family:*** **doughy** *adjective* of or like dough

doughnut *noun*
a round or ring-shaped cake, usually deep-fried and covered with sugar

dove (*say* duv) *noun*
a bird very like a pigeon, used as a symbol of peace

dovetail *noun*
1 a way of cutting and joining two pieces of wood together
dovetail *verb*
2 to join two pieces of wood using a dovetail joint 3 two make two things fit together neatly: *to dovetail a shopping trip and a visit to the cinema*

down (1) *adverb*
1 from a higher to a lower position, level or degree: *Slow down now. / Calm down!* 2 onto the ground: *to fall down* 3 on paper or in a book: *to write down*
down *preposition*
4 to or towards a lower place: *Go down the stairs.* 5 away from the beginning or source: *to row down the river*
down *adjective*
6 unhappy or depressed: *to feel rather down*
7 not operating properly: *The computers are down.*
down *noun*
8 a time when things are going badly: *the ups and downs of life* 9 a feeling of dislike: *to have a down on someone*
down *verb*
10 to put or throw something down: *The workers downed their tools and went on strike.*
11 to finish a drink: *Down your Coke and let's go.*
•***Word Family:*** **downward** *adjective* moving or pointing down **downwards** *adverb* to a lower place or position

down (2) *noun*
soft fine feathers or hair: *a duck's down / down on his cheeks*

downcast *adjective*
1 looking downwards: *downcast eyes* 2 sad or depressed: *to feel downcast*

downfall *noun*
1 someone's loss of happiness or success: *the mistake which led to his downfall* 2 the thing which causes this: *Carelessness was his downfall.*

download *verb*
to transfer information from one computer to another

downpour *noun*
a heavy shower of rain

downs *plural noun*
open, rolling, grassy country

Down's Syndrome *noun*
a disease caused by abnormal chromosomes, resulting in mental deficiency, slanted eyes and a broad, rather flat, face

dowry *noun*
property or money a bride in some cultures brings to her husband when she marries, usually provided by her father
•***Word Family:*** the plural is **dowries**

doze *verb*
1 to sleep lightly or for a short time: *to doze by the fire*
doze *noun*
2 a light, short sleep
•***Word Family:*** **dozy** *adjective* drowsy

dozen (*say* **duz**-en) *noun*
a group of twelve things: *a dozen eggs*
•***Word Family:*** the plural is **dozen** or **dozens** □ **baker's dozen** thirteen

drab *adjective*
1 having a dull, usually brown or greyish colour: *a drab uniform* 2 dull or boring: *a drab existence*
•***Word Family:*** other forms are **drabber, drabbest**

draft *noun*
1 the first rough version of a piece of writing: *the draft of an essay* 2 a written order for payment of money, especially from a bank 3 **the draft** conscription or making people join the armed forces
draft *verb*
4 to make a draft or outline of something: *His advisers drafted his speech.* 5 to conscript people

drag *verb*
1 to pull something along with difficulty: *They dragged the table over to the window.* 2 to pass slowly because of being boring or unpleasant: *Her hospital stay dragged by.*
drag *noun*
3 a very boring person or thing 4 a puff of a cigarette
•***Word Family:*** other verb forms are **drags, dragged, dragging**

dragnet *noun*
1 a net dragged through water to catch fish 2 any tricky system for catching or trapping, such as is used by the police force

dragon *noun*
1 an imaginary monster, usually pictured as a huge, winged, fire-breathing lizard with fierce claws and scaly skin 2 a strict or bossy woman
•***Word Origins:*** from a Greek word meaning "serpent"

dragonfly *noun*
a large brightly-coloured insect with a long, slender body and four delicate wings
•***Word Family:*** the plural is **dragonflies**

drain *verb*
1 to remove water or another fluid from somewhere: *to drain a swamp / to drain pus from a wound* 2 to flow away: *The floods drained away when the rain stopped. / The colour drained from her face.* 3 to empty a container: *to drain your glass* 4 to use something up: *to drain someone's energy*
drain *noun*
5 any pipe or channel that carries water away 6 something that causes loss or expense: *Going overseas was a drain on our savings.*
•***Word Family:*** **drainage** *noun*

drake *noun*
a male duck

drama (*say* **drah**-ma) *noun*
1 an exciting, sad or serious play for theatre, television or radio 2 an exciting or interesting event: *The drama of the election held everybody's attention.*
•***Word Family:*** **dramatist** *noun* someone who writes dramas **dramatic** *adjective* **dramatically** *adverb*

dramatize or **dramatise** *verb*
1 to rewrite a story or book in the form of a play 2 to express something in a dramatic or exaggerated way: *Why do you need to dramatize everything?*
•***Word Family:*** **dramatization** *noun*

drape *verb*
1 to hang something loosely in folds: *to drape a blanket around your shoulders* 2 to place something in a casual way: *to drape your arm along the back of the sofa*
drape *noun*
3 a curtain or length of cloth used to decorate

draper *noun*
someone who sells material, such as linen or cotton
•***Word Family:*** **drapery** *noun* (**draperies**)

drastic *adjective*
extremely strong or violent: *Drastic action is called for to deal with this crisis.*
• ***Word Family:*** **drastically** *adverb*

draught (*rhymes with* raft) *noun*
1 a breeze or current of cold air inside a room or building: *Close the door to keep out the draught.* 2 a drink: *a draught of water* 3 the depth of water a ship needs in order to float 4 **draughts** a game for two players, each with twelve pieces which are moved diagonally on a chequered board
draught *adjective*
5 drawn straight from the container without being bottled: *draught beer*
• ***Word Family:*** **draughty** *adjective* (**draughtier, draughtiest**) breezy

draughtsman *noun*
someone who draws detailed plans for buildings, roads and bridges

draw *verb*
1 to make a picture or outline with a pen or pencil 2 to pull or move something somewhere: *to draw your chair closer to the fire / to draw the curtains / to draw a gun* 3 to take in air: *to draw a deep breath* 4 to attract: *to draw a large audience* 5 to end a game with the same score as your opponent: *We drew 3-all.*
draw *noun*
6 a raffle, lottery or similar competition based on luck 7 the position reached at the end of a contest in which both sides are equal: *The game ended in a draw.* 8 an attraction: *The bouncy castle is quite a draw.*
• ***Word Family:*** other forms are **draws, drew, drawn, drawing** □ **drawn** *adjective*

drawback *noun*
a disadvantage

drawer *noun*
1 a sliding compartment for storing things in a piece of furniture 2 **drawers** baggy underpants

drawing *noun*
a picture or diagram done with a pencil, crayon and so on

drawl *verb*
to speak slowly so that the vowel sounds you make are very long

dread (*say* dred) *verb*
1 to be very afraid of something: *He dreads driving in heavy traffic.*
dread *noun*
2 a feeling of terror: *to face the examiners with dread*

dreadful *adjective*
1 causing dread or horror: *a dreadful accident / a dreadful monster* 2 unpleasant or bad: *a dreadful day / a dreadful movie*
• ***Word Family:*** **dreadfully** *adverb* **dreadfulness** *noun*

dream *noun*
1 what you imagine while you're asleep
2 something you imagine and hope for: *a dream of future peace*
dream *verb*
3 to have a dream 4 to imagine or hope for something: *to dream of fame* 5 **dream up** to invent something or make it up: *What mad idea will you dream up next?*
• ***Word Family:*** other verb forms are **dreams, dreamt** or **dreamed, dreaming** □ **dreamy** *adjective* (**dreamier, dreamiest**) vague, unreal or dreamlike **dreamer** *noun* **dreamless** *adjective*

Dreamtime *noun*
the time in which the Aboriginal people believe the earth was created along with the people, animals and plants that live on it

dreary *adjective*
dull or gloomy: *rows of dreary houses*
• ***Word Family:*** other forms are **drearier, dreariest** □ **dreariness** *noun* **drearily** *adverb*

dredge *noun*
1 a machine that is used to scoop up silt or mud from the bottom of a river or harbour
dredge *verb*
2 to use a dredge to remove silt and so on from the bottom of a river or habour
• ***Word Family:*** **dredger** *noun* a boat equipped with a dredge

dregs *plural noun*
1 the small solid bits that sink to the bottom of wine or other drinks 2 the most useless or unimportant people: *the dregs of society*

drench *verb*
to wet something completely: *We got drenched in the storm.*

dress *noun*
1 a piece of woman's clothing consisting of a one-piece skirt and top 2 clothes that are suitable for a particular occasion
dress *verb*
3 to put on clothes 4 to clean and bandage a wound 5 **dress up** (a) to wear clothes that make you look like someone else: *Let's dress up as pirates* (b) to wear formal clothes: *Do I need to dress up for dinner?*
• ***Word Family:*** the plural of the noun is **dresses** □ **dressy** *adjective* smart

dressage (*say* **dres**-ahj) *noun*
1 a method of training a horse to perform a series of steps to show its skill and obedience
2 a competition based on these skills

dresser *noun*
a piece of kitchen furniture with drawers and cupboards in the lower half and shelves in the upper half

dressing *noun*
1 a sauce to put on salad 2 a special bandage for covering and protecting a wound

dressing-gown *noun*
a loose coat, usually tied with a sash that you wear over your pyjamas or nightdress

dressing-table *noun*
a bedroom table with drawers and usually a mirror on top, used when dressing

dress rehearsal *noun*
the last rehearsal of a play which is like a real performance, with lights, scenery and costumes, but without an audience

dribble *verb*
1 to trickle or flow in slow, small drops: *Blood dribbled from the cut on her knee.* 2 to allow saliva to flow from your mouth as babies do 3 to move the ball in football and similar sports by tapping or kicking it with your feet as you run

drift *verb*
1 to be carried along in water or in the air: *The raft drifted downstream.* 2 to wander from place to place without any particular plan: *He drifted from country to country.*
drift *noun*
3 a movement or trend: *a drift from the cities to the countryside* 4 the general meaning in what someone is saying: *What was the main drift of his argument?* 5 a pile of snow that has been blown by the wind
•***Word Family:*** **drifter** *noun* someone who drifts through life without any plans

drill *noun*
1 a tool for making holes 2 a strict method of training in which you repeat the same task again and again until you can do it without thinking: *fire drill*
drill *verb*
4 to make holes with a drill 5 to train people by making them repeat something again and again

drink *verb*
1 to take liquid into your mouth and swallow it: *to drink milk* 2 to drink alcohol: *My parents don't drink.* 3 **drink in** to be absorbed by: *We drank in his every word.*
drink *noun*
4 liquid that you drink: *Would you like a drink of orange juice?* 5 an alcoholic drink: *Let's have a drink before dinner.*
•***Word Family:*** other verb forms are **drinks, drank, drunk, drinking** □ **drinkable** *adjective* fit for drinking **drinker** *noun*

drip *verb*
1 to fall in drops or let liquid fall in drops: *Raindrops dripped down my neck. / The leaking tap dripped noisily.*
drip *noun*
2 a drop of falling liquid or the noise it makes 3 a piece of equipment used in hospitals which sends liquid food into the veins of someone too ill to eat 4 a boring person
•***Word Family:*** other verb forms are **drips, dripped, dripping**

dripping *noun*
the fat that drips from cooking meat that can be used for frying

drive *verb*
1 to control a vehicle and make it move: *to drive a car* 2 to take someone somewhere in a vehicle: *Can you drive me into town?* 3 to force people or animals to go somewhere: *He's going to drive the cows into the next field.* 4 to provide the power that makes a machine work: *Steam drives that engine.* 5 to put someone into a particular state: *His chatter drives me mad.*
drive *noun*
6 a journey in a car: *Let's go for a drive in the country.* 7 a road from the street to a house 8 energy and determination: *She shows enormous drive at work.* 9 an organized attempt or effort to do something: *a drive to raise money for a new library*
•***Word Family:*** other verb forms are **drives, drove, driven, driving** □ **driver** *noun* someone or something that drives

drizzle *verb*
1 to rain in small, light drops
drizzle *noun*
2 light rain
•***Word Family:*** **drizzly** *adjective*

drone (1) *noun*
a male bee that grows from an unfertilized egg, does not produce honey, and dies or is killed soon after mating

drone (2) *verb*
1 to make a low, continuous sound: *to talk boringly for a long time / His voice droned on until there was no-one left in the room.*
drone *noun*
2 a low humming sound: *the drone of bees in the garden*

drool *verb*
1 to dribble saliva out of your mouth: *The dog drooled when it smelt the chicken.* 2 **drool over** to like something so much you wish you had it yourself: *She drooled over her sister's new clothes.*

A B C D E F G H I J K L M N O P Q R S T U V W X Y Z

droop *verb*
1 to hang down or bend down loosely: *Her head drooped wearily over her books.* 2 to become sad or without energy: *His spirits drooped after hours of waiting to be rescued.*
•*Word Family:* **droopy** *adjective* **(droopier, droopiest) drooping** *adjective*

drop *verb*
1 to fall or let something fall: *Water dropped from the branches. / I dropped the ball.* 2 to go to a lower level: *Prices dropped suddenly.* 3 to stop and let someone out of a car: *Please drop me at the corner.* 4 to stop including someone in a group: *to drop a player from a team* 5 **drop in** or **drop by** to visit someone casually
drop *noun*
6 a fall: *a drop in prices* 7 a very small amount of liquid: *a drop of water*
•*Word Family:* other verb forms are **drops, dropped, dropping**

drought (*rhymes with* out) *noun*
a long period without rain

drove *verb*
1 to move or drive cattle or sheep in a herd: *to drove in the outback*
drove *noun*
2 a large crowd of people
•*Word Family:* **drover** *noun* someone who droves cattle

drown *verb*
1 to die or make someone die because they are under water and cannot breathe: *The murderer drowned him in the pool.* 2 to make such a loud noise that another noise can't be heard: *The roars of the crowd drowned his voice.*

drowse (*rhymes with* cows) *verb*
to be half-asleep: *He was drowsing by the fire.*
•*Word Family:* **drowsy** *adjective* **(drowsier, drowsiest)** tired or half-asleep **drowsily** *adverb* **drowsiness** *noun*

drug *noun*
1 a chemical substance used to treat disease
2 a chemical substance that makes you feel different, for example excited or very calm
drug *verb*
3 to give someone a drug that makes them sleepy or unconscious: *to drug food / to drug a person*
•*Word Family:* other forms of the verb are **drugs, drugged, drugging**

drum *noun*
1 a percussion instrument with a tightly stretched skin or membrane on a round frame, that you strike with sticks or your hands 2 a drum-shaped container for holding liquid: *a petrol drum*
drum *verb*
3 to beat a drum or tap something repeatedly: *She drummed on the table with her fingers.* 4 to keep telling someone the same thing so that they remember it: *Saying 'please' and 'thank you' was drummed into me at an early age.*
•*Word Family:* other verb forms are **drums, drummed, drumming** □ **drummer** *noun* someone who plays a drum

drumstick *noun*
1 a stick used for beating a drum 2 the lower part of the leg of a chicken, duck or turkey

drunk *adjective*
1 having had too much alcohol to drink
drunk *noun*
2 someone who is often drunk
•*Word Family:* **drunkard** *noun* a drunk **drunken** *adjective*: *drunken snores*

dry *adjective*
1 not wet or damp: *Wood must be dry or it won't burn properly. / a dry summer* 2 boring and uninteresting: *a dry book* 3 funny in a clever and not very obvious way: *a dry sense of humour*
dry *verb*
4 to make something dry or to become dry: *to dry the dishes / The dam dried up.*
•*Word Family:* other adjective forms are **drier, driest** □ other verb forms are **dries, dried, drying** □ **drily** or **dryly** *adverb* **dryness** *noun*

dry-cleaning *noun*
the process of cleaning clothes with chemicals rather than water
•*Word Family:* **dry-clean** *verb* **dry-cleaner** *noun*

dual (*say* **dew**-el) *adjective*
having two parts or aspects: *This machine has a dual role—to wax and to polish.*

dual carriageway (*say* **dew**-al **car**-ij-way) *noun*
a road wide enough to have two lanes for traffic in each direction

dub *verb*
1 to give a name to someone or something: *He dubbed his skateboard "Speedster".* 2 to make someone a knight in a special ceremony: *The Queen dubbed him Sir Harold.*
•*Word Family:* other forms are **dubs, dubbed, dubbing** □ **dubbing** *noun*

dubious (*say* **dew**-bee-us) *adjective*
1 doubtful or uncertain: *I'm dubious about the possibility of ever becoming a model.* 2 not definitely good or honest: *The reasons for his generosity are rather dubious.*
•*Word Family:* **dubiously** *adverb* **dubiousness** *noun*

duchess (*say* **dutch**-ess) *noun*
1 the wife or widow of a duke 2 a woman with the same rank as a duke
•*Word Family:* the plural is **duchesses**

duck (1) *noun*
a waterbird with a broad, flat bill, short legs and webbed feet

duck (2) *verb*
1 to bend or move aside quickly so as not to get hit by something: *He ducked his head as the ball hurtled past.* 2 to avoid something difficult or unpleasant: *to duck responsibility* 3 to push someone under water

duco (*say* **dew**-ko) *noun*
a paint used on motor vehicles
•***Word Origins:*** this word is a trademark

duct *noun*
1 a tube through which gases or liquids are carried: *an air duct* 2 a tube in your body for carrying tears, bile or other liquids
•***Word Family:*** **ducting** *noun*

dud *noun*
someone or something that fails to work, such as a bomb that fails to explode

dude (*rhymes with* rude) *noun*
1 someone who is stylishly dressed in a rather showy way 2 any man or guy: *Hey dude!*
•***Word Origins:*** the origin is not known, but the word was first used in the United States

due *adjective*
1 expected to happen: *The rent is due next Wednesday. / The baby is due today.* 2 proper: *Take due care when driving on wet roads.* 3 **due to** caused by: *His stutter is due to extreme shyness.*
due *noun*
4 **give someone their due** to admit that someone has done something well: *To give her her due, she's worked hard.* 5 **dues** a membership fee or payment.
due *adverb*
6 directly or exactly: *We sailed due east.*

duel (*say* **dew**-el) *noun*
1 an arranged fight between two people, using guns or swords, to settle a quarrel 2 serious disagreement between two people or groups
duel *verb*
3 to fight a duel
•***Word Family:*** other verb forms are **duels, duelled, duelling** □ **duellist** *noun*

duet (*say* dew-**et**) *noun*
a piece of music sung or played by two people

duffel coat *noun*
a warm, heavy coat with a hood and buttons that are fastened with loops of thread

duke *noun*
1 a nobleman of the highest rank after a prince 2 a prince who rules a small country
•***Word Family:*** **dukedom** *noun*
•***Word Origins:*** from a Latin word meaning "leader"

dulcimer (*say* **dul**-si-ma) *noun*
an old-fashioned musical instrument, still used in traditional music, in which strings stretched over a sounding-board are struck with hammers

dull *adjective*
1 not bright, sharp or clear: *dull light / a dull day* 2 unintelligent or slow to learn: *a dull student* 3 not interesting: *a dull book*
dull *verb*
4 to become dull or make something dull
•***Word Family:*** **dullness** *noun* **dully** *adverb*

duly (*say* **dew**-lee) *adverb*
1 correctly: *She was duly voted captain.* 2 when expected: *The taxi duly arrived.*

dumb (*say* dum) *adjective*
1 not able to speak: *She was struck dumb with surprise.* 2 stupid
•***Word Family:*** **dumbly** *adverb* **dumbness** *noun*

dumbfound *verb*
to amaze someone so much that they cannot speak

dummy *noun*
1 an imitation of a person or thing made to look exactly like them 2 a rubber teat given to a baby to suck
•***Word Family:*** the plural is **dummies**

dump *verb*
1 to put something down carelessly 2 to leave something somewhere because you no longer want it: *to dump rubbish at the tip* 3 to stop going out with someone: *to dump your boyfriend*
dump *noun*
4 a place where things are dumped or stored: *a rubbish dump / an army supply dump for guns* 5 a copy of the data stored in a computer 6 a horrible place that no-one would want to live in

dumpling *noun*
a small ball of dough cooked in soup or a stew

dunce *noun*
an unintelligent or silly person
•***Word Origins:*** named for John *Duns* Scotus, a religious writer living from about 1265 to about 1308, whom critics attacked as being stupid

dune *noun*
a hill of sand built up by the wind

dung *noun*
animal manure

dungarees *plural noun*
a piece of clothing consisting of trousers, a square of material covering your chest and straps that go over your shoulders
•***Word Origins:*** this word comes from Hindi

A B C D E F G H I J K L M N O P Q R S T U V W X Y Z

dungeon (*say* **dun**-jen) *noun*
a dark cell especially one for holding prisoners underground

dunk *verb*
to dip something into a liquid: *to dunk biscuits into tea*

duo *noun*
two people or things: *a singing duo*

dupe *verb*
to trick someone: *He duped me into thinking that he was a millionaire.*

duple *adjective*
with two beats in each bar: *a melody written in duple time*

duplex (*say* **dew**-pleks) *noun*
a building containing two flats or home units

duplicate (*say* **dew**-pli-kat) *adjective*
1 made as an exact copy of something: *a duplicate key*
duplicate *noun*
2 an exact copy of something
duplicate (*say* **dew**-pli-kate) *verb*
3 to produce an exact copy
•***Word Family:*** **duplication** *noun*

durable (*say* **dew**-ra-bul) *adjective*
lasting a long time without wearing out: *I need a durable school bag.*
•***Word Family:*** **durability** *noun* **durably** *adverb*
•***Word Origins:*** from a Latin word meaning "hard"

duration (*say* dew-**ray**-shun) *noun*
the length of time that something exists or continues: *Smokers must not light cigarettes for the duration of the flight.*

duress (*say* dew-**ress**) *noun*
the use of force to achieve something, especially illegally: *The witness claimed his evidence was given under duress.*

during *preposition*
throughout a period of time

dusk *noun*
the time in the afternoon or evening when it is getting dark
•***Word Family:*** **dusky** *adjective* (**duskier, duskiest**) darkish or brownish in colour: *dusky skin* **duskiness** *noun*

dust *noun*
1 dirt and fluff that collects on a surface that hasn't been cleaned 2 a fine powder of earth or sand
dust *verb*
3 to remove dust from something: *to dust the furniture* 4 to sprinkle something dry and powdery onto something: *Dust the cake with sugar.*
•***Word Family:*** **duster** *noun* a cloth for removing dust **dusty** *adjective* (**dustier, dustiest**)

duty (*say* **dew**-tee) *noun*
1 a task that you have to do: *It's my duty to look after my sister on Saturday mornings.*
2 something you have to do as part of your job: *One of my duties is showing visitors round the factory.* 3 a government tax: *customs duty* 4 **off duty** not at work 5 **on duty** at work
•***Word Family:*** the plural is **duties** □ **dutiful** *adjective* doing your duty **dutifully** *adverb*

dux *noun*
the student who tops the exams in a school

dwarf (*say* dwawf) *noun*
1 a very small human-like being in fairy stories who sometimes has magical powers 2 a person, animal or plant much smaller or shorter than normal
dwarf *verb*
3 to be so much bigger than something that it looks quite small: *Huge multistorey buildings dwarfed the factory.*
•***Word Family:*** **dwarfish** *adjective* very small like a dwarf

dwell *verb*
1 to live in a particular place 2 **dwell on** to keep on thinking or talking about the same thing: *Let's not dwell on such an unpleasant topic.*
•***Word Family:*** other forms are **dwells, dwelt** or **dwelled, dwelling** □ **dwelling** *noun*

dwindle *verb*
to become smaller and smaller: *The food supply dwindled as the strike continued.*

dye *noun*
1 a liquid that will change the colour of your hair, a piece of material, shoes and so on
dye *verb*
2 to colour something with a dye: *to dye your hair pink*
•***Word Family:*** other verb forms are **dyes, dyed, dyeing** □ **dyer** *noun*

dyke (*say* dike) *noun*
a wall built along a river or the sea to stop the water flooding on to the land

dynamic (*say* die-**nam**-ik) *adjective*
1 to do with movement, force or energy
2 energetic and getting a lot of things done: *She succeeds because she's so dynamic.*
•***Word Family:*** **dynamically** *adverb* **dynamism** *noun*

dynamics *plural noun*
the scientific study of the forces that make things move

dynamite (*say* **die**-na-mite) *noun*
1 a powerful explosive made from nitroglycerine 2 something that will shock and excite people: *That news is dynamite.*
dynamite *verb*
3 to blow something up with dynamite

dynamo (*say* **die**-na-mo) *noun*
a generator used to produce electrical energy
• ***Word Family:*** the plural is **dynamos**

dynasty (*say* **din**-a-stee) *noun*
a series of rulers all belonging to the same family
• ***Word Family:*** the plural is **dynasties** □ **dynastic** *adjective*

dyslexia (*say* dis-**lek**-see-a) *noun*
extreme difficulty in learning to read
• ***Word Family:*** **dyslectic** *adjective* **dyslexic** *adjective*
• ***Word Origins:*** from Greek words meaning "bad speech"

dyspepsia (*say* dis-**pep**-si-a) *noun*
indigestion
• ***Word Family:*** **dyspeptic** *adjective* **(a)** suffering from indigestion **(b)** gloomy or pessimistic
• ***Word Origins:*** from Greek words meaning "bad" and "able to digest"

Ee

each *adjective*
1 every: *Each story had an interesting plot.*
each *pronoun*
2 every one: *Each of them enjoyed the film.*
each *adverb*
3 for every one: *There is one cake each.*

eager *adjective*
keen: *eager to finish her painting*
• ***Word Family:*** **eagerly** *adverb* **eagerness** *noun*
• ***Word Origins:*** from a Latin word meaning "sharp"

eagle *noun*
a large, strong, hunting bird with a hooked beak and sharp claws
• ***Word Family:*** **eaglet** *noun* a young eagle

ear (1) *noun*
1 one of the two parts of your body used for hearing 2 the ability to hear the difference between sounds: *String players need a good ear to play in tune.*

ear (2) *noun*
the part of a cereal plant such as wheat, that contains the seed or flowers

eardrum *noun*
a tightly stretched membrane inside your ear that vibrates as soundwaves strike it, allowing you to hear

early (*say* **er**-lee) *adverb*
1 near the beginning of a period of time: *early in the morning* 2 before the usual time or the time that was arranged: *I'll aim to arrive early.*
• ***Word Family:*** other forms are **earlier, earliest** □ **earliness** *noun*

earmark *verb*
to set something aside for a special purpose: *to earmark money for a holiday*

earn (*rhymes with* burn) *verb*
1 to get money as payment for your work: *to earn a good wage* 2 to get something because you deserve it: *She earned her reputation as a good teacher.* 3 to produce interest or profit: *Their investment earns 10 per cent interest.*
• ***Word Family:*** **earner** *noun* someone who earns **earnings** *noun* the money someone earns

earnest (*say* **er**-nest) *adjective*
serious and sincere
• ***Word Family:*** **earnestly** *adverb* **earnestness** *noun*

earphones *plural noun*
another name for **headphones**

earring *noun*
a piece of jewellery that you wear on your ear

earth (*say* erth) *noun*
1 the planet in the solar system on which we live 2 soil 3 a hole in the ground that a burrowing animal such as a fox lives in 4 a wire in a plug or piece of electrical equipment through which electricity can pass to the ground 5 **be down to earth** to be practical and sensible in your approach to life
earth *verb*
6 to connect a piece of electrical equipment to the ground with a wire, for extra safety

earthquake *noun*
a violent shaking of the ground caused when moving rocks under the earth's surface release built-up pressure in the form of shockwaves

earthworm *noun*
a worm which lives in the soil

A B C D E F G H I J K L M N O P Q R S T U V W X Y Z

ease (*say* eez) *noun*
1 freedom from pain, worry or difficulty: *His wealth allowed him to live a life of ease.* 2 **with ease** without any difficulty: *She passed the tests with ease.*
ease *verb*
2 to make something less severe or strong: *The tablet eased his headache.* 3 to move something very slowly and carefully: *I eased the picture out of the broken frame.*

easel *noun*
a frame used to put a picture on while it is being painted or drawn

east *noun*
1 the direction of the sun when it comes up in the morning
east *adjective*
2 coming from the east: *an east wind*
east *adverb*
3 towards or in the east: *The road went east.*
•***Word Family:*** **easterly** *adjective* **eastern** *adjective*

Easter *noun*
a Christian festival held each year to remember how Jesus Christ died, was buried and rose again from the dead

easy *adjective*
1 not difficult: *an easy exam* 2 relaxed and not worried: *Locking all the doors and windows made her feel easier.*
•***Word Family:*** other forms are **easier, easiest** □ **easily** *adverb* **easiness** *noun*

easygoing *adjective*
relaxed and not letting things bother you

eat (*rhymes with* feet) *verb*
1 to chew and swallow food: *All I ate for lunch was an apple.* 2 to have a meal: *We'll eat late tonight.*
•***Word Family:*** other forms are **eats, ate, eaten, eating**

ebb *verb*
1 to flow back from the shore: *The tide began to ebb.* 2 to fade away or get weaker: *His strength was ebbing fast.*
•***Word Family:*** **ebb** *noun: the ebb of the tide*

ebony (*say* **eb**-o-nee) *noun*
1 a very hard, black wood that comes from a tropical tree
ebony *adjective*
2 black

eccentric (*say* ek-**sen**-trik) *adjective*
unusual and different from normal: *an eccentric person / eccentric behaviour*
•***Word Family:*** **eccentric** *noun* an unusual person **eccentrically** *adverb* **eccentricity** *noun*

ecclesiastical (*say* e-kleez-ee-**as**-ti-kal) *adjective*
to do with the Church: *ecclesiastical robes*

echidna (*say* e-**kid**-na) *noun*
a spiny, egg-laying Australian mammal with strong claws and a slender, tube-like snout that it uses for digging up and eating ants

echo (*say* **ek**-o) *noun*
1 a repeat of a sound which happens when soundwaves bounce off a hard surface 2 a repeat of something which has already been said: *His words were an echo of my own.*
•***Word Family:*** the plural is **echoes** □ **echo** *verb* **(echoes, echoed, echoing)**

eclair (*say* e-**klair**) *noun*
a light, finger-shaped cake with a cream or custard filling and icing on the top
•***Word Origins:*** from a French word meaning "lightning", because it is eaten in a flash

eclipse (*say* e-**klips**) *noun*
1 a time when the moon passes between the sun and the Earth so that the sun seems to disappear and then reappear: *an eclipse of the sun* 2 a time when the Earth passes between the sun and the moon so that the moon seems to disappear and then reappear: *an eclipse of the moon*
eclipse *verb*
3 to be so successful or attractive that others don't get noticed: *She eclipsed all the other girls at the disco in that stunning outfit.*

ecology *noun*
the study of the way animals and plants relate to each other and to their environment
•***Word Family:*** **ecological** *adjective* **ecologically** *adverb* **ecologist** *noun*

economical (*say* ek-o-**nom**-i-kal or eek-o-**nom**-i-kal) *adjective*
1 using a small amount of something and not wasting it: *He's an economical user of paper.* 2 cheap to use or operate: *This car is quite economical to run.*
•***Word Family:*** **economically** *adverb*

economize or **economise** *verb*
to spend less money

economy (*say* e-**kon**-o-mee or ee-**kon**-o-mee) *noun*
1 the careful use of money or materials so they last as long as possible 2 the management of a country's money, industry and trade
•***Word Family:*** the plural is **economies** □ **economic** *adjective* **economics** *noun* the study of how money is used **economist** *noun*

ecosystem *noun*
all the plants and animals in an area and the environment that affects them

ecstasy (*say* **eks**-ta-see) *noun*
1 a sudden feeling of overwhelming joy 2 an illegal drug that makes you feel extremely happy and energetic and can have dangerous side effects
• ***Word Family:*** the plural is **ecstasies** □ **ecstatic** *adjective* **ecstatically** *adverb*
• ***Word Origins:*** from a Greek word meaning "trance"

eczema (*say* **ek**-sa-ma) *noun*
a skin disease that makes the skin dry, red and itchy

eddy *noun*
a current of liquid, smoke or air that goes round in circles
• ***Word Family:*** the plural is **eddies** □ **eddy** *verb* **(eddies, eddied, eddying)**

edge *noun*
1 a line that forms the outside of something: *the edge of the table* 2 the thin, sharp side of a blade, used for cutting 3 an advantage: *Because of his experience he has an edge over the other applicants.* 4 **on edge** nervous and uncomfortable: *The more the plane shook, the more on edge she felt.*
edge *verb*
5 to move very slowly and cautiously: *She edged her way up the face of the cliff.*
• ***Word Family:*** **edgy** *adjective* **(edgier, edgiest)** nervous and uncomfortable

edible *adjective*
all right to eat: *an edible plant*

edit *verb*
1 to be in charge of publishing a newspaper or magazine: *to edit a magazine* 2 to correct the mistakes in a piece of writing: *to edit a manuscript* 3 to arrange pieces of film or tape to make a film or TV or radio programme
• ***Word Family:*** other forms are **edits, edited, editing** □ **editor** *noun*

edition (*say* e-**dish**-on) *noun*
all the copies of a book or newspaper printed at one time: *The first edition of my novel had an error in it but that was corrected in the second edition.*

editorial (*say* ed-i-**tor**-i-al) *noun*
an article in a newspaper giving the opinion of the newspaper's editor on an issue

educate *verb*
to teach someone or give them information about something
• ***Word Family:*** **educated** *adjective* having a high level of education and culture **education** *noun* **educator** *noun*
• ***Word Origins:*** from a Latin word meaning "to lead out"

eel *noun*
a long, thin fish the same shape as a snake

eerie (*rhymes with* **cheery**) *adjective*
so strange that it makes you frightened: *An eerie light radiated from the alien craft.*
• ***Word Family:*** other forms are **eerier, eeriest** □ **eerily** *adverb* **eeriness** *noun*

effect (*say* e-**fekt**) *noun*
1 a direct result: *What effect will chlorine have on my new swimming costume? / Our arguments had no effect as he would not change his mind.*
effect *verb*
2 to bring something about

effective (*say* e-**fek**-tiv) *adjective*
producing the intended result: *Advertising is an effective way of getting people to buy a product.*
• ***Word Family:*** **effectively** *adverb*

effeminate (*say* e-**fem**-i-nate) *adjective*
acting or looking like a woman

effervescent (*say* ef-er-**ves**-ent) *adjective*
fizzy
• ***Word Family:*** **effervescence** *noun*

efficient (*say* e-**fish**-ent) *adjective*
able to do good work quickly and with no fuss: *an efficient secretary*
• ***Word Family:*** **efficiency** *noun* **efficiently** *adverb*

effluent (*say* **ef**-loo-ent) *noun*
the waste water from a sewage farm, factory or chemical works
• ***Word Family:*** **effluence** *noun*

effort *noun*
1 the use of your physical strength or mental energy: *It took a lot of effort to get the new bed up the stairs and into the bedroom.* 2 an attempt to do something: *Please make an effort to ice-skate without holding onto me.*
• ***Word Family:*** **effortless** *adjective* done easily

EFTPOS *noun*
a system that enables a customer to use a coded plastic card and PIN number to pay for goods in a shop

egg *noun*
1 the roundish object produced by a female bird, reptile, fish or insect in which their young develop 2 a hen's egg used for food 3 a cell produced inside the body of a female animal or human, which may develop into a baby if it's fertilized

ego (*say* **ee**-go) *noun*
your sense of your own importance as a person: *Their criticism of her story bruised her ego.*
• ***Word Family:*** the plural is **egos**
• ***Word Origins:*** from a Latin word meaning "I"

egotist (*say* **ee**-go-tist or **eg**-o-tist) *noun*
someone who is selfish and always talks and thinks about himself or herself
•***Word Family:*** **egotistic** *adjective* **egotism** *noun*

eiderdown (*say* **eye**-der-down) *noun*
a bed covering filled with feathers that goes on top of a sheet and blankets
•***Word Origins:*** from *eider*, a species of duck, whose breast feathers are so soft that they were originally used to fill eiderdowns

Eid-ul-Fitr (*say* eed-ool-**fee**-ta) *noun*
the Muslim festival to celebrate the end of Ramadan

eight (*rhymes with* **late**) *noun*
the number 8
•***Word Family:*** **eight** *adjective* **eighth** *noun* **eighth** *adjective*

eighteen (*say* ay-**teen**) *noun*
the number 18
•***Word Family:*** **eighteen** *adjective* **eighteenth** *noun* **eighteenth** *adjective*

eighty (*say* **ay**-tee) *noun*
the number 80
•***Word Family:*** the plural is **eighties** □ **eighty** *adjective* **eightieth** *noun* **eightieth** *adjective*

eisteddfod (*say* eye-**sted**-fod) *noun*
a Welsh festival for music, art, poetry and drama competitions
•***Word Family:*** plural is **eisteddfods** or **eisteddfodau** but the second one is less common
•***Word Origins:*** from a Welsh word meaning "session"

either (*say* **eye**-ther *or* **ee**-ther) *adjective*
1 one or the other of two things: *I don't like either colour very much.* 2 both of two: *There were guards on either side of the President.*
either *pronoun*
3 one or the other but not both: *I have two pens, so take either.*
either *conjunction*
4 used to show two equal choices: *Either ring me up or write a letter.*
either *adverb*
5 similarly or also: *Don't go and I won't either.*

ejaculation (*say* e-jak-yoo-**lay**-shon) *noun*
1 a sudden exclamation or shout, especially when you're surprised 2 the discharge of semen from the penis
•***Word Family:*** **ejaculate** *verb* **ejaculatory** *adjective*

eject (*say* ee-**jekt**) *verb*
1 to force someone to leave a place: *Police were called to eject the demonstrators from the building.* 2 to make something come out sharply, such as a tape from a tape deck
•***Word Family:*** **ejection** *noun*

elaborate (*say* e-**lab**-a-rit) *adjective*
1 complicated and with a lot of detail: *We drew an elaborate plan of the building.*
elaborate (*say* e-**lab**-a-rate) *verb*
2 **elaborate on** to give more details about something: *Please elaborate on your plans.*
•***Word Family:*** **elaborately** *adverb* **elaboration** *noun*

elapse *verb*
to pass: *A week elapsed before he rang again.*

elastic (*say* e-**las**-tik) *adjective*
1 able to go back to its shape after being pulled or stretched: *an elastic band* 2 easily changed if necessary: *Our schedule for the bike ride is quite elastic.*
elastic *noun*
3 a material that has rubber threads woven into it so that it can stretch and then go back to its original shape
•***Word Family:*** **elasticize** or **elasticise** *verb* to make elastic **elasticity** *noun*

elated (*say* e-**lay**-ted) *adjective*
extremely happy and in high spirits: *They were elated when they were rescued.*
•***Word Family:*** **elation** *noun* a feeling of great joy **elate** *verb* **elatedly** *adverb* **elatedness** *noun*

elbow *noun*
1 the joint in the middle of the arm
elbow *verb*
2 to push or nudge people with your elbow: *to elbow your way through the crowd*

elder *adjective*
1 older: *His elder brother is 19 now.*
elder *noun*
2 someone who is older: *She's my elder by four years.*
•***Word Family:*** for the other forms look at **old**

elderly *adjective*
rather old

eldest *noun*
the oldest person: *She's the eldest of five.*

elect *verb*
1 to choose someone by voting for them: *to elect a Member of Parliament*
elect *adjective*
2 elected to a job but not yet doing it: *She's our ambassador elect.*
•***Word Family:*** **elector** *noun* someone who votes in an election **electorate** *noun* an area with a representative

election *noun*
a time when people vote to decide who will do a particular job, such as be a Member of Parliament
•***Word Family:*** **electoral** *adjective* to do with political elections

electric (*say* e-**lek**-trik) *adjective*
1 worked by or producing electricity: *an electric guitar / an electric current* 2 thrilling or exciting: *The atmosphere was electric as the singer arrived on stage.*
• ***Word Family:*** **electrical** *adjective*: *an electrical engineer* **electrically** *adverb*

electrician (*say* el-ek-**trish**-un) *noun*
a person trained to set up, look after and mend electrical equipment

electricity (*say* el-ek-**tris**-i-tee) *noun*
the energy released when electrons move about, used to produce light and heat or to drive a machine

electrify *verb*
1 to make a system run on electricity: *electrifying the railways* 2 to make people feel thrilled and excited: *Her performance was electrifying.*
• ***Word Family:*** **electrification** *noun*: *the electrification of the railways*

electrocute (*say* e-**lek**-tra-kyoot) *verb*
to kill someone by sending an electric current through their body
• ***Word Family:*** **electrocution** *noun*

electrode *noun*
a conductor by which electrons enter or leave a battery, circuit or other electrical device

electrolysis *noun*
the process of passing an electrical current through something to cause chemical changes in it

electromagnet *noun*
a coil of wire around a soft iron core, which becomes a magnet when electricity flows through the coil
• ***Word Family:*** **electromagnetism** *noun* the magnetism caused by a moving electric charge **electromagnetic** *adjective*

electron *noun*
a tiny particle inside an atom which carries electricity

electronic (*say* el-ek-**tron**-ik) *adjective*
operated by changing an electric current with the help of transistors, silicon chips or valves
• ***Word Family:*** **electronically** *adverb*

electronic mail *noun*
the long form of **e-mail**

elegant *adjective*
tasteful and smart: *She wore an elegant dress.*
• ***Word Family:*** **elegance** *noun* **elegantly** *adverb*

elegy (*say* **el**-e-jee) *noun*
a sad song or poem in memory of someone who has died
• ***Word Family:*** the plural is **elegies**

element (*say* **el**-a-ment) *noun*
1 a basic and necessary part of something: *Trust is one of the elements of friendship.* 2 a substance that cannot be broken down chemically into anything simpler: *Iron and oxygen are two elements that can be combined to make the compound iron oxide.* 3 a wire in an electric kettle or similar electrical appliance which acts as a heating unit
• ***Word Family:*** **elemental** *adjective*

elementary (*say* el-e-**men**-tree) *adjective*
basic or simple: *an elementary course on computing*

elephant (*say* **el**-e-funt) *noun*
a very large mammal from Africa or India, with thick, leathery skin, a long trunk, curved tusks and big, fan-shaped ears
• ***Word Family:*** **elephantine** (*say* el-e-**fan**-tine) *adjective* large and slow-moving, like an elephant

elevate (*say* **el**-a-vate) *verb*
to raise or lift something up to a higher position
• ***Word Family:*** **elevation** *noun*

eleven *noun*
1 the number 11 2 the 11 players in a cricket, soccer or hockey team
• ***Word Family:*** **eleven** *adjective* **eleventh** *noun* **eleventh** *adjective*

elf *noun*
a small, mischievous fairy in tales, who enjoys tricking people
• ***Word Family:*** plural is **elves** □ **elfin** *adjective* small and attractive like an elf **elfish** *adjective*

eligible (*say* **el**-ij-a-bul) *adjective*
1 properly qualified: *Are you sure you're eligible for such a high-powered job?* 2 suitable for someone to marry: *an eligible bachelor*
• ***Word Family:*** **eligibility** (*say* el-i-ja-**bil**-a-tee) *noun* **eligibly** *adverb*

eliminate (*say* e-**lim**-in-ate) *verb*
to remove something: *We've eliminated several more names from the list.*
• ***Word Family:*** **elimination** *noun*

elite (*say* e-**leet**) *noun*
a small group of people who are richer, more powerful or cleverer than everyone else
• ***Word Family:*** **elitism** *noun* **elitist** *adjective*
• ***Word Origins:*** from a French word meaning "chosen"

elixir (*say* e-**liks**-a) *noun*
a potion or remedy, believed to lengthen your life or cure you of disease: *the elixir of eternal youth*

elk *noun*
the largest existing deer found in Europe, Asia and North America

A B C D E F G H I J K L M N O P Q R S T U V W X Y Z

ellipse *noun*
a regular oval shape
• ***Word Family:*** **elliptical** *adjective*

ellipsis *noun*
1 a meaning in speech or writing which you understand but which is not actually stated in words, as in *[You] Pick up the paper clips, please.* 2 a mark or marks in printing such as ..., used to show that some words have been left out
• ***Word Family:*** the plural is **ellipses**

elocution (*say* el-o-**kyoo**-shun) *noun*
speaking clearly and pronouncing words properly

elongate (*say* **ee**-long-gate) *verb*
to make something longer or to become longer
• ***Word Family:*** **elongation** *noun*

elope *verb*
to run away secretly to get married
• ***Word Family:*** **elopement** *noun*

eloquent (*say* **el**-a-kwent) *adjective*
speaking so well that you persuade or impress people: *His eloquent praise of the film made us all want to see it.*
• ***Word Family:*** **eloquence** *noun* **eloquently** *adverb*

else *adverb*
1 besides or instead: *Could someone else sing it?* 2 in addition or other: *Would you like something else to eat?* 3 otherwise: *We must leave now or else we'll be late.*

elude *verb*
to avoid someone who is trying to find you

elusive *adjective*
difficult to find or remember: *an elusive friend / an elusive melody*
• ***Word Family:*** **elusiveness** *noun*

e-mail (*say* **ee**-male) *noun*
messages that are sent from one computer to another rather than through the post

emancipate (*say* ee-**man**-sa-payt) *verb*
to set someone free: *to emancipate a slave*
• ***Word Family:*** **emancipation** *noun*

embalm (*say* em-**bahm**) *verb*
to preserve a dead body by treating it with chemicals

embankment *noun*
a wall or big mound of earth used to support a road or railway or to hold back water

embargo *noun*
a government order that stops trade in something: *an oil embargo*
• ***Word Family:*** the plural is **embargoes**

embark *verb*
1 to get on a ship: *They embarked at Liverpool for the journey to New York.* 2 to start something new: *Our class will embark on a new project.*
• ***Word Family:*** **embarkation** *noun*

embarrass *verb*
to make someone feel uncomfortable or self-conscious: *She was embarrassed by the pimples on her face.*
• ***Word Family:*** **embarrassment** *noun*

embassy (*say* **em**-ba-see) *noun*
the building where an ambassador works: *the British embassy in Moscow*
• ***Word Family:*** the plural is **embassies**

embed *verb*
to sink into something and get fixed firmly there: *We found the boulders embedded in soil.*
• ***Word Family:*** other forms are **embeds, embedded, embedding**

embers *plural noun*
burning pieces of wood or ash that remain in a fire after it has gone out

embezzle *verb*
to steal money from an organization that you work for
• ***Word Family:*** **embezzler** *noun* someone who embezzles **embezzlement** *noun*

emblem (say **em**-blem) *noun*
a design or object that stands for something: *The dove is an emblem of peace.*
• ***Word Family:*** **emblematic** *adjective*

emboss *verb*
to make a design on something that stands out slightly above a surface: *They embossed the name on the book's cover.*
• ***Word Family:*** **embossed** *adjective*

embrace *verb*
1 to put your arms around someone 2 to include: *Her speech embraced all aspects of education.*

embroider (*say* em-**broy**-der) *verb*
1 to sew stitches on something to make a design: *to embroider a pillow* 2 to add colourful details from your imagination to a story to make it more interesting
• ***Word Family:*** **embroidery** *noun*

embryo (*say* **em**-bree-o) *noun*
a young animal or baby in the early stages of growing in the womb from a fertilized egg
• ***Word Family:*** the plural is **embryos** □ **embryonic** (*say* em-bree-**on**-ik) *adjective*

emerald *noun*
a rare, bright green jewel

emerge (*say* i-**merj**) *verb*
1 to appear after being out of sight: *The sun emerged again from behind the clouds.* 2 to

become known: *Some new facts about the murder have just emerged.*
•***Word Family:*** **emergence** *noun*

emergency (*say* e-**mer**-jen-see) *noun*
a sudden and dangerous event that needs immediate action: *Ring this doctor if there's an emergency.*
•***Word Family:*** the plural is **emergencies**

emigrate (*say* **em**-i-grate) *verb*
to leave your own country to go and live in another: *Our family emigrated from Greece.*
•***Word Family:*** **emigration** *noun* the act of emigrating **emigrant** *noun* someone who emigrates

eminent *adjective*
well-known and very highly thought of: *An eminent professor gave a lecture to the school.*
•***Word Family:*** **eminence** *noun*

emit (*say* e-**mit**) *verb*
to give something out: *The sun emits light and heat.*
•***Word Family:*** other forms are **emits, emitted, emitting** □ **emission** *noun*

emotion (*say* e-**mo**-shon) *noun*
a strong feeling such as fear, joy or sorrow: *His voice expressed his intense emotion.*
•***Word Family:*** **emotional** *adjective*: *an emotional song / to become emotional* **emotionally** *adverb*

emperor *noun*
a man who rules an empire

emphasis (*say* **em**-fa-sis) *noun*
the importance attached to something: *We must put more emphasis on pollution in this election campaign.*
•***Word Family:*** the plural is **emphases** □ **emphatic** *adjective* full of force: *an emphatic answer* **emphasize** or **emphasise** *verb* to show up the importance of something **emphatically** *adverb*

empire *noun*
1 a group of countries ruled by a single person or government 2 a powerful group of companies run or owned by one person
•***Word Family:*** **emperor** *noun* **empress** *noun* **imperial** *adjective*

employ *verb*
1 to pay someone to work for you: *The bank employs 1300 people.* 2 to make use of something: *Why not employ your spare time reading?*
•***Word Family:*** **employee** *noun* a person paid to work by an employer **employer** *noun* a person other people work for **employment** *noun*

empress *noun*
a woman who rules an empire

empty *adjective*
1 with nothing inside: *He drank until the glass was empty.*
empty *verb*
2 to remove what was inside something so it is empty
•***Word Family:*** other adjective forms are **emptier, emptiest** □ other verb forms are **empties, emptied, emptying** □ **empties** *plural noun* empty bottles or containers

emu (*say* **ee**-myoo) *noun*
a large greyish-brown bird with long legs that cannot fly and lives in Australia
•***Word Family:*** the plural is **emus**
•***Word Origins:*** from a Portuguese word for "ostrich"

emulsion (*say* ee-**mul**-shon) *noun*
1 a mixture of two liquids that do not naturally mix completely, such as oil and water 2 a type of paint that is used on walls

enable *verb*
to make it possible to do something: *The fine weather enabled us to spend all our time outside.*

enact *verb*
to act something out as if it was a play: *She enacted the story of her life.*
•***Word Family:*** **enactment** *noun*

enamel *noun*
1 a hard, glassy coating used to decorate metal and pottery 2 a type of paint that is hard and shiny when it dries 3 the hard, white layer on the outside of teeth
enamel *verb*
4 to decorate something with enamel
•***Word Family:*** other verb forms are **enamels, enamelled, enamelling**

enchant *verb*
1 to charm or delight: *The tiny puppets enchanted us.* 2 to use magic or spells on someone
•***Word Family:*** **enchanter** *noun* someone who enchants **enchanting** *adjective* **enchantingly** *adverb* **enchantment** *noun*

encircle (*say* en-**ser**-kul) *verb*
to make a circle round something: *Enemy soldiers encircled the town.*

enclose *verb*
1 to surround a place with a wall or a fence completely: *A high brick wall enclosed the rose garden.* 2 to send something in an envelope with a letter or message: *He enclosed two tickets with a note.*
•***Word Family:*** **enclosure** *noun*

encore (*say* **on**-kor) *noun*
1 an extra piece performed at the end of a

A B C D E F G H I J K L M N O P Q R S T U V W X Y Z

concert because the audience has clapped so much
encore *interjection*
2 once more!
•***Word Origins:*** from a French word meaning "again"

encounter *verb*
1 to come across difficulties or problems: *We encountered some language problems when the Japanese students joined our class.*
encounter *noun*
2 an unexpected meeting

encourage (*say* en-**ku**-rij) *verb*
to help someone by giving them confidence that they can succeed: *Our cheers encouraged the team.*
•***Word Family:*** **encouragement** *noun* **encouraging** *adjective* **encouragingly** *adverb*

encroach *verb*
to intrude or go beyond the set limits: *to encroach on someone's land / to encroach on someone's hospitality by staying too long*
•***Word Family:*** **encroachment** *noun*

encyclopedia or **encyclopaedia** (*say* en-sigh-kla-**pee**-dee-a) *noun*
a book or set of books that gives information about many subjects, arranged in alphabetical order
•***Word Family:*** **encyclopedic** *adjective* knowing about or dealing with a wide variety of subjects

end *noun*
1 the farthest part of something: *You take the other end of the rope and tie it to a tree.* 2 the very last part of something: *What happened at the end of the film?* 3 an aim that someone is trying to achieve: *He's always working for his own ends.* 4 **make ends meet** to just about make enough money to live on: *After losing her job she found it difficult to make ends meet.*
end *verb*
5 to stop or finish
•***Word Family:*** **ending** *noun* the last or concluding part

endanger (*say* en-**dane**-jer) *verb*
to put a person or animal in danger of being hurt or destroyed: *Smoking can endanger your health. / Cutting down forests endangers many forms of wildlife.*
•***Word Family:*** **endangered** *adjective*

endangered species *noun*
a species of animal that is in danger of becoming extinct

endeavour or **endeavor** (*say* en-**dev**-or) *verb*
1 to try hard to do something: *She will endeavour to beat the world record.*
endeavour *noun*
2 an attempt to do something
•***Word Origins:*** from French words meaning "to do your best"

endorse *verb*
1 to write your signature or comment on: *to endorse a cheque* 2 to give approval or support to: *The Labor Party endorsed their new candidate for our seat in the state elections.*
•***Word Family:*** **endorsable** *adjective* **endorsement** *noun* **endorser** *noun*

endow *verb*
1 to give a lot of money to pay for something: *to endow a school* 2 **be endowed with** to have a natural ability for something: *to be endowed with a great singing voice*
•***Word Family:*** **endowment** *noun*

endure (*say* en-**dyoor**) *verb*
1 to put up with: *to endure pain* 2 to continue for a long time: *His fame endured long after his death.*
•***Word Family:*** **endurable** *adjective* able to be endured **endurance** *noun* the power to endure **enduring** *adjective* long-lasting

enemy (*say* **en**-a-mee) *noun*
1 someone who hates you 2 an army that is fighting your country's army in a war: *The enemy attacked at dawn.*
•***Word Family:*** the plural is **enemies**

energy (*say* **en**-a-jee) *noun*
1 the ability to do lots of things or to keep doing something without getting tired: *I felt full of energy.* 2 power, such as heat or electricity
•***Word Family:*** the plural is **energies** □ **energetic** *adjective* strong and active **energize** or **energise** *verb* to fill with energy **energetically** *adverb*

enforce *verb*
to make people obey a rule: *to enforce school rules*
•***Word Family:*** **enforcement** *noun* the act of enforcing **enforcer** *noun* someone who enforces **enforceable** *adjective*

engage (*say* en-**gayj**) *verb*
1 to take someone on to do a job: *They engaged a guide to lead them over the mountains.* 2 to keep busy or occupied: *She's engaged in building a model.* 3 to make two pieces of machinery fit together

engaged *adjective*
1 going to be married 2 already being used: *The phone line is engaged, I'll try again later.*

engagement *noun*
1 an agreement to get married 2 an arrangement to meet someone at a particular time

engine (*say* **en**-jin) *noun*
1 a machine that uses the energy it produces from petrol, steam or electricity to make something move: *a car engine* 2 the vehicle at the front of a train which pulls the train along

engineer (*say* **en**-ja-**neer**) *noun*
1 someone who is trained to design, build or look after machinery, bridges, chemical plants, roads and so on
engineer *verb*
2 to arrange that something will happen
•***Word Family:*** **engineering** *noun*

English *noun*
1 the language of England and other countries, such as Australia and New Zealand
English *adjective*
2 coming from England: *English people / English wool*
•***Word Family:*** **England** *noun*

engrave *verb*
1 to cut a pattern into a hard surface using a sharp tool: *Can you engrave my name on the bracelet?* 2 to fix something deeply in your memory so you will not forget it: *The sound of her voice is engraved on his memory.*
•***Word Family:*** **engraving** *noun* an engraved picture or design **engraver** *noun*

engross *verb*
to be so fascinating that it takes all your attention: *The new novel engrossed him for days.*

engulf *verb*
to surround and swallow it up completely: *Fire engulfed the timber cottage.*

enhance *verb*
to make something more valuable or attractive: *Lunch was greatly enhanced by our view of the sea.*
•***Word Family:*** **enhancement** *noun*

enigma (*say* e-**nig**-ma) *noun*
something very puzzling
•***Word Family:*** **enigmatic** *adjective*
•***Word Origins:*** from a Greek word meaning "riddle"

enjoy *verb*
1 to have a good time when you are doing something: *Enjoy the film!* 2 to have the benefit of something: *Granny still enjoys good health.*
•***Word Family:*** **enjoyable** *adjective: an enjoyable party* **enjoyably** *adverb* **enjoyment** *noun*

enlarge *verb*
1 to make something larger: *The photographer will enlarge the four best prints.* 2 to give more details about something: *Can you enlarge on that last point she mentioned?*
•***Word Family:*** **enlarger** *noun* a machine which enlarges photographs **enlargement** *noun*

enlighten *verb*
to make something clear so that you understand it: *I don't understand this paragraph — could you enlighten me?*
•***Word Family:*** **enlightened** *adjective* well-informed and free from prejudice
enlightenment *noun*

enlist *verb*
1 to join the army, navy or air force 2 to get someone to help you: *I enlisted her help.*

enmity *noun*
hatred between people who are enemies

enormous (*say* i-**nor**-mus) *adjective*
very large: *an enormous parcel*
•***Word Family:*** **enormity** *noun: the enormity of the tragedy* **enormously** *adverb*

enough (*say* i-**nuf**) *adjective*
as much or as many as needed: *Is there enough pie left for me to have some more?*
•***Word Family:*** **enough** *adverb: This meat isn't cooked enough.* **enough** *noun: Have you got enough to pay for the tickets?*

enquire (*say* en-**kwire**) *verb*
to ask about something
•***Word Family:*** **enquiry** *noun* (**enquiries**)

enrich *verb*
1 to improve something by adding something else: *We enriched the soil with compost.* 2 to make someone richer
•***Word Family:*** **enrichment** *noun*

enrol (*say* en-**role**) *verb*
to get your name on the list of people who will be in a club, school or class: *to enrol for judo lessons*
•***Word Family:*** other forms are **enrols, enrolled, enrolling** □ **enrolment** *noun*

ensign (*say* **en**-sine) *noun*
a flag, especially of a country or a particular group

ensue *verb*
to happen immediately after something: *Two or three people started shouting insults and a battle ensued.*

en suite (*say* on-**sweet**) *noun*
a bathroom which is attached to a bedroom
•***Word Origins:*** from French words meaning "following"

ensure *verb*
to make certain: *Please ensure that the dogs don't escape.*

enter *verb*
1 to go in: *Enter the cinema by the side door.* 2 to join an organization: *He entered the army when he was 18.* 3 to go in for a competition or race:

A B C D E F G H I J K L M N O P Q R S T U V W X Y Z

They entered and won all four events. 4 to write information in a book or key it into a computer: *I'll enter your name and age at the top.*

enterprise *noun*
1 a new or difficult job: *My dad's involved in a new business enterprise.* 2 energy and spirit that helps you do something new or difficult: *Her enterprise in raising the money was rewarded.*
• ***Word Family:*** **enterprising** *adjective*

entertain *verb*
1 to keep you interested and amused: *A magician entertained us before the concert.* 2 to have people round for a meal or a party: *Our parents entertained 12 people for dinner last night.*
• ***Word Family:*** **entertainer** *noun* **entertaining** *adjective* **entertainment** *noun*

enthusiasm (*say* en-**thew**-zi-az-um) *noun*
the feeling of being keen on something and excited about it: *The audience showed their enthusiasm by wild clapping and shouting.*
• ***Word Family:*** **enthuse** *verb* to show or inspire enthusiasm **enthusiast** someone who is enthusiastic about something **enthusiastic** *adjective: enthusiastic applause* **enthusiastically** *adverb*

entice *verb*
to get someone to do what you want by offering them something they want: *We enticed the cat down from the tree with a saucer of milk.*
• ***Word Family:*** **enticement** *noun* **enticing** *adjective* **enticingly** *adverb*

entire *adjective*
whole and complete: *His entire fortune was donated to a Lost Dogs' Home.*
• ***Word Family:*** **entirely** *adverb* completely **entirety** (*say* en-**tie**-ra-tee) *noun*

entitle *verb*
to give you the right to do something: *You are entitled to vote now.*

entomology (*say* ent-a-**mol**-o-jee) *noun*
the study of insects
• ***Word Family:*** **entomologist** *noun* a scientist who studies insects **entomological** *adjective*
• ***Word Origins:*** from a Greek word meaning "cut up", the way insects' bodies are in three sections

entourage (*say* **on**-too-rahj) *noun*
a group of attendants or followers: *The pop star arrived with his usual entourage.*
• ***Word Origins:*** from a French word meaning "surround"

entrance (1) (*say* **en**-trance) *noun*
1 someone's arrival at a place: *Her entrance was greeted with wild applause.* 2 the way into a place: *The entrance was blocked with cars.*

entrance (2) (*say* en-**trahnce**) *verb*
to fill you with wonder and delight: *The music entranced us.*
• ***Word Family:*** **entrancing** *adjective* **entrancingly** *adverb.*

entrant (*say* **en**-trant) *noun*
someone who officially enters a competition or organization: *The poetry competition had only 70 entrants.*

entreat *verb*
to beg for something you want very much: *I entreated her to stay but she just walked away.*

entree (*say* **on**-tray) *noun*
a dish served before the main course of a meal
• ***Word Origins:*** from a French word meaning "enter"

entrepreneur (*say* on-tra-pre-**ner**) *noun*
someone who starts up a new business, especially a risky one
• ***Word Family:*** **entrepreneurial** *adjective: entrepreneurial skills*

entry *noun*
1 going in to a place: *No-one noticed their entry into the house.* 2 the way in to a place: *A large horse blocked the entry to the stables.* 3 a piece of information that is recorded in a book or computer
• ***Word Family:*** the plural is **entries**

envelop (*say* en-**vel**-op) *verb*
to cover completely: *Clouds enveloped the tops of the mountains.*
• ***Word Family:*** **enveloping** *adjective* **envelopment** *noun*

envelope (*say* **en**-va-lope *or* **on**-va-lope) *noun*
the flat, folded sheet of paper you use to send letters in
• ***Word Origins:*** from a French word meaning "to wrap up"

environment (*say* en-**vy**-ron-ment) *noun*
1 the people, places and events that affect your life 2 the weather conditions, water supply and plants in a place
• ***Word Family:*** **environmentalist** *noun* someone concerned with the problems of the environment, especially the effects of pollution **environmental** *adjective* **environmentally** *adverb*

environmentally-friendly *adjective*
harmless to the world around us: *an environmentally-friendly detergent*

envoy (*say* **en**-voy) *noun*
an official representative sent to another country to negotiate or have talks

envy (*say* **en**-vee) *noun*
1 a feeling of discontent or resentment at

another person's possessions or good fortune
envy *verb*
2 to wish that you could have something that another person has
•***Word Family:*** other verb forms are **envies, envied, envying** □ **enviable** *adjective* worth envying **envious** *adjective* full of envy **enviably** *adverb*

enzyme (*say* **en**-zime) *noun*
a substance in people's and animals bodies that causes a chemical change: *The food we eat is broken down by enzymes so we can digest it.*

eon *noun*
another spelling of **aeon**

epic *noun*
1 a long poem about heroic events and actions 2 a long, dramatic book or film
epic *adjective*
3 grand or heroic: *an epic film about space*

epidemic (*say* ep-i-**dem**-ik) *noun*
the outbreak of a disease that spreads quickly among the people living in an area: *a flu epidemic*

epilepsy (*say* **ep**-i-lep-see) *noun*
an illness, caused by a disorder in the brain that makes someone suddenly lose consciousness or have fits
•***Word Family:*** **epileptic** *noun* someone who suffers from epilepsy **epileptic** *adjective*
•***Word Origins:*** from a Greek word for "an attack"

epilogue (*say* **ep**-i-log) *noun*
an extra part after the end of a play or book
•***Word Origins:*** from a Greek word meaning "conclusion"

episode (*say* **ep**-i-sode) *noun*
1 a time in someone's life when something important or memorable happens 2 one complete part of a serial: *an episode of a TV series*
•***Word Family:*** **episodic** (*say* ep-i-**sod**-ik) *adjective* **episodically** *adverb*

epistle (*say* e-**pis**-ul) *noun*
1 a letter 2 **Epistle** one of the apostles' letters in the New Testament of the Bible
•***Word Family:*** **epistolary** (*say* ee-**pist**-a-la-ree) *adjective* **epistolatory** *adjective*

epitaph (*say* **ep**-i-tahf) *noun*
words written about someone on their gravestone

epitome (*say* e-**pit**-a-mee) *noun*
the best example of something: *He's the epitome of success.*
•***Word Family:*** **epitomize** or **epitomise** *verb* to be typical or characteristic of

epoch (*say* **ee**-pok) *noun*
1 a particular period of time, especially one seen as a new or important beginning 2 the main division of a period in geology, during which certain rocks formed

equal (*say* **eek**-wal) *adjective*
1 the same in size, amount, degree or value: *We received equal shares of ice-cream.*
equal *verb*
2 to add up to the same number 3 to be as good as someone else or something else: *Can you equal his record?*
equal *noun*
4 a person who is as good as someone else: *He is her equal in every respect.*
•***Word Family:*** other verb forms are **equals, equalled, equalling** □ **equality** (*say* e-**kwol**-i-tee) *noun* **equally** *adverb*

equalize or **equalise** *verb*
1 to make things equal 2 to score a last goal in a sport like football which makes the score exactly equal
•***Word Family:*** **equalizer** *noun* a goal that equalizes

equation (*say* ee-**kway**-zhon) *noun*
an expression in maths showing one amount or set of values is equal to another
•***Word Family:*** **equate** *verb*

equator (*say* ee-**kway**-ta) *noun*
an imaginary circle drawn round the Earth, midway between the North and South Poles
•***Word Family:*** **equatorial** (*say* ek-wa-**taw**-ri-al) *adjective* near the equator: *equatorial rainforests*

equestrian (*say* e-**kwes**-tri-an) *noun*
1 a horserider
equestrian *adjective*
2 to do with horseriding: *an equestrian event at the show*
•***Word Origins:*** from a Latin word meaning "horse"

equilateral (*say* eek-wi-**lat**-er-al) *adjective*
with sides of equal length: *an equilateral triangle*

equilibrium (*say* eek-wi-**lib**-ri-um) *noun*
1 a balance between different forces 2 a calm and balanced state of mind: *It took a while for him to regain his equilibrium after the accident.*

equinox (*say* **ee**-kwi-noks) *noun*
one of the two days when the sun crosses the equator and day and night are of equal length
•***Word Origins:*** from a Latin word meaning "equal night"

equip (*say* e-**kwip**) *verb*
to provide tools, machines or other things that would be useful: *to equip a boat with radar*
•***Word Family:*** other forms are **equips, equipped, equipping** □ **equipment** *noun*

equivalent (*say* e-**kwiv**-a-lent) *adjective*
similar in value, effect or amount: *A mile is equivalent to 1.609 km.*

era (*rhymes with* nearer) *noun*
a long period of time: *the Christian era / an era of progress*

eradicate (*say* e-**rad**-i-kate) *verb*
to get rid of something completely so that it won't return: *The doctors have eradicated smallpox.*
•*Word Family:* **eradication** *noun*

erase (*say* e-**raze**) *verb*
to rub something out or remove it
•*Word Family:* **eraser** *noun* anything that erases, especially a rubber **erasure** *noun*

erect (*say* e-**rekt**) *adjective*
1 upright
erect *verb*
2 to build something: *We erected a monument in his honour.*
•*Word Family:* **erectly** *adverb* **erectness** *noun*

erection *noun*
the stiffening of a man's penis that happens when he is ready to have sex

ermine (*say* **er**-min) *noun*
the valuable, white, winter fur of a weasel or stoat

erode (*say* e-**rode**) *verb*
to wear something away: *Wind and water eroded the soil. / Support for the government was eroded by the mistakes they made.*
•*Word Family:* **erosion** *noun*

erotic (*say* e-**rot**-ik) *adjective*
to do with sexual love
•*Word Origins:* from the Greek word *Eros*, the god of love in Greek myths

err *verb*
to make a mistake
•*Word Family:* **erring** *adjective*

errand *noun*
a short trip you make to do a job for someone

erratic (*say* e-**rat**-ik) *adjective*
irregular so that you don't know what to expect: *erratic winds / erratic behaviour*
•*Word Family:* **erratically** *adverb*

error *noun*
a mistake
•*Word Family:* **erratum** *noun* a correction for a printed mistake **erroneous** *adjective* wrong **erroneously** *adverb*

erupt *verb*
1 to throw out lava and hot ash from the centre of a volcano 2 to burst out unexpectedly and violently: *Fighting erupted outside the pub.*
•*Word Family:* **eruption** *noun* **eruptive** *adjective*

escalate (*say* **es**-ka-late) *verb*
to increase or become more serious or more intense: *The war escalated on several fronts.*
•*Word Family:* **escalation** *noun*

escalator (*say* **es**-ka-lay-tor) *noun*
a moving staircase

escapade (*say* **es**-ka-pade) *noun*
a reckless or wild adventure

escape (*say* es-**kape**) *verb*
1 to get free from somewhere you were being held: *Two men escaped from prison yesterday.* 2 to avoid something dangerous or unpleasant: *She was lucky to escape injury.*
escape *noun*
3 escaping, or a way of escape
•*Word Family:* **escapee** *noun* someone who has escaped

escort (*say* **es**-kort) *noun*
1 a person or group that travels with someone: *The vehicle had an escort of motor cycles.*
escort (*say* es-**kort**) *verb*
2 to go with someone to keep them company or to protect them

especially *adverb*
particularly: *I love walking, especially in the spring.*

espionage (*say* **es**-pi-a-nahzh) *noun*
spying

esplanade (*say* **es**-pla-nahd *or* **es**-pla-nade) *noun*
a public path or road, usually by the sea

espresso *noun*
strong coffee made by forcing steam under pressure through ground coffee beans
•*Word Origins:* from an Italian word meaning "pressed out"

essay *noun*
a short piece of writing about a particular subject
•*Word Family:* **essayist** *noun* someone who writes essays

essence *noun*
1 the basic nature of a person or thing: *The essence of his character is kindness.* 2 a concentrated form of a substance: *vanilla essence*

essential (*say* e-**sen**-shal) *adjective*
absolutely necessary: *It's essential that you post this letter.*
•*Word Family:* **essentials** *plural noun* things that are basic and absolutely necessary **essentially** *adverb*

establish *verb*
1 to set something up and get it working: *The group established a new club in the area.* 2 to find

something out or show that something is true: *to establish why someone was angry*
•***Word Family:*** **establishment** *noun*

estate *noun*
1 a large piece of private land, especially in the country 2 an area of land on which a lot of houses or factories have been built 3 the money and possessions left by someone when they die

estate agent *noun*
a person whose job is selling flats, houses or land for people

esteem *verb*
1 to have great respect for someone you think highly of: *We've always esteemed your father for his dedication to our company.*
esteem *noun*
2 respect for someone you think highly of
•***Word Family:*** **esteemed** *adjective* respected

estimate (*say* **est**-i-mate) *verb*
1 to work something out approximately: *We estimate it will take two days.*
estimate (*say* **es**-ti-mit) *noun*
2 a rough guess or calculation: *What's your estimate of his abilities?*
•***Word Family:*** **estimation** *noun* your judgment or opinion

estuary (*say* **es**-choo-a-ree) *noun*
the wide mouth of a river where it meets the sea
•***Word Family:*** the plural is **estuaries** □ **estuarine** *adjective*

et cetera (*say* et **set**-er-a) *phrase*
and other similar things as well
•***Word Family:*** the short form is **etc.**
•***Word Origins:*** these words come from Latin

etch *verb*
1 to engrave a picture on a metal plate, by scratching the design through a layer of wax, and then letting acid eat into the exposed metal 2 to make prints from a picture that has been etched 3 to fix something clearly in your memory: *His face was etched in her memory.*
•***Word Family:*** **etching** *noun* a print made from a picture that has been etched

eternal (*say* e-**tern**-al) *adjective*
lasting for ever, with no beginning or end
•***Word Family:*** **eternally** *adverb*

eternity (*say* e-**ter**-na-tee) *noun*
1 time without beginning or end 2 time that seems endless: *It took an eternity for the doctor to arrive.*

ether (*say* **ee**-ther) *noun*
a liquid chemical once used as an anaesthetic to make patients sleep during operations, but now used to dissolve other substances
•***Word Origins:*** from a Greek word for "upper air"

ethics *plural noun*
the rules or principles that tell us what is right and what is wrong
•***Word Family:*** **ethic** *noun* **ethical** *adjective*

ethnic *adjective*
to do with people who belong to a particular national or racial group
•***Word Family:*** **ethnically** *adverb* **ethnicity** *noun*
•***Word Origins:*** from a Greek word meaning "nation"

ethnocentric (*say* eth-no-**sen**-trik) *adjective*
tending to believe that your own group or culture is the best and that all other groups are inferior
•***Word Family:*** **ethnocentrism** *noun*

etiquette (*say* **et**-i-ket) *noun*
rules for how to be polite

etymology (*say* et-i-**mol**-a-jee) *noun*
1 the study of the origin, history and changes in a word made over time 2 an account of the history of a particular word
•***Word Family:*** the plural is **etymologies** □ **etymological** *adjective* **etymologically** *adverb*

eucalyptus (*say* yoo-ka-**lip**-tus) *noun*
a type of tree that produces an oil used in medicine
•***Word Family:*** the plural is **eucalyptuses** or **eucalypti** □ **eucalyptus** *adjective*
•***Word Origins:*** from Greek words meaning "well covered" (as the flower bud is)

euphemism (*say* **yoo**-fem-iz-um) *noun*
a polite or pleasant-sounding word or phrase used instead of another word or phrase which is accurate but might shock or upset people: *To "pass away" is a euphemism for "to die".*
•***Word Family:*** **euphemistic** *adjective* **euphemistically** *adverb*

euphoria (*say* yoo-**faw**-ri-a) *noun*
a feeling of great joy or happiness that often doesn't last very long
•***Word Family:*** **euphoric** *adjective*

eureka (*say* yoo-**ree**-ka) *interjection*
an exclamation of triumph at a discovery

euthanasia (*say* yoo-tha-**nay**-zha) *noun*
the act of helping or letting someone die when they no longer wish to live, especially when they are suffering from a painful disease that cannot be cured

evacuate (*say* e-**vak**-yoo-ate) *verb*
to move people away from a dangerous

place: *to evacuate people from a flooded town*
•***Word Family:*** **evacuee** (*say* e-vak-yoo-**ee**) *noun* someone who is evacuated **evacuation** *noun*

evade *verb*
to cleverly avoid something
•***Word Family:*** **evasion** *noun* **evasive** *adjective* **evasively** *adverb*

evaluate (*say* e-**val**-yoo-ate) *verb*
to decide how important, useful or good something is: *We will evaluate your work at the end of term.*
•***Word Family:*** **evaluation** *noun*

evangelist (*say* e-**van**-ja-list) *noun*
a person who travels about teaching from the Bible and trying to persuade people to become Christians
•***Word Family:*** **evangelism** *noun* **evangelize** or **evangelise** *verb*

evaporate (*say* e-**vap**-a-rate) *verb*
to dry up and change into vapour: *Liquid begins to evaporate when it boils.*
•***Word Family:*** **evaporated** *adjective* dried or concentrated: *evaporated milk* **evaporation** *noun*

evasion (*say* e-**vay**-zhon) *noun*
escaping or avoiding something or someone: *evasion of income tax*
•***Word Family:*** **evasive** *adjective*: *an evasive answer* **evasively** *adverb* **evasiveness** *noun*

eve *noun*
the day or the night before a holiday or other important day: *New Year's Eve*

even (*say* **ee**-ven) *adjective*
1 able to be divided by two: *an even number such as two, four and six* 2 being the same in size or amount 3 equal: *The scores were even at half-time.* 4 calm and steady: *an even temper* 5 level or without bumps: *an even cricket pitch*
even *adverb*
6 still: *Their car is even bigger than ours.* 7 in spite of: *Even if it rains we'll still have our picnic.*
even *verb*
8 to make or become even
•***Word Family:*** **evenly** *adverb* **evenness** *noun*

evening (*say* **eev**-ning) *noun*
the part of the day between sunset and nightfall

event (*say* e-**vent**) *noun*
1 anything that happens or takes place, especially something important 2 any of the separate competitions in a sporting tournament or programme: *The long jump is the third event after lunch.*
•***Word Family:*** **eventful** *adjective* full of interesting or exciting events: *an eventful holiday*

eventual (*say* e-**ven**-tyoo-al) *adjective*
happening finally or in the end: *What was the eventual outcome of their argument?*
•***Word Family:*** **eventually** *adverb* **eventuality** *noun*

evergreen *noun*
1 a tree or plant that keeps its leaves throughout the year
evergreen *adjective*
2 having leaves all year long

every (*say* **ev**-ree) *adjective*
1 all the separate members of a group: *Every girl in my family has red hair.* 2 **every other** one out of every two: *He comes to clean the house every other week.* 3 **every so often** from time to time

everyday *adjective*
suitable for ordinary occasions: *everyday clothes*

everything *pronoun*
1 all 2 most important: *Her family is everything to her.*

evict (*say* e-**vikt**) *verb*
to force someone to move out of their home: *The landlord can evict you if you don't pay your rent.*
•***Word Family:*** **eviction** *noun*

evidence (*say* **ev**-i-dence) *noun*
1 anything you see or hear that makes you believe something 2 a sign or indication: *There was little evidence of suffering in his face.*
evidence *verb*
3 to show clearly

evident *adjective*
easily seen or understood: *It was evident that she was not amused.*
•***Word Family:*** **evidently** *adverb*

evil (*say* **ee**-vil) *adjective*
1 wicked or very bad: *evil deeds*
evil *noun*
2 anything that is evil or harmful

evolution *noun*
1 the idea that plants and animals have gradually changed and developed over time
2 gradual change
•***Word Family:*** **evolutionary** *adjective*

evolve *verb*
to change or develop gradually: *Humans evolved from apes.*

ewe (*say* yoo) *noun*
a female sheep

exact (*say* eg-**zakt**) *adjective*
precisely correct or accurate: *What is the exact time?*
•***Word Family:*** **exacting** *adjective* strict and demanding **exactly** *adverb*

exaggerate (*say* eg-**zaj**-a-rate) *verb*
to say that something is bigger, better, worse and so on than it really is
•***Word Family:*** **exaggeration** *noun* **exaggerated** *adjective*

examine (*say* eg-**zam**-in) *verb*
1 to inspect or test carefully: *to examine your teeth* 2 to test a person's knowledge or skill by questions or exercises
•***Word Family:*** **examination** *noun* a test of someone's understanding and knowledge of a subject **examinee** *noun* someone who is examined **examiner** *noun* someone who examines

example *noun*
1 something that shows what other things in its group or kind are like: *This house is a good example of Victorian architecture.* 2 something you learn from: *Let her success be an example to you.*

exasperate *verb*
to irritate or provoke someone very much
•***Word Family:*** **exasperation** *noun* **exasperating** *adjective*

excavate (*say* **eks**-ka-vate) *verb*
1 to make a hole by digging 2 to uncover by digging: *The archaeologists excavated several ancient bowls at the building site.*
•***Word Family:*** **excavation** *noun* a hole or site being excavated **excavator** *noun* a person or machine that excavates

exceed (*say* ek-**seed**) *verb*
to be greater than or go beyond something: *The party's great success exceeded our hopes.*
•***Word Family:*** **exceeding** *adjective* great or extreme **exceedingly** *adverb* extremely

excel (*say* ek-**sel**) *verb*
to be unusually talented or better than others: *She excels in all sports.*
•***Word Family:*** other forms are **excels, excelled, excelling**

excellent (*say* **ek**-sa-lent) *noun*
very good or of the best quality
•***Word Family:*** **excellence** *noun*

exception (*say* ek-**sep**-shon) *noun*
something or someone that is not included or does not follow a general rule
•***Word Family:*** **exceptional** *adjective* unusual or extraordinary **exceptionally** *adverb*

excerpt (*say* **ek**-serpt) *noun*
an extract or part from a book, speech or film

excess (*say* ek-**sess**) *noun*
1 too much of something, or more than you need: *an excess of enthusiasm.*

excess *adjective*
2 more than is usual or necessary
•***Word Family:*** **excessive** *adjective: excessive eating* **excessively** *adverb* **excessiveness** *noun*

exchange *verb*
1 to give or receive something in return for something else: *The family exchanged gifts on Christmas Day.*

exchange *noun*
2 exchanging: *Their exchange of angry words was heard by all the neighbours.* 3 a central office or building that connects things: *a telephone exchange* 4 a place for buying, selling or exchanging goods: *a stock exchange*

excite (*say* ek-**site**) *verb*
to make someone interested or lively: *We were all excited about the school trip.*
•***Word Family:*** **excitement** *noun* being excited, or anything that excites you **exciting** *adjective* **excitingly** *adverb*

exclaim (*say* eks-**klame**) *verb*
to speak out suddenly and loudly, often from surprise or pain
•***Word Family:*** **exclamation** *noun* a cry or other loud expression

exclamation mark *noun*
a punctuation mark (!), used to show a strong emphasis, as in *Stop thief!*

exclude (*say* eks-**klood**) *verb*
1 to leave out: *to exclude the last paragraph of a story* 2 to keep someone out: *He was excluded from membership.*
•***Word Family:*** **exclusion** *noun* excluding

exclusive (*say* eks-**kloo**-siv) *adjective*
1 fashionable or only allowing certain people in: *He belongs to an exclusive golf club.* 2 belonging solely to a single person or group: *We have exclusive rights to the book.*
•***Word Family:*** **exclusively** *adverb* **exclusiveness** *noun*

excrete (*say* eks-**kreet**) *verb*
to pass waste matter out of your body
•***Word Family:*** **excreta** *plural noun* excreted matter, such as faeces or sweat **excretion** *noun* excreting, or anything that is excreted **excretory** *adjective*

excruciating (*say* eks-**kroo**-shee-ayt-ing) *adjective*
causing very bad pain or suffering: *excruciating cramps*
•***Word Family:*** **excruciatingly** *adverb*
•***Word Origins:*** from a Latin word meaning "torture"

excursion (*say* eks-**ker**-shon) *noun*
a short trip or outing

A B C D E F G H I J K L M N O P Q R S T U V W X Y Z

excuse (*rhymes with* fuse) *verb*
1 to forgive or overlook: *Please excuse my lateness.* 2 to be allowed to leave: *She was excused from the room.*
excuse (*rhymes with* juice) *noun*
3 a reason that you give to explain why you were late or did something wrong: *What's your excuse this time?*
• ***Word Family:*** **excusable** *adjective* that can be excused

execute (*say* **ek**-si-kyoot) *verb*
1 to do or perform something: *The diver executed a perfect somersault in the air.* 2 to put someone to death as legal punishment
• ***Word Family:*** **executioner** *noun* a public official appointed to execute people **execution** *noun*

executive (*say* eg-**zek**-yoo-tiv) *noun*
1 someone with the power to make decisions, especially in a company
executive *adjective*
2 having the authority or power to carry out plans and make decisions: *The company has promoted her to an executive position.*

exempt (*say* eg-**zempt**) *verb*
to free or release someone from something they are supposed to do: *He was exempted from sport because of his broken leg.*
• ***Word Family:*** **exemption** *noun*

exercise (*say* **ek**-ser-size) *noun*
1 an activity that you do to make your body fitter and stronger 2 a set of questions in a text book or piece of work that you do
exercise *verb*
3 to do exercises, or make an animal do them: *to exercise a horse*

exert (*say* eg-**zert**) *verb*
to use or apply something, especially power or influence: *to exert pressure on a friend to do what you want*
• ***Word Family:*** **exertion** *noun* a vigorous effort

exhale (*say* eks-**hale**) *verb*
to breathe out air or smoke

exhaust (*say* eg-**zawst**) *verb*
1 to use up something completely: *The children exhausted their teacher's patience.* 2 to tire someone out: *The athlete was exhausted by the race.*
exhaust *noun*
3 the hot gases that come from an engine 4 the pipe or other outlet through which the hot gases are released
• ***Word Family:*** **exhaustion** *noun* great tiredness **exhaustive** *adjective* extremely thorough: *an exhaustive inquiry into the bombing*

exhibit (*say* eg-**zib**-it) *verb*
1 to show or display something: *The artist exhibited his works throughout Europe.*
exhibit *noun*
2 an object or collection of objects that are exhibited.
• ***Word Family:*** **exhibitor** *noun* someone who exhibits things **exhibition** (*say* ek-si-**bish**-on) *noun*

exhilarate (*say* eg-**zil**-a-rate) *verb*
to make someone lively or excited: *The sea air exhilarated us.*
• ***Word Family:*** **exhilarating** *adjective* **exhilaratingly** *adverb* **exhilaration** *noun*

exile *noun*
1 a punishment which means that you have to leave your home or country: *The defeated leader spent several years in exile.* 2 someone who has to leave their home or country in this way
exile *verb*
3 to force someone to leave their home or country

exist (*say* eg-**zist**) *verb*
1 to live or be real: *Does God exist?* 2 to occur: *This species of coral exists only on the Great Barrier Reef.*
• ***Word Family:*** **existence** *noun* **existent** *adjective*

exit *noun*
1 a way out 2 going out or leaving: *The actor made an exit from the stage.*
exit *verb*
3 to go out or away 4 to leave the file or document of a computer

exodus (*say* **eks**-o-dus) *noun*
the leaving of a large number of people: *a mass exodus*

exorcize or **exorcise** (*say* **ek**-sor-size) *verb*
to drive out an evil spirit using religious ceremonies: *The priest exorcized the ghost from the cellar.*
• ***Word Family:*** **exorcism** *noun* the words or ceremony used to exorcize evil spirits **exorcist** *noun* someone who exorcizes evil spirits

exoskeleton (*say* ek-so-**skel**-e-ton) *noun*
a hard, outer covering that gives protection, such as the shell of a tortoise

exotic (*say* eg-**zot**-ik) *adjective*
1 coming from a foreign country: *exotic fruit* 2 strikingly different or fascinating: *an exotic dress*
• ***Word Family:*** **exotically** *adverb*

expand *verb*
1 to make something larger or to become larger: *The company expanded its staff to cope with all the work.* 2 to express something in more detail:

Please expand your story by adding some facts about your trip. 3 to spread: *His face expanded into a broad, welcoming smile.*
• ***Word Family:*** **expansion** *noun*

expanse *noun*
a large or widespread area: *an expanse of grass*

expect *verb*
1 to believe that a particular thing will happen: *We expect him to come before lunch.* 2 to suppose or think something: *I expect that you are right.*
• ***Word Family:*** **expectant** *adjective* pregnant: *an expectant mother* **expectantly** *adverb* full of hope: *We waited expectantly for our presents.*
expectation *noun*

expedient (*say* eks-**pee**-di-ent) *adjective*
suitable or advisable under the circumstances: *It's expedient to go to school near your home.*
• ***Word Family:*** **expedience** or **expediency** *nouns* the quality of being expedient
expediently *adverb*

expedite (*say* **eks**-pa-dite) *verb*
to hasten the progress of
• ***Word Family:*** **expeditious** (*say* eks-pa-**dish**-us) *adjective* quick or prompt **expeditiously** *adverb*

expedition (*say* ek-spa-**dish**-on) *noun*
a trip made for a special purpose, such as to explore a place

expel *verb*
1 to force or send something out: *to expel air from your lungs* 2 to force someone to leave a school permanently: *John was expelled from school for smoking in class.*
• ***Word Family:*** other forms are **expels, expelled, expelling** □ **expulsion** *noun*

expense *noun*
1 cost 2 **expenses** the money spent, needed or provided for something: *travelling expenses*

expensive *adjective*
costing a lot of money
• ***Word Family:*** **expensively** *adverb*

experience (*say* eks-**peer**-i-ence) *noun*
1 an event or circumstance that happens to you or that you see 2 skill or knowledge you gain along the way
experience *verb*
3 to feel or go through something: *to experience pain*
• ***Word Family:*** **experienced** *adjective* wise

experiment (*say* eks-**pe**-ri-ment) *noun*
1 a test to examine an idea you have or discover something unknown
experiment *verb*
2 to try or test something in order to make a discovery
• ***Word Family:*** **experimentation** *noun* making experiments **experimental** *adjective*: *We're only at the experimental stage with this new drug.*
experimentally *adverb*

expert *noun*
1 someone who has special knowledge or training
expert *adjective*
2 having special skill or knowledge: *an expert witness*
• ***Word Family:*** **expertise** (*say* ek-sper-**teez**) *noun* the skill or knowledge that an expert has
expertly *adverb*: *He rode his horse expertly.*

expire *verb*
1 to come to an end: *The contract expired last week.* 2 to die: *The old man expired in his home.* 3 to breathe out
• ***Word Family:*** **expiry** *noun* **expiration** *noun*

explain *verb*
to make something clear and easy to understand: *He explained the meaning of the poem.*
• ***Word Family:*** **explanatory** *adjective* meant to explain: *explanatory notes* **explicable** *adjective* able to be explained **explanation** *noun*

explode *verb*
1 to burst or blow up 2 to show your feelings suddenly or noisily: *to explode into laughter*

exploit (*say* eks-**ployt**) *verb*
1 to use something or someone for your own advantage
exploit (*say* **eks**-ployt) *noun*
2 a brave or daring act: *We heard about his exploits during the battle.*
• ***Word Family:*** **exploitative** *adjective* exploiting someone **exploitation** *noun* exploiting
exploitable *adjective*

explore *verb*
1 to travel in order to discover a place 2 to examine closely: *We explored all possibilities before reaching a decision.*
• ***Word Family:*** **explorer** *noun* someone who explores **exploration** *noun* **exploratory** *adjective*: *an exploratory operation*

explosion (*say* eks-**plozh**-on) *noun*
1 the exploding of something, especially by a bomb 2 the loud sound this makes 3 a sudden outburst or increase: *a population explosion*
• ***Word Family:*** **explode** *verb*

export (*say* ex-**port**) *verb*
1 to send goods to another country
export (*say* **ex**-port) *noun*
2 something that is exported
• ***Word Family:*** **exporter** *noun* someone who exports goods

A B C D E F G H I J K L M N O P Q R S T U V W X Y Z

expose *verb*
1 to uncover, lay open or reveal something: *to expose your skin to the sun* 2 to let light on to a film to make a photograph

exposure *noun*
1 uncovering or revealing something: *exposure to radiation* 2 the effect of being in very cold weather for a long time: *The explorers suffered from exposure.* 3 letting light on to a film 4 the amount of film that you use to take one photograph

express *verb*
1 to show or reveal something, usually by putting it into words: *to express your feelings*
express *adjective*
2 definite or clear: *money set aside for an express purpose* 3 fast: *an express train / express post*
express *noun*
4 a fast train
•***Word Family:*** **expressive** *adjective* showing how you feel **expressively** *adverb* **expressly** *adverb* clearly

expression (*say* eks-**presh**-on) *noun*
1 the act of expressing in words: *an expression of opinion* 2 the look on your face 3 a phrase that has a special meaning

expressway *noun*
a freeway or motorway

expulsion *noun*
expelling or being expelled

exquisite (*say* eks-**kwiz**-it *or* **eks**-kwiz-it) *adjective*
1 extremely beautiful or delicate 2 intense or keen: *exquisite pleasure*
•***Word Family:*** **exquisitely** *adverb* **exquisiteness** *noun*

extend *verb*
1 to spread or stretch out: *The hills seemed to extend for ever.* 2 to make something bigger or longer: *to extend a road* 3 to offer something such as help or friendship: *to extend a welcome to someone*

extension (*say* eks-**ten**-shon) *noun*
1 extending or lengthening 2 an added part: *an extension to the house*
extension *adjective*
3 extending: *an extension lead*

extensive *adjective*
large or widespread: *An extensive search was made for the missing child.*

extent *noun*
1 the length or area that something covers: *We were shocked at the extent of the damage.* 2 the limits of something: *the full extent of someone's powers*

exterior (*say* eks-**tear**-i-a) *adjective*
1 outside: *exterior decoration / exterior influences*
exterior *noun*
2 the outer surface or view: *The exterior of the house is in bad repair.*

exterminate (*say* eks-**ter**-mi-nate) *verb*
to destroy completely: *Poison has exterminated thousands of cockroaches.*
•***Word Family:*** **extermination** *noun* exterminating **exterminator** *noun* someone who exterminates something

external *adjective*
1 on the outside or outer part: *The external appearance of a building.* 2 foreign: *Who's in charge of external affairs?*
•***Word Family:*** **externally** *adverb*

extinct *adjective*
1 no longer existing: *Dinosaurs are now extinct.* 2 no longer capable of erupting: *an extinct volcano*
•***Word Family:*** **extinction** *noun*

extinguish (*say* eks-**ting**-wish) *verb*
1 to put a fire or flame out: *Please extinguish your cigarettes.* 2 to bring something to an end: *All hope was extinguished when the crashed plane was found.*
•***Word Family:*** **extinguisher** *noun: a fire extinguisher*

extra *adjective*
1 more than is usual or necessary: *We need an extra plate for the baby.*
extra *noun*
2 something that is additional 3 a person hired for a very small part in a film, such as a member of a large crowd

extract (*say* eks-**trakt**) *verb*
1 to get something or someone out with difficulty or by force: *The dentist extracted my tooth. / The police extracted information from the suspect.*
extract (*say* **eks**-trakt) *noun*
2 something that is extracted: *vanilla extract*
3 a passage taken from a book

extraction *noun*
1 taking something out: *the extraction of oil from the sea* 2 where your family comes from originally: *I'm of Chinese extraction.*

extraordinary (*say* eks-**tror**-din-ree) *adjective*
unusual or remarkable
•***Word Family:*** **extraordinarily** *adverb*

extraterrestrial *adjective*
1 outside Earth: *extraterrestrial life forms*
extraterrestrial *noun*
2 a living creature from outside Earth

extravagant (*say* eks-**trav**-a-gant) *adjective*
1 wasteful, especially with money 2 too much or too high: *extravagant praise / extravagant prices*
•***Word Family:*** **extravagance** *noun* **extravagantly** *adverb*

extreme *adjective*
1 very great: *extreme danger* 2 going beyond the usual limits: *extreme views* 3 outermost: *the extreme edge of the paddock*
•***Word Family:*** **extremely** *adverb* very **extremity** *noun* (**extremities**) your hand or foot: *Frostbite had affected her extremities.*

eye *noun*
1 the organ or body part used for seeing
2 something like an eye, or with the shape of an eye: *the eye of a needle / an electronic eye* 3 the ability to notice: *She has an eye for detail.*
4 attention: *The teacher kept her eye on the students during the exam.*
eye *verb*
5 to look at something or someone closely: *The fox eyed the chickens.*
•***Word Family:*** other forms of the verb are **eyes, eyed, eying**

eyeball *noun*
the whole of the eye, including the part inside your head

eyebrow *noun*
one of the tufts of hair on your forehead just above each eye

eyelash *noun*
one of the fringe of hairs growing on the edge of each eyelid

eyelid *noun*
one of the folds of skin which you can close to protect each eye

eyesight *noun*
the power to see

eyesore *noun*
something that looks ugly

eyewitness *noun*
1 someone who has actually seen an event and can tell people what happened
eyewitness *adjective*
2 first-hand: *an eyewitness account*

eyrie (*say* **ee**-ri) *noun*
an eagle's nest, usually built on a mountain or cliff

fable *noun*
a short story that teaches a lesson or moral: *"The hare and the tortoise" is one of Aesop's fables.*

fabric *noun*
material or cloth made by weaving or knitting and used to make clothes, curtains and so on

fabulous (*say* **fab**-yoo-lus) *adjective*
1 very good or wonderful: *What a fabulous dress!*
2 appearing or happening in fables: *Dragons are fabulous beasts.*
•***Word Family:*** **fabulously** *adverb*

face *noun*
1 the front part of your head from your forehead to your chin 2 your expression: *a happy face*
3 the surface of anything: *They disappeared off the face of the earth.*
face *verb*
4 to look or turn towards someone or something
5 to meet or confront someone: *He turned to face the waiting reporters. / to face trouble*
•***Word Family:*** **facial** *adjective* (*say* **fay**-shul) to do with the face: *facial hair / a facial resemblance*

facility (*say* fa-**sil**-i-tee) *noun*
1 an ability to do something easily and well: *His facility with numbers pleased his teacher.*
2 something that makes it easier to do things: *The school has good facilities for music and drama.*
•***Word Family:*** the plural is **facilities** □ **facilitate** *verb* to make something easier

facsimile (*say* fak-**sim**-i-lee) *noun*
an exact copy, especially of a book or document
•***Word Family:*** **fax** *noun*
•***Word Origins:*** from Latin words meaning "to make like"

fact *noun*
1 something that we know is real or true 2 **in fact** really or indeed: *In fact, I meant to tell you myself.*
•***Word Family:*** **factual** *adjective* based on facts: *a factual account* **factually** *adverb*

factor *noun*
1 something that helps to bring about a result: *Hard work was a major factor in his success.*
2 one of the numbers that divide exactly into another number: *2 and 4 are factors of 8.*
•***Word Family:*** **factorize** or **factorise** *verb* to break up into factors

A B C D E F G H I J K L M N O P Q R S T U V W X Y Z

factory (*say* **fak**-ta-ree) *noun*
a building or group of buildings where something is made or put together
•***Word Family:*** the plural is **factories**

faculty (*say* **fak**-ul-tee) *noun*
1 an ability or talent for something: *the faculty for getting into mischief* 2 any of your mental or physical powers: *the faculty of reason / the faculties of sight and hearing* 3 the section or staff of a university or college where you study related subjects: *the arts faculty*
•***Word Family:*** the plural is **faculties**

fade *verb*
1 to lose brightness or colour or make something lose brightness and colour: *The curtains faded over the years. / Sunlight faded the curtains.* 2 to disappear gradually: *His smile faded when he heard the news.*

faeces (*say* **fee**-seez) *plural noun*
solid waste from digested food, that you get rid of when you go to the toilet

Fahrenheit (*say* **fa**-ren-hite) *adjective*
using a scale of temperature with the melting point of ice (0°C) set at 32°F and the boiling point of water (100°C) set at 212°F
•***Word Origins:*** thought of by Gabriel *Fahrenheit*, a German scientist who lived from 1686 to 1736

fail *verb*
1 to be unsuccessful in something: *to fail a test* 2 to lose strength or stop working: *Her health failed. / the brakes failed* 3 to not do something that you are supposed to do: *to fail to keep a promise* 4 **without fail** for certain
•***Word Family:*** **failing** *noun* a fault or weakness **failure** *noun*

faint *adjective*
1 weak or not clear: *a faint hope / a faint light* 2 dizzy and unsteady: *I was faint with hunger.*
faint *noun*
3 a sudden loss of consciousness
faint *verb*
4 to lose consciousness for a short time
•***Word Family:*** **faintly** *adverb* **faintness** *noun*

fair (1) *adjective*
1 honest or done according to the rules: *a fair trial / a fair fight* 2 quite good or quite large: *a fair knowledge of football* 3 pale or light in colour: *fair skin / fair hair* 4 fine and clear: *fair weather* 5 beautiful: *a fair maiden*
•***Word Family:*** **fairness** *noun*

fair (2) *noun*
1 a travelling amusement show, with stalls and fun rides 2 a place where goods are exhibited, bought and sold: *a book fair*

fairly *adverb*
1 quite: *He was fairly tall.* 2 in a fair way: *Share the chocolate fairly.*

fairy *noun*
a small imaginary creature with magical powers
•***Word Family:*** the plural is **fairies**

fairy tale *noun*
a story about fairies or magical events

faith *noun*
1 trust or confidence: *I have faith in you.* 2 a religion: *the Christian faith / the Islamic faith*

faithful *adjective*
1 loyal: *a faithful servant* 2 accurate or truthful: *a faithful description*
•***Word Family:*** **faithfully** *adverb* **faithfulness** *noun*

fake *verb*
1 to copy something so that people think it is real: *to fake someone's signature* 2 to pretend: *to fake illness*
fake *adjective*
3 not genuine: *fake diamonds*
fake *noun*
4 something faked, or someone who fakes or deceives: *That moustache is a fake. / What a fake that salesman is.*

falcon *noun*
a hunting bird often used to hunt other birds or small animals
•***Word Family:*** **falconry** *noun* the breeding and training of falcons **falconer** *noun*

fall *verb*
1 to move downwards: *A leaf fell from the tree. / Prices fell.* 2 to become less: *The wind has fallen.* 3 to become: *to fall asleep* 4 to be killed: *to fall in battle* 5 to land: *Bombs fell on the city. / His glance fell on me.* 6 **fall back** to retreat 7 **fall back on** to have someone or something as a backup: *If my boyfriend won't go, I'll fall back on my brother.* 8 **fall out** to quarrel 9 **fall through** to come to nothing: *Their plans fell through.*
fall *noun*
10 the act of falling or a time when you fall: *to have a bad fall* 11 **falls** a waterfall
•***Word Family:*** other verb forms are **falls, fell, fallen, falling**

fall-out *noun*
the radioactive dust that falls through the air after a nuclear explosion or accident

fallow *adjective*
left ploughed but with no crop sown: *a fallow field*

false *adjective*
1 not true or correct: *a false statement* 2 not genuine: *false teeth* 3 not faithful or loyal: *a false friend*

•*Word Family:* **falsify** *verb* (**falsifies, falsified, falsifying**) to make something false by changing it: *to falsify a certificate* **falsely** *adverb* **falseness** *noun*

falsehood *noun*
a lie

falter (*say* **fawl**-ter) *verb*
to hesitate or waver: *Her speech faltered. / His determination faltered.*
•*Word Family:* **falteringly** *adverb*

fame *noun*
being well known and talked about: *His fame spread far and wide.*

familiar (*say* fa-**mil**-i-a) *adjective*
1 well-known: *a familiar face* 2 **familiar with** having a thorough knowledge of: *Are you familiar with the rules?*
•*Word Family:* **familiarize** or **familiarise** *verb* to make yourself familiar with something **familiarity** *noun* **familiarly** *adverb*
•*Word Origins:* from a Latin word meaning "of the household"

family *noun*
1 parents and their children: *She comes from a large family. / a single parent family* 2 a group of related things, especially a species of animals and plants 3 all the people descended from the same ancestors, such as parents, children, aunts, uncles and cousins
•*Word Family:* the plural is **families**

family tree *noun*
a diagram that you can draw to show how all the members of your family are related

famine (*say* **fam**-in) *noun*
a widespread and serious shortage of food

famished *adjective*
extremely hungry

famous *adjective*
very well known

fan (1) *noun*
1 something that makes air move about, to cool you down
fan *verb*
2 to send air towards something: *to fan your face with a programme* 3 to spread like a fan: *The searchers fanned out across the countryside.*
•*Word Family:* other verb forms are **fans, fanned, fanning**

fan (2) *noun*
an enthusiastic follower or supporter: *He's a mad-keen football fan.*

fanatic (*say* fa-**nat**-ik) *noun*
someone who is too enthusiastic about something: *a recycling fanatic*
•*Word Family:* **fanatical** *adjective* **fanatically** *adverb* **fanaticism** *noun*
•*Word Origins:* from a Latin word meaning "frenzied" or "inspired by a god"

fancy *verb*
1 to imagine: *Fancy her saying that! / He fancied he saw a rat.* 2 to like or wish for something: *Do you fancy a cold drink?*
fancy *noun*
3 something you imagine: *The siren he thought he heard was only a fancy.* 2 a fondness or liking: *He's taken a fancy to you.*
fancy *adjective*
5 not plain or ordinary: *fancy dress*
•*Word Family:* other verb forms are **fancies, fancied, fancying** □ other adjective forms are **fancier, fanciest** □ **fancier** *noun* someone with a special interest: *a pigeon-fancier* **fanciful** *adjective* in your imagination: *fanciful ideas about building a castle*

fanfare *noun*
a loud, musical introduction, usually played on trumpets

fang *noun*
a long, pointed tooth: *a serpent's fang*

fantastic (*say* fan-**tas**-tik) *adjective*
1 wonderful: *What a fantastic party!* 2 strange or unusual: *a fantastic tale of adventure*
•*Word Family:* **fantastically** *adverb*

fantasy (*say* **fan**-ta-see) *noun*
1 wild imagination: *your own world of fantasy*
2 a daydream: *a fantasy about your future*
•*Word Family:* the plural is **fantasies** □ **fantasize** or **fantasise** *verb*

far *adverb*
1 to, from or at a considerable distance: *How far did you go?* 2 much: *She's far better now that she's fitter.* 3 **as far as** to the extent that: *As far as I know, he's honest.*
far *adjective*
4 distant: *a far country* 5 the more distant of two: *the far end of the street*
•*Word Family:* other forms are **further** or **farther, furthest** or **farthest**

farce *noun*
1 a ridiculous or absurd event: *The whole trial was a farce.* 2 an amusing comedy, often with an unlikely plot and slapstick humour
•*Word Family:* **farcical** *adjective* **farcically** *adverb*

fare *noun*
1 the money you pay when you go on a bus, train and so on 2 food
fare *verb*
3 to get on or manage: *How did you fare in your interview?*

farewell (*say* fair-**wel**) *interjection*
goodbye

farm *noun*
1 an area of land used to raise crops or animals
farm *verb*
2 to use land for growing crops or raising animals: *to farm land*
• ***Word Family:*** **farmer** *noun* **farming** *noun*

fascinate (*say* **fas**-i-nate) *verb*
to attract or interest someone very much: *We were fascinated by his daredevil stunts.*
• ***Word Family:*** **fascinating** *adjective* **fascinatingly** *adverb* **fascination** *noun*
• ***Word Origins:*** from a Latin word meaning "to cast a spell on"

Fascism (*say* **fash**-iz-um) *noun*
a system of government which is usually led by a dictator, does not allow people to have opposing political ideas and does not allow people of a different race or nationality to have rights
• ***Word Family:*** **Fascist** *noun* **Fascist** *adjective*

fashion (*say* **fash**-on) *noun*
1 a style of dress: *I follow the latest fashions.* 2 a way of doing something: *He settled down to work in a businesslike fashion.*
fashion *verb*
3 to form or mould: *to fashion a jug out of clay*
• ***Word Family:*** **fashionable** *adjective*

fast (1) *adjective*
1 swift or quick: *a fast car / fast food* 2 ahead of the correct time: *My watch is fast.* 3 firmly fixed: *The post is fast in the ground.* 4 close: *We were always fast friends.*
fast *adverb*
5 firmly, tightly or securely: *She was fast asleep.* 6 quickly: *Don't speak so fast.*

fast (2) *noun*
1 a time when someone eats no food, often as a religious duty or a protest
fast *verb*
2 to eat no food: *to fast for a day*

fasten (*say* **far**-sen) *verb*
to fix something to something else: *to fasten a coat*
• ***Word Family:*** **fastener** *noun* **fastening** *noun*

fastidious (*say* fas-**tid**-i-us) *adjective*
fussy or difficult to please: *He's fastidious about cleaning his car.*
• ***Word Family:*** **fastidiously** *adverb*

fast-track *verb*
to move through a system, bring about, or move towards unusually fast: *to fast-track your passport application / to fast-track a new runway*

fat *noun*
1 the greasy white or yellow substance in human and animal bodies, which is a store of food and provides protection from the cold
2 an oily substance such as butter or lard, that you use in cooking
fat *adjective*
3 plump: *a fat cat* 4 large: *a fat profit*
• ***Word Family:*** other adjective forms are **fatter, fattest** □ **fatten** *verb* to make someone or something fat **fatty** *adjective* **(fattier, fattiest)**

fatal (*say* **fay**-tal) *adjective*
1 causing death or disaster: *a fatal blow to the head* 2 likely to have bad results: *a fatal mistake*
• ***Word Family:*** **fatality** *noun* a death caused by an accident **fatally** *adverb*

fate *noun*
1 the power that controls what will happen to you: *We'll leave it to fate.* 2 the final state or condition of a person or thing: *What do you think the fate of the hostages will be?*
• ***Word Family:*** **fateful** *adjective* changing the future in a bad way: *a fateful decision to go by train* **fatefully** *adverb*

father *noun*
1 a male parent 2 a title for a priest or abbot in the Catholic and Anglican churches 3 **the Father** a name for the God that Christians believe in
father *verb*
4 to be the father of someone
• ***Word Family:*** **fatherhood** *noun* **fatherly** *adjective*

father-in-law *noun*
your husband's or wife's father
• ***Word Family:*** the plural is **fathers-in-law**

fathom (*say* **fath**-um) *noun*
1 an old-fashioned measure of the depth of water, equal to 6 feet or about 2 metres
fathom *verb*
2 to understand or work something out: *I can't fathom that riddle.*

fatigue (*say* fa-**teeg**) *noun*
1 tiredness of your mind or body, usually because you've been working hard 2 the weakness in a material, especially metal, caused by repeated stresses or vibrations
fatigue *verb*
3 to make someone tired
• ***Word Family:*** other verb forms are **fatigues, fatigued, fatiguing**

fatwa (*say* **fat**-wah) *noun*
a religious decision or ruling in a Muslim country

fault *noun*
1 something that spoils someone or something: *Although she has faults, she's a good worker.*

2 responsibility: *It's my fault we missed the train.* 3 an incorrect serve in tennis and similar games 4 a large crack or break in rock caused by movement of the earth's crust 5 **at fault** guilty or in the wrong
fault *verb*
6 to find a fault in something: *We couldn't fault his performance.*
•***Word Family:*** **faulty** *adjective* **(faultier, faultiest)** not working properly, or having a fault: *You should return that faulty CD.*

fauna (*say* **faw**-na) *noun*
all the animals of a certain area or period of time
•***Word Origins:*** named after *Fauna*, the Roman goddess of the earth

favour or favor *noun*
1 a helpful or considerate act: *Would you do me a favour?* 2 approval or good-will: *It didn't take him long to win her favour.* 3 **in favour of** in support of: *I'm in favour of accepting the offer.*
favour *verb*
4 to like or support someone: *I favour him for captain.* 5 to oblige someone: *She favoured me with a small loan.* 6 to treat a part of your body gently: *The horse favoured its sore leg.*
•***Word Family:*** **favourable** *adjective* helpful or approving: *favourable winds* **favourably** *adverb*

favourite (*say* **fay**-va-rit) *noun*
1 someone or something you like better than the rest: *This film is my favourite.* 2 someone who is treated specially: *the teacher's favourite* 3 the person or animal who is expected to win, for example in a race
favourite *adjective*
4 that is a favourite: *a favourite uncle*
•***Word Family:*** **favouritism** *noun* treating one person or group better than another

fawn (1) *noun*
1 a young deer 2 a light, yellowish-brown colour

fawn (2) *verb*
1 to try to win someone's favour by flattering them 2 to show pleasure and affection by tail-wagging or licking
•***Word Family:*** **fawning** *adjective* **fawningly** *adverb*

fax *noun*
1 a machine that sends documents or pictures along a telephone line 2 the exact copy of the material sent this way
fax *verb*
3 to send by fax: *to fax a letter to Spain*
•***Word Family:*** the plural is **faxes**
•***Word Origins:*** a respelling of the beginning of *facs(imile)*

fear *noun*
1 a feeling that danger or something frightening is near
fear *verb*
2 to be frightened of something or someone: *to fear the dark* 3 to feel worried: *to fear for his life* 4 to suspect: *to fear that you've been forgotten*
•***Word Family:*** **fearful** *adjective* **fearfully** *adverb* **fearless** *adjective* not afraid **fearsome** *adjective* frightening

feasible (*say* **fee**-zi-bul) *adjective*
possible, or able to be done: *a feasible plan*
•***Word Family:*** **feasibly** *adverb*

feast *noun*
1 a large, special meal for many people
feast *verb*
2 to take part in a feast

feat *noun*
a remarkable achievement that takes courage, strength or skill

feather *noun*
1 one of the light, fluffy parts that cover a bird's body 2 **a feather in your cap** an achievement to be proud of
•***Word Family:*** **feathered** *adjective* **feathery** *adjective*

feature (*say* **fee**-cher) *noun*
1 a very good or noticeable part of something 2 a part of your face: *My big nose is my worst feature.* 3 a special story, interview or programme in a newspaper, magazine, or on TV 4 the main film at a cinema
feature *verb*
5 to play an important part in something: *Wizards and dragons feature in most of his stories.* 6 to include as one of the main characters or stars: *This cartoon features Daffy Duck.*

February *noun*
the second month of the year, with 28 days, or 29 in leap years

federal *adjective*
to do with one central government, rather than a number of states each with a separate government
•***Word Family:*** **federation** *noun* the coming together of states to form a nation under a central government

fee *noun*
a charge or payment, especially when you are paying someone such as a doctor, lawyer or private teacher: *school fees*

feeble *adjective*
weak or ineffective: *feeble limbs / feeble light*
•***Word Family:*** **feebleness** *noun* **feebly** *adverb*

A B C D E F G H I J K L M N O P Q R S T U V W X Y Z

feed *verb*
1 to give food to a person, animal or plant 2 to supply something with what it needs to keep going: *to feed data into a computer* 3 to eat or get nourishment: *The lamb feeds from its mother.*
feed *noun*
4 food, especially for animals: *feed for hens*
•*Word Family:* other verb forms are **feeds, fed, feeding** □ **feeder** *noun*

feedback *noun*
information that helps you find out the results or success of something: *Have you heard any feedback about the concert?*

feel *verb*
1 to discover or examine something by touching it: *to feel your way downstairs in the dark / to feel a damaged leg* 2 to experience an emotion or a sensation: *to feel hot / to feel frightened* 3 to believe: *We felt it was time to leave.*
feel *noun*
4 the way something seems when you touch it: *a rough feel*
•*Word Family:* other verb forms are **feels, felt, feeling**

feeler *noun*
a long, thin part sticking out from an insect, used for sensing things around it

felafel (*say* fa-**lah**-fel) *noun*
a spicy Middle Eastern rissole made of chickpeas, chopped onions, hot peppers and chilli sauce

feline (*say* **fee**-line) *adjective*
1 to do with or like a cat or the cat family
feline *noun*
2 a cat or member of the cat family

fell *verb*
to cut something down or make it fall: *to fell an oak tree / to fell a warrior*

fellow *noun*
1 a man or boy 2 a member of an academic or professional society: *a Fellow of the Royal Academy*
fellow *adjective*
3 having the same job or occupation: *fellow workers*
•*Word Family:* **fellowship** *noun*

felony (*say* **fel**-a-nee) *noun*
any serious crime, such as murder or robbery
•*Word Family:* **felon** *noun* someone who has committed a felony **felonious** *adjective*

felt *noun*
a matted cloth made of bits of wool, fur or hair that are pressed tightly together: *a felt hat*

female *noun*
1 a person or animal of the sex able to give birth to young
female *adjective*
2 of the female sex

feminine (*say* **fem**-a-nin) *adjective*
1 female 2 like a woman, or thought to be suitable for a woman
•*Word Family:* **femininity** *noun*

feminism (*say* **fem**-a-niz-um) *noun*
the belief that women should have the same rights and opportunities as men
•*Word Family:* **feminist** *noun* a supporter of feminism

fence *noun*
1 a barrier or boundary around a house, garden and so on 2 someone who buys and sells stolen goods 3 **sit on the fence** to remain neutral or refuse to take sides in a debate
fence *verb*
4 to build or put a fence around land or property 5 to fight with a sword as a sport
•*Word Family:* **fencer** *noun*

fencing *noun*
1 material used for building fences 2 the sport of fighting with long, slender swords

fend *verb*
1 **fend off** to defend yourself from blows: *to fend off an attacker* 2 **fend for yourself** to take care of or provide for yourself: *to fend for yourself on the streets*

feral (*say* **fe**-ral *or* **fear**-al) *adjective*
wild, especially after once being tame or domestic: *feral cats*

ferment (*say* fer-**ment**) *verb*
1 to change sugar to gas and alcohol by adding yeast or bacteria: *Yeast ferments the juice from crushed grapes and turns it into wine.*
ferment (*say* **fer**-ment) *noun*
2 a state of excitement or agitation
•*Word Family:* **fermentation** *noun*

fern *noun*
a green plant with large, feather-like leaves and no flowers
•*Word Family:* **ferny** *adjective*

ferocious (*say* fe-**ro**-shus) *adjective*
extremely savage or cruel: *a ferocious lion*
•*Word Family:* **ferociously** *adverb* **ferocity** *noun*

ferret *noun*
1 a long, thin animal trained to drive rabbits and rats from their holes
ferret *verb*
2 **ferret out** to search out: *to ferret out criminals*

ferry *noun*
1 a boat used to carry passengers and vehicles across water

ferry *verb*
2 to transport from one place to another: *to ferry children to school*
• ***Word Family:*** the plural of the noun is **ferries** □ other verb forms are **ferries, ferried, ferrying**

fertile *adjective*
1 able to have young 2 producing good crops: *fertile soil* 3 full of ideas: *a fertile imagination*
• ***Word Family:*** **fertility** *noun*
• ***Word Origins:*** from a Latin word meaning "able to bear"

fertilize or **fertilise** *verb*
1 to start the process of reproducing or having babies: *A male sperm fertilizes a female egg to start a new life.* 2 to make soil more fertile by adding substances to enrich it: *to fertilize the roses with compost*
• ***Word Family:*** **fertilization** *noun*

fertilizer or **fertiliser** *noun*
a substance added to soil to make plants grow better

festival *noun*
a day or period of celebration or rejoicing: *the festival of Easter / a festival of plays, films and street performances*

festive *adjective*
full of joy and goodwill: *His birthday party was a festive occasion.*
• ***Word Family:*** **festivity** *noun* (**festivities**)

fetch *verb*
1 to go and get something or someone: *to fetch water / to fetch someone from the airport* 2 to sell for: *This old chair should fetch a good price.*

fetching *adjective*
attractive or charming: *a fetching hat / a fetching grin*
• ***Word Family:*** **fetchingly** *adverb*

fete (*say* fate) *noun*
a small fair held to raise money for a school or charity
• ***Word Origins:*** from a French word meaning "feast"

fetlock *noun*
the part of a horse's leg just above the hoof, often with a tuft of hair on it

feud (*say* fewd) *noun*
1 a long-lasting, bitter quarrel, especially between families
feud *verb*
2 to carry on a quarrel for a long time: *The brothers feuded over the land.*

feudalism (*say* **few**-da-li-zum) *noun*
the system of social and political organization that was common in medieval Europe, in which peasants farmed land and had to respect and serve their lord, especially by fighting for him
• ***Word Family:*** **feudal** *adjective: the feudal system*

fever *noun*
1 a very high body temperature caused by an illness 2 agitation or excitement: *The football fans worked themselves into a fever.*
• ***Word Family:*** **feverish** *adjective* hot and sweaty **feverishly** *adverb*

few *adjective*
1 not many: *Few people are chosen to become leaders.*
few *noun*
2 a small number: *The few who know him love him.* 3 **a good few** or **quite a few** a fairly large number

fez *noun*
a round hat with a flat top and no brim, worn by men in Muslim countries
• ***Word Family:*** the plural is **fezzes**

fiancé (*say* fee-**on**-say) *noun*
the man you are engaged to
• ***Word Origins:*** this word comes from French

fiancée (*say* fee-**on**-say) *noun*
the woman you are engaged to
• ***Word Origins:*** this word comes from French

fiasco (*say* fee-**as**-ko) *noun*
a complete or disastrous failure
• ***Word Family:*** the plural is **fiascos**

fib *noun*
1 a lie about something unimportant
fib *verb*
2 to tell a fib
• ***Word Family:*** other verb forms are **fibs, fibbed, fibbing** □ **fibber** *noun*

fibre (*say* **figh**-ber) *noun*
1 a thread of material such as wool or cotton 2 the part of food or roughage that your body can't digest: *Cereal has plenty of fibre.*
• ***Word Family:*** **fibrous** *adjective*

fibreglass *noun*
a material made from fine glass fibres, mixed with plastic and used to build car bodies, boats and surfboards

fibula (*say* **fib**-yoo-la) *noun*
the thinner of the two long bones between your knee and ankle
• ***Word Family:*** the plural is **fibulas** or **fibulae** □ **fibular** *adjective*

fickle *adjective*
not loyal, or often changing your mind: *a fickle nature*
• ***Word Family:*** **fickleness** *noun*

fiction (*say* **fik**-shon) *noun*
1 a novel, short story or other writing that is imaginary or made up 2 something imagined or invented: *The judge said the whole case was a fiction.*
• ***Word Family:*** **fictional** *adjective: a fictional character* **fictionally** *adverb* **fictitious** *adjective*

fiddle *noun*
1 a violin 2 **fit as a fiddle** very healthy
fiddle *verb*
3 to play a violin 4 to move your hands restlessly
• ***Word Family:*** **fiddly** *adverb* intricate and difficult **fiddler** *noun*

fidelity (*say* fi-**del**-i-tee) *noun*
1 faithfulness or loyalty: *fidelity to your wife / fidelity to your beliefs* 2 exactness or accuracy: *the fidelity of sound produced by a radio*

fidget (*say* **fij**-it) *verb*
1 to move about restlessly or impatiently: *to fidget in your seat*
fidget *noun*
2 someone who fidgets
• ***Word Family:*** **fidgety** *adjective*

field (*say* feeld) *noun*
1 an open, cleared area of land: *a field of corn / a hockey field* 2 a place where oil or minerals are found: *a gold field* 3 an area of interest: *the field of science* 4 the selected grouping of data in a computer to make it easy to find and sort
field *verb*
5 to stop or catch the ball in sports such as cricket or baseball
field *adjective*
6 not taking place on the running track: *Javelin throwing is a field event.*
• ***Word Family:*** **fielder** *noun*

fiend (*say* feend) *noun*
1 an evil spirit or devil 2 a wicked person 3 an addict: *a golf fiend*
• ***Word Family:*** **fiendish** *adjective* cruel or wicked **fiendishly** *adverb*

fierce *adjective*
1 angry, threatening or aggressive: *a fierce dog* 2 intense or severe: *fierce competition for the scholarship*
• ***Word Family:*** **fiercely** *adverb* **fierceness** *noun*

fiery (*say* **figh**-a-ree) *adjective*
1 like fire: *a fiery glow* 2 passionate or intense: *a fiery temper*

fiesta (*say* fee-**es**-ta) *noun*
a festival, especially a religious holiday
• ***Word Origins:*** this word comes from Spanish

fifteen *noun*
the number 15
• ***Word Family:*** **fifteen** *adjective* **fifteenth** *noun* **fifteenth** *adjective*

fifty *noun*
the number 50
• ***Word Family:*** the plural is **fifties** □ **fifty** *adjective* **fiftieth** *noun* **fiftieth** *adjective*

fifty-fifty *adjective* and *adverb*
shared equally between two: *a fifty-fifty chance / We split the money fifty-fifty.*

fig *noun*
a small soft fruit containing many seeds, eaten fresh, preserved or dried

fight *noun*
1 a struggle, quarrel or contest: *a playground fight / the fight against cancer*
fight *verb*
2 to take part in a fight: *to fight a battle / to fight in a boxing match* 3 to try hard to achieve: *to fight for freedom*
• ***Word Family:*** other verb forms are **fights, fought, fighting** □ **fighter** *noun*

figure (*say* **fig**-er) *noun*
1 a symbol that stands for a number: *the figure 7* 2 a form or shape: *He has geometrical figures on his tie. / an athlete's lean figure* 3 an amount or sum: *The house sold for a high figure.* 4 a person or character: *an important figure in film-making* 5 **figures** sums or calculations: *good at figures*
figure *verb*
6 to appear or take part in something: *to figure prominently in the programme* 7 **figure out** to work out or understand: *to figure out the meaning of a song*

figurehead *noun*
1 someone in a high position but having no real power 2 a carved model, usually of a woman or mermaid, that decorates the bow of sailing ships

figure of speech *noun*
an expression, such as a simile or metaphor, in which words are not used in their usual sense: *Saying that the sun is a ball of fire is a figure of speech.*

filament (*say* **fil**-a-ment) *noun*
a very fine thread or wire, such as the wire in a light bulb that heats as electricity passes through it

file (1) *noun*
1 a group of papers or records kept in order or the folder in which they are stored 2 a row or line of people or things placed one behind the other 3 an organized store of related data stored in a computer
file *verb*
4 to put papers in order, for easy access: *to file papers in alphabetical order* 5 to march or walk in a line: *We filed into the cinema.*

file (2) *noun*
1 a flat or rounded steel tool, covered with fine ridges or teeth, for smoothing metal or wood
file *verb*
2 to use a file

fill *verb*
1 to make something full or to become full: *Fill my glass. / The dam filled during the flood.* 2 to use all the space or time available: *to fill a room with books / to fill an afternoon with reading* 3 to occupy: *to fill a position at work* 4 **fill in** (a) to complete a form (b) to replace or stand in for someone: *to fill in for someone when they're sick*
fill *noun*
5 enough to make you full: *to drink your fill*
•***Word Family:*** **filling** *noun: the filling for a pie / a filling for a tooth* **filler** *noun* something that is used for filling

fillet *noun*
1 a slice of tender meat or fish without the bone
fillet *verb*
2 to cut fish into fillets

filly *noun*
a female horse or pony up to four years old
•***Word Family:*** the plural is **fillies**

film *noun*
1 a series of moving pictures with added sound, projected onto a cinema screen or shown on TV 2 a roll of thin, light-sensitive plastic, for loading into a camera and taking photographs 3 a very thin sheet, layer or coating: *a film of plastic / a film of oil on the water*
film *verb*
4 to cover something with a film: *His eyes filmed with tears.* 5 to record on film: *They filmed the first scenes at the beach.*
•***Word Family:*** **filmy** *adjective* (**filmier, filmiest**) thin and transparent **filminess** *noun*

filter *noun*
1 a device for removing unwanted material from liquid, air or other things: *The swimming pool filter cleans the water. / the filter on a camera lens for controlling the colours reaching the film*
filter *verb*
2 to remove or separate by a filter: *to filter coffee*
•***Word Family:*** **filtrate** *noun* the liquid that has passed through a filter **filtration** *noun* the process of filtering

filth *noun*
something that is disgustingly mucky, obscene or repulsive
•***Word Family:*** **filthy** *adjective* (**filthier, filthiest**): *filthy clothes* **filthiness** *noun*

fin *noun*
1 one of the thin parts sticking out from a fish's body, used to guide or move it through the water 2 a fin-shaped structure on a plane, submarine or surfboard for balancing or guiding it

final (*say* **figh**-nal) *adjective*
1 last or coming at the end: *My answer is final. / the final words in a book*
final *noun*
2 a contest or examination coming at the end of a series: *a tennis final at Wimbledon*
•***Word Family:*** **finalize** or **finalise** *verb* to make something final: *to finalize arrangements* **finalist** *noun* someone taking part in a final **finally** *adverb*

finale (*say* fin-**ah**-lee) *noun*
the last part of a piece of music or the last act of a play, ballet or opera: *All the performers came back on for the grand finale.*

finance (*say* **figh**-nance) *noun*
1 the management of money: *She's an expert in finance.* 2 **finances** money or funds: *The club's finances are running low.*
finance *verb*
3 to provide money for something: *to finance a holiday*
•***Word Family:*** **financier** *noun* someone whose business is finance **financial** *adjective* **financially** *adverb*

find *verb*
1 to come across something by chance: *to find a pound coin* 2 to get something by search or effort: *to find the answer to a problem* 3 to reach: *The arrow found its mark.* 4 to discover or learn: *I found that he was a good worker.*
find *noun*
5 something discovered, especially something valuable: *The table we bought was a real find.*
•***Word Family:*** other verb forms are **finds, found, finding** □ **findings** *plural noun* useful information that you have found out **finder** *noun*

fine (1) *adjective*
1 beautiful or of high quality: *a fine building / fine gold* 2 thin or slender: *a fine thread / a fine build* 3 sunny or without rain: *fine weather* 4 sharp: *a pencil with a fine point* 5 made of tiny particles: *fine dust* 6 with small holes: *a fine net*
fine *adverb*
6 well
•***Word Family:*** **finely** *adverb* **fineness** *noun*

fine (2) *noun*
1 a sum of money that you have to pay if you break a law or rule
fine *verb*
2 to give someone a fine

finger (*say* **fing**-ga) *noun*
1 one of the five long parts of your hand, especially one that's not your thumb 2 a piece

or part shaped like a finger: *the finger of a glove / a finger of toast*
finger *verb*
3 to touch or handle something lightly with your fingers

fingerprint *noun*
the pattern formed by the tiny ridges on the tips of your fingers
•***Word Family:*** **fingerprint** *verb*

finicky (*say* **fin**-i-kee) *adjective*
too fussy: *He's finicky about his food.*

finish *verb*
1 to bring something to an end or come to an end: *Finish the job quickly.* 2 **finish off** (a) to eat up: *Finish off your ice-cream.* (b) to kill
finish *noun*
3 the end or conclusion 4 a protective surface or coating: *The table has a very shiny finish.*

finite (*say* **figh**-nite) *adjective*
having an end or a limit: *There is a finite number of planets in our solar system.*

fiord (*say* fee-**ord**) *noun*
a long, deep, narrow inlet of the sea with very steep sides

fir *noun*
an evergreen tree with pointed cones and leaves shaped like needles

fire *noun*
1 the flame, heat and light produced by burning: *to see fire in the distance* 2 a pile of burning material: *to light a fire in the fireplace* 3 the shooting of guns: *to open fire*
fire *verb*
4 to shoot: *to fire a cannon* 5 to dismiss someone from a job: *to fire someone for shoddy work* 6 to harden pottery in a kiln by slow heating to a high temperature 7 to inspire: *to fire someone with enthusiasm*
•***Word Family:*** **fiery** *adjective* **(fierier, fieriest)**

firearm *noun*
any type of gun

fire-engine *noun*
a motor vehicle used for fighting fires with high-pressure hoses, ladders and pumps

fire-escape *noun*
an exit from a building that you can use if there is a fire, such as an outside staircase

firefighter *noun*
someone who is trained to fight fires

fireplace *noun*
the part of a chimney opening into a room, in which fires are lit

fireproof *adjective*
1 that does not burn
fireproof *verb*
2 to make something so that it cannot be burnt: *to fireproof a building*

firework *noun*
a cardboard tube filled with explosive powder, used to produce bright sparks of light or loud noise for a display at night

firm (1) *adjective*
1 solid or secure: *firm ground* 2 steady: *firm hands* 3 definite or fixed: *a firm decision*
firm *verb*
4 to make something firm or to become firm
•***Word Family:*** **firmly** *adverb* **firmness** *noun*

firm (2) *noun*
a business company or partnership

first *adjective*
1 being number one in a series 2 coming before all others in time, order or importance: *to have the first doctor's appointment*
first *adverb*
3 before anyone or anything else: *She left first.*
first *noun*
4 anything that is first in time, order or importance: *This model is a first in car design.*
•***Word Family:*** **firstly** *adverb*

first aid *noun*
emergency assistance given to a sick or injured person after an accident

first-class *adjective*
1 of the highest or best quality: *a first-class restaurant* 2 most expensive and luxurious: *first-class seats on a plane*

firsthand *adjective* and *adverb*
learnt directly, from the person who was there, not from someone else: *firsthand information*

fish *noun*
1 a cold-blooded animal that lives in water, has scales on its body and a backbone, breathes with gills and swims with fins
fish *verb*
2 to catch or try to catch fish 3 to search for and find something: *She fished a handkerchief out of her back pocket.*
•***Word Family:*** the plural of the noun is **fish** or **fishes** □ **fisherman** *noun* **(fishermen)** someone who fishes **fishmonger** *noun* someone who sells fish **fishing** *noun*

fishy *adjective*
1 like fish: *a fishy smell* 2 suspicious: *There is something fishy about the way he looked at us.*
•***Word Family:*** other forms are **fishier, fishiest**

fist *noun*
a tightly closed hand, with the fingers bent into the palm
•***Word Family:*** **fistful** *noun* a handful

fit (1) *verb*
1 to be the right shape or size for someone or to make something the right shape or size: *These shoes don't fit properly. / The salesman fitted the jacket.* 2 to put something carefully into place: *to fit new wheels on a car* 3 to be suitable for: *The punishment must fit the crime.* 4 to make room for: *to fit clothes in a wardrobe* 5 **fit out** to equip: *to fit out with camping gear*
fit *adjective*
6 suitable or right: *This burnt toast isn't fit to be eaten.* 7 healthy: *She's still not fit after her long illness.*
fit *noun*
8 the way in which something fits: *the fit of a coat*
•***Word Family:*** other forms of the verb are **fits, fitted, fitting** □ **fitness** *noun*

fit (2) *noun*
1 a sudden, violent outburst: *She threw the plate at the wall in a fit of rage.* 2 an attack caused by an illness, in which your muscles twitch uncontrollably and you can become unconscious: *an epileptic fit*
•***Word Family:*** **fitful** *adjective* interrupted: *a fitful sleep* **fitfully** *adverb*

fitting *noun*
1 the trying on and adjusting of clothes so that they fit 2 the size of clothes or shoes: *These shoes come in five width fittings.* 3 the equipment or furnishings provided for something, especially a house: *a light fitting*
fitting *adjective*
4 appropriate or suitable: *a fitting reply*
•***Word Family:*** **fittingly** *adverb*

five *noun*
the number 5
•***Word Family:*** **five** *adjective* **fifth** *noun* **fifth** *adjective*

fix *verb*
1 to make something secure: *The post was fixed into the ground.* 2 to repair or put in good condition: *Can you fix this broken light?* 3 to direct: *to fix your attention on a speaker*
fix *noun*
4 a difficult or awkward situation: *to be in a fix*
•***Word Family:*** **fixed** *adjective* **fixedly** *adverb: to stare fixedly*

fixture (*say* **fiks**-cher) *noun*
1 an object fixed into position, such as the lights in a house 2 a sporting event arranged to be held on a certain date

fizz *verb*
to hiss or bubble vigorously: *The lemonade fizzed everywhere when we took off the lid.*
•***Word Family:*** **fizzy** *adjective* (**fizzier, fizziest**)

fizzle *verb*
1 to splutter weakly: *The candle fizzled and went out.* 2 **fizzle out** to fail or end feebly: *The party fizzled out after the music stopped.*

fjord (*say* fee-**ord**) *noun*
another spelling for **fiord**

flabbergasted *adjective*
very shocked or astonished: *I'm flabbergasted by the news of their marriage.*

flabby *adjective*
with soft, loose, hanging flesh: *flabby arms*
•***Word Family:*** other forms are **flabbier, flabbiest** □ **flabbily** *adverb* **flabbiness** *noun*

flag (1) *noun*
1 a square or oblong cloth with a pattern, used as a symbol of a country, club or company, or as a signal 2 a marker in a computer given to an item of stored data
flag *verb*
3 to signal or mark something with a flag
•***Word Family:*** other verb forms are **flags, flagged, flagging**

flag (2) *verb*
to weaken or lose strength: *Our enthusiasm flagged when we saw the difficulty of the job ahead.*
•***Word Family:*** other forms are **flags, flagged, flagging**

flagrant (*say* **flay**-grant) *adjective*
outragious, or deliberately obvious: *flagrant disobedience*
•***Word Family:*** **flagrantly** *adverb*

flair *noun*
your natural ability or talent: *to have a flair for painting*

flake *noun*
1 a small piece or sliver of anything: *a flake of skin / a flake of snow / a flake of almond*
flake *verb*
2 to peel, separate or fall in flakes 3 **flake out** to collapse, faint or fall asleep
•***Word Family:*** **flaky** *adjective* (**flakier, flakiest**): *flaky pastry* **flakiness** *noun*

flamboyant (*say* flam-**boy**-ant) *adjective*
bold, elaborate or showy: *a flamboyant gesture*
•***Word Family:*** **flamboyance** *noun* **flamboyantly** *adverb*
•***Word Origins:*** from a French word meaning "flaming"

flame *noun*
1 a sheet or tongue of fire: *Flames raced through the house. / a candle flame*
flame *verb*
2 to burn or glow with flames 3 to become red: *Her face flamed with embarrassment.*

a b c d e f g h i j k l m n o p q r s t u v w x y z

A B C D E F G H I J K L M N O P Q R S T U V W X Y Z

flamenco (*say* fla-**men**-ko) *noun*
a fast, lively style of Spanish guitar music and dancing

flamingo (*say* fla-**ming**-go) *noun*
a long-legged, tropical wading bird with a long neck and pink or red feathers
•***Word Family:*** the plural is **flamingos** or **flamingoes**

flammable (*say* **flam**-a-bul) *adjective*
easy to set on fire and start burning

flank *noun*
1 the fleshy part of the side of animals, including humans 2 the side of anything: *the left flank of an army during battle*
flank *verb*
3 to be situated at the flank or side of someone, especially to provide protection: *Bodyguards flanked the President.*

flannel *noun*
1 a warm, soft woollen fabric: *flannel trousers*
2 a square of cloth that you use for washing

flannelette (*say* fla-na-**let**) *noun*
a soft, cotton fabric made to look and feel like flannel

flap *noun*
1 a loose piece of something, joined on one side: *the flap of an envelope / a tent flap* 2 a fuss or panic: *to get in a flap*
flap *verb*
3 to move up and down: *The bird flapped its wings.* 4 to swing or wave loosely: *The flag flapped in the breeze.*
•***Word Family:*** other verb forms are **flaps, flapped, flapping**

flare *verb*
1 to burst into a bright, strong flame: *The match flared in the darkness.* 2 to burst fiercely or erupt: *Tempers flared during the talks.* 3 to burn with an unsteady flame: *The candle flared in the breeze.*
4 to spread or curve outwards: *Her skirt flared from the waist.*
flare *noun*
5 a brilliant white or coloured light, used as a signal

flash *noun*
1 a sudden burst of light, fire or colour: *a flash of lightning* 2 a brief burst: *a flash of inspiration*
3 a short item of urgent news or information
flash *verb*
4 to give off or send a flash 5 to pass quickly and suddenly: *The idea flashed through his mind. / The car flashed by.*
•***Word Family:*** **flashy** *adjective* (**flashier, flashiest**) brilliant, smart or showy

flashback *noun*
a return to something that happened in the past, either in your mind or as part of a story in a film or novel

flask *noun*
a small, flat bottle

flat (1) *adjective*
1 level and smooth: *flat desert country* 2 not high or deep: *flat shoes* 3 deflated or with no air inside: *a flat tyre* 4 without bubbles: *flat lemonade* 5 absolute: *a flat refusal*
6 uninteresting: *a flat voice* 7 lowered in pitch by a semitone: *The musical note A flat is the black key on the piano below the white key A.*
flat *noun*
8 a flat surface or part: *the flat of your hand* 9 **(a)** a musical note lowered by one semitone from the main note **(b)** the sign (♭) placed next to a note that indicates this
flat *adverb*
10 in a flat position: *Lay the paper flat on the table.* 11 **flat out** as fast as possible: *to run flat out / working flat out*
•***Word Family:*** **flatly** *adverb* **flatness** *noun*

flat (2) *noun*
one or more rooms for living in, usually rented and part of a large building
•***Word Family:*** **flatmate** *noun* someone who shares a flat

flatter *verb*
1 to praise someone too much 2 to show or describe someone in a favourable way: *This photo really flatters you.*
•***Word Family:*** **flatterer** *noun* someone who flatters **flattery** *noun*

flaunt (*say* flawnt) *verb*
to display something that you have in a bold or showy way: *He flaunted his wealth by driving fast cars.*

flautist (*say* **flaw**-tist) *noun*
someone who plays the flute

flavour or flavor (*say* **flay**-va) *noun*
1 the taste that something has: *the strong flavour of garlic* 2 the character or nature of something: *The white-washed walls give the flavour of a Greek village.*
flavour *verb*
3 to give flavour to food: *We used fresh herbs to flavour the stew.*
•***Word Family:*** **flavouring** *noun*

flaw *noun*
1 a crack or break: *a flaw in an old cup* 2 a defect or fault: *Untidiness is the only flaw in her character.*
flaw *verb*
3 to spoil something
•***Word Family:*** **flawlessly** *adverb*

flax *noun*
a plant with narrow leaves and blue flowers, grown for its seeds that contain oil, and its fibre that is used to to make linen yarn

flea *noun*
a small, wingless, jumping insect that sucks blood from mammals and birds

fleck *noun*
1 a small spot or mark of colour or light
fleck *verb*
2 to mark something with flecks or spots

fledgling (*say* **flej**-ling) *noun*
1 a young bird just able to fly 2 someone who is young or inexperienced

flee *verb*
to run away: *The villagers fled as the troops invaded.*
•***Word Family:*** other forms are **flees, fled, fleeing**

fleece *noun*
1 the wool covering a sheep
fleece *verb*
2 to swindle or cheat someone by taking money from them: *The dishonest company fleeced the people who invested in it.*
•***Word Family:*** **fleecy** *adjective* (**fleecier, fleeciest**) woolly

fleet (1) *noun*
1 a large group of ships or other vehicles travelling together or organized by one company: *a fleet of taxis* 2 the largest organized unit of naval ships or warships commanded by one officer

fleet (2) *adjective*
swift or fast
•***Word Family:*** **fleeting** *adjective* very brief: *a fleeting glance*

flesh *noun*
1 the soft part of an animal's body 2 the soft part inside a fruit or vegetable
•***Word Family:*** **fleshy** *adjective* (**fleshier, fleshiest**) plump **fleshiness** *noun*

flex *verb*
1 to bend or stretch, especially something springy: *to flex a muscle*
flex *noun*
2 a length of wire covered with plastic, for carrying an electric current

flexible (*say* **flek**-si-bul) *adjective*
1 supple or easy to bend: *a flexible body*
2 adaptable or easy to change: *flexible plans*
•***Word Family:*** **flexibility** *noun* **flexibly** *adverb*

flick *verb*
1 to strike or touch quickly and lightly: *to flick dust off your coat*
flick *noun*
2 a quick, light movement or hit: *a flick of the wrist / a flick of a switch*

flicker *verb*
1 to burn, shine or move briefly and unsteadily: *The dying fire flickered gently.*
flicker *noun*
2 a brief, unsteady movement or light
•***Word Origins:*** from an Old English word meaning "to move the wings"

flight *noun*
1 flying 2 a journey made by air: *a flight across the desert* 3 a group of things flying together: *a flight of pelicans landing on water* 4 row of steps or stairs

flighty *adjective*
silly, frivolous or fickle: *a flighty child*
•***Word Family:*** other forms are **flightier, flightiest** □ **flightiness** *noun*

flimsy (*say* **flim**-zee) *adjective*
thin, weak and easily damaged or destroyed: *a flimsy box / a flimsy argument / a flimsy dress*
•***Word Family:*** other forms are **flimsier, flimsiest** □ **flimsiness** *noun*

flinch *verb*
to move back or away from something frightening, difficult or repulsive: *He did not flinch when they called him names.*

fling *verb*
1 to throw something violently: *to fling the door open*
fling *noun*
2 a pleasant time or spree: *Have a fling and buy some new clothes.*
•***Word Family:*** other verb forms are **flings, flung, flinging**

flint *noun*
a very hard and brittle stone that produces a spark when you strike it with steel

flip *verb*
1 to move or throw something with a snapping or jerking movement: *to flip a coin* 2 to strike or pick up lightly and quickly, especially when turning something over: *to flip a page with your finger* 3 to become angry or upset: *Dad will flip when I tell him the bad news.*
•***Word Family:*** other forms are **flips, flipped, flipping**

flipper *noun*
1 a broad, flat limb that whales and seals use for swimming 2 a rubber object shaped like an animal's flipper that you use on each foot to help you swim

flirt *verb*
1 to behave in a joking, sexy way towards someone for fun

A B C D E F G H I J K L M N O P Q R S T U V W X Y Z

flirt *noun*
2 someone who flirts
•***Word Family:*** **flirtation** *noun* **flirtatious** *adjective* liking to flirt **flirtatiously** *adverb*

float *verb*
1 to rest on, move or be held up in air or liquid: *She floated on her back in the pool. / The leaf floated through the air.* 2 to drift or move freely and easily: *The memory continued to float through his mind.*
float *noun*
3 something that floats or provides support for floating: *the float on a fishing line / a float to help you learn to swim* 4 a vehicle used for delivering milk to houses 5 a low cart or platform on wheels for carrying a display in a procession 6 a small amount of money in a shop or on a stall, for giving people change

flock *noun*
1 a group of birds, sheep or goats
flock *verb*
2 to go or gather in a flock: *People flocked to see the latest Batman film.*

flog *verb*
1 to strike or beat a person or animal with a whip or stick: *Criminals used to be flogged as a punishment.* 2 to sell: *to flog watches at a market*
•***Word Family:*** other forms are **flogs, flogged, flogging** □ **flogging** *noun* a punishment by whipping or beating

flood (*say* flud) *noun*
1 an overflowing of water, especially onto land which is usually dry 2 a large flow or stream of something: *a flood of tears*
flood *verb*
3 to rise or overflow in a flood 4 to come in great quantities: *Entries for the competition flooded in.*

floodlight *noun*
a light with a strong, broad beam, used to light up a sports ground or other building at night
•***Word Family:*** **floodlit** *adjective*

floor (*say* flor) *noun*
1 the lowest, flat part of a room or other place: *to smash a glass on the floor / to sink to the floor of the sea* 2 a storey or level of a building: *I live on the first floor.*
floor *verb*
3 to knock someone down: *The sumo wrestler floored his opponent.* 4 to stun or baffle someone: *I was quite floored by her sudden change of mood.*
•***Word Family:*** **flooring** *noun* the materials used to make a floor

flop *verb*
1 to fall, drop or collapse suddenly: *to flop onto your bed* 2 to fail: *The play flopped and the theatre closed down.*
flop *noun*
3 a failure: *The party was a complete flop.*
•***Word Family:*** other verb forms are **flops, flopped, flopping**

floppy *adjective*
hanging down or falling loosely
•***Word Family:*** other verb forms are **floppier, floppiest** □ **floppily** *adverb* **floppiness** *noun*

floppy disk *noun*
a thin, flexible, plastic disk on which computer data is stored

flora *noun*
all the plants of a certain area or period of time
•***Word Family:*** **floral** (*say* **floor**-al) *adjective*
•***Word Origins:*** named after *Flora*, the Roman goddess of flowers

florist (*say* **flo**-rist) *noun*
someone who sells flowers and indoor plants

flotilla (*say* flo-**til**-a) *noun*
a small group of boats, especially small naval ships: *a flotilla of tugs*

flotsam *noun*
wreckage or rubbish floating on the sea

flounce *verb*
to move or go with quick, impatient movements: *He flounced out of the room slamming the door behind him.*

flounder *verb*
to struggle helplessly or clumsily: *to flounder in the sea / to flounder through a speech*

flour *noun*
finely ground powder made from wheat or other grains and used in cooking
•***Word Family:*** **floury** *adjective* covered with flour

flourish (*say* **fluh**-rish) *verb*
1 to grow or be well, healthy or active: *The seedlings flourished. / Business flourished under the new boss.* 2 to wave about or display with pride: *She rushed in flourishing her first pay cheque.*
flourish *noun*
3 a wave or showy movement
•***Word Origins:*** from a Latin word meaning "bloom"

flout (*rhymes with* out) *verb*
to go against a rule or treat it with contempt: *to flout the school rules*

flow (*say* flo) *verb*
1 to move smoothly: *Blood flowed from the wound.* 2 to hang loosely: *Her hair flowed down her back.*

flow *noun*
3 a continuous movement: *We tried to stop the flow of blood.*

flower *noun*
1 the blossom or part of a plant that produces the seeds or fruit
flower *verb*
2 to produce blossoms or blooms

flowery *adjective*
1 covered with flowers: *flowery wallpaper*
2 using too many showy words: *a flowery poem*
•***Word Family:*** other forms are **flowerier, floweriest** □ **floweriness** *noun*

flu *noun*
a short form of **influenza**

fluctuate (*say* **fluk**-tyoo-ate) *verb*
to keep changing: *His moods fluctuate between happiness and sadness.*
•***Word Family:* fluctuation** *noun*
•***Word Origins:*** from a Latin word meaning "to move like the waves"

fluent (*say* **floo**-ent) *adjective*
1 able to express yourself clearly and easily: *to be fluent in Italian* 2 flowing smoothly and gracefully: *to speak fluent Italian*
•***Word Family:* fluency** *noun* **fluently** *adverb*

fluff *noun*
1 a light, downy substance: *fluff on the carpet*
fluff *verb*
2 to puff out: *Birds fluff their feathers.*
•***Word Family:* fluffy** *adjective* **(fluffier, fluffiest)** covered with fluff

fluid (*say* **floo**-id) *noun*
a substance that flows, either a liquid or gas

fluke (1) *noun*
one of the triangular halves of a whale's tail

fluke (2) *noun*
a stroke of good luck
•***Word Family:* fluky** *adjective* **(flukier, flukiest)**

fluorescent (*say* flor-es-ent) *adjective*
1 giving out a hard bright light: *a fluorescent lamp* 2 so bright that it seems to be shining itself when a light is shone on it: *a fluorescent strip on a school bag*
•***Word Family:* fluorescence** *noun*

fluoride (*say* **floor**-ide) *noun*
a chemical compound used to keep your teeth healthy and protect them from decay
•***Word Family:* fluoridate** *verb* to put fluoride in toothpaste or water **fluoridation** *noun*

flurry *noun*
1 a sudden whirling movement: *a flurry of snow*
2 a confused hurry: *a flurry of excitement*
•***Word Family:*** the plural of the noun is **flurries**

flush (1) *verb*
1 to blush or become red in the face: *The child flushed with embarrassment.* 2 to fill with water for cleaning: *to flush the toilet*
flush *noun*
3 a red or rosy glow of colour

flush (2) *adjective*
1 even or level: *The picture isn't flush with the top of the door.* 2 having plenty of money

flute *noun*
a musical instrument belonging to the woodwind family, consisting of a long tube with keys or fingerholes, played by blowing air across the mouthpiece

flutter *verb*
1 to move or flap quickly and lightly: *The moths fluttered around the light. / The flag fluttered in the wind.*
flutter *noun*
2 a flapping movement 3 a feeling of nervous excitement

fly (1) *verb*
1 to move or make something move through the air: *The bird flew overhead. / We flew a kite. / The astronauts flew the rocket to the moon.* 2 to move quickly: *The door flew open.*
fly *noun*
3 the front opening of a pair of trousers 4 a flap of cloth forming the door of a tent
•***Word Family:*** other forms of the verb are **flies, flew, flown, flying** □ the plural of the noun is **flies**

fly (2) *noun*
1 a two-winged insect 2 a fishhook made to look like a fly
•***Word Family:*** the plural is **flies**

flying doctor *noun*
a doctor who uses air transport to reach patients in outback areas of Australia

flying saucer *noun*
a flying, disc-shaped object that some people say they've seen in the sky and believe has come from outer space

foal *noun*
1 a young horse or donkey
foal *verb*
2 to produce a foal

foam (*say* fohm) *noun*
1 a collection of tiny bubbles of gas or liquid formed on a surface 2 a light, spongy material, used for padding chairs or in packaging
foam *verb*
3 to froth or make foam: *foaming at the mouth*
•***Word Family:* foamy** *adjective* **(foamier, foamiest)**

A B C D E F G H I J K L M N O P Q R S T U V W X Y Z

focus (*say* **foh**-kus) *noun*
1 the control used to make the image seen through a camera lens clear and sharp 2 the point at which converging rays of light meet 3 a central point of attention or attraction: *The TV star is the main focus of interest.*
focus *verb*
4 to bring something into focus: *to focus a camera* 5 to concentrate: *to focus your attention*
•***Word Family:*** the plural forms of the noun are **foci** or **focuses** □ other verb forms are **focuses, focused** or **focussed, focusing** or **focussing** □ **focal** *adjective*

fodder *noun*
food such as hay or oats, given to horses and cattle

foe (*rhymes with* mow) *noun*
an enemy or opponent

foetus (*say* **fee**-tus) *noun*
the young of a human or an animal as it grows in its mother's womb, especially in its later stages of development in the womb
•***Word Family:*** **foetal** *adjective*

fog *noun*
1 a thick mist of water droplets hanging in the air close to the ground, usually making it hard to see
fog *verb*
2 to become clouded with steam: *The car windscreen fogged up.*
•***Word Family:*** other verb forms are **fogs, fogged, fogging** □ **foggy** *adjective* **(foggier, foggiest) fogginess** *noun*

foil (1) *verb*
to prevent something from being successful: *His quick action foiled the attempted robbery.*

foil (2) *noun*
a thin sheet of metal: *aluminium foil*

foist *verb*
to force something on to someone: *to foist new ideas onto people*

fold (1) *verb*
1 to bend over on itself: *to fold a newspaper* 2 to cross: *to fold your arms* 3 to put or wrap: *to fold someone in your arms* 4 to mix cooking ingredients by slowly and gently turning one part over another: *to fold flour into the butter and sugar*
fold *noun*
5 the line or crease where something has been folded 6 a folded part

fold (2) *noun*
an enclosed area for keeping sheep

folder *noun*
a folded piece of cardboard or plastic for holding loose papers

foliage (*say* **foh**-lee-ij) *noun*
the leaves of a tree or plant

folk (*rhymes with* joke) *noun*
1 people: *old folk* 2 **your folks** your relatives, usually your parents
folk *adjective*
3 coming from the ordinary people of an area: *folk songs*
•***Word Family:*** the plural is **folk** or **folks**

folk dance *noun*
a traditional dance of a particular country or region

folklore *noun*
the traditional customs, legends and beliefs of the people of a particular country or region, passed down from parents to their children

follow *verb*
1 to come or go behind someone: *to follow the leader* 2 to go along: *Follow this path to the river.* 3 to obey: *to follow the teacher's instructions* 4 to come as a result of: *This punishment follows from your behaviour yesterday.* 5 to understand: *Can you follow my directions?* 6 to be interested in or watch the progress of someone: *to follow someone's career / to follow a local team*
•***Word Family:*** **follower** *noun*

following *noun*
a group of people who support someone: *The band has a large following in Japan.*

folly *noun*
a foolish or senseless act or idea
•***Word Family:*** the plural is **follies**
•***Word Origins:*** from a French word meaning "madness"

fond *adjective*
1 loving: *a fond glance* 2 **fond of** liking: *to be fond of reading*
•***Word Family:*** **fondly** *adverb* **fondness** *noun*

fondle *verb*
to handle or stroke with affection

font (1) *noun*
a basin, usually stone, that holds water for baptism in a church

font (2) *noun*
a complete range of type characters in one size and typeface, such as the ones you can choose for printing out your work on a computer

food *noun*
anything you eat to give your body the energy it needs to live and grow

food-chain *noun*
a series of plants and animals which are joined in an imaginary chain by each one eating the one before it, and being eaten by the one after it

fool *noun*
1 someone with no sense or judgment: *He was a fool to be talked into buying that old car.* 2 a pudding made from crushed fruit mixed with cream: *gooseberry fool*
fool *verb*
3 to trick or deceive someone: *to fool someone into believing something untrue* 4 to joke or play: *to fool around and waste time*
• ***Word Family:*** **foolery** *noun* silly behaviour **foolish** *adjective* silly **foolishly** *adverb* **foolishness** *noun*

foolhardy *adjective*
unwisely bold or rash: *a foolhardy action*
• ***Word Family:*** **foolhardiness** *noun*

foolproof *adjective*
so well designed or easy to follow that it cannot fail: *a foolproof plan*

foot *noun*
1 the lower end of the leg below the ankle: *to stand on one foot* 2 the lower end or bottom of something: *the foot of a hill / the foot of a page* 3 an old-fashioned measure of length equal to 12 inches or about 30 centimetres 4 the basic unit of rhythm in poetry equalling two or three syllables 5 **put your foot down** to be strict or firm
foot *verb*
6 to pay: *to foot the bill*
• ***Word Family:*** the plural of the noun is **feet**

football *noun*
1 a leather or plastic ball used in the game of football 2 a game played by two teams of 11 players using a round ball which they kick 3 an American game played with an oval ball which players kick, throw and handle
• ***Word Family:*** **footballer** *noun*

footlights *plural noun*
a row of lights set at the edge of the stage in a theatre

footnote *noun*
a note printed in smaller type at the bottom of a page in a book, that explains something in the main text more fully

for *preposition*
1 with the purpose or intention of: *Those shoes are made for rollerblading. / to fight for freedom* 2 in the direction of: *to leave for the city* 3 in order to have or get: *money for food* 4 at the price or cost of: *to buy an ice-cream for $2* 5 as far or long as: *to hike for a kilometre / to wait for an hour* 6 as a result of: *to praise for good work* 7 on behalf of or as a favour to: *Do it for me.* 8 in honour of: *The party is for her birthday.* 9 because of: *He cried for joy.*

forage (*rhymes with* porridge) *verb*
1 to hunt or search for food and supplies
forage *noun*
2 food or fodder for horses and cattle

forbid *verb*
1 to command someone not to do something: *I forbid you to go out.* 2 to not allow something: *Smoking is forbidden in this theatre.*
• ***Word Family:*** other forms are **forbids, forbade, forbidden, forbidding** □ **forbidding** *adjective* looking dangerous or unfriendly

force *noun*
1 strength or violence: *The force of the wind. / to use force to enter a building* 2 an organized body of people: *a police force* 3 **in force** (a) in large numbers: *to attack in force* (b) effective or in operation: *The new law is in force from today.*
force *verb*
4 to make someone do something, often using effort or strength: *She forced me to show her my homework.* 5 to break a lock open: *We had to force the lock because the key was lost.*
• ***Word Family:*** **forced** *adjective* not genuine: *a forced smile* **forceful** *adjective* powerful or vigorous **forcefully** *adverb* **forcible** *adjective* using force **forcibly** *adverb*

forceps *plural noun*
a pair of tongs for holding things, often used during operations

ford *noun*
1 a shallow part of a river where people or vehicles may walk or drive across
ford *verb*
2 to cross a river by walking or driving: *to ford a stream*

fore *adjective*
1 located at or towards the front
fore *adverb*
2 at or towards the bow of a ship
fore *noun*
3 **to the fore** in or to the front or most prominent position: *to push yourself to the fore*

forearm (*say* **for**-ahm) *noun*
the lower part of your arm between the wrist and the elbow

forecast (*say* **for**-cast) *verb*
1 to predict what will happen in the future: *The weather report forecasts gales for tomorrow.*
forecast *noun*
2 a prediction, usually about the weather
• ***Word Family:*** other verb forms are **forecasts, forecast, forecasting** □ **forecaster** *noun*

A B C D E F G H I J K L M N O P Q R S T U V W X Y Z

forecourt *noun*
a large open area in front of a building or a petrol station

forefather (*say* **for**-fath-a) *noun*
one of your ancestors

forefinger (*say* **for**-fing-ga) *noun*
the first finger, next to your thumb

forefront (*say* **for**-frunt) *noun*
the front place or position: *That reporter is always at the forefront of world affairs.*

forehead (*say* **for**-hed or **fo**-rid) *noun*
the part at the top of your face, above your eyes and below your hair

foreign (*say* **fo**-rin) *adjective*
1 from a country other than your own: *a foreign language* 2 not belonging in the place where it is found: *foreign matter in your eye*
• ***Word Family:*** **foreigner** *noun* someone from another country
• ***Word Origins:*** from a Latin word meaning "out of doors"

foreman *noun*
1 someone in charge of a group of workers
2 the person who speaks for a jury
• ***Word Family:*** the plural is **foremen** □ **forewoman** *noun* (**forewomen**)

foremost *adjective*
first in position or rank: *our foremost living author*

forensic (*say* fo-**ren**-zik) *adjective*
to do with the scientific examination of evidence found at the scene of a crime: *a forensic report*

foresee *verb*
to see or know beforehand: *to foresee that something will happen*
• ***Word Family:*** other forms are **foresees, foresaw, foreseen, foreseeing** □ **foreseeable** *adjective: the foreseeable future* **foresight** *noun* thought or planning for the future

forest (*say* **fo**-rest) *noun*
an area of land thickly covered with trees
• ***Word Family:*** **forester** *noun* a person who works in or looks after a forest **forestry** *noun*

forfeit (*say* **for**-fit) *noun*
1 a penalty or fine: *My forfeit for landing on that square is to lose my next turn in the game.*
forfeit *verb*
2 to lose as a forfeit: *to forfeit your pocket money*
• ***Word Family:*** **forfeiture** *noun*

forge (1) (*say* forj) *noun*
1 a furnace for heating and softening metal before it is shaped into tools and other things
forge *verb*
2 to shape or form something with great effort: *to forge horseshoes by hammering / to forge a partnership over the years* 3 to copy something illegally or in order to deceive people: *to forge the signature on a passport / to forge banknotes*
• ***Word Family:*** **forgery** *noun* (**forgeries**) the crime of forging imitations or fakes **forger** *noun*

forge (2) (*say* forj) *verb*
to move forward, especially with an abrupt increase of speed or power: *to forge ahead*

forget *verb*
1 to fail to remember: *I forgot her birthday.* 2 to stop thinking about something: *She tried to forget her troubles.*
• ***Word Family:*** other forms are **forgets, forgot, forgotten, forgetting** □ **forgettable** *adjective* able to be forgotten **forgetful** *adjective* tending to forget **forgetfulness** *noun*

forgive *verb*
to pardon or stop being angry with someone: *Please forgive me for losing my temper.*
• ***Word Family:*** other forms are **forgives, forgave, forgiven, forgiving** □ **forgiving** *adjective* willing to forgive **forgiveness** *noun*

fork *noun*
1 an instrument with two or more prongs, for eating, gardening and so on 2 a place where something divides into parts or branches: *a fork in the road*
fork *verb*
3 to lift, toss or pierce something with a fork: *to fork hay into a truck* 4 to divide into branches: *The river forked at the bend.* 5 **fork out** to spend money
• ***Word Family:*** **forked** *adjective*

forlorn *adjective*
sad, alone and uncared for
• ***Word Family:*** **forlornly** *adverb*

form *noun*
1 the shape or appearance of something: *the human form / Water in the form of steam.* 2 a class, especially in a secondary school 3 a printed piece of paper with spaces to be filled in with information 4 a long bench or seat 5 a kind or variety: *What a strange form of plant life!* 6 condition or fitness: *All the players will be in top form for the match.*
form *verb*
7 to shape, devise or organize: *to form an idea / to form a plan / to form a committee* 8 to develop: *to form bad habits*

formal *adjective*
1 following the accepted customs or rules: *Please*

make a formal application in writing. 2 stiff: *She greeted me in a formal manner.*
•***Word Family:*** **formally** *adverb*

formality *noun*
1 formal behaviour 2 something that you do to follow a custom or rule: *Filling in this form is just a formality.*
•***Word Family:*** the plural is **formalities**

format *noun*
1 the plan, style or layout of something: *the format of a new TV series*
format *verb*
2 to prepare a computer disk to receive or output data
•***Word Family:*** other verb forms are **formats, formatted, formatting**

formation *noun*
1 the process of forming or producing: *the formation of ice crystals* 2 the way in which something is formed or arranged: *The jets flew in close formation over the city.* 3 something that is formed: *a rock formation*

former *adjective*
1 coming before in time, place or order: *a former president* 2 being the first mentioned of two things: *Of pizza and spaghetti, I prefer the former.*
•***Word Family:*** **formerly** *adverb* at a past time

formidable (*say* **for**-mi-da-bul *or* for-**mid**-a-bul) *adjective*
1 difficult or needing great effort to do: *Cleaning up after the party was a formidable task.*
2 impressive and frightening: *a formidable opponent*
•***Word Family:*** **formidably** *adverb*

formula (*say* **for**-myoo-la) *noun*
1 a plan or rule for dealing with something: *The formula for curing tiredness is a good night's sleep.*
2 in chemistry, the representation of atoms in a molecule by using symbols for each atom: *The formula for water, H_2O, shows that a molecule of water is made up of two atoms of hydrogen (H) and one atom of oxygen (O).* 3 a liquid food or preparation, usually for a baby
•***Word Family:*** the plural is **formulae** or **formulas**

formulate *verb*
to work something out and put in a clear way: *to formulate a plan*
•***Word Family:*** **formulation** *noun*

forsake *verb*
to desert, abandon or give up someone or something
•***Word Family:*** other forms are **forsakes, forsook, forsaken, forsaking** □ **forsakenly** *adverb*

fort *noun*
a strongly-made building like a castle, able to withstand enemy attack

forte (*say* **for**-tay) *adverb*
played or sung loudly
•***Word Family:*** **fortissimo** *adverb* very loudly
•***Word Origins:*** this word comes from Italian

forthcoming *adjective*
1 taking place soon: *our forthcoming skiing trip*
2 ready or available when needed: *No answer was forthcoming.* 3 friendly or willing to talk: *He wasn't very forthcoming about his plans.*

forthright *adjective*
saying what you think in an honest and direct way
•***Word Family:*** **forthrightly** *adverb* **forthrightness** *noun*

fortify (*say* **for**-ti-figh) *verb*
to strengthen something so that it can resist damage or harm: *to fortify yourself against the cold with a warm jumper*
•***Word Family:*** other forms are **fortifies, fortified, fortifying** □ **fortifications** *plural noun* towers, walls and so on

fortnight *noun*
a period of two weeks
•***Word Family:*** **fortnightly** *adjective*

fortress *noun*
a castle or town that is strengthened to protect it from enemy attack
•***Word Family:*** the plural is **fortresses**

fortune *noun*
1 chance or luck: *What good fortune that the sun was shining for the picnic.* 2 wealth or riches: *They made a fortune from discovering oil on their land.* 3 **tell someone's fortune** to predict what will happen in a person's life
•***Word Family:*** **fortunate** *adjective* lucky or successful **fortunately** *adverb*

forty *noun*
the number 40
•***Word Family:*** the plural is **forties** □ **forty** *adjective* **fortieth** *noun* **fortieth** *adjective*

forum *noun*
1 a public meeting to discuss general issues
2 the public square in an ancient Roman town, used for business and meetings

forward *adjective*
1 near or moving towards the front: *She took up a forward position on the court. / a forward step*
2 bold or too eager to be noticed: *a forward young politician* 3 for the future: *forward planning*
forward *adverb*
4 toward the front: *Forward march!*

A B C D E F G H I J K L M N O P Q R S T U V W X Y Z

forward *noun*
5 a player in an attacking position in games like football
forward *verb*
7 to send on mail to a person's new address
•***Word Family:*** **forwards** *adverb*

fossick *verb*
1 to search or hunt: *to fossick in the cupboard for a sweater* 2 to search for gold in abandoned mines and in other places that others have worked before
•***Word Family:*** **fossicker** *noun*

fossil *noun*
the remains, impression or trace of a living thing, preserved as a rock
•***Word Family:*** **fossilized** or **fossilised** *adjective*
•***Word Origins:*** from a Latin word meaning "dug up"

foster *verb*
1 to bring up a child who is not your own son or daughter without adopting them officially 2 to encourage something: *to foster friendship*
•***Word Family:*** **foster-child** *noun* **foster-home** *noun* **foster-parent** *noun*

foul (*rhymes with* growl) *adjective*
1 very unpleasant: *a foul taste and smell* 2 offensive: *foul language* 3 stormy or disagreeable: *foul weather* 4 **foul play** violent crime or murder: *The police suspect foul play.*
foul *noun*
5 a breaking of the rules in a sport or game
foul *verb*
6 to make or become foul or dirty 7 to commit a foul against an opponent in sport

found *verb*
to set up or establish something: *to found a colony in a new land*
•***Word Family:*** **founder** *noun* **founding** *adjective*: *a founding member of a club*

foundation *noun*
1 the founding or establishing of something: *the foundation of a colony* 2 a base or basis of something: *the foundations of a building / the foundation of our beliefs*

founder *verb*
1 to fill with water and sink: *The ship foundered off the rocky shore.* 2 to fail: *The plan foundered because no-one was interested.*

foundry *noun*
a factory where metal is moulded and cast
•***Word Family:*** the plural is **foundries**

fountain (*say* **fown**-ten) *noun*
a structure that pumps water through a pipe and sprays it into the air

fountain pen *noun*
a pen which has a container of ink inside it that flows to the nib

four *noun*
1 the number 4 2 the score in cricket of four runs which a batsman gets when he or she hits the ball to the boundary
•***Word Family:*** **four** *adjective* **fourth** *adjective* **fourth** *noun*

fourteen *noun*
the number 14
•***Word Family:*** **fourteen** *adjective* **fourteenth** *noun* **fourteenth** *adjective*

fowl *noun*
a bird such as a hen, duck, turkey or goose, kept for its eggs or for eating
•***Word Family:*** the plural is **fowls** or, for a group of birds, **fowl**

fox *noun*
1 a small, wild animal like a dog, with reddish-brown fur, a pointed muzzle, upright ears and a bushy tail 2 someone who is sly and crafty
•***Word Family:*** the plural is **foxes** □ **foxy** *adjective* sly and crafty **foxily** *adverb* **foxiness** *noun*

foyer (*say* **foy**-ay) *noun*
an entrance hall, especially in a theatre, hotel or large building
•***Word Origins:*** from a French word meaning "home"

fraction (*say* **frak**-shon) *noun*
1 a part of a whole number: *$\frac{1}{2}$ and $\frac{1}{4}$ are both fractions* 2 a small part of something: *Only a fraction of our class escaped getting the flu.*
•***Word Family:*** **fractional** *adjective* **fractionally** *adverb*

fracture (*say* **frak**-cher) *noun*
1 a break or crack, especially a bone
fracture *verb*
2 to break or crack: *to fracture your wrist*

fragile (*say* **fra**-jile) *adjective*
easily broken or damaged: *a fragile vase*
•***Word Family:*** **fragility** *noun*

fragment (*say* **frag**-ment) *noun*
1 a small piece or part that is broken off something or is not complete: *a fragment of pottery / a fragment of conversation*
fragment (*say* frag-**ment**) *verb*
2 to break into fragments
•***Word Family:*** **fragmentary** *adjective* **fragmentation** *noun* **fragmented** *adjective*

fragrant (*say* **fray**-grent) *adjective*
having a pleasant smell: *a fragrant perfume*
•***Word Family:*** **fragrance** *noun* **fragrantly** *adverb*

frail *adjective*
feeble or weak: *a frail child / a frail invalid*
• ***Word Family:*** **frailty** *noun* (**frailties**) **frailness** *noun*

frame *noun*
1 a border for a picture 2 a supporting structure made up of parts joined together: *the steel frame of the shed / the human frame* 3 a small picture on a strip of film 4 **frame of mind** your mood or the way you are feeling
frame *verb*
5 to give a picture a frame 6 to arrange or give shape to your words: *to frame a question / to frame new laws* 7 to give false evidence against someone: *to frame someone for a crime*

framework *noun*
1 a frame that supports something: *a steel framework for a building* 2 the way something is arranged or planned

franchise (*say* **fran**-chize) *noun*
1 a citizen's right to vote in an election
2 permission given by a company for someone to sell its goods

frank *adjective*
open and straightforward in what you say: *to give someone a frank answer*
• ***Word Family:*** **frankly** *adverb* openly **frankness** *noun*

frankfurter *noun*
a long, thin, red sausage, usually boiled and eaten with sauce in a roll
• ***Word Origins:*** named after *Frankfurt-am-Main*, a German town

frantic *adjective*
nearly mad with grief, excitement, pain or worry
• ***Word Family:*** **frantically** *adverb*

fraternal (*say* fra-**tern**-al) *adjective*
to do with or like a brother
• ***Word Family:*** **fraternity** *noun* (**fraternities**) a group of people with something in common: *the medical fraternity* **fraternize** or **fraternise** *verb* to be friendly **fraternally** *adverb*

fraud (*say* frawd) *noun*
1 lying or being dishonest in order to get money or land 2 someone who pretends to be someone else
• ***Word Family:*** **fraudulent** *adjective*

fray (1) *noun*
a noisy dispute or fight: *More football supporters joined the fray.*

fray (2) *verb*
1 to become worn and ragged 2 to wear out someone's temper or nerves: *The stormy meeting frayed people's tempers.*

frazzle *noun*
1 the state of being exhausted: *worn to a frazzle*
2 a badly burnt state: *burnt to a frazzle*
• ***Word Family:*** **frazzled** *adjective* tired or worn out

freak *noun*
1 a very unusual animal, person or event: *The calf with five legs was a freak of nature. / By some freak the car stayed on the road after it skidded.*
2 someone who is very interested in or keen on something: *a health food freak*
freak *adjective*
3 unusual: *a freak storm*
freak *verb*
4 **freak out** to react violently: *to freak out over class tests*
• ***Word Family:*** **freakish** *adjective* **freakishly** *adverb*

freckle *noun*
a small brown spot on your skin, particularly your face, caused by the sun
• ***Word Family:*** **freckled** *adjective*

free *adjective*
1 able to do what you like or go where you like: *a free citizen / free choice* 2 not costing anything: *a free ride / free advice* 3 not being occupied or used: *Is the room free yet?*
free *verb*
4 to set or make someone free: *to free the captives*
• ***Word Family:*** other adjective forms are **freer, freest** □ other verb forms are **frees, freed, freeing** □ **freely** *adverb*

-free *suffix*
not containing or free from: *caffeine-free*

freedom *noun*
the right to say, behave or move about as you please: *to fight for freedom / freedom of speech*

freehand *adjective*
1 done by hand, without using rulers, compasses and other instruments: *a freehand sketch*
freehand *adverb*
2 without using rulers and so on: *Did you draw it freehand?*

free-range hen *noun*
a hen free to walk about looking for food
• ***Word Family:*** **free-range** *adjective: free-range eggs*

freestyle *noun*
1 the fastest swimming style, in which you use an overarm movement while kicking with your legs 2 a swimming race in which competitors may use any style they like, usually the freestyle as it is so fast

freeway *noun*
a divided highway with several lanes and limited entry and exit points, designed for traffic to travel fast

freeze *verb*
1 to change into ice: *The river froze.* 2 to be very cold: *You'll freeze without a coat.* 3 to be unable to move: *She froze with horror at the sight.* 4 to put food in a freezer to preserve it or keep it fresh: *We froze the peas.*
freeze *noun*
5 a time when something is fixed at a certain level: *a wage freeze* 6 a period of very cold weather when the temperature drops below 0°C
• ***Word Family:*** other verb forms are **freezes, froze, frozen, freezing** □ **frozen** *adjective*: *frozen peas*

freezer *noun*
a refrigerator or part of a refrigerator, usually with a temperature below –10°C, in which food may be frozen quickly and stored for a long time

freezing point *noun*
1 the temperature at which water turns to ice 2 the temperature at which any particular liquid freezes

freight (*say* frate) *noun*
1 goods transported as cargo by land, sea or air 2 the charge for this
• ***Word Family:*** **freighter** *noun* a ship or plane that carries freight

French horn *noun*
a brass instrument that you blow, with a long coiled tube ending in a flared bell

frenzy *noun*
great excitement, agitation or activity: *He went into a frenzy of cleaning when the baby was expected home.*
• ***Word Family:*** **frenzied** *adjective* very excited or maddened

frequency (*say* **free**-kwen-see) *noun*
1 the number of times something happens: *What is the frequency of earthquakes in this area?* 2 the fact of happening often: *The frequency of burglaries in our street is frightening.* 3 the number of vibrations per second of a sound, radio or light wave: *Animals hear higher frequency sounds than humans do.*
• ***Word Family:*** the plural is **frequencies**

frequent (*say* **free**-kwent) *adjective*
1 happening often or at short intervals: *frequent attacks of coughing* 2 regular or constant: *a frequent visitor*
frequent (*say* free-**kwent**) *verb*
3 to visit a place often: *to frequent the gym*
• ***Word Family:*** **frequently** *adverb*

fresco (*say* **fres**-ko) *noun*
a painting done on a freshly plastered wall or ceiling, usually while it is still damp to help the colours set
• ***Word Family:*** the plural is **frescos** or **frescoes**
• ***Word Origins:*** from an Italian word meaning "fresh"

fresh *adjective*
1 recently made, obtained or arrived: *fresh milk / fresh paint / a fresh group of students* 2 healthy or full of energy: *a fresh complexion / to feel fresh after a nap* 3 not salt: *fresh water* 4 bright: *fresh colours* 5 cool: *a fresh breeze* 6 cheeky: *Don't get fresh with me!*
• ***Word Family:*** **freshen** *verb* to make something fresh **freshly** *adverb* **freshness** *noun*

freshwater *adjective*
1 living in rivers or lakes, not the sea: *freshwater fish* 2 containing fresh water: *a freshwater lake*

fret (1) *verb*
to worry or be anxious, unhappy or irritable: *The cat fretted when her kittens were taken away.*
• ***Word Family:*** other forms are **frets, fretted, fretting** □ **fretful** *adjective* irritable **fretfully** *adverb*

fret (2) *noun*
one of the bars set across a stringed musical instrument, such as a guitar, to mark off the notes
• ***Word Family:*** **fretted** *adjective* having frets

friar *noun*
a member of a religious order, such as the Franciscans
• ***Word Family:*** **friary** *noun* a community of friars
• ***Word Origins:*** from a Latin word meaning "brother"

friction (*say* **frik**-shon) *noun*
1 the rubbing of one object or surface against another: *You use friction when you strike a match.* 2 conflict: *Her actions caused friction in the family.*

Friday *noun*
the sixth day of the week
• ***Word Origins:*** from an Old English word meaning "Freya's day", named after the Norse goddess of love

fridge *noun*
short for **refrigerator**

friend (*say* frend) *noun*
someone you know well and like
•***Word Family:*** **friendship** *noun*

friendly *adjective*
kind and pleasant
•***Word Family:*** **friendliness** *noun*

frieze (*say* freeze) *noun*
a decorative strip or band of pictures or designs around the top of a wall

fright *noun*
1 sudden, intense fear, usually as a reaction to something threatening: *He got a fright when he saw the huge shadow on the wall.* 2 a strange or unpleasant sight: *You look a fright with that mask.*
•***Word Family:*** **frighten** *verb* to make someone afraid **frightened** *adjective*

frightful *adjective*
shocking or unpleasant: *a frightful accident / frightful weather*
•***Word Family:*** **frightfully** *adverb* very

frigid (*say* **frij**-id) *adjective*
1 cold and unfriendly: *a frigid stare*
•***Word Family:*** **frigidity** *noun* coldness **frigidly** *adverb*

frill *noun*
a gathered strip or border, used for trimming or decorating something like the neck or hem of a dress
•***Word Family:*** **frilly** *adjective* (**frillier, frilliest**): *a frilly blouse*

fringe (*say* frinj) *noun*
1 an ornamental border with hanging threads, especially on a scarf, carpet or tablecloth 2 hair cut to hang across the forehead in a straight line 3 the edge of something: *The new housing estate is situated on the fringe of the city.*

frisbee *noun*
a brightly-coloured plastic toy shaped like a saucer, which flies through the air when you throw it
•***Word Origins:*** this is a trademark

frisk *verb*
1 to move about with quick, eager, playful movements: *The dogs frisked about the picnic area.* 2 to search someone for concealed weapons: *Security guards frisked the travellers by running their hands quickly over their clothes.*
•***Word Family:*** **frisky** *adjective* (**friskier, friskiest**) lively or playful **friskily** *adverb* **friskiness** *noun*

fritter (1) *verb*
to waste money or time little by little: *He frittered away his money on junk food.*

fritter (2) *noun*
a piece of food, such as a slice of meat or fruit, coated in a batter and deep-fried: *an apple fritter*

frivolous (*say* **friv**-a-lus) *adjective*
silly or flippant: *frivolous behaviour / a frivolous question*
•***Word Family:*** **frivolity** *noun* **frivolously** *adverb*

frizzy *adjective*
in tight, short curls: *frizzy hair*
•***Word Family:*** other forms are **frizzier, frizziest** □ **frizziness** *noun*

frock *noun*
a dress: *a cotton frock*

frog *noun*
a web-footed animal that moves by jumping and lives on land or in water

frogman *noun*
a diver trained and equipped with a wetsuit, flippers, a mask and an air tank for underwater work, such as finding things
•***Word Family:*** the plural is **frogmen**

frolic (*say* **frol**-ik) *verb*
to play merrily and joyfully: *The children frolicked in the garden.*
•***Word Family:*** other forms are **frolics, frolicked, frolicking** □ **frolicsome** *adjective* playful or full of fun

from *preposition*
1 starting at: *from Melbourne to Sydney / He improved his position from 8th to 2nd.* 2 not at: *She's away from school today.* 3 as opposed to: *I can't tell one twin from the other.* 4 out of: *a letter from his uncle* 5 because of: *Her mother suffered from bad eyesight.* 6 measured with reference to: *We are 10 minutes from the freeway.*

frond *noun*
the large, feather-like leaf of a fern or palm

front (*say* frunt) *noun*
1 the foremost or most important side, surface or part: *The entrance is at the front of the building. / The title is at the front of the book.* 2 the line or area between armies when fighting is taking place: *the battle front* 3 a boundary between two air masses: *The weather forecast is for a cold front.*
front *adjective*
4 at the front: *the front page / a front tooth*
•***Word Family:*** **frontal** *adjective*

frontier (*say* **frun**-tear) *noun*
1 the border between two countries or states 2 the end of a settled region: *The explorers reached the last frontier.*

frost *noun*
1 a covering of ice crystals formed when the air

in contact with the ground is below freezing point 2 weather when this happens
frost *verb*
3 to cover a cake with icing
•***Word Family:*** **frosted** *adjective*: *frosted glass* **frosty** *adjective* (**frostier, frostiest**): *a frosty morning* **frostily** *adverb* **frostiness** *noun*

frostbite *noun*
the damage done to your fingers, face and toes when they are frozen in extremely cold conditions
•***Word Family:*** **frostbitten** *adjective*

froth *noun*
1 a mass of small bubbles or foam
froth *verb*
2 to produce froth: *to froth at the mouth*
•***Word Family:*** **frothy** *adjective* (**frothier, frothiest**) **frothily** *adverb* **frothiness** *noun*

frown *verb*
1 to bring your brows together showing that you are thinking or feel cross 2 **frown on** to disapprove of something: *to frown on smoking*
frown *noun*
3 a cross expression on your face

frugal (*say* **froo**-gal) *adjective*
careful or economical so as not to waste things: *I'm frugal in my use of water.*
•***Word Family:*** **frugally** *adverb*

fruit (*rhymes with* hoot) *noun*
1 the part of a plant that develops from the flower and that you can eat, such as an apple or banana 2 the product or result of something: *His brilliant guitar playing is the fruit of many years of hard work.*
fruit *verb*
3 to bear fruit

fruitful *adjective*
successful or useful: *a fruitful discussion*
•***Word Family:*** **fruitfully** *adverb* **fruitfulness** *noun* **fruitless** *adjective* unsuccessful or useless

fruity *adjective*
1 tasting or smelling like fruit: *a fruity wine*
2 rich or deep: *a fruity voice*
•***Word Family:*** other forms are **fruitier, fruitiest** □ **fruitiness** *noun*

frustrate *verb*
to prevent or stop someone doing something: *Pouring rain frustrated her attempts to wash the car.*
•***Word Family:*** **frustrated** *adjective* **frustration** *noun*

fry (1) *verb*
to cook in hot fat or oil: *to fry bacon*
•***Word Family:*** other forms are **fries, fried, frying** □ **fried** *adjective*

fry (2) *noun*
1 newly hatched fishes 2 any young or small animals
•***Word Family:*** the plural is **fry**

fudge *noun*
a soft brown sweet made by boiling milk, sugar and butter

fuel (*say* **few**-el) *noun*
1 something, such as petrol, gas or wood, burned to produce heat and power
fuel *verb*
2 to provide something with fuel
•***Word Family:*** other verb forms are **fuels, fuelled, fuelling**

fugitive (*say* **few**-ji-tiv) *noun*
someone who is running away, usually to hide from the police

fugue (*say* fewg) *noun*
a piece of music in which a brief melody is played or sung once and then imitated or repeated to form an intricate pattern

fulcrum (*say* **full**-krum) *noun*
the point at which something pivots or balances
•***Word Family:*** the plural is **fulcrums** or **fulcra**

fulfil *verb*
1 to satisfy: *He fulfilled his desire for fame with the success of his first book.* 2 to carry out: *to fulfil a promise*
•***Word Family:*** other forms are **fulfils, fulfilled, fulfilling** □ **fulfilment** *noun*

full *adjective*
1 having or containing as many or as much as possible: *The glass is full of juice. / Your work is full of mistakes.* 2 complete: *It took a full day for us to paint our bedroom.* 3 having wide, loose folds: *a full skirt*
full *adverb*
4 completely: *The ball hit him full in the face.*
•***Word Family:*** **fully** *adverb*

full-blooded *adjective*
of pure and unmixed race: *a full-blooded Maori*

full moon *noun*
the moon when you see it as a complete circle

full stop *noun*
the dot (.) used to mark the end of a sentence or to show that a word has been abbreviated

fumble *verb*
to feel, grope about or handle something clumsily: *to fumble for a match / He fumbled his entrance and fell flat on his face.*

fume *noun*
1 **fumes** strong-smelling smoke or gas

fume *verb*
2 to give off fumes 3 to rage or be very angry: *to fume over the mess in the kitchen*
•***Word Family:*** **fuming** *adjective*

fun *noun*
1 playfulness: *to be full of fun* 2 amusing enjoyment: *The fun's about to begin.* 3 **make fun of** to ridicule or tease someone

function (*say* **funk**-shon) *noun*
1 the special purpose of someone or something: *Your function as captain is to lead and inspire the team.* 2 a formal ceremony or gathering, such as a wedding or ball 3 a basic operation that a calculator does
function *verb*
4 to work or perform your usual tasks: *The radio is functioning now. / He can't function in this tiny office.*
•***Word Family:*** **functional** *adjective* practical, useful or in working order **functionally** *adverb*

fund *noun*
1 a supply or stock of something, especially money: *He has an unlimited fund of silly jokes. / funds for your holiday*
fund *verb*
2 to find the money to pay for something: *How was the school hall funded?*

fundamental (*say* fun-da-**men**-tal) *adjective*
basic or central: *We need fundamental changes to the school rules.*
•***Word Family:*** **fundamentally** *adverb*

funeral (*say* **few**-na-ral) *noun*
a ceremony or church service held before the burial or cremation of someone who has died
•***Word Family:*** **funereal** (*say* few-**near**-ri-al) *adjective* gloomy or mournful

fungus *noun*
a simple plant, such as a mould, mushroom or toadstool, that grows best in dark, moist places
•***Word Family:*** the plural is **fungi** or **funguses**

funnel *noun*
1 a tube with a wide mouth or opening, often used to pour liquid into bottles 2 the metal chimney on ships and steam-engines
funnel *verb*
3 to direct or pour something into a narrow space: *The police funnelled the angry crowd through a back alley into the square.*
•***Word Family:*** other verb forms are **funnels, funnelled, funnelling**

funny *adjective*
1 making you laugh: *a funny comic* 2 strange or peculiar: *This cake has a funny taste.*
•***Word Family:*** other forms are **funnier, funniest** □ **funnily** *adverb*

fur *noun*
1 the soft, thick hair of some animals, such as rabbits or cats 2 the skin of animals, such as rabbits, foxes or minks, made into a coat
•***Word Family:*** **furrier** *noun* someone who makes or sells furs □ see also **furry**

furious (*say* **fyor**-ri-us) *adjective*
1 extremely or violently angry 2 intense or uncontrolled: *a furious storm*
•***Word Family:*** **furiously** *adverb*

furl *verb*
to roll up tightly: *to furl your umbrella*

furlong *noun*
an old-fashioned unit of distance equal to one-eighth of a mile or about 201 metres in length

furnace (*say* **fir**-nis) *noun*
a large, very hot fire in an enclosed structure, used for producing steam, making steel or heating a building

furnish *verb*
1 to put furniture in a room, house and so on: *to furnish your bedroom with a bunk bed* 2 to give someone what they need for a particular job or purpose: *We will furnish you with boots.*
•***Word Family:*** **furnishings** *plural noun* the fittings, furniture and so on for furnishing a room

furniture (*say* **fir**-na-cha) *noun*
movable objects used in buildings, such as chairs or tables

furrow *noun*
1 a narrow trench made in the ground by a plough
furrow *verb*
2 to wrinkle into grooves that look like furrows: *to furrow your brow*

furry *adjective*
covered with or like fur
•***Word Family:*** other forms are **furrier, furriest** □ **furriness** *noun*

further *adverb*
1 to or at a greater distance: *He threw the ball further than me. / The lake is further off than I'd expected.* 2 in addition
further *adjective*
3 more: *Do you expect further letters?*
further *verb*
4 to help something move forward or progress: *to further our friendship*
•***Word Family:*** other adverb and adjective forms are **far** and **furthest**

further education *noun*
education after you have left school, especially at a college

A B C D E F G H I J K L M N O P Q R S T U V W X Y Z

furtive *adjective*
secretive or sly: *a furtive glance to check that no-one could see*
• ***Word Family:*** **furtively** *adverb*
• ***Word Origins:*** from a Latin word meaning "stolen"

fury (*say* **fyor**-ree) *noun*
violent excitement or anger: *She smashed the mirror in her fury.*

fuse (1) (*say* fewz) *noun*
1 the safety wire that protects an electric circuit by melting and cutting off the power when the current is greater than it should be
2 the wick used to ignite explosives
fuse *verb*
3 to burn out and stop working: *The toaster fused when we turned it on.*

fuse (2) (*say* fewz) *verb*
to combine or join things by melting them together: *to fuse gold links together to make a necklace*
• ***Word Family:*** **fusion** *noun*: *nuclear fusion*

fuselage (*say* **few**-za-lahj) *noun*
the body of an aircraft

fuss *noun*
unnecessary excitement or anxiety: *She made such a fuss about what dress she was going to wear.*
• ***Word Family:*** **fussy** *adjective* (**fussier, fussiest**) **fussily** *adverb* **fussiness** *noun*

futile (*say* **few**-tile) *adjective*
useless or having no result: *She made a futile attempt to be heard amid the noise.*
• ***Word Family:*** **futilely** *adverb* **futility** *noun*

future (*say* **few**-cher) *noun*
1 the time or events still to come: *to predict the future*
future *adjective*
2 of or happening later: *future plans*
• ***Word Family:*** **futuristic** *adjective* so modern in its style that it seems to be from a future time

future tense *noun*
the form of a verb, using "will" and "shall", you use to show that something is going to happen in the future, such as "will sleep" in the sentence *He will sleep well tonight*.

fuzz *noun*
1 a fluffy or frizzy substance, especially hair
2 the police

fuzzy *adjective*
1 blurred or not clear: *The picture on the screen went fuzzy.* 2 like or covered with fuzz: *fuzzy hair*
• ***Word Family:*** other forms are **fuzzier, fuzziest, fuzzily** *adverb* **fuzziness** *noun*

Gg

gabardine or **gaberdine** (*say* gab-a-**deen**) *noun*
a woven fabric usually made from wool, cotton or viscose, often used for raincoats
• ***Word Origins:*** from an Old French word meaning a "pilgrim's robe"

gabble *verb*
to talk very quickly or unclearly

gable *noun*
a triangular section of an outside wall between the slopes of a roof
• ***Word Family:*** **gabled** *adjective*

gadget (*say* **gaj**-et) *noun*
a small, useful machine or tool designed to do a special job: *a gadget for shredding lettuce*
• ***Word Family:*** **gadgetry** *noun* gadgets

gag *noun*
1 something placed over your mouth to stop you talking 2 a joke, especially one that a comedian tells on stage
gag *verb*
3 to cough and choke: *He gagged on a fish bone.*
• ***Word Family:*** other verb forms are **gags, gagged, gagging**

gaggle *noun*
a flock of geese
• ***Word Origins:*** from an Old German word meaning "to cry like a goose"

gaiety (*say* **gay**-a-tee) *noun*
cheerfulness and liveliness
• ***Word Family:*** see also **gay**

gain *verb*
1 to get something: *to gain a baby brother* 2 to increase: *to gain weight* 3 to go ahead of the correct time: *My watch has gained five minutes.*
4 **gain on** to catch up with: *to gain on someone you are chasing*
gain *noun*
5 an increase, especially of money or possessions

gait *noun*
a way of moving, especially walking: *a shuffling gait*

gala (*say* **gah**-la) *noun*
1 a festival or other public entertainment: *a gala concert* 2 a sports meeting, especially in swimming: *a swimming gala*

galah (*say* ga-**lah**) *noun*
1 an Australian cockatoo with a pink chest and grey wings 2 a foolish or silly person
• ***Word Origins:*** from an Aboriginal language

galaxy (*say* **gal**-ak-see) *noun*
1 an enormous group of stars, dust and gas, separated from the millions of similar groups by vast expanses of space 2 our own galaxy, the Milky Way, which includes our solar system and billions of stars
• ***Word Family:*** the plural is **galaxies** □ **galactic** *adjective*
• ***Word Origins:*** from a Greek word meaning "milk"

gale *noun*
a very strong wind

gallant (*say* **gal**-ant) *adjective*
1 brave and daring: *a gallant rescue attempt* 2 polite and courteous: *a gallant escort*
• ***Word Family:*** **gallantry** *noun* chivalrous or heroic behaviour **gallantly** *adverb*

gall bladder *noun*
a small bag underneath your liver, that stores bile and releases it to help you digest fat

galleon (*say* **gal**-ee-on) *noun*
a large sailing ship with three masts, used by Spain and other countries during the 15th to 17th centuries

gallery (*say* **gal**-a-ree) *noun*
1 a room or building where works of art are displayed 2 an upper balcony, where the audience can sit in a theatre 3 a long narrow room: *a shooting gallery*
• ***Word Family:*** the plural is **galleries**

galley *noun*
1 the kitchen in a ship or aircraft 2 a long ship moved along by oars or by oars and sails, used in ancient times
• ***Word Family:*** the plural is **galleys**

gallon *noun*
an old-fashioned measure for liquids, equal to 8 pints or about 4.5 litres

gallop *noun*
1 the fastest movement a horse can make 2 a fast ride on a horse
gallop *verb*
3 to ride a horse at a gallop: *to gallop through the fields at breakneck speed*
• ***Word Family:*** other verb forms are **gallops, galloped, galloping**

gallows (*say* **gal**-oze) *noun*
a wooden frame with two upright posts and a crosspiece, on which criminals were once hanged

galore (*say* ga-**lor**) *adverb*
in abundance or large numbers: *There were books galore at the fair.*

galvanize or **galvanise** (*say* **gal**-va-nize) *verb*
1 to coat iron by dipping it in molten zinc to prevent rust 2 to stimulate or startle someone into doing something: *The shrill whistles galvanized the workers into action.*

gamble *verb*
1 to play a game for money 2 to take a risk or chance: *to gamble on the shop being open*
• ***Word Family:*** **gambler** *noun*

game *noun*
1 a form of sport or amusement that you can play, especially one with rules: *a tennis game / a card game* 2 wild animals, birds or fish hunted for sport or food
game *adjective*
3 plucky or courageous 4 willing or having the spirit to try something difficult or new: *She's game for anything.*
• ***Word Family:*** **gamely** *adverb* bravely

gander *noun*
a male goose

gang *noun*
1 a group of people working or getting together for a particular reason: *a gang of labourers / a gang of criminals*
gang *verb*
2 to act as a gang: *We ganged together to fight the proposed motorway.* 3 **gang up on** to join together against someone: *to gang up on a new kid*

gangling *adjective*
awkwardly tall and spindly: *a gangling teenager*

gangplank *noun*
a plank used as a bridge between a ship and the shore or another ship

gangrene (*say* **gang**-green) *noun*
the decay of flesh, usually of the limbs, due to the blood supply being cut off

gangster *noun*
a member of a gang of criminals

gangway *noun*
1 a passageway on a ship 2 a gangplank
gangway *interjection*
3 something you shout to tell people to get out of the way

gaol (*say* jale) *noun*
another spelling for **jail**

gap *noun*
1 a break or unfilled space: *a gap in the hedge / a gap between his front teeth* 2 a difference: *a wide gap between their opinions*

A B C D E F G H I J K L M N O P Q R S T U V W X Y Z

gape *verb*
1 to stare in amazement with your mouth wide open: *to gape at the strange sight* 2 to be open wide: *A large hole gaped in the roof.*
• ***Word Family:*** **gaping** *adjective* **gapingly** *adverb*

garage (*say* **ga**-rahj) *noun*
1 a building for sheltering cars and other vehicles 2 a place for mending cars and selling petrol and oil

garbage (*say* **gar**-bij) *noun*
any rubbish, especially household waste

garble *verb*
to distort or mix something up so that it's hard to understand: *to garble instructions*

garden *noun*
1 a piece of land where trees and grass grow, set aside for relaxing: *your back garden / public gardens* 2 a bed or piece of ground used for growing flowers, fruit or vegetables
garden *verb*
3 to work in a garden
• ***Word Family:*** **gardener** *noun* someone who looks after a garden **gardening** *noun*

gargle *verb*
to bubble liquid about inside your throat without swallowing

gargoyle (*say* **gar**-goil) *noun*
a rainwater spout on the side of a building, often in the shape of a grotesque animal or human head with its mouth open

garland *noun*
a wreath or ring of flowers used for decoration or as a token of honour

garlic *noun*
a plant like an onion, with strongly-flavoured bulbs used in cooking

garment *noun*
a piece of clothing

garnish *verb*
1 to decorate something so as to make it more tasty or inviting: *to garnish fish with wedges of lemon*
garnish *noun*
2 something added to garnish food: *Parsley is a common garnish.*

garrison *noun*
1 a group of soldiers who are based in and ready to defend a building or town 2 the strong fort or building where the soldiers are based

garter *noun*
a band of elastic you wear around your leg to keep a sock or stocking in place

gas *noun*
1 a substance like air, that completely fills any container in which it is kept 2 a gas or mixture of gases used as fuel: *natural gas / coal gas*
gas *verb*
3 to make someone sick or suffocate them with poisonous gas
• ***Word Family:*** the plural of the noun is **gases** □ other verb forms are **gases, gassed, gassing** □ **gaseous** *adjective* like gas **gassy** *adjective* full of gas.

gash *noun*
1 a large deep cut
gash *verb*
2 to make a large deep cut in something: *She gashed her arm on a rock.*

gasket *noun*
a rubber fitting used to seal joints and prevent gas escaping, especially in a car engine

gasp *verb*
1 to take in your breath noisily: *to gasp in amazement* 2 to breathe quickly or with difficulty: *to gasp for air* 3 to speak in a breathless way
gasp *noun*
4 an act of catching your breath

gastric *adjective*
to do with your stomach: *gastric juices / gastric flu*

gastroenteritis *noun*
an illness in which your stomach and intestines become inflamed

gate *noun*
1 a barrier, usually on hinges, that opens and closes an entrance 2 the number of people who pay admission to a sporting match or similar event

gatecrash *verb*
to go to a party or other gathering without being invited
• ***Word Family:*** **gatecrasher** *noun*

gather *verb*
1 to pick up or bring together: *to gather fallen fruit / to gather your thoughts* 2 to draw together in folds: *to gather a skirt at the waist* 3 to increase: *The car gathered speed along the road.* 4 to conclude or understand: *I gather you're not pleased.* 5 to come together: *They gathered to discuss the match.*
• ***Word Family:*** **gathering** *noun* a crowd of people

gauche (*say* gohsh) *adjective*
awkward or tactless: *gauche behaviour*
• ***Word Family:*** **gaucherie** *noun* awkwardness **gaucheness** *noun*
• ***Word Origins:*** from a French word meaning "left" or "left hand"

gaudy (*say* **gaw**-dee) *adjective*
bright or showy, often in a vulgar way
•***Word Family:*** other forms are **gaudier, gaudiest** □ **gaudily** *adverb* **gaudiness** *noun*

gauge (*say* gayj) *noun*
1 the thickness or diameter of something, such as wire 2 an instrument for measuring something, such as pressure or temperature 3 the distance between the rails of a railway track
gauge *verb*
4 to measure or estimate something: *to gauge the drop from the top floor / to gauge someone's feelings from their behaviour*

gaunt (*say* gawnt) *adjective*
thin or haggard in your appearance

gauze (*say* gawz) *noun*
1 thin, transparent cloth like a net for making bandages and other things 2 similar material consisting of crossed lines, such as wire

gay *adjective*
1 homosexual: *gay rights* 2 happy or bright: *a gay song / gay curtains*
•***Word Family:*** **gaiety** *noun* **gaily** *adverb*

gaze *verb*
1 to look with fixed attention or curiosity: *to gaze out of the window*
gaze *noun*
2 a long fixed look: *I couldn't meet his gaze.*

gazelle (*say* ga-**zel**) *noun*
a small African or Asian antelope

gazette (*say* ga-**zet**) *noun*
an official or government newspaper
•***Word Origins:*** from the Italian name for a Venetian coin (the price of a gazette)

GCSE *abbreviation*
short for General Certificate of Secondary Education

gear *noun*
1 the set of toothed wheels that work together in a machine, such as those affecting the wheels of a car or truck 2 tools or equipment: *fishing gear* 3 clothes: *football gear*
gear *verb*
4 to adjust or adapt something: *to gear your speech to your audience*

gearbox *noun*
the case containing the gears of a motor vehicle

gecko *noun*
a small flat lizard, usually with pads on its toes that stick to surfaces for climbing
•***Word Family:*** the plural is **geckos** or **geckoes**
•***Word Origins:*** from a Malay word that sounds like the noises these lizards make

Geiger counter (*say* **guy**-ga counter) *noun*
a portable instrument used for detecting and measuring radioactivity, especially after a nuclear blast
•***Word Origins:*** named after Hans *Geiger*, a German physicist who lived from 1882 to 1945

geisha (*say* **gee**-sha *or* **gay**-sha) *noun*
a Japanese woman trained to entertain with dancing, conversation, and so on
•***Word Origins:*** from Japanese

gel (*say* jel) *noun*
1 a substance like jelly: *hair gel / shower gel*
gel *verb*
2 to form or become a gel
•***Word Family:*** other verb forms are **gels, gelled, gelling**
•***Word Origins:*** a short form of *gelatine*

gelatine (*say* **jel**-a-teen) *noun*
a clear substance made from meat and bones, that dissolves in water and sets into a jelly, used in food, photography and medicine
•***Word Family:*** **gelatinous** *adjective*

gelato (*say* je-**lah**-to) *noun*
an ice-cream, usually made with water instead of milk
•***Word Family:*** the plural is **gelati**

geld *verb*
to remove the testicles of an animal: *to geld a stallion*
•***Word Family:*** **gelding** *noun* a male horse with its testicles removed

gelignite (*say* **jel**-ig-nite) *noun*
an explosive substance, used for blasting

gem (*say* jem) *noun*
a stone, cut and polished and used in jewellery to show off its beauty

gender (*say* **jen**-da) *noun*
1 one of the groups into which the nouns and pronouns of languages such as French are classed according to the sex of the person or thing described: *masculine gender / feminine gender* 2 the sex of a creature, either male or female

gene (*say* jeen) *noun*
one of the parts of a living cell whose job is to pass characteristics such as eye or hair colour from parents to their children
•***Word Family:*** **genetic** *adjective: genetic engineering* **genetics** *noun*

genealogy (*say* jee-ni-**al**-a-jee) *noun*
a family tree or the record of your ancestors and relatives
•***Word Family:*** the plural is **genealogies** □ **genealogical** *adjective* **genealogist** *noun*

general *adjective*
1 affecting everyone: *a general election / a general strike* 2 most common: *the general opinion* 3 not limited or restricted: *as a general rule*
general *noun*
4 an army officer of high rank 5 **in general** (a) as a whole and including everything: *We spoke about things in general.* (b) usually or as a rule: *In general, summer is a warm season.*
• ***Word Family:*** **generalize** or **generalise** *verb* to say that something is almost always true **generalization** *noun* **generally** *adverb*

general practitioner *noun*
a doctor who works in a local area, treating general medical problems

generate *verb*
1 to produce heat or electricity: *to generate electricity* 2 to produce or lead to ideas or feelings: *to generate interest*

generation (*say* jen-a-**ray**-shon) *noun*
1 all the people born at about the same time: *the older generation* 2 the average time between any two generations of a family, usually about 30 years 3 each stage in a family descent: *Three generations were present – mother, daughter and granddaughter.* 4 a period in the development of the computer in which one or more major breakthroughs occurred: *At the moment there are five computer generations.*

generator (*say* **jen**-a-ray-ter) *noun*
a machine that produces electricity from mechanical energy, using wind or water power and so on

generous (*say* **jen**-a-rus) *adjective*
1 ready to share or give to other people: *a generous person* 2 very large: *generous slices*
• ***Word Family:*** **generosity** *noun* **generously** *adverb*

genetics (*say* je-**net**-iks) *noun*
the science that studies the way certain characteristics are passed from one generation to another
• ***Word Family:*** **gene** *noun* **genetic** *adjective* **genetically** *adverb* **geneticist** *noun*

genial (*say* **jee**-nee-al) *adjective*
pleasant, kind and friendly: *a genial manner*
• ***Word Family:*** **genially** *adverb*

genie (*say* **jee**-nee) *noun*
a magical spirit in Arabian and Persian stories, especially one who changes into many different forms and obeys the commands of its owner
• ***Word Origins:*** from an Arabic word meaning "demon"

genesis (*say* **jen**-a-sis) *noun*
a beginning or creation: *the genesis of living creatures*
• ***Word Family:*** the plural is **geneses**

genitals (*say* **jen**-i-tals) *plural noun*
the organs of your body used to have sex and to reproduce, such as the penis and testes in males and the ovaries, uterus and vagina in females
• ***Word Family:*** **genital** *adjective*

genius (*say* **jee**-nee-us) *noun*
an exceptionally intelligent or creative person
• ***Word Family:*** the plural is **geniuses**

genocide (*say* **jen**-o-side) *noun*
the deliberate killing of everyone belonging to a particular race or nation

genre (*say* **zhon**-ra) *noun*
a style, variety or category, especially in art, film and writing: *Crime stories belong to the genre of fiction writing.*

genteel (*say* jen-**teel**) *adjective*
extremely polite and refined in your manners, speech or behaviour
• ***Word Family:*** **genteelly** *adverb* **gentility** *noun*

gentle *adjective*
1 kind or soft: *gentle words / a gentle touch*
2 moderate or not severe: *a gentle slope / a gentle breeze*
• ***Word Family:*** **gentleness** *noun* **gently** *adverb*

gentleman *noun*
1 a polite form of address for a man: *ladies and gentlemen* 2 a polite man with perfect manners: *He's a real gentleman.*
• ***Word Family:*** the plural is **gentlemen**

genuine (*say* **jen**-yoo-in) *adjective*
1 real or true: *genuine fear / a genuine antique*
2 sincere in what you say and feel: *a genuine person*
• ***Word Family:*** **genuinely** *adverb* **genuineness** *noun*

geography (*say* jee-**og**-ra-fee) *noun*
the study of the Earth's surface, including its land forms, climates, plants, soils and where its peoples live
• ***Word Family:*** **geographer** *noun* someone who studies geography **geographic** *adjective* **geographical** *adjective* **geographically** *adverb*
• ***Word Origins:*** from Greek words meaning "earth" and "write"

geology (*say* jee-**ol**-a-jee) *noun*
the study of the layers of rock that form the Earth
• ***Word Family:*** **geological** *adjective* **geologically** *adverb* **geologist** *noun*

geometry (*say* jee-**om**-a-tree) *noun*
the part of maths that studies lines, angles and shapes
• ***Word Family:*** **geometric** *adjective* **geometrical** *adjective* **geometrically** *adverb*

geranium (*say* je-**ray**-nee-um) *noun*
a garden shrub with red, pink or white flowers and leaves marked with different colours

gerbil *noun*
a small animal like a mouse, often kept as a pet

geriatrics (*say* je-ree-**at**-riks) *noun*
the medical care of old people
• ***Word Family:*** **geriatric** *adjective* to do with the care of old people **geriatric** *noun* an old person **geriatrician** *noun* a doctor who treats old people

germ (*say* jerm) *noun*
1 a living thing that is so tiny you can only see it with a microscope, and which may cause disease 2 the basis or beginning of something: *the germ of an idea*

German measles *noun*
a disease people catch that gives them red spots and a fever and which is dangerous to a pregnant woman as it may damage her unborn child

German shepherd *noun*
another name for an **Alsatian**

germinate (*say* **jer**-mi-nate) *verb*
to develop and grow, the way a plant grows from a seed
• ***Word Family:*** **germination** *noun*

gestation (*say* jes-**tay**-shon) *noun*
the time when a child or young animal is growing in its mother's womb

gesticulate (*say* jes-**tic**-u-late) *noun*
to wave your hands and arms while you talk

gesture (*say* **jes**-cher) *noun*
1 a movement of part of your body, such as your hands, that you make to express an idea or emotion 2 a way of showing your feelings: *She kissed me as a gesture of her friendship.*

get *verb*
1 to obtain: *She got the top mark in the test.* 2 to hit: *The ball got me in the back.* 3 to fetch or bring: *I'll go and get the book.* 4 to understand: *I don't get your meaning.* 5 to make or persuade someone to do something: *Can you get the car to start? / Can you get her to visit me?* 6 to prepare or make ready: *I'll get dinner now.* 7 to punish or kill: *I'll get you for that!* 8 to become: *He gets tired very easily.* 9 to travel on: *to get the train to work* 10 **get away with** to escape punishment for something you have done: *The robbers thought they would get away with their crime.* 11 **get by** to manage: *How will we get by without a car?* 12 **get off** to escape being punished 13 **get on** (a) to grow old (b) to make progress (c) to be friendly with 14 **get over** to recover from
• ***Word Family:*** other forms are **gets, got, getting**

geyser (*say* **gee**-za *or* **gy**-za) *noun*
a spring that sends up jets of hot water and steam into the air
• ***Word Origins:*** from an Icelandic word

ghastly (*say* **gahst**-lee) *adjective*
dreadful or unpleasant: *a ghastly sight / a ghastly smell*
• ***Word Family:*** other forms are **ghastlier, ghastliest** □ **ghastliness** *noun*

ghee (*say* gee) *noun*
a kind of butter used in Indian cooking, which has been made pure by heating

gherkin (*say* **ger**-kin) *noun*
a small cucumber that has been pickled

ghetto (*say* **get**-o) *noun*
an area of a city where a group of people lives separately from other groups in the community because they are poor or of a different race or religion
• ***Word Family:*** the plural is **ghettos** or **ghettoes**
• ***Word Origins:*** from an Italian word meaning "outside the city walls" and used for the Jewish quarter of Venice in the 16th century

ghost *noun*
1 the spirit of a dead person, believed to visit or haunt living people 2 a small trace of something: *the ghost of a grin*
• ***Word Family:*** **ghostly** *adverb* (**ghostlier, ghostliest**) **ghostliness** *noun*

ghoul *noun*
1 an evil spirit in stories, believed to eat dead bodies 2 someone who likes thinking about death or unpleasant things
• ***Word Family:*** **ghoulish** *adjective* **ghoulishly** *adverb* **ghoulishness** *noun*

giant (*say* **juy**-ant) *noun*
1 a huge imaginary person in fairy tales, who is often cruel and sometimes eats people
giant *adjective*
2 huge: *a giant pumpkin*
• ***Word Family:*** **giantess** a female giant

gibberish (*say* **jib**-er-ish) *noun*
a stream of rapid words that you can't understand
• ***Word Family:*** **gibber** (*say* **jib**-er) *verb* to talk very fast, in a way that people can't understand

gibbon (*say* **gib**-en) *noun*
a small, long-armed ape, living in the forests of tropical Asia

giddy (*say* **gid**-ee) *adjective*
having the feeling that everything is spinning
•*Word Family:* other forms are **giddier, giddiest** □ **giddily** *adverb* **giddiness** *noun*

gift *noun*
1 a present: *a birthday gift* 2 a special ability: *to have a gift for painting*
•*Word Family:* **gifted** *adjective* having a special ability or talent

gig *noun*
1 a performance by a band or a musician 2 an open, two-wheeled carriage pulled by one horse in olden times

gigabyte (*say* **gig**-a-bite) *noun*
a measurement of computer information equal to one thousand million bytes

gigantic (*say* jy-**gan**-tik) *adjective*
extremely large: *a gigantic sumo wrestler / gigantic shoes*
•*Word Family:* **gigantically** *adverb*

giggle *verb*
1 to laugh in a silly or nervous way
giggle *noun*
2 a joke: *to do something for a giggle* 3 **the giggles** a fit of giggling: *We got the giggles in our French lesson.*
•*Word Family:* **giggler** *noun* **giggly** *adjective*

gild *verb*
to cover with a fine layer of gold or a golden colour
•*Word Family:* other forms are **gilds, gilded** or **gilt, gilding** □ **gilding** *noun* a golden surface or coating

gill *noun*
the outside part of a fish's body, used for breathing

gimmick *noun*
a trick or unusual idea which is meant to grab your attention or make you buy something: *a sales gimmick*

gin (1) (*say* jin) *noun*
a strong alcoholic drink made from rye or other grain and flavoured with juniper berries

gin (2) (*say* jin) *noun*
a machine for separating the seeds from a cotton plant

ginger (*say* **jin**-ja) *noun*
1 the strong-smelling root of a tropical plant, used in cooking and medicine 2 a sandy-red colour
ginger *adjective*
3 sandy-red: *ginger hair*
•*Word Family:* **gingery** *adjective*

gingerbread *noun*
a treacle or honey cake flavoured with ginger

gingerly (*say* **jin**-ja-lee) *adverb*
with extreme caution or care: *to walk gingerly on the wet floor*

gingham (*say* **ging**-um) *noun*
a cotton cloth with a coloured check pattern

ginseng (*say* **jin**-seng) *noun*
a plant with a scented root, used as a medicine

gipsy (*say* **jip**-see) *noun*
someone who belongs to a race of nomadic wanderers, originally Hindu, now found mainly in Europe
•*Word Family:* the plural is **gipsies**
•*Word Origins:* from a short form of the word "Egyptian", because these people were thought to have come from Egypt

giraffe (*say* je-**raff**) *noun*
the tallest mammal, with a long neck and legs and a spotted skin, that feeds on leaves in African forests

girder *noun*
a large beam supporting a building or other similar structure

girdle *noun*
1 a belt or cord worn around your waist 2 a corset

girl *noun*
a female child
•*Word Family:* **girlhood** *noun* the time when a woman was a girl **girlish** *adjective* **girlishly** *adverb*

girlfriend *noun*
1 a female friend 2 the girl or woman that a boy or man regularly goes out with

girth *noun*
the measurement around something

gist (*say* jist) *noun*
the main or most important part of something: *But what's the gist of your argument?*

give *verb*
1 to provide or hand over something: *to give someone your help / to give a present* 2 to cause: *Does your leg give you pain?* 3 to result in: *My test marks give a gloomy picture of my progress.* 4 to make suddenly: *She gave a start when she saw him.* 5 to pay: *How much will you give me for my car?* 6 to present: *Did the newspaper give the whole story?* 7 **give away** (a) to give as a present (b) to betray: *Her smile gave her away.* 8 **give in** to accept defeat 9 **give out** (a) to

distribute: *to give out presents* **(b)** to wear out or become exhausted: *His voice gave out during the speech.* **10 give up (a)** to surrender: *to give yourself up* **(b)** to stop: *to give up smoking* **(c)** to lose hope: *Don't give up now.* **11 give way (a)** to collapse: *Her chair suddenly gave way.* **(b)** to let someone go in front: *Give way to other vehicles.*
•***Word Family:*** other forms are **gives, gave, given, giving** □ **gift** *noun* **giver** *noun*

glacial (*say* **glay**-shel *or* **glay**-see-el) *adjective*
1 to do with ice or glaciers 2 extremely cold or icy: *a glacial wind*
•***Word Family:*** **glacially** *adverb* **glaciation** *noun* the action of glaciers: *to be formed by glaciation*

glacier (*say* **glay**-see-a or **glas**-ee-a) *noun*
a large mass of ice, formed from compacted snow, that moves slowly downhill

glad *adjective*
pleased or happy: *I'm so glad you could visit me.*
•***Word Family:*** other forms are **gladder, gladdest** □ **gladden** *verb* to make someone glad **gladly** *adverb* **gladness** *noun*

glade *noun*
an open space in a forest

gladiator (*say* **glad**-ee-ay-ta) *noun*
someone trained to fight at shows in ancient Roman arenas
•***Word Origins:*** from a Latin word meaning "sword"

glamour or glamor (*say* **glam**-a) *noun*
an attractive charm or excitement: *the glamour of her fashionable clothes / the glamour of the stage*
•***Word Family:*** **glamorize** or **glamorise** *verb* to give glamour to something **glamorous** *adjective* **glamorously** *adverb*

glance *verb*
1 to look briefly 2 to hit something and then bounce off: *The bullet glanced off the tree and struck the wall.*
glance *noun*
3 a brief look: *to leave without a glance*

gland *noun*
a group of cells that produce a substance another part of your body needs to function: *Your salivary glands make the saliva you need to swallow.*
•***Word Family:*** **glandular** *adjective*

glandular fever *noun*
a disease you can catch, caused by a virus, making you feverish and your lymph glands swell

glare (*rhymes with* fair) *noun*
1 an angry or fixed look 2 a bright, intense light: *the glare of a spotlight*
glare *verb*
3 to look at someone angrily: *to glare at your mother* 4 to shine with a bright, intense light
•***Word Family:*** **glaring** *adjective* very obvious: *glaring mistakes* **glaringly** *adverb*

glass *noun*
1 a hard, brittle, usually transparent substance, used to make such things as windows and bottles 2 an object made of glass, such as a container for drinking or a mirror 3 **glasses** spectacles
•***Word Family:*** the plural is **glasses**

glassy *adjective*
1 like glass 2 fixed, or lifeless: *a glassy expression*
•***Word Family:*** other forms are **glassier, glassiest** □ **glassily** *adverb* **glassiness** *noun*

glaze *noun*
1 a smooth, glossy surface or coating: *the glaze on an iced bun* 2 a substance that produces a surface like this: *a pottery glaze*
glaze *verb*
3 to fit or cover with glass: *to glaze a window*
4 to cover pottery with a thin coat or smooth, glossy substance: *to glaze a pot*
•***Word Family:*** **glazier** *noun* someone who fits windows and doors with glass

gleam *noun*
1 a brief flash of light 2 a glow of soft light: *the gleam of polished metal* 3 a brief expression: *a gleam of love in his eyes* 4 a small amount: *a gleam of hope*
gleam *verb*
5 to shine: *Her hair gleamed in the sun.*
•***Word Family:*** **gleaming** *adjective*

glean *verb*
to collect or search out, slowly and steadily: *to glean the cut grain / to glean the facts of a situation*
•***Word Family:*** **gleaner** *noun*

glee *noun*
a feeling of joy or amusement
•***Word Family:*** **gleeful** *adjective* merry **gleefully** *adverb*

glen *noun*
a small, narrow valley

glide *verb*
1 to move or fly smoothly or effortlessly
glide *noun*
2 a smooth movement

glider *noun*
an aeroplane without an engine, that uses the action of air currents to help it fly

glimmer *noun*
1 a faint, wavering light: *a glimmer of moonlight through the trees* 2 a suggestion: *The news brought a glimmer of hope.*
glimmer *verb*
3 to gleam faintly

A B C D E F G H I J K L M N O P Q R S T U V W X Y Z

glimpse *noun*
1 a brief view or look: *to catch a glimpse of the film star*
glimpse *verb*
2 to see briefly: *to glimpse her face in the crowd*

glint *noun*
1 a quick, bright flash of light, especially off a metal surface
glint *verb*
2 to sparkle: *The buckle glinted in the sun.*

glisten (*say* **glis**-en) *verb*
to shine or sparkle, the way a wet or highly polished surface does

glitter *verb*
1 to sparkle with reflected light: *Her eyes glittered in the moonlight.*
glitter *noun*
2 sparkling flecks of colour you use to decorate things: *to put glitter on a birthday card*
• ***Word Family:*** **glittery** *adjective*

gloat (*rhymes with* boat) *verb*
to think about or gaze on something or someone with pleasure or evil delight: *The chess player gloated over his opponent's hopeless position.*

global *adjective*
1 to do with the whole world: *global warming*
2 to do with a whole computer file, program or operation: *a global command*
• ***Word Family:*** **globally** *adverb*

globe *noun*
1 a ball-shaped object 2 a map of the earth shaped like a ball or sphere 3 **the globe** the Earth: *to fly to the other side of the globe*

glockenspiel (*say* **glok**-en-shpeel) *noun*
a musical instrument with tuned, metal bars that you play with small hammers
• ***Word Origins:*** from the German words for "bell" and "play"

gloom *noun*
1 darkness, dimness or deep shadow 2 a feeling of great sadness or hopelessness
• ***Word Family:*** **gloomy** *adjective* (**gloomier, gloomiest**) □ **gloomily** *adverb* **gloominess** *noun*

glory (*say* **glaw**-ree) *noun*
1 praise, honour or fame: *the glory of winning the big match* 2 something that you are proud of: *Her beautiful red hair is only one of her glories.*
3 magnificence or splendour: *We could see the huge statue in all its glory.*
• ***Word Family:*** the plural is **glories** □ **glorify** *verb* (**glorifies, glorified, glorifying**) to praise or give glory **glorious** *adjective: a glorious sunset / a glorious win* **glorification** *noun*

gloss *noun*
1 a shine or lustre on the surface of something: *the gloss of satin sheets*
gloss *verb*
2 **gloss over** to try to cover up or disguise: *to gloss over your errors*

glossary (*say* **glos**-a-ree) *noun*
a list of special words with their explanations or definitions, usually found at the end of a book
• ***Word Family:*** the plural is **glossaries**

glossy *adjective*
smooth and shiny: *glossy hair*
• ***Word Family:*** the other forms are **glossier, glossiest** □ **glossily** *adverb* **glossiness** *noun*

glove (*say* gluv) *noun*
a covering for your hand, with a separate part for each finger

glow *verb*
1 to give off light and heat without flame: *The embers glowed in the hearth.* 2 to be red and shining: *The cold wind makes your cheeks glow.*
glow *noun*
3 light and heat without flames: *the glow from the fire* 4 a feeling of excitement
• ***Word Family:*** **glowing** *adjective* **glowingly** *adverb*

glower (*rhymes with* flower) *verb*
to glare or look angrily at someone

glow-worm *noun*
a beetle that comes out at night and produces a glowing light

glucose (*say* **gloo**-koze) *noun*
a natural sugar found in plants and used as a source of energy by animals and humans
• ***Word Origins:*** from a Greek word meaning "sweet"

glue (*say* gloo) *noun*
1 a sticky paste for holding things together
glue *verb*
2 to stick with glue
• ***Word Family:*** **gluey** *adjective* (**gluier, gluiest**)

glum *adjective*
unhappy or dejected: *a glum face*
• ***Word Family:*** other forms are **glummer, glummest** □ **glumly** *adverb* **glumness** *noun*

glut *noun*
a larger amount than you need: *A glut of tomatoes brought the price down sharply.*

glutton *noun*
someone who eats too much
• ***Word Family:*** **gluttonous** *adjective* **gluttonously** *adverb* **gluttony** *noun* the habit of eating too much

gnarled (*say* narld) *adjective*
knotty, twisted and rough: *a gnarled old tree*

gnash (*say* nash) *verb*
to grind your teeth together, especially in pain or rage

gnaw (*say* naw) *verb*
to chew or bite something for a long time: *to gnaw on a bone*
•*Word Family:* **gnawing** *adjective*: *a gnawing pain / a gnawing hunger*

gnome (*say* nome) *noun*
a small dwarf-like person in fairy stories, who lives in underground caves and often guards treasure

go *verb*
1 to move: *The car is going too fast.* 2 to become: *to go mad / to go cold at night* 3 to depart: *Tell them to go at once.* 4 to intend: *He is going to jump.* 5 to lead or run: *This road goes north.* 6 to work: *My watch has stopped going.* 7 to turn out: *How did everything go?* 8 to belong: *These dishes go there.* 9 to pass: *Time goes by.* 10 to attend: *We all go to school.* 11 to share: *Let's go halves in the cake.* 12 to fit or divide: *These sandwiches won't all go in my lunchbox. / 8 goes into 24 three times.* 13 **go off** (a) to explode: *The fireworks went off suddenly.* (b) to turn sour: *The milk has gone off.* (c) to stop liking
go *noun*
14 energy or liveliness: *to be full of go* 15 a try or turn: *to have a go at hang-gliding / It's your go.* 16 **on the go** very busy and active
•*Word Family:* other verb forms are **goes, went, gone, going** □ the plural of the noun is **goes**

goad *verb*
to anger or excite a person or an animal, often by teasing them: *to goad someone into a fury*

goal *noun*
1 something that you want to achieve: *My goal is to pass the exam.* 2 the basket, area or set of posts that you aim the ball towards in games such as football, hockey and basketball 3 the point or points that you get when you successfully move the ball into or through the goal
•*Word Family:* **goalkeeper** *noun* the player who tries to stop goals being scored **goalpost** *noun* an upright post marking a goal

goanna (*say* go-**an**-a) *noun*
an Australian lizard, with a long neck, loosely folded skin and a whip-like tail, growing up to about 7 feet or 2.5 metres long

goat *noun*
an animal with horns, shaggy hair and a beard, that chews its cud, climbs well and gives meat and milk
•*Word Family:* **goatherd** *noun* someone who looks after goats

gobble (1) *verb*
to eat and swallow food rapidly and greedily: *to gobble your dinner*

gobble (2) *verb*
to make the throaty sound of a turkey

gobbledegook *noun*
language that sounds important but is really meaningless or hard to understand

goblet *noun*
a large bowl-shaped cup for drinking, with a stem and a base but no handles

goblin *noun*
a mischievous, ugly elf in fairy stories

god *noun*
1 a powerful being who is worshipped: *In Greek myths, Eros is the god of love.* 2 the image of a god or an idol 3 someone or something that people worship like a god: *The sporting hero was his god.* 4 **God** the supreme creator and ruler of the universe, worshipped by Jews, Christians and Muslims who all believe in one god
•*Word Family:* **godly** *adjective* **(godlier, godliest)** pious: *a godly man* **goddess** *noun* a female god: *Diana is the goddess of the moon in Roman myths.* **godliness** *noun*

godparent *noun*
the person who promises at a child's baptism to help to bring him or her up as a Christian
•*Word Family:* **godchild** *noun* **god-daughter** *noun* **godfather** *noun* **godmother** *noun* **godson** *noun*

goggles *plural noun*
spectacles with special protective rims, worn by skin-divers, motorcycle riders and so on, to shield their eyes from water, dust, glare or wind
•*Word Family:* **goggle** *verb* to stare with your eyes wide open: *She goggled at the sight.*

gold *noun*
1 a precious yellow metal, used to make coins and jewellery 2 a yellowish colour, like gold 3 money or wealth 4 something that is very precious or rare: *She has a heart of gold.*
gold *adjective*
5 gold in colour 6 made of gold: *a gold brooch*
•*Word Family:* **goldsmith** *noun* someone who makes or sells gold things **goldmine** *noun*

golden *adjective*
1 made of gold: *The King wore a golden crown* 2 of the colour of gold: *golden curls* 3 favourable or precious: *a golden opportunity to get rich*

golden wedding *noun*
the special anniversary that you celebrate 50 years after your wedding

goldfish *noun*
a small fish, often golden in colour, kept in a pool or bowl
• ***Word Family:*** the plural is **goldfish** or **goldfishes**

golf *noun*
an outdoor game in which you try to hit a small ball into a series of holes with special clubs, using as few strokes as possible
• ***Word Family:*** **golfer** *noun* **golfing** *noun*

gondola (*say* **gon**-da-la) *noun*
1 a narrow boat with high pointed ends, used on canals in Venice 2 the passenger compartment hanging under an airship or balloon
• ***Word Family:*** **gondolier** *noun* someone who moves a gondola along with a long oar

gong *noun*
a bronze disc that rings when you strike it with a hammer, used to summon people to a meal and so on

good *adjective*
1 favourable or pleasant: *It's a good morning for a walk.* 2 kind or virtuous: *He's a good man.* 3 reliable: *She has a good reputation as a doctor.* 4 well-behaved: *Has the baby been good?* 5 competent: *You're a good musician.* 6 of a high standard: *We love good food.* 7 healthy: *Milk is good for you.* 8 large: *We walked a good distance.* 9 **as good as** almost: *It's as good as done.*
good *noun*
10 something that helps or makes things better for you: *Your attitude will do more harm than good. / You should have a holiday for your own good.* 11 **goods (a)** possessions **(b)** articles you can buy: *imported goods* 12 **for good** for ever: *She's given up netball for good.*
• ***Word Family:*** other adjective forms are **better, best** □ **goodness** *noun*

goodbye *interjection*
something you say when you leave someone or end a phone conversation
• ***Word Origins:*** a short form of "God be with you"

goodwill *noun*
good or kind feelings between people: *to show goodwill towards someone*

goose *noun*
a large, web-footed bird, often kept on farms to be fattened for eating
• ***Word Family:*** the plural is **geese**

gooseberry (*say* **gooz**-be-ree) *noun*
a round, green, sour-tasting berry, that grows on a prickly bush
• ***Word Family:*** the plural is **gooseberries**

goosestep *noun*
a way of marching without bending your knees, in which you kick each leg forward stiffly and sharply

gore (1) *noun*
clotted blood, especially from a cut or wound
• ***Word Origins:*** from an Old English word meaning "dirt" or "filth"

gore (2) *verb*
to wound or pierce with horns or tusks: *The matador was gored by a bull.*
• ***Word Origins:*** from an Old English word meaning "spear"

gorge (*say* gorj) *noun*
1 a narrow river valley with very steep sides
gorge *verb*
2 to stuff yourself with food or eat greedily: *to gorge yourself on chocolates*

gorgeous (*say* **gor**-jus) *adjective*
beautiful or splendid in appearance: *a gorgeous rainbow*
• ***Word Family:*** **gorgeously** *adverb*

gorilla *noun*
the largest kind of ape, found in the tropical forests of Africa

gory *adjective*
full of blood and violence: *a gory film*
• ***Word Family:*** other forms are **gorier, goriest**

gosling *noun*
a young goose

gospel *noun*
1 one of the first four books of the New Testament in the Christian bible, which describe Christ's life and teachings 2 something accepted as unquestionably true: *Take what he says as gospel.*
• ***Word Origins:*** from Old English words meaning "good news"

gossamer (*say* **gos**-a-ma) *noun*
1 a thread or web of the fine, silky substance made by spiders 2 an extremely delicate kind of material, such as gauze

gossip *noun*
1 unkind talk or rumours, especially about other people's private business 2 someone who talks about other people or lets out secrets
gossip *verb*
3 to spread gossip

gothic *adjective*
to do with a style of art and architecture which

had ornate lettering, pointed arches and high ceilings

gouge (*say* gawj) *verb*
to scoop something out by pressing hard with your fingers or something sharp: *They gouged his eyes out with their thumbs.*

gourmet (*say* **gaw**-may) *noun*
someone who knows a lot about good food and wine and how it should taste
•***Word Origins:*** from a French word meaning "wine-taster"

govern (*say* **guv**-en) *verb*
1 to rule and be in charge of: *to govern a country* 2 to fix or determine: *rules governing who may vote in the election*

governess (*say* **guv**-a-ness) *noun*
a woman employed to teach children in their own home
•***Word Family:*** the plural is **governesses**

government (*say* **guv**-an-ment) *noun*
the group of people chosen to govern a country or state
•***Word Family:*** **governmental** *adjective*

governor (*say* **guv**-er-na) *noun*
a person who governs a state or is in charge of an institution such as a bank or a prison: *a school governor / the governor of California*

governor-general *noun*
the person who represents the king or queen in Australia and some other countries that belong to the British Commonwealth
•***Word Family:*** the plural is **governor-generals** or **governors-general**

gown *noun*
1 a dress, especially a long or formal one
2 a long, loose cloak with wide sleeves, worn by judges, lawyers, priests and university graduates

GP *noun*
short for **general practitioner**

grab *verb*
to seize something or someone, especially roughly or hastily: *to grab a handful of chocolates / She grabbed me by the wrist.*
•***Word Family:*** other forms are **grabs, grabbed, grabbing**

grace *noun*
1 elegance or beauty of movement or expression: *to move with grace* 2 the mercy of God: *by the grace of God* 3 a short prayer said before or after a meal
grace *verb*
4 to honour someone by attending: *to grace the occasion with your presence* 5 to decorate or adorn: *a vase graced the table*
•***Word Family:*** **graceful** *adjective* **gracefully** *adverb*

gracious (*say* **gray**-shus) *adjective*
kind or courteous: *a gracious smile / a gracious host*
•***Word Family:*** **graciously** *adverb* **graciousness** *noun*

grade *noun*
1 a step or stage in rank, quality, value or skill: *I'll start work on the lowest grade.* 2 a student's mark for a test
grade *verb*
3 to arrange in grades or classes: *We grade our eggs by size.*

gradient (*say* **gray**-di-ent) *noun*
1 the steepness of the slope in a road or railway
2 a slope

gradual (*say* **grad**-yew-ul) *adjective*
taking place bit by bit: *a gradual rise in temperature*
•***Word Family:*** **gradually** *adverb*

graduate (*say* **grad**-yoo-at) *noun*
1 someone who has received a diploma or degree from a college or university
graduate (*say* **grad**-yoo-ate) *verb*
2 to receive an academic degree: *She graduated in law.* 3 to mark something with divisions or degrees for measuring: *a ruler graduated in centimetres*
•***Word Family:*** **graduation** *noun*: *a graduation ceremony*

graffiti (*say* gra-**fee**-tee) *plural noun*
drawings or words drawn or written on walls or in other public places
•***Word Family:*** the singular is **graffito**
•***Word Origins:*** from an Italian word meaning "a scratch"

graft (1) *noun*
1 a shoot or bud joined to another living plant to become part of it and form a new growth 2 the living tissue that is cut from one part of the body and used to replace diseased or damaged tissue in another part of the body: *a skin graft*
graft *verb*
3 to attach a graft: *to graft bone from your leg and use it in your skull*

graft (2) (*say* grahft) *noun*
1 the use of your position to gain profit or advantage 2 anything you gain by doing this
3 hard work
graft *verb*
4 to work hard
•***Word Family:*** **grafter** *noun*

grain *noun*
1 a cereal plant, such as wheat or barley 2 the small, hard seed of one of these plants: *a grain of*

A B C D E F G H I J K L M N O P Q R S T U V W X Y Z

rice 3 a small, hard particle: *a grain of sand* 4 a very small amount of something: *He doesn't have a grain of sense.* 5 the direction of the lines of fibre in wood or cloth
•***Word Family:*** **grainy** *adjective* (**grainier, grainiest**)

gram *noun*
a metric unit of mass equal to one thousandth of a kilogram

grammar (*say* **gram**-a) *noun*
the way that the words and sounds of a language work together to make phrases and sentences according to certain rules
•***Word Family:*** **grammarian** *noun* an expert in grammar **grammatical** *adjective* following the rules of grammar **grammatically** *adverb*

grammar school *noun*
a secondary school for children who are chosen if they pass a test

gramophone (*say* **gram**-a-fohn) *noun*
a rather old-fashioned word for **record-player**

granary (*say* **gran**-a-ree) *noun*
a building for storing grain
•***Word Family:*** the plural is **granaries**

grand *adjective*
1 magnificent or splendid: *a grand palace*
2 stately or dignified: *to make a grand entrance*
3 complete: *the grand total*
grand *noun*
4 one thousand pounds
•***Word Family:*** **grandly** *adverb* **grandness** *noun*

grandchild *noun*
a child of your son or daughter
•***Word Family:*** the plural is **grandchildren** □ **granddaughter** *noun* **grandson** *noun*

grandeur (*say* **gran**-dyer) *noun*
greatness or magnificence: *the grandeur of the Alps*

grandfather clock *noun*
a tall clock in a wooden case, which stands on the floor

grandiose (*say* **gran**-dee-ohs) *adjective*
being too grand or impressive: *a grandiose idea of his own importance*

grandparent *noun*
a parent of one of your parents
•***Word Family:*** **grandfather** *noun* **grandmother** *noun*

grand piano *noun*
a large piano with strings that are horizontal, not vertical

grandstand *noun*
a building with banks of seats for watching sporting events or outdoor entertainment

granite (*say* **gran**-it) *noun*
a hard, coarse rock used for building
•***Word Origins:*** from an Italian word meaning "grained"

grant *verb*
1 to give or allow something: *to grant permission to go home* 2 to agree to something that someone has asked for: *to grant a favour*
grant *noun*
3 something granted, especially money or land: *a grant to go to college*

granule (*say* **gran**-yool) *noun*
a small grain: *coffee granules*
•***Word Family:*** **granular** *adjective*

grape *noun*
a small, round green or purple fruit growing in clusters on vines, that is eaten fresh, dried as currants or raisins, or made into wine

grapefruit *noun*
a large, round, yellow citrus fruit with a thick skin and juicy, sour-tasting flesh

graph *noun*
a diagram that shows the relationship between two or more changing things by drawing lines, bars or dots, often on paper marked into squares

graphic (*say* **graf**-ik) *adjective*
1 vivid or life-like: *a graphic account of the play*
2 using lines, diagrams or graphs: *Show your results in graphic form.*
•***Word Family:*** **graphics** *plural noun* the art of drawing and making patterns, often on a computer **graphically** *adverb*

graphite (*say* **graf**-ite) *noun*
a soft, black, greasy form of carbon, used in lead pencils

grapple *verb*
to struggle or wrestle: *She grappled with the problem. / to grapple with an opponent*

grasp *verb*
1 to seize something firmly: *She grasped the shovel by its handle.* 2 to understand: *to grasp an argument*
grasp *noun*
3 a firm hold or grip 4 an understanding: *a good grasp of the subject*
•***Word Family:*** **grasping** *adjective* greedy for money

grass *noun*
1 a plant grown to make lawn or pasture 2 land covered by grass 3 any of a large group of plants such as wheat and other cereals 4 *another word for* **marijuana**
grass *verb*
5 to cover land with grass
•***Word Family:*** **grassy** *adjective* (**grassier, grassiest**)

grasshopper *noun*
a plant-eating insect with large hind legs for jumping

grate (1) *noun*
a metal framework used to hold fuel in a fireplace

grate (2) *verb*
1 to shred food into small particles, usually by rubbing it against a rough surface: *to grate cheese with a grater* 2 to rub things together to make a harsh rasping sound: *The knife grated on the stone.* 3 **grate on** to have an irritating effect on: *to grate on your nerves*
•***Word Family:*** **grater** *noun* a metal tool used for grating food **gratingly** *adverb*

grateful *adjective*
feeling or showing that you are pleased that someone has been kind to you
•***Word Family:*** **gratefully** *adverb* **gratefulness** *noun*

grating *noun*
a metal framework over a hole or window

gratitude *noun*
the feeling of being grateful

grave (1) *noun*
the burial place for a dead body, especially a hole dug in the ground

grave (2) *adjective*
1 serious: *a grave illness* 2 needing careful consideration: *a grave situation* 3 solemn: *a grave expression*
•***Word Family:*** **gravely** *adverb*

grave (3) (*say* grahv) *adverb*
played or sung very slowly
•***Word Origins:*** from Italian

gravel (*say* **grav**-el) *noun*
very small stones, often mixed with sand, used to make roads
•***Word Family:*** **gravelled** *adjective*: *a gravelled driveway* **gravelly** *adjective* harsh: *a gravelly voice*

gravity (*say* **grav**-i-tee) *noun*
1 the force that causes objects to fall towards the Earth 2 seriousness: *The gravity of this crime demands severe punishment.*
•***Word Family:*** **gravitate** *verb* to move towards something **gravitation** *noun* **gravitational** *adjective*: *a planet's gravitational field*

gravy (*say* **gray**-vee) *noun*
a sauce made from the juices produced when meat cooks, usually seasoned and thickened with flour

graze (1) *verb*
to eat grass, the way cattle and sheep do

graze (2) *verb*
1 to touch something lightly in passing 2 to scrape your skin: *to graze your knee*
graze *noun*
3 a slight scrape or scratch

grease (*say* greece) *noun*
1 melted animal fat 2 a soft oily or fatty substance 3 the substance you use to make machines run smoothly
grease *verb*
4 to put grease on or in something
•***Word Family:*** **greasy** *adjective* (**greasier, greasiest**) **greasily** *adverb* **greasiness** *noun*

great (*say* grate) *adjective*
1 large: *a great heap of sand* 2 considerable or more than usual: *great pain* 3 important or remarkable: *a great jazz musician* 4 very good: *a great party*
•***Word Family:*** **greatly** *adverb* **greatness** *noun*

greed *noun*
a strong desire for more food or money than you need
•***Word Family:*** **greedy** *adjective* (**greedier, greediest**) **greedily** *adverb* **greediness** *noun*

green *noun*
1 the colour of growing grass 2 the smooth grass that surrounds each hole on a golf course 3 the level lawn for playing bowls 4 **greens** green leafy vegetables
green *adjective*
5 of the colour green 6 not ripe: *green tomatoes* 7 inexperienced: *He was a bit green when he first arrived in the country.* 8 harmless to the environment: *green household products* 9 interested in looking after the environment
•***Word Family:*** **greenery** *noun* green leaves and plants **greenness** *noun*

greengrocer *noun*
someone who sells fresh fruit and vegetables

greenhouse *noun*
a glass building that stores heat from the sun, used for growing plants

greenhouse effect *noun*
the warming up of the Earth's surface that is caused by gases in the Earth's atmosphere trapping the sun's heat

greenie *noun*
someone who thinks that we should conserve the earth's energy and natural resources, care for our animals and vegetation, recycle our waste and live responsibly

Greenwich Mean Time (*say* **gren**-ich) *noun*
the time at Greenwich in London, used as a standard reference by people all over the world

greet *verb*
1 to meet and welcome someone: *to greet a visitor* 2 to receive or respond to something: *My efforts to cheer her up were greeted with silence.*
•***Word Family:*** **greetings** *plural noun* words of welcome

gregarious (*say* gre-**gair**-ri-us) *adjective*
enjoying being with others: *The gregarious boy had many friends.*
•***Word Origins:*** from a Latin word meaning "belonging to a flock"

grenade (*say* gre-**nayd**) *noun*
a small bomb thrown by hand or fired from a rifle

grey (*say* gray) *noun*
1 a colour between black and white or composed of a mixture of black and white
grey *adjective*
2 of the colour grey: *a grey coat*
grey *verb*
3 to become grey: *Her hair is greying.*
•***Word Family:*** **greyness** *noun*

greyhound *noun*
a fast, thin dog used in hunting and racing

grid *noun*
1 a framework of parallel or crossed bars, such as in a fire grate 2 a network of crossed lines on a map, used for reference

gridiron (*say* grid-**eye**-on) *noun*
1 a grill 2 a nickname for the game of American football, played on a field that looks like a grille or grid

grid reference *noun*
a set of numbers that allows you to find the precise place where something is on a map

grief (*say* greef) *noun*
1 very great sadness, sorrow or distress 2 **come to grief** to fail or end up in trouble

grievance (*say* **gree**-vance) *noun*
a feeling of resentment or annoyance because you think you've been treated unfairly

grieve *verb*
1 to be sad, especially because someone has died: *Give him time to grieve.* 2 to upset someone or make them very unhappy: *It grieves me to see you wasting your opportunities.*

grievous (*say* **gree**-vus) *adjective*
serious or causing suffering: *a grievous mistake / a grievous injury*

grill *noun*
1 the part of a cooker where food is cooked by heat coming down from above 2 food cooked under a grill: *a mixed grill*
grill *verb*
3 to cook food on a grill: *to grill chops* 4 to question or interrogate someone closely and intensely: *to grill a suspect*

grille (*say* gril) *noun*
a metal grating over a gate, window or the front of a car

grim *adjective*
1 severe or stern: *She had a grim expression.*
2 gloomy or worrying: *a grim prospect / grim news*
•***Word Family:*** other forms are **grimmer, grimmest** □ **grimly** *adverb* **grimness** *noun*

grimace *verb*
1 to twist or distort your face, with pain, anger, or some other strong feeling like this
grimace *noun*
2 a twisted expression

grime *noun*
dirt, especially on a surface
•***Word Family:*** **grimy** *adjective* (**grimier, grimiest**)

grin *verb*
1 to smile widely 2 **grin and bear it** to put up with something unpleasant
grin *noun*
3 a wide smile
•***Word Family:*** other verb forms are **grins, grinned, grinning**

grind (*rhymes with* kind) *verb*
1 to rub or crush a substance into a powder: *to grind coffee / to grind wheat into flour* 2 to sharpen something or make it smooth by rubbing it on something hard: *to grind a knife to sharpen it / to grind your teeth*
•***Word Family:*** other forms are **grinds, ground, grinding** □ **grinder** *noun* someone or something that grinds

grip *verb*
1 to take or hold something firmly: *to grip his hand* 2 to fascinate or capture someone's attention: *The new play gripped the audience.*
grip *noun*
3 a firm hold: *He lost his grip on the branch.*
•***Word Family:*** other verb forms are **grips, gripped, gripping** □ **gripping** *adjective* interesting or exciting: *a gripping story*

gripe *noun*
1 a complaint or grumble
gripe *verb*
2 to grumble or complain persistently: *Stop griping and help me.*
•***Word Family:*** this is a colloquial word

gristle (*say* **gris**-ul) *noun*
the firm rubbery tissue in meat, found near the bone
•***Word Family:*** **gristly** *adjective* containing gristle: *gristly meat*

grit *noun*
1 small, hard particles of stone: *grit in your eye* 2 strength or courage: *to show a lot of grit*
grit *verb*
3 to clench or grind: *to grit your teeth* 4 to put grit on a road
•***Word Family:*** other verb forms are **grits, gritted, gritting** □ **gritty** *adjective* (**grittier, grittiest**) **grittiness** *noun*

grizzle *verb*
to whine or cry
•***Word Family:*** **grizzler** *noun* someone who grizzles

grizzly bear *noun*
a very large brownish-grey bear that is found in North America

groan *verb*
1 to make a long low sound, of pain, sadness, or disapproval
groan *noun*
2 the sound you make when you groan

grocer (*say* **gro**-ser) *noun*
someone who sells food such as coffee, tinned meat and flour, and household goods such as soap
•***Word Family:*** **grocery** *noun* (**groceries**)

grog *noun*
any alcoholic drink, especially when cheap
•***Word Family:*** this word is colloquial

groggy *adjective*
feeling dazed and unsteady on your feet because you are sick or drunk
•***Word Family:*** other forms are **groggier, groggiest** □ **groggily** *adverb* **grogginess** *noun*

groin *noun*
the part of your body where your thighs join your abdomen

groom *noun*
1 *a shortened form of* **bridegroom** 2 someone who cares for horses
groom *verb*
3 to brush, comb and keep clean and tidy: *to groom a horse / to groom your hair*

groomsman *noun*
a man who helps and stands with the groom at his wedding
•***Word Family:*** the plural is **groomsmen**

groove *noun*
a long narrow channel, such as the track cut in a gramophone record for the needle to move in, or a notch cut in wood

grope *verb*
to feel about or search uncertainly: *I groped for the light switch in the dark. / I groped for his name all through our conversation.*

gross (*say* grohs) *adjective*
1 the total amount without anything deducted: *your gross salary* 2 vulgar and rough: *gross behaviour* 3 disgusting and unpleasant: *I can't eat that – it looks gross.* 4 fat or overfed 5 extreme or outrageous: *a gross injustice*
gross *noun*
6 twelve dozen or 144
gross *verb*
7 to earn a total of: *to gross £20 a week for delivering papers*
•***Word Family:*** the plural of the noun is **gross** □ **grossly** *adverb* **grossness** *noun*

grotesque (*say* groh-**tesk**) *adjective*
odd or unnatural in its shape, appearance or form: *a grotesque statue*
•***Word Family:*** **grotesquely** *adverb* **grotesqueness** *noun*

grotto *noun*
a cave
•***Word Family:*** the plural is **grottoes** or **grottos**

grouch *verb*
1 to complain or grumble
grouch *noun*
2 a complaint 3 someone who complains
•***Word Family:*** **grouchy** *adjective* (**grouchier, grouchiest**) **grouchily** *adverb* **grouchiness** *noun*

ground *noun*
1 the solid surface of the earth: *He fell to the ground.* 2 soil or earth: *stony ground* 3 an area used for a particular purpose or surrounding a building: *a cricket ground / hospital grounds* 4 a basis or reason: *Tell the court your grounds for the complaint.*
ground *verb*
5 to stop a plane from flying: *The plane was grounded while mechanics checked the engine.*

groundsman *noun*
someone whose job is to look after a sports field
•***Word Family:*** the plural is **groundsmen**

group *noun*
1 a number of people or things that are together 2 a number of singers and musicians: *a pop group*
group *verb*
3 to put people or things into groups: *Group the children according to age.*

grouse (*rhymes with* house) *noun*
a plump European bird with a short, curved bill, often shot for sport and eaten
•***Word Family:*** the plural is **grouse**

grout (*rhymes with* out) *noun*
1 thin cement used to fill or cover joints between tiles or bricks
grout *verb*
2 to fill gaps with grout

A B C D E F G H I J K L M N O P Q R S T U V W X Y Z

grove *noun*
a small group of trees: *an olive grove*

grovel (*say* **grov**-el) *verb*
1 to act in a very humble or undignified way: *You don't need to grovel – you can have the job.* 2 to lie or throw yourself on the ground, especially in fear
•*Word Family:* other forms are **grovels, grovelled, grovelling**

grow (*say* gro) *verb*
1 to become larger in size 2 to come or develop: *The tree grew from a seed.* 3 to make or let something grow: *to grow flowers / to grow a beard* 4 to become slowly: *to grow taller*
•*Word Family:* other forms are **grows, grew, grown, growing** □ **grower** *noun: a fruit grower*

growl *verb*
1 to make the deep, threatening, rumbling sound of a dog 2 to speak angrily: *She growled at us for being late.*
growl *noun*
3 the deep, rumbling sound that a dog makes

grown-up *noun*
1 an adult
grown-up *adjective*
2 adult: *grown-up behaviour*

growth *noun*
1 growing: *steady growth* 2 something that has grown 3 a tumour or lump in your body

grub *noun*
1 the larva or young of some insects 2 food

grubby *adjective*
dirty or untidy: *grubby hands*
•*Word Family:* other forms are **grubbier, grubbiest**

grudge *noun*
1 a feeling that you don't like someone because they have done something bad to you in the past: *to bear a grudge*
grudge *verb*
2 to be unwilling to give or let someone have something: *to grudge paying for service in a restaurant*
•*Word Family:* **grudgingly** *adverb*

gruelling (*say* **grew**-a-ling) *adjective*
exhausting or severe: *a gruelling hike*

gruesome (*say* **grew**-sum) *adjective*
horrible or sickening: *a gruesome picture*

gruff *adjective*
rough or unfriendly: *a gruff voice / a gruff manner*
•*Word Family:* **gruffly** *adverb* **gruffness** *noun*

grumble *verb*
to complain in a bad-tempered way
•*Word Family:* **grumbler** *noun* **grumblingly** *adverb*

grumpy *adjective*
bad-tempered or surly
•*Word Family:* other forms are **grumpier, grumpiest** □ **grump** *noun* a grumpy person **grumpily** *adverb* **grumpiness** *noun*

grunt *verb*
1 to make a low, harsh sound like a pig
grunt *noun*
2 a grunting sound

guarantee (*say* ga-ren-**tee**) *noun*
1 a written promise that something will be repaired or replaced if it breaks or goes wrong
2 an assurance: *Money is no guarantee of happiness.*
guarantee *verb*
3 to promise or assure something: *to guarantee safety*

guard (*say* gard) *verb*
1 to keep someone or something safe or in control: *to guard your house* 2 to take precautions: *to guard against the cold*
guard *noun*
3 someone who guards: *the guard on a train / a guard of honour* 4 careful watch: *The prisoner was kept under close guard.* 5 something used for protection against injury: *The footballer wore a shin guard.* 6 **be on your guard** to be prepared or cautious
•*Word Family:* **guarded** *adjective* careful **guardedly** *adverb*

guardian (*say* **gar**-dee-an) *noun*
1 someone who guards or protects someone or something 2 someone who has the legal duty to care for and protect another person and their property
•*Word Family:* **guardianship** *noun*

guerrilla (*say* ger-**ril**-a) *noun*
a member of a small band of revolutionary fighters who make surprise attacks on enemy positions, supplies and so on
•*Word Origins:* from a Spanish word meaning "little war"

guess (*say* gess) *verb*
1 to give an answer or opinion when you don't know if you are correct 2 to suppose: *I guess I'll be there.*
guess *noun*
3 an answer or opinion made without really knowing
•*Word Family:* **guesswork** *noun*

guest (*say* gest) *noun*
1 someone who comes to your house for a meal or a visit, or someone who goes to a party: *a dinner guest / a wedding guest* 2 someone staying at a hotel: *parking for hotel guests only*
3 someone making a special appearance on a TV or radio show

guest house *noun*
a small hotel

guide (*rhymes with* wide) *verb*
1 to show someone the way: *to guide the hikers to the hut*
guide *noun*
2 someone who guides, often as a job: *a tourist guide* 3 a book with useful advice or information for tourists or travellers 4 **Guide** a member of the Girl Guides Association
•***Word Family:*** **guidance** *noun* advice or instruction **guideline** *noun* a guiding suggestion or rule

guide dog *noun*
a dog trained to help a blind person

guild (*say* gild) *noun*
a group or society of people, such as weavers, who belong to the same trade

guile (*say* gile) *noun*
cunning or deceitfulness
•***Word Family:*** **guileless** *adjective* sincere and honest

guillotine (*say* **gil**-o-teen) *noun*
1 a machine that is used to behead people with a heavy blade 2 a machine with a long blade for trimming paper
•***Word Origins:*** named after the French doctor, J.I. *Guillotin*, who lived from 1738 to 1814 and recommended its use

guilt (*say* gilt) *noun*
1 the fact that you have done something wrong: *His guilt has been proved in court.* 2 the feeling of responsibility or shame you have when you've done something wrong: *Guilt made her confess.*
•***Word Family:*** **guilty** *adjective* **(guiltier, guiltiest) guiltily** *adverb* **guiltiness** *noun*

guinea (*say* **gin**-ee) *noun*
an old coin, worth 21 shillings or £1.05

guinea pig (*say* **gin**-ee-pig) *noun*
1 a small, short-eared, short-tailed animal kept as a pet and also sometimes used in laboratory experiments 2 someone used as the subject of an experiment: *I was one of the guinea pigs used to test the new toothpaste.*

guise (*say* gize) *noun*
an appearance that is meant to trick people: *The crook assumed the guise of a salesman.*

guitar (*say* gi-**tar**) *noun*
a musical instrument with six strings that you pluck using your fingers or a plectrum
•***Word Family:*** **guitarist** *noun*

gulf *noun*
1 a large bay or area of ocean partly surrounded by land 2 a wide gap or distance: *a huge gulf in the road / a wide gulf in age between the sisters*

gull *noun*
the short form of **seagull**

gullible *adjective*
easily cheated or tricked: *She's so gullible, she'll probably believe you.*
•***Word Family:*** **gullibility** *noun* **gullibly** *adverb*

gully *noun*
a small, steep-sided valley or gorge usually formed by running water or soil erosion
•***Word Family:*** the plural is **gullies**

gulp *verb*
1 to swallow in large amounts: *to gulp your food* 2 to gasp or choke: *to gulp for breath*
gulp *noun*
3 an amount you swallow at once: *She drank it in one gulp.*

gum (1) *noun*
1 a sticky substance that comes from plants 2 a soft sweet good for chewing 3 a type of glue
gum *verb*
4 to cover or stick together with gum or anything sticky like gum
•***Word Family:*** other verb forms are **gums, gummed, gumming** □ **gummy** *adjective*

gum (2) *noun*
the firm flesh in your mouth which holds your teeth firmly in place

gumboot *noun*
a waterproof rubber boot, usually reaching to your knee or thigh

gun *noun*
1 a weapon with a metal tube or barrel for firing bullets or shells 2 something shaped or used like a gun: *a spray gun for weedkiller*
gun *verb*
3 to shoot or kill with a gun: *to gun down*
•***Word Family:*** other verb forms are **guns, gunned, gunning** □ **gunfire** *noun* **gunsmith** *noun* a maker or seller of guns

gunpowder *noun*
a mixture of powdered chemicals, used as an explosive

gunya (*say* **gun**-ya) *noun*
an Aboriginal hut or bush shelter

guppy *noun*
a small fish that is often kept in home aquariums
•***Word Family:*** the plural is **guppies**

gurdwara (*say* **gord**-wah-ra or **gerd**-wah-ra) *noun*
a Sikh temple

gurgle *verb*
to make a bubbling sound: *Water gurgled down the drain. / The baby gurgled with joy.*

A B C D E F G H I J K L M N O P Q R S T U V W X Y Z

guru (*say* **goo**-roo) *noun*
1 a wise teacher who is interested in spiritual things 2 a Hindu or Sikh leader or religious teacher
•***Word Family:*** the plural is **gurus**

gush *verb*
1 to flow suddenly and with force: *Water gushed from the broken pipe.* 2 to talk with too much emotion or enthusiasm
•***Word Family:*** **gushing** *adjective* talking with too much emotion **gushy** *adjective* **(gushier, gushiest)**

gust *noun*
a sudden rush or burst: *a gust of wind*
•***Word Family:*** **gusty** *adjective* **(gustier, gustiest) gustily** *adverb*

gusto *noun*
great enjoyment: *to do something with gusto*
•***Word Origins:*** from an Italian word meaning "taste" or "relish"

gut *noun*
1 *another word for* **intestine** 2 the string made from the intestines of some animals, used for violin strings or tennis racquet strings 3 **guts** (a) your stomach (b) courage or endurance: *It takes guts to sail around the world alone.*
gut *verb*
4 to take out the guts of something: *to gut a fish* 5 to destroy the inside of something: *Fire gutted the house.*
•***Word Family:*** other verb forms are **guts, gutted, gutting** □ **gutless** *adjective* not brave **gutsy** *adjective* courageous

gutter *noun*
a channel for carrying off water, usually beside a road or at the edge of a roof

guy (1) (*rhymes with* high) *noun*
a man or boy

guy (2) (*rhymes with* high) *noun*
a rope or wire used to steady, guide or fix something firmly in place

guzzle *verb*
to eat or drink greedily
•***Word Family:*** **guzzler** *noun*

gym (*say* jim) *noun*
1 *short for* **gymnasium** 2 *short for* **gymnastics**

gymkhana (*say* jim-**kah**-na) *noun*
a horse-riding competition consisting of various events

gymnasium (*say* jim-**nay**-zee-um) *noun*
a building or room fitted with equipment for physical training and gymnastics
•***Word Family:*** the plural is **gymnasiums** or **gymnasia**

gymnastics (*say* jim-**nas**-tiks) *plural noun*
exercises that develop your agility, suppleness and strength
•***Word Family:*** **gymnast** *noun* someone trained or skilled in gymnastics **gymnastic** *adjective*

gynaecology or **gynecology** (*say* gigh-na-**kol**-a-jee) *noun*
the part of medicine concerned with women's diseases, especially those affecting the reproductive system
•***Word Family:*** **gynaecological** *adjective* **gynaecologist** *noun*

gypsy *noun*
another spelling of **gipsy**

gyrate (*say* jigh-**rate**) *verb*
to revolve or move in a circle
•***Word Family:*** **gyration** *noun* a turning or circular movement

gyroscope (*say* **jigh**-ra-skope) *noun*
a wheel that can spin inside its frame, used in instruments that guide ships and aircraft
•***Word Family:*** **gyroscopic** *adjective*

Hh

haberdasher (*say* **hab**-a-dash-a) *noun*
someone who sells things like ribbons, thread and needles
•***Word Family:*** **haberdashery** *noun*

habit *noun*
1 something you usually do 2 the robe worn by members of a religious order: *a monk's habit*
•***Word Family:*** **habitual** *adjective* done or used regularly **habitually** *adverb*

habitat *noun*
the place where a plant or animal usually grows or lives

habitation (*say* hab-i-**tay**-shon) *noun*
your home or place of living
•***Word Family:*** **habitable** *adjective*

hack *verb*
1 to cut roughly or clumsily: *to hack away at the tree trunk* 2 to use a computer illegally to get access to stored information

hacker *noun*
someone who uses a computer illegally to get

into the computer system of a government or business

hacksaw *noun*
a saw with a fine blade for cutting metal

haemoglobin (*say* hee-ma-**glo**-bin) *noun*
a red pigment or colouring found in red blood cells, that carries oxygen around the body

haemophilia (*say* hee-ma-**fil**-ee-a) *noun*
a serious disease in which blood doesn't clot properly and even small cuts bleed for a long time
• ***Word Family:*** **haemophiliac** *noun* someone with haemophilia

haemorrhage (*say* **hem**-a-rij) *noun*
a loss of blood, especially from a burst blood vessel inside your body

hag *noun*
an ugly old woman

haggis *noun*
a Scottish food like a large sausage, made of the internal organs of a sheep, minced with oatmeal, suet and flavourings and boiled in a sheep's stomach

haggle *verb*
to argue over the price of something

haiku (*say* **high**-koo) *noun*
a Japanese form of poem with three lines made up of five, seven and five syllables respectively

hail (1) *verb*
1 to greet or welcome someone: *to hail your friends* 2 to call out to someone: *to hail a taxi*

hail (2) *noun*
1 a shower of icy balls that fall from the sky like frozen raindrops 2 a shower of hard pellets: *a hail of bullets*
hail *verb*
3 to fall down as or like hail: *They hailed blows upon her back.*
• ***Word Family:*** **hailstone** *noun* **hailstorm** *noun*

hair (*rhymes with* chair) *noun*
1 a fine strand that grows from the skin of most people and animals 2 the mass of these strands on your head or on an animal's body
• ***Word Family:*** **hairy** *adjective* (**hairier, hairiest**) covered with hair

hair-raising *adjective*
exciting or terrifying

haka (*say* **hah**-ka) *noun*
a Maori war dance

hake *noun*
a sea-fish that you can eat

halal (*say* ha-**lal**) *adjective*
to do with meat that is prepared according to Muslim law: *halal meat / a halal butcher*

half (*say* harf) *noun*
1 one of two equal parts into which something is divided
half *adjective*
2 being about half of a whole amount: *half a bottle of juice*
half *adverb*
3 partly: *The sink is half full of dishes.*
• ***Word Family:*** the plural of the noun is **halves**

half-brother *noun*
a brother who shares one parent with you

half-caste *noun*
someone whose parents come from different races

half-hearted *adjective*
without much enthusiasm or interest: *a half-hearted attempt at singing*
• ***Word Family:*** **half-heartedly** *adverb*

halfpenny (*say* **hay**-pa-nee) *noun*
an old coin that was worth half a penny
• ***Word Family:*** the plural is **halfpennies** or **halfpence**

half-sister *noun*
a sister who shares one parent with you

half-term *noun*
a short holiday in the middle of a school term

half-time *noun*
the short break halfway through a game such as football

halibut *noun*
a large, flat sea-fish that you can eat

hall *noun*
1 a passage or corridor in a building 2 the entrance room of a building 3 a large building or room, especially one used for such things as public meetings and entertainment

hallelujah (*say* hal-a-**looh**-ya) *noun*
a song or exclamation of praise to God
• ***Word Origins:*** from a Hebrew word meaning "praise Jehovah" (a Jewish name for God)

hallo *interjection*
another spelling of **hello**

Halloween (*say* hal-ow-**een**) *noun*
a festival celebrated on 31 October each year, when people say you can see ghosts and witches

hallucination (*say* ha-loo-si-**nay**-shon) *noun*
something you see or hear that seems real but does not actually exist
• ***Word Family:*** **hallucinate** *verb* to experience hallucinations

halo (*say* **hay**-lo) *noun*
a brightness or circle of light around the head of religious figures and angels in paintings
• ***Word Family:*** the plural is **haloes** or **halos**

A B C D E F G H I J K L M N O P Q R S T U V W X Y Z

halt (*say* holt) *verb*
to make a temporary stop

halter (*say* **hol**-ta) *noun*
a strap that is put around a horse's head so that you can lead it

halve (*say* harv) *verb*
1 to divide into halves: *to halve an apple* 2 to reduce or cut down to half: *to halve the time a journey takes*

ham *noun*
1 the salted or smoked meat cut from the leg of a pig, usually eaten cold 2 an actor who overacts 3 someone who sends and receives messages from around the world on a radio
ham *verb*
4 to exaggerate or overact: *to ham up the part*
•***Word Family:*** other verb forms are **hams, hammed, hamming**

hamburger *noun*
a flat cake of seasoned, minced meat, usually served in a round bread roll
•***Word Origins:*** named after the town of *Hamburg* in Germany

hamlet *noun*
a small village or community, especially in the country

hammer *noun*
1 a tool with a handle and a heavy metal head for driving nails into wood and for beating things 2 something shaped or used like a hammer, such as the padded lever that strikes the strings in a piano
hammer *verb*
3 to strike something with a hammer or with something like a hammer: *to hammer a nail / to hammer the wall with your fist* 4 to defeat by a large amount in a game: *They hammered us.*

hammock *noun*
a hanging bed made of canvas or netting

hamper (1) *verb*
to get in the way or make things more difficult: *Her long skirt hampered her escape.*

hamper (2) *noun*
a large basket often used to carry food to a picnic

hamster *noun*
a small, short-tailed animal that looks like a guinea pig

hand *noun*
1 the part of your arm beyond the wrist, used for holding and grasping 2 something like a hand: *the hands of a clock* 3 a worker or helper: *a factory hand* 4 control: *The matter is out of my hands.* 5 applause: *Give the actors a big hand.* 6 help: *Can you give me a hand?* 7 a unit used to measure the height of horses, equal to about 10 centimetres 8 **at hand** near: *Help is at hand.*
hand *verb*
9 to give or pass with your hands: *Hand me a biscuit, please.*

handbag *noun*
a bag for carrying small articles such as a handkerchief, money or keys

handball *noun*
a game in which you bat a small ball against a wall with your hand

handbook *noun*
a book which tells you useful information about something: *a car handbook*

handcuffs *plural noun*
a pair of metal rings joined by a chain, for locking around a prisoner's wrists
•***Word Family:*** **handcuff** *verb*

handful *noun*
1 the amount you can hold in one hand: *a handful of beans* 2 a small number of things: *Only a handful of children turned up.* 3 someone, especially a child, who is difficult to control

handicap *noun*
1 a physical or mental disability 2 something that makes it more difficult for you to do something 3 a disadvantage or advantage that is given to competitors of different standards in a race or match, to try to make their chances of winning the same
handicap *verb*
4 to be a handicap to someone 5 to give a handicap to someone
•***Word Family:*** other verb forms are **handicaps, handicapped, handicapping** □ **handicapped** *adjective* disabled

handicraft *noun*
the art of making things with your hands: *My favourite handicraft is weaving.*

handkerchief (*say* **hang**-ka-cheef) *noun*
a small, square piece of cloth for wiping your nose or face
•***Word Family:*** the plural is **handkerchiefs** or **handkerchieves**

handle *noun*
1 the part of something you use to hold or open it
handle *verb*
2 to feel or touch something with your hands
3 to control: *to handle a difficult situation*
4 to use: *to handle your car with skill*

handlebars *plural noun*
the bars at the front of a bicycle or motorcycle, used for steering

handsome (*say* **han**-sum) *adjective*
1 looking attractive or pleasing: *a handsome man*
2 generous: *a handsome wedding present*
•***Word Family:*** **handsomely** *adverb*

hands-on *adjective*
learnt or shown through using: *hands-on computer experience*

handstand *noun*
an upside-down flip in which your hands are on the ground and your legs stretch up in the air

handwriting *noun*
writing done by hand, especially your own particular style of writing
•***Word Family:*** **handwritten** *adjective: a handwritten note*

handy *adjective*
1 nearby or easily reached: *Keep your weapons handy. / a handy corner shop* 2 skilful: *He's a handy carpenter.* 3 useful: *This is a very handy screwdriver.*
•***Word Family:*** other forms are **handier, handiest** □ **handily** *adverb* **handiness** *noun*

hang *verb*
1 to suspend or support something from above: *to hang your coat on a peg* 2 to kill someone by hanging them from a rope around their neck
3 to attach: *to hang wallpaper* 4 to grip or hold: *to hang on to my arm* 5 to lean or bend forward: *to hang out of the window / to hang your head*
6 **hang around** to pass time with nothing to do
7 **hang on** (a) to persevere or not give up
(b) to wait 8 **hang up** to end a telephone conversation by replacing the receiver
hang *noun*
9 **get the hang of** to learn the correct way of doing or using something: *I can't get the hang of this machine.*
•***Word Family:*** other verb forms are **hangs, hung, hanging**, except for definition 2, where we say **hanged** instead of **hung** □ **hanger** *noun* something on which you hang something: *a coat-hanger*

hangar (*say* **hang**-a) *noun*
a building in which planes and other aircraft are kept

hangover *noun*
the unpleasant feeling of sickness, dizziness and headache you get if you drink too much alcohol

hang-up *noun*
a worry or difficulty that you can't get rid of: *I have a hang-up about being too short.*

Hansard *noun*
the official published reports of debates in parliament
•***Word Origins:*** named after L. *Hansard* who printed and published British parliamentary debates from 1774

Hanukkah (*say* **hah**-nooh-kah) *noun*
a Jewish festival lasting eight days, when special candles are lit and children receive presents

haphazard (*say* hap-**haz**-ard) *adjective*
random or not planned: *He put his toys in the cupboard in a haphazard way.*
•***Word Family:*** **haphazardly** *adverb*

happen *verb*
1 to occur or take place: *The robbery happened while we were on holiday.* 2 to do something by chance: *I happened to meet her in the street.*
•***Word Family:*** **happening** *noun* something that happens

happy *adjective*
1 feeling contented or pleased about something: *She's happy at her new school.* 2 lucky or fortunate: *a happy decision / By a happy coincidence, we both booked our holidays at the same hotel.*
•***Word Family:*** other forms are **happier, happiest** □ **happily** *adverb* **happiness** *noun*

harangue (*say* ha-**rang**) *noun*
1 a long, passionate, lecturing speech
harangue *verb*
2 to make a speech like this to: *to harangue a crowd*
•***Word Family:*** other verb forms are **harangues, harangued, haranguing**

harass (*say* **ha**-ras *or* ha-**ras**) *verb*
to pester or torment someone: *The gang harassed all the passers-by.*
•***Word Family:*** **harassed** *adjective* worried or stressed **harassment** *noun*

harbour or **harbor** (*say* **har**-ba) *noun*
1 a sheltered area of water deep enough for ships to anchor
harbour *verb*
2 to give shelter to someone, especially a criminal

hard *adjective*
1 firm, solid or not easily cut: *hard wood*
2 needing great effort or endurance: *hard work / a hard climb* 3 difficult or not easy: *a hard problem in maths / to have a hard time*
4 energetic: *a hard worker* 5 **hard up** short of money
hard *adverb*
6 with a lot of energy: *Don't work too hard.*
•***Word Family:*** **hardness** *noun*

hardback *noun*
a book with a strong stiff cover

hard copy *noun*
anything printed out from a computer
•***Word Family:*** the plural is **hard copies**

a b c d e f g h i j k l m n o p q r s t u v w x y z

hard disk *noun*
the main storage disk inside a computer, made of metal

harden *verb*
to make or become hard: *This polish will harden my nails. / The glue will harden soon.*
•**Word Family:** **hardening** *noun*

hardly *adverb*
barely or not quite: *There's hardly any water. / It's hardly true to say that.*

hardship *noun*
difficulty or severe need: *Homeless people suffer great hardship.*

hardware *noun*
1 the tools and equipment you use in your home or garden 2 the mechanical parts of a computer

hardwood *noun*
strong heavy wood such as oak or mahogany

hardy *adjective*
strong, lasting and able to live in harsh conditions: *hardy desert plants*
•**Word Family:** other forms are **hardier, hardiest** □ **hardily** *adverb* **hardiness** *noun*

hare *noun*
1 an animal like a rabbit but with longer ears and stronger back legs
hare *verb*
2 to run or move very fast: *to hare down the path*

harebrained *adjective*
reckless or foolish: *a harebrained scheme*

harem (*say* **hair**-em *or* hah-**reem**) *noun*
1 the women of a Moslem household, including wives, female relatives and concubines, who live in a separate part of the house 2 the part of a house where the women live

hark *verb*
to listen

harm *noun*
1 damage or injury: *to cause grievous bodily harm*
harm *verb*
2 to damage or hurt someone or something: *The flowers weren't harmed in the storm. / This could harm your chances.*
•**Word Family:** **harmful** *adjective* **harmfully** *adverb* **harmless** *adjective* **harmlessly** *adverb*

harmonica (*say* har-**mon**-ik-a) *noun*
a small wind instrument with metal reeds, that you blow to make a sound

harmony (*say* **har**-ma-nee) *noun*
1 agreement and cooperation: *They live in perfect harmony.* 2 the pleasant effect made by musical notes played or sung at the same time
•**Word Family:** the plural is **harmonies** □ **harmonize** or **harmonise** *verb* **harmonization** *noun* **harmonic** (*say* har-**mon**-ik) *adjective* **harmonious** *adjective*
•**Word Origins:** from a Greek word meaning "a fitting together"

harness (*say* **har**-nis) *noun*
1 the straps and fittings used on a horse or other animal which is pulling a cart or other vehicle 2 straps used to attach or raise something: *a safety harness*
harness *verb*
3 to put a harness on an animal 4 to direct or control energy so that you can use it: *to harness the energy of running water to produce power*

harp *noun*
1 a large musical instrument with strings set in a triangular frame that you pluck with your fingers
harp *verb*
2 **harp on** to keep on talking about something in a boring way
•**Word Family:** **harpist** *noun* a harp player

harpoon *noun*
a spear attached to a line, thrown by hand or shot from a gun, used for catching whales or fish

harpsichord (*say* **harp**-si-kord) *noun*
a musical instrument like a piano, but with strings that are plucked rather than hit with hammers
•**Word Family:** **harpsichordist** *noun* a harpsichord player

harsh *adjective*
1 unpleasant, rough or painful to your senses: *a harsh wind / a harsh sound* 2 severe or cruel: *harsh treatment / a harsh ruler*
•**Word Family:** **harshly** *adverb* **harshness** *noun*

harvest *noun*
1 the gathering or picking of a crop, often grain
harvest *verb*
2 to gather or collect a crop: *to harvest wheat*
•**Word Family:** **harvester** *noun*

hash *noun*
1 a dish of small pieces of meat cooked or reheated with vegetables 2 **make a hash of** to ruin or do something badly

hassle *verb*
1 to annoy someone: *Stop hassling me!*
hassle *noun*
2 problem or nuisance: *Trying to park in town is a real hassle.*

haste *noun*
speed or hurry in your actions: *a letter written in haste*
•**Word Family:** **hasten** *verb* to hurry **hasty** *adjective* (**hastier, hastiest**) **hastily** *adverb*

hatch (1) *verb*
1 to break out of an egg: *The ducklings hatched last night.* 2 to produce: *to hatch a new scheme*
•***Word Family:*** **hatchery** *noun* (**hatcheries**) a place for hatching eggs

hatch (2) *noun*
1 an opening in a floor, wall or ceiling 2 a cover for such an opening
•***Word Family:*** the plural is **hatches** □ **hatchway** *noun*

hatch (3) *verb*
to draw many parallel lines close together, for shading or etching in art
•***Word Family:*** **hatching** *noun* a series of these lines

hatchet *noun*
1 a short-handled axe or tomahawk 2 **bury the hatchet** to make peace

hate *verb*
1 to dislike someone or something very strongly
hate *noun*
2 a feeling of strong dislike 3 something you hate: *My pet hate is tidying my room.*
•***Word Family:*** **hateful** *adjective* unpleasant or horrible **hatred** *noun*

haughty (*rhymes with* naughty) *adjective*
too proud of yourself and rude to others: *a haughty manner*
•***Word Family:*** other forms are **haughtier, haughtiest** □ **haughtily** *adverb* **haughtiness** *noun*

haul *verb*
1 to pull or drag something with all your strength: *to haul the children to safety*
haul *noun*
2 a hard pull 3 a quantity of something: *a haul of fish in the net* 4 **a long haul** a great distance

haunches (*say* **hawnch**-ez) *plural noun*
1 the tops of your legs and your buttocks: *to squat on your haunches* 2 the back parts of an animal

haunt *verb*
1 to visit a place as a ghost or spirit: *The spirit of the murdered prince haunts the castle.* 2 to worry or disturb someone: *The memory haunts her.*
haunt *noun*
3 a place you visit often: *a childhood haunt*
•***Word Family:*** **haunted** *adjective* worried, or visited by ghosts **haunting** *adjective* strange and fascinating, or staying in your thoughts: *haunting tunes / a haunting memory*

have *verb*
1 to possess, or own: *to have blue eyes / to have a brother / to have a guitar* 2 to take: *Do you have sugar?* 3 to obtain or receive: *to have someone's respect* 4 to suffer from: *to have a cold* 5 to enjoy or experience: *to have a game of chess* 6 to give birth to: *The cat had kittens.*
•***Word Family:*** other forms are **has, had, having**

haven (*say* **hay**-ven) *noun*
a place of shelter or safety, such as a harbour for ships

havoc (*say* **hav**-ak) *noun*
destruction, damage or chaos: *the havoc caused by the tornado*

hawk (1) *noun*
a bird of prey with large claws and a hooked beak, that hunts during the day

hawk (2) *verb*
to sell things by going from house to house
•***Word Family:*** **hawker** *noun*

hay *noun*
cut grass that is dried and used as animal food

hay fever *noun*
an allergy to pollen which makes you sneeze, gives you a blocked nose, and makes your eyes water

hazard (*say* **haz**-ard) *noun*
1 a risk or danger: *Smoking is a health hazard.*
hazard *verb*
2 to risk or chance: *to hazard a guess*
•***Word Family:*** **hazardous** *adjective* dangerous or risky **hazardously** *adverb*

haze *noun*
a mist of fine dust or smoke in the air, making it hard to see
•***Word Family:*** **hazy** *adjective* (**hazier, haziest**) misty

hazel (*say* **hay**-zel) *noun*
1 a small evergreen tree or shrub that produces nuts for eating 2 a light, greenish-brown colour
hazel *adjective*
3 of a hazel colour: *hazel eyes*
•***Word Family:*** **hazelnut** *noun*

he *pronoun*
the male you are talking about
•***Word Family:*** other forms are **his, him, they**

head (*say* hed) *noun*
1 the part of your body above the neck, containing your brain, eyes, mouth and so on 2 something with the shape or position of a head: *a head of cabbage / the head of a nail* 3 a leader, commander or chief 4 a person or animal being counted: *fifty head of sheep* 5 the front: *the head of a queue* 6 **come to a head** to come to a crisis point 7 **heads** the side of a coin showing a head: *Heads or tails?* 8 **lose your head** to panic

a b c d e f g h i j k l m n o p q r s t u v w x y z

A B C D E F G H I J K L M N O P Q R S T U V W X Y Z

head *verb*
9 to lead or be in front of: *to head the team*
10 to hit the ball with your head in football

headache *noun*
1 a pain in your head 2 a problem or a worry: *She's a real headache to her parents.*

heading *noun*
a group of words printed at the top of an article or the page of a book

headland *noun*
land that sticks out into the sea

headline *noun*
1 the title of a newspaper article or a news heading printed in large, bold type to grab your attention 2 **headlines** the most important news

headmaster *noun*
the male teacher in charge of a school

headmistress *noun*
the female teacher in charge of a school

headphones *plural noun*
a pair of small speakers, one for each ear, worn on a band over your head and connected to a radio or tape-recorder

headquarters *plural noun*
the central office or building where the head people of an organization work

headstand *noun*
balancing your body upside down, using your head and your arms as a support

headstrong *adjective*
obstinate or determined to have your own way

headteacher *noun*
the teacher in charge of a school

headword *noun*
the word that heads or begins a paragraph, chapter or dictionary entry

heal *verb*
to make someone healthy or to become healthy: *to heal the sick / The cut soon healed.*
•***Word Family:*** **healer** *noun*

health (*say* helth) *noun*
1 the normal working of your body and mind
2 your mental or physical state: *My health is no longer good.*

healthy *adjective*
1 not ill: *a healthy child* 2 good for you: *a healthy breakfast*
•***Word Family:*** other forms are **healthier, healthiest** □ **healthily** *adverb* **healthiness** *noun*

heap *noun*
1 a pile: *a heap of sand* 2 something very old or in bad condition, such as an old car 3 **heaps** plenty: *heaps of time*
heap *verb*
4 to pile up or put in a heap

hear *verb*
1 to pick up or sense sounds with your ears 2 to be told: *I hear that you're going away.* 3 to get news: *Do you ever hear from your brother?*
•***Word Family:*** other forms are **hears, heard, hearing**

hearing *noun*
1 the ability to hear: *His hearing isn't good.*
2 the opportunity of being heard: *Please give us a hearing.*

hearse (*rhymes with* nurse) *noun*
the special car for carrying the coffin to a funeral

heart *noun*
1 the organ in your chest that pumps the blood around your body 2 your emotions, affections or ability to love: *a kind heart* 3 courage or enthusiasm: *to have no heart for fighting* 4 the centre or most important part of anything: *the heart of a lettuce / the heart of the matter* 5 the red figure shaped like a heart, on a playing card 6 **by heart** from memory: *Please learn these rules by heart.*
•***Word Family:*** **heartache** *noun* painful sorrow **hearten** *verb* to cheer someone up

heart attack *noun*
a time when a person's heart stops working properly, which can sometimes cause death

hearth (*say* harth) *noun*
the floor of a fireplace and the area around it

heartless *adjective*
cruel: *The heartless thieves stole the children's toys.*

hearty (*say* **har**-tee) *adjective*
1 enthusiastic, friendly or sincere: *a hearty greeting*
2 large and satisfying: *a hearty bowl of soup*
•***Word Family:*** other forms are **heartier, heartiest** □ **heartily** *adverb* **heartiness** *noun*

heat *noun*
1 warmth or the feeling of being hot: *the heat of the day* 2 anger or excitement: *in the heat of an argument* 3 a first round in a race or contest
heat *verb*
4 to make something warm or hot, or to become hot: *Heat the soup.*
•***Word Family:*** **heated** *adjective* **heater** *noun*

heath (*rhymes with* teeth) *noun*
an area of flat land covered with low bushes and heather

heathen (*say* **hee**-then) *noun*
someone who does not worship God

heather (*rhymes with* feather) *noun*
a type of low evergreen shrub with purple or pink flowers, which grows on moors

heave *verb*
1 to lift or throw something you find heavy: *to heave the sack onto the truck* 2 to rise and fall: *His chest heaved as he coughed.* 3 to drag or pull something heavy: *The sailors heaved on the ropes.* 4 **heave a sigh** to utter a deep sigh

heaven (*rhymes with* seven) *noun*
1 the place where God and the angels are thought to live, and where people are thought to go when they die if they are good
2 something that pleases you greatly: *That meal was sheer heaven!* 3 **the heavens** the sky 4 **heavens!** something you say to show you are very surprised
• ***Word Family:*** **heavenly** *adjective*

heavy (*say* **hev**-ee) *adjective*
1 of great weight, size or force: *a heavy load*
2 sad or depressed: *a heavy heart* 3 more than usual: *a heavy smoker / heavy traffic* 4 difficult: *The climb was heavy going. / a heavy responsibility*
5 dark and cloudy: *a heavy sky*
• ***Word Family:*** **heavily** *adverb* **heaviness** *noun*

heckle *verb*
to interrupt someone by shouting and arguing all the time they are trying to speak
• ***Word Family:*** **heckler** *noun*

hectare *noun*
a metric unit of area used in land measurement, equal to 10 000 square metres, or about $2\frac{1}{2}$ acres

hectic *adjective*
very busy, especially when this involves lots of rushing about: *a hectic morning*
• ***Word Family:*** **hectically** *adverb*

hedge *noun*
1 a row of bushes grown close together to form a barrier
hedge *verb*
2 to surround somewhere with a hedge 3 to avoid giving direct answers to questions

hedgehog *noun*
a small animal, that looks for food at night and is covered in long spines

hedgerow *noun*
a long hedge, for example round a field

heed *verb*
1 to listen or pay attention to what someone is saying
heed *noun*
2 careful attention: *to pay heed to someone's advice*
• ***Word Family:*** **heedless** *adjective*

heel *noun*
1 the back part of your foot below the ankle
2 the part of a shoe or sock that covers the heel
3 **down at heel** shabby or untidy 4 **take to your heels** to run away fast
heel *verb*
5 to mend the heel of a shoe

hefty *adjective*
big or strong: *a hefty bill / a hefty policeman*

heifer (*say* **hef**-a) *noun*
a cow under three years of age, that has not yet had a calf

height (*rhymes with* light) *noun*
1 the distance from the bottom to the top of something 2 a high place, such as the top of a cliff 3 the highest extent or most important part of something: *the height of fashion*
• ***Word Family:*** **heighten** *verb* **high** *adjective*

heir (*say* air) *noun*
someone who inherits, or will inherit, the money, property or title of a dead person
• ***Word Family:*** **heiress** *noun*

heirloom (*say* **air**-loohm) *noun*
a valuable family possession passed down from generation to generation

helicopter *noun*
an aircraft without wings, that is lifted and moved forward by rotating blades on top

helium (*say* **hee**-lee-um) *noun*
a colourless gas that is much lighter than air and is often used in balloons
• ***Word Origins:*** from a Greek word meaning "sun"

hell *noun*
the place of fire and devils where wicked people are thought to go when they die
• ***Word Family:*** **hellish** *adjective*

hello *interjection*
the greeting you use when you meet someone

helm *noun*
1 the long handle or wheel you use for steering a boat 2 **at the helm** in charge of something
• ***Word Family:*** **helmsman** *noun*

helmet *noun*
a hard hat or covering to protect your head

help *verb*
1 to make something easier, better or less painful for someone or something: *May I help carry your bags?/ This medicine helps me to sleep.*
2 to stop yourself: *She couldn't help laughing.*
3 **help yourself to** to take something for yourself

help *noun*
4 someone or something that helps: *You've been a great help to us.*
•***Word Family:*** **helper** *noun* someone who helps **helping** *noun* a single serving of food

helpful *adjective*
1 willing to help: *She's very helpful.* 2 useful: *a helpful book*

helpless *adjective*
unable to do things for yourself or look after yourself
•***Word Family:*** **helplessly** *adverb* **helplessness** *noun*

hem *noun*
1 the edge of a piece of clothing or cloth that has been turned under and sewn down
hem *verb*
2 to fold back and sew down the edge of something: *to hem a skirt* 3 **hem in** to surround someone completely so they can't get out: *to be hemmed in on all sides by a crowd*
•***Word Family:*** other verb forms are **hems, hemmed, hemming**

hemisphere (*say* **hem**-is-fear) *noun*
half of a round shape or sphere, such as the Southern Hemisphere, which is the half of the Earth below the equator
•***Word Family:*** **hemispherical** *adjective*

hemp *noun*
a tall plant, originally from Asia, grown for its strong stem fibres which are used to make rope, and its leaves which people smoke as a drug

hen *noun*
a female bird, especially a chicken

hence *adverb*
1 from now: *two years hence* 2 therefore: *She got into a fight, hence the bruises.*

hepatitis (*say* hep-a-**tie**-tis) *noun*
a disease of the liver which causes fever and yellow skin

heptagon (*say* **hep**-ta-gon) *noun*
any flat shape with seven straight sides
•***Word Family:*** **heptagonal** *adjective*

heptathlon *noun*
a sports contest in which athletes compete in seven different events

her *pronoun*
1 the form of the pronoun **she** that comes after the verb or a preposition in a sentence and is its object: *He thanked her. / Give the cake to her.*
her *adjective*
2 the form of the pronoun **she** that shows something belongs to the female referred to: *It's her cake.*
•***Word Family:*** **hers** *pronoun: Which one is hers?* **herself** *pronoun: She loves herself to death.*

herald *noun*
1 a messenger
herald *verb*
2 to be a sign of something that is going to happen: *The killing heralds a full-scale war.*

heraldry (*say* **he**-ral-dree) *noun*
the study of coats of arms
•***Word Family:*** **heraldic** *adjective*

herb *noun*
a plant used as a medicine or to flavour food
•***Word Family:*** **herbal** *adjective: herbal tea* **herbalist** *noun* someone who uses herbs to treat diseases
•***Word Origins:*** from a Latin word meaning "grass"

herbivore (*say* **her**-be-vor) *adjective*
an animal that only eats plants
•***Word Family:*** **herbivorous** (*say* **her**-biv-er-us) *adjective: a herbivorous dinosaur.*

herd *noun*
1 a large group of animals, especially cattle
herd *verb*
2 to bring animals or people together as a group and move them somewhere: *The teachers herded us onto the bus.*
•***Word Family:*** **herdsman** *noun* the keeper of a herd of cattle or sheep

here *adverb*
1 at, in or to this place: *Put it here. / Come here.* 2 at this point: *Here I would like to stop and show a slide.*

hereditary (*say* ha-**red**-i-tree) *adjective*
inherited or coming from your parents or ancestors: *a hereditary disease / a hereditary title*

heredity (*say* ha-**red**-i-tee) *noun*
the passing on of characteristics from parents to children through their genes: *Heredity is responsible for their blood disease.*

heresy (*say* **he**-ra-see) *noun*
a belief or opinion that goes against what is usually taught or believed, especially by a religion
•***Word Family:*** the plural is **heresies** □ **heretic** *noun* someone who believes heresy **heretical** *adjective* expressing heresy

heritage (*say* **he**-ri-tij) *noun*
something precious passed on from one generation to the next: *Such beautiful beaches are part of our natural heritage.*

hermaphrodite (*say* her-**maf**-ra-dite) *noun*
an animal or plant with both male and female sex organs
•***Word Origins:*** named after *Hermaphrodites,*

the son of Hermes and Aphrodite in Greek myths, who became united in one body with a nymph

hermit *noun*
someone who lives alone, often for religious reasons
•***Word Family:*** **hermitage** *noun* a place where a hermit lives

hernia (*say* **her**-nee-a) *noun*
the pushing out of an organ in your body, such as the intestine, through a hole in the tissue that surrounds it

hero (*say* **hear**-ro) *noun*
1 someone, usually a man or boy, who has done something brave or noble 2 the main male character in a story, play or film
•***Word Family:*** the plural is **heroes** □ **heroic** *adjective* brave **heroically** *adverb* **heroism** *noun*

heroin (*say* **he**-ro-in) *noun*
a very powerful and addictive drug originally used as a painkiller and now mostly used illegally

heroine (*say* **he**-ro-in) *noun*
1 a woman or girl who has done something brave or noble 2 the main female character in a story, play or film

heron *noun*
a bird with long legs, a long neck and a long beak that lives near water

herpes (*say* **her**-peez) *noun*
a disease you catch from others, that produces cold sores or small blisters around your nose, mouth or sex organs

herring *noun*
a fish found in the Atlantic Ocean and eaten pickled, smoked (called a kipper) or cooked
•***Word Family:*** the plural is **herrings** or **herring**

hesitate (*say* **hez**-i-tate) *verb*
to pause before you do something, for example because you are nervous or uncertain: *to hesitate before answering*
•***Word Family:*** **hesitancy** *noun* **hesitant** *adjective* **hesitantly** *adverb* **hesitation** *noun*

hessian (*say* **hesh**-an) *noun*
a strong, coarse cloth made from jute and used for sacks

heterosexual (*say* het-a-roh-**sek**-shooh-al) *adjective*
1 sexually attracted to people of the opposite sex
heterosexual *noun*
2 a heterosexual person
•***Word Family:*** **heterosexuality** *noun*

hew *verb*
to cut wood or stone roughly and quickly
•***Word Family:*** other forms are **hews, hewed, hewn, hewing**

hexagon *noun*
a shape with six straight sides
•***Word Family:*** **hexagonal** *adjective*

hexagram *noun*
a six-pointed star, such as the Star of David

hibernate (*say* **high**-ber-nate) *verb*
to spend the winter hiding away and sleeping: *Squirrels store nuts in summer and hibernate in winter.*
•***Word Family:*** **hibernation** *noun*

hibiscus (*say* high-**bis**-kus) *noun*
a tropical shrub with brightly coloured flowers
•***Word Origins:*** from a Greek word meaning "marshmallow"

hiccup (*say* **hik**-up) *noun*
1 the short sharp sound you make when your chest moves suddenly and you are forced to take a quick breath
hiccup *verb*
2 to make this sound
•***Word Family:*** other verb forms are **hiccups, hiccupped, hiccupping**

hide (1) *verb*
to prevent someone or something from being seen or discovered: *to hide under the bed / to hide your true feelings*
•***Word Family:*** other forms are **hides, hid, hidden, hiding**

hide (2) *noun*
1 the skin of an animal, such as a cow 2 a special shelter used when you go bird-watching, so that birds won't see you

hideous (*say* **hid**-ee-us) *adjective*
ugly: *a hideous face / a hideous scar*
•***Word Family:*** **hideously** *adverb* **hideousness** *noun*

hiding *noun*
a beating or thrashing: *to give someone a good hiding*

hierarchy (*say* **high**-a-rah-kee) *noun*
the system that arranges or organizes people or things according to their rank, authority or importance: *The Prime Minister is at the top of the government hierarchy.*
•***Word Family:*** the plural is **hierarchies** □ **hierarchical** *adjective*

hieroglyphics (*say* high-ra-**glif**-iks) *plural noun*
writing in which pictures or symbols are used to represent words or sounds, as in the ancient Egyptian system of writing

A B C D E F G H I J K L M N O P Q R S T U V W X Y Z

higgledy-piggledy *adverb* and *adjective*
all mixed up and in a mess

high (*rhymes with* my) *adjective*
1 tall or a long way above the ground: *a high tower / a high throw* 2 of above average level or quantity: *a high temperature / high prices*
3 sounding shrill or sharp: *a high voice / a high note* 4 important: *a high rank* 5 beginning to go bad: *This fish is high.*
high *adverb*
6 in or to a high position or level: *The plane flew high overhead. / Aim high and you'll succeed.*
high *noun*
7 a high level: *Prices have reached a new high.*
• ***Word Family:*** see also **height** and **highly**

highlands *plural noun*
an area of hills or mountains: *the highlands of Scotland*
• ***Word Family:*** **highlander** *noun* someone from the highlands

highlight *noun*
1 the best or most interesting part of something: *The highlight of the concert was when the dancers came on. / to show the highlights of a football match*
highlight *verb*
2 to emphasize something or make it stand out

highlighter *noun*
a fluorescent pen used to make the important words in a piece of writing stand out clearly from the rest

highly *adverb*
1 very or extremely: *a highly dangerous drug* 2 in a way that shows how much you admire someone or something: *She thinks very highly of him.*

high-rise *adjective*
very tall, with lots of floors: *a high-rise office block*

high school *noun*
a secondary school

high-tech *adjective*
using or involving the latest designs or information that technology has produced: *high-tech office equipment*

highway *noun*
a main road

hijab (*say* he-**jab**) *noun*
the veil worn by some Muslim women

hijack *verb*
to take control of a plane or other vehicle and force the pilot or driver to take you somewhere: *to hijack a plane*
• ***Word Family:*** **hijacker** *noun* someone who hijacks a plane or vehicle

hike *verb*
1 to walk long distances through the country
hike *noun*
2 a long walk in the country
• ***Word Family:*** **hiker** *noun* someone who hikes

hilarious (*say* hi-**lair**-ree-us) *adjective*
extremely funny: *a hilarious comedy*
• ***Word Family:*** **hilariously** *adverb* **hilarity** *noun*

hilt *noun*
1 the handle of a sword or dagger 2 **to the hilt** fully or completely: *He was armed to the hilt.*

him *pronoun*
the form of the pronoun **he** that comes after the verb or a preposition in a sentence and is its object: *I hit him. / Give the cake to him.*
• ***Word Family:*** **himself** *pronoun: He's going by himself.*

hind (1) (*rhymes with* find) *adjective*
at the back: *Hares have long hind legs.*

hind (2) *noun*
a female deer

hinder (*say* **hin**-da) *verb*
to make something difficult or get in someone's way: *to hinder someone's progress*

Hindi (*say* **hin**-dee) *noun*
a language spoken in the north of India, and by many Indian people in the United Kingdom

hindsight *noun*
the ability to look back at what you did and understand what you should have done: *In hindsight, it was stupid to have a picnic in the rain.*

Hinduism (*say* **hin**-doo-iz-um) *noun*
the main religion of India, with many gods and goddesses
• ***Word Family:*** **Hindu** *noun* someone who follows Hinduism **Hindu** *adjective: the Hindu belief in reincarnation*

hinge (*say* hinj) *noun*
1 the movable joint on which a door or gate swings backwards and forwards
hinge *verb*
2 to attach something by a hinge 3 to depend: *It all hinges on whether you believe him or not.*

hint *noun*
1 a slight suggestion or clue: *to drop a hint about the way you feel* 2 a helpful tip or idea: *a book full of gardening hints*
hint *verb*
3 to suggest something without actually saying it: *to hint at what present you'd like*

hinterland *noun*
the land that lies inland from the coast

hip *noun*
the part sticking out from each side of your body between your waist and thighs

hippopotamus (*say* hip-a-**pot**-a-mus) *noun*
a heavy, thick-skinned, African mammal with a broad head, that lives near lakes and rivers
•***Word Family:*** the plural is **hippopotamuses** or **hippopotami**
•***Word Origins:*** from a Greek word meaning "a river-horse"

hire *verb*
to pay to employ someone or use something for a while: *to hire a waiter / to hire a TV*

his *adjective*
1 belonging to him: *It's his cake.*
his *pronoun*
2 the form of **he** you use for something belonging to him: *The cake is his.*

hiss *verb*
1 to make a long "sss" sound: *The snake hissed at the mouse.* 2 to express disapproval or dislike by making this sound: *The audience hissed when the witch came on.*

histogram (*say* **hiss**-toe-gram) *noun*
a graph that uses different sized bars or rectangles to show different amounts

historian (*say* his-**taw**-ree-un) *noun*
someone who writes or studies history

history *noun*
1 the study of the past 2 a record of past events relating to a particular period, country and so on: *the history of the motor car* 3 the past: *History has repeated itself.*
•***Word Family:*** the plural is **histories** □ **historic** *adjective* important in history **historical** *adjective* actually happening or existing in the past **historically** *adverb*

hit *verb*
1 to strike or knock against something: *She hit the ball over the fence. / The car hit the wall.* 2 to reach: *a singer who can't hit the high notes* 3 to have a bad effect on something: *The strike has hit prices.* 4 **hit it off** to get on well together: *The kids hit it off at once.* 5 **hit on** to discover or think of an idea or plan
hit *noun*
6 an impact or blow 7 something that is very successful or popular: *This song is sure to be a hit.*
•***Word Family:*** the verb form is **hits, hit, hitting** □ **hitter** *noun*

hitch *verb*
1 to fasten or tie something to something else: *to hitch a trailer to a car* 2 to hitchhike: *to hitch a ride* 3 **hitch up** to pull up: *to hitch up your skirt*
hitch *noun*
4 a kind of knot 5 a difficulty or problem: *a hitch in our plans*

hitchhike *verb*
to travel by getting free rides in passing cars and lorries
•***Word Family:*** **hitchhiker** *noun*

HIV *noun*
the name of the virus that weakens people's resistance to illness which, in turn, allows those infected to develop AIDS
•***Word Origins:*** made by using the first letters of *h*uman *i*mmunodeficiency *v*irus

hive *noun*
1 the home of bees 2 a busy place: *a hive of activity*

hoard (*say* hord) *noun*
1 a hidden store or fund
hoard *verb*
2 to save and store up something in a secret place: *to hoard sweets*
•***Word Origins:*** from a Middle English word meaning "treasure"

hoarding (*say* **hor**-ding) *noun*
1 a temporary fence, such as one around a building site 2 a board for putting up advertisements or posters

hoarse (*say* haws) *adjective*
rough or croaky: *a hoarse whisper*
•***Word Family:*** **hoarsely** *adverb* **hoarseness** *noun*

hoax (*say* hohks) *noun*
1 a trick played on people: *The bomb scare turned out to be a hoax.*
hoax *verb*
2 to trick someone
•***Word Family:*** **hoaxer** *noun*

hobby *noun*
an activity you enjoy doing in your spare time: *My hobby is watching birds.*
•***Word Family:*** the plural is **hobbies**

hockey *noun*
a game for two teams in which players use long-handled sticks with curved ends to try to hit the ball into their opponents' goal, played on a field or on ice

hoe *noun*
1 a long-handled tool used for loosening the soil
hoe *verb*
2 to dig with a hoe
•***Word Family:*** other verb forms are **hoes, hoed, hoeing**

hog *noun*
1 a pig 2 a greedy or dirty person

A B C D E F G H I J K L M N O P Q R S T U V W X Y Z

hog *verb*
3 to take more than your share of something: *to hog the TV*
•***Word Family:*** other verb forms are **hogs, hogged, hogging**

hoist *verb*
1 to raise or lift something: *to hoist a sail*
hoist *noun*
2 a machine for lifting heavy things off the ground

hold (1) *verb*
1 to have something in your hands or arms 2 to contain: *How much water does that jar hold?* 3 to apply: *That rule does not hold.* 4 to stay: *Hold still while I brush your hair.* 5 to support or carry someone or something: *That chair won't hold your weight.* 6 to consider: *to hold someone responsible* 7 **hold up** (a) to delay: *The train was held up.* (b) to rob: *A masked gunman held up the bank.*
hold *noun*
8 a grip: *He lost his hold on the rope.* 9 a strong influence or power: *to have a hold over someone*
•***Word Family:*** other forms are **holds, held, holding** □ **holder** *noun*

hold (2) *noun*
the inner part of a ship below the deck, where cargo is carried

hole *noun*
1 an opening in something 2 a burrow

Holi (*say* **hole**-ee) *noun*
a Hindu spring festival which is held towards the end of February

holiday (*say* **hol**-i-day) *noun*
1 a day off work or school: *a bank holiday* 2 a period of rest from work or school, usually a certain number of weeks in a year: *Where are you going on holiday this year?*
holiday *verb*
3 to go on holiday to a particular place: *to holiday in France*
•***Word Origins:*** from an Old English word meaning "holy day"

hollow (*say* **holl**-o) *adjective*
1 not solid or filled: *a hollow log* 2 worthless or insincere: *a hollow victory / a hollow promise*
hollow *noun*
3 a gap or dip in the ground
hollow *verb*
4 **hollow out** to make something hollow
•***Word Family:*** **hollowly** *adverb* **hollowness** *noun*

holly *noun*
an evergreen tree or shrub with red berries and sharp, pointed, shiny leaves used as a Christmas decoration

holocaust (*say* **hol**-a-caust) *noun*
1 great destruction, especially caused by fire
2 **the Holocaust** the mass murder of the Jews by the Nazis during World War II
•***Word Origins:*** from a Greek word meaning "burnt whole"

hologram (*say* **hol**-a-gram) *noun*
a three-dimensional image created using light from a laser
•***Word Family:*** **holographic** *adjective*

holy *adjective*
1 sacred: *a holy day* 2 dedicated to God or to a religion: *a holy person*
•***Word Family:*** other forms are **holier, holiest** □ **holiness** *noun*

homage (*say* **hom**-ij) *noun*
respect or honour: *to pay homage to the soldiers who died in battle*

home *noun*
1 the place where you live, belong or were born: *He left home to see the world. / Australia is the home of the kangaroo.* 2 a house or flat: *We aim to build hundreds of new homes.* 3 an institution where people are looked after: *an old people's home*
home *adverb*
4 in or to your own home or country: *Please come straight home after the party.*
home *adjective*
5 from your home: *a home office*
•***Word Family:*** **homing** *adjective: a homing device*

homesick *adjective*
depressed or sad because you long for home
•***Word Family:*** **homesickness** *noun*

homestead (*say* **home**-sted) *noun*
the main house on a farm or property

homicide (*say* **hom**-i-side) *noun*
the crime of deliberately killing someone

homogeneous (*say* ho-mo-**jee**-nee-us) *adjective*
made up of parts that are alike: *a homogeneous blend*
•***Word Family:*** **homogeneously** *adverb*

homogenize or **homogenise** (*say* ha-**moj**-a-nize) *verb*
to blend or mix something evenly so that all parts are alike
•***Word Family:*** **homogenized milk** milk treated to mix cream evenly throughout

homonym (*say* **hom**-a-nim) *noun*
a word that has the same sound, or the same spelling, as another but a different meaning

homophone *noun*
a word that has the same sound as another but a different meaning

homosexual (*say* ho-mo-**seks**-yew-al) *noun*
1 someone who is sexually attracted to people of their own sex
homosexual *adjective*
2 sexually attracted to people of your own sex
• ***Word Family:*** **homosexuality** *noun*

honest (*say* **on**-est) *adjective*
truthful or able to be trusted
• ***Word Family:*** **honestly** *adverb* **honesty** *noun*

honey (*rhymes with* funny) *noun*
a thick, sweet liquid made by bees from flower nectar

honeycomb *noun*
a structure of wax made by honeybees, containing rows of cells in which honey and pollen are stored, and eggs and larvae develop

honeymoon *noun*
the holiday taken by a couple who have just got married

honeysuckle *noun*
a climbing plant with sweet-smelling white, pink or yellow flowers

honk *noun*
1 the loud sound made by a car horn or by a goose
honk *verb*
2 to make this sound, or to sound the horn of your car

honorary (*say* **on**-a-ra-ree) *adjective*
given or received as an honour: *He received an honorary degree from the university.*

honour (*say* **on**-a) *noun*
1 respect: *to treat someone with honour* 2 glory, credit or fame: *to bring honour to your school* 3 good or noble character: *a man of honour* 4 a privilege: *It's an honour to serve you.*
honour *verb*
5 to show respect for someone or something
• ***Word Family:*** **honourable** *adjective* **honourably** *adverb*

hood *noun*
1 a soft, loose covering for your head and neck on a coat, jacket and so on 2 a folding roof, often canvas: *the hood of a pram*
• ***Word Family:*** **hooded** *adjective*: *hooded eyes*

hoodlum (*say* **hoohd**-lum) *noun*
a gangster or violent, destructive youth

hoof *noun*
the hard covering protecting the foot of animals, such as the ox and horse
• ***Word Family:*** the plural is **hoofs** or **hooves**

hook *noun*
1 a curved piece of metal or plastic for pulling or catching something 2 a short, swinging blow in boxing made with the arm bent 3 **by hook or by crook** by any means, however desperate
hook *verb*
4 to catch something with a hook 5 to hit a ball so that it curves away behind or to the side of the player
• ***Word Family:*** **hooked** *adjective* addicted: *hooked on drugs*

hooligan (*say* **hoo**-li-gan) *noun*
a rough and noisy person
• ***Word Family:*** **hooliganism** *noun*

hoop *noun*
a circular band or ring, sometimes used to support or strengthen something, or used as a child's toy

hoopla *noun*
a game in which you try to throw small hoops around objects offered as prizes

hoot *noun*
1 the sound made by an owl or a car horn 2 a loud laugh of delight or scorn: *The children broke out into hoots of laughter. / hoots of derision*
hoot *verb*
3 to make a sound like an owl, or to sound a car horn 4 to laugh or jeer loudly

hop *verb*
1 to jump, on all four feet if you are a rabbit or similar animal, or on one foot if you are a human
hop *noun*
2 a light springy jump on one foot
• ***Word Family:*** other verb forms are **hops, hopped, hopping**

hope *verb*
1 to wish for or look forward to something: *I hope you can come to my party.*
hope *noun*
2 wishing that something good will happen and expecting that it will: *Don't give up hope.* 3 a chance that something you want will happen: *There's little hope that the child will be found.*
• ***Word Family:*** **hopeful** *adjective* **hopefully** *adverb* **hopefulness** *noun* **hopeless** *adjective* **hopelessly** *adverb* **hopelessness** *noun*

horde *noun*
a large group of people, animals or insects

horizon (*say* ha-**rie**-zon) *noun*
1 the line where the sea or flat land seems to meet the sky 2 the limit of a person's knowledge or experience: *Travelling broadened my horizons.*

horizontal (*say* ho-ra-**zon**-tal) *adjective*
parallel to, or in line with, the ground or the horizon
• ***Word Family:*** **horizontally** *adverb*

hormone *noun*
a chemical substance produced by a gland in one part of the body and carried by the blood to another part where it controls various body functions
•***Word Family:*** **hormonal** *adjective*

horn *noun*
1 a hollow, pointed growth on the head of such animals as goats, sheep and cattle 2 a brass musical instrument: *the French horn* 3 a loud warning device: *a car horn*
•***Word Family:*** **horny** *adjective* (**hornier, horniest**) hard like a horn

hornet *noun*
a very large wasp with brown markings and a painful sting

horoscope (*say* **ho**-ra-skohp) *noun*
a prediction about someone's future based on the position of the stars when they were born
•***Word Origins:*** from a Greek word meaning "one who observes the hour of a birth"

horrible *adjective*
nasty or unpleasant: *a horrible smell*
•***Word Family:*** **horribly** *adverb*

horrid *adjective*
nasty or unpleasant: *a horrid little child*

horror *noun*
1 a strong feeling of disgust, shock or fear: *We looked in horror as the car went up in flames*
2 something or someone you really dislike: *That child is a real horror.*
•***Word Family:*** **horrific** *adjective* extremely shocking, violent or unpleasent: *a horrific accident* **horrify** *verb* (**horrifies, horrified, horrifying**) **horrifying** *adjective*

hors d'oeuvre (*say* or-**derv**) *noun*
a small portion of savoury food served before the main meal
•***Word Origins:*** from French words meaning "apart from the main work"

horse *noun*
1 a four-legged mammal with hoofs and a long mane and tail, used for riding or pulling a cart
2 a frame you sit on for doing exercises, or on which something is supported: *a vaulting horse / a clothes horse*
horse *verb*
3 **horse around** to play roughly or noisily

horsepower *noun*
a unit for measuring the power of engines

horticulture (*say* **hor**-ti-kul-cher) *noun*
the science or study of growing fruit, flowers and vegetables
•***Word Family:*** **horticultural** *adjective* **horticulturist** *noun*

hose *noun*
1 a flexible tube for carrying or spraying water
2 *a shortened form of* **hosiery**
hose *verb*
3 to spray or wet something or somewhere with water from a hose

hosiery (*say* **hoh**-zha-ree) *noun*
clothing for your feet or legs, such as socks or stockings

hospital (*say* **hos**-pit-al) *noun*
a place where sick or injured people are given medical treatment

host (1) (*rhymes with* most) *noun*
1 someone who entertains guests 2 an animal or plant on or in which a parasite lives
host *verb*
3 to introduce or present something: *to host a TV show*
•***Word Family:*** **hostess** *noun*

host (2) (*rhymes with* most) *noun*
a large group of people or things: *a host of angels / a host of invitations*

hostage (*say* **hos**-tij) *noun*
someone who is held as a prisoner until certain demands are met

hostel (*say* **hos**-tel) *noun*
a place where people such as students and tourists can stay cheaply

hostile (*say* **hos**-tile) *adjective*
unfriendly or willing to fight
•***Word Family:*** **hostility** *noun* (**hostilities**)

hot *adjective*
1 having or producing a high temperature: *a hot day / a hot stove* 2 passionate or violent: *a hot temper* 3 very spicy: *a hot curry* 4 skilled or clever: *not too hot at maths*
•***Word Family:*** other forms are **hotter, hottest**

hotel *noun*
a building where you pay to stay overnight and have meals
•***Word Family:*** **hotelier** *noun* the manager of a hotel

hound *noun*
1 a dog trained to hunt by following a scent
hound *verb*
2 to keep on following or bothering someone: *The landlord hounded us until we paid the rent.*

hour (*rhymes with* flower) *noun*
1 a unit of time measurement, equal to 60 minutes or one 24th part of a day 2 a time of day: *Who can be phoning at this hour?* 3 **hours** the usual time for work or school: *office hours*
•***Word Family:*** **hourly** *adjective* happening every hour

hourglass *noun*
an instrument for measuring time, consisting of two glass bulbs joined by a narrow passage through which sand runs

house *noun*
1 a building or part of a building where people live 2 a building or place that is used for a particular purpose: *a house of worship / a publishing house* 3 a family with all its ancestors and descendants: *The Queen belongs to the house of Windsor.* 4 the audience in a theatre: *a full house* 5 a parliament or government assembly: *the House of Commons* 6 one of the groups which pupils in many schools are divided into: *Which house are you in?*
house (*rhymes with* cows) *verb*
7 to contain or shelter things or people: *The new shelves house my books. / to house homeless people*
• ***Word Family:*** **housing** *noun*

household *noun*
all the people living together in a house or home
• ***Word Family:*** **householder** *noun* the person who is in charge of a particular household

house-train *verb*
to train a dog, cat or other pet not to use the house as a toilet
• ***Word Family:*** **house-trained** *adjective*

housework *noun*
the work such as cooking, washing and cleaning that needs to be done in a house

hovel (*say* **hov**-el) *noun*
a small, dirty house or hut

hover *verb*
1 to fly or stay in the same place in the air: *The bird hovered over the flower while it collected nectar.* 2 to wait close by: *We hovered near the food.*

hovercraft *noun*
a vehicle designed to travel over water or land, supported on a cushion of air

how *adverb*
1 in what manner, or condition: *How did you do it?* 2 to what extent: *How often do you see her?* 3 at what rate or price: *How much is it?*

however *adverb*
1 no matter how: *However hard he tried, he still couldn't do it.* 2 in whatever way: *Do it however you can.* 3 nevertheless: *I don't usually like curry, however, I'll give it a try.*

howl *verb*
1 to make a loud, long cry, like that of a dog or wolf 2 to cry loudly
• ***Word Family:*** **howler** *noun* a silly mistake

hub *noun*
1 the central part of a wheel 2 the centre or focus of activity: *The kitchen is the hub of our household.*

huddle *verb*
1 to crowd together: *to huddle up for warmth* 2 to curl or hunch yourself up: *to huddle in a corner*
huddle *noun*
3 a few people meeting together in private

hue *noun*
a colour

hug *verb*
1 to clasp someone tightly in your arms, usually with affection 2 to keep close to something or somewhere: *The boat hugged the shore.*
• ***Word Family:*** other verb forms are **hugs, hugged, hugging**

huge (*say* hewj) *adjective*
extremely large: *a huge elephant*
• ***Word Family:*** **hugely** *adverb* **hugeness** *noun*

hulk *noun*
1 the body or wreck of an old boat 2 someone or something that is bulky or awkward: *a hulk of a man*
• ***Word Family:*** **hulking** *adjective* heavy and clumsy

hull *noun*
the body of a boat

hum *verb*
1 to make a constant droning or buzzing sound, the way machines or bees do 2 to sing with your lips closed: *to hum a tune* 3 to be very busy: *The streets hummed with tourists.*
hum *noun*
4 a humming sound
• ***Word Family:*** other verb forms are **hums, hummed, humming**

human (*say* **hew**-man) *noun*
1 a person
human *adjective*
2 to do with people: *a human error*

humane (*say* hew-**mane**) *adjective*
feeling or showing kindness for those who are suffering: *a humane person / a humane action*
• ***Word Family:*** **humanely** *adverb*

humanity (*say* hew-**man**-i-tee) *noun*
1 everyone in the whole world: *the threat to humanity from pollution* 2 sympathy and kindness: *Show humanity to others.*
• ***Word Family:*** **humanitarian** *adjective* involving helping people, whoever they are

humble *adjective*
1 modest and aware of your failings: *a humble*

A B C D E F G H I J K L M N O P Q R S T U V W X Y Z

man 2 poor or unimportant: *to have humble beginnings*
•*Word Family:* **humbly** *adverb* **humility** *noun*

humid (*say* **hew**-mid) *adjective*
damp and warm: *humid air*
•*Word Family:* **humidity** *noun* **humidly** *adverb*

humiliate (*say* hew-**mil**-ee-ate) *verb*
to make someone feel silly and ashamed: *to humiliate someone in front of their friends*
•*Word Family:* **humiliation** *noun*

humour or **humor** (*say* **hew**-ma) *noun*
1 what makes people laugh: *We couldn't see the humour in his joke.* 2 a mood or state of mind: *He's not in a good humour today.* 3 **a sense of humour** the ability to see the funny side of life
humour *verb*
4 to keep someone happy by doing what they want or agreeing with them: *to humour a friend*
•*Word Family:* **humorous** *adjective* amusing or funny

hump *noun*
1 a rounded lump on the back: *a camel's hump* 2 a mound or bump: *a speed hump on the road*
hump *verb*
3 to carry something heavy, especially on your back or shoulders

humpy *noun*
an Aboriginal shelter built in the bush
•*Word Family:* the plural is **humpies**

humus (*say* **hew**-mus) *noun*
the dark, rich substance in soil that makes it more fertile, consisting of decaying animal and vegetable matter

hunch *verb*
1 to bend or draw up something in a hump: *to hunch your shoulders in the cold*
hunch *noun*
2 a feeling or suspicion about something: *I had a hunch that they'd get married.*
•*Word Family:* the plural of the noun is **hunches**

hundred *noun*
the number 100
•*Word Family:* **hundred** *adjective* **hundredth** *adjective*

hunger *noun*
the feeling in your stomach when you want to eat
•*Word Family:* **hungry** *adjective* (**hungrier, hungriest**) **hungrily** *adverb*

hunk *noun*
a large piece or chunk: *a hunk of bread*

hunt *verb*
1 to chase an animal in order to kill it: *to hunt rabbits* 2 to search for a particular thing: *to hunt for conkers*
hunt *noun*
3 the act of searching: *a treasure hunt* 4 an event at which people meet to hunt animals
•*Word Family:* **hunter** *noun* **hunting** *noun* **huntress** *noun* **huntsman** *noun*

hurdle *noun*
1 one of the barriers that stand on the track for athletes to jump over in certain races 2 an obstacle or difficult problem to be overcome
hurdle *verb*
3 to jump a hurdle
•*Word Family:* **hurdler** *noun* **hurdling** *noun*

hurl *verb*
to throw something with great force

hurricane (*say* **hur**-i-kan) *noun*
a violent storm with a very strong wind

hurry *verb*
1 to move or do things quickly to save time: *to hurry to the station to catch the train*
hurry *noun*
2 need for a particular thing to be done quickly: *What's the hurry? / no hurry* 3 **in a hurry** moving or working quickly because there's not enough time
•*Word Family:* other verb forms are **hurries, hurried, hurrying** □ **hurried** *adjective* **hurriedly** *adverb*

hurt *verb*
to cause injury or pain to someone: *to hurt your arm / Her nasty words hurt me.*
•*Word Family:* **hurtful** *adjective* **hurtfully** *adverb*

hurtle *verb*
to move very quickly, seeming out of control: *to hurtle downhill in a go-cart*

husband *noun*
the man to whom a woman is married

hush *noun*
1 silence: *Can we have some hush, please?*
hush *verb*
2 to make people quiet 3 **hush up** to keep something a secret: *The government has hushed up the results of the tests.*
hush *interjection*
4 something you say when you want people to be quiet: *Hush! I'm on the phone!*
•*Word Family:* **hushed** *adjective*: *to speak in a hushed voice*

husk *noun*
the dry, outer covering of a grain, especially of an ear of wheat

husky (1) *adjective*
dry, hoarse or whispering: *a husky voice*

•*Word Family:* other forms are **huskier, huskiest** □ **huskily** *adverb* **huskiness** *noun*

husky (2) *noun*
a large, sturdy dog with a thick coat, used to pull sledges
•*Word Family:* the plural is **huskies**

hustle (*say* **hus**-el) *verb*
1 to push or jostle someone roughly: *The men hustled him into the car.* 2 to hurry

hut *noun*
a simple house, usually having only one room

hutch *noun*
a box or cage, with wire mesh on one side, in which rabbits or other small animals are kept
•*Word Family:* the plural is **hutches**

hyacinth (*say* **hy**-a-sinth) *noun*
a plant which grows from a bulb and has lots of small, sweet-smelling flowers around the top of a single stem

hybrid (*say* **high**-brid) *noun*
an animal or plant that results from the breeding of parents of two different species

hydrant *noun*
an upright pipe connected to a water main and to which a hose can be attached

hydraulic (*say* high-**drol**-ik) *adjective*
operated by or using the force of a liquid such as water or oil: *hydraulic brakes*
•*Word Family:* **hydraulically** *adverb* **hydraulics** *noun*

hydro-electric *adjective*
to do with electricity produced by the energy or power of flowing water, such as from a dam
•*Word Family:* **hydro-electricity** *noun*

hydrofoil (*say* **high**-dra-foil) *noun*
a boat with ski-like parts attached, that support the hull above the water when the boat has reached a certain speed

hydrogen (*say* **high**-dra-jen) *noun*
a very light gas with no colour, taste or smell

hydroponics (*say* high-dra-**pon**-iks) *noun*
the growing of plants in water rather than soil

hyena (*say* high-**ee**-na) *noun*
a dog-like mammal with powerful jaws and short hind legs, that eats the remains of dead animals

hygiene (*say* **high**-jeen) *noun*
the cleanliness you need to keep healthy: *personal hygiene*
•*Word Family:* **hygienic** *adjective* **hygienically** *adverb*

hymn (*say* him) *noun*
a song of praise, especially one dedicated to God
•*Word Family:* **hymnal** *noun* a hymn book

hyperactive (*say* high-pa-**ak**-tiv) *adjective*
so restless, active and full of energy that you cannot relax: *hyperactive children*
•*Word Family:* **hyperactivity** *noun*

hypertension (*say* high-per-**ten**-shon) *noun*
an abnormally high blood pressure

hyphen (*say* **high**-fun) *noun*
a punctuation mark (-), used to join words or parts of words, as in "old-fashioned"
•*Word Family:* **hyphenate** *verb* to join words with a hyphen **hyphenation** *noun*

hypnosis (*say* hip-**no**-sis) *noun*
a sleep-like state that someone puts you into so they can affect the things you think and do
•*Word Family:* **hypnotic** *adjective* **hypnotism** *noun* **hypnotist** *noun* **hypnotize** or **hypnotise** *verb*
•*Word Origins:* from a Greek word meaning "sleep"

hypochondriac (*say* high-pa-**kon**-dree-ak) *noun*
someone who worries all the time about being ill or getting ill
•*Word Family:* **hypochondria** *noun*

hypocrite (*say* **hip**-a-krit) *noun*
someone who pretends to be much better or nicer than they really are
•*Word Family:* **hypocrisy** *noun* **hypocritical** *adjective*

hypodermic (*say* high-pa-**der**-mik) *adjective*
1 injecting under the skin: *a hypodermic syringe*
hypodermic *noun*
2 a hypodermic syringe or needle

hypotenuse (*say* high-**pot**-en-use) *noun*
the longest side, opposite the right angle, of a right-angled triangle

hypothermia (*say* high-po-**ther**-mee-a) *noun*
a dangerous condition that you can get when you are very cold, in which the temperature of your body falls below normal

hypothesis (*say* high-**poth**-a-sis) *noun*
an idea or theory which is used as a basis or starting point for a discussion or scientific experiment
•*Word Family:* the plural is **hypotheses** (*say* high-**poth**-a-seez) □ **hypothetical** (*say* high-per-**thet**-ic-cal) *adjective* imagined or assumed rather than real

hysterical (*say* his-per-**ter**-ik-al) *adjective*
1 extremely excited, upset or emotional 2 very funny: *hysterical jokes*
•*Word Family:* **hysterics** *plural noun* a hysterical outburst **hysteria** (*say* hiss-**teer**-ee-a)*noun* **hysterically** *adverb*

A B C D E F G H I J K L M N O P Q R S T U V W X Y Z

Ii

I *pronoun*
the word that the speaker of a sentence uses to refer to himself or herself: *I have a new book.*
•***Word Family:*** other singular forms are **my, mine, me** and the plural forms are **we, our, ours, us**

ibis (*say* **eye**-bis) *noun*
a large wading bird related to the heron
•***Word Family:*** the plural is **ibises**

ice *noun*
1 frozen water 2 **on thin ice** in a risky or uncertain position
ice *verb*
3 to freeze or become covered with ice: *The lake has iced over.* 4 to coat a cake with icing
•***Word Family:*** **icy** *adjective* (**icier, iciest**)

iceberg *noun*
a large mass of ice floating at sea, broken off from a glacier or an icecap
•***Word Origins:*** from Old Dutch words meaning "ice mountain"

ice-cream *noun*
a sweet, frozen food, made from cream, flavouring, eggs and sugar

icicle (*rhymes with* bicycle) *noun*
a long pointed piece of ice formed when dripping water freezes

icon (*say* **eye**-kon) *noun*
1 a picture of a religious subject 2 a small symbol or picture on a computer screen that you click on to do such things as open a file or carry out a command
•***Word Family:*** definition 1 is also spelt **ikon**

idea (*say* eye-**deer**) *noun*
a thought, belief or plan in your mind

ideal (*say* eye-**deel**) *adjective*
1 best, perfect or most suitable: *an ideal place for a picnic*
ideal *noun*
2 something or someone you copy or try to be like because you admire them so much: *She's my ideal of an artist.* 3 **ideals** the values or principles that you live your life by: *He can't live up to her ideals.*
•***Word Family:*** **ideally** *adverb* perfectly **idealism** *noun*

identical (*say* eye-**den**-ti-kal) *adjective*
exactly equal or the same: *identical twins*
•***Word Family:*** **identically** *adverb*

identify (*say* eye-**den**-ti-fie) *verb*
1 to recognize a particular thing or person: *He identified the ring as his mother's.* 2 **identify with** to think you feel the same way as someone else in a particular situation
•***Word Family:*** other forms are **identifies, identified, identifying** □ **identifiable** *adjective* **identification** *noun*

identity (*say* eye-**den**-ti-tee) *noun*
who you are: *I had to show my passport to prove my identity.*
•***Word Family:*** the plural is **identities**
•***Word Origins:*** from a Latin word meaning "the same"

idiom (*say* **id**-ee-um) *noun*
a phrase or expression whose meaning is different from that of the actual words used, as in: *He laughed his head off* for *He laughed a lot*
•***Word Family:*** **idiomatic** *adjective* **idiomatical** *adjective* **idiomatically** *adverb*

idiot *noun*
1 a very silly or foolish person 2 someone lacking the mental ability to learn things normally
•***Word Family:*** **idiotic** *adjective* **idiotically** *adverb*

idle (*say* **eye**-del) *adjective*
1 not busy, working or in use: *idle workers / idle machines* 2 useless: *idle gossip*
•***Word Family:*** **idler** *noun* an idle person **idleness** *noun* **idly** *adverb*

idol (*say* **eye**-dol) *noun*
1 a statue, picture, or image worshipped as a god 2 someone who other people greatly admire or adore: *a pop idol*
•***Word Family:*** **idolatry** *noun* **idolize** or **idolise** *verb*

Id-ul-Fitr *noun*
another spelling for **Eid-ul-fitr**

i.e. *abbreviation*
short for the Latin words id est *meaning* "that is": *Pack all the equipment you'll need for camping, i.e. tent, sleeping bag and torch.*

if *conjunction*
1 on condition that: *I'll be on time if you drive me.* 2 whether: *I'm not sure if I can come.*

igloo *noun*
a small dome-shaped house of snow blocks, built by the Inuit (once called Eskimos)

igneous (*say* **ig**-nee-us) *adjective*
formed from lava: *igneous rock*

ignite *verb*
to set something alight or on fire

ignition (*say* ig-**nish**-on) *noun*
1 setting something alight 2 the system for producing the electric sparks that start the fuel burning in a car engine

ignorant (*say* **ig**-na-runt) *adjective*
1 knowing little or nothing about something: *I'm completely ignorant of other languages.* 2 rude because of a lack of understanding or respect: *ignorant behaviour*
•***Word Family:*** **ignorance** *noun* **ignorantly** *adverb*

ignore *verb*
to pay no attention to a particular person or thing: *to ignore a person / to ignore a question*

iguana (*say* i-**gwah**-na) *noun*
a large tropical lizard found mainly in South America

ill *adjective*
1 sick 2 bad: *ill luck*
ill *noun*
3 something bad or unpleasant: *the ills of city life*
ill *adverb*
4 in a bad way: *to treat somebody ill*

illegal (*say* i-**lee**-gal) *adjective*
not allowed by law
•***Word Family:*** **illegality** *noun* **illegally** *adverb*

illegible (*say* i-**lej**-i-bul) *adjective*
not able to be read: *illegible handwriting*
•***Word Family:*** **illegibility** *noun* **illegibly** *adverb*

illegitimate (*say* il-a-**jit**-a-mit) *adjective*
1 not legal or allowed 2 born to parents who are not married: *illegitimate children*
•***Word Family:*** **illegitimacy** *noun* **illegitimately** *adverb*

illicit (*say* i-**lis**-it) *adjective*
not legal or permitted: *illicit gambling*

illiterate (*say* i-**lit**-a-rit) *adjective*
not able to read and write
•***Word Family:*** **illiteracy** *noun*

illuminate (*say* i-**loo**-ma-nate) *verb*
1 to light up a thing or place, especially using electricity 2 to make something clear, often by giving examples 3 to decorate a book or page the way monks in the Middle Ages used to
•***Word Family:*** **illuminated** *adjective: an illuminated manuscript* **illumination** *noun*

illusion (*say* i-**loo**-zhon) *noun*
1 a false belief: *an illusion of greatness*
2 something you think you see that does not really exist: *an optical illusion*

illustrate (*say* **il**-a-strate) *verb*
1 to add pictures or drawings to a story or a book: *to illustrate a book / a beautifully illustrated copy of "Peter Pan"* 2 to make something clear or explain it by using examples: *to illustrate an argument*
•***Word Family:*** **illustrator** *noun* an artist who illustrates books **illustration** *noun* **illustrative** *adjective*

illustrious (*say* i-**lus**-tree-us) *adjective*
very famous and respected: *an illustrious explorer*

image (*say* **im**-ij) *noun*
1 a picture, photograph or statue of someone or something: *images of the Queen / images of war*
2 an exact copy or likeness: *He's the image of his mother.* 3 the way a person appears to others: *The Prime Minister's public image has improved.*
4 a reflection formed by a lens or mirror

imagination (*say* im-aj-in-**ay**-shon) *noun*
the ability to form an image in your mind or to think of new ideas: *a vivid imagination*
•***Word Family:*** **imaginative** *adjective* able to think of new things or ideas easily

imagine (*say* i-**maj**-in) *adjective*
1 to form an image of something in your mind: *to imagine what job you'll do* 2 to suppose, or guess: *I can't imagine what he's up to.*
•***Word Family:*** **imaginary** *adjective* existing only in your mind

imam (*say* im-**am**) *noun*
a Muslim religious leader

imbecile (*say* **im**-ba-seel) *noun*
someone who is really stupid

imitate (*say* **im**-i-tate) *verb*
to copy someone or something: *to imitate a bird call*
•***Word Family:*** **imitation** *noun* **imitator** *noun*

immaculate (*say* i-**mak**-yoo-lit) *adjective*
perfectly clean or spotless
•***Word Family:*** **immaculately** *adverb*

immature (*say* im-a-**tyoor**) *adjective*
1 not fully grown or developed: *an immature plant* 2 acting in a childish way: *She's very immature sometimes.*
•***Word Family:*** **immaturity** *noun*

immediate (*say* i-**mee**-dee-it) *adjective*
done or happening without delay: *an immediate answer*
•***Word Family:*** **immediately** *adverb* at once **immediacy** *noun*

immense *adjective*
very large, or great: *an immense dog / immense pleasure*
•***Word Family:*** **immensely** *adverb* **immensity** *noun*

immerse (*say* im-**erse**) *verb*
to put something in or under a liquid: *to immerse lettuce leaves in water*
• ***Word Family:*** **immersion** *noun*

immigrate (*say* **im**-i-grate) *verb*
to enter and settle in a new country or region
• ***Word Family:*** **immigrant** *noun* someone who immigrates **immigration** *noun*

imminent (*say* **im**-i-nent) *adjective*
likely to happen soon: *an imminent arrival*
• ***Word Family:*** **imminence** *noun* **imminently** *adverb*

immoral (*say* i-**mo**-ral) *adjective*
wicked or not right: *an immoral act*
• ***Word Family:*** **immorality** *noun* **immorally** *adverb*

immortal (*say* i-**mor**-tal) *adjective*
lasting or living forever: *immortal fame / your immortal soul*
• ***Word Family:*** **immortality** *noun* **immortally** *adverb*

immune (*say* i-**myoon**) *adjective*
protected or safe, especially from a disease
• ***Word Family:*** **immunize** or **immunise** *verb* to make people or animals immune **immunization** *noun* **immunity** *noun*

imp *noun*
1 an elf 2 a mischievous or naughty child
• ***Word Family:*** **impish** *adjective* **impishly** *adverb*

impact *noun*
1 the striking of one thing against another: *The impact of the blow knocked him over.* 2 effect: *The news had little impact on us.*

impair *verb*
to spoil something or make it worse: *Pimples impaired her appearance.*
• ***Word Family:*** **impairment** *noun*

impartial *adjective*
fair or unwilling to take sides: *an impartial judge*
• ***Word Family:*** **impartiality** *noun* **impartially** *adverb*

impassive *adjective*
not showing emotion: *an impassive face*
• ***Word Family:*** **impassively** *adverb* **impassivity** *noun*

impatient (*say* im-**pay**-shent) *adjective*
unable to wait without getting annoyed: *impatient because of the delay*
• ***Word Family:*** **impatience** *noun* **impatiently** *adverb*

impeccable (*say* im-**pek**-a-bul) *adjective*
without faults: *impeccable behaviour*
• ***Word Family:*** **impeccably** *adverb*

impede *verb*
to obstruct something or someone or slow them down: *The parade impeded the flow of traffic.*
• ***Word Family:*** **impediment** *noun*

imperative (*say* im-**pe**-ra-tiv) *adjective*
essential: *It's imperative that we get there on time.*

imperceptible (*say* im-per-**sep**-tib-ul) *adjective*
extremely difficult to see or to notice: *imperceptible changes in the climate*

imperfect *adjective*
not perfect or complete
• ***Word Family:*** **imperfection** *noun* **imperfectly** *adverb*

imperial (*say* im-**pear**-i-al) *adjective*
1 of an empire or its ruler: *imperial Rome* 2 of the system of weights and measures such as inches, ounces or pints, used in the United Kingdom before the metric system
• ***Word Family:*** **imperialism** *noun* the rule of one country by another **imperious** *adjective* bossy

impersonal (*say* im-**per**-sa-nal) *adjective*
not expressing your personal feelings: *She gave me a cold impersonal stare.*
• ***Word Family:*** **impersonally** *adverb*

impersonate (*say* im-**per**-sa-nate) *verb*
to imitate or pretend to be a particular person: *The robber impersonated a police officer.*
• ***Word Family:*** **impersonator** *noun* someone, especially an actor, who impersonates others **impersonation** *noun*

impertinent (*say* im-**per**-ti-nant) *adjective*
rude or impudent: *an impertinent remark*
• ***Word Family:*** **impertinence** *noun* **impertinently** *adverb*

impetuous (*say* im-**pet**-yew-us) *adjective*
behaving in a hasty or rash way
• ***Word Family:*** **impetuosity** *noun* **impetuously** *adverb*

impetus (*say* **im**-pe-tus) *noun*
1 the energy or force of something that is moving 2 a stimulus or impulse: *We need an impetus to work harder.*
• ***Word Family:*** the plural is **impetuses**

implant (*say* im-**plant**) *verb*
1 to plant or fix something inside somewhere: *to implant an image in your mind*
implant (*say* **im**-plahnt) *noun*
2 something which is put inside your body to help it work properly or look better: *a breast implant*
• ***Word Family:*** **implantation** *noun*

implement (*say* **im**-pla-munt) *noun*
1 a tool

implement (*say* **im**-ple-ment) *verb*
2 to put something into use or carry it out: *to implement a new law*
•***Word Family:*** **implementation** *noun*

implicit (*say* im-**plis**-it) *adjective*
1 implied or suggested but not actually expressed: *implicit disapproval* 2 absolute or unquestioning: *to have an implicit belief in all you are taught*
•***Word Family:*** **implicitly** *adverb*

implore *verb*
to beg someone to do something

imply (*say* im-**ply**) *verb*
to suggest a feeling or idea without saying anything: *Your sighs imply that you are unhappy.*
•***Word Family:*** other forms are **implies, implied, implying** □ **implication** *noun*

import (*say* im-**port**) *verb*
1 to bring something in from a foreign country: *to import cars from Japan*
import (*say* **im**-port) *noun*
2 something that is imported

important (*say* im-**por**-tant) *adjective*
1 very valuable, significant or effective: *an important role in the play* 2 having great power or influence: *an important leader*
•***Word Family:*** **importance** *noun* **importantly** *adverb*

impose *verb*
1 to inflict something or force it to happen officially: *The judge imposed a heavy fine on the vandals.* 2 to take advantage of someone: *to impose on someone's hospitality*
•***Word Family:*** **imposition** *noun*

imposing *adjective*
impressive: *an impressive statue / an imposing speaker*

impossible *adjective*
1 not able to be believed, be done or happen: *an impossible tale* 2 annoying: *What an impossible person!*
•***Word Family:*** **impossibility** *noun* **impossibly** *adverb*

impostor (*say* im-**pos**-ta) *noun*
someone who deceives others by pretending to be someone else

impotent (*say* **im**-pa-tent) *adjective*
having no strength or power to act: *impotent in the face of danger*
•***Word Family:*** **impotence** *noun* **impotently** *adverb*

impoverish (*say* im-**pov**-a-rish) *verb*
to make poor: *The family was impoverished by years of medical bills.*
•***Word Family:*** **impoverishment** *noun*

impress (*say* im-**press**) *verb*
1 to make someone think well of you: *to be impressed by their fabulous singing* 2 to make someone understand something: *Try to impress on her the tragic effect of her actions*

impression (*say* im-**presh**-on) *noun*
1 a mark or shape made by pressing or stamping: *The dentist made a wax impression of her teeth.* 2 an effect made on your mind or feelings: *His rudeness creates a bad impression.* 3 an imitation: *to do impressions of famous people*
•***Word Family:*** **impressionable** *adjective* easily affected because of being young or naive

impressive *adjective*
having a strong and favourable effect: *an impressive piece of work*
•***Word Family:*** **impressively** *adverb*

imprint (*say* **im**-print) *noun*
1 a mark made by pressing or stamping something on something else
imprint (*say* im-**print**) *verb*
2 to fix something somewhere firmly: *to imprint something in your memory*

imprison *verb*
to put someone in prison
•***Word Family:*** **imprisonment** *noun*

improbable *adjective*
unlikely or doubtful

impromptu (*say* im-**promp**-tew) *adjective or adverb*
done or made without any preparation or practice: *an impromptu speech*
•***Word Origins:*** from a Latin word meaning "in readiness"

improper *adjective*
1 rude or indecent: *improper behaviour* 2 not right or fitting: *an improper use of government money*

improve (*say* im-**proov**) *verb*
to make or become better
•***Word Family:*** **improvement** *noun*

improvise (*say* **im**-pra-vize) *verb*
1 to create something quickly with whatever is available: *to improvise a costume from old clothes* 2 to invent and perform as you go along: *The guitarist improvised between the verses of the song.*
•***Word Family:*** **improvisation** *noun* **improviser** *noun*

impulse *noun*
a sudden urge or desire: *He had an impulse to dance on the sand. / to act on impulse*
•***Word Family:*** **impulsive** *adjective* **impulsively** *adverb*

in *preposition*
1 inside: *They're in school.* 2 at: *a house in the*

country 3 within: *in the record industry / Come in the morning.*
in *adjective*
4 available or in season: *When are artichokes in?* 5 most fashionable or up-to-date

inability *noun*
being unable to do something: *his inability to do what he was told*

inaccessible *adjective*
unable to be reached: *In winter the village is inaccessible for road vehicles.*
•**Word Family: inaccessibility** *noun*

inane *adjective*
silly or senseless: *an inane comment*
•**Word Family: inanity** *noun* **(inanities) inanely** *adverb*

inanimate (*say* in-**an**-a-mit) *adjective*
not alive: *Chairs are inanimate objects.*

inaudible (*say* in-**aw**-da-bul) *adjective*
not able to be heard
•**Word Family: inaudibly** *adverb*

inauguration (*say* in-aw-gya-**ray**-shon) *noun*
a formal or official introduction or opening ceremony: *Everyone watched the inauguration of the new president.*
•**Word Family: inaugural** *adjective* **inaugurate** *verb*

incandescent (*say* in-kan-**des**-ent) *adjective*
giving out light when it is heated: *an incandescent light bulb*
•**Word Family: incandescence** *noun*

incapacitate (*say* in-ka-**pas**-a-tate) *verb*
to take away someone's strength, power or ability: *The car accident incapacitated him for ages.*
•**Word Family: incapacitation** *noun*

incarcerate (*say* in-**kar**-sa-rate) *verb*
to shut in or confine: *to incarcerate a prisoner in a cell*
•**Word Family: incarceration** *noun*

incense (1) (*say* **in**-sense) *noun*
a substance that gives a pleasant smell when burnt, often used in religious ceremonies

incense (2) (*say* in-**sense**) *verb*
to enrage someone or make them angry

incentive *noun*
something which makes you want to do something or work harder

incessant (*say* in-**ses**-unt) *adjective*
going on and on: *the incessant racket of a burglar alarm*
•**Word Family: incessantly** *adverb*

incest (*say* **in**-sest) *noun*
sexual intercourse between people who are so closely related that the law forbids them to marry: *incest between a brother and sister*
•**Word Family: incestuous** *adjective*

inch *noun*
1 an old-fashioned unit of length equal to one-twelfth of a foot or about 2.54 centimetres 2 a very small distance or amount: *She escaped death by inches.*
inch *verb*
3 to move very slowly: *The traffic inched forwards.*
•**Word Family:** the plural of the noun is **inches** □ other verb forms are **inches, inched, inching**

incident (*say* **in**-si-dent) *noun*
an event or occurrence: *a nasty incident on the bus*
•**Word Family: incidental** *adjective* coinciding with something more important **incidentally** *adverb* by the way

incinerate (*say* in-**sin**-a-rate) *verb*
to destroy something by burning it
•**Word Family: incinerator** *noun* a container or device for burning rubbish **incineration** *noun*

incision (*say* in-**sizh**-on) *noun*
a cut or gash made with a sharp instrument such as a scalpel, for example during an operation

incisive (*say* in-**sigh**-siv) *adjective*
penetrating or keen: *incisive comments on a play*
•**Word Family: incisively** *adverb*

incisor (*say* in-**sigh**-za) *noun*
one of the sharp flat teeth at the front of your mouth, for cutting and biting food

incite (*say* in-**site**) *verb*
to stir up or provoke someone to action: *to incite a mob to riot*
•**Word Family: incitement** *noun*

incline (*say* in-**kline**) *verb*
1 to bend or lower something: *The road inclines to the left. / to incline your head* 2 to have a tendency: *I'm inclined to be lazy.*
incline (*say* **in**-kline) *noun*
3 a slope
•**Word Family: inclination** *noun* a liking: *an inclination to talk too much*

include *verb*
to contain or consider something or someone as part of a group or whole: *Don't forget to include her on the invitation list.*
•**Word Family: inclusion** *noun* **inclusive** *adjective* **inclusively** *adverb*

incognito (*say* in-kog-**nee**-toh) *adverb*
with your name, identity or appearance altered so nobody will recognize you: *to travel incognito*
•**Word Origins:** from a Latin word meaning "unknown"

income (*say* **in**-kum) *noun*
all the money you earn regularly in wages or investments, usually in a year
• ***Word Family:*** **income tax** *noun* the tax the government takes from your income each year

incompatible (*say* in-com-**pat**-ib-ull) *adjective*
unable to work together or live together: *She and I are incompatible. / incompatible machine parts*
• ***Word Family:*** **incompatibility** *noun*

incompetent *adjective*
unable to do a job properly: *an incompetent manager*
• ***Word Family:*** **incompetence** *noun*

incomprehensible (*say* in-con-pre-**hen**-sib-ull) *adjective*
unable to be understood

incongruous (*say* in-**kon**-grew-us) *adjective*
out of place or not appropriate: *Your sunglasses look incongruous in church.*
• ***Word Family:*** **incongruity** *noun* **incongruously** *adverb*

inconsiderate (*say* in-con-**sid**-er-ut) *adjective*
not at all considerate or thoughtful: *an inconsiderate place to park*

inconspicuous (*say* in-con-**spic**-you-us) *adjective*
not easily noticed, or easy to miss: *The bomb was left in an inconspicuous-looking van.*
• ***Word Family:*** **inconspicuously** *adverb*

incorporate (*say* in-**kor**-pa-rate) *verb*
to take in or include something as part of a whole: *to incorporate a new chapter into the book*
• ***Word Family:*** **incorporation** *noun*

incorrigible (*say* in-**ko**-rij-a-bul) *adjective*
unable to change or reform: *an incorrigible liar*
• ***Word Family:*** **incorrigibly** *adverb*

increase (*say* in-**kreece**) *verb*
1 to make or become greater or larger: *to increase your pocket money / The whale population is gradually increasing.*
increase (*say* **in**-kreece) *noun*
2 the amount of growth or addition: *an increase in house prices*
• ***Word Family:*** **increasingly** *adverb* more and more

incredible (*say* in-**kred**-a-bul) *adjective*
amazing or hard to believe: *What an incredible story!*
• ***Word Family:*** **incredibility** *noun* **incredibly** *adverb*

incredulous (*say* in-**kred**-ya-lus) *adjective*
unable to believe something: *I'm incredulous that you didn't even stop to help her.*
• ***Word Family:*** **incredulity** *noun* **incredulously** *adverb*

incubate (*say* **in**-kew-bate) *verb*
to hatch eggs by keeping them warm
• ***Word Family:*** **incubation** *noun*

incubator (*say* **in**-kew-bate-er) *noun*
1 a device for incubating eggs 2 a hospital machine in which babies who are born too early can be kept warm until they are stronger

incur (*say* in-**ker**) *verb*
to bring something upon yourself, usually something unpleasant: *to incur a fine*
• ***Word Family:*** other forms are **incurs, incurred, incurring**

indecent (*say* in-**dee**-sunt) *adjective*
offensive or not in good taste: *indecent language*
• ***Word Family:*** **indecently** *adverb*

indeed *adverb*
truly or really: *Indeed he was there. / She's very cross indeed.*

indelible (*say* in-**del**-a-bul) *adjective*
not able to be rubbed out or removed: *an indelible stain*
• ***Word Family:*** **indelibly** *adverb*

indent (*say* in-**dent**) *verb*
1 to set a new paragraph slightly further in or back from the margin 2 to form deep notches or recesses in something
• ***Word Family:*** **indentation** *noun*

independent (*say* in-di-**pen**-dent) *adjective*
1 able to make your own decisions 2 able to stand alone without help from others: *The colony fought to become independent of foreign control.*
independent *noun*
3 someone or something that is independent, especially a political candidate who does not belong to any political party
• ***Word Family:*** **independence** *noun* **independently** *adverb*

index *noun*
1 an alphabetical list of names, subjects or places at the end of a book, on cards or on computer in a library and so on
index *verb*
2 to give a book an index or put things into an index
• ***Word Family:*** the plural is **indexes** or **indices**
• ***Word Origins:*** from a Latin word meaning "forefinger" or "sign"

index finger *noun*
another name for your **forefinger**

indicate (*say* **in**-di-kate) *verb*
1 to show something or point it out: *The signpost indicates which street this is.* 2 to be a

A B C D E F G H I J K L M N O P Q R S T U V W X Y Z

sign of something: *His feeble voice indicates that he is unwell.*
•***Word Family:*** **indicative** *adjective* **indication** *noun*

indicator (*say* **in**-di-kay-ter) *noun*
something that shows or gives information, such as a flashing light used to show that a car is turning or changing lanes

indifferent *adjective*
1 having no interest in or care for: *to be indifferent to their suffering* 2 neither good nor bad: *an indifferent performance*
•***Word Family:*** **indifference** *noun* **indifferently** *adverb*

indigenous (*say* in-**dij**-a-nus) *adjective*
native to a particular place: *Wallabies are indigenous to Australia.*

indigestion (*say* in-da-**jes**-chen) *noun*
pain or discomfort in your stomach caused by difficulty in digesting food properly
•***Word Family:*** **indigestible** *adjective* unable to be digested

indignant (*say* in-**dig**-nant) *adjective*
angry at something you think is unfair
•***Word Family:*** **indignation** *noun* **indignantly** *adverb*

indignity (*say* in-**dig**-na-tee) *noun*
treatment that humiliates you or damages your self-respect: *Prisoners of war suffered many indignities.*
•***Word Family:*** the plural is **indignities**

indigo (*say* **in**-dig-o) *noun*
1 dark, purplish-blue colour 2 blue dye once extracted from plants, but now made artificially
indigo *adjective*
3 dark blue

indispensable *adjective*
absolutely essential: *Oxygen is indispensable to human life.*
•***Word Family:*** **indispensably** *adverb*

indisposed *adjective*
slightly sick or ill: *indisposed with a fever*
•***Word Family:*** **indisposition** *noun*

individual (*say* in-da-**vid**-yew-al) *adjective*
1 single or separate: *the individual members of a group* 2 for one person: *an individual portion of pizza*
individual *noun*
3 a single person or thing
•***Word Family:*** **individuality** *noun* **individually** *adverb*

indoctrinate *verb*
to fill someone's mind with a set of beliefs so that it is accepted as true
•***Word Family:*** **indoctrination** *noun*

induce (*say* in-**dewce**) *verb*
1 to persuade or influence someone to do something: *She induced me to stay another hour.* 2 to produce or cause something: *Being exposed to too much sun induces skin cancer.*
•***Word Family:*** **inducement** *noun*

indulge (*say* in-**dulj**) *verb*
to satisfy a particular wish or desire: *She likes to indulge her taste for ghost stories. / He always indulges his children's wishes.*
•***Word Family:*** **indulgence** *noun* **indulgent** *adjective* **indulgently** *adverb*

industrious (*say* in-**dus**-tree-us) *adjective*
hard-working: *an industrious worker*
•***Word Family:*** **industriously** *adverb*

industry (*say* **in**-dus-tree) *noun*
1 the production or manufacturing of goods: *a worldwide decline of industry* 2 a particular type of manufacturing or large-scale business: *the coal industry / the film industry* 3 hard work: *His quick success was due to his industry.*
•***Word Family:*** the plural is **industries** □ **industrial** *adjective* **industrially** *adverb* **industrialist** *noun*

inept *adjective*
awkward or without skill: *an inept remark / an inept manager*
•***Word Family:*** **ineptitude** *noun* **ineptly** *adverb* **ineptness** *noun*

inequality (*say* in-eek-**wal**-it-ee) *noun*
a lack of equality and fairness especially between different groups in society

inert (*say* in-**ert**) *adjective*
1 seeming dead, or not moving: *We covered the inert body with a blanket.* 2 not reacting with other substances: *an inert gas, such as neon*

inertia (*say* in-**er**-sha) *noun*
1 the way the speed an object is travelling remains the same unless the object is stopped by something: *The forward movement of people in a car when it stops suddenly is due to inertia.* 2 inactivity or sluggishness: *A feeling of inertia hit us after our meal.*

inevitable (*say* in-**ev**-it-a-bul) *adjective*
not able to be avoided or prevented: *an inevitable outcome*
•***Word Family:*** **inevitability** *noun* **inevitably** *adverb*

inexhaustible (*say* in-ex-**or**-stib-ull) *adjective*
unable to be used up or finished: *An inexhaustible supply of energy for industry does not exist.*

infallible *adjective*
never mistaken or wrong: *an infallible judge of character*
•***Word Family:*** **infallibility** *noun* **infallibly** *adverb*

infamous (*say* **in**-fa-mus) *adjective*
having a very bad reputation: *an infamous trouble-maker*
• ***Word Family:*** **infamously** *adverb* **infamy** *noun*

infant (*say* **in**-fant) *noun*
1 a baby or young child
infant *adjective*
2 to do with young children: *an infant school*
• ***Word Family:*** **infancy** *noun* the time when you are an infant **infantile** *adjective* babyish

infantry (*say* **in**-fan-tree) *noun*
the soldiers in an army who fight on foot with light weapons

infatuated (*say* in-**fat**-choo-ayt-ed) *adjective*
blinded with foolish love
• ***Word Family:*** **infatuate** *verb* **infatuation** *noun*

infect (*say* in-**fekt**) *verb*
to spread a disease or germs to other people, or to a part of your body: *He infected us all with the flu. / to infect a cut*
• ***Word Family:*** **infection** *noun* **infectious** *adjective*

infer (*say* in-**fer**) *verb*
to come to an opinion about something by considering the facts you know: *I infer from your rude comments that you don't like me.*
• ***Word Family:*** other forms are **infers, inferred, inferring** □ **inference** *noun* something that you infer

inferior (*say* in-**fear**-ree-a) *adjective*
1 of poor quality: *an inferior brand of peas* 2 lower in importance or rank: *an inferior crew member*
inferior *noun*
3 an inferior person in rank or importance: *He's your inferior in terms of experience.*
• ***Word Family:*** **inferiority** *noun*

infernal *adjective*
1 to do with hell 2 unpleasant and annoying: *Stop that infernal row!*

inferno (*say* in-**fer**-no) *noun*
a raging fire
• ***Word Family:*** the plural is **infernos**

infest *verb*
to spread over a place in unpleasantly large numbers: *Rats infested the city.*
• ***Word Family:*** **infestation** *noun*

infidel (*say* **in**-fa-del) *noun*
someone who does not believe in any religion, once used by Christians and Moslems when referring to each other

infiltrate *verb*
to enter into a place or organization secretly or in disguise: *The police spy infiltrated the drug ring.*
• ***Word Family:*** **infiltration** *noun* **infiltrator** *noun*

infinite (*say* **in**-fa-nit) *adjective*
having no boundaries or limits
• ***Word Family:*** **infinitely** *adverb* **infinity** *noun*

infinitive (*say* in-**fin**-a-tiv) *noun*
the basic form of a verb you use after the word "to" or after another verb, such as "go" in *She wants to go with me* and *Do you dare go?*

infirmary (*say* in-**firm**-a-ree) *noun*
a name for some hospitals
• ***Word Family:*** the plural is **infirmaries** □ **infirm** *adjective* weak

inflame *verb*
1 to make part of your body red or swollen: *The strong chlorine in the pool inflamed her eyes.* 2 to make people angry: *His passionate speech inflamed the crowd even more.*
• ***Word Family:*** **inflammatory** *adjective*

inflammable *adjective*
catching fire easily: *inflammable material*

inflammation (*say* in-fla-**may**-shon) *noun*
a painful redness on swelling of your body caused by an injury or infection

inflate *verb*
1 to fill or expand something with a gas, such as air: *to inflate a balloon / The air bed inflated.* 2 to make the price of something rise sharply: *to inflate the cost of petrol*
• ***Word Family:*** **inflatable** *adjective*

inflation *noun*
a general rise in prices and wages

inflict *verb*
to make someone suffer something unpleasant: *to inflict a wound / to inflict a punishment*
• ***Word Family:*** **infliction** *noun*

influence (*say* **in**-floo-ence) *noun*
1 the power to affect people or situations: *He's a good influence on me.*
influence *verb*
2 to have an effect on something or someone: *to influence your taste in music*
• ***Word Family:*** **influential** *adjective*

influenza (*say* in-floo-**en**-za) *noun*
an illness with symptoms such as aching muscles, fever, sneezing and sore eyes, caused by a virus

inform *verb*
to tell someone something or give them information: *Did you inform him that you were sick?*
• ***Word Family:*** **informant** *noun* someone who informs you of things **informer** *noun* someone who informs on others, often to the police **informative** *adjective* giving you useful information

A B C D E F G H I J K L M N O P Q R S T U V W X Y Z

informal *adjective*
casual or everyday: *informal language / informal clothes*
• ***Word Family:*** **informality** *noun*

information (*say* in-fa-**may**-shon) *noun*
knowledge, facts or news

information technology *noun*
the use of computers to store, organize and give out all kinds of information

infotainment *noun*
information intended to entertain as well as inform or teach you
• ***Word Origins:*** a blend of *information* and enter*tainment*

infra-red *noun*
1 an invisible part of the spectrum below red and with a longer wavelength than it
infra-red *adjective*
2 using infra-red radiation: *an infra-red camera*

infringe *verb*
to disobey, break or ignore a rule
• ***Word Family:*** **infringement** *noun*

infuriate (*say* in-**few**-ree-ate) *verb*
to make someone very angry
• ***Word Family:*** **infuriating** *adjective* **infuriatingly** *adverb* **infuriation** *noun*

infuse (*say* in-**fewz**) *verb*
to soak in hot water to release the flavour, smell or oils: *to infuse herbs*

ingenious (*say* in-**jee**-nee-us) *adjective*
1 cleverly or skilfully made: *an ingenious toy*
2 clever at inventing things
• ***Word Family:*** **ingeniously** *adverb* **ingenuity** *noun*

ingot (*say* **ing**-get) *noun*
a bar of metal, usually gold or silver, that has set in a mould

ingredient (*say* in-**gree**-dee-ent) *noun*
one of the parts of a mixture: *the ingredients of a cake*

inhabit (*say* in-**hab**-it) *verb*
to live in a particular place or area: *The early settlers inhabited inland areas.*
• ***Word Family:*** **inhabitable** *adjective* **inhabitant** *noun*

inhale *verb*
to breathe in
• ***Word Family:*** **inhaler** *noun* a device used to puff medicine into your mouth to help you breathe **inhalant** *noun* a medicine you inhale **inhalation** *noun*

inherit (*say* in-**he**-rit) *verb*
1 to receive something from someone who has died: *to inherit land* 2 to receive a family characteristic from your parents: *to inherit your father's big ears*
• ***Word Family:*** **inheritance** *noun* something you inherit

inhibited *adjective*
finding it difficult to show your feelings
• ***Word Family:*** **inhibit** *verb* **inhibition** *noun*

inhospitable *adjective*
1 unfriendly to strangers: *an inhospitable village*
2 without comfort or shelter: *an inhospitable area of desert*

inhuman *adjective*
extremely cruel or uncaring

iniquity (*say* in-**ik**-wa-tee) *noun*
wickedness: *He was feared for his iniquity.*
• ***Word Family:*** the plural is **iniquities** □ **iniquitous** *adjective*

initial (*say* in-**ish**-al) *adjective*
1 happening at the beginning: *our initial meeting*
initial *noun*
2 the first letter of a name or word
initial *verb*
3 to mark or sign something with your initials
• ***Word Family:*** other verb forms are **initials, initialled, initialling** □ **initially** *adverb*

initiate (*say* in-**ish**-ee-ate) *verb*
1 to begin or establish something: *to initiate peace talks between two countries* 2 to admit someone into a club, new school and so on, by a special ceremony
• ***Word Family:*** **initiation** *noun*

initiative (*say* in-**ish**-ee-a-tiv) *noun*
1 the ability to do things by yourself 2 a first act or step: *Take the initiative and start the dancing.* 3 a new scheme or project: *a government initiative to create jobs*

inject *verb*
to put a fluid into someone using a syringe: *The nurse injected me with a drug to make me sleep.*
• ***Word Family:*** **injection** *verb*

injure (*say* **in**-jer) *verb*
to hurt or harm someone: *to injure your leg / to injure someone's good name*
• ***Word Family:*** **injury** *noun* (**injuries**) **injured** *adjective* **injurious** *adjective*

injustice *noun*
behaviour or treatment which is not just: *to fight intolerance and injustice / to do someone an injustice*

ink *noun*
a strongly coloured liquid used for writing and printing
• ***Word Family:*** **inky** *adjective* (**inkier, inkiest**)

inkling *noun*
a hint or slight suggestion: *I had no inkling that there was a surprise party.*

inland *adjective*
1 situated in the middle part of a country away from the border or coast: *an inland sea*
inland *adverb*
2 in or to an inland part: *to travel inland*

inlet *noun*
a small narrow bay

inmate *noun*
someone living in a hospital or prison

inn *noun*
a small hotel, especially one where travellers stay
•***Word Family:*** **innkeeper** *noun*

innate (*say* in-**nate**) *adjective*
existing from birth rather than being learned: *an innate love of music*
•***Word Family:*** **innately** *adverb*

inner *adjective*
1 located further in: *an inner room* 2 private or secret: *He never revealed his inner thoughts to others.*
•***Word Family:*** **innermost** *adjective*

innings *noun*
the time in a cricket game in which a particular player or team is batting

innocent (*say* **in**-a-sent) *adjective*
1 pure or free from evil: *an innocent child* 2 not guilty: *The jury found him innocent.* 3 harmless: *innocent chatter*
•***Word Family:*** **innocence** *noun* **innocently** *adverb*

innocuous (*say* in-**ok**-yoo-us) *adjective*
harmless: *an innocuous remark*
•***Word Family:*** **innocuously** *adverb*

innovation (*say* in-a-**vay**-shon) *noun*
a new way of doing things: *an innovation in recycling water*
•***Word Family:*** **innovator** *noun* someone who makes innovations **innovate** *verb* **innovative** *adjective* new and clever: *an innovative design*
•***Word Origins:*** from a Latin word meaning "start again"

innuendo (*say* in-yoo-**en**-doh) *noun*
a comment that hints at something rude or unpleasant without actually saying it
•***Word Family:*** the plural is **innuendos** or **innuendoes**

innumerable (*say* in-**nyoo**-ma-ra-bul) *adjective*
more than you can count: *the innumerable stars in the heavens*

inoculate (*say* in-**ok**-yoo-late) *verb*
to inject germs into your body that give you a mild form of a disease, so that you won't get the disease again in its more serious form
•***Word Family:*** **inoculation** *noun*

input *noun*
1 whatever is put into something, especially the information fed into a computer
input *verb*
2 to put information into a computer
•***Word Family:*** other forms are **inputs, input, inputting**

inquest (*say* **in**-kwest) *noun*
an official inquiry, especially one to find out how someone died

inquire (*say* in-**kwire**) *verb*
1 to ask: *to inquire about someone's health* 2 to investigate: *to inquire into someone's disappearance*
•***Word Family:*** **inquirer** *noun* someone who inquires **inquiringly** *adverb*

inquiry (*say* in-**kwire**-ree) *noun*
an official investigation: *a court of inquiry*
•***Word Family:*** the plural is **inquiries**

inquisition (*say* in-kwa-**zish**-on) *noun*
a severe and harsh investigation or interrogation of a person
•***Word Family:*** **inquisitor** *noun*

inquisitive (*say* in-**kwiz**-a-tiv) *adjective*
1 fond of finding out about other people's business 2 eager to learn: *an inquisitive mind*
•***Word Family:*** **inquisitively** *adverb*

insane *adjective*
1 mad or mentally ill 2 very foolish
•***Word Family:*** **insanely** *adverb* **insanity** *noun*

inscribe *verb*
to write or carve something into a surface: *to inscribe words on a tombstone*
•***Word Family:*** **inscription** *noun* a message that has been inscribed

inscrutable (*say* in-**skroo**-ta-bul) *adjective*
not easily understood: *an inscrutable look on your face*
•***Word Family:*** **inscrutability** *noun* **inscrutably** *adverb*

insect (*say* **in**-sekt) *noun*
a small creature with its body divided into three parts (a head, a thorax and an abdomen), six legs and sometimes wings, such as an ant or a beetle

insecticide (*say* in-**sek**-ta-side) *noun*
a substance used to kill insects

insectivore *noun*
an animal or bird that eats insects
•***Word Family:*** **insectivorous** *adjective*

A B C D E F G H I J K L M N O P Q R S T U V W X Y Z

inseparable (*say* in-**sep**-er-a-bul) *adjective*
1 unable to be thought of separately: *Religion and politics are inseparable for some people.*
2 extremely good friends: *Ian and Andrew are inseparable.*

insert (*say* in-**sert**) *verb*
1 to put something inside or into something else: *to insert a bolt in a latch / to insert a notice in the paper*
insert (*say* **in**-sert) *noun*
2 something inserted, such as a leaflet in a magazine
•***Word Family:*** **insertion** *noun*

inside *noun*
1 the inner part or surface: *the inside of a suitcase / the inside of your hand* 2 **insides** the inner parts of your body, especially your stomach
inside *adjective*
3 inner or on the inside: *the inside pages of a newspaper* 4 done or coming from within a particular place or organization rather than from somewhere else: *The robbery was an inside job. / inside information*
inside *adverb*
5 into a particular house or building: *Please come inside.*

insight (*say* **in**-site) *noun*
an understanding of the truth about a person or thing: *The film gave us an insight into the lives of homeless people.*

insignia (*say* in-**sig**-nee-a) *plural noun*
official badges or markings on uniforms, vehicles and so on: *military insignia*

insincere (*say* in-sin-**sear**) *adjective*
pretending to have feelings you don't really have
•***Word Family:*** **insincerely** *adverb* **insincerity** *noun*

insinuate (*say* in-**sin**-yoo-ate) *verb*
1 to suggest something unpleasant in an indirect way: *He insinuated that I had copied his work.* 2 to introduce yourself slyly and gradually into a position or place: *to insinuate yourself into someone's confidence*
•***Word Family:*** **insinuation** *noun*

insist *verb*
to demand something firmly: *to insist on speaking to the manager*
•***Word Family:*** **insistence** *noun* **insistent** *adjective* **insistently** *adverb*

insolent (*say* **in**-sa-lent) *adjective*
insulting or rude
•***Word Family:*** **insolence** *noun* **insolently** *adverb*

insoluble (*say* in-**sol**-yew-bull) *adjective*
1 unable to be dissolved: *an insoluble chemical*
2 unable to be solved or sorted out: *an insoluble difficulty*
•***Word Family:*** **insolubility** *noun*

insomnia (*say* in-**som**-nee-a) *noun*
the inability to sleep, often because you are anxious or depressed
•***Word Family:*** **insomniac** *noun* someone who suffers from insomnia

inspect *verb*
to look at something carefully or officially to make sure everything is as it should be: *to inspect your makeup for smudges / to inspect a school*
•***Word Family:*** **inspection** *noun* **inspector** *noun*

inspire *verb*
to fill someone with good ideas or with a good feeling: *She inspired him to write his first novel. / His voice inspires confidence.*
•***Word Family:*** **inspiration** *noun*

install (*say* in-**stawl**) *verb*
1 to place or fix something in position so it is ready to be used: *The plumber installed a new shower.* 2 to establish someone in an important position with a ceremony: *to install a new president*
•***Word Family:*** **installation** *noun*

instalment (*say* in-**stawl**-ment) *noun*
1 one of a series of cash payments made to pay for something: *24 monthly instalments* 2 one of the parts of a longer story published by a magazine or shown on television over a period of time

instance (*say* **in**-stance) *noun*
a particular case or example: *In this instance he was right. / Give us an instance of his cruelty.*

instant (*say* **in**-stant) *adjective*
1 immediate: *an instant decision* 2 quickly prepared: *instant coffee*
instant *noun*
3 a specific point of time: *Come home this instant!* 4 a short space of time: *within an instant*
•***Word Family:*** **instantaneous** happening or done immediately *noun* **instantly** *adverb*

instead (*say* in-**sted**) *adverb*
in place of something else: *There was no fish, so we are having meat instead.*

instinct (*say* **in**-stinkt) *noun*
a natural way of feeling or behaving that you have without thinking and without being taught: *Birds learn to fly by instinct.*
•***Word Family:*** **instinctive** *adjective* **instinctively** *adverb*

institute (*say* **in**-sti-tyoot) *verb*
1 to establish something or set it up: *to institute a new law*

institute *noun*
2 an organization that is set up for a particular purpose: *the Royal National Institute for the Blind*

institution (*say* in-sti-**tyoo**-shon) *noun*
1 an organization, such as a hospital or university 2 the building or buildings used for this 3 a well-known person or thing: *Our long-serving postman is a local institution.* 4 a custom or habit: *The family's annual trip to the mountains has become an institution.*
• ***Word Family:*** **institutional** *adjective* **institutionalize** or **institutionalise** *verb* **institutionally** *adverb*

instruct (*say* in-**strukt**) *verb*
1 to give orders to someone: *The doctor instructed me to stay in bed.* 2 to teach someone: *He instructed my brother on how to drive.*
• ***Word Family:*** **instructive** *adjective* informative **instruction** *noun* **instructively** *adverb* **instructor** *noun*

instrument (*say* **in**-stra-ment) *noun*
1 a device or tool used for a particular purpose: *surgical instruments* 2 something for making music: *The bassoon is a woodwind instrument.* 3 a person or thing used for a particular purpose: *A bomb is an instrument of destruction.*
• ***Word Family:*** **instrumentalist** *noun* someone who plays a musical instrument

instrumental (*say* in-stra-**ment**-al) *adjective*
1 using musical instruments, especially without any singing: *an instrumental piece for piano and guitar* 2 extremely important, helpful or useful: *He was instrumental in arranging the deal.*
instrumental *noun*
3 a piece of instrumental music

insubordinate (*say* in-sa-**bor**-da-nit) *adjective*
disobedient: *insubordinate behaviour*
• ***Word Family:*** **insubordination** *noun*

insufferable (*say* in-**suf**-er-a-bul) *adjective*
unable to be tolerated: *an insufferable liar*
• ***Word Family:*** **insufferably** *adverb*

insulate (*say* **in**-syoo-late) *verb*
1 to cover something to stop electric current escaping: *to insulate electric wires* 2 to line a roof to prevent heat from entering in summer or from escaping in winter
• ***Word Family:*** **insulation** *noun* **insulator** *noun*

insulin (*say* **in**-syoo-lin) *noun*
a substance your body produces to control the amount of sugar coming into your blood from the food you eat

insult (*say* **in**-sult) *noun*
1 a rude remark or act
insult (*say* in-**sult**) *verb*
2 to speak to or treat someone rudely
• ***Word Family:*** **insulting** *adjective* **insultingly** *adverb*

insurance (*say* in-**shor**-ence) *noun*
an agreement under which you pay money regularly to a company that promises to pay you for any loss, damage, accident or fire you suffer
• ***Word Family:*** **insured** *noun* someone protected by insurance **insurer** *noun* the company issuing an insurance policy **insure** *verb* to protect something or someone by arranging insurance

intact (*say* in-**takt**) *adjective*
remaining whole, unchanged or undamaged: *The glasses were intact when we unpacked them.*

integer (*say* **in**-ta-ja) *noun*
a whole number without a fraction

integral (*say* **in**-ti-grul) *adjective*
being a necessary part of a whole: *Your arms and legs are integral parts of your body.*
• ***Word Family:*** **integrally** *adverb*

integrate (*say* **in**-ti-grate) *verb*
to combine parts into a whole: *to integrate people of different nationalities into the community*
• ***Word Family:*** **integration** *noun*

integrity (*say* in-**teg**-ra-tee) *noun*
honesty in your behaviour

intellect (*say* **in**-ta-lekt) *noun*
the power of your mind to understand and deal with ideas

intellectual (*say* in-ta-**lek**-tyoo-al) *adjective*
1 using your mind or intellect: *intellectual powers* 2 having a good mind: *an intellectual author*
intellectual *noun*
3 someone who spends time thinking about complex ideas
• ***Word Family:*** **intellectually** *adverb*

intelligence (*say* in-**tel**-i-jence) *noun*
1 the ability to understand ideas and solve problems 2 information, especially the kind that is useful to the army or police
• ***Word Family:*** **intelligent** *adjective* **intelligently** *adverb*

intend *verb*
to plan or mean to do something: *He intends to give up smoking. / It was intended to be a joke.*
• ***Word Family:*** **intention** *noun*

intense (*say* in-**tense**) *adjective*
1 very great or strong: *intense light / intense happiness* 2 having strong feelings and taking things very seriously: *an intense young man*
• ***Word Family:*** **intensify** (**intensifies, intensified, intensifying**) *verb* **intensely** *adverb* **intensity** *noun*

A B C D E F G H I J K L M N O P Q R S T U V W X Y Z

intensive (*say* in-**ten**-siv) *adjective*
1 needing a lot of work or effort in a short period or a small area: *an intensive course in first aid / intensive farming* 2 thorough: *an intensive search*
• ***Word Family:*** **intensively** *adverb*

intent (1) *noun*
a purpose or intention: *He acted with good intent.*

intent (2) *adjective*
1 firmly fixed or concentrated: *an intent gaze*
2 **intent on** determined to do something: *to be intent on causing trouble*
• ***Word Family:*** **intently** *adverb*

intention (*say* in-**ten**-shon) *noun*
a plan or purpose you have
• ***Word Family:*** **intentional** *adjective* deliberate: *an intentional insult* **intentionally** *adverb* deliberately

interaction (*say* in-ta-**rak**-shon) *noun*
the way two things act on or affect each other: *The interaction of sea water with metal causes metal to rust.*
• ***Word Family:*** **interact** *verb*

interactive *adjective*
allowing direct communication between the person using a computer program and the program itself: *an interactive language-learning program*

intercede (*say* in-ta-**seed**) *verb*
to speak or act for someone else in order to help or protect them

intercept (*say* in-ta-**sept**) *verb*
to stop something on its way somewhere: *to intercept a letter*
• ***Word Family:*** **interception** *noun* **interceptor** *noun*

interchange *verb*
1 to change things or people around: *to interchange guests at the dinner table*
interchange *noun*
2 interchanging things 3 a place where you can go from one motorway to another
• ***Word Family:*** **interchangeable** *adjective* **interchangeably** *adverb*

intercourse *noun*
1 the exchange of ideas, feelings or thoughts: *social intercourse between friends* 2 *a short way of saying* **sexual intercourse**

interest (*say* **in**-ta-rest) *noun*
1 the feeling that you want to learn about something: *He has an interest in pottery.*
2 something you enjoy doing or learning about: *Pottery is only one of his interests.* 3 importance: *Money is of no interest to her.* 4 the money a bank or building society pays you for your savings, or the money you pay in order to borrow money from a bank or building society
interest *verb*
5 to attract the attention of someone: *The old house interests me.*
• ***Word Family:*** **interested** *adjective* **interestedly** *adverb* **interesting** *adjective* **interestingly** *adverb*

interface *noun*
1 a surface that forms a boundary between two things 2 the link between any two computer systems or devices, or between the user and the computer

interfere (*say* in-ta-**fear**) *verb*
1 to get involved in other people's business without being asked 2 to get in the way: *His home life interferes with his work.*
• ***Word Family:*** other forms are **interferes, interfered, interfering** □ **interference** *noun*

intergalactic (*say* in-ta-ga-**lak**-tik) *adjective*
having to do with or between galaxies in space: *intergalactic travel*

interior (*say* in-**tear**-ree-a) *adjective*
1 inside: *interior organs in your body*
interior *noun*
2 an inner or inside part: *The interior of the building has not changed since the Middle Ages.*

interjection (*say* in-ta-**jek**-shon) *noun*
a word or phrase that expresses a strong feeling such as surprise, anger or pain

interlude *noun*
a relaxing break between one thing and another

intermediate (*say* in-ta-**mee**-dee-it) *adjective*
placed or happening between two other times, places or stages

interminable (*say* in-**term**-en-a-bul) *adjective*
seeming to have no end: *interminable fights*
• ***Word Family:*** **interminably** *adverb*

internal (*say* in-**tern**-al) *adjective*
to do with the inside or inner part of a thing or place: *internal body organs*
• ***Word Family:*** **internally** *adverb*

international (*say* in-ta-**nash**-en-al) *adjective*
between or among different countries: *an international trade agreement*
• ***Word Family:*** **internationally** *adverb*

Internet *noun*
an international network of computers that are linked together by telephone lines, so that people all over the world can exchange information and messages

interplay *noun*
the effect that two or more things have on each other

interpret (*say* in-**ter**-prit) *verb*
1 to explain the meaning of something: *We interpreted his reply as an apology.* 2 to translate what someone is saying into another language: *As she didn't understand English, I had to interpret for her.*
•*Word Family:* other forms are **interprets, interpreted, interpreting** □ **interpretation** *noun* **interpreter** *noun* someone who translates what people are saying

interrogate (*say* in-**te**-ra-gate) *verb*
to question someone closely or aggressively in order to discover something: *The soldiers interrogated their prisoners for hours.*
•*Word Family:* **interrogation** *noun* **interrogator** *noun*

interrupt (*say* in-ta-**rupt**) *verb*
to break or stop what is happening or what someone is saying: *to interrupt a journey / to interrupt a speech with shouts*
•*Word Family:* **interruption** *noun*

intersect (*say* in-ta-**sekt**) *verb*
to cut across or pass through something: *This line intersects the triangle.*
•*Word Family:* **intersection** *noun* a place where two streets intersect

intersperse (*say* in-ta-**sperse**) *verb*
to scatter or distribute unevenly among other things
•*Word Family:* **interspersion** *noun*

interstate *adjective*
1 in another state: *an interstate holiday*
2 between states: *interstate rivalry*
interstate *adverb*
3 to or from another state: *to fly interstate*

interval *noun*
1 the time that passes between events or meetings: *an interval of three years* 2 the difference in pitch between two musical notes 3 the time between two acts of a play or two parts of a film, when the audience leave their seats

intervene (*say* in-ta-**veen**) *verb*
to step in, in order to solve a problem or settle a disagreement: *to intervene in a dispute*
•*Word Family:* **intervention** *noun*

interview *noun*
1 a meeting between two people in which one questions the other about something: *a job interview / a radio interview with the author of a new book*
interview *verb*
2 to ask someone questions in a specially arranged meeting: *to interview a film star*
•*Word Family:* **interviewer** *noun* someone who asks the questions at an interview

intestine (*say* in-**tes**-tin) *noun*
the long tube that carries food from your stomach to your anus
•*Word Family:* **intestinal** *adjective*

intimate (*say* **in**-ti-mit) *adjective*
1 closely acquainted: *an intimate friend* 2 private and personal: *your intimate details* 3 thorough or detailed: *an intimate knowledge of Shakespeare*
•*Word Family:* **intimacy** *noun* **intimately** *adverb*

intimidate *verb*
to frighten someone, especially to force them to do something
•*Word Family:* **intimidation** *noun*

into *preposition*
1 towards or to the inside or inner part: *We went into the shop. / to be right into a book* 2 to a changed condition or result: *The rain turned into snow. / She burst into laughter.* 3 to be included in another number in maths: *2 into 6 goes 3.*
4 **be into** to be very keen on: *to be into rap music*
•*Word Family:* definition 4 is colloquial

intolerant (*say* in-**tol**-a-rant) *adjective*
not willing to accept people who are different from you
•*Word Family:* **intolerance** *noun* **intolerantly** *adverb*

intonation (*say* in-ta-**nay**-shon) *noun*
the pitch or tone of musical notes or of your voice when you speak

intoxicate (*say* in-**tok**-si-kate) *verb*
1 to make someone drunk 2 to make someone wildly excited: *to intoxicate with success*
•*Word Family:* **intoxicating** *adjective* **intoxication** *noun*

intravenous (*say* in-tra-**vee**-nus) *adjective*
into a vein: *an intravenous injection*
•*Word Family:* **intravenously** *adverb*

intrepid (*say* in-**trep**-id) *adjective*
fearless or bold: *an intrepid climber*
•*Word Family:* **intrepidly** *adverb*

intricate (*say* **in**-tra-kit) *adjective*
complicated, or with many fine details: *an intricate pattern*
•*Word Family:* **intricacy** *noun* **intricately** *adverb*
•*Word Origins:* from a Latin word meaning "entangled"

intrigue (*say* in-**treeg**) *verb*
1 to interest you or make you curious: *I'm intrigued by your suggestion.*
intrigue (*say* **in**-treeg) *noun*
2 a secret plot
•*Word Family:* other verb forms are **intrigues, intrigued, intriguing** □ **intriguing** *adjective*

A B C D E F G H I J K L M N O P Q R S T U V W X Y Z

introduce *verb*
1 to make something or someone known for the first time: *to introduce you to a friend / to introduce you to crime novels* 2 to start the use of something: *The government has introduced a new driving licence.* 3 to welcome viewers or listeners at the start of a television or radio programme
• ***Word Family:*** **introduction** *noun* **introductory** *adjective* only at the beginning: *a special introductory offer*

intrude *verb*
to force yourself in where you are unwelcome
• ***Word Family:*** **intruder** *noun* someone who intrudes **intrusion** *noun* **intrusive** *adjective* **intrusively** *adverb*

intuition (*say* in-tyoo-**ish**-on) *noun*
a powerful feeling you have about something without knowing why: *I have a strong intuition that he's in danger.*
• ***Word Family:*** **intuitive** *adjective* **intuitively** *adverb*

invade *verb*
to enter or attack a particular place as an enemy: *Britain was invaded by the Romans.*
• ***Word Family:*** **invader** *noun:* **invasion** *noun*

invalid (1) (*say* **in**-va-lid) *noun*
someone who is sick or disabled for a long period of time

invalid (2) (*say* in-**val**-id) *adjective*
not legally correct: *an invalid entry in a competition*
• ***Word Family:*** **invalidate** *verb* to make something invalid **invalidation** *noun*

invaluable *adjective*
extremely valuable or useful: *Her help has been invaluable.*
• ***Word Family:*** **invaluably** *adverb*

invent *verb*
to think of something for the first time or make something up: *to invent the telephone / to invent an excuse*
• ***Word Family:*** **invention** *noun* **inventive** *adjective* **inventively** *adverb* **inventor** *noun*

inventory (*say* **in**-ven-tree) *noun*
a list of things with the description and number of each, especially of all the stock in a factory or shop
• ***Word Family:*** the plural is **inventories**

inverse (*say* **in**-verse) *adjective*
1 reversed in order or turned in the opposite direction: *4321 is the inverse order of 1234*
inverse *noun*
2 the reverse or opposite of something
• ***Word Family:*** **invert** *verb* to turn something upside down or inside out **inversely** *adverb*

invertebrate (*say* in-**ver**-ti-brit) *noun*
an animal without a backbone, such as a worm

inverted commas *plural noun*
the punctuation marks (" " or ' ') used to show where speech begins and ends or if words are being quoted from somewhere else

invest *verb*
1 to put money into something so that you will make more money: *to invest in property* 2 to spend money or time on something: *to invest in a new camera / to invest a few hours a week on your hobby*
• ***Word Family:*** **investment** *noun* **investor** *noun*

investigate (*say* in-**ves**-ti-gate) *verb*
to examine or search into something thoroughly: *to investigate a robbery / to investigate a spooky noise*
• ***Word Family:*** **investigation** *noun* **investigator** *noun*

invigorate (*say* in-**vig**-a-rate) *verb*
to fill someone or something with energy: *Working out at the gym really invigorates me.*
• ***Word Family:*** **invigorating** *adjective*

invincible (*say* in-**vin**-sa-bul) *adjective*
not able to be beaten or conquered: *an invincible enemy*
• ***Word Family:*** **invincibility** *noun* **invincibly** *adverb*

invisible (*say* in-**viz**-a-bul) *adjective*
not able to be seen
• ***Word Family:*** **invisibility** *noun* **invisibly** *adverb*

invite (*say* in-**vite**) *verb*
1 to ask someone to do something or go somewhere, usually in a formal way: *to invite him to the party / to invite her to speak at the meeting* 2 to encourage something or make it likely to happen: *to invite trouble*
• ***Word Family:*** **invitation** *noun* **inviting** *adjective* attractive: *The water looks very inviting.*

in vitro fertilisation *noun*
the fertilisation of an egg by a sperm in artificial surroundings outside the mother's body, such as in a test tube

involve *verb*
1 to have or include something as a necessary part: *Being in the swimming squad involves daily training.* 2 to get someone into a complicated situation: *Don't involve me in your arguments.*
• ***Word Family:*** **involved** *adjective* **involvement** *noun*

inward *adjective*
1 towards the centre or the inside: *an inward breath* 2 inside but not showing on the surface: *an inward sense of anger*

•**Word Family: inwardly** *adverb: Inwardly she was furious.* **inwards** *adverb* moving or facing inside

iodine (*say* **eye**-o-deen) *noun*
a greyish-black chemical element that forms a thick purple vapour when heated and is widely used as an antiseptic

ion (*rhymes with* lion) *noun*
an atom or group of atoms with an electrical charge

IQ (*say* I-**kew**) *noun*
a way of measuring how intelligent someone is, according to specially designed tests: *to have a high IQ*
•**Word Origins:** from the initials of Intelligence Quotient

irate (*say* eye-**rate**) *adjective*
angry

iris (*say* **eye**-ris) *noun*
1 the coloured part of your eye, surrounding the pupil 2 a plant with sword-shaped leaves and colourful flowers
•**Word Origins:** from a Greek word meaning "rainbow"

iron (*say* **eye**-on) *noun*
1 a strong metallic element used to make tools and machines, and essential for the body to form blood 2 a metal device with a smooth flat bottom, that heats up so you can use it for smoothing clothes 3 a golf club, used mainly for short or high strokes
iron *verb*
4 to press or smooth clothes with an iron
5 **iron out** to sort out problems or difficulties in something
•**Word Family: ironing** *noun* the clothes that need to be ironed

ironbark *noun*
a gum tree with thick, black bark

ironic (*say* eye-**ron**-ik) *adjective*
speaking in a funny or mocking way in which your meaning is the opposite of what you are saying such as: *"Delicious!" she said, screwing up her face in disgust.*
•**Word Family: ironically** *adverb* **irony** *noun*

irradiate *verb*
to preserve something by exposing it to small amounts of radiation: *to irradiate food*
•**Word Family: irradiation** *noun*

irrational (*say* i-**rash**-a-nal) *adjective*
not logical or reasonable: *an irrational argument / an irrational fear of spiders*
•**Word Family: irrationally** *adverb*

irregular (*say* i-**reg**-yoo-la) *adjective*
1 not regular or consistent: *an irregular surface / an irregular heart beat* 2 not legal or right: *an irregular trade deal*
•**Word Family: irregularity** *noun* **irregularly** *adverb*

irrelevant (*say* i-**rel**-a-vant) *adjective*
having nothing to do with the subject being discussed: *an irrelevant interruption*
•**Word Family: irrelevance** *noun* **irrelevantly** *adverb*

irresistible (*say* ir-a-**zis**-ta-bul) *adjective*
so attractive that it overpowers you: *irresistible charm / an irresistible urge to laugh*
•**Word Family: irresistibly** *adverb*

irresponsible (*say* i-ra-**spon**-sa-bul) *adjective*
not sensible or trustworthy: *an irresponsible driver*
•**Word Family: irresponsibility** *noun* **irresponsibly** *adverb*

irreverent (*say* i-**rev**-er-unt) *adjective*
showing no respect for things people usually take seriously
•**Word Family: irreverence** *noun* **irreverently** *adverb*

irrigate *verb*
to supply a place or area with water using man-made channels and pipes: *to irrigate rice fields*
•**Word Family: irrigation** *noun*

irritable (*say* **ir**-i-ta-bul) *adjective*
easily made impatient, angry or irritated
•**Word Family: irritability** *noun* **irritably** *adverb*

irritate (*say* **ir**-i-tate) *verb*
1 to make someone impatient or angry: *to irritate his brother by being late* 2 to make part of your body sore or itchy
•**Word Family: irritant** *noun* something that irritates part of your body **irritating** *adjective* **irritation** *noun*

Islam (*say* **iz**-lahm) *noun*
the Muslim religion, based on belief in one supreme God, and the teachings of the prophet Mohammed as set down in the Koran, the holy book of Islam
•**Word Family: Islamic** *adjective*

island (*say* **eye**-land) *noun*
1 a piece of land completely surrounded by water 2 something that is like an island: *a traffic island*
•**Word Family: islander** *noun* someone who lives on an island

isle (*rhymes with* file) *noun*
a small island

isobar (*say* **eye**-sa-bar) *noun*
a line drawn on a weather map joining places of equal air-pressure

A B C D E F G H I J K L M N O P Q R S T U V W X Y Z

isolate *verb*
to separate someone or something or put them apart from others: *to isolate an infectious child*
•***Word Family:*** **isolated** *adjective* far from other places: *an isolated farm high in the hills* **isolation** *noun*

isosceles (*say* eye-**sos**-a-leez) *adjective*
having two sides equal: *an isosceles triangle*
•***Word Origins:*** from Greek words meaning "equal" and "leg"

issue (*say* **ish**-oo) *noun*
1 an important matter that needs to be discussed: *to consider an issue* 2 something published or produced at a particular time: *the June issue of a magazine* 3 something which is released or given out all at once: *an issue of new bank notes* 4 **take issue** to disagree
issue *verb*
5 to put out or deliver a message: *to issue a gale warning* 6 to publish or produce something: *to issue a newsletter* 7 to come out of somewhere: *Flames were seen issuing from an upstairs window.*
•***Word Family:*** other verb forms are **issues, issued, issuing**

isthmus (*say* **is**-mus) *noun*
a narrow strip of land joining two larger areas of land
•***Word Family:*** the plural is **isthmuses**

it *pronoun*
the person or thing being talked about whose sex is unknown or that has no sex: *Did you see who it was? / We saw who bought it.*
•***Word Family:*** other forms are **its:** *Its leg got caught.* and **they:** *They know me.*

italics (*say* i-**tal**-ik) *plural noun*
printing with characters sloping to the right, often used for emphasis
•***Word Family:*** **italicize** or **italicise** *verb* to print in italics

itch *noun*
1 a feeling of irritation on your skin causing you to scratch 2 a restless or continuing desire: *She has an itch to travel.*
itch *verb*
3 to have an itch
•***Word Family:*** **itchy** *adjective* **(itchier, itchiest) itchiness** *noun*

item *noun*
a single or separate thing in a list or series: *There are several valuable items for sale. / an important item of news*
•***Word Family:*** **itemize** or **itemise** *verb* to list every item

itinerant (*say* eye-**tin**-a-rant) *adjective*
1 travelling from place to place, usually to find work: *an itinerant shearer*
itinerant *noun*
2 someone who travels from place to place

itinerary (*say* eye-**tin**-a-ra-ree) *noun*
the route or plan of a journey, giving the places to be visited, the times of plane flights and so on
•***Word Family:*** the plural is **itineraries**

it's *contraction*
a short form of **it is** or **it has**, as in *It's a lovely day.*
•***Word Origins:*** **it's** sounds like **its** "used to express ownership", as in *Its burrow in the sand.*

ivory (*say* **eye**-va-ree) *noun*
1 the hard, creamy-white material that we get from the tusks of elephants 2 a creamy-white colour
ivory *adjective*
3 made of ivory

ivy (*say* **eye**-vee) *noun*
a climbing plant with dark, shiny, evergreen leaves

Jj

jab *verb*
1 to pierce something or poke someone with the end of something sharp: *to jab a needle into your arm*
jab *noun*
2 a sudden, sharp poke
•***Word Family:*** other verb forms are **jabs, jabbed, jabbing**

jabber *verb*
to chatter away without making any sense

jacaranda (*say* jak-a-**ran**-da) *noun*
a tall, tropical tree with bluish-purple flowers

jack *noun*
1 a tool for raising heavy objects, such as the one you use to hold up the car when you change a tyre 2 a playing card with a picture of a young man
jack *verb*
3 **jack up** to lift or move something with a jack

jackal *noun*
a wild dog of Africa and Asia that hunts in packs and feeds on dead meat

jackaroo *noun*
someone learning how to work on a sheep or cattle station

jackass *noun*
1 a male ass 2 a very stupid person

jacket *noun*
1 a short coat 2 an outer coat or covering around something: *a book jacket / potatoes cooked in their jackets*

jackhammer *noun*
a hammer-like drill operated by compressed air, for breaking up rocks or concrete

jackknife (*say* **jak**-nife) *noun*
1 a large knife with a blade that folds into its handle
jackknife *verb*
2 to fold or bend double like a jackknife: *A lorry has jackknifed on the main road.*
• ***Word Family:*** the plural is **jackknives**

jackpot *noun*
1 the largest prize you can win in a competition
2 **hit the jackpot** to be very successful or lucky

jacuzzi (*say* ja-**koo**-zee) *noun*
a large bath fitted with air jets that make water swirl around your body
• ***Word Origins:*** this word is a trademark

jade *noun*
a hard, usually green stone, used for carved statues or in jewellery

jaded *adjective*
tired or worn-out and bored

jaffle *noun*
a toasted sandwich cooked between two pieces of hot metal

jagged (*say* **jag**-ed) *adjective*
sharp and pointed: *jagged edges of broken glass*

jaguar (*say* **jag**-yoo-a) *noun*
a large, fierce, black-spotted cat, found in the forests of tropical America

jail *noun*
1 a prison
jail *verb*
2 to put someone in prison: *He was jailed for 10 years.*
• ***Word Family:*** **jailer** *noun* someone in charge of prisoners or a jail

Jainism (*say* **jie**-nism) *noun*
a Hindu religion whose followers believe in reincarnation and will not harm any living creatures, even insects
• ***Word Family:*** **Jain** *noun* a follower of Jainism

jam (1) *verb*
1 to squeeze something into a tight place: *to jam clothes into a drawer* 2 to push something suddenly or violently: *to jam on the brakes* 3 to become stuck: *The window's jammed and won't close.*
jam *noun*
4 things or people packed or crowded together: *a traffic jam* 5 a difficult situation: *I'm in a real jam.*
• ***Word Family:*** other verb forms are **jams, jammed, jamming**

jam (2) *noun*
a food for spreading on bread, made by boiling fruit with sugar

jamb (*sounds like* jam) *noun*
the upright frame at the sides of a door or window

jamboree *noun*
a large rally or gathering, usually of scouts

jangle *verb*
1 to make a loud, unpleasant ringing sound: *I could hear her bracelet's jangling.* 2 to have an unpleasant effect on you: *The accident has jangled my nerves a bit.*
jangle *noun*
3 a loud, unpleasant ringing sound

January *noun*
the first month of the year, with 31 days
• ***Word Origins:*** named after the ancient Roman god *Janus*, guardian of doors and gates, who had two faces looking in opposite directions

jar (1) *noun*
a glass container with an airtight lid, or its contents: *two jars of coffee / half a jar of honey*

jar (2) *verb*
1 to jolt or shock someone or something with a sudden movement: *The fall jarred us both.* 2 to irritate or grate on someone: *That screeching jars my nerves.*
• ***Word Family:*** other forms are **jars, jarred, jarring**

jargon *noun*
a way of talking used only by people in a particular job or group and not understood by other people: *medical jargon*

jarrah *noun*
a large tree found in Western Australia, with very hard, red wood

jasmine (*say* **jaz**-min) *noun*
a climbing plant with sweet-smelling, white, yellow or pink flowers

jaundice (*say* **jawn**-dis) *noun*
an illness of the liver in which your skin and the whites of your eyes turn yellow
• ***Word Family:*** **jaundiced** *adjective* (a) suffering

from jaundice (b) bitter and resentful
•*Word Origins:* from a French word meaning "yellow"

jaunty (*say* **jawn**-tee) *adjective*
cheerful and full of confidence: *a jaunty grin / Her hat was at a jaunty angle.*
•*Word Family:* other forms are **jauntier, jauntiest** □ **jauntily** *adverb* **jauntiness** *noun*

javelin *noun*
a light spear thrown in sporting competitions

jaw *noun*
either of two bones near your mouth, that hold your teeth

jazz *noun*
a style of music developed by Black Americans, which has swinging rhythms and which often allows the musicians to improvise as they go along
jazz *verb*
•*Word Family:* **jazzy** *adjective* (**jazzier, jazziest**) very bright or showy

jealous (*say* **jel**-us) *adjective*
resentful of another person's success, or careful to protect or guard what you already have: *I'm jealous of her good looks. / The dog was jealous of its huge bone.*
•*Word Family:* **jealously** *adverb* **jealousy** *noun*

jeans *plural noun*
trousers made of denim or a similar strong cloth

jeep *noun*
a small strong car used for driving over rough ground

jeer *verb*
to mock or laugh at someone rudely
•*Word Family:* **jeeringly** *adverb*

Jehovah (*say* ja-**hoh**-va) *noun*
a name for God used in the Old Testament of the Bible

Jehovah's Witness (*say* ja-ho-vaz **wit**-nes) *noun*
one of a group of Christians who are against war, do not follow the laws of their country when they think these conflict with God's laws and work to see God's rule established on earth

jelly *noun*
a soft but firm food made with gelatine or by boiling a liquid containing sugar until it sets
•*Word Family:* the plural is **jellies**

jellyfish *noun*
a soft, jelly-like sea creature, usually with an umbrella-like body and long tentacles
•*Word Family:* the plural is **jellyfishes** or **jellyfish**

jeopardize or **jeopardise** (*say* **jep**-a-dize) *verb*
to risk something or put it in danger: *to jeopardize your career*
•*Word Family:* **jeopardy** *noun* danger or peril

jerk *noun*
1 a quick, sharp or violent movement 2 an ignorant or unpleasant person
jerk *verb*
3 to move with a jerk
•*Word Family:* **jerky** *adjective* (**jerkier, jerkiest**) **jerkily** *adverb* **jerkiness** *noun*

jersey (*say* **jer**-zee) *noun*
1 a long-sleeved knitted sweater 2 **Jersey** a breed of small dairy cattle that produces rich milk
•*Word Origins:* named after the island of *Jersey* in the English Channel, where the cows came from and where knitted cloth was an important industry

jest *verb*
1 to speak jokingly or playfully
jest *noun*
2 a joke
•*Word Family:* **jester** *noun* a professional c lown in medieval times, who entertained at court

jet (1) *noun*
1 a stream of liquid or gas 2 a spout or tap that lets out a stream like this: *a gas jet* 3 an aeroplane that moves forward at high speed by sucking in air and forcing it out behind it
jet *verb*
4 to send a liquid or gas out in a jet 5 to travel in a jet
•*Word Family:* other verb forms are **jets, jetted, jetting**

jet (2) *noun*
a hard, black mineral that you can polish and use to make jewellery
•*Word Origins:* this word is a trademark

jettison *verb*
to throw something overboard from a ship or aircraft: *to jettison fuel*

jetty *noun*
a structure built from the land into water, used as a landing place for passengers from boats
•*Word Family:* the plural is **jetties**

Jew *noun*
1 someone who is descended from the Hebrews
2 someone whose religion is Judaism
•*Word Family:* **Jewish** *adjective*

jewel *noun*
1 a precious stone, such as a diamond, cut and polished and used in jewellery 2 an ornament,

such as a necklace or ring, containing precious stones
•*Word Family:* **jeweller** *noun* someone who makes or sells jewels **jewellery** *noun*

jig *noun*
1 a fast, lively dance
jig *verb*
2 to move up and down in a quick or jerky manner
•*Word Family:* other verb forms are **jigs, jigged, jigging**

jigsaw *noun*
a puzzle in which cardboard or wooden pieces are fitted together to form a picture

jingle *noun*
1 a tinkling sound 2 a short, cheerful song used to advertise products on TV or radio
jingle *verb*
3 to tinkle or clink: *to jingle your keys*

jinx *noun*
someone or something believed to bring bad luck
•*Word Family:* the plural is **jinxes** □ **jinxed** *adjective* bringing bad luck

jitters *plural noun*
a feeling of nervousness
•*Word Family:* **jittery** *adjective*

job *noun*
1 a piece of work or task that you have to do 2 paid employment: *your part-time job*

jockey *noun*
someone who rides racehorses as a profession

jodhpurs (*say* **jod**-pez) *plural noun*
riding trousers that are loose to the knees and then close-fitting to the ankle
•*Word Origins:* named after *Jodhpur* in India where these trousers were first worn

joey *noun*
a young kangaroo or wallaby

jog *verb*
1 to run at a slow, steady pace 2 to shake someone with a push or nudge: *to jog someone's arm* 3 **jog your memory** to remind you about something
jog *noun*
4 a slow run: *to move at a jog / to go for a jog*
•*Word Family:* other verb forms are **jogs, jogged, jogging** □ **jogger** *noun* someone who jogs

join *verb*
1 to come together or put things together 2 to become a member of a particular organization: *to join a club* 3 to meet other people: *Join us after the meal.*
join *noun*
4 a place where one thing joins another

joiner *noun*
someone who makes wooden furniture, doors or window frames
•*Word Family:* **joinery** *noun* the work a joiner produces

joint *noun*
1 a place where two or more parts or objects join: *Your knee is a joint in your leg.* 2 a cut of meat for roasting 3 a cigarette containing a drug such as marijuana
joint *adjective*
4 shared: *a joint project*
•*Word Family:* **jointly** *adverb*

joist *noun*
a wooden or metal beam, used as a support for a floor or ceiling

joke *noun*
1 something you say or do to make people laugh
joke *verb*
2 to make jokes
•*Word Family:* **jokingly** *adverb*

joker *noun*
1 a funny or amusing person 2 a playing card with a picture of a jester on it

jolly *adjective*
1 cheerful, amusing or pleasant: *a jolly old man*
jolly *adverb*
2 very: *jolly good*
•*Word Family:* **jolliness** *noun* **jollity** *noun*

jolt *verb*
1 to move or shake jerkily or roughly
jolt *noun*
2 a sudden rough movement

jostle (*say* **jos**-ul) *verb*
to push or knock someone roughly: *He was jostled by the crowd as he tried to leave.*

jot *verb*
1 to write something down briefly or quickly
jot *noun*
2 a small amount: *I don't care a jot.*
•*Word Family:* other verb forms are **jots, jotted, jotting** □ **jotter** *noun* a small notebook for jotting things down

joule (*rhymes with* tool) *noun*
a scientific unit for measuring work or energy
•*Word Origins:* named after the English scientist, J. P. *Joule*, who lived from 1818 to 1889

journal (*say* **jer**-nal) *noun*
1 a daily record or diary of what has happened 2 a newspaper or magazine

journalism (*say* **jer**-na-liz-um) *noun*
the work of writing, editing or publishing news

A B C D E F G H I J K L M N O P Q R S T U V W X Y Z

in newspapers and magazines, or on television or radio
•*Word Family:* **journalist** *noun* someone who gathers news

journey (*say* **jer**-nee) *noun*
1 a trip or expedition, especially by land: *a journey on camels into the desert*
journey *verb*
2 to travel somewhere: *to journey west*

jovial *adjective*
cheerful and friendly or pleasant
•*Word Family:* **joviality** *noun* **jovially** *adverb*

jowls *plural noun*
fat, sagging cheeks and chin

joy *noun*
happiness or great pleasure
•*Word Family:* **joyful** *adjective* **joyfully** *adverb* **joyous** *adjective* **joyously** *adverb*

joy-ride *noun*
a ride in a stolen car for fun
•*Word Family:* **joy-ride** *verb* **joy-rider** *noun* **joy-riding** *noun*

joystick *noun*
1 the pilot's control stick in an aircraft 2 a control stick that moves the position of the cursor on a computer

jubilant (*say* **joo**-bi-lant) *adjective*
joyful or triumphant: *to be jubilant at winning the match*
•*Word Family:* **jubilantly** *adverb* **jubilation** *noun*

jubilee (*say* joo-ba-**lee**) *noun*
a special anniversary or celebration: *A golden jubilee is a 50th anniversary.*
•*Word Origins:* from a Hebrew word meaning "ram's horn" (blown in a jubilee year)

Judaism (*say* **joo**-day-iz-um) *noun*
the religion of the Jewish people, based on a belief in one all-powerful God and the teachings and laws of the Old Testament
•*Word Family:* **Judaic** *adjective*

judge *noun*
1 someone who hears cases in a law court and decides how someone who is guilty of a crime should be punished 2 someone who decides the winner in a competition or contest
judge *verb*
3 to act as a judge: *to judge someone's character / to judge a flower show*

judgment or **judgement** *noun*
1 the ability to judge wisely: *What bad judgment he has in choosing girlfriends.* 2 the decision of a judge in a court case: *The judgment has been delayed.*

judicial (*say* joo-**dish**-al) *adjective*
to do with judges, justice or law courts: *a judicial inquiry*
•*Word Family:* **judiciary** *noun* the system of courts and judges

judicious (*say* joo-**dish**-us) *adjective*
sensible or wise
•*Word Family:* **judiciously** *adverb*

judo (*say* **joo**-doh) *noun*
a Japanese method of self-defence without weapons
•*Word Origins:* from Japanese words meaning "gentle way of life"

jug *noun*
a container with a spout and a handle, for holding or serving liquid

juggle *verb*
to toss several objects in the air one after the other and keep them moving without falling
•*Word Family:* **juggler** *noun*

jugular (*say* **jug**-yoo-la) *adjective*
1 having to do with the throat or neck: *the jugular veins*
jugular *noun*
2 any of several main veins in your neck

juice (*rhymes with* loose) *noun*
1 the liquid part of vegetables, fruit or meat: *carrot juice* 2 petrol
•*Word Family:* **juicy** *adjective* (**juicier, juiciest**) **juiciness** *noun*

jukebox *noun*
a coin-operated record or CD player

July (*say* joo-**lie**) *noun*
the seventh month of the year, with 31 days
•*Word Origins:* named after the Roman statesman, *Julius* Caesar, who was born in this month

jumble *noun*
1 confusion or disorder: *a jumble of paper*
2 things collected or gathered together for a jumble sale
jumble *verb*
3 to confuse or muddle things up

jumble sale *noun*
a sale of second-hand goods, home-made cakes and so on, to raise money

jumbo *adjective*
very large or outsize: *a jumbo jet*
•*Word Origins:* named after *Jumbo*, a famous 19th-century elephant

jump *verb*
1 to leap up from the ground 2 to move

suddenly from surprise or fear: *Oh! you made me jump!* 3 to increase: *The price of milk jumped yesterday.* 4 to change rapidly: *to jump from one subject to another*
jump *noun*
5 a leap 6 an obstacle to be leapt over
•***Word Family:*** **jumpy** *adjective* **(jumpier, jumpiest)** nervous

jumper *noun*
a knitted piece of clothing that you wear on the top part of your body

junction (*say* **junk**-shon) *noun*
a place where roads or railway lines join

June *noun*
the sixth month of the year, with 30 days
•***Word Origins:*** named after the Roman goddess *Juno*, the wife of Jupiter

jungle *noun*
a thick rainforest

junior *adjective*
1 younger or for young children: *a junior family member / a junior school* 2 lower in importance: *a junior staff member*
junior *noun*
3 a less important person: *the office junior*

junk (1) *noun*
old or worthless objects

junk (2) *noun*
a Chinese flat-bottomed ship with a high stern

Jupiter (*say* **joo**-pi-ter) *noun*
the largest planet in the solar system and fifth from the sun
•***Word Origins:*** named after the chief Roman god *Jupiter*

jurisdiction (*say* joo-ris-**dik**-shon) *noun*
1 power or authority: *He has no jurisdiction over my home life.* 2 the legal power of a court to make judgments

jury (*say* **joo**-ree) *noun*
1 a group of people chosen to hear a legal case in court and give a verdict 2 a group of people chosen to judge a competition
•***Word Family:*** **juror** *noun* a member of a jury

just *adjective*
1 fair or even-handed: *a just verdict*
just *adverb*
2 not long ago: *They've just left.* 3 by a small amount: *We just won.* 4 only: *She's just a baby.* 5 exactly: *That's just the point.*
•***Word Family:*** **justly** *adverb*

justice (*say* **jus**-tis) *noun*
1 right or fair treatment 2 the way the law is used in court to make fair judgments 3 a judge or magistrate

justify (*say* **just**-i-fie) *verb*
to show or prove that something is fair or right: *How can you justify spending so much money on a football kit?*
•***Word Family:*** other forms are **justifies, justified, justifying** □ **justifiable** *adjective* **justifiably** *adverb* **justification** *noun*

jut *verb*
to stick out: *The roof juts over the walls.*
•***Word Family:*** other forms are **juts, jutted, jutting**

juvenile (*say* **joo**-va-nile) *adjective*
1 to do with or for young people: *a juvenile court* 2 childish: *juvenile behaviour*
juvenile *noun*
3 a child or young person

juxtapose (*say* juk-sta-**poze**) *verb*
to place things side by side
•***Word Family:*** **juxtaposition** *noun*

Kk

kaleidoscope (*say* ka-**lie**-da-skope) *noun*
a toy consisting of a tube with mirrors and loose pieces of coloured glass that change pattern when the tube is turned
•***Word Family:*** **kaleidoscopic** *adjective* consisting of changing colourful patterns

kamikaze (*say* kam-a-**kah**-zee) *noun*
a member of a Japanese airforce corps in World War II who crashed their aircraft into enemy targets
•***Word Origins:*** from a Japanese word meaning "divine wind"

kangaroo *noun*
a large Australian animal growing up to about 2 metres high, with powerful back legs and a heavy tail
•***Word Origins:*** from an Aboriginal language

karaoke (*say* ka-ree-**oh**-kee) *noun*
an entertainment in which people take turns to sing along to recorded music using a microphone

A B C D E F G H I J K L M N O P Q R S T U V W X Y Z

karate (*say* ka-**rah**-tee) *noun*
a Japanese method of self-defence in which your hands, elbows, feet and knees are used as weapons
•***Word Origins:*** from a Japanese word meaning "empty hand"

karri *noun*
a Western Australian gum tree with hard, dark red wood used for building

kauri (*say* **kow**-ree) *noun*
a huge, New Zealand cone-bearing tree that grows to about 60 metres and has valuable wood
•***Word Origins:*** from a Maori word

kayak (*say* **kuy**-ak) *noun*
a small, lightweight canoe with a small opening for the rower

keel *noun*
1 the piece of wood or metal sticking out along the bottom of a boat to help keep it upright 2 **on an even keel** in a steady or balanced way
keel *verb*
3 **keel over** (a) to overturn or fall over: *The sailboard keeled over in the wind.* (b) to collapse suddenly: *to keel over and die*

keen *adjective*
1 intense or enthusiastic: *a keen football supporter* 2 well developed: *a keen sense of humour* 3 sharp: *a keen blade / a keen wind*
•***Word Family:*** **keenly** *adverb* **keenness** *noun*

keep *verb*
1 to continue: *to keep working* 2 to retain or continue to have: *Don't keep these clothes any longer.* 3 to have and look after: *to keep pets* 4 to stop: *to keep someone from leaving* 5 to do or carry out: *to keep a promise*
keep *noun*
6 the things you need to live, such as food, clothes and shelter: *to earn your keep*
•***Word Family:*** other verb forms are **keeps, kept, keeping**

keg *noun*
a small barrel, especially a metal one for beer

kelp *noun*
a type of large, brown seaweed

kennel *noun*
1 a house for a dog 2 **kennels** a place where dogs are kept or bred

kerb *noun*
the raised stone or concrete edge between a pavement and a road

kernel *noun*
the part of a nut inside the shell

kerosene (*say* ke-ra-**seen**) *noun*
a liquid fuel made from petroleum, used for heaters, lamps and jet engines

kettle *noun*
a container with a spout and a lid, in which water is boiled

kettledrum *noun*
a drum consisting of a basin-shaped brass or copper bowl with a skin stretched across it

key (*say* kee) *noun*
1 a small piece of metal cut or shaped to fit into and turn a lock 2 an explanation of symbols used on a map or to solve a puzzle or code 3 a button or part you press on a keyboard to work something such as a typewriter or a computer 4 one of the notes you press on a piano 5 a scale of notes related to each other and to one basic note, used to write or play music
key *adjective*
6 important: *to hold a key position in the school*
key *verb*
7 to enter data into a computer by using the keys

keyboard *noun*
a group or line of keys on a piano, typewriter, computer and so on

key signature *noun*
the sharps or flats coming after the clef to show in which key a piece of music is written

keystone *noun*
the middle stone of an arch, that holds it together

khaki (*say* **kah**-kee) *noun*
a dull, yellowish-brown colour especially used for army uniforms

kibbutz (*say* kib-**oots**) *noun*
a farm or settlement in Israel where people live together and share all the work, planning and income
•***Word Family:*** the plural is **kibbutzim**

kick *verb*
1 to strike or drive something with your foot: *to kick a ball* 2 to move your legs about a lot while lying down or being carried 3 to spring back the way a gun does when you fire it
kick *noun*
4 a hit with your foot 5 a pleasant or stimulating feeling: *to get a kick out of parachuting / This drink of punch has a real kick to it.* 6 **for kicks** for the thrill of it: *He did it for kicks.*
•***Word Family:*** definitions 5 and 6 are colloquial

kid (1) *noun*
1 a young goat 2 a child

kid (2) *verb*
to tease someone: *We're just kidding.*
• ***Word Family:*** other forms are **kids, kidded, kidding**

kidnap *verb*
to take someone away by force and demand money in exchange for their release
• ***Word Family:*** other forms are **kidnaps, kidnapped, kidnapping** □ **kidnapper** *noun*

kidney (*say* **kid**-nee) *noun*
one of the two organs in your body that removes waste from your blood and turns it into urine

kill *verb*
1 to make a person, animal or plant die 2 to pass or fill in time: *to have an hour to kill*
kill *noun*
3 the killing of an animal
• ***Word Family:*** **killer** *noun*

killing *noun*
a sudden large profit that is easily obtained: *to make a killing on the stock market*

kiln *noun*
a large oven for drying or baking bricks or pottery

kilo (*say* **kee**-lo) *noun*
a short form of **kilogram**
• ***Word Family:*** the plural is **kilos**

kilobyte *noun*
a measurement in computers of 1020 bytes, often used to indicate a thousand bytes

kilogram (*say* **kil**-o-gram) *noun*
a metric unit of mass measuring 1000 grams

kilojoule *noun*
one thousand joules, used to express the energy value of food, or how much food you have to eat to produce a unit of this energy

kilometre (*say* **kil**-a-mee-ta *or* kil-**om**-it-a) *noun*
a metric unit of length equal to 1000 metres

kilotonne (*say* **kil**-a-ton) *noun*
a metric unit for measuring the explosive force of nuclear weapons

kilowatt *noun*
a measurement of power equal to 1000 watts

kilt *noun*
a short pleated skirt, usually of tartan wool, sometimes worn by Scottish Highlanders

kimono (*say* ki-**mo**-no) *noun*
a loose Japanese robe, with wide sleeves and fastened with a sash

kin *plural noun*
your relatives: *My parents are my next of kin.*

kind (1) *adjective*
considerate, friendly or generous
• ***Word Family:*** **kindly** *adverb* **kindness** *noun*

kind (2) *noun*
a group, sort or type of similar or related things: *What kind of jam is this?*

kindergarten (*say* **kin**-da-gar-ten) *noun*
a school or class for very young children
• ***Word Origins:*** from the German words for "children" and "garden"

kindle (*say* **kin**-del) *verb*
1 to set something alight or to start burning: *to kindle the fire with dry twigs* 2 to excite a feeling in someone: *to kindle your imagination*

kindling (*say* **kin**-dling) *noun*
small pieces of wood or other material used to start a fire

kinetic (*say* kin-**et**-ik) *adjective*
to do with movement: *kinetic energy*

king *noun*
1 the royal, male ruler of a country who inherits his position from his mother or father
2 something or someone that is powerful or respected: *The lion is the king of beasts.*
3 a playing card with a picture of a king on it
• ***Word Family:*** **kingly** *adjective*

kingdom (*say* **king**-dum) *noun*
1 a country ruled by a king or queen 2 one of the large divisions in the natural world: *the plant and animal kingdoms*

kingfisher *noun*
a brightly coloured bird with a strong beak for catching fish or insects

kink *noun*
1 a short twist or curl in something 2 an unusual liking or quirk
• ***Word Family:*** **kinky** *adjective* **(kinkier, kinkiest)**

kinship *noun*
relationship by family ties or common interests

kiosk (*say* **kee**-osk) *noun*
1 a booth selling cigarettes, souvenirs, newspapers and so on 2 a telephone box

kiss *verb*
to touch someone with your lips as a sign of love

kit *noun*
1 the equipment or clothing for doing a

A B C D E F G H I J K L M N O P Q R S T U V W X Y Z

particular job: *a diving kit / a first-aid kit* 2 a set of parts made to be fitted together: *a table kit*

kitchen (*say* **kit**-chen) *noun*
a room for preparing and cooking food

kite *noun*
1 a light frame covered with fabric or paper, that you fly in the wind at the end of a string 2 a large hawk with long, pointed wings

kitten *noun*
the young of a domestic cat and of some other animals
•*Word Family:* **kittenish** *adjective* playful

kiwi (*say* **kee**-wee) *noun*
a flightless bird that is the national emblem of New Zealand

kiwi fruit *noun*
a small, hairy fruit with tender, green flesh

kleptomania (*say* klep-toe-**may**-nee-a) *noun*
an uncontrollable wish to steal things
•*Word Family:* **kleptomaniac** *noun*

knack (*say* nak) *noun*
an ability to do a particular thing well and easily: *a knack for finding bargains / a knack for getting into trouble*

knapsack (*say* **nap**-sak) *noun*
a light canvas or leather bag that hikers, climbers or other travellers carry on their backs for holding clothes and supplies

knave (*say* nave) *noun*
a dishonest or mischievous man or boy
•*Word Family:* **knavish** *adjective* **knavishly** *adverb*

knead (*say* need) *verb*
to press and squeeze dough or clay with your hands

knee (*say* nee) *noun*
the joint between the upper and the lower part of your leg

kneel (*say* neel) *verb*
to rest on or fall down onto your knees
•*Word Family:* other forms are **kneels, knelt** or **kneeled, kneeling**

knell (*say* nel) *noun*
the sound of a bell rung slowly to announce a death or funeral

knickers *plural noun*
underpants worn by women

knife (*say* nife) *noun*
1 a tool with a sharp blade set in a handle, used for cutting
knife *verb*
2 to cut or stab someone using a knife
•*Word Family:* the plural of the noun is **knives**

knight (*say* nite) *noun*
1 a nobleman in the Middle Ages, who was a solider and who usually fought on horseback wearing armour 2 a man who has been given the title "Sir", in return for serving his country 3 a chess piece shaped like a horse's head
knight *verb*
4 to officially give a man the title of knight
•*Word Family:* **knighthood** *noun* the title of knight, and being called "Sir"

knit (*say* nit) *verb*
1 to join loops of wool together using needles or a machine, in order to to make clothes 2 to join together or unite: *The broken bones will soon knit.* 3 to wrinkle together: *to knit your brow*
•*Word Family:* other forms are **knits, knitted, knitting** □ **knitting** *noun* a piece of knitted work

knob (*say* nob) *noun*
1 a round handle or control button: *a door knob / a TV knob* 2 a small amount: *a knob of butter*

knobbly (*say* **nob**-ull-ee) *adjective*
lumpy or bumpy: *a knobbly potato*
•*Word Family:* other forms are **knobblier, knobbliest**

knock (*say* nok) *verb*
1 to hit something with your hand or fist: *to knock on the door* 2 to strike or bump something: *to knock a hole in the wall / to knock over a vase*
knock *noun*
3 the act or sound of knocking

knockout *noun*
1 knocking someone unconscious, especially in a boxing match 2 something or someone who is very attractive or successful

knoll (*say* nol) *noun*
a small round hill

knot (*say* not) *noun*
1 a fastening made by passing the free end of a piece of string or rope through a loop in it and pulling tight 2 a group or cluster: *a small knot of people* 3 a hard lump in wood where a branch once joined a tree trunk 4 a measure for speed, used in air and sea navigation, equal to 1.85 kilometres per hour
knot *verb*
5 to make a knot in a piece of string or rope
•*Word Family:* other verb forms are **knots, knotted, knotting** □ **knotty** *adjective* (**knottier, knottiest**)

know (*say* noh) *verb*
1 to understand, or feel certain of something

because you have experienced or learnt it before: *I know what you mean*. 2 to be acquainted with a person or thing: *I know her well*. 3 to recognize someone: *I'd know you anywhere*.
•***Word Family:*** other forms are **knows, knew, known** □ **knowing** *adjective* shrewd **knowingly** *adverb*

know-how *noun*
the practical knowledge you need to do something

knowledge (*say* **nol**-ij) *noun*
what you know, or is possible to be known: *my knowledge of music / beyond human knowledge*
•***Word Family:*** **knowledgeable** *adjective* having knowledge

knuckle (*say* **nuk**-ul) *noun*
a finger joint, especially the joint where the base of a finger meets the hand

koala (*say* ko-**ah**-la) *noun*
an Australian animal with grey fur, a flat black nose and strong claws, living in and feeding only on eucalyptus trees
•***Word Origins:*** from an Aboriginal language

kookaburra *noun*
a brown and white Australian bird with blue markings on its wings, and an unusual, laughing cry
•***Word Origins:*** from an Aboriginal language

Koori (*say* **koo**-ree) *noun*
1 an Aboriginal person, especially of south-eastern Australia
•***Word Family:* Koori** *adjective*
•***Word Origins:*** from an Aboriginal language

Koran (*say* kor-**rahn**) *noun*
the sacred scriptures of Islam, believed by Muslims to be the words of Allah through the prophet Mohammed
•***Word Origins:*** from an Arabic word meaning "reading" or "recitation"

kosher (*say* -**koh**-sher) *adjective*
specially prepared according to Jewish religious law: *kosher meat*

Krishna *noun*
a popular Hindu god
•***Word Origins:*** from a Sanskrit (ancient Indian) word meaning "black"

kumquat (*say* **kum**-kwot) *noun*
another spelling for **cumquat**

kung fu *noun*
a Chinese form of karate used for excercise and self-defence

Ll

label (*rhymes with* table) *noun*
1 a piece of paper attached to an object to show where it is going, who it belongs to, or what it is: *a luggage label*
label *verb*
2 to mark or describe something with a label
•***Word Family:*** other verb forms are **labels, labelled, labelling**

laboratory (*say* la-**bo**-ra-tree) *noun*
a room or building with all the chemicals and instruments you need for doing scientific experiments
•***Word Family:*** the plural is **laboratories**

laborious (*say* la-**baw**-ree-us) *adjective*
needing effort or hard work: *a laborious task*
•***Word Family:* laboriously** *adverb*

labour or **labor** (*say* **lay**-ba) *noun*
1 hard work 2 the people paid to work at a particular type of job: *unskilled labour* 3 the time and effort involved in giving birth to a baby: *to be in labour for four hours*
labour *verb*
4 to work hard for a long time: *to labour in the garden*
•***Word Family:* labourer** *noun* a worker whose job needs strength rather than skill

labrador *noun*
a breed of large dog with smooth black or golden hair
•***Word Origins:*** named after *Labrador*, an area of Canada, from where the dogs first came

labyrinth (*say* **lab**-a-rinth) *noun*
a twisted maze of confusing paths from which it is hard to escape

lace *noun*
1 a fine, net-like material of threads woven together 2 a cord for fastening or tightening shoes or clothing
lace *verb*
3 to tie shoes or clothing together with laces: *to lace up your shoes*
•***Word Family:* lacy** *adjective* **(lacier, laciest)**

lack *noun*
1 an absence or shortage of something: *a widespread lack of food*
lack *verb*
2 to be without something: *to lack a job*

A B C D E F G H I J K L M N O P Q R S T U V W X Y Z

laconic *adjective*
using few words: *a laconic answer*
• ***Word Family:*** **laconically** *adverb*

lacquer (*say* **lak**-a) *noun*
1 a clear coating that protects a surface and makes it shiny
lacquer *verb*
2 to coat something with lacquer

lacrosse (*say* la-**kros**) *noun*
an outdoor game for two teams of players, whose aim is to force a ball into the goal, using long-handled racquets

lactate *verb*
to produce milk in your breasts or an animal's udder
• ***Word Family:*** **lactation** *noun*

lad *noun*
a boy or young man

ladder *noun*
1 a set of steps set into a frame, for climbing up and down 2 a line of stitches in a pair of tights or stockings, that have come undone
ladder *verb*
3 to tear tights or stockings and put a ladder in them

laden *adjective*
carrying a large heavy load: *a lorry laden with milk crates / a heavily laden lorry*

ladle (*say* **lay**-del) *noun*
1 a large, deep spoon with a long handle, normally used for serving liquids such as soup
ladle *verb*
2 to serve soup or other food using a ladle

lady (*say* **lay**-dee) *noun*
1 a polite word for a woman 2 **Lady** a form of address used for a countess, baroness or someone like this
• ***Word Family:*** the plural is **ladies**

ladybird *noun*
a beetle, often red with black spots, that feeds on insects

lag *verb*
1 to decrease: *My interest in shopping is lagging.* 2 to wrap pipes or a boiler with material to stop heat getting out 3 **lag behind** to fall behind or go more slowly than other people
• ***Word Family:*** other forms are **lags, lagged, lagging** □ **lagging** *noun* the material used to lag pipes or a boiler

lager (*say* **lah**-ga) *noun*
a light-coloured kind of beer

lagoon (*say* la-**goon**) *noun*
an area of salt water, often separated from the sea by a sandbank or coral reef

lair *noun*
the den or resting place of a wild animal

lake *noun*
a large area of water surrounded by land

lamb (*say* lam) *noun*
1 a young sheep, or its meat used as food
lamb *verb*
2 to give birth to lambs

lame *adjective*
1 crippled in one leg, so that you walk with a limp 2 weak: *What a lame excuse!*
lame *verb*
3 to make a person or animal lame
• ***Word Family:*** **lamely** *adverb* **lameness** *noun*

lament (*say* la-**ment**) *verb*
1 to feel or show sorrow or regret about something: *to lament the fact that you have spent all your money*
lament *noun*
2 a verse or song that expresses sorrow
• ***Word Family:*** **lamentable** *adjective* terrible: *a lamentable state of affairs* **lamentably** *adverb* **lamentation** *noun*

laminate (*say* **lam**-in-ate) *verb*
1 to split something such as wood into layers 2 to cover or overlay something with thin layers of something such as wood
laminate *noun*
3 a material consisting of lots of thin layers: *plastic laminate*
• ***Word Family:*** **laminated** *adjective* **lamination** *noun*

lamp *noun*
a light using oil, gas or electricity, often one that you can carry

lance *verb*
1 to cut open a boil or other swelling with a knife or scalpel: *The doctor lanced his abscess.*
lance *noun*
2 a long spear once used by soldiers on horseback

land *noun*
1 the part of the Earth's surface not covered by water 2 an area of ground: *The shed was on the land when we bought it.* 3 a country or nation: *to travel in foreign lands*
land *verb*
4 to come to land or shore: *The aircraft landed safely.* 5 to come to rest or arrive in a place or position: *Where did the kite land?*

landfill *noun*
garbage and building rubbish used to raise the level of a piece of land

landing *noun*
1 coming to land or shore: *a safe landing* 2 the

open area at the top of a flight of stairs, or between flights

landmark *noun*
1 an object you can easily recognize, which is used as a guide to travellers 2 an event marking an important stage of development: *The invention of gunpowder was a landmark in world history.*

land rights *plural noun*
the rights of the original people of a country to own land, especially their sacred or religious sites

landscape *noun*
1 the land in a particular area and what it looks like, especially how beautiful it is: *The landscape of the region has not changed for thousands of years.* 2 a painting or a photograph of a view, especially one of the countryside
landscape *verb*
3 to lay out a garden or similar place so that it looks attractive

landslide *noun*
1 a mass of soil and rocks sliding down a hillside 2 an easy victory: *He won the election in a landslide.*

lane *noun*
1 a narrow road or alley 2 a strip on a road marked with lines for a single line of traffic 3 a similar strip marked in a swimming pool or on a racetrack for a swimmer or runner

language (*say* **lang**-wij) *noun*
1 the words we speak or write 2 the sounds or words used by a particular country or group: *the Japanese language* 3 a system of signs or symbols used to communicate: *Deaf people use sign language.* 4 the code used to write a computer program

languish (*say* **lang**-gwish) *verb*
to become weak or feeble: *to languish in prison*

lank *adjective*
1 tall and lean: *a lank body* 2 straight and limp or flat: *lank hair*
•***Word Family:*** **lanky** *adjective* (**lankier, lankiest**) tall and thin

lantern *noun*
a light with a glass case around it to protect it from the wind

lap (1) *noun*
the front of your body from your waist to your knees, when sitting: *to hold a baby in your lap*

lap (2) *noun*
a single trip around a racetrack, or from one end of a swimming pool to the other

lap (3) *verb*
1 to drink a liquid with the tongue: *The kitten lapped the milk.* 2 to wash gently against something: *Water lapped against the wharf.*
•***Word Family:*** other forms are **laps, lapped, lapping**

lapel (*say* la-**pel**) *noun*
the part of a coat that comes down from the collar and folds back over your chest

lapidary (*say* **lap**-i-dree) *noun*
the art of cutting and polishing jewels

lapse (*say* laps) *noun*
1 a slight mistake or failure: *a lapse of memory* 2 a period of time that has passed
lapse *verb*
3 to slide or slip slowly: *to lapse into unconsciousness* 4 to be no longer valid

laptop *noun*
a small computer that you can carry around with you and rest on your lap

larceny (*say* **lar**-sa-nee) *noun*
the stealing of another person's things
•***Word Family:*** the plural is **larcenies** □ **larcenous** *adjective*

larder *noun*
a cupboard or room for keeping food

large *adjective*
1 bigger or greater than usual: *a large family*
large *noun*
2 **at large** (a) free: *The bandits are still at large.* (b) in general: *important information for tourists at large*
•***Word Family:*** **largely** *adverb* to a great extent

lark (1) *noun*
a type of small, brown bird, living mainly in northern parts of the world and known for its sweet song

lark (2) *noun*
an amusing prank or joke

larrikin *noun*
a wild, noisy person, usually young
•***Word Family:*** **larrikinism** *noun*

larva *noun*
the young of an insect at the stage when it has just come out of the egg and looks like a short, fat worm
•***Word Family:*** the plural is **larvae** (*say* **lar**-vee) □ **larval** *adjective*
•***Word Origins:*** from a Latin word meaning "ghost" or "mask"

laryngitis (*say* la-**rin**-juy-tis) *noun*
an infection in your larynx that makes your throat so red and sore that you can't speak

larynx (*say* **la**-rinx) *noun*
the box-shaped space in your neck, through which air passes from your nose to your lungs, and where speech sounds are produced by your vocal cords
• ***Word Family:*** the plural is **larynges** or **larynxes**

lasagne (*say* la-**san**-ya) *noun*
a type of pasta cut into flat rectangles and the dish made from this, usually with minced meat, tomato and cheese

laser (*say* **lay**-za) *noun*
a device for producing an extremely powerful beam of light, used in drilling steel, for some forms of surgery, or in communications
• ***Word Family:*** **laser printer** *noun* a printer linked to a computer, that uses laser beams
• ***Word Origins:*** an acronym from the first letter of the words light amplification by stimulated emission of radiation

lash *verb*
1 to strike someone or something with a whip 2 to beat or strike violently against something: *Heavy rain lashed the windows.* 3 to tie something securely with rope
lash *noun*
4 the cord of a whip 5 a blow with a whip: *The prisoner was sentenced to 16 lashes.* 6 a short form of **eyelash**
• ***Word Family:*** the plural of the noun is **lashes**

lass *noun*
a girl or young woman
• ***Word Family:*** the plural is **lasses**

lasso (*say* la-**soo**) *noun*
1 a long rope with a loop or noose at one end that you can pull tight, used to catch cattle, sheep or horses
lasso *verb*
2 to catch an animal with a lasso
• ***Word Family:*** the plural of the noun is **lassoes** or **lassos** □ other forms of the verb are **lassoes, lassoed, lassoing**

last (1) *adjective*
1 final or coming after all the others: *the last train* 2 most recent: *last week*
last *adverb*
3 after all the others: *to come last*
last *noun*
4 what comes at the very end: *We ate the last of the sandwiches.* 5 **at last** after much delay
• ***Word Family:*** **lastly** *adverb* finally

last (2) *verb*
to continue or endure: *The match lasted for two hours.*
• ***Word Family:*** **lasting** *adjective*

latch *noun*
1 a simple fastening with a bar that falls into a slot, for keeping a gate or door shut
latch *verb*
2 to fasten something with a latch 3 **latch on to** to understand something
• ***Word Family:*** the plural of the noun is **latches**

late *adjective*
1 coming after the usual or proper time: *a late breakfast / a late train* 2 near the end of a period of time: *late afternoon* 3 deceased or dead: *her late husband* 4 **of late** recently
• ***Word Family:*** **lately** *adverb* recently **lateness** *noun*

latent (*say* **lay**-tent) *adjective*
present but not active or easily seen: *latent talent*

lateral (*say* **lat**-a-ral) *adjective*
to do with the side: *the lateral branches on a tree trunk*
• ***Word Family:*** **laterally** *adverb*

lathe (*say* layth) *noun*
a machine that holds and turns a piece of wood, metal or other material while you are cutting or shaping it

lather *noun*
1 foam or froth: *soap lather / the lather on the skin of a hot horse*
lather *verb*
2 to make a lather on something: *He lathered his chin before shaving.*

Latin *noun*
the language of the ancient Romans

latitude (*say* **lat**-i-tewd) *noun*
1 distance north or south of the equator, measured in degrees 2 freedom to act or think as you like: *We are given latitude in what we wear to school.*

latter *adjective*
1 the second of two things being talked about: *Of meat pies and sausage rolls, I prefer the latter.* 2 belonging to or coming near the end of something: *the latter days of his life*
• ***Word Family:*** **latterly** *adverb* lately

lattice (*say* **lat**-iss) *noun*
a structure of crossed, wooden strips usually in a diamond pattern, used as a screen, or for supporting plants

laugh (*say* lahf) *verb*
1 to make sounds that show you are happy, amused or scornful 2 **laugh at** to make fun of
laugh *noun*
3 the sound, or act of laughing
• ***Word Family:*** **laughable** *adjective* amusing or silly **laughter** *noun*

launch (1) (*say* lawnch) *noun*
a large, sturdy, open boat, usually with an engine

launch (2) (*say* lawnch) *verb*
1 to put a boat into the water 2 to send a rocket into the air 3 to start something, or set it going: *to launch a book / to launch an attack*

laundry (*say* **lawn**-dree) *noun*
1 a room for washing clothes 2 the dirty clothes that are ready to be washed
• ***Word Family:*** **launder** *verb*

laurel (*say* **lo**-rel) *noun*
a small, evergreen tree with shiny leaves, once used to make the victory wreaths of ancient Greek and Roman heroes

lava (*say* **lah**-va) *noun*
1 the hot, liquid rock from inside the Earth that flows out through an erupting volcano 2 the solid rock that forms when this cools

lavatory (*say* **lav**-a-tree) *noun*
a toilet or the room it is in
• ***Word Family:*** the plural is **lavatories**

lavender *noun*
1 a pale, pinkish-violet colour 2 a shrub with spikes of pale purple flowers with a strong but pleasant smell

lavish (*say* **lav**-ish) *verb*
1 to give something abundantly or generously: *to lavish attention on a sick child*
lavish *adjective*
2 generous or plentiful: *lavish presents*
• ***Word Family:*** **lavishly** *adverb*
• ***Word Origins:*** from an Old French word meaning "a downpour of rain"

law *noun*
1 a rule or system of rules decided by a government or ruler, that the people of a country must keep 2 the profession that deals with these rules and the way they are used 3 the police force 4 a rule that helps us explain how and why things happen in the world around us: *the law of gravity*
• ***Word Family:*** **lawful** *adjective* allowed by law **lawless** *adjective* not obeying the law **lawfully** *adverb* **lawlessly** *adverb*

lawn *noun*
an area of neatly cut grass, usually in a private garden

lawsuit *noun*
a court case, for example when you sue someone, claim damages and so on

lawyer (*say* **loy**-a) *noun*
someone whose job is to advise people about the law and to represent and argue for them in a law court

lax *adjective*
not strict enough: *lax morals / lax discipline*
• ***Word Family:*** **laxity** *noun* **laxness** *noun*

laxative *noun*
medicine you take to help you pass waste matter from your bowels

lay *verb*
1 to put down or place something somewhere: *to lay a book on the table / to lay your head on a pillow* 2 to prepare or arrange something: *to lay plans / to lay the table* 3 to produce eggs 4 **lay off** (a) to dismiss someone from a job: *to lay off a worker* (b) to give up or stop doing something: *to lay off bullying someone* 5 **lay on** to arrange or provide something for people: *to lay on a meal for visitors*
• ***Word Family:*** the other verb forms are **lays, laid, laying**

layer *noun*
1 a single thickness or coating: *a layer of icing / a layer of dirt*
layer *verb*
2 to spread or arrange something in layers: *to layer his hair*

lazy *adjective*
1 unwilling to work or be active: *a lazy pupil / a lazy dog* 2 moving slowly: *a lazy stream*
• ***Word Family:*** other forms are **lazier, laziest** □ **laze** *verb* to be lazy or idle **lazily** *adverb* **laziness** *noun*

LCD *noun*
a way of displaying information continuously on watches, computers, calculators and other display screens, using a liquid-crystal film sealed between glass plates
• ***Word Origins:*** made from the first letters of the words Liquid Crystal Display

leach *verb*
to remove the parts that make up soil, ashes, and so on by the percolating action of water as it passes through

lead (1) (*say* leed) *verb*
1 to take or guide someone: *to lead him to the classroom* 2 to direct or command people: *to lead an army* 3 to spend or live: *to lead a dull life* 4 to be at the head of a group of people: *to lead a procession*
lead *noun*
5 the first or foremost place: *Who's in the lead?* 6 the distance ahead: *a lead of two metres* 7 a leash or strap: *a lead for holding a dog* 8 a clue: *a lead in the murder* 9 a cord for carrying electricity: *a guitar lead*
• ***Word Family:*** other verb forms are **leads, led, leading**

lead (2) (*say* led) *noun*
1 a soft heavy metal, used to make bullets and pipes 2 a long, thin piece of graphite used in pencils
•*Word Family:* **leaden** *adjective* heavy and bluish-grey like lead

leader (*say* **leed**-a) *noun*
1 someone or something that leads: *the leader of the tour* 2 a newspaper article written to express the opinion of the editor on current happenings

leaf *noun*
1 a flat, usually green, growth found on the stem of plants 2 a single sheet of paper forming two pages of a book 3 an extra panel used to make a table longer 4 a very thin metal sheet: *gold leaf* 5 **turn over a new leaf** to make a new and better start
•*Word Family:* the plural is **leaves** □ **leafy** *adjective* (**leafier, leafiest**)

leaflet *noun*
a flat or folded sheet with printed information on it

league (1) (*say* leeg) *noun*
1 a group of people, nations or organizations who have made an agreement for their common good 2 a group of sporting clubs that arranges matches between its member teams: *Rugby League football* 3 **in league with** working together with a particular group or person

league (2) (*say* leeg) *noun*
an old-fashioned measure of length, equal to about 5.5 kilometres or 3 miles

leak *verb*
1 to let liquid or gas enter or escape by accident: *The roof leaks.* 2 to give out secret information
leak *noun*
3 a hole or crack through which liquid or gas leaks 4 the amount that leaks: *a steady leak from the crack in the dam*
•*Word Family:* **leaky** *adjective* (**leakier, leakiest**) **leakiness** *noun*

lean (1) *verb*
1 to bend over from an upright position, or in a particular direction: *The waiter leaned over the table.* / *to lean out of the window* 2 to rest against or on something for support
•*Word Family:* other forms are **leans, leant** or **leaned, leaning**

lean (2) *adjective*
1 having little fat: *a lean man* / *lean meat* 2 when there is a shortage of food or money: *lean years*

leap *verb*
1 to spring or jump: *to leap off a fence* / *to leap back in fright*
leap *noun*
2 a spring or bound 3 a sharp rise: *a leap in prices*
•*Word Family:* other verb forms are **leaps, leapt** or **leaped, leaping**

leap year *noun*
a year that has 366 days, the extra day being 29 February, that occurs every four years

learn (*say* lern) *verb*
1 to gain knowledge or skill from instruction or practice: *to learn German* / *to learn the violin* 2 to be told or informed about something: *I was sorry to learn of your accident.*
•*Word Family:* other forms are **learns, learnt** or **learned, learning** □ **learning** *noun* knowledge **learner** *noun*

learned (*say* **ler**-ned) *adjective*
having a great deal of knowledge gained from years of study: *a learned judge*

lease *noun*
1 a contract that allows a person to use or live in a property in return for paying rent
lease *verb*
2 to give someone something or to use something by lease

leash *noun*
a strap or rope for holding a dog

least *noun*
1 the smallest in number, importance, cost or extent
least *adjective*
2 smallest: *She wears the least amount of makeup.*

leather (*say* **le**-dha) *noun*
the tanned and prepared skin of animals, used to make such things as bags and shoes
•*Word Family:* **leathery** *adjective*: *leathery skin*

leave (1) *verb*
1 to go away from a particular place: *to leave the country* 2 to cause or allow something to remain somewhere in a particular state: *Leave your hat in the hall.* / *Leave the radiator turned on.* 3 to entrust something or hand it over: *Leave the arrangements to me.* 4 to give someone something as an inheritance: *My father left me a fortune in his will.*
•*Word Family:* other forms are **leaves, left, leaving** □ **leaver** *noun*

leave (2) *noun*
1 permission: *Give me leave to depart.* 2 the time you are allowed to be absent: *four weeks' annual leave*

lecture (*say* **lek**-cher) *noun*
1 a formal talk given to teach or inform a group: *a lecture on health* 2 a long, boring telling-off: *Dad gave me a lecture when I got home late.*

lecture *verb*
3 to give a lecture to someone
• ***Word Family:*** **lecturer** *noun* someone who gives lectures

ledge *noun*
a narrow shelf: *a window ledge*

lee *noun*
the side of something that is sheltered or in a different direction from the wind: *the lee of a mountain*

leech *noun*
a small worm that lives in very damp places and sucks the blood of humans and animals
• ***Word Family:*** the plural is **leeches**

leek *noun*
a vegetable of the onion family, with a white bulb and broad flat leaves

leer *noun*
1 a nasty smile that shows you are thinking of sex or cunning things you could do to someone
leer *verb*
2 to make a leer

left *adjective*
1 to do with the side of a person or thing that faces west when their front is facing north: *your left leg*
left *noun*
2 the left side 3 **the left** the people or political groups who stand for the rights of the workers rather than the bosses of large companies and for wealth to be shared out more equally

left-handed *adjective*
using your left hand more than your right

leg *noun*
1 one of the parts of the body used for walking and carrying weight 2 something shaped or used like a leg: *a chair leg / a pyjama leg* 3 one of the distinct parts of a journey, course or race: *the first leg of an overseas tour*

legacy (*say* **leg**-a-see) *noun*
1 something handed down from people that lived or things that happened in the past: *The legacy of hatred that dates back to the war.* 2 a gift of money or property left to someone in a will
• ***Word Family:*** the plural is **legacies**

legal (*say* **lee**-gal) *adjective*
1 to do with the law: *legal matters* 2 lawful or allowed by law: *a legal business deal*
• ***Word Family:*** **legalize** or **legalise** *verb* to make something legal **legality** *noun* **legally** *adverb*

legend (*say* **lej**-end) *noun*
1 a tale from long ago about a famous hero or place, that is probably partly true 2 the key that explains the symbols on a map or diagram
• ***Word Family:*** **legendary** *adjective* famous

legible *adjective*
easy to read: *legible handwriting*
• ***Word Family:*** **legibility** *noun* **legibly** *adverb*

legion (*say* **lee**-jen) *noun*
1 a unit of soldiers in the Roman army, of more than 3000 men 2 a large unit of soldiers: *the Foreign Legion* 3 a huge number: *a legion of fans*
• ***Word Family:*** **legionary** *noun* a Roman soldier

legislation (*say* **lej**-is-lay-shon) *noun*
1 making laws 2 a law or group of laws: *new legislation to allow freedom of information*
• ***Word Family:*** **legislate** *verb* to make laws **legislator** *noun*

legitimate (*say* le-**jit**-a-mit) *adjective*
1 lawful: *a legitimate business* 2 born to parents who are legally married: *a legitimate child*
• ***Word Family:*** **legitimacy** *noun* **legitimately** *adverb*

leisure (*rhymes with* treasure) *noun*
1 the time free from work or duties: *How do you spend your leisure time?* 2 **at leisure** without hurrying
• ***Word Family:*** **leisurely** *adjective* without haste

lemon *noun*
1 a yellow fruit with a sour taste 2 a pale yellow colour
lemon *adjective*
3 pale yellow

lemonade *noun*
a fizzy drink made from lemons, sugar and water

lend *verb*
1 to give someone something that you expect to get back 2 **lend a hand** to help
• ***Word Family:*** other forms are **lends, lent, lending** □ **lender** *noun* **loan** *noun*

length *noun*
1 the distance from end to end: *What's the length of this room?* 2 a long piece of something: *a length of string* 3 **at length** in detail: *to describe the accident at length*
• ***Word Family:*** **lengthen** *verb* **lengthy** *adjective*

lengthways *adverb*
from end to end, or along the longest part: *to fold a piece of paper lengthways*

lenient (*say* **lee**-nee-ent) *adjective*
mild, merciful or gentle in the treatment of others: *a lenient captain / a lenient punishment*
• ***Word Family:*** **lenience** *noun* **leniency** *noun* **leniently** *adverb*

lens (*say* lenz) *noun*
a curved piece of glass or plastic that makes

A B C D E F G H I J K L M N O P Q R S T U V W X Y Z

objects look bigger when you look through it, or is used in a pair of glasses to help you see better
•*Word Family:* the plural is **lenses**

Lent *noun*
a period of forty days before Easter, when some Christians give up something they enjoy

leopard (*say* **lep**-ed) *noun*
a large, spotted, meat-eating animal of the cat family that comes from Asia or Africa

leotard (*say* **lee**-o-tard) *noun*
a close-fitting piece of clothing worn for dancing, gymnastics or other exercise
•*Word Origins:* named after Jules *Léotard*, a French acrobat, who died in 1870

leprosy (*say* **lep**-ra-see) *noun*
a disease spread from one person to another, that causes sores on your skin, and loss of feeling in your nerve ends, sometimes leading to loss of your fingers and toes
•*Word Family:* **leper** (*say* **lep**-a) *noun*

lesbian *noun*
a woman who is sexually attracted to other women
•*Word Family:* **lesbianism** *noun*
•*Word Origins:* named after *Lesbos*, the Greek island home of Sappho, an ancient poet who wrote of lesbian love

less *adjective*
1 smaller or not as much in amount, size or extent: I get *less pocket money than my sister.*
less *adverb*
2 in a smaller amount: *Do you have any less expensive meat?*
•*Word Family:* this is a form of **little** □ **lessen** *verb* to make or become less

lesson *noun*
1 something you learn, or from which you learn: *a lesson in ice-skating / The crash taught me a lesson.* 2 a period of time in which a pupil or class is taught one particular subject: *a maths lesson* 3 a passage from the Bible read aloud during a church service

let *verb*
1 to allow or permit someone to do something: *Let me come!* 2 to rent or hire a place to someone: *We let the house to a French family.*
3 **let down** (a) to lower something: *to let down the blinds* (b) to fail or disappoint someone: *to let someone down*
•*Word Family:* other forms are **lets, let, letting**

lethal (*say* **lee**-thal) *adjective*
able to cause death: *a lethal drug*
•*Word Family:* **lethally** *adverb*

lethargic (*say* le-**thar**-jik) *adjective*
sleepily lazy or inactive: *to feel lethargic in the heat*
•*Word Family:* **lethargically** *adverb* **lethargy** *noun*

letter *noun*
1 a written symbol for a speech sound: "Z" *is the last letter in the alphabet.* 2 a written or printed message addressed to a person or group

lettuce (*say* **let**-iss) *noun*
a large, green vegetable with leaves that are used in salads

leukaemia or leukemia (*say* loo-**kee**-mee-a) *noun*
a disease that makes your body produce too many white blood cells and that may cause death

levee (*say* **lev**-ee) *noun*
1 a river bank formed when a river leaves layers of sandy earth during floods 2 a bank built around irrigated fields, or to protect land from possible floodwater

level *noun*
1 a position in relation to others: *the highest level of power* 2 a horizontal line or position 3 an instrument used to check or indicate if something is flat or horizontal: *a spirit level*
4 **on the level** honest: *Is he really on the level?*
level *adjective*
5 straight or even: *a level shelf* 6 equal: *They're level in most subjects.*
level *verb*
7 to make or become level or equal 8 to aim or point a weapon at someone: *The hijacker levelled a gun at the hostage.* 9 to be honest or truthful: *to level with your parents*
•*Word Family:* other verb forms are **levels, levelled, levelling** □ **leveller** *noun* **levelly** *adverb*

lever (*say* **lee**-va) *noun*
1 a bar supported somewhere along its length, that you use to lift or move a weight 2 a handle for working a machine
lever *verb*
3 to move a weight with a lever
•*Word Family:* **leverage** *noun*

levy (*say* **lev**-ee) *verb*
1 to impose or collect money by law: *to levy a new tax on alcohol*
levy *noun*
2 a tax or fee which must be paid by law
•*Word Family:* other verb forms are **levies, levied, levying** □ the plural of the noun is **levies**

liability (*say* lie-a-**bil**-i-tee) *noun*
1 a legal obligation or responsibility: *to deny*

liability for the accident 2 something that makes things difficult or dangerous rather than helping you: *These shoes are a liability in wet weather.*
• ***Word Family:*** the plural is **liabilities**

liable (*say* **lie**-a-bul) *adjective*
1 legally responsible: *The company was declared liable and had to repay all the money.* 2 likely: *He's liable to throw a tantrum if he doesn't get his own way.*

liaison (*say* lee-**ay**-zon) *noun*
someone who brings about contact, connection or communication between people or groups: *There is a close liaison between the police and the local schools.*
• ***Word Family:*** **liaise** *verb* to meet and work with a particular person or group

liar *noun*
someone who tells lies

libel (*say* **lie**-bel) *noun*
1 a written, broadcast or printed statement that is untrue and damages someone's good name
libel *verb*
2 to use libel against someone
• ***Word Family:*** other verb forms are **libels, libelled, libelling** □ **libeller** *noun* **libellous** *adjective* **libellously** *adverb*

liberal (*say* **lib**-a-ral) *adjective*
1 in favour of progress, reform and individual freedom, especially in social or religious matters
2 generous: *a liberal serving of chips*
liberal *noun*
3 a person with liberal, tolerant views
• ***Word Family:*** **liberality** *noun* (**liberalities**) **liberalism** *noun* **liberally** *adverb*

liberate *verb*
to set a person or place free: *to liberate the hostages from the rebel forces*
• ***Word Family:*** **liberation** *noun* **liberator** *noun*

liberty (*say* **lib**-a-tee) *noun*
1 freedom from confinement, or from the control of a foreign army: *to gain your liberty after twenty years in prison* 2 the right to do, act or think as you choose 3 a rude act or remark: *What a liberty!* 4 **at liberty** permitted, or free to do something: *You are at liberty to leave whenever you wish.*
• ***Word Family:*** the plural is **liberties**

library (*say* **lie**-bra-ree) *noun*
1 a room or building where a collection of books is kept for people to read or borrow 2 a collection of books, or of records, films or music: *She has a huge library of ghost stories.*
• ***Word Family:*** the plural is **libraries** □ **librarian** *noun* someone in charge of a library

licence (*say* **lie**-sense) *noun*
1 official permission to do something 2 a document showing this permission: *a driving licence* 3 freedom you are given to do what you like: *The young teacher allowed his students too much licence.*

license *verb*
to give official permission to someone to do something: *This store is licensed to sell alcohol.*
• ***Word Family:*** **licensee** *noun* someone issued with a licence, usually to sell alcohol

lichen (*say* **lie**-ken) *noun*
a plant like moss, often appearing as a light green growth on tree trunks and rocks

lick *verb*
1 to pass the tongue over something: *The dog licked the plate clean.* 2 to touch something lightly: *The flames licked the side of the house.* 3 to defeat someone easily or by a large amount: *We licked the opposing team.*
lick *noun*
4 a stroke of the tongue, or a similar light touch

licorice (*say* **lik**-a-rish) *noun*
another spelling for **liquorice**

lid *noun*
1 a movable cover that fits on top of a container 2 a short form of **eyelid**

lie (1) *noun*
1 a deliberately told untrue statement: *to tell a lie*
lie *verb*
2 to say something you know is untrue
• ***Word Family:*** other verb forms are **lies, lied, lying**

lie (2) *verb*
1 to rest in a flat or horizontal position: *The book lay on the table. / You can't lie in bed all day.* 2 to remain: *The money lay in the bank for ten years.* 3 to extend, or exist: *The future lies before you. / The fault lies with the government.*
• ***Word Family:*** other verb forms are **lies, lay, lain, lying**

lieutenant (*say* lef-**ten**-ent) *noun*
1 an officer in the army or navy, ranking under a captain 2 a person's chief assistant or deputy

life *noun*
1 the state of being alive, growing and reproducing, which makes plants and animals different from earth or stones 2 your own existence, or the time you are alive, from when you are born to when you die: *He worked hard all his life. / Life has been difficult for us recently.* 3 all living things: *There's no evidence of life on Mars.* 4 activity or interest: *a spark of life* 5 the time that something lasts or works for: *Most computers have a life of about three years.* 6 the

A B C D E F G H I J K L M N O P Q R S T U V W X Y Z

punishment of being sent to prison for the rest of your life or for a very long time
•***Word Family:*** the plural is **lives**

lifeboat *noun*
1 a boat based on the coast and equipped to rescue people or ships in trouble at sea 2 a boat carried on deck and used to escape from a sinking ship

life cycle *noun*
the changes a living thing goes through from the start of its life to its adult or completed form and then to its death

life insurance *noun*
insurance which pays a person's husband, wife and so on a large amount of money if the person dies

lifesaver *noun*
someone who rescues and gives first aid to swimmers in danger of drowning

lifespan *noun*
the length of time that a person, animal or plant lives for

lifestyle *noun*
the way people live, what they like doing and what they spend their money on

lift *verb*
1 to raise something to a higher position or level: *to lift a box from the floor onto the table / She tried to lift our spirits.* 2 to clear away: *The mist should lift soon.* 3 to remove something: *to lift a ban*
4 to steal something: *to lift goods from a store*
lift *noun*
5 a box-like cage for moving people or goods from one level of a building to another 6 a ride: *Give me a lift in your car.*

ligament (*say* **lig**-a-ment) *noun*
a band of tough tissue in your body that connects your bones

light (1) *noun*
1 the radiation from the sun, a fire or some similar source, that lets us see things
2 something that gives out light, such as an electric light: *Put the light on.* 3 one of the set of coloured traffic lights that tells cars when to stop or go: *a red light* 4 a match or flame: *to give someone a light*
light *adjective*
5 with plenty of light: *a light room* 6 pale in colour: *I used light green for the living room.*
light *verb*
7 to give light to someone: *The moon will light your way.* 8 to start something burning: *to light a match* 9 **light up** to brighten something: *His face lit up in a huge grin. / The church was lit up at night by floodlights.*
•***Word Family:*** other verb forms are **lights, lit** or **lighted, lighting** □ **lighting** *noun* **lightness** *noun*

light (2) *adjective*
1 having little weight or not heavy: *a light bag*
2 not large, long or strong: *a light meal / a light sleep / light rain* 3 not serious: *some light reading*
4 cheery or carefree: *a light laugh*
•***Word Family:*** **lightly** *adverb* **lightness** *noun*

lighthouse *noun*
a tower, clearly seen from the sea, with a strong light to guide passing ships and keep them away from rocks

lightning *noun*
a brilliant flash of light in the sky caused by the release of natural electricity in the air during a thunderstorm

like (1) *preposition*
1 in the same way as, or looking similar to: *to grow like a weed / She's like her mother.*
like *noun*
2 something which is the same as or equal to something else: *I've never heard the like before.*
3 a similar thing: *tables, chairs and the like*
like *adjective*
4 similar: *They are of like mind.*
•***Word Family:*** **liken** *verb* **likeness** *noun*

like (2) *verb*
1 to find a person or thing agreeable or pleasant: *Do you like the new boy? / We like movies.* 2 to wish: *Come whenever you like.*
•***Word Family:*** **likeable** *adjective* easily liked **liking** *noun*: *to have a liking for pizza*

likely *adjective*
1 probable: *to be likely to rain*
likely *adverb*
2 probably: *I'll very likely be there.*
•***Word Family:*** **likelihood** *noun* probability

likeness *noun*
a similarity between two things or people: *to notice a likeness between two sisters / Do you think the photograph is a good likeness?*

lilac (*say* **lie**-luk) *noun*
1 a pale purple colour 2 a garden shrub with spikes of fragrant purple or white flowers
lilac *adjective*
3 pale purple

lily (*say* **lil**-lee) *noun*
a plant with trumpet-shaped flowers of various colours, growing from a bulb
•***Word Family:*** the plural is **lilies**

limb (*say* lim) *noun*
1 your arm or leg 2 a similar part of an animal's body, including a wing 3 a branch of a tree

lime (1) *noun*
a white, chalky powder used to make cement and mortar, or as a fertilizer

lime (2) *noun*
1 a small, green fruit, similar to a lemon 2 a greenish-yellow colour

limerick (*say* **lim**-a-rik) *noun*
a nonsense poem with five lines and strict rules about its rhythm and rhyme
•*Word Origins:* from an Irish chorus, 'will you come up to *Limerick?*', a county in the Republic of Ireland

limestone *noun*
a soft, white, chalky rock made from the shells and bodies of sea creatures that died millions of years ago

limit *noun*
1 the furthest point that is possible or allowable: *a limit to what we may spend / What's the speed limit?* 2 a boundary: *This is the limit of my land.*
limit *verb*
3 to make sure something doesn't go over what is allowed: *to limit your speed to 30 miles per hour*
•*Word Family:* **limitation** *noun* (a) limiting something (b) a restriction or shortcoming: *This scheme has a number of serious limitations.*

limited *adjective*
1 small in amount or extent: *to have only limited success / a limited choice* 2 part of the name of a business or company whose owners are not responsible for all of its debts: *a limited company / Computer Supplies Limited.*

limousine (*say* **lim**-a-zeen) *noun*
a large, luxurious car, especially if driven by a paid driver or chauffeur

limp (1) *verb*
1 to walk unevenly because you have hurt your leg or foot
limp *noun*
2 a lame walk: *to walk with a limp*

limp (2) *adjective*
not stiff or firm: *limp celery*
•*Word Family:* **limply** *adverb* **limpness** *noun*

limpid *adjective*
clear or transparent: *a limpid pool / limpid eyes*
•*Word Family:* **limpidly** *adverb*

line (1) *noun*
1 a long narrow mark made on a surface: *He drew a line across the page.* 2 a row of something: *a line of trees / a line of people waiting* 3 a row of words written or printed on a page: *to read a few lines of a poem* 4 length of cord, wire or rope: *a telephone line / a clothes line* 5 a wrinkle on your face 6 a type of goods: *The shop doesn't sell that line of clothes any more.* 7 the strip of rails a train moves along: *the railway line* 8 **lines** the words an actor says in a play or film
line *verb*
9 to form a line along something or somewhere: *Rubbish bins lined the footpath.* 10 **line up** (a) to take position in a line (b) to arrange or organize things or people: *Have you lined anyone up to take to the party?'*

line (2) *verb*
to cover the inner side of something: *The coat was lined with fur.*
•*Word Family:* **lining** *noun* an inner covering

linen (*say* **lin**-in) *noun*
1 cloth made from flax 2 clothes or other articles, such as sheets, made from linen

linger (*say* **ling**-ga) *verb*
to remain somewhere because you don't want to leave
•*Word Family:* **lingering** *adjective* drawn out **lingeringly** *adverb*

lingerie (*say* **lon**-zha-ree) *noun*
women's underwear
•*Word Origins:* from a French word meaning "linen goods"

linguist (*say* **ling**-wist) *noun*
someone who studies language or is good at foreign languages
•*Word Family:* **linguistics** *noun* the study of language **linguistic** *adjective*

link *noun*
1 a loop or ring forming part of a chain 2 bond or connection: *a link between music and art*
link *verb*
3 to join things together: *to link hands*
•*Word Family:* **link-up** *noun* a connection **linkage** *noun*

lintel *noun*
a horizontal support over a door or window

lion *noun*
a large Asian or African member of the cat family, the male having a shaggy mane around its neck and shoulders

lip *noun*
1 one of the two fleshy parts forming the front of your mouth 2 something shaped or used like a lip: *the lip of a jug*

lipstick *noun*
a cosmetic for colouring your lips

liquefy (*say* **lik**-wa-fuy) *verb*
to make or become liquid
•*Word Family:* other forms are **liquefies, liquefied, liquefying** □ **liquefier** *noun*

a b c d e f g h i j k l m n o p q r s t u v w x y z

A B C D E F G H I J K L M N O P Q R S T U V W X Y Z

liquid (*say* **lik**-wid) *noun*
1 a substance that flows, such as water or oil
liquid *adjective*
2 flowing like water: *liquid food / liquid movements*
•***Word Family:*** **liquidly** *adverb* **liquidness** *noun* **liquidize** or **liquidise** *verb*

liquidate (*say* **lik**-wi-date) *verb*
1 to pay or settle: *to liquidate a debt* 2 to close down and use the remaining goods or assets to pay the debts: *to liquidate a business* 3 to murder: *The assassin liquidated the gang's enemies*.
•***Word Family:*** **liquidation** *noun* **liquidator** *noun*

liquor (*say* **lick**-er) *noun*
a strong alcoholic drink such as whisky

liquorice (*say* **lick**-a-rish) *noun*
1 a plant with blue flowers and a sweet flavoured root 2 the black sweet made from this root

lisp *noun*
1 the pronunciation of the speech sounds "s" and "z" as "th" so that *sing* sounds like *thing*
lisp *verb*
2 to speak with a lisp

list *noun*
a number of things, such as names or numbers, set down or stated one after the other: *to make a list of things to buy*
•***Word Family:*** **list** *verb*

listen (*say* **lis**-en) *verb*
to pay attention to sound in order to hear: *to listen to music*
•***Word Family:*** **listener** *noun*

listless *adjective*
having no interest or energy: *a listless reply*
•***Word Family:*** **listlessly** *adjective*

literal (*say* **lit**-a-ral) *adjective*
1 matching the original exactly: *The literal translation of the French word for potato is "earth apple"*. 2 meaning exactly what the words say: *a literal fight for survival*
•***Word Family:*** **literally** *adverb*
•***Word Origins:*** from a Latin word meaning "letter of the alphabet"

literary (*say* **lit**-er-a-ree) *adjective*
to do with books or literature: *literary criticism*

literate (*say* **lit**-a-rut) *adjective*
able to read and write
•***Word Family:*** **literacy** *noun*

literature (*say* **lit**-er-a-cher) *noun*
1 poems, novels, plays and other similar forms of writing: *to study English literature* 2 books, magazines and so on about a particular subject: *travel literature*

lithe *adjective*
able to move or bend easily
•***Word Family:*** **lithely** *adverb* **litheness** *noun*

litmus *noun*
a substance, often made into paper, that turns red when dipped in an acid, and blue in an alkali
•***Word Family:*** **litmus paper** *noun*

litre (*say* **lee**-ta) *noun*
a unit for measuring the volume of liquids in the metric system
•***Word Origins:*** from a Greek word meaning "pound"

litter *noun*
1 rubbish or untidy mess, especially in a public place 2 a number of baby animals born together to the same mother: *a litter of puppies*
litter *verb*
3 to scatter rubbish around somewhere

little *adjective*
1 small: *a cosy little room / a little child* 2 short: *a little while* 3 not much: *little chance of survival* 4 a small amount of something: *Would you like a little tea?*
little *adverb*
5 not much: *Things have improved little since yesterday*.
•***Word Family:*** other forms for definition 1 **littler, littlest** □ other forms for definitions 2 and 3 **less, least**

live (1) (*rhymes with* give) *verb*
1 to have life or be alive 2 to continue to exist or remain in a particular place: *to live in my memory* 3 to have your home in a particular place: *Where do you live? / to live on the streets*
•***Word Family:*** **living** *adjective* alive, or still in use

live (2) (*rhymes with* hive) *adjective*
1 alive, not dead: *a live spider* 2 broadcast on radio or television while it is actually happening: *a live concert* 3 carrying electricity: *a live wire* 4 not exploded: *a live bullet*

livelihood *noun*
the way you earn money to live: *to make a livelihood from singing in a band*

lively *adjective*
full of energy or enthusiasm: *a lively song*
•***Word Family:*** other forms are **livelier, liveliest** □ **liven** *verb* **liveliness** *noun*

liver (*say* **liv**-a) *noun*
the large organ in your abdomen, that makes the bile used to help you digest food

livestock (*say* **live**-stok) *noun*
all the horses, cattle, sheep and other animals kept on a farm

living *noun*
1 the way you earn money: *What do you do for a living? / to earn a living as a writer* 2 the way that someone lives: *a good standard of living*

lizard (*say* **liz**-ud) *noun*
a reptile with four legs, a slender body and a long tail

llama (*say* **lah**-ma) *noun*
a camel-like, South American animal with thick wool, used for carrying loads

load *noun*
1 something carried or supported: *a load of bricks* 2 a large amount: *I've got loads of work to do.*
load *verb*
3 to put a load onto something such as a lorry 4 to fill a gun with bullets 5 to put something into something else ready to be used: *to load a program into a computer / to load film into a camera*
•***Word Family:*** **loaded** *adjective*: *a loaded rifle*

loaf (1) *noun*
a whole lump of bread that has been baked in the oven
•***Word Family:*** the plural is **loaves**

loaf (2) *verb*
to be lazy or idle: *to loaf about the house*

loam (*rhymes with* home) *noun*
a rich, fertile soil

loan *noun*
1 the giving of something that must be returned to its owner after it has been used: *the loan of a library book* 2 a sum of money you borrow and pay back at a fixed rate of interest
loan *verb*
3 to lend something to someone: *to loan someone your skis*

loath (*rhymes with* oath) *adjective*
unwilling or reluctant: *I am loath to lend him my hat.*

loathe (*rhymes with* clothe) *verb*
to feel intense hatred and disgust for someone or something
•***Word Family:*** **loathing** *noun* disgust **loathsome** *adjective* disgusting

lob *noun*
1 the slow, rising, curved flight of a ball hit high in the air
lob *verb*
2 to throw or hit a ball high in the air
•***Word Family:*** other verb forms are **lobs, lobbed, lobbing**

lobby *noun*
1 an entrance hall in a building 2 a group of people trying
to get support for something: *the environmental lobby*
lobby *verb*
3 to try to influence or get the support of someone: *to lobby your member of parliament*
•***Word Family:*** other verb forms are **lobbies, lobbied, lobbying** □ **lobbyist** *noun*

lobe *noun*
a soft, rounded part of something, such as the lower part of your ear

lobster *noun*
a large shellfish, with two large pincers, eight legs and a long tail, that turns pink when you cook it

local (*say* **lo**-kal) *adjective*
1 to do with a particular place or area: *a local resident / a local tradition* 2 to do with a particular part of your body: *a local anaesthetic / a local infection*
local *noun*
3 someone who lives in a particular place or area: *Ask one of the locals.*
•***Word Family:*** **localize** or **localise** *verb* **locally** *adverb*

locality (*say* lo-**kal**-i-tee) *noun*
a particular place or district
•***Word Family:*** the plural is **localities**

locate (*say* lo-**kate**) *verb*
1 to find the position of someone or something: *to locate a friend / to locate a hole in the roof* 2 to put something in a particular place: *to locate a school at the crossroads*
•***Word Family:*** **location** *noun*

loch (*sounds like* lock) *noun*
a Scottish word for a lake: *Loch Ness*

lock (1) *noun*
1 a fastening device that is opened with a key 2 an enclosed section of a river or canal with gates at each end, in which boats are raised or lowered from one level to another by altering the depth of the water
lock *verb*
3 to fasten something or to become fastened with a key: *to lock the front door*

lock (2) *noun*
a bunch or curl of hair

locker *noun*
a small cupboard or compartment with a lock, used for storing your things

locket (*say* **lok**-it) *noun*
a small case to hold a photograph or other

A B C D E F G H I J K L M N O P Q R S T U V W X Y Z

keepsake, usually worn on a chain around your neck

locomotive (*say* lo-ko-**mo**-tiv) *noun*
a railway engine
•***Word Family:*** **locomotion** *noun* moving around from place to place

locust (*say* **lo**-kust) *noun*
a type of large grasshopper that moves about in large swarms, eating all the crops in its path

lodge *noun*
1 a small house such as one used for holidays: *a ski lodge* 2 a small house set in the grounds of a larger house: *the gatekeeper's lodge*
lodge *verb*
3 to live or board in a house belonging to someone else 4 to stick or stay somewhere: *The bullet lodged in his leg.*
•***Word Family:*** **lodger** *noun* someone who rents a room in another's house **lodgings** *noun* a room you rent in someone else's house

loft *noun*
the space between the ceiling of a room and the roof above it

lofty *adjective*
1 towering high into the air: *lofty mountains* 2 noble or dignified: *lofty feelings* 3 proud and haughty: *a lofty manner*
•***Word Family:*** other forms are **loftier, loftiest**

log *noun*
1 a length of wood cut from the trunk or branch of a tree 2 the daily record of progress kept by the captain of a ship or plane
log *verb*
3 to record something in a log: *to log a journey*
•***Word Family:*** other verb forms are **logs, logged, logging** □ **logging** *noun* the industry that cuts down trees for timber **logger** *noun*

logbook *noun*
1 the book for entering details of a ship or plane's journey 2 a document or book used to record official information about a car or other vehicle, such as who owns it

logic (*say* **loj**-ik) *noun*
1 reasoning based on carefully organized arguments: *to use logic to convince someone you are right* 2 correctness and reasonableness: *to see the logic of a decision*
•***Word Family:*** **logical** *adjective* **logically** *adverb*

logo (*say* **low**-go) *noun*
a symbol used to identify a product or company
•***Word Family:*** the plural is **logos**

loin *noun*
1 the lower part of your body, between your ribs and your hips 2 the similar part of a four-legged animal 3 **gird your loins** to prepare for action

loiter *verb*
to stand or move about aimlessly: *to loiter at street corners*

lone *adjective*
alone or solitary: *a lone cowboy*
•***Word Family:*** **loner** *noun* someone who likes to be alone

lonely *adjective*
1 feeling sad or depressed because you are alone: *Were you lonely while we were away?* 2 remote or isolated: *lonely hills / a lonely house in the country*
•***Word Family:*** **loneliness** *noun*

long (1) *adjective*
1 having a great distance or length from end to end: *a long walk / long hair* 2 continuing on and on: *a long time*
long *adverb*
3 for a great amount of time 4 for a certain amount of time: *How long did he stay?* 5 **so long** goodbye
long *noun*
6 a long time: *The job won't take long.*
•***Word Family:*** **length** *noun*

long (2) *verb*
to wish for something strongly: *to long for summer*
•***Word Family:*** **longing** *noun* a strong wish or desire for something **longingly** *adverb*

long division *noun*
dividing one number into another, and writing the process down as you go

longitude (*say* **long**-gi-tewd) *noun*
a distance east or west of Greenwich in England, measured in degrees
•***Word Family:*** **longitudinal** *adjective* **longitudinally** *adverb*

long jump *noun*
a competition in athletics, in which you run and then jump as far as you can

long-sighted *adjective*
not being able to see things that are very close

look *verb*
1 to direct your eyes towards a particular thing, place and so on in order to see 2 to try to find someone or something: *to look for your friend* 3 to seem: *to look happy* 4 to face in a particular direction: *The town looks north.* 5 **look after** to mind or take care of someone or something 6 **look down on** to regard someone with contempt 7 **look out** to be careful 8 **look up to** to admire someone

look *noun*
9 looking: *to have a quick look* 10 a particular appearance: *He has the look of his father.* / *the look of a worried man*
•*Word Family:* **looks** *plural noun* your appearance

loom *verb*
to appear, often in a huge, distorted or frightening shape: *A tree loomed out of the fog.*

loop *noun*
1 a curve doubling over itself so that it leaves an opening in the middle: *a loop of ribbon*
2 something shaped like this: *the loop in a road*
loop *verb*
3 to fasten something using a loop

loophole *noun*
a way of getting round a law, rule and so on

loose *adjective*
1 free from being fastened, held and so on: *loose hair* / *loose papers* 2 not firm: *a loose grip on the rope* / *a loose tooth* 3 unpacked: *loose potatoes*
4 baggy: *a loose sweater*
loose *verb*
5 to let someone or something loose
•*Word Family:* **loosen** *verb* to make or become looser **loosely** *adverb*

loot *noun*
1 stolen money or goods
loot *verb*
2 to rob somewhere during a battle or riot

lop *verb*
to cut something off, such as a branch from a tree
•*Word Family:* other forms are **lops, lopped, lopping**

lope *verb*
to run with long, bounding strides
•*Word Origins:* from an Icelandic word meaning "to leap"

lopsided *adjective*
uneven or not straight: *a lopsided smile*
•*Word Family:* **lopsidedly** *adverb* **lopsidedness** *noun*

lord *noun*
1 a British nobleman or peer with a title before his name 2 someone with authority or power over others: *a feudal lord* 3 **Lord** a form of address: *the Lord Mayor of Perth* 4 **the Lord** God or Jesus Christ
•*Word Family:* **lordly** *adjective*
•*Word Origins:* from an Old English word meaning "the keeper of the bread"

lore *noun*
the knowledge about a subject, especially of a traditional or popular nature: *the lore of herbalists*

lose (*say* looz) *verb*
1 to part with something, by chance or carelessness, and be unable to find it: *She lost her purse.* 2 to be deprived of something or have it taken away: *to lose your life in an accident* 3 to be beaten in a game or competition 4 to get rid of something: *to lose weight*
•*Word Family:* other forms are **loses, lost, losing** □ **loser** *noun*

loss *noun*
1 the losing of something: *the loss of a puppy* / *the loss of a game* 2 something or someone that is lost 3 **be at a loss** to be puzzled or uncertain

lotion (*say* **lo**-shon) *noun*
a liquid you dab on your skin to clean, heal or protect it: *sun lotion*

lottery *noun*
a kind of gambling in which people buy numbered tickets or chose a group of numbers hoping to win money
•*Word Family:* the plural is **lotteries**

loud *adjective*
1 noisy or producing a lot of sound: *loud music*
2 having colours that are too bright and showy: *loud tights*
•*Word Family:* **loudly** *adverb* **loudness** *noun*

lounge *verb*
1 to stand, sit, lie or move in a lazy or relaxed manner
lounge *noun*
2 a room in a house or hotel for relaxing and entertaining

louse (*rhymes with* house) *noun*
1 a small, flattened, wingless insect that lives on your body and sucks your blood 2 a nasty, untrustworthy person
•*Word Family:* the plural is **lice**

lousy *adjective*
1 of very poor quality: *a lousy play* 2 unpleasant: *lousy weather* 3 ill: *to feel lousy*
•*Word Family:* other forms are **lousier, lousiest**

lout *noun*
a rough, rude, aggressive young man
•*Word Family:* **loutish** *adjective*

love *verb*
1 to have a strong affection for someone or something: *to love your mother* 2 to like a particular thing very much: *to love ice-cream*
love *noun*
3 a strong feeling of affection 4 passion or sexual desire 5 a score of nil in tennis or similar games 6 **in love with** feeling deep passion for
7 **make love** to have sexual intercourse
•*Word Family:* **lovable** *adjective* **lover** *noun* **loving** *adjective*

lovely *adjective*
1 charming or delightful: *a lovely picnic*
2 looking beautiful: *a lovely young woman*
•***Word Family:*** other forms are **lovelier, loveliest** □ **loveliness** *noun*

low (1) (*say* lo) *adjective*
1 not tall or high: *a low shelf / to have a low opinion of yourself* 2 not shrill, sharp or loud: *a low hum* 3 small in amount or degree: *a low number / a low temperature* 4 of inferior rank or importance: *low birth* 5 mean and nasty: *a low trick*
low *adverb*
6 at or to a low position: *to aim low*

low (2) (*say* lo) *verb*
to make the hollow, bellowing sound of cattle

lower (*say* **lo**-a) *verb*
to let or bring something down: *Lower the blinds. / Lower the rent. / Lower your voice.*

lower case *noun*
small rather than capital letters

lowest common denominator *noun*
the smallest number into which the bottom part of all of a series of fractions can be divided: *The lowest common denominator of* $\frac{1}{2}$ *and* $\frac{1}{3}$ *is 6*

lowest common multiple *noun*
the smallest number into which a group of numbers can be divided: *The lowest common multiple of 7 and 3 is 21*

loyal *adjective*
remaining true and faithful to your friends
•***Word Family:*** **loyally** *adverb* **loyalty** *noun*

lozenge (*say* **loz**-inj) *noun*
a sweet tablet sucked to make a sore throat or cold feel better

lubricate (*say* **loo**-bri-kate) *verb*
to apply oil or grease to something, in order to make it move or run smoothly: *to lubricate an engine*
•***Word Family:*** **lubricant** *noun* a substance that lubricates **lubrication** *noun*
•***Word Origins:*** from a Latin word meaning "to make slippery"

lucerne (*say* **loo**-sern) *noun*
a plant with bluish-purple flowers, used to feed cattle, sheep and horses

lucid (*say* **loo**-sid) *adjective*
1 easy to understand: *a lucid explanation* 2 able to think clearly: *to be very sick but quite lucid*
•***Word Family:*** **lucidity** *noun* **lucidly** *adverb*

Lucifer (*say* **loo**-si-fa) *noun*
an angel who led the revolt in heaven and was cast into hell

luck *noun*
1 something that happens by chance: *bad luck*
2 success or good fortune: *to wish someone luck / a stroke of luck*
•***Word Family:*** **lucky** *adjective* (**luckier, luckiest**) **luckily** *adverb*

lucrative (*say* **loo**-kra-tiv) *adjective*
making a profit: *a small but lucrative business*

ludicrous (*say* **loo**-di-krus) *adjective*
so silly that you can't help laughing: *a ludicrous story*

lug *verb*
to pull or drag something heavy using all your strength
•***Word Family:*** other forms are **lugs, lugged, lugging**

luggage (*say* **lug**-ij) *noun*
the bags or suitcases you take on a journey

lukewarm *adjective*
1 only just warm: *lukewarm tea* 2 not very enthusiastic: *a lukewarm reaction to our plan*

lull *verb*
1 to soothe or calm someone: *Her singing lulled me off to sleep. / His explanation lulled my suspicions.*
lull *noun*
2 a brief time of calm: *a lull in the storm*

lullaby (*say* **lul**-a-by) *noun*
a soothing song to put a baby to sleep
•***Word Family:*** the plural is **lullabies**

lumber *noun*
1 sawn timber
lumber *verb*
2 to burden someone with something unpleasant or useless: *He lumbered me with the task of firing a friend.*

lumberjack *noun*
someone whose job is cutting down trees and bringing them out of the forest

luminous (*say* **loo**-mi-nus) *adjective*
shining or glowing, especially in the dark: *a luminous watch*
•***Word Family:*** **luminosity** *noun* **luminously** *adverb*

lump *noun*
1 a solid mass: *a lump of clay* 2 a swelling: *a lump on your head*
lump *verb*
3 to put people or things together carelessly in one group: *to lump all the slow readers together*
•***Word Family:*** **lumpily** *adverb* **lumpiness** *noun* **lumpy** *adjective* (**lumpier, lumpiest**)

lunar (*say* **loo**-na) *adjective*
to do with the moon: *lunar exploration*

lunatic (*say* **loo**-na-tik) *noun*
1 someone who is mad or insane
lunatic *adjective*
2 to do with lunatics: *a lunatic asylum* 3 crazy: *a lunatic scheme*
• ***Word Origins:*** from a Latin word meaning "moon", because in the past madness was thought to be brought on by changes in the moon

lunch *noun*
1 your midday meal
lunch *verb*
2 to have lunch: *to lunch at the pub*
• ***Word Family:*** the plural of the noun is **lunches**

luncheon (*say* **lun**-chen) *noun*
a more formal word for **lunch**

lung *noun*
one of the two, large, spongy parts of your body found in your chest and used for breathing

lunge (*say* lunj) *noun*
1 a sudden forward movement, such as one made in order to attack someone
lunge *verb*
2 to make a lunge

lurch *noun*
1 a sudden rolling or swaying to one side: *The train gave a lurch and I fell over.*
lurch *verb*
2 to stagger from side to side: *He lurched across the room towards me.*
• ***Word Family:*** the plural of the noun is **lurches**

lure *noun*
1 something used to attract an animal, such as a worm used to attract fish
lure *verb*
2 to attract or entice a person or animal: *to lure him away with the promise of sweets*

lurid (*say* **loo**-rid) *adjective*
1 involving a lot of details of violence, sex and so on: *a lurid film / a lurid description* 2 brightly coloured in a tasteless or garish way: *lurid purple wallpaper*

lurk *verb*
to creep about in a secretive way: *A man was lurking in the shadows.*

luscious (*say* **lush**-us) *adjective*
tasting delicious: *a luscious strawberry*
• ***Word Family:*** **lusciously** *adverb* **lusciousness** *noun*

lush *adjective*
with healthy plants growing thickly: *a lush rainforest*
• ***Word Family:*** **lushly** *adverb* **lushness** *noun*

lust *noun*
1 a strong desire, especially a powerful desire for sex
lust *verb*
2 to have feelings of lust: *to lust for power / to lust after someone's body*
• ***Word Family:*** **lustful** *adjective* **lustfully** *adverb*

lustre (*say* **lust**-er) *noun*
a soft, gleaming brightness or brilliance: *the lustre of pearls / the lustre of her eyes*
• ***Word Family:*** **lustrous** *adjective*

lute (*rhymes with* hoot) *noun*
an old-fashioned musical instrument a bit like a guitar with strings you pluck with your fingers

Lutheran (*say* **loo**-tha-ran) *noun*
a member of the Protestant Church based on the teachings of its German founder, Martin Luther, who lived from 1483 to 1546
• ***Word Family:*** **Lutheranism** *noun*

luxury (*say* **luk**-sha-ree) *noun*
1 the comfort and ease possible when you are surrounded by expensive things: *a life of luxury* 2 something that is pleasing or enjoyable, but is not really necessary: *Their budget allows few luxuries.*
• ***Word Family:*** the plural is **luxuries** □ **luxuriate** *verb* to indulge yourself in a luxury **luxurious** *adjective* **luxuriously** *adverb*

lychee (*say* **lie**-chee) *noun*
a small, Chinese fruit with a firm shell and a soft, jelly-like middle

lynch (*say* linch) *verb*
to kill someone, usually by hanging, without giving them a proper trial
• ***Word Family:*** **lynching** *noun*
• ***Word Origins:*** first used as a form of rough justice by Captain William *Lynch*, a United States magistrate in Virginia, about 1780

lyre (*say* **lie**-a) *noun*
a stringed musical instrument of ancient Greece

lyrebird (*say* **lire**-bird) *noun*
a type of Australian bird that can mimic other birds and sounds, the male of which spreads his tail feathers into the shape of a lyre to dance and court a female bird

lyric (*say* **li**-rik) *noun*
1 a short poem which expresses feelings or emotions 2 **lyrics** the words of a song
lyric *adjective*
3 to do with or like a lyric: *lyric poetry*
• ***Word Family:*** **lyrical** *adjective* poetic or romantic: *a lyrical film*

Mm

macabre (*say* ma-**kah**-bra) *adjective*
ghastly, horrible or gruesome
•***Word Origins:*** from an Arabic word meaning "graveyard"

macadamia (*say* mak-a-**day**-mee-a) *noun*
a hard-shelled, edible Australian nut
•***Word Origins:*** named after John *Macadam*, died 1865, an Australian chemist

macaroni (*say* mak-a-**ro**-nee) *noun*
a type of pasta shaped like short, hollow tubes
•***Word Origins:*** this word comes from Italian

macaw (*say* ma-**kaw**) *noun*
a large, long-tailed, South American parrot, with brightly coloured feathers and a harsh cry

mace *noun*
a club-like weapon, usually with sharp spikes on the end

machete (*say* ma-**shet**-ee) *noun*
a large, heavy chopping-knife
•***Word Origins:*** this word comes from Spanish

machine (*say* ma-**sheen**) *noun*
a mechanical device designed to do a particular job: *a sewing machine*
•***Word Family:*** **machinist** *noun* someone who operates a machine **machinery** *noun*
•***Word Origins:*** from a Greek word meaning "a device"

machine-gun *noun*
a gun which fires bullets continuously for as long as the trigger is pressed

macho (*say* **mat**-cho) *adjective*
behaving in a strongly masculine way, especially by showing a lot of aggression

mackerel *noun*
a slender, bluish-green sea fish that is used for food
•***Word Family:*** the plural is **mackerel** or **mackerels**

macramé (*say* ma-**krah**-may) *noun*
the craft of knotting thread or cord together to make decorative patterns
•***Word Origins:*** from a Turkish word meaning "towel"

macrocosm (*say* **mak**-ro-koz-um) *noun*
the world or universe as a whole
•***Word Origins:*** from Greek words meaning "large" and "world"

mad *adjective*
1 insane 2 angry: *I was mad with them for teasing me.* 3 excited or uncontrolled: *There was a mad rush for seats.*
•***Word Family:*** **madden** *verb* **madly** *adverb* **madness** *noun*

madam *noun*
a polite form of address for a woman
•***Word Origins:*** from French words meaning "my lady"

made *verb*
the past tense and past participle of the verb **make**

mademoiselle (*say* ma-dum-wa-**zel**) *noun*
a French title for an unmarried woman

maestro (*say* **my**-stro) *noun*
someone who is very skilful at something, especially conducting or playing music
•***Word Origins:*** from an Italian word meaning "master"

magazine (*say* mag-a-**zeen**) *noun*
1 a publication with a paper cover containing stories and pictures, which comes out regularly 2 the part of a gun where the ammunition is stored
•***Word Origins:*** from an Arabic word meaning "storehouse"

maggot *noun*
a small, white grub that grows into a fly

magic *noun*
1 the power to use supernatural forces to control people and events and make impossible things happen 2 tricks done for entertainment
•***Word Family:*** **magician** (*say* ma-**jish**-un) *noun* someone who does magic **magic** or **magical** *adjectives* **magically** *adverb*

magistrate (*say* **maj**-is-trate) *noun*
a judge in a local court with the power to decide some less important cases
•***Word Origins:*** from a Latin word meaning "master"

magma *noun*
a layer of hot melted rock beneath the solid surface of the earth

magnanimous (*say* mag-**nan**-i-mus) *adjective*
generous, forgiving and unselfish
•***Word Family:*** **magnanimity** (*say* mag-na-**nim**-i-tee) *noun* **magnanimously** *adverb*
•***Word Origins:*** from Latin words meaning "great" and "spirit"

magnate *noun*
someone who has wealth and power from

success in business: *a newspaper magnate*
•*Word Origins:* from a Latin word meaning "great"

magnet *noun*
1 a piece of metal, usually iron, that draws iron objects to it 2 something that acts like a magnet: *The jam was a magnet to wasps.*
•*Word Family:* **magnetize** or **magnetise** *verb* to make something into a magnet

magnetic tape *noun*
a narrow, plastic tape coated with a magnetic substance which is used for recording sounds, pictures or computer information

magnificent (*say* mag-**nif**-i-sunt) *adjective*
splendid or very fine: *a magnificent view*
•*Word Family:* **magnificence** *noun* **magnificently** *adverb*
•*Word Origins:* from a Latin word meaning "grand, on a large scale"

magnify (*say* **mag**-ni-fie) *verb*
to make something appear larger: *A microscope magnifies objects.*
•*Word Family:* other forms are **magnifies, magnified, magnifying** □ **magnifier** *noun* **magnification** *noun*

magnitude *noun*
1 size or extent 2 importance: *events of great magnitude*
•*Word Origins:* from a Latin word meaning "greatness"

magpie *noun*
a large, black and white bird

maharajah or maharaja (*say* mah-ha-**rah**-ja) *noun*
a king or prince in India
•*Word Family:* **maharani** or **maharanee** *noun* a queen in India, or the wife of a maharajah

Mahabharata (*say* mah-har-**bar**-ah-tah) *noun*
a long, Indian poem of around 200,000 lines, which contains many Hindu legends and religious teachings
•*Word Origins:* from Sanskrit (Indian) words meaning "great" and "story"

mahogany (*say* ma-**hog**-u-nee) *noun*
a hard, reddish-brown wood which is used to make furniture

maid *noun*
1 a girl or unmarried woman 2 a female servant

maiden *noun*
1 a girl or young unmarried woman 2 an over in cricket in which no runs are scored
maiden *adjective*
3 unmarried: *a maiden aunt* 4 first: *a maiden speech*

mail (1) *noun*
1 letters and parcels sent or delivered by post
mail *verb*
2 to send something by post

mail (2) *noun*
armour made from lots of very small metal rings joined together, worn by soldiers in the past
•*Word Origins:* this is a short form of **chain mail**

maim *verb*
to cripple or damage a person or animal

main *adjective*
1 chief or most important: *the main thing to remember is to smile*
main *noun*
2 the largest pipe or cable in a water, gas or electrical system 3 **in the main** mostly
•*Word Family:* **mainly** *adverb* chiefly

mainland *noun*
a large land mass, as distinguished from the islands around it

mainsail (*say* **main**-sul) *noun*
the large sail on the tallest mast on a ship

mainstay *noun*
the most important thing or part: *Wheat farming is the mainstay of the district.*

maintain *verb*
1 to keep a thing or place in good order: *My job is to maintain the house and gardens.* 2 to continue to have something or keep it up: *to maintain good relations with friends* 3 to firmly state a belief: *She still maintained that she was innocent.*
•*Word Family:* **maintenance** *noun*
•*Word Origins:* from Latin words meaning "to hold in the hand"

maize *noun*
a cereal plant with large spikes of yellow grain

majesty (*say* **maj**-es-tee) *noun*
1 grandness and dignity: *The procession continued with great majesty.* 2 **Majesty** the title given to a king or queen: *Her Majesty Queen Elizabeth*
•*Word Family:* the plural is **majesties** □ **majestic** *adjective* **majestically** *adverb*

major (*say* **may**-ja) *noun*
1 an officer in the army
major *adjective*
2 greater or important: *The major part of my money goes on rent.* / *He is a major artist.* 3 in the musical scale that has a semitone between the third and seventh notes: *C major*

majority (*say* ma-**jo**-ri-tee) *noun*
1 the greater part or number: *The majority of*

students work hard. 2 the difference between a larger and a smaller group of voters: *a majority of 16.*
•***Word Family:*** the plural is **majorities**

make *verb*
1 to produce something: *I made you an apple pie. / You make too much noise.* 2 to force someone to do something, or cause something to happen: *They made me clean up the mess. / What makes a car go?* 4 to perform an action: *to make trouble.* 5 to become: *She will make an excellent doctor.* 6 to reach a particular place by a particular time: *We hope to make your place by midnight.* 7 to earn a particular amount of money: *We made a fortune selling horses.* 8 to add up to a particular amount: *If we include you it makes eight of us.* 9 **make off** to leave quickly 10 **make out** to manage to see, hear or understand something, especially when it is difficult: *I could just about make out the lights of the village.* 11 **make up** (a) to invent a story, situation and so on: *He made up the whole story.* (b) to become friends again after a disagreement
make *noun*
12 a type or brand: *What make is your car?*
•***Word Family:*** other forms of the verb are **makes, made, making** □ **maker** *noun*

makeshift *adjective*
made from whatever you can lay your hands on and only meant to be used for a short time: *We made a makeshift shelter for the night.*

make-up *noun*
1 lipstick, eyeshadow and so on 2 a person's character or personality: *Being afraid isn't part of her make-up.*

maladjusted (*say* mal-a-**just**-id) *adjective*
behaving in a way that is not acceptable to most people, especially because of being unhappy or finding things difficult

malady (*say* **mal**-a-dee) *noun*
a disease or illness

malapropism (*say* **mal**-a-prop-iz-um) *noun*
a word used by mistake for another word that has a similar sound but a different meaning so that the effect is amusing as in *the squaw on the hippopotamus* instead of *the square of the hypotenuse*
•***Word Origins:*** named after *Mrs Malaprop*, a character in a play who confused words in this way

malaria (*say* ma-**lair**-ree-a) *noun*
an illness causing fevers and chills, that is spread by mosquitoes
•***Word Origins:*** from the Italian words for "bad" and "air"

malcontent (*say* **mal**-kon-tent) *noun*
someone who is dissatisfied and likely to make trouble

male *noun*
1 an animal of the sex that does not give birth 2 a man or boy

malevolent (*say* mal-**ev**-o-lunt) *adjective*
intending to hurt or upset other people
•***Word Family:*** **malevolence** *noun* **malevolently** *adjective*

malice (*say* **mal**-is) *noun*
a desire to hurt people or cause suffering
•***Word Family:*** **malicious** *adjective* **maliciously** *adverb* **maliciousness** *noun*

malignant (*say* ma-**lig**-nant) *adjective*
1 full of hate and a desire to harm 2 likely to cause death because of spreading rapidly: *a malignant tumour*
•***Word Family:*** **malignancy** *noun* **malignantly** *adverb*

mall (*say* mawl *or* mal) *noun*
a shopping area where cars are not allowed

mallard *noun*
the common wild duck of Europe

malleable (*say* **mal**-ee-a-bul) *adjective*
easy to hammer into thin sheets or roll into a different shape: *Gold is a malleable metal.*
•***Word Family:*** **malleability** *noun*
•***Word Origins:*** from a Latin word meaning "a hammer"

mallee *noun*
a small Australian gum tree that grows in dry areas

mallet *noun*
1 a hammer with a wooden head 2 a long-handled wooden stick used to hit the ball in polo and croquet

malnutrition (*say* mal-new-**trish**-on) *noun*
poor health caused by not eating enough good food
•***Word Family:*** **malnourished** *adjective*

malt (*rhymes with* salt) *noun*
grain used in making beer and whisky

mammal *noun*
an animal whose young feeds on milk from its mother's breast
•***Word Origins:*** from a Latin word meaning "breast"

mammary gland *noun*
the gland in female mammals that produces milk

mammoth *noun*
1 a hairy elephant, that lived on earth a long time ago

mammoth *adjective*
2 huge or gigantic: *a mammoth cleaning-up job*

man *noun*
1 an adult male human being 2 all human beings: *Man has always dreamed of travelling to the stars.* 3 one of the pieces used in playing certain games, such as chess
man *verb*
4 to supply with workers: *to man a factory*
• ***Word Family:*** the plural of the noun is **men** □ other forms of the verb are **mans, manned, manning**

manage (*say* **man**-ij) *verb*
1 to control or be in charge of something: *to manage a business* 2 to succeed in doing something: *She managed to sell her car.*
• ***Word Family:*** **manageable** *adjective*

management *noun*
1 the running of something such as a business 2 the people or group in charge of a business

manager *noun*
someone who is in charge of a business or a group of people at work
• ***Word Family:*** **managerial** *adjective*

manchester *noun*
goods such as sheets, pillowcases, towels and tablecloths
• ***Word Origins:*** named after the city of *Manchester*, in England, where goods like these are made

mandarin *noun*
a small, sweet, orange-coloured citrus fruit

mandate *noun*
1 an order 2 the right or power to do something: *The voters have given the Government a mandate to carry out its policies.*
• ***Word Family:*** **mandatory** *adjective* compulsory

mandir (*say* **man**-deer) *noun*
a Hindu or Jain temple

mandolin (*say* man-da-**lin**) *noun*
a musical instrument with a wooden body and eight metal strings that are plucked

mane *noun*
the long hair on the neck of animals such as horses and lions

mange (*rhymes with* strange) *noun*
a skin disease, mainly of animals, causing red sores and loss of hair or fur
• ***Word Family:*** **mangy** (*say* **mane**-jee) *adjective*

manger (*say* **mane**-ja) *noun*
a box from which cattle or horses eat

mangle *verb*
to bend, twist or damage something badly

mango (*say* **man**-go) *noun*
a tropical fruit with juicy yellow flesh
• ***Word Family:*** the plural is **mangoes** or **mangos**

mangrove *noun*
a low tree with roots that are above the ground, growing close together with others on mudflats along the coast

mania (*say* **may**-nee-a) *noun*
1 a passionate enthusiasm for something: *a mania for football* 2 a serious mental illness that makes someone extremely anxious or excited
• ***Word Family:*** **manic** (*say* **man**-ik) *adjective*

maniac (*say* **may**-nee-ak) *noun*
someone who is violent and dangerous
• ***Word Family:*** **maniacal** (*say* ma-**nie**-a-kul) *adjective*

manicure *verb*
to care for someone's hands and cut and polish their fingernails
• ***Word Family:*** **manicure** *noun* **manicurist** *noun* someone whose job is to look after your hands and fingernails
• ***Word Origins:*** from Latin words meaning "hand" and "care"

manifesto *noun*
a statement by a group of people, especially a political party, explaining their aims and setting out their policies
• ***Word Family:*** the plural is **manifestos**

manipulate (*say* ma-**nip**-yoo-late) *verb*
1 to do something skilfully, especially with your hands 2 to control or influence someone indirectly: *He manipulates people for his own ends.*
• ***Word Family:*** **manipulation** *noun* **manipulative** *adjective*

mankind *noun*
all living people

manly *adjective*
having qualities that people admire in men, such as being brave and strong

mannequin (*say* **man**-u-kin) *noun*
1 someone, usually a woman, whose job is to wear new clothes to show them to customers 2 a model of the human body used by dressmakers and to display clothes in a shop window

manner *noun*
1 the way in which something happens or is done: *cooked in the Chinese manner* 2 **manners** ways of behaving politely or rudely towards other people: *He has good manners.*

mannerism (*say* **man**-u-riz-um) *noun*
a particular way of behaving or speaking that can sometimes be a little odd: *He has a mannerism of rubbing his chin while thinking.*

manoeuvre (*say* ma-**noo**-va) *noun*
1 a movement which takes skill or care
2 **manoeuvres** military exercises
manoeuvre *verb*
3 to move something skilfully: *She manoeuvred the car into an awkward parking space.*
•***Word Family:*** **manoeuvrable** *adjective*

manor *noun*
a large country house and the land belonging to it

mansion (*say* **man**-shon) *noun*
a large, grand house usually with a lot of land around it

manslaughter (*say* **man**-slaw-ta) *noun*
the accidental killing of someone

mantle *noun*
1 a cloak 2 something that covers or conceals: *a mantle of fog*

mantra *noun*
a word or phrase which is repeated to help a person concentrate on religious thoughts and used by Hindus and Buddhists

manual *adjective*
1 done with the hands: *manual labour*
manual *noun*
2 a book giving information about how to use a machine: *the instruction manual for the camera*
•***Word Family:*** **manually** *adverb*
•***Word Origins:*** from a Latin word meaning "of the hand"

manufacture (*say* man-yoo-**fak**-cher) *noun*
1 the making of large numbers of goods
manufacture *verb*
2 to make large numbers of a product, usually in a factory: *to manufacture car parts* 3 to invent
•***Word Family:*** **manufacturer** *noun*
•***Word Origins:*** from Latin words meaning "by hand" and "made"

manure (*say* ma-**nyoor**) *noun*
waste matter from animals that is spread on the ground to make plants grow better

manuscript (*say* **man**-yoo-skript) *noun*
a handwritten or typed copy of a piece of writing before it is printed: *She sent the manuscript of her first novel to a publisher.*
•***Word Origins:*** from Latin words meaning "hand" and "writing"

many *adjective*
1 large in number: *many hours / Many people died in the war.*
many *noun*
2 a large number of people or things: *Many would agree with his ideas.* 3 a quantity: *How many came to the party?*
•***Word Family:*** other forms of the adjective are **more, most**

Maori (*rhymes with* dowry) *noun*
someone descended from the people who lived in New Zealand before the arrival of white people
•***Word Origins:*** from a Maori word meaning "of the usual kind"

map *noun*
1 a diagram of a place showing the position of rivers, cities, borders and so on as if seen from above
map *verb*
2 to make a map of a place
•***Word Family:*** other forms of the verb are **maps, mapped, mapping**

marathon *noun*
1 a long-distance race in which people run about 42 kilometres or 26 miles: *the London marathon*
marathon *adjective*
2 long and difficult: *a marathon effort*
•***Word Origins:*** from the running of a messenger from the plain of *Marathon* to Athens, 42 kilometres away, with news of a Greek victory in 490 BC

marble *noun*
1 a hard limestone which can be polished to make a smooth surface and is used to make statues and in buildings 2 a small, coloured, glass ball which is used in a children's game

March *noun*
the third month of the year, with 31 days
•***Word Origins:*** named after the ancient Roman god *Mars*

march *verb*
1 to walk with regular steps, like soldiers 2 to make someone walk somewhere: *The prisoners were marched to their cells.*
march *noun*
3 a large group of people marching in a procession or demonstration: *We watched the march go by.* 4 a piece of music for marching to

mare (*rhymes with* air) *noun*
a fully grown female horse or pony

margarine (*say* mar-ja-**reen**) *noun*
a spread made from vegetable oils and used like butter

margin (*say* **mar**-jin) *noun*
1 the space at the side of a page between the printing or writing and the edge 2 an amount

which is the difference between two quantities or numbers: *She won the election by a narrow margin.*
•***Word Family:*** **marginal** *verb* **marginally** *adverb*

marijuana or **marihuana** (*say* ma-ru-**wah**-na) *noun*
a drug made from the leaves and flowers of the hemp plant
•***Word Origins:*** from the Spanish words *Maria Juana* or "Mary Jane"

marina (*say* ma-**reen**-a) *noun*
a small harbour for small boats and yachts
•***Word Origins:*** this word comes from Italian

marinate (*say* **ma**-ri-nate) *verb*
to soak meat in a spicy liquid before cooking it to increase the flavour and make it more tender
•***Word Family:*** **marinade** *noun* a liquid, such as wine, in which meat can be soaked
•***Word Origins:*** from a Spanish word meaning "pickle"

marine (*say* ma-**reen**) *adjective*
1 living in the sea or to do with the sea: *marine life / marine navigation*
marine *noun*
2 a soldier who serves on ships as well as on land
•***Word Origins:*** from a Latin word meaning "of the sea"

maritime (*say* **ma**-ri-time) *adjective*
to do with the sea or ships

mark *noun*
1 a spot, stain or scratch on a surface that would otherwise be plain and clean: *a finger mark / a dirty mark* 2 a number or letter of the alphabet used to show how good your work is: *I got a bad mark in the maths test.* 3 **make your mark** to be successful 4 **on your marks** get ready to start a race
mark *verb*
5 to spoil something by getting a mark on it
6 to put a symbol, stamp or official words on something: *The cattle were marked with a brand.*
7 to be a feature of something: *The day was marked by brilliant sunshine.* 8 to judge somebody's worth and give it a mark: *The teacher is marking exam papers.*
•***Word Family:*** **marked** *adjective* very noticeable **marking** *noun* a mark or a series of marks for example on the skin of an animal **marker** *noun*

market *noun*
1 a place where people buy and sell goods 2 the demand for goods: *There is no market for cars here.* 3 **on the market** for sale
market *verb*
4 to sell
•***Word Family:*** **marketable** *adjective* fit or easy to sell

marksman *noun*
someone who can shoot guns and other firearms accurately: *a police marksman*
•***Word Family:*** the plural is **marksmen** □ **marksmanship** the ability to shoot accurately

marlin *noun*
a large, strong fish with a snout shaped like a spear

marmalade *noun*
a jam made from oranges or other citrus fruit
•***Word Origins:*** this word comes from Portuguese

maroon (1) (*say* ma-**roon**) *noun*
a brownish-red colour
•***Word Origins:*** from a French word meaning "chestnut" (a nut with a brownish-red skin)

maroon (2) (*say* ma-**roon**) *verb*
to leave someone in a place from which it is difficult to leave: *Rising floodwaters marooned the sheep on a hilltop.*

marquee (*say* mar-**kee**) *noun*
a large tent used for outdoor shows and parties

marriage *noun*
the relationship between two people who are married to each other: *My parents had a good marriage.*

marrow *noun*
1 the soft substance that fills the hollow spaces within bones 2 a large, long, round green vegetable

marry *verb*
1 to join together as husband and wife: *We have been married for a year.* 2 to become someone's husband or wife: *She is marrying my cousin.*
•***Word Family:*** other forms are **marries, married, marrying**

marsh *noun*
low flat land that is wet and muddy
•***Word Family:*** **marshy** *adjective* **(marshier, marshiest)**

marshal *verb*
1 to organize a group of people or things and get them in the right place: *Police marshalled the crowd behind a roped-off area.*
marshal *noun*
2 someone who helps to organize a public event
3 an officer of high rank in the army
•***Word Family:*** other forms of the verb are **marshals, marshalled, marshalling**

marsupial (*say* mar-**soo**-pi-ul) *noun*
a mammal whose young live and feed in a pouch on their mother until they are old enough to look after themselves
•***Word Origins:*** from a Greek word meaning "a purse or bag"

A B C D E F G H I J K L M N O P Q R S T U V W X Y Z

martyr (*say* **mar**-ta) *noun*
1 someone who goes through great suffering or dies rather than give up their political or religious beliefs 2 **make a martyr of yourself** to suffer unnecessarily in the hope that you will get sympathy or praise
martyr *verb*
3 to kill someone or make them suffer because of their beliefs
• ***Word Family:*** **martyrdom** *noun*

marvel *verb*
1 to wonder at something or be very surprised
marvel *noun*
2 something that causes wonder
• ***Word Family:*** other forms of the verb are **marvels, marvelled, marvelling** □ **marvellous** *adjective* wonderful
• ***Word Origins:*** from Latin words meaning "wonderful things"

mascara (*say* mas-**kar**-a) *noun*
a coloured substance which you put on your eyelashes to make them darker and thicker
• ***Word Origins:*** from a Spanish word meaning "mask"

mascot *noun*
someone or something that brings you good luck

masculine (*say* **mas**-kew-lin) *adjective*
1 having the qualities thought to be typically male 2 using the form of a word that has to do with males: *"He" is a masculine pronoun.*
• ***Word Family:*** **masculinity** *noun*

mash *verb*
1 to crush food to a soft mass: *to mash potatoes*
mash *noun*
2 mashed potato

mask *noun*
1 a covering that you wear over your face to protect it or as a disguise
mask *verb*
2 to hide or disguise something

mason *noun*
someone who carves stone
• ***Word Family:*** **masonry** *noun*

masquerade (*say* mas-ka-**rade**) *noun*
1 a dance at which people wear masks and disguises
masquerade *verb*
2 to pretend to be someone or something

mass *noun*
1 a large quantity or amount of something: *a mass of spectators* 2 a lump or heap of something 3 the amount of physical matter that something has: *The mass of a litre of water is greater than the mass of a litre of gas.* 4 **the masses** the ordinary people
mass *verb*
5 to gather together in large numbers: *The refugees massed at the border.*
• ***Word Family:*** the plural is **masses**

Mass *noun*
a religious ceremony in the Roman Catholic and some other Christian churches

massacre (*say* **mas**-i-ka) *noun*
1 the cruel killing of large numbers of people
massacre *verb*
2 to kill large numbers of people cruelly

massage (*say* **mas**-arzh) *verb*
to rub and press a person's muscles and joints to take away their pain or stiffness
• ***Word Family:*** **massage** *noun*

massive (*say* **mas**-iv) *adjective*
1 very large, heavy and solid: *a massive oak table*
2 large and very serious: *a massive haemorrhage*
• ***Word Family:*** **massively** *adverb* **massiveness** *noun*

mast *noun*
1 a long pole on the deck of a boat that the sails are attatched to 2 a tall pole: *a radio mast*

mastectomy (*say* mas-**tek**-ta-mee) *noun*
a surgical operation to remove someone's breast usually because they have cancer
• ***Word Origins:*** from Greek words for "breast" and "a cutting out"

master *noun*
1 someone who has control or authority over people, animals, or things: *the master of a ship*
2 a male teacher: *the geography master* 3 an expert at something: *a master of disguise*
master *verb*
4 to learn something so that you know it thoroughly: *She had finally mastered French.*
• ***Word Family:*** **masterly** *adjective* skilful
mastery *noun*

masterpiece *noun*
1 a very great work of art 2 the best work that an artist or writer has done: *Some people say "Hamlet" is Shakespeare's masterpiece.*

masticate (*say* **mas**-ta-kate) *verb*
to chew thoroughly
• ***Word Family:*** **mastication** *noun*
• ***Word Origins:*** from a Greek word meaning "to gnash the teeth"

masturbate (*say* **mas**-ta-bate) *verb*
to rub your genitals to get sexual pleasure
• ***Word Family:*** **masturbation** *noun*

mat *noun*
1 a piece of heavy cloth used to cover the floor

2 a small piece of thick, stiff material that you put under hot dishes, glasses and so on to protect a table
• ***Word Family:*** other forms of the verb are **mats, matted, matting** □ **matting** *noun*

matador *noun*
a bullfighter who teases the bull with a red cape and then tries to kill it with a sword

match (1) *noun*
a short stick of wood covered at one end with a chemical substance that produces fire when it is rubbed on a rough surface
• ***Word Family:*** the plural is **matches**

match (2) *noun*
1 someone or something that is like another person or thing in some way: *Can you find a match for this saucer?* 2 a game in a sport: *a cricket match*
match *verb*
3 to go well with something and look good together: *I bought a jumper to match my new skirt.* 4 to compete against someone: *The best runners will be matched in the final.*
• ***Word Family:*** the plural of the noun is **matches** □ **matchless** *adjective* without equal

mate *noun*
1 a friend or fellow worker: *They have been mates for years.* 2 one of a pair of animals who produce young together
mate *verb*
3 to have sex in order to produce young

material (*say* ma-**teer**-i-ul) *noun*
1 anything that is used to make something else: *building materials / writing materials* 2 fabric or cloth: *Velvet is a heavy material.*
material *adjective*
3 to do with money, possesions and the needs of the body rather than the mind or soul: *Food and shelter are material necessities.*
• ***Word Family:*** **materially** *adverb*

materialize or materialise *verb*
to become visible: *Three figures materialized out of the fog.*

materialism *noun*
a way of living in which money and possessions are thought to be more important than anything else
• ***Word Family:*** **materialist** *noun* **materialistic** *adjective*

maternal *adjective*
to do with a mother: *maternal love*
• ***Word Family:*** **maternity** *noun*

mathematics *noun*
a subject that involves the study of numbers and shapes
• ***Word Family:*** **mathematical** *adjective* **mathematically** *adverb* **mathematician** *noun*
• ***Word Origins:*** from a Greek word meaning "to do with science"

matinee (*say* **mat**-in-ay) *noun*
a daytime performance of a play or film
• ***Word Origins:*** from a French word meaning "morning"

matriarch (*say* **may**-tree-ark) *noun*
a woman who is the head of a family or ruler of a group
• ***Word Family:*** **matriarchy** *noun* a system in which a woman has the most power in a family or group **matriarchal** *adjective*
• ***Word Origins:*** from a Latin word meaning "mother" and a Greek word meaning "leader"

matriculate (*say* ma-**trik**-yoo-late) *verb*
to be accepted as qualified to enter a university
• ***Word Family:*** **matriculation** *noun*
• ***Word Origins:*** from a Latin word meaning "a public register or roll"

matrimony (*say* **mat**-ri-mo-nee) *noun*
marriage
• ***Word Family:*** **matrimonial** *adjective*

matrix *noun*
a set of numbers or symbols arranged in rows and columns, used in mathematics

matt *adjective*
not shiny

matted *adjective*
in a thick, tangled mass: *matted hair*

matter *noun*
1 the substance that physical things are made of 2 a particular kind of substance: *vegetable matter* 3 a subject, situation or affair that has to be discussed or dealt with: *It's a serious matter.* 4 **the matter** a problem: *What's the matter with you today?*
matter *verb*
5 to be important: *Will it matter if we are late?*

mattress *noun*
a long, flat bag filled with feathers, foam rubber or springs and used on a bed to sleep on
• ***Word Origins:*** from an Arabic word meaning "cushion or mat"

mature (*say* ma-**tyoor**) *adjective*
1 fully grown or developed: *a mature plant* 2 behaving in a sensible, grown-up way: *a mature decision*
mature *verb*
3 to reach a stage of development
• ***Word Family:*** **maturity** *noun*
• ***Word Origins:*** from a Latin word meaning "ripe"

A B C D E F G H I J K L M N O P Q R S T U V W X Y Z

matzo *noun*
a piece of unleavened bread eaten during the Jewish Passover

maul (*say* mawl) *verb*
to badly injure someone by handling them roughly and tearing their flesh: *The bear mauled the zoo keeper.*

mauve (*rhymes with* stove) *noun*
a light, pinkish-purple colour

maximum *noun*
the greatest amount possible: *We can invite a maximum of 25 people.*
•***Word Family:*** **maximize** or **maximise** *verb* to increase something to the greatest possible amount
•***Word Origins:*** from a Latin word meaning "greatest"

may *verb*
1 to be allowed: *You may leave now.* 2 to be possible: *That story may be totally wrong.*
•***Word Family:*** another form is **might**

May *noun*
the fifth month of the year, with 31 days

maybe *adverb*
perhaps: *Maybe you're right.*

Mayday *noun*
the word used internationally over a plane's or ship's radio to say you are in great danger and need help

mayhem *noun*
great disorder and confusion

mayonnaise (*say* may-on-**aze**) *noun*
a creamy, cold sauce made from eggs and oil and used on salads

mayor (*say* mare) *noun*
someone elected to represent a city or town
•***Word Family:*** **mayoress** *noun* the wife of a mayor

maze *noun*
a complicated arrangement of passages and paths which are meant to confuse someone trying to find a way through

me *pronoun*
a word that the speaker of a sentence uses to refer to himself or herself: *She hit me.*
•***Word Family:*** the plural is **us** □ the form of **I** used after a verb

meadow (*say* **med**-oh) *noun*
an area of grassy land
•***Word Family:*** **meadowy** *adjective*

meagre (*say* **mee**-ga) *adjective*
too small in amount to be enough
•***Word Origins:*** from a Middle English word meaning "lean"

meal *noun*
the food eaten at one of the usual daily eating times, such as breakfast, lunch and dinner

mean (1) *verb*
1 to intend something or do it deliberately: *Is this meant to be a joke?* 2 to convey or indicate: *What does this word mean?*
•***Word Family:*** other forms are **means, meant** (*say* ment), **meaning**

mean (2) *adjective*
1 unkind or nasty: *It is a mean trick to hide her toys.* 2 not generous: *Although he is wealthy he is very mean with money.*
•***Word Family:*** **meanness** *noun*

mean (3) *noun*
the average: *The mean of 7, 4, 3 and 6 is 5.*
•***Word Origins:*** from a Latin word meaning "in the middle"

meander (*say* mee-**and**-a) *verb*
1 to wander somewhere slowly and without any particular aim 2 to follow an indirect route with a lot of bends: *The stream meandered through the woods.*
•***Word Origins:*** from *Meander*, the Greek name for a winding river in Turkey

meaning *noun*
what is intended to be understood by words, symbols and so on: *What is the meaning of this word?*

means *plural noun*
wealth or property: *a person of private means*

meanwhile *adverb*
1 during the time in between: *The accident was yesterday; meanwhile I have been in bed.* 2 at the same time: *Meanwhile, back at the ranch, our hero was in trouble.*

measles (*say* **mee**-zels) *noun*
an infectious disease that causes fever and small red spots on the skin
•***Word Origins:*** from a German word meaning "spot"

measly (*say* **meez**-lee) *adjective*
miserably small

measure (*rhymes with* treasure) *noun*
1 a unit in a measuring system: *A metre is a measure of length.* 2 an action taken to achieve a particular result: *The council took measures to keep cars out of the town centre.*
measure *verb*
3 to find how long, heavy, high and so on something is using an instrument such as a ruler or scales

•*Word Family:* **measured** *adjective* careful or deliberate **measurement** *noun*

meat *noun*
the flesh of an animal used for food

mechanic (*say* me-**kan**-ik) *noun*
someone whose job is to make, use or repair machines: *a car mechanic*
•*Word Family:* **mechanical** *adjective* worked by machinery
•*Word Origins:* from a Greek word meaning "ingenious or inventive"

mechanics *noun*
the science of how forces affect objects

mechanism (*say* **mek**-a-niz-um) *noun*
the part of a machine that moves to make the machine work

medal *noun*
a small, metal disc given to someone for bravery, especially in a battle, or as a prize in a sport
•*Word Family:* **medallist** *noun*

medallion (*say* me-**dal**-yon) *noun*
a round metal disk that is worn on a chain round the neck as a piece of jewellery

meddle *verb*
to interfere in someone else's business without being asked to do so
•*Word Family:* **meddler** *noun* **meddlesome** *adjective*
•*Word Origins:* from an Old French word meaning "to mix"

media (*say* **mee**-di-a) *plural noun*
all the ways news may be spread to a large number of people, including radio, television, newspapers and magazines
•*Word Family:* this is the plural of **medium**

medial (*say* **mee**-di-ul) *adjective*
1 in the middle 2 of average size or amount

median (*say* **mee**-di-un) *noun*
the middle of a series of numbers or values: *The median of 2, 5, 9, 12, 17, 18, 25, is 12.*
•*Word Origins:* from a Latin word meaning "in the middle"

mediate (*say* **mee**-di-ate) *verb*
to settle an argument between two groups by talking to both sides to find out the things that they agree on
•*Word Family:* **mediation** *noun* **mediator** *noun*

medical (*say* **med**-i-kul) *adjective*
to do with medicine
•*Word Family:* **medically** *adverb*
•*Word Origins:* from a Latin word meaning "of healing"

medication (*say* med-i-**kay**-shon) *noun*
pills or medicine used to treat an illness
•*Word Origins:* from a Latin word meaning "to cure"

medicine (*say* **med**-i-sun *or* **med**-sun) *noun*
1 a substance containing a drug that you drink or swallow to treat an illness 2 the study of diseases and ways of treating them
•*Word Family:* **medicinal** (*say* me-**dis**-a-nul) *adjective*

medieval (*say* med-i-**ee**-vul) *adjective*
to do with the Middle Ages, that is, from the fifth to the fifteenth century

mediocre (*say* mee-di-**oh**-ka) *adjective*
not awful but not particularly good: *a mediocre soap opera*
•*Word Family:* **mediocrity** *noun*
•*Word Origins:* from a Latin word meaning "average"

meditate (*say* **med**-i-tate) *verb*
to think deeply and seriously about something
•*Word Family:* **meditation** *noun* deep thought

medium (*say* **mee**-di-um) *adjective*
1 average in size or quality: *of medium height*
medium *noun*
2 the way in which something is expressed or shown: *She prefers film to theatre as a medium for getting her ideas across.* 3 someone through whom the spirits of the dead are said to be able to communicate
•*Word Family:* the plural of definition 2 is **media** □ the plural of definition 3 is **mediums**
•*Word Origins:* from a Latin word meaning "middle"

medley (*say* **med**-lee) *noun*
a mixture of things: *a medley of songs from different lands*
•*Word Origins:* from an Old French word meaning "a mixing"

meek *adjective*
humble and gentle and likely to obey other people
•*Word Family:* **meekly** *adverb* **meekness** *noun*

meet *verb*
1 to come face to face with: *I met Mrs Smith at the shop.* 2 to come together because you have arranged to: *Meet me at six o'clock.* 3 to join: *where the river meets the sea* 4 to pay: *Who will meet the cost of the expedition?*
meet *noun*
5 a sports event with races
•*Word Family:* other forms of the verb are **meets, met, meeting**

meeting *noun*
a gathering of people who meet to discuss something

A B C D E F G H I J K L M N O P Q R S T U V W X Y Z

mega- *prefix*
great: *megaphone*

megalomania (*say* meg-a-lo-**may**-nee-a) *noun*
a mental illness in which the patients falsely believe they are powerful or important
• ***Word Family:*** **megalomaniac** *noun* someone who constantly seeks power and personal glory
• ***Word Origins:*** from Greek words meaning "great" and "madness"

melancholy (*say* **mel**-un-kol-ee) *adjective*
1 sad, gloomy or depressing: *The funeral was a melancholy occasion.*
melancholy *noun*
2 sadness or depression

melee (*say* **mel**-ay) *noun*
a confused fight or struggle
• ***Word Origins:*** this word comes from French

mellow *adjective*
1 rich, soft and smooth in sound, colour or flavour: *the mellow notes of the harp / mellow afternoon light / mellow wine* 2 made more pleasant by age: *My father became mellow in his old age.*
mellow *verb*
3 to become more pleasant as you get older
• ***Word Family:*** **mellowness** *noun*

melodrama *noun*
a play with an exciting plot and characters who behave very dramatically
• ***Word Family:*** **melodramatic** *adjective*: *His melodramatic speech was delivered with passionate and exaggerated gestures.*

melody *noun*
a pleasant tune
• ***Word Family:*** **melodious** (*say* me-**loh**-dee-us) *adjective* producing a pleasant sound
• ***Word Origins:*** from a Greek word meaning "singing"

melon *noun*
a large, round, sweet fruit with many seeds inside

melt *verb*
1 to change from a solid to a liquid when heated: *The ice melted in the sun.* 2 to fade or disappear: *She melted into the darkness.*
• ***Word Family:*** other forms are **melts, melted** or **molten, melting**

meltdown *noun*
the failure of the cooling system of a nuclear reactor that causes the nuclear fuel to overheat and melt, and may allow dangerous radioactive material to escape

member *noun*
someone or something that belongs to a group
• ***Word Family:*** **membership** *noun*

Member of Parliament *noun*
someone who has been elected to represent an area of the country in parliament

membrane *noun*
a soft, thin piece of skin which covers or connects parts of an animal or plant
• ***Word Origins:*** from a Latin word meaning "skin"

memento (*say* me-**men**-toe) *noun*
something that reminds you of an event or person: *Keep this rose as a memento of the dance.*
• ***Word Family:*** the plural is **mementos** or **mementoes**
• ***Word Origins:*** from a Latin word meaning "remember!"

memoirs (*say* **mem**-wahz) *plural noun*
a book written by someone about their own life and times

memorable *adjective*
special or unusual enough to be remembered
• ***Word Family:*** **memorably** *adverb*

memorandum (*say* mem-a-**ran**-dum) *noun*
a note of something to be remembered
• ***Word Family:*** the plural is **memoranda** or **memorandums**
• ***Word Origins:*** from a Latin word meaning "that is to be remembered"

memorial (*say* me-**maw**-ri-ul) *noun*
1 something that is built to remind people of a historical event or famous person
memorial *adjective*
2 in memory of someone: *A memorial service was held for the dead soldiers.*

memorize or **memorise** (*say* **mem**-a-rize) *verb*
to learn something and remember it exactly

memory (*say* **mem**-a-ree) *noun*
1 the ability to remember things 2 something that you remember 3 the part of a computer in which information is stored
• ***Word Family:*** the plural is **memories**

menace (*say* **men**-is) *noun*
1 a threat or danger: *Crop failure is a menace in underdeveloped countries.*
menace *verb*
2 to threaten: *He menaced me with a knife.*
• ***Word Origins:*** from a Latin word meaning "a threat"

mend *verb*
to work on something so that it works properly and is no longer broken

meningitis (*say* men-in-**jie**-tis) *noun*
a serious illness in which the outer part of the brain is swollen, causing headaches, vomiting, fever and a stiff neck

menopause (*say* **men**-o-pawz) *noun*
the time when a woman stops having monthly periods
• ***Word Origins:*** from Greek words meaning "of a month" and "stopping"

menorah (*say* men-**aw**-ra) *adjective*
a candlestick with several branches that is lit during the Jewish festival of Hannukah

menstruation (*say* men-stroo-**ay**-shon) *noun*
the monthly flow of blood from the uterus in a woman who is not pregnant
• ***Word Family:*** **menstrual** *adjective* **menstruate** *verb*
• ***Word Origins:*** from a Latin word meaning "monthly"

mental *adjective*
1 to do with the mind or with thinking: *mental arithmetic / a mental illness* 2 insane, mad
• ***Word Family:*** **mentality** (*say* men-**tal**-i-tee) *noun* the powers of the mind **mentally** *adverb*
• ***Word Origins:*** from a Latin word meaning "of a mind"

mention (*say* **men**-shon) *verb*
1 to speak or write about something briefly
mention *noun*
2 a short remark mentioning someone or something
• ***Word Origins:*** from a Latin word meaning "a calling to mind"

menu (*say* **men**-yoo) *noun*
1 a list of things to eat available at a restaurant
2 a list of options in a computer program shown on the screen of a computer
• ***Word Origins:*** from a French word meaning "a detailed list"

mercenary (*say* **mer**-sun-ree) *adjective*
1 interested only in the money that can be got from someone or something
mercenary *noun*
2 a soldier willing to fight for any country or group that will pay
• ***Word Family:*** the plural is **mercenaries**
• ***Word Origins:*** from a Latin word meaning "hired for pay"

merchandise (*say* **mer**-chen-dice) *noun*
goods for sale

merchant *noun*
someone who buys and sells goods: *a fish merchant*

merciful (*say* **mer**-si-ful) *adjective*
showing mercy
• ***Word Family:*** **merciless** *adjective*

mercurial (*say* mer-**kew**-ri-ul) *adjective*
quickly changing in mood: *a lively and mercurial personality*

mercury (*say* **mer**-kew-ree) *noun*
a silvery, metal element which is a liquid at normal temperatures and is used in thermometers

mercy (*say* **mer**-see) *noun*
kindness and forgiveness that you show by not punishing someone
• ***Word Family:*** the plural is **mercies** □ See also **merciless** and **merciful** *adjective*

mere *adjective*
nothing more than: *a mere three years of age*
• ***Word Family:*** **merely** *adverb* only or simply

merge (*say* merj) *verb*
1 to blend in with something: *Twilight merged gradually into darkness.* 2 to bring together two or more files on a computer to make one larger file
• ***Word Family:*** **merger** *noun* a joining of two or more business companies into one

meridian (*say* me-**rid**-i-an) *noun*
a line on a map that runs from the North pole to the South pole

meringue (*say* me-**rang**) *noun*
a mixture of sugar and beaten egg whites baked in the oven and used in cakes and puddings

merino (*say* me-**ree**-no) *noun*
a breed of sheep with long fine wool, originally from Spain
• ***Word Origins:*** this word comes from Spanish

merit *noun*
1 excellence or value: *a film of great artistic merit*
2 **merits** good points: *Let us discuss the merits of the production.*
merit *verb*
3 to deserve: *Her suggestions merit serious thought.*
• ***Word Family:*** other forms of the verb are **merits, merited, meriting**
• ***Word Origins:*** from a Latin word meaning "deserved or earned"

mermaid *noun*
an imaginary creature with a woman's body and a fish's tail, supposed to live in the sea
• ***Word Family:*** **merman** *noun*
• ***Word Origins:*** from "maid" and a Middle English word meaning "lake or pond"

merry *adjective*
cheerful and happy
• ***Word Family:*** **merriment** *noun* **merrily** *adverb*

mesh *noun*
1 a material like net with open spaces between the wire or threads: *wire mesh*
mesh *verb*
2 to fit together closely

A B C D E F G H I J K L M N O P Q R S T U V W X Y Z

mesmerise or **mesmerize** (*say* **mez**-ma-rize) *verb*
to fascinate or hold the attention of: *We were mesmerised by the beauty of the ballet.*
•*Word Family:* **mesmerism** *noun* an old fashioned word for hypnotism
•*Word Origins:* from F. A. Mesmer, 1734 to 1815, an Austrian doctor who studied hypnotism

mess *noun*
1 a dirty or untidy state: *His desk was in a mess.* 2 a difficult, awkward or confused state: *a financial mess / Her life is a mess.* 3 the room where officers in the armed forces eat
mess *verb*
4 **mess up** to make a place dirty or untidy
5 **mess around** or **mess about** to waste time doing things slowly and without any plan
•*Word Family:* the plural of the noun is **messes** □ **messy** *adjective* **(messier, messiest)** **messily** *adverb*

message (*say* **mess**-ij) *noun*
1 information sent to someone or left for them
2 **get the message** to understand
•*Word Family:* **messenger** *noun* someone who carries a message
•*Word Origins:* from a Latin word meaning "sent"

messiah (*say* mes-**eye**-a) *noun*
a great religious leader who will save the world
•*Word Origins:* from a Hebrew word meaning "the anointed"

metabolism (*say* me-**tab**-a-liz-um) *noun*
the chemical processes in your body which turn food into energy
•*Word Family:* **metabolic** *adjective*
•*Word Origins:* from a Greek word meaning "change"

metal *noun*
an element, such as copper or iron, which can be shaped and moulded and conducts heat and electricity
•*Word Family:* **metallic** *adjective* **metallically** *adverb*
•*Word Origins:* from a Greek word meaning "a mine"

metallurgy (*say* met-**al**-er-jee) *noun*
the study of metals
•*Word Family:* **metallurgist** *noun* someone whose job is to study metals

metamorphosis (*say* met-a-**mor**-fa-sis) *noun*
a change from one form to another, such as a caterpillar into a butterfly and a tadpole into a frog
•*Word Family:* the plural is **metamorphoses** □ **metamorphic** *adjective* **metamorphose** *verb*
•*Word Origins:* from a Greek word meaning "transformation"

metaphor (*say* **met**-a-for) *noun*
a figure of speech in which one thing is described as if it were something else, without using the word "like" as in *She was a tower of strength during the crisis.*
•*Word Family:* **metaphorical** (*say* met-a-**fo**-ri-kul) or **metaphoric** *adjective* **metaphorically** *adverb*
•*Word Origins:* from a Greek word meaning "to transfer"

meteor (*say* **mee**-ti-or) *noun*
a small piece of rock or metal from space which burns brightly as it falls into the Earth's atmosphere. A meteor which reaches the Earth's surface is called a **meteorite**
•*Word Family:* **meteoric** (*say* mee-ti-**or**-ik) *adjective* rising swiftly: *a meteoric rise to power* **meteorically** *adverb*
•*Word Origins:* from a Greek word meaning "high in the air"

meteorology (*say* mee-tee-a-**rol**-a-jee) *noun*
the study of climate and weather
•*Word Family:* **meteorologist** *noun* **meteorological** *adjective* **meteorologically** *adverb*

meter *noun*
an instrument that measures the amount of something used: *a gas meter*

methane (*say* **mee**-thane) *noun*
a colourless gas that can be used as a fuel

method *noun*
a way of doing something: *a new teaching method*
•*Word Family:* **methodical** *adjective* in a careful, orderly way **methodically** *adverb*

Methodism *noun*
a branch of the Christian church which follows the teachings of John and Charles Wesley, 18th-century preachers
•*Word Family:* **Methodist** *noun* a member of such a church

methylated spirits *noun*
a colourless, poisonous liquid used for cleaning and as a fuel

meticulous (*say* me-**tik**-yoo-lus) *adjective*
extremely careful and precise: *drawn with meticulous attention to detail*
•*Word Family:* **meticulously** *adverb*
•*Word Origins:* from a Latin word meaning "fearful"

metre (1) (*say* **mee**-ta) *noun*
a unit of length
•*Word Origins:* from a Greek word meaning "measure"

metre (2) (*say* **mee**-ta) *noun*
a pattern of rhythms in poetry
•***Word Family:*** **metrical** *adjective* **metrically** *adverb*

metric system *noun*
a decimal system of weights and measures based on the metre and the kilogram

metro *noun*
an underground railway system: *the Paris metro*

metronome (*say* **met**-ra-nome) *noun*
an instrument which can be set to sound out the number of beats per minute at which a piece of music should be played

metropolis (*say* me-**trop**-u-lis) *noun*
the most important, and usually the largest, city of a country or state
•***Word Origins:*** from a Greek word meaning "mother state or city"

metropolitan (*say* met-ra-**pol**-i-tun) *adjective*
to do with a large city

mew (*say* myoo) *verb*
to make the sound of a cat

mia-mia (*say* **my**-a-my-a) *noun*
a temporary shelter made of branches, bark and so on

miaow (*say* mee-**ow**) *noun*
the sound that a cat makes
•***Word Family:*** **miaow** *verb*

microbe *noun*
a living thing that is so tiny it can only be seen with a microscope

microchip *noun*
a very small piece of silicon inside a computer that contains electronic circuits needed for the computer to function

microcomputer *noun*
a small computer designed to be used by one person at a time such as in the home or at school

microcosm (*say* **mike**-ro-koz-um) *noun*
a system or world where everything is on a small scale

microfiche (*say* **mike**-ro-feesh) *noun*
a sheet of transparent plastic containing very small photographs of many pages of text that can be read using a special projector

microfilm *noun*
a photographic film with information photographed at greatly reduced size

microphone *noun*
a device that changes soundwaves into electrical waves, used to make sounds louder, to record on tape or a computer, or to broadcast sounds

microscope (*say* **my**-kra-skope) *noun*
an instrument that makes very small objects look larger
•***Word Family:*** **microscopic** extremely tiny
•***Word Origins:*** from Greek words meaning "very small" and "to look at"

microsurgery (*say* my-kro-**sir**-ja-ree) *noun*
surgery performed on very small parts of the body, such as blood vessels or nerve fibres, using microscopes and special instruments

microwave *noun*
1 a type of oven that cooks food very quickly by electric waves rather than by heat
microwave *verb*
2 to cook food in a microwave

mid *adjective*
in the middle of

midday (*say* **mid**-day) *noun*
1 12 noon: *The train leaves at midday.* 2 the middle of the day

middle *noun*
1 the point or part that is furthest from the edges or ends: *the middle of the room / the middle of the week*
middle *adjective*
2 in or near the centre: *the middle row*

Middle Ages *noun*
the period of history between about 1000AD and 1500AD

Middle East *noun*
the countries between the eastern Mediterranean and India, including Israel and the Arab countries
•***Word Family:*** **Middle Eastern** *adjective*

middle school *noun*
a school for children between the ages of 8 or 9 and 12 or 13

midget *noun*
a very small person or thing

midnight *noun*
1 12 o'clock at night: *The boat sails at midnight.*
2 the middle of the night

midst *noun*
the middle of something

midway *adverb*
halfway: *Midway through my favourite TV programme, the electricity went off.*

midwife *noun*
a specially trained nurse who helps a mother during childbirth
•***Word Family:*** **midwifery** (*say* mid-**wif**-a-ree) *noun* the work of a midwife

might (1) *verb*
the past tense of the verb **may**

A B C D E F G H I J K L M N O P Q R S T U V W X Y Z

might (2) *noun*
strength or power
•***Word Family:*** **mighty** *adjective* (mightier, mightiest) **mightily** *adverb* **mightiness** *noun*

mighty *adjective*
1 powerful: *a mighty ruler* 2 great or huge: *a mighty mountain range*
mighty *adverb*
3 very: *You seem mighty pleased with yourself.*
•***Word Family:*** other adjective forms are **mightier, mightiest** □ **mightily** *adverb* extremely **mightiness** *noun*

migraine (*say* **my**-grane) *noun*
a very painful headache that is often accompanied by a feeling of sickness and blurred vision
•***Word Origins:*** from a Greek word meaning "a pain on one side of the head"

migrate (*say* my-**grate**) *verb*
1 to move regularly from one part of the world to another: *Some birds migrate every winter.* 2 to move to a new area or country to live or find work
•***Word Family:*** **migration** *noun* **migratory** (*say* **my**-gra-tree) *adjective*

mild *adjective*
1 gentle or calm: *a mild voice* 2 not strong or severe: *He had a look of mild surprise on his face. / mild weather* 3 not strong in flavour: *a mild cheese*
•***Word Family:*** **mildly** *adverb* **mildness** *noun*

mildew (*say* **mil**-dew) *noun*
a powdery mould that appears in warm and moist conditions on the surface of food, leather, paper, plants and so on

mile *noun*
a unit of length equal to about 1.6 kilometres
•***Word Family:*** **mileage** *noun* the number of miles travelled in a journey
•***Word Origins:*** from a Latin word meaning "one thousand paces"

militant *adjective*
eager to fight, especially for a political cause: *a militant trade unionist*
•***Word Family:*** **militancy** *noun*

military (*say* **mil**-i-tree) *adjective*
to do with soldiers

militia (*say* mil-**ish**-a) *noun*
a group of men trained to fight but not part of the regular army

milk *noun*
1 the white liquid produced by female mammals to feed their young, and, in the case of cows and goats, used by people for food
milk *verb*
2 to take milk from a cow or goat
•***Word Family:*** **milky** *adjective* (**milkier, milkiest**)

Milky Way *noun*
a white band of stars stretching across the night sky and formed by the stars of our galaxy

mill *noun*
1 a building with machinery for grinding grain into flour 2 a device for grinding or crushing things: *a pepper mill / a coffee mill* 3 a factory in which cloth is made
mill *verb*
4 to grind grain to make flour
•***Word Family:*** **miller** *noun*

millennium (*say* mi-**len**-i-um) *noun*
a period of 1000 years

milli- *prefix*
one thousandth: *millimetre*

millibar *noun*
a unit of measurement for air pressure, especially in the atmosphere

milligram *noun*
a unit of measurement equal to 1000th of a gram

millilitre *noun*
a unit of measurement equal to 1000th of a litre

millimetre *noun*
a unit of measurement equal to 1000th of a metre

milliner *noun*
someone who makes or sells hats for women

million (*say* **mil**-yun) *noun*
the number 1 000 000 or 10^6

millionaire (*say* mil-yun-**air**) *noun*
someone who has a million pounds or dollars

millipede *noun*
a small animal rather like a worm whose body is made up of many segments, each with two pairs of legs
•***Word Origins:*** from Latin words meaning "thousand" and "of a foot"

mime *noun*
1 a form of acting in which the actors use actions and gestures, but not words
mime *verb*
2 to act using actions or gestures but not words or sounds

mimic *verb*
1 to imitate or copy someone or something
mimic *noun*
2 someone or something that imitates the sound or movements of someone or something else: *Some parrots are good mimics.*

•*Word Family:* other forms of the verb are **mimics, mimicked, mimicking** □ **mimicry** *noun* the act of mimicking

minaret *noun*
a tall thin tower on a mosque which the muezzin stands in to call Muslims to prayer

mince *verb*
1 to cut food into very small pieces 2 **not mince your words** to speak in a direct and blunt manner 3 to walk with small steps in a dainty way
mince *noun*
4 finely chopped meat

mind *noun*
1 the part of someone that thinks, reasons, remembers and so on: *Keep your mind on the job!* 2 intelligence or mental ability: *a good mind for figures* 3 what someone thinks or feels: *He doesn't know his own mind. / to change your mind*
mind *verb*
4 to pay attention to something: *Mind your manners! Mind the step.* 5 to take care of someone or something: *Will you mind the house while I'm away?* 6 to be bothered or annoyed by something: *Do you mind if I open the window?*
•*Word Family:* **mindful** *adjective* thoughtful or careful **mindless** *adjective* senseless or careless

mine *noun*
1 a large hole dug under the ground so that minerals or gems can be taken out 2 a rich source of something: *a mine of information*
3 a small bomb hidden in the ground or floating in the sea to destroy enemy troops or ships
mine *verb*
4 to remove minerals or gems from under the ground 5 to place military mines in the ground or at sea

miner *noun*
someone who works in a mine

mineral *noun*
a substance that is formed naturally in rocks and earth, such as coal, tin and salt

mineral water *noun*
water that comes from a natural source of water in the ground and contains dissolved minerals and gases

minestrone (*say* min-a-**stroh**-nee) *noun*
a soup containing vegetables and pasta
•*Word Origins:* this word comes from Italian

mingle *verb*
to mix: *The prince mingled with the crowd.*

mini *noun*
a thing which is small, such as a short skirt
•*Word Origins:* this is an abbreviation of the word "miniature"

miniature (*say* **min**-u-cher) *adjective*
1 being a much smaller version of something bigger: *a miniature railway / miniature roses*
miniature *noun*
2 a very small painting
•*Word Family:* **miniaturize** or **miniaturise** *verb* to make small, or on a small scale

minibus *noun*
a small bus

minim *noun*
a note in music equal in length to half a semibreve
•*Word Origins:* from a Latin word meaning "smallest"

minimal *adjective*
as small or little as possible: *He showed minimal interest in his work.*

minimum *noun*
the least amount: *It requires a minimum of two crew to operate the plane.*
•*Word Family:* □ **minimize** or **minimise** *verb* to reduce to the smallest possible amount
•*Word Origins:* from a Latin word meaning "least"

minister *noun*
1 a member of the clergy who conducts services in a church: *a Baptist minister* 2 a Member of Parliament who is in charge of a government department: *the Minister for Education*
minister *verb*
3 **minister to** to look after and help: *He ministered to the sick.*
•*Word Family:* **ministerial** *adjective* **ministry** *noun*
•*Word Origins:* from a Latin word meaning "servant"

mink *noun*
1 a small, cat-like mammal with a long, pointed nose 2 the valuable shiny brown fur of the mink

minor (*say* **my**-na) *adjective*
1 smaller, or less important: *Luckily he suffered only minor injuries. / a minor poet* 2 in the musical scale that has a semitone between the second and third notes: *B minor*
minor *noun*
3 someone who has not reached the legal age of adulthood
•*Word Origins:* from a Latin word meaning "less"

minority (*say* my-**no**-ra-tee) *noun*
1 a small group within a much larger group: *We were a minority, so our idea was rejected by the meeting.* 2 a group of people whose beliefs, race, religion and so on are different from the larger community in which they live
•*Word Family:* the plural is **minorities**

A B C D E F G H I J K L M N O P Q R S T U V W X Y Z

mint (1) *noun*
1 a herb with strong-flavoured leaves, used in cooking 2 a sweet flavoured with peppermint

mint (2) *noun*
1 a place where the government makes money, notes and coins
mint *verb*
2 to make money in a mint
•***Word Origins:*** from a Latin word meaning "money"

minuet (*say* min-yoo-**et**) *noun*
a slow piece of music, originally for a dance from France
•***Word Origins:*** from an Old French word meaning "very small", because of the small steps taken in the dance

minus (*say* **my**-nus) *preposition*
less or without: *Two minus one equals one.*

minute (1) (*say* **min**-it) *noun*
1 a unit of time equal to 60 seconds or one 60th of an hour 2 a very short time: *I'll only be a minute.* 3 **minutes** the official written record of what was said at a meeting
•***Word Origins:*** from a Latin word meaning "little"

minute (2) (*say* my-**newt**) *adjective*
extremely small: *Some insects are minute. / minute details*
•***Word Family:*** **minutely** *adverb* **minuteness** *noun*

miracle (*say* **mi**-ri-kul) *noun*
1 an event that is not possible under the normal laws of nature: *the miracle of turning water into wine* 2 a wonderful and surprising event: *It's a miracle they saw the lifeboat.*
•***Word Family:*** **miraculous** (*say* mir-**rak**-yoo-lus) *adjective* **miraculously** *adverb*

mirage (*say* mi-**rahzh**) *noun*
an illusion sometimes experienced in hot deserts, in which distant objects appear to be close or you see things which are not there
•***Word Origins:*** from a French word meaning "to look in a mirror"

mirror *noun*
1 a shiny surface, usually glass with a metal backing, that reflects images
mirror *verb*
2 to be very similar to something else

mirth *noun*
laughter
•***Word Family:*** **mirthless** *adjective*

misadventure *noun*
bad luck: *death by misadventure*

miscarriage *noun*
1 the birth of a baby before it has developed enough to live 2 a wrong legal decision: *a miscarriage of justice*
•***Word Family:*** **miscarry** *verb* (**miscarries, miscarried, miscarrying**)

miscellaneous (*say* mis-u-**lay**-nee-us) *adjective*
made up of different kinds of things
•***Word Family:*** **miscellany** (*say* mi-**sel**-u-nee) *noun*
a mixed collection

mischief (*say* **mis**-chif) *noun*
naughtiness that is not very serious: *stirring up mischief in the classroom*
•***Word Family:*** **mischievous** (*say* **mis**-chiv-us) *adjective* **mischievousness** *noun*

misconduct (*say* mis-**kon**-dukt) *noun*
wrong or unacceptable behaviour: *The solicitor was guilty of professional misconduct.*

miser (*say* **my**-za) *noun*
someone who is mean with money
•***Word Family:*** **miserliness** *noun* **miserly** *adjective*

miserable (*say* **miz**-ra-bul) *adjective*
1 very unhappy or uncomfortable 2 making you feel unhappy or uncomfortable: *a miserable cold* 3 small or stingy: *a miserable wage*

misery (*say* **miz**-u-ree) *noun*
great unhappiness
•***Word Family:*** the plural is **miseries**

misfit *noun*
someone who does not get on with the people they live and work with

misfortune *noun*
bad luck

misgiving *noun*
a slight worry that something may not be all right

mishap *noun*
something that goes wrong but not very badly

mislay *verb*
to lose something for a time because you've forgotten where you put it
•***Word Family:*** other forms of the verb are **mislays, mislaid, mislaying**

mislead *verb*
to give someone the wrong idea about something
•***Word Family:*** other forms are **misleads, misled, misleading** □ **misleading** *adjective* **misleadingly** *adverb*

misprint *noun*
a mistake in a word printed in a book, newspaper or magazine

Miss *noun*
the title put before the surname of an unmarried woman

miss *verb*
1 to fail to do something, for example to see something, hear something, catch a ball, hit a target and so on: *She missed her appointment. / I missed the ball.* 2 to feel sad because someone or something is not with you or because you are away from a place: *She misses her homeland. / I miss my old friend.*

missile *noun*
1 a weapon which can be fired to fly for long distances and which explodes on landing 2 an object which is thrown as a weapon
•***Word Origins:*** from a Latin word meaning "that may be thrown"

missing *adjective*
lost or not in its usual place

mission (*say* **mish**-un) *noun*
1 a group of people sent to another country to carry out a particular duty, usually government or religious work 2 a task that someone is sent to carry out
•***Word Family:*** **missionary** *noun* someone sent overseas to spread the teaching of a religion
•***Word Origins:*** from a Latin word meaning "a sending"

mist *noun*
a mass of water droplets in the air which makes it difficult to see far
•***Word Family:*** **mistily** *adverb* **mistiness** *noun* **misty** *adjective*

mistake *noun*
1 a wrong idea or action: *It was a mistake to leave my umbrella behind. / I made a mistake in my addition and got the wrong answer.*
mistake *verb*
2 to understand wrongly: *I mistook the meaning of her words.* 3 to wrongly think that a person or thing is someone or something else: *I sometimes mistake Joe for Sam.*
•***Word Family:*** other forms of the verb are **mistakes, mistook, mistaken, mistaking** □ **mistaken** *adjective* **mistakenly** *adverb*

Mister *noun*
a title for a man

mistletoe (*say* **mis**-ul-toe) *noun*
a plant with green leaves and white berries that does not have roots in the ground, but instead feeds and grows on the branches of trees

mistress *noun*
1 a female teacher: *the geography mistress* 2 a woman who has a sexual relationship with a married man
•***Word Family:*** the plural is **mistresses**

misunderstanding *noun*
1 a failure to understand something: *Due to a misunderstanding we ended up at the wrong house.* 2 a disagreement: *a misunderstanding with the landlord*

misuse (*say* mis-**yooz**) *verb*
to use something for the wrong reason or in the wrong way
misuse (*say* mis-**yoos**) *noun*
3 a bad or wrong use of something: *a misuse of power*

mite *noun*
1 a tiny insect-like creature 2 a young child you are sorry for: *poor little mite*

mitigate (*say* **mit**-i-gate) *verb*
to make less serious
•***Word Family:*** **mitigation** *noun*

mitten *noun*
a glove that covers your thumb separately and your other four fingers together

mix *verb*
1 to combine things together: *Mix the flour, sugar and salt in a large bowl.* 2 to talk to lots of different people and get on well with them
mix *noun*
3 a prepared mixture of the things you need to make something: *a cake mix / cement mix*
•***Word Family:*** **mixed** *adjective* made up of different types **mixer** *noun*

mixture *noun*
a combination of different things: *This stew is a mixture of meat and vegetables.*

moa *noun*
a large flightless bird that once lived in New Zealand
•***Word Origins:*** this is a Maori word

moan *noun*
1 a long, low, soft sound: *a moan of pain / the moan of the wind*
moan *verb*
2 to make a long, soft sound 3 to complain: *He's always moaning about the government.*

moat *noun*
a deep, wide ditch, usually filled with water, around a castle or fort that protects it against invaders

mob *noun*
1 a large crowd who may become dangerous or violent: *An angry mob waited at the courthouse.*
mob *verb*
2 to crowd around someone in great numbers: *Fans mobbed the pop star.*
•***Word Family:*** other forms of the verb are **mobs, mobbed, mobbing** □ **mobster** *noun* a criminal
•***Word Origins:*** from a Latin word meaning "fickle or excitable crowd"

a b c d e f g h i j k l m n o p q r s t u v w x y z

A B C D E F G H I J K L M N O P Q R S T U V W X Y Z

mobile (*say* **moh**-bile) *adjective*
able to move or be moved easily: *a mobile crane / a mobile phone*
• ***Word Family:*** **mobility** (*say* mo-**bil**-a-tee) *noun*
• ***Word Origins:*** from a Latin word meaning "easy to move"

mobilise or **mobilize** (*say* **mo**-bu-lize) *verb*
to get people ready for an activity: *to mobilise troops / to mobilise supporters*
• ***Word Family:*** **mobilisation** *noun*

moccasin (*say* **mok**-a-sin) *noun*
a very soft leather shoe
• ***Word Origins:*** from a Native American language

mock *verb*
1 to make fun of someone
mock *adjective*
2 pretend: *a mock battle*
• ***Word Family:*** **mockery** *noun* **mockingly** *adverb*

mode *noun*
a way of doing something: *Buses and trains are different modes of transport.*

model *noun*
1 a small copy of something: *a model of the Tower of London* 2 something which is an example to be copied 3 someone who poses for a painter or photographer 4 someone employed to wear and display new clothes to customers 5 a particular design: *the latest model of that car*
model *verb*
6 to work as a model 7 to make a model of something: *She was modelling animals from clay.* 8 to copy: *He models himself on his father.*
model *adjective*
9 excellent: *a model parent*
• ***Word Family:*** other forms of the verb are **models, modelled, modelling**
• ***Word Origins:*** from a Latin word meaning "a small measure"

modem *noun*
a device that changes information from one computer into a form that can be sent through the telephone to another computer

moderate (*say* **mod**-u-rit) *adjective*
1 not great or extreme: *a moderate income / to cook at a moderate heat*
moderate *noun*
2 someone whose ideas are not extreme
moderate (*say* **mod**-u-rate) *verb*
3 to make something less severe: *to moderate rules on school uniform*
• ***Word Family:*** **moderation** *noun: He shows moderation in his eating.* **moderately** *adverb*

modern *adjective*
happening in the present or most recent times: *modern history / modern forms of transport*
• ***Word Family:*** **modernize** or **modernise** *verb* to make something more modern
• ***Word Origins:*** from a Latin word meaning "lately"

modest *adjective*
1 not boastful: *She is very modest about her success.* 2 not particulary large, expensive or high in value: *a modest income / He drives a very modest car for someone of his wealth.*
• ***Word Family:*** **modestly** *adverb* **modesty** *noun*

modify (*say* **mod**-i-fie) *verb*
1 to change something slightly: *The car was modified to include a sun roof.* 2 to add to or limit the meaning of another word: *Adverbs modify verbs.*
• ***Word Family:*** other forms are **modifies, modified, modifying** □ **modifier** *noun* **modification** *noun*

module (*say* **mod**-yool) *noun*
a part that can be used either on its own or combined with others in various ways to form a larger thing
• ***Word Family:*** **modular** *adjective*

mohair *noun*
a soft cloth made from the silky fleece of an Angora goat

moist *adjective*
slightly wet
• ***Word Family:*** **moisten** *verb* to make moist **moistness** *noun*

moisture *noun*
tiny droplets of liquid in the air or on a surface: *The rocks glistened with moisture.*
• ***Word Family:*** **moisturize** or **moisturise** *verb* to give moisture to: *to moisturize skin* **moisturizer** *noun*

molar (*say* **mole**-a) *noun*
one of the 12 square teeth at the back of your mouth

molasses *noun*
a thick syrup obtained from raw sugar

mole (1) *noun*
a small, dark spot on the skin

mole (2) *noun*
a small, furry mammal that eats insects and lives mainly underground

molecule (*say* **mol**-u-kewl) *noun*
the smallest unit of a chemical substance that can exist by itself without changing or breaking apart
• ***Word Family:*** **molecular** (*say* mo-**lek**-yoo-la) *adjective*
• ***Word Origins:*** from a Latin word meaning "a mass"

molest (*say* mo-**lest**) *verb*
to attack or harm someone, especially sexually
• ***Word Family:*** **molestation** *noun* **molester** *noun*

mollusc *noun*
an animal such as a slug, snail, oyster or octopus that has a soft body and no backbone. Most molluscs have a shell to protect their bodies
• ***Word Origins:*** from a Latin word meaning "soft"

molten *adjective*
turned into liquid by heat: *molten iron*

moment *noun*
1 a short space of time: *Wait a moment.* 2 a particular time: *At that moment the rain stopped and the sun came out.* 3 **at the moment** now
• ***Word Family:*** **momentous** *adjective* of great importance

momentary (*say* **moh**-men-tree) *adjective*
lasting only a moment: *a momentary glimpse*
• ***Word Family:*** **momentarily** *adverb* for a moment

monarch (*say* **mon**-ark) *noun*
a ruler of a country who inherits the position, such as a king or queen
• ***Word Family:*** **monarchy** *noun* the system of rule by a king or queen **monarchist** *noun* a supporter of the monarchy
• ***Word Origins:*** from Greek words meaning "alone" and " to rule"

monastery (*say* **mon**-u-stree) *noun*
the buildings in which a group of monks live
• ***Word Family:*** the plural is **monasteries** □ **monastic** (*say* mo-**nas**-tik) *adjective*
• ***Word Origins:*** from a Greek word meaning "to live alone"

Monday *noun*
the second day of the week
• ***Word Origins:*** from Old English words meaning "moon" and "day"

money (*say* **mun**-ee) *noun*
1 coins and paper notes 2 wealth
• ***Word Family:*** the plural is **monies** or **moneys** □ **monetary** *adjective* to do with money, currency or finance **moneyed** *adjective* wealthy

monger (*say* **mung**-ga) *noun*
someone who sells something: *fishmonger*

mongolism (*say* **mon**-gul-iz-um) *noun*
another word for **Down's Syndrome**

mongoose *noun*
a small, furry animal found in Africa and Asia, that kills venomous snakes
• ***Word Family:*** the plural is **mongooses**

mongrel (*say* **mung**-grel) *noun*
a dog that is a mixture of different breeds

monitor (*say* **mon**-i-ta) *noun*
1 a pupil in a school who has certain duties: *Joe is blackboard monitor this week.* 2 something used to control or check what is happening 3 a computer's screen where text and graphics are displayed
monitor *verb*
4 to check what is happening

monk (*say* munk) *noun*
a member of an all-male group who live a life of religious devotion, own nothing and often are not in contact with the rest of the world
• ***Word Origins:*** from a Greek word meaning "solitary"

monkey (*say* **mung**-kee) *noun*
a tree-climbing animal with a long tail found in tropical regions.
• ***Word Family:*** the plural is **monkeys**

mono- *prefix*
one or single: *monologue*

monocle (*say* **mon**-u-kul) *noun*
a lens for one eye only
• ***Word Origins:*** from a Greek word meaning "single" and a Latin word meaning "eye"

monogamy (*say* mon-**og**-a-mee) *noun*
marriage to one person at a time
• ***Word Family:*** **monogamist** *noun* **monogamous** *adjective*

monologue (*say* **mon**-u-log) *noun*
a long speech by one person, for example in a play
• ***Word Origins:*** from Greek words meaning "single" and "a word"

monopoly (*say* mo-**nop**-u-lee) *noun*
complete control over making or selling a particular product so that other companies can't compete
• ***Word Family:*** the plural is **monopolies** □ **monopolize** or **monopolise** *verb*

monosyllable (*say* **mon**-o-sil-a-bul) *noun*
a word of one syllable
• ***Word Family:*** **monosyllabic** *adjective: a monosyllabic reply*

monotone *noun*
a series of sounds that all have the same pitch: *He talked in a monotone.*
• ***Word Family:*** **monotonous** *adjective* boring and never changing

monsoon *noun*
a strong wind in the Indian Ocean and southern Asia, which brings heavy rain in summer
• ***Word Origins:*** from an Arabic word meaning "fixed season"

A B C D E F G H I J K L M N O P Q R S T U V W X Y Z

monster *noun*
1 a large, frightening, imaginary creature
2 someone or something that is extremely large
3 a cruel or wicked person
monster *adjective*
4 huge
•***Word Family:*** **monstrosity** *noun* something big and very ugly **monstrous** *adjective*

month (*say* munth) *noun*
one of the twelve parts into which the calendar year is divided
•***Word Family:*** **monthly** *noun* a magazine or publication produced once a month **monthly** *adjective* **monthly** *adverb*

monument *noun*
a building or statue built in memory of a person or event
•***Word Family:*** **monumental** *adjective* huge
•***Word Origins:*** from a Latin word meaning "to remind"

mood *noun*
the way someone feels at a particular time: *He was in a good mood.*
•***Word Family:*** **moody** *adjective* (**moodier, moodiest**) gloomy or sulky **moodily** *adverb* **moodiness** *noun*

moon *noun*
the satellite that goes around the Earth every month and is seen at night shining in the sky

moor (1) *noun*
an open area of land covered with coarse grasses and heather

moor (2) *verb*
to tie up a boat or anchor it so that it stays in one place

moose *noun*
a large member of the deer family with a big head and very large antlers
•***Word Family:*** the plural is **moose**
•***Word Origins:*** this is a Native American word

mop *noun*
1 a bundle of thick strings or a sponge attached to a long handle and used for cleaning floors
mop *verb*
2 to clean something with a mop 3 to clean or wipe: *She mopped the sweat from her brow.*
•***Word Family:*** other forms of the verb are **mops, mopped, mopping**

mope *verb*
to be miserable and not interested in doing things

mopoke *noun*
a kind of owl found in Australia and New Zealand
•***Word Origins:*** named for the sound it makes

moraine *noun*
a mass of earth and stones that have been left by a glacier

moral *adjective*
1 to do with knowing what is right and wrong: *She has a moral objection to the death penalty. / a moral responsibility* 2 behaving in a way that is believed to be right or good
moral *noun*
3 a piece of advice on how to behave taught by a story or experience: *The moral of the story is "Never give up hope!"* 4 **morals** behaviour based on what is right or good: *high morals*
•***Word Family:*** **moralize** or **moralise** *verb* **moralist** *noun* **moralistic** *adjective* **morally** *adverb*
•***Word Origins:*** from a Latin word meaning "customs"

morale (*say* ma-**rahl**) *noun*
the amount of confidence and optimism someone has: *low morale / high morale*

morality (*say* mo-**ral**-i-tee) *noun*
knowledge of what is right and wrong

moratorium (*say* mo-ra-**taw**-ri-um) *noun*
an official halt or delay
•***Word Family:*** the plural is **moratoria** or **moratoriums**
•***Word Origins:*** from a Latin word meaning "to delay"

morbid *adjective*
showing an unhealthy interest in unpleasant things, especially things concerned with death
•***Word Family:*** **morbidly** *adverb*
•***Word Origins:*** from a Latin word meaning "disease"

more *adjective*
1 in greater quantity or to a greater degree: *More rain is needed.*
more *adverb*
2 to a greater extent or degree: *more difficult / I like football more than cricket.*
•***Word Family:*** for other forms of the adjective look up **much**

moreover *adverb*
in addition or as well

morgue (*say* morg) *noun*
a place where dead bodies are kept before being buried or cremated

morning *noun*
the early part of the day before midday

moron (*say* **maw**-ron) *noun*
a very stupid person
•***Word Family:*** **moronic** (*say* maw-**ron**-ik) *adjective*
•***Word Origins:*** from a Greek word meaning "foolish"

morphine (*say* **mor**-feen) *noun*
a powerful drug used to stop pain and to help people sleep
•***Word Origins:*** named after *Morpheus*, the ancient Greek god of dreams

morse code *noun*
a way of sending messages using a combination of short and long signals for each letter of the alphabet
•***Word Origins:*** after Samuel *Morse*, 1791 to 1872, the United States inventor of the telegraph system

morsel *noun*
a small piece or amount

mortal (*say* **mor**-tul) *adjective*
1 not living forever: *All living creatures are mortal.* 2 causing death: *a mortal illness.*
mortal *noun*
3 a human being
•***Word Family:*** **mortally** *adverb*
•***Word Origins:*** from a Latin word meaning "of death"

mortality (*say* mor-**tal**-i-tee) *noun*
1 the fact of having to die 2 death

mortar *noun*
a mixture of cement or lime, sand and water that sets hard and is used for joining bricks together

mortgage (*say* **mor**-gij) *noun*
1 a loan from a bank or building society to buy a house. If the loan is not repaid the bank or building society takes the house back
mortgage *verb*
2 to borrow money using a house as a guarantee that the money will be repaid
•***Word Origins:*** from French words meaning "dead" and "a pledge"

mortuary (*say* **mort**-tyoo-ree) *noun*
a place in a hospital where bodies are kept before burial or cremation
•***Word Family:*** the plural is **mortuaries**
•***Word Origins:*** from a Latin word meaning "dead"

mosaic (*say* moh-**zay**-ik) *noun*
a pattern made from small pieces of coloured glass, stone or tiles
•***Word Origins:*** from a Greek word meaning "of the Muses"

Moslem (*say* **moz**-lem) *noun*
another spelling of **Muslim**

mosque (*say* mosk) *noun*
a building in which Muslims worship

mosquito (*say* mo-**skee**-toh) *noun*
a small, flying insect, the female of which sucks the blood of humans and other animals
•***Word Family:*** the plural is **mosquitos** or **mosquitoes**
•***Word Origins:*** from a Spanish word meaning "little fly"

moss *noun*
a plant with very small leaves, that grows in moist areas and on damp rocks, walls and tree trunks and looks like a green mat

most *adjective*
1 greatest: *the most money / the most harm*
2 nearly all: *He ate most of the apple.*
most *adverb*
3 to the greatest degree: *most beautiful*
•***Word Family:*** for other forms of the adjective look up **much** □ **mostly** *adverb* mainly or usually

moth *noun*
an insect similar to a butterfly but which flies mainly at night and is not so brightly coloured

mother *noun*
1 a female parent 2 the head of a convent of nuns
mother *verb*
3 to care for someone and protect them like a mother
•***Word Family:*** **motherly** *adverb* kind, like a caring mother **motherhood** *noun*

mother-in-law *noun*
the mother of your husband or wife
•***Word Family:*** the plural is **mothers-in-law**

mother-of-pearl *noun*
the pearly lining of some shells, used to make ornaments

motif *noun*
an idea or theme repeated throughout a piece of music or writing or throughout a design
•***Word Family:*** the plural is **motifs**

motion (*say* **moh**-shon) *noun*
1 movement: *The branches were in constant motion.* 2 a movement that you make: *He dismissed us with a motion of his hand.* 3 a suggestion made formally at a meeting
motion *verb*
4 to move your hand or head as a way of telling someone something: *She motioned us to be quiet.*
•***Word Family:*** **motionless** *adjective* still

motivate *verb*
to encourage someone to try harder: *If he can motivate the team they will do well.*
•***Word Family:*** **motivated** *adjective* **motivation** *noun*

motive (*say* **moh**-tiv) *noun*
something that causes a person to act in a particular way: *a motive for murder*
•***Word Family:*** **motivated** *adjective* **motivation** *noun*

a b c d e f g h i j k l m n o p q r s t u v w x y z

motley *adjective*
made up of many different types of people or things: *a motley crowd*

motor *noun*
1 a machine that uses electricity or fuel to make something work or move: *The lawnmower has an electric motor.*
motor *adjective*
2 using a motor: *a motor vehicle*
• ***Word Family:*** **motorist** *noun* someone who drives a car

motorcycle *noun*
a vehicle similar to a heavy bicycle that has an engine
• ***Word Family:*** **motorcyclist** *noun*

motorway *noun*
a wide road for people to drive long distances fast and with no bicycles or pedestrians

mottled *adjective*
covered with patches of different colours

motto *noun*
a short sentence that sums up the aims and beliefs of a person or organization: *His motto is "Never say die".*
• ***Word Origins:*** from an Italian word meaning "word"

mould (1) (*rhymes with* old) *noun*
1 a hollow container into which a liquid is poured and left to harden into the shape of the container: *a jelly mould*
mould *verb*
2 to make something into a particular shape: *She moulded a head from clay.*

mould (2) (*rhymes with* old) *noun*
a furry layer of tiny fungi that grows on old food and damp walls, clothes and leather
• ***Word Family:*** **mouldy** *adjective* **(mouldier, mouldiest)**

moult (*say* mohlt) *verb*
to shed old feathers, skin or fur that will be replaced by new ones

mound *noun*
1 a large heap of earth, sand, stones and so on 2 a small hill

mount *verb*
1 to get on a horse or bicycle that you are going to ride 2 to fix something into a position: *to mount photographs in an album* 3 to increase in amount: *Costs were mounting rapidly.*
mount *noun*
4 a horse for riding 5 a mountain: *Mount Everest*

mountain *noun*
1 an area of very high land rising to a point 2 a large pile: *a mountain of letters*
• ***Word Family:*** **mountainous** *adjective*

mountaineer *noun*
someone who climbs mountains

mourn (*say* morn) *verb*
to feel deep sadness because someone you love has died
• ***Word Family:*** **mourner** *noun* someone who attends a funeral **mourning** *noun* deep sadness at someone's death **mournful** *adjective* very sad

mouse *noun*
1 a small, furry animal with a pointed nose, sharp teeth and a long tail 2 a small object which, when you move it on a flat surface, makes the cursor on a computer screen move in the same direction
• ***Word Family:*** the plural is **mice** ☐ **mousy** *adjective* **(mousier, mousiest)** dull and uninteresting

mousse (*say* moose) *noun*
1 a light, fluffy food made with whipped cream, beaten eggs, gelatine and a sweet or savoury flavouring: *chocolate mousse / salmon mousse* 2 a frothy substance that you put on your hair to style it
• ***Word Origins:*** from a French word meaning "froth"

moustache (*say* ma-**stahsh**) *noun*
the hair that grows above a man's upper lip
• ***Word Origins:*** from a Greek word meaning "of the upper lip"

mouth *noun*
1 the part of your face used for eating, drinking and speaking 2 an entrance to something: *the mouth of a cave / the mouth of a river*
mouth *verb*
3 to form words with your lips without making any sound

mouth organ *noun*
another word for **harmonica**

mouthpiece *noun*
the part of something like a musical instrument that you put in your mouth or the part of the telephone that you speak into

move *verb*
1 to change position or change the position of something: *Move this table into the next room / Don't move or I'll shoot!* 2 to make you feel strong emotions: *Her sad story moved us greatly.* 3 to make a formal request at a meeting: *I move that Jane be appointed treasurer.*
move *noun*
4 a movement: *One move and I'll shoot!* 5 a turn in a game made by moving a piece
• ***Word Family:*** other forms of the verb are **moves, moved, moving** ☐ **movable** or **moveable** *adjective* **moving** *adjective* making you feel strong emotions **movingly** *adverb*

movement *noun*
1 a changing of position: *the movement of the waves* 2 an organized group of people working towards a goal: *the anti-smoking movement* 3 one of the main parts of a long piece of music

movie *noun*
a film

mow (*say* moh) *verb*
to cut grass with a machine: *to mow the lawn*
• ***Word Family:*** other forms are **mows, mowed, mown, mowing** ☐ **mower** *noun*

MP *noun*
a Member of Parliament

much *adjective*
1 a lot of: *I had much trouble hiring the camels.*
much *noun*
2 a lot: *Much of the work was difficult.*
much *adverb*
3 a lot: *It was much more interesting than I expected.*
• ***Word Family:*** other forms of the adjective are **more, most**

muck *noun*
dirt or rubbish

mucus (*say* **mew**-kus) *noun*
a thick, slimy liquid made in your body, such as the liquid which builds up in your nose and throat when you have a cold
• ***Word Family:*** **mucous** *adjective*
• ***Word Origins:*** this word comes from Latin

mud *noun*
soft, wet earth
• ***Word Family:*** **muddy** *adjective* **(muddier, muddiest)**

muddle *verb*
1 to confuse things or mix them up
muddle *noun*
2 a jumble or confused mess: *My mind is in a muddle.*
• ***Word Family:*** **muddler** *noun*

mudguard *noun*
a cover above the wheel of a truck, car or bicycle to stop mud or water flying up from the wheels

muesli (*say* **mewz**-lee) *noun*
a breakfast food made with whole-grain cereals, nuts and dried fruits
• ***Word Origins:*** from the German that is spoken in Switzerland

muezzin *noun*
a man who calls Muslims to pray at certain times during the day

muffin *noun*
a small flat, round, bread-like cake, eaten toasted and buttered

muffle *verb*
to make a sound more difficult to hear: *A thick hedge muffled the noise of the traffic.*

muffler *noun*
1 a thick scarf 2 a device fitted to the exhaust pipe of a car to reduce the noise of the engine

mug *noun*
1 a large cup with straight sides 2 someone who is easily fooled
mug *verb*
3 to attack someone violently, and rob them: *The old man was mugged in the dark alley.*
• ***Word Family:*** other forms of the verb are **mugs, mugged, mugging** ☐ **mugger** *noun* someone who attacks and robs people

muggy *adjective*
unpleasantly warm and humid: *a muggy day*
• ***Word Family:*** other forms are **muggier, muggiest**

mulberry *noun*
1 a tree with juicy purple berries and leaves that are fed to silkworms 2 the berries of this tree
• ***Word Family:*** the plural is **mulberries**

mulch (*say* mulsh) *noun*
a mixture of decaying leaves, grass clippings, straw and so on spread on gardens to retain moisture and feed plants

mule *noun*
an animal whose father is a donkey and whose mother is a horse
• ***Word Family:*** **muleteer** *noun* a driver of mules **mulish** *adjective* stubborn

mulga *noun*
a type of wattle that grows in the drier parts of Australia

mull *verb*
mull over to think about

mullet *noun*
a small fish found in seaside rivers, lakes and bays

multicultural *adjective*
to do with people who come from different countries and who have different traditions: *a multicultural society*
• ***Word Family:*** **multiculturalism** *noun*

multilingual (*say* mul-ti-**ling**-wul) *adjective*
able to speak several languages

multimedia *noun*
1 involving several different types of media, such as television, radio and newspapers: *a multimedia advertising campaign* 2 a mixture of text, graphics, animation, video and sound in a computer program

A B C D E F G H I J K L M N O P Q R S T U V W X Y Z

multiple (*say* **mul**-ti-pul) *adjective*
1 having many parts or elements: *a multiple car accident / a multiple fracture*
multiple *noun*
2 a number formed by multiplying one number by another

multiple sclerosis (*say* mul-ti-pul skler-**roh**-sis) *noun*
a disease of the nervous system which can affect a person's sight, control of movement and memory

multiply *verb*
1 to increase greatly: *His debts have multiplied.*
2 to add a number to itself a given number of times to get a total: *2 multiplied by 4 (2 × 4 or 2 + 2 + 2 + 2) equals 8*
•*Word Family:* other forms are **multiplies, multiplied, multiplying** □ **multiplication** *noun*

multitude *noun*
a large number of people or things

mumble *verb*
to speak unclearly without opening your mouth properly

mummy *noun*
a dead body that has been preserved by wrapping it in bandages and treating it with oils and spices
•*Word Family:* the plural is **mummies**
•*Word Origins:* from an Arabic word meaning "embalming wax"

mumps *plural noun*
an infectious disease, usually in children, which makes the glands around the neck and face swell

munch *verb*
to chew steadily and rather noisily

mundane *adjective*
ordinary and unexciting: *a very mundane job*

municipality (*say* mew-nis-i-**pal**-i-tee) *noun*
a district with its own local government, such as a town or city
•*Word Family:* **municipal** *adjective*: *the municipal swimming pool*

mural (*say* **myoor**-rul) *noun*
a picture painted on a wall
•*Word Origins:* from a Latin word meaning "wall"

murder *noun*
1 the deliberate killing of someone
2 something that is extremely difficult or unpleasant: *It was murder trying to park near the concert hall.*
murder *verb*
3 to kill someone deliberately
•*Word Family:* **murderer** *noun* **murderous** *adjective*

murky *adjective*
dark and gloomy
•*Word Family:* other forms are **murkier, murkiest** □ **murk** *noun* darkness **murkiness** *noun*

murmur *verb*
1 to speak very quietly: *He murmured gently in her ear.*
murmur *noun*
2 a quiet, low continuous sound: *a murmur of disapproval*
•*Word Family:* other forms of the verb are **murmurs, murmured, murmuring** □ **murmuring** *adjective*
•*Word Origins:* from a Greek word meaning "to roar" (of water)

Murri *noun*
an Aboriginal person, especially of Queensland

muscle (*say* **mus**-ul) *noun*
1 one of the parts of your body that gives it the power to move: *arm muscles* 2 strength or power: *It will take some muscle to move these boxes.*
muscle *verb*
3 to force your way into a situation where you are not wanted: *He muscled in on the meeting.*
•*Word Family:* other forms of the verb are **muscles, muscled, muscling** □ **muscular** *adjective*
•*Word Origins:* from a Latin word for "little mouse", because of the shape of some muscles

muse *verb*
to think deeply

museum *noun*
a building where rare, valuable and interesting things are kept and shown to the public

mush *noun*
a thick, soft mass of food
•*Word Family:* **mushy** *adjective* (**mushier, mushiest**)

mushroom *noun*
1 a fungus that grows in damp places and is the shape of a small, flat umbrella. Many types of mushroom can be eaten
mushroom *verb*
2 to appear and grow up quickly: *Courses in media studies have mushroomed recently.*

music *noun*
1 a combination of sounds played on musical instruments or sung to make tunes or sound patterns 2 printed notes and signs that stand for sounds and can be played on a musical instrument or sung

musical *adjective*
1 to do with the playing or studying of music: *a musical instrument / a musical sound* 2 good at music and interested in it: *She is very musical.*
musical *noun*
3 a play or film with singing and dancing
• ***Word Family:*** **musically** *adverb*

musician (*say* mew-**zish**-un) *noun*
someone trained in music, especially someone whose job is to play a musical instrument

musk *noun*
a strong-smelling powder used in making some perfumes and obtained from a type of deer
• ***Word Family:*** **musky** *adjective* (**muskier, muskiest**)

musket *noun*
an old-fashioned type of gun
• ***Word Family:*** **musketeer** *noun* a soldier armed with a musket

Muslim (*say* **muz**-lim) *noun*
a follower of Islam, the religion based on the teachings of Mohammed

mussel *noun*
a type of shellfish with a black shell made of two parts that fit tightly together and a soft body that can be eaten

must *verb*
1 to have to: *You must leave before midnight.*
must *noun*
2 something that is necessary: *Don't miss that film, it's a must!*
• ***Word Family:*** this verb helps other verbs

mustard *noun*
a hot-tasting yellow powder or paste made from the seeds of a herb and used as a spice in cooking

muster *verb*
to gather together: *The general mustered his troops. / He mustered all his strength.*

musty *adjective*
smelling stale and damp: *a musty old building*
• ***Word Family:*** other forms are **mustier, mustiest**

mutation *noun*
a change in the genes of a plant or animal, which may cause the development of a new sort of plant or animal with different features
• ***Word Family:*** **mutate** *verb* to change **mutant** *adjective* changing **mutant** *noun*
• ***Word Origins:*** from a Latin word meaning "to change"

mute *noun*
1 someone who cannot speak or make sounds
2 something that can be put on a musical instrument to soften the sound
mute *adjective*
3 silent, not speaking or unable to speak
• ***Word Family:*** **mutely** *adverb* **muteness** *noun*

mutilate (*say* **mew**-ti-late) *verb*
to seriously damage someone or something
• ***Word Family:*** **mutilation** *noun*

mutiny (*say* **mew**-ti-nee) *noun*
1 a rebellion by soldiers or sailors against their officers
mutiny *verb*
2 to take part in a mutiny
• ***Word Family:*** the plural is **mutinies** □ other forms of the verb are **mutinies, mutinied, mutinying** □ **mutinous** *adjective* rebellious **mutineer** *noun* someone who takes part in a mutiny

mutter *verb*
to speak in a low voice that is not easy to hear

mutton *noun*
the meat of a fully grown sheep

mutual *adjective*
shared by two people or felt by two people about each other: *a mutual respect / a mutual enemy*
• ***Word Family:*** **mutually** *adverb*
• ***Word Origins:*** from a Latin word meaning "reciprocal"

muzzle *noun*
1 the front part of an animals face, including its mouth and nose 2 a covering of straps or wire put over a dog's mouth to prevent it from biting someone 3 the front end of a gun barrel

my *possessive pronoun*
1 belonging to me: *This is my book.*
my *interjection*
2 an exclamation of surprise: *My! What big teeth!*
• ***Word Family:*** the plural is **our**

myopia (*say* my-**oh**-pee-a) *noun*
an inability to see things that are far away
• ***Word Family:*** **myopic** (*say* my-**op**-ik) *adjective*
• ***Word Origins:*** from Greek words meaning "to shut" and "eye"

myriad (*say* **mi**-ree-ad) *noun*
a very great number
• ***Word Origins:*** from a Greek word meaning "ten thousand"

myrrh (*rhymes with* fur) *noun*
a sweet-smelling gum obtained from a shrub and used in making perfume

mystery (*rhymes with* history) *noun*
something that is puzzling, unknown or unexplained: *The disappearance of the money is a mystery.*
• ***Word Family:*** **mysterious** *adjective*

mystify (*say* **mis**-ti-fie) *verb*
to puzzle you so you cannot understand what is happening: *She was mystified by his strange behaviour.*
• ***Word Family:*** **mystifies, mystified, mystifying** □ **mystification** *noun*

mystique (*say* mis-**teek**) *noun*
a quality that makes someone or something seem fascinating and mysterious

myth (*say* mith) *noun*
1 an ancient story, usually about gods and magical events 2 a story which a lot of people believe but which is not true
• ***Word Family:*** **mythical** *adjective* imaginary
• ***Word Origins:*** from a Greek word meaning "a story"

mythology (*say* mith-**ol**-u-jee) *noun*
all the ancient stories of a particular country or time: *Greek mythology*
• ***Word Family:*** **mythological** *adjective*

Nn

nag *verb*
1 to continue finding fault, complaining or requesting
nag *noun*
2 a person who nags
• ***Word Family:*** other verb forms are **nags, nagged, nagging**

nail *noun*
1 a metal pin with a point and a flat end, usually hammered into place to join two or more things together 2 the tough horny tip of your fingers and toes
nail *verb*
3 to fasten with nails

naive (*say* nigh-**eev**) *adjective*
not experienced in the ways of the world
• ***Word Family:*** **naively** *adverb* **naivety** *noun*
• ***Word Origins:*** this word comes from French

naked (*say* **nay**-kid) *adjective*
1 having no clothing or covering: *a naked man / a naked wound* 2 blunt or plain: *the naked truth*
• ***Word Family:*** **nakedly** *adverb* **nakedness** *noun*

name *noun*
1 what a person or thing is called 2 reputation: *a good name as a drummer* 3 someone famous: *a big name*
name *verb*
4 to give a name to: *to name the child Julia* 5 to give the correct name of: *Can you name all the US States?*
• ***Word Family:*** **namely** *adverb* that is to say

nanny *noun*
a person whose job is to look after small children in their home
• ***Word Family:*** the plural is **nannies**

nanny-goat *noun*
a female goat

nap *verb*
1 to have a short sleep
nap *noun*
2 a short sleep
• ***Word Family:*** other verb forms are **naps, napped, napping**

nape *noun*
the back of your neck

napkin *noun*
a square piece of cloth or paper used to protect your clothes during a meal

nappy *noun*
a piece of replaceable towel or paper pad worn by a baby around its bottom until it is old enough to use a potty
• ***Word Family:*** the plural is **nappies**

narcissism (*say* nar-**sis**-iz-um) *noun*
an extreme form of self-love, often of the way you look
• ***Word Family:*** **narcissistic** *adjective*
• ***Word Origins:*** named after *Narcissus*, a beautiful youth in Greek myths who fell in love with his own reflection

narcotic (*say* nar-**kot**-ik) *noun*
a drug that relieves pain or helps you sleep, sometimes causing addiction

narrate (*say* na-**rate**) *verb*
1 to tell a story 2 to provide spoken comments for a film or television show: *to narrate a documentary*
• ***Word Family:*** **narrative** *noun* a story **narration** *noun* **narrator** *noun*

narrow *adjective*
1 not broad or wide: *a narrow corridor* 2 limited in your opinions or outlook: *a narrow mind* 3 close: *a narrow escape*
• ***Word Family:*** **narrowly** *adverb* **narrowness** *noun*

nasal (*say* **nay**-zal) *adjective*
1 to do with your nose: *your nasal passages*

2 sounded through your nose: *a nasal voice*
• ***Word Family:*** **nasally** *adverb*

nasturtium (*say* na-**ster**-shum) *noun*
a garden plant with bright, yellow, red or orange flowers and large leaves sometimes used in salads

nasty (*say* **nah**-stee) *adjective*
1 disgusting or unpleasant: *a nasty smell*
2 unkind or cruel: *a nasty person* 3 severe: *a nasty cut*
• ***Word Family:*** other forms are **nastier, nastiest** □ **nastily** *adverb* **nastiness** *noun*

natal (*say* **nay**-tal) *adjective*
having to do with your birth

nation (*say* **nay**-shon) *noun*
a large group of people living in one country and sharing their history, government and main language
• ***Word Family:*** **national** *adjective* **nationally** *adverb*

nationalism (*say* **nash**-a-na-liz-um) *noun*
1 love of your own country 2 a wish for your country or nation to become independent
• ***Word Family:*** **nationalist** *noun* **nationalistic** *adjective*

nationality (*say* nash-a-**nal**-a-tee) *noun*
the fact of belonging to or being born in a particular country or nation: *She has Italian nationality.*
• ***Word Family:*** the plural is **nationalities**

nationalize or nationalise (*say* **nash**-a-na-lize) *verb*
to make privately owned companies or industries the property of the nation
• ***Word Family:*** **nationalization** *noun*

native (*say* **nay**-tiv) *adjective*
1 of your birth: *your native country* 2 belonging to the place where it is growing: *a native plant*
3 belonging to the place of your birth: *Greek is my native language.*
native *noun*
4 one of the people who first settled in a country 5 someone born in a particular place: *Ken is a native of Liverpool.* 6 a plant or animal living in its own country

native title *noun*
the giving back of land to its original owners who had the right to claim it because their ancestors lived there first or because it contained their sacred sites

nativity (*say* na-**tiv**-i-tee) *noun*
1 *an old-fashioned word for* **birth** 2 **the Nativity** the birth of Jesus Christ
• ***Word Family:*** the plural is **nativities**

natural *adjective*
1 found in or produced by nature: *a natural desert / a natural ability* 2 open and relaxed: *a natural manner* 3 normal or expected: *It's only natural that he should be upset.*
natural *noun*
4 (a) a musical note that is neither a sharp nor a flat (b) the sign (♮) placed in front of a note to show this
• ***Word Family:*** **naturally** *adverb*

natural history *noun*
the study of animals and plants

naturalized or naturalised *adjective*
having become a full citizen of a country
• ***Word Family:*** **naturalization** *noun*

nature (*say* **nay**-cher) *noun*
1 the world and all the animals, plants and landforms it contains, except those made by human beings: *forces of nature* 2 the basic character or qualities of a person or thing: *to have a forgiving nature* 3 sort: *music of a similar nature*
• ***Word Family:*** **naturalist** *noun* someone who studies nature

naturopathy (*say* nat-yer-**op**-a-thee) *noun*
a way of treating disease in which herbal remedies and vitamins help the body's own natural healing forces
• ***Word Family:*** **naturopath** *noun*

naughty (*say* **naw**-tee) *adjective*
behaving badly
• ***Word Family:*** other forms are **naughtier, naughtiest** □ **naughtiness** *noun* **naughtily** *adverb*

nausea (*say* **naw**-see-a) *noun*
a feeling in your stomach that you are going to vomit
• ***Word Family:*** **nauseous** *adjective*

nautical (*say* **naw**-ti-kal) *adjective*
to do with sailors, ships or sailing
• ***Word Family:*** **nautically** *adverb*

naval (*say* **nay**-val) *adjective*
to do with or belonging to a navy: *naval warfare / a naval uniform*

nave *noun*
the main part of a church between the aisles, stretching from the entrance to where the clergy and choir sit

navel (*say* **nay**-val) *noun*
the small round pit in the centre of your stomach, left when your umbilical cord was cut at birth

navigate (*say* **nav**-i-gate) *verb*
to guide the direction and speed of a ship or plane
• ***Word Family:*** **navigation** *noun* **navigator** *noun*

navy (*say* **nay**-vee) *noun*
the part of a country's armed forces organized and trained for fighting at sea
• ***Word Family:*** the plural is **navies**

NB *abbreviation*
short for nota bene, *Latin words meaning* "note well"

near *adverb*
1 at or to a short distance: *to live near / to come near*
near *adjective*
2 not far away: *The station's near. / The holidays are near.* 3 closely related: *a near relative*
near *verb*
4 to come within a short distance of: *The boat neared the jetty.*
• ***Word Family:*** **nearby** *adjective*

nearly *adverb*
1 almost: *He nearly died.* 2 not distantly: *nearly related*

neat *adjective*
1 tidy or orderly: *a neat desk* 2 clever: *a neat trick* 3 not mixed with anything else: *to drink neat gin*
• ***Word Family:*** **neatly** *adverb* **neatness** *noun*

nebula (*say* **neb**-yoo-la) *noun*
a cloudy patch of pale light, made up of gas and dust in the night sky
• ***Word Family:*** the plural is **nebulae** or **nebulas**

nebulous (*say* **neb**-yoo-lus) *adjective*
vague, unclear, or cloudy: *a nebulous idea / a nebulous image*
• ***Word Family:*** **nebulously** *adverb*

necessary (*say* **nes**-a-se-ree *or* **nes**-es-ree) *adjective*
1 essential or needed: *Food is necessary for life.* 2 certain or inevitable: *a necessary part of growing old*
• ***Word Family:*** **necessarily** *adverb*

necessity (*say* na-**ses**-i-tee) *noun*
1 something that is essential: *Food is a necessity for life.* 2 the state of being in need: *Necessity forced her to steal.*
• ***Word Family:*** the plural is **necessities** □ **necessitate** *verb*

neck *noun*
1 the part of your body that joins your head to your shoulders 2 something shaped like a neck: *the neck of a bottle / the neck of a violin*

necklace *noun*
a string of beads, pearls or other ornaments worn around your neck

nectar *noun*
the sweet, sugary substance produced by many flowers, that attracts insects and birds

nectarine *noun*
a fruit with a smooth yellow and red skin, looking a bit like a firm peach

need *verb*
1 to have to have: *to need love / to need help* 2 to have to do something: *You need to sleep.*
need *noun*
3 a demand or necessity: *a need for urgent help / Their main need is food.* 4 a situation or time of difficulty: *a friend in need*
• ***Word Family:*** **needy** *adjective* (**needier, neediest**)

needle *noun*
1 a small, slender steel object used for sewing, pointed at one end and with a hole at the other for carrying thread 2 a long thin plastic or metal rod used for knitting 3 a tube holding a drug, with a sharp end for injecting into one of your veins 4 something shaped like a needle: *a pine needle* 5 a pointer on a dial, that moves to show measurement: *a compass needle*

needless *adjective*
not necessary

negative (*say* **neg**-a-tiv) *adjective*
1 meaning or saying no: *a negative answer*
2 smaller or less than zero: *a negative number*
3 having the same kind of electric charge as an electron: *the negative pole of a battery*
negative *noun*
4 an image on a developed photographic film in which the dark parts are light and the light parts dark
• ***Word Family:*** **negate** *verb* **negation** *noun* **negatively** *adverb*

neglect (*say* ne-**glekt**) *verb*
1 to ignore or disregard: *to neglect your homework*
2 to leave something uncared for: *to neglect your garden*
• ***Word Family:*** **neglectful** *adjective*

negligent (*say* **neg**-li-jent) *adjective*
not taking enough care: *a negligent driver*
• ***Word Family:*** **negligence** *noun*

negligible (*say* **neg**-li-ja-bul) *adjective*
so little that it seems unimportant: *a negligible sum of money*
• ***Word Family:*** **negligibly** *adverb*

negotiate (*say* ne-**go**-shee-ate) *verb*
to bargain or discuss something until you reach an agreement: *The companies negotiated a deal.*
• ***Word Family:*** **negotiable** *adjective* **negotiation** *noun*

neigh (*say* nay) *noun*
1 the loud cry of a horse
• ***Word Family:*** **neigh** *verb*

neighbour or **neighbor** (*say* **nay**-ba) *noun*
someone who lives next door or close to you
• ***Word Family:*** **neighbourhood** *noun* **neighbourly** *adjective*

neither (*say* **nee**-tha *or* **nigh**-tha) *adjective*
1 not one or the other of two things: *Neither twin can sing in tune.*
neither *pronoun*
2 not the one or the other: *Neither of the kids likes meat.*
neither *conjunction*
3 not either: *Neither you nor I know his name.*

neon (*say* **nee**-on) *noun*
a colourless gas found in tiny amounts in the earth's atmosphere and used in some electric lights

nephew (*say* **nef**-yoo) *noun*
the son of your brother or sister, or of your husband's or wife's brother or sister

nepotism (*say* **nep**-a-tiz-um) *noun*
unfair favour or advantage shown to your relatives or friends by giving them good jobs

nerd *noun*
an unfashionable, uninteresting or foolish person, often used about people who have unusual or obsessive interests that seem strange or uncool to most people: *a computer nerd*

nerve *noun*
1 a cord-like bundle of fibres carrying messages from your brain to other parts of your body in order for you to move and feel 2 courage or calmness: *It took a lot of nerve to climb that cliff.* 3 cheek or rudeness: *You've got a nerve, telling me to work harder!* 4 **nerves**: nervousness: *to suffer from nerves*

nervous *adjective*
1 anxious or easily frightened 2 to do with the nerves: *the human nervous system.*
• ***Word Family:*** **nervously** *adverb* **nervousness** *noun*

nest *noun*
1 a home, often of twigs and grass, made or used by birds for hatching and rearing their young
nest *verb*
2 to make a nest and lay eggs in it

nestle (*say* **nes**-ul) *verb*
1 to settle down comfortably: *to nestle down in the armchair* 2 to cuddle: *to nestle the baby in your arms*

net (1) *noun*
1 material made of knotted threads or strings with holes in between: *a mosquito net / a fishing net* 2 a barrier of net used in sports such as tennis
net *verb*
3 to catch something in a net: *to net a crab*
• ***Word Family:*** other verb forms are **nets, netted, netting**

net (2) *adjective*
1 remaining after deductions or expenses are paid: *your net income* 2 counting the contents only and not the packaging: *What's the net weight of the peas?*

netball *noun*
a game played on a court, between two teams of seven players who try to throw a ball through a net attached to a high pole

nettle *noun*
1 a small, wild plant with stinging hairs on its leaves and stem
nettle *verb*
2 to irritate or provoke: *His rude comments nettled us.*

network *noun*
1 a system with lots of connected lines, passages and so on: *a network of caves / the rail network* 2 a group of radio or television stations linked so they can broadcast the same programmes, often with the same owner 3 a system of linked computers, which are sometimes far apart from one another, that share information

neurotic (*say* new-**rot**-ik) *adjective*
1 having unreasonable fears, often because you have a mind disorder
neurotic *noun*
2 a neurotic person
• ***Word Family:*** **neurotically** *adverb*

neuter *adjective*
not masculine or feminine

neutral (*say* **new**-tral) *adjective*
1 not taking part in an argument, dispute or war: *a neutral country* 2 of no definite colour: *a neutral shade of grey*
neutral *noun*
3 a person or country taking no sides in a war 4 the position of gears in a car when they are not connected to the engine and so cannot transmit any power
• ***Word Family:*** **neutralize** or **neutralise** *verb*

neutron *noun*
a tiny particle inside an atom with no electric charge

never *adverb*
not ever or at no time: *I've never seen him before.*

nevertheless *adverb*
in spite of that

new *adjective*
1 recently born, arrived, made or discovered: *a*

new baby / a new style / new clothes / a new star
2 fresh or not used before: *Start on a new page.*
•***Word Family:*** **newly** *adverb* **newness** *noun*

news *noun*
1 a report of events given each day by newspapers, television or radio: *The news is all bad.* 2 information you didn't know before: *That's news to me.*

newspaper *noun*
a publication, usually daily or weekly, printed on large sheets of paper, that describes and comments on news and contains articles and advertisements

newt *noun*
a small animal that can live both in and out of water, with short legs and a long tail

newton *noun*
a unit for measuring force

next *adjective*
1 immediately following: *the next page*
2 nearest: *the next house*
next *adverb*
3 in the nearest place: *I'll stand next to you.*
4 at the nearest time: *Who goes next?*
•***Word Family:*** **next of kin** *noun* your closest relative

nib *noun*
the writing point of a pen

nibble *verb*
1 to take small bites from: *The rabbit nibbled the lettuce.*
nibble *noun*
2 a small bite

nice *adjective*
1 pleasant or good: *a nice day / a nice taste*
2 friendly or kind: *a nice person* 3 precise or subtle: *a nice distinction*
•***Word Family:*** **nicely** *adverb* **niceness** *noun*

niche (*say* nitch *or* neesh) *noun*
1 a small hollow in a wall for keeping ornaments, and other similar things 2 a comfortable position that suits a person or thing: *He's found a niche in the school.*
•***Word Origins:*** from a Latin word meaning "nest"

nick *verb*
1 to make a small cut or notch in 2 to steal
nick *noun*
3 a notch or groove

nickel *noun*
a hard, whitish metal used in coins and for protective plating

nickname *noun*
the name people call you instead of your real name: *Eddie King's nickname was Spud.*

nicotine (*say* **nik**-a-teen) *noun*
a poisonous substance found in tobacco
•***Word Origins:*** introduced to France by Jacques *Nicot* in 1560

niece (*say* neece) *noun*
the daughter of your brother or sister, or the daughter of your husband's or wife's brother or sister

nigh *adverb, adjective*
an old word meaning near or nearly: *The end of the world is nigh.*

night *noun*
the dark time between two days, from sunset to sunrise
•***Word Family:*** **nightly** *adjective* coming, happening or active at night **nightly** *adverb* every night

nightingale *noun*
a small, brown bird known for the beautiful singing of the male at night

nightmare *noun*
1 a frightening dream 2 a very frightening experience: *Driving through the blizzard was a nightmare.*
•***Word Family:*** **nightmarish** *adjective*
•***Word Origins:*** named after the Old English word *mare*, an evil spirit supposed to suffocate people while they slept

nil *noun*
nothing

nimble *adjective*
quick in movement or understanding: *nimble fingers / a nimble mind*
•***Word Family:*** **nimbleness** *noun* **nimbly** *adverb*

nimbus *noun*
1 a rain cloud 2 a halo
•***Word Family:*** the plural is **nimbi** or **nimbuses**
•***Word Origins:*** from a Latin word meaning "a thunder cloud"

nine *noun*
the number 9
•***Word Family:*** **nine** *adjective* **ninth** *adjective* **ninth** *noun*

nineteen *noun*
the number 19
•***Word Family:*** **nineteen** *adjective* **nineteenth** *adjective* **nineteenth** *noun*

ninety *noun*
the number 90
•***Word Family:*** the plural is **nineties** □ **ninetieth** *adjective* **ninetieth** *noun*

nip *verb*
1 to pinch, bite or squeeze 2 to go quickly, especially for a reason: *to nip down to the shop*

nip *noun*
3 a light pinch or bite 4 a cold, stinging feeling: *a nip in the air*
•***Word Family:*** other verb forms are **nips, nipped, nipping** □ **nippy** *adjective*

nipple *noun*
one of the two small, pointed parts on a person's chest, used by a baby to suck its mother's milk

nit *noun*
1 the egg of an insect such as the louse, especially when attached to your hair or clothing 2 a stupid person

nitrogen (*say* **nigh**-tra-jen) *noun*
a colourless gas forming about 78 per cent of the Earth's atmosphere

no *interjection*
1 used to deny or refuse something: *No! Go away!*
no *adjective*
2 not any: *to have no money*

noble *adjective*
1 belonging to the aristocratic class of a country: *a noble family* 2 honest, brave and generous: *a noble sacrifice* 3 grand and stately: *a noble monument*
noble *noun*
4 an aristocrat
•***Word Family:*** **nobility** *noun* the aristocracy **nobleman** *noun* **noblewoman** *noun* **nobly** *adverb*

nobody *pronoun*
1 no-one: *Nobody came to the party.*
nobody *noun*
2 a person of no importance: *She is a nobody.*

nocturnal (*say* nok-**ter**-nal) *adjective*
1 happening at night: *a nocturnal visit* 2 active at night: *a nocturnal animal*

nod *verb*
to move your head up and down, usually to show you agree or to say yes
•***Word Family:*** other forms are **nods, nodded, nodding**

node *noun*
1 a lump, knot or knob 2 a joint on a stem of a plant from which a leaf grows
•***Word Family:*** **nodal** *adjective*

nodule (*say* **nod**-yool) *noun*
a knob or small rounded lump
•***Word Family:*** **nodular** *adjective*

noise (*rhymes with* boys) *noun*
any sound, especially a loud, unpleasant or confused one
•***Word Family:*** **noisy** *adjective* **(noisier, noisiest) noisily** *adverb* **noisiness** *noun*

nomad (*say* **no**-mad) *noun*
1 a member of a tribe that moves from place to place hunting, gathering food or feeding animals 2 a wandering person
•***Word Family:*** **nomadic** *adjective*

nominate (*say* **nom**-i-nate) *verb*
to put forward a person's name for an election or a position
•***Word Family:*** **nomination** *noun* **nominee** *noun*

nonagon (*say* **non**-a-gon) *noun*
a flat shape with nine straight sides

nonchalant (*say* **non**-sha-lant) *adjective*
unconcerned, cool or indifferent: *a nonchalant approach to exams*
•***Word Family:*** **nonchalance** *noun*

non-committal *adjective*
not letting anyone know what you really think or have decided about something: *a non-committal reply*

nonconformist *noun*
someone who rebels against what is usual or expected and lives life according to his or her own rules
•***Word Family:*** **nonconformity** *noun*

nondescript (*say* **non**-da-skript) *adjective*
dull and uninteresting in the way it looks: *It was such a nondescript dress that I don't remember what colour it was.*

none (*rhymes with* sun *or* gone) *pronoun*
1 not any: *That's none of your business.* 2 not one: *None of them would help.*

nonentity (*say* non-**en**-ta-tee) *noun*
a person or thing of no importance

non-fiction *noun*
writing that is about facts and real people, rather than about imaginary or made-up things

nonsense *noun*
words that are silly or make no sense
•***Word Family:*** **nonsensical** *adjective*

noodles *plural noun*
pasta cut in long, flat and narrow pieces

nook *noun*
a small, sheltered place or corner: *a shady nook*

noon *noun*
midday or twelve o'clock in the middle of the day

noose *noun*
a loop with a sliding knot that tightens when the rope is pulled

norm *noun*
a model or standard that you use to measure, assess or judge everything else

A B C D E F G H I J K L M N O P Q R S T U V W X Y Z

normal *adjective*
usual, typical or expected: *normal behaviour / normal growth*
•*Word Family:* **normally** *adverb* usually **normality** *noun*

north *noun*
the direction to your right as you face the west where the sun sets
•*Word Family:* **north** *adjective* **north** *adverb* **northern** *adjective*

nose (*say* noze) *noun*
1 the part of your face above your mouth, used for smelling and breathing 2 a sense of smell: *to have a good nose for selecting wine*
nose *verb*
3 to move slowly: *to nose into the heavy traffic*
4 to pry: *to nose into other people's affairs*
•*Word Family:* **nosy** *adjective* **(nosier, nosiest)** prying **nasal** *adjective*

nostalgia (*say* nos-**tal**-ja) *noun*
a longing for the past and the way things once were
•*Word Family:* **nostalgic** *adjective* **nostalgically** *adverb*

nostril *noun*
one of the two openings in your nose

notable (*say* **no**-ta-bul) *adjective*
1 important or worthy of notice: *a notable artist*
notable *noun*
2 an important person
•*Word Family:* **notability** *noun* **notably** *adverb*

notation (*say* no-**tay**-shon) *noun*
a system of symbols or signs used to write down such things as the sounds of music or the movements of dance, that you can't express in words
•*Word Family:* **notate** *verb*

notch *noun*
a V-shaped cut in a surface, sometimes used as a record or to keep count
•*Word Family:* the plural is **notches**

note *noun*
1 a short message or letter 2 a written reminder of something you don't want to forget 3 paper money: *a ten pound note* 4 a single musical sound, or the symbol you use to write it down 5 importance: *a writer of note* 6 **take note of** pay attention to: *Take note of our new opening times.*
note *verb*
7 to watch or notice carefully: *Note the way she walks.* 8 to write down: *Note the date on your calendar.*
•*Word Family:* **noted** *adjective* famous

notebook *noun*
1 a book with blank pages, used for writing notes 2 a small, light computer that you can carry around with you

nothing (*say* **nuth**-ing) *noun*
1 no thing: *This carton has nothing in it.*
2 nought

notice (*say* **no**-tiss) *noun*
1 attention or awareness: *Your lateness has come to my notice.* 2 a written or printed announcement: *a notice about a new play*
3 a formal statement that a job or some other agreement is ending: *to give notice*
notice *verb*
4 to be aware of or pay attention to: *Did you notice that strange smell?*
•*Word Family:* **noticeable** *adjective* easily seen **noticeably** *adverb*

notify (*say* **no**-ti-fie) *verb*
to inform someone officially about something
•*Word Family:* the other forms are **notifies, notified, notifying** □ **notification** *noun*

notion (*say* **no**-shon) *noun*
1 a general idea or feeling: *I have a notion that we've been here before.* 2 an opinion or belief: *His notions about friendship are very strange.*

notorious (*say* no-**taw**-ree-us) *adjective*
well-known for something bad: *a notorious thief*
•*Word Family:* **notoriety** *noun* **notoriously** *adverb*

nought (*rhymes with* port) *noun*
zero, or the symbol "0"

noun *noun*
a word that names something, divided into common nouns such as "girl" or "dog", proper nouns such as "Tom" or "Newcastle", abstract nouns such as "beauty" and "anger" or collective nouns such as "herd" or "flock"

nourish (*say* **nur**-ish) *verb*
to feed a person, animal or plant so that they will grow or remain healthy
•*Word Family:* **nourishing** *adjective* **nourishment** *noun*

novel (1) (*say* **nov**-el) *noun*
a long story about imaginary people and events
•*Word Family:* **novelist** *noun* someone who writes novels

novel (2) (*say* **nov**-el) *adjective*
new, unusual or different: *a novel experience*

novelty *noun*
1 strangeness or newness: *the novelty of snow in*

summer 2 something new or interesting 3 a small, unusual toy or gimmick
•*Word Family:* the plural is **novelties**

November *noun*
the eleventh month of the year, with 30 days

novice (*say* **nov**-is) *noun*
1 someone who is new to the job or activity they are doing 2 someone who is training to become a monk or nun

nowhere *adverb*
1 not anywhere: *He's nowhere to be found.*
2 **get nowhere** to achieve nothing

noxious (*say* **nok**-shus) *adjective*
harmful or poisonous: *a noxious weed / a noxious gas*
•*Word Family:* **noxiously** *adverb*

nozzle *noun*
the end of a pipe or hose through which water is sprayed

nuance (*say* **new**-ons) *noun*
a slight difference in tone, colour, meaning or feeling: *to imitate the nuances of his brother's voice*

nuclear (*say* **new**-klee-a) *adjective*
1 to do with or powered by nuclear energy: *a nuclear test / a nuclear reactor* 2 armed with nuclear weapons: *France is a nuclear power.* 3 to do with a nucleus: *a nuclear family*

nuclear energy *noun*
power produced by splitting atoms

nuclear reactor *noun*
a machine that produces nuclear energy, for example to generate electricity

nuclear waste *noun*
dangerous radioactive products formed when nuclear energy is produced

nucleus (*say* **new**-klee-us) *noun*
1 the central part of something around which other things are grouped: *The three of us form the nucleus of the band.* 2 the main part or core of an atom made up of protons and neutrons
•*Word Family:* the plural is **nuclei** or **nucleuses**

nude (*say* newd) *adjective*
1 naked or without clothes
nude *noun*
2 a naked human figure, or a drawing, painting or photograph of one
•*Word Family:* **nudist** *noun* **nudity** *noun*

nudge *verb*
to push gently, especially with your elbow, in order to attract attention
•*Word Family:* **nudge** *noun*

nugget *noun*
a small lump, especially of gold dug from the ground

nuisance (*say* **new**-sence) *noun*
an annoying person or thing

null *adjective*
null and void having no legal force: *Their marriage was proclaimed to be null and void.*

numb (*say* num) *adjective*
1 unable to feel or move: *His toes were numb with cold. / to be numb with shock*
numb *verb*
2 to make numb

number (*say* **num**-ba) *noun*
1 a symbol or figure that shows how many of something there is or what its position is in a series: *the number 9* 2 a particular number given to something to fix its place in a series and so on: *The number of your locker is 5. / your telephone number* 3 a quantity, total or amount: *the number of kids in our class* 4 a large quantity: *A number of spectators were injured.* 6 a song played during a concert: *The band played the next number.*
number *verb*
7 to give a number to: *to number the pages*
8 to amount to in number: *The protesters numbered several thousand.*

numberplate *noun*
a metal strip attached to your car with the registration number on it

numeral *noun*
the letter, figure or word that represents a number: *The Roman numeral for two is II.*

numerate *adjective*
able to do basic arithmetic
•*Word Family:* **numeracy** *noun*

numerator *noun*
the number written above the line in a fraction, such as 3 in $\frac{3}{4}$, showing how many parts of the whole there are

numerical *adjective*
to do with numbers

numerous (*say* **new**-ma-rus) *adjective*
existing in great numbers
•*Word Family:* **numerously** *adverb*

nun *noun*
a woman who lives in a convent, belongs to a religious order and has vowed to live for God

nuptials (*say* **nup**-shels) *plural noun*
a marriage ceremony or wedding
•*Word Family:* **nuptial** *adjective*

A B C D E F G H I J K L M N O P Q R S T U V W X Y Z

nurse *noun*
1 someone trained to care for sick people, usually in hospital 2 someone trained to care for young children
nurse *verb*
3 to care for or look after: *to nurse the sick* 4 to breastfeed: *to nurse a baby* 5 to hold gently, especially in your arms: *to nurse a sore leg / to nurse a puppy* 6 to feel something strongly for a long time: *to nurse a grudge / to nurse an ambition*

nursery *noun*
1 a school where very young children are looked after 2 a room in a house for children to sleep and play 3 a place where you can buy plants
• ***Word Family:*** the plural is **nurseries**

nurture (*say* **ner**-cha) *verb*
to feed and look after a young child or plant when it is still growing

nut *noun*
1 a dry fruit with a tasty kernel enclosed in a hard shell 2 the kernel of the fruit that you eat 3 a piece of metal with a hole in the centre for screwing on to the end of a bolt 4 an odd or eccentric person 5 your head
• ***Word Family:*** **nutty** *adjective* (**nuttier, nuttiest**)

nutmeg *noun*
a sweet spice made from the dried seed of a tropical tree and used in cooking

nutrient (*say* **new**-tree-ent) *noun*
a substance, such as a vitamin or mineral, that gives the energy needed for growth when it is eaten

nutrition (*say* new-**trish**-on) *noun*
1 your eating habits: *poor nutrition* 2 the taking in, changing and absorbing of food so that it nourishes us
• ***Word Family:*** **nutritious** *adjective* providing a lot of nourishment **nutritionist** *noun*

nuzzle *verb*
to push against with your nose: *The puppy nuzzled its mother's teat to get more milk.*

nylon *noun*
1 a strong, synthetic material made from coal, with flexible threads used to make yarn, fabric, fishing line and so on 2 **nylons** stockings made of nylon

nymph (*say* nimf) *noun*
1 a beautiful young goddess who lived in the sea, woods or meadows in ancient myths 2 a young, wingless insect

oaf *noun*
a stupid or clumsy person

oak *noun*
a large tree that produces acorns and hard wood that is used for making furniture or building

oar (*rhymes with* door) *noun*
a long, wooden pole with a flat blade at one end, used to row a boat

oasis (*say* o-**ay**-sis) *noun*
a place in a desert where there is a source of water and trees can grow
• ***Word Family:*** the plural is **oases**

oath *noun*
1 a serious promise 2 the words you say in a law court when you promise to tell the truth 3 a swearword

oats *plural noun*
grain used to make porridge and flapjacks, and fed to animals

obedient (*say* o-**bee**-dee-ent) *adjective*
willing to do what you are told: *She's obedient at school but a rebel at home. / an obedient horse*
• ***Word Family:*** **obedience** *noun* **obediently** *adverb*

obelisk (*say* **ob**-a-lisk) *noun*
a stone column with a pyramid-shaped top, built as a monument in praise of a person or event

obese (*say* o-**beece**) *adjective*
extremely fat
• ***Word Family:*** **obesely** *adverb* **obesity** *noun*

obey (*say* o-**bay**) *verb*
to do what you are told

obituary (*say* o-**bit**-cha-ree) *noun*
a short account of someone's life and the things they have achieved that is published or broadcast after they have died

object (*say* **ob**-ject) *noun*
1 anything that you can see or touch: *I tripped over a large object in the dark.* 2 an aim or purpose: *The object of the meeting is to elect a captain.* 3 the person you are thinking about: *He's the object of our pity.* 4 the person or thing that the action that a verb describes is done to, such as "brother" in *Jill kissed her brother.*

object (*say* ob-**jekt**) *verb*
5 **object to** to say you dislike something or disagree with it
•***Word Family:*** **objection** *noun* an argument against something **objector** *noun*

objectionable (*say* ob-**jek**-shon-a-bul) *adjective*
unpleasant and offensive: *an objectionable person*
•***Word Family:*** **objectionably** *adverb*

objective *noun*
1 an aim that you plan to achieve: *My objective is to make a million pounds by the time I'm thirty.*
objective *adjective*
2 based on facts and not on someone's feelings or opinions
•***Word Family:*** **objectively** *adverb* **objectivity** *noun*

objective case *noun*
the form that a noun or pronoun takes when it is the object of a verb, such as "them" in *He hates them.*

obligation (*say* ob-li-**gay**-shon) *noun*
something you feel it is your duty to do: *I have an obligation to visit my auntie in hospital.*
•***Word Family:*** **obligatory** *adjective* required or compulsory

oblige *verb*
be obliged to **(a)** to have to: *We are obliged to wear school uniform.* **(b)** to be grateful for something: *I'm much obliged to you for all your help.*
•***Word Family:*** **obliging** *adjective* helpful **obligingly** *adverb*

oblique (*say* o-**bleek**) *adjective*
1 sloping: *an oblique line* 2 indirect: *to give an oblique answer to a question*
•***Word Family:*** **obliquely** *adverb*

obliterate (*say* o-**blit**-a-rate) *verb*
to destroy so completely there is nothing left: *The whole building was obliterated by the fire.*
•***Word Family:*** **obliteration** *noun*

oblivion (*say* o-**bliv**-ee-on) *noun*
1 complete unawareness of your surroundings: *to sink into oblivion* 2 **in oblivion** forgotten: *Her past life is in oblivion.*
•***Word Family:*** **oblivious** *adjective* forgetful

oblong *noun*
1 a flat shape with four sides and four right angles, with two sides longer than the other two
oblong *adjective*
2 having an oblong shape

obnoxious (*say* ob-**nok**-shus) *adjective*
really horrible: *an obnoxious boy*

oboe *noun*
a woodwind instrument that you play by blowing through a double reed
•***Word Family:*** **oboist** *noun* an oboe player

obscene (*say* ob-**seen**) *adjective*
so rude that it is shocking or offensive: *obscene videos*
•***Word Family:*** **obscenity** *noun* **(obscenities)** **obscenely** *adverb*

obscure (*say* ob-**skew**-er) *adjective*
1 not well known or hardly known at all 2 hard to understand: *an obscure idea*
obscure *verb*
3 to make something hard to see or understand: *A high wall obscured her view of the palace.*
•***Word Family:*** **obscurely** *adverb* **obscurity** *noun*

observant (*say* ob-**zer**-vant) *adjective*
quick to notice things

observatory (*say* ob-**zerv**-a-tree) *noun*
a place with telescopes for observing stars, planets and the weather
•***Word Family:*** the plural is **observatories**

observe (*say* ob-**zerv**) *verb*
1 to watch: *I'll do the experiment first while you observe then you can try it.* 2 to celebrate a traditional holiday: *to observe Christmas* 3 to obey a rule or law: *I am observing the speed limit.* 4 to comment on something: *She observed how hot it was.*
•***Word Family:*** **observation** *noun* **observer** *noun*

obsess *verb*
to fill your thoughts most of the time: *She is obsessed by her fear of burglars.*
•***Word Family:*** **obsession** *noun* **obsessive** *adjective* **obsessively** *adverb*

obsolete (*say* **ob**-sa-leet) *adjective*
out-of-date and no longer used: *an obsolete computer*
•***Word Family:*** **obsolescent** *adjective* becoming obsolete **obsolescence** *noun*

obstacle (*say* **ob**-sti-kul) *noun*
something that is in your way

obstetrics (*say* ob-**stet**-riks) *noun*
the part of medicine that studies and cares for women during pregnancy and childbirth
•***Word Family:*** **obstetric** *adjective* **obstetrician** *noun*

obstinate (*say* **ob**-sti-nit) *adjective*
1 stubborn and unwilling to change your mind: *an obstinate refusal* 2 difficult to control or get rid of: *an obstinate patch of weeds in the flower bed*
•***Word Family:*** **obstinacy** *noun* **obstinately** *adverb*

A B C D E F G H I J K L M N O P Q R S T U V W X Y Z

obstruct *verb*
1 to block a place so that you can't get past: *Fallen rocks obstructed our path.* 2 to make something difficult to do: *He was obstructing my attempts to build a new fence.*
• ***Word Family:*** **obstruction** *noun*

obtain *verb*
to get something: *Did you obtain the information you needed?*

obtuse (*say* ob-**tewce**) *adjective*
1 stupid and not able to understand something
2 between 90° and 180°: *an obtuse angle*
• ***Word Family:*** **obtusely** *adverb* **obtuseness** *noun*

obvious *adjective*
easily seen or understood
• ***Word Family:*** **obviously** *adverb* clearly

occasion (*say* o-**kay**-zhon) *noun*
1 a particular time: *We've met on several occasions.* 2 a special or important event: *Their wedding was a special occasion.* 3 an opportunity

occasional (*say* o-**kay**-zhon-al) *adjective*
happening from time to time but not often: *occasional laughter*
• ***Word Family:*** **occasionally** *adverb*

occult (*say* **ok**-ult) *noun*
1 the study or practice of magic and the supernatural
occult *adjective*
2 to do with the magic or the supernatural
• ***Word Origins:*** from a Latin word meaning "hidden"

occupant (*say* **ok**-yoo-pant) *noun*
someone who is in a place or building
• ***Word Family:*** **occupancy** *noun*

occupation (*say* ok-yoo-**pay**-shon) *noun*
1 a job: *Write down your name, age and occupation.* 2 a hobby: *Gardening is my usual occupation.* 3 the taking over of a place by force: *We are resisting the enemy occupation of our country.*
• ***Word Family:*** **occupational** *adjective* to do with an occupation or activity

occupy (*say* **ok**-yoo-puy) *verb*
1 to fill your time and keep you busy: *Playing computer games occupies my spare time.* 2 to live in a place: *The house has not been occupied for years.* 3 to seize control of a place by force: *The army has moved in to occupy the country.*
• ***Word Family:*** other forms are **occupies, occupied, occupying** □ **occupier** *noun*

occur (*say* o-**ker**) *verb*
1 to happen: *The accident occurred yesterday.*
2 **occur to** to come into your mind as a thought: *It occurs to me that the shop will be closed.*
• ***Word Family:*** other forms are **occurs, occurred, occurring** □ **occurrence** *noun*

ocean (*say* **o**-shen) *noun*
one of the areas of salt water covering the parts of the Earth's surface between the continents: *the Atlantic Ocean*
• ***Word Family:*** **oceanography** *noun* the study of oceans **oceanic** *adjective*

ochre (*rhymes with* poker) *noun*
a pale yellowish or reddish-brown clay used to colour paint or dye

o'clock *adverb*
what you say after the hour when giving the time: *It's two o'clock.*

octagon *noun*
a shape that has eight straight sides
• ***Word Family:*** **octagonal** *adjective*

octahedron (*say* ok-ta-**hee**-dron) *noun*
a solid or hollow form with eight plane faces

octave (*say* **ok**-tiv) *noun*
the eight note interval between one musical note and another of the same name but of a higher or lower pitch

octet *noun*
a group of eight people who play or sing together, or a musical piece for eight players or singers

October *noun*
the tenth month of the year, with 31 days

octopus *noun*
a sea animal with a soft body and eight long tentacles with suckers
• ***Word Family:*** the plural is **octopuses**
• ***Word Origins:*** from a Greek word meaning "eight feet"

odd *adjective*
1 puzzlingly different from what is usual or normal: *an odd noise* 2 not matching: *odd socks*
3 having a remainder of one when divided by two: *Three and seven are odd numbers.*
4 occasional or casual: *odd jobs* 5 **odds** the probability of something happening: *What are the odds on that horse winning the race?*
• ***Word Family:*** **oddity** *noun* (**oddities**) **oddly** *adverb*

ode *noun*
a poem written in praise of something: *an ode to beauty*

odious (*say* **o**-dee-us) *adjective*
hateful or repulsive: *an odious human being*
• ***Word Family:*** **odium** *noun* intense hatred or disgust felt for someone

odour or **odor** (*say* **oh**-da) *noun*
a smell or scent

odyssey (*say* **od**-i-see) *noun*
a long and exciting journey

•***Word Origins:*** named after *Odysseus*, a hero in Greek myths, who wandered for ten years

oesophagus (*say* a-**sof**-a-gus) *noun*
the tube connecting your mouth with your stomach through which food passes
•***Word Family:*** the plural is **oesophagi** (*say* a-**sof**-a-guy)

offence *noun*
1 a crime: *a parking offence* 2 something that makes people feel insulted or upset: *The book gave offence to many religious people.*

offend *verb*
1 to hurt someone or upset them 2 to commit a crime
•***Word Family:*** **offender** *noun* someone who breaks the law

offensive *adjective*
1 rude or upsetting: *an offensive comment / an offensive gesture* 2 attacking: *an offensive campaign*
offensive *noun*
3 an attack by soldiers: *a dawn offensive against the city*
•***Word Family:*** **offensively** *adverb*

offer *verb*
1 to be willing to give something or do something if the other person would like it: *He offered me a cup of tea. / I offered to do the washing up.* 2 to say what you would be willing to give or pay for something
offer *noun*
3 a bid to buy something: *We've put in an offer for the house.*
•***Word Family:*** **offering** *noun*

offhand *adjective*
1 without really knowing: *an offhand guess*
2 rudely abrupt or unfriendly: *an offhand response*

office *noun*
1 a place where people work usually at desks
2 an important job: *the office of Minister of Education* 3 a place where people can go for tickets, information or other services

officer *noun*
someone who holds a position of authority in the army, navy, air force or police force

official (*say* o-**fish**-al) *adjective*
1 approved of by someone with authority: *an official dinner / an official report*
official *noun*
2 a person who holds a position of authority, especially in a large organization: *a government official*
•***Word Family:*** **officially** *adverb*

officious *adjective*
telling you what to do in a self-important and superior way

off-line *adjective*
not having direct access to a computer: *This branch of the bank is off-line.*

off-putting *adjective*
making you dislike it or feel uncomfortable about it: *I find the smell a bit off-putting.*

off-side *adjective*
in a position in a sport where you are not allowed to play the ball

offspring *noun*
the young of an animal, human or plant

ogre (*say* **o**-ga) *noun*
a cruel giant in myths and fairy stories, said to like eating humans

ohm *noun*
a unit in measuring the amount of resistance something has to an electric current

oil *noun*
1 a greasy liquid made from plants and used for cooking: *olive oil* 2 a smooth thick liquid used to make machinery run smoothly and as a fuel
3 a black, sticky liquid that we get from under the ground and use to make oil and petrol
oil *verb*
4 to put oil on something
•***Word Family:*** **oily** *adjective* **(oilier, oiliest)**

oil rig *noun*
a large structure on a platform that is used to drill for oil under the sea or under the ground

oilskin *noun*
a cloth treated with oil to make it waterproof so it can be worn in the rain

ointment *noun*
a soft thick paste or cream you put on your skin as a medicine

OK or okay (*say* o-**kay**) *adjective*
1 all right: *He's OK now.*
OK *adverb*
2 well or correctly: *I did OK in the test.*
OK *verb*
3 to accept that something is all right: *to OK a passport*
OK *noun*
4 approval: *He gave it his OK.*

old *adjective*
1 having existed or lived for a long time: *old forests / an old man* 2 grown-up: *He's old for his age.* 3 from a long time ago: *an old school friend*
4 of a particular age: *three years old*
•***Word Family:*** **olden** *adjective* long ago

Old English *noun*
the form of the English language used from the 5th to the 12th century

A B C D E F G H I J K L M N O P Q R S T U V W X Y Z

old-fashioned *adjective*
out-of-date and no longer fashionable: *old-fashioned shoes*

Old French *noun*
the language used in France before AD 1400

olive (*say* **ol**-iv) *noun*
1 a small, green or black fruit with a stone, that is eaten or crushed for its oil 2 a deep, yellowish-green or brownish-green colour
olive *adjective*
3 yellowish-green or brownish-green

olfactory (*say* ol-**fak**-ta-ree) *adjective*
having to do with your sense of smell

ombudsman (*say* **om**-budz-man) *noun*
a government official appointed to investigate people's complaints against the government or a public service

omelette (*say* **om**-let) *noun*
a food made from eggs that have been beaten and then lightly fried in a pan

omen (*say* **oh**-men) *noun*
a sign of what will happen in the future: *a bad omen*

ominous (*say* **om**-i-nus) *adjective*
making you think that something unpleasant is coming: *ominous clouds / an ominous silence*
• ***Word Family:*** **ominously** *adverb*

omit (*say* o-**mit**) *verb*
1 to leave someone or something out 2 to not do something: *He omitted to tell me his name.*
• ***Word Family:*** other forms are **omits, omitted, omitting** □ **omission** *noun*

omnipotent (*say* om-**nip**-a-tent) *adjective*
having absolute and unlimited power: *omnipotent gods*
• ***Word Family:*** **omnipotence** *noun*

omnivore *noun*
an animal that eats plants and other animals
• ***Word Family:*** **omnivorous** *adjective: Humans are omnivorous.*

on *preposition*
1 at or resting over the surface of something that supports it: *a scar on his face / to scribble on the wall / a book on the desk* 2 at the time or occasion of: *on Monday / on my arrival home* 3 about or concerning: *a talk on conservation* 4 near or close to: *a town on the river / just on a year ago*
on *adverb*
5 attached to or in contact with yourself or itself: *Put your coat on. / to turn the radio on*
6 further or onwards: *to hurry on*

once *adverb*
1 in the past: *a once powerful nation* 2 at a single time: *once a week*
once *noun*
3 a single occasion: *Once is enough.*
• ***Word Family:*** **once** *conjunction* whenever

one *noun*
1 the number 1 2 a single person or thing: *Please give me one of those.*
• ***Word Family:*** **one** *adjective*

ongoing *adjective*
continuing: *ongoing discussions about peace*

onion (*say* **un**-yon) *noun*
a round, white vegetable with a brown skin that has a strong taste and smell

on-line *adjective*
directly connected to or using a computer

only (*rhymes with* lonely) *adjective*
1 being the single one: *an only child / the only cat I have*
only *adverb*
2 just one person or thing and no others: *Only Jill was late.* 3 no more than: *He can only crawl. / He's only ten years old.*
only *conjunction*
4 except: *I like that car, only it's too expensive.*

onomatopoeia (*say* on-a-mat-a-**pee**-a) *noun*
the use of a word whose sound suggests its meaning, as in "hiss", "buzz", "croak"
• ***Word Family:*** **onomatopoeic** *adjective*

onset *noun*
the beginning of something: *the onset of rain*

onslaught (*say* **on**-slawt) *noun*
a fierce or violent attack

onward *adjective*
going forward: *We stop off in Los Angeles and then continue on the onward journey to Hawaii.*
• ***Word Family:*** **onwards** *adverb: He lived in Liverpool from the age of twelve onwards.*

ooze *verb*
to flow very slowly: *Hot mud oozed from the volcano. / Blood oozed from the wound.*

opal (*say* **o**-pal) *noun*
a whitish gem with streaks of colour in it

opaque (*say* o-**pake**) *adjective*
not able to be seen through: *an opaque bathroom window*
• ***Word Family:*** **opacity** *noun*

open *adjective*
1 allowing you to go through: *an open gate*
2 not closed, covered or enclosed: *an open jar / open countryside* 3 ready for business: *The shop is open.* 4 friendly and relaxed: *an open manner*
5 honest and not hiding anything: *She was quite open with me.* 6 unfolded or spread out: *The book was open at the chapter on volcanoes.*

open *verb*
7 to become open or make something become open: *The door opened when we pushed it. / She opened the window.* 8 to take off the cover, lid, top and so on: *She's opening her presents now.*
open *noun*
9 a clear area: *We spent the day in the open.*
• ***Word Family:*** **opener** *noun* a device that opens **openly** *adverb* not hiding anything

opening *noun*
1 a hole or space: *The dogs squeezed through an opening in the fence.*
opening *adjective*
2 first: *the opening match of the season*

open-minded *adjective*
willing to consider new ideas or arguments

opera (*say* **op**-er-a) *noun*
a play that is set to music and sung by trained singers
• ***Word Family:*** **operatic** *adjective*
• ***Word Origins:*** from a Latin word meaning "labour"

operate *noun*
1 to make something work: *to operate a computer* 2 to cut open someone's body in order to repair it inside: *The surgeon will operate on his appendix.*
• ***Word Family:*** **operational** *adjective* working

operation (*say* op-a-**ray**-shon) *noun*
1 a complicated activity involving a lot of people: *a rescue operation* 2 working: *There are three machines in operation.* 3 a medical treatment in which a surgeon operates on someone's body
• ***Word Family:*** **operational** *adjective*

operator (*say* **op**-a-ray-ta) *noun*
1 someone who operates a machine: *a telephone operator / a computer operator* 2 someone who runs a business: *a tour operator*

opinion (*say* o-**pin**-yon) *noun*
your idea about something: *What's your opinion of the new headteacher?*
• ***Word Family:*** **opinionated** *adjective* convinced your own ideas are right

opium (*say* **oh**-pee-um) *noun*
a drug made from the juice of certain poppies, used in medicine to relieve pain or help you sleep

opponent (*say* a-**po**-nent) *noun*
someone who is on the opposite side to you in a contest or argument: *your opponent in chess*

opportunity (*say* op-a-**tew**-na-tee) *noun*
a chance to do something: *She had the opportunity to appear on TV.*
• ***Word Family:*** the plural is **opportunities**

oppose *verb*
to be against something: *I'm opposed to fox-hunting.*

opposite *adjective*
1 directly facing someone or something: *She sat at the opposite end of the table to me.* 2 entirely different: *in the opposite direction*
opposite *noun*
3 something as different as possible: *You just said the opposite.*

opposition (*say* op-a-**zish**-on) *noun*
1 very strong disagreement with something: *There was a lot of opposition to the new motorway.* 2 **the Opposition** the party or parties in parliament who are not in power and who usually criticize the Government

oppress *verb*
1 to treat someone cruelly or unjustly 2 to make you feel gloomy and depressed
• ***Word Family:*** **oppression** *noun* **oppressive** *adjective* **oppressor** *noun*

opt *verb*
1 to choose: *I opted to do French rather than German.* 2 **opt out** to decide not to join in

optical *adjective*
to do with the eye or with seeing: *an optical lens / an optical illusion*

optician (*say* op-**tish**-on) *noun*
someone who makes and sells glasses

optimism (*say* **op**-ti-miz-um) *noun*
the tendency to look on the bright side
• ***Word Family:*** **optimist** *noun* someone who is full of optimism **optimistic** *adjective* **optimistically** *adverb*

option (*say* **op**-shon) *noun*
1 the right to make a choice: *You have no option but to accept my offer.* 2 a choice: *We have two options.*
• ***Word Family:*** **optional** *adjective* open to choice

optometry (*say* op-**tom**-a-tree) *noun*
the job of testing your eyesight and prescribing suitable glasses
• ***Word Family:*** **optometrist** *noun* someone who tests eyes and makes glasses

opulent (*say* **op**-yoo-lent) *adjective*
rich and comfortable: *an opulent lifestyle*
• ***Word Family:*** **opulence** *noun* wealth

opus (*say* **o**-pus) *noun*
a musical composition.

or *conjunction*
used to connect or link alternatives: *red or white flowers / Either that dog goes, or I go.*

oracle (*say* **o**-ra-kul) *noun*
1 a holy person in ancient Greece who guarded the shrine of a god or goddess and helped interpret

A B C D E F G H I J K L M N O P Q R S T U V W X Y Z

their answers to questions about the future 2 a wise or puzzling saying given by an oracle

oral (*say* **o**-rul) *adjective*
1 spoken rather than written: *an oral test in French* 2 to do with, used in or taken through the mouth: *oral medicine*
•***Word Family:*** **orally** *adverb*

orange (*say* **o**-rinj) *noun*
1 a reddish-yellow colour 2 a round, medium-sized, orange-coloured fruit
orange *adjective*
3 reddish-yellow

orang-outang (*say* a-**rang**-a-tang) *noun*
a large, long-armed ape with reddish-brown hair, that lives in the forests of Indonesia
•***Word Origins:*** from a Malay word meaning "man of the woods"

oration (*say* or-**ray**-shon) *noun*
a formal speech made in public
•***Word Family:*** **orator** *noun* a skilful public speaker **oratorical** *adjective*

orbit *noun*
1 the curved path that a satellite or planet follows around the Earth or sun
orbit *verb*
2 to travel in an orbit

orbital *adjective*
going round the outside of a city: *an orbital road*

orchard (*say* **or**-ched) *noun*
an area of land planted with fruit trees

orchestra (*say* **or**-kes-tra) *noun*
a large group of musicians who play woodwind, brass, percussion and string instruments together
•***Word Family:*** **orchestral** *adjective*

orchid (*say* **or**-kid) *noun*
a colourful and unusually shaped plant with flowers

ordain *verb*
1 to appoint someone to the church as a bishop, priest or deacon 2 to order that something should happen
•***Word Family:*** **ordination** *noun*

ordeal *noun*
a very unpleasant and difficult experience

order *noun*
1 a command to do something 2 the way things are arranged: *alphabetical order* 3 a situation in which people are behaving properly and obeying the rules: *Our teacher can't keep order.* 4 a request to supply something: *I've put in an order for the book.* 5 a particular group or kind, usually of plants or animals 6 a group of religious people living together and following the same rules: *an order of nuns*
order *verb*
7 to give an order or make an order
•***Word Family:*** **orderly** *adjective*

ordinal number *noun*
a number that tells what order something comes in a series, such as "first" in *their first record* or "tenth" in *the tenth month*

ordinary (*say* **or**-din-ree) *adjective*
normal or usual: *an ordinary school day*
•***Word Family:*** **ordinarily** *adverb* usually

ore *noun*
a rock or mineral containing metal

organ *noun*
1 a musical instrument with pipes, one or more keyboards you play like a piano and pedals you work with your feet 2 a part of your body with its own job to do, such as your kidneys which clean the blood 3 a newsletter or magazine that gives information for a particular organization or group
•***Word Family:*** **organist** *noun* someone who plays the organ

organic (*say* or-**gan**-ik) *adjective*
1 to do with living things: *organic remains*
2 produced or grown without pesticides and artificial fertilizers: *organic vegetables*
3 organized in a planned way
•***Word Family:*** **organically** *adverb*

organism *noun*
a living plant or animal

organization or **organisation** (*say* or-ga-nigh-**zay**-shon) *noun*
1 the planning arrangments made for something: *A huge amount of organization is needed for a successful tour.* 2 a group, society or business that runs something: *We all work for the same organization.*
•***Word Family:*** **organizational** *adjective*

organize or **organise** (*say* **or**-ga-nize) *verb*
1 to plan and make arrangements for something: *They organized a surprise party.* 2 to put things in a sensible order: *to organize your desk*

orgasm (*say* **or**-gaz-um) *noun*
the climax of excitement or pleasure in sexual intercourse

orgy (*say* **or**-jee) *noun*
a wild party with a lot of drinking and sex
•***Word Family:*** the plural is **orgies**

orient (*say* **or**-ee-ent) *verb*
1 *another word for* **orientate**
orient *noun*
2 **the Orient** the countries of eastern Asia including China and Japan
•***Word Family:*** **oriental** *adjective* to do with or from an Asian country

orientate (*say* **or**-ee-en-tate) *verb*
1 to work out your position and what direction you are facing: *I had to look at the map to orientate myself.* 2 to adjust to a new situation: *It takes time to orientate yourself in a new job.*
• ***Word Family:*** **orientation** *noun*

orienteering (*say* or-ee-en-**teer**-ring) *noun*
the sport of cross-country running over a set course using a map and a compass

orifice (*say* **o**-ra-fis) *noun*
an opening or hole, especially in your body

origami (*say* o-ra-**gah**-mee) *noun*
the Japanese art of folding paper to make models

origin (*say* **o**-ra-jin) *noun*
where something or someone begins, comes from or is born: *the origin of a song / of Jamaican origin*

original (*say* o-**rij**-a-nal) *adjective*
1 earliest or existing from the beginning: *The old house has its original windows.* 2 new and different from what has been done before: *an original design* 3 producing new ideas: *an original thinker*
original *noun*
4 the first one produced rather than a copy: *This is a photograph of Raphael's painting; the original is in the National Gallery.*
• ***Word Family:*** **originality** *noun* **originally** *adverb*

originate (*say* o-**rij**-a-nate) *verb*
to begin: *The quarrel originated with him. / He originated the quarrel.*

ornament *noun*
1 a small, attractive object that you display in a house
ornament *verb*
2 to decorate something
• ***Word Family:*** **ornamental** *adjective* **ornamentation** *noun*

ornate (*say* or-**nate**) *adjective*
decorated with complicated patterns: *ornate gold plaster*
• ***Word Family:*** **ornately** *adverb*

ornithology (*say* or-na-**thol**-a-jee) *noun*
the study of birds and the way birds live
• ***Word Family:*** **ornithologist** *noun*

orphan (*say* **or**-fan) *noun*
1 someone, especially a child, whose parents are dead
orphan *verb*
2 to become an orphan: *She was orphaned when both her parents were killed in a plane crash.*
• ***Word Family:*** **orphanage** *noun* a place where orphans live

orthodontist (*say* or-tho-**don**-tist) *noun*
someone whose job is to straighten crooked teeth
• ***Word Family:*** **orthodontics** *noun*

orthodox (*say* **or**-tho-doks) *adjective*
1 accepted as normal: *orthodox schooling*
2 believing in the traditional beliefs or forms of your religion or political group: *orthodox Jews*
• ***Word Family:*** **orthodoxy** *noun*

orthopaedics or **orthopedics** (*say* or-tha-**pee**-diks) *noun*
medical treatment for your bones
• ***Word Family:*** **orthopaedic** *adjective*

oscillate (*say* **os**-a-late) *verb*
to move back and forth between two positions
• ***Word Family:*** **oscillation** *noun* **oscillator** *noun*

osmosis (*say* oz-**mo**-sis) *noun*
the movement of water from a weak solution across a barrier or membrane to a strong solution, so that both solutions end up being of equal strength. This process can happen through the walls of animal or plant cells

ostentatious *adjective*
intended to impress other people because it is so expensive: *an ostentatious watch*
• ***Word Family:*** **ostentation** *noun*

osteopath (*say* **os**-tee-o-path) *noun*
someone who treats illnesses by pressing or manipulating your spine and other bones

ostracize or **ostracise** (*say* **ost**-ra-size) *verb*
to keep someone out of a group: *He was ostracized by the whole class.*
• ***Word Family:*** **ostracism** *noun*

ostrich *noun*
an African bird, the largest in the world, with long legs and two toes needed for running as it cannot fly

other (*rhymes with* mother) *adjective*
1 different: *in the other street / any other way*
2 extra or more: *We need one other person.*

otherwise *adverb*
1 if not: *Athletes should be careful with their training otherwise they're likely to get injuries.*
2 apart from that: *The music was a bit loud but otherwise I enjoyed it.*

otter *noun*
a furry mammal with webbed feet and a long rudder-like tail that lives near water

ought *verb*
should: *You ought to be nicer to your brother.*

ounce *noun*
1 a unit of weight equal to about 29 grams or one sixteenth of a pound 2 a very small amount: *Don't you have an ounce of sense?*

A B C D E F G H I J K L M N O P Q R S T U V W X Y Z

our *pronoun*
belonging to us: *our books*
•***Word Family:*** **ours** *pronoun: Those books are ours.*

out *adverb*
1 not in a place: *to run out* 2 into the open, or into view: *to go out to play / The sun came out.* 3 no longer burning or shining: *The fire went out.* 4 not at home: *I called round but he was out.*
out *adjective*
5 outside the boundary lines of a court or field during a game: *The ball's out.* 6 not fashionable: *Those shorts are out this season.*

outback *noun*
the remote, inland parts of Australia where few people live

outbreak *noun*
a sudden start of something nasty: *an outbreak of rioting / an outbreak of flu*

outburst *noun*
a sudden expression of strong feeling: *an outburst of anger*

outcast *noun*
someone who is rejected by other people

outcome *noun*
a result: *the outcome of the peace talks*

outcry *noun*
a protest: *There was an outcry against atomic tests in the Pacific Ocean.*
•***Word Family:*** the plural is **outcries**

outer *adjective*
on or towards the outside of something: *the outside walls of the castle*

outfit *noun*
1 a set of clothes that are worn together 2 a group or organization
outfit *verb*
3 to provide the equipment needed to do a job
•***Word Family:*** other verb forms are **outfits, outfitted, outfitting**

outgoing *adjective*
1 about to leave a job: *the outgoing president*
2 friendly: *an outgoing nature*

outing *noun*
a short trip just for pleasure

outlaw *noun*
1 a criminal who is wanted by the police
outlaw *verb*
2 to make something illegal

outlet *noun*
1 a pipe through which liquid or gas goes out
2 a shop for selling goods made by a particular company 3 a way of expressing your feelings, ideas or energy

outline *noun*
1 a line showing the basic shape of something: *an outline of the house* 2 a brief summary giving only the main points: *an outline of the story*
outline *verb*
3 to make an outline or give an outline

outlook *noun*
1 your attitude to things in general: *an optimistic outlook* 2 the future: *Their outlook was grim.*

outnumber *verb*
to be more in number than another group: *Girls outnumber boys in the club by 2 to 1.*

outpatient *noun*
someone who has treatment in a hospital during the day but does not stay there at night

outpost *noun*
a group of people living far away from the main places where people live

output *noun*
1 the amount that a person or company produces: *We will only raise wages if output increases.* 2 the information a computer gives, such as printouts, files and text shown on screen

outrage *noun*
1 the anger you feel at something dreadful and shocking 2 something that makes people feel shocked and angry: *The bombing was the latest outrage from the terrorists.*
•***Word Family:*** **outrageous** *adjective*

outright *adverb*
1 completely or openly: *to agree outright / to lie outright* 2 at once: *The blow killed him outright.*
outright *adjective*
3 absolute, or clear: *an outright criminal / an outright winner*

outset *noun*
the beginning: *We've been friends from the outset.*

outside *noun*
1 the outer side or part: *The outside of the house needs painting.*
outside *adjective*
2 on the outer edge or side: *the outside lane of traffic* 3 not in your area or group: *the outside world* 4 unlikely: *an outside chance of defeat*
outside *adverb*
5 out of a building or house: *She looked outside. / Go and play outside.*
•***Word Family:*** **outsider** *noun* someone who doesn't belong to a group

outskirts *plural noun*
the outer districts of a town

outspoken *adjective*
frank and direct in what you say, even though it might offend people

outstanding *adjective*
1 extremely impressive: *an outstanding success / outstanding bravery* 2 not paid or settled: *outstanding debts*

outward *adjective*
1 away from a place: *the outward journey*
2 showing on the surface but not true inside: *Her outward happiness hid a lot of worry.*
• ***Word Family:*** **outwardly** *adverb*: *He was outwardly calm, but shaking inside.* **outwards** *adverb* towards the outside

outweigh *verb*
to be more important than something else: *The advantages outweigh the disadvantages.*

outwit *verb*
to get the better of someone by being more clever or cunning
• ***Word Family:*** other forms are **outwits, outwitted, outwitting**

oval (*say* **o**-vul) *adjective*
1 egg-shaped: *an oval mirror*
oval *noun*
2 an oval shape

ovary (*say* **o**-va-ree) *noun*
either of the two small parts of a woman's body, on each side of the uterus, that produce eggs
• ***Word Family:*** the plural is **ovaries** □ **ovarian** *adjective*

ovation (*say* o-**vay**-shon) *noun*
a long burst of enthusiastic applause: *The audience gave the singer a standing ovation.*

oven (*say* **uv**-en) *noun*
the enclosed part in a cooker, in which food is heated, baked or roasted

overall *adjective*
1 including everything
overall *adverb*
2 taking everything into account

overawe *verb*
to fill you with fear, respect or wonder: *The prospect of meeting a film star overawed her.*

overbearing *adjective*
dominating or bossy: *an overbearing aunt*
• ***Word Family:*** **overbearingly** *adverb*

overboard *adverb*
1 over the side of a boat and into the water
2 **go overboard** to be too enthusiastic

overcast *adjective*
dark and cloudy: *an overcast day*

overcome *verb*
1 to control a feeling or sort out a problem: *to overcome your fears* 2 to make you helpless: *to be overcome with laughter*
• ***Word Family:*** other forms are **overcomes, overcame, overcoming**

overdo *verb*
to do or have more than you should: *I think I overdid the chocolate biscuits.*
• ***Word Family:*** other forms are **overdoes, overdid, overdone, overdoing** □ **overdone** *adjective* cooked for too long: *overdone steak*

overdose *noun*
a larger dose of a drug than is safe to use, often causing death or illness: *a heroin overdose*

overdue *adjective*
late: *overdue rent*

overhaul *verb*
to examine something carefully and make sure it works properly: *The plumber is going to overhaul the washing machine.*

overhead *adjective*
1 above your head: *overhead wires*
overhead *adverb*
2 over your head or in the air: *The jet flew high overhead.*
overhead *noun*
3 **overheads** the general costs of running a business, such as rent and electricity

overhear *verb*
to hear someone else's conversation
• ***Word Family:*** other forms are **overhears, overheard, overhearing**

overjoyed *adjective*
very happy indeed

overlap *verb*
1 to lie over part of something else: *One rug overlaps the other.* 2 to be about the same subject or at the same time
• ***Word Family:*** other forms are **overlaps, overlapped, overlapping**

overlook *verb*
1 to miss something or ignore it: *to overlook an error / to overlook bad manners* 2 to have a view of a place: *Our room overlooks the garden.*

overpass *noun*
a bridge to take cars, pedestrians or cyclists over a busy road
• ***Word Family:*** the plural is **overpasses**

overpower *verb*
to defeat someone because you are stronger than they are
• ***Word Family:*** **overpowering** *adjective* extremely strong: *an overpowering scent*

overrule *verb*
to officially say that a decision or a person's ideas are wrong: *The judge overruled the barrister's objections.*

overrun *verb*
1 to take over a place in great numbers: *Enemy soldiers overran the country.* 2 to spread everywhere: *Weeds started to overrun the garden.*
• ***Word Family:*** other forms are **overruns, overran, overrun, overrunning**

overseas *adverb*
abroad: *He spent a year travelling overseas.*

oversee *verb*
to supervise other people's work
• ***Word Family:*** other forms are **oversees, oversaw, overseen, overseeing** □ **overseer** *noun* someone who oversees other people's work

overshadow *verb*
1 to cast a shadow over a place 2 to make a person or thing seem much less important or interesting by comparison: *She overshadowed him with her bubbly personality.*

oversight *noun*
an accidental failure to notice something or do something: *Not locking the door was a bad oversight.*

overt (*say* o-**vert**) *adjective*
open and not hidden: *an overt attack*
• ***Word Family:*** **overtly** *adverb*

overtake *verb*
1 to catch up with another vehicle and pass it
2 to come upon you without warning: *The storm overtook us as we climbed the mountain.*
• ***Word Family:*** other forms are **overtakes, overtook, overtaken, overtaking**

overthrow *verb*
to use force to remove a government or leader
• ***Word Family:*** other forms are **overthrows, overthrew, overthrown, overthrowing**

overtime *noun*
work done outside normal working hours

overture (*say* o-ver-**tyoor**) *noun*
1 the music played at the beginning of an opera, ballet or musical show 2 a first offer of friendship between people or nations

overturn *verb*
1 to turn something over or upside down: *He overturned the jug and milk went everywhere.* 2 to defeat or conquer: *to overturn a ruling*

overwhelm *verb*
1 to overcome you completely: *Grief overwhelmed them.* 2 to completely defeat a group of people: *They overwhelmed the sentries and then attacked the town.*
• ***Word Family:*** **overwhelming** *adjective*

ovulate (*say* **ov**-yoo-late) *verb*
to release eggs from the ovary: *Women ovulate once a month.*
• ***Word Family:*** **ovulation** *noun*

ovum (*say* **o**-vum) *noun*
one of the female cells that can join with a male sperm to produce young
• ***Word Family:*** the plural is **ova**
• ***Word Origins:*** from a Latin word meaning "egg"

owe (*rhymes with* go) *verb*
1 to have to pay money to someone that they are waiting for 2 to feel grateful for the kindness and help someone has given you: *I owe a lot to my music teacher.*
• ***Word Family:*** **owing to** *adjective* on account of: *The match was postponed owing to rain.*

owl *noun*
a bird with large eyes, a short hooked beak and a hooting cry, that hunts for small animals at night
• ***Word Family:*** **owlet** *noun* a young owl

own (*rhymes with* bone) *verb*
1 to have something which belongs to you
2 **own up** to confess: *He owned up to breaking the window.*
own *adjective*
3 belonging to yourself: *That's my own bike.*
own *noun*
4 **get your own back** to get revenge
• ***Word Family:*** **owner** *noun* **ownership** *noun*

ox *noun*
a bull that has been castrated, especially a large one used to pull a cart or carry loads
• ***Word Family:*** the plural is **oxen**

oxide *noun*
a compound of oxygen and another chemical element

oxidize or **oxidise** *verb*
to change chemically because of the effect of oxygen

oxygen (*say* **ok**-sa-jen) *noun*
a colourless gas with no smell that forms about a third of the air we breathe

oyster *noun*
a shellfish which is often eaten raw and which sometimes has a pearl inside

ozone (*say* **o**-zone) *noun*
a bluish, poisonous kind of oxygen formed in the atmosphere during electrical storms when you can detect its strong smell
• ***Word Origins:*** from a Greek word meaning "smell"

ozone layer *noun*
a layer of ozone in the outer atmosphere, that acts as a shield to block most of the sun's harmful rays

Pp

pace *noun*
1 the rate of movement: *I was jogging at a slow pace. / to live life at a hectic pace* 2 a single step: *Take one pace forward.*
pace *verb*
3 to walk backwards and forwards: *He paced up and down the station platform.* 4 to measure an area by counting up the steps you take to walk it: *She paced out the distance from the house to the back fence.*

pacemaker *noun*
1 someone who sets a fast pace in a race
2 a small medical machine put inside someone's body next to the heart to help it beat at the right speed

pacific (*say* pa-**sif**-ik) *adjective*
peace-loving

pacifism *noun*
an opposition to all war or violence
•***Word Family:*** **pacifist** *noun*

pacify (*say* **pas**-i-fie) *verb*
to calm and satisfy someone who is angry and upset: *It is difficult to pacify a crying baby.*
•***Word Family:*** other verb forms are **pacifies, pacified, pacifying**

pack *noun*
1 a bundle of things tied up for carrying
2 a bag, often with a stiff frame, for carrying belongings or other goods on your back
3 a group of animals hunting together: *a pack of dogs* 4 a group of people or things: *a pack of thieves / a pack of lies* 5 a complete set of playing cards
pack *verb*
6 to put things into a box, parcel or suitcase: *to pack food for a picnic* 7 to crowd together in a place: *People packed the store for the sale.*

package *noun*
1 a small parcel 2 a group of ideas or things which are offered together and which must be accepted together

packet *noun*
a small box or bag of something: *a packet of chewing gum*

pact *noun*
an agreement

pad (1) *noun*
1 a thick, flat piece of soft material: *The hockey players wore pads to protect their shins. / shoulder pads* 2 a number of sheets of paper held together at one edge: *a note pad* 3 the soft, underneath part of the foot of such animals as dogs and cats
pad *verb*
4 to fill something with soft material: *He padded the seat of the chair with foam rubber.*
•***Word Family:*** other verb forms are **pads, padded, padding** □ **padding** *noun* soft material put in something or on something

pad (2) *verb*
to walk with quick, light footsteps: *She was padding around the house in bare feet.*
•***Word Family:*** other forms are **pads, padded, padding**

paddle (1) *noun*
1 a short pole with a flat blade at one end, used to move a boat or canoe through water
paddle *verb*
2 to move a boat or canoe with a paddle.

paddle (2) *verb*
to walk or play in shallow water

paddock *noun*
a large enclosed area of land, usually used for grazing sheep or cattle

paddy field *noun*
a flooded field for growing rice

padlock *noun*
1 a lock with a U-shaped metal bar that you snap into a metal block and release with a key
padlock *verb*
2 to lock something with a padlock: *Padlock the back gate. / Padlock the bike to the fence.*

paediatrics (*say* pee-di-**at**-riks) *noun*
the study and treatment of diseases in young children: *Paediatrics is a rewarding profession.*
•***Word Family:*** **paediatrician** *noun* a doctor who specializes in the diseases of children

pagan (*say* **pay**-gan) *noun*
someone who does not follow one of the main religions of the world
•***Word Family:*** **paganism** *noun*

page *noun*
1 a sheet of paper making up a book, newspaper or letter 2 one side of one of these sheets

pageant (*say* **paj**-unt) *noun*
a grand public show, especially one with a procession of people in costume
•***Word Family:*** **pageantry** *noun*

pager (*say* **pay**-ja) *noun*
a small, electronic machine that makes a high-

A B C D E F G H I J K L M N O P Q R S T U V W X Y Z

pitched sound when someone is trying to contact the person carrying it

pagoda (*say* pa-**go**-da) *noun*
a decorated Buddhist or Hindu temple shaped like a pyramid or tower

pail *noun*
a bucket

pain *noun*
1 the sensation you get when you are hurt or injured 2 suffering or unhappiness 3 an annoying task or person: *Homework is a pain.* 4 **take pains** to do something with great care
•***Word Family:*** **painful** *adjective* **painfully** *adverb* **painless** *adjective* **painlessly** *adverb*

painstaking *adjective*
taking very great care, especially with all the details of something

paint *noun*
1 a coloured liquid used to give colour to a surface
paint *verb*
2 to decorate something with paint: *Mum's upstairs painting the bathroom.* 3 to make a picture with paint: *He paints portraits.*
•***Word Family:*** **painting** *noun* a picture made with paint

painter *noun*
1 an artist who paints pictures 2 someone whose work is decorating walls and houses with paint

pair *noun*
1 a set of two people or things that are the same or go together: *a pair of shoes / a matching pair* 2 two parts joined together to make a single thing: *a pair of trousers*

pakeha (*say* **pah**-kee-a) *noun*
the Maori word for a white person

Pakistani *adjective*
to do with or coming from Pakistan

pal *noun*
a friend

palace (*say* **pal**-is) *noun*
a large, grand building used as the official home of a king, queen, bishop or other important person
•***Word Family:*** **palatial** *adjective* like a palace

palaeontology (*say* pa-li-on-**tol**-a-jee) *noun*
the study of fossils
•***Word Family:*** **palaeontologist** *noun*

palate (*say* **pal**-it) *noun*
1 the top part of the inside of your mouth 2 your sense of taste: *The fine wine pleased his palate.*
•***Word Family:*** **palatable** (*say* **pal**-it-a-bul) *adjective* pleasant to taste

pale (1) *adjective*
1 whitish or without much colour: *pale skin*
pale *verb*
2 to become pale
•***Word Family:*** **palely** *adverb* **paleness** *noun*

pale (2) *noun*
a post, often pointed at the top, used for fences

palette (*say* **pal**-et) *noun*
a small, thin board with a hole for the thumb, on which a painter mixes colours

palindrome *noun*
a word or words that are spelt the same backwards as they are forwards: *"Madam" and "was it a cat I saw" are palindromes.*
•***Word Origins:*** from a Greek word meaning "running back again"

paling (*say* **pay**-ling) *noun*
a strip of metal or wood used as part of a fence

pall (1) (*say* pawl) *noun*
1 a cloth for spreading over a coffin 2 a dark or gloomy covering: *A pall of smoke hung over the industrial town.*
•***Word Origins:*** from a Latin word meaning "covering or cloak"

pall (2) (*say* pawl) *verb*
to become boring: *After listening to him for two hours, his monotonous voice began to pall on me.*

pallbearer *noun*
someone who helps to carry the coffin at a funeral

pallet *noun*
1 a tool with a flat blade and a handle used in pottery-making 2 a movable platform on which goods are stacked when being stored, especially one designed to be lifted and moved by a fork-lift truck 3 *another spelling of* **palette**

palm (1) (*say* pahm) *noun*
1 the inner surface of your hand from your wrist to the beginning of your fingers
palm *verb*
2 to hide something in your hand: *The magician palmed the coin.*

palm (2) (*say* pahm) *noun*
a tropical plant with a tall trunk without branches and with long pointed leaves at the top

palmistry (*say* **pah**-mis-tree) *noun*
the art of telling what someone is like and what will happen in their future by looking at the pattern of lines on the palm of their hand
•***Word Family:*** **palmist** *noun*

palpitate *verb*
1 to tremble or shake: *His body palpitated with*

terror. 2 to beat very quickly: *Her heart was palpitating after running up the steep hill.*
•*Word Family:* **palpitation** *noun* a medical condition in which the heart beats quickly and irregularly

palsy (*say* **pawl**-zee) *noun*
another word for **paralysis**

paltry (*say* **pawl**-tree) *adjective*
very small and not worth much: *a paltry price*

pamper *verb*
to go to a lot of trouble to make someone or something feel comfortable and happy: *They really pamper their guests at that hotel. / to pamper yourself with a long, hot bath*

pamphlet (*say* **pam**-flit) *noun*
a booklet in paper covers: *They have pamphlets on how to look after different animals.*

pan *noun*
1 a round container used to cook food in
pan *verb*
2 to separate pieces of gold from sand and gravel by swirling the lot in a type of sieve with water 3 to criticize a film, book, play and so on severely: *All the critics panned his new film.*
•*Word Family:* other forms of the verb are **pans, panned, panning**

panacea (*say* pan-a-**see**-a) *noun*
something that is supposed to fix all troubles and cure all illnesses

pancake *noun*
a thin, flat cake made by frying a batter of eggs, milk and flour

pancreas (*say* **pan**-kree-us) *noun*
a part of the body behind the stomach that makes the hormone insulin and also helps with digestion

panda *noun*
a large, black and white bear-like animal found mainly in China

pandemonium (*say* pan-da-**moh**-nee-um) *noun*
wild and noisy confusion: *There was pandemonium as fans raced onto the field at the end of the match.*
•*Word Origins:* from Greek words meaning "all the demons"

pander *verb*
to give someone everything they want: *They pandered to their child's every wish.*

pane *noun*
a single sheet of glass: *a window pane*

panel *noun*
1 a separate part of a door, ceiling or wall, usually raised above or sunk below the rest of the surface 2 a separate piece of material, sometimes of a different colour, set into a dress 3 a thin, flat piece of wood 4 a group of people gathered together to take part in a discussion or to judge something: *a panel of experts* 5 a board or surface that contains the switches and instruments which control a machine: *a control panel*
•*Word Family:* **panellist** *noun* a member of a panel

pang *noun*
a sudden sharp feeling: *a pang of regret / hunger pangs*

panic *noun*
1 sudden great fear: *There was panic when the theatre caught fire.*
panic *verb*
2 to be suddenly very frightened: *I panicked when I thought I was drowning.*
•*Word Family:* other verb forms are **panics, panicked, panicking** □ **panicky** or **panic-stricken** *adjectives* full of panic
•*Word Origins:* from a Greek word meaning "caused by *Pan*" (a god who was believed to be the cause of sudden fear)

pannier *noun*
one of two bags or boxes hung over the sides of a bicycle's or motorcycle's back wheels

panorama (*say* pan-a-**rah**-ma) *noun*
1 a view over a wide area: *the panorama from the top of the tower* 2 a continuously changing scene: *She watched the panorama of seething city life.*
•*Word Family:* **panoramic** *adjective*

pansy (*say* **pan**-zee) *noun*
a small plant with brightly coloured flowers
•*Word Family:* the plural is **pansies**

pant *verb*
to breathe quickly and loudly with the mouth open

panther *noun*
a leopard, especially the black leopard

pantomime *noun*
a play with songs, usually based on a fairy story or nursery rhyme, and put on at Christmas

pantry *noun*
a room or large cupboard, usually near the kitchen, where food is stored
•*Word Family:* the plural is **pantries**
•*Word Origins:* from an old French word meaning "a servant in charge of bread"

pants *plural noun*
1 a piece of underwear that covers your hips and bottom 2 another name for **trousers**

pantyhose *noun*
stockings and underpants in one piece
•***Word Family:*** the plural is **pantyhose**

papacy (*say* **pay**-pa-see) *noun*
1 the position of Pope in the Roman Catholic Church 2 the length of time a particular Pope rules

paper *noun*
1 a thin sheet of material, usually made from wood, and used to write or print things on or wrap things in 2 a newspaper 3 a written examination 4 **papers** official documents which say who you are and where you were born
paper *verb*
5 to put wallpaper on the walls: *She's papering the dining room.*
•***Word Family:*** **papery** *adjective* thin and delicate
•***Word Origins:*** from the word "papyrus"

paperback *noun*
a book with a paper cover

pappadum *noun*
another spelling for **poppadom**

paprika (*say* pa-**pree**-ka) *noun*
a mild-tasting red spice made from ground sweet pepper

papyrus (*say* pa-**pie**-rus) *noun*
1 a tall water plant that grows in Egypt 2 a material made from this plant which was used for writing on in ancient times
•***Word Family:*** the plural is **papyri** (*say* pa-**pie**-ree)

par *noun*
1 the average standard: *The quality of your work is well above par.* 2 **on a par** the same standard or level: *Your work is on a par with mine.*
•***Word Origins:*** a Latin word meaning "equal"

parable (*say* **pa**-ru-bul) *noun*
a short story about everyday things, which teaches a moral lesson

parabola (*say* pa-**rab**-u-la) *noun*
the kind of curve an object makes when it is thrown into the air and comes down in a different place

parachute (*say* **pa**-ra-shoot) *noun*
1 a large dome of fabric which, when it fills with air, lets a person or cargo drop safely to the ground from an aircraft
parachute *verb*
2 to drop from a plane using a parachute
•***Word Family:*** **parachutist** *noun*

parade (*say* pu-**rade**) *noun*
1 a procession to celebrate a special day or event 2 a ceremony in which soldiers stand in line or march and are inspected
parade *verb*
3 to march in a procession

paradise (*say* **pa**-ru-dice) *noun*
1 heaven 2 a wonderful or perfect place
•***Word Origins:*** from an ancient Persian word meaning "an enclosed garden"

paradox (*say* **pa**-ru-doks) *noun*
a statement which seems to contradict itself, such as "the more things change, the more they stay the same"
•***Word Family:*** **paradoxical** *adjective* **paradoxically** *adverb*

paragon (*say* **pa**-ra-gon) *noun*
a perfect example of a good quality: *a paragon of virtue*

paragraph (*say* **pa**-ru-graf) *noun*
a group of sentences placed together in a piece of writing and beginning on a new line

parallel (*say* **par**-ru-lel) *adjective*
1 being the same distance apart along all their length: *parallel lines / The road runs parallel to the river.*
parallel *noun*
2 a line that is parallel with another line
3 something that is very similar to another thing: *There are many parallels between his career and that of his mother.*
•***Word Origins:*** from a Greek word meaning "side by side"

parallelogram (*say* pa-ru-**lel**-u-gram) *noun*
a four-sided shape whose opposite sides are equal, such as a rhombus or square

paralyse or **paralyze** (*say* **pa**-ru-lize) *verb*
to make someone unable to move: *The accident paralysed his legs. / She was paralysed with terror when she saw the ghost.*
•***Word Family:*** **paralysis** *noun* an inability to move

paramedical *adjective*
helping with medical work: *first aid officers and other paramedical services*
•***Word Family:*** **paramedic** *noun*

paramount (*say* **pa**-ru-mount) *adjective*
more important than anyone or anything else: *Her wishes are paramount. / Our paramount concern is the environment.*

paranoid (*say* pa-ru-**noyd**) *adjective*
being more suspicious, fearful and distrustful of other people than is normal

parapet *noun*
a low wall around the edge of a balcony or bridge or the top of a building

paraphernalia (*say* pa-ru-fu-**nay**-lee-a) *plural noun*
all the belongings or equipment needed for something

paraphrase (*say* **par**-a-fraze) *verb*
to say what someone else has said only in different words

paraplegic (*say* par-ru-**plee**-jik) *adjective*
1 unable to feel anything or to move the muscles in the lower part of your body
paraplegic *noun*
2 someone who does not have the use of the lower part of their body
•***Word Family:*** **paraplegia** *noun*

parasite (*say* **pa**-ru-site) *noun*
1 a plant or animal that gets its food by living in or on a plant or animal of a different kind: *Fleas and ticks are parasites of dogs.* 2 someone who takes food and shelter from others and gives nothing in return
•***Word Family:*** **parasitic** *adjective* **parasitically** *adverb* **parasitism** *noun*
•***Word Origins:*** from a Greek word meaning "dinner guest"

parasol *noun*
a small, light umbrella to protect you from the sun

parcel (*say* **par**-sel) *noun*
1 something wrapped up in paper, usually so that it can be sent through the post
parcel *verb*
2 **parcel up** to wrap something up as a parcel
•***Word Family:*** other forms of the verb are **parcels, parcelled, parcelling**

parch *verb*
to make very dry: *The long drought parched the fields.*

parched *adjective*
1 very dry: *The fields were parched after the long drought.* 2 very thirsty

parchment *noun*
1 an animal skin made into a material for writing on in ancient times 2 a kind of thick, good quality, yellowish paper

pardon *noun*
1 you say "Pardon" or "I beg your pardon" as a polite apology 2 forgiveness for a crime
pardon *verb*
3 to excuse: *Pardon my interruption.* 4 to officially forgive someone for a crime
•***Word Family:*** **pardonable** *adjective* able to be pardoned

pare *verb*
1 to cut off the outer layer of something: *Pare the rind from the orange.* 2 to reduce: *You must pare down your expenses.*

parent (*say* **pair**-ent) *noun*
a mother or father
•***Word Family:*** **parental** *adjective* **parenthood** *noun*

parenthesis (*say* pu-**ren**-thu-sis) *noun*
1 words separated from the rest of a sentence by commas, dashes or brackets, for example "the large one" in *Can you bring the hammer—the large one—from the garage?* 2 brackets ( ) used in writing
•***Word Family:*** the plural is **parentheses** (*say* pu-**ren**-thu-seez)

parish *noun*
1 a district with its own church and clergyman
2 a small area, usually a village, with its own council
•***Word Family:*** **parishioner** *noun*

park *noun*
1 an area of public land, usually with trees and flowers, where people can go to relax and enjoy themselves: *jogging in the park*
park *verb*
2 to stop a car or other vehicle and leave it in a particular place: *I'll park in the shade.*

parka *noun*
a waterproof jacket with a hood

parley (*say* **par**-lee) *noun*
an informal discussion between people or groups who are fighting but who want to stop
•***Word Family:*** the plural is **parleys**

parliament (*say* **par**-la-munt) *noun*
a group of people elected to make the laws for a country
•***Word Family:*** **parliamentarian** *noun* **parliamentary** *adjective*

parlour or parlor (*say* **par**-la) *noun*
1 a sitting room where visitors are entertained
2 a business with a comfortably furnished area for customers: *a beauty parlour*

parmesan *noun*
a hard Italian cheese with a strong smell, that is often grated and sprinkled on food

parochial (*say* pu-**roh**-kee-ul) *adjective*
1 to do with a parish 2 only interested in local issues, not things outside the local area

parody (*say* **pa**-ra-dee) *noun*
a funny imitation of a serious piece of writing or film-making and so on
•***Word Family:*** the plural is **parodies**

parole (*say* pa-**role**) *noun*
the early release of a prisoner who promises to behave well: *He was on parole.*

paroxysm (*say* **pa**-rok-sizm) *noun*
a sudden, uncontrolled fit or spasm: *a paroxysm of coughing*

parrot *noun*
1 a brightly coloured bird with a hooked bill that can be taught to imitate human speech
parrot *verb*
2 to repeat words without really understanding them: *Having no original ideas, he parrots what others say.*

parry *verb*
to avoid answering a question: *She parried the reporter's questions about her private life.*
•*Word Family:* other forms are **parries, parried, parrying**

parse (*say* parz) *verb*
to give each word in a phrase or sentence its part of speech

parsley (*say* **par**-slee) *noun*
a herb with crinkled green leaves, used in cooking

parsnip *noun*
a white, carrot-shaped root vegetable

parson *noun*
a vicar in the Church of England
•*Word Family:* **parsonage** (*say* **par**-sa-nij) *noun* a house built for a parson to live in

part *noun*
1 a piece of a whole: *Part of this book is missing.* 2 a replacement piece: *I need some new parts for my sewing machine.* 3 a role in a play
part *verb*
4 to separate two things or to separate: *At last the clouds parted. / The twins could not be parted.*

partial (*say* **par**-shul) *adjective*
1 not total or complete: *The meeting was only a partial success.* 2 biased or prejudiced in favour of one side: *It's useless having the dispute decided by a partial judge.* 3 fond of something: *He's very partial to honey.*
•*Word Family:* **partially** *adverb* **partiality** *noun*

participate (*say* par-**tiss**-u-pate) *verb*
to take part: *We participated in the discussions.*
•*Word Family:* **participant** *noun* **participation** *noun*

participle (*say* par-**tiss**-ip-ul) *noun*
1 a word formed from a verb and used in compound verbs such as "laughing" in *The girl had been laughing* and "rescued" in *The man has been rescued.* 2 a word formed from a verb and used as an adjective, such as "laughing" in *the laughing girl* and "rescued" in *the rescued man*

particle *noun*
a very small piece or amount of something

particular (*say* par-**tik**-yoo-la) *adjective*
1 to do with one person, group or thing rather than all: *I haven't heard that particular song.*
2 fussy and wanting everything exactly right: *She's very particular about her clothes.*
particular *noun*
3 a detail: *You are correct in every particular.*
4 **in particular** especially
•*Word Family:* **particularly** *adverb* especially

parting *noun*
1 leaving a person 2 the line in your hair where the hair is brushed different ways on each side

partition *noun*
1 the division of a country into separate parts or nations: *the partition of India* 2 a wall or screen that separates one part of a room from the rest
partition *verb*
3 to divide a room or country into separate parts

partly *adjective*
to some extent but not completely: *The window was partly open. / I was partly sorry and partly relieved that I couldn't go.*

partner *noun*
1 someone who does something with another person: *a tennis partner / a business partner*
2 a person's husband, wife or lover
•*Word Family:* **partnership** *noun*

partridge *noun*
a fat, brown bird with a short tail that is hunted and eaten

part-time *adjective*
taking up less than the normal hours: *a part-time job*
•*Word Family:* **part-timer** *noun*

party *noun*
1 a social gathering, usually to celebrate something: *a birthday party* 2 an organization of people with the same political beliefs
•*Word Family:* the plural is **parties**

pass *verb*
1 to go by or go past: *I slowed to let the car behind pass me.* 2 to move from one place to another
3 to hand someone something: *Pass me the butter.* 4 to get through a test: *to pass an exam*
5 to officially make a new law 6 **pass away** to die 7 **pass out** to faint
pass *noun*
8 the handing, throwing or kicking of a ball from one player to another in a sport such as football 9 a narrow road through a low part of a mountain range 10 a piece of paper that officially says you are allowed to do something or go somewhere 11 success in passing an examination

• ***Word Family:*** other verb forms are **passes, passed** or **past, passing** □ **passable** *adjective* adequate or acceptable

passage *noun*
1 a narrow space between walls or a corridor 2 part of a story, poem or piece of music: *I'd like to read you this passage again.*

passbook *noun*
a book which shows what's been paid in and what's been paid out of an account, for example a building society account

passenger (*say* **pas**-in-ja) *noun*
someone who travels in a car, boat, train or plane and so on who is not the driver

passer-by *noun*
someone who is walking past

passion (*say* **pash**-on) *noun*
1 a very strong feeling, such as love, hate, anger, hope or grief 2 a strong interest or enthusiasm for someone or something: *a passion for poetry*
• ***Word Family:*** **passionate** *adjective*

passionfruit *noun*
a small, round, purple fruit with sweet-tasting seeds and pulp
• ***Word Family:*** the plural is **passionfruit**

passive (*say* **pas**-iv) *adjective*
1 accepting what happens to you without taking any action yourself 2 to do with the form of the verb in which the action is done to the subject, rather than the subject doing the action, for example "was eaten" is the passive form of "eat"
• ***Word Family:*** **passively** *adverb*

passive smoking *noun*
the breathing in of smoke from someone else's cigarette

Passover (*say* **pahs**-over) *noun*
a religious festival in the Jewish religion

passport *noun*
an official document that shows who a person is and what country they come from which they take with them when they travel in foreign countries

password *noun*
a secret word that allows someone who knows it to go somewhere or use a computer

past *adjective*
1 having occurred in a time before the present: *the past month*
past *noun*
2 a time before the present: *History is a study of the past.*
past *preposition*
3 after a particular time: *It is past 6 o'clock.*
4 further than: *The shop is past the corner.*

pasta *noun*
a food made from flour, water and eggs in different shapes, for example macaroni and spaghetti

paste *noun*
1 a soft, sticky mixture used for sticking paper to things 2 a soft smooth mixture: *toothpaste / fish paste*
paste *verb*
3 to stick paper to something using paste or glue

pastel (*say* **pas**-tul) *noun*
1 a pale colour 2 a crayon or a picture drawn with crayons

pasteurize or pasteurise (*say* **pahs**-chu-rize) *verb*
to destroy bacteria in a liquid such as milk by heating at a high temperature
• ***Word Family:*** **pasteurization** *noun*
• ***Word Origins:*** named after Louis *Pasteur*, a French chemist who lived from 1822 to 1895

pastime *noun*
a hobby or similar activity that helps time pass pleasantly

pastor *noun*
a vicar or member of the clergy in some Christian churches

pastoral *adjective*
to do with the countryside or farming
• ***Word Family:*** **pastoralist** *noun*

pastry (*say* **pay**-stree) *noun*
1 a mixture of flour, water and fat used as the base or crust of a pie 2 a small, sweet cake made with pastry
• ***Word Family:*** the plural is **pastries**

past tense *noun*
the form of the verb that shows the action has already taken place, as in I *went*, she *ran*

pasture (*say* **pahs**-cher) *noun*
grass land suitable for grazing cattle or sheep

pasty (*say* **pas**-tee) *noun*
a small pie made of pastry folded around meat and vegetables
• ***Word Family:*** the plural is **pasties**

pat *verb*
1 to touch something lightly with your hand: *She patted the dog.*
pat *noun*
2 a light touch with the hand
• ***Word Family:*** other forms of the verb are **pats, patted, patting**

patch *noun*
1 a piece of cloth used to cover a hole 2 a piece of cloth used to cover an injured eye 3 a small area: *a patch of land*

patch *verb*
4 to mend something with a patch
•***Word Family:*** the plural is **patches** □ **patchy** *adjective* **(patchier, patchiest)**

patchwork *noun*
a type of needlework in which small pieces of different coloured fabric are sewn together

pâté (*say* **pat**-ay) *noun*
a paste made from finely chopped meat, fish or vegetables: *liver pâté / mushroom pâté*
•***Word Origins:*** this word comes from French

paternal *adjective*
to do with or like a father: *He treats us in a paternal way.*
•***Word Family:*** **paternalism** *noun* **paternally** *adverb*

path (*say* pahth) *noun*
a track that you can walk along

pathetic (*say* pa-**thet**-ik) *adjective*
1 making you feel pity or sympathy: *The starving kitten was a pathetic sight.* 2 useless or weak: *a pathetic effort / a pathetic joke*
•***Word Family:*** **pathetically** *adverb*

pathology (*say* pu-**thol**-u-jee) *noun*
the study of diseases and their effects
•***Word Family:*** **pathologist** *noun* a doctor who studies the effects of diseases

patient (*say* **pay**-shunt) *adjective*
1 calm and tolerant when things are irritating or take too long: *I'm only a beginner so you'll have to be patient with me.*
patient *noun*
2 someone who is being treated by a doctor or dentist or is in a hospital
•***Word Family:*** **patience** *noun* the ability to wait calmly **patiently** *adverb*

patio *noun*
a paved area near a house where you can sit and eat

patriarch (*say* **pay**-tree-ark *or* **pat**-ree-ark) *noun*
a man who is the head of a family or ruler of a group
•***Word Family:*** **patriarchy** *noun* a system in which a man has the most power in a family or group **patriarchal** *adjective*

patriot (*say* **pat**-ree-ot *or* **pay**-ree-ot) *noun*
someone who loves their country deeply
•***Word Family:*** **patriotic** *adjective* **patriotically** *adverb* **patriotism** *noun*
•***Word Origins:*** from a Greek word meaning "fatherland"

patrol (*say* pu-**trole**) *verb*
to go round an area to guard it: *Guards with dogs patrol the grounds.*
•***Word Family:*** other forms are **patrols, patrolled, patrolling**

patron (*say* **pay**-trun) *noun*
1 someone who gives help or support to a person or group: *a patron of the arts* 2 a regular customer
•***Word Family:*** **patronage** *noun*

patronize or **patronise** (*say* **pat**-ru-nize) *verb*
1 to treat someone as if they were inferior or less intelligent 2 to be a customer of a hotel or shop
•***Word Family:*** **patronizingly** *adverb*

patter *noun*
1 a series of quick, light, tapping sounds: *the patter of rain*
•***Word Family:*** **patter** *verb*

pattern *noun*
1 a design used as a decoration: *The carpet had a flower pattern.* 2 a shape you use as a guide for making something: *Cut the fabric using the paper pattern.*

paunch (*say* pawnch) *noun*
a large, fat stomach
•***Word Family:*** **paunchiness** *noun* **paunchy** *adjective*

pauper (*say* **paw**-pa) *noun*
a very poor person

pause (*say* pawz) *noun*
1 a short stop before continuing with something
pause *verb*
2 to stop briefly and then carry on: *I paused before knocking.*

pave *verb*
to make a hard surface using stones, bricks, concrete or bitumen
•***Word Family:*** **paving** *noun* the material used to pave **paving** *adjective: a paving stone*
•***Word Origins:*** from a Latin word meaning "to beat down"

pavement *noun*
a path for pedestrians at the side of a road

pavilion (*say* pu-**vil**-yon) *noun*
1 a building at the edge of a sports ground where the players can change, rest and so on 2 a large temporary building or tent used for entertainment or exhibitions
•***Word Origins:*** from a Latin word meaning "tent"

pavlova (*say* pav-**loh**-va) *noun*
a dessert made of meringue filled with fruit and whipped cream

paw *noun*
1 the foot of an animal with claws such as a cat or dog

paw *verb*
2 to scrape something with a paw or hoof: *The horse pawed the ground.*

pawn (1) *verb*
to leave an object you own with a pawnbroker in return for a loan. The pawnbroker gives the object back when the loan is repaid

pawn (2) *noun*
the smallest and least valuable chess piece
• ***Word Origins:*** from a Medieval Latin word meaning "foot soldier"

pawnbroker *noun*
someone who lends money in return for an object you own. You get the object back when you have repaid the money
• ***Word Family:*** **pawnshop** *noun*

pawpaw *noun*
a large, yellow, tropical fruit

pay *verb*
1 to give someone money to buy something or because they work for you 2 to give an advantage: *It pays to be honest.* 3 to suffer: *You'll pay for that remark.*
pay *noun*
4 the money you earn when you work
• ***Word Family:*** other forms of the verb are **pays, paid, paying** □ **payment** *noun*

payroll *noun*
1 a list of people in a company or business who are paid wages 2 the total amount of money paid out as wages

PC *noun*
a personal computer

PE *noun*
sport and athletics that you learn at school

pea *noun*
a small, round, green vegetable that grows in pods

peace *noun*
1 a time when there is no war 2 calmness or stillness
• ***Word Family:*** **peaceful** *adjective*

peach *noun*
a yellowish-red round, juicy fruit with a large stone and furry skin
• ***Word Family:*** the plural is **peaches**
• ***Word Origins:*** from a Greek word meaning "Persian apple"

peacock *noun*
a large bird with green and blue feathers and a large and brightly coloured tail that the male spreads out like a fan
• ***Word Family:*** the plural is **peacock** or **peacocks**

peak *noun*
1 the pointed top of a mountain 2 the highest or most successful point of something: *She reached her peak at the Olympics.*
peak *adjective*
3 highest in level: *peak fitness* 4 busiest: *peak season / peak hour*

peal *noun*
a long, loud sound: *a peal of bells / a peal of thunder*

peanut *noun*
a small nut that grows in a pod underground and is often eaten as a snack

pear *noun*
a juicy fruit with green skin that is wider at the bottom and gets narrower towards the stalk

pearl (*say* perl) *noun*
a small, hard, shiny white ball that grows in an oyster shell and is used in jewellery: *a string of pearls*
• ***Word Family:*** **pearly** *adjective*

peasant (*say* **pez**-unt) *noun*
someone who farms a small piece of land

peat *noun*
a kind of soil found near swamps, made of rotted plants and used as a fuel or as a garden fertilizer

pebble *noun*
a small, rounded stone
• ***Word Family:*** **pebbly** *adjective*

peck *verb*
1 to quickly bite at something with the beak: *The bird was pecking a hole in the tree.* 2 to only eat a little food, quite slowly: *She pecked at her food.*
peck *noun*
3 a hasty kiss: *a peck on the cheek*

peckish *adjective*
a little bit hungry

peculiar (*say* pu-**kew**-li-a) *adjective*
strange or unusual
• ***Word Family:*** **peculiarity** *noun* **peculiarly** *adverb*

pedal *noun*
1 a lever you work with your foot: *a bicycle pedal / the brake pedal in a car*
pedal *verb*
2 to ride a bicycle: *She pedalled up the hill as fast as she could.*
• ***Word Family:*** other verb forms are **pedals, pedalled, pedalling**

pedant (*say* **ped**-unt) *noun*
someone who pays far too much attention to minor details
• ***Word Family:*** **pedantic** *adjective* **pedantically** *adverb* **pedantry** *noun*

A B C D E F G H I J K L M N O P Q R S T U V W X Y Z

pedestal *noun*
a base that a statue or column stands on

pedestrian (*say* pu-**des**-tree-un) *noun*
1 someone who is walking: *Cars have been banned from the city centre to make it safer for pedestrians.*
pedestrian *adjective*
2 for pedestrians: *a pedestrian crossing*
•***Word Origins:*** from a Latin word meaning "on foot"

pedigree *noun*
a list of ancestors, especially one showing that an animal's ancestors are of the same breed

peek *verb*
to take a very quick look

peel *noun*
1 the skin of a fruit
peel *verb*
2 to take off the skin of a fruit: *to peel an orange* 3 to come off in strips: *My face peeled after a day in the sun.*

peep (1) *noun*
1 a short, quick look
peep *verb*
2 to take a peep at 3 to come into view partly or briefly: *The sun peeped through the clouds.*

peep (2) *noun*
the weak, high cry made by young birds or mice

peer (1) *noun*
1 someone of the same age as you 2 a nobleman or noblewoman
•***Word Family:*** **peerage** *noun*

peer (2) *verb*
to look hard at something trying to see it clearly: *to peer through the fog*

peg *noun*
1 a piece of wood, metal or plastic used to fasten things or hang things on: *a clothes peg*
peg *verb*
2 to fasten something with pegs: *to peg down a tent*
•***Word Family:*** other verb forms are **pegs, pegged, pegging**

pelican *noun*
a large, white seabird that keeps the fish it catches in the bottom part of its bill which is shaped like a big bag

pellet *noun*
a small, round ball of something: *a pellet of paper*

pelt *verb*
1 to throw a lot of things: *The boys were pelting each other with stones.* 2 to rain heavily: *It's pelting down.*

pelvis *noun*
the strong, bowl-shaped frame of bones formed by your lower back and your hipbones
•***Word Family:*** **pelvic** *adjective*

pen (1) *noun*
1 an instrument used for writing or drawing with ink
pen *verb*
2 to write something: *to pen a letter*
•***Word Family:*** other verb forms are **pens, penned, penning**

pen (2) *noun*
1 a small, fenced-off area for farm animals
pen *verb*
2 to put farm animals in a pen
•***Word Family:*** other verb forms are **pens, penned, penning**

penal (*say* **pee**-nul) *adjective*
to do with the punishment of criminals: *the penal system*

penalty (*say* **pen**-ul-tee) *noun*
1 a punishment for breaking a rule or law: *The penalty for murder may be death.* 2 a free kick in a sporting game given because a player on the other side has broken a rule
•***Word Family:*** **penalize** or **penalise** *verb* to punish someone for breaking a rule

penance (*say* **pen**-ance) *noun*
a punishment willingly accepted by someone to show they are sorry for doing wrong

pencil (*say* **pen**-sil) *noun*
1 a thin piece of wood with a central rod of graphite used for writing or drawing
pencil *verb*
2 to write something or mark something with a pencil
•***Word Family:*** other verb forms are **pencils, pencilled, pencilling**

pendulum (*say* **pen**-dew-lum) *noun*
a hanging weight that swings evenly backwards and forwards to make a clock work

penetrate (*say* **pen**-u-trate) *verb*
to go into or through: *A piece of flying glass penetrated her arm. / A beam of light penetrated the darkness.*
•***Word Family:*** **penetration** *noun*

penfriend *noun*
someone, usually in another country, who has become a friend by writing letters rather than meeting

penguin (*say* **pen**-gwin) *noun*
a seabird that cannot fly and has webbed feet and small wings that look like flippers

penicillin (*say* pen-u-**sil**-in) *noun*
a medicine used to treat illnesses that are caused by bacteria

peninsula *noun*
a long piece of land jutting out into the water

penis (*say* **pee**-nus) *noun*
the part of the male body that he uses to urinate and to have sexual intercourse

penitentiary (*say* pen-i-**ten**-sha-ree) *noun*
a prison or gaol

penknife *noun*
a small knife with a blade that folds back into the handle

pennant *noun*
a long, triangular flag

penny *noun*
a British coin worth one hundredth of a pound
• ***Word Family:*** **penniless** *adjective* without any money

pension (*say* **pen**-shon) *noun*
a sum of money paid regularly by the government to someone who is old or by an employer to someone who used to work for them and is now retired
• ***Word Family:*** **pensioner** *noun*

pensive (*say* **pen**-siv) *adjective*
thoughtful in a serious or sad way
• ***Word Family:*** **pensively** *adverb*

pentagon *noun*
a flat shape with five straight sides

pentahedron (*say* pen-tu-**hee**-drun) *noun*
a shape with five flat sides

pentathlon (*say* pen-**tath**-lon) *noun*
a sporting competition in which the athletes compete in five different events
• ***Word Origins:*** from a Greek word meaning "five contests"

penthouse *noun*
a luxurious flat on the top storey of a tall building

people *noun*
1 human beings in general 2 all the men, women and children in a place or country: *desert people / the British people* 3 human beings who have something in common: *medical people* 4 relatives: *my father's people*
• ***Word Family:*** the plural is **people** or **peoples**

pepper *noun*
1 a hot-tasting spice made from dried berries that are ground to a powder 2 a green, red or yellow vegetable that is hollow in the middle
pepper *verb*
3 to sprinkle: *a face peppered with freckles*
• ***Word Family:*** **peppery** *adjective*

peppermint *noun*
1 a strong-smelling mint that is used to flavour sweets 2 a sweet with this flavour

per *preposition*
for each: *We've enough for two sandwiches per person.*

perambulate (*say* per-**ram**-bew-late) *verb*
to stroll about
• ***Word Family:*** **perambulation** *noun*

per annum *adverb*
yearly: *What do you earn per annum?*
• ***Word Origins:*** these words come from Latin

per capita *adverb*
per person in the population: *a country with a high per capita income*
• ***Word Origins:*** these words come from Latin

perceive (*say* per-**seev**) *verb*
1 to notice something, especially by seeing, hearing or feeling it: *I could just perceive the shape of a person in the distance.* 2 to understand: *I perceived a change in his attitude.*
• ***Word Family:*** **perceivable** *adjective*

per cent *adverb*
in every hundred: *$\frac{3}{100}$ is 3 per cent and is written 3%*
• ***Word Origins:*** these words come from Latin

percentage (*say* per-**sen**-tij) *noun*
1 a number that shows the rate per hundred 2 a part or proportion: *a small percentage of the population*

perception (*say* per-**sep**-shon) *noun*
1 the ability to notice or understand things that are not obvious to others 2 an idea you have about something based on what you know or notice: *He gave us his perceptions on what it means to be a teenager today.*
• ***Word Family:*** **perceptive** *adjective* able to notice or understand things that are not obvious **perceptiveness** *noun*

perch *noun*
1 a short rod on which a bird can rest
perch *verb*
2 to sit or stand on something for a short time: *An owl perched on her shoulder.*
• ***Word Origins:*** from a Latin word meaning "measuring rod"

percolate (*say* **per**-ku-late) *verb*
1 to make coffee by dripping hot water slowly through ground coffee beans 2 to spread slowly among people: *New ideas percolated throughout the community.*
• ***Word Family:*** **percolater** *noun*

percussion (*say* per-**kush**-on) *noun*
musical instruments such as drums, cymbals or xylophones which are played by being hit

a b c d e f g h i j k l m n o p q r s t u v w x y z

perennial (*say* pu-**ren**-ee-ul) *adjective*
1 lasting for a long time: *a perennial joke* 2 with a life cycle that lasts for more than two years: *a perrenial plant*
• ***Word Family:*** **perennially** *adjective*

perfect (*say* **per**-fikt) *adjective*
1 without any mistakes, faults or flaws 2 exactly right: *a house that's just perfect for us* 3 complete or absolute: *perfect strangers / perfect sense* 4 to do with the tense of a verb that shows the action has been completed, for example *have spoken*, *had spoken* or *will have spoken*
perfect (*say* per-**fekt**) *verb*
5 to make something perfect or as excellent as possible: *to perfect a technique*
• ***Word Family:*** **perfection** *noun* the quality of being perfect **perfectionist** *noun* someone who tries to do everything perfectly **perfectly** *adverb*

perforate (*say* **per**-fa-rate) *verb*
to make small holes in something: *Tear off the bottom part of the form where the paper has been perforated.*
• ***Word Family:*** **perforation** *noun*

perform *verb*
1 to carry something out: *to perform an operation* 2 to act, sing or dance in front of an audience
• ***Word Family:*** **performance** *noun* **performer** *noun*

perfume (*say* **per**-fewm) *noun*
1 a pleasant-smelling liquid that you put on your skin: *a bottle of perfume* 2 a pleasant smell
perfume (*say* per-**fewm**) *verb*
3 to give out a pleasant smell: *The roses perfumed the air.*

pergola (*say* **per**-gu-la *or* per-**gole**-a) *noun*
a framework of posts supporting a roof over which vines or other plants may be grown
• ***Word Origins:*** from a Latin word meaning "shed"

perhaps *adverb*
possibly

peril *noun*
great danger: *Her life was in peril.*

perimeter (*say* per-**rim**-u-ta) *noun*
1 the distance round the edge of a flat shape or area: *the perimeter of a circle* 2 the boundary round a large area: *the airport perimeter*

period *noun*
1 a length of time: *a period of rest / geological and historical periods* 2 the time taken for a lesson or a single activity in school or college: *a maths period* 3 the monthly flow of blood from the uterus in a woman who is not pregnant
• ***Word Family:*** **periodic** *adjective* appearing or happening at regular intervals **periodical** *noun* a magazine which is published regularly **periodically** *adverb*

peripheral (*say* per-**rif**-ah-rul) *adjective*
of little importance or not central: *peripheral issues*
• ***Word Family:*** **peripherally** *adverb* **periphery** *noun*

periscope *noun*
an instrument made of mirrors and a tube used to see something that is above you or out of your sight: *the periscope in a submarine*

perish *verb*
1 to die: *Many people perished in the fire.* 2 to rot or decay: *These old rubber tyres have perished.*
• ***Word Family:*** **perishables** *plural noun* food that goes bad quickly **perishable** *adjective*

perjury (*say* **per**-ja-ree) *noun*
the crime of lying in a court of law after you have taken an oath to tell the truth
• ***Word Family:*** **perjure** *verb* **perjurer** *noun*

permafrost *noun*
ground that is permanently frozen to a great depth

permanent *adjective*
lasting forever or for a very long time
• ***Word Family:*** **permanence** *noun* **permanently** *adverb*

permission (*say* per-**mish**-on) *noun*
being allowed to do something: *Can I have permission to leave early?*
• ***Word Family:*** **permissible** *adjective* allowed

permissive *adjective*
allowing people freedom to choose how to behave, especially sexually and morally: *a permissive society*
• ***Word Family:*** **permissiveness** *noun*

permit (*say* per-**mit**) *verb*
1 to allow: *Smoking is not permitted.*
permit (*say* **per**-mit) *noun*
2 an official document giving permission to do something
• ***Word Family:*** other verb forms are **permits, permitted, permitting**

permutation (*say* per-mew-**tay**-shon) *noun*
one of the different ways in which things can be arranged in order
• ***Word Family:*** **permutate** *verb*

perpendicular (*say* per-pun-**dik**-yoo-la) *adjective*
1 vertical or upright 2 meeting a line or surface at a right angle
perpendicular *noun*
3 a perpendicular line or surface

A B C D E F G H I J K L M N O P Q R S T U V W X Y Z

perpetrate (*say* **per**-pu-trate) *verb*
to do something which is bad or against the law: *to perpetrate a crime*
•***Word Family:*** **perpetrator** *noun*

perpetual (*say* per-**pet**-choo-ul) *adjective*
1 lasting for ever: *the perpetual snow on the mountain peak* 2 continuous: *a perpetual stream of phone calls*
•***Word Family:*** **perpetually** *adverb* **perpetuate** *verb* to make something continue **perpetuation** *noun*

perplex (*say* per-**pleks**) *verb*
to puzzle and confuse you
•***Word Family:*** **perplexing** *adjective* **perplexity** *noun*

persecute (*say* **per**-sa-kewt) *verb*
to keep on treating someone cruelly and unfairly
•***Word Family:*** **persecution** *noun* **persecutor** *noun*

persevere (*say* per-sa-**vear**) *verb*
to keep on doing something even though it is very difficult: *I'm going to persevere with German—I shall learn it eventually.*
•***Word Family:*** **perseverance** *noun*

persist *verb*
1 to continue doing something, even though it is difficult or other people are against it: *The residents persisted with their demands for a new bus shelter.* 2 to last for a long time: *The bruise persisted for weeks.*
•***Word Family:*** **persistence** *noun* **persistency** *noun* **persistent** *adjective*

person *noun*
1 a human being 2 **in person** actually present: *She delivered the news in person.*

personal *adjective*
1 for or belonging to a particular person: *a personal letter / personal belongings* 2 insulting to a particular person: *personal remarks*
•***Word Family:*** **personally** *adverb*

personal computer *noun*
a computer that can be used by one person at a time, such as in the home or in a small business

personal identification number *noun*
a secret number used with a plastic card to operate an automatic teller machine or EFTPOS terminal

personality (*say* per-sa-**nal**-a-tee) *noun*
1 the qualities that make someone individual and unique: *a strong personality* 2 someone who is well-known: *a sporting personality*
•***Word Family:*** the plural is **personalities**

personify *verb*
1 to give human feelings or form to animals or objects 2 to be a good example of: *She is goodness personified.*
•***Word Family:*** other forms are **personifies, personified, personifying** □ **personification** *noun*

personnel (*say* per-sa-**nel**) *noun*
all the people employed in a particular business or work

perspective (*say* per-**spek**-tiv) *noun*
1 a way of drawing or painting objects in a picture so that they seem to be the correct distance, height and width in relation to each other 2 **in perspective** in proper proportion or balance

perspex *noun*
a colourless, transparent plastic that can be used as a substitute for glass
•***Word Origins:*** this is a trademark

perspire *verb*
to give out moisture through pores in your skin in order to cool your body
•***Word Family:*** **perspiration** *noun*
•***Word Origins:*** from a Latin word meaning "to breathe through"

persuade (*say* per-**swade**) *verb*
to make someone willing to do or believe something by giving a good reason: *She persuaded me I was wrong.*
•***Word Family:*** **persuasive** *adjective* **persuasively** *adverb*

persuasion *noun*
1 the act of persuading: *I used all my powers of persuasion, but he wouldn't change his mind.* 2 a religious belief: *people of different persuasions*

pertain *verb*
having to do with: *the files that pertain to the investigation*

pertinent *adjective*
relevant or to the point: *a pertinent remark*
•***Word Family:*** **pertinence** *noun*

perturb (*say* per-**terb**) *verb*
to disturb or worry greatly: *The anonymous telephone calls perturbed us.*
•***Word Origins:*** from a Latin word meaning "to throw into confusion"

peruse (*say* per-**rooz**) *verb*
to read through carefully: *I'll peruse your application at my leisure.*
•***Word Family:*** **perusal** *noun*

pervert (*say* per-**vert**) *verb*
1 to make something bad, wrong or unnatural: *to pervert the course of justice / to pervert the mind of a child* 2 to make someone do things that are wrong or unacceptable, especially to do with sex

A B C D E F G H I J K L M N O P Q R S T U V W X Y Z

pervert (say **per**-vert) *noun*
3 someone who behaves unnaturally or wrongly, especially in a sexual way
•***Word Family:*** **perversion** *noun* **perverted** *adjective*

Pesach (*say* **pay**-sak) *noun*
the Jewish word for the festival of Passover

pessimism *noun*
the habit of expecting things to turn out badly
•***Word Family:*** **pessimist** *noun* **pessimistic** *adjective*

pest *noun*
an annoying or harmful person or thing: *What a pest you are!*

pester *verb*
to keep annoying someone

pesticide (*say* **pes**-ti-side) *noun*
a substance used to destroy pests, especially insect pests
•***Word Origins:*** from Latin words meaning "plague" and "kill"

pestle (*say* **pes**-ul) *noun*
a tool shaped like a small club, used for crushing food, medicines and so on in a mortar (a special bowl)

pet *noun*
1 a tame animal that you keep and look after
2 a favourite: *teacher's pet*
pet *verb*
3 to stroke or touch affectionately: *to pet the dog*
pet *adjective*
4 kept as a pet: *a pet dog*
•***Word Family:*** other verb forms are **pets, petted, petting**

petal *noun*
one of the coloured or white outer parts of a flower
•***Word Origins:*** from a Greek word meaning "leaf"

petite (*say* pe-**teet**) *adjective*
small and delicate

petition *noun*
a written request, usually signed by many people, which you give to a group or person in power, to ask them to do something or to show them that you feel strongly about something

petrify *verb*
1 to be unable to move because you are scared
2 to turn into stone: *The passage of time has petrified these trees.*
•***Word Family:*** other forms are **petrifies, petrified, petrifying** □ **petrification** *noun*
•***Word Origins:*** from a Greek word meaning "rock"

petrol *noun*
a liquid made from petroleum and special additives, used as a fuel for motor vehicles

petroleum (*say* pe-**tro**-lee-um) *noun*
an oil which is found under the ground and is used to make petrol, oils, waxes and other substances

petticoat *noun*
a thin skirt or dress that girls and women wear underneath their clothes

petty *adjective*
1 small and unimportant: *petty details* 2 mean and unkind: *petty criticism / petty jealousy*
•***Word Family:*** other forms are **pettier, pettiest** □ **pettily** *adverb* **pettiness** *noun*

pew *noun*
a long, wooden seat in a church

pewter *noun*
a mixture of tin and other metals used to make dishes, plates and mugs

pH *noun*
a measure of how acid or alkaline a solution is

phantom (*say* **fan**-tum) *noun*
1 a ghost 2 something that is not real

pharmacy (*say* **far**-ma-see) *noun*
a shop where medicines are prepared and sold
•***Word Family:*** the plural is **pharmacies** □ **pharmaceutical** (*say* far-ma-**syoo**-ti-kul) *adjective* to do with medicines **pharmacist** *noun* a person trained to prepare medicines

pharynx (*say* **fa**-rinks) *noun*
the wide air passage that connects your nose to your throat

phase (*say* faze) *noun*
1 a stage of development or change: *the adolescent phase / the phases of the moon*
phase *verb*
2 to carry out or do something gradually: *to phase in a new method*

pheasant (*say* **fez**-unt) *noun*
a large, long-tailed bird often eaten for food

phenomenon (*say* fe-**nom**-a-non) *noun*
1 a thing that you can see and observe directly
2 someone or something that is remarkable or extraordinary
•***Word Family:*** the plural is **phenomena** □ **phenomenal** *adjective*

phial (*say* **fy**-ul) *noun*
a small, glass container for storing liquids, especially medicines

philanthropy (*say* fil-**an**-thro-pee) *noun*
a love of humanity, especially as shown by acts of goodness or kindness

•*Word Family:* **philanthropic** *adjective* **philanthropist** *noun*

philately (*say* fil-**at**-a-lee) *noun*
the study and collecting of postage stamps
•*Word Family:* **philatelist** *noun*

philharmonic (*say* fil-har-**mon**-ik) *adjective*
fond of music

philistine (*say* **fil**-is-tine) *noun*
someone who does not like or does not understand good art, music, literature or architecture
•*Word Family:* **philistinism** *noun*
•*Word Origins:* this word comes from the name of a race who, in Biblical history, fought against Saul and David and who were wrongly said to be uncivilised

philosophy (*say* fi-**los**-u-fee) *noun*
1 the search for answers to questions like "What is the meaning of life?" 2 a particular theory or set of ideas about how to live and behave: *What is your philosophy of life?*
•*Word Family:* the plural is **philosophies** □ **philosophical** *adjective* calm and accepting when disappointing things happen **philosopher** *noun* **philosophically** *adverb* **philosophize** or **philosophise** *verb*

phobia (*say* **fo**-bee-a) *noun*
an overwhelming fear of a particular thing: *a phobia about heights*
•*Word Family:* **phobic** *adjective* **phobic** *noun*

phone (*say* fone) *noun, verb*
a short form of **telephone**

phonetics (*say* fo-**net**-iks) *noun*
the study of sounds used in speech
•*Word Family:* **phonetic** *adjective: a phonetic system of spelling* **phonetically** *adverb*

phoney (*say* **fo**-nee) *adjective*
false or counterfeit: *a phoney name / phoney money*

phonology (*say* fo-**nol**-a-jee) *noun*
the study of the way in which sounds are made into words

phospherescent (*say* fos-for-**ess**-ent) *adjective*
shining or glowing in the dark
•*Word Family:* **phosphorescence** *noun*

phosphorus (*say* **fos**-fa-rus) *noun*
a chemical element which is used in fertilizers, detergents and the heads of matches
•*Word Family:* **phosphate** *noun* a fertilizer made from phosphorus
•*Word Origins:* from a Greek word meaning "bringing light"

photo (*say* **fo**-toe) *noun*
a short form of **photograph**

photocopy *noun*
1 an exact copy of a page of writing or a picture made by a special photographic machine
photocopy *verb*
2 to make a copy of a page in this way
•*Word Family:* the plural is **photocopies** □ other verb forms are **photocopies, photocopied, photocopying** □ **photocopier** *noun* the special photographic machine that makes a photocopy

photograph (*say* **fo**-ta-graf) *noun*
1 a picture made by exposing a film in a camera to light and then printing the images made on the film onto special paper
photograph *verb*
2 to use a camera to make a picture in this way
•*Word Family:* **photographic** *adjective* to do with photography

photography (*say* fo-**tog**-ra-fee) *noun*
the art of taking photographs
•*Word Family:* **photographer** *noun*

photosynthesis (*say* fo-toe-**sin**-tha-sis) *noun*
the process by which green plants use the energy from sunlight to make sugar and starch from water and carbon dioxide

phrase (*say* fraze) *noun*
1 a group of words, usually without a verb, that form part of a sentence 2 a small group of notes that form part of a melody
phrase *verb*
3 to say or write in words: *If you don't understand, I'll phrase it another way.*
•*Word Origins:* from a Greek word meaning "speech"

phylum (*say* **fuy**-lum) *noun*
a classification used by biologists to group together animals they think are related: *All animals with backbones are in the phylum called Chordata.*
•*Word Family:* the plural is **phyla**

physical (*say* **fiz**-i-kul) *adjective*
1 to do with the body: *physical exercise* 2 to do with the structure, shape or size of things that can be seen or touched: *physical geography*
•*Word Family:* **physically** *adverb*

physician (*say* fiz-**ish**-un) *noun*
a doctor who treats diseases with medicine, not surgery

physics (*say* **fiz**-iks) *noun*
the science which studies natural forces such as heat, light, sound, pressure, gravity and electricity
•*Word Family:* **physicist** (*say* **fiz**-i-sist) *noun*
•*Word Origins:* from a Greek word meaning "natural"

physiology (*say* fiz-i-**ol**-a-jee) *noun*
the study of how the bodies of living things work
•***Word Family:*** **physiological** *adjective* **physiologically** *adverb* **physiologist** *noun*

physiotherapy (*say* fiz-i-o-**the**-ra-pee) *noun*
the use of exercises, massages, and so on to treat injuries or diseases of the body
•***Word Family:*** **physiotherapist** *noun*

physique (*say* fiz-**eek**) *noun*
the shape and appearance of your body

pi (*say* pie) *noun*
the symbol π, used for the number 3.141592...., which is always the answer when the circumference of a circle is divided by its diameter
•***Word Origins:*** a letter of the Greek alphabet

piano (1) (*say* pee-**an**-oh) *noun*
a large, musical instrument played by pressing black or white bars (keys) which make small hammers hit metal strings
•***Word Family:*** **pianist** (*say* **pee**-a-nist) *noun* someone who plays the piano

piano (2) (*say* pee-**ahn**-oh) *adverb*
softly
•***Word Family:*** **pianissimo** *adverb* very softly
•***Word Origins:*** this word comes from Italian

picador (*say* **pik**-a-dor) *noun*
a bullfighter on horseback who uses a stick like a spear to annoy and weaken the bull
•***Word Origins:*** from a Spanish word meaning "to pierce"

piccolo (*say* **pik**-a-lo) *noun*
a small flute that makes very high notes
•***Word Family:*** the plural is **piccolos**
•***Word Origins:*** from the Italian word for "small"

pick (1) *verb*
1 to choose or select: *to pick which cake you want* 2 to gather or collect: *to pick flowers* 3 to touch or remove: *to pick off flakes of paint* 4 to dig into with something sharp and pointed: *He picked a hole in the desk with his compass.* 5 to open a lock without using the key 6 **pick on** to blame or criticize
pick *noun*
7 a choice or selection: *Take your pick.*

pick (2) *noun*
a tool with a wooden handle and a pointed iron bar, used to break up hard soil and rock

picket *noun*
1 a post with a pointed end, driven into the ground as part of a fence 2 a group of people protesting about something, especially people who stand guard outside their workplace to stop people from going into work during a strike
picket *verb*
3 to protest outside a workplace and try to stop people going in when there is a strike
•***Word Family:*** other verb forms are **pickets, picketed, picketing**

pickle *noun*
1 a vegetable, such as an onion or cucumber, which has been preserved in salt water or vinegar 2 a difficult or tricky situation
pickle *verb*
3 to preserve vegetables in salt water or vinegar

pickpocket *noun*
someone who steals from people's pockets or handbags in a public place

picnic *noun*
1 an outing where you take food to eat outdoors
picnic *verb*
2 to eat food outdoors on an outing: *to picnic by the river*
•***Word Family:*** other forms of the verb are **picnics, picnicked, picnicking** □ **picnicker** *noun*

picture *noun*
1 a painting, drawing or photograph 2 a beautiful sight: *The twins looked a picture in their new outfits.* 3 **the pictures** the cinema
picture *verb*
4 to imagine: *picture the excitement*
•***Word Family:*** **pictorial** *adjective* illustrated **pictorially** *adverb*

picturesque (*say* pik-cher-**esk**) *adjective*
charming or attractive to look at: *a picturesque village*
•***Word Family:*** **picturesquely** *adverb*

pidgin (*say* **pij**-in) *noun*
a language based on a mixture of languages, used when people from different countries have no other language in common

pie *noun*
a pastry case with a sweet or savoury filling and usually a crust of pastry on top, which is baked in the oven

piebald *adjective*
having patches of different colours, especially black and white: *a piebald pony*

piece (*say* peece) *noun*
1 a part or fragment: *a piece of pie / an interesting piece of news* 2 an individual part: *How many pieces are in the chess set?*
piece *verb*
3 to assemble something by joining parts together: *to piece together the clues to a murder*

piecemeal *adverb*
gradually or piece by piece

pie chart *noun*
a circle divided into sectors, used to show information: *Draw a pie chart to show how you spend your day.*

pier (*rhymes with* fear) *noun*
a structure built from the land into water, used for tying boats to, and to fish from

pierce *verb*
1 to make a hole in: *to pierce your ears / The thorn pierced my thumb.* 2 to cut through sharply: *Spine-chilling screams pierced the air.*
•**Word Family: piercing** *adjective* **piercingly** *adverb*

piety (*say* **pie**-a-tee) *noun*
respect for religion
•**Word Family:** □ See also **pious**

pig *noun*
1 a farm animal with short legs, bristly hair and a snout 2 someone who is greedy or dirty
pig *verb*
3 **pig out** to eat a great deal on a particular occasion or of a particular food
•**Word Family: piggy** *adjective*

pigeon (*say* **pij**-in) *noun*
a bird with a plump, grey body, small head and short legs, that makes a cooing sound

pig face *noun*
a low-growing plant with thick, pale leaves and bright flowers

pig-headed *adjective*
stupidly stubborn

piglet *noun*
a young pig

pigment *noun*
1 a coloured powder that is mixed with water or oil to make paint 2 the substance that gives plants and animals particular colours
•**Word Family: pigmentation** *noun* the natural colouring of a plant or animal

pigmy *noun*
another way of spelling **pygmy**

pigsty *noun*
1 a building or area where pigs are kept 2 an untidy room
•**Word Family:** the plural is **pigsties**

pile (1) *noun*
1 a number of things heaped together: *a pile of papers* 2 a large quantity or amount
pile *verb*
3 to make into a pile: *Pile up the papers.*
4 **pile up** to accumulate: *His debts piled up.*

pile (2) *noun*
a raised surface on a carpet, towel, and so on made of loops of yarn or fibre
•**Word Origins:** from a Latin word meaning "a hair"

pile (3) *noun*
a large post of wood, concrete or steel, put upright in the ground to support a bridge or a house

pilfer *verb*
to steal in small quantities

pilgrim *noun*
someone who travels a long distance to a holy place
•**Word Family: pilgrimage** *noun* a journey made by a pilgrim
•**Word Origins:** from a Latin word meaning "foreigner"

pill *noun*
a form of medicine in a hard, usually round shape, that you swallow: *vitamin pills*

pillage *verb*
to rob in a rough, violent way, especially in war

pillar *noun*
a column that supports part of a building

pillion (*say* **pil**-yun) *noun*
a seat for a passenger behind the driver on a motorcycle

pillow *noun*
a bag filled with soft material, used to rest your head on when you sleep

pilot *noun*
1 someone who controls an aircraft 2 someone who guides a ship through a difficult area of water, such as the entrance to a busy harbour
3 something used as an experiment or to test a future project, such as a sample film for a television series
4 **pilot** *verb*
to steer, guide or conduct

pimple *noun*
a small swelling on your skin, usually containing pus
•**Word Family: pimply** *adjective* having many pimples

pin *noun*
1 a small piece of metal with a sharp, pointed end, used to fasten or join things: *sewing pins / safety pins / drawing pins*
pin *verb*
2 to fasten or attach something with a pin 3 to hold securely: *The climber was pinned under the fallen rocks.*
•**Word Family:** other verb forms are **pins, pinned, pinning**

A B C D E F G H I J K L M N O P Q R S T U V W X Y Z

PIN *noun*
a secret number used with a plastic card in a cashpoint machine
•***Word Origins:*** an acronym from the first letter of the words *P*ersonal *I*dentification *N*umber

pinafore *noun*
1 an apron with a top part 2 **pinafore dress** a dress without sleeves, worn over a blouse or jumper

pinball *noun*
a game played by pulling levers and pushing buttons to move a ball around a sloping board

pincers *plural noun*
1 the claws of crabs, lobsters and some insects 2 a tool with a pair of jaws for gripping nails to pull them out of wood

pinch *verb*
1 to squeeze tightly, especially between the thumb and finger: *She pinched his arm. / I pinched my finger in the door.* 2 to steal: *Who's pinched my ruler?*
pinch *noun*
3 a squeeze 4 a very small amount, such as that held between your finger and thumb: *a pinch of salt*

pine (1) *noun*
an evergreen tree with cones and long leaves like needles

pine (2) *verb*
1 to long for something or someone greatly: *The prisoner pined for his freedom.* 2 **pine away** to become weak and die because you are very sad

pineapple *noun*
a large, tropical fruit with a tough, brown, prickly skin and juicy yellow flesh

ping-pong *noun*
another name for **table tennis**

pinion (1) *noun*
a small wheel with cogs, that locks together with a larger, similar wheel

pinion (2) *noun*
the end of a bird's wing

pink *noun*
pale red

pinking shears *plural noun*
a pair of scissors with notches along the blades, which cut material so that it has a zigzag edge

pinnacle (*say* **pin**-a-kul) *noun*
1 the highest part of something: *a mountain pinnacle* 2 the most successful part of something: *the pinnacle of her career*

pinpoint *verb*
to show or explain exactly: *Can you pinpoint where you lost the money?*

pint *noun*
an eighth of a gallon, about 568 millilitres

pioneer (*say* pie-a-**near**) *noun*
1 someone who is the first to enter, explore or settle in a new region
pioneer *verb*
2 to explore or settle for the first time 3 to try out or do something for the first time

pious (*say* **pie**-us) *adjective*
very religious
•***Word Family:*** **piously** *adverb* **piousness** *noun*
☐ see also **piety**

pip (1) *noun*
a small seed found in fruit such as apples or grapes

pip (2) *noun*
a short, high sound, such as a time signal heard on a radio

pipe *noun*
1 a hollow tube for carrying fluids: *a water pipe / a gas pipe* 2 an object consisting of a hollow tube with a small bowl at one end, used for smoking tobacco 3 a simple wind instrument consisting of a tube with holes, that you blow through 4 **pipes** *short for* bagpipes
pipe *verb*
5 to carry or send by a pipe: *to pipe water to the fields* 6 to play a musical pipe
•***Word Family:*** **piper** *noun* someone who plays a pipe, especially the bagpipes

piping *adverb*
piping hot very hot

pique (*say* peek) *noun*
a feeling of slight annoyance

piranha (*say* puh-**rah**-na) *noun*
a small, fierce, South American fish, which attacks in groups and eats flesh
•***Word Origins:*** from Portuguese words meaning "fish" and "tooth"

pirate *noun*
1 someone who attacks and robs ships at sea
pirate *verb*
2 to copy and use someone else's work without permission: *to pirate videos*
•***Word Family:*** **piracy** *noun*

pirouette (*say* pi-rooh-**et**) *noun*
a spinning step done on one foot, especially on the tips of your toes, as in dancing
•***Word Family:*** **pirouette** *verb*
•***Word Origins:*** from a French word meaning "to whirl"

pistil *noun*
the part of a flower which produces the seeds

pistol *noun*
a small gun that can be held and fired with one hand

piston *noun*
a short cylinder or disc that slides up and down inside a tube and is used to make parts of an engine move

pit (1) *noun*
1 a hole in the ground 2 a coal-mine 3 a shallow hole in a surface: *Acne left many pits in her skin.* 4 an area beside a car racetrack where a car may stop for repairs or petrol during a race 5 the area in a theatre below and in front of the stage: *the orchestra pit*
pit *verb*
6 to make holes or hollows in: *Meteors have pitted the moon with craters.* 7 to compete with: *They pitted their strength against the raging winds.*
•***Word Family:*** other verb forms are **pits, pitted, pitting**

pit (2) *noun*
1 the stone of a fruit such as a cherry or plum
pit *verb*
2 to remove the stone from a fruit
•***Word Family:*** other verb forms are **pits, pitted, pitting**

pitch (1) *verb*
1 to throw or toss 2 to put up a tent 3 to fall or plunge: *He pitched headlong down the slope.* 4 to rock violently: *The ship pitched in the rough seas.*
pitch *noun*
5 the highness or lowness of a sound or musical note 6 a throw or toss 7 an area marked out for playing a game in sport, such as cricket, football or hockey 8 the angle of slope: *The roof has a steep pitch.*
•***Word Family:*** **pitcher** *verb* the player who throws the ball to the batter in a game of baseball

pitch (2) *noun*
a thick, black, sticky substance used for making paths and roads

pitcher *noun*
a jug with a spout and a handle

pitfall *noun*
a hidden trap or danger

pith *noun*
a soft, spongy substance, such as that between the flesh and rind of an orange
•***Word Family:*** **pithy** *adjective* concise and full of meaning: *a pithy statement*

pitiable *adjective*
making you feel pity

pitiful *adjective*
1 making you feel pity: *The starving sheep were a pitiful sight.* 2 not deserving respect, or not being taken seriously: *a pitiful display of cowardice*
•***Word Family:*** **pitifully** *adverb* **pitifulness** *noun*

pitiless *adjective*
cruel, showing no pity or mercy
•***Word Family:*** **pitilessly** *adverb*

pittance *noun*
a very small amount of money: *They paid him a pittance.*

pity *noun*
1 a feeling of deep sympathy for the suffering of other people 2 something that makes you sad or sorry: *What a pity that it is raining.*
pity *verb*
3 to feel very sorry for someone who is suffering
•***Word Family:*** other verb forms are **pities, pitied, pitying**

pivot *noun*
1 a point on which something balances or turns
pivot *verb*
2 to turn on or balance as if on a pivot
•***Word Family:*** **pivotal** *adjective*

pixel *noun*
a tiny square that makes up a picture on a screen

pixie *noun*
a small fairy, especially one that plays tricks on people

pizza (*say* **peet**-sa) *noun*
a flat, round piece of dough covered with tomato, cheese, and other toppings and cooked quickly in a very hot oven
•***Word Origins:*** the Italian word for "pie"

pizzicato (*say* pit-si-**kah**-toe) *adjective*
played by plucking the strings of a violin or cello with a finger instead of using a bow
•***Word Origins:*** from an Italian word meaning "to pinch"

placard (*say* **plak**-ard) *noun*
a large poster or notice

placate (*say* pla-**kate**) *verb*
to make someone calm: *She tried to placate the screaming child.*

place *noun*
1 a particular area of space where something is or where something goes: *Please put that book back in its right place. / a good place to stop / Have dinner at our place.* 2 a situation or circumstances: *I wish I could swap places with the Prime Minister for a day.* 3 a short street or square in a town or city 4 a position in a race: *The horse finished in third place.* 5 a particular

passage or page in a book: *I've lost my place.* **6 go places** to be very successful: *If she carries on like this I think she might go places.* **7 in place of** instead of: *May I go in place of you?* **8 out of place (a)** not appropriate **(b)** not in the right place **9 take place** to happen: *The accident took place on the corner.*
place *verb*
10 to put something in a particular place: *Place the chops in the casserole dish. / Place your trust in me.* 11 to remember: *His face is familiar, but I just can't place him.*
•*Word Family:* **placement** *noun*

placenta (*say* pla-**sen**-ta) *noun*
the organ that supplies food and oxygen from the mother's blood to a baby in the womb
•*Word Family:* the plural is **placentas** or **placentae** □ **placental** *adjective*

placid (*say* **plas**-id) *adjective*
calm
•*Word Family:* **placidly** *adverb*

plagiarist (*say* **play**-ja-rist) *noun*
someone who copies or takes another's work or ideas and pretends they are his or her own
•*Word Family:* **plagiarism** *noun* **plagiarize** or **plagiarise** *verb*
•*Word Origins:* from a Latin word meaning "kidnapper"

plague (*say* playg) *noun*
1 an infectious disease that spreads quickly and kills many people 2 a large number of unpleasant things: *a plague of mosquitoes*
plague *verb*
3 to trouble, annoy or bother someone: *plagued by problems*
•*Word Family:* other verb forms are **plagues, plagued, plaguing**

plain *adjective*
1 simple and uncomplicated: *plain food / Give us the plain facts.* 2 easily seen: *Their embarrassment was plain to all.* 3 easily heard or understood: *Her meaning was plain.* 4 not beautiful
plain *noun*
5 an area of low, flat land
•*Word Family:* **plainly** *adverb* **plainness** *noun*

plaintiff *noun*
someone who brings a case to a court of law, such as a person demanding payment of a debt

plaintive *adjective*
sounding or looking sad: *a plaintive smile*
•*Word Family:* **plaintively** *adverb* **plaintiveness** *noun*

plait (*say* plat) *noun*
1 a length of hair divided into three strands that are woven together and tied at the end
plait *verb*
2 to weave something such as hair or ribbons into a plait

plan *noun*
1 something that you are going to do, worked out beforehand: *What are your plans for the holidays?* 2 a drawing or diagram of a building: *May we see a plan of the house?*
plan *verb*
3 to decide on a plan for something: *to plan a party / to plan your route*
•*Word Family:* other verb forms are **plans, planned, planning** □ **planner** *noun*

plane (1) *noun*
1 a flat or level surface 2 *a short form of* **aeroplane**
plane *adjective*
3 flat: *a plane shape*

plane (2) *noun*
a tool with a sharp blade for shaping or smoothing the surface of wood

planet *noun*
a large body in space that revolves around a star, especially the nine planets of our solar system
•*Word Family:* **planetary** *adjective*

plank *noun*
a long, flat piece of cut timber

plankton *noun*
very tiny animals and plants that drift in water
•*Word Origins:* from a Greek word meaning "wandering"

plant *noun*
1 a living thing with roots, a stem and leaves, that grows in the ground 2 the buildings and equipment for a particular industry: *an electrical plant*
plant *verb*
3 to place a seed or young plant in the ground so it will grow 4 to hide something illegal on someone else's property so that they will get into trouble: *She said that the drugs had been planted in her flat.*

plantation (*say* plan-**tay**-shon) *noun*
1 a farm, especially in tropical regions, where tobacco, coffee, and sugar are grown 2 a group of planted trees

plaque (*say* plahk) *noun*
1 a flat piece of metal or smooth stone which has writing on it and is attached to a wall: *a plaque showing that a famous person had lived there* 2 a white substance that forms on your teeth and causes decay

plasma *noun*
the liquid part of blood, that contains the corpuscles and blood cells

plaster (*say* **plahs**-ta) *noun*
1 a paste of lime, sand and water, that hardens as it dries and is used to cover walls and ceilings 2 a white powder that swells and quickly hardens when mixed with water and is used for making moulds 3 a bandage soaked in such a mixture, wrapped around a broken limb as a support 4 a piece of sticky material used for covering small cuts
plaster *verb*
5 to cover a wall with plaster 6 to cover something with something messy: *to plaster yourself with face paints*
•***Word Family:*** **plasterer** *noun*

plastic *noun*
1 a man-made substance that may be shaped when soft and then hardened
plastic *adjective*
2 made of plastic: *a plastic bag*

plastic surgery *noun*
an operation to change the shape of part of someone's body, or to make someone look better after an accident
•***Word Family:*** **plastic surgeon** *noun*

plate *noun*
1 a flat dish for food 2 a thin, flat, smooth sheet or piece of metal or glass 3 a full-page colour illustration in a book 4 a piece of metal or plastic with false teeth attached
plate *verb*
5 to coat something with a thin layer of metal: *The nickel was plated with silver.*
•***Word Family:*** **plating** *noun* a thin coating or layer, as on metal **plate glass** *noun* a thick, clear glass used for windows and mirrors

plateau (*say* **plat**-oh) *noun*
a large, fairly flat area of high ground
•***Word Family:*** the plural is **plateaus** or **plateaux**

platform *noun*
a raised floor or surface, such as a stage in a theatre or the area beside a railway line at a railway station

platinum *noun*
a greyish or bluish-white metal used in scientific equipment and jewellery
•***Word Origins:*** from a Spanish word meaning "silver"

platitude (*say* **plat**-i-tewd) *noun*
a remark that has been made many times before, especially when said as if it is wise and new
•***Word Family:*** **platitudinous** *adjective*

platonic (*say* pla-**ton**-ik) *adjective*
having to do with a feeling of great affection that does not involve sex: *a platonic relationship*
•***Word Family:*** **platonically** *adverb*
•***Word Origins:*** named after *Plato*, an ancient Greek philosopher who spoke in favour of pure, non-sexual love

platoon *noun*
a small group of soldiers

platter *noun*
a large, shallow dish for serving food

platypus (*say* **plat**-ee-puss) *noun*
an Australian mammal that has brown fur, webbed feet and a bill like a duck's, and lays eggs and feeds its young with its own milk
•***Word Family:*** the plural is **platypuses**
•***Word Origins:*** from Greek words meaning "flat" and "foot"

plausible (*say* **plaw**-zi-bul) *adjective*
reasonable or easy to believe: *His alibi sounded quite plausible to the jury. / a plausible explanation*
•***Word Family:*** **plausibility** *noun* **plausibly** *adverb*

play *verb*
1 to take part in a game, sport or amusement: *to play tennis / to play a trick* 2 to produce music on an instrument: *to play the guitar* 3 to act a part in a play or film: *He's playing the King.*
play *noun*
4 a story written to be acted in a theatre
5 something done for fun or relaxation 6 the way someone plays a game: *There was some good play today.* 7 a quick, irregular movement: *the play of sunlight on water*

playful *adjective*
wanting to play; joking: *a playful puppy*
•***Word Family:*** **playfully** *adverb*

playgroup *noun*
a place like a nursery school, where helpers do activities with children who are too young for school

playwright (*say* **play**-rite) *noun*
someone who writes plays

plaza *noun*
a public square in a city or town

plea *noun*
1 an emotional and sincere request: *a plea for peace* 2 a statement made by someone in a court of law: *a plea of not guilty*

plead *verb*
1 to make an emotional and sincere request: *I pleaded with him to stay.* 2 to say whether you are guilty or innocent of a crime

pleasant (*say* **plez**-unt) *adjective*
enjoyable or pleasing
•***Word Family:*** **pleasantly** *adverb*

A B C D E F G H I J K L M N O P Q R S T U V W X Y Z

please *verb*
to make someone happy or satisfied: *She was pleased to see us.*
•***Word Family:*** **pleasingly** *adverb*

pleasure (*say* **plezh**-a) *noun*
1 something that makes you happy or satisfied
2 being pleased: *His face lit up with pleasure.*
•***Word Family:*** **pleasurable** *adjective*

pleat *noun*
a fold in cloth, paper and so on
•***Word Family:*** **pleated** *adjective*: *a pleated skirt*

pledge *noun*
1 a solemn promise or vow: *a pledge of loyalty*
pledge *verb*
2 to give or make a pledge

plenty *noun*
1 an abundant supply: *food in plenty*
plenty *adjective*
2 ample or enough: *No more, this is plenty.*
•***Word Family:*** **plentiful** *adjective* **plentifully** *adverb*

pliable (*say* **ply**-a-bul) *adjective*
flexible or easily bent
•***Word Family:*** **pliability** *noun*

pliant *adjective*
1 flexible or easily bent 2 easy to influence

pliers (*say* **ply**-erz) *plural noun*
a small, metal tool with long jaws for holding small objects and for bending and cutting wire

plight *verb*
a dangerous, distressing or difficult situation

plod *verb*
1 to walk slowly and heavily 2 to work at something in a steady way
•***Word Family:*** other forms are **plods, plodded, plodding** □ **plodder** *noun*

plop *noun*
1 a sound like something dropping into liquid
plop *verb*
2 to fall with a plop
•***Word Family:*** other forms are **plops, plopped, plopping**

plot (1) *noun*
1 a secret plan: *a plot to murder the president*
2 the story of a novel, play or film
plot *verb*
3 to plan secretly: *The prisoners plotted their escape.* 4 to mark a route on a map or points on a graph or a chart
•***Word Family:*** other verb forms are **plots, plotted, plotting** □ **plotter** *noun*

plot (2) *noun*
a small area of ground: *a garden plot*

plough (*rhymes with* cow) *noun*
1 a tool for digging or turning the soil
plough *verb*
2 to turn soil with a plough 3 **plough through** to carry on with something boring or difficult: *to plough through a book*

plover (*rhymes with* lover) *noun*
a wading bird with long legs
•***Word Family:*** the plural is **plover** or **plovers**

ploy *noun*
a scheme or trick

pluck *verb*
1 to pull at something in order to remove it: *to pluck the feathers from a turkey / to pluck an apple from a tree* 2 to make musical notes by pulling at the strings of an instrument with your fingers or a plectrum
pluck *noun*
3 courage: *She's full of pluck and daring.*
•***Word Family:*** **plucky** *adjective* (**pluckier, pluckiest**) brave **pluckily** *adverb* **pluckiness** *noun*

plug *noun*
1 a piece of metal or rubber used to block up a hole, such as in a bath 2 a small plastic device at the end of an electrical wire that is put into a power point to connect an appliance with a supply of electricity 3 an advertisement for something
plug *verb*
4 to stop up something with a plug: *to plug a leak* 5 to mention or praise something in order to encourage people to buy it
•***Word Family:*** other verb forms are **plugs, plugged, plugging**

plum *noun*
a small, round, juicy fruit with a large stone in the centre

plumage (*say* **ploo**-mij) *noun*
the feathers on a bird's body

plumb (*say* plum) *noun*
a lead weight on a string, used to check that something such as a wall is vertical or to find out how deep something is
•***Word Family:*** **plumb** *verb* **plumb** *adverb*: *plumb in the middle*

plumber (*say* **plum**-a) *noun*
someone who puts in or repairs pipes for water and drainage systems and baths and toilets
•***Word Family:*** **plumbing** *noun* the system of pipes and drains in a building

plummet *verb*
to fall downwards suddenly and very quickly: *The eagle plummeted from the heavens.*

plump *adjective*
fat and rounded: *plump chickens*
•*Word Family:* **plumpness** *noun*

plunder *verb*
to rob or steal, especially in war: *to plunder a town*
•*Word Family:* **plunderer** *noun*

plunge (*say* plunj) *verb*
1 to push or thrust suddenly: *He plunged his hand into the water.* 2 to fall quickly and sharply: *The car plunged off the cliff.*
•*Word Family:* **plunge** *noun* a sudden fall

plural *adjective*
1 consisting of more than one person or thing
plural *noun*
2 a word that means more than one of something: *"Geese" is the plural of "goose"*

plus *preposition*
1 also or in addition to: *One plus one equals two.*
plus *noun*
2 the plus sign (+) 3 a positive amount
4 something that is extra or additional

plutonic (*say* ploo-**ton**-ik) *adjective*
having to do with rocks such as granite, formed deep below the earth's surface

plutonium (*say* ploo-**toe**-nee-um) *noun*
a radioactive metal used in nuclear weapons and as a fuel in nuclear power stations

plywood *noun*
board made of thin sheets of wood glued together

p.m. *abbreviation*
short for post meridiem, *Latin words meaning* "after noon"

pneumatic (*say* new-**mat**-ik) *adjective*
1 powered by compressed air: *a pneumatic drill*
2 filled with air: *pneumatic tyres*

pneumonia (*say* new-**mone**-yuh) *noun*
a serious illness of the lungs, that makes it difficult to breathe

poach (1) *verb*
to cook food by gently simmering it in liquid: *to poach fish in milk*

poach (2) *verb*
to hunt or fish on someone else's land without permission
•*Word Family:* **poacher** *noun*

pocket *noun*
1 a small bag sewn into clothing for holding small things such as money or keys 2 a small, isolated area: *a pocket of rainforest* 3 **be out of pocket** to lose money
pocket *verb*
4 to put something in a pocket: *I pocketed the money.*
•*Word Family:* **pocketful** *noun*

pocket money *noun*
an amount of money that children get regulary from their parents

pod *noun*
a long container in which seeds grow: *a pea-pod*

podgy *adjective*
short and fat: *podgy hands*
•*Word Family:* other forms are **podgier, podgiest** □ **podginess** *noun*

podium (*say* **poe**-dee-um) *noun*
a small platform used by the conductor of an orchestra or for making speeches
•*Word Family:* the plural is **podia** or **podiums**

poem *noun*
a piece of writing, often with short lines that have the same rhythm or that end with words that rhyme
•*Word Family:* **poet** *noun* someone who writes poems **poetic** *adjective* **poetry** *noun: to write poetry*

poignant (*say* **poyn**-yunt) *adjective*
sad and distressing: *a poignant tale of an unhappy childhood*
•*Word Family:* **poignancy** *noun* **poignantly** *adverb*

point *noun*
1 a sharp end: *the point of a needle* 2 the most important part: *Get to the point of the story.* 3 a unit of scoring in games such as football or cards 4 the exact level or place in a process at which a certain thing happens: *the boiling point of water* 5 a compass position 6 a written dot, such as a full stop or a decimal point
point *verb*
7 to indicate or show the direction of something: *He pointed to the car. / The needle pointed north.* 8 to aim: *to point a camera*
9 **point out** to explain or show someone something

point-blank *adjective*
1 aimed or fired at very close range 2 blunt and direct: *a point-blank refusal*

pointed *adjective*
1 shaped with a point at one end: *a pointed stick*
2 done in a way that someone will notice, as a way of telling them something: *She made a pointed remark about people who were always late.*
•*Word Family:* **pointedly** *adverb: to look pointedly at the clock*

pointer *noun*
1 something that you can use to point with 2 a helpful piece of advice or information: *She gave me a few pointers on how to do it.* 3 a kind of hunting dog

A B C D E F G H I J K L M N O P Q R S T U V W X Y Z

pointless *adjective*
with no sense or purpose: *a pointless remark*
•***Word Family:*** **pointlessly** *adverb* **pointlessness** *noun*

poise (*say* poyz) *noun*
1 a calm and confident manner: *She handled the situation with great poise.*
poise *verb*
2 to hold yourself or an object steady and balanced: *He poised on the board before diving.*
•***Word Family:*** **poised** *adjective* dignified, calm and self-controlled

poison (*say* **poy**-zun) *noun*
1 a substance that causes death or illness if it is breathed in or eaten
poison *verb*
2 to kill or harm someone or something with poison: *to poison weeds*
•***Word Family:*** **poisoner** *noun* **poisonous** *adjective*

poke *verb*
1 to jab or push: *He poked me in the ribs with his finger.* 2 to appear suddenly, especially through or from behind something: *Poke your head out of the window.*
poke *noun*
3 a jab or push

poker (1) *noun*
a metal rod for stirring a fire

poker (2) *noun*
a card game in which the players bet on the cards they have in their hand

poky *adjective*
small and cramped: *a poky room*
•***Word Family:*** other forms are **pokier, pokiest**

polar *adjective*
to do with the North or South Poles of the Earth: *polar icecaps*

polar bear *noun*
a large, white bear that lives near the North Pole

pole (1) *noun*
a long, rounded piece of wood or metal

pole (2) *noun*
1 either of the two opposite ends or forces: *the North and South Pole / the poles of a battery / the poles of a magnet* 2 **poles apart** completely different: *Our views on most things are poles apart.*

pole-vault *noun*
a jump over a very high bar, using a long pole to help you
•***Word Family:*** **pole-vault** *verb* **pole-vaulter** *noun*

police *noun*
1 the people whose job is to make sure that people obey the laws of a country, to protect people and property and to arrest criminals
police *verb*
2 to keep order: *to police a football match*
•***Word Family:*** **police officer** *noun*

policy (*say* **pol**-i-see) *noun*
a general plan of action: *the school's policy on homework / a country's foreign policy*
•***Word Family:*** the plural is **policies**

polio (*say* **pole**-ee-oh) *noun*
a serious infectious disease, now rare, which can paralyse you
•***Word Origins:*** this is a short form of *poliomyelitis*

polish *verb*
1 to make something smooth and shining by rubbing it: *Polish those shoes.* 2 to improve something: *He went through his speech again to polish it.* 3 **polish off** to finish or get rid of something: *We soon polished off the cakes.*
polish *noun*
4 the act of polishing: *to give the car a polish*
5 the substance used to make a surface smooth and shiny: *furniture polish* 6 refinement or elegance
•***Word Family:*** **polisher** *noun*

polished *adjective*
1 shiny: *polished furniture.* 2 well practised: *a polished performance* 3 graceful and elegant: *polished manners*

polite *adjective*
having good manners and behaviour: *a polite request*
•***Word Family:*** **politely** *adverb* **politeness** *noun*

politics *plural noun*
1 the matters connected with the government of a country 2 someone's beliefs on how a country should be managed: *What are her politics?* 3 the methods used to get power in a country, organization or group: *office politics*
•***Word Family:*** **politician** *noun* someone taking an active part in politics: *politicians in Westminster* **political** *adjective* **politically** *adverb*
•***Word Origins:*** from a Greek word meaning "of citizens"

polka dot *noun*
a dot that is part of a pattern of dots on material

poll (*sounds like* **pole**) *noun*
1 a counting of people, votes or opinions 2 **the polls** a place where voting is held
poll *verb*
3 to receive votes: *Our candidate polled the*

highest number of votes. 3 to take a survey of opinion
•***Word Family:*** **poll tax** *noun* a tax that all adults have to pay

pollen *noun*
the yellow seed powder found in flowers, which is carried to another flower to make new seeds
•***Word Family:*** **pollinate** *verb* to move pollen from one flower to another to cause a seed to be formed: *Bees pollinate flowers*. **pollination** *noun*

pollen count *noun*
a measurement of how much pollen there is in the air, to warn people who get asthma or hay fever

pollute *verb*
to make air, water and so on dirty or impure
•***Word Family:*** other forms are **pollutes, polluted, polluting** □ **pollution** *noun*

polo *noun*
a ball game played on horseback using long-handled mallets and a small wooden ball
•***Word Origins:*** from a Tibetan word for "ball"

polo neck *noun*
a high rolled collar: *a polo-neck sweater*

polygon *noun*
a flat shape with at least five straight sides, such as an octagon

polyhedron (*say* pol-i-**hee**-drun) *noun*
a solid figure with many flat sides
•***Word Family:*** the plural is **polyhedrons** or **polyhedra** □ **polyhedral** *adjective*

polystyrene (*say* pol-i-**sty**-reen) *noun*
a stiff, plastic foam used to make insulating material, cups and as a packing material

polythene (*say* **pol**-i-theen) *noun*
a tough, thin plastic used to make bags and as wrapping

pomegranate (*say* **pom**-i-gran-it) *noun*
a round, red fruit with a tough skin and lots of seeds inside
•***Word Origins:*** from an Old French word meaning "many-seeded fruit"

pomp *noun*
solemn and splendid show, especially at an official ceremony: *The coronation was conducted with great pomp*.

pompom *noun*
a ball of coloured wool often used as decoration on a hat or cap

pompous *adjective*
behaving as if you are more important than you are
•***Word Family:*** **pompously** *adverb* **pomposity** *noun*

poncho *noun*
a cloak with a hole in the middle for your head to go through
•***Word Family:*** the plural is **ponchos**
•***Word Origins:*** this word comes from Native American

pond *noun*
a small area of water, surrounded by land: *a fish pond in the garden*

ponder *verb*
to think about something carefully

pontificate (*say* pon-**tif**-i-kit) *noun*
1 the time during which a pope holds office
pontificate (*say* pon-**tif**-i-kate) *verb*
2 to give opinions as if they are the only correct ones

pontoon (1) *noun*
a floating platform used to support a temporary bridge or pier

pontoon (2) *noun*
a card game where you have to try to get closest to twenty-one points

pony *noun*
a small horse
•***Word Family:*** the plural is **ponies**

ponytail *noun*
a hairstyle in which your hair is pulled back and tied so it hangs like a horse's tail

poodle *noun*
a breed of dog with thick, curly hair

pool (1) *noun*
1 a small area of still water: *a swimming pool* 2 a small amount of liquid lying on a surface: *a pool of blood*

pool (2) *noun*
1 something that is shared by several people or organizations: *a typing pool / a car pool* 2 the prize that can be won in some gambling games 3 a game similar to billiards **4 the pools** a way of gambling by guessing the results of football matches: *to do the pools*
pool *verb*
5 to put things together so that everyone can share them: *Three of us pooled our savings to buy an old car*.

poop *noun*
a deck or cabin at the back part of a boat
•***Word Origins:*** from a Latin word for "the stern"

poor *adjective*
1 having very little money or property: *a poor shoemaker* 2 not very good: *poor soil / poor health / a poor excuse* 3 not many or not much: *a poor*

A B C D E F G H I J K L M N O P Q R S T U V W X Y Z

attendance / a poor wage 4 unfortunate: *The poor cat got locked out all night.*
•***Word Family:*** **poorly** *adjective* unwell

pop (1) *verb*
1 to make a short explosive sound: *The champagne cork popped loudly.* 2 to move, come or go suddenly or quickly: *A rabbit popped out of its hole. / Pop the book straight into the bag.* 3 **pop in** to make a brief visit, often unexpected
pop *noun*
4 a short explosive sound: *The balloon burst with a pop.* 5 a fizzy drink
•***Word Family:*** other forms of the verb are **pops, popped, popping**

pop (2) *adjective*
to do with popular music: *a pop song*
•***Word Origins:*** short for *popular*

popcorn *noun*
the burst, puffed kernels of maize grain after they have been heated

Pope *noun*
the bishop of Rome as the head of the Roman Catholic Church
•***Word Origins:*** from a Greek word meaning "father"

poplar *noun*
a tall, straight, thin tree

poppadom *noun*
a thin, crispy circle made from flour, that you eat with Indian food

poppy *noun*
a flower with large red or purple petals
•***Word Family:*** the plural is **poppies**

popular *adjective*
1 liked by many people: *She is very popular. / a popular film* 2 to do with the general public: *popular opinion*
•***Word Family:*** **popularity** *noun* **popularly** *adverb*

populate *verb*
to fill a place with people: *a town populated by miners*

population *noun*
all the people, animals or plants living in a certain area

porcelain (*say* **por**-sa-lin) *noun*
fine china: *a porcelain plate*

porch *noun*
a covered area at the entrance to a building
•***Word Family:*** the plural is **porches**

porcupine (*say* **pork**-yoo-pine) *noun*
a small animal covered with long, thin spines
•***Word Origins:*** from Old French words meaning "pig" and "spiny"

pore (1) *verb*
to study or look at something closely and carefully: *She pored over the map.*

pore (2) *noun*
a very small opening in your skin, through which sweat can pass
•***Word Family:*** **porous** *adjective* allowing liquid or air to pass through

pork *noun*
the meat of a pig

pornography (*say* por-**nog**-ra-fee) *noun*
magazines, videos and so on that show sexual material in a way that many people find offensive
•***Word Family:*** **pornographic** *adjective*

porpoise (*say* **por**-pus) *noun*
a large, sea mammal, related to the whale, which has a short, round snout and swims about in groups
•***Word Family:*** the plural is **porpoise** or **porpoises**
•***Word Origins:*** from Latin words for "pig" and "fish"

porridge *noun*
oats cooked in milk or water until thick and creamy and often eaten for breakfast

port (1) *noun*
1 a town with a harbour and docks where ships load and unload cargo 2 the harbour itself

port (2) *noun*
the left side of a boat or aeroplane when you are facing the front

port (3) *noun*
a strong, sweet, dark-red wine
•***Word Origins:*** first shipped from *Oporto*, a city in Portugal

port (4) *noun*
a small opening on a computer where another piece of equipment, such as a printer, is plugged in

portable *adjective*
able to be carried: *a portable television set*

portcullis *noun*
a strong gate at the entrance to a castle, which can be raised and lowered

porter *noun*
1 someone whose job is to carry luggage, such as at an airport or hotel 2 someone who looks after the entrance to a building, such as a hotel or a college

portfolio *noun*
a flat case for carrying papers
•***Word Family:*** the plural is **portfolios**

porthole *noun*
a small, circular window in the side of a ship

portion *noun*
a segment or share

portrait *noun*
1 a painting, drawing or photograph of someone, usually showing their face 2 a description: *The book gives a vivid portrait of life in medieval times.*
• ***Word Family:*** **portraiture** *noun* the art of painting portraits

portray *verb*
1 to make a painting or drawing of someone
2 to describe something or someone in words
• ***Word Family:*** **portrayal** *noun*

pose *verb*
1 to stand or sit in a particular way, as in front of a camera 2 to pretend to be someone: *The man posed as a doctor.* 3 to ask a question: *The examiner posed several difficult questions.*
pose *noun*
4 a position that your body is in: *a relaxed pose*

poser *noun*
1 a problem or tricky question 2 someone who does things just to get attention

posh *adjective*
fashionable, expensive or upper-class: *a posh hotel / a posh accent*

position (*say* po-**zish**-on) *noun*
1 the place where something is: *We had a good position right at the front.* 2 the way in which something is arranged: *to sit in a cramped position*
3 situation: *You put me in a difficult position.* 4 a job: *to apply for a position in an office* 5 a point of view: *What's your personal position on this?*
position *verb*
6 to put someone or something in a particular position: *The general positioned his troops.*

positive *adjective*
1 meaning or saying yes: *a positive reply to the invitation* 2 absolutely certain: *positive proof*
3 optimistic or hopeful: *a positive attitude*
4 greater than zero 5 lacking electrons: *a positive electrical charge*
• ***Word Family:*** **positively** *adverb* **positiveness** *noun*

posse (*say* **poss**-ee) *noun*
a group of volunteers who help an officer of the law find a criminal or keep order

possess *verb*
to own or have something: *Do you possess many books? / to possess a sense of humour*

possession *noun*
something you own: *The house is my most valuable possession.*

possessive *adjective*
not wanting to share things with other people

possible *adjective*
1 able to be done or happen: *Is it possible to cure such a disease?* 2 likely to be true: *It is possible that she forgot.*
• ***Word Family:*** **possibility** *noun* **possibly** *adverb*

possum *noun*
a small, furry, Australian marsupial with strong arms and legs and a long tail, that lives in trees and is active at night

post (1) *noun*
1 an upright piece of wood or metal used as a support 2 the place where a race starts or finishes: *the winning post*
post *verb*
3 to put up a notice for people to see: *to post advertisements on a wall*

post (2) *noun*
1 the system of sending and delivering letters and parcels 2 a collection or delivery of letters: *the second post*
post *verb*
3 to send letters and parcels by post
• ***Word Family:*** **postage** *noun* the cost of sending letters and parcels by post **postal** *adjective: the postal service*

post (3) *noun*
1 a position or appointment 2 the place where a job or duty is done: *a guard post*

postcard *noun*
a card, usually with a picture on one side and space for a message on the other side, that you can send to someone

postcode *noun*
a group of letters and numbers that are part of your address

poster *noun*
a large picture or printed sheet put up on a wall

posterior *adjective*
1 situated at the back or behind
posterior *noun*
2 the buttocks

posterity (*say* pos-**te**-ri-tee) *noun*
the future generations: *to preserve the environment for posterity*

posthumous (*say* **pos**-tew-mus) *adjective*
happening after someone's death: *a posthumous award for bravery*
• ***Word Family:*** **posthumously** *adverb*

postmark *noun*
an official mark that is stamped on an envelope after it is posted

A B C D E F G H I J K L M N O P Q R S T U V W X Y Z

post-mortem *noun*
a medical examination of a dead body to find out why the person died

postnatal *adjective*
happening soon after the birth of a baby: *a postnatal check-up*

post office *noun*
a place where you can buy stamps, send parcels and so on

postpone *verb*
to move something to a later time: *to postpone the trip for a week*
• ***Word Family:*** **postponement** *noun*

postscript *noun*
a message added at the end of a letter after it has been signed
• ***Word Origins:*** from Latin words meaning "written after"

posture (*say* **pos**-cher) *noun*
the position of your body when you are standing, walking or sitting: *an awkward posture*

posy *noun*
a small bunch of flowers
• ***Word Family:*** the plural is **posies**

pot *noun*
1 a round, deep container: *a cooking pot*
pot *verb*
2 to plant something in a pot: *to pot seedlings*
• ***Word Family:*** other verb forms are **pots, potted, potting**

potassium *noun*
a soft, metallic substance that all living things need

potato *noun*
a round, white plant root eaten as a vegetable
• ***Word Family:*** the plural is **potatoes**

potent *adjective*
full of power or strength: *a potent remedy*
• ***Word Family:*** **potency** *noun* **potently** *adverb*

potential (*say* po-**ten**-shul) *adjective*
1 possible: *your potential classmates*
potential *noun*
2 the possibility of developing or becoming good at something in the future: *to show great potential as a singer*
• ***Word Family:*** **potentially** *adverb*

pothole *noun*
1 a hole in the road 2 a deep hole in the ground

potholing *noun*
exploring underground by climbing down potholes

potion *noun*
a liquid used as a medicine or believed to have magic powers

potpourri (*say* po-**poo**-ree *or* po-poor-**ee**) *noun*
a mixture of dried petals with herbs or spices, which smells nice

potter (1) *verb*
to spend time doing unimportant things in a calm, relaxed manner: *to potter in the garden*

potter (2) *noun*
someone who makes pots from clay

pottery *noun*
1 pots, bowls and plates made by shaping and baking clay 2 a place where pottery is made
• ***Word Family:*** the plural is **potteries**

potty (1) *adjective*
mad or foolish
• ***Word Family:*** other forms are **pottier, pottiest**

potty (2) *noun*
a small pot used as a toilet by young children
• ***Word Family:*** the plural is **potties**

pouch *noun*
1 a small bag 2 a pocket of skin on an animal: *a kangaroo's pouch*
• ***Word Family:*** the plural is **pouches**

poultry (*say* **pole**-tree) *noun*
large birds such as chickens, ducks and turkeys, used as food or kept to supply eggs
• ***Word Family:*** the plural is **poultry**

pounce *verb*
to suddenly leap at and seize something: *The cat pounced on the trembling mouse.*

pound (1) *verb*
1 to hit loudly many times: *He pounded desperately on the door.* 2 to crush: *Pound the garlic to a paste.* 3 to run with heavy, noisy steps: *They pounded up the stairs.*

pound (2) *noun*
1 a measure of weight about equal to half a kilogram 2 a unit of money equal to 100 pence

pound (3) *noun*
1 a place where lost animals are kept 2 a place where cars or bicycles that have been found or towed away are taken, until the owner comes to get them back

pour (*rhymes with* door) *verb*
1 to make something flow or stream: *Pour that milk into a cup.* 2 to rain heavily: *It is pouring outside, so take your coat.* 3 to come in large amounts: *Complaints poured in*

pout (*rhymes with* out) *verb*
to push out your lips as a way of showing that you are cross or sulking

poverty (*say* **pov**-a-tee) *noun*
having little or no money: *to live in poverty*

powder *noun*
1 very small bits of something that has been crushed or ground: *curry powder / talcum powder*
powder *verb*
2 to crush something or make it into powder
3 to cover something with powder: *She powdered her face.*
• *Word Family:* **powdery** *adjective*: *powdery snow*

power *noun*
1 the ability to do something: *Most birds have the power of flight.* 2 control over other people or activities: *She has the power to sack me.*
3 force or strength: *the power of the wind* 4 force or energy that can be used for doing work: *solar power / electrical power* 5 a number written in a small size above and to the right of another number showing how many times that number must be multiplied by itself to get a particular result: *two to the power of three is eight*
power *verb*
6 to supply something, such as a machine, with the force or energy needed to do work: *The machines are all powered by electricity.*
• *Word Family:* **powerful** *adjective* **powerfully** *adverb*

powerless *adjective*
not able to stop something from happening
• *Word Family:* **powerlessness** *noun*

power station *noun*
a large building where electricity is produced

practical *adjective*
1 to do with real situations rather than ideas: *practical experience / Does your invention have any practical value?* 2 good at doing useful jobs: *a practical person* 3 sensible and realistic: *a practical solution to a problem*
• *Word Family:* **practically** *adverb* nearly or almost: *We're practically there now.*

practical joke *noun*
a trick that you play on someone

practice *noun*
1 the actual doing of something, rather than the idea of it: *How will your plan turn out in practice?* 2 doing something many times so that you get better at it: *It takes years of practice to play golf well.* 3 the usual way that something is done: *It is the practice in that country to marry young.* 4 the business of a professional person: *a legal practice*

practise *verb*
1 to do something many times so that you get better at it: *Practise the piano and you'll quickly improve.* 2 to do something as a usual habit: *to practise what you preach* 3 to work at a profession: *to practise medicine*
• *Word Family:* **practised** *adjective* experienced: *The baker kneaded the dough with practised hands.*

practitioner (*say* prak-**tish**-en-a) *noun*
someone who practises a profession: *A doctor is a medical practitioner.*

prairie *noun*
a wide, grassy, treeless plain

praise (*say* praze) *verb*
1 to say that you like or admire someone or something
praise *noun*
2 strong approval
• *Word Family:* **praiseworthy** *adjective* admirable

pram *noun*
a cot on wheels for carrying a baby

prance *verb*
to walk with high quick steps: *The horse pranced around the circus ring.*

prank *noun*
a practical joke

prattle *verb*
1 to chatter about things that aren't important
prattle *noun*
2 meaningless chatter

prawn *noun*
a small shellfish that you can eat

pray *verb*
to talk to a god or saint to ask for something or to give praise or thanks: *to pray for a miracle*
• *Word Family:* **prayer** *noun*

prayer mat *noun*
a mat used by Muslims to pray on

praying mantis *noun*
a large insect that presses its front legs together as if it is praying

preach *verb*
1 to give a sermon 2 to give someone advice that they don't want: *to preach about tidiness*
• *Word Family:* **preacher** *noun*

precarious (*say* pre-**care**-i-us) *adjective*
not at all safe or secure: *a precarious hold on a slippery cliff*
• *Word Family:* **precariously** *adverb*

precaution (*say* pre-**kaw**-shon) *noun*
something that you do to stop something unpleasant or dangerous from happening in the future: *Lock the house as a precaution against thieves.*
• *Word Family:* **precautionary** *adjective*

A B C D E F G H I J K L M N O P Q R S T U V W X Y Z

precede (*say* pree-**seed**) *verb*
to come or go in front of or before something or someone: *Spring precedes summer.*
•***Word Family:*** **precedence** (*say* **pree**-si-dunce *or* **pres**-i-dunce) *noun*

precinct (*say* **pree**-sinkt) *noun*
1 the area immediately around a place, such as the grounds of a church 2 an area that can only be used by a particular group or for a particular activity: *a pedestrian precinct*

precious (*say* **presh**-us) *adjective*
very valuable: *A diamond is a precious stone. / to spend a few precious moments together*

precipice (*say* **pres**-i-pis) *noun*
the very steep edge of a cliff

precipitate (*say* pre-**sip**-i-tate) *verb*
1 to make something happen more quickly: *Swearing at the boss precipitated your dismissal.*
2 to change from water-vapour into rain, hail or dew
•***Word Family:*** **precipitately** *adverb*

precipitation (*say* pre-sip-i-**tay**-shon) *noun*
moisture falling from the sky as rain, snow or hail

precis (*say* **pray**-see) *noun*
a short piece of writing which contains the most important points of a longer piece

precise (*say* pre-**sice**) *adjective*
1 accurate: *Give me precise directions.* 2 exact: *At that precise moment, the siren blew.*
•***Word Family:*** **precisely** *adverb* **precision** *noun*

precocious (*say* pre-**koe**-shus) *adjective*
more developed or advanced than others of the same age: *a precocious child*
•***Word Family:*** **precociously** *adverb*

predator (*say* **pred**-a-ter) *noun*
an animal that lives by feeding on other animals
•***Word Family:*** **predatory** *adjective*

predecessor (*say* **pree**-da-ses-a) *noun*
a person who did the job before: *My predecessor retired after 40 years in office.*

predicament (*say* pre-**dik**-a-ment) *noun*
a difficult or unpleasant situation

predict *verb*
to say in advance that something will happen: *The weather bureau predicts rain.*
•***Word Family:*** **predictable** *adjective: I knew you'd choose that meal—you're so predictable!* **prediction** *noun: The fortune-teller's prediction came true.*

preen *verb*
1 to clean and smooth the feathers with the beak, as birds do 2 to make your hair and clothes look neat and tidy

prefabricate (*say* pree-**fab**-ri-kate) *verb*
to make in parts in a factory so they can be easily carried and put together later at any place: *to prefabricate a shed*
•***Word Family:*** **prefabrication** *noun*

preface (*say* **pref**-is) *noun*
1 a note by the author at the beginning of a book explaining why it was written and what it is about
preface *verb*
2 to write or say something before the main part of a book or speech: *to preface your remarks*

prefect (*say* **pree**-fekt) *noun*
a senior pupil with certain powers to help keep order in a school

prefer *verb*
to like something or someone better: *Do you prefer tea or coffee?*
•***Word Family:*** other verb forms are **prefers, preferred, preferring** □ **preferable** *adjective* **preferably** *adverb* **preference** *noun*

prefix (*say* **pre**-fiks) *noun*
a word part which is added at the beginning of a word to make a new word, such as "re-" in *revisit* and "mis-" in *misfire*

pregnant *adjective*
having a baby growing in your womb
•***Word Family:*** **pregnancy** *noun*

prehistoric (*say* pree-his-**to**-rik) *adjective*
to do with the time before events were written down
•***Word Family:*** **prehistory** *noun*

prejudice (*say* **prej**-a-dis) *noun*
1 an opinion that someone has without a good reason, or without knowing about something: *Although he has never met one, he has a prejudice against Australians.*
prejudice *verb*
2 to influence: *Her actions prejudiced me in her favour.*
•***Word Family:*** **prejudiced** *adjective* **prejudicial** *adjective: Smoking can be prejudicial to your health.*

preliminary (*say* pre-**lim**-in-aree) *adjective*
coming before the main activity: *First I shall make a preliminary statement.*

prelude (*say* **prel**-yood) *noun*
1 something that comes before the main event or action 2 a short piece of music for the piano or organ
•***Word Origins:*** from a Latin word meaning "to play beforehand"

premature (*say* **prem**-a-cha *or* **prem**-a-tyor) *adjective*
happening before the proper or usual time: *a premature baby*
•*Word Family:* **prematurely** *adverb*

premier (*say* **prem**-ee-a) *noun*
1 the leader of a government
premier *adjective*
2 most important: *the premier university in the country* 3 winning or champion: *the premier team*
•*Word Family:* **premiership** *noun*

premiere (*say* prem-ee-**air**) *noun*
the first public performance of a play or film

premises (*say* **prem**-i-ses) *plural noun*
a building and the land belonging to it: *Be off the school premises by 6 o'clock.*

premium *noun*
1 a payment for insurance: *monthly premiums*
2 **at a premium** rare or above normal price

premium bond *noun*
a ticket for a special lottery run by the government, which you keep for a long time

prenatal (*say* pree-**nay**-tul) *adjective*
to do with the time before birth: *prenatal tests*

preoccupy (*say* pree-**ok**-yoo-pie) *verb*
to take up all your attention: *Thoughts of the holidays preoccupy my mind.*
•*Word Family:* other verb forms are **preoccupies, preoccupied, preoccupying** □ **preoccupation** *noun* **preoccupied** *adjective*

preparatory (*say* pri-**pa**-ra-ter-i) *adjective*
preparing for something

prepare *verb*
to get or make ready: *Prepare to leave at once. / We all prepared lunch.*
•*Word Family:* **preparation** *noun*

preposition (*say* prep-pa-**zish**-on) *noun*
a word used before a noun or pronoun to show how it connects with other words in the sentence, such as "on" in *The book is on the table*, and "by" in *I need the book by tomorrow.*

preposterous (*say* pre-**pos**-tu-rus) *adjective*
totally unreasonable or absurd: *a preposterous price*
•*Word Family:* **preposterously** *adverb*

prerogative (*say* pre-**rog**-u-tiv) *noun*
a special privilege or power that someone has because of the position they hold: *The King has the prerogative to free the prisoners.*

prescribe *verb*
to order something as a treatment for illness: *She prescribed several months' rest. / to prescribe antibiotics*
•*Word Family:* **prescription** *noun* a written instruction from a doctor to a chemist for a particular medicine

presence (*say* **prez**-unce) *noun*
being in a particular place: *The show will be in the presence of the Queen. / Don't say that in his presence.*

present (1) (*say* **prez**-unt) *adjective*
1 being or happening now: *the present headmaster / the present time* 2 being in a place: *Were you present at the meeting?*
present *noun*
3 the present time
•*Word Family:* **presently** *adverb* soon

present (2) (*say* **prez**-unt) *noun*
1 something that you give someone: *a birthday present*
present (*say* pri-**zent**) *verb*
2 to give or award someone something: *He was presented with first prize.* 3 to show or introduce someone or something: *to present a report / I'd like to present a great new pop group!*
•*Word Family:* **presentable** *adjective* fit to be seen **presenter** *noun* someone who introduces people or items on a television show **presentation** *noun*

present tense *noun*
the form of the verb that shows the action is taking place at the present time, as in "go" in *I go.* and "is running" in *She is running.*

preservative *noun*
a chemical added to a food to make it last longer

preserve (*say* pre-**zerv**) *verb*
1 to keep something whole or safe: *to preserve wilderness* 2 to treat food so that it will last longer: *to preserve fruit in bottles*
preserve *noun*
3 jam: *raspberry preserve*
•*Word Family:* **preservation** *noun*

president *noun*
1 someone chosen or elected to lead a group or meeting: *the president of a company* 2 the elected leader of a republic, as in France or the United States
•*Word Family:* **presidency** *noun* **presidential** *adjective*

press *verb*
1 to put steady weight or force on somerthing: *She pressed the doorbell impatiently.* 2 to make something flat by putting weight on it: *to press flowers* 3 to iron clothes: *to press a shirt*
press *noun*
4 newspapers and magazines and the people who write for them 5 a machine for printing on

paper **6** a machine that presses or squeezes: *a garlic press*

press-up *noun*
an excercise in which you lie face down and push yourself up using your arms

pressure (*say* **presh**-a) *noun*
1 the action of putting weight or force onto something **2** the amount of this weight or force in a particular area: *air pressure* **3** worry and difficulty: *The pressures of work were exhausting.*
pressure *verb*
4 to make someone do something: *He pressured us to sign the contract.*

pressurize or **pressurise** *verb*
1 to keep the normal air pressure in an enclosed space, such as in the cabin of an aeroplane **2** to try to force someone to do something

prestige (*say* pres-**teezh**) *noun*
respect or admiration that something has because it is very good, successful or expensive
• ***Word Family:*** **prestigious** *adjective*: *a prestigious company to work for*

presumably *adverb*
probably: *Presumably, he didn't want to come.*

presume *verb*
1 to believe something is a fact: *I presume that this is your mother.* **2** to dare: *I would not presume to contradict you.*

presumptuous *adjective*
too bold or cheeky

pretence *noun*
1 a false display: *His pretence of anger was not very convincing.* **2** claim: *I make no pretence to cleverness.*

pretend *verb*
1 to act in a way that will trick or mislead someone: *I'm sure she's only pretending to be sick.* **2** to make believe: *Let's pretend we're rich.*
pretend *adjective*
3 make believe or imaginary: *We're in a pretend ship.*

pretentious (*say* pre-**ten**-shus) *adjective*
making false or exaggerated claims of wealth, importance or merit: *a pretentious film / What a pretentious name for a cat!*
• ***Word Family:*** **pretentiousness** *noun*

pretty *adjective*
1 pleasing in appearance: *a pretty design / a pretty child*
pretty *adverb*
2 reasonably or moderately: *She paints pretty well for a beginner.*
• ***Word Family:*** other forms of the adjective are **prettier, prettiest**

prevail *verb*
to win through after a struggle: *Finally sense prevailed and the trees were saved.*

prevalent (*say* **prev**-a-lunt) *adjective*
widespread or common: *diseases prevalent in past times*

prevent *verb*
to stop something from happening: *It was difficult to prevent a fight.*
• ***Word Family:*** **prevention** *noun* **preventive** or **preventative** *adjective*: *Take preventative measures to stop your house being burgled.*

preview *noun*
1 a viewing of something before it is officially open to the public: *a film preview*
preview *verb*
2 to give a preview of a film, play and so on

previous (*say* **pree**-vi-us) *adjective*
earlier or former: *at a previous meeting / the previous bank manager*
• ***Word Family:*** **previously** *adverb*

prey (*say* pray) *noun*
1 an animal killed by another animal for food
2 a victim: *Tourists were the unsuspecting prey of local shopkeepers.*
prey *verb*
3 **prey on (a)** to hunt for prey: *Tigers prey on smaller animals.* **(b)** to make you worried: *Don't let it prey on your mind.*

price *noun*
1 the amount of money that something costs
price *verb*
2 to put a price on something
• ***Word Family:*** **pricey** *adjective* expensive **(pricier, priciest)**

priceless *adjective*
very valuable: *priceless rubies*

prick *verb*
1 to make a small hole with a sharp point: *to prick your finger with a pin*
prick *noun*
2 a hole or mark made by pricking **3** the feeling of being pricked: *He felt a sharp prick.*

prickle *noun*
1 a small, sharp point or thorn: *prickles on a hedgehog*
prickle *verb*
2 to give a sharp, tingling sensation: *This jumper prickles me.*
• ***Word Family:*** **prickly** *adjective* **(pricklier, prickliest)**

pride *noun*
1 a feeling of pleasure or satisfaction when you have done something well: *She felt great pride on*

receiving the award. 2 a feeling of being better than other people: *His pride and arrogance lost him many friends.* 3 a group of lions 4 **pride of place** the most important position: *He gave the trophy pride of place on the mantelpiece.*
pride *verb*
5 **pride yourself on** to be pleased with, or proud of something you have done

priest *noun*
someone whose job is to perform religious duties and ceremonies
•***Word Family:*** **priestess** *noun* the feminine form of priest □ **priesthood** *noun: to train for the priesthood*

prim *adjective*
neat and proper; not liking rudeness
•***Word Family:*** **primly** *adverb* **primness** *noun*

primary (*say* **pry**-ma-ree) *adjective*
first, chief or main: *primary education / of primary importance*
•***Word Family:*** **primarily** *adverb*

primary colour *noun*
red, yellow or blue, the colours which you can use to mix all the other colours

primary school *noun*
a school for children aged between 5 and 11

primate (*say* **pry**-mate) *noun*
1 a mammal of the group that includes humans, monkeys and apes 2 the main bishop of a Christian church in a country or region

prime *adjective*
most important or best: *prime minister / prime reason / prime beef*

prime minister *noun*
the leader of the government

prime number *noun*
a number that can only be divided exactly by itself and the number 1: *13 is a prime number.*

primer (*say* **pry**-ma) *noun*
a coat of paint used to prepare a bare surface for the main coat of paint

primeval or **primaeval** (*say* pry-**mee**-vul) *adjective*
to do with the earliest period of the Earth

primitive (*say* **prim**-i-tiv) *adjective*
1 in the earliest stage or form of something: *primitive technology / primitive life* 2 rough, simple or crude: *She built a primitive shelter of bark and foliage.*

primrose *noun*
a pale, yellow flower

prince *noun*
a son or other male relation of a king or queen
•***Word Family:*** **princely** *adjective* (**a**) to do with a prince (**b**) splendid or generous: *a princely sum*

princess *noun*
1 a daughter or other female relation of a king or queen 2 the wife of a prince

principal (*say* **prin**-si-pul) *adjective*
1 first in order of importance: *our principal problem*
principal *noun*
2 someone in charge of a school or college
•***Word Family:*** **principally** *adverb*

principle (*say* **prin**-si-pul) *noun*
1 a rule or truth: *a scientific principle* 2 a belief you have about how you should behave: *a man of principle*

print *noun*
1 a mark made on a surface by pressing on it: *a footprint* 2 a copy made by pressing an inked surface on to paper or other material
print *verb*
3 to make a number of copies by pressing such things as inked type, a design or a picture on to a surface 4 to write with separated letters, rather than joined-up letters

printed circuit *noun*
an electric circuit which has a thin line of metal on a board

printer *noun*
someone or something that prints: *a book printer / a computer printer*

printout *noun*
information from a computer printed on paper by a machine attached to the computer

prior (*say* **pry**-or) *adjective*
coming before something else in time, order or importance: *She couldn't come, because she had a prior engagement.*

priority (*say* pry-**o**-ri-tee) *noun*
1 something that is important or urgent: *Getting food is a priority.* 2 the right to go first because of importance or urgency: *His age gives him priority over us.*

priory *noun*
a place where a group of monks or a group of nuns lives
•***Word Family:*** the plural is **priories**

prise *verb*
to move or force something up with a lever: *to prise off the lid*

prism (*say* **priz**-um) *noun*
a solid, transparent object made of glass or plastic, usually with a triangular base and many flat sides, able to separate light into the colours of the rainbow

A B C D E F G H I J K L M N O P Q R S T U V W X Y Z

prison *noun*
a place where criminals are locked up as punishment
•***Word Family:*** **prisoner** *noun* someone who is kept in captivity or in a prison □ see also **imprison**

pristine (*say* **pris**-teen) *adjective*
undamaged or as new: *in pristine condition*

private (*say* **pry**-vit) *adjective*
1 not seen, used or shared by other people: *a private discussion / private property* 2 to do with your personal life: *It is his private affair and has nothing to do with us. / a private opinion*
private *noun*
3 the lowest rank in the army
•***Word Family:*** **privacy** *noun* **privately** *adverb*

private school *noun*
a school which does not get money from the government but charges its pupils fees instead

privatize or **privatise** *verb*
to sell a company or business owned by the government to private buyers: *to privatize a government-owned airline*

privilege *noun*
a special advantage that a person has
•***Word Family:*** **privileged** *adjective: a privileged childhood*

prize (1) *noun*
something that you get as a reward for winning a race or competition

prize (2) *verb*
to value something highly: *I prize these books above all my possessions.*

pro (1) *noun*
1 **pros and cons** the facts and arguments for and against something: *The pros and cons of living in the country.*
pro *preposition*
2 in favour of: *He is pro the government.*

pro (2) *noun*
a professional

probability *noun*
1 something that is likely to happen: *There is a probability that the aeroplane will be late.* 2 the chance of something happening: *the probability of throwing a six*

probable *adjective*
expected to happen or be true
•***Word Family:*** **probably** *adverb*

probation (*say* pro-**bay**-shon) *noun*
1 a trial period, such as for a new employee
2 the system of letting someone who has broken the law stay out of prison if they promise to behave well in the future
•***Word Family:*** **probationary** *adjective: a probationary teacher*

probe *noun*
1 a close examination or investigation
probe *verb*
2 to examine something closely

problem *noun*
1 someone or something that causes difficulties: *the problem of pollution / The leaking roof is a problem. / a weight problem* 2 a question to be solved: *a maths problem*
•***Word Family:*** **problematic** *adjective*

procedure (*say* pro-**seed**-yer) *noun*
a way of doing something: *Is there a set procedure for this type of job?*

proceed (*say* pro-**seed**) *verb*
to continue, especially after you have stopped

proceedings *plural noun*
1 a series of events happening in one place: *They watched the proceedings from an upstairs window.* 2 a record of the activities of a club or society 3 a lawsuit: *to start legal proceedings*

proceeds (*say* **pro**-seeds) *plural noun*
money from an activity: *The proceeds from the sale will go to charity.*

process *noun*
1 a series of actions or changes that are part of doing something: *the process of digestion / Packing the glasses was a slow process.*
process *verb*
2 to treat or prepare something, especially to make products that can be used or sold: *to process film / to process food*

procession (*say* pro-**sesh**-on) *noun*
a line or group of people or vehicles moving along as part of a ceremony or public entertainment

proclaim *verb*
to announce something in public
•***Word Family:*** **proclamation** *noun*

procrastinate (*say* pro-**kras**-ti-nate) *verb*
to put off doing something
•***Word Family:*** **procrastination** *noun*

prod *verb*
1 to poke or push something or someone with a pointed object
prod *noun*
2 a pointed instrument used for prodding: *a cattle prod*
•***Word Family:*** other verb forms are **prods, prodded, prodding**

prodigal (*say* **prod**-i-gul) *adjective*
carelessly wasteful

prodigy (*say* **prod**-i-jee) *noun*
someone, especially a child, who is extraordinarily clever or talented
• ***Word Family:*** the plural is **prodigies**

produce (*say* pro-**dewce**) *verb*
1 to make, create or show something: *The rabbit produced five offspring. / The novelist produced a new book. / The defence lawyer produced new evidence.*
produce (*say* **prod**-yooce) *noun*
2 something that has been produced: *potatoes and other farm produce*
• ***Word Family:*** **producer** *noun*

product *noun*
1 something made 2 the result of multiplying two or more numbers together: *20 is the product of 4 and 5.*

production *noun*
1 making, creating or showing something 2 the amount that is produced 3 a play, film or show

productive *adjective*
1 producing a lot 2 useful: *a productive meeting*
• ***Word Family:*** **productively** *adverb*
productivity *noun* the amount that is produced: *The factory will have to improve its productivity.*

profess *verb*
to declare, often insincerely: *She professes to be a friend.*

profession *noun*
1 a job, especially one that you train for: *She is a dentist by profession.* 2 all the people working at such a job: *the teaching profession*

professional *adjective*
1 to do with a profession: *to get professional advice* 2 doing a job for money, rather than as a hobby: *a professional photographer*
professional *noun*
3 someone who does a job for money, rather than as a hobby 4 someone who does something to a high standard, with great skill
• ***Word Family:*** **professionalism** *noun* **professionally** *adverb: to take up boxing professionally*

professor (*say* pro-**fes**-a) *noun*
an important teacher in a university

proficient (*say* pro-**fish**-unt) *adjective*
skilled or expert in something: *a proficient teacher*
• ***Word Family:*** **proficiency** *noun: a test of cycling proficiency* **proficiently** *adverb*

profile *noun*
1 an outline showing the side view of a face 2 an article about someone in a magazine or newspaper

profit *noun*
1 an advantage or benefit: *His trip overseas was of great profit to his studies.* 2 an amount of money that you make by selling something for more than it cost
profit *verb*
3 to get a profit or benefit: *to profit from experience*
• ***Word Family:*** **profitable** *adjective: The school tuck-shop is very profitable.* **profitably** *adverb*

profound *adjective*
1 very deep: *profound knowledge* 2 thoughtful: *a profound remark*
• ***Word Family:*** **profoundly** *adverb*

profuse (*say* pro-**fewce**) *adjective*
abundant: *profuse apologies*
• ***Word Family:*** **profusely** *adverb* **profusion** *noun*
• ***Word Origins:*** from a Latin word meaning "poured forth"

prognosis *noun*
a forecast or prediction, especially a doctor's opinion on how a disease will develop
• ***Word Family:*** the plural is **prognoses** (*say* prog-**no**-seez) □ **prognostic** *adjective*

program *noun*
1 a list of instructions given to a computer to make it perform certain tasks
program *verb*
2 to give instructions to a computer
• ***Word Family:*** other verb forms are **programs, programmed, programming** □ **programmer** *noun*

programme *noun*
1 a performance or show: *a television programme* 2 a list of events: *a concert programme* 3 a plan of activities: *a full programme of events*

progress (*say* **pro**-gress) *noun*
1 working towards achieving or completing something: *The builder is making good progress with the house.* 2 **in progress** under way or taking place: *The meeting is in progress.*
progress (*say* pro-**gress**) *verb*
3 to move forward, advance or develop
• ***Word Family:*** **progression** *noun* **progressive** *adjective*

prohibit *verb*
to forbid something: *Smoking is prohibited.*
• ***Word Family:*** **prohibition** *noun*

project (*say* **proj**-ekt) *noun*
1 a scheme or plan: *a project for building houses where the old factory stood* 2 a special piece of school work where you try to find out about a subject: *a project on the discovery of gold*

project (*say* pro-**jekt**) *verb*
3 to jut out: *The shelf projected from the wall.* 4 to throw your voice 5 to show a film or picture on a screen: *to project slides onto a wall*

projectile *noun*
1 something fired from a gun 2 something thrown

projector *noun*
a machine for showing films or slides on a screen
• ***Word Family:*** **projectionist** *noun* someone who operates a projector

prolific *adjective*
producing things in large amounts: *a prolific writer / a prolific grape vine*

prologue (*say* **pro**-log) *noun*
1 the part that introduces a play or a book 2 an act or event that introduces something else

prolong *verb*
to make something last longer: *to prolong your stay*

promenade (*say* prom-a-**nahd**) *noun*
1 a slow walk for pleasure 2 a public place for walking, especially along a waterfront
promenade *verb*
3 to take a slow walk

prominent *adjective*
1 standing out so that you can easily see it: *a prominent peak in the mountain range / a prominent nose* 2 important or well-known: *a prominent artist*
• ***Word Family:*** **prominence** *noun* **prominently** *adverb*: *to display your photo prominently*

promise (*say* **prom**-is) *noun*
1 saying that you will do something 2 a sign of future success: *The child shows great promise.*
promise *verb*
3 to say that you will do something
• ***Word Family:*** **promising** *adjective*

promontory (*say* **prom**-en-te-ree) *noun*
a high piece of land which juts out into the sea or a lake
• ***Word Family:*** the plural is **promontories**

promote *verb*
1 to move someone to a more important job: *to be promoted to chief accountant* 2 to advertise something so that you can sell it more easily: *She promotes a pop group.*
• ***Word Family:*** **promoter** *noun* **promotion** *noun*

prompt *adjective*
1 without delay: *a prompt reply*
prompt *verb*
2 to encourage or inspire you to do something: *Mum prompted me to say "thank you".* 3 to remind an actor of the next lines in a play
prompt *noun*
4 a message on a computer screen that shows the computer is waiting for further instructions
• ***Word Family:*** **promptly** *adverb* **promptness** *noun*

prone *adjective*
1 likely to do or have something: *He is prone to accidents.* 2 lying flat or still, especially face downwards

pronoun *noun*
a word used in place of a noun: *"It", "that", "they" and "she" are pronouns.*

pronounce *verb*
1 to make the sounds of a word or phrase: *How do you pronounce your last name?* 2 to state or declare something officially or formally: *The judge pronounced the death sentence.*
• ***Word Family:*** **pronouncement** *noun* **pronunciation** *noun*

proof *noun*
1 evidence that shows for certain that something is true: *The police have proof that he committed the crime.*
proof *adjective*
2 giving protection against: *proof against fire*

prop (1) *verb*
1 to support or hold something in a particular position: *Prop that chair against the door to keep it open.*
prop *noun*
2 something that acts as a support: *a prop for a clothes line*
• ***Word Family:*** other verb forms are **props, propped, propping**

prop (2) *noun*
an object or piece of furniture used on stage in a play or opera
• ***Word Origins:*** a short form of **property**

propaganda *noun*
information, often biased, which is spread to try to make people believe something

propagate (*say* **prop**-a-gate) *verb*
to increase, grow or spread: *to propagate the species / to propagate tomatoes / to propagate rumours*
• ***Word Family:*** **propagation** *noun* **propagator** *noun*

propel (*say* pro-**pel**) *verb*
to push or drive something forward
• ***Word Family:*** other verb forms are **propels, propelled, propelling**

propellant (*say* pro-**pel**-unt) *noun*
something used to push another thing forwards, such as an explosive in a gun or the compressed gas in an aerosol container

propeller *noun*
a device with blades that spin, used to drive a ship or aircraft forward

proper *adjective*
1 suitable or correct: *the proper way to do it / Jeans aren't the proper thing to wear to a wedding.* 2 real: *Is this a proper compass?* 3 respectable 4 complete or thorough: *a proper fool*
• *Word Family:* **properly** *adverb*

proper noun *noun*
a noun that is the name of a person or place, such as *Joe* or *Newcastle*

property (*say* **prop**-a-tee) *noun*
1 all the things that belong to someone 2 a particular piece of land that someone owns: *railway property* 3 a characteristic that something has: *to investigate the properties of salt*
• *Word Family:* the plural is **properties**

prophecy (*say* **prof**-a-see) *noun*
a prediction
• *Word Family:* the plural is **prophecies**

prophesy (*say* **prof**-a-sigh) *verb*
to predict or forecast something: *to prophesy an earthquake*
• *Word Family:* other verb forms are **prophesies, prophesied, prophesying**

prophet (*say* **prof**-it) *noun*
1 someone who can predict future events 2 a religious leader or great teacher

proportion *noun*
1 a part: *A large proportion of the class failed the exam.* 2 the relationship between one thing and another according to size, quantity or importance: *What is the proportion of flour to water in this dough?* 3 a correct or balanced relationship: *The size of the house is not in proportion to the garden.*
• *Word Family:* **proportional** *adjective* **proportionally** *adverb* **proportionate** *adjective*

propose *verb*
to suggest something: *to propose a new law*
• *Word Family:* **proposal** *noun* **proposition** *noun*

proprietor *noun*
an owner of a business

propulsion (*say* pro-**pul**-shon) *noun*
the power or force that drives something forward

prose (*say* proze) *noun*
ordinary writing with no rhythm or pattern, in contrast to poetry

prosecute (*say* **pros**-i-kewt) *verb*
to take legal action against someone
• *Word Family:* **prosecution** *noun* **prosecutor** *noun*

prospect (*say* **pros**-pekt) *noun*
1 a future possibility or chance: *There is little prospect of the weather improving.* 2 a wide view
prospect (*say* pro-**spekt**) *verb*
3 to search for gold or other valuable minerals
• *Word Family:* **prospector** *noun* someone who searches for valuable minerals

prosper *verb*
to be successful: *The company prospered under the new director.*
• *Word Family:* **prosperity** *noun* success or wealth **prosperous** *adjective* rich and successful

prostate gland *noun*
a gland at the base of the bladder in males

prostitute *noun*
someone who has sex in return for money
• *Word Family:* **prostitution** *noun*

protagonist *noun*
the main character in a story or play

protect *verb*
to keep or guard someone or something from harm or attack
• *Word Family:* **protection** *noun* **protective** *adjective* **protectively** *adverb* **protector** *noun*

protectorate (*say* pro-**tek**-ta-rit) *noun*
a country protected and partly controlled by a stronger country

protégé (*say* **pro**-ta-zhay) *noun*
someone who is helped and looked after by someone more powerful or important
• *Word Origins:* from a French word meaning "protected"

protein (*say* **pro**-teen) *noun*
a substance found in foods, that helps to make your body strong and healthy

protest (*say* pro-**test**) *verb*
1 to object: *I must protest at such rudeness.* 2 to declare: *to protest your innocence*
protest (*say* **pro**-test) *noun*
3 a demonstration of disapproval: *a protest against nuclear testing*
• *Word Family:* **protester** *noun* **protestation** *noun*

Protestant (*say* **prot**-is-tunt) *noun*
a member of one of the Christian Churches that separated from the Roman Catholic Church from the 16th century onwards
• *Word Family:* **Protestantism** *noun*

protocol *noun*
rules about the correct way to behave at important official occasions, such as meeting a king or prime minister

proton *noun*
a tiny, positively charged particle inside an atom

A B C D E F G H I J K L M N O P Q R S T U V W X Y Z

protoplasm *noun*
the colourless substance like jelly from which animal and plant cells are made

prototype *noun*
the first example of something, from which other forms are developed

protractor *noun*
a device for measuring angles, usually in the shape of a semi-circle

protrude *verb*
to jut out: *Her lower lip protruded sulkily.*
•***Word Family:*** **protrusion** *noun*

proud *adjective*
1 feeling very pleased or satisfied: *He was very proud of his daughter's success.* 2 feeling more important than others: *too proud to help in the kitchen*
•***Word Family:*** **proudly** *adverb* ☐ see also **pride**

prove *verb*
1 to show that something is true or genuine: *Can you prove that you are 18?* 2 to turn out: *It proved to be a terrible mistake.*
•***Word Family:*** other forms of the word are **proves, proved, proved** or **proves, proven, proving**

proverb *noun*
a short saying, usually containing a useful or well-known belief or truth, such as *An apple a day keeps the doctor away.*
•***Word Family:*** **proverbial** *adjective* **proverbially** *adverb*

provide *verb*
to supply something
•***Word Family:*** **provider** *noun* someone who earns money to support a family

provided *conjunction*
on the condition that: *You may come provided you don't mess about.*

province *noun*
1 a part or division of a country 2 a special area of knowledge: *That problem is outside my province.*

provincial (*say* pro-**vin**-shul) *adjective*
1 to do with a province or provinces away from the main cities: *provincial newspapers*
2 narrow-minded

provision *noun*
1 supplying or providing something: *Let's organize the provision of food.* 2 **provisions** supplies, especially of food: *provisions for the trip*
•***Word Family:*** **provisional** *adjective* temporary: *a provisional driving licence* **provisionally** *adverb*

provoke *verb*
1 to annoy someone: *His teasing provoked me to hit him.* 2 to lead to something: *to provoke a reaction*
•***Word Family:*** **provocation** *noun* **provocative** *adjective*: *provocative remarks*

prowess (*say* **prow**-ess) *noun*
great skill or ability

prowl *verb*
to move about in a quiet, careful way, especially when searching for prey or for something to steal
•***Word Family:*** **prowler** *noun* someone who prowls

proximity (*say* prok-**sim**-i-tee) *noun*
1 nearness 2 **in the proximity of** near

proxy *noun*
someone who is allowed to do something on behalf of someone else, such as to vote
•***Word Family:*** the plural is **proxies**

prude *noun*
someone who is easily shocked by rude or embarrassing things
•***Word Family:*** **prudish** *adjective* **prudishly** *adverb*

prudent *adjective*
acting in a cautious, sensible way: *It was a prudent decision to save the money.*
•***Word Family:*** **prudence** *noun* **prudently** *adverb*

prune (1) *noun*
a purplish-black dried plum

prune (2) *verb*
to cut branches or parts off plants to make them grow better

pry *verb*
to try to find out about someone else's business or look at their personal things: *I don't mean to pry, but are you O.K?*
•***Word Family:*** other forms are **pries, pried, prying**

PS *abbreviation*
short for postscript

psalm (*say* sarm) *noun*
a religious song or poem, especially from the Bible

pseudonym (*say* **syoo**-du-nim) *noun*
a name used by an author instead of his or her real name: *Charlotte Brontë wrote under the pseudonym of Currer Bell.*

psychiatry (*say* sigh-**kie**-a-tree) *noun*
the study and treatment of mental illness
•***Word Family:*** **psychiatric** (*say* sigh-kee-**at**-rik) *adjective* **psychiatrist** *noun* a doctor who treats mental illness

psychic (*say* **sigh**-kik) *adjective*
to do with such powers as being able to read someone's mind or tell the future

psychology (*say* sigh-**kol**-a-jee) *noun*
the study of people's minds and the way people behave
• ***Word Family:*** **psychological** *adjective* to do with how your mind works **psychologically** *adverb* **psychologist** *noun* someone who studies how people's minds work

pub *noun*
a building where alcoholic drinks are served
• ***Word Origins:*** short for "public house"

puberty (*say* **pew**-ba-tee) *noun*
the time when you start to become an adult, and your body starts to change
• ***Word Origins:*** from a Latin word meaning "adult"

pubic (*say* **pew**-bik) *adjective*
to do with the part of your body near your sexual organs: *pubic hair*

public *adjective*
1 for all the people of a place or country: *public transport* 2 open to all people: *a public meeting*
public *noun*
3 all the people in a particular community or country 4 **in public** in front of other people

publication (*say* pub-li-**kay**-shon) *noun*
1 something that is published, such as a book or magazine 2 the publishing of something

publicity (*say* pub-**lis**-i-tee) *noun*
information or advertisements that tell you about something and make you want to see it or buy it
• ***Word Family:*** **publicize** or **publicise** *verb* to tell people about something: *to publicize the school fair*

public relations *plural noun*
the methods that companies use to make a good impression on the public

publish *verb*
1 to print a book, magazine or newspaper 2 to be the author of a book: *She has published five books so far.*
• ***Word Family:*** **publisher** *noun*

puce (*say* **pewce**) *noun*
a dark, purplish-brown colour

pucker *verb*
to gather something into wrinkles or folds: *to pucker up your lips / The fabric became puckered.*

pudding *noun*
1 a soft sweet food served as dessert 2 the dessert course of a meal 3 a savoury food made with pastry or flour: *a steak and kidney pudding / Yorkshire pudding*

puddle *noun*
a small pool of liquid, such as muddy rainwater

puff *noun*
1 a short, quick blowing of breath, air or smoke: *a puff of wind*
puff *verb*
2 to blow out or breathe with puffs: *She puffed after running uphill. / The train puffed along.*
3 **puff up** to swell
• ***Word Family:*** **puffed** *adjective* out of breath

puffin *noun*
a black and white sea bird with a large, colourful beak, which is found in the North Atlantic

pugnacious (*say* pug-**nay**-shus) *adjective*
quarrelsome or aggressive
• ***Word Family:*** **pugnaciously** *adverb*

pull (*rhymes with* wool) *verb*
1 to move something by tugging it: *The horse pulled a cart.* 2 to move in a particular direction: *The car pulled out onto the road.*
3 to strain a muscle: *I've pulled a muscle in my leg.* 4 **pull apart** to divide or separate into pieces 5 **pull out** to say that you won't take part in something 6 **pull through** to recover from an illness or difficult time

pulley *noun*
a wheel with a rope around it, used for lifting heavy things

pullover *noun*
a warm garment for your top half that you can wear over other clothes

pulp *noun*
1 the fleshy part of a fruit 2 any soft, moist mass of substance, such as wood which is treated to be made into paper
pulp *verb*
3 to make something into pulp: *to pulp old newspapers*

pulpit (*say* **pull**-pit) *noun*
a small, high platform where a priest can stand to talk to the people in a church

pulsate (*say* pul-**sate**) *verb*
to beat regularly, like the heart
• ***Word Family:*** **pulsation** *noun*

pulse (1) *noun*
1 a regular movement in your arteries, caused by the beating of your heart as it pumps the blood through them
pulse *verb*
2 to throb, especially strongly

pulse (2) *noun*
the seeds of plants such as peas, beans and lentils which are eaten as food

pulverize or **pulverise** *verb*
to crush or grind something into a powder

puma (*say* **pew**-ma) *noun*
an American mammal of the cat family, with a tawny coat

pumice (*say* **pum**-is) *noun*
a light, spongy rock that comes from a volcano, used for smoothing things

pummel *verb*
to hit or beat someone or something many times with the fists
• ***Word Family:*** other word forms are **pummels, pummelled, pummelling**

pump (1) *noun*
1 a machine for making a liquid or a gas move through a pipe: *a petrol pump / a bicycle pump*
pump *verb*
2 to move air or liquids with a pump: *to pump air into the tyres / to pump water out of the well*
3 to move something up and down: *He pumped my hand vigorously.*

pump (2) *noun*
a light shoe for dancing or sport

pumpkin *noun*
a large vegetable with firm orange flesh

pun *noun*
1 a clever or funny joke using words that sound or look similar, such as *"Did you hear about the bald man who put some rabbits on his head? He thought they were hairs!"*
pun *verb*
2 to make a pun or puns
• ***Word Family:*** other verb forms are **puns, punned, punning**

punch (1) *verb*
1 to hit someone or something hard with your fist
punch *noun*
2 a blow with your fist

punch (2) *noun*
1 a tool or machine for cutting holes or stamping designs: *a paper punch*
punch *verb*
2 to make a hole with a punch

punch (3) *noun*
a drink made of water, fruit juice, pieces of fruit and sometimes wine or spirits

punctual (*say* **punk**-tew-ul) *adjective*
coming at the correct time: *Please be punctual in your payments.*
• ***Word Family:*** **punctuality** *noun* **punctually** *adverb*

punctuate (*say* **punk**-tew-ate) *verb*
to use marks, such as full stops and commas, in a piece of writing to make the meaning clearer
• ***Word Family:*** **punctuation** *noun* marks such as full stops and commas
• ***Word Origins:*** from a Latin word meaning "a point"

puncture (*say* **punk**-cher) *noun*
1 a small hole made by a sharp object: *He mended the puncture in his bicycle tyre.*
puncture *verb*
2 to prick or pierce something with a sharp object

pungent (*say* **pun**-junt) *adjective*
sharp in taste or smell: *a pungent salad dressing*
• ***Word Family:*** **pungency** *noun* **pungently** *adverb*

punish *verb*
to make someone suffer in some way because they have done something wrong or against the law
• ***Word Family:*** **punishment** *noun* **(a)** punishing someone **(b)** the way that someone is punished: *A fair punishment would be for you to mend the window that you broke.* **punishable** *adjective*

punk *adjective*
having to do with a style of rock music which has a strong fast beat
• ***Word Family:*** **punk** *noun* **punk rock** *noun* **punk rocker** *noun*

punnet *noun*
a small box made of thick card, such as those used to hold strawberries

punt *noun*
1 a narrow, flat-bottomed boat that you move along by pushing a long pole against the bottom of the river 2 a kick in which you drop and kick a football before it reaches the ground
punt *verb*
3 to use a pole to push a punt along 4 to kick a football after dropping it, before it reaches the ground

punter *noun*
1 someone who gambles or bets, especially on a horserace 2 a customer

pup *noun*
a young dog or seal

pupa (*say* **pew**-pa) *noun*
an insect at the stage of development between a larva and an adult
• ***Word Family:*** the plural is **pupae** (*say* **pew**-pee) □ **pupate** *verb* to become a pupa

pupil (1) (*say* **pew**-pil) *noun*
someone who is learning, especially in a school

pupil (2) (*say* **pew**-pil) *noun*
the small, dark hole in the iris or coloured part of your eye

puppet *noun*
1 a doll attatched to a glove so that you can move its head and arms with your fingers 2 a doll whose legs and arms are moved with strings or sticks
•*Word Family:* **puppeteer** *noun* someone who makes puppets move, dance and so on
puppetry *noun*

puppy *noun*
a young dog
•*Word Family:* the plural is **puppies**

purchase (*say* **per**-chus) *verb*
1 to buy something
purchase *noun*
2 something that you have bought: *He unloaded his purchases onto the table.*

pure *adjective*
1 not mixed with any other substance: *pure orange juice* 2 clear and clean: *pure fresh water*
•*Word Family:* **purity** *noun* how pure something is: *to test the purity of the water*
purely *adverb* only

puree (*say* **pew**-ray) *noun*
fruit or vegetables mashed or sieved into a smooth, thick liquid

purgatory (*say* **per**-ga-ta-ree) *noun*
a place where some Christians believe that the souls of dead people go before they go to heaven

purge (*say* perj) *verb*
1 to get rid of unwanted people or things: *to purge the body with medicine / to purge the group of traitors*
purge *noun*
2 a cleansing or purifying: *A political purge took place after the revolution.*

purify *verb*
to make something pure: *to purify salt*
•*Word Family:* other forms are **purifies, purified, purifying** □ **purification** *noun*
purifier *noun*

puritan (*say* **pew**-ri-tan) *noun*
someone who is very strict about the way they behave and thinks that people should live a simple life
•*Word Family:* **puritanical** *adjective*

purple *noun*
a reddish-violet colour

purpose (*say* **per**-pus) *noun*
1 the reason that something is done: *What is the purpose of your visit?* 2 **on purpose** deliberately: *Did you trip her up on purpose?*
•*Word Family:* **purposeful** *adjective* determined
purposefully *adverb* **purposely** *adverb*

purr *verb*
to make a low, murmuring sound, as a cat does when it is happy

purse *noun*
1 a small bag for carrying money
purse *verb*
2 to pull your lips together in folds: *to purse your lips in disgust*

pursue *verb*
1 to chase someone: *The bank robbers were pursued by the police.* 2 to try hard to do something: *to pursue your studies* 3 to carry on with something: *Let's not pursue that matter any further.*

pursuit *noun*
1 chasing: *Police followed in hot pursuit. / They ran off in pursuit of the ball.* 2 a hobby: *leisure pursuits*

pus *noun*
a thick, yellowish-white liquid in pimples and sores

push *verb*
1 to move something or someone by force: *Help me push the car uphill.* 2 to press: *Push the button.* 3 to force a way: *The army pushed into the enemy territory.* 4 to encourage or persuade: *She pushed him to take the job.* 5 **push off** to move away or leave 6 **push on** to continue
push noun
7 a pushing movement: *Give the car a push.* 8 **at a push** if necessary: *We can fit three in the back at a push.*
•*Word Family:* **pushy** *adjective* (**pushier, pushiest**) assertive or aggressive

pushchair *noun*
a folding chair with wheels, for pushing a small child

push-over *noun*
something very easy to do

put *verb*
1 to move something to a particular position: *Let's put the picture here. / Put that chair down. / She put money in the bank.* 2 to make someone be in a certain situation: *They were put to death. / We were put to work. / You put me to a lot of trouble.* 3 to express: *Put your request in writing.* 4 **put down** to kill or destroy an animal because it is old or sick: *The old horse was put down.* 5 **put off** (a) to postpone: *The meeting was put off until tomorrow.* (b) to make you stop wanting

A B C D E F G H I J K L M N O P Q R S T U V W X Y Z

something: *His manners put me off my dinner.*
•***Word Family:*** other forms are **puts, put, putting**

putrid (*say* **pew**-trid) *adjective*
rotten or decaying, and smelling bad

putt *verb*
to hit a golfball gently towards the hole
•***Word Family:*** **putter** *noun* a straight club used for putting **putting green** *noun*

putty *noun*
a paste that goes hard when it is dry, used for fixing window panes in place or filling holes in wood

puzzle *noun*
1 a toy or game such as a crossword or jigsaw
2 something that is hard to understand
puzzle *verb*
3 to be difficult to understand: *Her strange behaviour puzzled me.* 4 to think deeply and work something out: *to puzzle over a problem*
•***Word Family:*** **puzzlement** *noun: She stared at the clues in puzzlement.*

pygmy (*say* **pig**-mee) *noun*
a very small person or thing
•***Word Family:*** the plural is **pygmies**

pyjamas (*say* pa-**jah**-mas) *plural noun*
a top and trousers for sleeping in
•***Word Origins:*** from a Persian word meaning "leg clothes"

pylon *noun*
1 a tall, steel tower that supports electric cables high above the ground 2 a tower, such as at either end of a bridge

pyramid (*say* **pir**-a-mid) *noun*
1 an object on a square base with sloping triangular sides that come together at a point
2 a massive structure with this shape, such as one built above the tombs of the ancient Egyptian queens and kings
•***Word Family:*** **pyramidal** *adjective* like a pyramid

pyre (*say* **pie**-a) *noun*
a large pile of firewood used to burn a dead body in some countries

Pyrex (*say* **pie**-reks) *noun*
a strong glass that does not break when heated, is used to make cooking pots, jugs and so on
•***Word Origins:*** a trademark

python (*say* **pie**-thon) *noun*
a large, non-venomous snake found mostly in Africa and western Asia, that coils around and crushes its victims
•***Word Origins:*** named after *Python*, a huge monster in Greek myths

Qq

quack (1) (*say* kwak) *noun*
1 the loud, harsh sound a duck makes
quack *verb*
2 to make this sound

quad (*say* kwod) *noun*
1 a quadrangle 2 a quadruplet

quadrangle (*say* **kwod**-rang-gal) *noun*
a rectangular courtyard surrounded by buildings, such as in a college or school

quadrant (*say* **kwod**-rant) *noun*
a quarter of a circle, or something with this shape
•***Word Origins:*** from a Latin word meaning "a fourth part"

quadrilateral (*say* kwod-ra-**lat**-a-ral) *noun*
1 a flat shape with four straight sides
quadrilateral *adjective*
2 having four sides

quadriplegic (*say* kwod-ra-**plee**-jik) *noun*
someone whose arms and legs are paralysed, usually due to an accident
•***Word Family:*** **quadriplegia** *noun*

quadruped (*say* **kwod**-ra-ped) *noun*
1 an animal with four feet
quadruped *adjective*
2 having four feet

quadruple (*say* kwad-**roo**-pel) *verb*
1 to multiply by four
quadruple *adjective*
2 having four parts 3 being four times as big

quadruplet *noun*
one of four children born at the same time to the same mother

quagmire (*say* **kwog**-my-a) *noun*
an area of soft, muddy ground

quail (1) (*say* kwale) *noun*
a small, brown bird that lives and nests on the ground

quail (2) (*say* kwale) *verb*
to feel afraid or show fear

quaint (*say* kwaint) *adjective*
1 old-fashioned in an attractive way: *a quaint cottage* 2 curiously strange or unusual: *a quaint child*
•***Word Family:*** **quaintly** *adverb* **quaintness** *noun*

quake (*say* kwake) *verb*
1 to shake or tremble: *to quake with fear*
quake *noun*
2 an earthquake

Quaker *noun*
someone who belongs to a religious group called the Society of Friends

qualify (*say* **kwol**-i-fie) *verb*
1 to have the qualities or training necessary for something: *to qualify for a student grant / to qualify as a doctor* 2 to change or limit the meaning of something: *Please qualify your statement. / Adverbs qualify verbs.*
•***Word Family:*** other forms are **qualifies, qualified, qualifying** □ **qualification** *noun*

quality (*say* **kwol**-i-tee) *noun*
1 a characteristic: *I look for qualities such as loyalty in my friends.* 2 value: *Meat of good quality is very expensive.*
•***Word Family:*** the plural is **qualities**

qualm (*rhymes with* farm) *noun*
a sudden feeling or pang of guilt: *to have qualms about skipping school*

quandary (*say* **kwon**-daree) *noun*
not knowing, or being confused about what you should do: *He's in a quandary about whether to join the club.*
•***Word Family:*** the plural is **quandaries**

quantity (*say* **kwon**-ti-tee) *noun*
an amount of something: *to discover a large quantity of gold*
•***Word Family:*** the plural is **quantities**

quarantine (*say* **kwo**-ren-teen) *noun*
1 putting people, animals or plants with a disease on their own so they don't spread the infection to others: *to put a dog into quarantine to make sure that it hasn't got rabies*
quarantine *verb*
2 to put someone or something in quarantine
•***Word Origins:*** from an Italian word meaning "40 days" (the original period of isolation)

quarrel (*say* **kwo**-rel) *noun*
1 an angry argument
quarrel *verb*
2 to argue angrily
•***Word Family:*** other verb forms are **quarrels, quarrelled, quarrelling** □ **quarrelsome** *adjective*

quarry (1) (*say* **kwo**-ree) *noun*
1 an open pit, formed when stone or slate is dug or blasted out of the ground
quarry *verb*
2 to obtain stone from, or dig a quarry: *to quarry sandstone*
•***Word Family:*** the plural of the noun is **quarries** □ other verb forms are **quarries, quarried, quarrying**

quarry (2) (*say* **kwo**-ree) *noun*
the animal or bird that you are hunting or chasing: *to startle your quarry*
•***Word Family:*** the plural is **quarries**

quart (*rhymes with* port) *noun*
two pints

quarter (*say* **kwor**-ta) *noun*
1 one of the four equal parts into which you can divide something: *a quarter of an orange*
2 a district in a city: *to work in the old quarter*
3 **quarters** your lodgings or where you live
quarter *verb*
4 to divide something into four equal parts

quartet (*say* kwor-**tet**) *noun*
1 a group of four people, especially musicians
2 a musical composition for four instruments or voices
•***Word Family:*** **string quartet** *noun* a group of four players, with two violins, a viola and a cello

quartz (*say* kworts) *noun*
a very common mineral that is often used to make electronic equipment, especially accurate clocks and watches

quaver (*say* **kway**-va) *verb*
1 to shake or tremble
quaver *noun*
2 a shaking sound: *to speak with a quaver* 3 a musical note that is half as long as a crotchet
•***Word Family:*** **quavery** *adjective* trembling

quay (*say* kee) *noun*
a place for tying up and loading and unloading boats

queasy (*say* **kwee**-zee) *adjective*
feeling sick: *The boat trip made me a bit queasy.*
•***Word Family:*** other forms are **queasier, queasiest** □ **queasily** *adverb* **queasiness** *noun*

queen (*say* kween) *noun*
1 a woman who rules a country throughout her lifetime 2 the wife of a king 3 a playing card with a picture of a queen on it 4 the most powerful piece in chess 5 a large female ant, termite or bee, that lays eggs
•***Word Family:*** **queenly** *adverb*

queer *adjective*
1 strange or unusual: *queer ideas / queer noises*
2 faint or unwell: *to feel queer* 3 homosexual

quell (*say* kwel) *verb*
to stop or overcome something: *to quell someone's doubt / to quell an uprising by force*

quench (*say* kwench) *verb*
1 to put out or stop a fire burning 2 **quench your thirst** satisfy your thirst

query (*say* **kweer**-ee) *noun*
1 a question or inquiry
query *verb*
2 to ask questions about or doubt something: *to query his fitness*
•***Word Family:*** the plural of the noun is **queries** □ other forms of the verb are **queries, queried, querying**

quest (*say* kwest) *noun*
a search or pursuit: *a quest for gold / a quest for fame*

question (*say* **kwes**-chon) *noun*
1 a sentence that asks for information: *I asked her questions about her childhood.* 2 a problem: *She raised the question of where to hold the party.* 3 debate: *Your argument is open to question.*
4 **out of the question** impossible
question *verb*
5 to ask questions
•***Word Family:*** **questionable** *adjective* open to question **questionably** *adverb*

question mark *noun*
a punctuation mark (?) used at the end of a written question

questionnaire (*say* kwes-chen-**air**) *noun*
a set of questions printed on a form, with spaces included so that you can write the answers underneath each one

queue (*say* kew) *noun*
1 a line of people, cars and so on waiting for their turn: *a queue at the tuckshop*
queue *verb*
2 to stand in a line and wait: *to queue for bread*
•***Word Family:*** other verb forms are **queues, queued, queueing** or **queuing**

quibble (*say* **kwib**-el) *verb*
to argue about unimportant things: *to quibble over how to tie shoelaces*

quiche (*say* keesh) *noun*
a tart filled with a cooked mixture of cream, cheese and eggs, often with such things as bacon added and eaten hot or cold

quick (*say* kwik) *adjective*
1 moving rapidly: *a quick stride* 2 done in a short time: *a quick meal* 3 impatient: *a quick temper*
quick *noun*
4 the tender skin under your nails: *Her nails were bitten to the quick.*
•***Word Family:*** **quickly** *adverbs*

quicksand *noun*
wet sand that sucks you down if you fall into it or try to walk on it

quid *noun*
a pound (£1)
•***Word Family:*** the plural is **quid**

quiet (*say* **kwy**-et) *adjective*
1 making little or no sound or movement
2 calm and peaceful: *a quiet afternoon reading*
quiet *noun*
3 peace or calmness: *The teacher appealed for quiet.*
•***Word Family:*** **quieten** *verb* to make someone or something quiet or to become quiet **quietly** *adverb*

quill (*say* kwil) *noun*
1 a large wing or tail feather 2 an old-fashioned pen, made from a feather and dipped in ink for writing 3 one of the spines of a hedgehog or porcupine

quilt (*say* kwilt) *noun*
a bed-cover filled with soft padding
•***Word Family:*** **quilted** *adjective* sewn with padding inside: *a quilted jacket*

quin *noun*
a quintuplet

quintet (*say* kwin-**tet**) *noun*
1 a group of five people, especially musicians
2 a musical piece for five instruments or singers

quintuplet (*say* kwin-**tup**-let) *noun*
one of five children born at the same time to the same mother

quip (*say* kwip) *noun*
1 a funny or sarcastic remark
quip *verb*
2 to make a quip
•***Word Family:*** other forms are **quips, quipped, quipping**

quirk (*say* kwerk) *noun*
1 an odd or strange habit that someone has: *a quirk of her personality / We're used to her funny quirks.* 2 a sudden twist or turn: *a quirk of fate*
•***Word Family:*** **quirky** *adjective* (**quirkier, quirkiest**) odd

quit (*say* kwit) *verb*
1 to leave or go away from somewhere: *to quit your job / to quit the city and live on a farm* 2 to stop: *Quit talking and work.*
•***Word Family:*** other forms are **quits, quit** or **quitted, quitting** □ **quitter** *noun: He won't give up; he's not a quitter.*

quite *adverb*
1 completely or entirely: *She has quite recovered.*
2 fairly: *It's quite a scary film.*

quiver (1) (*say* **kwiv**-a) *verb*
to tremble: *to quiver with excitement*

quiver (2) (*say* **kwiv**-a) *noun*
a container for holding arrows

quiz (*say* kwiz) *verb*
1 to question someone closely

quiz *noun*
2 a test, especially of general knowledge
•***Word Family:*** other verb forms are **quizzes, quizzed, quizzing** □ the plural of the noun is **quizzes**

quoits (*say* koyts) *plural noun*
a game in which rings made of rope are aimed and thrown around a peg on the ground

quorum (*say* **kwor**-rum) *noun*
the number of people that must be at a meeting if proper decisions are to be made

quota (*say* **kwo**-ta) *noun*
a share of something: *What's your quota of work?*

quotation (*say* kwo-**tay**-shon) *noun*
a passage from a book or speech copied exactly as it first appeared

quotation marks *noun*
one of the punctuation marks (" " or ' ') used to show where speech begins and ends or if words are quoted

quote (*say* kwote) *verb*
1 to repeat or copy words exactly: *to quote a verse from the Bible* 2 to state a price of goods or services: *They quoted for the repair.*
quote *noun*
3 a quotation

quotient (*say* **kwo**-shent) *noun*
the result you get when you divide one number by another: *In the sum 10 ÷ 5, the quotient is 2.*
•***Word Origins:*** from a Latin word meaning "how many times?"

Rr

rabbi (*say* **rab**-eye) *noun*
a Jewish religious leader or teacher
•***Word Family:*** the plural is **rabbis**
•***Word Origins:*** from a Hebrew word meaning "my master"

rabbit *noun*
a small, furry, long-eared animal that lives in a burrow and is also kept as a pet

rabble *noun*
a noisy crowd

rabies (*say* **ray**-beez) *noun*
a disease of dogs and other animals, that makes them go mad and die and can be passed on to people by the bite of an infected animal
•***Word Family:*** **rabid** *adjective: a rabid dog*
•***Word Origins:*** from a Latin word meaning "madness" or "rage"

raccoon or racoon (*say* ra-**koon**) *noun*
a small animal of North America, which has a bushy white tail with black rings
•***Word Origins:*** from Native American words meaning "he scratches with his hands"

race (1) *noun*
1 a contest of speed 2 any kind of competition or contest: *the race for the presidency*
race *verb*
3 to compete in a race 4 to run or move quickly: *I raced to the gate. / His pulse raced.*
•***Word Family:*** **racer** *noun* someone or something that races

race (2) *noun*
a nation or large group of people with the same culture and skin colour
•***Word Family:*** **racial** (*say* **ray**-shul) *adjective: racial equality*

racism (*say* **ray**-sizm) *noun*
1 thinking that your race is better than other races. 2 treating people of a different race unfairly or badly
•***Word Family:*** **racist** *noun* **racist** *adjective*

rack *noun*
1 a shelf or container made of a framework of metal or wood: *a luggage rack in a train / a magazine rack* 2 a machine used in the past, to torture people by stretching their bodies: *to put someone on the rack*
rack *verb*
3 to torment or cause distress: *She was racked with pain.* 4 **rack your brain** to think deeply: *I racked my brain for the answer.*

racket (1) *noun*
1 a loud, unpleasant noise 2 a dishonest scheme or activity to make money

racket (2) *noun*
another spelling of **racquet**

racquet (*say* **rak**-it) *noun*
a bat with a long handle and nylon strings stretched across an oval frame, which is used for hitting the ball in games of tennis and squash

radar (*say* **ray**-dah) *noun*
a method of finding or tracking a ship or aeroplane, by sending out radio waves and measuring the time taken for the radio wave to bounce off the object and return
•***Word Origins:*** an acronym from the first letter of the words *r*adio *d*etection *a*nd *r*anging

A B C D E F G H I J K L M N O P Q R S T U V W X Y Z

radial (*say* **ray**-dee-al) *adjective*
arranged like a wheel, with rays or spokes coming out from the centre
• ***Word Origins:*** from a Latin word meaning "a wheel spoke, a ray"

radiant (*say* **ray**-dee-ant) *adjective*
1 sending out heat or light: *the radiant sun*
2 bright or lit up: *a radiant smile*
• ***Word Family:*** **radiance** *noun* **radiantly** *adverb*

radiator (*say* **ray**-dee-ay-tuh) *noun*
1 a room heater through which hot water is pumped 2 a device that cools the engine of a motor vehicle

radical (*say* **rad**-i-kul) *adjective*
1 wanting great social or political change: *His radical ideas upset his conservative parents.* 2 to do with the most important or basic qualities of a situation or thing: *The plan failed because of a radical fault. / We need to make radical changes.*
radical *noun*
3 someone who believes in great social or political change
• ***Word Family:*** **radically** *adverb*

radio *noun*
1 the sending or receiving of sounds through the air by electric waves 2 an instrument for receiving sounds sent in this way.
radio *verb*
3 to send a message by radio: *to radio for help*
• ***Word Family:*** the plural of the noun is **radios** □ other forms of the verb are **radios, radioed, radioing**

radioactivity (*say* ray-dee-o-ak-**tiv**-i-tee) *noun*
the ability of some substances, such as uranium, to give out powerful atomic rays that can be harmful
• ***Word Family:*** **radioactive** (*say* ray-dee-o-**ak**-tiv) *adjective*

radish (*say* **rad**-ish) *noun*
a small, round, white root with a red skin and a sharp taste, which is usually eaten raw in salads

radium (*say* **ray**-dee-um) *noun*
a radioactive element

radius (*say* **ray**-dee-us) *noun*
1 a straight line drawn from the centre of a circle to any point on its circumference
2 a circular area measured from its centre: *a 10 kilometre radius of the city*
• ***Word Family:*** the plural is **radii** (*say* **ray**-dee-eye)
• ***Word Origins:*** from a Latin word meaning "a spoke" (as in a wheel)

raffia *noun*
a fibre that comes from a palm tree and can be woven into baskets, hats and so on

raffle *noun*
1 a kind of lottery, usually held to raise money for a charity, school and so on, with prizes
raffle *verb*
2 to offer something as a prize in a raffle

raft *noun*
a floating platform used for moving people or things over water

rafter *noun*
one of the pieces of timber that support a roof

rag *noun*
1 an old or torn scrap of fabric 2 **rags** old or torn clothes

rage *noun*
1 violent anger: *to fly into a rage* 2 **the rage** something that is popular or fashionable: *Short skirts are the rage this summer.*
rage *verb*
3 to act or speak angrily 4 to move with great violence or intensity: *The fire raged out of control.*

ragged (*say* **rag**-id) *adjective*
1 old and torn: *a ragged coat* 2 wearing old and torn clothes: *a ragged beggar*

raid *noun*
1 a sudden surprise attack
raid *verb*
2 to attack or invade

rail *noun*
1 a bar of metal or wood: *fence rail / stair rail*
2 either of two bars of steel on which a train or tram travels 3 the railway: *We travelled by rail.*

railway *noun*
1 a track consisting of parallel steel rails with sleepers for trains to run on 2 a system of these tracks with their trains, land and buildings

rain *noun*
1 drops of water which fall to the ground from the clouds
rain *verb*
2 to fall from the sky in drops of water: *It has started to rain.* 3 to come down in large numbers: *They rained blows upon his head.*

rainbow *noun*
an arc of colours seen in the sky when the sun shines through rain

rainfall *noun*
the amount of rain that falls somewhere: *heavy annual rainfall*

rainforest *noun*
the thick, steamy forest found in tropical areas which have heavy rainfall

raise *verb*
1 to move something to a higher position: *Raise*

your hand. 2 to increase: *to raise the rent* 3 to bring up: *to raise a family* 4 to collect or gather together: *to raise money for the Red Cross / to raise an army* 5 to make something appear: *The car raised a cloud of dust. / to raise a laugh*
raise *noun*
6 an increase in salary

raisin (*say* **ray**-zun) *noun*
a dried grape

rake *noun*
1 a long-handled garden tool with a row of prongs, which you use for levelling the ground, gathering cut grass and so on
rake *verb*
2 to gather or smooth leaves, earth and so on with a rake: *to rake up leaves*

rally *verb*
1 to bring or come together to do something: *to rally for peace* 2 to improve or recover strength: *to rally after weeks of fever / Their spirits rallied with the good news.* 3 **rally round** to come together to help someone
rally *noun*
4 a large public meeting: *a peace rally* 5 an exchange of strokes between players in tennis 6 a race for motor cars on public roads
•***Word Family:*** other forms of the verb are **rallies, rallied, rallying** □ the plural of the noun is **rallies**

ram *noun*
1 a male sheep 2 a device for pushing something with great force: *a battering ram*
ram *verb*
3 to strike or force something with heavy blows: *The ferry rammed into the wharf.*
•***Word Family:*** other forms of the verb are **rams, rammed, ramming**

RAM *abbreviation*
a short form of **random access memory**

Ramadan *noun*
the ninth month of the Muslim year, during which Muslims do not eat or drink during daylight hours

ramble *verb*
1 to wander in a slow, relaxed way: *to ramble through the park* 2 **ramble on** to talk or write for a long time in a confused way
ramble *noun*
3 a long walk in the country

ramp *noun*
a sloping surface connecting two different levels
•***Word Origins:*** from a French word meaning "to creep or crawl"

rampage (*say* ram-**page**) *verb*
1 to move about or act in a violent or furious manner: *The gang rampaged through the town.*
rampage *noun*
2 violent or wild behaviour: *The gang went on a rampage.*

rampant *adjective*
wild or uncontrolled: *rampant weeds*

ramshackle *adjective*
badly made or likely to collapse: *a ramshackle shed*

ranch *noun*
a large farm, especially one for cattle or horses
•***Word Family:*** the plural is **ranches** □ **rancher** *noun*

rancid (*say* **ran**-sid) *adjective*
having an unpleasantly stale smell or taste: *rancid butter*
•***Word Family:*** **rancidness** *noun* **rancidity** *noun*
•***Word Origins:*** from a Latin word meaning "stinking"

random *adjective*
1 without any definite order, plan or method: *a random selection*
random *noun*
2 **at random** without a method or plan: *I chose a book at random.*
•***Word Family:*** **randomly** *adverb*

random access memory *noun*
the memory in a computer in which information can be stored or recalled equally quickly

range *noun*
1 the difference between the highest and the lowest, top and bottom and so on: *a range of prices / a range of colours / the range of a singing voice* 2 a line or group of mountains 3 an area of land used for shooting practice: *a rifle range* 4 the distance to which something can travel: *the range of an aircraft / the range of a bullet* 5 a collection of different things of the same general kind: *our new range of toys / a range of objections* 6 a cooking stove
range *verb*
7 to vary within set limits 8 to move or travel about: *Wild herds ranged across the land.*
•***Word Family:*** **ranger** *noun* (a) someone who looks after a national park or similar public area (b) **Ranger** a senior Guide
•***Word Origins:*** from an Old French word meaning "arrange in a line"

rank (1) *noun*
1 a position in society or any group or organization: *a poet of the highest rank / to be promoted to the rank of general* 2 a row, line or series: *ranks of flowers lined the path / a taxi-rank*
rank *verb*
3 to have or hold a particular position: *to be ranked fourth in the class* 4 to arrange something or put it in order

A B C D E F G H I J K L M N O P Q R S T U V W X Y Z

rank (2) *adjective*
having an unpleasant smell

ransack *verb*
to search thoroughly or violently, especially when robbing a house

ransom *noun*
1 money paid so that someone who has been kidnapped or captured in battle will be given back
ransom *verb*
2 to pay money to free someone who has been kidnapped or captured 3 to get a ransom for someone
•***Word Family:*** other forms of the verb are **ransoms, ransomed, ransoming**

rant *verb*
to speak loudly in a wild way

rap (1) *verb*
1 to hit something with a sharp, quick blow
rap *noun*
2 a sharp, quick knock or blow
•***Word Family:*** other forms of the verb are **raps, rapped, rapping**

rap (2) *verb*
1 to have a relaxed, friendly conversation
rap *noun*
2 a kind of pop music in which someone speaks the words in a rhythmic way
•***Word Family:*** other forms are **raps, rapped, rapping**

rape *noun*
1 the crime of forcing someone to have sexual intercourse when they do not want to
rape *verb*
2 to force someone to have sexual intercourse when they do not want to
•***Word Family:*** **rapist** (*say* **ray**-pist) *noun*
•***Word Origins:*** from a Latin word meaning "to seize or carry off"

rapid *adjective*
1 with great speed
rapid *noun*
2 **rapids** a part of a river where it flows swiftly over rocks
•***Word Family:*** **rapidity** *noun* **rapidly** *adverb*

rapport (*say* ra-**por**) *noun*
a feeling of agreement and understanding: *Our teacher has a good rapport with the class.*

rapt *adjective*
deeply absorbed or fascinated: *She listened with rapt attention.*

rapture (*say* **rap**-cher) *noun*
great joy and delight
•***Word Family:*** **rapturous** *adjective*: *a rapturous welcome*

rare (1) *adjective*
not found or happening often: *a rare disease / a rare plant*
•***Word Family:*** **rarely** *adverb* **rareness** *noun* **rarity** (*say* **rair**-i-tee) *noun*
•***Word Origins:*** from a Latin word meaning "thin, not dense"

rare (2) *adjective*
cooked very lightly: *a rare steak*

rascal (*say* **rahs**-kul) *noun*
1 someone who is dishonest 2 a mischievous child

rash (1) *adjective*
done quickly without thinking: *a rash decision*
•***Word Family:*** **rashly** *adverb* **rashness**, *noun.*

rash (2) *noun*
spots or patches of red on your skin

rasp (*say* rahsp) *verb*
1 to make a harsh, scraping sound
rasp *noun*
2 a file with a coarse, pointed surface, used for smoothing wood

raspberry (*say* **rahz**-bree) *noun*
a small, juicy, red berry
•***Word Family:*** the plural is **raspberries**

Rastafarian *noun*
someone who belongs to a religious group from Jamaica, who often wear their hair in dreadlocks

rat *noun*
1 a long-tailed animal similar to a mouse, but larger 2 someone who is nasty or sneaky
3 **smell a rat** to be suspicious

rate *noun*
1 speed: *at the rate of 60 kilometres an hour*
2 a charge or payment: *What is the interest rate on the loan?* 3 **at any rate** anyhow
rate *verb*
4 to give an opinion about the price or quality of something: *How do you rate this painting?*
to think of or consider someone in a particular way: *I rate him as a highly intelligent child.*

rather (*rhymes with* father) *adverb*
1 preferably or more willingly: *I would rather go for a swim than watch television.* 2 to a certain degree: *It's rather old.*

rating *noun*
the value or position that someone or something has when compared to others: *the popularity rating of a television show*

ratio (*say* **ray**-she-o) *noun*
the relationship between two amounts or measurements, given in the lowest possible

whole numbers: *The ratio of males to females in the town is 5 to 3 because for every five males, there are three females.*

ration (*say* **rash**-on) *noun*
1 a fixed amount of something that a person is allowed: *our weekly ration of eggs*
ration *verb*
2 to give something out in limited amounts: *Petrol was rationed during the strike.*
•***Word Family:*** **rationing** *noun*

rational *adjective*
1 sensible, reasonable or logical: *a rational explanation* 2 able to think clearly and make sensible decisions
•***Word Family:*** **rationally** *adverb*

rattle *verb*
1 to make short, sharp sounds: *The wind rattled the windows.* 2 to confuse or upset someone: *He was rattled by the unexpected questions.* 3 **rattle off** to say something quickly: *She rattled off a list of things to buy.*
rattle *noun*
4 a series of short, sharp sounds: *a rattle of pots and pans* 5 a child's toy that rattles when you shake it

rattlesnake *noun*
a venomous American snake which makes a rattling sound by shaking its tail when angry

raucous (*say* **raw**-kus) *adjective*
loud and harsh-sounding: *a raucous shout*
•***Word Family:*** **raucously** *adverb* **raucousness** *noun*

rave *verb*
1 to talk in a wild and confused way 2 to talk or write with great enthusiasm: *She raved about her new car.*
rave *noun*
3 a party or dance for many people, with fast pop music and special lighting effects
•***Word Family:*** **ravings** *plural noun*: *the ravings of a madman* **raving** *adjective*

raven (*say* **ray**-vun) *noun*
a large bird similar to the crow, with shiny, black feathers

ravenous (*say* **rav**-en-us) *adjective*
very hungry
•***Word Family:*** **ravenously** *adverb*

ravine (*say* ra-**veen**) *noun*
a long, narrow and deep valley

ravishing *adjective*
very beautiful
•***Word Family:*** **ravishingly** *adverb*

raw *adjective*
1 not cooked: *raw meat* 2 not processed or treated: *raw sugar* 3 painful because the covering of skin has been removed: *raw hands from pulling in the rope* 4 harsh and cold: *a raw wind*
•***Word Family:*** **rawly** *adverb* **rawness** *noun*

ray (1) *noun*
1 a narrow beam of light or heat: *a ray of sunlight* 2 a very small bit: *a ray of hope*

ray (2) *noun*
a large fish with a flat body, eyes on the top of the body and a long tail

rayon *noun*
a man-made fabric that looks like silk

raze *verb*
to destroy something, such as a building or a town, so that nothing is left standing: *to raze the building to the ground*

razor (*say* **ray**-za) *noun*
a sharp cutting instrument for shaving hair from the skin
•***Word Origins:*** from a Latin word meaning "scraped"

reach *verb*
1 to get to a place: *We reached Manchester at midnight.* 2 to go as far as or touch something: *The coat reaches her ankles.* 3 to stretch to: *I couldn't reach the apple on the tree.*
reach *noun*
4 the distance someone or something can reach: *The grapes were hanging just out of his reach.* 5 a straight part of a river

react *verb*
to act in response to something: *Police reacted quickly to the call for help. / She reacted angrily to his question.*

reaction (*say* ree-**ak**-shon) *noun*
1 something that is done or happens after another action or situation: *When I saw the snake my first reaction was to run.* 2 a chemical change that happens when two or more substances are combined
•***Word Family:*** **reactionary** *adjective* not wanting change

reactor *noun*
a large machine that produces nuclear power

read *verb*
1 to look at and understand written words: *Can you read?* 2 to say written words aloud: *Read me the first paragraph.* 3 to record or indicate: *The thermometer reads 7°.* 4 to take in information from a computer memory or computer disk
•***Word Family:*** other forms of the verb are **reads, read** (*say* red)**, reading** □ **readable** *adjective* easy or interesting to read **reading** *noun*

A B C D E F G H I J K L M N O P Q R S T U V W X Y Z

(a) a piece of writing read aloud: *a poetry reading* **(b)** the amount that is recorded on a measuring instrument: *Check the readings.*

read only memory *noun*
a permanent memory in a computer which can be read but not changed

ready *adjective*
1 prepared, or prepared to do something: *ready for school / Is dinner ready yet?* 2 available for immediate use: *ready cash* 3 quick: *a ready wit* 4 likely to happen: *The bag is full and ready to burst.*
ready *noun*
5 **at the ready** ready for action
ready *verb*
6 to prepare: *She readied herself to serve the ball.*
•***Word Family:*** other forms of the adjective are **readier, readiest** □ other forms of the verb are **readies, readied, readying** □ **readily** (*say* **red**-i-lee) *adverb* willingly or quickly: *to agree readily* **readiness** *noun*

real *adjective*
1 actual: *in real life* 2 true: *real love* 3 not artificial: *real diamonds*
•***Word Family:*** **reality** (*say* ree-**al**-i-tee) something which is real or exists in fact: *His dream of success had become a reality.* **really** *adverb: really hot*

realism (*say* **ree**-a-liz-um) *noun*
1 dealing with things in a practical, sensible way 2 a style of writing or painting about life as it really is
•***Word Family:*** **realist** *noun* **realistic** *adjective*

realize or **realise** (*say* **ree**-a-lize) *verb*
1 to understand fully: *Do you realize what you have done?* 2 to make something real or a fact: *to realize an ambition*
•***Word Family:*** **realization** *noun*

realm (*say* relm) *noun*
1 a kingdom 2 an area of activity or study: *the realm of biology*

reap *verb*
1 to cut and harvest grain 2 to gain something as a return for work or actions: *to reap the benefits of hard work*
•***Word Family:*** **reaper** *noun* someone or something that reaps

rear (1) *noun*
1 the back part of something: *the rear of the shop* 2 the buttocks
rear *adjective*
3 to do with the back of something: *a rear wheel*

rear (2) *verb*
1 to care for and bring up a child or young animal 2 to rise up on the back legs: *My horse reared and I fell off.*

rearrange *verb*
to arrange something differently: *to rearrange the furniture*
•***Word Family:*** **rearrangement** *noun*

reason (*say* **ree**-zun) *noun*
1 the cause of something that happens: *What are her reasons for leaving?* 2 the ability to use your mind 3 good sense
reason *verb*
4 to form an opinion based on the facts
•***Word Family:*** **reasoned** *adjective* logically argued or thought out **reasoning** *noun*

reasonable (*say* **ree**-zun-a-bul) *adjective*
showing good judgment or common sense: *The plan sounds quite reasonable.*
•***Word Family:*** **reasonably** *adverb* **reasonableness** *noun*

reassure (*say* ree-a-**shor**) *verb*
to say or do something to stop someone worrying: *She was reassured by her mother's smile.*
•***Word Family:*** **reassurance** *noun* **reassuringly** *adverb*

rebate (*say* **ree**-bate) *noun*
a sum of money that you get back, such as a discount or a tax refund

rebel (*say* **reb**-ul) *noun*
1 someone who fights against people in authority
rebel (*say* re-**bel**) *verb*
2 to fight against people in authority: *She rebelled against her parents' strict rules.*
•***Word Family:*** other forms of the verb are **rebels, rebelled, rebelling**

rebellion (*say* re-**bel**-yun) *noun*
organized fighting against the government of a country

rebound (*say* ree-**bound**) *verb*
1 to bounce or spring back after hitting something: *The ball rebounded from the wall and broke a window.*
rebound (*say* **ree**-bound) *noun*
2 the action of bouncing or springing back

rebuff (*say* re-**buff**) *verb*
1 to refuse or reject something in an unfriendly way: *She rebuffed my offer of help.*
rebuff *noun*
2 a refusal or defeat

rebuke *verb*
to tell someone off: *to rebuk for being late*

recall *verb*
1 to remember: *Can you recall her name?* 2 to order someone to return: *The king recalled his*

ambassadors. 3 to get back a faulty product after people have bought it: *They had to recall the cars after a fault was discovered.*
recall (*say* **ree**-kawl) *noun*
4 the ability to remember: *the gift of total recall*

recap *verb*
1 to recapitulate
recap *noun*
2 an example of recapitulation: *Can you give me a quick recap?*

recapitulate (*say* ree-ka-**pit**-yoo-late) *verb*
to repeat the main points of an argument or explanation
•***Word Family:*** **recapitulation** *noun*

recapture *verb*
to capture something or someone again

recede (*say* re-**seed**) *verb*
to move back or away: *We were able to cross when the tide receded. / His hair had begun to recede.*
•***Word Origins:*** from a Latin word meaning "to go back"

receipt (*say* re-**seet**) *noun*
1 a written statement saying that payment has been made 2 the receiving of something: *I am in receipt of your letter.*
•***Word Origins:*** from a Latin word meaning "recovered"

receive (*say* re-**seev**) *verb*
1 to get something: *I received a letter this morning. / He received the bad news.* 2 to admit or welcome someone: *to receive into the group*

receiver *noun*
1 someone who receives something: *a receiver of stolen goods* 2 a radio or television set 3 the part of a telephone that you hold

recent (*say* **ree**-sunt) *adjective*
made or happening not long ago: *a recent illness / a recent photo*
•***Word Family:*** **recently** *adverb*

receptacle (*say* re-**sep**-ti-kul) *noun*
anything that holds or contains something

reception (*say* re-**sep**-shon) *noun*
1 a welcome: *My idea met with a cold reception.* 2 the area of a hotel or office where visitors are met 3 a formal party: *a wedding reception* 4 the quality of signals received by a radio or television set: *bad reception*
•***Word Family:*** **receptionist** someone whose job is to welcome and help visitors or clients in an office or hotel

receptive (*say* re-**sep**-tiv) *adjective*
able to take in knowledge and new ideas: *a receptive mind*

recess (*say* re-**sess** *or* **ree**-sess) *noun*
1 a part of a room that is set back from the main wall 2 a period of time when work stops
•***Word Family:*** the plural is **recesses**

recession (*say* re-**sesh**-on) *noun*
a period when the economy of a country becomes less successful and people find it hard to get jobs, but not as bad as a depression

recharge *verb*
to fill a battery with electricity

recipe (*say* **res**-uh-pee) *noun*
a list of ingredients and instructions for cooking a particular dish

reciprocal (*say* re-**sip**-ra-kul) *adjective*
given or done in return for something else that is given to or done for you: *a reciprocal baby-sitting arrangement*
•***Word Family:*** **reciprocate** *verb* to do something in return: *I invited her to my party, but she didn't reciprocate.*

recital (*say* re-**sigh**-tul) *noun*
a performance of music or poetry

recite *verb*
to say something, such as a poem, out loud

reckless *adjective*
not thinking or caring about what might happen: *reckless driving*
•***Word Family:*** **recklessly** *adverb* **recklessness** *noun*

reckon *verb*
1 to think or suppose: *I reckon it will rain later.* 2 to believe: *She is reckoned to be the best in the country.* 3 to count up or calculate: *I reckon we should have five pounds left.*
•***Word Family:*** **reckoning** *noun* a calculation: *By my reckoning we're lost.*

reclaim *verb*
1 to make land useful or productive: *The swamp was reclaimed by draining.* 2 to get something back: *I reclaimed my camera from the lost property office.*
•***Word Family:*** **reclamation** (*say* rek-la-**may**-shon) *noun: a land reclamation project*

recline *verb*
to lean back in a resting position

recluse (*say* re-**kloose**) *noun*
someone who lives apart from others
•***Word Family:*** **reclusive** *adjective*
•***Word Origins:*** from a Latin word meaning "shut up"

recognize or recognise (*say* **rek**-ug-nize) *verb*
1 to know something or someone again: *I recognize that tune. / Would you recognize me*

a b c d e f g h i j k l m n o p q r s t u v w x y z

without a beard? 2 to understand and accept something: *She recognized the truth of his words.*
•***Word Family:*** **recognition** (*say* rek-ug-**nish**-un) *noun: My recognition of him was immediate.* **recognizable** *adjective* **recognizably** *adverb*
•***Word Origins:*** from a Latin word meaning "to call to mind again"

recoil (*say* re-**koil**) *verb*
1 to jump or spring back: *The gun recoiled after being fired / to recoil in horror*
recoil (*say* **ree**-koil) *noun*
2 the act of recoiling, such as the backward movement of a gun when it is fired

recollect (*say* rek-uh-**lekt**) *verb*
to remember
•***Word Family:*** **recollection** (*say* rek-uh-**lek**-shun) *noun* memory: *I had no recollection of having been there before.*

recommend *verb*
to suggest that someone or something would be good to have or do: *Can you recommend a good school? / We've recommended you for the job.*
•***Word Family:*** **recommendation** *noun*

reconcile (*say* **rek**-un-sile) *verb*
to make things or people agree: *The enemies reconciled their differences.*
•***Word Family:*** **reconciliation** (*say* rek-un-sil-i-**ay**-shun) *noun*

reconnaissance (*say* re-**kon**-uh-sance) *noun*
the gathering of useful information about an area or situation before taking action, as soldiers do
•***Word Origins:*** from a French word meaning "recognition"

reconnoitre (*say* rek-uh-**noy**-ta) *verb*
to send a small group to gather useful information about an area, situation or opponent before taking action

reconsider (*say* ree-kun-**sid**-a) *verb*
to think about something again and perhaps change a decision
•***Word Family:*** **reconsideration** *noun*

reconstruction *noun*
1 building something again: *the reconstruction of a damaged city* 2 acting out something that happened: *Police carried out a reconstruction of the crime to jog people's memories.*

record (*say* re-**kord**) *verb*
1 to write down information so it will be known in the future: *This book records the history of cinema.* 2 to put music, other sounds or images on tape, disc or film: *The concert was recorded for television.*
record (*say* **rek**-ord) *noun*
3 a written account: *a record of the early history of the town* 4 a thin disc, usually plastic, for recording and reproducing sounds 5 the facts known about the past of someone or something: *This airline has a good safety record. / a criminal record* 6 the best so far: *The time for this race is a new record.* 7 the basic unit of information storage on a computer
•***Word Family:*** **recording** *noun*

recorder *noun*
1 someone who keeps official records 2 a simple wind instrument similar to a flute

record-player *noun*
a machine that reproduces the sounds on a record

recount (*say* ruh-**kownt**) *verb*
to tell about or describe something: *He recounted his adventures.*

recover *verb*
1 to get something back again: *The police recovered the stolen goods. / He recovered his wits after the accident.* 2 to return to a healthy or normal situation: *I've recovered from my illness.*
•***Word Family:*** **recovery** *noun*

recreation (*say* rek-ri-**ay**-shon) *noun*
a relaxing pastime, hobby or sport
•***Word Family:*** **recreational** *adjective*

recruit (*say* re-**kroot**) *verb*
1 to get new people to join a club, army and so on: *to recruit new members for a club*
recruit *noun*
2 someone who has recently joined an organization, especially a new soldier

rectangle (*say* **rek**-tang-gul) *noun*
a flat shape with four sides and four right angles
•***Word Family:*** **rectangular** *adjective*

rectify (*say* **rek**-ti-fie) *verb*
to put something right: *It will take days to rectify the damage.*
•***Word Family:*** other forms of the verb are **rectifies, rectified, rectifying** □ **rectification** *noun*

rector *noun*
a clergyman in charge of a parish, congregation or certain colleges
•***Word Family:*** **rectory** (*say* **rek**-ta-ree) *noun* (**rectories**) the house where a rector lives

rectum *noun*
the short end part of the large intestine, connected to the anus

recuperate (*say* re-**koo**-pa-rate) *verb*
to get well again after an illness
•***Word Family:*** **recuperation** *noun*

recur (*say* re-**ker**) *verb*
to repeat or happen again: *If this behaviour recurs*

I'll be angry. / Her back trouble often recurs.
•***Word Family:*** other forms of the verb are **recurs, recurred, recurring** ☐ **recurrence** (*say* ree-**kur**-ence) *noun: a recurrence of bad weather* **recurrent** *adjective*

recycle *verb*
to change waste or unwanted products into something that can be used again
•***Word Family:* recycling** *noun*

red *adjective*
1 having a colour like that of fresh blood
2 having left-wing political views
red *noun*
3 a Communist or left-wing person **4 in the red** in debt **5 see red** to become extremely angry
•***Word Family:* redden** *verb* to make or become red: *His face reddened.* **reddish** *adjective* slightly red

redeem (*say* re-**deem**) *verb*
1 to get something back by paying for it: *She redeemed her ring from the pawnbroker.* 2 to get back into favour: *He redeemed himself for past rudeness.*
•***Word Family:* redemption** *noun*

red-handed *adverb*
while doing something wrong or bad: *to catch someone red-handed*

redhead *noun*
someone with ginger hair

reduce (*say* re-**dewce**) *verb*
1 to make something smaller, lower or less: *The car reduced speed / I'd like to reduce my weight!*
2 to make something change into another condition: *The fire reduced the house to ashes.*
3 to force someone to be in a bad situation: *reduced to begging in the street*
•***Word Family:* reduction** (*say* re-**duk**-shon) *noun: a 10 per cent reduction on all goods in the sale*

redundant (*say* re-**dun**-dunt) *adjective*
1 not needed or unnecessary **2 be made redundant** to lose your job because your employer no longer needs you
•***Word Family:* redundancy** *noun: With his redundancy payment, Dad set up his own business.*
•***Word Origins:*** from a Latin word meaning "overflowing"

reed *noun*
1 a tall, straight grass growing in a marshy area
2 the stalk of such a grass 3 a thin piece of cane or plastic in the mouthpiece of a musical instrument such as the clarinet and oboe, that produces sound by vibrating
•***Word Family:* reedy** *adjective* **(reedier, reediest)**

reef *noun*
a line of rocks or coral near the surface of the sea

reek *verb*
to have a strong, unpleasant smell: *to reek of cigar smoke*

reel (1) *noun*
1 a cylinder on which a fishing line, cotton thread and so on may be wound: *a reel of film*
reel *verb*
2 to wind something onto a reel

reel (2) *verb*
1 to stagger or sway: *to reel down the street* 2 to be dizzy: *His head was reeling.*

reel (3) *noun*
a fast and lively Scottish dance

refer (*say* re-**fer**) *verb*
1 to look at something for information: *to refer to the telephone book* 2 to go or send to for help: *to refer a patient to a specialist* **3 refer to (a)** to talk or write about: *Please do not refer to this matter again.* **(b)** to be connected with: *Does this diagram refer to this example?.*
•***Word Family:*** other forms of the word are **refers, referred, referring** ☐ **referral** *noun: a referral to a specialist*

referee *noun*
1 someone who judges whether rules have been broken and who settles disagreements, especially in some sporting games
referee *verb*
2 to act as a referee: *to referee a football match*
•***Word Family:*** other forms of the verb are **referees, refereed, refereeing**

reference (*say* **ref**-runce) *noun*
1 a source of information: *List your references at the end of the essay.* 2 a mention 3 a letter about the character and abilities of someone: *My boss gave me a good reference.*
reference *adjective*
4 used for information: *a reference book*

referendum (*say* ref-a-**ren**-dum) *noun*
a vote by all the people in a country to decide a question of government or law
•***Word Family:*** the plural is **referenda** or **referendums**

refine (*say* re-**fine**) *verb*
1 to make something pure or clean: *to refine sugar* 2 to improve: *The design has been refined during the last 20 years.*
•***Word Family:* refined** *adjective* polite, elegant or tasteful **refinement** *noun* ☐ **refinery** *noun* **(refineries)** a factory where something is refined: *an oil refinery*

reflect (*say* re-**flekt**) *verb*
1 to throw back light or sound from a surface: *The moon was reflected in the still water.* 2 to be a sign of: *His good marks reflect his hard work.* 3 to think carefully: *Before I can answer I must reflect upon what you have told me.*
•***Word Family:*** **reflection** *noun* □ **reflective** *adjective* **reflectively** *adverb* **reflector** *noun*
•***Word Origins:*** from a Latin word meaning "to bend back"

reflex (*say* **ree**-fleks) *noun*
1 an uncontrollable movement or action made in response to something: *Sneezing is a body reflex.*
reflex *adjective*
2 made in response: *Shivering is a reflex action to cold.*
•***Word Family:*** the plural is **reflexes**

reflex angle *noun*
an angle between 180 and 360 degrees

reform *verb*
1 to improve something or someone by changing or removing what is wrong or bad
reform *noun*
2 an improvement: *law reforms*
•***Word Family:*** **reformer** *noun* someone who works to change something: *a prison reformer*

refraction (*say* re-**frak**-shon) *noun*
the change in direction of a light wave when it passes from one kind of matter to another. A straw in a glass of water will look bent because light travels slower in water than in air
•***Word Family:*** **refract** *verb* to cause to change direction by refraction

refrain (1) (*say* re-**frane**) *verb*
to stop someone from doing or saying something: *Please refrain from talking during the performance.*

refrain (2) *noun*
a part of a song that is repeated

refresh *verb*
to make someone fresh and strong again: *I felt refreshed after my sleep.*
•***Word Family:*** **refreshing** *adjective*: *a refreshing drink*

refreshment *noun*
food or drink

refrigerate (*say* re-**frij**-uh-rate) *verb*
to make or keep something cool or cold
•***Word Family:*** **refrigeration** *noun*
•***Word Origins:*** from Latin words meaning "to make cool again"

refrigerator (*say* re-**frij**-uh-ray-tuh) *noun*
a large cabinet in which food and drink can be stored at a low temperature without being frozen

refuel *verb*
to put fuel in an aeroplane, car and so on
•***Word Family:*** other forms are **refuels, refuelled, refuelling**

refuge (*say* **ref**-yooj) *noun*
shelter or protection from danger or trouble: *refuge from the freezing wind / to take refuge in a castle*

refugee (*say* ref-yoo-**jee**) *noun*
someone who has gone to another country for safety because of some danger or disaster in their own country, such as a war or an earthquake

refund (*say* re-**fund**) *verb*
1 to give money back: *The shop will refund the full price if you are not happy with the chair.*
refund (*say* **ree**-fund) *noun*
2 a repayment of money: *We got a refund because the chair was faulty.*

refuse (1) (*say* re-**fewz**) *verb*
to say that you will not do, accept, give or allow something
•***Word Family:*** **refusal** *noun*

refuse (2) (*say* **ref**-yooce) *noun*
rubbish or waste material

regain (*say* re-**gane**) *verb*
1 to get something back again: *to regain health* 2 to reach somewhere again: *to regain the safety of the shore*

regal (*say* **ree**-gul) *adjective*
to do with a king or queen: *a regal visit*
•***Word Family:*** **regally** *adverb*

regard (*say* re-**gard**) *verb*
1 to think of someone or something in a particular way: *to regard as the best / to regard with affection* 2 to have to do with: *a matter regarding the new law* 3 to look at in a particular way: *She regarded him with a hostile stare.*
regard *noun*
4 concern or attention: *He carries on with no regard for my wishes.* 5 respect: *I have great regard for the leader.* 6 **in regard to** concerning or to do with: *in regard to the money you owe* 7 **regards** kind wishes: *Please send my regards to your parents.*
•***Word Family:*** **regardless** *adjective* without care, consideration or thought: *I asked them to stop, but they carried on regardless.* **regardlessly** *adverb*

regatta (*say* re-**gat**-a) *noun*
a gathering of boats at which contests or races are held

regenerate (*say* ree-**jen**-a-rate) *verb*
1 to give new life and strength to something: *to*

regenerate old inner-city suburbs 2 to grow again: *forest regenerated after the fires*
•*Word Family:* **regeneration** *noun*

regent (*say* **ree**-junt) *noun*
someone who rules a country for a king or queen who is too young or ill to rule
•*Word Family:* **regency** *noun*

reggae (*say* **reg**-ay) *noun*
a type of music from the West Indies, with a strong, regular beat

regime (*say* ray-**zheem**) *noun*
1 a system of rule or government: *Things will be different under the new regime.* 2 a particular government

regiment (*say* **rej**-i-munt) *noun*
1 a large division of the army consisting of two or more battalions
regiment *verb*
2 to control people with strict discipline, as if they are in the army
•*Word Family:* **regimental** (*say* rej-i-**men**-tul) *adjective* **regimentation** *noun*

region (*say* **ree**-jun) *noun*
1 an area of land with features that make it different from another area: *desert regions* 2 a part of the country: *Southern regions will have rain tomorrow.* 3 an area or part: *The pain is in the lower region of my back.*
•*Word Family:* **regional** *adjective: a regional accent*

register (*say* **rej**-is-ter) *noun*
1 an official list: *a register of historic houses / the class register* 2 a machine that can calculate and record numbers: *a cash register* 3 the musical range of a voice or instrument
register *verb*
4 to write something down in a register: *to register a birth* 5 to show or indicate something: *A thermometer registers temperature. / Shock registered on her face.*
•*Word Family:* **registration** *noun: a registration number on a car* **registry** *noun* **(registries)**

registrar (*say* **rej**-i-strar) *noun*
1 someone who keeps records 2 a doctor in a hospital who is training to be a specialist

regret *verb*
1 to feel sorry or unhappy about something: *She regretted her harsh words.*
regret *noun*
2 a feeling of loss, sorrow or disappointment: *Much to his regret the horse lost. / I have no regrets.* 3 **regrets** a polite expression of disappointment: *Joe is unable to join us and sends his regrets.*
•*Word Family:* other forms of the verb are **regrets, regretted, regretting** □ **regretful** *adjective* **regretfully** *adverb* **regretfulness** *noun* **regrettable** *adjective* causing regret: *a regrettable incident at the match* **regrettably** *adverb*

regular (*say* **reg**-yoo-la) *adjective*
1 normal or usual 2 evenly shaped: *regular teeth* 3 following a rule or pattern 4 happening often, usually at fixed times: *regular meals*
regular *noun*
5 a regular customer or visitor
•*Word Family:* **regularity** (*say* reg-yoo-**lar**-i-tee) *noun* **regularly** *adverb*

regulate (*say* **reg**-yoo-late) *verb*
1 to control something, especially by rules 2 to adjust a machine so that it works at a certain speed
•*Word Family:* **regulator** *noun* **regulatory** *adjective* **regulation** *noun*

rehabilitate (*say* ree-ha-**bil**-i-tate) *verb*
to help someone return to a state of health, well-being or usefulness
•*Word Family:* **rehabilitation** *noun*

rehearse (*say* re-**herse**) *verb*
to practise a play, piece of music, speech and so on before giving a public performance
•*Word Family:* **rehearsal** *noun*

reign (*say* rane) *noun*
1 the length of time that a king or queen rules
reign *verb*
2 to rule as a king or queen 3 to be dominant or in control: *Fear reigned while the monster was at large.*

reimburse (*say* ree-im-**berse**) *verb*
to pay someone back the money they have spent: *Do they reimburse you for your travelling expenses?*
•*Word Family:* **reimbursement** *noun*

rein (*say* rane) *noun*
1 a long, leather strap used to control and guide a horse 2 **give free rein to** to allow complete freedom to something 3 **keep a tight rein on** to control something closely

reincarnation (*say* ree-in-kar-**nay**-shon) *noun*
the belief that after someone dies their soul moves into a new body or form
•*Word Family:* **reincarnate** (*say* ree-in-kar-**nate**) *verb: to be reincarnated as a fish*

reindeer (*say* **rane**-deer) *noun*
a large deer with branched antlers, that lives in the cold northern parts of the world
•*Word Family:* the plural is **reindeer** or **reindeers**

reinforce (*say* ree-in-**force**) *verb*
to make something stronger, especially by adding someone or something

A B C D E F G H I J K L M N O P Q R S T U V W X Y Z

•***Word Family:*** **reinforcements** *plural noun* someone or something used to add strength or support, such as extra troops

reiterate (*say* ree-**it**-a-rate) *verb*
to repeat something several times
•***Word Family:*** **reiteration** *noun*

reject (*say* re-**jekt**) *verb*
1 to refuse to accept or use something or someone: *The committee rejected our proposal / The mother panda rejected her baby.*
reject (*say* **ree**-jekt) *noun*
2 something that is rejected, refused or thrown away: *These plates were cheap because they were rejects.*
•***Word Family:*** **rejection** *noun*
•***Word Origins:*** from a Latin word meaning "thrown back"

rejoice *verb*
to be glad or joyful
•***Word Family:*** **rejoicing** *noun*: *There was great rejoicing when the war was over.*

rejuvenate (*say* re-**joov**-i-nate) *verb*
to make someone feel young or something look new again
•***Word Family:*** **rejuvenation** *noun*

relapse (*say* re-**laps**) *verb*
to become ill again when you have been getting better
•***Word Family:*** **relapse** (*say* **ree**-laps) *noun*

relate *verb*
1 to tell or describe: *He related his adventures.* 2 to be connected or associated: *The falling number of road deaths is related to the latest road safety campaign.* 3 to get on well and understand each other: *He relates well to children.*
•***Word Family:*** **related** *adjective* part of the same family: *We are related.*

relation (*say* re-**lay**-shon) *noun*
1 the way that things or people are connected: *What is the relation between these two numbers? / Personal relations are not good between them.* 2 a relative: *She is a distant relation of my mother's.*

relationship *noun*
1 the way that things or people are connected 2 the way that you get on with someone: *I have a good relationship with my father.* 3 a strong friendship between two people: *The relationship ended when she fell in love with someone else.*

relative *adjective*
1 compared or connected with something else: *They live in relative luxury for such a large family.*
relative *noun*
2 someone who is related to you by blood or marriage
•***Word Family:*** **relatively** *adverb*: *a relatively easy exam*

relax *verb*
1 to become looser or less firm: *to relax your grip* 2 to make or become less strict: *to relax the rules* 2 to rest and feel less worried: *to relax on holiday*
•***Word Family:*** **relaxation** *noun*

relay (*say* **ree**-lay) *noun*
1 a group or team that takes turns with others in keeping an activity going 2 a race that is divided into four or more parts with each part run or swum by one member of a team
relay (*say* re-**lay** *or* **ree**-lay) *verb*
3 to pass or carry something from one person to another: *Please relay this message to her.*

release *verb*
1 to set free or let go: *to release from prison* 2 to make public: *to release information*
release *noun*
3 something that sets free or releases something: *I find that shouting is a great release for tension.*
4 something put out for people to see or buy: *the release of his new film / the group's latest release*

relegate (*say* **rel**-uh-gate) *verb*
to put someone or something in a lower or worse place
•***Word Family:*** **relegation** *noun*
•***Word Origins:*** from a Latin word meaning "to send into retirement"

relent *verb*
to become less angry or severe
•***Word Family:*** **relentless** *adjective* without pity **relentlessly** *adverb*

relevant (*say* **rel**-a-vunt) *adjective*
connected to a particular subject: *Your suggestion is not relevant to our discussion.*
•***Word Family:*** **relevance** *noun* **relevantly** *adverb*

reliable (*say* re-**lie**-a-bul) *adjective*
able to be trusted: *The witness is not reliable.*
•***Word Family:*** **reliability** *noun* **reliably** *adverb*

reliant (*say* re-**lie**-ant) *adjective*
having trust in or depending on someone or something: *She is still reliant on her mother.*
•***Word Family:*** **reliance** *noun*

relic *noun*
something that has survived from a past time

relief (*say* re-**leef**) *noun*
1 a feeling of pleasure after worry, discomfort or pain: *What a relief to see the road again! / The cool verandah provided relief from the heat.*
2 something or someone that gives help or comfort: *Please send relief to the flood victims.*
3 someone who replaces someone else: *The*

doctor waited for her relief to arrive. 4 a part or figure in a map or sculpture that is carved so that it stands out from the surface 5 differences in height between hills and valleys: *A relief map shows different heights in different colours.*

relieve (*say* re-**leev**) *verb*
1 to make pain or boredom better: *to relieve a headache* 2 to take over someone's duties: *to relieve the exhausted fire-fighters*

religion (*say* re-**lij**-on) *noun*
1 a belief in and worship of a supernatural power that made the world and can control it 2 a particular system of belief and worship: *the Christian religion*
• ***Word Family:*** **religious** *adjective*

relinquish (*say* re-**ling**-kwish) *verb*
to let something go or give it up: *to relinquish control*
• ***Word Family:*** **relinquishment** *noun*
• ***Word Origins:*** from a Latin word meaning "to leave behind"

relish *noun*
1 pleasure or enjoyment: *He watched the exciting contest with relish.* 2 a savoury food, such as a pickle or sauce, added to a meal
relish *verb*
3 to take pleasure in or enjoy: *I relish the thought of a week relaxing at the lake.*

reluctant (*say* re-**luk**-tunt) *adjective*
not eager: *I'm reluctant to lend you my new game.*
• ***Word Family:*** **reluctance** *noun* **reluctantly** *adverb*

rely *verb*
rely on to depend on someone or something: *He relies on a walking stick to get around. / You can rely on me to get the tickets.*
• ***Word Family:*** other forms are **relies, relied, relying**

remain *verb*
1 to stay or continue: *Remain in your seats. / The horses remained calm during the storm.* 2 to be left: *Much work remains to be done.*
• ***Word Family:*** **remainder** *noun* the part that is left: *If you take 6 from 10 the remainder is 4.*

remains *plural noun*
1 parts that are left after use: *the remains of dinner* 2 a dead body: *We buried her remains.* 3 ruins: *the remains of the abbey*

remark (*say* re-**mark**) *verb*
1 to say something casually
remark *noun*
2 a comment or casual expression
3 commenting or noticing: *The event was scarcely worthy of remark.*
• ***Word Family:*** **remarkable** *adjective* unusual or worthy of comment **remarkably** *adverb*

remedial (*say* re-**mee**-di-ul) *adjective*
helping to improve something: *remedial teaching*

remedy (*say* **rem**-a-dee) *noun*
1 something that cures: *a remedy for a sore throat* 2 something that puts right: *a remedy for street crime*
remedy *verb*
3 to fix or put right
• ***Word Family:*** other forms of the verb are **remedies, remedied, remedying** □ the plural is **remedies**

remember *verb*
1 to keep something in your mind: *Please remember to bring your coat.* 2 to think of something that you knew before: *I can't remember his name.*
• ***Word Family:*** **remembrance** *noun*

remind *verb*
to help someone remember: *Please remind me to buy the meat.*
• ***Word Family:*** **reminder** *noun*

reminiscence (*say* rem-i-**nis**-unce) *noun*
1 a memory 2 **reminiscences** descriptions of past experiences and events
• ***Word Family:*** **reminisce** *verb* to think or talk about past experiences or events **reminiscent** *adjective: a smell reminiscent of spring*

remission (*say* re-**mish**-on) *noun*
1 a pardon or release from punishment: *remission for good behaviour* 2 a time when a disease gets better for a while: *a temporary remission of the cancer*

remnant *noun*
a small part or amount that is left: *fabric remnants*

remorse *noun*
a feeling of regret for something bad that you have done: *He felt remorse for his crimes.*
• ***Word Family:*** **remorseless** *adjective* without pity **remorseful** *adjective* **remorsefully** *adverb* **remorsefulness** *noun* **remorselessly** *adverb*

remote *adjective*
far away or distant: *a remote town / the remote past*
• ***Word Family:*** **remotely** *adverb* **remoteness** *noun*

remote control *noun*
a device or system for controlling something from some distance away
• ***Word Family:*** **remote-controlled** *adjective: a remote-controlled car*

remove (*say* re-**moov**) *verb*
to take something or someone off or away: *Remove your shoes before entering.*
• ***Word Family:*** **removal** (*say* re-**moo**-vul) *noun*

render *verb*
1 to give: *to render assistance* 2 to make: *to be rendered speechless* 3 to represent: *The artist rendered the scene in great detail.* 4 to perform: *to render a song* 5 to coat a wall with a layer of plaster or mortar
• ***Word Family:*** **rendering** *noun* **rendition** *noun: a rendition of a song*

rendezvous (*say* **ron**-day-voo) *noun*
1 an arranged meeting 2 a meeting place
rendezvous *verb*
3 to meet with someone by arrangement
• ***Word Family:*** other forms of the verb are **rendezvous, rendezvoused, rendezvousing**
• ***Word Origins:*** from a French word meaning "to present yourself"

renegade (*say* **ren**-a-gade) *noun*
someone who leaves or betrays a group, belief or cause

renew *verb*
to begin again, or make something new: *to renew a friendship. / to renew a library book*
• ***Word Family:*** **renewal** *noun*

renewable energy *noun*
energy from the sun, wind and waves

renounce *verb*
to give up or reject: *I renounce all claim to the inheritance.*
• ***Word Family:*** **renunciation** *noun*

renovate (*say* **ren**-a-vate) *verb*
to repair a house or other building
• ***Word Family:*** **renovation** *noun* **renovator** *noun*

renown (*say* ree-**noun**) *noun*
fame: *an artist of great renown*
• ***Word Family:*** **renowned** *adjective*

rent *noun*
1 regular payment for the use of something, usually a building, that belongs to someone else
rent *verb*
2 to pay for the use of property that belongs to someone else: *to rent a television* 3 to let someone use your property in return for payment: *We rented our house to friends when we went overseas.*
• ***Word Family:*** **rental** *adjective*

repair (*say* re-**pair**) *verb*
1 to mend something: *We repaired the hole in the roof.*
repair *noun*
2 repairing: *a house in need of repair* 3 condition: *to be in good repair*
• ***Word Family:*** **repairable** (*say* **rep**-ar-a-bul) *adjective* **repairer** *noun: a shoe repairer*

repatriate (*say* ree-**pat**-ri-ate) *verb*
to send someone back to their own country
• ***Word Family:*** **repatriation** *noun*

repay *verb*
1 to pay back: *repay a loan* 2 to return: *How can I ever repay your kindness?*
• ***Word Family:*** other forms of the verb are **repays, repaid, repaying** □ **repayment** *noun*

repeal *verb*
to cancel or withdraw: *Parliament has repealed the law.*

repeat *verb*
1 to say or do something again: *Repeat the poem until you know it by memory.*
repeat *noun*
2 something which is repeated, such as a television programme
• ***Word Family:*** **repeated** *adjective* done or said again and again **repeatedly** *adverb* **repetition** *noun*

repel *verb*
1 to force someone or something back: *to repel an invasion of mice* 2 to disgust someone: *The filthy kitchen repelled her.* 3 to keep something away: *This spray will repel insects.*
• ***Word Family:*** other forms of the verb are **repels, repelled, repelling** □ **repellent** *adjective* □ see also **repulsion**

repent (*say* re-**pent**) *verb*
to feel sad or sorry that you have done something: *He repented his crimes.*
• ***Word Family:*** **repentance** *noun* **repentant** *adjective*

repercussion (*say* ree-pa-**kush**-on) *noun*
something that happens because of something else: *The tragedy had many repercussions.*

repertoire (*say* **rep**-a-twa) *noun*
the songs, musical pieces, plays and so on presented by a performer or group
• ***Word Origins:*** this word comes from French

replace *verb*
1 to put something back: *Please replace books on the correct shelves.* 2 to take the place of something: *We planted a new tree to replace the one that died.* 3 to put something new in instead of something old: *to replace the water in the fishtank*
• ***Word Family:*** **replacement** *noun*

replay (*say* ree-**play**) *verb*
1 to play a sports match over again because of a draw 2 to play a recording again: *to replay the tape*
replay (*say* **ree**-play) *noun*
3 a repeat, on television or on a screen at a

sports ground, of important parts of a sports game, sometimes immediately after they have happened: *Let's see that catch on the replay.* 4 a sports match played again because of a draw

replica (*say* **rep**-li-ka) *noun*
an exact copy
•***Word Family:*** **replicate** *verb* to make an exact copy of something: *The thief tried to replicate my signature.* **replication** *noun*

reply *verb*
1 to say or do something in return: *Have you replied to his letter yet?*
reply *noun*
2 something said or done in return
•***Word Family:*** other forms of the verb are **replies, replied, replying** □ the plural is **replies**

report *noun*
1 an account of a particular subject: *a report on the latest developments in Bosnia / a report on a student's progress at school* 2 a loud bang or explosion
report *verb*
3 to give an account of something: *His speech was reported in the newspapers.* 4 to make a complaint about: *to report noisy neighbours to the police* 5 to appear for duty: *Report for work at noon.*
•***Word Family:*** **reporter** *noun* someone whose job is to gather and describe the news

repossess (*say* re-po-**zes**) *noun*
to take property back again, usually because payments have not been made: *The car company repossessed their car.*
•***Word Family:*** **repossession** *noun*

represent (*say* rep-ri-**zent**) *verb*
1 to stand for something: *The red lines on the map represent main roads.* 2 to act on behalf of someone: *That MP represents our town.* 3 to describe or give a picture of something: *a painting representing rural life*
•***Word Family:*** **representative** *noun* **representation** *noun*

repress *verb*
to hold back or control something or someone: *to repress a smile / to repress opposition*
•***Word Family:*** **repression** (*say* re-**presh**-on) *noun* **repressive** *adjective*: *to live under a repressive regime*

reprieve (*say* re-**preev**) *verb*
1 to delay or cancel someone's punishment
reprieve *noun*
2 a delay or postponement of a punishment
3 a temporary relief or release

reprimand (*say* **rep**-ri-mahnd) *verb*
1 to scold or criticize someone severely
reprimand *noun*
2 a spoken or written criticism

reprint (*say* re-**print**) *verb*
1 to print something again
reprint (*say* **re**-print) *noun*
2 something that has been printed again, such as a new edition of a book

reprisal (*say* re-**pry**-zul) *noun*
an act of revenge

reproach *verb*
1 to blame someone in a way that shows that you are disappointed in them
reproach *noun*
2 blame or disapproval
•***Word Family:*** the plural is **reproaches** □ **reproachful** *adjective* **reproachfully** *adverb*

reproduce (*say* re-pro-**dewce**) *verb*
1 to give birth to offspring 2 to copy: *to reproduce a painting from the original.*
•***Word Family:*** **reproduction** *noun* **(a)** something that is produced again or in an identical form **(b)** producing offspring **reproductive** *adjective*

reptile *noun*
a cold-blooded animal, such as the snake, turtle or crocodile, that lays eggs and usually has scales or tough skin.
•***Word Family:*** **reptilian** (*say* rep-**til**-i-an) *adjective*
•***Word Origins:*** from a Latin word meaning "creeping"

republic (*say* re-**pub**-lik) *noun*
a country with an elected government and a president instead of a king or queen
•***Word Family:*** **republican** *adjective* wanting a republic as the form of government **republican** *noun* someone who wants a republic as the form of government **republicanism** *noun*

repugnant *adjective*
distasteful or unpleasant
•***Word Family:*** **repugnance** *noun*

repulsion (*say* re-**pul**-shon) *noun*
1 strong dislike: *a feeling of repulsion* 2 resisting or repelling

repulsive *adjective*
disgusting: *Please get rid of that repulsive smell!*

reputable (*say* **rep**-yoo-ta-bul) *adjective*
honest, dependable and trustworthy
•***Word Family:*** **reputably** (*say* rep-**yoo**-ta-blee) *adverb*

reputation (*say* rep-yoo-**tay**-shon) *noun*
the opinion that most people have about someone or something: *a reputation for cheating customers / a good reputation*

A B C D E F G H I J K L M N O P Q R S T U V W X Y Z

repute (*say* re-**pewt**) *noun*
1 fame or reputation: *a man of evil repute / The company is held in high repute.*
repute *verb*
2 to consider or regard someone as something: *She's reputed to be a witch.*
•***Word Family:*** **reputed** *adjective: She spent a reputed fortune on the house.* **reputedly** *adverb*

request (*say* re-**kwest**) *verb*
1 to ask for something
request *noun*
2 the act of asking 3 something that is asked for

requiem (*say* **rek**-wi-em) *noun*
1 a service in the Roman Catholic Church for the peace of the dead 2 a ceremony for the dead
•***Word Origins:*** from a Latin word meaning "rest"

require (*say* re-**kwire**) *verb*
1 to need something: *All visitors require permission to enter.* 2 to want or wish for something: *Do you require anything else?*
•***Word Family:*** **requirement** *noun* something that is necessary

rescue (*say* **res**-kew) *verb*
1 to save someone or something from danger, imprisonment or unpleasantness
rescue *noun*
2 the act of rescuing
•***Word Family:*** **rescuer** *noun*

research *noun*
1 study to find new facts or learn more about a subject
research *verb*
2 to investigate a subject thoroughly
•***Word Family:*** **researcher** *noun*

resemble (*say* re-**zem**-bul) *verb*
to be or look like: *She resembles her grandmother.*
•***Word Family:*** **resemblance** *noun: There is little resemblance between the two languages.*

resent (*say* re-**zent**) *verb*
to feel hurt or angry about something: *I resent those rude comments.*
•***Word Family:*** **resentful** *adjective* **resentfully** *adverb* **resentment** *noun*
•***Word Origins:*** from a Latin word meaning "to feel"

reservation (*say* rez-uh-**vay**-shon) *noun*
1 an arrangement in advance to keep something, such as a hotel room or seat in an aeroplane for someone 2 an uncertainty: *You seem to have reservations about parts of our agreement.* 3 an area of land set aside for a group of people to live on: *a Navaho reservation*

reserve (*say* re-**zerv**) *verb*
1 to keep something back or save it for later: *We must reserve some water for the horses.* 2 to book or organize in advance: *We reserved a seat for you on tomorrow's train.*
reserve *noun*
3 something that is kept, saved or set aside: *a reserve of food* 4 an extra member of a sports team 5 an area of public land set aside for a particular purpose: *a wildlife reserve*

reserved *adjective*
shy and not liking to show your feelings

reservoir (*say* **rez**-a-vwa) *noun*
1 a place or container for storing water 2 a large supply or store: *reservoirs of oil / a vast reservoir of knowledge*
•***Word Origins:*** this word comes from French

reside (*say* re-**zide**) *verb*
to stay in one place or home for a particular time: *She now resides in Italy.*

residence (*say* **rez**-i-dence) *noun*
1 the place where someone lives 2 a large house

resident (*say* **rez**-i-dunt) *noun*
1 someone who lives in a particular place
2 a doctor who lives in a hospital
•***Word Family:*** **residency** *noun* **residential** *adjective*

residue (*say* **rez**-i-dew) *noun*
something that remains or is left over

resign (*say* re-**zine**) *verb*
1 to give up a position or job: *She resigned her job. / He resigned as president of the club.* 2 **resign yourself to something** to accept that something will happen
•***Word Family:*** **resignation** (*say* rez-ig-**nay**-shon) *noun*

resilient (*say* re-**zil**-yunt) *adjective*
able to recover quickly from something bad: *Her resilient nature helped her to get better quickly.*
•***Word Family:*** **resilience** *noun* **resiliently** *adverb*

resin (*say* **rez**-in) *noun*
a thick, sticky sap produced by some plants, used for making polish and varnish

resist (*say* re-**zist**) *verb*
to fight against something: *to resist arrest / I could not resist a smile.*
•***Word Family:*** **resistance** *noun* **(a)** fighting back: *Resistance is useless.* **(b)** the slowing or stopping of an object by another object: *wind resistance* **resistant** *adjective*

resolute (*say* **rez**-a-loot) *adjective*
very determined: *resolute opposition*
•***Word Family:*** **resolutely** *adverb*

resolution (*say* rez-a-**loo**-shon) *noun*
1 a firm decision: *a resolution not to swear any more* 2 being determind or firm 3 a solution or answer: *Resolution of this problem is going to be difficult.*

resolve (*say* re-**zolv**) *verb*
1 to make a firm decision: *I resolved never to do it again.* 2 to solve or settle a problem or argument: *to resolve the dispute*
resolve *noun*
3 a firm determination: *She was filled with resolve to succeed.*

resonant (*say* **rez**-a-nant) *adjective*
1 vibrating or echoing: *the resonant sound of a bell* 2 deep and rich: *a resonant voice*
• ***Word Family:*** **resonate** *verb* to resound or echo **resonance** *noun* **resonantly** *adverb*

resort (*say* re-**zort**) *verb*
1 to turn to or use something: *We resorted to walking during the bus strike.*
resort *noun*
2 a place that people visit or use often: *a popular beach resort* 3 **the last resort** someone or something used when all else has failed

resound (*say* re-**zound**) *verb*
to echo loudly: *The tunnel resounded with the rumble of the train.*
• ***Word Family:*** **resounding** *adjective* (a) loud and clear: *a resounding knock* (b) complete: *a resounding success*

resource (*say* re-**sorce** *or* re-**zorce**) *noun*
1 a source or supply: *resources of food.*
2 something that helps or comforts you in a difficult situation: *Her great resource is her optimism.* 3 **resources** the supplies of things that a country can use: *natural resources*
• ***Word Family:*** **resourceful** *adjective* good at thinking of ways to solve difficulties **resourcefully** *adverb* **resourcefulness** *noun*

respect *noun*
1 admiration of someone, or appreciation of their abilities, qualities and so on: *We have great respect for him as a leader. / Please show your mother more respect.* 2 a detail: *Our opinions differ in some respects.* 3 **respects** polite good wishes: *Mother sends her respects.*
respect *verb*
4 to feel respect for someone: *We respect him as a leader.*
• ***Word Family:*** **respectful** *adjective* showing respect **respectfully** *adverb* **respectfulness** *noun*

respectable *adjective*
1 living your life or behaving in a way that most people think is suitable or decent: *a respectable suburb / a respectable skirt / a respectable job* 2 quite good: *a respectable performance*
• ***Word Family:*** **respectably** *adverb* **respectability** (*say* ree-spek-ta-**bil**-i-tee) *noun*

respective *adjective*
to do with each individual person or thing: *We split up and went back to our respective homes.*

respiration (*say* resp-i-**ray**-shon) *noun*
breathing

respirator (*say* **res**-pi-ray-ta) *noun*
1 a device worn over your face to help you breathe if there is smoke or dangerous gas present 2 a machine to help you breathe if you are too ill or injured to breathe on your own

respond (*say* re-**spond**) *verb*
to speak or act in return: *She responded to the joke with a smile.*

response *noun*
something said or done in return
• ***Word Family:*** **responsive** *adjective* **responsively** *adverb* **responsiveness** *noun*

responsible (*say* re-**spon**-si-bul) *adjective*
1 in the position of looking after someone or something: *Parents are responsible for their children.* 2 being the cause of or being to blame for something: *the person responsible for the accident / Who is responsible for these beautiful flowers?* 3 reliable or capable: *a responsible child*
• ***Word Family:*** **responsibility** (*say* re-spon-si-**bil**-i-tee) *noun* (**responsibilities**) a duty or care **responsibly** *adverb*

rest (1) *noun*
1 a break from work 2 a short sleep 3 a pause, such as a silence between musical notes or a break in a line of poetry 4 a support: *an armrest*
rest *verb*
5 to relax or sleep: *They rested from digging for a while. / Rest on the bed.* 6 to lean or be supported: *Her chin rested on her hands.* 7 to depend: *The success of the party rests on good music.* 8 to leave alone: *let the matter rest*

rest (2) *noun*
someone or something that remains or is left over: *Some of us stayed at home while the rest went out. / Where is the rest of the cake?*

restaurant (*say* **rest**-a-ront) *noun*
a place where you can go for a meal: *a Chinese restaurant*

restless *adjective*
unable to keep still
• ***Word Family:*** **restlessly** *adverb* **restlessness** *noun*

restore (*say* re-**stor**) *verb*
1 to put or bring something back: *to restore order after the riot / to restore stolen property to its owner*

A B C D E F G H I J K L M N O P Q R S T U V W X Y Z

2 to bring something back to good condition: *to restore vintage cars*
•**Word Family: restoration** *noun* restoring: *the restoration of an old house to its original condition / the restoration of peace after war*

restrain *verb*
to control or hold something back: *Please restrain your dog.*
•**Word Family: restraint** *noun* something that controls or restricts: *physical restraint / wage restraint / to keep a dog under restraint*

restrict *verb*
to limit or confine someone or something: *Her movements are restricted by her injured leg. / Restrict your questions to the main topic.*
•**Word Family: restricted** *adjective: This is a restricted area—entry to authorized personnel only.* **restriction** *noun* **restrictive** *adjective*

result *noun*
1 something that happens because of an action or event 2 the answer to a sum 3 the outcome of a game or contest: *the election result*
result *verb*
4 to happen because of something else: *The crash resulted from careless driving.* 5 **result in** to end in a particular way: *to result in an agreement*

resume *verb*
to continue: *We will resume this lesson tomorrow.*
•**Word Family: resumption** (*say* re-**zump**-shon) *noun: the resumption of peace talks*

résumé (*say* **rez**-yoo-may) *noun*
a short account of a speech, book or other piece of writing: My *teacher asked me to write a résumé of the book I'd been reading.*
•**Word Origins:** from a French word meaning "summed up"

resurrect (*say* rez-a-**rekt**) *verb*
to bring someone back to life or something back into use: *to resurrect an old friendship*
•**Word Family: resurrection** (*say* rez-a-**rek**-shon) *noun: the resurrection of Christ*

resuscitate (*say* re-**sus**-i-tate) *verb*
to revive someone who has collapsed or become unconscious
•**Word Family: resuscitator** *noun* a machine used to try to revive someone **resuscitation** *noun*

retail *noun*
1 the selling of small quantities of goods to the public, usually in a shop
retail *verb*
2 to sell goods in a shop: *to retail books* 3 to be sold: *This book retails at £15.*
•**Word Family: retailer** *noun*

retain *verb*
1 to keep or hold onto something: *She retained her dignity despite the embarrassing mistake.* 2 to remember: *He retains everything he reads.*
•**Word Family: retention** *noun*

retaliate (*say* re-**tal**-i-ate) *verb*
to repay an injury or wrong with a similar act: *The bombed troops retaliated with a surprise attack.*
•**Word Family: retaliation** *noun*

retard (*say* re-**tard**) *verb*
to slow down or delay the progress of: *Frosts retarded the growth of the vegetables.*
•**Word Family: retarded** *adjective: mentally retarded* **retardant** *noun a fire retardant* **retardation** (*say* re-tar-**day**-shon) *noun*

retch *verb*
to try to vomit
•**Word Origins:** from an Old English word meaning "a clearing of the throat"

retina (*say* **ret**-i-na) *noun*
the coating on the back of the eye which receives light and sends an image of what is seen through nerves to the brain
•**Word Family:** the plural is **retinas** or **retinae** (*say* **ret**-i-nee)

retire *verb*
1 to go away to another place: *She retired to her office to think about the proposal. / to retire to bed*
2 to give up paid work permanently: *to retire at 65*
•**Word Family: retiring** *adjective* shy **retirement** *noun*

retort *verb*
1 to reply quickly and sharply
retort *noun*
2 a quick or sharp reply

retract *verb*
to withdraw or take something back: *The tortoise retracted its head. / to retract an accusation*
•**Word Family: retractable** *adjective* **retraction** *noun*

retreat *noun*
1 moving back to safety away from danger: *The soldiers made a retreat to the waiting boats.* 2 a quiet, peaceful place: *a holiday retreat*
retreat *verb*
3 to move back away from danger

retrench *verb*
to dismiss staff in order to save money
•**Word Family: retrenchment** *noun*
•**Word Origins:** from an Old French word meaning "to cut back"

retrieve (*say* re-**treev**) *verb*
1 to bring something back: *The dog retrieved the stick.* 2 to put something right: *It's too late to retrieve the situation now.*
•**Word Family: retriever** *noun* a type of dog that

can be trained to bring shot birds and small animals back to the hunter **retrieval** *noun*
•***Word Origins:*** from an Old French word meaning "to find again"

retrospective *adjective*
1 having to do with or looking back to the past: *a retrospective exhibition* 2 having effect from a past date: *to make a law retrospective*
•***Word Family:*** **retrospection** *noun* a survey of the past

return *verb*
1 to come or go back: *to return home / He has returned to his old habits.* 2 to send or give something back: *to return the ball with a powerful stroke / Please return the money I lent you.*
return *noun*
3 the act of returning: *On my return, I went to bed. / The tennis player hit a splendid return.*
4 something received as a profit: *What return did you get on your investment?* 5 a return ticket: *a day return to London* 6 an official statement or report: *a tax return* 7 **many happy returns** a birthday greeting 8 **return ticket** a ticket for a journey to a place and back

reunion (*say* re-**yoon**-yon) *noun*
a special meeting of people who have not seen each other for a period of time: *a class reunion*

rev *verb*
1 to increase engine speed quickly
rev *noun*
2 a revolution of an engine
•***Word Family:*** other forms of the verb are **revs, revved, revving**
•***Word Origins:*** short for **revolution**

reveal *verb*
1 to show something: *This dress reveals my horrible knees.* 2 to make something known: *to reveal a secret*
•***Word Family:*** **revealing** *adjective* **revelation** *noun*

revenge (*say* re-**venj**) *noun*
1 harm you do to someone to repay them for harming or injuring you: *I'll get revenge for that insult!*
revenge *verb*
2 to take revenge: *to revenge a defeat*
•***Word Family:*** **revengeful** *adjective* **revengefully** *adverb*

revenue (*say* **rev**-uh-new) *noun*
income, especially money that a government gets from taxes

reverberate (*say* re-**ver**-ba-rate) *verb*
to echo again and again: *His screams reverberated in the empty theatre.*
•***Word Family:*** **reverberation** *noun*

revere (*say* re-**vear**) *verb*
to feel great respect for
•***Word Family:*** **reverence** (*say* **rev**-a-runce) *noun* a feeling of deep respect and awe **reverent** *adjective* **reverential** *adjective*

Reverend (*say* **rev**-a-rund) *adjective*
a title for a member of the clergy: *the Reverend Mr Hudson*

reverse *adjective*
1 opposite to the usual: *reverse order*
reverse *noun*
2 the opposite: *The reverse of what she says is true.* 3 a setback or defeat: *Our plans suffered a major reverse.* 4 a gear which makes a vehicle move backwards 5 the back of a coin, medal or postage stamp
reverse *verb*
6 to turn something round in direction, order or position: *to reverse a decision / to reverse the car into the parking space*
•***Word Family:*** **reversal** *noun: a reversal of the usual order* **reversible** *adjective: a reversible coat*
•***Word Origins:*** from a Latin word meaning "turned about"

revert *verb*
to return to a particular state: *He quickly reverted to his old ways.*

review (*say* re-**vew**) *noun*
1 a general survey or inspection: *a review of the year's work* 2 a short article giving an opinion about a new book, film, play, and so on 3 a magazine which contains articles about recent happenings
review *verb*
4 to write about a new book, film, and so on, giving your opinion of it 5 to reconsider: *The court reviewed the earlier judgment.*
•***Word Family:*** **reviewer** *noun* someone who reviews books, films, and so on

revise (*say* re-**vize**) *verb*
1 to check, alter or change something: *I have revised my opinion. / Revise the text before you print it out.* 2 to read or study something again, especially before an examination
•***Word Family:*** **revision** (*say* re-**vizh**-on) *noun*

revive *verb*
to bring someone or something back to life or use: *She was revived after being pulled from the sea. / The government revived an old law.*
•***Word Family:*** **revival** *noun*

revolt *verb*
1 to fight against authority 2 to disgust or horrify someone: *I was revolted by the terrible crime.*
revolt *noun*
3 a fight against authority
•***Word Family:*** **revoltingly** *adverb*

revolution (*say* rev-a-**loo**-shon) *noun*
1 the turning of a circle around a central point
2 a complete change, such as that caused by the overthrow of a government
•*Word Family:* **revolutionize** or **revolutionise** *verb* to bring about a complete change

revolutionary (*say* rev-a-**loo**-shon-ree) *noun*
1 someone who wants a complete change in society
revolutionary *adjective*
2 causing a great change in the way things are done or made: *revolutionary teaching methods / a revolutionary building material*
•*Word Family:* the plural is **revolutionaries**

revolve *verb*
to turn around a central point: *The Earth revolves around the sun.*

revolver *noun*
a pistol with a revolving container for bullets, allowing a number of shots to be fired without reloading

revue (*say* re-**vew**) *noun*
a show with short acts and songs which usually makes fun of people and recent happenings

reward *noun*
1 something you are given as a way of thanking you for something you have done
reward *verb*
2 to give someone something in return for help or work: *She was rewarded with a friendly smile.*
•*Word Family:* **rewarding** *adjective* satisfying

rewind *verb*
to make a tape go backwards
•*Word Family:* other forms are **rewinds, rewound, rewinding**

rhapsody (*say* **rap**-sa-dee) *noun*
1 a feeling of great delight: *They are in rhapsodies about the new house.* 2 a short piece of romantic music

rheumatism (*say* **room**-a-tiz-um) *noun*
a disease that causes pain and stiffness in joints and joint-muscles
•*Word Family:* **rheumatic** (*say* roo-**mat**-ik) also called **rheumatoid** (*say* **roo**-ma-toyd) *adjective*

rhinoceros (*say* rye-**nos**-a-rus) *noun*
a large, heavy, thick-skinned animal with one or two horns on its snout, found in Africa and Asia
•*Word Family:* the plural is **rhinoceroses** (*say* rye-**nos**-a-rus-ez) □ the short form is **rhino**
•*Word Origins:* from Greek words meaning "nose" and "horn"

rhododendron (*say* ro-da-**den**-drun) *noun*
a shrub with large clusters of pink, purple or white flowers

rhombus (*say* **rom**-bus) *noun*
a shape with four equal, parallel sides and angles that are not right angles
•*Word Family:* the plural is **rhombuses** or **rhombi**

rhubarb (*say* **roo**-barb) *noun*
a plant with thick, long, red stalks, usually cooked with sugar as a dessert

rhyme (*say* rime) *noun*
1 the repeating of similar or identical sounds such as *park, mark* and *lark* 2 a verse or poem in which the last words of each line sound alike
rhyme *verb*
3 to sound alike: *"dog" rhymes with "log"*

rhythm (*say* **rith**-um) *noun*
1 the pattern of strong and weak beats in music or speech 2 a regular pattern: *the rhythm of the seasons*
•*Word Family:* **rhythmic** *adjective* **rhythmical** (*say* **rith**-mi-kul) *adjective* **rhythmically** *adverb*

rib *noun*
1 one of the thin, curved bones that form a cage around your heart and lungs 2 the main vein of a leaf

ribbon *noun*
1 a band of fabric used for tying or decorating
2 something that is long and thin like a ribbon: *a ribbon of flowerbed along the fence / My coat was torn to ribbons.*

rice *noun*
a cereal plant which is an important food, often grown in water in warmer climates

rich *adjective*
1 having a lot of money, property or resources
2 deep, strong and attractive: *a rich voice / a rich red* 3 made with a lot of cream, eggs and so on: *a rich sauce* 4 expensive or luxurious: *rich tapestries* 5 abundant: *a rich supply of paintings*
•*Word Family:* **riches** *plural noun* wealth **richly** *adverb* **richness** *noun*

rickety *adjective*
unsteady or unsafe: *a rickety old bridge*

rickshaw *noun*
a small, two-wheeled cart pulled by one or two people and used in some Asian countries to carry goods or passengers
•*Word Origins:* from a Japanese word meaning "people-power-vehicle"

ricochet (*say* **rik**-o-shay) *verb*
to hit a surface, bounce off and continue travelling
•*Word Family:* other forms of the word are **ricochets, ricocheted** (*say* rik-o-**shade**) **ricocheting** (*say* rik-o-**shay**-ing)
•*Word Origins:* this word comes from French

rid *verb*
1 to make someone or something free of something unwanted: *to rid the dog of fleas / to rid the country of terrorists* 2 **get rid of** to remove something or throw it away
•***Word Family:*** other forms of the word are **rids, rid** or **ridded, ridding**

riddle *noun*
1 a question asked as a puzzle, with a clever or amusing answer 2 someone or something that is puzzling

ride *verb*
1 to travel on a horse, bicycle and so on 2 to be carried as a passenger in a vehicle or on someone's back: *to ride in a bus*
ride *noun*
3 a journey on horseback, a bicycle or in a vehicle: *a ride in a bus*
•***Word Family:*** other forms of the verb are **rides, rode, ridden, riding** □ **rider** *noun*

ridge *noun*
1 a long, narrow area of raised land 2 a long, narrow raised line: *the ridge of the roof*

ridicule (*say* **rid**-i-kewl) *verb*
1 to make fun of someone or something: *The papers ridiculed the design of the new bridge.*
ridicule *noun*
2 words, actions or unkind laughter meant to make someone or something look foolish

ridiculous (*say* re-**dik**-yoo-lus) *adjective*
silly or foolish: *a ridiculous hat / a ridiculous idea*
•***Word Family:*** **ridiculously** *adverb* **ridiculousness** *noun*

rife *adjective*
widespread or common: *Corruption was rife in the country.*

rifle (1) (*say* **rye**-ful) *noun*
a gun with a long barrel that is supported on the shoulder to be fired

rifle (2) (*say* **rye**-ful) *verb*
to search through in order to steal something: *The desk had been rifled by a thief.*

rift *noun*
1 a split 2 a disagreement: *to heal the rift between two people*

rig *noun*
1 the arrangement of masts and sails on a boat 2 equipment for a particular purpose, such as the machinery for drilling an oil well
rig *verb*
3 to provide a boat with the necessary masts, sails, ropes and so on 4 to manipulate or control something dishonestly: *The election was rigged.* 5 **rig up** to assemble: *to rig up an aerial*
•***Word Family:*** other forms of the verb are **rigs, rigged, rigging** □ **rigging** *noun* the ropes on a ship that support the sails

right *adjective*
1 opposite to left: *my right arm* 2 good or fair: *It's not right to cheat.* 3 true, correct or accurate: *What is the right time?*
right *noun*
4 that which is good, fair, proper and correct: *He can't tell the difference between right and wrong.* 5 something that people are allowed to do or have: *the right to vote* 6 a fair claim: *I have a right to be here.* 7 something opposite the left: *the girl on the right* 8 a political party or group which generally believes in the private ownership of business and property rather than the equal distribution of wealth
right *adverb*
9 towards the right 10 straight or directly: *Go right home. / Get right to the point.* 11 correctly or properly: *I can't do a thing right today.* 12 at once: *I'll come right away.*
right *verb*
13 to correct: *These mistakes must be righted.*
14 to put something upright: *to right your canoe*
•***Word Family:*** **rightly** *adverb* **rightness** *noun*

right angle *noun*
an angle of 90°

righteous (*say* **rye**-chus) *adjective*
doing what is right: *The righteous person obeyed all the laws.*
•***Word Family:*** **righteously** *adverb* **righteousness** *noun*

right-handed *adjective*
using your right hand more than your left

rigid (*say* **rij**-id) *adjective*
1 stiff or unbending: *a rigid pole* 2 strict or severe: *rigid discipline*
•***Word Family:*** **rigidity** *noun* **rigidly** *adverb*

rigour or **rigor** (*say* **rig**-a) *noun*
severity or harshness: *the rigour of a long winter*

rim *noun*
the outer edge or margin, especially of a curved or circular object: *the rim of a wheel*

rind (*rhymes with* find) *noun*
a hard, outer skin: *orange rind / cheese rind*
•***Word Origins:*** from an Old English word meaning "bark"

ring (1) *noun*
1 a circular band, especially one that you wear on your finger: *a wedding ring* 2 a circular area, often enclosed, used for a particular purpose: *a circus ring / a boxing ring* 3 a circular shape: *She drew a ring around the number.*

A B C D E F G H I J K L M N O P Q R S T U V W X Y Z

ring *verb*
4 to surround something with a ring
•***Word Family:*** other forms of the verb are **rings, ringed, ringing**

ring (2) *verb*
1 to make a clear musical sound when struck, such as a bell makes 2 to use a bell, especially to ask for something: *to ring for service* 3 to telephone: *I'll ring you tonight.*
ring *noun*
4 the act or sound of ringing: *the ring of a bell*
5 a telephone call: *I'll give you a ring tonight.*
•***Word Family:*** other forms of the verb are **rings, rang, rung, ringing**

ringbark *verb*
to cut away a ring of bark from around a branch or trunk of a tree in order to kill it by cutting off the flow of sap

ringleader *noun*
someone who leads a small group, especially a group of troublemakers or a gang

ringlet *noun*
a curly piece of someone's hair

ringmaster *noun*
someone in charge of the performances in the ring of a circus

ringworm *noun*
a skin infection causing an itchy, circular rash, often on the scalp

rink *noun*
a smooth, artificial surface of ice for ice-skating
2 a flat surface for roller-skating

rinse *verb*
1 to wash lightly: *She rinsed the sand from her feet.* 2 to use clean water to remove soap: *He rinsed the shampoo from his hair.*
rinse *noun*
3 a non-permanent colouring for the hair: *a blue rinse*

riot (*say* **rye**-ot) *noun*
1 a noisy, uncontrolled and often violent disturbance caused by a large group of people
riot *verb*
2 to join with others in wild and violent behaviour: *The crowd rioted.*
•***Word Family:*** **rioter** *noun* **riotous** *adjective* noisy and wild **riotously** *adverb*

rip (1) *verb*
1 to tear or be torn roughly: *He ripped open the parcel.* / *Her dress was ripped to shreds.* 2 **rip off** to cheat someone by charging them too much for something
rip *noun*
3 a tear
•***Word Family:*** other forms of the verb are **rips, ripped, ripping**

rip (2) *noun*
a strong, dangerous current, especially near a beach: *to be swept out in a rip*

ripe *adjective*
mature or fully developed: *a ripe apple* / *a ripe old age*
•***Word Family:*** **ripen** *verb* to become ripe **ripeness** *noun*

ripple *noun*
1 a small wave: *ripples in a still pond* 2 a sound or movement that flows in small waves: *a ripple of laughter*
ripple *verb*
3 to make small waves on something: *A gust of wind rippled the lake.* 4 to flow in small waves: *Laughter rippled through the room.*

rise (*say* rize) *verb*
1 to stand up: *All rise please.* 2 to get out of bed: *to rise early* 3 to increase: *The temperature has risen.* / *His voice rose to a shout.* 4 to extend upwards: *The building rises to a height of 50 metres.* 5 to rebel: *to rise against the government*
rise *noun*
6 an increase: *a rise in temperature* / *a rise in salary*
7 an upward slope: *The house is just over the rise.*
8 **give rise to** to cause or produce something
•***Word Family:*** other forms of the verb are **rises, rose, risen, rising** □ **riser** *noun*

risk *noun*
1 a danger 2 the possibility of being injured or losing something: *There is a great risk involved in the parachute drop.*
risk *verb*
3 to put something in danger 4 to take the chance of being injured or losing something
•***Word Family:*** **risky** *adjective* (**riskier, riskiest**)
•***Word Origins:*** from an Italian word meaning "to run into danger"

risqué (*say* **ris**-kay) *adjective*
close to being rude or shocking: *a risqué joke*
•***Word Origins:*** this word comes from French

rissole *noun*
a fried ball of minced meat or vegetables

ritual (*say* **rit**-yew-ul) *noun*
1 a ceremony that follows a set pattern
ritual *adjective*
2 to do with such a ceremony
•***Word Family:*** **ritualistic** *adjective* **ritually** *adverb*

rival (*say* **rye**-vul) *noun*
1 a competitor: *They are rivals for the prize.*
rival *verb*
2 to be as good as: *This meal rivals my mother's cooking.*

•*Word Family:* other forms of the verb are **rivals, rivalled, rivalling** □ **rivalry** *noun* competition
•*Word Origins:* from a Latin word meaning "those living near the same stream"

river *noun*
a large stream of water in a natural channel with banks, that flows into the sea or a lake

rivet (*say* **riv**-it) *noun*
1 a bolt used to hold metal plates together
rivet *verb*
2 to hold metal plates together with a rivet 3 to hold your attention strongly or fascinate you: *We were riveted by the acrobats' performance.*
•*Word Family:* other forms of the verb are **rivets, riveted, riveting** □ **riveter** *noun*

road *noun*
a specially-made track for motor vehicles, people or animals to travel along
•*Word Family:* **roadworthy** *noun* fit for use on the road

roam (*rhymes with* home) *verb*
to travel about with no particular purpose: *to roam the countryside*

roar *verb*
1 to make a loud, deep sound: *to roar with laughter / The lion roared.*
roar *noun*
2 a loud, deep sound: *the roar of the wind*

roast (*rhymes with* most) *verb*
1 to cook food in an oven 2 to be very hot
roast *noun*
3 a meal of roasted meat and vegetables

rob *verb*
to take something that belongs to someone else, often using force
•*Word Family:* other forms of the verb are **robs, robbed, robbing** □ **robber** *noun* someone who robs **robbery** *noun* **(robberies)**
•*Word Origins:* from an Old French word meaning "booty"

robe *noun*
a long, loose piece of clothing, such as a dressing-gown

robin *noun*
a small bird with a red breast

robot (*say* **ro**-bot) *noun*
a machine, sometimes made in the shape of a human, that can do jobs usually done by people

robust (*say* ro-**bust** *or* **ro**-bust) *adjective*
strong and healthy
•*Word Family:* **robustly** *adverb* **robustness** *noun*
•*Word Origins:* from a Latin word meaning "an oak"

rock (1) *noun*
1 a large stone or mass of stone 2 a stick of a hard kind of sweet

rock (2) *verb*
1 to sway back and forth or from side to side: *The boat was gently rocked by the waves.* 2 to shock someone: *We were rocked by the news of his death.*
rock *noun*
2 *another word for* **rock-and-roll:** *a rock band*

rock-and-roll *noun*
a form of modern music with a strong, loud beat

rock-bottom *adjective*
very low: *rock-bottom prices*

rocker *noun*
1 a rocking chair 2 one of the curved pieces on which a cradle, rocking horse or rocking chair rocks

rockery *noun*
an area in a garden where plants grow in small patches of earth between rocks
•*Word Family:* the plural is **rockeries**

rocket *noun*
1 an object, usually shaped like a cylinder, which is pushed up into the air by burning gases shooting out from the back: *a space rocket* 2 a firework that rises into the air and then explodes

rocking chair *noun*
a chair that you can rock while you are sitting in it

rod *noun*
a stick or pole made of wood or metal: *a curtain rod / a fishing rod*

rodent (*say* **ro**-dent) *noun*
an animal such as a beaver, squirrel, mouse or rat, with strong, sharp, long front teeth for gnawing

rodeo (*say* ro-**day**-o *or* **ro**-dee-o) *noun*
an entertainment consisting of a display of cowboy skills, such as riding wild horses and lassoing cattle
•*Word Origins:* from a Spanish word meaning "cattle ring"

roe *noun*
the eggs of a female fish

rogue (*say* rohg) *noun*
1 someone who is dishonest 2 someone who plays harmless tricks
•*Word Family:* **roguish** *adjective* **roguishly** *adverb*

role *noun*
1 the character or part performed by an actor, dancer or singer in a film, play, ballet, musical

or opera 2 someone's job or function: *What is my role in this office?*

roll *verb*
1 to move by turning over and over: *The ball rolled along the floor. / He rolled the dice.* 2 to move on wheels: *The car rolled backwards.* 3 to rock from side to side: *The ship rolled in the rough seas.* 4 to flatten or spread something with a special tube-shaped tool: *Roll the dough very thinly.* 5 to form dough, clay and so on into a ball 6 to make a vibrating sound like drums or thunder 7 **roll up** (a) to make something into the shape of a tube: *Roll up your towel.* (b) to arrive or gather round
roll *noun*
8 something made into the shape of a tube: *a roll of film* 9 a list of people in a class or group: *to call the roll* 10 a very small loaf of bread 11 a long, low noise: *a roll of drums*

roller *noun*
1 a tube-shaped object, especially one that is rolled over and over to flatten something
2 a long wave in the sea

Rollerblade *noun*
1 a roller-skate with the wheels in a single line
Rollerblade *verb*
2 to move using Rollerblades

roller-coaster *noun*
a small railway with steep slopes and sharp turns, that you ride on for fun at fairs and amusement parks

roller-skate *noun*
1 a shoe or skate with four small wheels or rollers allowing you to move quickly over a smooth surface
roller-skate *verb*
2 to move using roller-skates

rolling pin *noun*
a heavy cylinder, usually made of wood, that you use for rolling pastry or dough

ROM *abbreviation*
this is the short form of **read only memory**

Roman Catholicism *noun*
the branch of the Christian church which has the Pope as its head
• ***Word Family:*** **Roman Catholic** a member of such a church

romance (*say* ro-**mance** *or* **ro**-mance) *noun*
1 a story about love 2 a story about unusual or exciting adventures 3 a love affair
• ***Word Family:*** **romantic** *adjective* **romantically** *adverb*
• ***Word Origins:*** from tales of love and exciting adventures written in the *Romance* languages (the languages that developed from Latin, such as French and Italian)

Roman numerals *plural noun*
the letters used in the ancient Roman system of counting and sometimes still used on monuments, for chapter headings and so on: *In Roman numerals, X = 10.*

romp *verb*
to play in a noisy or lively way

roo *noun*
a short form of **kangaroo**

roof *noun*
1 a cover over a building, supported by the walls and usually made of tiles, iron or timber
2 something similar, such as the top of a car
3 the upper surface of a hollow space: *the roof of your mouth*
• ***Word Family:*** the plural is **roofs**

rook (1) *noun*
a black bird like a crow

rook (2) *noun*
a chess piece shaped like a castle which can only move in a straight line

rookery *noun*
a breeding place for birds or other animals
• ***Word Family:*** the plural is **rookeries**

room *noun*
1 a division of a building with its own walls and ceiling 2 the space taken up by or available for something: *There's not much room in this car.*
• ***Word Family:*** **room-mate** *noun* someone who shares a room with you **roomy** *adjective* (**roomier, roomiest**) having plenty of space

roost *noun*
1 a place such as a branch or short rod on which birds may rest at night
roost *verb*
2 to rest on a branch or rod for the night

rooster *noun*
a male, domestic fowl

root *noun*
1 the part of the plant that grows down into the ground where it gets water and food from the soil 2 the basic or essential part of something: *the root of the problem* 3 a number which, when multiplied by itself a certain number of times, gives another number: *3 is the square root of 9 (3 × 3), written* $\sqrt{9}$ *and the cube root of 27 (3 × 3 × 3), written* $\sqrt[3]{27}$.
root *verb*
4 to send out roots and begin to grow 5 to become fixed or established 6 **root out** to remove completely

rope *noun*
a strong, thick cord made from twisted strands of fibre or wire

rort *noun*
a dishonest scheme or trick: *a tax rort*

rosary (*say* **ro**-za-ree) *noun*
a string of beads that people use to count when they are reciting a certain series of prayers in the Roman Catholic Church
•***Word Family:*** the plural is **rosaries**

rose (*say* roze) *noun*
1 a bush grown in the garden, with thorny stems and attractive, sometimes sweet-smelling, flowers
rose *adjective*
2 pinkish-red

rosella (*say* ro-**zel**-a) *noun*
a brightly coloured Australian parrot

rosemary *noun*
a shrub with strong-smelling leaves that are used as a herb in cooking
•***Word Origins:*** from Latin words meaning "dew of the sea"

rosette (*say* ro-**zet**) *noun*
1 a badge made of ribbons arranged in the shape of a rose 2 a decoration in the shape of a rose
•***Word Origins:*** from a French word meaning "little rose"

Rosh Hashana *noun*
the Jewish new year

roster *noun*
a list of names and when it is each person's turn to do a job: *a cleaning roster*

rostrum *noun*
a raised platform for a speaker or a conductor of an orchestra to stand on
•***Word Family:*** the plural is **rostrums** or **rostra**

rosy (*say* **ro**-zee) *adjective*
1 pink or pinkish-red: *rosy cheeks* 2 promising or hopeful: *The future looks rosy.*
•***Word Family:*** other forms are **rosiest, rosier** □ **rosiness** *noun*

rot *verb*
1 to make something go bad, or to go bad: *Sugar will rot your teeth. / Meat rots in the sun.*
rot *noun*
2 decay: *an old tree full of rot* 3 nonsense: *He talks a lot of rot.*
•***Word Family:*** other forms of the verb are **rots, rotted, rotting**

rotate (*say* ro-**tate**) *verb*
1 to turn or spin like a wheel 2 to go in a series of turns: *to rotate crops through the year*

rotation *noun*
1 rotating something: *The rotation of the big wheel made me dizzy.* 2 taking turns to do something: *The seasons follow in rotation.*

rotisserie (*say* ro-**tis**-a-ree) *noun*
a skewer which turns round and round in an oven or above a fire, for cooking meat, poultry and so on
•***Word Origins:*** from a French word meaning "roasting place"

rotor *noun*
something that goes round, especially a blade on a helicopter

rotten *adjective*
1 bad or decayed: *a rotten egg* 2 mean or nasty: *What a rotten thing to do!* 3 bad or unfortunate: *What rotten luck!*
•***Word Family:*** **rottenness** *noun*

rotund (*say* ro-**tund**) *adjective*
plump or rounded

rouge (*say* roozh) *noun*
a red cream or powder used to colour the cheeks
•***Word Origins:*** a French word meaning "red"

rough (*say* ruf) *adjective*
1 uneven: *rough ground* 2 violent or stormy: *rough seas* 3 not properly finished: *a rough draft of the speech / The rough diamond doubled in value after it was cut.* 4 not exact: *a rough idea* 5 difficult or unpleasant: *a rough time* 6 unwell: *to feel rough*
rough *noun*
7 a part of a golf course with uneven ground and long grass or trees
•***Word Family:*** **roughly** *adverb* approximate **roughen** *verb* **roughness** *noun*

roughage (*say* **ruff**-ij) *noun*
the fibre in food that does not actually feed you but helps digestion and makes your bowels work better: *Cereal has plenty of roughage in it.*

roulette (*say* roo-**let**) *noun*
a gambling game in which you bet on where a small ball will come to rest on a spinning wheel with numbered divisions
•***Word Origins:*** from a French word for "little wheel"

round *adjective*
1 shaped like a ball, ring or circle 2 exact or complete: *a round dozen* 3 completed by returning to the starting point: *a round trip*
round *noun*
4 one stage of a competition: *We were knocked out in the first round.* 5 a complete course or series: *a round of Christmas parties* 6 a course of usual actions or duties: *The doctor did her round of the wards.* 7 an outburst: *a round of applause* 8 a song in which each singer or group of singers begins the song at a different time 9 a slice of bread, or two together as a sandwich: *a round of toast / a round of sandwiches*

round *verb*
10 to go or pass around: *to round a corner*
round *adverb*
11 on every side of: *They swarmed round us.* 12 here and there: *His clothes were scattered round.* 13 throughout: *the year round* 14 in a circle: *the wheels go round* 15 to someone's house: *I'll come round later.*
•***Word Family:*** **rounded** *adjective* **roundness** *noun*

roundabout *noun*
1 a road junction where traffic moves round in a circle
roundabout *adjective*
2 indirect: *It was a roundabout way of saying he didn't want to come.*

rouse (*rhymes with* cows) *verb*
to wake someone up
•***Word Family:*** **rousing** *adjective* lively or exciting: *a rousing speech*

rout (*rhymes with* out) *verb*
1 to completely defeat your enemy and make them run away: *to rout an army*
rout *noun*
2 an overwhelming defeat

route (*say* root) *noun*
a way or road for travelling between one place and another

routine (*say* roo-**teen**) *noun*
1 a usual way of doing something
routine *adjective*
2 regular or according to what is usually done: *a routine inspection*
•***Word Family:*** **routinely** *adverb*

rove *verb*
to wander around freely or without any particular purpose
•***Word Family:*** **rover** *noun*

row (1) (*say* ro) *noun*
a line of people or things: *a row of seats in a theatre*

row (2) (*say* ro) *verb*
to use oars to move a boat through water
•***Word Family:*** **rower** *noun* **rowing** *noun*

row (3) (*rhymes with* cow) *noun*
1 a noisy quarrel 2 a loud noise

rowdy (*rhymes with* cloudy) *adjective*
noisy and rough
•***Word Family:*** other forms of the adjective are **rowdier, rowdiest** □ **rowdily** *adverb* **rowdiness** *noun*

royal *adjective*
1 to do with a king or queen: *a royal tour*
2 magnificent: *His mother gave us a royal welcome.*
royal *noun*
3 a member of a royal family
•***Word Family:*** **royally** *adverb*

royalty *noun*
1 kings and queens and their families 2 a regular payment to an inventor, author or composer from the profits made from their work
•***Word Family:*** for definition 1 the plural is **royalty** for definition 2 the plural is **royalties**

rub *verb*
1 to move backwards and forwards over a surface while pressing down: *to rub a blackboard clean / I have blisters where my new shoes have been rubbing my heels.* 2 **rub out** to remove a mistake by rubbing
rub *noun*
3 the act of rubbing: *to give the table a rub*
•***Word Family:*** other forms of the verb are **rubs, rubbed, rubbing**

rubber *noun*
1 a srong elastic substance that is made from the sap of a tropical tree or is manufactured from chemicals, and is used to make things such as car tyres and elastic bands 2 a piece of soft rubber used to remove pencil or pen marks

rubbish *noun*
1 unwanted or worthless material 2 nonsense: *You're talking utter rubbish!*
•***Word Family:*** **rubbishy** *adjective* worthless

rubble *noun*
small pieces of broken stone or bricks

rubella (*say* roo-**bel**-a) *noun*
a mild, infectious disease that gives you a temperature and small, red spots on the skin and is usually not serious, but can damage an unborn baby if a pregnant woman catches it
•***Word Origins:*** from the Latin word for "reddish"

ruby (*say* **roo**-bee) *noun*
1 a red gemstone 2 a rich, deep red
•***Word Family:*** the plural is **rubies**

rucksack *noun*
a bag with shoulder straps and a supporting frame for wearing on the back
•***Word Origins:*** from the German word for "back" and the English word "sack"

rudder *noun*
a blade at the back of a boat or aeroplane which is moved from side to side for steering

ruddy *adjective*
reddish in colour: *a ruddy complexion*
•***Word Family:*** other forms are **ruddier, ruddiest**

rude *adjective*
1 impolite or bad-mannered: *How rude not to answer your letter!* 2 improper or obscene: *a rude word / a rude joke* 3 roughly made: *We quickly built a rude shelter for the night.*
•***Word Family:*** **rudely** *adverb* **rudeness** *noun*

ruffian *noun*
someone who is violent or rough

ruffle *verb*
to disturb the smoothness or calmness of something: *The bird ruffled its feathers. / Their harsh words ruffled her.*

rug *noun*
1 a small, thick carpet 2 a thick, warm blanket

rugby *noun*
a ball game played with an oval ball between two teams on a pitch with H-shaped goals

rugged (*say* **rug**-id) *adjective*
1 rough or uneven: *a rugged mountain side / a rugged, weather-beaten face* 2 tough or strong: *rugged clothes*
•***Word Family:*** **ruggedly** *adverb* **ruggedness** *noun*

ruin (*say* **roo**-in) *noun*
1 the loss of a person's happiness, success and everything else they value: *Gambling bought about his ruin.* 2 a state of collapse, destruction or decay: *The castle fell into ruin.* 3 a building that has collapsed or been destroyed: *The castle is now a ruin.* 4 **in ruins** collapsed or destroyed
ruin *verb*
5 to severely damage or destroy something: *Rain ruined the harvest.*
•***Word Origins:*** from a Latin word meaning "a tumbling down"

rule *noun*
1 an instruction that tells you what you must or must not do, which you have to obey: *Do you know the rules of the game?* 2 authority or control: *India was once under British rule.* 3 **as a rule** usually: *I go to bed early as a rule.*
rule *verb*
4 to control or direct something: *to rule a country / His heart rules his head.* 5 to make an official decision or judgement: *The court ruled that the will was invalid.* 6 to draw lines with a ruler 7 **rule out** to dismiss or decide to ignore a particular idea or suggestion: *The government has ruled out the possibility of a November election.*
•***Word Family:*** **ruling** *noun* a judgment or decision **ruling** *adjective* in charge: *the ruling party*

ruler *noun*
1 someone who governs or rules 2 a strip of wood, metal or plastic with straight edges and marked with measurements, used for measuring and drawing straight lines

rum *noun*
a strong, alcoholic drink made from sugar cane

rumble *verb*
1 to make a low, continuous, heavy sound, such as distant thunder 2 to move with this sound: *The heavy truck rumbled down the lane.*

rummage (*say* **rum**-ij) *verb*
to look for something, especially by moving things around: *She rummaged through the drawers of the desk for a pencil.*

rummy *noun*
a card game in which players try to match cards or make sets

rumour or **rumor** (*say* **roo**-ma) *noun*
a story that may or may not be true: *There is a rumour that you are going away.*

rump *noun*
the fleshy back-part of an animal, just above the hind legs

rumple *verb*
to crush or crease your clothes: *My dress was rumpled in the crowded train.*

rumpus *noun*
a noisy disturbance
•***Word Family:*** the plural is **rumpuses**

run *verb*
1 to move quickly on foot: *Run and answer the telephone.* 2 to go or make to go: *The train is running late. / The ship ran aground.* 3 to pass or move quickly: *She ran her eyes over the page.* 4 to move or operate: *This engine runs quietly. / I run this business myself. / Run this program on the computer.* 5 to continue or extend: *This fence runs down to the river. / The play ran for six weeks.* 6 to flow or make flow: *to leave a tap running / My nose is running.* 7 **run out** to be all used up: *Time has run out.* 8 **run through** to rehearse something
run *noun*
9 the act of running: *to go for a run in the park / The play had a six week run.* 10 a journey: *a run in the car* 11 a particular thing happening over and over again: *a run of bad luck* 12 a point in cricket 13 **in the long run** in the end
•***Word Family:*** other forms of the verb are **runs, ran, running** □ **running** *adjective: running water* **runny** *adjective* **runner** *noun*

rung (1) *verb*
the past participle of the verb **ring (2)**

rung (2) *noun*
a step on a ladder
•***Word Origins:*** from an Old English word meaning "a pole"

runner-up *noun*
someone who comes second in a competition
•***Word Family:*** the plural is **runners-up**

run-of-the-mill *adjective*
neither good nor bad, but ordinary: *a run-of-the-mill film*

rupee (*say* roo-**pee**) *noun*
the basic unit of money in India and Pakistan

A B C D E F G H I J K L M N O P Q R S T U V W X Y Z

rupture (*say* **rup**-cher) *verb*
1 to break or burst: *She ruptured a blood vessel. / The dam ruptured, flooding the whole valley.*
rupture *noun*
2 a breaking or bursting, especially in a part of your body: *a rupture in the bowel*

rural (*say* **roo**-rul) *adjective*
to do with farming or the countryside
•***Word Family:*** **rurally** *adverb*
•***Word Origins:*** from a Latin word meaning "of the countryside"

ruse (*say* rooz) *noun*
a trick or a dishonest scheme

rush (1) *verb*
1 to go or move quickly: *The crowd rushed forward. / Tears rushed to his eyes.* 2 to do something very quickly: *The new law was rushed through parliament.*
rush *noun*
3 a hurried or forceful movement: *a rush for seats / a gold rush / the rush of water from a burst pipe*

rush (2) *noun*
a tall, thin, grass-like plant that grows in marshy areas and is used in weaving baskets

rusk *noun*
a crisp, dry biscuit, given to babies to help them when they are teething

rust *noun*
1 a flaky, reddish-brown coating that forms on iron left in damp air. 2 reddish-brown
rust *verb*
3 to form rust: *Your bike will rust if you leave it in the rain.*
•***Word Family:*** **rusty** *adjective* (**rustier, rustiest**)

rustle (*say* **rus**-ul) *verb*
1 to make soft, quiet sounds: *The leaves rustled in the wind.* 2 to move with such a sound: *A fox rustled through the undergrowth.* 3 to steal cattle or sheep
rustle *noun*
4 a soft, quiet sound: *I heard a rustle in the bushes.*
•***Word Family:*** **rustler** *noun* a cattle or sheep thief

rut *noun*
1 a deep, narrow track in the ground, especially one made by the wheels of vehicles 2 **in a rut** having a fixed and boring way of life

ruthless (*say* **rooth**-less) *adjective*
pitiless or merciless
•***Word Family:*** **ruthlessly** *adverb* **ruthlessness** *noun*

rye *noun*
a cereal plant used to make flour and whisky, and as food for cattle

Ss

Sabbath *noun*
the day of the week kept as a day of rest and worship in some religions. The Jewish Sabbath is Saturday, while the Christian Sabbath is Sunday

sabotage (*say* **sab**-a-tahzh) *noun*
1 deliberate and secret damaging of machinery or buildings, especially during a war or an industrial dispute
sabotage *verb*
2 to damage or ruin something deliberately
•***Word Family:*** **saboteur** *noun* someone who commits sabotage

sabre (*say* **say**-ba) *noun*
a heavy sword with a slightly curved blade and one cutting edge

saccharin (*say* **sak**-a-rin) *noun*
1 a chemical used for sweetening, about 400 times sweeter than cane sugar
saccharine *adjective*
2 sickeningly sweet: *a saccharine smile*
•***Word Origins:*** from a Greek word meaning "sugar"

sachet (*say* **sash**-ay) *noun*
a small, sealed envelope or packet used to hold small amounts of such things as sugar, perfume or shampoo
•***Word Origins:*** this word comes from French, which is why we don't sound the "t"

sack *noun*
1 a large, strong bag, for carrying wood, potatoes and so on 2 **the sack** dismissal from your job 3 **hit the sack** to go to bed
sack *verb*
4 to dismiss someone from their job: *My boss sacked me today.*

sacrament (*say* **sak**-ra-ment) *noun*
an important Christian ceremony such as baptism or communion

sacred (*say* **say**-krid) *adjective*
holy, or to do with religion: *a sacred relic / sacred music*

sacrifice (*say* **sak**-ri-fice) *noun*
1 giving up something you love for the sake of something you think is even more important
2 killing an animal or person as an offering to a god 3 the thing you give up or kill

sacrifice *verb*
4 to give something up for the sake of something you think is even more important
5 to offer an animal or person as a sacrifice to a god
• ***Word Family:*** **sacrificial** *adjective*

sad *adjective*
1 sorrowful or unhappy: *a sad face* 2 causing sorrow: *sad news*
• ***Word Family:*** **sadden** *verb* to make or become sad

saddle *noun*
1 a padded leather seat for a rider on a horse
2 a similar seat on a bicycle
saddle *verb*
3 to put a saddle on a horse or other animal
4 to load or burden someone with difficulties or problems
• ***Word Family:*** **saddler** *noun* **saddlery** *noun*

sadhu (*say* **sah**-doo) *noun*
a wandering Hindu holy man

sadist (*say* **say**-dist) *noun*
someone who enjoys hurting or being cruel to other people
• ***Word Family:*** **sadism** *noun* **sadistic** *adjective*

safari (*say* sa-**far**-ree) *noun*
an expedition, especially for hunting or looking at wild animals
• ***Word Family:*** the plural is **safaris**
• ***Word Origins:*** from a Swahili (an African language) word meaning "journey"

safe *adjective*
1 free from danger, injury or risk: *The missing children were found safe and well.* 2 unable to do any further harm: *He's safe in gaol.* 3 not dangerous: *to drive at a safe speed*
safe *noun*
4 a strong, metal box with a special lock, in which money, jewellery and other valuable things are kept
• ***Word Family:*** **safely** *adverb* **safety** *noun*

safe sex *noun*
the wearing of condoms and other sensible sexual practices, to stop the spread of AIDS and other diseases you can catch during sexual intercourse

sag *verb*
1 to sink or bend downwards, especially in the middle, due to weight or pressure: *The mattress sagged under our weight.* 2 to droop: *Her shoulders sagged when she heard the news.*
• ***Word Family:*** other forms are **sags, sagged, sagging**

saga (*say* **sah**-ga) *noun*
1 a long, complicated story 2 a long poem or story about the adventures of heroes from Iceland and Norway long ago
• ***Word Origins:*** from an Old Norse word meaning "story" or "narrative"

sage (1) (*say* sayj) *noun*
1 a very wise person
sage *adjective*
2 wise: *sage advice*

sage (2) (*say* sayj) *noun*
a herb with strongly flavoured greyish-green leaves

sago (*say* **say**-go) *noun*
a starchy, rice-like food obtained from some palm trees, used in puddings and soups

sail *noun*
1 a sheet of nylon or canvas, fastened to a mast so that it catches the wind and moves a boat along 2 something that looks or acts like a sail: *the sails of a windmill* 3 a trip in a sailing boat: *to go for a sail*
sail *verb*
4 to move or be carried across the surface of water: *In the afternoon we sailed on the lake.* 5 to travel by water: *We sailed all the way to Bali in a luxury cruise ship.* 6 to manage a sailing boat: *to learn how to sail* 7 to move quickly: *He sailed past us without saying a word.*
• ***Word Family:*** **sailor** *noun* a member of the crew of a boat or ship

sailboard *noun*
a shaped board with a movable sail on it, used for windsurfing

saint *noun*
1 someone who is honoured by some Christian churches because of their holy life and the miracles they are believed to have performed
2 a very good or unselfish person
• ***Word Family:*** **sainthood** *noun* **saintly** *adjective*

sake (*rhymes with* lake) *noun*
1 benefit: *Do it for my sake.* 2 purpose: *For the sake of hygiene, always wash your hands before you eat.*

salaam (*say* sal-**ahm**) *interjection*
a word used as a greeting by Muslims

salad *noun*
1 a dish of raw or cooked vegetables, sometimes mixed with meat, fish, rice or pasta, usually served cold with a dressing 2 **fruit salad** a dessert of chopped fruit
• ***Word Origins:*** from a Latin word meaning "salt"

salami (*say* sa-**lah**-mee) *noun*
a spicy, cooked sausage

salary (*say* **sal**-a-ree) *noun*
the pay you receive every month or fortnight for doing your job
• ***Word Family:*** the plural is **salaries**
• ***Word Origins:*** from a Latin word for "the money paid to Roman soldiers to buy salt"

sale *noun*
1 the act of selling something: *the sale of a flat* 2 a special selling of goods at lower prices than usual: *the department store's summer sale*

saline (*say* **say**-line) *adjective*
containing or tasting of salt: *a saline solution*

saliva (*say* sa-**lie**-va) *noun*
the watery liquid produced by glands in your mouth, that helps you swallow and begin to digest food
• ***Word Family:*** **salivate** *verb* to produce saliva

salmon (*say* **sam**-on) *noun*
a fish with pink flesh, that lives in the sea but goes up rivers to lay its eggs
• ***Word Family:*** the plural is **salmon**

salmonella (*say* sal-ma-**nel**-a) *noun*
a group of bacteria, many of which cause diseases, including typhoid and food poisoning
• ***Word Origins:*** named after D. E. *Salmon*, an American vet who lived from 1861 to 1914

salon *noun*
a fashionable shop: *a beauty salon / a salon for designer clothes*

salt (*rhymes with* malt) *noun*
1 white crystals found in sea water and certain rocks, used to flavour and preserve food 2 a chemical compound formed by the action of an acid on a metal or base
• ***Word Family:*** **salty** *adjective* **(saltier, saltiest)** □ **saltiness** *noun*

salt cellar *noun*
a small container, used for sprinkling salt on your food

salute (*say* sa-**loot**) *verb*
1 to greet someone 2 to make a sign of respect, such as to raise your hand to the side of your forehead as soldiers do
salute *noun*
3 a sign of respect 4 a series of guns fired as a sign of respect on official occasions: *a 21-gun salute*

salvage (*say* **sal**-vij) *verb*
1 to rescue things from a shipwreck, fire and so on so that they can be used again
salvage *noun*
2 the rescue of things from a shipwreck, fire and so on so that they can be used again

salvation (*say* sal-**vay**-shon) *noun*
1 saving or delivering someone from such things as harm, evil or sin 2 a means of saving someone or something: *The quick arrival of the rescue helicopter was his salvation.*

salwar kamees (*say* **sal**-wah kam-**eez**) *noun*
an outfit consisting of a long, loose top and loose trousers, worn by some Muslim women

same *adjective*
matching, or unchanged: *He's the same age as me. / to get up at the same time each morning*

samosa *noun*
an Indian snack that consists of a triangular envelope of pastry filled with spicy meat or vegetables

sample (*say* **sahm**-pul *or* **sam**-pul) *noun*
1 a small part of something that shows what the whole thing is like: *to taste a sample of ice-cream*
sample *verb*
2 to test or try something by taking a sample: *to sample the ice-cream* 3 to record sounds or parts of songs and use these recordings to create a new piece of music

samurai (*say* **sam**-yoo-rye) *noun*
a member of the Japanese warrior class in medieval times
• ***Word Family:*** the plural is **samurai**

sanatorium (*say* san-a-**taw**-ree-um) *noun*
a type of nursing home where people go to recover after an illness or operation, especially in a place with a good climate
• ***Word Family:*** the plural is **sanatoriums** or **sanatoria**

sanction (*say* **sang**-shon) *verb*
1 to approve or allow something officially: *to sanction a request*
sanction *noun*
2 permission granted by authority: *to receive official sanction to travel in the war zone* 3 an official punishment or threat: *a trade sanction in protest at nuclear testing*

sanctuary (*say* **sang**-cha-ree) *noun*
1 a sacred or holy place 2 protection or refuge given to someone in trouble: *to offer the refugees sanctuary* 3 a place that provides protection: *a wildlife sanctuary*
• ***Word Family:*** the plural is **sanctuaries**

sand *noun*
1 the fine, loose grains of rocks that have been worn down by wind and water
sand *verb*
2 to smooth or polish something using sandpaper
• ***Word Family:*** **sander** *noun* a machine that sands **sandy** *adjective* **(sandier, sandiest)**

sandal *noun*
a light shoe with a leather, wooden or plastic sole and straps around your foot

sandalwood *noun*
the sweet-smelling wood of an Asian tree, used for carving, or burnt as incense

sandpaper *noun*
1 a sheet of heavy paper coated with sand, used for making rough surfaces smooth
sandpaper *verb*
2 to smooth something with sandpaper

sandshoe *noun*
a light canvas shoe with rubber soles, used for tennis and other sports

sandstone *noun*
a rock formed of layers of sand pressed together

sandwich *noun*
1 two pieces of buttered bread with a filling in between them
sandwich *verb*
2 to put or squeeze something between two other things: *She was sandwiched between two huge men.*
•***Word Family:*** the plural of the noun is **sandwiches**
•***Word Origins:*** invented by the fourth Earl of *Sandwich*, 1718 to 1792, so that he could eat meals while he gambled

sane *adjective*
1 having a normal, healthy mind 2 sensible: *That's a very sane idea.*
•***Word Family:*** **sanely** *adverb* **sanity** *noun*

sanitary (*say* **san**-i-tree) *adjective*
so clean and healthy that germs and disease don't spread
•***Word Family:*** **sanitation** *noun* the use of clean water, good drains and so on

sanitary towel *noun*
a paper pad worn by a woman during her period

sap (1) *noun*
the watery liquid inside a plant

sap (2) *verb*
to break down or weaken someone's strength bit by bit: *Her illness sapped her energy.*
•***Word Family:*** other forms are **saps, sapped, sapping**

sapling *noun*
a young tree

sapphire (*say* **saf**-eye-a) *noun*
a deep blue stone used as a gem

sarcastic *adjective*
saying the opposite of what you mean in a mocking or rude way in order to hurt someone's feelings
•***Word Family:*** **sarcasm** *noun* **sarcastically** *adverb*

sarcophagus (*say* sar-**kof**-a-gus) *noun*
a stone coffin
•***Word Family:*** the plural is **sarcophagi** or **sarcophaguses**

sardine (*say* sar-**deen**) *noun*
a small, tasty seafish often cooked in oil and canned

sari (*say* **sar**-ee) *noun*
a long piece of silk or cotton cloth that Indian women wear by winding it around their body with one end over their shoulders or head

sarong (*say* sa-**rong**) *noun*
a piece of cloth that Malaysian men and women wind around the lower half of their body like a skirt and tuck in at the waist

sash *noun*
a wide strip of cloth worn around your waist or over your shoulder
•***Word Family:*** the plural is **sashes**

Satan (*say* **say**-tan) *noun*
the devil
•***Word Family:*** **satanic** *adjective* wicked or evil

satchel *noun*
a school bag with shoulder-straps, for carrying books on your back

satellite (*say* **sat**-a-lite) *noun*
1 a moon or a similar natural object in space, that moves around a larger object such as a planet or a star 2 an object sent into space to orbit around the Earth or another planet, gathering and sending back information
•***Word Origins:*** from a Latin word meaning "a bodyguard"

satellite dish *noun*
a dish-shaped aerial used to receive radio, television and microwave signals beamed from a satellite

satin *noun*
a smooth, shiny type of cloth

satire *noun*
1 the use of mocking or exaggerated humour to make fun of foolish or wicked people or things 2 a book, song, play or poem that does this
•***Word Family:*** **satiric** *adjective* **satirical** *adjective* **satirically** *adverb* **satirize** or **satirise** *verb* **satirist** *noun*

satisfy (*say* **sat**-is-fie) *verb*
1 to make someone happy, especially by giving them what they want or need: *to satisfy your curiosity / to satisfy your thirst* 2 to convince someone about something: *to satisfy someone that you're telling the truth*

A B C D E F G H I J K L M N O P Q R S T U V W X Y Z

•***Word Family:*** other forms are **satisfies, satisfied, satisfying** □ **satisfaction** *noun* **satisfactory** *adjective* good enough

saturate (*say* **satch**-a-rate) *verb*
to wet something thoroughly: *Heavy rain saturated the dry earth.*
•***Word Family:*** **saturation** *noun*

Saturday *noun*
the seventh day of the week
•***Word Origins:*** from a Latin word meaning "the day of Saturn"

sauce (*rhymes with* horse) *noun*
1 a thick liquid, served with food to give it extra flavour 2 rudeness or impertinence
•***Word Family:*** **saucy** *adjective* (**saucier, sauciest**) rude or impertinent

saucepan *noun*
a metal cooking-pot with a lid and a handle

saucer (*say* **saw**-sa) *noun*
a small dish for putting under a cup

sauerkraut (*say* **sow**-a-krowt) *noun*
shredded cabbage that has been preserved in salty water or vinegar
•***Word Origins:*** from the German words for "sour" and "cabbage"

sauna (*say* **saw**-na) *noun*
a closed, heated room in which you go to have a steam bath to make you sweat in order to clean your skin

saunter (*say* **sawn**-ta) *verb*
1 to stroll or wander slowly along
saunter *noun*
2 a gentle stroll

sausage (*say* **sos**-ij) *noun*
minced meat mixed with spices and packed into a skin

sauté (*say* **soh**-tay) *verb*
to fry food lightly in a small amount of oil: *to sauté vegetables*
•***Word Family:*** other forms are **sautés, sautéed, sautéeing**
•***Word Origins:*** this word comes from French, which is why the "e" has an accent over it

savage (*say* **sav**-ij) *adjective*
1 wild, untamed or uncivilized: *a savage tribe*
2 fierce or vicious: *a savage glare*
savage *verb*
3 to injure someone viciously: *He was savaged by a huge guard dog.*
savage *noun*
4 a wild or uncivilized person
•***Word Family:*** **savagely** *adverb* **savagery** *noun* savage behaviour

savanna (*say* sa-**van**-a) *noun*
grassland where not many trees grow, for example in parts of Africa

save *verb*
1 to rescue or keep someone or something safe from danger, harm or loss: *to save someone from drowning* 2 to not waste something: *to save time* 3 to keep something for future use: *to save money for a holiday*

saviour or **savior** (*say* **save**-yer) *noun*
1 someone who has rescued or saved people
2 **the Saviour** Jesus Christ

savour or **savor** (*say* **say**-va) *noun*
1 taste, smell or flavour
savour *verb*
2 to enjoy the taste or smell of a particular food: *He savoured the aroma of the spicy cheese.* 3 to enjoy a particular feeling or achievement: *to savour your victory in the cup final*

savoury or **savory** (*say* **say**-va-ree) *noun*
1 a small piece of tasty food, especially served at the beginning of a meal
savoury *adjective*
2 smelling or tasting good 3 sharp or spiced and salty rather than sweet: *a savoury biscuit*
•***Word Family:*** the plural of the noun is **savouries**

saw *noun*
1 a tool with a sharp-toothed blade for cutting
saw *verb*
2 to use or cut something with a saw
•***Word Family:*** other verb forms are **saws, sawed, sawn or sawed, sawing**

sawdust *noun*
the bits of wood and powder that come from wood when you saw it

saxophone (*say* **sak**-sa-fone) *noun*
a wind instrument with a single reed and a metal body
•***Word Family:*** **saxophonist** *noun* a saxophone player
•***Word Origins:*** named after A. *Sax*, its Belgian inventor who lived from 1814 to 1894

say *verb*
1 to speak, or express something in words: *What did you say? / to say you are sorry* 3 to state something with certainty: *I can't say who is right.*
say *noun*
4 your turn to speak: *Be quiet, let him have his say!*
•***Word Family:*** other verb forms are **says, said, saying**

saying *noun*
something wise or well-known that people often say

scab *noun*
the dry crust that forms over a wound or sore as it heals

scabbard (*say* **skab**-ud) *noun*
a sheath or cover for the blade of a sword or dagger

scaffold *noun*
1 a raised platform on which criminals were executed 2 the raised framework you stand on when you are working on the outside of a building

scald (*say* skawld) *verb*
1 to burn or hurt someone with hot liquid or steam
2 to heat a liquid to just below boiling point
scald *noun*
3 a burn caused by hot liquid or steam

scale (1) *noun*
1 any of the thin, flat pieces forming the skin covering of certain animals, such as fish and snakes 2 any small, flat flake or piece that peels off
•*Word Family:* **scaly** *adjective* (**scalier, scaliest**)

scale (2) *noun*
1 a set of points at regular intervals along a line, used for measuring temperature, distance and so on: *the scale on a thermometer / the scale on a map*
2 a series of musical notes going up or down in fixed intervals, especially a series like this beginning on a particular note 3 the size or importance of something when you compare it to other similar things: *a small-scale business / to spend money on a grand scale*
scale *verb*
4 to climb up or over something: *to scale a ladder / to scale a mountain* 5 to increase or decrease something according to a fixed scale: *You can scale up your drawing using a grid.*

scales *plural noun*
a device or machine for weighing things

scallop (*say* **skol**-op) *noun*
1 a tasty shellfish with two fan-shaped shells
2 a wavy edge on pastry, cloth or a garment

scalp *noun*
1 the skin covering your head, usually covered with hair
scalp *verb*
2 to cut off someone's scalp

scalpel *noun*
a small knife with a thin, sharp blade, used by surgeons in operations

scamp *noun*
a mischievous person, especially a child

scamper *verb*
to run or move lightly and quickly

scan *verb*
1 to examine something closely: *He scanned her face for signs of tears.* 2 to pass a beam of light or X-rays over something, for example a bar code, in order to examine it 3 to glance at something: *to scan the morning newspaper*
scan *noun*
4 a search or examination using a scanner: *a brain scan*
•*Word Family:* other verb forms are **scans, scanned, scanning** □ **scanner** *noun* a machine that scans things, for example the inside of people's bodies

scandal (*say* **skan**-dal) *noun*
1 a shameful or disgraceful action or situation: *It's a scandal that the murderer was set free.*
2 sensational gossip that damages someone's good name: *Have you heard the latest scandal about her?*
•*Word Family:* **scandalize** or **scandalise** *verb* to shock people

scant *adjective*
very little or barely enough: *She paid scant attention to my advice.*
•*Word Family:* **scanty** *adjective* (**scantier, scantiest**)

scapegoat *noun*
someone blamed or punished for things that other people have done

scar *noun*
1 a mark left on your skin by a cut or wound that has healed
scar *verb*
2 to mark with a scar
•*Word Family:* other verb forms are **scars, scarred, scarring**

scarce (*say* skairs) *adjective*
not enough for everyone: *Tomatoes were scarce during the summer.*
•*Word Family:* **scarcely** *adverb* barely or hardly **scarcity** *noun*

scare (*rhymes with* air) *verb*
1 to frighten someone
scare *noun*
2 a feeling of fear or alarm about something: *a bomb scare*
•*Word Family:* **scary** *adjective* (**scarier, scariest**)

scarecrow *noun*
a human figure dressed in old clothes, set up to scare birds away from crops

scarf *noun*
a strip or square of cloth worn around your head or neck, often to keep you warm
•*Word Family:* the plural is **scarves** or **scarfs**

A B C D E F G H I J K L M N O P Q R S T U V W X Y Z

scarlet *noun*
a bright reddish-orange colour

scarlet fever *noun*
a disease that spreads quickly and gives you a sore throat, a high fever and a red rash

scathing (*say* **skay**-dhing) *adjective*
very critical or scornful: *a scathing film review*
•***Word Family:*** **scathingly** *adverb*

scatter *verb*
to throw or send something, or to move in many different directions: *to scatter seed on ploughed land / The crowd scattered at the sound of sirens.*
•***Word Family:*** **scattering** *noun* a scattered number or quantity: *a scattering of farm houses*

scavenger (*say* **skav**-in-ja) *noun*
1 an animal that lives on the rotting flesh of dead animals 2 someone who searches in rubbish bins for leftover food or who uses things that other people don't want
•***Word Family:*** **scavenge** *verb*

scene (*say* seen) *noun*
1 a place or area where action occurs: *The scene of the crime.* 2 a view: *This painting shows a scene of the river.* 3 a noisy outburst: *There was a terrible scene when I came home late.* 4 a particular area of activity: *the music scene* 5 one of the parts of an act in a play, usually set in one place: *act four, scene three*
•***Word Family:*** **scenic** *adjective* having a pleasant view or beautiful scenery: *a scenic route*

scenery (*say* **see**-na-ree) *noun*
1 the natural features of a place: *impressive mountain scenery* 2 the painted backgrounds and other structures used in a play or film

scent (*say* sent) *noun*
1 a perfume, or a pleasing smell: *What scent are you wearing? / the scent of roses* 2 the smell left behind by someone or something, that an animal can follow
scent *verb*
3 to detect or find something by or as if by smelling: *The dogs scented a rabbit. / to scent trouble*

sceptic (*say* **skep**-tik) *noun*
someone who doubts the truth of things that others believe
•***Word Family:*** **sceptical** *adjective* **sceptically** *adverb* **scepticism** (*say* **skep**-ti-sism) *noun*

schedule (*say* **shed**-yool *or* **sked**-yool) *noun*
1 a plan that sets out how and when to do something 2 a list of things you have to do
schedule *verb*
3 to arrange or put people or events in a schedule: *You are scheduled to visit the museum next.*

scheme (*say* skeem) *noun*
1 a plan to help you get something done 2 an arrangement or system: *a colour scheme*
scheme *verb*
3 to plan or plot, especially dishonestly: *to scheme against the government*

scholar (*say* **skol**-a) *noun*
1 someone who knows a lot about a particular subject: *a Greek scholar* 2 a pupil or student, especially one who has won an award
•***Word Family:*** **scholarly** *adjective* involving a lot of detailed knowledge of a particular subject **scholastic** (*say* sko-**las**-tik) *adjective* having to do with education, schools or students

scholarship (*say* **skol**-a-ship) *noun*
1 a sum of money a student wins to pay for books and school or university fees 2 the knowledge or skill you gain from studying: *The professor is a woman of great scholarship.*

scholastic (*say* sko-**las**-tik) *adjective*
having to do with education, schools or students: *your scholastic record*

school (1) (*say* skool) *noun*
1 a place where students are trained or instructed: *primary school / art school* 2 the students who attend a school 3 the lessons you have at school: *There's no school today.*
school *verb*
4 to train or instruct someone: *to school a child in gymnastics*
•***Word Family:*** **schooling** *noun* education or training

school (2) *noun*
a large group of fish swimming together

schooner (*say* **skoo**-na) *noun*
a sailing ship with two or more masts

science (*say* **sigh**-ence) *noun*
1 the study of the natural world or the knowledge obtained by observing, measuring and testing 2 a branch of this knowledge or study, such as chemistry or botany
•***Word Family:*** **scientist** *noun* someone skilled or trained in science **scientific** *adjective*

science fiction *noun*
stories about the future, and what it might be like

scissors (*say* **siz**-ers) *plural noun*
a cutting instrument made of two sharp blades with handles, joined at the centre

scoff (1) *verb*
to jeer at someone or something or treat them with contempt: *He scoffed at my fears.*

scoff (2) *verb*
to eat food greedily and quickly

scold *verb*
to criticize or find fault with someone angrily

scone (*say* skon) *noun*
a small, light cake which is usually cut open and spread with butter

scoop *noun*
1 a cup-like spoon for lifting or measuring such things as flour or sugar 2 a bucket-like shovel 3 an important news item that a reporter or publisher gets before anyone else
scoop *verb*
4 to lift things with or as though with a scoop: *to scoop coal on to the fire / to scoop up a pile of toys*

scooter *noun*
1 a two-wheeled vehicle, used by children, with a flat board to stand on and a handlebar 2 a motorcycle with small wheels, that you ride with your legs together, like sitting on a chair

scope *noun*
1 the range something covers: *That's within the scope of his knowledge.* 2 opportunity or room: *There's still scope for improvement.*
• ***Word Origins:*** from a Greek word meaning "a target"

scorch *verb*
1 to burn something slightly: *to scorch a shirt with an iron / The blistering sun scorched the grass.*
scorch *noun*
2 a slight burn
• ***Word Family:*** **scorcher** *noun* a very hot day

score *noun*
1 all the points or goals that the players or teams get in a game 2 a line or scratch, usually made in metal or wood 3 written or printed music, showing the parts for each musician 4 a group of twenty: *to live for four score years*
score *verb*
5 to get points or goals in a game, or to keep a record of these

scorn *noun*
1 great contempt or lack of respect for someone or something
scorn *verb*
2 to feel or show scorn for someone or something: *to scorn all your rivals*

scorpion *noun*
a spider-like creature with eight legs and a long, narrow tail with a sting at the end

scoundrel (*say* **skown**-drel) *noun*
a wicked or dishonourable person

scour (1) (*rhymes with* power) *verb*
to clean or polish something by rubbing hard: *to scour saucepans*

scour (2) (*rhymes with* power) *verb*
to search a place or area thoroughly and energetically: *She scoured the garden looking for snail shells.*

scout *noun*
1 someone sent out to gather information, especially about what your enemies are doing 2 a member of the Scout Association: *a Boy Scout*

scowl *verb*
to have an angry or bad-tempered expression on your face

scramble *verb*
1 to move, crawl or climb as fast as you can: *to scramble up rocks* 2 to cook beaten eggs gently 3 to jumble up a radio or telephone message so that it can only be understood by someone using a special device
scramble *noun*
4 a confused or wild struggle: *There was a violent scramble to get the last two seats.*
• ***Word Family:*** **scrambler** *noun* a device for scrambling radio or telephone messages

scrap *noun*
1 a small piece or fragment left over: *a scrap of material* 2 something useless or unwanted, especially metal that can be used again 3 **scraps** leftover food: *The dog refuses to eat scraps.*
scrap *verb*
4 to get rid of something as useless or unwanted: *Let's scrap that idea and start again.* 5 to make something into scrap: *to scrap a car*
• ***Word Family:*** other verb forms are **scraps, scrapped, scrapping** □ **scrappy** *adjective* untidy or messy

scrape *verb*
1 to rub or scratch something, especially in order to remove an outer layer: *We scraped the burnt food off the saucepan. / I scraped my knee on the concrete.* 2 **scrape through** to only just succeed in something: *He managed to scrape through his exams.* 3 **scrape up** to collect money with difficulty: *I managed to scrape up enough for a ticket.*
scrape *noun*
4 a mark made by scraping: *a scrape on the side of the car* 5 a difficult or embarrassing situation: *to get yourself into a scrape*

scratch *verb*
1 to mark, cut or tear something with something sharp or rough: *The fork scratched the table. / The rose thorn scratched my arm.* 2 to rub something using claws or fingernails to stop it itching 3 to rub something with a grating sound: *The dog scratched at the door.* 4 to erase

A B C D E F G H I J K L M N O P Q R S T U V W X Y Z

or cross out some writing: *We scratched your name from our records.* 5 to withdraw from a competition: *Those horses were scratched from the race.*
scratch *noun*
6 the act of scratching: *to have a scratch* 7 a mark left by scratching: *The kitten gave me this scratch.*
•***Word Family:*** the plural of the noun is **scratches**

scrawl *verb*
to write carelessly or untidily
Word Family: **scrawl** *noun*

scrawny *adjective*
thin or bony: *a scrawny chicken*
•***Word Family:*** other forms are **scrawnier, scrawniest**

scream *verb*
1 to make a loud, sharp or violent cry or sound: *The child screamed with pain.*
scream *noun*
2 a loud, piercing sound or cry 3 someone or something that is very funny

screech *verb*
1 to make a harsh, shrill cry or sound
screech *noun*
2 a harsh sound like this
•***Word Family:*** the plural of the noun is **screeches**

screen *noun*
1 a smooth surface on which films or slides are shown using a projector 2 the part of a TV set or a computer on which the pictures or words appear 3 a frame covered with wire mesh, set in a window to keep out insects 4 something that divides, protects or shelters a particular place or area: *The nurse placed a screen around my bed. / A screen of trees sheltered the house from the wind.*
screen *verb*
5 to show a film or TV programme 6 to cover or divide somewhere using a screen, wall and so on: *The house is screened from the main road by the trees* 7 to test people for a particular disease: *to screen women for breast cancer*

screen saver *noun*
a computer program consisting of a moving pattern, designed to protect the screen from damage

screw *noun*
1 a metal pin with a slot or cross in its flat top and a spiral thread ending in a point
screw *verb*
2 to twist something open or shut: *Screw the lid on the jar.* 3 **screw up** to twist something up into a tight ball: *She screwed up the letter and threw it into the bin.*

screwdriver *noun*
a tool that fits into the slot in the top of a screw to tighten or loosen it

scribble *verb*
1 to write or draw something carelessly 2 to make meaningless marks or lines with a pen or pencil
scribble *noun*
3 careless writing

script *noun*
1 handwriting 2 a copy of the words the actors say in a play or film

scripture (*say* **skrip**-cha) *noun*
1 religious writing 2 **Scripture** the Bible
•***Word Family:*** **scriptural** *adjective*
•***Word Origins:*** from a Latin word meaning "written"

scroll (*rhymes with* hole) *noun*
1 a roll of paper, especially parchment, used for writing
scroll *verb*
2 to move your cursor up or down so that you move through the text or images on a computer screen
•***Word Family:*** **scrolling** *noun*

scrotum (*say* **skro**-tum) *noun*
the soft pouch of skin in males that hangs between their legs and contains their testicles
•***Word Family:*** the plural is **scrota**

scrounge *verb*
to get something by begging or borrowing: *to scrounge a meal*
•***Word Family:*** **scrounger** *noun*

scrub (1) *verb*
1 to rub something hard with a brush and soapy water, in order to clean it 2 to remove or cancel something: *to scrub a player from the team*
scrub *noun*
3 a hard rub
•***Word Family:*** other verb forms are **scrubs, scrubbed, scrubbing**

scrub (2) *noun*
an area covered with low trees or bushes

scruff *noun*
the back of your neck

scruffy *adjective*
untidy or dirty: *scruffy clothes*
•***Word Family:*** other forms are **scruffier, scruffiest**

scrum *noun*
1 a stage in the game of rugby when the forwards from both teams bend over and push against each other with their shoulders while trying to get the ball with their feet 2 a group

of people who are all pushing or struggling with each other: *pushing your way through a scrum of reporters*

scrumptious (*say* **skrum**-shus) *adjective*
delicious or splendid: *a scrumptious meal*

scrupulous (*say* **skroop**-ya-lus) *adjective*
1 careful to do the right thing 2 paying careful attention to every detail: *She copied the poem with scrupulous care.*
•***Word Family:*** **scruple** *noun* **scrupulously** *adverb*

scrutinize or **scrutinise** (*say* **skroo**-tin-ize) *verb*
to examine something very closely or carefully
•***Word Family:*** **scrutiny** *noun*

scuba diving (*say* **skoo**-ba) *noun*
the sport of swimming underwater while breathing from an air tank on your back
•***Word Origins:*** an acronym from the first letter of the words *s*elf *c*ontained *u*nderwater *b*reathing *a*pparatus

scuff *verb*
1 to mark or scratch something: *to scuff your shoes / to scuff the furniture* 2 to scrape or shuffle your feet along the ground as you walk

scuffle *verb*
1 to struggle or fight in a confused way
scuffle *noun*
2 a confused struggle

scull *noun*
1 a racing boat for one person with a pair of oars 2 one of the oars used in a scull
scull *verb*
3 to row a boat using sculls

sculpture (*say* **skulp**-cher) *noun*
1 making figures, animals or shapes in clay, bronze, marble and so on 2 an object or objects created in this way
•***Word Family:*** **sculpt** *verb* to carve **sculptor** *noun* someone who makes sculptures **sculptural** *adjective*

scum *noun*
1 a layer of froth or dirt on top of a liquid
2 someone you feel contempt for

scurry *verb*
to move or rush somewhere quickly: *I scurried past the huge dog.*
•***Word Family:*** other verb forms are **scurries, scurried, scurrying**

scurvy (*say* **sker**-vee) *noun*
a disease due to a lack of vitamin C in your diet, that causes swollen gums, pale skin and bruising

scuttle *verb*
to run or move somewhere very fast using lots of very small steps: *The lizard scuttled under the rock.*

scythe (*say* sithe) *noun*
a long-handled farm tool with a long, thin, slightly curved blade for cutting grass

sea *noun*
1 the salt water that covers most of the Earth's surface 2 a large area of water: *the Red Sea*
3 a large number or area of things: *a sea of faces*
4 at sea puzzled or bewildered

sea-anemone (*say* **see**-a-nem-a-nee) *noun*
a sea animal that lives stuck to a rock and has a small round body, with tentacles on top

seagull *noun*
a long-winged seabird with a harsh cry and webbed feet, often white with grey wings

seahorse *noun*
a small fish with a long, curved tail and a head that looks like a horse's head

seal (1) *noun*
1 a mark, sticker or design used on official documents 2 the piece of wax that closes a document or envelope and that must be broken before it can be opened and read 3 something that is designed to close something completely
seal *verb*
4 to fix or close something completely so that force is needed to open or enter: *to seal an envelope / to seal a cave* 5 to fix a situation in a particular way: *The accident sealed her fate.*

seal (2) *noun*
a large, fish-eating, sea mammal with a smooth, furry body and flippers for swimming
•***Word Family:*** the male animal is a **bull**; the female is a **cow**; the young is a **pup**

sea-level *noun*
the average level of the sea, halfway between high and low tide, used to measure how high things such as mountains or aircraft are: *We are 50 metres above sea-level.*

sea-lion *noun*
a type of large seal found in the Pacific Ocean

seam *noun*
1 a line of sewing joining two pieces of cloth together 2 a thin layer of a rock or mineral, such as coal in between other types of rock

seance (*say* **say**-ons) *noun*
a meeting of people who wish to communicate with the spirits of dead people

seaplane *noun*
a plane with floats, able to take off or land on water

a b c d e f g h i j k l m n o p q r s t u v w x y z

A B C D E F G H I J K L M N O P Q R S T U V W X Y Z

sear *verb*
1 to burn or scorch the surface of something
2 to brown and seal the surface of meat

search (*say* serch) *verb*
1 to look carefully or thoroughly in order to find something 2 to examine a person or look through a house, car and so on when looking for something such as stolen goods, weapons or drugs
search *noun*
3 searching or examining: *a thorough search*
•*Word Family:* the plural of the noun is **searches** ☐ **searching** *adjective* thorough: *a searching look*

seasick *adjective*
feeling sick or vomiting because of the movement of a ship at sea
•*Word Family:* **seasickness** *noun*

season (*say* **see**-zon) *noun*
1 one of the four divisions of the year into spring, summer, autumn and winter 2 the time of year when something
usually happens: *the football season / the season for apples*
season *verb*
3 to add salt and pepper to food
•*Word Family:* **seasonal** *adjective* **seasonally** *adverb*

seasoning (*say* **seez**-ning) *noun*
salt and pepper added to food

seat *noun*
1 something, such as a chair, for sitting on
2 the part of a piece of clothing for sitting on: *the seat of your pants* 3 a centre or location: *the seat of local government* 4 a position in parliament and the constituency it represents: *to win a seat in the election / a safe seat* 5 a large house or estate: *their country seat*
seat *verb*
6 to sit in or on a seat: *to seat yourself for dinner*
7 to have room for a particular number of people: *This hall seats 700.*

seat belt *noun*
a harness in a car or aircraft designed to keep a traveller safely seated in a crash or in rough conditions

secateurs (*say* sek-a-**terz** *or* **sek**-a-terz) *plural noun*
gardening shears with short blades for pruning trees and plants

secluded (*say* se-**kloo**-did) *adjective*
quiet and hidden
•*Word Family:* **seclusion** *noun*

second (1) (*say* **sek**-und) *adjective*
1 being number two in order or a series
2 another: *a second chance* 3 alternate: *every second day*
second *noun*
4 someone who aids or assists someone else if needed: *He's my second in the fight.* 5 **seconds** (a) a second helping or course of a meal (b) slightly damaged products being sold at a reduced price
second *verb*
6 to support someone or back them up: *David proposed the motion and Nicola seconded it.*
•*Word Family:* **seconder** *noun* someone who seconds a suggestion or nomination **secondly** *adverb*

second (2) (*say* **sek**-und) *noun*
the basic unit for measuring time, which is a sixtieth part of a minute

secondary (*say* **sek**-un-dree) *adjective*
1 coming second in importance, time or place: *a secondary concern / an idea of secondary importance* 2 involving education for children between the ages of 11 and 18: *secondary education / secondary pupils* 3 happening as a result of something else of the same kind: *a secondary infection*

secondary school *noun*
a school for pupils aged between 11 and 18

second-hand (*say* sek-und-**hand**) *adjective*
once owned or used by someone else: *a second-hand bike / second-hand clothes*

secret (*say* **see**-krit) *adjective*
1 kept hidden from others: *a secret meeting / secret cupboard*
secret *noun*
2 something kept secret or hidden 3 a hidden reason or cause: *Hard work is the secret of his success.*
•*Word Family:* **secretive** *adjective* liking to keep secrets **secrecy** *noun* **secretly** *adverb*

secretary (*say* **sek**-ra-tree) *noun*
someone whose job is to write letters, keep records, make phone calls and so on for their employer
•*Word Family:* the plural is **secretaries** ☐ **secretarial** *adjective*

secrete (*say* se-**kreet**) *verb*
1 to produce a substance in the way a gland does: *to secrete adrenalin* 2 to hide or conceal something: *to secrete money under the mattress*
•*Word Family:* **secretion** *noun*

sect *noun*
a religious group that has broken away from a larger group
•*Word Family:* **sectarian** *adjective*

section (*say* **sek**-shon) *noun*
1 a separate part or division: *This section of the book is boring.* 2 a drawing or diagram of what

something would look like if you cut it through the middle to show the inside

sector (*say* **sek**-ta) *noun*
1 a wedge-shaped part of a circle, looking like a slice of cake 2 a division or department of something larger: *the business sector of society*

secular (*say* **sek**-yoo-la) *adjective*
not connected at all with religious or spiritual matters: *We live in a secular society.*

secure (*say* se-**kew**-er) *adjective*
1 feeling safe and confident 2 firmly fastened in place: *The ladder is secure now.* 3 certain or sure to last a long time: *a secure job*
secure *verb*
4 to fasten something firmly: *to secure a new tree to a stake* 5 to obtain something: *to secure good seats for the concert* 6 to make something safe: *to secure a room*
•***Word Family:*** **securely** *adverb* **security** *noun*

sedate (*say* se-**date**) *adjective*
1 calm and dignified: *to take a sedate stroll*
sedate *verb*
2 to quieten a person or animal by giving them a sedative
•***Word Family:*** **sedately** *adverb* **sedation** *noun*

sedative (*say* **sed**-a-tiv) *noun*
a drug used to calm people or animals down and make them relax

sediment (*say* **sed**-i-ment) *noun*
the solid material that falls to the bottom of a liquid
•***Word Family:*** **sedimentary** *adjective*

seduce (*say* se-**dewce**) *verb*
1 to persuade someone to have sex 2 to lead someone into doing something wrong: *He's seduced me into bad habits.*
•***Word Family:*** **seducer** *noun* **seduction** *noun* **seductive** *adjective* **seductively** *adverb*

see *verb*
1 to take things in with your eyes 2 to experience or find out about something: *to see a bit of life / to see how other people live* 3 to realize or understand something: *to see the error of your ways / I see what you mean.* 4 to consider or regard things in a particular way: *to see things differently from my parents* 5 to find something out: *See who's at the door.* 6 to visit someone: *to go to see a friend* 7 to escort or go with someone: *Let me see you to the door.* 8 **see through** (a) to realize that something is a trick or a lie: *We saw through your disguise.* (b) to help or support someone for a while: *to see someone through a difficult time* 9 **see you** goodbye
•***Word Family:*** other forms are **sees, saw, seen, seeing**

seed *noun*
1 the part of a plant from which a new plant grows 2 a tennis player ranked according to skill: *The first and second seeds played in the final.* 3 **seeds** beginnings: *the seeds of unhappiness*

seedling *noun*
a young plant

seek *verb*
1 to try to find or obtain something: *to seek friends / to seek support* 2 **be sought after** to be in demand
•***Word Family:*** other forms are **seeks, sought, seeking**

seem *verb*
to appear: *He seems sad. / It seems wrong.*
•***Word Family:*** **seeming** *adjective* apparent: *Her seeming lack of enthusiasim annoyed me.* **seemingly** *adverb*

seep *verb*
to leak or ooze slowly: *Water seeped through the roof. / Blood seeped from the wound.*
•***Word Family:*** **seepage** *noun*

seesaw *noun*
a plank fastened in the middle, so that the child sitting on one end goes up while the child at the other end goes down

seethe *verb*
1 to bubble and foam as if boiling 2 to be agitated or excited: *to seethe with rage*

segment (*say* **seg**-ment) *noun*
1 a part into which something separates naturally: *the segments of an orange*
segment (*say* seg-**ment**) *verb*
2 to separate something into segments
•***Word Family:*** **segmentation** *noun*

segregate (*say* **seg**-ra-gate) *verb*
to separate or keep apart, especially people or groups from each other
•***Word Family:*** **segregation** *noun*

seismograph (*say* **size**-ma-graf) *noun*
an instrument for measuring the vibrations caused by earthquakes
•***Word Family:*** **seismic** *adjective* caused by an earthquake **seismologist** *noun* **seismology** *noun*

seize (*say* seez) *verb*
1 to take hold of someone or something firmly: *to seize someone by the arm* 2 **seize on** or **seize upon** to show great interest in something: *to seize upon an idea* 3 **seize up** to become jammed, the way an engine does when it overheats
•***Word Family:*** **seizure** *noun* a fit

seldom *adverb*
not often: *She seldom sings.*

A B C D E F G H I J K L M N O P Q R S T U V W X Y Z

select (*say* se-**lekt**) *verb*
1 to choose something: *to select your favourite song on a jukebox*
select *adjective*
2 carefully chosen or very special: *a select group of friends*
• ***Word Family:*** **selection** *noun* **selective** *adjective* **selector** *noun*

self *noun*
your own person, nature or character
• ***Word Family:*** the plural is **selves**

self- *prefix*
1 of or over yourself: *self-control* 2 by or in yourself: *self-evident* 3 to or for yourself: *self-addressed*

self-centred *adjective*
selfish or too concerned with yourself

self-confidence *noun*
belief in your own abilities, worth, judgment and so on
• ***Word Family:*** **self-confident** *adjective*

self-conscious *adjective*
too concerned with how you appear to other people
• ***Word Family:*** **self-consciously** *adverb*

self-contained *adjective*
1 keeping your thoughts to yourself 2 having all the things you need, such as a flat with its own bathroom, laundry and kitchen

self-control *noun*
the ability to control what you do: *Don't eat so much—show a little self-control.*
• ***Word Family:*** **self-controlled** *adjective*

self-defence *noun*
defending yourself from attack: *self-defence classes / She shot him in self-defence.*

self-esteem *noun*
a good opinion of yourself

selfish *adjective*
caring too much for yourself and too little for others
• ***Word Family:*** **selfishly** *adverb* **selfishness** *noun*

selfless *adjective*
unselfish
• ***Word Family:*** **selflessly** *adverb* **selflessness** *noun*

self-raising flour *noun*
flour already containing baking powder to make cakes rise

self-respect *noun*
a feeling of confidence and pride in your own character and the way you behave
• ***Word Family:*** **self-respecting** *adjective*

self-righteous (*say* self-**rie**-chus) *adjective*
sure that you are better and more virtuous than everyone else, in an annoying way
• ***Word Family:*** **self-righteously** *adverb*

self-service *adjective*
served, worked or carried out partly or wholly by the customer, passenger and so on: *a self-service restaurant*

self-sufficient *adjective*
1 able to look after yourself without help from others 2 able to grow the food you need and to make the things you need without having to buy anything: *a self-sufficient farm*
• ***Word Family:*** **self-sufficiency** *noun*

sell *verb*
1 to exchange something for money: *He sold his bike and bought a better one.* 2 to offer something for sale as a way of making money, or as your job: *She sells cars.*
• ***Word Family:*** other forms are **sells, sold, selling**

semaphore (*say* **sem**-a-for) *noun*
a method of signalling messages in which flags held in different positions represent the letters of the alphabet

semen (*say* **see**-mun) *noun*
the white fluid produced by a male's sex organs
• ***Word Origins:*** from a Latin word meaning "seed"

semibreve (*say* **sem**-i-breev) *noun*
a long, musical note that is equal in time value to four crotchets

semicircle (*say* **sem**-i-sir-kul) *noun*
a half of a circle
• ***Word Family:*** **semicircular** *adjective*

semicolon (*say* sem-i-**kole**-on) *noun*
a punctuation mark (;), used in a sentence to separate clauses or introduce a pause longer than that of a comma

semidetached *adjective*
partly detached or separated, as a pair of houses that are separated from other buildings but share a common wall

semifinal (*say* sem-i-**fie**-nul) *noun*
one of the contests or matches that take place to decide who will play in the final
• ***Word Family:*** **semifinalist** *noun* a person or team that competes in a semifinal

seminary (*say* **sem**-in-ree) *noun*
a training college for priests
• ***Word Family:*** the plural is **seminaries**

semiquaver (*say* **sem**-i-kway-va) *noun*
a short, musical note equal to half of the time value of a quaver

semitone *noun*
the smallest musical interval in western music, equal to half a tone, represented on the piano as the difference between any note and the one next to it

semolina (*say* sem-a-**lee**-na) *noun*
the hard parts of wheat grain left after separating the fine flour, used to make pasta or puddings

senate *noun*
the upper house of parliament in countries such as the United States, with members representing each of the individual states
• ***Word Family:*** **senator** *noun* a member of the senate

send *verb*
1 to make someone or something go somewhere: *to send him into the room / to send a letter* 2 to transmit a radio signal or message 3 to cause a person or animal to behave in a particular way: *to send the bull into a frenzy* 4 **send for** to ask for a particular person to come and see you: *to send for the doctor* 5 **send up** to make fun of a person or their behaviour by copying them: *We sent up the way she walks.*
• ***Word Family:*** other forms are **sends, sent, sending** □ **sender** *noun*

senile (*say* **see**-nile) *adjective*
weak in your mind because you are old
• ***Word Family:*** **senility** *noun*

senior (*say* **seen**-ya) *adjective*
1 older or more important: *a senior student / a senior manager*
senior *noun*
2 a senior person or student
• ***Word Family:*** **seniority** *noun*

sensation (*say* sen-**say**-shon) *noun*
1 a feeling: *a tingling sensation in your leg / to have the sensation that someone is watching you* 2 someone or something that causes great excitement: *The pop group was a sensation. / The film caused a sensation.*
• ***Word Family:*** **sensational** *adjective* **sensationally** *adverb*

sense *noun*
1 your ability to see, hear, smell, touch or taste: *a good sense of smell* 2 a feeling: *There was a sense of menace in his voice.* 3 the ability to understand a particular thing, or deal with it well: *a sense of humour / a sense of adventure* 4 the ability to act and think in a sensible way: *to have sense* 5 meaning: *In what sense are you using the word?*
sense *verb*
6 to be or become aware of something: *I sensed that someone was looking at me.*

sensible (*say* **sen**-sa-bul) *adjective*
1 having or showing good sense: *sensible behaviour* 2 aware: *He's sensible of the danger of his situation.*
• ***Word Family:*** **sensibility** *noun* (**sensibilities**) **sensibly** *adverb*

sensitive (*say* **sen**-sa-tiv) *adjective*
1 easily affected by something: *Her skin is sensitive to hot sun.* 2 easily offended or hurt: *She's sensitive about being so tall.* 3 able to measure finely and exactly: *a sensitive thermometer*
• ***Word Family:*** **sensitivity** *noun* (**sensitivities**) **sensitively** *adverb*

sensory (*say* **sen**-sa-ree) *adjective*
having to do with feeling or experiencing heat, light, sound, and so on

sensual (*say* **sens**-yew-al) *adjective*
having to do with feeling and your senses rather than your mind: *the sensual rhythm of the pounding drums*
• ***Word Family:*** **sensuous** *adjective* **sensualist** *noun* **sensuality** *noun* **sensually** *adverb*

sentence *noun*
1 a group of words that together express a complete thought, beginning with a capital letter and ending with a full stop, question mark or exclamation mark, as in *The man bought a book.* 2 the punishment of a convicted criminal: *a life sentence*
sentence *verb*
3 to officially give someone a punishment: *to sentence a murderer*

sentiment (*say* **sen**-ti-ment) *noun*
1 a tender feeling or emotion 2 an opinion or attitude: *I agree with his sentiments on this issue.*

sentimental (*say* sen-ti-**men**-tal) *adjective*
having or showing too much emotion: *a sentimental film*
• ***Word Family:*** **sentimentality** *noun* **sentimentally** *adverb*

sentry *noun*
a soldier keeping guard
• ***Word Family:*** the plural is **sentries**

separate (*say* **sep**-a-rate) *verb*
1 to remove parts so that they are no longer together: *to separate the milk from the cream* 2 to stop living with your husband or wife but not get a divorce
separate (*say* **sep**-ret) *adjective*
3 not shared or joined: *to sleep in separate rooms*
• ***Word Family:*** **separately** *adverb* **separation** *noun* **separator** *noun*

sepia (*say* **see**-pi-a) *noun*
a deep brown colour: *a sepia photograph*

A B C D E F G H I J K L M N O P Q R S T U V W X Y Z

September *noun*
the ninth month of the year, with 30 days
• ***Word Origins:*** from a Latin word for the seventh month of the Roman calendar

septet *noun*
1 any group of seven people or things 2 a piece of music for seven musicians

septic *adjective*
infected with germs: *a septic wound*

sequel (*say* **see**-kwel) *noun*
1 a book or film that continues the story begun in an earlier book or film 2 something that follows as a result or consequence of something else

sequence (*say* **see**-kwence) *noun*
1 the order in which one or more things follow each other: *to arrange the numbers in sequence*
2 a connected series of things: *a strange sequence of events*
• ***Word Family:*** **sequential** *adjective* **sequentially** *adverb*

sequin (*say* **see**-kwin) *noun*
a small, coloured, shining disc, used to decorate bags or clothes
• ***Word Family:*** **sequined** *adjective*

serenade (*say* se-ra-**nade**) *noun*
1 music of the kind originally sung or played by a lover under his loved one's window at night
serenade *verb*
2 to sing or play a serenade to

serene (*say* se-**reen**) *adjective*
calm and tranquil: *a serene smile*
• ***Word Family:*** **serenely** *adverb* **serenity** *noun*

serf *noun*
a labourer in the Middle Ages, who was forced to work on the land owned by the lord of the manor and who could be sold with the land
• ***Word Family:*** **serfdom** *noun*

sergeant (*say* **sar**-jent) *noun*
1 a soldier ranking above a corporal 2 a police officer ranking between a constable and an inspector

sergeant major *noun*
a soldier who is one rank above a sergeant

serial (*say* **sear**-ree-ul) *noun*
a story presented in parts, usually week by week in a magazine or on television or radio
• ***Word Family:*** **serialize** or **serialise** *verb* to publish or broadcast in the form of a serial **serialization** *noun*

series (*say* **sear**-reez) *noun*
1 a number of related things or events that happen one after another: *a series of accidents*
2 a number of television or radio shows with the same name, subject matter, characters or story: *a nature series*
• ***Word Family:*** the plural is **series**

serious (*say* **sear**-ree-us) *adjective*
1 thoughtful or solemn: *a serious face*
2 important: *a serious decision* 3 very bad or worrying: *a serious accident / a serious illness*
4 sincere or meaning what you say: *Please be serious.*
• ***Word Family:*** **seriously** *adverb*

sermon *noun*
a serious talk or speech, especially one based on the Bible and given by a priest or minister

serpent *noun*
a snake
• ***Word Family:*** **serpentine** *adjective* twisting like a snake

serrated (*say* se-**ray**-tid) *adjective*
having a sharply notched or grooved edge, as a saw does
• ***Word Family:*** **serration** *noun*

servant *noun*
1 someone, such as a maid, who works in the household of another 2 someone employed by the government: *a public servant*

serve *verb*
1 to perform useful work or duties: *to serve your country / to serve in the army* 2 to be of use for a particular purpose: *This box will serve as a table.*
3 to work as an assistant: *to serve in a bar / to serve customers in a shop* 4 to give people food or drink at a meal: *May I serve dinner now?* 5 to spend time doing something: *to serve a prison sentence / to serve an apprenticeship* 6 to hit a ball into play in tennis
serve *noun*
7 serving a ball in tennis

service (*say* **ser**-vis) *noun*
1 a useful act: *to perform a service for your country* 2 something provided for and needed by many people: *a bus service* 3 a regular check-up for equipment or machinery: My *car needs a service.* 4 a religious meeting or ceremony: *the marriage service* 5 a set of objects used for a special purpose: *a dinner service* 6 a government department or the people in it: *the diplomatic service* 8 serving a ball in tennis 9 **the services** the army, navy and air force
service *verb*
10 to give equipment or machinery a check-up: *to service a car*

serviceable (*say* **ser**-vis-a-bul) *adjective*
useful because it is strong and lasting: *serviceable clothes*
• ***Word Family:*** **serviceably** *adverb*

serviette (*say* ser-vi-**et**) *noun*
a piece of cloth or paper you use at a table to protect your clothes or wipe your mouth

serving *noun*
1 a portion or helping of food
serving *adjective*
2 used for serving food: *a serving spoon*

session (*say* **sesh**-on) *noun*
1 the meeting together of a court, council or parliament 2 the time during which an activity takes place: *a recording session*

set *verb*
1 to put something somewhere: *to set the bowl on the table* 2 to behave in a particular way: *to set a good example to your friends* 3 to give people work to do: *to set homework* 4 to arrange things: *to set the table with cutlery* 5 to adjust something so that it is ready to work: *to set your alarm clock* 6 to become hard or firm: *The ice-cream set quickly in the freezer.* 7 to start someone doing something: *That book set me thinking.* 8 to sink below the horizon: *The sun began to set.* 9 **set out** (a) to aim to do a particular thing: *to set out to become a pilot* (b) to state a particular thing clearly: *Set out your request in writing.* (c) to begin a journey
set *noun*
10 a number of things that form a complete collection: *a set of dinner plates* 11 a radio or television receiver: *a TV set* 12 the scenery used to represent a particular place during a play or film 13 the area where filming takes place 14 a major division in a tennis match where one player has won at least six games 15 a collection of similar numbers or objects in maths
set *adjective*
16 fixed: *a set smile / a set time* 17 ready: *I'm set to leave.*
• ***Word Family:*** other verb forms are **sets, set, setting**

setback *noun*
something that delays or slows down your progress

set square *noun*
a flat instrument in the shape of a right-angled triangle, used for drawing such things as the plans for houses

settee *noun*
a covered seat or sofa for two or more people

setting *noun*
1 what surrounds a particular thing: *a diamond in a gold setting / a restaurant in a mountain setting* 2 the time and place in which a play or film occurs 3 the arrangement of someone's cutlery, napkin, glasses on a table

settle *verb*
1 to agree: *to settle on where to spend the holidays* 2 to pay what you owe: *to settle a bill* 3 to put an end to a disagreement: *to settle an argument* 4 to make a particular country or area your home: *to settle on the coast* 5 to sink down or rest: *Mud settled on the river bottom.* 6 to get used to something new: *to settle into your new house*
• ***Word Family:*** **settlement** *noun*

settler *noun*
someone who settles in a new country or area

seven *noun*
the number 7
• ***Word Family:*** **seven** *adjective* **seventh** *noun* **seventh** *adjective*

seventeen *noun*
the number 17
• ***Word Family:*** **seventeen** *adjective* **seventeenth** *noun* **seventeenth** *adjective*

seventy *noun*
the number 70
• ***Word Family:*** the plural is **seventies** □ **seventy** *adjective* **seventieth** *noun* **seventieth** *adjective*

sever (*say* **sev**-a) *verb*
1 to cut off or cut right through something: *to sever an artery* 2 to end a connection with someone: *to sever your ties with your old friends*

several *adjective*
1 more than two or three, but not many
2 individual or respective: *The delegates returned to their several countries.*

severe (*say* se-**veer**) *adjective*
1 stern or strict: *a severe look* 2 very bad or serious: *severe damage / a severe illness*
• ***Word Family:*** **severely** *adverb* **severity** *noun*

sew *verb*
to join, mend, decorate or make something using a needle and thread, either by hand or machine
• ***Word Family:*** other forms are **sews, sewed, sewn** or **sewed, sewing**

sewage (*say* **soo**-ij) *noun*
waste matter carried away in drains and sewers

sewer (*say* **soo**-a) *noun*
a pipe, usually underground, for carrying waste water and human waste away from buildings

sewerage (*say* **soo**-a-rij) *noun*
the removal of waste matter and waste water by sewers

sex *noun*
1 one of the two groups, male and female, into which humans and animals are divided: *to find*

out what sex your hamster is / the opposite sex 2 the condition of being either male or female: *She was left out of the team because of her sex. / sex discrimination* 3 the instinct that makes two people physically attracted to each other 4 the act of sexual intercourse 5 sexual activity in books, films or on TV: *The film is full of sex.*

sexism *noun*
an attitude that judges people by their sex rather than by their own personal qualities or on how qualified or experienced they are
•***Word Family:*** **sexist** *noun* **sexist** *adjective*

sextet *noun*
1 a group of six people, especially musicians 2 a musical composition for six instruments or voices

sextuplet *noun*
one of six children born to the same mother at the same time

sexual (*say* **seks**-yew-al) *adjective*
1 to do with sex: *sexual attraction* 2 to do with the difference between males and females: *sexual equality*
•***Word Family:*** **sexuality** *noun* **sexually** *adverb*

sexual intercourse *noun*
a sexual act between two people, usually one in which a man puts his penis into a woman's vagina

sexy *adjective*
1 sexually attractive or exciting 2 concerned with sex: *a sexy film*
•***Word Family:*** other forms are **sexier, sexiest**

shabby *adjective*
1 worn-out: *a shabby old coat* 2 dressed in old, worn-out clothes: *shabby kids* 3 mean or unfair: *What a shabby way to treat a friend!*
•***Word Family:*** other forms are **shabbier, shabbiest**

shack *noun*
a small, roughly-built hut

shackle *noun*
1 one of a pair of iron rings joined by a chain, fastened around a prisoner's wrists or ankles 2 anything that stops you or holds you back: *to escape the shackles of poverty*

shade *noun*
1 the area of darkness and coolness caused by cutting off the sun's rays: *the shade of a tree* 2 a lighter or darker form of one colour: *a vivid shade of blue* 3 something, such as a window blind, used to protect you against bright light
shade *verb*
4 to protect or cover a person, thing or area from bright light 5 to draw or paint light and dark sections in a sketch

shadow *noun*
1 a dark shape or figure formed when something blocks the light: *the shadow of a man* 2 any dark area: *shadows under your eyes* 3 shade or darkness caused when light doesn't reach a place: *the trees were in shadow*
shadow *verb*
4 to cast shade or shadow 5 to follow someone secretly and watch them closely: *The detective shadowed the suspect.*
•***Word Family:*** **shadowy** *adjective*

shady *adjective*
1 giving shade: *a shady tree* 2 away from sunlight: *a shady corner* 3 dishonest or illegal: *a shady business deal*
•***Word Family:*** other forms are **shadier, shadiest**

shaft (*say* shahft) *noun*
1 the rod or pole of a tool or weapon, such as an axe or an arrow 2 a beam or ray: *a shaft of sunlight* 3 a very deep, narrow hole with staight sides: *a mine shaft / a lift shaft*

shaggy *noun*
1 covered with long, untidy hair: *a shaggy dog* 2 rough and untidy: *a shaggy mane*
•***Word Family:*** other forms are **shaggier, shaggiest**

shake *verb*
1 to move something from side to side or to and fro with short, sharp, quick movements: *The wind shook the branches. / Shake your head now.* 2 to affect someone badly by frightening or upsetting them: *The news shook me.* 3 to waver or tremble: *Her voice shook with fear.* 4 **shake hands** to clasp hands when you meet someone or agree with them
shake *noun*
5 a shaking movement: *Give the bottle a good shake.* 6 a drink made by shaking or whisking the ingredients together: *a milk shake*
•***Word Family:*** other verb forms are **shakes, shook, shaken, shaking** □ **shaky** *adjective* **(shakier, shakiest) shakily** *adverb*

shale (*rhymes with* male) *noun*
a soft, flaky rock formed when layers of mud and clay were pressed together

shallot (*say* sha-**lot**) *noun*
a small, thin, onion-like plant that you can eat raw or cooked

shallow (*say* **shal**-oh) *adjective*
1 not deep: *shallow water* 2 insincere or without serious thought: *a very shallow person*
•***Word Family:*** **shallowness** *noun*

sham *noun*
1 a fake or pretence: *His illness was only a sham.*

sham *verb*
2 to pretend: *to sham an illness*
•***Word Family:*** other verb forms are **shams, shammed, shamming**

shamble *verb*
to shuffle or walk clumsily

shambles *noun*
a confused muddle: *My room is a shambles.*

shame *noun*
1 the guilt or embarrassment you feel when you do or say something silly or wrong 2 dishonour or disgrace: *She has brought shame on her family.* 3 a pity or something that makes you sorry: *What a shame!*
shame *verb*
4 to disgrace someone or make them feel ashamed
•***Word Family:*** **shameful** *adjective* **shamefully** *adverb* **shameless** *adjective* **shamelessly** *adverb*

shampoo *noun*
1 a liquid soap, especially for washing hair or carpets
shampoo *verb*
2 to wash something with shampoo
•***Word Family:*** other verb forms are **shampoos, shampooed, shampooing**

shamrock *noun*
a small, clover-like plant with three, bright green leaves on each stem

shanty (1) *noun*
a roughly-built shack
•***Word Family:*** the plural is **shanties**

shanty (2) *noun*
a sailors' song, often sung in time with their work
•***Word Family:*** the plural is **shanties**

shape *noun*
1 the outline or form of something: *a circular shape* 2 condition: *The garden is in poor shape.*
shape *verb*
3 to make or fashion a material into an object: *to shape the wood into a vase* 4 **shape up** to develop: *The new players are shaping up well.*
•***Word Family:*** **shapely** *adjective* **(shapelier, shapeliest)** having an attractive shape **shapeless** *adjective*

share (*rhymes with* air) *noun*
1 a part of something that has been divided out among several people: *You'll have to do your share of the work.* 2 one of the equal parts into which the ownership of a company is divided, which returns to the holder a proportion of the profits: *to hold shares in an oil company*
share *verb*
3 to use, do or have something together: *to share a room with your sister* 4 to give or receive a part of: *to share sweets with your friends*
•***Word Family:*** **shareholder** *noun*

shareware *noun*
computer software that is available to all users free of charge either on a disk or on the Internet

shark *noun*
large, powerful sea-fish with sharp teeth

sharp *adjective*
1 having a thin edge or fine point that can cut things or make a hole in them: *a sharp sword / a sharp pencil* 2 abrupt or sudden: *a sharp corner / a sharp rise in temperature* 3 distinct or easy to see: *a sharp outline* 4 harsh or biting: *a sharp reply / a sharp taste / a sharp wind* 5 alert: *to keep a sharp lookout* 6 dishonest: *a sharp practice* 7 clever: *to be very sharp* 8 raised in pitch by a semitone, or above proper pitch: C *sharp*
sharp *adverb*
9 exactly, or punctually: *Come at six o'clock sharp.*
sharp *noun*
10 **(a)** a musical note raised by one semitone from the main note **(b)** the sign (♯) placed next to a note that indicates this
•***Word Family:*** **sharpen** *verb* **sharply** *adverb* **sharpness** *noun*

shatter *verb*
1 to break violently into fragments: *The bullet shattered the glass.* 2 to make someone very upset or distressed: *The news of his death shattered me.*

shave *verb*
1 to remove hair with a razor 2 to remove something in layers or thin slices: *to shave wood* 3 to scrape against something: *The car shaved the fence.*
shave *noun*
3 the act of shaving, especially your face: *to need a shave* 4 **a close shave** a narrow escape
•***Word Family:*** other verb forms are **shaves, shaved, shaved** or **shaven, shaving**

shavings *noun*
thin, small pieces of wood: *pencil shavings*

shawl *noun*
a large, often thick scarf you wear around your shoulders

she *pronoun*
the female you are talking about
•***Word Family:*** other forms are **her, hers, they**

sheaf *noun*
1 a small bundle of cut cereal plants: *a sheaf of wheat* 2 a small bundle or pile: *a sheaf of papers*
•***Word Family:*** the plural is **sheaves**

shear *verb*
to cut the wool off a sheep
•***Word Family:*** other forms are **shears, sheared, shorn, shearing** □ **shearer** *noun* someone who shears sheep

shears *plural noun*
a pair of large scissors with long, heavy blades

sheath (*say* sheeth) *noun*
1 a case for the blade of a knife or something similar 2 a closely fitting cover 3 *another name for a* **condom**
•***Word Family:*** the plural is **sheaths**

sheathe (*say* sheedh) *verb*
1 to replace something in its sheath: *to sheathe a knife* 2 to cover something with a protective layer

shed (1) *noun*
a simple building for storage or shelter

shed (2) *verb*
1 to lose something or let it fall off: *The cattle shed their winter coats. / The trees are shedding their leaves.* 2 to give out light: *The lamp sheds light onto my book.* 3 **shed blood** to injure or kill people 4 **shed tears** to cry
•***Word Family:*** other forms are **sheds, shed, shedding**

sheen *noun*
a soft shine or glossy brightness

sheep *noun*
1 a grass-eating animal kept for its wool and meat 2 a meek or timid person
•***Word Family:*** the plural is **sheep**

sheepish *adjective*
embarrassed or timid: *a sheepish smile*

sheer *adjective*
1 so thin that you can see right through: *sheer silk* 2 pure or absolute: *She laughed for sheer joy.* 3 steep: *sheer cliffs*

sheet *noun*
1 a large rectangle of thin cloth used on a bed 2 a thin piece of something: *a sheet of paper* 3 a broad area of something: *a sheet of flame*
•***Word Family:*** **sheeting** *noun*

Sheikh (*say* shake) *noun*
a male Arab ruler or chief

shelf *noun*
1 a piece of wood or glass, fixed to a wall or as part of a cupboard and used to stand things on 2 a ledge on a cliff face
•***Word Family:*** the plural is **shelves**

shell *noun*
1 the hard covering or case of animals such as mussels and snails 2 an outer covering, usually hard: *the shell of an egg or nut* 3 the outside walls of a house or other building: *Only the shell of the house remained after the fire.* 4 a hollow case containing an explosive charge, designed to be fired from a large gun
shell *verb*
5 to remove the shell of something: *to shell peas* 6 to fire shells or explosives at someone or something: *to shell enemy forces*

shellfish *noun*
a water-living animal, such as an oyster or crayfish, with a shell around its soft body
•***Word Family:*** the plural is **shellfishes** or **shellfish**

shelter *noun*
1 a place or structure that provides protection, covering or safety: *a bomb shelter / a bus shelter* 2 protection: *to provide shelter from the storm*
shelter *verb*
3 to find or provide people with a shelter

shelve *verb*
1 to place things on a shelf or shelves 2 to postpone something or put it aside: *to shelve your plans until next week*

shepherd (*say* **shep**-erd) *noun*
1 someone who guards or herds sheep
shepherd *verb*
2 to protect, guard or watch over someone: *His minders shepherded him to his car.*

sherbet *noun*
a sweet, fizzy powder used in drinks and sweets
•***Word Origins:*** from an Arabic word meaning "a drink"

sheriff (*say* **she**-rif) *noun*
1 an officer appointed to enforce the law in a United States county 2 the chief judge in a Scottish county

sherry *noun*
a strong, sweet or dry wine, first made in Spain
•***Word Family:*** the plural is **sherries**

shield (*say* sheeld) *noun*
1 a flat piece of metal, wood or leather, that soldiers once carried for protection in battle 2 something used to protect, hide or defend something else: *His dark glasses provided a shield from the sun.*
shield *verb*
3 to protect or hide something or someone

shift *verb*
1 to move from one place or position to another: *Shift the logs into the yard.*
shift *noun*
2 a movement or change to another place or position 3 a period of working time, especially in a factory: *to work the night shift* 4 the

employees who work during this time: *the morning shift* 5 a loose, sleeveless dress

shifty *adjective*
looking uncomfortable or as if you are hiding something
•***Word Family:*** other forms are **shiftier, shiftiest** □ **shiftily** *adverb*

shilling *noun*
a silver coin used in the United Kingdom before the introduction of decimal currency, and worth 5 pence

shimmer *verb*
to shine with a faintly flickering light

shin *noun*
1 the front of your leg between your knee and your ankle
shin *verb*
2 to climb up something by gripping with your arms and legs: *He shinned up the palm tree.*
•***Word Family:*** other verb forms are **shins, shinned, shinning**

shine *verb*
1 to give out light or brightness 2 to clean or polish something: *to shine your shoes* 3 to be very good at something: *to shine at netball* 4 to aim or point the light at something: *Shine the torch over here.*
shine *noun*
5 light or brightness
•***Word Family:*** other verb forms are **shines, shone** or **shined, shining** □ **shiny** *adjective* (**shinier, shiniest**) bright or glossy

shingle *noun*
the pebbles found on a beach

Shinto *noun*
the earliest religion of Japan, in which people worship nature and the spirits of their ancestors
•***Word Family:*** **Shintoist** *noun*

ship *noun*
1 a large sea-going boat for carrying people and cargo
ship *verb*
2 to send or transport things by ship, rail or truck
•***Word Family:*** other verb forms are **ships, shipped, shipping**

shipment *noun*
a load made up of all the goods shipped at a particular time

shipshape *adjective*
neatly arranged or in order

shiralee (*say* **shi**-ra-lee) *noun*
another name for **swag**

shire *noun*
a county, or local government area

shirk (*say* sherk) *verb*
to avoid or put off something you should be doing: *to shirk your responsibilities*
•***Word Family:*** **shirker** *noun* someone who shirks
•***Word Origins:*** from a German word meaning "a scoundrel or parasite"

shirt (*say* shert) *noun*
a light piece of clothing, usually reaching to your waist, having sleeves, a collar and fastening down the front

shiver (*say* **shiv**-a) *verb*
to shake or tremble with cold or fear
•***Word Family:*** **shivery** *adjective* shaking

shoal (1) *noun*
a sandbank on the bottom of a sea or river, forming an area of shallow water

shoal (2) *noun*
a large group of fish swimming together

shock (1) *noun*
1 a sudden, violent surprise or upset: *to get a shock* 2 a sudden state of weakness caused when you are hurt or unpleasantly surprised: *to be in shock* 3 the painful effect caused by an electric current passing through you: *an electric shock*
shock *verb*
4 to greatly surprise or upset people: *The news shocked the world.*
•***Word Family:*** **shocking** *adjective* very bad, or disgusting

shock (2) *noun*
a thick, bushy mass: *a shock of red hair*

shoddy *adjective*
of very poor quality: *a shoddy piece of work*
•***Word Family:*** other forms are **shoddier, shoddiest** □ **shoddily** *adverb* **shoddiness** *noun*

shoe (*say* shoo) *noun*
1 one of a pair of strong coverings for your feet 2 something that is like a shoe: *horseshoe*

shoot (*rhymes with* boot) *verb*
1 to fire something from a weapon: *to shoot an arrow* 2 to wound or kill someone with a bullet or arrow from a weapon: *The police shot the hijacker.* 3 to move or send something quickly: *He shot inside to answer the phone. / to shoot out a leg to trip someone* 4 to kick or hit a ball towards a goal 5 to photograph or film something: *to shoot a movie* 6 to grow new buds or shoots 7 to grow very quickly: *He's really shot up.*
shoot *noun*
8 a new or young growth on a plant
•***Word Family:*** other verb forms are **shoots, shot, shooting**

A B C D E F G H I J K L M N O P Q R S T U V W X Y Z

shop *noun*
1 a place where goods are sold
shop *verb*
2 to visit shops and buy things
•***Word Family:*** other verb forms are **shops, shopped, shopping** □ **shopkeeper** *noun* **shopper** *noun*

shoplifter *noun*
someone who steals goods from a shop
•***Word Family:* shoplift** *verb* **shoplifting** *noun*

shopping *noun*
1 buying things from shops: *to go shopping*
2 what you buy: *a trolley full of shopping*

shore *noun*
the land along the edge of a sea, lake or river

short *adjective*
1 not long, or tall: *a short distance / a short man*
2 low in amount: *Food is in short supply.* 3 rude or abrupt: *to be short with someone* 4 rich, crumbly and containing a lot of fat: *short pastry*
5 **short for** being a shorter form of: *"TV" is short for "television".*
short *adverb*
6 abruptly or suddenly: *The horse stopped short.*
7 before reaching the right place: *The ball fell short.*
short *noun*
8 a short film shown before the feature film at a cinema 9 **shorts** short trousers usually reaching to somewhere above your knees
•***Word Family:* shortly** *adverb* soon **shorten** *verb*

shortage (*say* **shor**-tij) *noun*
a time when there's not enough of a particular thing: *a petrol shortage*

shortbread (*say* **short**-bred) *noun*
a rich, crumbly biscuit made with flour, sugar and butter

short circuit *noun*
a fault in an electric circuit, in which two points of different voltage become connected, causing the current to flow directly between them rather than through the complete circuit

shortcoming (*say* **short**-kum-ing) *noun*
a flaw or weakness: *Greediness is my worst shortcoming.*

short cut *noun*
a quicker way to get somewhere

shorthand *noun*
a way of writing things down very quickly, by using symbols instead of words and phrases

shorthanded *adjective*
not having enough workers or helpers

short-sighted *adjective*
1 not able to see far 2 not concerned with what might happen in the future: *a short-sighted plan*
•***Word Family:* short-sightedly** *adverb*

short-tempered *adjective*
irritable or easily made angry

short-wave *adjective*
having a radio wavelength of less than 100 metres, used for long-range radio broadcasts

shot *noun*
1 the firing of a gun: *a shot rang out* 2 a hit or stroke: *a shot at goal* 3 a try or attempt: *Have a shot at this puzzle.* 4 an injection: *a tetanus shot*
5 ammunition such as pellets or bullets
6 someone who shoots a gun, especially accurately: *She's a good shot.* 7 a photograph: *I managed to get a shot of the children dancing.* 8 the heavy iron ball thrown in shot-put contests

shotgun *noun*
a sporting gun with one or two barrels, used to fire small shot or pellets

shot-put *noun*
the sport of throwing a heavy metal ball as far as you can
•***Word Family:* shot-putter** *noun*

should (*rhymes with* good) *verb*
1 to have a duty to or ought to: *You should apologize for your rudeness.* 2 to be likely to: *They should get there before dark.*

shoulder (*rhymes with* folder) *noun*
1 the upper part of your body between your arm and your neck
shoulder *verb*
2 to push with your shoulders: *to shoulder your way through the crowd* 3 to put or lift something onto your shoulders: *to shoulder a bag of sand*
4 to carry or bear: *to shoulder a burden of care*

shoulder-blade *noun*
the flat bone at the back of your shoulder

shout *verb*
1 to call or cry out loudly
shout *noun*
2 a loud call or cry

shove (*say* shuv) *verb*
to push rudely or roughly
•***Word Family:* shove** *noun*

shovel (*say* **shuv**-ul) *noun*
1 a spade with a wide scooped blade for moving such things as soil and coal
shovel *verb*
2 to lift or move something with a shovel
•***Word Family:*** other verb forms are **shovels, shovelled, shovelling**

show (*say* sho) *verb*
1 to allow something to be seen: *Show me the*

book you are reading. 2 to lead or direct someone: *Show them out, please!* 3 to be able to be seen: *Once you've washed your shirt these stains won't show.* 4 to instruct someone: *I'll show you how to do it.* 5 **show off** (a) to show or display something you are proud of: *to show off your new roller-blades* (b) to try to impress other people 6 **show up** (a) to reveal something or make it obvious: *to show up your ignorance* (b) to arrive: *He didn't show up until lunchtime.*
show *noun*
7 a public performance or exhibition: *a new TV show / a fashion show* 8 a pretence: *Her tears were all show.*
•***Word Family:*** other verb forms are **shows, showed, shown** or **showed, showing**

showdown *noun*
a big argument or fight which is meant to settle a disagreement once and for all

shower (*rhymes with* flower) *noun*
1 a brief fall of rain or snow 2 something that falls like rain: *a shower of sparks* 3 a device attached to the wall of a bathroom, used to spray water onto someone standing under it 4 a wash taken using this device: *I need a shower!*
shower *verb*
5 to fall in or as if in a shower: *Bullets showered down on the soldiers.* 6 to have a shower
•***Word Family:*** **showery** *adjective* having a lot of showers: *showery weather / a showery day*

show-off *noun*
someone who is trying to impress other people

showroom *noun*
a place used for displaying goods for people to look at and buy

showy *adjective*
meant to attract people's attention and impress them: *a large, showy, gold watch*
•***Word Family:*** other forms are **showier, showiest** □ **showily** *adverb*

shrapnel *noun*
the fragments from an exploding cannon shell
•***Word Origins:*** invented by H. *Shrapnel*, a British army officer who lived from 1761 to 1842

shred *noun*
1 a small, narrow strip cut or torn off: *The dog tore my slippers to shreds.* 2 a piece or particle: *There's not a shred of evidence to support your story.*
shred *verb*
3 to reduce something to shreds
•***Word Family:*** other verb forms are **shreds, shredded, shredding** □ **shredder** *noun* a device for shredding things: *a paper shredder*

shrewd (*say* shrood) *adjective*
clever or showing good judgment, often in a sharp way: *a shrewd politician*
•***Word Family:*** **shrewdly** *adverb* **shrewdness** *noun*

shriek (*say* shreek) *noun*
1 a loud, shrill cry: *the shriek of owls / a shriek of terror*
shriek *verb*
2 to utter a shriek: *to shriek with pain*

shrill *adjective*
high-pitched and piercing: *a shrill whistle*
•***Word Family:*** **shrilly** *adverb* **shrillness** *noun*

shrimp *noun*
a small, tasty, prawn-like shellfish

shrine *noun*
a sacred or holy place: *a Buddhist shrine*

shrink *verb*
1 to become smaller or make something smaller: *Woollen clothes shrink in hot water.* 2 to move quickly back from something: *to shrink back in fear*
•***Word Family:*** other forms are **shrinks, shrank, shrunk, shrinking** □ **shrinkable** *adjective* **shrinkage** *noun*

shrivel (*say* **shriv**-ul) *verb*
to shrink and become wrinkled, especially by drying out
•***Word Family:*** other forms are **shrivels, shrivelled, shrivelling**

shroud (*rhymes with* loud) *noun*
1 a cloth in which a dead person is wrapped for burial
shroud *verb*
2 to wrap a body in a shroud 3 to cover or hide something

shrub *noun*
a woody plant, smaller than a tree and without a main trunk
•***Word Family:*** **shrubbery** *noun* an area of shrubs in a garden or park

shrug *verb*
1 to lift and lower your shoulders to show that you don't know or you don't care
shrug *noun*
2 a movement like this
•***Word Family:*** other verb forms are **shrugs, shrugged, shrugging**

shrunken *adjective*
smaller than it used to be: *a few shrunken old vegetables*

shudder *verb*
1 to shiver violently with cold, fear, disgust or horror

shudder *noun*
2 a shivering movement

shuffle *verb*
1 to walk with dragging or scraping steps 2 to mix a pack of cards, especially before dealing 3 to move things about: *to shuffle papers*

shun *verb*
to deliberately avoid something or someone all the time: *He shuns all publicity.*
•*Word Family:* other forms are **shuns, shunned, shunning**

shunt *verb*
1 to move people or things to a different place 2 to move trains or carriages from one railway line to another

shut *verb*
1 to close or block an opening: *Please shut the window. / Shut your eyes.* 2 to bring something together or fold it up: *Shut the blinds. / to shut an umbrella* 3 **shut down** to close or stop operating for a time: *The factory has shut down for the summer.* 4 **shut off** to stop the flow of something: *to shut off water* 5 **shut up** (a) to confine or imprison someone (b) to stop talking (c) to make somewhere secure by fastening windows and doors: *to shut up your house*
shut *adjective*
6 closed
•*Word Family:* other verb forms are **shuts, shut, shutting**

shutter *noun*
1 a hinged, wooden cover for a window 2 the part of a camera that opens and shuts to let light pass through the lens onto the film

shuttle *noun*
1 the part of a loom used for carrying the threads backwards and forwards in weaving 2 a bus, plane and so on which travels backwards and forwards between two places 3 *the short form of* **space shuttle**

shuttlecock *noun*
a piece of cork or plastic stuck with feathers and used instead of a ball in badminton

shy *adjective*
1 uneasy or lacking confidence when meeting or talking to others: *Don't be shy.* 2 timid or easily startled: *Deer are quite shy creatures.*
shy *verb*
3 to jump suddenly in fright: *The horse shied at the tractor.* 4 to avoid doing something through fear or lack of confidence: *to shy away from making a decision*
•*Word Family:* other adjective forms are **shyer, shyest** or **shier, shiest** □ other verb forms are **shies, shied, shying**

sibling *noun*
a brother or sister

sick *adjective*
1 ill or affected by a disease 2 vomiting or feeling like vomiting 3 for sick people: *sick leave* 4 deliberately disgusting: *sick jokes* 5 **be sick** to vomit 6 **be sick of** to be tired of something or someone: *I'm sick of work.*
•*Word Family:* **sicken** *verb* to make someone sick or to become sick **sickening** *adjective* disgusting or revolting **sickness** *noun*

sickle *noun*
a short-handled tool with a curved blade for cutting or trimming plants

sickly (*say* **sik**-lee) *adjective*
1 not strong or healthy: *a sickly child* 2 pale or weak, and so associated with sickness: *a sickly colour* 3 very sweet or rich: *a sickly cheesecake*
•*Word Family:* other forms are **sicklier, sickliest** □ **sickliness** *noun*

side *noun*
1 a surface of an object or a solid: *the side of a box* 2 an edge of something: *How many sides does a triangle have? / to stand at the side of the road* 3 a surface between the front and back, and between the top and bottom: *Go round the side of the house.* 4 one of the surfaces of something flat: *both sides of a piece of paper* 5 the part of your body around your hip: *to have a pain in your side* 6 the space next to someone: *to stand at someone's side* 7 a particular part of something: *the east side of the city* 8 a group of people with a particular opinion in a discussion or argument: *Whose side are you on?*
side *adjective*
9 at or on one side: *a side door* 10 from or to one side: *a side glance*
side *verb*
11 **side with** to support a particular opinion or group of people in a disagreement

sideboard *noun*
a piece of furniture with drawers and shelves for holding such things as cups and plates, or for serving food

sideline *noun*
1 an extra job or activity done to raise money 2 **sidelines** the lines along the sides of a football pitch, tennis court and so on

sidelong *adjective*
directed to one side: *a sidelong glance*

sideshow *noun*
a small show or exhibition that is part of a fair or circus

sidetrack *verb*
to make someone change the topic away from what was being discussed

sideways *adjective*
1 towards or from one side 2 with one side towards the front

sidle (*say* **sigh**-del) *verb*
to move sideways, hoping not to attract attention to yourself: *to sidle into a back seat*

SIDS *noun*
a condition experienced by some babies under the age of about two years, in which they stop breathing when they are asleep and often die
• ***Word Origins:*** an acronym made from the first letters of the words Sudden Infant Death Syndrome

siege (*say* seej) *noun*
the surrounding of a place by an army wanting to capture it

siesta (*say* see-**es**-ta) *noun*
a rest or short sleep, especially one taken after lunch

sieve (*say* siv) *noun*
1 a round container made of wire mesh or with small holes in its metal bottom, used for straining or sifting
sieve *verb*
2 to put or force something through a sieve

sift *verb*
1 to separate fine particles from coarse ones using a sieve 2 to scatter something with a sieve: *to sift sugar over the plums* 3 to sort through information carefully: *The detective sifted through all the evidence.*
• ***Word Family:*** **sifter** *noun*

sigh *verb*
1 to give out a deep, long, loud breath, when you are tired, sad or relieved
sigh *noun*
2 a deep, long, loud breath

sight *noun*
1 the ability to see: *to lose your sight*
2 something that is seen, or is worth seeing: *What a beautiful sight! / the sights of New York*
3 something that looks odd or unattractive: *He looked a sight in his tattered old coat.*
sight *verb*
4 to get a glimpse or view of something: *to sight a school of whales*
• ***Word Family:*** **sighted** *adjective* not blind **sightless** *adjective* blind **sighting** *noun* an occasion when something is seen

sight-read *verb*
to be able to read, play or sing from written music without previous practice or rehearsal

sightseeing *noun*
looking at interesting places and things, especially as a tourist
• ***Word Family:*** **sightseer** *noun*

sign (*say* sine) *noun*
1 something that shows that something exists or is likely to occur: *He gave no sign of pain. / Dark clouds are a sign of rain.* 2 an action or gesture that expresses an idea, information and so on: *Holding her finger to her lips was a sign to be quiet.* 3 a board or poster that warns or displays information or advertising: *The sign said "Keep Out".* 4 a mark, symbol or figure that stands for a word, mathematical operation and so on: *a dollar sign / a minus sign*
sign *verb*
5 to write your signature on something: *to sign a cheque* 6 to communicate by a sign: *He signed to me to follow him.* 7 to hire someone by writing a contract: *The team has just signed a new player.* 8 **sign up** to join the armed forces

signal (*say* **sig**-nal) *noun*
1 an action, message or object that gives an order, a warning or a message: *a traffic signal / Give the signal to begin.* 2 a wave that carries sound or pictures to a radio or television
signal *verb*
3 to make a signal to someone: *to signal someone to follow you* 4 to make something known by signals or signs: *Her face signalled her distress.*
• ***Word Family:*** other verb forms are **signals, signalled, signalling**

signature (*say* **sig**-na-cher) *noun*
1 your own name as written by yourself 2 a sign written at the beginning of a piece of music used to show its key or time

significant (*say* sig-**nif**-i-kunt) *adjective*
1 important or notable: *a significant victory*
2 full of meaning: *a significant glance*
• ***Word Family:*** **significance** *noun* **significantly** *adverb*

signify (*say* **sig**-ni-fie) *verb*
1 to be a sign of a particular thing: *Raised eyebrows signify surprise.* 2 to make something known by signs: *He signified his approval by nodding his head.*
• ***Word Family:*** other forms are **signifies, signified, signifying** □ **signification** *noun*

sign language *noun*
a way of communicating with your hands, used mainly by deaf people

Sikh (*say* seek) *noun*
a member of an Indian religion founded in the 16th century that developed from Hinduism and is based on a belief in a single god
• ***Word Family:*** **Sikhism** *noun*

silence (*say* **sigh**-lence) *noun*
1 the absence of sound
silence *verb*
2 to make someone or something silent

silent (*say* **sigh**-lent) *adjective*
1 making no sound or noise: *Please be silent!*
2 having no sound: *a silent night / a silent movie*
3 not pronounced: *The word "knock" begins with the silent letter "k".*
• ***Word Family:*** **silently** *adverb*

silhouette (*say* sil-oo-**et**) *noun*
1 the dark outline of something when it is seen against a light background
silhouette *verb*
2 to show up something as a silhouette: *Branches were silhouetted against the moonlit sky.*

silicon (*say* **sil**-i-kon) *noun*
an element found in minerals and rocks, used to make such things as glass and computer chips

silk *noun*
a soft, shiny cloth made from the fine thread of a silkworm's cocoon
• ***Word Family:*** **silken** *adjective* made of silk **silky** *adjective* as smooth and glossy as silk **silkiness** *noun*

silk screen *noun*
a way of printing in which ink is pressed through a stencil stuck on a screen of fine cloth

silkworm *noun*
a caterpillar that spins a cocoon of silk threads

sill *noun*
a long, flat piece of wood or stone across the bottom of a door or window

silly *adjective*
lacking good sense
• ***Word Family:*** other forms are **sillier, silliest**

silt *noun*
very fine sand, carried by running water and left on the bottom of a river or lake

silver *noun*
1 a useful white metal, used for making such things as jewellery and ornaments 2 a shiny white or whitish-grey colour 3 objects made from silver, such as goblets, knives and forks: *to give the silver a good polish*
silver *adjective*
4 made of or containing silver: *a silver ring / a silver mine* 5 shiny whitish-grey
• ***Word Family:*** **silvery** *adjective*

silver wedding *noun*
the special anniversary that you celebrate 25 years after your wedding

similar (*say* **sim**-i-la) *adjective*
alike or of the same kind: *Our noses are similar. / You have similar shoes to mine.*
• ***Word Family:*** **similarity** *noun*

simile (*say* **sim**-a-lee) *noun*
a figure of speech in which two unlike things are compared using "like" or "as", as in *He chattered like a magpie.*

simmer *verb*
1 to cook something gently in a liquid just below boiling point 2 to be filled with strong feelings you manage to control: *to simmer with fury* 3 **simmer down** to become calm or calmer

simper *verb*
to smile in a silly or self-conscious way

simple *adjective*
1 easy to do, use or understand: *a simple test / a simple recipe / simple instructions* 2 plain or not elaborate: *a simple style of writing / a simple black dress* 3 uncomplicated: *a simple way of life* 4 not intelligent: *Do you think I'm simple?*
• ***Word Family:*** **simplify** *verb* (**simplifies, simplified, simplifying**) to make something more simple **simplification** *noun* **simplicity** *noun*

simply *adverb*
1 in a simple way: *They decorated the house simply but imaginatively.* 2 merely or only: *It's simply a question of money.* 3 absolutely: *She's simply great as a teacher.*

simulate (*say* **sim**-yoo-late) *verb*
1 to imitate something: *The computer game simulated a real battle.* 2 to pretend to have a particular emotion: *to simulate enthusiasm*
• ***Word Family:*** **simulator** *noun* a machine that simulates movement or flight, used to train astronauts and similar people **simulation** *noun* a computer model of an event or situation

simultaneous (*say* sim-ul-**tay**-nee-us) *adjective*
happening, existing or done at the same time
• ***Word Family:*** **simultaneously** *adverb*

sin *noun*
1 the breaking of one of God's laws 2 a wicked or immoral act
sin *verb*
3 to commit a sin
• ***Word Family:*** other verb forms are **sin, sinned, sinning** □ see also **sinful, sinner**

since *adverb*
1 between a particular past time and the present: *He left school and I haven't heard from him since.*
since *preposition*
2 from a particular time: *We've been working since daybreak.*

since *conjunction*
3 from the time when: *He hasn't written since he left home last February.* 4 because: *Since it is late, I'll go home now.*

sincere (*say* sin-**seer**) *adjective*
honest, or expressing your true feelings: *sincere congratulations / a sincere smile*
•***Word Family:*** **sincerely** *adverb* **sincerity** *noun*

sinew (*say* **sin**-yoo) *noun*
the tough tissue in your body that connects a muscle to a bone

sinful *adjective*
wicked or immoral: *sinful actions*
•***Word Family:*** **sinfully** *adjective*

sing *verb*
1 to make musical sounds with your voice 2 to make a humming or whistling sound: *Bullets were singing past me.*
•***Word Family:*** other verb forms are **sings, sang, sung, singing** □ **singer** *noun*

singe (*say* sinj) *verb*
to burn slightly
•***Word Family:*** other forms are **singes, singed, singeing**

single *adjective*
1 separate or one only: *Every single seat was empty. / Not a single person came.* 2 unmarried: *a single man* 3 for one person: *a single bed* 4 for a journey to somewhere but not back again: *a single ticket*
single *verb*
5 **single out** to choose or pick a particular thing or person out from others
single *noun*
6 a single thing, such as a one-way rail ticket
•***Word Family:*** **singly** *adverb* one by one

single-handed *adjective* or *adverb*
working or done alone or without help: *to paint the house single-handed*
•***Word Family:*** **single-handedly** *adverb*

singular (*say* **sing**-yoo-la) *adjective*
1 extraordinary, strange or remarkable: *to have a singular way of dressing* 2 indicating one person, action or thing, as the words "he", "buys" and "book" do in the sentence *He buys the book.*
•***Word Family:*** **singularly** *adverb* **singularity** *noun*

sinister (*say* **sin**-is-ta) *adjective*
seeming evil or threatening: *a sinister figure*
•***Word Origins:*** from a Latin word meaning "left-hand side", as the left side was thought to be unlucky

sink *verb*
1 to go down or cause something to go down, especially in water: *The stone sank below the surface. / Enemy aircraft sank the destroyer.* 2 to fall slowly: *She sank weakly to her knees.* 3 to drill or dig something: *to sink a well* 4 **sink in** to be fully understood: *The news hasn't sunk in yet.*
sink *noun*
5 a kitchen basin with a drain, used for washing dishes
•***Word Family:*** other verb forms are **sinks, sank, sunk, sinking**

sinker *noun*
a weight attached to a fishing line or net to make it sink in the water

sinuous (*say* **sin**-yew-us) *adjective*
1 having lots of smooth curves and bends: *a sinuous mountain road* 2 moving in a winding way, like a snake

sinus (*say* **sigh**-nus) *noun*
one of the spaces in the bones of your skull just behind your nose
•***Word Family:*** the plural is **sinuses**

sip *verb*
1 to drink a little at a time
sip *noun*
2 a small mouthful
•***Word Family:*** other verb forms are **sips, sipped, sipping**

siphon (*say* **sigh**-fon) *noun*
1 a tube through which a liquid may flow up out of a container and down to a lower level
siphon *verb*
2 to pass liquid down through a siphon

sir *noun*
a respectful form of address used when speaking to a man

sire (*rhymes with* fire) *noun*
1 a male parent, especially of horses and dogs
sire *verb*
2 to produce offspring

siren (*say* **sigh**-ren) *noun*
a device that produces a loud, wailing sound, such as the one on ambulances and police cars

sister *noun*
1 a girl or woman with the same parents as you 2 a nun belonging to a religious order 3 a fully trained nurse
•***Word Family:*** **sisterhood** *noun*

sister-in-law *noun*
1 the sister of your husband or wife 2 the wife of your brother 3 the wife of your husband's or wife's brother
•***Word Family:*** the plural is **sisters-in-law**

sit *verb*
1 to rest with your body supported on your bottom 2 to make someone sit in a particular

place: *I sat her in the chair.* 3 to meet or hold a meeting: *Parliament sat every day last week.* 4 to pose: *to sit for a portrait* 5 to perch: *The bird sat on a branch.* 6 to enter an exam or test
•***Word Family:*** other forms are **sits, sat, sitting**

sitar (*say* sit-**ar**) *noun*
a long, guitar-like, Indian musical instrument with three plucked strings

site *noun*
1 a particular place or piece of land used or set aside for a special purpose: *a building site / the site of a battle*
site *verb*
2 to locate or place something somewhere

sit-in *noun*
a protest in which lots of people sit down and refuse to move
•***Word Family:*** the plural is **sit-ins**

situate (*say* **sit**-yoo-ate) *verb*
to place something in a particular position

situation (*say* sit-yoo-**ay**-shon) *noun*
1 a location: *The situation of the new house is close to the town.* 2 a state of affairs, or the way things are: *The situation could easily lead to war.*

six *noun*
1 the number 6 2 a score of six runs in cricket, obtained by a batsman hitting the ball over the boundary of the field without it bouncing
•***Word Family:*** **six** *adjective* **sixth** *noun* **sixth** *adjective*

sixteen *noun*
the number 16
•***Word Family:*** **sixteen** *adjective* **sixteenth** *adjective* **sixteenth** *noun*

sixty *noun*
the number 60
•***Word Family:*** the plural is **sixties** □ **sixty** *adjective* **sixtieth** *adjective* **sixtieth** *noun*

size *noun*
1 how big or small something is: *hailstones the size of golf-balls* 2 a way of measuring how big clothes or shoes are: *What size shoes do you take?*
size *verb*
3 **size up** to look at something carefully before deciding what to do next

sizeable (*say* **size**-a-bul) *adjective*
quite large: *a sizeable fortune*

sizzle *verb*
to make a hissing sound, as in frying or burning: *Bacon sizzling in the pan.*

skate *noun*
1 a boot with a blade attached to the bottom, worn for moving over ice 2 *a short form of* **roller-skate**
skate *verb*
3 to move about on ice-skates or roller-skates

skateboard *noun*
a flat board with roller-skate wheels attached to the bottom, usually ridden standing up

skeleton (*say* **skel**-a-ton) *noun*
1 all the bones of your body joined together
2 a supporting framework
skeleton *adjective*
3 made up of the smallest number needed to run something: *a skeleton staff*

sketch *noun*
1 a quickly drawn picture 2 a brief outline or description of something 3 a short, comic play
sketch *verb*
4 to make a sketch
•***Word Family:*** the plural is **sketches** □ **sketchy** *adjective* **(sketchier, sketchiest)**

skewer *noun*
a long pin of wood or metal, especially one put through meat during cooking to hold it in shape

ski (*say* skee) *noun*
1 a long, narrow strip of wood, metal or plastic turned up at the front and usually attached to a boot, used for travelling over snow or water
ski *verb*
2 to travel on or use skis
•***Word Family:*** other verb forms are **skis, skied** or **ski'd, skiing** □ **skier** *noun*

skid *verb*
1 to slide or slip sideways because the wheels of your car or bike are no longer gripping the road surface
skid *noun*
2 skidding over a surface: *The car went into a skid.*
•***Word Family:*** other verb forms are **skids, skidded, skidding**

skill *noun*
1 the ability to do something well: *His skill as a footballer is well-known.* 2 a particular type of work that needs special training: *to learn a new skill*
•***Word Family:*** **skilled** *adjective* trained or experienced **skilful** *adjective* **skilfully** *adverb*

skim *verb*
1 to move or glide lightly over or along a surface: *Birds skimmed over the pond.* 2 to read something quickly without taking in the full meaning: *to skim a magazine* 3 to remove floating matter from the surface of something with a spoon: *to skim a stew*
•***Word Family:*** other forms are **skims, skimmed, skimming**

skimmed milk *noun*
milk from which the cream has been removed

skimpy *adjective*
1 not big enough: *a skimpy swimming costume*
2 mean: *a skimpy helping*
• ***Word Family:*** other forms are **skimpier, skimpiest** □ **skimp** *verb* **skimpily** *adverb* **skimpiness** *noun*

skin *noun*
1 the outer covering of an animal body, fruit and so on 2 a layer or coating on a surface: *A skin formed on the boiled milk.*
skin *verb*
3 to remove skin from something: *to skin a rabbit*
4 to cut or injure the skin or surface of a part of your body: *to fall and skin your knee*
• ***Word Family:*** other verb forms are **skins, skinned, skinning**

skin-diver *noun*
someone who swims under water with light breathing equipment but not a wet-suit
• ***Word Family:*** **skin-dive** *verb*

skinny *adjective*
very thin
• ***Word Family:*** other forms are **skinnier, skinniest**

skip (1) *verb*
1 to jump lightly from one foot to another, or over a twirling rope 2 to leave parts of something out: *to skip the scary parts in the book*
skip *noun*
3 a skipping movement
• ***Word Family:*** other verb forms are **skips, skipped, skipping**

skip (2) *noun*
a large container attached to a crane, or designed to be picked up by a special truck

skipper *noun*
the captain of a ship or team

skirmish (*say* **sker**-mish) *noun*
a small, unexpected fight or battle

skirt *noun*
1 a piece of clothing that women and girls wrap around the lower half of their bodies
skirt *verb*
2 to pass or go around the edge of a particular place: *We skirted the city to avoid the traffic.*

skirting board *noun*
a strip of wood around the base of a wall where it joins the floor

skit *noun*
a short play or piece of writing that makes fun of something

skite *verb*
1 to boast or brag
skite *noun*
2 someone who skites

skulk *verb*
to stay near a place or in the background hoping that nobody will notice you

skull *noun*
the framework of bones which forms the head of a person or animal and which holds the brain

skunk *noun*
a small, black, North American animal with a white stripe down its back, that lets out a strong-smelling liquid when in danger

sky *noun*
the upper air, seen as blue where there are no clouds
• ***Word Family:*** the plural is **skies**

sky-diving *noun*
the sport of jumping from an aircraft, and opening the parachute late in your fall
• ***Word Family:*** **sky-dive** *verb* **sky-diver** *noun*

skylight *noun*
a window or glass-lined opening in a roof, that lets in light

skyscraper *noun*
a very tall building with lots of floors, usually used as an office block

slab *noun*
a wide, flat piece: *a slab of stone*

slack *adjective*
1 loose: *a slack rope* 2 careless or lazy: *slack work*
slack *noun*
3 the loose or slack part of something: *to take up the slack of a rope*
slack *verb*
4 to be lazy when you should be working: *No slacking!*
• ***Word Family:*** **slackly** *adverb* **slackness** *noun*

slacken *verb*
1 to loosen something tight: *Slacken the rope or it will break.* 2 to go at slower pace, or with less energy: *She slackened her speed so that he could catch up. / He slackened off when he got tired.*

slacks *plural noun*
long trousers

slag *noun*
waste matter from mining, or from when metal has been melted down
• ***Word Family:*** **slagheap** *noun* a mound of waste matter from mining or a similar process

slalom (*say* **slah**-lum) *noun*
a downhill skiing race in and out of a line of posts
• ***Word Origins:*** from a Norwegian word meaning "a sloping track"

A B C D E F G H I J K L M N O P Q R S T U V W X Y Z

slam *verb*
1 to shut something violently and noisily: *to slam a door* 2 to put something down somewhere violently and noisily: *to slam money onto the table*
•***Word Family:*** other forms are **slams, slammed, slamming**

slander *noun*
1 a false spoken statement that damages someone's good name
slander *verb*
2 to spread slander about someone
•***Word Family:*** **slanderer** *noun* **slanderous** *adjective*

slang *noun*
everyday or colloquial language consisting of words used in an informal rather than a formal way
•***Word Family:*** **slangy** *adjective*

slant *verb*
1 to slope or lean at an angle: *My writing slants forwards.*
slant *noun*
2 a leaning or sloping position: *the slant of a roof* 3 your point of view: *The news gave a new slant to the situation.*

slap *verb*
1 to strike or smack someone, especially with your open hand: *He slapped my face.* 2 to put something down somewhere loudly and forcefully: *He slapped his wallet onto the counter.*
slap *noun*
3 a quick blow or smack
•***Word Family:*** other verb forms are **slaps, slapped, slapping**

slapstick *noun*
loud or rowdy comedy, such as between circus clowns

slash *verb*
1 to cut something with long, sweeping strokes: *to slash the grass with a scythe* 2 to reduce an amount greatly: *to slash prices*
slash *noun*
3 a sweeping stroke, cut or gash

slat *noun*
a long, thin, narrow piece of wood or metal: *the slats of a blind*

slate *noun*
a dark, bluish-grey, fine-grained rock, that splits easily into layers and is used to make floors and roofs

slaughter (*say* **slaw**-ta) *noun*
1 the killing of animals for food 2 a brutal killing: *the slaughter of civilians in a war*
slaughter *verb*
3 to kill animals for food 4 to kill people or animals brutally in large numbers 5 to defeat someone completely

slave *noun*
1 someone who is the property or prisoner of another person and who works without pay or rights
slave *verb*
2 to work very hard: *I slaved all night on my essay.*
•***Word Family:*** **slavery** *noun* **slavish** *adjective*

slay *verb*
to kill a person or animal: *The knight slayed the dragon.*
•***Word Family:*** other forms are **slays, slew, slain, slaying**

sledge *noun*
a vehicle mounted on runners and used for travelling over snow and ice

sledge-hammer *noun*
a large, heavy hammer

sleek *adjective*
soft, smooth and glossy: *The cat has a sleek coat.*

sleep *noun*
1 the condition in which your body rests, your mind is unconscious and your eyes are closed: *to get some sleep* 2 the time during which you do this: *I need a sleep.*
sleep *verb*
3 to rest by having a sleep 4 to have beds for a particular number of people: *This hotel sleeps 60 people.*
•***Word Family:*** other verb forms are **sleeps, slept, sleeping** □ **sleepy** *adjective* (**sleepier, sleepiest**) **sleepiness** *noun* **sleepless** *adjective*

sleeper *noun*
1 a railway carriage where you can sleep 2 a beam or slab forming part of the foundation for a railway track 3 a ring worn in the ear after it has been pierced, to stop the hole closing
4 someone who is asleep

sleet *noun*
a mixture of falling rain and snow

sleeve *noun*
1 the part of a piece of clothing that covers all or part of your arm 2 a record cover

sleigh *noun*
a sledge used to carry people and pulled by animals

slender *adjective*
attractively thin
•***Word Family:*** **slenderness** *noun*

sleuth (*say* slooth) *noun*
a detective or investigator
•***Word Origins:*** from an Icelandic word meaning "track"

slice *noun*
1 a thin, flat and wide piece cut off from something: *a slice of bread* 2 a stroke that causes the ball to spin away to the right of a right-handed player
slice *verb*
3 to cut something up into slices 4 to hit a slice: *He sliced his second shot into the bushes.*

slick (1) *adjective*
1 smooth and clever rather than pleasant or friendly: *a slick shop assistant* 2 smart or quick: *a slick answer*
slick *noun*
3 an area of oil floating on water

slick (2) *verb*
to make something sleek or smooth: *to slick back your hair with gel*

slide *verb*
1 to move smoothly over a polished or slippery surface: *The car slid on the icy road.*
slide *noun*
2 a sliding movement 3 a children's play structure with a smooth, sloping surface for sliding down 4 a small piece of film or a see-through photograph, shown on a screen with a projector 5 a small, oblong piece of glass on which objects are placed for study under a microscope 6 a device for keeping your hair in place
•*Word Family:* other verb forms are **slides, slid, sliding**

slight *adjective*
1 small: *a slight smile / a slight improvement*
2 slender or frail-looking: *a child with a slight build*
slight *verb*
3 to insult someone by ignoring them: *to slight someone by not inviting them to your party*
slight *noun*
4 a snub or insult
•*Word Family:* **slightly** *adverb* to a small degree: *slightly tired*

slim *adjective*
1 attractively thin: *She's tall and slim with dark hair.* 2 small: *a slim chance*
slim *verb*
3 to lose weight by dieting
•*Word Family:* other adjective forms are **slimmer, slimmest** □ other verb forms are **slims, slimmed, slimming**

slime *noun*
unpleasant, wet, slippery stuff
•*Word Family:* **slimy** *adjective* (**slimier, slimiest**) **sliminess** *noun*

sling *noun*
1 a cloth bandage looped over your shoulder to support a broken arm 2 a strap with a string attached to each end from which you can hurl a stone by whirling it around your head and releasing one of the strings
sling *verb*
3 to hang something somewhere, or carry it loosely: *He slung the bag over his shoulder.*
•*Word Family:* other verb forms are **slings, slung, slinging**

slingshot *noun*
another name for a **catapult**

slink *verb*
to creep slowly and quietly so that you won't be noticed: *The fox slunk into its den.*
•*Word Family:* other forms are **slinks, slunk, slinking**

slip (1) *verb*
1 to lose your balance or fall over: *to slip on the slimy seaweed* 2 to fall or escape from a particular place, usually by not being held firmly: *The glass slipped from my hand.* 3 to move smoothly and gently: *The boat slipped through the water.*
slip *noun*
4 a mistake, especially a careless one 5 a petticoat 6 **give someone the slip** to get away from someone who is following you
•*Word Family:* other verb forms are **slips, slipped, slipping**

slip (2) *noun*
a small piece of paper printed for a particular purpose: *a bank deposit slip*

slipper *noun*
a loose, light shoe you wear in the house

slippery (*say* **slip**-a-ree) *adjective*
so smooth or wet that you can't hold it or walk on it: *a slippery fish / a slippery floor*

slit *noun*
1 a long, narrow cut or opening
slit *verb*
2 to make a long cut or opening in something: *She slit open the letter with a paperknife.*
•*Word Family:* other verb forms are **slits, slit, slitting**

slither *verb*
1 to slide or slip unsteadily 2 to move as a snake does

sliver (*say* **sliv**-a) *noun*
a small, thin piece broken or split off from a larger piece: *a sliver of glass*

slob *noun*
a clumsy, lazy and untidy person

slobber *verb*
to let saliva run from the mouth the way a dog does

slog *verb*
1 to hit something hard: *to slog a ball* 2 to work hard and steadily 3 to trudge or walk heavily
slog *noun*
4 a strong, heavy blow 5 hard work 6 a long, hard walk
•***Word Family:*** other verb forms are **slogs, slogged, slogging**

slogan (*say* slo-gun) *noun*
a clever, easily remembered phrase used to advertise something

slop *verb*
to spill or splash liquid somewhere: *Water slopped out of the bucket.*
•***Word Family:*** other forms are **slops, slopped, slopping**

slope *verb*
1 to lean or be at an angle: *The roof slopes downwards.*
slope *noun*
2 a sloping surface, or the amount something slopes 3 **slopes** a hilly area: *Snow blanketed the mountain slopes.*
•***Word Family:*** **sloping** *adjective*

sloppy *adjective*
1 wet, muddy or slushy 2 careless or untidy: *sloppy homework* 3 foolishly sentimental: *a sloppy love song*
•***Word Family:*** other forms are **sloppier, sloppiest**

slosh *verb*
to pour or splash liquid messily: *to slosh water over your dirty feet*

slot *noun*
1 a narrow groove or opening into which something is put or fitted: *Put a coin in the slot.* 2 a particular position in a schedule or timetable: *The new gardening programme will fill the midday slot.*

sloth (*say* slohth) *noun*
1 extreme laziness 2 a slow-moving, South American mammal that hangs upside down from tree branches
•***Word Family:*** **slothful** *adjective* **slothfully** *adverb*

slouch (*rhymes with* ouch) *verb*
to sit, stand or move with your head and shoulders drooping forward

slovenly (*say* **sluv**-en-lee) *adjective*
dirty, careless or untidy
•***Word Family:*** **slovenliness** *noun*

slow (*say* sloh) *adjective*
1 taking a long time: *a slow train / a slow reader* 2 behind the correct time: *The clock is slow.*
slow *verb*
3 to make something slow or slower or to become slow or slower
•***Word Family:*** **slowly** *adverb* **slowness** *noun*

sludge (*say* sluj) *noun*
thick, mud-like stuff

slug *noun*
1 a slimy, snail-like animal without a shell 2 a small bullet

sluggish *adjective*
moving or acting slowly and without energy
•***Word Family:*** **sluggishly** *adverb*

sluice (*say* sloose) *noun*
1 a water channel with a gate to control how much water flows through
sluice *verb*
2 to wash something with running water or by pouring water over it

slum *noun*
a dirty, poor and overcrowded part of a city

slumber *verb*
1 to sleep deeply
slumber *noun*
2 deep sleep

slump *verb*
1 to fall or drop heavily: *to slump into a chair / Prices slumped.* 2 to lean on or across something, for example because you have fallen asleep: *to slump over a book*
slump *noun*
3 a heavy or sudden fall

slur *verb*
1 to pronounce words unclearly by running them together
slur *noun*
2 slurring: *to speak with a slur* 3 a remark or suggestion which damages someone's good name
•***Word Family:*** other verb forms are **slurs, slurred, slurring**

slurp *verb*
to eat or drink noisily

slush *noun*
soft, melting snow

slushy *adjective*
1 consisting of slush: *slushy snow* 2 soppy and sentimental: *a slushy film*

sly *adjective*
1 secretive and cunning: *a sly pickpocket*
2 playful or mischievous: *sly humour*

smack (1) *verb*
1 to hit someone or something sharply with the palm of your hand

smack *noun*
2 a sharp, quick stroke or blow

smack (2) *verb*
1 to have a trace or suggestion of a particular quality: *Your behaviour smacks of rudeness.*
smack *noun*
2 a slight flavour or trace

small *adjective*
1 not big or large: *a small house / a small problem* 2 mean and petty: *a small mind* 3 ashamed or humble: *to feel small*
small *adverb*
4 into small pieces: *to cut an apple up small*

small-minded *adjective*
selfish or petty

smallpox *noun*
a serious, infectious disease causing blisters that often form scars

smart *adjective*
1 clever or bright 2 brisk, vigorous or lively: *to walk at a smart pace* 3 neat or fashionable: *a smart outfit*
smart *verb*
4 to sting or hurt: *This cut smarts. / to smart from a cruel joke*
•***Word Family:*** **smarten** *verb* **smartly** *adverb*

smash *verb*
1 to break violently into pieces: *to smash a windscreen* 2 to crash or hit hard: *The car smashed into the wall. / to smash a ball*
smash *noun*
3 a loud crash 4 a very successful record, film or play 5 a very hard, downward stroke in tennis
•***Word Family:*** **smashing** *adjective* very good

smear *verb*
1 to rub or spread something: *to smear suncream on your body* 2 to unfairly damage someone's good name or reputation
smear *noun*
3 a greasy mark or smudge 4 a remark or suggestion that damages your good name

smell *verb*
1 to sense with your nose 2 to give off an odour: *The roses smell lovely. / That cheese smells!* 3 to feel that something is about to happen: *I smell trouble.*
smell *noun*
4 the ability to smell things 5 an odour or scent: *perfume with a sickly smell*
•***Word Family:*** other verb forms are **smells, smelt** or **smelled, smelling** □ **smelly** *adjective* **(smellier, smelliest)**

smelt *verb*
to extract a metal from its ore by heating or melting

smile *verb*
1 to show pleasure, amusement or kindness by curving the corners of your mouth upwards
smile *noun*
2 a pleased or amused expression on your face

smirk *verb*
1 to smile in a sneering, smug or annoying way
smirk *noun*
2 an annoying smile

smith *noun*
someone who works with metals, especially a blacksmith
•***Word Family:*** **smithy** *noun* **(smithies)** a blacksmith's forge

smock *noun*
a loose dress or apron, sometimes worn to protect your clothes

smog *noun*
a dirty mixture of fog and smoke
•***Word Family:*** **smoggy** *adjective* **(smoggier, smoggiest)**
•***Word Origins:*** a blended word made from *smoke* and *fog*

smoke *noun*
1 the cloud of fine, solid particles and gas, that is given off when things burn 2 time spent smoking a cigarette: *to have a smoke*
smoke *verb*
3 to give off smoke the way a chimney does 4 to breathe in and blow out the smoke of a cigarette 5 to preserve and flavour food by drying it in smoke: *to smoke herrings*
•***Word Family:*** **smoky** *adjective* **(smokier, smokiest)**

smooth (*rhymes with* soothe) *adjective*
1 without bumps, lumps or jolts: *smooth skin / smooth seas / a smooth paste / a smooth ride* 2 too pleasant to be sincere: *smooth manners*
smooth *verb*
3 to make something smooth or to become smooth: *He smoothed out the crumpled paper.*
•***Word Family:*** **smoothly** *adverb* **smoothness** *noun*

smother (*rhymes with* mother) *verb*
1 to choke someone from lack of air 2 to put a fire out by covering it in sand or foam 3 to cover something thickly: *to smother potatoes in butter*

smoulder (*say* **smole**-da) *verb*
to burn slowly with smoke but without a flame: *The embers smouldered in the grate.*

smudge (*say* smuj) *noun*
1 a dirty mark or smear
smudge *verb*
2 to make a smudge or smudges on something

smug *adjective*
too satisfied or pleased with yourself

smuggle *verb*
to bring or carry things somewhere secretly and illegally: *to smuggle drugs / to smuggle a gun into a jail*
•*Word Family:* **smuggler** *noun*

smut *noun*
1 a piece of soot or dirt that makes a black, dirty mark 2 offensive or indecent language or writing
•*Word Family:* **smutty** *adjective* (**smuttier, smuttiest**)

snack *noun*
a small, quick meal

snag *noun*
1 an unexpected or hidden difficulty: *a snag in our plans* 2 a small hole or ladder in clothes such as stockings, caused by catching them on a sharp object
snag *verb*
3 to catch and tear your clothes on something sharp
•*Word Family:* other verb forms are **snags, snagged, snagging**

snail *noun*
a slimy, air-breathing animal with a soft body and a coiled shell

snake *noun*
1 a reptile without legs, that slithers along the ground
snake *verb*
2 to move, wind or curve like a snake: *The river snaked through the valley.*
•*Word Family:* **snaky** *adjective* (**snakier, snakiest**) spiteful

snap *verb*
1 to make or cause something to make a sudden, sharp sound: *to snap your fingers* 2 to break suddenly with a sharp sound: *to snap a twig / the sound of a twig snapping* 3 to make a sudden, quick bite: *The dog snapped at my ankles.* 4 to speak sharply: *to snap angrily in reply* 5 to take a photograph of someone or something
snap *noun*
6 a sudden, sharp sound 7 a simple game in which each player throws cards onto a pile aiming to win by being the first to notice two matching cards
snap *adjective*
8 sudden: *a snap decision*
•*Word Family:* other verb forms are **snaps, snapped, snapping** □ **snappy** *adjective* (**snappier, snappiest**) **snappily** *adverb*

snare (*rhymes with* air) *noun*
1 a trap for catching animals
snare *verb*
2 to catch an animal in a snare

snarl *verb*
1 to make a harsh, angry growl: *The dog snarled at the strangers.*
snarl *noun*
2 a fierce growl

snatch *verb*
1 to seize something suddenly: *to snatch a wallet from someone*
snatch *noun*
2 a small fragment: *to hear a snatch of a tune*

sneak *verb*
1 to move in a sly way: *He sneaked down the hall.*
sneak *noun*
2 an unpleasant telltale whom you can't trust
•*Word Family:* **sneaky** *adjective* (**sneakier, sneakiest**) mean or tricky **sneakily** *adverb*

sneer *verb*
to show contempt by curling your lip or saying scornful things

sneeze *verb*
1 to let air out through your nose and mouth in a sudden, explosive action
sneeze *noun*
2 the act or sound of sneezing

snide *adjective*
sly and nasty: *snide remarks*
•*Word Family:* **snidely** *adverb*

sniff *verb*
1 to draw air into your nose in short, sharp breaths: *to sniff loudly after you stop crying*
sniff *noun*
2 the act or sound of sniffing

sniffle *verb*
1 to sniff repeatedly as you do when you have a cold
sniffle *noun*
2 a slight cold

snigger *noun*
1 a rude or mocking laugh that you are trying to hide
snigger *verb*
2 to give a laugh like this

snip *verb*
1 to cut something with a small, quick stroke or strokes: *to snip someone's fringe*
snip *noun*
2 the act or sound of snipping
•*Word Family:* other verb forms are **snips, snipped, snipping**

sniper *noun*
someone who shoots at people from a hiding place
•*Word Family:* **snipe** *verb*

snivel (*say* **sniv**-ul) *verb*
to cry and sniff in an annoying way
•***Word Family:*** other verb forms are **snivels, snivelled, snivelling**

snob *noun*
someone who admires upper-class or rich people and looks down on everyone else
•***Word Family:*** **snobbery** *noun* **snobbish** *adjective*

snooker *noun*
a game similar to billiards, using 22 balls of different colours

snoop *verb*
to go around prying into things that don't concern you

snooze *verb*
1 to doze or rest: *to snooze in the sun*
snooze *noun*
2 a short doze or rest

snore *verb*
1 to breathe while you're asleep with a harsh, rough sound
snore *noun*
2 the noise of a snore

snorkel *noun*
1 a breathing tube you hold in your mouth, so that it sticks up into the air and lets you breathe when you're swimming with your face in the water
snorkel *verb*
2 to swim under water with a snorkel
•***Word Family:*** other verb forms are **snorkels, snorkelled, snorkelling**

snort *verb*
1 to force breath through your nostrils with a loud, harsh sound
snort *noun*
2 the act of snorting: *She gave an angry snort and stormed out.*

snout (*say* snowt) *noun*
the nose of an animal, often including its jaws

snow (*say* snoh) *noun*
1 ice crystals formed in clouds that fall to the ground as flakes
snow *verb*
2 to fall as snow: *It's been snowing.*
•***Word Family:*** **snowy** *adjective* (**snowier, snowiest**) (a) covered in snow (b) white as snow

snowball *noun*
1 a ball of snow pressed together for throwing
snowball *verb*
2 to grow rapidly: *The band's popularity continues to snowball.*

snowman *noun*
the shape of a man, made in snow
•***Word Family:*** the plural is **snowmen**

snowshoe *noun*
one of a pair of devices shaped like tennis racquets, that you wear on your feet so that you don't sink in deep snow

snub *verb*
1 to treat someone with contempt, especially by ignoring them
snub *noun*
2 an insulting remark or an unfriendly act
snub *adjective*
3 short and turned up at the point: *a snub nose*
•***Word Family:*** other verb forms are **snubs, snubbed, snubbing**

snuff *verb*
to put out a flame: *to snuff a candle*

snug *adjective*
cosy: *a snug corner beside the fire*
•***Word Family:*** other forms are **snugger, snuggest**

snuggle *verb*
to cuddle up closely, for warmth, comfort or affection

so *adverb*
1 just as said, directed, suggested or implied: *Hold your arm out so.* 2 in the same way: *I think so too.* 3 to that degree or extent: *I didn't realise the plains stretched so far.* 4 very or extremely: *You are so helpful.* 5 **just so** in perfect order

soak *verb*
1 to lie or leave something in a liquid until clean: *to soak in a bubble bath / to soak dirty football socks* 2 to make people or things very wet: *We got soaked waiting for the taxi.* 3 **soak up** to take in or absorb liquid: *Blotting paper soaks up ink.*
soak *noun*
4 soaking: *Give the sheets a good soak.*

soap *noun*
1 a substance used for washing or cleaning
soap *verb*
3 to rub or cover something with soap
•***Word Family:*** **soapy** *adjective* (**soapier, soapiest**)

soap opera *noun*
a radio or television serial which deals with a group of people's everyday lives and problems
•***Word Origins:*** the name came about because this type of story was once sponsored by advertisers of soap and detergents

soar *verb*
1 to rise or fly upwards, like a bird: *The kite soared up on a gust of wind.* 2 to glide at a great

A B C D E F G H I J K L M N O P Q R S T U V W X Y Z

height: *an eagle soaring high above* 3 to rise steeply: *The mountain soars into the clouds. / The price of coffee has soared.*

sob *verb*
1 to cry with gulping catches of breath
sob *noun*
2 a sobbing sound
•***Word Family:*** other verb forms are **sobs, sobbed, sobbing**

sober (*say* **so**-ba) *adjective*
1 not drunk 2 quiet and serious: *a sober mood*
sober *verb*
3 to make someone sober or to become sober
•***Word Family:* sobriety** *noun*

soccer (*say* **sok**-a) *noun*
football

sociable (*say* **so**-sha-bul) *adjective*
friendly or enjoying being with other people
•***Word Family:* sociability** *noun* **sociably** *adverb*

social (*say* **so**-shul) *adjective*
1 living in a community rather than alone: *Bees are social insects.* 2 to do with life within a society: *social justice* 3 to do with wealthy or famous people: *the magazine's social pages*
4 organized for friendly purposes, rather than for business: *a social function*
social *noun*
5 a party or friendly gathering: *the school social*
•***Word Family:* socially** *adverb*

socialism (*say* **so**-sha-liz-um) *noun*
the political belief that the government should own and control important industries on behalf of the public and distribute wealth fairly
•***Word Family:* socialist** *noun*

socialize or socialise (*say* **so**-sha-lize) *verb*
to mix with others in a friendly way: *to socialise at a party*

society (*say* so-**sigh**-a-tee) *noun*
1 all people thought of as a whole: *20th-century society* 2 the organization, culture and way of life of a particular group of people: *Western society* 3 rich or famous people and the things they do 4 an organization or club for people with similar jobs or interests: *The Cactus Society*
•***Word Family:*** the plural is **societies**

sociology (*say* so-see-**ol**-a-jee) *noun*
the study of human society
•***Word Family:* sociologist** *noun*

sock *noun*
1 a short stocking, usually of nylon or wool, that reaches to your ankle or knee 2 **pull your socks up** to try to improve

socket *noun*
a hollow part or opening, especially one into which something fits: *your eye socket / a plug socket / a light socket*

sod *noun*
a square or oblong piece of turf

soda (*say* **so**-da) *noun*
1 *a short form of* **soda-water** 2 a simple chemical compound containing sodium: *baking soda / washing soda*

soda-water *noun*
water made fizzy with bubbles of carbon dioxide

sodden *adjective*
completely soaked or wet

sodium (*say* **so**-dee-um) *noun*
a silvery-white metallic element found in salt

sofa *noun*
a long, padded seat, with a back and armrests

soft *adjective*
1 not firm, hard or stiff: *a nice soft peach / soft toilet paper* 2 pleasant or smooth to touch: *soft skin* 3 low or soothing in sound: *a soft voice*
4 tender: *a soft glance* 5 weak: *to be too soft with bullies* 6 not bright or harsh: *soft lights* 7 **soft water** water without the mineral salts that prevent soap from lathering
•***Word Family:* soften** *verb* **softly** *adverb* **softness** *noun*

softball *noun*
a game similar to baseball, played with a larger, softer ball and a wider bat

soft drink *noun*
a drink without any alcohol in it

software *noun*
computer programs, rather than the machines they run on

softwood *noun*
wood that is easy to saw, such as pine or fir

soggy *adjective*
wet through: *soggy ground*
•***Word Family:*** other forms are **soggier, soggiest**

soil (1) *noun*
the top layer of the Earth's surface where plants grow

soil (2) *verb*
to make something dirty: *to soil your soccer gear*

solar (*say* **sole**-a) *adjective*
1 to do with the sun: *a solar eclipse* 2 using or operated by energy from the sun's rays: *solar energy / solar panels*

solar system *noun*
the sun together with the nine planets, the

comets and the asteroids that travel or orbit around it

solder *noun*
1 an alloy that melts quickly, used to join pieces of metal together
solder *verb*
2 to join things with solder

soldering iron *noun*
an electrical tool, used when you solder things

soldier *noun*
someone who serves in an army

sole (1) *adjective*
the only one: *I'm the sole owner of this go-cart.*
• ***Word Family:*** **solely** *adverb*

sole (2) *noun*
the underneath or bottom of your foot or shoe

solemn (*say* **sol**-em) *adjective*
serious and formal: *a solemn occasion*
• ***Word Family:*** **solemnity** *noun* **solemnly** *adverb*

solenoid (*say* **sol**-i-noyd) *noun*
a tightly wound coil or wire through which an electric current flows to produce a magnetic field

solicitor (*say* so-**lis**-i-ta) *noun*
a lawyer who advises clients, prepares legal documents and usually works in the lower courts

solid *adjective*
1 having a fixed shape and volume rather than being a liquid or a gas: *Ice is solid water.*
2 having the inside filled rather than being hollow: *a solid rock* 3 firm and closely packed rather than being loose and crumbly: *a solid stone wall* 4 full or complete: *a solid day's work*
solid *noun*
5 something which is solid
• ***Word Family:*** **solidify** *verb* **(solidifies, solidified, solidifying) solidity** *noun* **solidly** *adverb*: *I worked solidly all weekend.*

solidarity (*say* sol-i-**da**-ri-tee) *noun*
a show of unity or support by members of a group who share things in common

soliloquy (*say* so-**lil**-a-kwee) *noun*
a speech made by a character in a play when alone on the stage
• ***Word Family:*** the plural is **soliloquies**

solitary (*say* **sol**-i-tree) *adjective*
1 single: *a solitary lighthouse on the cliffs* 2 on your own or alone: *to live a solitary life*

solitude (*say* **sol**-i-tewd) *noun*
being alone: *to enjoy a time of peace and solitude*

solo *noun*
1 a song or piece of music performed by one person
solo *adjective*
2 performed or performing alone: *a solo flight*
solo *adverb*
3 alone: *to perform solo*
• ***Word Family:*** the plural is **solos** □ **soloist** *noun* someone who performs a solo

solstice (*say* **sol**-stis) *noun*
either of two times, about 21 June or 21 December, when the sun is furthest from the equator and the shortest or longest day of the year occurs
• ***Word Origins:*** from Latin words meaning "sun to stand still"

soluble *adjective*
1 able to be dissolved: *soluble aspirin* 2 able to be solved or explained: *a soluble puzzle*

solution (*say* so-**loo**-shon) *noun*
1 an answer or explanation: *What's the solution to this problem?* 2 a liquid in which a solid substance has been dissolved: *a solution of salt and water*

solve *verb*
to find an answer or explanation for a problem or puzzle: *to solve a riddle*

solvent *noun*
a liquid which can dissolve other substances: *A solvent is used in dry cleaning to remove grease.*

sombre (*say* **som**-ba) *adjective*
1 dark in a gloomy or dull way: *a sombre room*
2 serious or gloomy: *a sombre expression*

sombrero (*say* som-**brair**-o) *noun*
a pointed hat with a very wide, upturned brim, worn in Mexico, Spain and other countries
• ***Word Family:*** the plural is **sombreros**
• ***Word Origins:*** from a Spanish word meaning "shade"

some *adjective*
1 not knowing or naming which one: *Some day you'll understand. / Some people were late.*
2 fairly long: *to remain silent for some time*
3 great or remarkable: *That was some jump!*

somehow *adverb*
in a way that is not known or understood: *I'll get my revenge somehow.*

somersault (*say* **sum**-a-solt) *noun*
1 a complete, circular roll of your body head over heels, either forwards or backwards
somersault *verb*
2 to make this movement

sometimes *adverb*
at times: *Sometimes I think you're silly.*

somewhat *adverb*
rather: *I find this situation somewhat annoying.*

somewhere *adverb*
1 in, at or to a place not exactly known: *to be somewhere in the garden* 2 at some time: *The train arrives somewhere between six and seven o'clock.*

son (*say* sun) *noun*
someone's male child

sonar (*say* **so**-nar) *noun*
an electronic device or system using echoes from underwater soundwaves for finding the position of such things as submarines, mines and shoals of fish
• ***Word Origins:*** an acronym from the first letters of the words *so*und *n*avigation *a*nd *r*anging

sonata *noun*
a musical composition with three or four movements, often played by a solo instrument accompanied by the piano
• ***Word Origins:*** from an Italian word meaning "sounded"

song *noun*
1 a short, musical composition with words
2 the musical sound made by some birds

songbird *noun*
a bird such as a thrush or a lark which is well-known for its song

sonic (*say* **son**-ik) *adjective*
to do with sound: *a sonic boom*

sonic boom *noun*
an explosion caused by an aircraft flying faster than the speed of sound

son-in-law *noun*
the husband of your daughter
• ***Word Family:*** the plural is **sons-in-law**

sonnet *noun*
a poem of 14 lines, normally with ten syllables in each line and a set way of rhyming

soon *adverb*
1 in the near future: *Write to me soon.* 2 a short time: *Soon afterwards, it started raining.* 3 **as soon as** straight after something else: *I'll ring you as soon as I get home.*

soot (*rhymes with* foot) *noun*
a black, powdery substance left behind in the chimney or grate when coal, wood and other fuel is burned
• ***Word Family:*** **sooty** *adjective* (**sootier, sootiest**)

soothe *verb*
1 to make someone feel much less angry or upset: *to soothe a crying baby.* 2 to make a part of your body feel less sore: *a cream to soothe your sunburn.*
• ***Word Family:*** **soothing** *adjective*

sophisticated (*say* so-**fis**-ti-kay-tid) *adjective*
1 refined or cultured in your habits and tastes because you are used to lots of different things
2 complex and advanced: *a sophisticated computer*
• ***Word Family:*** **sophistication** *noun*

sopping *adjective*
extremely wet

soprano (*say* so-**prah**-no) *noun*
1 the range of musical notes sung by the highest singing voice in women and boys 2 a singer or musical instrument that has this range: *She's singing soprano.*
• ***Word Family:*** the plural is **sopranos** or **soprani** □ **soprano** *adjective: a soprano saxophone*
• ***Word Origins:*** from an Italian word meaning "above"

sorbet (*say* **saw**-bay) *noun*
a frozen dessert made from fruit mixed with water, sugar and egg white

sorcerer (*say* **sor**-sa-ra) *noun*
someone who does magic, especially witchcraft
• ***Word Family:*** **sorceress** *noun* a female sorcerer **sorcery** *noun* black magic or witchcraft

sordid *adjective*
1 dirty and depressing: *a sordid slum* 2 dishonest and immoral: *living a sordid existence*

sore *adjective*
1 tender or painful: *a sore knee* 2 annoyed or irritated: *Don't get sore at me.*
sore *noun*
3 an injured or inflamed place on your body

sorrow *noun*
unhappiness, grief or regret
• ***Word Family:*** **sorrowful** *adjective* **sorrowfully** *adverb*

sorry *adjective*
1 feeling regret for doing something wrong, or sympathy for someone: *I'm sorry for my rudeness. / I'm sorry you've been ill.* 2 old, damaged or worn out: *The old minibus was in a sorry condition.*
• ***Word Family:*** other forms are **sorrier, sorriest**

sort *noun*
1 a particular kind or type: *What sort of music do you like?* 2 **of sorts** poor or disappointing in quality: *They provided food of sorts.* 3 **out of sorts** not in good health or a good mood 4 **sort of** more or less
sort *verb*
5 to arrange or separate things into groups: *Sort these eggs into different sizes.*

SOS *noun*
a distress signal or call for help

•*Word Origins:* probably an acronym made from the first letter of the words save our souls

soufflé (*say* **soo**-flay) *noun*
a light, fluffy, baked dish made of savoury or sweet ingredients mixed with beaten eggwhites
•*Word Origins:* this word came from French which is why it has an accent above the "e"

soul (*say* sole) *noun*
1 the invisible spiritual part of someone which is thought to survive after death 2 a person: *There wasn't a soul in sight.* 3 a type of pop music, originally played by black American singers and groups

sound (1) *noun*
1 vibrations travelling through the air, that you hear when they hit your eardrum: *the sound of music from an open window*
sound *verb*
2 to make or give out a sound: *The trumpets sounded.* 3 to cause something to make a sound: *Sound the bells.* 4 to give a certain feeling or impression: *Your story sounds odd.*

sound (2) *adjective*
1 in good or healthy condition: *sound teeth*
2 reasonable or reliable: *sound advice*

sound (3) *verb*
1 to test or measure the depth of water, by dropping a weighted line or by sending down sonar signals 2 **sound out** to ask someone questions to see what they think about something: *Sound him out about going to the party.*

soundproof *adjective*
1 not allowing any sound to come in
soundproof *verb*
2 to make somewhere soundproof

soundtrack *noun*
1 the speech, sound effects and music of a film, television programme or a video 2 the music from a film, released on a CD, cassette or record

soundwave *noun*
a wave by which sound is carried

soup (*say* soop) *noun*
a liquid food made from boiled meat, fish or vegetables and usually served hot

sour *adjective*
1 having a sharp, acid taste, such as that of vinegar, lemons or unripe fruit 2 bad-tempered or surly: *a sour expression*
sour *verb*
3 to make something sour or to become sour
•*Word Family:* **sourly** *adverb* **sourness** *noun*

source (*rhymes with* horse) *noun*
1 a place or thing from which something comes: *My news is from a reliable source.* 2 the place where a river starts: *the source of the Nile*

south *noun*
the direction to your left when you face the west where the sun sets
•*Word Family:* **south** *adjective* **south** *adverb* **southern** *adjective*

souvenir (*say* **soo**-va-near) *noun*
an object given or kept to help you remember someone or something

sovereign (*say* **sov**-rin) *noun*
1 a king or queen 2 an old, gold coin that was worth £1
•*Word Family:* **sovereignty** *noun*

sow (1) (*say* so) *verb*
1 to plant or scatter seeds 2 to introduce or spread a particular feeling: *to sow unhappiness*
•*Word Family:* other forms are **sows, sowed, sown, sowing**

sow (2) (*rhymes with* cow) *noun*
an adult female pig

soya bean *noun*
a kind of seed that you can cook and eat as a bean or crush to make oil

soy sauce *noun*
a rich, salty, brown sauce used in Chinese and Japanese cooking

spa *noun*
1 a mineral spring flowing from the earth 2 a health resort where there is a mineral spring
•*Word Origins:* named after *Spa*, a resort town in Belgium

space *noun*
1 wherever is empty or gives you more room: *There's not enough space for my books in here.*
2 a place or area that's empty or can be used: *a parking space / Leave a space for your name and address.* 3 where all the stars and planets are: *space travel* 4 a period of time: *We've been away twice in the space of a year.*
space *verb*
5 to fix, divide or separate things into spaces: *Space your words further apart.*

spacecraft *noun*
a vehicle designed to travel outside the Earth's atmosphere

space shuttle *noun*
a spaceship that is designed to be used many times to carry people and equipment backwards and forwards between Earth and space

spacious (*say* **spay**-shus) *adjective*
roomy: *a spacious house*
•*Word Family:* **spaciousness** *noun*

spangle *noun*
a small thin disc of glittering metal, used to decorate dresses
•***Word Family:*** **spangled** *adjective* covered with spangles

spade *noun*
a long-handled tool with a broad, flat blade for digging

spaghetti (*say* spa-**get**-i) *noun*
a type of pasta made into long, thin rods or threads
•***Word Origins:*** from an Italian word meaning "little cords"

span *noun*
1 the distance between two places such as the tips of a pair of wings or two supports of a bridge: *a bird with a wing span of 2 metres* 2 the amount of time that someone lives for, or that something lasts for: *Most cars have a lifespan of about 10 years.*
span *verb*
3 to extend over or across somewhere: *A bridge spanned the river.* 4 to last over a particular period of time: *His life spans two world wars.*
•***Word Family:*** other verb forms are **spans, spanned, spanning**

spaniel (*say* **span**-yul) *noun*
a kind of small, long-haired dog with drooping ears

spank *verb*
to slap or hit someone on the bottom with the open hand
•***Word Family:*** **spanking** *noun*

spanner *noun*
a metal tool with a space at each end for holding and turning nuts or bolts
•***Word Origins:*** from a German word meaning "to tighten up"

spar (1) *noun*
a strong pole, such as a mast or a boom supporting a ship's sails

spar (2) *verb*
to box with light punches, usually for exercise or practice: *The boxers sparred in the ring.*
•***Word Family:*** other forms are **spars, sparred, sparring**

spare (*rhymes with* air) *adjective*
1 extra: *spare time / a spare tyre* 2 small or meagre: *a spare diet* 3 thin or lean: *a spare frame*
spare *verb*
4 to deliberately avoid hurting, damaging or destroying a person, animal, place and so on: *The general spared the man's life.* 5 to have enough to give some of what you've got to someone else: *Can you spare me some milk?*
spare *noun*
6 something extra or in reserve
•***Word Family:*** **sparing** *adjective* careful or economical

spark *noun*
1 a tiny, glowing particle that is thrown out by a fire 2 a tiny flash of electricity 3 a slight bit: *a spark of kindness*
spark *verb*
4 to produce or throw out sparks 5 to make something start happening: *to spark some interest*

sparkle *verb*
1 burn or shine with sparks or little flashes of light 2 to be lively and intelligent: *His conversation sparkled with wit.*
sparkle *noun*
3 a small spark or gleam

sparrow *noun*
a small, brown bird

sparse *adjective*
thin or thinly scattered: *a sparse beard / the sparse population in a desert*
•***Word Family:*** **sparsely** *adverb* **sparseness** *noun* **sparsity** *noun*

spasm *noun*
1 a sudden, uncontrolled movement of your muscles 2 a short, sudden burst: *He only works in spasms.*
•***Word Family:*** **spasmodic** *adjective* **spasmodically** *adverb*

spastic *noun*
someone whose brain is damaged and is partly paralysed or suffers from muscle spasms they cannot control

spate *noun*
a sudden flood or rush: *a spate of present buying before Christmas*

spatter *verb*
to splash tiny drops of liquid everywhere

spatula (*say* **spat**-yoo-la) *noun*
a tool with a flat blade for lifting, mixing or spreading food, paint and so on

spawn *noun*
the egg cells produced by fish, frogs and so on.

spay *verb*
to remove the ovaries of a female animal to stop it having young

speak *verb*
1 to produce words using your voice: *Can your baby speak yet?* 2 to have a conversation with someone: *She wants to speak to you.* 3 to give a lecture or talk: *He spoke for four hours on the Roman Empire.* 4 to know and be able to use a particular language: *to speak Spanish*

•*Word Family:* other verb forms are **speaks, spoke, spoken, speaking**

speaker *noun*
1 someone who speaks, especially to an audience 2 *the short form of* **loudspeaker** 3 **Speaker** the person who has been chosen to control debates in the House of Commons, and other parliaments

spear *noun*
1 a weapon with a pointed blade on a long pole
spear *verb*
2 to pierce or wound someone with or as if with a spear

special (*say* **spesh**-ul) *adjective*
1 of a particular kind: *special boots for hiking / special cream for fading freckles* 2 more important or better than usual: *a special treat / a special offer*
special *noun*
3 something special, usually something for sale cheaply
•*Word Family:* **specially** *adverb* particularly

specialist *noun*
someone, especially a doctor, who studies or is skilled in one particular subject or type of work: *a skin specialist*

speciality (*say* spesh-i-**al**-i-tee) *noun*
something special or distinct, such as a product or job that a person or business specializes in: *The chef's speciality is curried beef.*

specialize or **specialise** (*say* **spesh**-a-lize) *verb*
to concentrate on or put all your energy into one particular type of study or activity: *She specializes in working with dolphins.*
•*Word Family:* **specialization** *noun*

species (*say* **spee**-sheez) *noun*
one of the groups used for classifying or dividing animals, the members of which have similar characteristics and are able to breed with each other
•*Word Family:* the plural is **species**

specific (*say* spe-**sif**-ik) *adjective*
1 particular: *to buy a specific type of bread*
2 precise or exact: *to give a specific description*
•*Word Family:* **specifically** *adverb*

specify (*say* **spes**-i-fie) *verb*
to name or mention something clearly and precisely: *Please specify your time of arrival.*
•*Word Family:* **specification** *noun*

specimen (*say* **spes**-i-mun) *noun*
a single part or thing used to find out or show people what the rest is like: *to test a specimen of urine*

speck *noun*
a very small spot or particle
•*Word Family:* **specked** *adjective* marked with specks

speckle *noun*
1 a small mark or spot
speckle *verb*
2 to mark something or somewhere with speckles

spectacle (*say* **spek**-ti-kul) *noun*
1 a strange or interesting sight: *The sunset made a fine spectacle.* 2 an impressive or large-scale public show or display 3 **spectacles** a pair of glass lenses in a frame that rests on your nose and ears, that you wear to improve your eyesight
•*Word Family:* **spectacular** *adjective*

spectator (*say* spek-**tay**-ta) *noun*
someone who watches or looks on: *spectators at a cricket match*

spectre (*say* **spek**-ta) *noun*
a ghost

spectrum *noun*
1 the band of colours, red, orange, yellow, green, blue, indigo and violet, into which white light is divided 2 a range of kinds, ideas or beliefs: *the spectrum of musical instruments*
•*Word Family:* the plural is **spectra** or **spectrums**

speculate (*say* **spek**-yoo-late) *verb*
1 to think or form opinions without evidence to back them up: *He speculated endlessly about what presents he'd get.* 2 to undertake risky business deals in the hope of making a lot of money
•*Word Family:* **speculator** *noun* someone who speculates **speculation** *noun* **speculative** *adjective*

speech *noun*
1 the ability to speak: *to lose the power of speech*
2 a formal talk given to a group of people: *an after-dinner speech* 3 a way of speaking: *Her speech is slow and difficult to hear.*
•*Word Family:* the plural is **speeches**

speed *noun*
1 swiftness in moving, travelling or doing 2 **at full speed** as fast as possible
speed *verb*
3 to move or cause to move swiftly: *He sped past.* 4 to increase the rate of progress: *We must speed up production.* 5 to drive a car faster than the speed-limit
•*Word Family:* other verb forms are **speeds, sped** or **speeded, speeding** □ **speedy** *adjective* **(speedier, speediest) speedily** *adverb*

speed-limit *noun*
the fastest legal speed at which you are allowed to drive on a particular road

speedometer (*say* spee-**dom**-it-a) *noun*
an instrument on a vehicle for measuring how fast it is travelling

spell (1) *verb*
1 to say or write the letters of a word correctly 2 to be the letters of a word: *"C-a-t" spells "cat"*. 3 to signify or mean a particular thing: *The huge waves spell disaster for the rowing boat*.
• ***Word Family:*** other forms are **spells, spelt** or **spelled, spelling** □ **spelling** *noun*

spell (2) *noun*
1 a word or words believed to have magic power: *The wizard chanted a spell and the cat turned into a broom*. 2 any magical or fascinating power: *to be under someone's spell*

spell (3) *noun*
1 a short period of time: *to go away for a spell* 2 a period of weather: *a hot spell* 3 a short turn of work: *to take a spell at the wheel so that the driver can rest*

spellchecker *noun*
a computer program that checks your spelling when you write things using a word processor

spelling *noun*
1 the way letters are arranged to spell particular words: *to check spellings in a dictionary* 2 how well someone can spell: *His spelling is awful*.

spend *verb*
1 to pay out money 2 to use up all the power or energy: *The storm had spent its fury*. 3 to pass or make use of time in a particular way: *She spent the weekend in the country*.
• ***Word Family:*** other forms are **spends, spent, spending** □ **spender** *noun*

spendthrift *noun*
someone who wastes their money

sperm *noun*
a cell produced by a male's sex organs, that joins with a female's egg or ovum to grow into a new creature
• ***Word Family:*** the plural is **sperm**

spew *verb*
1 to vomit 2 **spew out** to come out of somewhere quickly and in large amounts: *Smoke was spewing out of the exhaust*.

sphere (*say* sfeer) *noun*
1 a completely round shape, such as a ball 2 an area of activity or interest
• ***Word Family:*** **spherical** *adjective* round

spice *noun*
1 a substance from a plant, such as pepper, used to add flavour to food 2 something that is interesting or adds excitment: *Variety is the spice of life*.
• ***Word Family:*** **spicy** *adjective* (**spicier, spiciest**) **spiciness** *noun*

spider *noun*
an eight-legged creature without wings, that usually spins a web
• ***Word Family:*** **spidery** *adjective* long and thin

spike *noun*
a strong, pointed piece of metal
• ***Word Family:*** **spiky** *adjective* (**spikier, spikiest**)

spill *verb*
1 to run or fall out from a container, or to make this happen: *The juice spilt*. / *He spilt the juice*.
spill *noun*
2 something which has been spilt or the occasion when this happens: *an oil spill at sea*
• ***Word Family:*** other verb forms are **spills, spilt** or **spilled, spilling**

spin *verb*
1 to make yarn by twisting and winding fibres into a long thread 2 to make a web or cocoon by giving out a sticky substance from the body the way spiders do: *to spin a web* 3 to rotate rapidly: *to spin a coin on the table*
spin *noun*
4 a rapid turning movement 5 a short journey: *to take the car for a spin*
• ***Word Family:*** other verb forms are **spins, spun, spinning**

spinach (*say* **spin**-itch) *noun*
a green, leafy vegetable

spinal cord *noun*
a cylinder of nerve tissue extending from the base of your brain all the way down the inside of your backbone

spindly *adjective*
long and thin: *spindly legs*

spin-dry *verb*
to squeeze or wring most of the water from wet clothes by spinning them rapidly in a machine
• ***Word Family:*** other forms are **spin-dries, spin-dried, spin-drying** □ **spin-drier** or **spin-dryer** *noun* a machine for spin-drying clothes

spine *noun*
1 your backbone or the ridge of bones running down your back 2 something shaped like this: *the rocky spine of a mountain* 3 the pointed part on an animal or plant, such as a quill or thorn 4 the part of a book's cover that holds the pages together
• ***Word Family:*** **spinal** *adjective* to do with your spine **spiny** *adjective* (**spinier, spiniest**) having spines or spine-shaped leaves

spinning wheel *noun*
a machine for spinning flax or wool into

threads, consisting of a spindle driven by a wheel which is worked by your foot or hand

spin-off *noun*
an unexpected benefit that comes from research and development in a particular field: *Pocket calculators are a spin-off from space research.*

spinster *noun*
an unmarried woman

spiral (*say* **spy**-rul) *noun*
1 a curve winding round and round itself
spiral *verb*
2 to move in a spiral shape: *Smoke spiralled up from the bushfires.*
spiral *adjective*
3 shaped like a spiral: *a spiral staircase*
•***Word Family:*** other verb forms are **spirals, spiralled, spiralling**

spire *noun*
the tall, pointed part on top of a church tower or other building

spirit *noun*
1 *another name for* **soul** 2 a supernatural being, such as a ghost 3 your character or outlook on the world: *Such a hard life has broken her spirit.* 4 courage or liveliness: *We like him for his intelligence and spirit.* 5 the general mood: *to join in the spirit of Christmas* 6 the general meaning: *to grasp the spirit of her letter* 7 **spirits** (a) your state of mind: *to be in good spirits* (b) strong alcoholic drink such as whisky, gin and so on
spirit *verb*
8 to carry someone or something off secretly or mysteriously: *to spirit away the loot before the police came*
•***Word Family:*** **spirited** *adjective* lively or courageous

spiritual (*say* **spi**-ri-tewl) *adjective*
1 dealing with ideas about your soul rather than your body: *spiritual art and poetry* 2 to do with supernatural, religious or sacred things: *the spiritual world*
spiritual *noun*
3 a religious folk song first sung by Black Americans
•***Word Family:*** **spirituality** *noun*

spit (1) *verb*
1 to force saliva from your mouth: *to spit on the ground* 2 to send something out from your mouth: *to spit out a tablet* 3 to fall in light, scattered drops: *Rain spat on the windscreen.* 4 to make a spitting noise: *The wet wood hissed and spat as it started to burn.*
spit *noun*
5 saliva which has been spat from your mouth
•***Word Family:*** other verb forms are **spits, spat, spitting**

spit (2) *noun*
1 a pointed, revolving rod for roasting food over a grill or fire 2 a narrow ridge of land that sticks out into the sea

spite *noun*
1 a malicious or nasty wish to hurt or annoy someone else: *He did it out of spite.* 2 **in spite of** even though a particular thing has happened or been said: *I'll do it in spite of her warning.*
spite *verb*
3 to deliberately annoy or hurt someone because of spite: *She did it to spite him.*
•***Word Family:*** **spiteful** *adjective* full of spite **spitefully** *adverb*

splash *verb*
1 to wet or dirty someone or something with drops of water, or with mud 2 to fly about and fall in drops 3 to display information somewhere in an obvious way: *Did you see the news splashed across the front page of the newspaper?*
splash *noun*
4 the act or sound of splashing: *to have a splash about in the paddling pool / He fell in the river with a loud splash.* 5 a mark or spot made by splashing 6 a patch or small area: *a splash of colour*
•***Word Family:*** the plural is **splashes** □ **splashy** *adjective*

spleen *noun*
the large organ in your body, that lies between your stomach and your left kidney

splendid *adjective*
superb or brilliant: *a splendid sunset / a splendid idea*
•***Word Family:*** **splendidly** *adverb* **splendour** *noun*

splice *verb*
to make two lengths of rope, magnetic tape, film and so on into a single piece by cutting them and joining them together

splint *noun*
a thin piece of wood, metal or leather used to keep an injured bone or joint fixed in position

splinter *noun*
1 a sharp, narrow piece of wood, metal or glass, split or broken off from the rest
splinter *verb*
2 to split or break something into splinters

split *verb*
1 to break or divide something, especially from one end to the other: *to split a log in two / to split your trousers* 2 to divide or separate in any way: *to split the sweets between the three children / Opinions were split over the matter.* 3 to leave 4 **split up** to part or or stop living together

A B C D E F G H I J K L M N O P Q R S T U V W X Y Z

split *noun*
5 a crack, break or division caused by splitting: *a split in the screen / a split in a skirt / a split in the opinion of a committee* 6 **do the splits** to spread your legs along the floor until they form a straight line at right angles with your body
•***Word Family:*** other verb forms are **splits, split, splitting**

splutter *verb*
1 to talk so fast that you can't be understood properly: *to splutter with excitement* 2 to spit drops of liquid noisily the way boiling fat does

spoil *verb*
1 to damage or ruin something: *The rain spoilt our holiday.* 2 to damage someone's character or nature by always letting them have what they want: *to spoil a child* 3 to go bad: *The meat spoilt in the sun.*
•***Word Family:*** other verb forms are **spoils, spoilt** or **spoiled, spoiling**

spoke *noun*
1 one of the rods that connect the hub or centre of a bike or steering wheel to the rim or outside 2 any similar rod, such as one on an umbrella

spokesperson *noun*
someone who speaks on behalf of someone else
•***Word Family:*** **spokesman** *noun* **spokeswoman** *noun*

sponge (*say* spunj) *noun*
1 a sea creature with a light, absorbent skeleton that can be used for washing or cleaning 2 a cloth like this, with holes for soaking up water or other liquids 3 a light, fluffy cake
sponge *verb*
4 to wash, wipe, clean or absorb something using a sponge 5 to take things from other people and never give anything back
•***Word Family:*** **spongy** *adjective*

sponsor *verb*
1 to help to pay for something in return for publicity or advertising: *The festival was sponsored by Coca-Cola.* 2 to give someone money to walk, swim and so on as a way of raising money for charity: *I'll sponsor you £1 a mile in the fun run.*
sponsor *noun*
3 a person or organization who sponsors someone or something
•***Word Family:*** **sponsorship** *noun* **sponsored** *adjective: a sponsored walk*

spontaneous (*say* spon-**tay**-nee-us) *adjective*
happening naturally rather than being planned: *spontaneous growth / a spontaneous laugh*
•***Word Family:*** **spontaneity** *noun* **spontaneously** *adverb*

spoof *noun*
a clever or funny imitation meant to make people laugh: *The TV show is a spoof on Star Trek.*

spook *noun*
a ghost
•***Word Family:*** **spooky** *adjective* (**spookier, spookiest**) scary or frightening

spool *noun*
a cylinder onto which tape, thread or film is wound

spoon *noun*
a kitchen utensil with a handle and small bowl-shaped end that you use for eating, measuring, stirring or serving

spoor (*say* spore) *noun*
the tracks left by wild animals

sporadic (*say* spo-**rad**-ik) *adjective*
happening or appearing occasionally: *sporadic bursts of gunshots / sporadic trees in a landscape*

spore *noun*
a seed or germ cell that separates from its parent before it begins to develop

sporran *noun*
a fur or leather pouch hung at the front of a belt as part of Scottish Highland costume

sport *noun*
1 a game involving physical effort and skill, organized with a set of rules 2 all these games: *I'm no good at sport.* 3 someone who is fair and honest rather than selfish: *She's a good sport.*
•***Word Family:*** **sporty** *adjective* (**sportier, sportiest**)

sporting *adjective*
1 to do with sport: *sporting activities* 2 fair, honest and unselfish: *That's very sporting of you.*

spot *noun*
1 a round, usually small, mark on a surface, having a different colour from its surroundings 2 a pimple on your skin 3 a place: *a good spot to fish* 4 **on the spot** (**a**) here, at once: *mend shoes on the spot.* (**b**) in a difficult or embarrassing situation: *That tricky question put her on the spot.*
spot *verb*
5 to mark or stain something with spots: *to spot your hands with paint* 6 to find or discover something: *Spot the hidden apple on this page.*
•***Word Family:*** other verb forms are **spots, spotted, spotting** □ **spotty** *adjective* (**spottier, spottiest**)

spotlight *noun*
1 a light or lamp with a strong, narrow beam, used in a theatre or attached to a car 2 **in the spotlight** receiving a lot of attention and interest

spotlight *verb*
3 to draw something to the public's attention: *to spotlight a problem*
• ***Word Family:*** other verb forms are **spotlights, spotlit** or **spotlighted, spotlighting**

spouse (*rhymes with* house) *noun*
your husband or wife

spout *noun*
1 a pipe or tube, usually with a lip-like end attached to a container, for pouring
spout *verb*
2 to pour out in gushes 3 to talk rubbish for a long time

sprain *verb*
1 to twist or strain a part of your body without breaking it: *to sprain your wrist*
sprain *noun*
2 a twisting or straining of part of your body without breaking it

sprawl *verb*
1 to stretch out in a careless or ungraceful way: *to sprawl in your chair* 2 to straggle or spread out: *The suburbs sprawled across the countryside.*

spray (1) *noun*
1 a liquid blown or forced through the air as fine drops: *sea spray*
spray *verb*
2 to apply a liquid as a spray: *to spray yourself with perfume* 3 to move or fall as a spray

spray (2) *noun*
a small, fine branch with leaves, flowers or berries, often used for decoration

spread (*say* spred) *verb*
1 to make or become larger, wider or more full: *The eagle spread its wings. / He spread the map out on the table.* 2 to cover, distribute or extend something evenly over an object, period of time, place and so on: *to spread butter on the bread / to spread payments over 12 months / The disease spread throughout the country.* 3 to make something widely known: *The news spread rapidly.* 4 to lay something out: *Spread your clothes by the fire to dry.*
spread *noun*
5 something you can spread on bread: *cheese spread* 6 a feast
• ***Word Family:*** other verb forms are **spreads, spread, spreading**

spreadsheet *noun*
a computer program for arranging and calculating tables of figures, charts and so on

spree *noun*
a time of fun when you do a lot of something you don't usually do very much: *a shopping spree*

sprightly (*say* **sprite**-lee) *adjective*
lively or energetic: *a sprightly dance*
• ***Word Family:*** **sprightliness** *noun*

spring *verb*
1 to rise or move lightly and suddenly: *to spring up the steps / to spring into the air* 2 to rush or come quickly: *The words sprang to her lips.* 3 to come from: *Their quarrel sprang from a misunderstanding.*
spring *noun*
4 a leap or pounce 5 a wire coil that bounces back into shape after it has been stretched 6 the season of the year between winter and summer 7 a stream
• ***Word Family:*** other verb forms are **springs, sprang, sprung, springing** □ **springiness** *noun* **springy** *adjective*

springbok *noun*
a small, South African antelope

spring-clean *verb*
to clean or tidy somewhere thoroughly, especially as an annual clean-up of your whole house in spring
• ***Word Family:*** **spring-cleaning** *noun*

sprinkle *verb*
1 to scatter something or fall in drops or small particles: *to sprinkle water on seeds / to sprinkle salt on your dinner*
sprinkle *noun*
2 a small quantity: *a sprinkle of salt*
• ***Word Family:*** **sprinkler** *noun* **sprinkling** *noun: to add a sprinkling of chilli to your stew*

sprint *verb*
1 to run or race at full speed, especially over a short distance
sprint *noun*
2 a short race at top speed
• ***Word Family:*** **sprinter** *noun* someone who sprints

sprocket *noun*
one of the pointed teeth on a wheel, that fits into the links of a chain, such as on a bicycle

sprout *verb*
1 to begin to grow or develop: *to sprout new shoots*
sprout *noun*
2 a young growth or shoot 3 *a short name for a* **brussels sprout**

spud *noun*
a potato

spunk *noun*
courage or spirit: *to have a lot of spunk*
• ***Word Family:*** **spunky** *adjective* **(spunkier, spunkiest)**

A B C D E F G H I J K L M N O P Q R S T U V W X Y Z

spur *noun*
1 a sharp, metal point strapped to the heel of a rider's boot, used to make the horse go faster 2 anything that inspires you or urges you on 3 a part jutting out, such as a ridge on the side of a hill or a horny growth on the leg of some birds or animals 3 **on the spur of the moment** suddenly or all of a sudden
spur *verb*
4 to prick or strike an animal, using a spur: *to spur a horse* 5 to encourage someone to move faster, work harder and so on
•***Word Family:*** other verb forms are **spurs, spurred, spurring**

spurn *verb*
to treat or reject someone with scorn or contempt: *She spurned his attempts to make friends.*

spurt *noun*
1 a sudden flow or rush: *a spurt of water from the burst pipe / a spurt of blood from a wound* 2 a sudden burst of speed
spurt *verb*
3 to flow or release suddenly

spy *noun*
1 someone sent to gather information secretly or to watch and report on the activities of others
spy *verb*
2 to act as a spy 3 to catch sight of or see someone or something: *She can't spy him anywhere.*
•***Word Family:*** the plural of the noun is **spies** □ other verb forms are **spies, spied, spying**

squabble (*say* **skwob**-ul) *noun*
1 a small, silly argument
squabble *verb*
2 to argue about trivial things

squad (*say* skwod) *noun*
a small group chosen for a particular purpose: *a squad of soldiers / a swimming squad*
•***Word Origins:*** from an Old French word meaning "a square", because soldiers use a square formation

squadron (*say* **skwod**-run) *noun*
a fighting unit of the airforce, cavalry or tank regiments

squalid (*say* **skwol**-id) *adjective*
dirty and depressing
•***Word Family:*** **squalor** *noun*

squall (*say* skwawl) *noun*
a sudden gust of strong wind

squander (*say* **skwon**-da) *verb*
to waste your money, time and so on

square (*say* skwair) *noun*
1 a shape with four equal sides and four right angles 2 a number in maths multiplied by itself: *The square of 2, written* 2^2*, is* $2 \times 2 = 4$. 3 a measuring instrument used to draw and check right angles 4 an open area in a town or city 5 someone you think is boring and old-fashioned
square *verb*
6 to put something at right angles to something else 7 to agree: *His story doesn't square with yours.* 8 to multiply a number by itself
square *adjective*
9 having four sides and four right angles: *a square box* 10 in the form of a right angle: *a square corner* 11 measured as a unit of area in the form of a square: *a square metre* 12 settled or paid up: *Our accounts are square now.* 13 honest and fair: *a square deal* 14 satisfying or filling enough: *a square meal* 15 boring and old-fashioned
square *adverb*
16 in a square form or at right angles
•***Word Family:*** **squarely** *adverb*

square root *noun*
the number which, when multiplied by itself, equals a particular number: *The square root of 16 is 4.*

squash (*say* skwosh) *verb*
1 to press or beat something down into a flat mass: *I sat on the tomato and squashed it.* 2 to stop or prevent something: *to squash an uprising*
squash *noun*
3 a game played by two or four players in a walled court, with racquets and a small rubber ball 4 a drink made with fruit juice or cordial and water: *orange squash*

squat (*say* skwot) *verb*
1 to sit on your heels or in a crouching position 2 to live somewhere without permission and without paying rent
squat *noun*
3 a place where people are squatting: *to share a squat*
squat *adjective*
4 short and thick: *squat fingers*
•***Word Family:*** other verb forms are **squats, squatted, squatting** □ **squatter** *noun*

squawk (*say* skwawk) *verb*
1 to utter a harsh cry, as chickens do when they are frightened
squawk *noun*
2 a harsh cry

squeak (*say* skweek) *verb*
1 to make a short, high-pitched cry or creak: *The mouse squeaked. / The door squeaked.*

squeak *noun*
2 a short, high-pitched cry or creak
•***Word Family:*** **squeaky** *adjective* (**squeakier, squeakiest**) making squeaks **squeakily** *adverb*

squeal (*say* skweel) *verb*
1 to make a long, loud, high-pitched cry or sound in pain, surprise or fright
squeal *noun*
2 a squealing sound

squeamish (*say* **skwee**-mish) *adjective*
easily sickened or shocked

squeeze (*say* skweez) *verb*
1 to press something or someone firmly: *to squeeze someone's hand / to squeeze someone tight* 2 to crush or force something out: *to squeeze the juice from a lemon* 3 to fit or force something somewhere: *to squeeze six people onto a settee / to squeeze through a hole in the fence*
squeeze *noun*
4 a crush or squash: *We managed to get into the bus, but it was a tight squeeze.*

squelch *verb*
to make a sticky, wet sound like walking in deep mud: *to squelch through a puddle*

squid (*say* skwid) *noun*
a sea creature with a long, soft body and ten arms or tentacles, two longer than the others

squint (*say* skwint) *verb*
1 to look with your eyes partly closed or screwed up 2 to be cross-eyed, with your eyes turning in towards your nose

squire (*say* skwire) *noun*
1 a country land-owner 2 a young man serving as attendant to a knight in the Middle Ages

squirm (*say* skwerm) *verb*
to wriggle or twist your body about because you feel embarrassed or uncomfortable

squirrel (*say* **skwi**-rul) *noun*
a small animal with reddish-brown or grey fur and a bushy tail, usually living in trees and storing nuts for the winter

squirt (*say* skwert) *verb*
1 to wet something or someone with a quick stream of liquid: *to squirt water*
squirt *noun*
2 a thin, fast stream or jet of liquid

stab *verb*
1 to pierce or wound someone or something with or as if with a knife: *He was stabbed in the fight. / to stab yourself with a fork*
stab *noun*
2 a sudden, painful feeling: *a stab of pain* 3 an attempt or guess: *to have a stab at the answer*
•***Word Family:*** other verb forms are **stabs, stabbed, stabbing**

stabilize *verb*
to make something stable, or to become stable: *to stabilize prices / Her illness has stabilized.*

stable (1) *noun*
1 a building in which horses are kept
stable *verb*
2 to put or keep horses in a stable

stable (2) *adjective*
steady and not likely to fall, collapse or fail: *a stable bridge / a stable relationship*
•***Word Family:*** **stability** *noun*

staccato (*say* sta-**kah**-toe) *adverb*
short and abrupt

stack *noun*
1 a large pile, often arranged in layers: *haystack*
2 a large number: *I have a stack of things to do.*
3 a tall chimney
stack *verb*
4 to place or arrange things in a stack: *to stack chairs*

stadium (*say* **stay**-dee-um) *noun*
a sports ground surrounded by raised banks of seats for spectators
•***Word Family:*** plural is **stadiums** or **stadia**

staff (*say* stahf) *noun*
1 the group of people working together in an organization, business, school or hospital 2 a rod, pole or stick used as a weapon, flagpole and so on
staff *verb*
3 to provide a place, building and so on with staff

stag *noun*
a male deer

stage *noun*
1 the raised platform on which actors perform, especially in a theatre 2 a single step in a development or series: *The first stage of our project is finished. / the larval stage of an insect.*
3 a powered section of a rocket, that is ejected after firing
stage *verb*
4 to put on a play or other performance: *to stage an opera* 5 to arrange and carry out something: *The workers staged a strike.*

stagecoach *noun*
an enclosed carriage with the driver's seat outside at the front, once used to carry passengers or mail over a set route and changing horses along the way
•***Word Family:*** the plural is **stagecoaches**

stagger *verb*
1 to walk or move unsteadily: *to stagger with*

A B C D E F G H I J K L M N O P Q R S T U V W X Y Z

exhaustion 2 to amaze people: *to stagger everyone with your brilliant exam results* 3 to arrange things in alternating or overlapping periods or intervals: *Workers should stagger their lunchtimes so that the office is never empty.*

stagnant *adjective*
stale or dirty because no movement occurs: *a stagnant pool*
• ***Word Family:*** **stagnate** *verb* **stagnation** *noun*

stain (*say* stane) *noun*
1 a mark: *a coffee stain* 2 a liquid dye that soaks into and colours wood
stain *verb*
3 to make a stain upon something 4 to colour wood or furniture with a liquid dye

stair *noun*
one of a series of steps leading from one level of a building to another

staircase *noun*
a series of fixed steps and its banister or handrail

stake (1) *noun*
1 a pointed stick or post, usually made of wood or metal, driven into the ground as a support or marker 2 **the stake** execution by being burnt to death

stake (2) *noun*
1 the money or any other thing promised as payment for a bet 2 an interest or involvement: *He has a personal stake in this matter.* 3 **at stake** at risk: *There's too much at stake for us to fail.*
stake *verb*
4 to bet

stalactite (*say* **stal**-ak-tite) *noun*
a spike of limestone that forms on the roof of a cave

stalagmite (*say* **stal**-ag-mite) *noun*
a spike of limestone that forms on the floor of a cave
• ***Word Origins:*** from a Greek word meaning "a dripping"

stale *adjective*
not fresh or new: *stale bread*

stalemate *noun*
1 a position in chess in which neither player can move without putting their king in check, resulting in a draw 2 a situation in which no-one can win or get what they want

stalk (1) (*say* stawk) *noun*
the stem of a plant, flower, leaf or fruit

stalk (2) (*say* stawk) *verb*
1 to follow another animal or person stealthily: *The cat stalked the mouse.* 2 to walk slowly and stiffly: *She stalked off in a huff.*

stall (1) *noun*
1 a section of a barn or stable for keeping one animal 2 a stand, bench or table used to display goods for sale, such as at a market 3 **the stalls** the seats on the ground floor of a theatre
stall *verb*
4 to stop a car engine suddenly by mistake: *The learner driver stalled the car.*

stall (2) *verb*
to put off doing something: *Stop stalling and answer the question.*

stallion (*say* **stal**-yun) *noun*
a male horse, especially one used for breeding

stamen (*say* **stay**-mun) *noun*
the part of a flower that produces pollen

stamina (*say* **stam**-i-na) *noun*
the strength and power to keep going, especially when you are tired or sick

stammer *noun*
1 a stutter
stammer *verb*
2 to talk with a stammer

stamp *noun*
1 the act of bringing your foot down hard: *to give a stamp of impatience* 2 a small piece of paper with a design on it, that you stick on a letter before you post it 3 a block of rubber, used to produce a shape, design or mark on something 4 the mark this makes: *a stamp on your passport*
stamp *verb*
5 to put your foot down hard 6 to walk with heavy or violent steps: *He stamped across the room.* 7 to put a mark on something to show that it is official or has been paid: *to stamp a passport*

stampede (*say* stam-**peed**) *noun*
1 a sudden, uncontrolled rush by a large group of horses, cattle or people
stampede *verb*
2 to rush or cause others to rush in a stampede

stand *verb*
1 to keep or take an upright position on your feet: *He was standing by the table. / She stood and walked across the room.* 2 to be or to put something in an upright position: *Stand the bottle on the table.* 3 to be placed or remain in a particular place: *The shop stood on the corner for 60 years. / Not many buildings are still standing after the bomb blast.* 4 to tolerate or put up with something you don't like: *I can't stand the noise.* 5 to be a candidate: *to stand for parliament* 6 **stand by** (a) to wait and be ready (b) to support: *He stood by me when I was in trouble.* (c) to stick to what you have already said: *to*

stand by an agreement 7 **stand for** (a) to tolerate or put up with something: *I won't stand for your nonsense.* (b) to mean: *What does the abbreviation 'St' stand for?* 8 **stand in** to be a substitute for someone else 9 **stand out** to be easily noticed or recognized because of being so different
stand *noun*
10 a position you take, either for or against something: *What's your stand on making some drugs legal?* 11 a platform or other structure for people to watch sports and so on 12 a piece of furniture or other support on or in which something is placed: *an umbrella stand / to have a stand at an exhibition*
• ***Word Family:*** other verb forms are **stands, stood, standing**

standard *noun*
1 a grade or level, especially of achievement or excellence: *high standards of behaviour*
2 something which other things are measured against or compared with: *By modern standards, these old computers seem very slow.* 3 a flag used as an emblem for a nation or an army
standard *adjective*
4 seen or used as the best or most correct: *standard spelling* 5 accepted or normal: *a standard shoe size / Follow the standard first-aid procedure.*

Standard English *noun*
the way of speaking and writing English that is thought of by most people as acceptable and correct

standing *noun*
1 your reputation or status: *a family of good standing in the neighbourhood* 2 the time that something has existed: *a quarrel of long standing*
standing *adjective*
3 continuing or permanent: *a standing quarrel*
4 done in or from an upright position: *a standing jump*

standstill *noun*
a halt or stop: *The strike brought public transport to a standstill.*

stanza *noun*
one of the groups of lines or verses into which a poem is divided

staple (1) *noun*
1 a U-shaped piece of wire or metal for fastening or joining things
staple *verb*
2 to secure or fasten things with a staple
• ***Word Family:*** **stapler** *noun* a machine for driving staples into a surface

staple (2) *noun*
1 the main food item produced or used in a particular country or a region
staple *adjective*
2 chief or most important: *Their staple food is rice.*

star *noun*
1 a large body of burning gas in space that from Earth looks like a tiny point of light in the night sky 2 a figure, shape or design, usually with five or six points 3 a famous or very talented person, such as a leading actor or sporting figure
star *verb*
4 to be a star in a film, TV show and so on: *to star in a new movie*
star *adjective*
5 famous or important: *a star attraction / a star performer*
• ***Word Family:*** other forms are **stars, starred, starring** □ **starry** *adjective* **stellar** *adjective* to do with stars in space

starboard *noun*
the right side of a boat or aeroplane when looking towards the front

starch *noun*
1 a white substance found in food such as potatoes, rice and cereals 2 a form of this substance, that is used to make linen and other cloth stiff
starch *verb*
3 to stiffen things with starch

stare (*rhymes with* air) *verb*
1 to look right at someone or something for a long time
stare *noun*
2 a long, fixed look

starfish *noun*
a sea animal with its body in the shape of a star

stark *adjective*
1 complete or utter: *stark madness* 2 harsh or desolate: *a stark landscape*
stark *adverb*
3 utterly or absolutely: *stark naked*

start *verb*
1 to begin to or to make something move: *The car started first time. / I can't start the car.* 2 to begin: *Start work now. / It's starting to rain.* 3 to leave: *to start for Egypt* 4 to make a sudden movement because you are surprised or frightened
start *noun*
5 the beginning or the first part: *The start of the film was boring.* 6 a lead or advantage, such as one given to weaker competitors at the beginning of a race: *We gave them a 10-second start.*
• ***Word Family:*** **starter** *noun*

A B C D E F G H I J K L M N O P Q R S T U V W X Y Z

startle *verb*
to alarm or surprise someone

starve *verb*
1 to suffer or die from hunger 2 to stop people or animals from getting anything to eat: *The army starved the rebels by cutting off their food supplies.*
•***Word Family:*** **starvation** *noun*

stash *verb*
1 to hide or store things away
stash *noun*
2 a secret or hidden store of things

state *noun*
1 the condition of someone or something: *The house was in a filthy state. / How's your state of health?* 2 a tense, nervous or excited frame of mind: *The sick child was in quite a state.* 3 the form of something: *The ice melted to a liquid state.* 4 a division or area of a country, which has its own government: *the six States of Australia* 5 **the state** the government and official organizations of a country, and the people who work for them
state *verb*
6 to say something clearly: *The barrister stated her client's case.*
state *adjective*
7 to do with the government, especially in the case of ceremonies or special occasions: *a state funeral*

statement *noun*
1 an official description or declaration: *The police took a statement of what he had seen. / The Prime Minister will be making a statement this afternoon.* 2 a report showing the amount of money owed or in credit in a bank account

static (*say* **stat**-ik) *adjective*
1 not active, moving or changing
static *noun*
2 a release of electricity in the atmosphere, causing a radio or television receiver to crackle

static electricity *noun*
electricity produced in some materials by rubbing

station (*say* **stay**-shon) *noun*
1 a place or position occupied or equipped for a particular job: *a police station / a television station* 2 a place where a train stops 3 a TV or radio channel
station *verb*
4 to put people in particular places: *Sentries were stationed at each gate.*
•***Word Origins:*** from a Latin word meaning "a standing still"

stationary (*say* **stay**-shun-ree) *adjective*
1 not moving: *a stationary tram* 2 not movable: *a stationary crane*

stationery (*say* **stay**-shun-ree) *noun*
writing paper and related materials such as pens, rubbers or pencils
•***Word Family:*** **stationer** *noun* someone who sells stationery

statistics (*say* sta-**tis**-tiks) *plural noun*
facts and figures collected, analysed and used to give information in the form of figures, charts or graphs
•***Word Family:*** **statistical** *adjective*

statue (*say* **stat**-yoo) *noun*
a sculpture or image of a person or animal made from wood, stone or metal

stature (*say* **stat**-yoor) *noun*
1 your height 2 importance: *He's a person of great stature in the music world.*

status (*say* **stay**-tus) *noun*
1 how important a person or group is compared to other people or groups 2 something's condition or state: *What is the status of this information—is it confidential?*

staunch (*say* stawnch) *adjective*
firmly loyal: *She's a staunch supporter of the government.*

stave *noun*
1 the five parallel lines on which music is written and printed
stave *verb*
2 to crush something inwards or make a hole in it 3 **stave off** to delay something or keep it away: *It was impossible to stave off disaster.*
•***Word Family:*** other verb forms are **staves, staved** or **stove, staving**

stay *verb*
1 to continue to be in a place or condition: *to stay in bed / to stay tidy* 2 to live somewhere for a while: *to stay at a hotel*
stay *noun*
3 a period of staying in a place: *He had a short stay in Boston.*

steadfast (*say* **sted**-fahst) *adjective*
firm, steady or strong: *steadfast loyalty / a steadfast gaze*

steady (*say* **sted**-ee) *adjective*
1 not likely to fall over or topple: *a steady ladder* 2 not easily disturbed or upset: *steady nerves* 3 constant or regular: *a steady breeze / a steady worker*
steady *adverb*
4 in a steady manner: *to hold something steady* 5 **go steady** to go out regularly with one girlfriend or boyfriend
steady *verb*
6 to make something steady or to become steady

steady *noun*
7 your regular girlfriend or boyfriend
• ***Word Family:*** other verb forms are **steadies, steadied, steadying** □ the plural form of the noun is **steadies** □ **steadily** *adverb*

steak (*say* stake) *noun*
a thick slice of meat or fish

steal (*say* steel) *verb*
1 to take something that belongs to someone else, usually secretly 2 to move about quietly or secretly: *I stole into the house at midnight.* 3 to take or do something secretly or quickly: *to steal a glance / to steal a kiss*
• ***Word Family:*** other verb forms are **steals, stole, stolen, stealing**

stealth (*say* stelth) *noun*
quiet secrecy or cunning
• ***Word Family:*** **stealthily** *adverb* **stealthy** *adjective* (**stealthier, stealthiest**)

steam *noun*
1 water in the form of a colourless gas or vapour, caused by boiling 2 **let off steam** to release stored up energy or feelings, for example by running about or making a noise
steam *verb*
3 to give off steam: *The kettle has begun to steam.* 4 to move or work using steam: *The ship steamed into port.* 5 to cook, soften or clean something using steam: *to steam vegetables* 6 **steam up** to become covered with water-vapour: *The kitchen windows are all steamed up.*
• ***Word Family:*** **steamy** *adjective* (**steamier, steamiest**)

steamroller *noun*
a heavy vehicle with large rollers for levelling roads

steed *noun*
an old-fashioned word for a horse, especially a fast one

steel *noun*
1 iron mixed with carbon and various other metals to make it harder and stronger
steel *verb*
2 to make someone hard or determined: *to steel yourself against fear*
• ***Word Family:*** **steely** *adjective* (**steelier, steeliest**) looking hard or cruel: *a steely gaze*

steep (1) *adjective*
1 rising or falling sharply: *a steep flight of stairs*
2 unreasonable because it is too high: *The price is too steep.*
• ***Word Family:*** **steeply** *adverb*

steep (2) *verb*
1 to soak something thoroughly in a liquid
2 **steeped in** filled with: *an area steeped in history*

steeple *noun*
the tower and spire on top of a church

steeplechase *noun*
1 a horserace over ditches or hedges, either on a racetrack or across country 2 a similar race for athletes

steer (1) *verb*
1 to guide a vehicle, boat and so on using a wheel or rudder 2 to take a particular route: *to steer a path between the trees*

steer (2) *noun*
a castrated bull

stem (1) *noun*
1 the part of a plant that is normally above ground and carries the leaves and buds
2 something that is shaped like the stem of a plant: *the stem of a pipe / the stem of a wineglass*
stem *verb*
3 to start or develop from a particular time in the past: *His love of flying stems from his childhood.*
• ***Word Family:*** other verb forms are **stems, stemmed, stemming**

stem (2) *verb*
to stop or hold back something that is flowing in or out of somewhere: *to stem the flow of blood*
• ***Word Family:*** other forms are **stems, stemmed, stemming**

stench *noun*
a nasty smell

stencil (*say* **sten**-sil) *noun*
1 a sheet of paper or other material with a pattern or letters cut out of it 2 the letters or patterns produced
stencil *verb*
3 to produce patterns or letters using a stencil
• ***Word Family:*** other verb forms are **stencils, stencilled, stencilling**

step *noun*
1 a movement made by lifting your foot and putting it down in another place 2 the distance covered by such a movement: *She moved back a step.* 3 the sound of such a movement: *I heard a step on the gravel.* 4 a stair: *to climb the steps to the balcony* 5 a move, especially one that is part of a series: *the first step towards peace* 6 **watch your step** to take care
step *verb*
7 to walk or tread: *Please step this way. / to step on a piece of glass* 8 **step on it** to hurry
• ***Word Family:*** other verb forms are **steps, stepped, stepping**

stepchild *noun*
a husband's or wife's child from a previous marriage
• ***Word Family:*** **stepdaughter** *noun* **stepson** *noun*

A B C D E F G H I J K L M N O P Q R S T U V W X Y Z

stepfather *noun*
a man who is not your father, but who is married to your mother

stepladder *noun*
a folding ladder with flat steps and a hinged support to keep it upright

stepmother *noun*
a woman who is not your mother, but who is married to your father

steppe (*say* step) *noun*
a wide plain, the climate of which generally allows grass but not trees to grow
•***Word Origins:*** from a Russian word meaning "lowland"

stereo (*say* **ste**-ree-o) *noun*
1 a machine such as a radio, television, CD or record player which produces stereophonic sound
stereo *adjective*
2 stereophonic: *a stereo tape-recorder*
•***Word Family:*** the plural is **stereos**

stereophonic (*say* ste-ree-o-**fon**-ik) *adjective*
to do with sound which can be split into two and played on two separate speakers
•***Word Origins:*** from Greek words meaning "solid sound"

sterile (*say* **ste**-rile) *adjective*
1 unable to have children 2 free from germs: *a sterile bandage*
•***Word Family:*** **sterility** *noun*

sterilize or **sterilise** (*say* **ste**-ri-lize) *verb*
1 to operate on a person or animal and make them infertile or unable to have young: *The vet sterilized the young cat.* 2 to destroy the germs in something, usually by boiling
•***Word Family:*** **sterilization** *noun*

sterling *noun*
the British currency with the pound as its basic unit
•***Word Origins:*** probably from an Old English word meaning "a coin with a star on it"

stern (1) *adjective*
1 grave or harsh: *a stern warning* 2 very strict: *a stern teacher*
•***Word Family:*** **sternly** *adverb*

stern (2) *noun*
the back of a boat

steroid (*say* **ste**-royd *or* **steer**-oyd) *noun*
a chemical found naturally in your body, sometimes prescribed by doctors in drug form

stethoscope (*say* **steth**-a-skope) *noun*
an instrument used for listening to the sounds of the heart and lungs

stew *verb*
1 to cook food slowly by simmering it in liquid
2 to fret or worry
stew *noun*
3 food, usually a combination of meat and vegetables, cooked slowly in liquid 4 a state of agitation or uneasiness

steward *noun*
1 someone who waits on passengers in a ship, aeroplane or train 2 an official who organizes, arranges or manages things
•***Word Family:*** **stewardess** *noun*

stick (1) *noun*
1 a long, slender piece of wood, especially a tree branch 2 something looking like this: *a walking stick / a hockey stick*

stick (2) *verb*
1 to pierce something with a pointed instrument: *to stick a skewer into meat* 2 to attach or fasten something by gluing it on: *to stick a stamp on an envelope* 3 to put or place something in a particular position: *He stuck his hands in his pockets. / Stick the kettle on the stove.* 4 to be at or come to a standstill: *to get stuck in traffic* 5 to stay or remain: *The thought stuck in my mind.* 6 to do what you say: *to stick to a promise*
•***Word Family:*** other forms are **sticks, stuck, sticking**

sticker *noun*
a sticky label

stick insect *noun*
an insect with a long, slender, twig-like body

sticky *adjective*
1 tending to stick to things 2 hot and humid: *sticky weather* 3 difficult or awkward: *a sticky problem*
•***Word Family:*** other forms are **stickier, stickiest**

stiff *adjective*
1 not easily bent or changed in shape: *stiff cardboard* 2 hard to move or work: *The new car had stiff gears. / to have stiff muscles* 3 difficult: *a stiff exam* 4 too formal: *to give a stiff bow*
5 strong: *to have a stiff drink* 6 severe: *The judge gave him a stiff sentence.*
stiff *adverb*
7 extremely or completely: *to be bored stiff / to be frozen stiff*
•***Word Family:*** **stiffen** *verb* **stiffness** *noun*

stifle (*say* **sty**-ful) *verb*
1 to suffocate or smother someone 2 to suppress or try to stop something: *to stifle a yawn*
•***Word Family:*** **stifling** *adjective* suffocating

stigma *noun*
a feeling of shame or disgrace: *the stigma of receiving a prison sentence*

stile *noun*
a group of steps on both sides of a fence allowing people to climb over

stiletto (*say* stil-**let**-o) *noun*
1 a dagger with a slender, tapering blade 2 a high, narrow heel on a woman's shoe

still *adjective*
1 free from movement 2 free from sound or disturbance: *a still night* 3 not fizzy: *still orange juice*
still *noun*
4 a photograph showing a scene from a film
5 silence or calm
still *adverb*
6 without sound or movement: *to sit still* 7 now as before: *She's still away.*
still *verb*
8 to make or become silent
•*Word Family:* **stillness** *noun*

stilt *noun*
either of two long poles with supports for your feet, used for walking high above the ground

stilted *adjective*
stiffly or unnaturally formal: *to talk in a stilted way*

stimulant (*say* **stim**-ya-lunt) *noun*
a substance, such as caffeine, that makes you more active for a while

stimulate (*say* **stim**-ya-late) *verb*
1 to make a person or situation more active
2 to give a person or situation new ideas or more excitement
•*Word Family:* **stimulation** *noun*

stimulus *noun*
something that causes something else to begin or develop: *a stimulus for growth*
•*Word Family:* the plural is **stimuli**

sting *noun*
1 the sharp or poisonous part of an insect or plant that can hurt you 2 a wound or pain caused by stinging
sting *verb*
3 to hurt someone, using a sting: *I was stung by a bee.* 4 to cause someone to suffer: *Their jeers stung him.*
•*Word Family:* other verb forms are **stings, stung, stinging**

stingy (*say* **stin**-jee) *adjective*
mean and unwilling to give away or spend your money
•*Word Family:* other forms are **stingier, stingiest**

stink *verb*
1 to give off a bad smell
stink *noun*
2 a bad smell 3 a scandal or fuss: *They made a stink about my exam results.*
•*Word Family:* other verb forms are **stinks, stank, stunk, stinking**

stint *noun*
an amount or period of work to be done: *We all did a stint in the garden.*

stir *verb*
1 to mix something round and round with a spoon: *to stir soup* 2 to move something or cause it to move, especially slightly: *The breeze stirred the leaves. / She didn't stir all afternoon.*
3 to rouse or excite you: *The story stirred my imagination.* 4 to mention things in order to make trouble: *to stir up trouble / to stir it*
stir *noun*
5 the act of stirring: *Give the paint a stir.*
6 a commotion: *to cause a stir*
•*Word Family:* other verb forms are **stirs, stirred, stirring**

stirrup *noun*
one of the two metal loops hanging from a horse's saddle on straps and into which the rider's foot is placed

stitch *noun*
1 one complete movement of the needle in knitting, sewing or crocheting 2 the loop of cotton or wool left by the movement of a needle 3 a sudden sharp pain in your side
4 **in stitches** laughing so much that you cannot stop
stitch *verb*
5 to fasten, join or decorate something using stitches
•*Word Family:* the plural is **stitches**

stoat (*say* stote) *noun*
a type of weasel that has brown fur during the summer

stock *noun*
1 the complete supply of goods kept for selling
2 a supply of something kept for future use: *to keep a stock of petrol for the tractor* 3 *another word for* **livestock** 4 the shares of a company
5 your ancestry, tribe, or race: *Lee Yan comes from Chinese stock.* 6 the clear liquid obtained by boiling bones, meat or vegetables, used as a base for soups or sauces 7 **stocks** a heavy, wooden frame locking someone by their ankles, used in the past as a public punishment
stock *adjective*
8 kept readily available for sale or use: *stock items* 9 ordinary or usual: *She received a stock reply to her question.*

stock *verb*
10 to provide or fill a place with stock: *to stock a farm with chickens* 11 to have a particular product as part of your stock: *to stock the latest computers*
•***Word Family:*** **stockist** *noun*

stockade (*say* stok-**ade**) *noun*
a wall of posts set in the ground and used as a fortification

stockbroker *noun*
a member of a stock exchange, who buys and sells stocks and shares on behalf of clients for a commission

stock exchange *noun*
a place where stocks or shares may be bought and sold

stocking *noun*
a light, tightly fitting piece of clothing worn on your foot and leg

stockpile *verb*
1 to build up a supply of raw materials, arms and so on for future use
stockpile *noun*
2 a supply of goods or materials

stocky *adjective*
short, strong and solidly built
•***Word Family:*** other forms are **stockier, stockiest**

stodgy *adjective*
1 very thick and heavy: *a stodgy meal* 2 not very interesting or easy to follow: *a stodgy book*
•***Word Family:*** other forms are **stodgier, stodgiest**

stoke *verb*
to stir or add fuel to a fire

stole *noun*
a long strip of silk, cotton or wool worn over your shoulders

stomach (*say* **stum**-ik) *noun*
1 a thick-walled bag-like organ in your body, where food is mixed with your gastric juices to start digesting it
stomach *verb*
2 to put up with or tolerate a particular thing or person: *I can't stomach violence on TV.*

stone *noun*
1 the hard substance of which rocks are made 2 a small piece of rock 3 a gem 4 a unit of weight, equal to 14 pounds or just over 6 kilograms 5 the hard, central seed of many fruits, such as peaches or apricots
stone *verb*
6 to remove stones from fruit: *to stone peaches* 7 to throw stones at a person or thing

stone-deaf *adjective*
completely deaf

stony *adjective*
1 covered with stones: *a stony beach* 2 showing no friendship or sympathy: *a stony silence / a stony expression*
•***Word Family:*** other forms are **stonier, stoniest**

stool *noun*
a small seat without armrests or a back

stoop *verb*
1 to bend forwards 2 to reach a low standard of behaviour: *to stoop to lying to get what you want*

stop *verb*
1 to end or finish: *to stop crying* 2 to bring something to a halt or to come to a halt: *Please stop the car here. / The car has stopped.* 3 to fill or cover an opening or a hole: *to stop a leak* 4 to prevent something from happening: *to stop them coming* 5 to stay: *to stop at home*
stop *noun*
6 a finish or end: *to bring the fight to a stop* 7 the place where something stops: *a bus-stop*
•***Word Family:*** other verb forms are **stops, stopped, stopping** □ **stoppage** an obstruction

stopper *noun*
a plug or cork used to block a hole

stopwatch *noun*
an accurate watch that you can start or stop whenever you want, used for timing races and other events

store *noun*
1 something that has been kept or saved for another time: *to have a store of pens in your bag* 2 a place where goods are kept 3 a shop, often a large one: *to buy some eggs at the store* 4 **in store** coming very soon: *There's a surprise in store for you.*
store *verb*
5 to collect and keep something for future use: *to store coal for the winter*
•***Word Family:*** **storage** *noun* **storekeeper** *noun*

storey (*say* **stor**-ee) *noun*
any of the levels of a building above the ground floor

stork *noun*
a large, black and white wading bird with long legs, neck and bill

storm *noun*
1 a disturbance in the weather bringing winds, with rain, thunder and lightning 2 a violent outburst: *a storm of tears*
storm *verb*
3 to go about angrily and violently: *He stormed*

out of the room. 4 to capture a place by a sudden and violent attack: *to storm a castle*
•***Word Family:*** **stormy** *adjective*

story *noun*
1 the telling of something that has happened, either true to life or made up 2 a lie or an excuse
•***Word Family:*** the plural is **stories**

stout *adjective*
1 rather fat or bulky: *a stout little man* 2 strongly made: *a castle with stout walls* 3 brave, bold or stubborn: *a stout heart*
stout *noun*
4 a dark beer flavoured with roasted malt

stove *noun*
a device for cooking or heating, powered by gas, wood or electricity

stow (*say* stoh) *verb*
1 to pack things away or store them: *to stow the chairs below deck* 2 **stow away** to hide yourself on a ship or aeroplane, to get a free trip
•***Word Family:*** **stowaway** *noun*

straddle *verb*
to stand or sit with one leg or part on either side: *to straddle a horse / The bridge straddles the river.*

straggle *verb*
1 to stray or lag behind the rest 2 to grow or spread in a messy or rambling way: *Ivy straggled all over the wall.*
•***Word Family:*** **straggler** *noun* **straggly** *noun*

straight (*say* strate) *adjective*
1 without bends or curves: *a straight line* 2 level: *Is the picture straight?* 3 honest and open: *a straight answer* 4 without waves or curls: *to have straight black hair*
straight *adverb*
5 in a straight line or way 6 directly: *Come straight home.* 7 tidy: *to put your room straight*
•***Word Family:*** **straighten** *verb*

straightforward *adjective*
1 open and honest 2 easy or simple: *straightforward language*

strain *verb*
1 to draw tight or stretch, sometimes too far: *to strain a muscle* 2 to pull hard: *The dog strained at his lead.* 3 to pour through a sieve: *to strain lemon juice*
strain *noun*
4 great force, weight or effort 5 an injury to your body caused by too much effort 6 **strains** musical sounds or a tune: *the distant strains of a waltz*
•***Word Family:*** **strained** *adjective* tense **strainer** *noun* a small sieve

strait *noun*
a narrow strip of water between two pieces of land

straitjacket *noun*
a tight, canvas jacket sometimes put on violent, mentally ill patients or prisoners to keep them still

strand *noun*
1 a single piece of fibre, thread, string or yarn, twisted together to form a cord or rope 2 a lock of hair

stranded *adjective*
1 washed up on a beach: *a stranded whale*
2 helpless or in difficulties: *a stranded motorist on a lonely road*

strange *adjective*
1 odd or unusual: *What a strange thing to do.*
2 not previously known: *to move to a strange area*
•***Word Family:*** **strangely** *adverb* **strangeness** *noun*

stranger (*say* **strane**-jer) *noun*
1 someone you've never met or seen before
2 someone who is new to a place: *I'm a stranger to your city.*

strangle *verb*
to choke someone to death
•***Word Family:*** **strangler** *noun* **stranglehold** *noun* a tight hold around the neck **strangulation** *noun*

strap *noun*
1 a strip of leather or cloth for supporting, fastening or holding things together: *the straps on a bag*
strap *verb*
2 to fasten with a strap
•***Word Family:*** other verb forms are **straps, strapped, strapping**

strapping *adjective*
tall, strong and healthy: *a strapping rower*

strategy (*say* **strat**-a-jee) *noun*
1 planning, especially in a military campaign
2 a plan or trick, especially for deceiving your enemies or winning a game
•***Word Family:*** the plural is **strategies** □ **strategist** *noun* an expert in strategy **strategic** *adjective*

stratum (*say* **strah**-tum) *noun*
a horizontal layer or level, especially of rock
•***Word Family:*** the plural is **strata**

straw *noun*
1 the dried, cut stems of grain such as wheat or corn, used for animal bedding 2 a hollow tube for sucking up drink

A B C D E F G H I J K L M N O P Q R S T U V W X Y Z

strawberry *noun*
a small, red, juicy fruit with small seeds on the outside
•***Word Family:*** the plural is **strawberries**

stray *verb*
1 to wander or lose your way: *to stray from the path*
stray *noun*
2 a pet animal that has wandered away from home
stray *adjective*
3 lost or out of place: *a stray hair*

streak *noun*
1 a long, thin line or mark: *a streak of lightning / a streak of dirt*
streak *verb*
2 to mark with a streak or streaks 3 to move very fast: *The runner streaked past the finishing line.* 4 to run naked in public
•***Word Family:*** **streaky** *adjective* **(streakier, streakiest)** □ **streaker** *noun*

stream *noun*
1 a small river or creek 2 a steady flow: *a stream of cold air / a stream of letters* 3 a group of children in a school who work together for a subject or subjects
stream *verb*
4 to flow in or as if in a stream: *Water streamed down the window. / The crowd streamed through the stadium gates.*
5 to divide or group children into classes according to their ability

streamer *noun*
a long, narrow strip of material: *to decorate a hall with streamers*

streamlined *adjective*
1 shaped so that it can skim through air or water
2 efficient: *our new streamlined admissions system*
•***Word Family:*** **streamline** *verb*

street *noun*
a road lined with houses, shops and so on

strength *noun*
1 power of your body or muscles: *Superman had the strength to lift cars.* 2 something that you are good at: *Make a list of your strengths.*
•***Word Family:*** **strengthen** *verb* to make something strong or to become strong

strenuous (*say* **stren**-yew-us) *adjective*
needing great effort: *a strenuous climb*
•***Word Family:*** **strenuously** *adverb*

stress *noun*
1 great importance: *to lay stress on the need to be fit* 2 the extra force or accent placed on a word or syllable, such as in the pronunciations of this dictionary 3 pressure or tension: *The court case placed him under a lot of stress.*
stress *verb*
4 to lay or put stress on someone or something
•***Word Family:*** the plural of the noun is **stresses**

stretch *verb*
1 to pull in order to make or become longer, wider, larger or tighter: *to stretch new shoes to make them pinch less / Stretch the balloon before you blow it up.* 2 to lay out full length, or extend your body: *to stretch out on the sofa / The cat yawned and stretched.* 3 to strain: *The constant chatter stretched my patience.* 4 to continue: *The hills stretch for miles.*
stretch *noun*
5 the act of stretching: *She gave a stretch and got up.* 6 a continuous length, distance or period: *a stretch of shallow water / a stretch without food*
•***Word Family:*** the plural of the noun is **stretches** □ **stretchy** *adjective* **(stretchier, stretchiest)**

stretcher *noun*
a piece of material supported by two long poles, used to carry sick or injured people

strew *verb*
to spread something about loosely or at random: *to strew papers over the floor*
•***Word Family:*** other forms are **strews, strewed, strewn, strewing**

stricken *adjective*
afflicted or affected by: *a town stricken by fever / to be stricken by fear*

strict *adjective*
1 demanding that you behave properly: *a strict teacher* 2 harsh: *strict discipline* 3 exact: *My watch doesn't keep strict time.* 4 absolute or complete: *to tell something in strict confidence*
•***Word Family:*** **strictly** *adverb* **strictness** *noun*

stride *verb*
1 to walk with long steps
stride *noun*
2 a long step forward or the space covered by such a step
•***Word Family:*** other verb forms are **strides, strode, stridden, striding**

strife *noun*
angry fighting or quarrelling

strike *verb*
1 to hit: *I struck him on the chin.* 2 to crash into: *The ship struck a reef.* 3 to attack: *The villians struck at dusk.* 4 to light or ignite: *to strike a match* 5 to chime: *The clock struck four.* 6 to come upon or discover: *The miners finally struck*

gold. 7 to affect in some way: *The news struck me speechless.*
strike *noun*
8 a hit: *a strike at tenpin bowling* 9 the discovery of oil or gold 10 a time when workers refuse to work in protest against low wages or unsafe working conditions
•***Word Family:*** other verb forms are **strikes, struck, striking** □ **striking** *adjective* attractive or interesting

string *noun*
1 a cord or thread used for tying 2 a set of objects threaded together: *a string of pearls*
3 a series or collection: *a string of questions*
4 a tightly stretched length of catgut or wire stretched across such musical instruments as violins and guitars, which produce a note when you pluck them or draw a bow across them
5 **strings** instruments with strings, especially those of the violin family
string *verb*
6 to hang or thread something on a string
7 **string out** to spread out, or lengthen: *The horses were strung out all over the field. / to string out a discussion*
•***Word Family:*** other verb forms are **strings, strung, stringing** □ **stringed** *adjective: a stringed instrument* **stringy** *adjective* **(stringier, stringiest)** (a) tough: *stringy meat* (b) like string: *stringy hair*

stringent (*say* **strin**-junt) *adjective*
strict: *stringent laws*

strip (1) *verb*
1 to remove or take the covering from: *to strip the bark from trees / to strip the paint from wood*
2 to undress, or make bare or naked: *to strip and search police suspects* 3 to take something away from someone: *She was stripped of her gold medal.*
•***Word Family:*** other forms are **strips, stripped, stripping** □ **stripper** *noun*

strip (2) *noun*
1 a long, narrow piece: *a strip of land* 2 **comic strip** a series of funny pictures telling a story

stripe *noun*
1 a long, narrow piece or section, with a different colour or texture from its surroundings
2 a piece of cloth worn on an army uniform to show rank
•***Word Family:*** **striped** *adjective* **stripy** *adjective* **(stripier, stripiest)**

strive *verb*
to try hard: *He strove for success.*
•***Word Family:*** other forms are **strives, strove, striven, striving**

stroke (1) *noun*
1 a blow or strike: *the stroke of an axe / a stroke of lightning* 2 a mark made by one movement of a pen, pencil or brush 3 a piece or dash: *a stroke of good luck / a stroke of genius* 4 a sudden blockage in one of the blood vessels that supply blood to part of your brain, leaving you unconscious and sometimes paralysed 5 a style of rowing, swimming or hitting the ball in tennis

stroke (2) *verb*
1 to pass your hand over something gently or lovingly: *to stroke a cat*
stroke *noun*
2 a caress or pat

stroll *verb*
1 to walk in a slow or casual way
stroll *noun*
2 a relaxed walk

strong *adjective*
1 powerful: *a strong man / a cup of strong coffee*
2 lasting or not breaking easily: *strong cloth*
strong *adverb*
3 in a strong way: *to be still going strong* 4 in number: *The new religion is 200 000 strong.*
•***Word Family:*** **strongly** *adverb*

stronghold *noun*
a fortress

stroppy *adjective*
causing trouble or complaining: *to be in a stroppy mood*
•***Word Family:*** other forms are **stroppier, stroppiest**

structure (*say* **struk**-cher) *noun*
1 the way something is put together: *the structure of a story* 2 something that has been built or constructed, such as a bridge or building
•***Word Family:*** **structural** *adjective* **structurally** *adverb*

struggle *verb*
1 to work or fight very hard: *to struggle to open a jammed door / to struggle to make a living / to struggle through the jungle*
struggle *noun*
2 the act of struggling: *She lost her glasses in the struggle.* 3 a great effort: *the struggle for peace*

strum *verb*
to sound a guitar by running your fingers across the strings
•***Word Family:*** other forms are **strums, strummed, strumming**

strut *verb*
1 to walk in a stiff-legged, proud way with your chest puffed out and your head or chin pushed forward
strut *noun*
2 a strutting way of walking
•***Word Family:*** other verb forms are **struts, strutted, strutting**

A B C D E F G H I J K L M N O P Q R S T U V W X Y Z

stub *noun*
1 the short, blunt end of something that has been worn down, used up or cut: *the stub of a pencil*
stub *verb*
2 to hit against something hard: *to stub your toe / to stub out a cigarette*
•*Word Family:* other verb forms are **stubs, stubbed, stubbing**

stubble *noun*
1 the cut stalks of wheat and corn, left in the ground after a harvest 2 the unshaven growth of beard on a man's face
•*Word Family:* **stubbly** *adjective* (**stubblier, stubbliest**)

stubborn (*say* **stub**-un) *adjective*
unwilling to give way or change your mind
•*Word Family:* **stubbornly** *adverb* **stubbornness** *noun*

stubby *adjective*
short and thick: *stubby fingers*
•*Word Family:* other forms are **stubbier, stubbiest**

stuck-up *adjective*
conceited or superior

stud (1) *noun*
1 a small, metal button, or knob: *a stud for fastening a shirt / the studs on the bottom of football boots or running shoes*
stud *verb*
2 to set or decorate something with or as if with studs: *a shield studded with jewels*
•*Word Family:* other verb forms are **studs, studded, studding**

stud (2) *noun*
a farm where horses or cattle are kept for breeding

student (*say* **stew**-dunt) *noun*
someone who is studying, especially at a school, college or university

studio (*say* **stew**-dee-o) *noun*
1 the workroom of an artist or photographer
2 a room or building with equipment for broadcasting television and radio programmes or making films
•*Word Family:* the plural is **studios**

studious (*say* **stew**-dee-us) *adjective*
liking to study
•*Word Family:* **studiously** *adverb*

study *noun*
1 the learning of a subject through reading, investigation or thinking 2 a room with a desk and books for studying, reading or writing 3 a musical piece for practising your technique
study *verb*
4 to spend time learning: *to study for a test* 5 to examine: *to study someone's face*
•*Word Family:* the plural of the noun is **studies** □ other verb forms are **studies, studied, studying**

stuff *verb*
1 to cram or fill something tightly: *to stuff yourself with food / to stuff a cushion with down*
stuff *noun*
2 belongings: *Pack up your stuff and go.*
3 a substance: *What's that stuff?*

stuffing *noun*
1 a tasty mixture of seasoned breadcrumbs used to stuff meat or poultry before you cook it 2 the soft material used to stuff something such as a cushion

stuffy *adjective*
1 not having enough fresh air: *a stuffy room*
2 blocked: *a stuffy nose* 3 prim or easily shocked
4 formal and boring
•*Word Family:* other forms are **stuffier, stuffiest** □ **stuffily** *adverb* **stuffiness** *noun*

stumble *verb*
1 to trip and almost fall 2 to walk or move in an unsteady or blundering way 3 **stumble upon** to come across something accidentally or unexpectedly: *to stumble upon a new drug*

stump *noun*
1 the short, remaining part of something: *a tree stump / the stump of a leg* 2 one of the three upright wooden pegs set at either end of a cricket pitch
stump *verb*
3 to baffle someone or leave them at a loss: *The last question stumped all the students.*
•*Word Family:* **stumpy** *adjective* (**stumpier, stumpiest**) short and thick

stun *verb*
1 to knock someone unconscious: *Did the blow stun him?* 2 to shock or astonish
•*Word Family:* other forms are **stuns, stunned, stunning** □ **stunning** *adjective* strikingly attractive

stunt (1) *verb*
to stop something or someone growing properly: *The cold winters have stunted the trees.*
•*Word Family:* **stunted** *adjective*

stunt (2) *noun*
1 a bold, daring, dangerous or unusual deed
2 an action meant to attract attention: *It was an advertising stunt.*
•*Word Family:* **stunt man** *noun* someone paid to perform stunts, especially as a substitute for an actor in dangerous scenes

stupa (*say* **stoo**-pa) *noun*
a round building used as a shrine by Buddhists

stupendous (*say* stew-**pen**-dus) *adjective*
amazing or astounding: *The Grand Canyon is a stupendous sight.*
• ***Word Family:*** **stupendously** *adverb*

stupid (*say* **stew**-pid) *adjective*
1 slow to grasp or understand: *a stupid boy*
2 unthinking or silly: *That was a stupid thing to say.*
• ***Word Family:*** **stupidity** *noun* dullness or lack of intelligence **stupidly** *adverb*

sturdy (*say* **ster**-dee) *adjective*
strong and unlikely to be damaged or injured: *a sturdy chair / a child's sturdy little legs*
• ***Word Family:*** other forms are **sturdier, sturdiest** □ **sturdily** *adverb* **sturdiness** *noun*

stutter *noun*
1 a speech problem in which you find it difficult to speak smoothly and you repeat the first consonant or sound of a word
stutter *verb*
2 to speak with a stutter

sty (1) *noun*
a place where pigs live
• ***Word Family:*** the plural is **sties**

sty (2) *noun*
a small swelling, like a boil, on the edge of your eyelid
• ***Word Family:*** the plural is **sties**

style (*say* stile) *noun*
1 the way something looks or is done: *a new style of shoes / The author writes in a natural style.*
2 the way of making or doing something at a particular time: *the Gothic style of building churches* 3 an elegant manner: *to live in style*
style *verb*
4 to design or give a style to something: *She cut and styled his hair.*
• ***Word Family:*** **stylish** *adjective* elegant or fashionable **stylishly** *adverb*

stylus (*say* **sty**-lus) *noun*
1 a pointed tool for writing or engraving 2 the diamond-tipped needle of a record-player

suave (*say* swahv) *adjective*
sophisticated or smoothly pleasant in the way you act: *a suave movie star*

sub *noun*
1 a submarine 2 a subscription 3 a substitute

subconscious *noun*
the part of your mind under or below your immediate consciousness or awareness: *to dream using your subconscious*
• ***Word Family:*** **subconsciously** *adjective* **subconsciousness** *noun*

subcontinent *noun*
a large area of land that is part of a continent
• ***Word Family:*** **subcontinental** *adjective*

subdivide *verb*
to divide again or into smaller parts: *to subdivide land for a housing estate*
• ***Word Family:*** **subdivision** *noun*

subdue (*say* sub-**dew**) *verb*
1 to conquer or overcome: *to subdue your fears*
2 to soften something or tone it down
• ***Word Family:*** other forms are **subdues, subdued, subduing** □ **subdued** *adjective* quiet and depressed

subject (*say* **sub**-jekt) *noun*
1 a topic or main theme: *What's the subject of your talk?* 2 an area of study: *What's your favourite subject?* 3 something represented in or used as the model for a painting or sculpture
4 someone who is ruled by a sovereign or a government: *a British subject* 5 the word or words in a sentence about which something is said, such as "the girl in the red dress" in *The girl in the red dress ran across the road.*
subject (*say* sub-**jekt**) *verb*
6 **subject to** to make someone or something undergo or experience something: *to subject a patient to massive doses of drugs / to subject the new material to thorough testing*
subject (*say* **sub**-jekt) *adjective*
7 **subject to (a)** open or liable to: *The decision is subject to appeal.* **(b)** dependent upon: *The street fair is subject to the council's approval.*

subjective (*say* sub-**jek**-tiv) *adjective*
influenced by your personal interests, emotions or prejudices: *to take a subjective view of the problem*

subjective case *noun*
the form of a noun or pronoun that shows it as the subject of a verb, such as "the dog" in *The dog slobbered on my dress.*

sublime (*say* sa-**blime**) *adjective*
grand or noble: *sublime music / sublime mountain scenery*
• ***Word Family:*** **sublimely** *adverb*

submarine (*say* sub-ma-**reen**) *noun*
a ship designed and equipped to travel and operate both on and below water

submerge (*say* sub-**merj**) *verb*
to plunge or make something sink under water or some other liquid: *The submarine submerged. / I submerged my hands in soap suds.*
• ***Word Family:*** **submerged** *adjective* **submersion** *noun*

submit (*say* sub-**mit**) *verb*
1 to surrender and let yourself be led or controlled: *I submit to your better judgment.* 2 to give or send something to be judged: *to submit a manuscript to a publisher*
• ***Word Family:*** other forms are **submits, submitted, submitting** □ **submission** *noun* **submissive** *adjective* meek and obedient

subordinate (*say* su-**bor**-di-nit) *adjective*
1 belonging to a lower rank or status: *a subordinate worker*
subordinate (*say* su-**bor**-di-nate) *verb*
2 to make someone subordinate
subordinate (*say* su-**bor**-di-nit) *noun*
3 a subordinate person or thing: *He's my subordinate.*
• ***Word Family:*** **subordination** *noun*

subscribe *verb*
1 to pay money so that you receive a certain number of issues of a regular magazine or to be a member of something and so on 2 to promise or contribute a sum of money: *to subscribe to the hospital appeal*
• ***Word Family:*** **subscriber** *noun* someone who subscribes to something **subscription** *noun*

subsequent (*say* **sub**-sa-kwent) *adjective*
following or coming after or later: *Subsequent discoveries changed our minds about the murder.*
• ***Word Family:*** **subsequently** *adverb*

subside (*say* sub-**side**) *verb*
to sink to a lower level: *The road began to subside.* / *The noise of the storm gradually subsided.*
• ***Word Family:*** **subsidence** (*say* **sub**-si-dans)*noun*

subsidy (*say* **sub**-si-dee) *noun*
money given by a government or organization to support someone or something that needs help: *a subsidy to farmers during the drought*
• ***Word Family:*** the plural is **subsidies** □ **subsidize** or **subsidise** *verb*

subsist (*say* sub-**sist**) *verb*
to continue to stay alive especially without much food or water
• ***Word Family:*** **subsistence** *noun*

substance *noun*
1 what something consists of or is made of 2 a particular kind of this: *Oil is a greasy substance.* 3 the main or essential part: *I've reported the substance of what he said.*

substantial (*say* sub-**stan**-shul) *adjective*
large, important or solid: *a substantial pay rise* / *a substantial bridge*

substitute (*say* **sub**-sti-tewt) *noun*
1 someone or something that acts or stands in place of another
substitute *verb*
2 to put someone or something in the place of another person or thing: *to substitute red for green* / *to substitute a player in a basketball game*
• ***Word Family:*** **substitution** *noun*

subterranean (*say* sub-ta-**ray**-nee-un) *adjective*
underground: *a subterranean stream*

subtitle *noun*
1 a second or alternative title of a book or poem, sometimes used to explain the first title 2 a short sentence shown on the screen during a foreign film or opera to translate the soundtrack, or for deaf people
subtitle *verb*
3 to give something a subtitle or subtitles

subtle (*say* **sut**-ul) *adjective*
1 so faint or slight that it is difficult to find: *a subtle perfume* / *a subtle distinction* 2 using clever or indirect methods to express something: *subtle humour*
• ***Word Family:*** **subtlety** *noun* (**subtleties**) **subtly** *adverb*

subtract *verb*
to take away, especially one quantity from another: *If you subtract 3 from 4, you get 1.*
• ***Word Family:*** **subtraction** *noun*

subtropical *adjective*
growing or happening in the regions near the tropics

suburb (*say* **sub**-erb) *noun*
an area or district of a city with its own shops, school and so on
• ***Word Family:*** **suburbia** *noun* the suburbs **suburban** *adjective*

subway *noun*
an underground passage, tunnel or railway

succeed (*say* suk-**seed**) *verb*
1 to achieve something that you have attempted to do: *to succeed in blowing up the balloon* 2 to come after someone and take their place: *Who will succeed the king when he dies?*
• ***Word Family:*** for definition 2 **succession** *noun* **successor** *noun* a person who comes after another and takes their place

success (*say* suk-**ses**) *noun*
1 the result that you wanted: *Did you have success with your plan?* 2 someone who has achieved an important position, become wealthy and so on
• ***Word Family:*** the plural is **successes** □ **successful** *noun* **successfully** *adverb*

successive (*say* suk-**ses**-iv) *adjective*
following in an uninterrupted order: *It rained for four successive days.*
• ***Word Family:*** **successively** *adverb*

succulent (*say* **suk**-yoo-lunt) *adjective*
fleshy or full of juice: *A cactus has a succulent stem. / succulent roast lamb*

such *adjective*
1 so much: *It's such an interesting novel.*
2 similar: *nuts, dried fruits and other such foods*

suck *verb*
1 to draw something up or in: *The vacuum cleaner sucks up dirt. / to suck lemonade through a straw*
2 to hold food and move it about in your mouth until it is melted or dissolved: *to suck sweets*
suck *noun*
3 the act or sound of sucking

suckle *verb*
to allow a young baby or a young animal to take milk at the breast: *My mother suckled our new baby. / The mother cat suckled her six kittens.*

suction (*say* **suk**-shon) *noun*
the force of sucking produced when you remove, or try to remove, gas from an enclosed space

sudden *adjective*
done or happening quickly and unexpectedly: *a sudden storm*
• ***Word Family:*** **suddenly** *adverb* **suddenness** *noun*

sudden infant death syndrome *noun*
the long form of **SIDS**

suds (*say* sudz) *plural noun*
soapy water with bubbles

sue (*say* soo) *verb*
to take someone to court to try to get money from them: *He sued the doctor who gave him the wrong drug.*
• ***Word Family:*** other forms are **sues, sued, suing**

suede (*say* swade) *noun*
leather with a soft, furry surface

suet (*say* **soo**-it) *noun*
the fat from sheep and cattle, often used in boiled or baked puddings

suffer *verb*
1 to feel the bad or unpleasant effects of something: *to suffer from a cold / The country suffered from bad government.* 2 to tolerate or put up with something: *I won't suffer rudeness.*
• ***Word Family:*** **sufferer** *noun* **suffering** *noun*

sufficient (*say* se-**fish**-unt) *adjective*
as much as is needed: *Do you have sufficient time to catch the train?*
• ***Word Family:*** **sufficiently** *adverb*

suffix *noun*
a word part added to the end of a word, such as "-ful" in *helpful* or "-est" in *greatest*
• ***Word Family:*** the plural is **suffixes**

suffocate (*say* **suf**-a-kate) *verb*
1 to die from lack of air 2 to kill someone by cutting off their air supply
• ***Word Family:*** **suffocation** *noun*

suffrage (*say* **suf**-rij) *noun*
the right to vote in elections

sugar *noun*
a sweet, grainy substance obtained from sugar cane or sugar beet
• ***Word Family:*** **sugary** *adjective*

sugar beet *noun*
a variety of beet with white roots, from which sugar is obtained

sugar cane *noun*
a tall, tropical grass with thick stems divided into segments, from which sugar is obtained

suggest (*say* se-**jest**) *verb*
1 to offer or put something forward as an idea: *May I suggest a better way of painting?* 2 to show, or give a sign: *This work suggests that you don't really understand.*
• ***Word Family:*** **suggestion** *noun*

suicide (*say* **soo**-i-side) *noun*
killing yourself deliberately: *to commit suicide*
• ***Word Family:*** **suicidal** *adjective* **(a)** feeling so depressed that you want to kill yourself **(b)** very dangerous

suit (*rhymes with* boot) *noun*
1 a set of matching clothes 2 one of the four sets of cards in a pack (clubs, diamonds, hearts or spades) 3 a legal action taken by one person against another in a court of law
suit *verb*
4 to be acceptable or appropriate for someone's needs: *I hope this room will suit you.* 5 to look good on: *Does this colour suit me?*

suitable (*say* **soo**-ta-bul) *adjective*
correct or adequate for a particular position or occasion: *You're not suitable for the job. / Those jeans aren't suitable for school.*
• ***Word Family:*** **suitability** *noun* **suitably** *adverb*

suitcase *noun*
a strong bag for carrying clothes and other things when you are travelling

suite (*sounds like* sweet) *noun*
a set or group: *a suite of furniture / a suite of rooms*

suitor *noun*
a man who is trying to get a woman to love him or marry him

sulk *verb*
to be silent and moody, or cross because you think that someone has treated you unfairly
• ***Word Family:*** **sulky** *adjective* **(sulkier, sulkiest) sulkily** *adverb* **sulkiness** *noun*

A B C D E F G H I J K L M N O P Q R S T U V W X Y Z

sullen *adjective*
silent in a rude and angry way
• ***Word Family:*** **sullenly** *adverb* **sullenness** *noun*

sulphur or **sulfur** (*say* **sul**-fa) *noun*
a yellow non-metallic element essential for living tissue and used in making such things as gunpowder and matches
• ***Word Family:*** **sulphuric** *adjective* containing sulfur: *sulfuric acid* **sulphurous** *adjective*

sultan *noun*
the ruler of a Muslim city or country
• ***Word Family:*** **sultanate** *noun* a country or state ruled by a sultan

sultana (*say* sul-**tah**-na) *noun*
1 a small, sweet, seedless grape 2 the raisin or dried fruit made from it

sultry *adjective*
unpleasantly hot and humid: *sultry weather*

sum *noun*
1 the total or amount that you get when you add: *The sum of 7 and 10 is 17.* 2 an amount of money: *She inherited a huge sum from her father.* 3 a problem in maths
sum *verb*
4 to add together 5 **sum up (a)** to make or give a summary of **(b)** to assess or describe: *I find it difficult to sum her up.*
• ***Word Family:*** other verb forms are **sums, summed, summing**

summary (*say* **sum**-a-ree) *noun*
a short statement of the important points or details of a speech or piece of writing
• ***Word Family:*** the plural is **summaries** □ **summarize** or **summarise** *verb* to make a summary of something

summer *noun*
the warmest season of the year, between spring and autumn
• ***Word Family:*** **summery** *adjective* like or suitable for summer **summertime** *noun*

summit *noun*
the highest point or top: *the summit of a hill*

summon *verb*
1 to send for someone officially or ask them to appear: *They summoned him to appear before a committee of politicians.* 2 **summon up** to call up or gather: *I summoned up courage to speak to him.*

summons *noun*
an order to go somewhere, especially to appear in court
• ***Word Family:*** the plural is **summonses**

sumo (*say* **soo**-moh) *noun*
a type of Japanese wrestling

sumptuous (*say* **sump**-chew-us) *adjective*
expensive or grand: *a sumptuous meal*

sun *noun*
1 the star around which the Earth and the other eight planets of the solar system revolve 2 the energy, especially heat and light, given out by the sun: *Go out and play in the sun.*

sunburn *noun*
reddening or blistering of the skin due to being burnt by the sun's rays
• ***Word Family:*** **sunburned** *adjective* **sunburnt** *adjective*

sundae (*say* **sun**-day) *noun*
a serving of ice-cream with fruit and sauce, often topped with chopped nuts and whipped cream

Sunday *noun*
the first day of the week, kept as a day of rest or worship by many Christians

sundial (*say* **sun**-dile) *noun*
an instrument with a flat base and upright rod, that shows the time by the position of the shadow made by the sun

sunflower *noun*
a tall, garden plant with large, yellow flowers, and whose seeds are pressed to make oil

sunglasses *plural noun*
spectacles with tinted lenses, worn to protect your eyes from the sun

sunlight *noun*
the light from the sun
• ***Word Family:*** **sunlit** *adjective*

sunny *adjective*
1 full of sunlight: *a sunny kitchen* 2 cheerful: *a sunny smile*
• ***Word Family:*** other forms are **sunnier, sunniest**

sunrise *noun*
the rising of the sun above the horizon in the morning, or the time at which this happens

sunset *noun*
the passing of the sun below the horizon in the evening, or the time at which this happens

sunshine *noun*
the direct light or brightness of the sun

sunspot *noun*
a dark patch on the surface of the sun, thought to affect things on Earth, such as stormy weather

sunstroke *noun*
an illness with headaches, faintness and high temperatures, caused by spending too long in the sunshine

suntan *noun*
brownness of the skin caused by the sun
•*Word Family:* **suntanned** *adjective*

super (*say* **soo**-pa) *adjective*
extremely pleasing or excellent

superb (*say* soo-**perb**) *adjective*
very good indeed: *superb writing / superb beauty*

superficial (*say* soo-pa-**fish**-ul) *adjective*
1 to do with the surface: *a superficial cut* 2 not deep or thorough: *a superficial understanding of black holes*
•*Word Family:* **superficially** *adverb* **superficiality** *noun*

superfluous (*say* soo-**per**-floo-us) *adjective*
more than you need: *a superfluous remark*

super highway *noun*
a global network of computers, telephones and televisions that carries large amounts of information, such as the Internet and cable TV, into your home

superimpose (*say* soo-per-im-**poze**) *verb*
to put something on top of something else: *to superimpose a map of France on the map of Britain to show their relative sizes*

superintendent (*say* soo-per-in-**tend**-unt) *verb*
1 a supervisor in charge of work, a building or a business 2 a police officer above the rank of inspector

superior (*say* soo-**peer**-ree-a) *adjective*
1 higher or more important: *your superior officer* 2 greater in amount: *a superior number of enemy forces* 3 better: *a superior brand of soap* 4 conceited or proud: *a superior smile*
superior *noun*
5 someone or something that is superior
•*Word Family:* **superiority** *noun*

superlative (*say* soo-**per**-la-tiv) *adjective*
1 of the very best kind: *superlative computer skills* 2 to do with the form of an adjective or adverb that expresses the greatest degree of comparison: *"Fluffiest" is the superlative of "fluffy" and "most readily" is the superlative of "readily".*
•*Word Family:* **superlative** *noun* **superlatively** *adverb*

supermarket *noun*
a large, self-service shop selling food, things for the home, and sometimes clothes

supernatural (*say* soo-pa-**natch**-a-rul) *adjective*
1 not belonging to the natural world or its laws: *Ghosts are supernatural beings.*
supernatural *noun*
2 supernatural beings or forces

superpower *noun*
an extremely powerful country with a lot of influence on world affairs

supersede (*say* soo-pa-**seed**) *verb*
to replace: *Our new uniform supersedes the old one.*
•*Word Origins:* from a Latin word meaning "sit above"

supersonic (*say* soo-pa-**son**-ik) *adjective*
moving or able to move faster than the speed of sound: *a supersonic jet*

superstar *noun*
a famous person such as a singer or actor

superstition (*say* soo-pa-**stish**-on) *noun*
a belief or practice based on faith in magic or chance: *Do you believe in the superstition that Friday the 13th is an unlucky day?*
•*Word Family:* **superstitious** *adjective* **superstitiously** *adverb*

supervise (*say* **soo**-pa-vize) *verb*
to direct or manage someone or something: *to supervise work or workers*
•*Word Family:* **supervisor** *noun* someone who supervises **supervision** *noun* **supervisory** *adjective*

supper *noun*
a late-night snack, or evening meal

supple *adjective*
easily bent or bending: *The gymnast had supple limbs.*
•*Word Family:* **suppleness** *noun*

supplement (*say* **sup**-li-munt) *noun*
1 something added to improve or complete something: *The dictionary had a supplement of special new words and their meanings.* 2 an extra part of a newspaper on a particular subject: *a sporting supplement*
supplement (*say* **sup**-li-ment) *verb*
3 to complete or add to something: *I supplement my pocket money by working in a shop.*
•*Word Family:* **supplementary** *adjective*

supply (*say* su-**ply**) *verb*
1 to provide something or make it available: *The chickens supply us with all the eggs we need.*
supply *noun*
2 an amount of what is provided: *We'll have a fresh supply of eggs tomorrow.* 3 **supplies** a store of materials or food: *army supplies*
•*Word Family:* other verb forms are **supplies, supplied, supplying** □ the plural of the noun is **supplies** □ **supplier** *noun*

support *verb*
1 to hold something up or add strength to it: *Tall columns support the roof. / Support your plans with action.* 2 to be loyal to or help: *to support a children's charity / to support United* 3 to look

a b c d e f g h i j k l m n o p q r s t u v w x y z

after someone by earning money for their food, house and so on: *She supports two children.*
support *noun*
4 the providing of support: *Can I rely on your support?* 5 someone or something that supports: *He's the main support of his family. / The supports of the bridge collapsed.*
•***Word Family:*** **supporter** *noun* **supportive** *adjective*

suppose (*say* su-**poze**) *verb*
1 to assume: *Let's suppose that his advice is sensible.* 2 to think, believe or guess: *I suppose that flying saucers from other planets exist.*
•***Word Family:*** **supposed** *adjective* believed to be: *supposed experts* **supposition** *noun* the act of supposing, or a guess based on this: *They said she did it, but it was only supposition.*

suppress *verb*
1 to end or abolish: *The army suppressed the rebellion.* 2 to prevent something from being seen, known, read and so on: *to suppress a smile / to suppress news of his assassination*
•***Word Family:*** **suppression** *noun* **suppressor** *noun*

supreme (*say* su-**preem**) *adjective*
1 with the highest rank or power: *the supreme commander / the supreme ruler* 2 greatest: *I have supreme confidence in you.*
•***Word Family:*** **supremacy** (*say* su-**prem**-a-see) *noun* supreme power or authority **supremely** *adverb*

sure (*say* shore) *adjective*
1 convinced, certain or confident: *to be sure of your facts / She is sure to be late.* 2 careful: *Be sure to lock the door.* 3 solid, tested or reliable: *sure ground / a sure remedy for headache* 4 never missing: *a sure aim*
sure *adverb*
5 certainly or surely: *You sure were lucky.*
•***Word Family:*** **surely** *adverb* almost without doubt: *It will surely rain tomorrow.*

surf *noun*
1 the waves, especially large ones, that break into foamy water on the shore
surf *verb*
2 to ride a surfboard 3 **surf the Net** to explore the Internet on a computer
•***Word Family:*** **surfer** *noun* **surfing** *noun*

surface (*say* **sir**-fis) *noun*
1 the outside or outer boundary of something: *a smooth surface / A cube has six surfaces.* 2 the top of a liquid: *The ship sank beneath the sea's surface.* 3 your outward appearance: *Beneath the surface he's a nice kid.*
surface *verb*
4 to rise to the surface: *The submarine surfaced.* 5 to give a surface to a road: *to surface a road with tar*

surfboard *noun*
a narrow board on which you balance to ride to shore on the crest of a wave

surge (*say* serj) *verb*
1 to rush or swell strongly like rolling waves: *The crowd surged forward.*
surge *noun*
2 a sudden rush or strong forward or upward movement: *a surge of anger / a surge of power*

surgeon (*say* **sir**-jun) *noun*
a doctor who performs operations

surgery (*say* **sir**-ja-ree) *noun*
1 the treating of diseases or injuries by a surgeon using cutting and other instruments to operate on your body 2 an operation done by a surgeon 3 the room or building in which a doctor or dentist treats patients
•***Word Family:*** the plural is **surgeries** □ **surgical** *adjective* **surgically** *adverb*

surly *adjective*
rude, bad-tempered or unfriendly
•***Word Family:*** other forms are **surlier, surliest**

surname *noun*
the name of your family: *My first name is Jody and my surname is Lee.*

surpass *verb*
to be better or greater than someone or something else: *His new book surpasses all his earlier ones.*

surplice (*say* **sir**-plis) *noun*
a loose, white, linen robe with wide sleeves, worn by clergy and the choir during religious services

surplus (*say* **sir**-plus) *noun*
1 something left over when you have used all that you need: *The good wheat harvest resulted in a surplus of grain.*
surplus *adjective*
2 left-over: *surplus wheat*

surprise (*say* sir-**prize**) *noun*
1 something sudden or unexpected: *What a pleasant surprise to see you again.* 2 the feeling of shock or wonder caused by this: *He almost fainted with surprise.*
surprise *verb*
3 to shock or startle someone: *Her unkind remark surprised me.* 4 to come upon someone suddenly and without warning: *I surprised him in the act of stealing fruit.*
•***Word Family:*** **surprising** *adjective* **surprisingly** *adverb*

surrender (*say* su-**ren**-da) *verb*
to give up or give in to someone: *The criminals refused to surrender themselves to the police. / Don't surrender to despair.*

surrogate (*say* **su**-ra-git) *noun*
a substitute or person standing in for another: *His aunt became a surrogate for his mother when she went overseas.*
• ***Word Family:*** **surrogacy** *noun*

surround *verb*
to enclose or go around something or someone completely: *The house is surrounded by trees. / We surrounded the escaped lion.*

surroundings *plural noun*
everything around a person, thing or place: *Where can I see lions in their natural surroundings?*

surveillance (*say* sir-**vay**-lance) *noun*
a close watch or guard: *Keep the prisoner under surveillance.*

survey (*say* sir-**vay**) *verb*
1 to look over something: *You can survey the whole town from this lookout.* 2 to ask people's opinions: *to survey passers-by* 3 to inspect, plot or measure buildings, land and so on: *to survey a plot of land*
survey (*say* **sir**-vay) *noun*
4 a record or report written after surveying: *a survey that shows what people think of the Olympics* 5 a look or inspection
• ***Word Family:*** the plural of the noun is **surveys** □ **surveyor** *noun* someone who surveys land

survive (*say* sir-**vive**) *verb*
to stay alive or carry on living, especially after something awful has happened: *Everyone survived the earthquake. / We managed to survive our father's death.*
• ***Word Family:*** **survivor** *noun* someone or something that survives **survival** *noun*

susceptible (*say* sa-**sep**-ti-bul) *adjective*
likely to be affected by something: *The cats are susceptible to the cold.*
• ***Word Family:*** **susceptibility** *noun*

suspect (*say* sus-**pekt**) *verb*
1 to think that something is likely or possible: *I suspect it will rain soon.* 2 to consider someone to be guilty without having proof: *I suspect her of lighting the fire.*
suspect (*say* **sus**-pekt) *noun*
3 someone who may be guilty: *The police have caught a suspect in the murder case.*
suspect (*say* **sus**-pekt) *adjective*
4 thought to have something wrong with it: *The suspect meat may have caused food poisoning.*

suspend *verb*
1 to attach or hang something from above: *The light bulb was suspended from the ceiling.* 2 to put something off or postpone it until later: *The bank will suspend payment for a month.* 3 to stop someone working or doing something because of bad behaviour: *The football player was suspended for three matches for fighting on the field.*

suspense *noun*
a feeling of being anxious or excited about something that is going to happen: *The film kept us in suspense about the killer's identity.*
• ***Word Family:*** **suspenseful** *adjective*

suspension (*say* sus-**pen**-shon) *noun*
1 suspending, or being suspended: *The suspension of our best player is a disaster. / He's under suspension from school.* 2 the springs, shock absorbers and so on, of a vehicle used to absorb jolting and protect it from damage 3 a liquid in which very small, solid bits are mixed but not dissolved: *Milk is a suspension.*

suspicion (*say* sus-**pish**-on) *noun*
1 a feeling that something is likely or possible: *I had a suspicion you'd be late.* 2 a belief or feeling that someone is guilty: *She was arrested on suspicion of the murder.* 3 doubt or mistrust: *to gaze at someone with suspicion* 4 a suggestion or slight taste: *a suspicion of garlic in the soup*
• ***Word Family:*** **suspicious** *adjective* **suspiciously** *adverb*

sustain *verb*
1 to support something or bear the weight of it: *Will this chair sustain my weight?* 2 to maintain or keep something up: *It's hard to sustain a conversation with her.* 3 to suffer an injury: *The victim sustained a broken arm.*

sustenance (*say* **sus**-ta-nence) *noun*
the things you need to live, such as food, clothes and money

sutra *noun*
a piece of Hindu holy writing

swab (*say* swob) *noun*
1 a small piece of cloth, sponge or cottonwool, used to clean parts of your body, apply a medicine or take samples of fluid to be analysed

swaddle (*say* **swod**-ul) *verb*
to wrap or bind a baby with long strips of cloth

swagger *verb*
to walk or strut proudly or smugly

swallow (1) (*say* **swol**-oh) *verb*
1 to take something into your stomach through your throat: *to swallow food* 2 to make something disappear: *The clouds swallowed the mountain completely. / Buying CDs swallows up*

all my money. 3 to accept, or believe: *You're not going to swallow that excuse, are you?*
swallow *noun*
4 the act of swallowing, or the amount swallowed at one time

swallow (2) (*say* **swol**-oh) *noun*
a long-winged, graceful, migrating bird that catches insects while flying

swami (*say* **swah**-mee) *noun*
a title for a Hindu religious teacher

swamp (*say* swomp) *noun*
1 an area of soft, wet ground
swamp *verb*
2 to flood or soak with water 3 to overwhelm: *The firm was swamped with job applications*.
•***Word Family:*** **swampy** *adjective* (**swampier, swampiest**)

swan (*say* swon) *noun*
a large, graceful water bird with a long, slender neck and white feathers

swap (*say* swop) *verb*
to exchange one thing for another: *to swap football cards*
•***Word Family:*** other forms are **swaps, swapped, swapping**

swarm *noun*
1 a large group of bees or other insects moving together 2 a large group of people or things moving together
swarm *verb*
3 to move in large numbers: *Crowds swarmed to the beach in the hot weather*. 4 **swarm with** to abound or be covered with: *The beach was swarming with sunbathers*.

swarthy (*say* **swor**-thee) *adjective*
having a dark complexion or skin colour
•***Word Family:*** other forms are **swarthier, swarthiest** □ **swarthiness** *noun*

swashbuckling (*say* **swosh**-buk-ling) *adjective*
daring, swaggering or showy

swastika (*say* **swos**-tik-a) *noun*
an ancient symbol or ornament in the shape of a cross with its arms extended and bent at right angles: *Adolf Hitler adopted the swastika as the emblem of the Nazi party*.

swat (*say* swot) *verb*
1 to hit or slap something with a sharp blow: *to swat flies*
swat *noun*
2 a sharp blow
•***Word Family:*** other verb forms are **swats, swatted, swatting** □ **swatter** *noun*

swathe (*rhymes with* bathe) *verb*
to wrap or bind someone or something in bandages or something like bandages: *The baby was swathed in blankets*.

sway *verb*
1 to swing or make something swing from side to side: *She swayed with tiredness. / Wind swayed the trees*. 2 to change someone's mind: *Her passionate speech swayed me*.
sway *noun*
3 a swaying movement 4 rule, control or influence: *He holds sway over his gang of friends*.

swear (*say* swair) *verb*
1 to promise or declare something solemnly: *He swore he'd be on time*. 2 to take an oath to tell the truth: *The witness swore on the Bible*. 3 to curse or use unpleasant or rude language
•***Word Family:*** other forms are **swears, swore, sworn, swearing** □ **swearer** *noun* **swearword** *noun*

sweat (*say* swet) *verb*
1 to give out a salty liquid through the pores of your skin 2 to work very hard: *I really sweated over that assignment*. 3 to worry or suffer: *to make someone sweat for three weeks before telling them they'd passed the exam*
sweat *noun*
4 the salty fluid given out when you sweat
•***Word Family:*** **sweaty** *adjective* (**sweatier, sweatiest**)

sweater (*say* **swet**-a) *noun*
a knitted jumper

swede *noun*
a round, yellow root vegetable

sweep *verb*
1 to clean or clear with a broom: *He swept the floor*. 2 to touch lightly: *Her dress swept the floor as she walked*. 3 to pass quickly: *His eyes swept over the page*. 4 to carry: *The floods swept away houses and trees*.
sweep *noun*
5 the act of sweeping: *Give the room a sweep*. 6 a long stroke or movement: *She cleared his desk with a sweep of her arm*. 7 an unbroken stretch: *We gazed at the long sweep of coastline*. 8 someone who cleans soot from chimneys
•***Word Family:*** other verb forms are **sweeps, swept, sweeping** □ **sweeping** *adjective* wide-ranging **sweeper** *noun*

sweet *adjective*
1 tasting pleasant and sugary: *I don't like my coffee too sweet*. 2 pleasant in any way: *sweet singing / a sweet child*
sweet *noun*
3 a piece of sweet food, such as a chocolate or toffee 4 a dessert
•***Word Family:*** **sweeten** *verb* to make sweet **sweetly** *adverb* **sweetness** *noun*

sweet corn *noun*
the small, yellow kernels or seeds of maize, which can be taken off the cob and eaten as a vegetable

sweetheart *noun*
a person that you love, especially a boyfriend or girlfriend

sweet pea *noun*
a climbing, garden plant with sweet-smelling, brightly coloured flowers

sweet potato *noun*
the tasty root of a plant, eaten as a vegetable
•*Word Family:* the plural is **sweet potatoes**

swell *verb*
1 to get bigger, stronger or louder: *The wood swelled after being soaked with rain. / The noise swelled until it was unbearable.* 2 to make something bulge out: *The wind swelled the sails.*
swell *noun*
3 an increase in size, force or strength: *There was a swell in the music.* 4 the regular movement of the surface of the sea
swell *adjective*
5 excellent or first-rate: *What a swell idea.*
•*Word Family:* other verb forms are **swells, swelled, swelled or swollen, swelling** □ **swelling** *noun* a swollen part on your body

swelter *verb*
to feel very hot: *to swelter during summer*
•*Word Family:* **sweltering** *adjective*

swerve *verb*
to turn aside suddenly or sharply: *The bike swerved to miss the old lady.*

swift *adjective*
fast or quick: *a swift train / Her swift fingers raced up and down the piano keys.*
•*Word Family:* **swiftly** *adverb* **swiftness** *noun*

swill *noun*
1 a rinse: *I gave the barrel a swill with water.* 2 a mixture of liquid and solid food, especially as a food for pigs
swill *verb*
3 to drink greedily or too much 4 to clean something by flooding it with water

swim *verb*
1 to move through water by moving arms, legs, fins, tails and so on: *Everyone should learn to swim. / He swam across the river.* 2 to cross a stretch of water by moving yourself through it: *to swim a river* 3 to seem to whirl: *The room swam before her eyes. / My head swims and I feel sick.* 4 to overflow: *His eyes swam with tears.*
swim *noun*
5 the act of swimming: *to go for a swim*
•*Word Family:* other verb forms are **swims, swam, swum, swimming** □ **swimmer** *noun* someone who swims **swimmingly** *adverb* easily or with great success: *The party went swimmingly.*

swimsuit *noun*
a piece of clothing you wear for swimming

swindle *verb*
to cheat someone out of money or property
•*Word Family:* **swindle** *noun* **swindler** *noun*

swine *noun*
1 a pig 2 a nasty, stupid or greedy person
•*Word Origins:* definition 2 is colloquial

swing *verb*
1 to move or make something move back and forth: *The pendulum swung slowly. / He swung his arms as he walked.* 2 to move or make something move in a circular or sweeping motion: *He swung his sword above his head. / The car swung round the corner.*
swing *noun*
3 a swinging movement: *a golfer's swing* 4 a hanging seat, on which children swing to and fro 5 a ride on a swing
•*Word Family:* other verb forms are **swings, swung, swinging**

swipe *noun*
1 a long, sweeping blow or stroke: *She took a swipe at the ball.*
swipe *verb*
2 to hit something with a sweeping blow 3 to steal 4 to slide a card that has a magnetic strip through the slot of a magnetic strip reader

swirl *verb*
to move or make something move in a twisting or whirling motion: *The leaves swirled around the foot of the tree.*

swish *verb*
1 to move or make something move through the air with a hissing or whistling sound: *The horse swished its tail.*
swish *adjective*
2 smart or fashionable: *a swish restaurant*

switch *noun*
1 a button for turning electricity on or off 2 a turning, shifting or changing: *a switch in their policy* 3 a flexible rod or cane, used for whipping
switch *verb*
4 to connect or disconnect something by a switch: *Switch off that fan!* 5 to shift or change something: *Let's switch the conversation to something else. / The train was switched to another track.* 6 to exchange: *Let's switch rooms.*
•*Word Family:* the plural of the noun is **switches**

switchboard *noun*
a panel which has switches for connecting telephone calls

swivel (*say* **swiv**-ul) *verb*
to turn round: *He swivelled round to look.*
• *Word Family:* other forms are **swivels, swivelled, swivelling**

swoon *verb*
to faint, usually from pain, shock or strong feelings

swoop *verb*
1 to sweep down through the air, usually from a great height: *The eagle swooped down on the rabbit.* 2 to take or seize something suddenly: *He swooped up his trophy and marched off.*
swoop *noun*
3 a swooping movement **4 at one fell swoop** all at once

swop *verb*
another spelling of **swap**
• *Word Family:* other forms are **swops, swopped, swopping**

sword (*say* sord) *noun*
a weapon with a long, sharp blade and a handle

swot *verb*
1 to study hard **2 swot up** to learn something for a test
swot *noun*
3 a person who works hard at school
• *Word Family:* other forms are **swots, swotted, swotting**

syllable (*say* **sil**-a-bul) *noun*
the small part of a word that contains a vowel sound and sometimes consonant sounds around the vowel: *The word "asleep" (say a-sleep) contains two syllables.*

syllabus (*say* **sil**-a-bus) *noun*
the set programme or outline of what is taught in a classroom
• *Word Family:* the plural is **syllabuses**

symbol (*say* **sim**-bul) *noun*
something that is used to suggest or represent something else: *A dove is a symbol of peace. / The symbol for addition is +.*
• *Word Family:* **symbolic** *adjective* **symbolize** or **symbolise** *verb* **symbolism** *noun*
• *Word Origins:* from a Greek word meaning "a token"

symmetry (*say* **sim**-a-tree) *noun*
an exact match or balance between the opposite halves of a figure, form, line or pattern, on either side of an axis or centre
• *Word Family:* **symmetrical** *adjective*

sympathy (*say* **sim**-pa-thee) *noun*
1 a feeling of being sorry for someone or sharing their feelings 2 sharing someone else's opinions or ideas: *We are in sympathy on many this issue.*
• *Word Family:* **sympathize** or **sympathise** *verb* to feel or express sympathy for someone **sympathetic** *adjective* **sympathetically**

symphony (*say* **sim**-fa-nee) *noun*
a long, musical composition for a complete orchestra, usually having four movements or large sections
• *Word Family:* the plural is **symphonies** □ **symphonic** *adjective* **symphony orchestra** *noun* an orchestra large enough to play a symphony
• *Word Origins:* from Greek words meaning "sounds together"

symptom (*say* **simp**-tum) *noun*
1 an obvious change in the way your body or mind is working that shows you have a disease: *Tell the doctor your symptoms.* 2 a sign that shows something exists: *The riots were the most obvious symptom that people were unhappy.*

synagogue (*say* **sin**-a-gog) *noun*
a building where Jewish people worship

synchronize or **synchronise** (*say* **sing**-kra-nize) *verb*
1 to occur or make something occur at the same time: *His arrival synchronized with my departure.* 2 to make watches or clocks agree in time: *They synchronized their watches before the attack.*
• *Word Family:* **synchronization** *noun*

syncopate (*say* **singk**-a-pate) *verb*
to place the stress on beats that are normally unstressed in order to change the rhythm of the music
• *Word Family:* **syncopation** *noun*

syndicate (*say* **sin**-di-kit) *noun*
a group of people or companies formed to carry out an expensive project, such as a newspaper organization that sells news or an article to several publications at once

synonym (*say* **sin**-a-nim) *noun*
a word with the same or almost the same meaning as another: *"Happy" is a synonym of "glad".*

synopsis (*say* se-**nop**-sis) *noun*
a summary, especially of the plot of a novel or play
• *Word Family:* the plural is **synopses** (*say* se-**nop**-seez)

syntax (*say* **sin**-taks) *noun*
the arrangement and relationships between words in phrases and sentences

synthesis (*say* **sin**-tha-sis) *noun*
the combination or blend of parts or elements

into a whole: *Our project was a synthesis of all our ideas and work.*

synthetic (*say* sin-**thet**-ik) *adjective*
artificially made: *synthetic rubber*
• ***Word Family:*** **synthetically** *adverb*

syphon *noun*
another spelling of **siphon**

syringe (*say* se-**rinj**) *noun*
1 a hollow tube with a plunger, fitted on to a hypodermic needle and used to inject fluids into, or take them out of, your body
syringe *verb*
2 to clean or inject using a syringe: *to have your ears syringed*
• ***Word Origins:*** from a Greek word meaning "a (musical) pipe"

syrup (*say* **si**-rup) *noun*
a thick, sweet liquid made by boiling sugar, water and often flavouring
• ***Word Family:*** **syrupy** *adjective*
• ***Word Origins:*** from an Arabic word meaning "a drink"

system (*say* **sis**-tum) *noun*
1 a group of things or parts forming a whole: *a railway system / your digestive system* 2 an organized way of running things: *a system of government* 3 an organized way of doing things: *There's no system in the way he works.*
• ***Word Family:*** **systematic** *adjective* arranged in or using a system **systematically** *adverb*

Tt

tabby *noun*
a cat with grey, brown or black stripes on its fur
• ***Word Family:*** the plural is **tabbies**

table *noun*
1 a piece of furniture which has a flat top and is supported by legs 2 a column or list of information or numbers arranged in order: *a book's table of contents / a multiplication table*

tablespoon *noun*
a large, oval spoon used to serve food or measure ingredients

tablet *noun*
1 a small, round pill 2 a block of soap 3 a slab of stone meant for writing on

table tennis *noun*
a game played indoors on a table, using small bats and a light ball

tabloid (*say* **tab**-loyd) *noun*
a newspaper with small pages, short, popular news stories and many pictures

taboo (*say* ta-**boo**) *adjective*
banned or forbidden: *Sex is a taboo topic in some homes. / In the Jewish religion, eating pork is taboo.*

tack *noun*
1 a short, sharp nail with a large, flat top 2 a long, loose stitch used to fasten seams before you sew them properly 3 a particular approach or way of doing things: *Humour didn't work so he tried a different tack.*
tack *verb*
4 to fasten or attach something with a tack
5 to sew loosely with long stitches 6 to sail a boat in a series of zigzags to take advantage of the wind

tackle *noun*
1 equipment, especially the rods, reels and so on used in fishing 2 blocks and ropes for moving heavy objects
tackle *verb*
3 to try to grab and pull someone down by force: *to tackle the escaping robber* 4 to try to deal with something: *to tackle a tricky problem*
5 to try to stop or take the ball from someone: *to tackle a player on the other team*

tacky *adjective*
1 sticky 2 cheap and not tasteful: *tacky Christmas decorations*
• ***Word Family:*** other forms are **tackier, tackiest**

tact *noun*
being able to deal with people without upsetting them
• ***Word Family:*** **tactful** *adjective* **tactfully** *adverb* **tactless** *adjective* **tactlessly** *adverb*

tactics (*say* **tak**-tiks) *plural noun*
a plan for achieving something, especially by using troops, ships and weapons in a battle
• ***Word Family:*** **tactical** *adjective* **tactically** *adverb* **tactician** *noun*

tadpole *noun*
a young frog or toad in an early stage of its development, having fins and a tail for swimming rather than legs, and not able to live on land

tag (1) *noun*
1 a strip of paper or metal attached to something as a label
tag *verb*
2 to attach a tag to something 3 to follow

someone closely, usually without being asked: *His little brother tagged after him everywhere.*
•***Word Family:*** other verb forms are **tags, tagged, tagging**

tag (2) *noun*
a children's game in which one person chases the other players

tagliatelle (*say* tag-lee-a-**tel**-ee) *noun*
a type of pasta cut into long, thin strips

tai chi (*say* **tie** chee) *noun*
a set of exercises developed from martial arts that teach you how to balance and to stay alert

tail *noun*
1 the end part of an animal that sticks out of the end of its body 2 something with the shape or position of a tail: *the tail of a comet* 3 the bottom part of anything: *a coat tail*
4 **tails** (a) a man's formal suit with a long-tailed coat (b) the side of a coin that does not have a picture of a head on it
tail *verb*
5 to follow and watch someone: *The detective tailed the robber to his den.*

tailback *noun*
a very slow queue of traffic: *a tailback because of roadworks*

tailor *noun*
1 someone who makes clothes, especially for men
tailor *verb*
2 to make, adapt or fit clothes for individual customers 3 to adjust, adapt or make something for a particular purpose: *We'll tailor the job to your experience.*

taint *verb*
1 to spoil slightly with something unpleasant: *My memory of the holiday was tainted by the nightmare plane journey.* 2 to infect or spoil something: *The chemicals tainted the water supply.*

take *verb*
1 to get something into your hands, possession or control: *Take this hammer. / The army took the city.* 2 to catch: *You took me by surprise.* 3 to become: *She took ill last week.* 4 to make use of: *We took shelter under a tree.* 5 to carry or let in: *The car takes six passengers.* 6 to feel: *to take pleasure in being nasty* 7 to lead or make someone go to another place: *The bus will take you to the city. / Who took you to the cinema?*
8 to perform or do something: *We took a walk. / Take careful aim. / I took revenge.* 9 to understand or interpret: *Don't take his words the wrong way.* 10 to require or need: *It takes courage to do what she did.* 11 to subtract: *If you take 3 from 6 you have 3.* 12 **take after** to look like your mother, father, grandparents and so on
13 **take in** (a) to cheat or swindle (b) to reduce or make smaller: *to take in a dress at the waist*
14 **take off** (a) to leave the ground (b) to imitate or mimic someone: *to take off your teacher* (c) to remove: *Take off your shoes.*
take *noun*
15 an amount taken: *The take in the shop was £5000.* 16 a scene filmed without stopping the camera: *They had to do five takes.*
•***Word Family:*** other verb forms are **takes, took, taken, taking**

takeaway *noun*
food that you buy and eat away from the shop
•***Word Family:*** also called **fast food**

takings *plural noun*
money received by a shop: *to count the week's takings*

talcum powder *noun*
a white, sweet-smelling powder you use on your skin to dry and soothe it

tale *noun*
1 a story: *a tale of adventure* 2 a deliberate lie or unkind account of what has happened: *Don't tell tales.*

talent *noun*
natural skill or ability: *a talent for dancing*
•***Word Family:*** **talented** *adjective* having talent

talk *verb*
1 to say things: *We talked about her trip.* 2 to gossip: *People will talk if they see us together.* 3 to reveal information: *The baddies made the spy talk.* 4 to discuss: *to talk business* 5 to persuade: *The salesman talked me into buying a new car.*
talk *noun*
6 a conversation: *There was a lot of talk about the film.* 7 a short speech: *to give a talk about Rome*
•***Word Family:*** **talkative** *adjective* liking to talk **talkatively** *adverb* **talkativeness** *noun*

tall *adjective*
1 higher than usual: *a tall man* 2 having a particular height: *He's 1.73 metres tall.* 3 **tall story** a story that is hard to believe
•***Word Family:*** **tallness** *noun*

tally *noun*
1 a score or account of something you count or owe: *Keep a tally of all the pocket money I owe you.*
tally *verb*
2 to reckon or count 3 to agree or correspond: *Do their answers tally?*
•***Word Family:*** other verb forms are **tallies, tallied, tallying**

Talmud *noun*
a book which contains rules for Jewish people to follow

talon (*say* **tal**-on) *noun*
a claw, especially of a bird of prey

tambourine (*say* tam-ba-**reen**) *noun*
a small, flat, one-sided drum with small metal plates set in the side, which you beat or shake to make a rattling sound

tame *adjective*
1 used to living with humans: *a tame rabbit*
2 dull: *This story has a tame ending.*
tame *verb*
3 to make an animal used to being with people: *to tame a wild pony*
•*Word Family:* **tamer** *noun* someone who tames animals **tamely** *adverb* **tameness** *noun*

tamper *verb*
to interfere or meddle with something

tampon *noun*
a cotton plug used by a woman who is having her period, to soak up the blood

tan *verb*
1 to make an animal hide into leather 2 to brown your skin in the sun or with a sunlamp
tan *noun*
3 a light, reddish-brown colour 4 a suntan
•*Word Family:* other verb forms are **tans, tanned, tanning**

tandem *noun*
1 a bicycle for two riders
tandem *adverb*
2 one behind the other: *to ride in tandem*

tandoori (*say* tan-**door**-ee) *noun*
a style of Indian food cooked in a round, clay oven: *tandoori chicken*

tang *noun*
a sharp or salty flavour or smell: *the tang of the ocean*
•*Word Family:* **tangy** *adjective* (**tangier, tangiest**)

tangent (*say* **tan**-junt) *noun*
1 a straight line touching a curve 2 a sudden change of course: *She went off at a tangent and talked about her aunt.*

tangerine (*say* tan-ja-**reen**) *noun*
1 a type of small orange 2 a reddish-orange colour

tangible (*say* **tan**-ja-bul) *adjective*
1 real or definite: *We need tangible evidence, not just ideas.* 2 able to be touched

tangle (*say* **tang**-gul) *verb*
1 to mix things up or twist them together in a confused mass: *The kitten tangled the wool.*
tangle *noun*
2 a confused mass or state: *tangles in your hair*

tango (*say* **tang**-goh) *noun*
a Spanish-American ballroom dance

tank *noun*
1 a large container for holding a liquid or gas
2 a heavily armoured fighting vehicle with tracks and a powerful gun

tankard *noun*
a large mug, usually for drinking beer, with a handle

tanker *noun*
a ship, aircraft or road vehicle designed to carry large quantities of oil or other liquids

tantalize *or* **tantalise** *verb*
to make someone want something by dangling it out of their reach
•*Word Family:* **tantalizing** *adjective* **tantalizingly** *adverb*

tantrum *noun*
a sudden, violent fit of bad temper

Taoist (*say* tow-ist) *noun*
a member of one of the main religions of China
•*Word Family:* **Taoism** *noun*

tap (1) *verb*
1 to strike something gently
tap *noun*
2 a gentle blow, or the sound this makes
•*Word Family:* other verb forms are **taps, tapped, tapping**

tap (2) *noun*
1 a device for controlling the flow of a liquid: *a bath tap*
tap *verb*
2 to use or draw upon something: *The reporter tapped all his usual news sources.* 3 to listen to someone secretly: *The enemy agents tapped my phone conversation.*
•*Word Family:* other verb forms are **taps, tapped, tapping**

tap-dancing *noun*
dancing in special shoes that make a clicking noise on the floor
•*Word Family:* **tap-dancer** *noun*

tape *noun*
1 a narrow strip of fabric or paper 2 a plastic ribbon coated with a magnetic substance and used to record sounds and video signals and to store computer information
tape *verb*
3 to tape-record or video-tape 4 to stick something with tape
•*Word Family:* **tape measure** *noun* a long strip or ribbon, marked with centimetres and millimetres and used for measuring

A B C D E F G H I J K L M N O P Q R S T U V W X Y Z

taper *verb*
1 to get gradually narrower at one end: *The blade tapered to a sharp point.*
taper *noun*
2 a very slender candle 3 a piece of string used for lighting lamps, candles and so on
•***Word Family:*** **tapering** *adjective*

tape recorder *noun*
a machine used to record and reproduce sound
•***Word Family:*** **tape recording** *noun* a magnetic tape on which sound has been recorded **tape-record** *verb*

tapestry (*say* **tap**-a-stree) *noun*
a fabric on which coloured threads are woven or stitched by hand to make a design, often used as a wall-hanging or to cover cushions or screens
•***Word Family:*** the plural is **tapestries**

tapeworm *noun*
a long, flat worm living as a parasite in the intestine of animals and humans

tapioca (*say* ta-pi-**oh**-ka) *noun*
floury grains made by drying cassava starch and used to thicken puddings and soups

taproot *noun*
the large main root of a plant from which smaller roots branch

tar *noun*
1 a black, sticky substance obtained from coal and wood, used to make roads
tar *verb*
2 to smear or cover something with tar
•***Word Family:*** other verb forms are **tars, tarred, tarring** □ **tarry** *adjective*

tarantula (*say* ta-**ran**-chew-la) *noun*
a large, hairy poisonous spider

target *noun*
1 something that you aim at, such as the object marked with circles or numbers in archery
target *verb*
2 to aim at: *The shop will target overseas visitors.*
•***Word Origins:*** from an Old French word meaning "little shield"

tariff *noun*
1 a government charge for bringing goods into a country 2 a list of prices or charges for a hotel room
•***Word Origins:*** from an Arabic word meaning "notification"

tarmac (*say* **tar**-mak) *noun*
1 a mixture of tar and very small stones, used for making road surfaces 2 an area of tarmac, such as an airport runway

tarnish *verb*
1 to become dull or discoloured: *The silver cutlery tarnished quickly in the salty air.* 2 to spoil something: *The crime tarnished the school's reputation.*

tarpaulin (*say* tar-**paw**-lin) *noun*
a large piece of canvas or waterproof covering

tart (1) *adjective*
sharp, sour or bitter: *the tart taste of lemon / Her tart reply brought tears to my eyes.*
•***Word Family:*** **tartly** *adverb* **tartness** *noun*

tart (2) *noun*
a sweet fruit or jam pie, especially one without a top crust

tartan *noun*
a woven, woollen cloth with checks of different colours and sizes, originally in the colours of the different Scottish Highland clans

task (*say* tahsk) *noun*
1 a piece of work, especially a difficult one
2 **take someone to task** to blame or scold someone

tassel *noun*
a knot of threads or cords with the ends left hanging, used for decoration

taste *noun*
1 the sense that helps you experience flavour
2 the flavour that something has: *a salty taste*
3 an understanding of what matches or is beautiful or excellent: *to have good taste in clothes*
4 a liking or preference: *She's developed quite a taste for tomato sauce.* 5 a sample: *These warm spring days are just a taste of our summer weather.*
taste *verb*
6 to experience, especially with your sense of taste: *Can you taste the carrot in this cake? / She tasted success when she made the team.* 7 to try or have some of something: *to taste the bread to see if you like it*
•***Word Family:*** **tasteful** *adjective* showing good taste or judgment **tasteless** *adjective* **tastelessly** *adverb* **tastelessness** *noun* **tasty** *adjective* **(tastier, tastiest)** having a pleasant or rich taste **tastiness** *noun*

tattered *adjective*
torn and ragged

tatters *plural noun*
torn pieces hanging loose, especially of clothes

tattoo (1) *noun*
1 a permanent picture or design put on your body by pricking your skin with a needle and marking it with dyes
tattoo *verb*
2 to mark your skin with a tattoo
•***Word Family:*** other verb forms are **tattoos, tattooed, tattooing** □ **tattooist** *noun*

tattoo (2) *noun*
1 a signal beaten on a drum 2 a public military display, usually outdoors

taunt (*say* tawnt) *verb*
1 to insult or mock someone hoping to make them angry
taunt *noun*
2 an insulting remark or action

taut *adjective*
tightly stretched
•***Word Family:*** **tautly** *adverb* **tautness** *noun*

tavern *noun*
a place where food and alcohol are served

tawny *adjective*
yellowish-brown in colour
•***Word Family:*** other forms are **tawnier, tawniest**

tax *noun*
1 the sum of money you pay each year to help the government provide such things as roads and hospitals
tax *verb*
2 to make someone pay a tax 3 to put a tax on something 4 to put great demands on someone: *The race taxed his strength.*
•***Word Family:*** the plural of the noun is **taxes** □ **taxable** *adjective* subject to tax **taxation** *noun*

taxi (*say* **tak**-see) *noun*
1 a car you hire for a journey, with a driver
taxi *verb*
2 to move slowly along the runway, before take-off or after landing
•***Word Family:*** the plural of the noun is **taxis** □ other verb forms are **taxis, taxied, taxiing**

tea *noun*
1 the dried leaves of a shrub grown in China, India and Ceylon 2 a drink made from these leaves brewed in water 3 a meal in the late afternoon or evening: *to have tea at five*
•***Word Origins:*** from the Chinese word *ch'a*

teach *verb*
to give lessons, or explain how to do something: *He teaches a class of 30 pupils. / She teaches ballet.*
•***Word Family:*** other forms are **teaches, taught, teaching** □ **teacher** *noun* someone who teaches **teaching** *noun*

teak *noun*
a hard wood that is used for furniture

team *noun*
1 an organized group of people doing something together: *a football team* 2 two or more animals harnessed together to do such work as pulling a plough: *a team of oxen*
team *verb*
3 **team up** to work together
•***Word Family:*** **team-mate** *noun* someone belonging to your team

tear (1) (*say* teer) *noun*
1 a drop of salty water that falls from your eye when you cry 2 **in tears** weeping
•***Word Family:*** **tearful** *adjective* **tearfully** *adverb*

tear (2) (*rhymes with* air) *verb*
1 to rip or force something apart: *He tore the page in two. / The branch tore her shirt.* 2 to pull something violently: *He tore the book from his brother's hands.* 3 to race or rush: *They tore out of the house.*
tear *noun*
4 a rip: *a tear in your shorts*
•***Word Family:*** other verb forms are **tears, tore, torn, tearing**

tease (*say* teez) *verb*
1 to mock, annoy or make fun of someone 2 to separate the strands of wool, hair and so on
tease *noun*
3 someone or something that teases, puzzles or annoys you
•***Word Family:*** **teasingly** *adverb*

teaspoon *noun*
a small, oval-shaped spoon used for stirring drinks or for measuring quantities

teat *noun*
1 the nipple-shaped mouthpiece of a baby's bottle 2 the nipple of an animal

tea towel *noun*
a piece of cloth for drying dishes

technical (*say* **tek**-ni-kul) *adjective*
1 to do with the machines and processes used in industry or practical sciences: *Building is a technical skill.* 2 using the correct words that people only know if they know a subject well: *That's getting a bit technical. / The technical term for German measles is rubella.*
•***Word Family:*** **technically** *adverb* **technician** *noun*

technique (*say* tek-**neek**) *noun*
1 a particular way of doing something: *The champion has an unusual swimming technique.*
2 practical skill in doing something: *The young pianist's technique is perfect.*

technology (*say* tek-**nol**-a-jee) *noun*
the study or use of science and scientific knowledge in industry
•***Word Family:*** **technological** *adjective* **technologist** *noun*

tedious (*say* **tee**-di-us) *adjective*
boring and going on for a long time
•***Word Family:*** **tediously** *adverb*

tee *noun*
1 a level area of ground on a golf course from

which the player first hits the ball for each hole 2 a wooden or plastic peg on which the ball is placed for the first stroke
tee *verb*
3 **tee off** to hit a golf ball from a tee
• ***Word Family:*** other verb forms are **tees, teed, teeing**

teem *verb*
1 to rain heavily 2 to be full: *The playground teemed with shouting children.*

teenager *noun*
someone who is over 12 but less than 20 years old
• ***Word Family:*** **teens** *plural noun* the years of being a teenager **teenage** *adjective*

teetotal *adjective*
never drinking alcohol
• ***Word Family:*** **teetotalism** *noun* **teetotaller** *noun*

telecast *noun*
a television broadcast

telecommunications (*say* tel-i-ko-mew-ni-**kay**-shonz) *noun*
the science or technology of sending signals or messages by telephone, radio or satellite

telegram *noun*
a message sent by telegraph

telegraph (*say* **tel**-i-grahf) *noun*
1 a system for sending messages from a transmitter to a receiver along electrical wires or with radio signals used especially before telephones became common
telegraph *verb*
2 to send a message by telegraph
• ***Word Family:*** **telegraphic** *adjective* **telegraphy** *noun*

telepathy (*say* ta-**lep**-a-thee) *noun*
the communication of thoughts between two people without them looking, speaking or writing to each other
• ***Word Family:*** **telepathic** *adjective* **telepathically** *adverb*

telephone (*say* **tel**-i-fone) *noun*
1 a device for talking to someone who is in a different place from you
telephone *verb*
2 to speak to someone on the telephone
• ***Word Family:*** **telephonist** *noun* someone who works at a telephone switchboard or a telephone exchange

telephoto lens *noun*
a camera lens that makes distant things look bigger so that you can take pictures of things that are far away

telescope (*say* **tel**-i-skope) *noun*
a tube-like instrument with powerful lenses, used for making distant objects appear nearer and larger
• ***Word Family:*** **telescopic** *adjective*

teletext *noun*
words that are broadcast and can be decoded and read as text on your television screen

television (*say* **tel**-i-vizh-on) *noun*
1 the use of cables or radio waves to send moving pictures to a receiving set for viewing 2 the viewing set you use to watch the pictures
• ***Word Family:*** **televise** *verb*

tell *verb*
1 to give information to someone: *Tell me your name. / She told me the news.* 2 to say something: *Don't tell lies.* 3 to know: *How can you tell for certain?* 4 to order: *I told you to be quiet.* 5 to have a bad effect: *The effort told on her health.* 6 **tell apart** to tell which of two similar things or people is which: *Can you tell the twins apart?* 7 **tell off** to scold severely 8 **tell on** to let someone else know about something someone has done wrong: *I'm going to tell on you.*
• ***Word Family:*** other forms are **tells, told, telling**

teller *noun*
someone who receives or pays out money at a bank

telling *adjective*
effective and showing you more about something than you would expect: *a telling comment*

telltale *noun*
1 someone who tells secrets or informs on others
telltale *adjective*
2 giving away something that is supposed to be secret: *A telltale sneeze let us know that someone was hiding in the cupboard.*

temper *noun*
1 the particular state of mind you are in: *He's in a good temper.* 2 an angry mood: *She's always in a temper.*
temper *verb*
3 to make something less severe or strong: *to temper your anger* 4 to heat and then cool steel quickly to make it hard enough

temperament (*say* **tem**-pra-munt) *noun*
your usual nature or personality: *He had a nervous temperament.*
• ***Word Family:*** **temperamental** *adjective* moody and easily upset or made angry **temperamentally** *adverb*

temperate (*say* **tem**-pa-rut) *adjective*
moderate and not getting either extremely hot or extremely cold: *a temperate climate*

temperature (*say* **tem**-pra-cher) *noun*
1 a measure of how hot or cold someone or something is 2 an unusually high body temperature: *She's in bed with a temperature.*

tempest *noun*
a violent storm
• ***Word Family:*** **tempestuous** *adjective* passionate and dramatic **tempestuously** *adverb*

template (*say* **tem**-plet) *noun*
1 a thin plate of card or metal, used as a guide or pattern when doing such things as patchwork or mechanical work 2 a pattern or form used in a computer software program to help you find and simplify a task

temple (1) *noun*
a large building used for worship

temple (2) *noun*
the part on each side of your forehead, just next to your eyes

tempo *noun*
speed: *Play the music at a brisk tempo.*
• ***Word Family:*** the plural is **tempos** or **tempi**
• ***Word Origins:*** from a Latin word meaning "time"

temporary (*say* **temp**-a-ra-ree) *adjective*
lasting for a short time only: *a temporary job*
• ***Word Family:*** **temporarily** *adverb*

tempt *verb*
to try to persuade or attract someone, especially to do something that they ought not to do
• ***Word Family:*** **temptation** *noun*
• ***Word Origins:*** from a Latin word meaning "to test by probing"

ten *noun*
the number 10
• ***Word Family:*** **ten** *adjective* **tenth** *noun* **tenth** *adjective*

tenacious (*say* te-**nay**-shus) *adjective*
persistent and determined
• ***Word Family:*** **tenaciously** *adverb* **tenacity** *noun*

tenant (*say* **ten**-unt) *noun*
someone who rents a house or flat from the owner
• ***Word Family:*** **tenancy** *noun*

tend *verb*
to happen usually: *It tends to get quite hot in the early afternoon.*

tendency *adjective*
a likelihood that something will keep happening: *She has a tendency to get the giggles.*

tender (1) *adjective*
1 gentle or affectionate: *a tender touch / a tender smile* 2 painful and sensitive: *The injury is still quite tender.* 3 not hard or tough: *tender meat*
• ***Word Family:*** **tenderly** *adverb* **tenderness** *noun*

tender (2) *verb*
to offer something formally: *to tender your resignation*

tendon *noun*
a thick cord of body tissue joining a muscle to a bone

tendril *noun*
a small, curling stem that a climbing plant curls around to hold itself up

tenement (*say* **ten**-a-munt) *noun*
a large house or building divided into many flats

tennis *noun*
a ball game for two or four people played on a court divided by a central net over which they hit the ball with racquets
• ***Word Origins:*** from an Old French word meaning "receive!"

tenor *noun*
1 the range of musical notes sung by a man with a high voice: *to sing tenor* 2 a singer or instrument that has this range
• ***Word Family:*** **tenor** *adjective: a tenor saxophone*

tense (1) *adjective*
1 tightly stretched: *tense muscles* 2 feeling worried, nervous and unable to relax: *She was tense for days before the concert.*
tense *verb*
3 to make something become stiff or tense
• ***Word Family:*** **tensely** *adverb* **tenseness** *noun* **tension** *noun*

tense (2) *noun*
the form of a verb that shows whether the action the verb describes takes place in the past, present or future

tent *noun*
a shelter, usually made of waterproof canvas or plastic, which is held up by poles and has the sides pinned to the ground with ropes and pegs

tentacle (*say* **ten**-ti-kul) *noun*
one of the long, thin, bendy parts attached to an animal such as an octopus, which are used for grasping and feeling

tentative (*say* **ten**-ta-tiv) *adjective*
acting or speaking cautiously because you are uncertain or afraid: *The baby took a tentative step.*
• ***Word Family:*** **tentatively** *adverb*

tepee (*say* **tee**-pee) *noun*
a tent usually made of animal skins on a cone-shaped frame, once used by Native Americans

A B C D E F G H I J K L M N O P Q R S T U V W X Y Z

tepid *adjective*
slightly warm: *tepid milk / a tepid greeting*

term *noun*
1 a fixed period of time: *a term of imprisonment / The school year is divided into three or four terms.* 2 the word for something: *The technical terms are too difficult to learn.* 3 **terms (a)** conditions that are agreed to: *The contract was signed when the author and the publisher finally agreed on its terms.* **(b)** relations: *She's on excellent terms with her neighbours.*

terminal *noun*
1 a building where passengers and goods begin and end a journey: *an air terminal* 2 either of the points at which electric current enters or leaves an electrical device 3 a machine with a screen and a keyboard linked to a computer system and used for entering or giving information
terminal *adjective*
4 ending in death: *The patient had a terminal disease.*

terminate *verb*
to come to an end or bring something to an end: *The tram terminates here.*
• ***Word Family:*** **termination** *noun*

terminology (*say* ter-mi-**nol**-a-jee) *noun*
the special words used in a particular field: *computer terminology*

terminus *noun*
the last stop or station at the end of a railway line or bus route
• ***Word Family:*** plural is **termini** or **terminuses**

termite *noun*
a white, tropical insect that causes damage to wooden buildings or furniture

terrace (*say* **ter**-us) *noun*
1 a row of joined houses or a house in a row like this 2 an open area outside a house or restaurant where you can sit: *We sat on the terrace and had a drink.* 3 a narrow strip of land cut into a hillside

terracotta (*say* ter-a-**kot**-a) *noun*
1 a type of reddish-brown, unglazed pottery 2 a strong, reddish-brown colour.
• ***Word Origins:*** from an Italian word meaning "baked earth"

terrain (*say* te-**rane**) *noun*
the typical features of an area of land: *rocky terrain*

terrestrial *adjective*
to do with or living on the Earth

terrible *adjective*
1 causing great fear, shock, distress or discomfort: *He died in terrible agony.* 2 very bad: *My old shoes are in a terrible state.*
• ***Word Family:*** **terribly** *adverb*

terrier *noun*
a type of small dog originally used in hunting to chase an animal into its hole or burrow

terrific (*say* te-**rif**-ik) *adjective*
1 very great: *She drove at a terrific speed.* 2 very good: *The book was really terrific.*
• ***Word Family:*** **terrifically** *adverb*

terrify (*say* **ter**-i-fie) *verb*
to make someone extremely afraid: *The sound of thunder terrified him.*
• ***Word Family:*** other forms are **terrifies, terrified, terrifying**

territory (*say* **te**-ri-tree) *noun*
land under the control of a particular government, ruler or army: *We were in enemy territory.*
• ***Word Family:*** the plural is **territories** □ **territorial** *adjective*

terror *noun*
fear so great that it almost overpowers you: *The trapped animal bristled with terror.*

terrorism (*say* **te**-ra-riz-um) *noun*
the use of violent acts, such as setting off bombs, to put pressure on a government so that it will do what you want
• ***Word Family:*** **terrorist** *noun* someone who uses terrorism

terrorize or **terrorise** (*say* **te**-ra-rize) *verb*
to deliberately make someone feel terrified

terse *adjective*
short and sticking to the point: *a terse answer*
• ***Word Family:*** **tersely** *adverb* **terseness** *noun*

test *noun*
1 a trial use of something or check on something to find out if it is working properly: *a blood test* 2 a set of questions to find out something such as how much you know about a subject
test *verb*
3 to give a test to someone or something

Testament *noun*
either of the collections of books, the Old Testament and the New Testament, which form the Bible

testicle (*say* **test**-i-kul) *noun*
either of the two rounded male sex organs in the scrotum that produce sperm

testify (*say* **test**-i-fie) *verb*
1 to give a statement in a court of law that you swear is true: *The witness testified that she saw the*

killing. 2 to be a sign that shows something: *The drooping flowers testify to a severe drought*.
•*Word Family:* other forms are **testifies, testified, testifying**

testimony (*say* **test**-i-mo-nee) *noun*
a statement given in a court of law by a witness who swears that what they say is true
•*Word Family:* the plural is **testimonies** □ **testimonial** *noun* an expression of appreciation

test tube *noun*
a long, thin, glass tube with a rounded bottom used as a container in scientific experiments

tetanus (*say* **tet**-nus) *noun*
an infectious, sometimes fatal, disease that makes your muscles stiff and paralysed, especially your jaw muscles

tether *noun*
a rope or chain for tying up an animal
•*Word Family:* **tether** *verb*: *He tethered the dog to the railings*.

text *noun*
words, for example the words in a book, speech or computer file
•*Word Family:* **textual** *adjective*

textbook *noun*
a book that gives the information you need in order to study a particular subject: *a history textbook*

textile *noun*
woven cloth or fabric used to make such things as clothes or curtains

texture (*say* **teks**-cher) *noun*
the way something feels, for example whether it is rough or smooth

thank *verb*
1 to say how grateful you are to someone
thank *noun*
2 **thanks** words expressing how grateful you are
•*Word Family:* **thankful** *adjective* **thankless** *adjective*

that *pronoun*
1 *used to refer to something or someone pointed out*: *That is so rude*. / *That is my sister*. 2 which or who: *This is the CD that I wanted*.
that *conjunction*
3 *used to introduce a noun clause*: *I thought that I was late*.
that *adjective*
5 *used to show someone or something pointed out*: *That man saw the accident*.

thatch *noun*
1 a roof covering made from straw or reeds
thatch *verb*
2 to put thatch on a roof

thaw *verb*
1 to melt: *The ice thawed*.
thaw *noun*
2 a period during which ice and snow melt

theatre *noun*
1 a building where plays, ballet or opera are performed on a stage 2 a room in a hospital where surgeons perform operations
•*Word Family:* **theatrical** *adjective*
•*Word Origins:* from a Greek word meaning "seeing place"

theft *noun*
the crime of stealing

their *adjective*
belonging to them: *It is their cake*.
•*Word Family:* this is a possessive form of **they** □ the singular is **his, her, its** □ **theirs** *pronoun*

them *pronoun*
those ones: *We hit them*. / *Give the cake to them*.
•*Word Family:* this is a form of **they** used after the verb □ the singular is **him, her, it**

theme (*say* theem) *noun*
the central subject of an essay, book, film, idea, piece of music and so on
•*Word Family:* **thematic** *adjective*

theme park *noun*
an outdoor place with rides, games and other activities which are all linked to one idea

theology (*say* thee-**ol**-a-jee) *noun*
1 the study of God and religion 2 the set of beliefs held by a particular religion
•*Word Family:* the plural is **theologies** □ **theologian** *noun* someone who knows about theology **theological** *adjective* **theologically** *adverb*

theorem (*say* **theer**-rum) *noun*
a statement in maths that you can prove

theory (*say* **theer**-ree) *noun*
1 an idea based on reasoning and observation that is used to explain something: *the theory of evolution* 2 the part of a subject that deals with the basic principles and ideas behind it: *We have to learn the theory as well as doing practical experiments*. 3 an idea about something which has not been proved: *I've got a theory about why you are always late*.
•*Word Family:* the plural is **theories** □ **theoretical** *adjective* **theoretically** *adverb*
•*Word Origins:* from a Greek word meaning "a spectator"

therapy (*say* **the**-ra-pee) *noun*
the treatment of illness, often without using drugs: *speech therapy*
•*Word Family:* the plural is **therapies** □

A B C D E F G H I J K L M N O P Q R S T U V W X Y Z

therapist *noun* someone trained to treat disease
therapeutic *adjective*
•***Word Origins:*** from a Greek word meaning "healing"

there *adverb*
1 in or at that place: *The book is there, where I left it.* 2 to, into or towards that place: *Let's go there now.*

thermal *adjective*
to do with heat or caused by heat: *thermal energy*

thermometer (*say* ther-**mom**-i-ta) *noun*
an instrument used to measure temperature

thermos flask *noun*
a container with double walls of silvered glass or stainless steel with a vacuum between them used to keep hot drinks or food hot and cold drinks or food cold
•***Word Origins:*** this word is a trademark

thermostat *noun*
a device used to control temperature: *the thermostat for a microwave oven*

thesaurus (*say* tha-**saw**-rus) *noun*
a book of words and phrases grouped into sets with similar meanings
•***Word Family:*** the plural is **thesauruses**
•***Word Origins:*** from a Greek word meaning "treasure"

they (*rhymes with* hay) *pronoun*
a word used to indicate people or things, used before a verb, as in They ate the cake.
•***Word Family:*** the singular is **he, she**, or **it**

thick *adjective*
1 measuring a lot from one surface or side to the other: *the thick wall of a castle* 2 measuring that particular amount: *a wall one metre thick*
3 dense or closely packed: *We had to crawl through the thick undergrowth.* 4 filling a place and hard to see through: *thick fog / The room was thick with smoke.* 5 not very runny: *We spilt the thick, sticky syrup all over the floor.*
thick *noun*
6 the most active or intense part: *I was caught in the thick of the crowd.*
•***Word Family:*** **thicken** *verb* **thickly** *adverb* **thickness** *noun*

thief (*say* theef) *noun*
someone who steals something, especially without using force
•***Word Family:*** the plural is **thieves** □ **thieve** (*say* theev) *verb* to steal

thigh *noun*
the upper part of your leg between your knee and your hip

thimble *noun*
a small, metal or plastic cap used to protect the end of your finger when sewing.

thin *adjective*
1 measuring very little from one surface or side to the other: *The thin ice cracked under her weight.* 2 without any extra fat on your body: *thin legs / a thin child* 3 scattered or not closely packed: *The audience was quite thin. / His hair is getting very thin.* 4 very runny or watery
5 weak: *a thin excuse*
thin *verb*
6 to make something thinner or to become thinner: *You can thin the soup by adding water.*
•***Word Family:*** other adjective forms are **thinner, thinnest** □ other verb forms are **thins, thinned, thinning** □ **thinly** *adverb* **thinness** *noun*

thing *noun*
1 a real object that is not alive or conscious: *A chair is a thing, a cat is not.* 2 something that cannot be described or named exactly 3 an aspect or area: *Many things about the affair were not thought of.*

think *verb*
1 to form ideas or judgments with your mind: *I thought about the holiday. / You have to think what to do next.* 2 to bring something into your mind: *I can't think of his name.* 3 to believe: *He thought you were joking.* 4 to expect: *I never thought to find you here.* 5 to imagine: *Think how good it would be to go swimming.*
•***Word Family:*** other forms are **thinks, thought, thinking** □ **thinker** *noun*

thirst *noun*
1 dryness of your mouth and throat that makes you feel you need a drink 2 a strong desire for something: *A thirst for adventure.*
•***Word Family:*** **thirsty** *adjective* (**thirstier, thirstiest**) **thirstily** *adverb* **thirstiness** *noun*

thirteen *noun*
the number 13
•***Word Family:*** **thirteen** *adjective* **thirteenth** *adjective* **thirteenth** *noun*

thirty *noun*
the number 30
•***Word Family:*** the plural is **thirties** □ **thirty** *adjective* **thirtieth** *adjective* **thirtieth** *noun*

this *pronoun*
1 the person, place or thing present, nearby or just mentioned: *Was this the boy you wanted to see?*
this *adjective*
2 having to do with the one here: *This chair is nicer than that one over there.*
•***Word Family:*** plural is **these**

thistle (*say* **this**-ul) *noun*
a wild plant with prickly leaves and fluffy purple or white flowers

thong *noun*
a narrow strip of leather used for fastening things

thorax (*say* **thor**-aks) *noun*
the part of an insect between its head and abdomen
•***Word Family:*** the plural is **thoraces** or **thoraxes**
•***Word Origins:*** from a Greek word meaning "chest" or "breastplate"

thorn *noun*
a small, sharp-pointed prickle on a plant's stem
•***Word Family:*** **thorny** *adjective* (**thornier, thorniest**)

thorough (*say* **thu**-ra) *adjective*
complete and leaving no part untouched: *a thorough search / Give the back of your ears a thorough scrubbing.*
•***Word Family:*** **thoroughly** *adverb* **thoroughness** *noun*

thoroughbred *noun*
a pure breed of horse used for racing

thoroughfare *noun*
a main road through a town or village

though (*rhymes with* no) *conjunction*
1 in spite of the fact that: *I disagree, though I see your point.* 2 if: *Act as though you didn't hear.*

thought (*say* thawt) *noun*
1 the forming of ideas in your mind: *She was deep in thought.* 2 one of the ideas you form: *a clever thought* 3 care or concern: *to do something without thought for the consequences* 4 an intention: *I had no thought of going.*
•***Word Family:*** **thoughtful** *adjective* **thoughtfully** *adverb*

thoughtless (*say* **thawt**-less) *adjective*
acting carelessly without thinking about the effect on other people

thousand *noun*
the number 1000
•***Word Family:*** **thousand** *adjective* **thousandth** *adjective* **thousandth** *noun*

thrash *verb*
1 to beat someone soundly, especially as a punishment 2 to defeat an opposing team easily: *We thrashed them by six goals.*

thread (*say* thred) *noun*
1 a long, thin piece of cotton, wool or silk used for sewing or weaving 2 a thin strand: *a thread of colour* 3 a connecting link: *I lost the thread of the story.* 4 a spiral ridge cut around the length of a bolt or screw
thread *verb*
5 to pass a thread through something: *to thread a needle* 6 to move in a twisting or winding way: *They had to thread their way through the crowd.*

threat (*rhymes with* met) *noun*
1 a warning that someone will hurt or punish you if you don't do what they want: *Frightened by their threats, he gave the thugs the money.* 2 a warning or sign: *a threat of rain*
•***Word Family:*** **threaten** *verb*

three-dimensional *adjective*
being or appearing solid rather than flat: *a three-dimensional sculpture*

thresh *verb*
to separate the grain from the rest of a plant such as corn or wheat by beating it
•***Word Family:*** other forms are **threshes, threshed threshing**

thrift *noun*
careful use of money and supplies
•***Word Family:*** **thrifty** *adjective* (**thriftier, thriftiest**) □ **thriftily** *adverb* **thriftiness** *noun*

thrill *noun*
1 a sudden feeling of great excitement: *It gave him a thrill to ride the horse.* 2 an experience causing this feeling: *It's a thrill to meet you.*
thrill *verb*
3 to feel a strong feeling of excitement and pleasure or to make someone feel this: *Winning the race thrilled me.*
•***Word Family:*** **thrilling** *adjective*

thriller *noun*
a book, play or film dealing with exciting or mysterious events, usually involving crime, war or spying

thrive *verb*
1 to grow strong and healthy: *The garden cannot thrive in this drought.* 2 to enjoy something and succeed in it: *to thrive in business / The kittens thrived on the love and attention.*
•***Word Family:*** other forms are **thrives, thrived** or **throve, thrived** or **thriven, thriving**

throat *noun*
1 the passage stretching from your mouth to your voicebox and the start of the tube that goes down into your stomach 2 the front part of your neck, under your chin

throb *verb*
1 to beat with a strong rhythm
throb *noun*
2 a strong beat or rhythm: *the throb of an engine*
•***Word Family:*** other verb forms are **throbs, throbbed, throbbing**

throne *noun*
1 a raised, ornamental chair used by kings, queens or bishops on important occasions 2 the position of a king or queen: *the heir to the throne*
• ***Word Origins:*** from a Greek word meaning "a high seat"

throng *noun*
1 a crowd
throng *verb*
2 to go to a place in very large numbers: *Thousands of people thronged the streets.*

throttle *verb*
1 to choke or strangle someone
throttle *noun*
2 the device that controls the amount of petrol flowing into an engine

through (*say* throo) *preposition*
1 in one side and out the other: *He climbed through the hole in the hedge. / The road goes through the jungle.* 2 by means of something: *She passed her exams mainly through hard work.*

throw *verb*
1 to make something move from your hand through the air: *He was throwing stones into the pond.* 2 to start behaving in a particular way: *She threw a tantrum.* 3 to arrange: *to throw a party* 4 **throw up** to vomit
• ***Word Family:*** other verb forms are **throws, threw, thrown, throwing**

thrush *noun*
a brown bird that sings sweetly
• ***Word Family:*** the plural is **thrushes**

thrust *verb*
to push quickly and hard: *She thrust the bag into my hands and started to run. / They thrust their way through the crowd.*
• ***Word Family:*** other forms are **thrusts, thrust, thrusting**

thud *noun*
1 a heavy, bumping sound: *There was a thud as the book fell.*
thud *verb*
2 to hit something or fall somewhere with a thud
• ***Word Family:*** other verb forms are **thuds, thudded, thudding**

thug *noun*
a violent man
• ***Word Origins:*** from a Hindi word meaning "robber" or "swindler"

thumb (*say* thum) *noun*
1 the short, thick, inner part of your hand that is set apart from your four other fingers and used for grasping
thumb *verb*
2 to turn pages over quickly: *I thumbed through the book to see what it was like.* 3 to hold up your thumb to show you want to hitchhike a ride: *He thumbed a ride home.*

thump *verb*
1 to beat heavily, especially with a thick, dull sound: *Her heart thumps with fright. / to thump someone on the back*
thump *noun*
3 the sound of a heavy blow

thunder *noun*
1 the loud, booming noise produced when the heat from lightning causes the air to expand suddenly 2 a loud noise: *a thunder of applause*
thunder *verb*
3 to speak or do something very loudly or violently: *She thundered on the door with her fists.*
• ***Word Family:*** **thunderous** *adjective* **thunderously** *adverb* **thundery** *adjective*

thunderbolt *noun*
1 a flash of lightning and thunder 2 an unexpected disaster or unpleasant surprise: *The news came as a thunderbolt.*

Thursday *noun*
the fifth day of the week
• ***Word Origins:*** named after *Thor*, the ancient Scandinavian god of thunder

thyme (*say* time) *noun*
a low-growing plant with sweet-smelling leaves used as a herb in cooking

tick (1) *noun*
1 the clicking sound made by a mechanical clock 2 a small written mark (✓) to show that something is correct or noted 3 a moment: *Wait here, I'll only be a tick.*
tick *verb*
4 to make a ticking sound: *The old clock ticked away quietly.* 5 to mark something as correct with a tick 6 **tick off** to scold
• ***Word Family:*** definitions 3 and 6 are colloquial

tick (2) *noun*
a small, blood-sucking creature that attaches itself to humans and animals and can cause disease

ticket *noun*
1 a small piece of cardboard or paper showing that you have paid for something: *a train ticket / a theatre ticket* 2 a label showing how much something costs
• ***Word Family:*** **ticket** *verb*

tickle *verb*
to touch someone lightly, usually making them laugh: *to tickle the sensitive parts of your skin*

•**Word Family: ticklish** *adjective* sensitive: *She is ticklish under her arms.*

tidal wave *noun*
a huge, ocean wave produced by an earthquake at sea

tide *noun*
1 the rise and fall of the level of the sea, caused twice a day by the pull of the sun and moon
tide *verb*
2 **tide over** to help someone during a difficult time: *Can you lend me some money to tide me over until next week?*
•**Word Family: tidal** *adjective*

tidings *plural noun*
news or information: *glad tidings of comfort and joy*

tidy *adjective*
1 neat and with everything in its right place: *a tidy child / a tidy drawer*
tidy *verb*
2 to make a place neat by putting everything away in its right place
•**Word Family:** other adjective forms are **tidier, tidiest** □ other verb forms are **tidies, tidied, tidying** □ **tidily** *adverb* **tidiness** *noun*

tie *verb*
1 to fasten things using string or rope: *He tied the prisoner's hands. / Tie this label to his coat.*
2 to make a knot or bow: *Please tie my shoelaces for me.* 3 to score equally in a contest: *The swimmers tied for second place.*
tie *noun*
4 a close connection: *the ties of friendship* 5 a narrow piece of cloth worn around the neck under a collar and knotted at the front
•**Word Family:** other verb forms are **ties, tied, tying**

tier (*rhymes with* fear) *noun*
a row or level which is one of a series rising one above the other, like the seats in a theatre or the parts of a wedding cake

tiger *noun*
a large, meat-eating, Asian mammal of the cat family that has a tawny coat with black stripes

tight *adjective*
1 fitting closely or too closely: *These shoes are a bit tight.* 2 stingy: *She's tight with her money.*
3 in short supply: *Money is tight this month.*
4 difficult or demanding: *to be in a tight spot / to have a tight schedule* 5 drunk
•**Word Family: tighten** *verb* to make something tight or to become tight **tightly** *adverb* **tightness** *noun*

tightrope *noun*
a rope or wire stretched high above the ground on which an acrobat walks or performs tricks

tights *plural noun*
stockings stretching from your waist to your feet

tile *noun*
1 a flat piece of baked clay used to cover roofs, floors or walls
tile *verb*
2 to stick tiles on a roof, floor or wall

till (1) *preposition* or *conjunction*
until

till (2) *verb*
to get the ground ready for planting crops: *to till the soil*

till (3) *noun*
1 a drawer in a shop's cash register where the money is kept 2 the place in a shop or restaurant with a cash register where you pay: *There were queues at all the tills.*

tiller *noun*
the handle attached to a ship's rudder that is used for steering

tilt *verb*
1 to slope or lean or to make something slope or lean: *If you tilt the table, the plates will fall off.*
tilt *noun*
2 the movement made when something tilts
3 a tilting position

timber *noun*
wood that has been cut and made ready for building

timbre (*say* **tam**-ba) *noun*
the quality of sound made by a musical instrument or a voice: *The double bass and the oboe have different timbres.*

time *noun*
1 the passing of seconds, minutes, hours, days, weeks, months and years in a continuous progression 2 a definite moment or period: *The time is 12 midday. / in the time of the ancient Greeks* 3 an experience: *Did you have a good time?* 4 an occasion when something happens: *How many times do I have to tell you?* 5 (a) the number of beats in a bar in a piece of music: *three four time* (b) the length of a musical note
6 **on time** at the time something is supposed to happen: *The train arrived on time.* 7 **times** multiplied by: *5 times 5 equals 25*
time *verb*
8 to measure the time or speed of something: *We timed the race with a stopwatch.* 9 to arrange to do something at a particular time: *We timed our holidays to coincide with the good weather.*
•**Word Family: timeless** *adjective* lasting for ever

time signature *noun*
the sign with two numbers at the beginning of a

piece of music that shows the type and number of notes to be played in each bar

timetable *noun*
a list showing the times that things are going to happen: *a train timetable*

timid *adjective*
easily frightened or made nervous: *a timid kitten*
• ***Word Family:*** **timidity** *noun* **timidly** *adverb*

timing *noun*
knowing the right moment to do something: *The actor's timing was wrong and he messed up the whole scene.*

timorous (*say* **tim**-a-rus) *adjective*
timid or full of fear
• ***Word Family:*** **timorously** *adverb*

timpani (*say* **tim**-pa-nee) *plural noun*
a set of kettledrums
• ***Word Family:*** **timpanist** *noun* someone who plays the timpani

tin *noun*
1 a soft, silvery-white metal used especially to coat other metals 2 a metal container: *a tin of soup / a baking tin*
tin *verb*
3 to pack food in tins: *to tin tomatoes*
tin *adjective*
4 made of tin
• ***Word Family:*** other verb forms are **tins, tinned, tinning**

tinder *noun*
dry twigs and bits of paper used for lighting fires

tingle *verb*
to have a slight pricking or prickling feeling: *Her face tingled with cold.*

tinker *verb*
to fiddle with something, trying to mend it: *to tinker with a broken watch*

tinkle *noun*
1 a light, high-pitched ringing sound
tinkle *verb*
2 to make a sound like this: *A bell tinkles when the shop door opens.*

tinny *adjective*
making a grating, high-pitched sound: *a tinny radio*
• ***Word Family:*** other forms are **tinnier, tinniest**

tinsel *noun*
thin, glittering, metal strips used for decoration: *to put tinsel on a Christmas tree*

tint *noun*
1 a small amount of a colour 2 a hair dye used to change the colour of someone's hair slightly
tint *verb*
3 to slightly change the colour of someone's hair with hair dye: *to tint your hair*

tiny *adjective*
very small: *The flea is a tiny insect.*
• ***Word Family:*** other forms are **tinier, tiniest**

tip (1) *noun*
the pointed end of something: *the tip of an iceberg / the tip of your nose*

tip (2) *verb*
1 to go over at an angle or to make something do this: *I tipped the bucket over and water spilled out.*
tip *noun*
2 a rubbish dump
• ***Word Family:*** other forms of the verb are **tips, tipped, tipping**

tip (3) *noun*
1 a small gift of money given to someone such as a waiter or a taxi driver who has done something for you 2 a piece of advice about what you should do or how you should do it: *a betting tip*
tip *verb*
3 to give a tip to someone 4 **tip off** to inform someone in advance about what is going to happen: *He tipped off the police about the robbery.*
• ***Word Family:*** other verb forms are **tips, tipped, tipping** □ **tip-off** *noun*

tip (4) *verb*
to strike with a light, glancing blow: *The ball tipped her bat and flew into the keeper's hands.*
• ***Word Family:*** other forms are **tips, tipped, tipping**

tipsy *adjective*
slightly drunk
• ***Word Family:*** the other forms are **tipsier, tipsiest**

tiptoe *verb*
to walk very quietly and carefully on your toes
• ***Word Family:*** other forms are **tiptoes, tiptoed, tiptoeing**

tirade (*say* tie-**rade**) *noun*
a long speech, usually an angry or critical one

tire *verb*
to use up your energy and make you feel tired: *Such a long swim tired us. / I tire easily after having the flu.*
• ***Word Family:*** **tiring** *adjective*

tired *adjective*
1 needing to rest or sleep 2 bored and fed up with something you don't want to do any longer: *I'm tired of staying indoors.*

tiresome *adjective*
annoying and making you feel impatient

tissue (*say* **tish**-oo) *noun*
1 the substance that a living thing is made of: *bone tissue* 2 a thin, soft, paper handkerchief 3 **tissue paper** light, see-through paper used for wrapping or protecting something

titan (*say* **tie**-tan) *noun*
an extremely strong or important person
•*Word Family:* **titanic** *adjective* very large or strong

titbit *noun*
a small, tasty piece of food

title (*say* **tie**-tul) *noun*
1 the name of a book, play, painting or piece of music 2 a name showing someone's occupation, rank or social position, such as *Sir*, *Dr* or *Mrs* 3 championship: *The young boxer won the world title.* 4 the legal right to own a particular piece of land or property
title *verb*
5 to give something a title

titter *verb*
to giggle in a nervous or embarrassed way

to *preposition*
1 towards or in the direction of: *from Sydney to Singapore* 2 with the aim or intention of: *Let's go to see a film.*
to *adverb*
3 into a closed position: *Pull that door to behind you.* 4 **to and fro** backwards and forwards

toad *noun*
an animal like a frog but with warty skin

toadstool *noun*
a type of fungus similar to a mushroom but often poisonous, with a stalk and umbrella-like cap

toast (1) *noun*
1 a slice of bread grilled so that it becomes crisp and brown
toast *verb*
2 to grill a slice of bread 3 to sit near a fire to get warm: *to toast yourself in front of the fire*
•*Word Family:* **toaster** *noun* a machine into which slices of bread are put to be toasted

toast (2) *verb*
1 to take a drink in honour of someone: *to toast the bride and groom*
toast *noun*
2 the act of toasting someone, or the words you say when you toast them: *I propose a toast to the new Prime Minister.* 3 someone who becomes so famous and popular that everyone is praising him or her: *She's the toast of London.*

tobacco (*say* te-**bak**-o) *noun*
1 the dried leaves of a plant used for smoking or as snuff 2 the plant that tobacco comes from

toboggan (*say* te-**bog**-an) *noun*
1 a light kind of sledge that you use to slide downhill on snow
toboggan *verb*
2 to ride on a toboggan

today *noun*
this day

toddle *verb*
to walk with short, unsteady steps
•*Word Family:* **toddler** *noun* a young child who has just learned to walk

toe *noun*
one of the five separate parts at the end of your foot

toffee *noun*
a chewy sweet made by boiling sugar or treacle with butter and water

toga (*say* **toe**-ga) *noun*
a long, loose robe worn by people living in ancient Rome

together *adverb*
1 with someone else, or as one group: *Let's go there together. / He weighs more than all of us together.* 2 so as to be joined, near or in contact: *Stick the two parts together. / to clap your hands together* 3 by each other: *Multiply these two numbers together.*
•*Word Family:* **togetherness** *noun* a feeling of closeness or friendship

toggle *noun*
a fastener consisting of a short rod that fits through a loop such as you get on a duffel coat

toil *verb*
1 to work hard, without stopping: *He was toiling at mending the shed roof all day.* 2 to walk somewhere slowly and with difficulty: *The hikers toiled up the steep hill.*

toilet (*say* **toy**-let) *noun*
1 a bowl fitted with a device to flush it clean with water and connected by a pipe to the drains, used for getting rid of urine and waste matter from the bowels 2 a room where people go to use the toilet
•*Word Family:* **toiletries** *plural noun* soap, toothpaste, and so on
•*Word Origins:* from a French word meaning "a cloth"

token (*say* **toe**-ken) *noun*
1 a symbol or sign of something: *A kiss is a token of affection.* 2 a ticket, voucher or stamped piece of metal used instead of money to pay for things: *a book token*

tolerance (*say* **tol**-a-rance) *noun*
1 the ability to cope with something painful,

nasty or bad: *He has a low tolerance to infection.* 2 the ability to resist the effects of a drug 3 acceptance of beliefs, customs, food and so on that are different from yours: *religious tolerance*
• ***Word Family:*** **tolerant** *adjective* showing or feeling tolerance **tolerantly** *adverb*

tolerate (*say* **tol**-a-rate) *verb*
to allow or put up with something that you don't like: *I will not tolerate such rudeness.*
• ***Word Family:*** **tolerable** *adjective* able to be tolerated **tolerably** *adverb* quite or fairly **toleration** *noun*

toll (1) *verb*
to ring slowly and regularly: *The bell tolled.*

toll (2) *noun*
1 a charge people have to pay for driving on a major road or crossing a bridge 2 the number of people who have been killed in a particular way or during a particular time: *The toll from the earthquake is high.*
• ***Word Family:*** **tollgate** *noun* a gate or barrier at which a toll is collected

tom *noun*
a male cat

tomahawk (*say* **tom**-a-hawk) *noun*
a small axe that was used as a weapon by Native Americans
• ***Word Origins:*** from a Native American word meaning "war club" or "ceremonial object"

tomato *noun*
a juicy, red fruit that can be eaten raw or cooked
• ***Word Family:*** the plural is **tomatoes**

tomb (*rhymes with* zoom) *noun*
a large grave, usually for an important person to be buried
• ***Word Family:*** **tombstone** *noun* a stone set above a grave with the name and dates of birth and death of the dead person carved on it

tomboy *noun*
a girl who enjoys doing the things that boys traditionally do, especially energetic, outdoor activities

tomorrow (*say* to-**mor**-roh) *noun*
the day after today

tom-tom *noun*
a small drum that is usually beaten with your hands

tone *noun*
1 a particular quality that a sound has: *the clear tones of a church bell / The furious tone of her voice made me apologize nervously.* 2 a mood: *There was a light-hearted tone to the meeting.* 4 a difference in pitch between two musical notes that is the same as two semitones 5 a shade of a colour: *painted in several different tones of blue*
tone *verb*
6 **tone down** to make something more moderate: *Please tone down your language.*

toner *noun*
a powdered colouring that is used as ink in various types of printers and photocopiers

tongs *plural noun*
a tool with two hinged arms, for picking up or holding something

tongue (*say* tung) *noun*
1 the muscle in your mouth that helps you taste and eat things and also helps you speak 2 your language: *He speaks fluent Japanese but English is his native tongue.* 3 the flap of material under the laces of a shoe

tonic *noun*
something that cheers you up and makes you feel stronger and healthier

tonic water *noun*
a clear, fizzy drink that is often mixed with alcoholic drinks

tonight *noun*
this present or coming night

tonne (*say* tun) *noun*
a metric measure of mass, equal to 1000 kilograms

tonsil *noun*
either of two groups of white body cells at the very back of your throat
• ***Word Family:*** **tonsillitis** *noun* an infection that makes your tonsils red and sore

too *adverb*
1 also: *Are you coming too?* 2 more than you can cope with: *The box is too heavy to lift.* 3 **only too** extremely: *I'm only too glad to help.*

tool *noun*
an object, such as a hammer or a drill, that you hold in your hands and that helps you work

tooth *noun*
1 one of the hard enamel-covered parts fixed in rows in human and animal mouths and used for chewing and biting 2 one of the parts of a comb, saw or rake that is fixed to it in rows, like teeth
• ***Word Family:*** the plural is **teeth**

toothpaste *noun*
a flavoured paste used for cleaning your teeth

top (1) *noun*
1 the highest place, surface or position: *Climb to the top of the hill. / Start at the top of the page.* 2 someone or something that has the highest place or position: *She's top of the class.* 3 the

highest point or pitch: *to scream at the top of your voice* 4 a lid or covering: *Put the top back on the bottle.* 5 a piece of clothing you wear on the top half of your body
top *verb*
6 to be on the top or to put something on the top: *A massive tower topped the building.*
top *adjective*
7 highest: *the top drawer* 8 best or excellent: *She's a top model.*
•***Word Family:*** other verb forms are **tops, topped, topping**

top (2) *noun*
a spinning toy shaped like a cone

topic *noun*
the subject of a discussion, conversation or piece of writing

topical (*say* **top**-i-kul) *adjective*
interesting because it is happening now
•***Word Family:* topically** *adverb*

topography (*say* top-**og**-ra-fee) *noun*
the hills, rivers and other geographical features of an area
•***Word Family:* topographically** *adverb*

topping *noun*
some food that you put on top of another food: *a pizza with a cheese and tomato topping*

topple *verb*
to become unsteady and fall over: *That pile of boxes could easily topple over.*

Torah (*say* **taw**-ra) *noun*
a scroll with the first five books of the Old Testament on it used in religious services in a synagogue

torch *noun*
1 a small, electric lamp you can carry around that is powered by batteries 2 a burning flame on a long stick that is carried to give light
•***Word Family:*** the plural is **torches**
•***Word Origins:*** from an Old French word meaning "handful of twisted straw"

toreador (*say* **tor**-ree-a-dawr) *noun*
a bullfighter

torment (*say* **tor**-ment) *noun*
1 great pain, suffering or worry: *the torments of toothache* 2 a cause of suffering: *That child is a torment to his parents.*
torment (*say* tor-**ment**) *verb*
3 to worry or annoy someone: *Stop tormenting her with your silly questions.*
•***Word Origins:*** from a Latin word meaning "a torture rack"

tornado (*say* tor-**nay**-doe) *noun*
a very strong wind with a whirlwind at its centre
•***Word Family:*** the plural is **tornadoes** or **tornados**

torpedo (*say* tor-**pee**-doe) *noun*
1 a self-propelled, underwater missile filled with explosives that is used to destroy ships and submarines
torpedo *verb*
2 to attack or destroy a ship with a torpedo
•***Word Family:*** the plural of the noun is **torpedoes**

torrent *noun*
a lot of water flowing very fast

torso *noun*
the human body without the head, arms and legs
•***Word Family:*** the plural is **torsos**

tortoise (*say* **tor**-tus) *noun*
a reptile, usually living on land, whose body is covered by a thick shell which it can pull its legs and head under

torture (*say* **tor**-cher) *noun*
1 making someone feel extreme pain, often in order to get information 2 the pain and suffering of torture
torture *verb*
3 to deliberately make someone feel extreme pain: *to torture a prisoner-of-war to find out enemy plans*
•***Word Family:* torturer** *noun* **torturous** *adjective*

toss *verb*
1 to throw something through the air: *Toss me the newspaper.* 2 to mix, or move around: *to toss the lettuce in a salad / The man tossed in his sleep.* 3 to decide by throwing a coin into the air and seeing which side it comes down on: *We'll toss for who gets the top bunk.*
•***Word Family:* toss** *noun*

total (*say* **toe**-tal) *noun*
1 the amount you get when you add everything together
total *adjective*
2 adding everything together: *the total amount*
3 complete or absolute: *a total failure*
total *verb*
4 to add up or add up to: *Total the bill, please. / The bill totals £60.*
•***Word Family:*** other verb forms are **totals, totalled, totalling** □ **totality** *noun* the whole of something **totally** *adverb* completely

totalitarian (*say* toe-tal-i-**tair**-ree-an) *adjective*
to do with a government that has all the power in a country and does not permit anyone to disagree with its ideas or allow any other political parties
•***Word Family:* totalitarianism** *noun*

totter *verb*
to move unsteadily as if you are just about to fall over

toucan (*say* **too**-kan) *noun*
a large, tropical, American bird with a huge beak

touch (*say* tutch) *verb*
1 to feel something with your finger or some other part of your body: *Touch the paint and see if it's still wet.* 2 to come into contact with something: *The car just touched me as I crossed the road.* 3 to make you feel sad: *The story touched his heart.*
touch *noun*
4 touching something 5 close communication: *We keep in touch by letter.* 6 the one of your five senses that lets you feel things

touchy (*say* **tutch**-ee) *adjective*
easily upset or offended
•*Word Family:* other forms are **touchier, touchiest**

tough (*say* tuf) *adjective*
1 not easily cut, broken or worn out: *steak too tough to chew* 2 rough or likely to be violent: *The gang leader was a tough character.* 3 difficult to do or answer: *tough questions*
•*Word Family:* **toughen** *verb* to make something tough or tougher or to become tough **toughly** *adverb* **toughness** *noun*

tour (*say* toor) *noun*
1 a journey in which you visit a number of different places: *a tour of Africa*
tour *verb*
2 to travel to a number of different places: *The band toured Scotland.*

tourist *noun*
someone who travels for sightseeing and pleasure
•*Word Family:* **tourism** *noun*

tournament (*say* **tor**-na-ment) *noun*
1 a competition in which a lot of players or teams play a series of games or matches against each other 2 a contest between two medieval knights on horseback armed with blunted weapons

tourniquet (*say* **tor**-ni-kay) *noun*
a tight bandage that is twisted around your leg or arm to stop bleeding

tow (*say* toe) *verb*
1 to pull a vehicle by attaching it to another vehicle with a rope or chain: *I'll tow your car to a garage.*
tow *noun*
2 towing a vehicle by pulling it along behind another vehicle: *to give a car a tow*

towel *noun*
a thick, cotton cloth for drying things
•*Word Family:* **towelling** *noun* the cloth used for making towels

tower (*rhymes with* flower) *noun*
1 a tall, narrow structure, sometimes forming part of another building such as a church or castle
tower *verb*
2 **tower over** to be much higher than something close by

town *noun*
1 a large area with many streets, houses, shops, offices and businesses where people live and work, smaller than a city and larger than a village 2 the people who live in a town: *The whole town came out to meet the Pope.* 3 the business or shopping centre of such an area, rather than the suburbs
•*Word Family:* **town hall** *noun* the main public building of a town

toxic (*say* **tok**-sik) *adjective*
poisonous: *a toxic chemical*
•*Word Family:* **toxin** *noun* a poison

toy *noun*
an object made for children to play with

trace *noun*
1 a sign that something has happened or that someone has been in a place: *The wanted man has disappeared without a trace.* 2 a very small amount: *You have a trace of an American accent.*
trace *verb*
3 to find out the origin or source of something: *He's tracing the history of his family.* 4 to copy a picture by putting a transparent sheet on top of it and drawing the outlines that show through: *to trace a map for school* 5 to try and find someone or something: *Police are trying to trace the woman last seen on Tuesday.*
•*Word Family:* **tracing** *noun* **tracing paper** *noun* transparent paper for tracing a picture

track *noun*
1 a rough road or path: *a track through the forest* 2 the set of metal rails and sleepers on which a train runs 3 a mark or series of marks left by anything that has passed along: *He left a track of footprints on the beach.* 4 an area of ground laid out for racing 5 one of the songs or separate pieces of music on a CD, tape or record
track *verb*
6 to follow the tracks of someone or something: *She was able to track the animal to its den.*

traction (*say* **trak**-shon) *noun*
1 the power used in pulling something heavy along a surface 2 the grip that wheels have on

the ground **3 in traction** having a broken leg raised and supported, usually with pressure applied by a series of pulleys

tractor *noun*
a motor vehicle with very big, back wheels and heavy tyres, used for pulling farm machinery or heavy loads

trade *noun*
1 the business of buying, selling or exchanging goods 2 the people involved in a particular business: *Discounts are available only to the trade.* 3 a swap: *I got these stamps as a trade.* 4 work that involves skilled knowledge and practical ability: *the trade of a plumber*
trade *verb*
5 to buy, sell or exchange goods: *to trade in oil* 6 **trade in** to give something you own as part of the payment for something new that you are buying: *to trade in your old car for a new one*
• ***Word Family:*** **trader** *noun* someone who buys, sells or exchanges goods

trademark *noun*
a name or symbol a manufacturer always uses to show that particular goods have been made by them

trade union *noun*
an organized group of workers set up to help all the workers in a particular industry with such things as wage disputes with bosses, working hours and work safety
• ***Word Family:*** **trade unionism** *noun* **trade unionist** *noun*

tradition (*say* tra-**dish**-on) *noun*
1 the passing down of customs, culture or beliefs from generation to generation 2 something that is passed on in this way
• ***Word Family:*** **traditional** *adjective*

traffic *noun*
1 the movement of people or goods in cars, trains, ships or planes: *air traffic* 2 all the cars, lorries and so on travelling on the roads
3 trading in illegal goods: *the traffic in drugs*
traffic *verb*
4 **traffic in** to trade illegal goods
• ***Word Family:*** other verb forms are **traffics, trafficked, trafficking** □ **trafficker** *noun*

tragedy (*say* **traj**-a-dee) *noun*
1 a sad, serious story or play, usually ending with the death of the hero 2 a disastrous, fatal or dreadful event
• ***Word Family:*** the plural is **tragedies** □ **tragic** *adjective* **tragically** *adverb*

trail *verb*
1 to drag something along the ground behind you 2 to follow slowly behind someone: *He trailed behind them with his sore leg.* 3 to grow along the ground or up a fence, wall and so on: *The rose trails over the balcony.* 4 to follow someone secretly: *Police had trailed the suspect*
trail *noun*
5 a track or marks left behind by something: *a trail of blood led to the door / The invaders left a trail of destruction.* 6 a track or scent left behind: *The hounds quickly found the deer's trail.* 7 a path or track made through rough country

trailer *noun*
1 a short film made from scenes taken from a new film, used as an advertisement for the new film 2 a vehicle for carrying loads, designed to be pulled behind a lorry or car

train *noun*
1 a set of railway vehicles connected to an engine 2 a line of vehicles, people or animals travelling together: *a camel train* 3 a series of connected things or thoughts: *a strange train of events* 4 an extra long part at the back of a long, formal dress that lies on the ground
train *verb*
5 to teach a person or animal a particular skill or job: *She trained the dog to walk to heel.* 6 to learn how to do a job: *He's training to be a doctor.* 7 to make a plant grow in a particular place 8 to aim or point something in a particular direction: *She trained the camera at the pride of lions.*
• ***Word Family:*** **trainer** *noun* someone who trains others **trainee** *noun* someone being trained **training** *noun*

trainers *noun*
sports shoes with a thick sole to protect your feet when running

traitor (*say* **tray**-ta) *noun*
someone who betrays their country or another person or a belief
• ***Word Family:*** **traitorous** *adjective* disloyal or treacherous

tram *noun*
a passenger vehicle running on rails in the street and usually powered by electricity from an overhead wire

tramp *verb*
1 to walk with steady or heavy steps.
tramp *noun*
2 someone, with no home and usually little or no money, who travels about on foot 3 the sound of heavy, firm steps

trample *verb*
to walk on something such as plants that you damage by crushing them: *The children are trampling over the flower beds.*

trampoline (*say* **tram**-pa-leen) *noun*
1 a tightly stretched canvas sheet attached by springs to a frame above the ground on which you bounce and do acrobatic jumps
trampoline *verb*
2 to jump on a trampoline

trance *noun*
1 a state in which you are only partly conscious
2 a state in which you are completely absorbed in thinking about something

tranquil (*say* **trang**-kwil) *adjective*
calm and peaceful: *a tranquil sleep*
•***Word Family:*** **tranquillity** (*say* trang-**kwil**-i-tee) *noun* **tranquilly** *adverb*

tranquillizer or **tranquilliser** (*say* **trang**-kwa-lie-za) *noun*
a drug that makes you very calm without putting you to sleep
•***Word Family:*** **tranquillize** or **tranquillise** *verb* to give someone a tranquillizer

transaction (*say* tran-**zak**-shon) *noun*
a piece of business that involves money, such as the sale of something
•***Word Family:*** **transact** *verb* to carry out business

transatlantic *adjective*
1 across the Atlantic Ocean: *a transatlantic flight*
2 on the other side of the Atlantic Ocean

transfer (*say* trans-**fer**) *verb*
1 to go or move something from one place to another: *He transferred his savings to another bank.*
transfer (*say* **trans**-fer) *noun*
2 the movement of something from one place to another: *The transfer of the money was handled by a foreign bank.* 3 a design on a piece of paper that can be pressed or ironed onto a surface: *to put transfers on a model plane*
•***Word Family:*** other verb forms are **transfers, transferred, transferring** □ **transference** *noun* **transferral** *noun*

transfix *verb*
to make someone unable to move because they are so amazed or afraid

transform *verb*
to change something completely: *The ugly duckling was transformed into a swan.*
•***Word Family:*** **transformation** *noun* a complete change in something

transformer *noun*
a device used for changing the voltage of an electric current

transfusion (*say* tranz-**few**-zhon) *noun*
the process of putting blood into someone's body that has been taken from another person

transistor *noun*
1 an electronic device used to control the flow of current in a machine such as a computer or radio 2 a small, portable radio that uses transistors

transit (*say* **tran**-zit) *noun*
the state of being carried or taken from one place to another: *The package was lost in transit.*

transition *noun*
a change from one situation to another
•***Word Family:*** **transitional** *adverb*

translate (*say* tranz-**late**) *verb*
to change speech or writing from one language to another: *to translate English into Japanese*
•***Word Family:*** **translation** *noun* **translator** *noun*

translucent (*say* tranz-**loo**-sent) *adjective*
allowing some light to pass through but not clear like glass: *a translucent type of plastic*
•***Word Family:*** **translucence** *noun* **translucently** *adverb*
•***Word Origins:*** from a Latin word meaning "shining through"

transmission (*say* tranz-**mish**-on) *noun*
1 passing something from one person or place to another 2 the broadcasting of radio or television programmes 3 the parts of a vehicle that carry the power from the engine to the wheels

transmit (*say* tranz-**mit**) *verb*
1 to pass something on: *Metal transmits heat.*
2 to broadcast: *to transmit radio messages* 3 to pass a disease on to someone: *Fleas transmitted the disease.*
•***Word Family:*** other forms are **transmits, transmitted, transmitting** □ **transmitter** *noun*

transparency (*say* tranz-**par**-ren-see) *noun*
1 the quality of being transparent 2 a small piece of photographic film with a picture on it which can be projected onto a screen or viewed by shining light through it from behind
•***Word Family:*** the plural is **transparencies**

transparent (*say* trans-**par**-ent) *adjective*
1 allowing light to pass through so that you can see the objects on the other side clearly
2 obvious or easily seen: *Her fear was transparent although she tried to hide it.*
•***Word Family:*** **transparently** *adverb*

transplant (*say* tranz-**plahnt**) *verb*
1 to remove something from one place and put it in another: *to transplant a tree* 2 to remove a diseased organ from somebody's body and put in a new one from someone else's body

transplant (*say* **tranz**-plahnt) *noun*
3 an operation to transplant an organ in someone's body: *a heart transplant*

transport (*say* tran-**sport**) *verb*
1 to carry people or goods from one place to another 2 to affect someone very strongly: *The wonderful music transported him.* 3 to send someone to another country far away as a punishment for a crime: *In the eighteenth century some thieves were transported to Australia.*
transport (*say* **tran**-sport) *noun*
4 a system for carrying passengers or goods from one place to another: *public transport* 5 a vehicle used for transporting people or goods
• ***Word Family:*** **transportation** *noun*

transvestite (*say* tranz-**ves**-tite) *noun*
someone who likes to dress in the clothing of the opposite sex

trap *noun*
1 a device for catching animals, such as a cage with a door that snaps shut when the animal enters it 2 a trick designed to catch someone or to catch them out 3 a light, two-wheeled carriage, pulled by a pony
trap *verb*
4 to catch an animal in a trap 5 to trick someone: *He trapped them into telling their secrets.*
• ***Word Family:*** other verb forms are **traps, trapped, trapping**

trapdoor *noun*
a door cut into a floor, ceiling or roof

trapeze (*say* tra-**peez**) *noun*
a short bar, with a long rope attached to each end, hung above the ground and used by acrobats and gymnasts

trapezium (*say* tra-**pee**-zi-um) *noun*
a four-sided figure with two parallel sides
• ***Word Family:*** the plural is **trapezia** or **trapeziums**

trash *noun*
something of very poor quality: *That film was trash.*

trauma (*say* **traw**-ma) *noun*
1 a very upsetting or shocking experience 2 an injury to your body
• ***Word Family:*** **traumatic** *adjective* **traumatize** or **traumatise** *verb*

travel (*say* **trav**-el) *verb*
1 to go from one place to another: *to travel across Europe / He's travelling back from Perth tomorrow.* 2 to move from one place to another: *Light travels faster than sound.*
travel *noun*
3 travelling: *a book about travel*
• ***Word Family:*** other verb forms are **travels, travelled, travelling** □ **traveller** *noun*

trawl *verb*
1 to fish by dragging a net along the seabed
trawl *noun*
2 a strong net used for trawling
• ***Word Family:*** **trawler** *noun* a fishing boat used to trawl

tray *noun*
a flat board with a higher part around the edge used for carrying things

treacherous (*say* **tretch**-a-rus) *adjective*
not to be trusted because it hides danger for you: *a treacherous smile / a treacherous current*
• ***Word Family:*** **treacherously** *adverb* **treachery** *noun*

treacle (*say* **tree**-kul) *noun*
a dark, sticky syrup made when sugar cane is being refined
• ***Word Family:*** **treacly** *adjective*

tread (*say* tred) *verb*
1 to walk or put your foot on something: *Don't tread on the carpet wearing those muddy boots.*
2 **tread water** to float in an upright position by moving your arms and legs in the water
tread *noun*
3 the sound of someone walking: *She could hear his tread on the path outside.* 4 the part of a tyre that touches the road and has a pattern cut into it to improve its grip 5 the part of a step where you put your foot
• ***Word Family:*** other verb forms are **treads, trod, trodden** or **trod, treading**

treason (*say* **tree**-zun) *noun*
the crime of betraying your country, especially by giving secret information to another country
• ***Word Family:*** **treasonable** *adjective*

treasure (*say* **trezh**-a) *noun*
1 any very valuable possession, especially gems or gold 2 a very helpful person: *Our babysitter is a real treasure.*
treasure *verb*
3 to have something which is very special or important to you: *to treasure a memory*

treasurer (*say* **trezh**-a-ra) *noun*
someone who is in charge of the money of a club, company or city

treasury (*say* **trezh**-a-ree) *noun*
1 a place where money and other valuable things are kept 2 **Treasury** the department of a government that controls what a country earns, borrows, lends and spends

treat (*say* treet) *verb*
1 to behave towards someone in a particular way: *He treated her with kindness.* 2 to deal with something in a particular way: *They treated the*

A B C D E F G H I J K L M N O P Q R S T U V W X Y Z

idea as a joke. / The police are treating the death threats seriously. 3 to give medical care to someone: *The doctor is treating me for chickenpox.* 4 to protect something using chemicals or other processes: *This wood should be treated for woodworm.* 5 to give someone something special: *They treated her to lunch in her favourite restaurant.*
treat *noun*
6 something that is arranged or bought for you that gives you great pleasure: *It was a treat for the kids to go to the beach.* 7 **my treat** I will pay
•***Word Family:*** **treatment** *noun*

treatment *noun*
1 the way you behave towards someone: *His treatment of her is cruel.* 2 medical care: *He's getting treatment for his asthma.* 3 a process of putting chemicals on something to protect it

treaty (*say* **tree**-tee) *noun*
a formal agreement between countries: *a peace treaty*
•***Word Family:*** the plural is **treaties**

treble (*say* **treb**-ul) *adjective*
1 being three times as big or having three parts: *to buy treble the amount* 2 high-pitched: *a treble recorder*
treble *noun*
3 the range of musical notes sung by a boy before his voice breaks 4 singer or instrument with this range of notes: *He's a treble in the church choir.*
treble *verb*
5 to multiply by three

tree *noun*
a plant with a woody trunk, branches, leaves and roots

trek *verb*
1 to travel for long distances over rough ground
trek *noun*
2 a long, difficult journey
•***Word Family:*** other verb forms are **treks, trekked, trekking**
•***Word Origins:*** this word comes from Afrikaans, a language spoken by Dutch settlers in South Africa

trellis *noun*
a frame made of crossed wooden or metal strips, used for supporting climbing plants

tremble *verb*
to shake, usually from fear, cold or weakness: *His hands were trembling.*

tremendous (*say* tre-**men**-dus) *adjective*
1 enormous or very great: *a runner of tremendous stamina* 2 wonderful: *What a tremendous concert!*
•***Word Family:*** **tremendously** *adverb*

tremor (*say* **trem**-a) *noun*
a shaking: *a tremor in your voice / an earth tremor*

trench *noun*
a long, deep ditch
•***Word Family:*** the plural is **trenches**

trend *noun*
a general tendency to change towards something different or new: *a trend towards eating less junk food*
•***Word Family:*** **trendy** *adjective* (**trendier, trendiest**) fashionable **trendiness** *noun*

trespass *verb*
to go onto someone's property without permission
•***Word Family:*** **trespasser** *noun*

trestle (*say* **tres**-ul) *noun*
a narrow piece of wood with sloping legs at each end that is used to support a board to make a rough table

triad (*say* **try**-ad) *noun*
a group of three similar things, such as the three musical notes in a chord

trial (*say* trile) *noun*
1 the hearing of the facts by a judge and jury in a law court, followed by a decision as to whether the person accused of a crime is guilty or innocent 2 a test, or an experiment to test something: *the trial of a new drug* 3 a nuisance: *My stutter is a bit of a trial.*
trial *verb*
4 to try something out or test it: *to trial a new sportscar*

triangle (*say* **try**-ang-ul) *noun*
1 a flat shape with three straight sides 2 a musical instrument in the shape of a thin steel bar bent into a triangle that you hit with a small steel rod
•***Word Family:*** **triangular** *adjective* shaped like a triangle

triathlon *noun*
a sporting contest involving the three different sports of swimming, cycling and running

tribe *noun*
a group of people, usually living in the same area, and sharing a common ancestor, leadership or customs
•***Word Family:*** **tribal** *adjective*

tribunal (*say* try-**bew**-nal) *noun*
a special court or committee that is set up to hear and settle disputes

tributary (*say* **trib**-yoo-tree) *noun*
a river or stream that flows into a larger one
•***Word Family:*** the plural is **tributaries**

tribute (*say* **trib**-yoot) *noun*
something you say or do to show respect and admiration for someone

trice *noun*
a very short time

triceps (*say* **try**-seps) *noun*
the large muscle at the back of your upper arm that you use to straighten your arm at your elbow

trick *noun*
1 something you do to deceive someone or get an advantage over them 2 a skilful act: *a card trick* 3 something you do as a habit: *She has an odd trick of stroking her elbow when she's thinking.* 4 **do the trick** to achieve the result you want: *That should do the trick.*
trick *verb*
5 to deceive someone or cheat them using a trick
• ***Word Family:*** **tricky** *adjective* (**trickier, trickiest) trickery** *noun* **trickster** *noun*

trickle *verb*
1 to flow slowly in drops: *Raindrops trickled down her back.* 2 to move slowly: *The cars trickled through the city at peak hour.*
trickle *noun*
3 a few drops of a liquid moving slowly: *a trickle of blood*

tricycle (*say* **try**-sik-ul) *noun*
a cycle with three wheels, one at the front and two at the back

trifle (*say* **try**-ful) *verb*
1 **trifle with** to treat someone as if they had no value or importance: *to trifle with someone's affections*
trifle *noun*
2 a small, unimportant or worthless thing: *Don't get upset over trifles.* 3 a dessert made from sponge cake, fruit, cream, custard and sometimes jelly
• ***Word Family:*** **trifling** *adjective* small or unimportant

trigger *noun*
1 the lever on a gun that you press to release a spring and fire a bullet
trigger *verb*
2 to start something happening: *The blast triggered a series of smaller explosions.*

trill *noun*
1 the very fast repetition one after the other of two musical notes either a tone or a semitone apart
trill *verb*
2 to sing using short, high, repeated notes, the way a bird does

trillion *noun*
a million times a million (1000 000 000 000)
• ***Word Family:*** **trillionth** *noun* **trillionth** *adjective*

trilogy (*say* **tril**-a-jee) *noun*
a series of three related novels or plays with the same characters
• ***Word Family:*** the plural is **trilogies**

trim *verb*
1 to make something neat or tidy by cutting the ends off or pruning: *The barber trimmed his beard.* 2 to decorate the edge of something: *to trim a hat with feathers* 3 to change the position of the sails on a boat to catch the wind
trim *noun*
4 a haircut that makes your hair neat without altering its style
trim *adjective*
5 neat and smart: *a trim suit*
• ***Word Family:*** other verb forms are **trims, trimmed, trimming** □ **trimly** *adverb* **trimness** *noun*

trimaran (*say* **try**-ma-ran) *noun*
a sailing boat or raft with three hulls that are parallel and joined above the water

trinity (*say* **trin**-i-tee) *noun*
1 a group of three things or people 2 **the Trinity** the Father, the Son and the Holy Spirit, as one God in the Christian religion

trinket *noun*
a small, cheap ornament

trio (*say* **tree**-oh) *noun*
1 a group of three people, especially musicians 2 a musical piece for three instruments or voices
• ***Word Origins:*** this word comes from Italian

trip *verb*
1 to stumble, or make someone fall: *I tripped over the step. / I put out my foot and tripped him.* 2 to walk quickly and with short, light steps 3 to experience the effects of a drug that makes you see things differently or see things that aren't there 4 **trip up** to cause someone to make a mistake
trip *noun*
5 a journey, especially one you go on for pleasure 6 the effects of a drug that makes you see things differently or see things that aren't there
• ***Word Family:*** other verb forms are **trips, tripped, tripping**

tripe *noun*
1 the flat, white stomach-lining of cattle, that can be cooked and eaten 2 nonsense: *Don't talk tripe.*

triple (*say* **trip**-ul) *adjective*
1 being three times as big or having three parts: *triple the size / a triple ice-cream cone*
triple *verb*
2 to make, or to become, three times as many or as large

triplet *noun*
1 one of three children born to the same mother at the same time 2 a group of three equal musical notes performed in the time of two

tripod (*say* **try**-pod) *noun*
a stand with three legs used to support a camera

trite *adjective*
so common that it sounds dull or unoriginal: *a trite comment*
•***Word Family:*** **tritely** *adverb*

triumph (*say* **try**-umf) *noun*
1 a victory or success
triumph *verb*
2 to win a victory over: *to triumph over evil*
•***Word Family:*** **triumphant** *adjective* victorious **triumphantly** *adverb*

trivial (*say* **triv**-i-al) *adjective*
unimportant: *trivial objections*
•***Word Family:*** **trivialize** or **trivialise** *verb* **triviality** *noun* **trivially** *adverb*

troll *noun*
an imaginary being in myths, sometimes believed to be a giant and sometimes a mischievous dwarf, who lives underground

trolley *noun*
1 a small table on wheels, for carrying dishes or food 2 a small truck running on rails, such as the ones that carry coal in a mine 3 a wire cart on wheels for carrying goods in a supermarket

trombone *noun*
a brass wind instrument a bit like a trumpet, on which you change the note by moving a slide to lengthen or shorten the tube
•***Word Family:*** **trombonist** *noun*

troop *noun*
1 a group of people or animals: *a troop of admirers* 2 **troops** many soldiers
troop *verb*
3 to go somewhere in a large group: *The children trooped out of the school gates.*
•***Word Family:*** **trooper** *noun*

trophy (*say* **troh**-fee) *noun*
1 something you keep in memory of a success in war or in hunting animals 2 a prize, especially for the winner of a sporting competition

tropic *noun*
1 the line of latitude at about $23\frac{1}{2}°$ north of the equator, known as the *Tropic of Cancer* 2 the line of latitude at about $23\frac{1}{2}°$ south of the equator, known as the *Tropic of Capricorn*
3 **the tropics** the area of the Earth lying between these two lines
•***Word Family:*** **tropical** *adjective* to do with the tropics or in the tropics: *a tropical rainforest*

trot *noun*
1 the movement of a horse between a walk and canter, in which you can hear two groups of hoof-beats as a front leg moves in time with the opposite back leg 2 a run using quick, short steps
trot *verb*
3 to move or run at a trot
•***Word Family:*** other verb forms are **trots, trotted, trotting**

troubadour (*say* **troo**-ba-dor) *noun*
a travelling musician, poet and singer in medieval France and Italy

trouble (*say* **trub**-ul) *verb*
1 to cause worry or anxiety: *My mother's strange behaviour troubles me.* 2 to bother: *Don't trouble to meet me at the station.* 3 to disturb someone: *I'm sorry to trouble you.*
trouble *noun*
4 worry, anxiety or problems: *You never cause any trouble. / Strikes are a sign of industrial trouble.* 5 **in trouble** likely to get punished for what you have done
•***Word Family:*** **troublesome** *adjective* causing trouble

trough (*say* trof) *noun*
1 a container used for food or water for animals 2 an area of low pressure shown on a weather map 3 a long, narrow channel such as the low point between ocean waves

troupe (*say* troop) *noun*
a group of actors or performers who work together
•***Word Family:*** **trouper** *noun*

trousers *plural noun*
a piece of clothing that covers the lower half of your body from waist to ankle with a separate part for each leg

trout *noun*
a freshwater fish related to the salmon and caught for sport and food
•***Word Family:*** plural is also **trout**

trowel *noun*
a short-handled tool, with either a flat blade for spreading mortar, or a curved blade for gardening

truant *noun*
someone who has stayed away from school with no excuse
• ***Word Family:*** **truancy** *noun*

truce (*say* troos) *noun*
an agreement to stop fighting for a period of time

truck *noun*
1 a lorry 2 a railway carriage used for carrying heavy goods not people

trudge *verb*
to walk heavily or wearily: *He trudged up the hill in the rain.*

true (*say* troo) *adjective*
1 matching what really happened: *a true story* 2 real, not artificial or fake: *true gold* 3 accurate: *Does the thermometer give true temperature readings?* 4 loyal or faithful: *a true companion*

trump *noun*
1 **trumps** the suit of cards in a card game that has the highest value 2 a card that belongs to the suit that is trumps
trump *verb*
3 to win a round of cards by playing a trump: *Your ace trumped my queen.* 4 **trump up** to make something up in order to get someone into trouble
• ***Word Family:*** **trumped-up** *adjective*

trumpet *noun*
1 a high-pitched, brass instrument with a bell-shaped end 2 **blow your own trumpet** to praise yourself
trumpet *verb*
3 to make the loud sound of an elephant 4 to tell something to many people: *She trumpeted the news all over town.*
• ***Word Family:*** **trumpeter** *noun* someone who plays the trumpet

truncheon (*say* **trun**-chon) *noun*
a short club used by police to protect themselves or to keep back angry crowds

trunk *noun*
1 the main, woody stem of a tree without the roots and branches 2 the main part of your body not including your head, neck, arms and legs 3 a large box with a hinged lid, for carrying or storing clothes 4 the long, flexible nose of an elephant
trunk *adjective*
6 made over a telephone line connecting two distant exchanges: *a trunk call*

trunk road *noun*
a main road

truss *verb*
to tie something up or bind: *to truss a chicken / to truss someone's legs*

trust *noun*
1 a firm belief in something: *I have complete trust in you* 2 responsibility: *To be treasurer of the club is a position of trust.* 3 money or property held and looked after by one person for the benefit of another 4 **on trust** without proof: *You'll have to take my word on trust.*
trust *verb*
5 to have trust in: *I don't trust his promises.* 6 to hope: *I trust you'll have a pleasant journey.*
• ***Word Family:*** **trusting** *adjective* ready to trust **trustworthy** *adjective* able to be trusted **trusty** *adjective* reliable and able to be trusted **trustworthiness** *noun*

truth (*say* trooth) *noun*
1 the true facts about something: *Are you telling the truth?* 2 a fact or principle that everyone agrees is true: *a scientific truth* 3 the quality of being true: *There is no truth in that rumour.*
• ***Word Family:*** **truthful** *adjective* telling the truth **truthfully** *adverb*

try *verb*
1 to attempt: *Try to speak quietly.* 2 to test: *Try the hamburger and see whether it's spicy enough.* 3 to use something to see what it is like: *to try a new pen* 4 to hear evidence about a case in a law court and decide whether someone is guilty or innocent
try *noun*
5 an attempt 6 the action of carrying the ball over the opposing team's goal line in rugby and touching the ground with it
• ***Word Family:*** other verb forms are **tries, tried, trying** □ the plural of the noun is **tries**

tsar (*say* zar) *noun*
the title given to the kings of Russia between 1547 and 1917
• ***Word Family:*** **tsarina** (*say* zar-**ree**-na) *noun* the wife of a tsar

T-shirt *noun*
a cotton top with no collar
• ***Word Origins:*** from the shape of a shirt with short sleeves when you spread it out

tub *noun*
a deep container: *a tub of margarine*

tuba (*say* **tew**-ba) *noun*
a low-pitched, brass, musical instrument with valves, that you blow

tubby *adjective*
short, round and fat
• ***Word Family:*** other forms are **tubbier, tubbiest** □ **tubbiness** *noun*

tube *noun*
1 a long, hollow pipe made from glass, metal or rubber 2 a long, thin container with a lid at one end: *a tube of toothpaste* 3 an underground railway: *to travel on the Tube*

tuber (*say* **tew**-ba) *noun*
a rounded or thickened underground stem of a plant such as a potato that can be eaten

tuberculosis (*say* tu-**berk**-yoo-**lo**-sis) *noun*
a serious disease affecting lungs, causing small swellings or lumps to appear
•***Word Family:*** **tubercular** *adjective* **tuberculous** *adjective*

tubing *noun*
long pieces of rubber or plastic in the shape of a tube

tubular *adjective*
shaped like a tube

tuck *noun*
1 a narrow fold you stitch in cloth to give it a better shape
tuck *verb*
2 to fold material under something or press in a loose edge of it: *to tuck the blankets under the mattress / Comb your hair and tuck in your shirt.* 3 to move something so that it is under something else: *He tucked his legs under the bench.* 4 **tuck in** to eat hungrily

Tuesday *noun*
the third day of the week
•***Word Origins:*** named after the ancient German god *Tiw*, identified with Mars

tuft *noun*
a bunch of feathers, hair or grass, growing upright or held together at the base
•***Word Family:*** **tufted** *adjective* containing tufts

tug *verb*
1 to pull hard: *Stop tugging my hair.*
tug *noun*
2 a hard pull: *Give the rope a tug.* 3 a small boat with a powerful engine used to tow other ships
•***Word Family:*** other verb forms are **tugs, tugged, tugging**

tuition (*say* tew-**ish**-on) *noun*
teaching: *She needs tuition for the test.*

tulip (*say* **tew**-lip) *noun*
a garden plant with a single, bright, cup-shaped flower growing from a bulb

tumble *verb*
1 to fall with a bouncing movement: *She tumbled down the hill.*
tumble *noun*
2 a fall

tumbler *noun*
1 a flat-bottomed drinking glass 2 an acrobat who performs somersaults in the air and other gymnastic feats before an audience

tummy *noun*
your stomach
•***Word Family:*** the plural is **tummies**

tumour or **tumor** (*say* **tew**-ma) *noun*
an abnormal mass of cells that grows in someone's body, sometimes causing death

tuna (*say* **tew**-na) *noun*
a large, seafish with pink flesh that can be eaten

tundra *noun*
a large area of flat land in the Artic where the frozen conditions mean that only plants such as mosses and lichens can grow
•***Word Origins:*** this word comes from a Russian word meaning "marshy plain"

tune *noun*
1 a series of different musical sounds that form the melody of a song or other piece of music
2 correct pitch: *You sing out of tune.*
tune *verb*
3 to adjust a musical instrument so that it is at the proper musical pitch: *She's tuning her violin.* 4 to adjust a radio so that it receives a strong, incoming signal from a particular station 5 to make an engine run smoothly: *Your car engine needs tuning.*
•***Word Family:*** **tuneful** *adjective* having a good tune **tunefully** *adverb* **tuner** *noun* the part of a radio you adjust when you tune it

tunic (*say* **tew**-nik) *noun*
1 a short, loose, sleeveless dress, often with a belt: *a school tunic* 2 a jacket worn as part of a police or military uniform

tunnel *noun*
1 an underground passage, especially one trains and cars can go through
tunnel *verb*
2 to make a tunnel: *to tunnel under the water*
•***Word Family:*** other verb forms are **tunnels, tunnelled, tunnelling**

turban *noun*
a head covering consisting of a long strip of cloth wound around the head worn especially by Muslim men in Asia and Africa and by Sikhs

turbine (*say* **ter**-bine) *noun*
a revolving motor in which the shaft is turned by water, steam or gas passing over blades set in a wheel

turbo *noun*
a fan in an engine which is driven by the

engine's exhaust and which improves the engine's performance
•*Word Family:* **turbo-charged** *adjective* fitted with a turbo

turbulent (*say* **ter**-bew-lunt) *adjective*
violent or uncontrolled: *The diver drowned in the turbulent waters of the whirlpool.*
•*Word Family:* **turbulence** *noun* violent currents of air near the ground **turbulently** *adverb*

turf *noun*
1 a layer of earth containing grass and its roots 2 a square piece of this
•*Word Family:* the plural of the noun is **turfs** or **turves** □ **turf** *verb*

turkey (*say* **ter**-kee) *noun*
a large bird, found in the wild originally in North America and now bred for eating

turmoil *noun*
great confusion or worry: *The government was in a turmoil over the scandal.*

turn *verb*
1 to spin round: *The wheels turned as the car rolled forward.* 2 to go round: *to turn the corner* 3 to move so as to face in a particular direction: *She turned her head to see.* 4 to move something so that it is the other way round or from one side to the other: *Turn the pancakes before they burn.* 5 to become something different: *She turned blue with cold.* 6 to make something change into something different: *The witch turned the prince into a frog.* 7 to move a switch or dial on a machine to change it: *Turn the TV off. / Can you turn the sound up?* 8 to perform: *The acrobat turned somersaults.* 9 **turn on** (a) to attack someone very suddenly (b) to make you feel excited: *The new band really turns me on.* 10 **turn out** (a) to turn something off: *Turn out the lights.* (b) to make something in large numbers: *The factory turns out 50 chocolate eggs a minute.* (c) to empty something: *Turn out your pockets.* (d) to go somewhere to see a public event: *Crowds turned out to see the fireworks.* 11 **turn up** (a) to arrive: *Visitors turned up without warning.* (b) to be found: *Has your lost dog turned up yet?*
turn *noun*
12 a turning movement: *Give the key a hard turn.* 13 a change in direction: *There were many turns in the road.* 14 your chance or right to do something: *Wait for your turn.* 15 a sudden feeling of being unwell: *The bad news gave me quite a turn.*

turnip *noun*
a plant with a white, round root used as a vegetable

turnstile *noun*
a revolving gateway that only allows one person through at a time

turntable *noun*
the part of a record-player on which the record sits and goes around

turpentine (*say* **ter**-pen-tine) *noun*
an oil used for things such as cleaning or thinning oil paints, which once came from fir trees but which is now made from petroleum

turquoise (*say* **ter**-koyz) *noun*
1 a hard, blue or blue-green mineral used as a gem 2 a bright, greenish-blue colour

turret *noun*
a small tower, often on the corner of a castle

turtle *noun*
a reptile that has a hard, round shell covering its body and lives in the sea or fresh water using its flippers for swimming

tusk *noun*
one of a pair of very long teeth coming right outside the mouth that mammals such as boars, elephants and walruses have

tussle *verb*
1 to struggle with someone in a fight
tussle *noun*
2 a fight, struggle or argument between two people for something that they both want

tutor (*say* **tew**-ta) *noun*
a teacher, especially a private one for a single pupil, or one at a university
•*Word Origins:* from a Latin word meaning "guardian"

tutorial (*say* tew-**taw**-ri-ul) *noun*
a period of being taught alone or in a small group by a university tutor

tutu *noun*
a flared skirt made of layers of net worn by female ballet dancers

TV *noun*
the short form of **television**

tweed *noun*
a type of heavy, woollen cloth

tweezers *plural noun*
a small tool with two parts that can be used as pincers for pulling out hairs or picking up small objects

twelve *noun*
the number 12
•*Word Family:* **twelve** *adjective* **twelfth** *noun* **twelfth** *adjective*

twenty *noun*
the number 20
•***Word Family:*** the plural is **twenties** □ **twenty** *adjective* **twentieth** *noun* **twentieth** *adjective*

twice *adverb*
two times

twiddle *verb*
to twist something or turn it over and over: *to twiddle the knobs on a radio / He is twiddling his thumbs.*

twig (1) *noun*
a small, woody shoot at the end of a branch or stem

twig (2) *verb*
to suddenly realize or understand something
•***Word Family:*** other forms are **twigs, twigged, twigging**

twilight (*say* **twy**-lite) *noun*
the period of dim light just after the sun sets

twin *noun*
1 one of two people or animals born to the same mother at the same time
twin *adjective*
2 matching: *twin beds*

twinge (*say* twinj) *noun*
a sudden, sharp pain

twinkle *verb*
1 to sparkle with a flickering light
twinkle *noun*
2 sparkle or brightness

twirl *verb*
to spin round

twist *verb*
1 to wind something in a particular way: *You twist strands of fleece together to make wool.* 2 to bend something into a different shape 3 to turn something round: *She twisted her head to look at him.* 4 to turn in a series of curves: *The stream twisted through the valley.* 5 to give a different, unfair meaning to something: *The newspapers twisted his words.*
twist *noun*
6 a twisting movement 7 a bend or curve

twitch *noun*
1 a short, jerky movement in part of your body
twitch *verb*
2 to make a short, jerky movement: *His mouth twitched with laughter.*
•***Word Family:*** the plural of the noun is **twitches**

twitter *verb*
1 to make the high-pitched, chirping sounds of a bird 2 to talk quickly about things that are silly or unimportant

two (*say* too) *noun*
the number 2
•***Word Family:*** **two** *adjective*

two-dimensional *adjective*
having the two dimensions height and width but no depth

twosome (*say* **too**-sum) *noun*
two people together

tycoon (*say* tie-**koon**) *noun*
a very wealthy and powerful owner of a business
•***Word Origins:*** from a Japanese word meaning "great prince"

type *noun*
1 a kind or sort: *What type of cheese is this?*
2 printed letters: *a headline in huge type*
type *verb*
3 to write something using a typewriter or a computer keyboard

typewriter *noun*
a machine with keys that you press down to print letters or symbols on paper
•***Word Family:*** **typist** *noun* someone who uses a typewriter

typhoid (*say* **tie**-foyd) *noun*
a disease spread by eating food and water with bacteria in it that causes fever and sometimes death

typhoon (*say* tie-**foon**) *noun*
a very violent storm
•***Word Origins:*** from Chinese words meaning "big wind"

typical (*say* **tip**-i-kul) *adjective*
usual or expected: *a typical family car / It's typical of you to be late.*
•***Word Family:*** **typically** *adverb*

tyrannosaurus (*say* te-ran-a-**saw**-rus) *noun*
a very large, meat-eating dinosaur that walked upright on its hind legs

tyrant (*say* **tie**-runt) *noun*
1 a ruler with total power who uses it cruelly and unjustly 2 anyone with power who acts like this
•***Word Family:*** **tyranny** *noun* a cruel or unjust use of power **tyrannical** *adjective* **tyrannically** *adverb* **tyrannize** or **tyrannise** *verb*

tyre *noun*
a band of hollow, inflated rubber around the rim of a vehicle's wheel that grips the road and cuts down vibration in the vehicle

Uu

udder *noun*
the bag-like part of animals such as goats and cows that produces milk

UFO *noun*
something unusual seen in the sky, often thought to be an alien spaceship
• ***Word Origins:*** short for the words *u*nidentified *f*lying *o*bject

ugly (*say* **ug**-lee) *adjective*
1 unpleasant in appearance: *an ugly face*
2 unpleasant or bad: *an ugly temper*
• ***Word Family:*** other forms are **uglier, ugliest** □ **ugliness** *noun*

ukulele (*say* yoo-ka-**lay**-lee) *noun*
an instrument like a small guitar with four strings

ulcer (*say* **ul**-sa) *noun*
a sore area on your skin or on the inner surface of an organ, such as your stomach, which heals very slowly

ultimate (*say* **ul**-ti-mit) *adjective*
1 final or eventual: *Our ultimate aim is to have a computer for every child.* 2 the maximum or greatest possible: *the ultimate luxury*
• ***Word Family:*** **ultimately** *adverb* finally or at last

ultimatum (*say* ul-ti-**may**-tum) *noun*
a warning that unless someone does what you want, you will take action against them

ultrasonic (*say* ul-tra-**son**-ik) *adjective*
too high for humans to hear: *ultrasonic sounds*

ultrasound *noun*
the use of ultrasonic waves or sound vibrations to produce pictures of the inside of your body

ultraviolet *adjective*
beyond the violet end of the light spectrum and unable to be seen by humans: *This cream protects your skin from the sun's ultraviolet rays.*

umbilical cord (*say* um-**bil**-i-kul *or* um-bi-**lie**-kul kord) *noun*
the tube that connects an unborn baby to the lining of its mother's womb and through which it gets food and oxygen

umbrella *noun*
a folding, circular frame covered in waterproof material with a handle used to protect you from the rain
• ***Word Origins:*** from an Italian word meaning "a little shade"

umpire *noun*
1 someone whose job is to make decisions on whether the rules have been obeyed during a competition or sports match
umpire *verb*
2 to act as an umpire for a competition or sports match

unanimous (*say* yoo-**nan**-i-mus) *adjective*
with every single person agreeing: *a unanimous vote*
• ***Word Family:*** **unanimously** *adverb* **unanimity** (*say* yoo-na-**nim**-i-tee) *noun*

unawares *adverb*
unexpectedly: *We caught them unawares by creeping up behind them.*

unbalanced *adjective*
1 not balanced 2 slightly mad

unbearable *adjective*
so unpleasant or upsetting you feel unable to put up with it any longer: *unbearable pain*
• ***Word Family:*** **unbearably** *adverb*

uncanny *adjective*
strange and difficult to explain
• ***Word Family:*** **uncannily** *adverb* **uncanniness** *noun*

uncle *noun*
1 your mother's or father's brother 2 the husband of your aunt

uncomfortable *adjective*
1 not comfortable: *an uncomfortable seat*
2 uneasy: *He made me feel uncomfortable.*
• ***Word Family:*** **uncomfortably** *adverb*

unconscious (*say* un-**kon**-shus) *adjective*
1 having lost consciousness: *They carried the unconscious boxer away.* 2 not aware of what is going on around you: *She was completely unconscious of her surroundings.*
unconscious *noun*
3 the part of your mind that contains feelings that you are unaware of and cannot control
• ***Word Family:*** **unconsciously** *adverb*

uncover *verb*
1 to take a cover off something 2 to discover something which had been secret or hidden: *Police uncovered a drug-smuggling ring.*

uncouth (*say* un-**kooth**) *adjective*
rude and rough
• ***Word Family:*** **uncouthly** *adverb* **uncouthness** *noun*

undaunted (*say* un-**dawn**-tid) *adjective*
not discouraged or dismayed

underarm *adjective*
1 to do with your armpit: *an underarm deodorant* 2 thrown or hit with your arm below your shoulder

undercarriage *noun*
the parts of an aeroplane under its body that support it when it is on the ground and when it takes off and lands

undercover *adjective*
keeping your real identity secret while trying to get information: *an undercover agent*

underdog *noun*
the person or team that is expected to lose

undergo *verb*
to experience or go through something: *He had to undergo major heart surgery.*
•*Word Family:* other forms are **undergoes, underwent, undergone, undergoing**

undergraduate *noun*
a student who has not yet received a university degree

underground *adjective*
1 below the earth's surface: *an underground cave* 2 secret and not official or not legal: *an underground movement working for democracy*

undergrowth *noun*
the small trees and plants growing under larger trees

underhand *adjective*
secret and dishonest: *underhand tactics*

underline *verb*
1 to draw a line under words 2 to emphasize something: *He hit the desk to underline his point.*

undermine *verb*
1 to take away the earth underneath a building or structure 2 to take actions which gradually make something or someone less strong or less confident

underneath *preposition*
1 beneath or below: *Your bunk is underneath mine.*
underneath *adjective*
2 lower: *Your bunk is the underneath one.*
underneath *noun*
3 a lower part or surface: *the underneath of the car*

underpass *noun*
a road that goes under another road or railway line
•*Word Family:* the plural is **underpasses**

understand *verb*
1 to grasp the meaning of something or know what it is like: *I can't understand the problem. / You can understand why he was upset.* 2 to know the meaning of something: *Do you understand Vietnamese?* 3 to have been told: *I understand that you've just arrived.*
•*Word Family:* other forms are **understands, understood, understanding** □ **understandable** *adjective* easy to understand **understandably** *adverb*

understanding *noun*
1 the ability or power to understand: *I think I have a clear understanding of the problem.* 2 sympathy: *All I was asking for was a little understanding.* 3 an agreement: *We came to a friendly understanding.*

understudy *noun*
1 someone prepared to take over an important role in a play, ballet and so on if the actor, dancer and so on is unable to perform
understudy *verb*
2 to act as an understudy
•*Word Family:* the plural of the noun is **understudies** □ other forms of the verb are **understudies, understudied, understudying**

undertake *verb*
to promise to do something: *I'll undertake to be there on time.*
•*Word Family:* other forms are **undertakes, undertook, undertaken, undertaking** □ **undertaking** *noun* a promise to do something

undertaker *noun*
someone who prepares bodies for burial or cremation and arranges funerals

underwear *noun*
clothing such as pants or a bra that you wear next to your skin under other clothes

undesirable *adjective*
unpleasant, unwanted or likely to cause harm: *The plan may have some undesirable results.*

undo (*say* un-**doo**) *verb*
1 to unfasten something: *Can you undo the zip?* 2 to do something which gives the opposite effect from what was done before: *You've undone all our good work on the project.*
•*Word Family:* other forms are **undoes, undid, undone, undoing** □ **undoing** *noun* ruin or downfall

undoubted (*say* un-**dow**-ted) *adjective*
accepted as true or real: *her undoubted genius*
•*Word Family:* **undoubtedly** *adverb*

undress *verb*
to take your clothes off or another person's clothes off

unearth *verb*
to dig something up or find something: *The detective unearthed new clues.*

uneasy *adjective*
slightly worried and uncertain: *She felt uneasy about singing to a strange audience.*
• *Word Family:* **uneasily** *adverb* **uneasiness** *noun*

unemployment *noun*
1 not having a job 2 the number of people who cannot get a job: *The level of unemployment rose at the end of the year.*
• *Word Family:* **unemployed** *adjective*

uneven *adjective*
1 not level or flat: *an uneven surface* 2 not equal or balanced: *an uneven contest / a book of uneven quality* 3 odd: *an uneven number*
• *Word Family:* **unevenly** *adverb*

unexpected *adjective*
coming without warning: *an unexpected visitor*
• *Word Family:* **unexpectedly** *adverb*

unfair *adjective*
not fair or just
• *Word Family:* **unfairly** *adverb* **unfairness** *noun*

unfamiliar *adjective*
1 not known or seen before: *an unfamiliar part of town* 2 not having any knowledge of something: *He's unfamiliar with my novels.*
• *Word Family:* **unfamiliarity** *noun*

unfit *adjective*
1 not in good physical condition 2 not good enough for something: *This food is unfit to eat.*
• *Word Family:* **unfitness** *noun* **unfitted** *adjective*

unfold *verb*
1 to open out something that has been folded 2 to become known or to become visible bit by bit: *The news story was gradually unfolding. / The landscape unfolded before us.*

unforeseen *adjective*
not expected: *an unforeseen problem*
• *Word Family:* **unforeseeable** *adjective*

unfortunate *adjective*
1 not lucky: *The unfortunate driver has had three accidents this week.* 2 not likely to turn out well: *She made the unfortunate decision to resign.*
• *Word Family:* **unfortunately** *adverb*

ungainly *adjective*
clumsy or awkward: *an ungainly walk*
• *Word Family:* **ungainliness** *noun*

unhealthy (*say* un-**helth**-ee) *adjective*
1 not very well: *She looks thin and pale and quite unhealthy.* 2 likely to make you unwell eventually: *unhealthy foods*

unicorn (*say* **yoo**-ni-korn) *noun*
an imaginary creature similar to a horse but with one long horn in the centre of its forehead
• *Word Origins:* from a Latin word meaning "a horn"

unicycle (*say* **yoo**-ni-sigh-kul) *noun*
a cycle with a single wheel that clowns or acrobats ride

uniform (*say* **yoo**-ni-form) *noun*
1 the special clothes worn by members of a particular group of people to make them look different from others: *a police uniform / a school uniform*
uniform *adjective*
2 exactly the same throughout without varying: *Mix the ingredients to a uniform thickness.*
• *Word Family:* **uniformity** *noun* sameness **uniformly** *adverb*

unify (*say* **yoo**-ni-fy) *verb*
to bring separate things together to make one whole thing
• *Word Family:* other forms are **unifies, unified, unifying** □ **unification** *noun*

uninhibited *adjective*
freely behaving as you want to without caring what other people think

union (*say* **yoon**-yon) *noun*
1 two or more things or people that are joined together to become one thing: *the union of East and West Germany* 2 *short for* **trade union**
• *Word Family:* **unionize** *verb* to organize into a trade union **unionist** *noun* a member of a trade union

unique (*say* yoo-**neek**) *adjective*
being the only one of its kind
• *Word Family:* **uniquely** *adverb*

unisex (*say* **yoo**-ni-sex) *adjective*
for both men and women: *a unisex hairdresser*

unison (*say* **yoo**-ni-sun) *noun*
in unison all together at the same time: *The class recited the poem in unison.*

unit (*say* **yoo**-nit) *noun*
1 a thing, group or person considered as a single thing but forming part of a larger group or whole: *a unit of soldiers in the army* 2 a quantity or amount used as a standard of measurement: *A litre is a unit of volume.* 3 a separate part of a machine that has a particular use

unite (*say* yoo-**nite**) *verb*
to join together so as to become one thing or group: *The states united to form a single country.*
• *Word Family:* **unity** *noun* being united **united** *adjective*

A B C D E F G H I J K L M N O P Q R S T U V W X Y Z

universal (*say* yoo-ni-**ver**-sal) *adjective*
including or affecting all people, things or places: *universal peace*
•***Word Family:*** **universality** *noun* **universally** *adverb*

universe (*say* **yoo**-ni-vers) *noun*
1 all the space, matter and energy that is thought to exist 2 the world and all its people

university (*say* yoo-ni-**ver**-si-tee) *noun*
a place where students can go after they've left school to study for a degree or do research
•***Word Family:*** the plural is **universities**

unjust *adjective*
unfair: *an unjust decision*.
•***Word Family:*** **unjustly** *adverb*

unkind *adjective*
nasty or a bit cruel: *an unkind thing to say*
•***Word Family:*** **unkindly** *adverb*

unleaded *adjective*
containing no lead: *unleaded petrol*

unleavened *adjective*
not made with yeast to make it rise: *unleavened bread*

unlikely *adjective*
1 probably not true or likely to happen: *an unlikely tale / It's unlikely to snow in summer.*
2 surprising or strange: *What an unlikely pair!*
•***Word Family:*** **unlikelihood** *noun*

unmistakable *adjective*
so clear, obvious or well-known that it could not be mistaken for anything else: *the unmistakable smell of curry*
•***Word Family:*** **unmistakably** *adverb*

unnatural *adjective*
not natural or normal: *There was an unnatural quiet in the classroom.*
•***Word Family:*** **unnaturally** *adverb*

unnecessary (*say* un-**nes**-is-ree *or* un-**nes**-a-se-ri) *adjective*
1 not necessary or not needed: *It was unnecessary for you to come.* 2 more than is necessary or needed: *He acted with unnecessary caution.*
•***Word Family:*** **unnecessarily** *adverb*

unorthodox *adjective*
different from the usual: *an unorthodox view*
•***Word Family:*** **unorthodoxy** *noun*

unpalatable (*say* un-**pal**-it-a-bul) *adjective*
unpleasant, or hard to accept: *unpalatable food / an unpalatable decision*

unquestioning *adjective*
without any questions or protest: *unquestioning obedience*
•***Word Family:*** **unquestioningly** *adverb*

unreal *adjective*
1 imaginary: *unreal fears* 2 not true to life: *unreal characters in a story*
•***Word Family:*** **unrealistic** *adjective* **unreality** *noun*

unrest *noun*
anger and unhappiness in a group of people

unruly *adjective*
noisy and uncontrollable: *an unruly child*

unscrew *verb*
1 to remove something by taking out the screws that are holding it in place 2 to remove a lid, cap and so on by turning it round and round

unseemly *adjective*
not becoming or in good taste: *unseemly behaviour*

unsettle *verb*
to make you feel disturbed or upset: *The fireworks unsettled the baby.*

unsightly *adjective*
not pleasant to look at

unskilled *adjective*
1 not trained to do a job: *unskilled workers*
2 not needing special training: *unskilled work*

unsuitable *adjective*
not right or appropriate for something

unthinkable *adjective*
1 too terrible to think about: *unthinkable horrors*
2 outrageous or out of the question: *That's unthinkable!*

until *preposition*
1 up to a particular time: *We'll wait until midday.*
2 before: *The dance doesn't start until ten.*
until *conjunction*
3 to the time when: *I'll stay here until I get better.*
4 before: *I couldn't leave until my teacher left.*

untold *adjective*
1 not told: *an untold secret* 2 too much or too many to be calculated: *untold damage*

untruth *noun*
a lie
•***Word Family:*** **untrue** *adjective* **untruthful** *adjective* **untruthfully** *adverb*

unused (*say* un-**yoozd**) *adjective*
1 not having been used: *Find an unused glass and I'll pour you some punch.* 2 **unused to** (*say* un-**yoost**) not used to something: *He's unused to the cold.*

unusual *adjective*
not seen or done very often
•***Word Family:*** **unusually** *adverb* particularly

unwaged *plural noun*
people who do not earn money from a job
•***Word Family:*** **unwaged** *adjective*

unwieldy *adjective*
difficult to move or manage because it is very big or has a strange shape: *an unwieldy package*

unwind (*say* un-**wined**) *verb*
1 to undo something which was wound round something else: *She unwound the bandage from her arm.* 2 to relax: *It takes me a couple of hours to unwind after school.*
•***Word Family:*** other forms are **unwinds, unwound, unwinding**

unwitting *adjective*
not intended: *an unwitting insult*
•***Word Family:*** **unwittingly** *adverb*

up *adverb*
1 to or towards a higher place: *Carry the pillow up the stairs.* 2 out of bed: *to get up*
up *preposition*
3 to or towards a higher place: *up a tree*
4 further along: *up the road*
up *adjective*
5 occurring or happening: *What's up?*

Upanishad *noun*
one of a collection of ancient writings that form the basis of Hinduism

upbringing *noun*
the way a person is brought up as a child

update *verb*
1 to make something up-to-date by adding new information or parts: *to update a computer program* 2 to give the latest news to someone: *I'll update you on what's been happening.*

upgrade *verb*
1 to give someone a better or more important job 2 to improve something: *I need to upgrade my word processor.*

upheaval *noun*
a lot of disturbance caused by a change: *Our house is in a state of upheaval because we have just moved.*

uphill *adjective*
1 going up a hill or slope: *an uphill climb*
2 difficult: *It'll be an uphill job to convince him.*

uphold *verb*
1 to support something so that it stays strong: *We need to uphold our laws.* 2 to say officially that a legal decision was correct: *The appeal court upheld the judge's ruling.*
•***Word Family:*** other forms are **upholds, upheld, upholding** □ **upholder** *noun*

upholster *verb*
to fit a chair with stuffing, springs, cushions and coverings
•***Word Family:*** **upholsterer** *noun* **upholstery** *noun*

upkeep *noun*
the cost or work involved in looking after a person, place or thing: *the upkeep of a car*

upper *adjective*
1 higher than something else: *the upper lip / the upper floors of a building* 2 facing upwards: *the upper surface of the table*
upper *noun*
3 the part of a shoe or boot above the sole.

upper case *noun*
capital letters

upright *adjective*
1 standing or sitting with your back straight
2 honest and moral: *an upright man*
upright *adverb*
3 standing or sitting with your back straight

uproar *noun*
noisy excitement and confusion: *The meeting ended in an uproar.*

upset (*say* up-**set**) *verb*
1 to make you feel unhappy: *The news really upset me.* 2 to knock something over: *He upset his glass of lemonade in his lap.*
upset (*say* **up**-set) *noun*
3 a short illness affecting your stomach and digestive system: *a tummy upset*
upset (*say* up-**set**) *adjective*
4 unhappy because of something that has happened
•***Word Family:*** other verb forms are **upsets, upset, upsetting**

upshot *noun*
the end result

upside down *adverb*
with the top at the bottom and the bottom at the top: *You're holding the picture upside down.*
•***Word Family:*** **upside down** *adjective*

uptight *adjective*
tense and worried: *He's uptight about playing in the concert tonight.*

up-to-date *adjective*
1 modern or fashionable: *an up-to-date computer*
2 containing the latest information or improvements: *an up-to-date atlas*

uranium (*say* yoo-**ray**-ni-um) *noun*
a white, radioactive metal used in nuclear reactors and as the basis of the first atomic bombs

A B C D E F G H I J K L M N O P Q R S T U V W X Y Z

urban *adjective*
to do with cities and large towns

urchin (*say* **er**-chin) *noun*
a small, mischievous, shabbily dressed child: *a street urchin*

Urdu *noun*
the official language of Pakistan which is also spoken in parts of India

urge *verb*
1 to try to make a person or animal go somewhere: *He urged his horse on with a whip.*
2 to encourage or persuade someone to do something: *He urged me to buy his old watch.*
urge *noun*
3 a strong desire: *I had a sudden urge for chocolate.*

urgent (*say* **er**-jent) *adjective*
needing immediate attention or action: *an urgent message*
•***Word Family:*** **urgency** *noun* **urgently** *adverb*

urinal (*say* yoor-**rye**-nal) *noun*
a bowl or trough fixed to a wall in a public toilet for men to urinate in

urinate (*say* **yoor**-in-ate) *verb*
to pass urine from your body
•***Word Family:*** **urination** *noun*

urine (*say* **yoor**-in) *noun*
a fluid produced by your kidneys and passed from your body when you go to the toilet
•***Word Family:*** **urinary** *adjective* to do with producing and passing urine

urn (*say* ern) *noun*
1 a vase, usually with a base or stem, used for storing the ashes of a cremated person 2 a large, metal container in which tea or coffee are made and kept hot

use (*say* yooz) *verb*
1 to put something into action or service: *We use the front room to watch TV.* 2 to take advantage of someone for selfish reasons: *She used me to get close to my best friend.* 3 **use up** to finish up all there is of something
use (*say* yooce) *noun*
4 the action or fact of using something: *The use of e-mail is gradually increasing.* 5 being used: *Is that custom still in use?* 6 the way that something is used: *A dictionary has many uses.* 7 the right or ability to use something: *I've lost the use of one eye.* 8 the need to use something: *Do you have any further use for this book?* 9 the continued practice of using something: *It's a custom that has become established with use.*
•***Word Family:*** **usage** *noun* **usable** *adjective* **useful** *adjective* **usefulness** *noun* **useless** *adjective* **user** *noun*

used *adjective*
1 (*say* yoozd) having already been used or owned by someone else: *a used car*
2 **used to** (*say* yoost) known because you've done it or seen it often before: *I'm used to the noise.*

user-friendly *adjective*
designed to be easy to use

usher *noun*
1 someone who shows other people to their seats in a cinema, church or theatre
usher *verb*
2 to show someone the way to a place and take them there
•***Word Family:*** **usherette** *noun* a woman who works as an usher in a cinema
•***Word Origins:*** from a Latin word meaning "doorman"

usual *adjective*
expected because you have used it or it has happened before: *your usual desk / your usual music lesson*
•***Word Family:*** **usually** *adverb*

utensil (*say* yoo-**ten**-sil) *noun*
a tool used in the kitchen
•***Word Origins:*** from a Latin word meaning "fit for use"

uterus (*say* **yoo**-ta-rus) *noun*
the part of a woman's body in which a baby grows
•***Word Family:*** the plural is **uteri** or **uteruses**

utilize or **utilise** (*say* **yoo**-ti-lize) *verb*
to make use of something: *The system utilizes the sun's rays to heat the building.*
•***Word Family:*** **utilization** *noun*

utility (*say* yoo-**til**-i-tee) *noun*
1 being useful 2 a useful service provided for the public such as water, electricity and gas

utmost *adjective*
1 greatest possible: *These exams are of the utmost importance.*
utmost *noun*
2 the greatest possible extent: *He tried his utmost to win.*

utter (1) *verb*
to say out loud: *The mouse uttered a squeak.*
•***Word Family:*** **utterance** *noun*

utter (2) *adjective*
total: *They lived in utter misery for years.*
•***Word Family:*** **utterly** *adverb*

vacant (*say* **vay**-kant) *adjective*
1 not occupied: *vacant seats* 2 vague: *a vacant stare*
•***Word Family:*** **vacancy** *noun* **vacantly** *adverb*

vacation (*say* vay-**kay**-shon *or* va-**kay**-shon) *noun*
1 a holiday 2 the time of the year between terms at a university or college: *summer vacation*

vaccine (*say* **vak**-seen) *noun*
a medicine made from the germs that produce a disease, given to people to stop them from catching the disease
•***Word Family:*** **vaccinate** *verb* to give a vaccine to someone **vaccination** *noun*

vacuum (*say* **vak**-yoom) *noun*
1 an empty space from which air and all other gases have been removed 2 a machine that sucks up dirt from floors
vacuum *verb*
3 to clean something using a vacuum cleaner

vagina (*say* va-**jie**-na) *noun*
the passage in a female's body that connects her womb to the sex organs outside her body

vagrant (*say* **vay**-grunt) *noun*
someone who wanders from place to place and has no settled home or job

vague (*say* vaig) *adjective*
1 not clear or distinct: *a vague, shadowy figure / a vague memory* 2 not concentrating, or thinking about something else: *a vague expression*
•***Word Family:*** **vaguely** *adverb* **vagueness** *noun*

vain *adjective*
1 too proud of your looks, abilities and so on
2 hopeless or useless: *She made a vain attempt to stop the baby crying.*
vain *adverb*
2 **in vain** without having any success: *I tried in vain to call her.*
•***Word Family:*** **vainly** *adverb*
•***Word Origins:*** from a Latin word meaning "empty"

valentine (*say* **val**-en-tine) *noun*
1 a card sent to someone you love or someone you fancy on St Valentine's Day (February 14th) 2 the person you send the card to

valiant (*say* **val**-i-unt) *adjective*
very brave: *a valiant soldier / She made a valiant effort to finish on time.*
•***Word Family:*** **valiantly** *adverb*

valid *adjective*
1 officially usable: *The ticket is only valid for one month.* 2 reasonable enough to be accepted: *Do you have a valid excuse?*
•***Word Family:*** **validity** *noun*

valley *noun*
a low stretch of land between hills or higher land, often with a river flowing through it

valour or **valor** (*say* **val**-a) *noun*
very great courage

valuable (*say* **val**-yoo-bul) *adjective*
1 worth a lot of money or very important: *a valuable painting / valuable friends*
valuable *noun*
3 **valuables** any objects such as jewellery, that are worth a lot of money

value (*say* **val**-yoo) *noun*
1 the fact of being worthwhile or useful: *What's the value of all the reading you've done?* 2 the amount of money something is worth: *the value of your car* 3 **values** a person's ideas about what is right and wrong and how people should behave: *We have similar values.*
value *verb*
4 to work out how much something could be sold for: *to value a house* 5 to think highly of something: *I value your friendship.*
•***Word Family:*** **valuation** *noun* **valuer** *noun*

valve *noun*
1 the part attached to a pipe for controlling the flow of liquids or gases 2 one of the parts in your heart or your veins that control the flow of blood

vampire *noun*
an imaginary character, who is a dead person who has returned to life, thought to leave its grave at night and suck the blood of sleeping people

van *noun*
a vehicle between a car and a lorry in size that is used for carrying goods

vandal *noun*
someone who destroys or damages things on purpose
•***Word Family:*** **vandalize** or **vandalise** *verb* **vandalism** *noun*
•***Word Origins:*** named after the *Vandals*, a Germanic tribe that destroyed Rome in AD 455

vanilla *noun*
a flavouring for food made from a pod-like fruit: *vanilla ice-cream*

A B C D E F G H I J K L M N O P Q R S T U V W X Y Z

vanish *verb*
to disappear completely, especially quickly: *He vanished into the night.*

vanity *noun*
being too proud of your looks, abilities and so on

vanquish (*say* **vang**-kwish) *verb*
to conquer: *He vanquished his enemies.*

vaporize or **vaporise** (*say* **vay**-pa-rize) *verb*
to change a liquid or something solid into steam or gas
• *Word Family:* **vaporization** *noun*

vapour or **vapor** (*say* **vay**-pa) *noun*
a gas-like substance, such as mist or steam, which some substances turn into when you heat them

variable (*say* **vair**-i-a-bul) *adjective*
likely to change: *variable weather*
• *Word Family:* **variably** *adverb*

variation (*say* vair-ri-**ay**-shon) *noun*
1 a slight change: *variations in temperature from the expected spring weather* 2 a simple tune repeated in different keys, tempos or rhythms: *variations on a theme of Beethoven*

variety (*say* va-**rye**-a-tee) *noun*
1 differences or different parts to something: *I want a job with variety not dull routine.* 2 a different kind of something: *We have 37 varieties of ice-cream.* 3 a number of different things: *She gave a variety of reasons to support her argument.*
• *Word Family:* the plural is **varieties**

various (*say* **vair**-i-us) *adjective*
1 different: *We have this skirt in various colours.* 2 several: *He spoke to various guests.*
• *Word Family:* **variously** *adverb*

varnish *noun*
1 a liquid coating that dries and leaves a glossy, transparent look when you put it on a surface
varnish *verb*
2 to put varnish on something

vary (*say* **vair**-ree) *verb*
1 to change: *The quality of our product never varies.* 2 to make changes in something: *You should vary your diet more.*
• *Word Family:* other forms are **varies, varied, varying**

vase (*say* vahz) *noun*
a special container for flowers

vassal *noun*
someone in feudal times who lived and worked on the land on a nobleman's estate and had to provide food and be prepared to fight for the nobleman in exchange

vast (*say* vahst) *adjective*
very great: *a vast desert* / *vast sums of money*
• *Word Family:* **vastly** *adverb* **vastness** *noun*

vat *noun*
a large container for liquids

vault (1) (*say* volt) *noun*
1 an underground room, such as a burial place under a church, or a room for storing valuable objects in a bank 2 an arched roof: *the vault of a cathedral*

vault (2) (*say* volt) *verb*
to jump over something using your hands or a pole as support

VCR *noun*
a video tape-recorder that records both images and sounds
• *Word Origins:* short for video cassette recorder

VDU *noun*
the short form of **visual display unit**

veal *noun*
the meat of a calf

Veda *noun*
one of the oldest of the holy writings in Hinduism

veer *verb*
to change direction: *The bus veered to the right.*

vegetable (*say* **vej**-ta-bul) *noun*
a plant or part of a plant that is used as food, such as a carrot, pea or bean

vegetarian (*say* vej-a-**tair**-ri-un) *noun*
someone who eats vegetable foods only except, usually, for eggs and dairy produce
• *Word Family:* **vegetarianism** *noun*

vegetation (*say* ve-ja-**tay**-shon) *noun*
the plants that grow in a certain area

vehement (*say* **vee**-a-ment) *adjective*
strongly passionate: *a vehement speech against nuclear weapons*
• *Word Family:* **vehemence** *noun* **vehemently** *adverb*

vehicle (*say* **vee**-ik-ul) *noun*
a car, truck, bike or another form of transport used for carrying people or goods

veil (*say* vale) *noun*
1 a piece of cloth, often a transparent one, that is worn by a woman on her head and hanging over her face or shoulders 2 a layer of something which conceals something: *a veil of mist over the mountains*
• *Word Origins:* from a Latin word meaning "curtain"

vein (*say* vane) *noun*
1 one of the thin-walled tubes carrying blood around your body and back to your heart 2 a thin line on a leaf or an insect's wing 3 a strip of coal, gold or another metal in a crack in between rocks

Velcro *noun*
a type of fastener made with strips of small nylon threads and hooks, that stick together when pressed firmly together
•***Word Origins:*** this word is a trademark

velocity (*say* ve-**los**-i-tee) *noun*
the speed at which something is moving in a certain direction: *the velocity of wind*
•***Word Family:*** the plural is **velocities**

velvet *noun*
a soft, thick material that hangs in heavy folds
•***Word Family:*** **velvety** *adjective*

veneer (*say* ve-**near**) *noun*
1 a thin layer of wood or plastic used to cover a surface 2 a pleasant appearance covering what is hidden underneath: *Under a veneer of meekness he's really a vicious person.*

venerable (*say* **ven**-ra-bul) *adjective*
worthy of great respect: *a venerable old artist*
•***Word Family:*** **venerate** *verb*

venereal disease (*say* ve-**neer**-ree-al diz-eez) *noun*
any disease other than HIV that is spread by having sexual intercourse with an infected person

vengeance (*say* **ven**-jence) *noun*
1 harming someone who has harmed you
2 **with a vengeance** much more strongly than you would expect: *The hail was coming down with a vengeance.*

venison *noun*
the meat of a deer
•***Word Origins:*** from a Latin word meaning "hunting"

Venn diagram *noun*
a drawing in maths using circles to show the relationships of one set to another

venom *noun*
1 a poison made by certain animals, such as spiders and snakes, and injected into their victims by a bite or sting 2 spiteful anger: *The critic's attack was full of venom.*
•***Word Family:*** **venomous** *adjective*

vent *noun*
1 an opening that allows air or smoke to escape from a room, or lava to escape from a volcano
vent *verb*
2 to let out strong feelings: *She vented her anger on the unfortunate bystanders.*

ventilate (*say* **vent**-i-late) *verb*
to allow fresh air to flow around a room: *Ventilate the room by opening all the windows.*
•***Word Family:*** **ventilation** *noun* **ventilator** *noun*

ventriloquist (*say* ven-**tril**-a-kwist) *noun*
someone able to produce sounds or voices that seem to come from somewhere else: *a ventriloquist's dummy*
•***Word Family:*** **ventriloquism** *noun*

venture *noun*
1 something you decide to do that may involve risk or danger
venture *verb*
2 to go somewhere risky: *to venture up the steep cliffs* 3 to dare to suggest: *Might I venture a suggestion?*

venue (*say* **ven**-yoo) *noun*
the place where an event takes place: *The new stadium is the venue for the football final.*

verandah or **veranda** (*say* ve-**ran**-da) *noun*
an open area with a floor and roof on the outside of a house

verb *noun*
a word that expresses what someone or something does or feels, such as "sang" and "was" in *The boy sang because he was happy.*
•***Word Family:*** **verbally** *adverb*

verbal *adjective*
1 expressed in spoken words: *a verbal agreement*
2 to do with words and how they are used: *verbal skills*
•***Word Family:*** **verbally** *adverb*

verbatim (*say* ver-**bay**-tim) *adverb*
using exactly the same words: *to quote from the poem verbatim*

verdict *noun*
a judge's or jury's decision about whether someone is guilty or innocent in a court case

verge (*say* verj) *noun*
1 a strip of grass beside a road 2 **on the verge of** just about to: *on the verge of leaving home*
verge *verb*
3 **verge on** to be almost: *He must be verging on 60.*

verify (*say* **ve**-ri-fie) *verb*
to make sure that something is the truth: *We can verify your alibi by asking your witnesses.*
•***Word Family:*** other forms are **verifies, verified, verifying** □ **verification** *noun* proof or confirmation

vermin *noun*
harmful or dirty pests that damage food or carry disease, such as rats or cockroaches

a b c d e f g h i j k l m n o p q r s t u v w x y z

A B C D E F G H I J K L M N O P Q R S T U V W X Y Z

•*Word Family:* the plural is **vermin** □ **verminous** *adjective*
•*Word Origins:* from a Latin word meaning "worm"

versatile (*say* **ver**-sa-tile) *adjective*
able to do different things well and to change from one to the other: *a versatile performer on violin, viola and cello*
•*Word Family:* **versatility** *noun*

verse *noun*
1 a part of a poem or song 2 poetry: *a child's book of verse* 3 a short, numbered division of a chapter in the Bible

version (*say* **ver**-zhon) *noun*
1 someone's own account of an event: *Don't believe his version of the accident.* 2 a different form of something: *the film version of a novel*

versus *preposition*
against: *Manchester United versus Newcastle*

vertebra (*say* **ver**-ta-bra) *noun*
one of the chain of bones that form your spine
•*Word Family:* the plural is **vertebrae** (*say* **ver**-ti-bray *or* **ver**-ta-bree)

vertebrate (*say* **ver**-ta-brit) *noun*
an animal with a backbone: *A crocodile is a vertebrate but a slug is not.*

vertex *noun*
a point where two or more lines meet or three or more sides meet
•*Word Family:* the plural is **vertices** (*say* **ver**-ti-seez) or **vertexes**

vertical *adjective*
upright or at right angles to the horizon: *a vertical pole*
•*Word Family:* **vertically** *adverb*

vertigo *noun*
dizziness and loss of balance that some people get when they are high up
•*Word Origins:* from a Latin word meaning "whirling"

vessel *noun*
1 a ship or large boat 2 a container for liquids, such as a bottle 3 a tube in your body that blood flows through

vestibule (*say* **vest**-i-bewl) *noun*
an entrance hall or lobby

vestry *noun*
the part of a church where the clergy change into their robes
•*Word Family:* the plural is **vestries**

vet *verb*
1 to check something carefully: *The security guards vetted the passengers boarding the plane.*
vet *noun*
2 *a short form of* **veterinary surgeon**
•*Word Family:* other verb forms are **vets, vetted, vetting**

veteran (*say* **vet**-a-run) *noun*
1 someone who has been doing something for a long time and has a lot of experience at it: *a veteran war reporter*
veteran *adjective*
2 built before 1918: *a veteran car*

veterinary surgeon (*say* **vet**-er-in-ree sur-jen) *noun*
someone trained to treat and operate on sick animals

veto (*say* **vee**-toe) *noun*
1 the right to prevent something from going ahead
veto *verb*
2 to refuse to agree to: *to veto a treaty*
•*Word Family:* the plural of the noun is **vetoes** □ other verb forms are **vetoes, vetoed, vetoing**
•*Word Origins:* from a Latin word meaning "I forbid"

vex *verb*
to irritate someone
•*Word Family:* **vexation** *noun* **vexatious** *adjective* **vexed** *adjective*

VHF *noun*
a waveband which many radio stations are broadcast on

via (*say* **vie**-a) *preposition*
by way of: *We flew to Australia via Thailand.*

viaduct (*say* **vie**-a-dukt) *noun*
a long bridge with many arches spanning a valley and carrying a road or railway across it

vibrant (*say* **vie**-brant) *adjective*
1 lively and energetic: *She has a vibrant personality.* 2 rich and strong: *The painting was done in vibrant colours.*
•*Word Family:* **vibrancy** *noun* **vibrantly** *adverb*

vibrate (*say* vie-**brate**) *verb*
to throb or shake: *The drill vibrated in my hand.*
•*Word Family:* **vibration** *noun*

vibrato (*say* vi-**brah**-toe) *noun*
a slight variation or trembling in the pitch of a note produced by a singer or musician to make the sound fuller and richer

vicar (*say* **vik**-a) *noun*
a member of the Anglican clergy in the Christian church who is in charge of a parish
•*Word Family:* **vicarage** *noun* the home of a vicar

vice (1) *noun*
1 a bad habit: *Smoking is one of his vices.*
2 wicked or criminal behaviour: *a den of vice*

vice (2) *noun*
a tool with two strong jaws that you tighten to hold an object firmly

vice versa (*say* vie-sa **ver**-sa) *adverb*
the other way around. *He doesn't like Susan and vice versa* means *He doesn't like Susan and Susan doesn't like him.*

vicinity (*say* va-**sin**-i-tee) *noun*
the area near a place: *Look in the vicinity of the swings.*
•*Word Family:* the plural is **vicinities**

vicious (*say* **vish**-us) *adjective*
1 fierce: *a vicious animal* 2 spiteful or cruel: *a vicious lie*
•*Word Family:* **viciously** *adverb*

victim *noun*
someone who is harmed or injured: *an accident victim*

victimize or **victimise** *verb*
to deliberately treat someone unfairly
•*Word Family:* **victimization** *noun*

victory (*say* **vik**-ta-ree) *noun*
a win against an opponent in a contest or war
•*Word Family:* the plural is **victories** □ **victor** *noun* the winner **victorious** *adjective*

video (*say* **vid**-ee-o) *noun*
1 a machine that records both pictures and sounds and can play them back when connected to your television set 2 a film or recorded TV programme that you can play back on a television using a video 3 a video cassette
video *verb*
4 to record a TV programme to play back later using a video
•*Word Family:* **videotape** *noun* magnetic tape onto which pictures and sounds are recorded
•*Word Origins:* from a Latin word meaning "I see"

video cassette *noun*
a video recording inside a box that you can insert into a video

video game *noun*
an electronic game played with images on a visual display screen

view *noun*
1 what you can see when you look in a particular direction or from a particular place: *The view out over the valley was breathtaking.*
2 an opinion: *What are your views on junk food?*
3 **in view of** considering: *In view of the bad weather we'll stay in.* 4 **on view** shown or exhibited for everyone to see
view *verb*
5 to look at something: *to view a building site*
6 to consider something: *I view your conduct with disgust.*
•*Word Family:* **viewer** *noun*

vigil (*say* **vij**-il) *noun*
staying quietly in a place to keep watch: *to keep vigil by a dying man*

vigilant (*say* **vij**-i-lunt) *adjective*
alert and watchful
•*Word Family:* **vigilance** *noun* **vigilantly** *adverb*

vigour or **vigor** (*say* **vig**-a) *noun*
energetic strength or force
•*Word Family:* **vigorous** *adjective* strong and lively **vigorously** *adverb*

Viking
one of the Scandinavian sailors who raided and traded with people in north west Europe between the 8th and the 11th centuries

vile *adjective*
repulsive or disgusting: *I'm shocked at your vile language.*
•*Word Family:* **vilely** *adverb* **vileness** *noun*

village (*say* **vil**-ij) *noun*
a group of houses and shops in the country, smaller than a town
•*Word Family:* **villager** *noun* someone who lives in a village

villain (*say* **vil**-un) *noun*
a wicked person
•*Word Family:* **villainous** *adjective* wicked **villainy** *noun* wickedness

vindicate (*say* **vin**-di-kate) *verb*
to show that a person is right or innocent after all
•*Word Family:* **vindication** *noun*

vindictive (*say* vin-**dik**-tiv) *adjective*
spiteful and wanting revenge
•*Word Family:* **vindictively** *adverb*

vine *noun*
a plant, such as a grape, that climbs by winding tendrils around or over a support

vinegar (*say* **vin**-i-ga) *noun*
a sour liquid made from wine or cider that is used for flavouring or pickling food
•*Word Family:* **vinegary** *adjective*
•*Word Origins:* from French words meaning "wine" and "sour"

vineyard *noun*
a farm for growing grapevines

A B C D E F G H I J K L M N O P Q R S T U V W X Y Z

vintage (*say* **vin**-tij) *noun*
1 the year that a good quality wine was made
vintage *adjective*
2 especially good: *This has been a vintage year for travel books.* 3 built between 1918 and 1930: *a vintage car*

vinyl (*say* **vie**-nil) *noun*
a kind of plastic: *vinyl chairs*

viola (*say* vee-**ole**-a) *noun*
a stringed, musical instrument played with a bow and which is slightly larger than, and has a lower pitch than, a violin

violate (*say* **vie**-a-late) *verb*
1 to break a promise, law or agreement 2 to treat a person or place with disrespect and violence: *to violate a temple*
•***Word Family:*** **violation** *noun*

violent (*say* **vie**-a-lent) *adjective*
1 using force to hurt or injure someone 2 strong and forceful: *a violent temper / a violent headache*
•***Word Family:*** **violence** *noun* **violently** *adverb*

violet (*say* **vie**-a-let) *noun*
1 a small plant with fragrant, dark purple flowers and bright green leaves 2 a purplish-blue colour

violin (*say* vie-a-**lin**) *noun*
a stringed, high-pitched, musical instrument held under your chin and played with a bow
•***Word Family:*** **violinist** *noun* someone who plays the violin

violoncello (*say* vie-a-lin-**chel**-oh) *noun*
the long form of **cello**

VIP *noun*
an important person
•***Word Origins:*** short for *v*ery *i*mportant *p*erson

viper *noun*
a venomous snake with a thick body found in Europe, Africa and Asia

virgin (*say* **ver**-jin) *noun*
1 someone who has never had sexual intercourse
virgin *adjective*
2 pure or untouched: *virgin snow*
•***Word Family:*** **virginity** *noun*

virile (*say* **vi**-rile) *adjective*
strong and manly
•***Word Family:*** **virility** (*say* vi-**ril**-itee) *noun*
•***Word Origins:*** from a Latin word meaning "like a man"

virtual (*say* **ver**-tew-ul) *adjective*
as if it were actually the case: *He's the virtual head of the company even though he isn't the chairman.*
•***Word Family:*** **virtually** *adverb* essentially

virtual reality *noun*
a made-up world created using powerful computer-assisted machines, a hand-held control and an encasing headset which presents the user with 3D images

virtue (*say* **ver**-tew) *noun*
1 goodness 2 a good quality in your character: *Patience is a virtue.*
•***Word Family:*** **virtuous** *adjective* honourable and obedient **virtuously** *adverb*

virtuoso (*say* ver-tew-**oh**-so) *noun*
a musician who displays dazzling skill when he or she performs
•***Word Family:*** the plural is **virtuosi** or **virtuosos** □ **virtuosity** *noun* the skill of a virtuoso

virus (*say* **vie**-rus) *noun*
1 a tiny organism, too small to be seen with an ordinary microscope, which may cause disease 2 an illness caused by a virus 3 a hidden computer program which is introduced into a computer on a floppy disk and which can spread to other computers and destroy files or software
•***Word Family:*** **viral** *adjective*

visa (*say* **vee**-za) *noun*
an official stamp or written permit, from a foreign country, in your passport that allows you to visit that country for a certain time

visible (*say* **viz**-i-bul) *adjective*
able to be seen: *The road was scarcely visible through the fog.*
•***Word Family:*** **visibility** *noun* **visibly** *adverb*

vision (*say* **vi**-zhon) *noun*
1 the ability to see: *to have excellent vision* 2 a mental picture: *a vision of angels / visions of grandeur* 3 imaginative understanding: *Leaders need real vision.*
•***Word Family:*** **visionary** *adjective* **visionary** *noun*

visit (*say* **viz**-it) *verb*
1 to go to see someone or something: *Have you visited the art show yet?* 2 to stay with someone: *We spent last month visiting relations.*
•***Word Family:*** **visitor** *noun*

visor (*say* **vie**-zor) *noun*
1 the movable part of a helmet that protects your face 2 a small, movable shield set above the windscreen of a car to protect the driver's eyes from the sun

visual (*say* **viz**-yew-al) *adjective*
to do with sight: *Visual aids for teaching include maps and films.*
•***Word Family:*** **visually** *adverb*

visual display unit *noun*
a computer terminal that shows information on a screen

visualize or **visualise** (*say* **viz**-yoo-al-ize) *verb*
to form a mental image of something: *Try to visualize the scene of the accident.*

vital (*say* **vie**-tal) *adjective*
1 necessary for life: *Your heart is a vital organ.*
2 essential or very important: *Pollution control is vital for the survival of our environment.*
3 vigorous and full of life: *a vital child*
•***Word Family:*** **vitally** *adverb*

vitality (*say* vie-**tal**-i-tee) *noun*
energy and enthusiasim for life

vitamin (*say* **vie**-ta-min *or* **vit**-a-min) *noun*
one of a number of substances found in some foods that are essential for our life and growth but only needed in very small amounts

vivacious (*say* vi-**vay**-shus) *adjective*
full of life and spirit
•***Word Family:*** **vivaciously** *adverb* **vivacity** *noun*

vivid *adjective*
1 intense or bright: *vivid blue / vivid sunlight*
2 giving a clear and detailed mental picture: *You certainly have a vivid imagination.*
•***Word Family:*** **vividly** *adverb* **vividness** *noun*

vivisection *noun*
the use of living animals in experiments by scientists and medical researchers

vixen (*say* **vik**-sen) *noun*
a female fox

vocabulary (*say* vo-**kab**-yoo-la-ree) *noun*
the whole range of words known and used by a person or group of people: *to have a huge vocabulary*

vocal (*say* **vo**-kul) *adjective*
1 to do with your voice 2 sung or meant for singing 3 outspoken or talkative: *She is vocal on the topic of clothes.*
•***Word Family:*** **vocalist** *noun* a singer

vocational (*say* voh-**kay**-shun-al) *adjective*
designed to teach you how to do a particular job: *vocational training*

vodka *noun*
a strong, alcoholic drink made from rye, corn or potatoes and originally made in Russia from wheat

vogue *noun*
the current fashion

voice *noun*
1 the sounds you make with your mouth and vocal chords when you speak or sing 2 your opinion: *She insists on a voice in this matter.*
voice *verb*
3 to express something in words: *to voice your opinion*

void *noun*
1 an empty space: *The spaceship was swallowed up in the void.*
void *adjective*
2 empty: *Her face was void of expression.*
3 having no legal power: *The court declared the contract void.*

volatile (*say* **vol**-a-tile) *adjective*
1 changing rapidly from one mood, idea or state to another: *a volatile personality* 2 easily changing from a liquid into a vapour: *a volatile substance*

volcano (*say* vol-**kay**-no) *noun*
a mountain with an opening at the top through which lava, hot gases and ash are forced when it erupts
•***Word Family:*** the plural is **volcanoes** □ **volcanic** *adjective*
•***Word Origins:*** named after *Vulcan*, the ancient Roman god of fire

volley (*say* **vol**-ee) *noun*
1 the firing of a number of weapons at the same time: *a volley of machine-gun fire* 2 the return of a tennis ball before it hits the ground
volley *verb*
3 to hit the ball before it hits the ground or bounces

volleyball *noun*
a game played on a court with a high net, usually between two teams of six players, in which you try to stop the ball touching the ground by hitting it over the net with your hand

voltage (*say* **vole**-tij *or* **vol**-tij) *noun*
the force of an electric current measured in volts
•***Word Family:*** **volt** *noun* a measurement of electric force

volume (*say* **vol**-yoom) *noun*
1 the amount of space a body or substance takes up: *Work out the volume of this container.* 2 a quantity or amount, especially a large quantity: *Our volume of business is steadily increasing. / Volumes of smoke billowed from the tyre factory.*
3 a book, especially one of a set of books
4 loudness: *Please turn up the volume of the TV.*

voluntary *adjective*
1 done because you want to do it: *to make a voluntary statement to the police* 2 unpaid: *voluntary work*
•***Word Family:*** **voluntarily** *adverb*

volunteer (*say* vol-un-**teer**) *noun*
1 someone who offers to do something of his or her own free will, such as a soldier who is not forced to join up 2 someone who does work for which they are not paid

A B C D E F G H I J K L M N O P Q R S T U V W X Y Z

volunteer *verb*
3 to offer to do something without anyone asking you: *to volunteer to help at the fête* 4 to join the army as a volunteer

vomit *verb*
to bring up the contents of your stomach through your mouth

vote *noun*
1 a way of choosing someone or something by putting your hand up or writing your choice on a piece of paper: *We chose our school council representative by a vote.* 2 the total number of votes: *The Green vote was lower than last year's.* 3 an expression: *a vote of thanks*
vote *verb*
4 to cast a vote: *to vote for your friend*
•***Word Family:*** **voter** *noun* someone who votes or has the right to vote

vouch *verb*
to guarantee something: *I can vouch for the truth of his story.*

voucher (*say* **vow**-cha) *noun*
1 a document or receipt that proves how you have spent money 2 a ticket or form used instead of cash to buy goods: *a gift voucher*

vow *verb*
1 to make a solemn promise
vow *noun*
2 a solemn promise: *a marriage vow*

vowel *noun*
1 a speech sound made without using your tongue or lips to block your breath 2 a letter, *a*, *e*, *i*, *o* or *u*, used to express these sounds

voyage (*say* **voy**-ij) *noun*
1 a journey, especially one in a ship
voyage *verb*
2 to go on a voyage
•***Word Family:*** **voyager** *noun*

vulgar *adjective*
rude: *He told a vulgar story at dinner.*
•***Word Family:*** **vulgarity** *noun*

vulnerable (*say* **vul**-na-ra-bul) *adjective*
capable of being hurt, damaged or attacked: *a vulnerable young child / The house was in a vulnerable position on the edge of a cliff.*
•***Word Family:*** **vulnerability** *noun* **vulnerably** *adverb*

vulture (*say* **vul**-cher) *noun*
a large bird of prey that feeds on dead flesh

vulva *noun*
the outer part of a woman or girl's sexual organs
•***Word Family:*** the plural is **vulvae** (*say* **vul**-vee) or **vulvas**

Ww

wad (*say* wod) *noun*
1 a soft mass: *a wad of tissue* 2 a roll: *a wad of banknotes*

waddle (*say* **wod**-ul) *verb*
to walk with short, swaying steps like a duck

wade *verb*
to walk through water

wafer *noun*
1 a sweet, thin biscuit

waffle (1) (*say* **wof**-ul) *noun*
a flat cake made from batter, cooked in a special mould

waffle (2) (*say* **wof**-ul) *noun*
1 vague or silly talk or writing
waffle *verb*
2 to talk or write a lot without expressing anything clearly: *The politician didn't answer the question, he just waffled.*

waft (*say* woft) *verb*
to blow or float lightly, especially through the air: *The leaves wafted down from the trees.*

wag *verb*
to move from side to side or up and down, especially quickly: *The dog wagged its tail.*
•***Word Family:*** other forms are **wags, wagged, wagging**

wage *noun*
1 money paid to someone for their work usually on an hourly or weekly rate
wage *verb*
2 to carry on a war or a campaign

wager *noun*
a bet

waggle *verb*
to wag with quick, short movements

wagon *noun*
a strong cart, or railway carriage for carrying heavy loads

wail *verb*
1 to give a long, high, mournful cry
wail *noun*
2 a long, sad cry

waist *noun*
the part of your body between your ribs and your hips

waistcoat *noun*
a closely fitting, sleeveless jacket reaching to your waist, sometimes worn under a jacket

wait *verb*
1 to stay or rest before going on: *Wait here till I return.* 2 **wait on** to serve or attend someone personally: *to wait on someone in a shop*
wait *noun*
3 the act or time of waiting: *a long wait for the bus* 4 **lie in wait** to wait in ambush

waiter *noun*
someone who brings food and drink to your table in a restaurant

waiting-room *noun*
a room where you can wait, such as on a station or in a clinic

waitress *noun*
a girl or woman who brings food and drink to your table in a restaurant

waive (*say* wayv) *verb*
to give something up, or not insist on it: *to waive your right to inherit his land*

wake (1) *verb*
1 to stop sleeping or stop someone sleeping: *I woke late. / Don't wake the baby.* 2 **wake up** to stop sleeping
wake *noun*
3 a party held after a funeral
• ***Word Family:*** other verb forms are **wakes, woke, woken, waking**

wake (2) *noun*
1 the pattern or track of disturbed water left behind a moving ship 2 something that follows something else: *The car left a cloud of dust in its wake.*

waken *verb*
to wake

walk *verb*
1 to go along, putting one foot in front of the other
walk *noun*
2 a journey on foot 3 the way that someone walks 4 a path or way that you can walk along: *a cliff-top walk*

walkie-talkie *noun*
a light radio you can carry and operate while moving, that sends and receives messages

walking stick *noun*
a stick that you lean on as you walk

wall *noun*
1 a solid, upright structure used for supporting, surrounding or dividing something: *the brick walls of a house / the wall surrounding the old city* 2 something that closes off or divides something, like a wall: *a wall of fire*

wallaby (*say* **wol**-a-bee) *noun*
an Australian marsupial, similar to a kangaroo but smaller and furrier
• ***Word Family:*** the plural is **wallabies**
• ***Word Origins:*** from an Aboriginal language

wallet (*say* **wol**-it) *noun*
a small, folding holder for such things as banknotes, cards and stamps, that you carry in your pocket or handbag

wallop (*say* **wol**-up) *verb*
1 to beat or strike a person or an animal hard
wallop *noun*
2 a heavy blow
• ***Word Family:*** other forms of the verb are **wallops, walloped, walloping**

wallow (*say* **wol**-oh) *verb*
1 to roll about: *The children wallowed happily in the pool.* 2 to enjoy or take great pleasure in something: *The rich man wallowed in luxury.*

wallpaper *noun*
any paper, usually with a pattern, for covering the inside walls of a room

walnut *noun*
a nut that has a wrinkled surface, like a brain

walrus (*say* **wawl**-rus) *noun*
an arctic sea-living animal, related to the seal, which has flippers and two long tusks
• ***Word Family:*** the plural is **walruses**

waltz (*rhymes with* false *or* faults) *noun*
1 a ballroom dance in which partners revolve in circles to a one-two-three rhythm 2 the music for a dance like this
waltz *verb*
3 to dance a waltz 4 to move lightly and quickly

wan (*rhymes with* on) *adjective*
pale or sickly: *a wan complexion / a wan grin*

wand (*say* wond) *noun*
a stick, such as one used by a conjurer performing magic tricks or a fairy making spells

wander (*say* **won**-da) *verb*
1 to walk around aimlessly or casually: *We got lost when we wandered away from the path.* 2 to move away from something else: *Her eyes wandered towards the new boy.*
• ***Word Family:*** **wanderer** *noun*

wane *verb*
1 to decrease in size the way the moon's face does when it changes from a full moon to a new moon 2 to decrease in power or strength: *My good spirits waned when I saw the mess.*

A B C D E F G H I J K L M N O P Q R S T U V W X Y Z

wangle *verb*
to get or accomplish something by scheming and trickery: *to wangle a free dinner*

want (*rhymes with* font) *verb*
1 to desire: *I want a bicycle for Christmas.* 2 to need: *Your hair wants a cut.*
want *noun*
3 a lack: *I'm reading this old book for want of anything better.*

wanted *adjective*
being looked for by the police: *a wanted man*

war (*say* wor) *noun*
1 serious fighting between countries or groups of people in one country 2 a conflict: *a war of words*
war *verb*
3 to engage in war or conflict
•*Word Family:* other verb forms are **wars, warred, warring**

warble *verb*
to sing with trills, the way a bird does

ward (*rhymes with* ford) *noun*
1 a division or part of a local council area, city or town, used to group people in elections 2 a room or division in a hospital, usually for a particular type of patient: *the cancer ward* 3 a young person under the protection or control of a guardian: *a ward of court*
ward *verb*
4 **ward off** to keep away: *to ward off an attack*

warden (*say* **wor**-den) *noun*
1 someone who is in charge of a building: *a prison warden* 2 a traffic warden

warder *noun*
a prison officer

wardrobe (*say* **wawd**-robe) *noun*
1 a large cupboard for storing and hanging clothes 2 a collection of clothes: *an actor's wardrobe*

warehouse *noun*
a large building where goods are stored

wares *plural noun*
goods for sale: *to sell your wares door-to-door*

warfare *noun*
fighting or war

warhead *noun*
the front part of a bomb or missile: *nuclear warheads*

warlock (*say* **wor**-lok) *noun*
a wizard or sorcerer

warm *adjective*
1 fairly hot: *a warm day* 2 lively or enthusiastic: *a warm welcome* 3 protecting you from the cold: *a warm blanket*
warm *verb*
4 to make something or to become warm: *to warm your hands by the fire* 5 **warm up** to practise or do exercises before a game or performance
•*Word Family:* **warmly** *adverb* **warmth** *noun*

warm-blooded *adjective*
having a body temperature that stays pretty much the same no matter how cold or hot the surrounding temperature is

warn *verb*
to tell someone about something dangerous or bad that is going to happen or that might happen: *The weather bureau warned of a coming hurricane. / Dad warned us not to talk to strangers.*
•*Word Family:* **warning** *noun*

warp (*say* worp) *verb*
1 to twist or bend something out of shape: *The sun warped the plastic.*
warp *noun*
2 a bend, twist or distortion 3 the yarn placed lengthwise in a loom in weaving

warrant (*say* **wo**-runt) *noun*
1 a legal document signed by a magistrate giving a police officer authority to take certain actions: *a warrant to search someone's house*
warrant *verb*
2 to justify or demand something: *The situation warrants the actions we took.*
•*Word Family:* **warranty** *noun* (**warranties**) a guarantee of reliability

warren *noun*
a series of connected burrows where rabbits live and breed

warrior (*say* **wo**-ree-a) *noun*
a soldier or fighter

warship *noun*
a ship that is built for use in war, especially one that has guns

wart (*say* wort) *noun*
a small, hard swelling on the skin, caused by a virus

wary (*say* **wair**-ree) *adjective*
careful, watchful or on your guard
•*Word Family:* other forms are **warier, wariest** □ **warily** *adverb* **wariness** *noun*

wash *verb*
1 to clean something with water and soap or detergent: *to wash your hair* 2 to flow: *The waves washed against the cliff.* 3 to carry along with water: *The river washed away the hillside.* 4 **to be washed out** to be abandoned due to rain

wash *noun*
5 an act or instance of washing: *Give your hair a good wash.* 6 clothes that are waiting to be washed: *Put your dirty socks in the wash.* 7 the pattern of waves made by a moving boat
• ***Word Family:*** **washable** *adjective* **wash-out** *noun*: *The match was a wash-out.*

washer (*say* **wosh**-a) *noun*
a flat, circular piece of metal, rubber or leather with a hole in the centre, used with a nut and bolt to seal a joint tightly

washing *noun*
clothes or laundry that are waiting to be washed or being washed
• ***Word Family:*** **washing-line** *noun* **washing-machine** *noun* **washing-powder** *noun*

washing-up *noun*
1 washing dishes and so on: *to do the washing-up* 2 dishes and so on that are waiting to be washed: *There's too much washing-up.*

wasp (*say* wosp) *noun*
a stinging insect, often found living in a colony with other wasps

waste *verb*
1 to use something up without a good reason: *to waste money* 2 to fail to use something: *He wasted the perfect opportunity.* 3 to kill 4 to become feeble and run down: *Disease has wasted his body.*
waste *noun*
5 the act of wasting: *a waste of time* 6 an area of desert or frozen land: *Arctic wastes*
waste *adjective*
7 no longer wanted or useful: *waste paper*
• ***Word Family:*** **wastage** *noun* **wasteful** *adjective* **wastefully** *adverb* **wastefulness** *noun*

watch (*say* wotch) *verb*
1 to look at or look out attentively: *to watch a play / Watch you don't trip on the step.* 2 to mind or guard something: *to watch the shop for five minutes* 3 **watch over** to protect, or keep your eye on someone: *to watch over a child*
watch *noun*
4 a guard: *Keep a watch on the house.* 5 a small clock that you wear on your wrist
• ***Word Family:*** the plural of the noun is **watches** □ **watchful** *adjective* alert: *The cat kept a watchful eye on the dog.* **watchfully** *adverb*

water (*say* **waw**-ta) *noun*
1 a liquid with no colour, taste or smell, that falls from the sky as rain 2 **waters** the water or liquid of a river, sea, mineral spring or tide: *coastal waters*
water *verb*
3 to wet something with water: *to water the flowers* 4 to give water to an animal: *to water a horse* 5 to fill with water: *The smoke made his eyes water.*
• ***Word Family:*** **watery** *adjective*

watercolour or watercolor *noun*
1 colour mixed with water to make paint 2 a painting done with this sort of paint

water cycle *noun*
the way that water falls as rain, forms rivers and seas, evaporates to form clouds, falls as rain and so on

waterfall *noun*
a steep fall or flow of water from a high cliff down to the ground below

waterlogged *adjective*
filled, soaked or flooded with water

watermark *noun*
a mark or design in paper, seen when you hold it up to the light, showing who made it and whether or not it is genuine

watermelon *noun*
a very large, green fruit with a hard skin and juicy red flesh with many pips

water-polo *noun*
a game played in a swimming-pool in which one team tries to throw the ball into the opponent's goal

waterproof *adjective*
letting no water get in or out: *a waterproof jacket*

water-skiing *noun*
the sport of skimming over water on skis while you are being towed by a motor boat
• ***Word Family:*** **water-ski** *verb* **(water-skis, water-skied, water-skiing)**

watertight *adjective*
1 made so that water cannot enter or leak through 2 foolproof or without mistakes or doubts: *She had a watertight excuse.*

waterway *noun*
part of a river that ships or boats can travel along

waterworks *plural noun*
buildings and pipes that supply water to houses and other buildings

watt (*say* wot) *noun*
a unit of electrical power
• ***Word Family:*** **wattage** *noun* the amount of electrical power expressed in watts
• ***Word Origins:*** named after James Watt, a Scottish inventor who lived from 1736 to 1819

wattle (*say* **wot**-ul) *noun*
1 any of the Australian acacias 2 a fold of skin, often brightly coloured, hanging from the throat of such birds as the turkey

wave *noun*
1 a ridge or swell moving on the surface of water, especially the sea 2 a piece of hair that curves and curls 3 a surging or swelling movement: *A wave of relief passed over him.* 4 the up-and-down or to-and-fro movement you make with your hand when you are greeting someone or saying goodbye 5 a regular vibration of light, sound or heat energy travelling through air and water
wave *verb*
6 to move something up-and-down or to-and-fro: *to wave a flag* 7 to show something by waving your hand: *She waved me to a seat.*
• ***Word Family:*** **wavy** *adjective* **(wavier, waviest)**: *wavy hair / wavy lines*

waveband *noun*
sound waves of similar length, used for putting out radio programmes

wavelength *noun*
1 one complete wave movement, such the distance between two crests or tops of waves at sea 2 the size of a radio wave or electric wave 3 **on the same wavelength** in harmony or agreement

waver *verb*
to be uncertain or unsteady: *He wavered: should he go or not? / the wavering light of a candle*

wax (1) *noun*
1 a solid, shiny substance that is easy to melt, used to make crayons, candles and polish
wax *verb*
2 to rub, cover or polish something with wax
• ***Word Family:*** **waxy (waxier, waxiest)** *adjective*: *Oranges have a waxy skin.*

wax (2) *verb*
to increase in size the way the moon's face does when it changes from a new moon to a full moon

waxwork *noun*
a model of a person or person's head, made out of wax: *a waxwork of the Queen*

way *noun*
1 the manner of doing something: *the correct way to knit* 2 distance: *It's a long way to school.* 3 direction: *Which way did they go?* 4 a road or a path 5 room or space: *Make way for the girl holding the balloons.* 6 **no way!** absolutely impossible!

wayward (*say* **way**-wud) *adjective*
wanting your own way: *a wayward child*
• ***Word Family:*** **waywardness** *noun*

we *pronoun*
the plural form of **I:** *We are having lunch.*
• ***Word Family:*** other forms are **our** and **ours**

weak *adjective*
1 without much strength: *a weak voice* 2 likely to break or fail: *a weak link* 3 taking too much notice of what others think: *a weak leader*
• ***Word Family:*** **weaken** *verb* to make something weak or to become weak or weaker **weakly** *adverb* **weakness** *noun*

weakling *noun*
a feeble person or animal

wealth (*say* welth) *noun*
1 a large amount of goods, property or money that someone owns 2 a great deal of something: *The painter uses a wealth of bright colours.*
• ***Word Family:*** **wealthy** *adjective* **(wealthier, wealthiest)**

wean *verb*
to start giving food to a baby or young animal other than its mother's milk: *to wean a baby*

weapon (*say* **wep**-on) *noun*
an instrument used for fighting
• ***Word Family:*** **weaponry** *noun* weapons

wear (*say* wair) *verb*
1 to have or carry something on your body or face: *to wear a beard and spectacles / to wear a frown* 2 **wear away** to get rid of something slowly, over time: *The wind and rain wore the rock away.* 3 **wear off** to get less: *The pain began to wear off.* 4 **wear out (a)** to use something so much that it becomes thin, broken and weak: *to wear out your shoes* **(b)** to exhaust something or someone: *to wear out someone's patience*
wear *noun*
5 damage caused by using something: *There's quite a bit of wear on that front tyre.* 6 things to wear: *beach wear*
• ***Word Family:*** other verb forms are **wears, wore, worn, wearing** □ **wearable** *adjective* **wearer** *noun*

weary (*say* **wear**-ree) *adjective*
very tired
• ***Word Family:*** other forms are **wearier, weariest** □ **wearily** *adverb* **weariness** *noun*

weasel (*say* **wee**-zel) *noun*
a small, fierce mammal with yellowish-brown fur, which can squeeze down burrows looking for rabbits and other food

weather (*say* **wedh**-a) *noun*
1 sunshine, cold, rain, snow, wind and so on 2 **under the weather** not feeling very well.
weather *verb*
3 to safely come through something bad: *The ship weathered the storm.* 4 to show the effects of weather: *Granite weathers slowly.*
• ***Word Family:*** **weathering** *noun* the action of the weather on rock or other materials

weathervane *noun*
a device consisting of a pole with a piece of metal, often in the shape of a cockerel, that spins in the wind and indicates its direction

weave *verb*
1 to intertwine threads to make such things as cloth or baskets 2 to move in a twisting and turning path
•*Word Family:* other forms are **weaves, wove, woven, weaving** □ **weaver** *noun*

web *noun*
1 the fine, sticky thread spun by spiders to catch insects 2 a complex network: *a web of roads across the country* 3 a piece of skin joining two toes on the foot of some animals and birds that swim, such as ducks
•*Word Family:* **webbed** *adjective: webbed feet* **web-footed** *adjective*

wedding *noun*
a marriage ceremony
•*Word Family:* **wed** *verb* (**weds, wed** *or* **wedded, wedding**) to marry
•*Word Origins:* from an Old English word meaning "pledge"

wedge *noun*
1 a solid, triangular piece of wood or metal, used to split a piece of wood or to fix something firmly 2 something shaped like a wedge: *a wedge of pie / potato wedges*
wedge *verb*
3 to fix something in place with a wedge: *to wedge the wheels of a car* 4 to crowd or force something into a narrow space: *to wedge tightly into a lift*

wedlock *noun*
the state of marriage

Wednesday *noun*
the fourth day of the week
•*Word Origins:* named after the ancient German god *Woden*

weed *noun*
1 a troublesome or useless plant, especially one growing where it is not wanted
weed *verb*
2 to remove weeds from a garden or flowerbed
3 **weed out** to remove something bad: *to weed out trouble makers*
•*Word Family:* **weedy** *adjective* (**weedier, weediest**) **(a)** full of weeds **(b)** thin and unhealthy

week *noun*
a period of seven days

weekday *noun*
any day of the week except Saturday and Sunday

weekend *noun*
Saturday and Sunday, when most people have time off work

weekly *adjective*
1 happening once a week: *a weekly piano lesson*
weekly *adverb*
2 once a week: *The magazine comes out weekly.*
weekly *noun*
3 a newspaper or magazine published once a week
•*Word Family:* the plural form of the noun is **weeklies**

weep *verb*
to shed tears or cry because you are sad or hurt
•*Word Family:* other forms are **weeps, wept, weeping**

weeping willow *noun*
a willow tree with long branches that hang down to the ground

weigh (*say* way) *verb*
1 to measure how heavy something or someone is: *to weigh fruit on a pair of scales* 2 to have a certain weight: *She weighs six stone.* 3 to consider something: *to weigh your decision carefully* 4 to be a burden to you: *The situation weighed on her mind.* 5 **weigh anchor** to pull up the anchor and start sailing 6 **weigh down** **(a)** to hold down **(b)** to trouble you 7 **weigh up** to think about or consider a decision

weight (*say* wate) *noun*
1 how heavy something is 2 a heavy object
3 a heavy burden: *a weight off my mind*
•*Word Family:* **weightless** *adjective* **weightlessness** *noun* **weighty** *adjective* (**weightier, weightiest**) **(a)** heavy **(b)** important

weir (*rhymes with* fear) *noun*
a small dam across a river, over which the water may flow

weird (*say* weerd) *adjective*
odd or strange
•*Word Family:* **weirdo** *noun* a strange person **weirdly** *adverb* **weirdness** *noun*

welcome (*say* **wel**-kum) *adjective*
1 received with pleasure: *a welcome guest / a welcome letter* 2 allowed to have or do something: *You're welcome to stay.*
welcome *verb*
3 to give a welcome to someone
welcome *noun*
4 a friendly greeting: *a warm welcome*

weld *verb*
to join two things by heating and melting them together: *to weld metal*
•*Word Family:* **welder** *noun*

welfare (*say* **wel**-fair) *noun*
1 health, comfort and happiness 2 help given to people who are poor or have social problems

well (1) *adverb*
1 in a good, pleasing or satisfactory way: *to ride well / The party went well.* 2 completely or thoroughly: *Stir the soup well.* 3 comfortably: *to live well* 4 intimately: *I don't know him well.* 5 kindly: *to treat someone well*
well *adjective*
6 in a satisfactory state: *All is well.* 7 in good health: *to feel well*
•***Word Family:*** other forms are **better, best**

well (2) *noun*
a hole dug in the ground to obtain oil or water
well *verb*
2 to rise or flow up like water in a spring: *Tears welled up in her eyes.*

well-being *noun*
good health and happiness

wellington boots *plural noun*
rubber or plastic knee-length boots

well-off *adjective*
quite wealthy

werewolf (*say* **ware**-wolf *or* **weer**-wolf) *noun*
someone who, in folktales, changed into a wolf when the moon was full
•***Word Family:*** the plural is **werewolves**
•***Word Origins:*** from the Old English word for "man" added to **wolf**

west *noun*
1 the direction of the sun at sunset 2 **the West** the countries of western Europe and North America
•***Word Family:*** **west** *adjective* **west** *adverb* **westward** *adjective*

western *noun*
a film or book about cowboys and American Indians in the west of the United States

wet *adjective*
1 covered or soaked with water or some other liquid 2 still in a liquid state: *wet paint* 3 having a rainy climate
wet *verb*
4 to make something wet: *Wet your hair.*
•***Word Family:*** other adjective forms are **wetter, wettest** □ other verb forms are **wets, wet, wetting** □ **wetly** *adverb* **wetness** *noun*

wet suit *noun*
a garment worn by divers and surfers, keeping a warm layer of water around the wearer

whack *noun*
1 a hard hit or blow
whack *verb*
2 to hit something hard

whale (*say* wale) *noun*
a very large, sea mammal found in all oceans and hunted for their oil, bone and flesh
•***Word Family:*** **whaler** *noun* a ship that is used for hunting whales **whaling** *noun*

wharf (*say* worf) *noun*
a permanent landing place in a harbour, where ships are loaded and unloaded
•***Word Family:*** the plural is **wharves** (*say* worvz)

what (*say* wot) *pronoun*
1 which particular thing: *What do you want to eat?* 2 that which or the thing that: *This is what I think.*
what *adjective*
3 which one of a number: *What dress did you buy?*

wheat (*say* weet) *noun*
a cereal plant used to make flour

wheedle *verb*
to persuade someone or obtain something by flattery

wheel *noun*
1 a circular disc or frame, such as on a car or machine, that turns on an axle
wheel *verb*
2 to push something on wheels: *to wheel a pram* 3 to turn or whirl around: *The starlings wheeled about in the sky.*

wheelbarrow *noun*
a small vehicle, usually with a single wheel at one end and handles at the other, used to carry goods

wheelchair *noun*
a chair with wheels, used by people who cannot walk

wheel clamp *noun*
a metal device which can be fixed onto a car's wheel to stop the driver moving away, for example if it is parked in the wrong place

wheeze (*say* weez) *verb*
to breathe with difficulty, producing a whistling sound
•***Word Family:*** **wheezy** *adjective* (**wheezier, wheeziest**) **wheezily** *adverb* **wheeziness** *noun*

when (*say* wen) *adverb*
1 at what time: *When will breakfast be ready?*
when *pronoun*
2 what or which time: *Since when have you been in charge?*
•***Word Family:*** **whenever** *conjunction*

where (*say* wair) *adverb*
1 at or in what place: *Where could they be? / Where did you hear that?* 2 to what place: *Where are you going now?*

whereupon *adverb*
and at that point: *She opened the oven door, whereupon the gingerbread man jumped out.*

wherever *adverb*
in or to whatever place: *The cat sleeps wherever she likes.*

whet *verb*
to sharpen: *to whet steel / to whet your hunger*
•***Word Family:*** other forms are **whets, whetted, whetting**

whether (*say* **we**-*dha*) *conjunction*
1 if: *Tell me whether you are thirsty.* 2 either: *Whether by luck or skill, she got the right answer.*

whey (*say way*) *noun*
the watery part of milk that separates from the curd when you make cheese

which *adjective*
1 what particular one: *Which kitten do you like best?*
which *pronoun*
2 what person or thing: *I didn't know which to choose.*
•***Word Family:*** **whichever** *pronoun*

whiff (*say* wif) *noun*
1 a faint smell carried in the air: *a whiff of lavender* 2 a puff: *a whiff of smoke*

while (*say* wile) *noun*
1 a period of time: *a while ago*
while *conjunction*
2 during or in the time that: *While you are here I'll show you my video game.*
while *verb*
3 to spend time pleasantly or idly: *to while away the day*

whim *noun*
a sudden desire or fancy: *to buy something on a whim*

whimper (*say* **wim**-pa) *verb*
1 to cry with low, broken sounds
whimper *noun*
2 a weak cry

whine (*say* wine) *verb*
1 to make a long, piercing sound 2 to make an annoying, complaining cry or sound

whinge (*say* winj) *verb*
to complain in an annoying or tiring way

whinny (*say* **win**-ee) *noun*
1 the happy, neighing sound that a horse makes
whinny *verb*
2 to make this sound
•***Word Family:*** the plural of the noun is **whinnies** □ other forms of the verb are **whinnies, whinnied, whinnying**

whip (*say* wip) *verb*
1 to mix something with quick, repeated strokes: *to whip cream* 2 to hit someone as a punishment 3 **whip up** (a) to create something quickly: *to whip up a cake for unexpected visitors* (b) to arouse something: *to whip up fury*
whip *noun*
4 a long cord or leather lash with a handle, for striking or beating people or animals: *The jockey whipped the racehorse on to victory.*
•***Word Family:*** other verb forms are **whips, whipped, whipping**

whiplash *noun*
1 the lash of a whip 2 a sudden, jerking movement, such as when your head is thrown backwards or forwards in a car crash

whirl (*say* werl) *verb*
1 to spin or turn around rapidly
whirl *noun*
2 a whirling movement 3 a state of confusion: *My head's in a whirl.*

whirlpool *noun*
a circular movement in water, produced by two currents meeting

whirlwind *noun*
a very strong wind blowing in a spiral

whirr *verb*
to move quickly with a vibrating or buzzing sound: *the whirring of a humming-bird's wings*

whisk *noun*
1 a light, wire tool for beating or mixing eggs, cream and so on
whisk *verb*
2 to mix or beat food with a whisk: *to whisk eggs*
3 to move quickly and lightly: *to be whisked off*

whisker *noun*
1 one of the long, stiff, bristly hairs growing around the mouth of animals such as cats and rats 2 a very small amount: *She won by a whisker.* 3 **whiskers** the hair on a man's face

whisky or **whiskey** (*say* **wis**-kee) *noun*
a strong, alcoholic drink made from grain
•***Word Origins:*** from a Gaelic word meaning "water of life"

whisper (*say* **wis**-pa) *verb*
1 to speak very softly 2 to talk secretly or privately 3 to rustle: *The leaves whispered in the breeze.*
whisper *noun*
4 a whispering sound or voice: *to talk in a whisper*

whistle (*say* **wis**-ul) *verb*
1 to produce a musical sound by forcing air through your teeth or lips 2 to produce a similar sound: *The wind whistled down the chimney. / The steam-train whistled.*

whistle *noun*
3 a small instrument that produces whistling sounds 4 a sound produced by whistling or by a whistle

white *noun*
1 the lightest colour, or the opposite of black 2 something with this colour, such as the part of an egg surrounding the yolk or the part of an eye surrounding the pupil 3 **White** a member of one of the white or light-skinned races of Europe 4 white clothes: *dressed in white* 5 **whites** cricket or tennis clothes
white *adjective*
6 of the colour white: *white snow* 7 light in colour: *white wine / white bread* 8 with milk or cream: *white coffee*
•***Word Family:*** **whiten** *verb* to make something white or to become white or whiter **whiteness** *noun*

white-hot *adjective*
so hot that it glows with a bright white light
•***Word Family:*** **white heat** *noun*

white lie *noun*
a harmless lie that you tell when you don't want to hurt someone's feelings

whitewash *noun*
1 a white liquid used to paint surfaces white 2 anything used to disguise or cover faults

whittle (*say* **wit**-ul) *verb*
1 to trim or shape by cutting off small pieces with a knife 2 to cut or reduce: *How can we whittle down the cost of the trip?*

whiz (1) (*say* wiz) *verb*
1 to make a hissing or whirring sound, like something moving quickly through the air 2 to move with such a sound
•***Word Family:*** other forms are **whizzes, whizzed, whizzing**

whiz (2) *noun*
someone who is extremely skilled or clever: *a whiz at maths*

whiz-kid *noun*
a young person who is very clever or successful

who (*say* hoo) *pronoun*
1 which person or people: *Who told you that?* 2 a person already mentioned: *Is that the teacher who makes films?*
•***Word Family:*** **whoever** *pronoun*

whole (*say* hole) *adjective*
1 entire, or including all its parts: *a whole set of CDs* 2 all in one piece: *to swallow a grape whole*
whole *noun*
3 a whole thing or amount 4 **on the whole** generally
•***Word Family:*** **wholeness** *noun*

wholemeal *adjective*
made with complete wheat grains: *wholemeal flour / a wholemeal loaf*
•***Word Family:*** also called **wholewheat**

whole number *noun*
a number with no fractions, such as 1, 2, 3, 4 and so on

wholesale *noun*
1 the selling of goods in large quantities to shop owners rather than to the general public
wholesale *adjective*
2 sold in large quantities: *wholesale jeans* 3 on a large scale: *wholesale slaughter*
wholesale *adverb*
4 sold in large quantities: *He buys his equipment wholesale.*
•***Word Family:*** **wholesaler** *noun*

wholesome (*say* **hole**-sum) *adjective*
good for your health: *a wholesome breakfast*

wholly (*say* **hole**-ee) *adverb*
to the fullest or whole amount: *I wholly agree with you.*

whom (*say* hoom) *pronoun*
which person or people: *With whom do you wish to speak?*
•***Word Family:*** **whomever** *pronoun*

whoop (*say* woop) *noun*
1 a hooting shout or cry: *a whoop of laughter*
whoop *verb*
2 to make a hooting sound

whooping cough (*say* **hoo**-ping kof) *noun*
a disease usually caught by children, which makes them take long, noisy breaths

whose (*say* hooz) *possessive pronoun*
1 belonging to which person: *Whose shoes are these?* 2 of whom: *That's the boy whose book I borrowed.* 3 of which: *a tree whose leaves had fallen off*

why *adverb*
for what reason: *Why did she go?*

wick *noun*
a piece of cord in a candle or lamp through which the fuel soaks up to the flame

wicked (*say* **wik**-id) *adjective*
1 evil or sinful: *a wicked crime* 2 mischievous: *a wicked smile* 3 very good: *Their new song is wicked!*
•***Word Family:*** **wickedly** *adverb* **wickedness** *noun*

wicker *noun*
thin branches or reeds woven together, used to make baskets, furniture and so on
•***Word Family:*** **wicker** *adjective* **wickerwork** *noun*

wicket *noun*
1 three stumps joined across the top by the bails, at which the bowler aims the ball in cricket 2 the pitch or playing area in cricket: *The ball hardly bounced because the wicket was so wet.* 3 when a batsman's turn is over

wicket-keeper *noun*
a fielder who stands behind the batsman in cricket

wide *adjective*
1 large from side to side: *a wide river* 2 fully open: *Her eyes were wide with fear.* 3 having a particular measurement from side to side
wide *adverb*
4 fully, or as much as possible: *Open your mouth wide.* 5 to one side: *Her first shot went wide.*
•*Word Family:* **widely** *adverb* **widen** *verb*

widespread (*say* **wide**-spred) *adjective*
existing or scattered over a wide area or amongst many people: *widespread beliefs*

widow *noun*
a woman whose husband has died

widowed *adjective*
left alone after your husband or wife has died

widower *noun*
a man whose wife has died

width *noun*
how wide something is: *Measure the width of the room.*

wield (*say* weeld) *verb*
to handle, manage or use something, such as a weapon: *to wield a sword / to wield power*

wife *noun*
the woman to whom a man is married
•*Word Family:* the plural is **wives**

wig *noun*
real or artificial hair used instead of your own hair, or on top of it: *a clown's wig*

wiggle *verb*
to move with quick movements from side to side: *to wiggle your hips when you walk*

wigwam (*say* **wig**-wam) *noun*
a hut or tent used by Native Americans, made of bark or animal hides stretched over a cone-shaped frame of poles

wild *adjective*
1 living, growing or existing in a natural state without human care: *wild animals*
2 uncontrolled, or violent: *wild curly hair / a wild crowd of spectators* 3 unlikely or unconsidered: *a wild guess*
wild *noun*
5 **the wilds** areas far away from cities and towns, where few people live: *the wilds of Africa*
•*Word Family:* **wildly** *adverb* **wildness** *noun*

wilderness *noun*
1 an area of land where no-one lives and no crops are grown 2 a wild area: *The garden has turned into a wilderness.*

wildfire *noun*
like wildfire with great or uncontrollable speed: *The news spread like wildfire.*

wildlife *noun*
animals, birds and insects living in their natural environment

wilful *adjective*
1 planned, or done on purpose: *He was charged with wilful murder.* 2 stubborn, or determined to get your own way: *wilful disobedience*
•*Word Family:* **wilfully** *adverb* **wilfulness** *noun*

will (1) *verb*
1 to be going to: *We will come afterwards.* 2 to be willing to: *Will you do my shopping?* 3 to be used to, or in the habit of: *She would work late every night.*

will (2) *noun*
1 the power or ability of choosing how you will act: *a weak will* 2 what you want to do: *He went to the party against his will.* 3 determination to do something: *She has a strong will to succeed.*
4 a document stating what someone wants done with his or her money and property after death

willing *adjective*
agreeing, or saying you will do something: *I'm willing to babysit.*
•*Word Family:* **willingly** *adverb* **willingness** *noun*

willow *noun*
a tree with slender, drooping branches and strong, light wood used for weaving and making cricket bats
•*Word Family:* **willowy** *adjective* gracefully slender

willpower *noun*
strength or control over your wishes or actions: *You need great willpower to stay on a diet.*

wilt *verb*
to become limp and drooping: *The flowers wilted in the hot sun.*

wily (*say* **wye**-lee) *adjective*
cunning or full of crafty tricks: *a wily fox*
•*Word Family:* other forms are **wilier, wiliest** □ **wiliness** *noun*

wimp *noun*
a weak person who is bossed about by others
•*Word Family:* **wimpish** *adjective* **wimpy** *adjective*

win *verb*
1 to do best when competing against others: *to win a race / to win a battle* 2 to receive something as a reward for effort: *to win first prize*
win *noun*
3 the act of winning
• ***Word Family:*** other verb forms are **wins, won, winning**

wince *verb*
to flinch in pain

winch *noun*
1 a lifting or pulling device, often with several gearwheels attached to it and a crank handle or motor for turning it
winch *verb*
2 to hoist or pull something up using a winch: *to winch a boat out of the water*

wind (1) (*rhymes with* skinned) *noun*
1 moving air 2 breath: *She ran out of wind after three laps.* 3 a build-up of gases coming from your stomach: *Brown rice always gave him wind.* 4 wind instruments
wind *verb*
5 to take away your breath: *Running up the steep hill winded me.*
• ***Word Family:*** **winded** *adjective* temporarily out of breath

wind (2) (*rhymes* with mined) *verb*
1 to twist and turn the way a snake does: *The river winds down the valley.* 2 to wrap around in coils or rolls: *to wind string around a yoyo* 3 to tighten the spring of a clock or watch: *to wind a watch*
• ***Word Family:*** other forms are **winds, wound, winding**

windfall *noun*
1 a piece of unexpected good luck, especially money 2 a ripe fruit blown down off the tree by the wind

wind instrument *noun*
a musical instrument that you play by blowing through it, such as a trumpet or a recorder

windmill *noun*
a machine with large vanes or sails fixed on to an axle and powered by wind, used to grind grain, pump water and so on

window *noun*
1 an opening in a wall to let in light and air, usually consisting of a frame, into which glass is set 2 a window-shaped part of a computer screen in which you can program text or graphics to appear

windpipe *noun*
the tube or passage that carries air from your throat to your lungs

wind power *noun*
energy that comes from the wind

windscreen *noun*
the window at the front of a car or other vehicle

windsock *noun*
a device for showing wind direction at airports, consisting of an open sleeve-like flag flown from a pole

windsurfing *noun*
a sport in which you ride on a sailboard in the sea
• ***Word Family:*** **windsurfer** *noun*

windy *adjective*
with much wind: *a windy day*
• ***Word Family:*** other forms are **windier, windiest**

wine *noun*
the red or white alcoholic drink made from grape skins and the fermented juice of grapes

wing *noun*
1 the part of a bird or insect that it uses for flying 2 the long, flat, horizontal parts on either side of an aeroplane 3 the section of a building joined to the main part 4 the backstage areas on either side of the stage in a theatre 5 a section or group within a political party or organization: *the left wing of the Labour Party* 6 the area along the edges of a sports field on which you play hockey, football and other games 7 someone who plays in this position on the field 8 the side part of a car above the wheel: *a dent in the wing*
wing *verb*
9 to fly: *The plane winged its way to New York.*
• ***Word Family:*** **winged** *adjective* **wingless** *adjective*

wingspan *noun*
the distance across a bird's wings, or the wings of an aeroplane

wink *verb*
1 to open and close one eye quickly, often as a signal 2 to flash or twinkle: *The city lights winked in the fog.*
wink *noun*
3 a winking movement or action

winner *noun*
1 someone who wins 2 something good or successful

winning *adjective*
1 being the one that wins: *the winning team* 2 charming: *a winning smile*
winning *noun*
3 **winnings** money that you win

winter *noun*
the coldest season of the year, between autumn and spring
•***Word Family:*** **wintertime** *noun* **wintry** *adjective: wintry weather*

wipe *verb*
1 to rub or pass over something lightly with a cloth, in order to clean or dry it: *Wipe your sticky hands!* 2 to remove something: *Please wipe that smile off your face.* 3 **wipe out** to destroy something completely: *The earthquake wiped out the village.*
wipe *noun*
4 the act of wiping: *Give the table a wipe.*

wire *noun*
1 a long, thin, bendy piece of metal, usually used for carrying electricity, or for making fences
wire *verb*
2 to fasten something with wire 3 to fit something with a system of wires to provide electricity: *to wire a sound system*
•***Word Family:*** **wiring** *noun* a system of wires providing electricity

wireless *noun*
a radio

wiry *adjective*
1 like wire in shape or stiffness: *wiry grass*
2 slender but strong: *He has a wiry build.*
•***Word Family:*** other forms are **wirier, wiriest**

wisdom (*say* **wiz**-dom) *noun*
1 the good judgment or understanding to know what is right or true 2 learning or knowledge: *to gain wisdom through reading*

wise *adjective*
1 able to use your knowledge and experience to make sensible decisions: *a wise grandmother*
2 sensible: *Is it wise to go out in the storm?*
3 **wise to** aware of: *I think the police are wise to our disguise.*
•***Word Family:*** **wisely** *adverb*

wish *verb*
1 to want or long for something: *I wish it would rain.* 2 to say that you hope someone will have something: *Wish your brother goodnight.* 3 to hope that you get something, usually without telling anyone: *What did you wish for as you blew out the candles?*
wish *noun*
4 a desire or longing: *a wish for peace*
5 something you wish for: *What is your wish?*
•***Word Family:*** the plural of the noun is **wishes**

wishbone *noun*
a Y-shaped bone in front of the breast of birds such as chickens

wisp *noun*
a small, fine bunch of strands: *a wisp of hair*
•***Word Family:*** **wispy** *adjective* **(wispier, wispiest)**

wistful *adjective*
thoughtful and sad: *a wistful smile*
•***Word Family:*** **wistfully** *adverb* **wistfulness** *noun*

wit *noun*
1 the ability to say things which are clever and funny 2 someone who can do this: *She's a real wit!* 3 **wits** sense or intelligence: *to have your wits about you*
•***Word Family:*** see also **witty**

witch *noun*
a woman who practises magic, especially bad magic
•***Word Family:*** the plural is **witches** □ **witchcraft** *noun*

witchdoctor *noun*
a powerful member of a tribe thought to possess magical powers of healing or harming

with *preposition*
1 in someone's company: *Come with me.*
2 combined or connected: *Stir the flour with the butter.* 3 by means of: *Cut it with this knife.*
4 having or possessing: *the girl with green eyes*

withdraw *verb*
1 to take something away or out: *to withdraw money from a bank* 2 to take something back: *Please withdraw that remark.* 3 to go or move away: *He withdrew to his bedroom.*
•***Word Family:*** other forms are **withdraws, withdrew, withdrawn, withdrawing** □ **withdrawn** *adjective* lost in your own thoughts **withdrawal** *noun: to make a withdrawal from your account*

wither *verb*
to become faded, dry and shrunken: *The leaves withered and fell from the tree.*

withhold *verb*
to hold something back or refuse to give it: *The police withheld the victim's name.*
•***Word Family:*** other forms are **withholds, withheld, withholding**

within *preposition*
1 inside
within *adverb*
2 in or inside

without *preposition*
not having something

withstand *verb*
to stand up against something: *These plants can withstand drought.*
•***Word Family:*** other forms are **withstands, withstood, withstanding**

A B C D E F G H I J K L M N O P Q R S T U V W X Y Z

witness *noun*
1 someone who is present when something happens: *He was a witness to the attack.* 2 someone who makes a statement or gives evidence, especially in a court case 3 someone who signs a document swearing that what it says is true
witness *verb*
4 to be a witness or perform the duties of a witness: *to witness a crime / to witness someone's will*
•***Word Family:*** the plural is **witnesses**

witty *adjective*
clever and amusing
•***Word Family:*** other forms are **wittier, wittiest** □ **writtily** *adverb* **wittiness** *noun*

wizard (*say* **wiz**-ud) *noun*
1 a magician or sorcerer 2 a very clever or skilled person: *She's a wizard at chess.*
•***Word Family:*** **wizardry** (*say* **wiz**-ud-ree) *noun* magic or witchcraft
•***Word Origins:*** from a Middle English word meaning "wise one"

wobble *verb*
1 to move or make something move unsteadily from side to side: *The loose tooth wobbled and fell out.* 2 to tremble or quiver: *Her voice wobbled with emotion.*
•***Word Family:*** **wobbly** *adjective* unsteady

woe *noun*
1 sorrow or misery: *to be full of woe* 2 trouble or misfortune: *Woe to the enemy.*
•***Word Family:*woeful** *adjective* **woefully** *adverb*

wok *noun*
a large, bowl-shaped metal pan, used for Chinese cooking, especially stir-frying
•***Word Origins:*** this word comes from Chinese

wolf (*say* woolf) *noun*
a large animal like a dog, that hunts in packs and is found in the northern parts of Europe, Asia and America
•***Word Family:*** the plural is **wolves**

woman (*say* **wum**-un) *noun*
an adult female human being
•***Word Family:*** the plural is **women** (*say* **wim**-in) □ **womanhood** *noun* **womanly** *adjective*

womb (*rhymes with* boom) *noun*
another name for **uterus**

wombat *noun*
a heavily built, burrowing and grazing animal with a small pouch, found in south-eastern Australia

wonder (*say* **wun**-da) *verb*
1 to think about something with curiosity or doubt: *I wonder if they are as weird as people say.* 2 to think about something with awe or admiration: *to wonder at the Pyramids*
wonder *noun*
3 something that causes awe or admiration: *Space travel is one of the wonders of the 20th century.* 4 the feeling caused by such a thing: *I was filled with wonder when they landed on the moon.*

wonderful (*say* **wun**-da-ful) *adjective*
extremely good or fine: *She's a wonderful friend.*
•***Word Family:*** **wonderfully** *adverb*

woo *verb*
to try to persuade someone to love or marry you: *He wooed her with flowers.*
•***Word Family:*** other forms are **woos, wooed, wooing** □ **wooer** *noun*

wood *noun*
1 the hard substance of tree trunks or branches 2 this substance cut up for use in carpentry or for building houses 3 an area of land covered with trees
•***Word Family:*** another name for definition 2 is **timber** □ **wooded** *adjective*: *wooded hillsides* **wooden** *adjective* (a) made of wood (b) stiff and awkward: *She gave a wooden performance.*

woodland *noun*
an area of land covered in trees, with some grass but no shrubs

woodlouse *noun*
a small creature with 14 legs which lives under stones, wood and so on, and can roll itself up into a ball
•***Word Family:*** the plural is **woodlice**

woodpecker *noun*
a bird which uses its long beak to make holes in trees to find insects

woodwind *noun*
the group of musical wind instruments that includes flutes, clarinets, oboes and bassoons, that are sounded by blowing onto a reed or blowing across a hole

woodwork *noun*
work done with wood

woodworm *noun*
the larva of a kind of beetle, which makes holes in wood

woody *adjective*
1 like wood 2 full of trees
•***Word Family:*** other forms are **woodier, woodiest**

wool *noun*
1 the soft, curly hair of sheep and other similar animals 2 the thread or cloth made from this hair and used for knitting or weaving

• ***Word Family:*** **woollen** *adjective* made from wool **woolly** *adjective* (**woollier, woolliest**) (a) covered with wool (b) like wool, or made with wool: *woolly socks*

word *noun*
1 a combination of sounds that means something and is one of the basic units of our language 2 a remark or expression: *a word of warning before you begin* 3 a command or signal: *Give the word and a hundred men will arrive.*
4 a speech or a talk: *May I have a word with you?*
5 a promise or assurance: *I'll keep your secret, I give you my word.* 6 news: *Have you had word of their whereabouts?* 7 **words** the sounds spoken or sung in a song: *I've forgotten the words.*
word *verb*
8 to express something in words: *How should I word my letter?*
• ***Word Family:*** **wording** *noun* the words you use to say something

word processing *noun*
writing, editing, storing and printing documents using a computer
• ***Word Family:*** **word processor** *noun* a computer with a visual display unit, programmed for word processing

wordy (*say* **wer**-dee) *adjective*
using more words than you need: *a wordy answer*
• ***Word Family:*** **wordily** *adverb* **wordiness** *noun*

work (*say* werk) *noun*
1 effort you make to do something: *The hard work had made my back ache.* 2 something produced by effort: *Her embroidered jacket is a work of art.* 3 something you undertake to do: *I must finish this work today.* 4 the job you do to earn money 5 **the works** the whole lot: *a pizza with the works*
work *verb*
6 to do work: *to work in the garden / to work in a shop* 7 to use, operate or function: *to work a machine / This machine won't work.* 8 to prove successful, or turn out as planned: *Did your plan work or was it a failure?* 9 to cause or bring about: *to work a miracle* 10 **work out** (a) to solve: *to work out a problem* (b) to train or practise, especially as an athlete: *to work out in the gym*
11 **work up** (a) to excite or arouse something: *to work up interest in a project / to work yourself up into a rage* (b) to make something increase: *to work up an appetite for dinner*
• ***Word Family:*** **workable** *adjective* able to be operated or used **workout** *noun* a session in the gym

worker *noun*
1 someone who works, especially at a particular job: *a factory worker / an office worker* 2 a bee or ant that does the work in a hive or colony

workmanship *noun*
the skill involved in making something

workshop *noun*
a room or place where things are made or repaired

world (*say* werld) *noun*
1 the Earth and all the people who live on it
2 a particular part of the Earth: *the western world*
3 a particular group of the Earth's creatures: *the animal world* 4 a sphere or area of life: *the world of dreams*
• ***Word Family:*** **worldwide** *adjective* extending throughout the world

worldly *adjective*
1 not interested in religious or spiritual things but only about life on Earth 2 experienced in the ways of the world
• ***Word Family:*** other forms are **worldlier, worldliest** □ **worldliness** *noun*

worm (*say* werm) *noun*
1 a long, thin, soft animal with no legs
worm *verb*
2 to get something out of someone: *He managed to worm my secret out of me.*

worn *adjective*
1 damaged by wear or use 2 very tired or old

worry (*say* **wu**-ree) *verb*
1 to feel uneasy or slightly fearful: *to worry about walking home in the dark* 2 to disturb or bother someone: *Don't worry me when I'm in the shower.*
3 to pull, bite or tear at something: *The dog worried the bone.*
worry *noun*
4 being worried: *He was frantic with worry.*
5 something that makes you worried: *worries about your future*
• ***Word Family:*** other verb forms are **worries, worried, worrying** □ **worrisome** *adjective* troublesome **worrier** *noun*

worse (*say* werse) *adjective*
1 more bad: *The pain is worse than I expected.*
2 more ill: *She gradually got worse.*
• ***Word Family:*** **worsen** *verb* to make something worse or to become worse: *The situation worsened.*

worship (*say* **wer**-ship) *noun*
1 giving praise or honour to God or gods using ceremonies or rites 2 a deep honour or love
worship *verb*
3 to show your love and respect for someone: *to worship God*
• ***Word Family:*** other verb forms are **worships, worshipped, worshipping** □ **worshipper** *noun*

A B C D E F G H I J K L M N O P Q R S T U V W X Y Z

worst (*say* werst) *adjective*
most bad: *the worst drought in recorded history*

worth (*say* werth) *noun*
1 the value or importance of something or someone: *a necklace of untold worth / the worth of a painting* 2 the amount of something you can buy for a certain amount of money: *a pound's worth of sweets*
worth *adjective*
3 deserving of or good enough for something: *a place worth a visit* 4 having a value of: *What is this house worth?*
• ***Word Family:*** **worthless** *adjective*

worthwhile (*say* werth-**wile**) *adjective*
good or important enough to be worth doing: *Chess is a worthwhile hobby.*

worthy (*say* **wer**-dhee) *adjective*
1 deserving your support or respect: *a worthy cause* 2 **worthy of** good enough to have something: *a person worthy of respect*
• ***Word Family:*** other forms are **worthier, worthiest** □ **worthiness** *noun*

wound (*rhymes with* spooned) *noun*
1 an injury caused by a cut, blow or burn rather than by a disease
wound *verb*
2 to hurt or damage someone or something: *to wound someone with a knife / to wound someone's pride*

wrap (*say* rap) *verb*
1 to cover or enclose something with paper or material: *to wrap a present* 2 to fold, coil or clasp about something: *to wrap the blanket around the baby / to wrap your arms about someone*
wrap *noun*
3 a stole, shawl or rug
• ***Word Family:*** other verb forms are **wraps, wrapped, wrapping** □ **wrapper** *noun* a covering

wrath (*say* roth) *noun*
violent or resentful anger
• ***Word Family:*** **wrathful** *adjective* **wrathfully** *adverb*

wreath (*say* reeth) *noun*
a circular band of flowers or leaves, often sent to a funeral or put on a grave

wreathe (*say* reedh) *verb*
to encircle or surround something: *Smoke wreathed the house.*

wreck (*say* rek) *verb*
1 to destroy or spoil something completely: *The ship was wrecked in the storm. / You've wrecked my party.*
wreck *noun*
2 the remains of something that has been wrecked: *Divers examined the wreck.*
• ***Word Family:*** **wreckage** *noun* the remains of something which has been wrecked **wrecker** *noun*

wren (*say* ren) *noun*
a tiny, brown bird

wrench (*say* rench) *verb*
1 to twist something suddenly and violently: *to wrench open the drawer / to wrench your ankle*
wrench *noun*
2 a sudden, violent twist 3 a kind of spanner
• ***Word Family:*** the plural of the noun is **wrenches**

wrestle (*say* **res**-ul) *verb*
1 to struggle with and try to throw your opponent to the ground 2 to struggle and try to deal with something: *He wrestled with the problem all night.*
• ***Word Family:*** **wrestler** *noun* **wrestling** *noun* a contest between two opponents who wrestle as a sport

wretch (*say* retch) *noun*
someone who is unfortunate or unhappy
• ***Word Family:*** the plural is **wretches** □ **wretched** (*say* **retch**-id) *adjective* poor and unhappy

wriggle (*say* **rig**-ul) *verb*
1 to twist or turn your body with winding movements: *to wriggle through the grass on your stomach* 2 **wriggle out of** to get out of something using cunning
• ***Word Family:*** **wriggler** *noun* **wriggly** *adjective*

wring (*say* ring) *verb*
to twist and squeeze something: *He wrung water out of the towels. / to wring your hands in grief*
• ***Word Family:*** other forms are **wrings, wrung, wringing** □ **wringing wet** *adjective* extremely wet

wrinkle (*say* **rink**-ul) *noun*
1 a small furrow or ridge on a normally smooth surface: *a wrinkle in the wallpaper*
wrinkle *verb*
2 to form into a furrow or crease: *to wrinkle your nose*
• ***Word Family:*** **wrinkly** *adjective*

wrist (*say* rist) *noun*
the movable part or joint between your arm and your hand

write (*say* rite) *verb*
1 to form letters or words on a surface using a pen, pencil or something similar 2 to compose or produce something using words: *to write a poem* 3 to fill in the blank spaces of something: *He wrote a cheque.* 4 to record or copy

computer information from its main storage area onto a disc or tape **5 write off** to damage a vehicle so that it cannot be mended
• ***Word Family:*** other forms are **writes, wrote, written, writing** □ **writer** *noun* **writing** *noun*

writhe (*say* rithe) *verb*
to twist or squirm, as if in pain

wrong (*say* rong) *adjective*
1 not correct: *She gave the wrong answer. / We took the wrong turn and arrived late.* 2 bad or immoral: *It is wrong to steal.* 3 not in good condition or not working properly: *What's wrong with your hand?*
wrong *verb*
4 to treat someone unfairly or unjustly: *She felt that she had been wronged.*
wrong *noun*
5 something that is wrong: *to know right from wrong* **6 in the wrong** mistaken, or having done something wrong
• ***Word Family:*** **wrongly** *adverb*

wry (*rhymes with* dry) *adjective*
bitter in a rather humorous way and showing dislike: *to give a wry smile*
• ***Word Family:*** other forms are **wrier, wriest** □ **wryly** *adverb*

xenophobia (*say* zen-a-**fo**-bee-a) *noun*
a strong fear or dislike of foreigners
• ***Word Family:*** **xenophobic** *adjective*

Xmas (*say* **Kris**-mas *or* **eks**-mas)
Christmas

X-ray *noun*
1 a ray that can pass through solid things such as wood or human flesh 2 a photograph of the inside of your body, taken by a machine using X-rays, used to detect fractured bones and so on
X-ray *verb*
3 to examine someone using an X-ray

xylophone (*say* **zye**-la-fone) *noun*
a musical instrument consisting of tuned, wooden bars of different lengths that you strike with small hammers
• ***Word Origins:*** from the Greek words for "wood" and "sound"

Yy

yacht (*say* yot) *noun*
a sailing boat used for cruising or racing, usually with an engine
• ***Word Family:*** **yachting** *noun* **yachtsman** *noun* (**yachtsmen**) **yachtswoman** *noun* (**yachtswomen**)

yak *noun*
a large animal like an ox with long hair, found in the mountains of Tibet, and often kept as a work animal

yam *noun*
a starchy root grown in warm tropical areas, similar to a potato

yank *verb*
1 to pull with a sudden jerking movement
yank *noun*
2 a sudden, rough pull

yap *verb*
to bark with sharp, high-pitched sounds
• ***Word Family:*** other forms are **yaps, yapped, yapping**

yard (1) *noun*
an old-fashioned unit of length equal to about 91 centimetres

yard (2) *noun*
1 the fenced area of ground or garden around a house 2 a fenced area used for a particular purpose: *a schoolyard / a shipyard*

yardstick *noun*
a standard of measurement

yarn *noun*
1 a thread made by twisting cotton, woollen or nylon strands together, used for weaving or knitting 2 a long story, especially about events that probably never happened

yawn *verb*
1 to open your mouth and take a deep breath, usually when you are drowsy or bored 2 to open wide like a mouth: *The hole yawned before us.*
yawn *noun*
3 the action of yawning: *I tried to hide my yawns.*

year *noun*
1 a period of 12 months or 365 days, starting on 1 January and ending on 31 December 2 any period of 12 months, such as from March to March: *The school year begins in September.*
• ***Word Family:*** **yearly** *adjective*

yearn (*say* yern) *verb*
to long for something or someone: *They yearn to see their daughter again.*
•***Word Family:*** **yearning** *noun*

yeast *noun*
a substance used for making dough rise and in making wine or beer

yell *verb*
1 to cry out or shout with fright, surprise or anger
yell *noun*
2 a loud shout or cry

yellow *noun*
1 the colour of lemons
yellow *adjective*
2 of or to do with the colour yellow 3 cowardly
•***Word Family:*** **yellowish** *adjective*

yellow fever *noun*
an infectious disease spread by mosquitoes, causing fever, aching limbs, yellow skin and sometimes death

yelp *verb*
1 to give a quick, sharp cry or bark: *to yelp with pain / The puppy yelped when we sprayed it with water.*
yelp *noun*
2 a quick, sharp cry or bark

yen *noun*
a desire or longing: *I have a yen to visit Paris.*

yes *adverb*
what you say when you are agreeing with someone, accepting something, or saying that something is true or correct

yesterday *noun*
1 the day before today 2 the time recently past: *The cars of yesterday still have their own charm.*

yeti (*say* **yet**-ee) *noun*
the large, hairy creature believed to live in the snows of the Himalayas in Tibet
•***Word Family:*** the plural is **yetis**

yield (*say* yeeld) *verb*
1 to produce or give forth: *The farm yielded a good wheat crop.* 2 to give in: *They yielded to the enemy and lost the battle. / I yielded to the force of their arguments.*
yield *noun*
3 something that is yielded, such as a crop

yodel (*say* **yo**-dul) *noun*
1 a style of singing, with some normal notes and some very high notes, popular in the Austrian and Swiss mountains
yodel *noun*
2 to sing in this way
•***Word Family:*** other verb forms are **yodels, yodelled, yodelling** □ **yodeller** *noun*

yoga (*say* **yoe**-ga) *noun*
a system of exercises in which you learn to hold your body in certain positions and breathe deeply so that you can relax completely and control your mind
•***Word Family:*** **yogi** *noun* someone who teaches and practises yoga
•***Word Origins:*** from a Sanskrit word meaning "union"

yoghurt (*say* **yog**-ert) *noun*
a thick, liquid food made from fermented or curdled milk, sometimes with fruit added
•***Word Origins:*** this word comes from Turkish

yoke *noun*
1 a crossbar with two U-shaped pieces that are placed around the necks of a pair of oxen or carthorses pulling a load 2 a shaped part of a garment from which the rest of the garment hangs: *the yoke of a dress*

yolk (*rhymes with* poke) *noun*
the yellow centre of an egg

Yom Kippur (*say* yom **ki**-poor) *noun*
a Jewish day of fasting and prayers
•***Word Origins:*** this name comes from Hebrew

you *pronoun*
the person or group to whom you are speaking: *Are you coming to my party tonight?*

young (*say* yung) *adjective*
1 in the early stage of life, growth or development: *a young child*
young *noun*
2 young people: *The young have so much to look forward to.* 3 young animals or birds: *A bird's young are its chicks.*

youngster (*say* **yung**-sta) *noun*
a child or young person

your *possessive adjective*
belonging to you: *It is your book.*
•***Word Family:*** the form of the pronoun **you** used before a noun

yours *possessive pronoun*
belonging to you: *The book is yours.*
•***Word Family:*** a form of the pronoun **you**

youth *noun*
1 a young man 2 young people thought of as a group: *the youth of today* 3 the time when you were young: *I was a good rider in my youth.*
•***Word Family:*** **youthful** *adjective*

youth hostel *noun*
a place where you can stay when you are on a walking holiday

yoyo (*say* **yoh**-yoh) *noun*
a round toy containing string around its centre,

so that it spins up and down as the string winds and unwinds
•*Word Family:* the plural is **yoyos**

yummy *adjective*
tasting delicious: *a yummy chocolate*
•*Word Family:* other forms are **yummier, yummiest**

Zz

zany (*say* **zay**-nee) *adjective*
odd, funny or ridiculous: *a zany sense of humour*
•*Word Family:* other forms are **zanier, zaniest**
•*Word Origins:* from an Italian word meaning "clown"

zap *verb*
1 to hit or shoot something or someone: *to zap an alien with a ray gun* 2 to do or make something quickly: *to zap through your chores*
•*Word Family:* other forms are **zaps, zapped, zapping**

zebra *noun*
a wild, African animal like a horse, with brown or black stripes on its white body

zero (*say* **zeer**-oh) *noun*
1 the number 0 2 nothing or nil: *After Christmas, my bank balance was zero.*
zero *verb*
3 **zero in** to approach a target, accurately
•*Word Family:* the plural is **zeros** or **zeroes**
•*Word Origins:* from an Arabic word meaning "empty"

zest *noun*
1 great enjoyment or excitement: *She ate the meal with zest.* / *to have a zest for life* 2 a piece of citrus rind used as a flavouring: *the zest of lemons*
•*Word Family:* **zestful** *adjective* **zestfully** *adverb*

zigzag *noun*
1 a line or path that turns sharply right and left
zigzag *verb*
2 to move in a zigzag
•*Word Family:* other verb forms are **zigzags, zigzagged, zigzagging**

zinc (*say* zink) *noun*
a bluish-white metal, used in making alloys, especially brass, and as a coating for other metals so that they don't rust

zip *noun*
1 a long, narrow fastener consisting of two rows of interlocking teeth which can be joined or separated by a small bar pulled between them
2 liveliness or energy: *to have plenty of zip*
3 a zipping sound
zip *verb*
4 to fasten something with a zip: *She zipped her pencil case shut* 5 to move quickly or energetically: *to zip between the lines of traffic in your car* 6 to move with a sharp, hissing sound like a bullet: *to zip through the air*
•*Word Family:* other verb forms are **zips, zipped, zipping** □ **zippy** *adjective* lively or energetic

zodiac (*say* **zoh**-di-ak) *noun*
a part of the sky through which the sun, moon and main planets seem to travel, and which is divided into the 12 groups of stars used in astrology
•*Word Origins:* from a Greek word meaning "a sculpture of an animal"

zombie *noun*
1 a dead body supposed to be brought to life by witchcraft or other supernatural methods
2 someone who looks and acts like a zombie because they are very tired
•*Word Origins:* named after *Zombi*, a West African snake god

zone *noun*
an area marked off in some way from other areas: *a military zone* / *a residential zone*
•*Word Origins:* from a Greek word meaning "a girdle"

zoo *noun*
a place where many types of live animals are kept so that people can go and look at them

zoology (*say* zoo-**ol**-a-jee) *noun*
the study of animals
•*Word Family:* **zoological** *adjective* **zoologist** *noun*

zoom *verb*
1 to move quickly and sharply: *The aircraft zoomed into the clouds.* 2 to use a camera to make what you are filming appear to come closer or move away: *to zoom in on his face*

APPENDIX

Prefixes and suffixes

Prefixes

Prefixes are small words which can be added to root words to change their meanings.

Some common prefixes are:

anti	against, opposite, or opposed to	e.g.	**anti**clockwise
ex	former	e.g.	**ex**-husband
bi	two, twice	e.g.	**bi**centenary, **bi**annual
mis	mistaken or wrongly	e.g.	**mis**spell
tri	three	e.g.	**tri**cycle
pre	before	e.g.	**pre**view

These prefixes always change the meaning of a word to the opposite:

de	e.g. **de**forestation
in	e.g. **in**tolerant
dis	e.g. **dis**agreeable
un	e.g. **un**believable

Suffixes

A suffix is a small word which can be added to the end of a root word and changes the way it is used. For example, a suffix might change a noun into an adjective or a verb into an adverb.

Make root words into nouns by adding:

er	**hood**	**age**
or	**ness**	**ance**
eer	**ism**	**ence**
ist	**ment**	**ation**
ship	**ice**	**ition**

e.g. celebrate celebr**ation**

Make root words into adjectives by adding:

able	**ish**	**ary**
ible	**ous**	**cry**
al	**less**	**ory**
y	**ful**	**ic**

e.g. help help**ful**

Change adjectives to adverbs by adding "**ly**":

e.g. nice nice**ly**

Spelling tips

Vowels

The vowels are **a**, **e**, **i**, **o**, **u**.
All words have at least one vowel.
Every syllable in a word usually has a vowel.
Sometimes "**y**" can also act as a vowel, e.g. "hymn".

Suffixes

Sometimes the spelling of the end of a root word changes when a suffix is added.
Watch out for:

Doubling consonants

Double the last letter when the vowel is short.

e.g. **stop** — the vowel is short, so the past tense is "**stop*ped***"

walk — the vowel is long, so the past tense is "**walk*ed***"

Silent "e"

Keep the "**e**" when the suffix begins with a consonant.

e.g. **state** **state*ment***

Drop the "**e**" when the suffix begins with a vowel.

e.g. **hope** **hop*ing***

"Y" endings

Adding "***ing***" to a root word ending with "**y**" does not change the spelling.

e.g. **cry** **cry*ing***

Any suffix can be added to words ending with a vowel followed by a "**y**".

e.g. **play** **play*er***

In one syllable words change "**y**" to "**i**" before adding a suffix.

e.g. **day** **dai*ly***

When the root word ends with a consonant , change "**y**" to "**i**" before adding any suffix except "***ing***"

e.g. **happy** **happi*ness***

BUT

cry **cry*ing***

a b c d e f g h i j k l m n o p q r s t u v w x y z

A B C D E F G H I J K L M N O P Q R S T U V W X Y Z

SINGULAR AND PLURAL

Most singular words can be changed to plural by adding "**s**":

e.g.	dog	dog**s**

Words ending in "s", "sh", "tch", "x", and "z" need an "**es**" added so that they can be said easily:

e.g.	bus	bus**es**
	bush	bush**es**
	match	match**es**
	box	box**es**

Words ending in a "ch" that are pronounced "tch" need an "**es**" added:

e.g.	lunch	lunch**es**

Words ending in "y" which have a consonant before the "y" need the "y" changed to "**i**" and the "**es**" added:

e.g.	pony	pon**ies**

Some words ending in "o" need "**es**" added:

e.g.	torpedo	torpedo**es**

CHECKING YOUR WRITING

Follow these rules when you have finished a piece of writing!

1 Reread your writing to check that no words have been left out.

2 Reread your writing *backwards* for spelling.

3 Circle words that do not look correct and those you are not sure about.

4 Check these circled words in the dictionary.

5 When you find each word *look* at it and picture the whole word in your mind.

6 *Write* the word from memory and then check it in the dictionary.

7 Replace circled words with correctly spelled words to complete your writing.

LISTS OF USEFUL WORDS

DAYS OF THE WEEK

Sunday
Monday
Tuesday
Wednesday
Thursday
Friday
Saturday

MONTHS OF THE YEAR

January
February
March
April
May
June
July
August
September
October
November
December

NUMBERS

1 one
2 two
3 three
4 four
5 five
6 six
7 seven
8 eight
9 nine
10 ten
11 eleven
12 twelve
13 thirteen
14 fourteen
15 fifteen
16 sixteen
17 seventeen
18 eighteen
19 nineteen
20 twenty
30 thirty
40 forty
50 fifty
60 sixty
70 seventy
80 eighty
90 ninety
100 hundred
1000 thousand
1 000 000 million

FESTIVALS

Christmas
Diwali
Easter
Eid-ul-Fitr
Hanukkah
Ramadan

PLANETS

Mercury
Venus
Earth
Mars
Jupiter
Saturn
Uranus
Neptune
Pluto

(*Note*: The planets are listed according to their distance from the sun. Mercury is the planet closest to the sun.)

d e f g h i j k l m n o p q r s t u v w x y z

OVERUSED WORDS

Overused Words	Alternatives
angry	furious, livid, mad
bad	awful, atrocious
beautiful	gorgeous, lovely, stunning
believe	assume, imagine, think
big	gigantic, huge, massive
boring	dull, monotonous, tedious
careful	attentive, diligent, intent
careless	lax, negligent, slack
dangerous	perilous, risky, unsafe
difficult	arduous, complicated, hard
easy	effortless, simple
excellent	ace, first-class
exciting	exhilarating, mind-blowing,
fine	fantastic, smashing, terrific
get	collect, obtain, receive
give	award, bestow, provide
good	decent, satisfactory
great	amazing, fabulous, sensational
happy	delighted, glad, thrilled
hate	abhor, detest, dislike, loathe
important	celebrated, distinguished, prominent
like	admire, delight in, enjoy
lot (a lot)	heaps, loads, many, masses, piles
love	adore, be soft on, care for
mad	(1) foolish, idiotic, silly (2) angry, cross, furious
nice	magnificent, marvellous, splendid
normal	average, ordinary, standard
right	accurate, correct, true
sad	dejected, glum, miserable
safe	all right, safe and sound, secure
say (said)	comment(ed), observe(d), remark(ed)
sacred	hallowed, heavenly, holy, sacrosanct
see	notice, observe, spot

Overused Words	Alternatives
simple	easy, foolproof, uncomplicated
small	minute, petite, slight, tiny
strange	different, odd, peculiar
strong	muscular, powerful, sturdy
stupid	dense, dumb, foolish, ridiculous
suddenly	abruptly, all at once, unexpectedly
terrible	awful, disastrous, dreadful
ugly	hideous, grotesque, repulsive, unsightly
use	exercise, employ, wield
want	feel like, need, require
weak	feeble, frail, helpless
well	fit, hale and hearty, strong
wonderful	heavenly, unreal
wrong	false, improper, incorrect